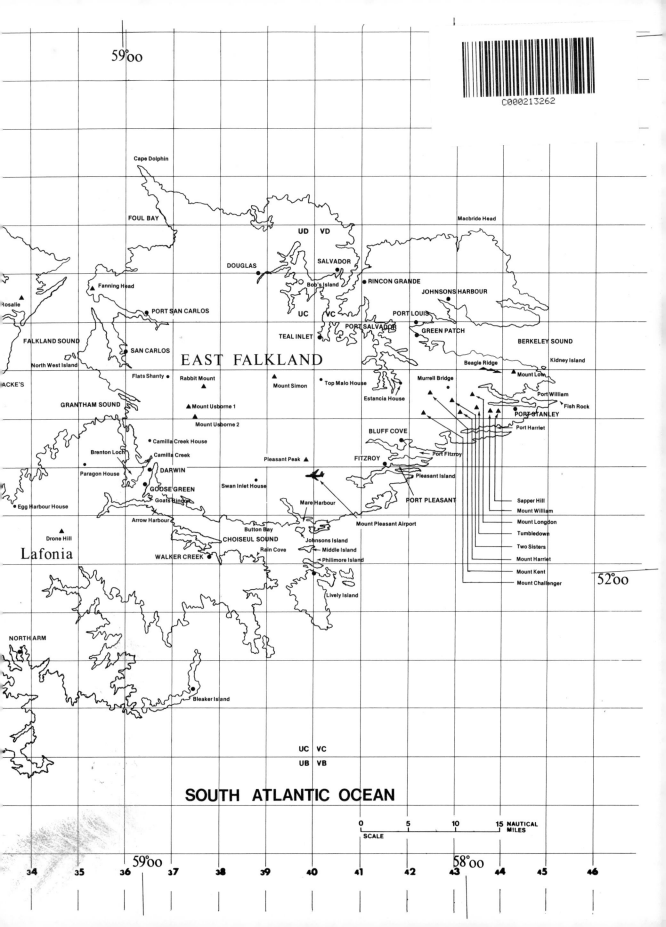

# FALKLANDS
## The
# AIR WAR

# FALKLANDS
# The
# AIR WAR

by

Rodney A Burden
Michael I Draper
Douglas A Rough
Colin R Smith
David L Wilton

a&ap

ARMS AND ARMOUR PRESS

Published in Great Britain in 1986 by Arms and Armour Press Limited,
Link House, West Street, Poole, Dorset BH15 1LL

Distributed in the USA by Sterling Publishing Co. Inc., 2 Park Avenue,
New York, NY 10016.

Distributed in Australia by Capricorn Link (Australia) Pty. Ltd.,
P.O. Box 665, Lane Cove, New South Wales 2066, Australia.

First published 1986 by the British Aviation Research Group

Reprinted 1987

ISBN 0-85368-842-7

Text data-transferred and typeset in the UK by Blackmore Press,
Shaftesbury, Dorset. Photograph captions typeset by Millbrook Press,
Southampton, Hampshire. Captions for maps and diagrams typeset by
Solent Typesetting Ltd., Otterbourne, Hampshire. Printed and bound
in Great Britain by R. J. Acford, Chichester.

*This book is dedicated to*

*the dead and injured of the 1982 South Atlantic conflict,*
*regardless of nationality,*

*and the late*

*A H V Hillier FRSA MInstPI AMRAeS*
*Design and Research consultant to the Fleet Air Arm Museum, RNAS Yeovilton.*

# FOREWORD

Janet W. McLeod
Goose Green
East Falkland
Falkland Islands
South Atlantic

Although my husband Bob and I have tried, with some success, to answer at least a few of the many questions put to us by Douglas Rough on behalf on all of the authors, it came as a bit of a shock to be asked to compile the "Foreword" to this book. For a while I was completely at a loss as to what to write! However, following my guidelines of simplicity and sincerity, I finally decided to relate some of the events of April, May and June 1982 which affected my family, and others, at Goose Green and Darwin, and our reactions to them.

**************

We lay awake all night after listening to the Governor's announcement that the Argentines were most probably going to invade the Falklands by dawn. For us at Goose Green the most frightening moments were before it happened, the uncertainty, even disbelief. However, the reality came with their arrival at Goose Green, creeping around behind the hedges at first, slowly gaining confidence. They were left with no provisions for the first week, but were too proud to admit it, although we could see them gathering mussels off the beach each day.

We could do nothing but bear their presence, watching the Chinooks bringing in more troops and equipment until the Darwin Boarding School was filled to overflowing. By then the Argentines had erected a huge tent village beside it. A few people left the settlement for unoccupied places, fearing being caught in the middle of a battlefield, but they were told to come back. On the evening before the first air strike about a dozen Pucaras flew in and lined up on the grass airstrip.

Our family arose in time to listen to the 7 o'clock news on the 1st of May, and had not long finished cheering at the news of the strike on Stanley airfield when we heard the now unmistakeable sound of Harriers coming over low. I was too slow getting to the window, but other members of the family saw some of the planes disappearing over the hill on their way to attack our airstrip. I later found some diaries written by Argentine soldiers which told of their terror and confusion during and immediately after the raid. The Argentines would not admit to us for some weeks that they had suffered any losses.

Some time after the strike, a Land Rover came to take us from Darwin to Goose Green for "a meeting to advise us of what to do in the case of another air raid". The "meeting" lasted until 2 PARA fought to free us!

6

Many of the other residents of Darwin and Goose Green had been taken from their homes with no explanation, and were not even given time to change from their slippers or put on coats. On the way to the Social Club we passed the airfield and had the satisfaction of seeing many of the Pucaras with tails and wings at all angles in the air. No helicopters were damaged as they had been moved down close to the houses after the attack on Stanley.

Gradually we became used to the attacks, and while some people stood at the windows cheering, to the annoyance of the Argentines, the children became expert at diving onto the floor, away from any glass, at the first sign of either an alarm or a jet engine. While this went on, we got into a routine, doing the tasks necessary to live as best we could cramped up in the Social Club building, like taking turns at jobs from cooking to unblocking drains.

As time went on, we grew accustomed to sleeping through naval shelling, and early mornings we could see the shells exploding in precise rows, the dull thumps coming at regular intervals. Most of us went under the floor after seeing 2 PARA coming down over the hill, seeming to walk steadily and unfalteringly through a continuous barrage. The foundations of the building might have offered some protection from the odd bullet, but not much else. We just resigned ourselves to wait for the outcome. Everything went quiet at dusk, and fear spread among us when we saw Argentines still walking around outside, while the radio was announcing that Goose Green had been recaptured by the British! The next morning we asked the guard at the door what had happened, and he said he didn't really know, but thought that his side had lost. Eventually, he abandoned his post and followed the other Argentines lining up on the Green. We caught the odd word of a speech by their Lieutenant Colonel, then they split up to pick up one or two items they treasured. Many passed us smiling and chatting amongst themselves, obviously glad it was over.

Then 2 PARA came into the settlement, tired and quiet, and spent the next few days unwinding and resting, getting ready for the next step - Stanley. After they moved on, the war seemed over to us. The relief was immense. All we could find out about the progress of the battles near Stanley was coming to us via the BBC and, when the news came that Stanley had fallen, we all met for a celebration drink. We were all very grateful to the Army, Navy and Air Force personnel who had liberated our normally quiet and peaceful Islands.

The Falklands are gradually being cleared of war debris - you can still hear explosions as shells and mines are disposed of, but most danger areas are well marked and fenced off. Now we look forward to a brighter future with much needed development just around the corner. Hopefully we will never have the uncertainty of whether or not to invest our money in a place which may be taken from under our feet at any moment. Our way of life is totally different from Latin America. We are British and proud to remain so.

Janet M°Leod.

# CONTENTS

## Royal Navy Fleet Air Arm

## Army Air Corps & Royal Marines

## Royal Air Force

## Appendices

## Part 3:  FALKLAND ISLANDS, THE DEPENDENCIES & BRITISH ANTARCTIC TERRITORY

## GLOSSARY

# INTRODUCTION

*FALKLANDS - THE AIR WAR* is an account of the air battle fought by Argentina and the United Kingdom during 1982. It is presented in a style which provides a balanced summary of the activities of every flying unit involved and which records their achievements against a common measure.

On 5 April 1982 two of the eventual Authors of this book stood amongst thousands of onlookers at Portsmouth, watching the aircraft-carriers 'Hermes' and 'Invincible' pass, with their escorts, slowly through the morning sunshine on the first stage of their journey to the South Atlantic and the Falkland Islands. It was an emotional moment for all present but the excitement of the occasion did not prevent the two friends engaging in objective conversation about the Task Force, its composition and, indeed, its prospects of success. Their interest was more than casual; professionally involved in aviation and regular contributors to specialist magazines devoted to current military matters, they were faced with an immediate problem. That problem was quickly and simply resolved by a self-imposed moratorium, subsequently extended by agreement with the publishers of responsible specialist magazines, to refrain from printing any data explicitly identifying aircraft, by unit or individual details, that were or would be involved in Operation "Corporate". It was assumed that, once "Corporate" had been successfully concluded, an interesting series of articles could be published and that, more or less, would be that.

By July 1982 the climate had changed. The Falklands War had been fought and won and, by and large, our two Authors and their associates thought that they were well aware of which elements of the British forces had been involved. A simple decision was made: a group of long-standing friends with a common interest in military aviation and, more specifically, much experience of aviation research and the possessors of some useful "contacts", would spend a few months of their free time producing a fairly modest, self-financed account of those aircraft and organisations that had been deployed to the Falklands' theatre. It was also hoped that, with a little work and good fortune, some Argentine-supplied data might become available. The monograph was to be aimed primarily at enthusiasts and aircraft-modellers.

By early 1983 it was apparent that much, much more was necessary. The complexity of the conflict had been such that any research undertaken revealed vast quantities of fascinating detail, much of it completely overlooked by the plethora of publications that were by then appearing. Worse still, many errors were being made in those books. Research continued, more and more data became available and, gradually, Argentine material began to appear. By 1984 the project had almost run beyond control and more urgent decisions had to be taken. Fortunately, our publishers, the British Aviation Research Group, continued to back us and make available the materials and resources (at some cost to their other commitments) without which *FALKLANDS - THE AIR WAR* could not have appeared in this format.

The decision to write a book, rather than a monograph of more limited scope, was taken when the Authors could no longer ignore a number of factors. We have already referred to the mass of data being unearthed at every turn and, not unnaturally, the Authors felt that much of it deserved publication. At the same time many of those involved in the conflict, both servicemen and Falkland Islanders, were universally enthusiastic to help us with a project that was seen to have the attributes of presenting an objective account of their efforts without having an overtly mercenary motive. While they answered our questions we became more conscious of the need to do justice to their accounts. They might, we reasoned, be unlikely to give anyone a second chance if we failed and, should they eventually decide to do so, there was doubt as to whether their memories would then be quite so vivid. As other books appeared we continued to work at data collection, interviewing and letter writing until we had a format clearly in mind. We resolved to write a book, directed at a mature readership, which would not only present a precise account of the air war in such a way that would be a "good read" but one that would have equal appeal to the serious historian as well as the aviation "buff".

*FALKLANDS - THE AIR WAR* is published by the British Aviation Research Group, an organisation of which the team of Authors are all members. The Project Co-ordinator was Douglas Rough and without his commitment and determination it is probable that the book would never have been completed. Douglas, with Rod Burden, was also responsible for much of the research and writing of those sections concerned with the Fleet Air Arm. Michael Draper, research consultant to the Museum of Army Flying at Middle Wallop, produced the Army Air Corps and Royal Marines section while Dave Wilton undertook the Royal Air Force section and Colin Smith tackled the Argentine section — or so the theory goes! In reality we all worked in one another's "territory" and hopefully we have combined our talents and knowledge to the extent that the book does not read like a collection of essays by individuals. Douglas Rough became the Falklands historian and "expert" on local civilian aviation ("somebody had to do it"), others were dragooned into writing shipping histories, glossary and link-notes; all of us suffered with photo-captions. David Allen and Peter Cooper (the Production Team) were responsible for artwork, layout and printing liaison, the former having the unenviable task of laying up nearly 500 pages of text and artwork. Peter's primary functions were to guide five indisciplined Authors in their selection of nearly 300 photographs and then to present them to David in print-ready format. Ian Carroll undertook research for the glossary and other sections. The production team was supported by Raymond Smith, the proprietor of DPR Marketing & Sales, who provided invaluable technical and commercial advice during the latter stages of the project. For his guidance and considerable patience, we thank him.

Elsewhere we acknowledge the assistance of the many people who have provided us with the material to write this book. Several of those named are Falkland Islanders. From the outset of the project we were always careful not to lose sight of the reason for the conflict, nor to forget the weeks of deprivation endured by the Islanders while the battle was fought around them. Janet McLeod, a resident of Goose Green and one who experienced occupation, incarceration, bombing, shelling and finally a major battle, was an early contact who galvanised many friends and neighbours into coming to our aid, particularly when field-work was required! It seemed wholly appropriate that we should ask our new friend to write the foreword to this book and, to our pleasure, she did so. To Janet, and all of her friends who helped us, we offer special thanks.

*FALKLANDS - THE AIR WAR* attempts to tell the story of an air war in an unprejudiced and objective fashion. We have endeavoured to investigate the operations of both sides to equal depth and to make judgements, on those rare occasions when such judgements are appropriate to this work, from a neutral position. We should perhaps apologise now to those who might consider our coverage of the land and naval war inadequate but, unless airpower was involved, we have arbitrarily considered certain otherwise significant events to warrant but passing mention. We make no apology for the omission of virtually all political background, historic or current. Such matters are clearly beyond the scope of this book. We have not ventured into the realms of conjecture or sensationalism and have also refrained from wandering into the nether regions of "contingency plans" or seeking to investigate covert assistance provided — to both sides — by third parties.

The book is structured in what we came to believe could be the only possible format for a work of this nature and size. Any attempt to combine all elements of the conflict into one grotesque chronological account was unthinkable and thus a structure was devised in which three major sections appeared. Two of them deal with the protagonists while the third, considerably smaller, is concerned with aviation in the Falkland Islands. Both major sections present an account of the War as it was conducted by each of their involved units: every first-line aviation unit in each of the Argentine armed services and all of those involved in the United Kingdom's Operation "Corporate". These two sections are each prefaced by a brief account of the total conduct of the respective campaigns. The overview of Argentina's war is, however, considerably larger than is that of the United Kingdom's and a few words of explanation are necessary.

We have assumed that the typical reader will be familiar not only with the circumstances and major events of the Falklands War but also with the broad composition of the British armed forces and their approximate orders of battle during 1982. If he is not, there are many specialist publications commercially available to provide useful background material. We have therefore limited ourselves in this preface ("United Kingdom's War") to a brief resume of events, all of which are considerably expounded on in the subsequent pages of unit histories. It would be unreasonable, however, to expect the reader to possess the same degree of background knowledge of the Argentine forces, nor indeed is it likely that all readers will have a clear understanding of how Argentina conducted her war in terms of overall strategy or contiguous operations. The opening section ("Argentina's War") is therefore intended to draw together all those elements that played significant parts in the campaign in order that the reader may then possess adequate basic knowledge to digest the subsequent, and far more detailed, accounts of the activities of the combat units. The Argentine elements of the book are further reinforced by appendices designed to provide the reader with additional reference material. Such appendices are inappropriate to the United Kingdom section and, in general terms, have not been included. However, because of the considerable involvement in the War of warships and merchant vessels, substantial appendices containing relevant shipping details have been included in both sections.

The third section covers aviation in the Falkland Islands and associated territories and, although some of it has little direct relevance to the conflict of 1982, the Authors believe it to be an important section in its own right. An understanding of the history and significance of aviation in the Falklands will give the reader further insight into the events that led to the invasion of April 1982.

It was decided not to attempt to index the book in conventional fashion. The nature of the text made that an overwhelmingly complex task and it was never seriously contemplated. A detailed glossary of terms is, however, provided and some effort has gone into ensuring that full explanations of all abbreviations and acronyms are included. A full list of rank equivalents is contained within the glossary. It was reluctantly decided not to include details of military decorations awarded to individual Argentine servicemen because we were unable to obtain such data for all elements of the armed forces. Such information is, of course, readily available for all British servicemen and details of awards, where appropriate to individuals within the scope of the book, are included in the text.

We have used a considerable number of photographs to illustrate our work, but those included have been chosen for their particular relevance to the text and not necessarily for the quality of the print. Naturally, we consider each to be of at least adequate standard for reproduction, but the reader will be aware of the circumstances under which some photographs were taken!

As explained earlier, this book has been written and published by a private organisation, the British Aviation Research Group. While such an arrangement has had the benefit of enabling the Authors to work without some of the constraints normally imposed by commercial publishing houses, it has also, to some extent, dictated the style and format of the book. The entire work was input on the Group's own word-processors by Dave Wilton and Colin Smith and disc-to-disc reproduction techniques have been employed to produce the final typeface. The combined limitations of our budget and the technology of the word-processors have led to a few shortcomings which we would have wished to avoid. Perhaps the most regrettable of them is our inability to do full justice to the Spanish language.

There are a few idiosyncrasies in our choice of terminology which also require some words of explanation. Throughout the book we have used "Zulu" or Greenwich Mean Time (GMT) for all events, irrespective of theatre. The use of such a convention, incomprehensible though it may be to some, was the only way to avoid completely confusing ourselves, never mind our anticipated readers. British Summer Time in the United Kingdom was GMT plus one hour throughout the campaign, Ascension Island time was GMT, while Argentine (Buenos Aires) time was GMT minus four hours although a local zone of minus three hours existed in the Rio Grande area. Falkland Islands time was GMT minus four hours but, to complicate matters, Port Stanley observed a "summer" time of GMT minus three hours to coincide with British Summer Time although this was widely ignored in the "Camp" (Goose Green, for example, remained at GMT minus four hours). Argentine time thus coincided with Port Stanley time but not with that of the rest of the Falkland Islands!

Throughout the book, we have used the word "mile" to indicate one nautical mile. All "miles" are therefore nautical miles! Finally, we must recommend the reader to arm himself with a quality map of the Falkland Islands. By its very nature, the book makes frequent reference to place-names and features of the landscape which are too insignificant for inclusion on any map that we could reasonably incorporate. Nevertheless, every effort has been made to identify to the reader the general locality of such isolated spots but, where appropriate, we have resorted to the use of Grid References. However, we have recognised that the indiscriminate use of such references would not help the reader, so they have been kept to a minimum.

Finally, we would like to remind the reader that we are not military men, nor do we have access to state secrets. We will have made mistakes and for those we apologise.

The Authors and Production Team
October 1985

# ACKNOWLEDGEMENTS

The preparation of *FALKLANDS - THE AIR WAR* required the considerable help of a very large number of people. We would like to acknowledge the assistance given by the Royal Navy (in particular the Fleet Air Arm), the Army (in particular the Army Air Corps), the Royal Marines and the Royal Air Force. Without their help our task would have been impossible.

Amongst the many individuals who have contributed to the project are:

John Ayers, John Bater, Andrew Bell, Martin Bishop, W.G. "Pip" Calvert, Alastair Cameron, Dugald Cameron, Sukey Cameron, Julian Cathrew, Steve Chollerton, Richard Coates, Paul Crickmore, Sam Drennan, Kensuke Ebata, Griff Evans, Wally Felton, Jeremy Flack, Richard Foster, John Gammon, David Gaunt, Steve George, Ron Goddard, Kevin Gollop, José Luis González Serrano, Jim Gosling, John Greenhalgh, Richard Griffiths, Mark Harrison, Pete Hellier, Mike Hill, Kath Hoare, Chris Hobson, Mike Hockley, John Huckle, Ian Hunter, Jan Hunter, Tony Hyatt, Graeme Hyde, Paul Jackson, Mel James, Tony Merton-Jones, Jim Kerr, D.W. "Doc" Knights, John Leonard, Pete Longley, Alan Macey, Salvador Mafé Huertas, Steve Martin, Alan Mawman, Mike McEvoy, Janet McLeod, Bob McLeod, Tony Merton-Jones, Peter Middlebrook, Steve Mills, Trevor StJ Murphy, Eric Myall, Jeff Niblett, Ian O'Neill, Lesley Pearson, Chris Pocock, Dave Pope, Alfred Price, Martin Ray, Elfan ap Rees, Julian "Jay" Rigg, Ian Roy, Neill Rush, Eric Salmon, Graham Sheppard, Mike Sharpe, Maurice Smith, Ray Smith, Vic Spencer, Vernon Steen, Trevor Stone, Ann Todd, Simon Van Tromp, Alec Tweedie, Geoff Wakeham, Robin Walker, Richard Leask Ward, Paul Whiteman, Alan Williams, Chris Wilson, Alessandro De Witt and John Wright.

To those mentioned above, and to those we have declined to mention, we offer our profound thanks. Each will be aware of his, or her, contribution and of its significance.

Finally, we offer simple thanks to our "better halves", who have suffered the tribulations of the past three years with much stoicism. Thank-you Bella, Carol, Dawne, Linda, Shan, Sonia, Val and Vicki.

# Part 1
# ARGENTINA

# ARGENTINA'S WAR

# RECOVERY OF THE ISLAS MALVINAS

It has been suggested by informed sources in Argentina that it was on 19 January 1982 that the three armed services were instructed to meet with each other, in considerable secrecy, in order to convert one of the several "textbook" Malvinas invasion plans into a realistic 1982 operation. The accuracy of this assertion is, however, arguably unimportant to this account of the War because we are here concerned with operational issues rather than with the political aspects that led to it. 19 January 1982 does, however, provide a most appropriate starting point for our account.

The visit of a Fuerza Aerea Argentina Boeing 707 to Stansted, Essex on 27 January 1982 was not, in itself, unusual. Argentina was a useful customer of the British arms industry, indeed at that moment aircraft and missiles were on several British production lines in various stages of completion and her warships were using British range facilities to work-up their air defence systems. After a two day stopover the Grupo 1 Boeing 707 left for Las Palmas and Buenos Aires. The inbound cargo had been of a general nature, it carried home "explosives". Other flights were to follow.

If, as has been suggested by many sources, the decision to capture the Falkland Islands by military means was taken in late January (and that the British diplomatic services were given every opportunity to appreciate the intention), it is clear that the plan itself was not revealed to more than a handful of senior Argentine officers. It was to be essentially a naval operation and one that the Armada, with its amphibious marine forces and air support, would be well able to undertake with little assistance from the Ejercito or the Fuerza Aerea. Once the Islands were recaptured both would be required to establish a permanent Argentine presence.

Throughout February and March the serious planning continued. The Grupo 1 707's ranged far and wide garnering weapons, ammunition and other equipment. While support from the the United States was still denied them, several trips were made to Europe and Israel (including four more visits to Stansted) as Argentina urgently augmented her existing stocks. Intriguingly, the last notified flight through Stansted (from Tel Aviv) was scheduled to arrive in Britain on 5 April!

The arrival of 'Bahia Buen Suceso' at Leith, South Georgia on 19 March with a cargo of civilian demolition workers was probably no part of the military master plan. The indignant reaction of Britain and the Falkland Islands to their arrival was, of course, predictable enough but it appears to have been a fortuitous event — as was the "LADE incident" at Port Stanley — that was to provide Argentina with an element of public justification for the planned Operacion "Rosario". It has been suggested in Argentina that the firm decision to invade the Falklands on 29/30 March was made by 22 March, using the annual naval exercises with neighbouring Uruguay as cover for the mobilising of the task force. From such limited evidence that is available, this would seem to have been the case. It was on 23 March that 'Bahia Paraiso' was diverted from her routine Antarctic duties, patently unconnected with subsequent events, to make her way to South Georgia to offer assistance to the threatened Argentine civilians. Her combat marine force, in much the same way as those of 'Endurance', was prepared for any eventuality.

What, therefore, was the general state of Argentine military awareness when the Armada's Task Forces 20 and 40 put to sea on 28 March? How much was known of Operacion "Rosario"? The Armada was fully alerted and the senior commanders of all operational elements, directly involved or not, were aware of the undertaking. Briefings to the more junior officers, which came as a surprise to most, were made at sea after the fleet sailed on 28 March. The Ejercito had at that time been little involved and, if some reports are to be believed, little informed. Only a minimum, perhaps token, force of soldiers had embarked with Task Force 40, accompanied by one Puma helicopter. The FAA, least enthusiastic of the services for the adventure, appears to have kept all but those directly involved completely unaware of the Armada's operation. The Grupo 1 Boeing 707's and C-130's had already played an extensive role in the general preparations (the latter in the long-range reconnaissance role over the Falklands and South Georgia) but it is unlikely that their crews had any official knowledge of "Rosario". It was not until 29 March that Grupo 2 de

Vigilancia y Control (G2VYCA, the FAA's mobile radar unit) was briefed that it was to deploy to Port Stanley and there is much evidence that other early FAA arrivals there were given only the vaguest of briefings until the last possible moment. For the majority of the FAA, including the combat units, news of the recovery of the Islands came as a complete surprise, through public channels, on 2 April.

The invasion fleet was composed of two major elements, Task Force 20 and Task Force 40. Task Force 20 was the covering and supporting force and comprised the aircraft carrier '25 de Mayo', the destroyers 'Comodoro Py', 'Hipolito Bouchard', 'Piedra Buena' and 'Segui', the fleet support tanker 'Punta Medanos' and the patrol vessel 'Alferez Sobral'. Task Force 40, the amphibious element, comprised the destroyers 'Hercules' and 'Santisima Trinidad', the frigates 'Drummond' and 'Granville', the submarine 'Santa Fe', the tank landing craft 'Cabo San Antonio', the polar ship 'Almirante Irizar' and the transport 'Isla de los Estados'. The complete force was commanded by Vicealmirante Juan Lombardo on '25 de Mayo' and his senior subordinates were Contraalmirante Gualter Allara on 'Santisima Trinidad', commander of the Task Force 40, and Contraalmirante de IM Carlos Busser on 'Cabo San Antonio', commander of the landing force, Task Group 40.1. Once ashore, and with the Islands secure, General de Division Osvaldo Garcia of the Ejercito would assume the theatre command. The small force that eventually secured South Georgia on 3 April was hastily designated Task Force 60 and comprised 'Bahia Paraiso' and the frigate 'Guerrico'. Capitan de Navio C.Trombeta, the captain of 'Bahia Paraiso', was appointed force commander.

South Atlantic storms thwarted the planned landings on East Falkland on 30 March and the amphibious force did not arrive off Port Stanley until the evening of 1 April, the invasion itself commencing in the early hours of the next day. At 0015Z the first marine commando forces were put ashore and by 1215Z they had complete control of the Port Stanley area including the Airport and all British military facilities. The formal surrender of the Governor, Rex Hunt, was accepted at about 1300Z.

The forces used in the amphibious landings had comprised 800 marines, many of whom were from the Batallon de Infanteria de Marina 2 (BIM2), and at 1700Z on 2 April BIM2 passed the operational control of the Falkland Islands to the Ejercito's Regimiento de Infanteria 25 (RgtInf25). Although 39 of its men had accompanied the marines ashore (they had been given a low-key role in "Rosario") the bulk of the unit was flown in to Port Stanley by the FAA C-130's as soon as the airfield had been secured. The first of those flights had landed at 1130Z that morning.

# CONSOLIDATION ON THE ISLANDS

For the purposes of controlling military operations on the Falklands the Argentine senior commanders created an organisation known as the Teatro de Operaciones Malvinas (TOM) — the Malvinas Operational Theatre. It was anticipated that TOM would be short-lived and quickly replaced by a local military governing body once the immediate commotion of the occupation had been accepted by the indigenous population. TOM was commanded by General de Division Osvaldo Garcia (the erstwhile commander of the Ejercito's V Cuerpo) and his three subordinate field commanders in Port Stanley, each representing the interests of his service, were Contraalmirante Gualter Allara, General de Brigada Americo Daher and Brigadier Luis Castellanos. TOM's sojourn in Port Stanley was brief, however, and on 5 April it was relocated on the mainland at Comodoro Rivadavia.

The early establishment of a military air component at Port Stanley was an integral part of "Rosario" and within hours of the surrender the first aircraft had arrived at the rapidly established BAM Malvinas (Stanley Airport). The initial force comprised four Grupo 3 Pucaras that arrived on 2 April, a Grupo 7 Bell 212 that was delayed until 5 April and a single CAB601 Puma which, having arrived by sea in a damaged state, was eventually made airworthy on 3 April. Two Escuadrilla Antisubmarina S-2E Trackers were deployed from '25 de Mayo' on 3 April to serve in the reconnaissance role for a ten-day period. In addition to this mixed force — which does not seem to have operated under a unified command — several CANA aircraft visited Port Stanley in the few days following the landings, while the FAA's transports became routine sights.

By 7 April it was clear to the senior military staff in Buenos Aires that a serious misjudgement had been made by the Argentine diplomatic service and that a British military response to their action was a real possibility. All senior officers of Argentina's armed forces were accordingly alerted and a full-scale mobilisation and emergency deployment programme was rapidly created. It was reasoned that any combat in the region would probably not be limited to the Falklands but would embrace the surrounding ocean area and outlying islands, indeed it might involve mainland Argentina, and thus TOM, having outlived its usefulness, was replaced by the Teatro de Operaciones del Atlantico Sur (TOAS) — the South Atlantic Theatre of Operations. TOAS was established on 7 April at Comodoro Rivadavia and was commanded by Vicealmirante Juan Lombardo. His theatre commander was Contraalmirante Alberto Padilla — the Armada was clearly in control — and his component commanders were Contraalmirante Allara, General de Brigada Julio Ruiz and Brigadier Mayor Hellmuth Weber. Simultaneously General de Brigada Mario Menendez was appointed Gobernador Militar de las Islas Malvinas; islas Georgias de Sur e islas Sandwich del Sur (Military Governor of the Falkland, South Georgia and South Sandwich Islands).

The mobilisation of Argentina's forces was no less dramatic than was that of their British counterparts and on 7 April most of their units were frantically recalling personnel, servicing equipment and formulating plans to meet the wholly unexpected demands of the circumstances. The wholesale reorganisation of FAA and CANA forces on the mainland is considered shortly but it is first apposite to consider events on the Falklands.

It was recognised that the defence of the Islands against a well-equipped British military force would be no simple matter but the task was by no means impossible, indeed there were several available options that could be successfully embraced. Accordingly Argentina increased her land forces on the Islands (slowly establishing garrisons at all the major centres of population), provided them with a rudimentary air defence umbrella and readied the mainland and naval forces for combat. However, the purpose of this book is not to consider at great length the events of the War that were not aviation-related and the reader must thus excuse the authors if relatively little attention is paid here to Argentine land and naval forces deployed to the Falklands.

The largest single element of the occupation forces was the Ejercito (some 9,804 soldiers were deployed) and it is appropriate to consider its contribution first, limiting ourselves to broad details. The structure that eventually emerged under the combined military command comprised three territorial commands and a group of headquarters and mobile organisations. Those forces centred on Port Stanley were commanded by General de Brigada Oscar Jofre, the erstwhile commander of X Brigada de Infanteria Mecanizada, many elements of which were deployed to the Falklands. Jofre was installed as the supreme commander of all land forces on the Falklands on 7 April but, although his troops at Port Stanley remained the greater part of the whole, the subsequently established commands at Darwin and on West Falkland were given to General de Brigada Omar Parada, commander of III Brigada de Infanteria. Parada does not appear to have been subordinate to Jofre. On 16 April General de Brigada Daher, the commander of IX Brigada de Infanteria, returned to Port Stanley to resume his involvement on the Islands as senior military advisor to the Military Governor (General de Brigada Menendez)! Several non-Ejercito units were subordinate to the three area commands and they included Marina combat troops and Marina and FAA anti-aircraft batteries. Even a small unit of the Gendarmeria Nacional was among the independent organisations deployed to Port Stanley.

FAA movements into Stanley Airport continued at their "post-invasion" level until about 10 April, at which time the first of the emergency supplies began to appear and the tempo of the airlift rapidly increased. The situation was confused and aggravated by the British announcement of a Maritime Exclusion Zone (MEZ) round the Falklands which became effective at 0400Z on 12 April. While that had little effect on the airlift of personnel it caused havoc, particularly for the Ejercito, to the carriage of all supplies and heavy equipment, practically all of which was being shipped into Port Stanley. The MEZ was absolutely observed by Argentina — the Armada had no illusions about the damage that British

submarines could cause — and virtually all cargo vessels were kept away from the Falklands.

The carriage of vital items including helicopters, field guns, anti-aircraft guns and radars was halted and, wherever possible, the equipment was dismantled and taken to Comodoro Rivadavia for airfreighting to Port Stanley by Grupo 1 C-130's. The helicopters of CAB601 were typically delayed. Following the early delivery of its first Puma, three more Pumas, two A-109A's and a UH-1H were flown to Port Stanley via the deck of 'Bahia Paraiso' and other ships between 7 and 11 April. The next arrival, a UH-1H, had, however, to be airfreighted in knocked-down condition by a C-130 and was not received until 18 April. The final batch of seven UH-1H's was airfreighted in between 21 and 29 April and, with two Chinooks and another Puma managing to fly in, CAB601 achieved a final strength of 19 helicopters on 30 April, perhaps two weeks later than had been anticipated. Equally affected by the shortage of C-130 capacity were the anti-aircraft units GADA101 and GADA601 whose weapons and radars were actually loaded onto a ship at Mar del Plata on 13 April and then off-loaded for air carriage, eventually arriving piecemeal at Port Stanley after 18 April. In spite of the problems, however, most of the vital Ejercito equipment, including such items as the Roland unit and the 105mm artillery pieces, were in place by 29 April and only a few very high priority items (such as the 155mm guns) were to arrive after that.

The massive airlift of mid and late April was organised and undertaken by the FAA and it is appropriate that we now return to 2 April and the arrival at Stanley Airport at 1900Z of a Grupo 1 C-130. It contained the AN/TPS-43F surveillance radar with which the FAA intended to enhance local ATC. This single piece of equipment was to play a substantial, and at times highly dramatic, role in the weeks to follow and its ultimate survival until 14 June enabled Argentina to deal Britain serious military damage. It was set-up and operated adjacent to the airfield by a detachment of G2VYCA and, once the British Task Force had sailed, it became arguably the most vital component of the Argentine command, control and communications centre at Port Stanley.

The establishment of a consolidated FAA presence on the Falklands followed a similar timetable to that of the Ejercito. We have already discussed the establishment of the small force of Grupo 3 Pucaras and the Grupo 7 Bell 212 in early April and Brigadier Luis Castellanos remained at Port Stanley in command of this air component after 7 April and the creation of TOAS. He was responsible to both the local military command and to TOAS itself although after the local fighting commenced on 1 May his operational links were with the FAA at Comodoro Rivadavia (CdoFAS) as much as with his local command. His immediate subordinates were Comodoro Hector Destri, the commander of BAM Malvinas, and Comodoro Wilson Pedrozo who, on 11 April, was appointed commander of the newly established BAM Condor at Goose Green. The creation of a second FAA base on East Falkland was an urgent necessity once a British military response became probable because Stanley Airport was both congested and vulnerable to air and naval attack. Goose Green was not an ideal site but it was arguably the best of those strategically acceptable to the FAA and work commenced in mid-April to make it suitable for Pucara operations. BAM Condor became operational on 14 April when two Chinooks and two Bell 212's of Grupo 7 (a second Bell 212 had by then arrived) were transferred from Port Stanley. These four helicopters were collectively, and formally, identifed as the "Escuadron de Helicopteros Malvinas". It was not until 29 April that the Grupo 3 Pucaras, which by then had been increased to a strength of 12, were also transferred to Goose Green. They, too, had received a new name by then, the "Escuadron Pucara Malvinas".

The security of Goose Green was to be a problem for the FAA throughout their occupation and ultimately it required a company of the Ejercito's RgtInf25 (the original troops sent to garrison Darwin) and two companies of RgtInf12. The latter were flown in from Port Stanley after 1 May (other troops were flown in during the battle for Darwin and Goose Green later that month). The FAA contingent comprised support elements for the aircraft and two companies of officer cadets from the FAA's Escuela de Aviacion Militar (EAM) at Cordoba. These cadets, variously described as "lookouts" and "riflemen" appear to have been deployed as observers in some of the remote areas of East Falkland that were beyond the range of the Port Stanley surveillance radars. In the latter part of May they were equipped with the SA-7 "Strela" portable SAM's. The cadets had been flown into Port Stanley from the mainland, en masse, on 14 April.

The service most heavily involved in Operacion "Rosario" had been the Armada; indeed the recovery of the Falklands had been undertaken almost exclusively by naval and amphibious forces. It had immediately established a naval base and an air station at Port Stanley (the Apostadero Naval Malvinas and the Estacion Aeronaval Malvinas were both created at 1430Z on 2 April) but the fleet and the bulk of the Marina forces were rapidly withdrawn from the Islands after 3 April. The task of routine maritime security was put into the hands of a new local coastguard detachment and, to that end, the Prefectura Naval Argentina (PNA) deployed two Z28 patrol craft, 'Islas Malvinas' and 'Rio Iguazu', to Port Stanley in early April. They were later joined by a small air component comprising two Skyvan transport aircraft and a Puma helicopter.

With the exception of the two S-2E Trackers already mentioned, CANA did not place any aircraft onto the Falkland Islands until obliged to do so when Britain's intentions had become clear. No plans had existed to base CANA combat aircraft on the Falklands, primarily because there had been no need for them, but after 5 April the situation suddenly changed. Not only was there a real prospect of air combat in the Falklands theatre but the inadequacies of the local airfields precluded the use of any of the FAA's fast jets from any base on the Islands. The FAA had always recognised that fact but had believed that its Pucaras were ideally suited for Island operations (although not in the air superiority or anti-shipping roles!). Thus CANA was left to establish which of its carrier and land based types might be most appropriately deployed to Port Stanley. By mid-April Stanley Airport had been fully evaluated for possible use by the A-4Q

Skyhawks and Super Etendards but CANA reluctantly concluded that their operation was impossible in all but exceptionally good weather conditions. One item that could not be relied upon in the Falklands was, of course, the weather. However, CANA's MB-339A light attack aircraft did meet the marginal conditions offered by Stanley Airport and they eventually became the only Argentine combat jets to be based on the Falkland Islands.

During their 10 day stay at Port Stanley the Trackers of the Escuadrilla Antisubmarina had photographed the tiny airstrip on Pebble Island with a view to its adoption by the FAA as their second base on the Falklands. However, the FAA was unimpressed with this remote grass strip and considered it to be even less acceptable for Pucara operations than was Goose Green, which they subsequently adopted in its place. Pebble Island could not handle any jet aircraft, nor indeed any large propeller types, but it was strategically attractive and so CANA decided to use the strip which was then grandly established as the Estacion Aeronaval Calderon. It became operational on 29 April when the first of four 4 Escuadrilla de Ataque T-34C Mentors were deployed there, having reached Port Stanley from Rio Grande some days before. They had arrived at Stanley with two 1 Escuadrilla de Ataque MB-339A's, the latter soon to be joined by a second pair. By the end of the month CANA thus had four Mentors deployed to Pebble Island and four MB-339A's at Stanley. The Prefectura Skyvans and the Puma were available for general purposes work.

There being no Falkland Islands-based air defence aircraft available to protect the local installations against any British air attack, Argentina considered it imperative that as many anti-aircraft guns and SAM's as possible should be taken to the Islands. Consequently substantial quantities of weapons were moved to Port Stanley during early April. They were provided by all three services and, following early confusion, were integrated into a fairly well organised system by late April.

The anti-aircraft guns were only deployed in two areas, Port Stanley and its environs and Goose Green. The most modern weapons were twin-barrel 35mm Oerlikons that were linked to Skyguard and Superfledermaus fire-control radars. The Ejercito deployed three batteries to Port Stanley (one from GADA101 and two from GADA601, the latter with elements of GADA602) and one section (of three GADA601 guns) to Goose Green. One section of FAA 35mm guns was deployed to Stanley Airport (the Ejercito 35mm guns were linked to Skyguard and the FAA's to Superfledermaus). Two batteries of the FAA twin-barrel 20mm Rhinemetall guns were initially deployed to Stanley Airport and six of them, linked to an Elta short-range radar, were removed to Goose Green by 22 April. All the FAA anti-aircraft guns are thought have been operated by Escuadrones Antiaereos I and II of Grupo 1 de Artilleria Antiaerea (Escuadron II certainly deployed its 20mm guns to the mainland bases in southern Argentina and a battery of 35mm guns is known to have gone to Rio Gallegos). A single battery of 12 single-barrel 30mm Hispano-Suiza guns (no fire-control radar) was deployed by the Marina to Port Stanley. From a command post, initially in West Road, the 35mm guns of GADA601 were deployed to the south-western approaches of the town and to the western side of Stanley Airport. Those of GADA101 were sited on the promontory of land on the north side of Stanley Harbour. The 30mm guns were deployed by the Marina to the Stanley Airport and Wireless Ridge areas while the 20mm guns were positioned close in to the Airport, specifically for its defence (by the later stages of the War many of these guns had been repeatedly moved).

Relatively few SAM's were deployed by the Argentine forces and all of those that were, with the exception of the portable Blowpipes and SA-7's, went to the Port Stanley area. The most efficacious of them, the single Roland unit, was eventually found between town and Airport near the Cable and Wireless building and it is presumed to have operated in that area. Three Marina Tigercat batteries were deployed in the same area as their protecting 30mm gun battery. The portable Blowpipe was universally deployed by the Ejercito to all its garrisons, including those on West Falkland, and in the later stages of the war SA-7's were issued to both the Ejercito and the FAA for use in those areas particularly vulnerable to British attack.

The successful integration of Argentine forces on the Falklands depended upon the early establishment of an efficient command, control and communications centre on the Islands. The FAA created a Centro de Informaccion y Control (CIC), under the command of Vicecomodoro Luis Aranda, at Port Stanley on 6 April to provide its own command and control as a matter of routine and it was this CIC that subsequently became the core of the combined services control organisation. The CIC relied heavily on inputs from the AN/TPS-43F search radar of G2VYCA (later renamed "Escuadron G2VYCA Malvinas" under the command of Mayor Silva) which had initially been placed on a high point near the Airport. On 13 April it was removed to the relative safety of the western suburbs of Port Stanley (it was found by the British in Port Street) and a replica was left in its place. This invaluable piece of equipment, with a range (subject to the curvature of the earth) of 225 miles interrupted only by some of the peaks to the west of Port Stanley, continued to operate throughout the War and was still functional when Argentine forces surrendered on 14 June. A TPS-44 tactical surveillance radar (believed to have been deployed by the Ejercito) provided an element of support for the FAA radar in the later stages of the War and was eventually found by the British on the Airport road some 1,000 yds from the G2VYCA AN/TPS-43F installation.

The Port Stanley air defences were thus marshalled by an integrated command structure whose primary resources were the FAA CIC (with naval input), a Marina-established communications network and the anti-aircraft guns and missiles of all three services controlled by the Ejercito.

It was on 27 April that the CIC detected the distant presence of the British Task Force away to the north-east of the Islands. Argentina believed that Britain's long-awaited assault would take place fairly rapidly and in anticipation of that there was yet another organisational change in Port Stanley. A new combined command, the Comando Conjunto Malvinas, was established on 29 April under the command of General de Brigada Daher. This command structure incorporated all the operational functions such as intelligence, logistics, internal security and communications but two key military advisory positions were also established. Contraalmirante Edgardo Otero was appointed Asesor Naval and Brigadier Castellanos became Asesor Aereo. The former had been the Armada's chief of operations during the planning of "Rosario", while the latter had been the senior FAA officer on the Falklands since the landings.

As open warfare with Britain drew nearer, these men had 46 aircraft in place on their three Falklands airfields and several helicopter landing zones (19 CAE helicopters, 12 FAA Pucaras and four helicopters, eight CANA light attack aircraft and two PNA Skyvans and one PNA helicopter had been deployed). Of the local light aircraft, only an Islander was used operationally. During May these 46 aircraft were to be reinforced with 12 more Pucaras and two more MB-339A's. Of the 60 deployed aircraft only three would eventually return to Argentina.

# MAINLAND MOBILISATION

The FAA's role in Operacion "Rosario" had been extremely low-key and very much supportive to the Armada's landings on the Falklands and South Georgia. It had been limited to an air transport role — although a most vital one — and to the provision of a tiny force of aircraft that had established an FAA presence at Port Stanley. A few ancilliary tasks had been performed by other FAA units but, in essence, the recovery of the Falkland Islands was of little operational consequence to the combat commands, Comando de Operaciones Aereas and Comando Aereo de Defensa, and had involved little of their time.

In the hours following the capture of Port Stanley the situation scarcely changed. The FAA's position in TOM has been explained and under the guidance of that body various consolidating tasks took place. The FAA carried in a quantity of urgent military hardware but otherwise its most important task was to integrate the Islands into Argentina's air defence network. This was a priority task because of fears of possible Chilean interference in the region and between 3 and 6 April two complete mobile radars of G2VYCA were set in place at Comodoro Rivadavia and Rio Grande, joining the unit already established at Rio Gallegos and the one that was about to go on-line at Port Stanley on 6 April. These four radars and their CIC's were overlapping and thus provided the local regional command, Comando de la Fuerza Aerea Sur (CdoFAS) — Southern Air Force Command — with full medium and high-level and limited low-level coastal air defence warning from Trelew in the north to Cape Horn in the south. It further encompassed all of Tierra del Fuego, the Falklands and much of Patagonia. It was anticipated that the integrity of this airspace would continue to be enforced by the periodic deployments to Rio Gallegos of tactical aircraft from the northern based combat units. The recently created Pucara unit at Comodoro Rivadavia, Grupo 4 de Ataque, would be strengthened and may have been intended to provide detachments to Rio Gallegos and Port Stanley.

The departure from Portsmouth of the British Task Force on 5 April changed all these unhurried plans and, with considerable urgency, the FAA prepared itself for a possible air war with one of the world's stronger military nations. Every element of the FAA was involved in the struggle to reorganise to meet the needs of the situation. It was reasoned that although any potential war would probably be fought in the area of the Falklands, the British might reasonably be expected to attack key mainland installations — even Buenos Aires itself. In the south the FAA's only base, Rio Gallegos, was austere and incomplete and the Falklands possessed no base capable of safely supporting its combat jets. Very few aircraft were capable of night combat and many did not possess inflight refuelling equipment. The FAA's problems were many and daunting.

The FAA began by establishing a revised command structure to meet the circumstances of the emergency. The existing structure was not well suited to this special task and thus key FAA personnel were given new commands for the duration of the crisis. Comando Aereo de Defensa (CdoAeDef) — Air Defence Command — was not much affected by the reorganisation but simply expanded its area of activity. Its standing responsibility for all the FAA radars, anti-aircraft systems and air defence fighters ensured that the primary concern was the optimum deployment of this equipment.

Two new commands were established early in April and both were given powerful terms of reference. Comando Aereo Estrategico (CdoAeEstr) — Strategic Air Command — was made responsible for planning the FAA's military reaction to the British Task Force, monitoring the size and progress of the fleet as it sailed south, assessing Britain's preparations for war and the creation of the FAA's own battle plans. To enable CdoAeEstr to achieve this the command was given its own reconnaissance capability using aircraft drawn from regular FAA units. The second new command, Comando Aereo de Transporte (CdoAeTr) — Air Transport Command — was created to reorganise all of Argentina's air transport to meet the requirements of the situation. It, too, was given wide powers that enabled it to mobilise the civilian air transport industry. Responsible for all international, domestic and Falklands "air bridge" operations, CdoAeTr functioned throughout the war.

The fourth component of the emergency FAA structure was the Comando de la Fuerza Aerea Sur (CdoFAS) — Southern Air Force Command — that was headquartered at Comodoro Rivadavia. Already one of the FAA's regional commands, CdoFAS had its terms of reference expanded to assume the day to day operational control of any air war in its region. It was clear that CdoFAS would be vitally important to the success of such a war and much

effort was spent in ensuring that its chain of command and control was rapidly and well established early on. The command was given to Brigadier Ernesto Crespo, the commander of IV Brigada Aerea, and he was charged with executing the orders given him by the co-located TOAS (after 20 May TOAS was superseded by Centro de Operaciones Conjuntas — CEOPECON). Crespo was expected to maintain close operational links with the Armada and Ejercito commanders.

The redeployment of FAA and other resources to the CdoFAS region began in earnest in mid-April after several days of energetic preparation. The FAA's revised order of battle was considerably influenced by many factors and it is much to the credit of the FAA that all available aircraft were actually in place and ready when the British Task Force eventually arrived off the Falkland Islands. The relocation of each combat unit is explained in detail in subsequent sections of this book, as is the emergency order of battle, but it is appropriate that their collective redeployment be considered now.

CdoFAS effectively utilised seven major bases during the War including its headquarters at Comodoro Rivadavia, since 1975 the established home of IX Brigada Aerea and the most southerly of the fully developed FAA airfields. The only other regular FAA base available was Rio Gallegos in Santa Cruz province but, although the home of X Brigada Aerea, its operational state in April 1982 was far from ideal for the task in hand. The gestation to Brigada Aerea status had been slow and, although G2VYCA had set up and operated a permanent radar establishment since 1980, the only combat aircraft based there were the temporary deployments from the northern airfields. Rio Gallegos was, in reality, still very much in a state of development with limited accommodation and tiny air terminal facilities. Above all else, its windswept open expanses provided practically no shelter for combat aircraft and the few small hangars could not support large quantities of redeployed aircraft.

CdoFAS was thus obliged to use the CANA facilities at Trelew, which was really too far removed from the Falklands for normal combat operations, and Rio Grande, which was in the right location but possessed a somewhat short runway and fairly limited facilities. From available evidence it appears that relations between the CANA and FAA personnel at the latter base were to become rather strained as the War progressed. In addition to these four established military bases CdoFAS adopted three civilian airfields in Santa Cruz province; Puerto Deseado, San Julian and Santa Cruz. The first was little used during the fighting and served primarily as a diversion field but San Julian was extensively used for combat operations. Santa Cruz saw no direct operations but was used by the FAA as a mainland support establishment for the Grupo 3 de Ataque Pucaras deployed to the Falklands.

The broad strategy of deployment was that each combat Grupo worked-up an Escuadron at the home base (the parent Brigada Aerea) and, once ready, the aircraft were ferried to their temporary home where the unit was re-titled for the duration of the War. As well as aircraft and their support equipment other units, such as anti-aircraft batteries, were also brought south from the parent Brigada Aerea. Most deployments were undertaken between 14 and 26 April and the major transfers were those of the Grupo 2 de Bombardeo Canberras to Trelew, Grupo 4 de Caza A-4C Skyhawks to San Julian, Grupo 5 de Caza A-4B Skyhawks to Rio Gallegos, Grupo 6 de Caza Daggers to Rio Grande and San Julian and Grupo 8 de Caza Mirages to Comodoro Rivadavia. As explained above, the transfer of the Grupo 3 de Ataque Pucaras to Santa Cruz was made for a different purpose.

CdoAeEstr had, as described earlier, been issued with its own reconnaissance aircraft and the unit was formally constituted on 4 April (presumably only on paper at that time) at Comodoro Rivadavia as Grupo Aereo de Exploracion y Reconocimiento 1 (GrAeExplRec1). It drew on the Boeing 707's and C-130's of Grupo 1 de Transporte Aereo and Learjets of Grupo 1 de Aerofotografico as required.

Two other flying units were created within CdoFAS to meet the extraordinary needs of the situation. It was appreciated that an extensive SAR network would probably be vital and thus, making full use of suitable impressed civilian helicopters and fixed-wing aircraft to augment the FAA helicopters, the Seccion Operativa de Busqueda y Salvamento (SOBS) was formed on 5 April at Comodoro Rivadavia. It had detachments, known as Sub-Centros de Control de Busqueda y Salvamento (SCCBS), at all the CdoFAS bases except Rio Grande where the existing CANA facilities were adequate (CdoFAS did not, of course, in any way control the CANA bases nor indeed the use of naval aircraft on them).

The second of the new units was the Escuadron Fenix. This peculiar organisation, administered from Comodoro Rivadavia, is fully discussed elsewhere but, in essence, it was a collection of impressed civilian executive aircraft gathered to provide the FAA, and in particular CdoFAS, with abundant communications aircraft that could be used throughout the country on ad hoc tasks.

Extensive use was naturally made of the existing local resources and, in particular, the aircraft of the resident general purposes unit at Comodoro Rivadavia, Grupo 9 de Transporte Aereo (the LADE aircraft). The recently created Pucara unit, Grupo 4 de Ataque, was also to see local operational use during the war.

During the period of FAA mobilisation the Armada and the Ejercito were similarly engaged in moving men,

equipment and materials to where they would be needed in combat. The latter's efforts were almost entirely devoted to the garrisoning of the Falklands and to that end virtually all available transport helicopters and some of the attack helicopters were despatched to the Islands. The story of CAB601's mobilisation and deployment is told in a later section of this book and little more need be said of it here.

Throughout the emergency period the Armada demonstrated considerable independence of the other services and in April its preparations for war were conducted in some isolation from those of the FAA. The provision of base facilities for the FAA at Trelew and Rio Grande was perhaps the most obvious evidence of what little inter-service co-operation existed but there were other, perhaps unavoidable, instances of joint ventures. One such example was the use of the Grupo 1 KC-130H tankers to support the CANA Super Etendards in their Exocet anti-shipping role.

There was no reorganisation of CANA to meet the emergency for the simple reason that it was unnecessary. Apart from the deployment of the Exocet-equipped Super Etendards of 2 Escuadrilla de Caza y Ataque from Espora to Rio Grande on 19 and 20 April, there was no major move of a combat unit on the Argentine mainland until 9 May when the A-4Q Skyhawks of 3 Escuadrilla de Caza y Ataque moved to Rio Grande.

By the final week of April Argentina was in no doubt that, unless a political resolution to the problem was quickly achieved, Britain would use her Task Force within the next few days to attempt to recapture the Falkland Islands. The style of the recovery of South Georgia on 25 April had left her with little doubt that Britain possessed the political will to fight. After the Task Force was detected by the Port Stanley search radar on 27 April the situation became extremely tense and FAA and CANA aircraft were constantly airborne in an attempt to monitor the fleet's movements. All air transport flights from Argentina to Port Stanley were suspended from 29 April and the mainland bases braced themselves for possible air attack as British aircraft briefly appeared on their air defence radar screens. Finally, on 30 April, CdoAeEstr was stood down by the FAA, its task completed, and its resources were transferred to CdoFAS.

# AIR COMBAT

By the evening of 30 April the Argentine forces on the Falklands were in no doubt that a British assault was imminent, perhaps only hours away. The mainland and naval forces were equally tense and, although there was no clear indication as to what form it would take, a consensus of military opinion suggested that a series of diversionary attacks would probably be the prelude to large-scale landings somewhere on East Falkland.

The FAA and CANA reconnaissance aircraft had endeavoured to keep as much of the British fleet as possible under distant surveillance but their combined re-

sources were inadequate for the task. CdoFAS was thus resigned to a situation in which it would probably have to react to the first overt enemy action rather than act in anticipation of the event.

According to the FAA Comandante en Jefe, Brigadier General Basilio Lami Dozo, CdoFAS had, by 30 April, assembled 82 serviceable FAA combat aircraft on its mainland bases. Only a few machines had been held in reserve, mainly for training purposes, although others that had been in maintenance and storage were, wherever possible, being returned to airworthiness. As will become apparent from the later unit histories some of these aircraft, particularly the Skyhawks, would be returned to operational use without items of avionics and, in some instances, still fitted with time-expired components.

The FAA has never precisely explained the composition of its force of 82 aircraft but it is reasonable to assume that it was in the order of six Canberra B.62's at Trelew, 14 A-4C Skyhawks at San Julian, 18 A-4B Skyhawks at Rio Gallegos, 24 Daggers at Rio Grande and San Julian and eight Mirage IIIEA's at Rio Gallegos and Comodoro Rivadavia. The total included Pucaras which were presumably the 12 or so at Comodoro Rivadavia and perhaps Santa Cruz. CdoFAS, working on the assumption that the Royal Navy was planning its amphibious assault for somewhere on East Falkland, had established a carefully considered programme of retaliatory air-strikes. These attacks would be directed at the warships, by definition close inshore and probably fairly near to Port Stanley. Using all available aircraft CdoFAS thus held its force on full alert, ready for a maximum-effort, anti-shipping strike. The plan, publicly revealed post-war by the FAA, was to launch 16 A-4B and 12 A-4C Skyhawk sorties, six Canberra sorties, 12 Dagger sorties and ten Mirage IIIEA sorties. What has not been stated, but is evident from other information, is that the Skyhawks were to be launched as seven flights of four, the Canberras as two flights of three with Daggers and Mirages operating, in pairs, in an escort role. Although, as will be seen, this plan went somewhat awry on the day, it should be realised that CdoFAS had no intention of trying to establish air superiority over the Islands as such — the FAA interceptors were to be used solely in the escort role. On the Falklands, those aircraft capable of offensive use — the Pucaras, MB-339A's and Mentors — would be used on an ad hoc basis against targets as they presented themselves. Only the MB-339A's were anticipated to have an anti-shipping role.

The arrival of the 101 Sqdn Vulcan overhead Stanley Airport at 0746Z on the morning of 1 May was the long-awaited trigger to the CdoFAS counter strike but the isolated, single aircraft attack on Port Stanley confused the Argentines and their immediate response was cautious. Two of the Rio Grande Daggers, due to have performed a routine escort sortie for a CANA SP-2H Neptune mission, were, in effect, diverted to perform a somewhat nebulous "top-cover" sortie to East Falkland. It is indicative of the FAA's general confusion that morning (both on East Falkland and at Comodoro Rivadavia) that these Daggers took-off well before the first Sea Harrier attacks on Stanley and Goose Green airfields and with no clear idea of what to expect over the Falkland Islands. In fact it was not until late in the day that the TOAS command staff at Comodoro Rivadavia were finally agreed that there had been no large-scale British landings on the Islands. Unfortunately, by then CdoFAS had executed its carefully considered retaliation plan.

For all its daring and resolution displayed in the later stages of the War and its undoubted successes, CdoFAS badly bungled its operation on 1 May. The anti-shipping sorties dispatched to attack British warships which were not within 100 miles of the identified target area were naturally doomed to failure, but it was the nature of the failure that must have most alarmed the FAA's commanders. Of the 56 planned sorties only 35 "reached targets" and while Argentina has never been specific about those targets it is clear that none of the Skyhawks, and only three Daggers, actually found and attacked British warships. Indeed, some of the Skyhawks that did reach East Falkland were involved in hair-raising and ludicrous incidents that might well have ended in disaster. The Canberras were found to be dreadfully vulnerable and as a result of their experience on 1 May virtually all future missions were conducted at night. What was probably the FAA's greatest shock, however, was the discovery that the new R530/Magic-equipped Mirages were no match for the Sea Harriers in air combat. The events of the day are fully described elsewhere but, in summary, it is fair to say that all aspects of the Sea Harrier operation — its performance and weapons, the quality of the pilots and its utilisation — were underestimated by the FAA. After 1 May a complete reappraisal of the Mirage's role was undertaken and it was never again hazarded in combat against the Sea Harrier. The Dagger had also suffered at the hands of the Sea Harrier on 1 May and it was immediately withdrawn from escort work over the Falklands. Although no official comment has been forthcoming it is apparent that the FAA found the performance of their Shafrir AAM's disappointing. On 1 May the FAA lost two Mirage IIIEA's, one Dagger and a Canberra in air combat. On the Falklands the air attack on Goose Green effectively destroyed three Pucaras.

While the CdoFAS fighter-bombers and interceptors laboured above the Falkland Islands on 1 May the embarked aircraft and helicopters of Task Force 79 spent a tense day probing for the enemy. Although briefed to seek and attack the British fleet, '25 de Mayo' and her escorts were understandably cautious, having no wish to be subjected to a submarine attack. It has been suggested that a signal sent at 2307Z from Viceaalmirante Lombardo at Comodoro Rivadavia clearly instructed Contraalmirante Allara on '25 de Mayo' to withdraw all elements of Task Force 79 from their positions and to discontinue offensive operations. That message was allegedly reiterated at 0419Z on 2 May in a further signal that provided Allara with Lombardo's reasoning for the decision. It is clear, however, that the carrier's S-2E Trackers were airborne for much of the night and, far from breaking off his search for the British carrier group, Allara briefed his Skyhawk pilots between 0500Z and 0700Z to prepare for a dawn attack on 'Invincible'. The strike was never launched but it was not aborted until about 0900Z after a Tracker (launched from '25 de Mayo' at 0828Z) had failed to relocate the British warships in the area in which they had been found some hours before. The Tracker eventually returned to the carrier at about 1200Z after an extensive sea search and '25 de Mayo' did not leave the area until after she was made aware of the loss of 'General Belgrano'. The cruiser was torpedoed at 1858Z and, from the evidence of the operational activity on '25 de Mayo' during the morning of 2 May, the withdrawal of the northern elements of Task Force 79 to home waters was a reaction to that event rather than to a direct order allegedly received some 20 hours earlier.

The events of early May were dramatic and it probably took CdoFAS some days to fully appraise the situation. The loss of 'General Belgrano' was rapidly followed by the spectacular destruction of the destroyer 'Sheffield' by a CANA Super Etendard from Rio Grande and both sides by then were viewing each other with some respect. Gradually the situation became clearer. It was realised that the British were waiting for reinforcements before making an amphibious landing and in the meantime the Task Force was engaged in sundry "softening-up" activities. These frequently took the form of the night bombardment of troop concentrations and the airfield installations. Coastal shipping was attacked whenever caught and the Sea Harriers' aerial domination of the Falklands restricted Pucara and helicopter movements to low level, often in poor visibility. Fortunately for the Argentine forces the CIC at Port Stanley, well served by G2VYCA's radar, was able to provide adequate early warning of the approaching Sea Harrier Combat Air Patrols and local losses were few during early May.

The FAA has published statistics indicating that it planned 19 attack sorties from the mainland for 2 May, all of which were cancelled because of poor weather conditions, and that a further 85 were intended for the period from the 3 to 20 May. Of these 85 only 16 actually reached their targets with the balance cancelled or aborted because of bad weather and technical difficulties. The cancelled sorties of 2 May probably resulted from the realisation that there had been no major landings on the Falklands on the previous day, but the high number of cancelled missions during the following three weeks is intriguing. Argentina has published detailed data on the perceived weather situation in the area for the entire War period and it makes interesting reading. For the 44 days until 13 June, 17 were adjudged to have had weather bad enough to prevent flying on either the mainland or over the Falklands. A further six allowed limited flying (although "limited" was not defined) but the rest were regarded as being fair to good. This apparently meant that Argentina regarded the continental weather as operable on 41 days but for only 30 days on the Falklands. On only two occasions did the weather prevent en route sorties from reaching the Falklands. Thus to lose 69 of 85 sorties to weather and "technical" reasons seems rather odd. Without access to the detail of the CdoFAS plans it is, of course, impossible to do more than guess at its strategy during this period.

However, the events of two days, 9 and 12 May, are significant. On 9 May CdoFAS made a definite effort to reach British warships in the Port Stanley area using A-4C Skyhawks but, in rapidly deteriorating weather, two were lost en route and no attack was made. On 12 May, eight A-4B Skyhawks attacked two British warships off Port Stanley and succeeded in damaging the destroyer 'Glasgow', thus achieving the first real success of the war for the CdoFAS squadrons. The mission also cost CdoFAS four aircraft and pilots and confirmed the lethality of the British Seawolf missile system.

On the Falklands further heavy losses were sustained early on 15 May when 11 aircraft were destroyed on the ground at Pebble Island during an attack by British Special Forces. By 20 May 19 aircraft of all services had been destroyed or damaged beyond repair on the Falklands.

As the days slipped by it became clear that the British were close to making their major assault on East Falkland. CdoFAS had used the first three weeks of May to fully review its early experiences and, by 20 May, it was in a considerably better situation to meet its next major obligation. Since 30 April it had lost 10 combat jets from the mainland squadrons and with them, depressingly, all but one of their pilots. Each major unit had suffered at least one loss but some valuable lessons had been learned in the process. Lami Dozo's original 82 aircraft, despite the losses, had been reinforced by more Daggers and Skyhawks and several more Pucaras had been brought into the region. The mainland fighter-bomber strength had been further boosted on 9 May by the arrival at Rio Grande of eight A-4Q Skyhawks from Espora, recently disembarked from '25 de Mayo'.

The role of each CdoFAS unit had been more clearly defined by 20 May and it is important that the operational parameters of their aircraft should be clearly appreciated. The all-weather, interceptor-configured Mirage IIIEA's (although effectively withdrawn from the theatre by 20 May), were limited, even with underwing tanks, to a 12 to 15 minute loiter at medium to high altitude over East Falkland when operating from Rio Gallegos. Once the tanks were jettisoned and the afterburner used the Mirage pilot would probably be thinking of going home! The Daggers, their escort/interceptor role also abandoned after 1 May, were even more restricted and with a typical war-load of two 500lb or one 1,000lb bomb and underwing tanks they were effectively limited to a straight out-and-back mission to the Port Stanley area or one to Falkland Sound with a few minutes holding time available. Sustained low-level or supersonic flight would rapidly exhaust limited fuel reserves. Unlike the Mirages, the Daggers were not all-weather aircraft and were restricted to daylight operations.

The Skyhawks carried a similar bomb-load to that of the Daggers but, although their in-flight refuelling capability theoretically allowed them to operate comfortably to virtually any target in the Falklands, in practice they, too, were often range-limited. Much depended on the availability of the two KC-130H's and their early priority seems to have been to the CANA Super Etendards. That problem does not appear to have been resolved until 21 May when the first air-refuelled Skyhawk sorties were undertaken. Once that procedure was adopted the Skyhawks were able to venture beyond Falkland Sound with more confidence, secure in the knowledge that the tankers were waiting for any aircraft in trouble. It rapidly became standard procedure to refuel every Skyhawk sortie some 15 minutes after departure and again on the way home should it prove necessary. Like the Daggers, the Skyhawks were day fighter-bombers. The Canberras, of course, had sufficient range for virtually any envisaged mission but, after 1 May, daylight operations were out of the question because of their demonstrated vulnerability.

In the coming days the CdoFAS aircraft were to fly only clear-weather, daylight missions invariably without the benefit of fighter escorts or their own AAM's. The pilots were to learn to rely on the Stanley CIC and other ad hoc radio means for warning of the presence of Sea

Harriers. They would fly "hi-lo-hi" profiles to avoid the British radars and, once attacked, their flying skill and superior airspeed were often the only means of salvation.

# THE BRITISH LANDINGS

As had been the case on 30 April, Argentina was, on 20 May, well aware that the next British move was imminent. In response to the changing circumstances TOAS was stood down that day and replaced by CEOPECON — the Combined Operations Centre. Its senior triumverate of Garcia, Lombardo and Weber assumed operational control of the War until the eventual surrender on 14 June.

The first reports of the British landings at San Carlos Water were received at Comodoro Rivadavia between 1115Z and 1130Z on the morning of 21 May. They were incomplete and CEOPECON was not immediately convinced that they did not simply relate to diversionary landings. The probable British landing areas had earlier been identified by TOAS as Fitzroy/Port Pleasant and San Carlos but the former had always been considered the more likely of the two and CEOPECON was reluctant to accept that it was actually the latter. The San Carlos reports did, however, explain the earlier shelling of Goose Green and by about 1300Z the FAA's own intelligence from the first Pucara sorties confirmed the earlier naval reports that these were indeed full-scale landings.

The FAA had always appreciated that should the landings take place, as they ultimately did, in the San Carlos area then the Ejercito would probably be unable to stop the British advance once the beach-head had been properly established. Under the circumstances the FAA and CANA aircraft had to prevent the consolidation ashore of the British forces by inflicting maximum damage as quickly as possible. This damage would be best inflicted on the troopships and supply vessels in San Carlos Water. Thus the CdoFAS strategy was a simple one. It had to launch a maximum-effort air-strike against the transports and their protecting warships. To its credit CdoFAS wasted no time in getting the first aircraft airborne soon after 1230Z, their pilots relying on updated target information being passed to them en route. Following a lone CANA MB-339A of 1 Escuadrilla, up from Port Stanley, that had attacked 'Argonaut' a few minutes earlier, the first waves of Daggers and Skyhawks arrived over Falkland Sound shortly before 1330Z and, within moments, the bitter and bloody struggle for supremacy over the beach-heads had begun.

CdoFAS had pre-planned (much as it had done for 1 May) 63 fighter-bomber sorties for the 21 May and 54 of them were successfully dispatched. 12 CANA Skyhawk sorties were also planned but the first six, launched to be overhead Falkland Sound at 1315Z, were recalled en route because of vague target information at that stage. A total of 60 Dagger and Skyhawk sorties thus reached at least as far east as West Falkland in pursuit of the "maximum-effort" strategy. With the exception of the MB-339A sortie mentioned earlier (which was essentially only a reconnaissance mission), no Falklands-based aircraft were tasked with, nor undertook, any anti-shipping sorties on 21 May.

Some British accounts of the day's action, and in particular those of certain journalists, create an impression of unending waves of Argentine aircraft appearing overhead the warships throughout the daylight hours. The reality was rather different. CdoFAS reasoned that it would create maximum confusion in the British defences if they were flooded with aircraft. Not only would the SAM's and anti-aircraft guns have problems following several fast-moving aircraft approaching from different headings but the Sea Harrier CAP's, for which there was by now widespread respect, could not simultaneously chase multiple targets. From limited Argentine evidence it seems that four main strikes, each involving at least 12 aircraft from mixed units, were planned for arrival at San Carlos at approximately 1330Z, 1600Z, 1650Z and 1810Z. However, as the day progressed, fewer aircraft tended to get through the outer British defences. As feared by CdoFAS, the British soon discovered that, because of the combined limitations of fuel, safe altitude and topography, all the incoming aircraft were limited to using only three tracks across West Falkland and the Sea Harriers were vectored accordingly. Individual CdoFAS sorties are fully discussed elsewhere but it is clear that the early attacks, and in particular the first combined Dagger and Skyhawk strike at 1330Z, were unlucky not to inflict more damage than they did. With the early chances missed, later sorties, although much benefitting from the experience and reconnaissance data of their colleagues, were to suffer more severely as the British anti-aircraft defences were progressively strengthened.

The day closed with seven FAA and three mainland-based CANA combat jets lost. With the single exception of a Dagger brought down by a SAM, probably a Seawolf, all were caught by Sea Harriers. Fortunately, six of the pilots survived but that was not known at the time and initially most were thought to be lost.

Although none of the thousands of rounds of gunfire and only one of the dozens of British SAM's launched actually brought down an aircraft, considerable damage was inflicted by this fire and many machines required repair in Argentina that night. Had the following day's weather permitted operations, very few sorties would have been launched because of unrepaired battle damage. The CdoFAS aircraft had been forced by geography and British strategy into attacking her warships and had suffered in the process.

There were, of course, considerable Argentine successes on 21 May and, with a little more luck, her aircraft might have crippled the British operation. Argentine aircraft had sunk 'Ardent', seriously damaged 'Argonaut' and, to a lesser extent, 'Antrim', 'Brilliant' and 'Broadsword' but, most frustratingly for the FAA, several 500lb and

1,000lb bombs had failed to detonate on impact because of the way that they had been fused. In an effort to ensure that aircraft were not destroyed by the blast of their own bombs beneath them, delayed action fuses were fitted to allow the low-flying fighter-bombers to get clear of their targets. The explosions were thus always expected to occur after the aircraft were clear and many pilots counted the seconds elapsing from launch to detonation. The strategy was a complete success in one respect, for no Argentine aircraft was lost in an accident involving its own ordnance, but several bombs either tore their way through the thin-skinned ships without exploding or, after lodging in the structure, simply failed to detonate because of a fuse malfunction.

It was not until early afternoon on 23 May that the fighter-bombers were able to attack the warships a second time and, by then, the air battle had effectively been lost. For 60 hours the British had been disembarking, advancing and digging-in. Vast quantities of men, weapons and general supplies had been taken ashore unimpeded. Nevertheless, CdoFAS planned 46 FAA sorties for the day and although the poor early weather reduced the number actually launched, about half of the planned total were able to find their way into the San Carlos Water area. There they found reinforced gun and SAM defences and, nearby, the inevitable Sea Harrier CAP's. Surprisingly, only two FAA aircraft were lost; a Dagger to a Sea Harrier and a Skyhawk to a SAM. Both pilots were lost, as was a CANA Skyhawk pilot in a bizarre landing incident at Rio Grande that left his aircraft with only minor damage.

On the following day, 24 May, even fewer FAA aircraft, 12, reached their targets and one of them, a Skyhawk, was lost with its pilot after it had taken multiple hits over San Carlos Water. Three Daggers were also lost when caught unawares by Sea Harriers over West Falkland. Two of the pilots ejected safely. For all their efforts on 23 and 24 May the CdoFAS pilots only succeeded in sinking 'Antelope' and caused no serious damage to any other ships.

By the evening of 24 May the hopelessness of the situation was abundantly evident both to the Escuadrones and to the CdoFAS commanders. The British had not only turned San Carlos Water into one of the world's most heavily defended anchorages but they had stationed picket ships and ESM helicopters so that most approaching FAA fighters were seen on radar before they reached the west coast of West Falkland. Even worse was the realisation that the Sea Harriers were, by then, operating below the level at which G2VYCA's radar at Port Stanley could detect them. Without this vital intelligence from the CIC the Argentine fighters were decidedly vulnerable to the Sea Harrier CAP's.

Target information was also lacking for, by 24 May, there were virtually no scouts or forward air controllers close to San Carlos Water and useful aerial reconnaissance, despite occasional efforts by the high-flying FAA Learjets, was very limited. CdoFAS generally reckoned that its best target information was some 90 minutes old when its aircraft arrived overhead. In an effort to reduce this delay to a minimum, fighter-bombers were launched in response to "Fragmentary Orders" from Comodoro Rivadavia that required only a minimal briefing for the crews before take-off. They were then updated en route (another FAA statistic reveals that on 13 days no missions were undertaken because of a lack of suitable target information).

On 25 May CdoFAS tried new tactics that were designed to eliminate one of the radar picket ships operating to the north of Falkland Sound. They were ultimately successful and although 'Coventry' accounted for two of the three Skyhawks lost to SAM's that day, it was the Skyhawks that eventually sank her to the north of Pebble Island. Far to the north-east CANA was equally successful, celebrating Argentina's National Day with the destruction of 'Atlantic Conveyor' by the devastatingly successful Exocet/Super Etendard combination. 22 FAA anti-shipping sorties were planned for the day, 17 of them accomplishing their missions. For the first time in the War, an Argentine pilot, one of three Skyhawk casualties and the only survivor, was recovered from the sea by the British. With a fine sense of occasion he went into San Carlos Water in front of television cameras!

Consolidated FAA statistics for the period 21 to 25 May show that 167 combat sorties were dispatched from the mainland bases, primarily Rio Gallegos, Rio Grande and San Julian, and that 106 of them reached targets in the Falklands. 16 FAA aircraft were lost in these attacks as were three CANA aircraft. By 26 May the struggle was effectively over and CdoFAS had lost its battle for the beach-heads and probably the War itself. Subsequent attacks on troop positions at San Carlos, initially by Skyhawks and then by Canberras, were eventually abandoned when the futility of these highly dangerous missions became clear to all. The San Carlos gun and SAM defences were to bring down a Skyhawk on 27 May, a Dagger on 29 May and a high-flying reconnaisssance Learjet on 7 June.

# DEFEAT

On the Falkland Islands themselves Argentine aircraft had been lost in many and varied ways since 1 May. The intricacies of their destruction by other aircraft, by shelling, by SAM's, in commando attacks and in accidents are detailed elsewhere, but by the time British forces began their assault on Darwin and the abandoned Goose Green airstrip on 28 May few of the 60 deployed aircraft were still airworthy. The battle for Goose Green saw the destruction of two more Pucaras and an MB-339A, one of the former and the latter being brought down near the airfield in the evening murk. It required virtually all the remaining airworthy Ejercito and FAA helicopters to carry in overnight reinforcements from Port Stanley but the effort was in vain and on 29 May Comodoro Pedrozo, the senior military officer at Darwin, surrendered his forces to the British.

By 30 May the need for dramatic success was vital to rekindle Argentine hope at home and on the Islands. It came in almost bizarre fashion that day in the form of a desperate operation that combined a cold-blooded and potentially successful CANA Super Etendard mission against the British carrier group with a near-suicidal FAA plan to achieve the same result. The circumstances surrounding the mission, which led Argentina to believe that serious damage had been inflicted on 'Invincible', are described in detail in other sections of this book but it must be recorded here that the FAA and CANA scored a domestic propaganda coup of some substance with the claim. The FAA also lost two Skyhawks and their courageous pilots in the process. However, while the Royal Navy escaped with no more than another nasty fright, and Argentina rejoiced at their "success", the British forces on East Falkland continued to consolidate their positions.

On 1 June the Sea Harriers at last destroyed an FAA C-130 when its crew misjudged their distance from the CAP. There were no survivors.

The first week of June was notable for its generally poor weather and few CdoFAS missions were undertaken from the mainland. The few Pucaras that remained at Port Stanley in airworthy condition were equally quiet. Between 26 May and 7 June, 110 mainland FAA fighter-bomber sorties were planned but only 57, mainly those of late May, were adjudged to have reached their targets. As noted earlier, three Skyhawks and a Dagger had been lost. That they were all lost to SAM's is indicative that, late in the day, the FAA had nearly perfected the art of avoiding the Sea Harrier CAP's (it should also be recognised that there were fewer CAP's over the Falklands in early June and that when on station they were obliged to leave sooner to return to their carriers that had, for much of the time, been stationed well to the east of the Islands).

The events of 8 June sharply reminded both sides of the other's capabilities. Following the inactivity of early June CdoFAS was alerted to the presence that morning of British Fleet Auxiliary vessels disembarking troops in the area of Fitzroy. At last a good, poorly defended target had presented itself and after a long spell of inactivity the FAA was only too anxious to take advantage of such unexpected British carelessness. With the aid of excellent intelligence, provided by Argentine observation posts near the Fitzroy anchorage, CdoFAS rapidly planned and launched a maximum-effort strike. A complex series of interrelated sorties involving Mirages, Canberras, Daggers, Skyhawks and even Learjet lead-ships were used in the attack and, perhaps with more luck than the FAA would care to acknowledge, they succeeded in destroying 'Sir Galahad' and seriously damaging 'Sir Tristram' and 'Plymouth', the latter in Falkland Sound.

Sadly for one of the Skyhawk squadrons CdoFAS made the unwise decision to return in strength to the scene of these triumphs in the closing minutes of daylight and as one flight was decimated by Sea Harriers another was all but destroyed by curtains of SAM's and anti-aircraft gunfire. However, despite the loss of three Skyhawks and their pilots, CdoFAS regarded the loss of 'Sir Galahad' in Port Pleasant as a considerable triumph, grossly overestimating the number of British casualties, if not the damage to British morale. The FAA's effort on 8 June had indeed been considerable, with 31 of the 37 planned sorties adjudged to have reached targets.

The successes of 8 June were to be the last enjoyed by the FAA over the Falklands. By then the Argentine forces on East Falkland could do little but fight a desperate rearguard action and on 9 June both the FAA Chinooks were successfully evacuated from Port Stanley to the mainland. A further 65 attack sorties were planned by CdoFAS after 8 June before the surrender but only 27, many of them by nocturnal Canberras, reached targets.

The last serious damage to be inflicted on a British warship occurred in the early hours of 12 June when, after at least one earlier unsuccessful attempt, an MM.38 Exocet was fired from a makeshift launch vehicle at 'Glamorgan'. The destroyer was returning from a night bombardment in support of British troops and, when struck by the missile, was some 15 miles offshore. The damage was severe and had not the crew reacted as well as they did, the ship might have been lost.

A final flurry of activity by FAA Skyhawks startled the British near Port Stanley on 13 June but no damage resulted. These Skyhawks again survived heavy SAM and anti-aircraft fire to return safely but a Canberra was brought down that night by a Sea Dart at 0155Z and, in the process, became the final casualty of the air war.

In cold statistical terms the air war cost the FAA 36 mainland-based aircraft in combat, at least one in an operational accident and a further 26 were lost or abandoned on the Falkland Islands. These 63 aircraft and helicopters were lost with the associated deaths of 41 flight crew, officers and men, as well as a further 14 killed on the ground on the Falklands (the frequently quoted FAA total of "36 pilots" killed is, in reality, the total number of officers killed).

The Armada lost a total of 14 aircraft and helicopters in all theatres with the loss of four pilots while 20 Ejercito helicopters were lost in action and another in a mainland training accident. The Prefectura lost three aircraft on the Falklands. Thus, exactly 100 Argentine aircraft were lost in circumstances directly attributable to the War with Britain and 57 of those were aircraft deployed to the Falklands.

Significant among the welter of published FAA statistics are those relating to operational flight hours. Throughout the operational period 12,454 hours were flown, of which 2,782 were by the combat jets, 7,719 by the transports and 1,953 by other aircraft including the impressed civilian machines. A total of 505 combat missions were, according to the statistics, planned and 445 of them were launched. Of these, approximately 280 reached their targets.

# ARGENTINA'S AIRCRAFT LOSSES

*To be read in conjunction with the appropriate Individual Aircraft Details and Unit Histories. Losses of each type are listed in date and time order. The number in the left-hand column is cumulative, leading to the final total of Argentine aircraft losses.*

## DAGGER A                                      Losses 11

| 1  | C-433 | Grupo 6 de Caza | 1.5.82  | 1941Z  |
|----|-------|-----------------|---------|--------|
| 2  | C-428 | Grupo 6 de Caza | 21.5.82 | 1330Z  |
| 3  | C-409 | Grupo 6 de Caza | 21.5.82 | 1735Z  |
| 4  | C-404 | Grupo 6 de Caza | 21.5.82 | c1750Z |
| 5  | C-403 | Grupo 6 de Caza | 21.5.82 | c1750Z |
| 6  | C-407 | Grupo 6 de Caza | 21.5.82 | c1750Z |
| 7  | C-437 | Grupo 6 de Caza | 23.5.82 | c1900Z |
| 8  | C-419 | Grupo 6 de Caza | 24.5.82 | c1415Z |
| 9  | C-430 | Grupo 6 de Caza | 24.5.82 | c1415Z |
| 10 | C-410 | Grupo 6 de Caza | 24.5.82 | c1415Z |
| 11 | C-436 | Grupo 6 de Caza | 29.5.82 | 1500Z  |

## MIRAGE IIIEA                                  Losses 2

| 12 | I-015 | Grupo 8 de Caza | 1.5.82 | 1910Z  |
|----|-------|-----------------|--------|--------|
| 13 | I-019 | Grupo 8 de Caza | 1.5.82 | c1915Z |

## A-4B/A-4C SKYHAWK                             Losses 19

| 14 | C-303 | Grupo 4 de Caza | 9.5.82  | unknown |
|----|-------|-----------------|---------|---------|
| 15 | C-313 | Grupo 4 de Caza | 9.5.82  | unknown |
| 16 | C-246 | Grupo 5 de Caza | 12.5.82 | 1644Z   |
| 17 | C-208 | Grupo 5 de Caza | 12.5.82 | 1644Z   |
| 18 | C-206 | Grupo 5 de Caza | 12.5.82 | 1644Z   |
| 19 | C-248 | Grupo 5 de Caza | 12.5.82 | 1725Z   |
| 20 | C-309 | Grupo 4 de Caza | 21.5.82 | 1605Z   |
| 21 | C-325 | Grupo 4 de Caza | 21.5.82 | 1605Z   |
| 22 | C-242 | Grupo 5 de Caza | 23.5.82 | 1650Z   |
| 23 | C-305 | Grupo 4 de Caza | 24.5.82 | c1630Z  |
| 24 | C-244 | Grupo 5 de Caza | 25.5.82 | c1230Z  |
| 25 | C-319 | Grupo 4 de Caza | 25.5.82 | c1530Z  |
| 26 | C-304 | Grupo 4 de Caza | 25.5.82 | 1544Z   |
| 27 | C-215 | Grupo 5 de Caza | 27.5.82 | c2000Z  |
| 28 | C-301 | Grupo 4 de Caza | 30.5.82 | c1735Z  |
| 29 | C-310 | Grupo 4 de Caza | 30.5.82 | c1736Z  |
| 30 | C-226 | Grupo 5 de Caza | 8.6.82  | 1945Z   |
| 31 | C-228 | Grupo 5 de Caza | 8.6.82  | c1946Z  |
| 32 | C-204 | Grupo 5 de Caza | 8.6.82  | c1947Z  |

## CANBERRA B.62                                 Losses 2

| 33 | B-110 | Grupo 2 de Bombardeo | 1.5.82  | 2047Z |
|----|-------|----------------------|---------|-------|
| 34 | B-108 | Grupo 2 de Bombardeo | 14.6.82 | 0155Z |

## PUCARA                                        Losses 25

| 35 | A-527 | Grupo 3 de Ataque | 1.5.82  | c1125Z |
|----|-------|-------------------|---------|--------|
| 36 | A-506 | Grupo 3 de Ataque | 1.5.82  | c1125Z |
| 37 | A-517 | Grupo 3 de Ataque | 1.5.82  | c1125Z |
| 38 | A-502 | Grupo 3 de Ataque | 15.5.82 | c0740Z |
| 39 | A-520 | Grupo 3 de Ataque | 15.5.82 | c0740Z |
| 40 | A-523 | Grupo 3 de Ataque | 15.5.82 | c0740Z |
| 41 | A-529 | Grupo 3 de Ataque | 15.5.82 | c0740Z |
| 42 | A-552 | Grupo 3 de Ataque | 15.5.82 | c0740Z |
| 43 | A-556 | Grupo 3 de Ataque | 15.5.82 | c0740Z |
| 44 | A-531 | Grupo 3 de Ataque | 21.5.82 | c1300Z |
| 45 | A-511 | Grupo 3 de Ataque | 21.5.82 | c1510Z |
| 46 | A-537 | Grupo 3 de Ataque | 28.5.82 | c1500Z |
| 47 | A-555 | Grupo 3 de Ataque | 28.5.82 | 2009Z  |
| 48 | A-509 | Grupo 3 de Ataque | 14.6.82 | 2359Z  |
| 49 | A-513 | Grupo 3 de Ataque | 14.6.82 | 2359Z  |
| 50 | A-514 | Grupo 3 de Ataque | 14.6.82 | 2359Z  |
| 51 | A-515 | Grupo 3 de Ataque | 14.6.82 | 2359Z  |
| 52 | A-516 | Grupo 3 de Ataque | 14.6.82 | 2359Z  |
| 53 | A-522 | Grupo 3 de Ataque | 14.6.82 | 2359Z  |
| 54 | A-528 | Grupo 3 de Ataque | 14.6.82 | 2359Z  |
| 55 | A-532 | Grupo 3 de Ataque | 14.6.82 | 2359Z  |
| 56 | A-533 | Grupo 3 de Ataque | 14.6.82 | 2359Z  |
| 57 | A-536 | Grupo 3 de Ataque | 14.6.82 | 2359Z  |

| | | | | |
|---|---|---|---|---|
| 58 | A-549 | Grupo 3 de Ataque | *14.6.82* | *2359Z* |
| 59 | A-540 | Grupo 4 de Ataque | *unknown* | *unknown* |

## C-130E HERCULES — Loss 1

| | | | | |
|---|---|---|---|---|
| 60 | TC-63 | Grupo 1 de Transporte Aereo (Escuadron I) | *1.6.82* | *1346Z* |

## LEARJET 35A — Loss 1

| | | | | |
|---|---|---|---|---|
| 61 | T-24 | Grupo 1 de Aerofotografico | *7.6.82* | *1203Z* |

## BELL 212 — Losses 2

| | | | | |
|---|---|---|---|---|
| 62 | H-83 | Grupo 7 de COIN Escuadron Helicopteros | *14.6.82* | *2359Z* |
| 63 | H-85 | Grupo 7 de COIN Escuadron Helicopteros | *14.6.82* | *2359Z* |

## A-4Q SKYHAWK — Losses 3

| | | | | |
|---|---|---|---|---|
| 64 | 0660 | 3 Escuadrilla de Caza y Ataque | *21.5.82* | *c1812Z* |
| 65 | 0667 | 3 Escuadrilla de Caza y Ataque | *21.5.82* | *c1812Z* |
| 66 | 0665 | 3 Escuadrilla de Caza y Ataque | *21.5.82* | *c1830Z* |

## MB-339A — Losses 5

| | | | | |
|---|---|---|---|---|
| 67 | 0764 | 1 Esc de Ataque | *3.5.82* | *c1900Z* |
| 68 | 0765 | 1 Esc de Ataque | *28.5.82* | *c2000Z* |
| 69 | 0761 | 1 Esc de Ataque | *14.6.82* | *2359Z* |
| 70 | 0763 | 1 Esc de Ataque | *14.6.82* | *2359Z* |
| 71 | 0767 | 1 Esc de Ataque | *14.6.82* | *2359Z* |

## T-34C MENTOR — Losses 4

| | | | | |
|---|---|---|---|---|
| 72 | 0719 | 4 Esc de Ataque | *15.5.82* | *c0740Z* |
| 73 | 0726 | 4 Esc de Ataque | *15.5.82* | *c0740Z* |
| 74 | 0729 | 4 Esc de Ataque | *15.5.82* | *c0740Z* |
| 75 | 0730 | 4 Esc de Ataque | *15.5.82* | *c0740Z* |

## ALOUETTE III — Loss 1

| | | | | |
|---|---|---|---|---|
| 76 | 0649 | 1 Escuadrilla de Helicopteros | *2.5.82* | *1858Z* |

## LYNX HAS.23 — Loss 1

| | | | | |
|---|---|---|---|---|
| 77 | 0735 | 1 Escuadrilla de Helicopteros | *2.5.82* | *unknown* |

## SKYVAN — Losses 2

| | | | | |
|---|---|---|---|---|
| 78 | PA-54 | Prefectura Naval | *3/4.5.82* | *unknown* |
| 79 | PA-50 | Prefectura Naval | *15.5.82* | *c0740Z* |

## SA.330L PUMA — Loss 1

| | | | | |
|---|---|---|---|---|
| 80 | PA-12 | Prefectura Naval | *14.6.82* | *2359Z* |

## A-109A HIRUNDO — Losses 3

| | | | | |
|---|---|---|---|---|
| 81 | AE-337 | CAB601 Ca de Ataque | *23.5.82* | *c1330Z* |
| 82 | AE-331 | CAB601 Ca de Ataque | *14.6.82* | *2359Z* |
| 83 | AE-334 | CAB601 Ca de Ataque | *14.6.82* | *2359Z* |

## UH-1H IROQUOIS — Losses 9

| | | | | |
|---|---|---|---|---|
| 84 | AE-406 | CAB601 Ca de Asalto B | *14.6.82* | *2359Z* |
| 85 | AE-409 | CAB601 Ca de Asalto B | *14.6.82* | *2359Z* |
| 86 | AE-410 | CAB601 Ca de Asalto B | *14.6.82* | *2359Z* |
| 87 | AE-412 | CAB601 Ca de Asalto B | *14.6.82* | *2359Z* |
| 88 | AE-413 | CAB601 Ca de Asalto B | *14.6.82* | *2359Z* |
| 89 | AE-417 | CAB601 Ca de Asalto B | *14.6.82* | *2359Z* |
| 90 | AE-418 | CAB601 Ca de Asalto B | *14.6.82* | *2359Z* |
| 91 | AE-422 | CAB601 Ca de Asalto B | *14.6.82* | *2359Z* |
| 92 | AE-424 | CAB601 Ca de Asalto B | *14.6.82* | *2359Z* |

## SA.330L PUMA — Losses 6

| | | | | |
|---|---|---|---|---|
| 93 | AE-504 | CAB601 Ca de Asalto A | *3.4.82* | *1505Z* |
| 94 | AE-505 | CAB601 Ca de Asalto A | *9.5.82* | *1907Z* |
| 95 | AE-501 | CAB601 Ca de Asalto A | *21.5.82* | *c1100Z* |
| 96 | AE-503 | CAB601 Ca de Asalto A | *23.5.82* | *c1330Z* |
| 97 | AE-500 | CAB601 Ca de Asalto A | *23.5.82* | *c1330Z* |
| 98 | AE-508 | CAB601 Ca de Asalto A | *30.5.82* | *c1230Z* |

## CH-47C CHINOOK — Losses 2

| | | | | |
|---|---|---|---|---|
| 99 | AE-521 | CAB601 Ca de Asalto A | *21.5.82* | *c1100Z* |
| 100 | AE-520 | CAB601 Ca de Asalto A | *14.6.82* | *2359Z* |

*Initially immobilised by cannon-fire from the 1(F) Squadron Harrier XZ963 of Flt Lt Mark Hare on 21.5.82, the CAB601 Puma AE-501 was subsequently demolished five days later in a CBU attack by Sqdn Ldr Jerry Pook in XZ988.* (815 Sqdn 'Exeter' Flight)

*Close inspection of the inverted boom of AE-501 revealed the Aerospatiale construction number "1540". Lying adjacent to a mined area near Mount Kent, the wreckage was difficult to reach on foot and, probably because of its inaccessibility, it was still there in early 1985.* (SAC K. Gollop, RAF)

*The fuselage of the Grupo 6 de Caza Dagger C-403 remained substantially intact after it was brought down by an AIM-9L from the 801 Squadron Sea Harrier ZA190 of Lt Steve Thomas near Green Hill Bridge, West Falkland on 21.5.82. It was later retrieved and temporarily "displayed" at RAF Kelly's Garden near San Carlos settlement.* (815 Sqdn 'Exeter' Flight)

*This Grupo 6 de Caza Dagger wreck, lying to the north-east of First Mount, Pebble Island, is thought to be that of C-410, brought down by the 800 Squadron Sea Harrier ZA193 of Lt Dave Smith on 24.5.82. Teniente Carlos Castillo was killed in the incident.* (815 Sqdn 'Exeter' Flight)

*The rotor-blades were virtually all that remained recognisable of the CAB601 Chinook AE-521 after Flt Lt Mark Hare's cannon attack on 21.5.82. The incinerated wreckage was still visible in early 1985, some 300 yards from the Puma AE-501.* (SAC K. Gollop, RAF)

*Little remained of the CAB601 Puma AE-508 after its loss in mysterious circumstances on 30.5.82. The wreckage (seen here on 3.9.84) lies about two miles north-east of the summit of Mount Kent.* (Fg Off S. Martin, RAF)

*Luna's crater. The remains of the Grupo 6 de Caza Dagger C-409, from which Primer Teniente Hector Luna successfully ejected on 21.5.82 near Teal River Inlet. He had fallen victim to a Sidewinder launched by Lt Cdr Rod Frederiksen of 800 Squadron in Sea Harrier XZ455.* (815 Sqdn 'Exeter' Flight)

*Brought down by a Stinger SAM on 21.5.82, Capitan Jorge Benitez of Grupo 3 de Ataque ejected safely from his Pucara and walked to safety. The wreckage of A-531 was little disturbed and was still in evidence near Flat Shanty settlement in early 1985.* (815 Sqdn 'Exeter' Flight)

# MB-339

# 1 ESCUADRILLA DE ATAQUE

For many years 1 Escuadrilla de Ataque had served CANA in the dual roles of jet training and light attack. It had long been established at Punta Indio, Buenos Aires and in March 1982 was the sole flying element of its parent wing, the 4 Escuadra Aeronaval. At that time it was equipped with the Italian manufactured MB-326GB and MB-339A light attack aircraft, universally known to their crews as "Aermacchis". The MB-326GB's had served the unit well for many years, but the 10 MB-339A's had not been taken on CANA charge until 1980/81 and, in early 1982, their pilots and support staff were still engaged in some development work with the aircraft.

1 Escuadrilla's initial involvement in the campaign was, perhaps, curious but eventually it proved to be substantial and as bitter as that of any of the recognised first-line combat units. It would appear that during the early planning of Operacion "Rosario" it was realised that there might be a military reaction from the neighbouring state of Chile to the recovery of the Falklands. In anticipation of that, or perhaps simply as part of a general naval alert, the entire Squadron was deployed on 2 April "along the whole Argentine coast". 16 aircraft, presumed to have been all the MB-339A's and six of the MB-326GB's, were thus detached in flights to bases such as Trelew, Espora and Rio Grande. It is thought that the camouflage that replaced the bright red and white training colours of the MB-339A's may have been applied for that exercise, rather than as a later reaction to the possibility of battle on the Falklands. The Aermacchis remained briefly on station before returning to Punta Indio, leaving only a small detachment of MB-339A's at Rio Grande. It remained there throughout the subsequent War, flying reconnaissance sorties in the area of the Chilean border and acting in support of the aircraft later deployed to the Falklands.

The decision to place a small force of MB-339A's on the Islands was made in early April when it became apparent that the British were threatening to recover them by military means. It had always been fully understood by the military authorities that no FAA combat jets could safely operate from Stanley Airport's short runway and thus CANA would have to deploy the only attack jets in its own inventory that were capable of the operation. Four aircraft were thus detached to Rio Grande in early April for a short period of working-up before final deployment to Stanley. Although an agile and advanced training aircraft, the MB-339A was a fairly modest warplane and CANA prudently, if belatedly, asked the crews to establish exactly how best it should be used in the anti-shipping role. The unit's commander, Capitan de Corbeta Carlos Molteni, was thus given that unenviable task in the knowledge that he might have to put his new theories into practice against a British carrier battle group that was perhaps only two weeks' sailing time away. The evaluation established that all attacks would have to be made low and fast and that only the 30mm cannon and 5in rockets would be used. Because the MB-339A's unsophisticated bomb release mechanism was considered potentially dangerous (it could only release all bombs simultaneously while the aircraft flew an unacceptably hazardous line), the use of iron bombs against warships was never entertained. However, despite that considerable shortcoming, the unit believed that, in the right circumstances, the combination of twin cannon and four rocket pods could cause considerable damage, and that the anti-shipping mission was realistic.

The first pair of aircraft, thought to have been 0764/4-A-113 and 0767/4-A-116, were ferried from Rio Grande to Stanley Airport at 1200Z on 24 April soon after a pair of 4 Escuadrilla Mentors. The MB-339A's were escorted by a CANA King Air 200 that had left Rio Grande a few minutes earlier. With good route and destination weather, the deployment was undertaken without incident and a second pair of aircraft followed within a day or so. The third, and final, pair of MB-339A's are believed to have been deployed to Stanley Airport some three weeks later, on 14 May. The precise sequence of aircraft delivery is not known but the six deployed aircraft were:

| | | |
|---|---|---|
| 0761/4-A-110 | 0764/4-A-113 | 0766/4-A-115 |
| 0763/4-A-112 | 0765/4-A-114 | 0767/4-A-116 |

The 1 Escuadrilla detachment was allocated a small, improvised parking area on the southern side of the runway, towards the eastern threshold and away from the con-

This anonymous and ambulance-configured Alouette III of 1 Escuadrilla de Helicopteros made several brief visits to 'Uganda' in 6.82, usually carrying International Red Cross Commission personnel on inspection duties. Like the similarly-used CAB601 Puma, the Alouette wore none of its normal external markings during the seven-week deployment on the hospital ship 'Bahia Paraiso'. (Capt J. G. Clark)

When seen here at Stanley Airport shortly after the surrender, MB-339A 0767/4-A-116 of 1 Escuadrilla de Ataque had been on the Falklands for more than seven weeks. Although certainly not airworthy since late 5.82, all British efforts to destroy it during the fighting had clearly failed and, apart from some minor shrapnel punctures, the aircraft was in generally good condition – until the souvenir hunters arrived! The 30mm DEFA553 cannon pods and underwing auxiliary fuel tanks are still fitted.
(Paul R. G. Haley, 'SOLDIER')

RAF personnel quickly and somewhat crudely made safe the ejection seats in all three MB-339A's and eventually their undercarriages were intentionally collapsed as well. Sadly, vandals and souvenir hunters ignored all instructions to stay away from the aircraft and very soon the hulks were in such a state that they were regarded, by the British, simply as rubbish, there being no initial thoughts of preservation or restoration. 0761/4-A-110 is seen here before dismantling in early 1983.
(Richard Gardner)

gested main apron area. However, the location was dreadfully vulnerable to air attack.

The unit flew several armed reconnaissance and terrain familiarisation sorties during its early days on the Islands, but had made no contact with the British Task Force by 1 May when Stanley Airport was attacked for the first time. An attack had been anticipated but, unlike the FAA, CANA had not had the luxury of a suitable dispersal airstrip for its MB-339A jets and thus the unit was extremely fortunate to survive the initial 800 Sqdn Sea Harrier air raid without damage, suffering only a showering of earth when a CBU fell in its area.

During early May the line-astern attack technique that had been evolved at Rio Grande was practised under simulated combat conditions. At any moment the unit was liable to have been asked to perform such a mission against the enemy and the exercises had real urgency. It was during such an armed reconnaissance mission on 3 May that the unit suffered its first aircraft loss. At 1806Z two aircraft, piloted by Capitan de Corbeta Molteni and Teniente de Fragata Carlos Benitez, took-off to investigate and attack a ship at sea, some 60 miles south-east of Port Stanley. The flight departed through a 900ft overcast with initial cruise visibility of about three miles and although that deteriorated en route a thorough search of the target area was, nevertheless, still possible. Unfortunately, nothing was found. The mission had been undertaken in radio-silence and Molteni and Benitez returned to Port Stanley without any discussion. Molteni landed safely but, behind him, Benitez drifted away from the centre-line while low on the final approach. His aircraft, 0764/4-A-113, clipped the rocks located several hundred yards short of the runway's eastern threshold and, with a wing torn off, the MB-339A crashed into the cliffs. Benitez did not eject and was killed in the immediate explosion and fire.

It was not until 21 May that 1 Escuadrilla finally met the enemy in combat. A two-aircraft mission had been planned on the previous day to depart at first light on 21 May to reconnoitre the eastern side of Falkland Sound, in particular the San Carlos Water and Grantham Sound areas. Naval intelligence was of the view that it might be in that locality that the imminently expected British landings would be attempted. Thus the MB-339A's were to fly at low level overland to Port San Carlos and then follow the coast south to Darwin, before turning east for Port Stanley and home. Their mission was delayed while early morning reports of landings were assessed, and then again when the aircraft of Teniente de Navio Horacio Talarico became unserviceable when it was due to leave the apron for the runway. The importance of the mission was such that Teniente de Navio Guillermo Crippa was instructed to continue on his own and, at 1304Z, he took-off in 0766/4-A-115 (the launch time, from CANA, seems suspect — the aircraft probably left several minutes earlier). When he reached Falkland Sound mist and glare caused him to change his mind about entering the area from overhead Port San Carlos and he thus turned north towards Foul Bay, preferring to make his run from the north with the sun behind him. Crippa expected to meet the British fleet further north than their actual position but he quickly found the outer escorting warships off Jersey

Point, West Falkland. He continued his run-in towards San Carlos Water at a height of 500ft and was about to make an easy cannon attack on an unsuspecting Lynx when he noticed a frigate, beyond the helicopter, directly in his path. He thus ignored the Lynx and made a somewhat rushed cannon and rocket attack on 'Argonaut', causing minor damage and some crew injuries. By that time Crippa was under fire from several warships and he was obliged to follow a low zig-zag track through the hills behind Ajax Bay until he reached Port Sussex. He then turned north again in order to count the ships that he had seen, although he kept well clear of their gunfire! Finally, he turned south for Darwin and then east for Port Stanley (where he was equally anxious to avoid any over-zealous Argentine anti-aircraft gunfire). At that moment Crippa's objective assessment of the British naval strength in the San Carlos area was of fundamental value to Argentina and he was to be subsequently decorated for the mission.

Little is known of 1 Escuadrilla's activities in the immediate aftermath of the British landings and it is possible that no sorties were launched for some days. The unit suffered many technical problems during May and operations were seriously affected at that time. Condensation inside the aircraft wings badly affected electrical circuits and, as the winter hardened, freezing temperatures exacerbated the problem. In such conditions batteries would not hold an adequate start-up charge overnight and thus they were removed from the aircraft every night for warm storage — with consequential operational delays! After 21 May Stanley Airport was subjected to repeated air and naval attack but, in spite of several near misses, it appears that the unit survived until 28 May without further serious damage. The greatest problem facing 1 Escuadrilla continued to be the serviceability state of the MB-339A's.

By 28 May the Argentine situation at Darwin and Goose Green had reached a critical stage and all available air power was mustered to slow the progress of the advancing British forces. The FAA's Grupo 3 Pucara and the MB-339A crews were briefed accordingly, but dreadful weather over the Darwin and Port Stanley areas severely restricted operations. After some early Pucara sorties were successfully launched, Capitan de Corbeta Molteni and Teniente de Fragata Daniel Miguel took-off for Goose Green during the afternoon. However, shortly before they reached Darwin, they were told by the FAA commander at Goose Green to abandon the attack because of low cloud and limited local visibility. Both aircraft thus returned to Stanley Airport and were readied for a second mission when the weather improved. By 1830Z the aircraft were ready but high cross-winds at the Airport prevented both the MB-339A's and a pair of Pucaras from departing until shortly before 2000Z. After following a low-level course across East Falkland, both MB-339A's were able to make low, fast cannon and rocket attacks on the British positions in the vicinity of Darwin School. The two aircraft both received considerable ground fire from a variety of weapons and it was a Blowpipe round fired by Marine Strange of 3 Cdo Bde Air Defence Troop that destroyed 0765/4-A-114. As Miguel was rocketing British positions his aircraft was hit and it dived into the ground from low level and exploded. The pilot did not eject and was killed in the crash. Molteni, initially unaware of the loss of his wingman, returned safely to Port Stanley at full power while following a low-level, zig-zag course in the hope of evading any searching Sea Harriers.

In the mistaken belief that Super Etendards had been deployed to Port Stanley, 801 Sqdn Sea Harriers attacked the 1 Escuadrilla area with 1,000lb bombs on 29 May. On the following day 1(F) Sqdn Harriers attacked the unit and although the small detachment apparently suffered no serious damage in either assault it would appear that CANA then took the decision to terminate the 1 Escuadrilla operation. What would seem to have been the only airworthy aircraft, 0766/4-A-115, was flown out to Rio Grande on 30 May and the other three were left to their fate. There have been unconfirmed reports that 0763/4-A-112 received minor damage on 29 May, but early British inspection after the surrender of 14 June indicated that, with the exception of some minor shrapnel damage to 0767/4-A-116, the three surviving MB-339A's were in excellent condition. Their fate was probably sealed by technical and support shortcomings, rather than by battle damage. After capture, the RAF took the immediate (and unnecessary) precaution of firing their ejec-

It could be said that the decision to deploy MB-339A's to Stanley Airport was a mistake, for the aircraft was "lightweight" and far from ideal from the task in hand or the weather encountered. Nevertheless a 1 Escuadrilla de Ataque machine caught 'Argonaut' unawares on 21.5.82 and, with better luck, the unit might have caused damage to other isolated warships earlier in the conflict. Here 0763/4-A-112 lies forlornly at RAF Stanley on 19.10.82.          (Richard Gardner)

Both sides suffered fatal operational accidents. The wreckage of the MB-339A 0764/4-A-113 of Teniente de Fragata Carlos Benitez could still be seen in early 1985 lying among the rocks to the north of Christina Bay. It had crashed well over a mile short of the Stanley Airport runway on 3.5.82.

(Flt Lt R. Robinson, RAF)

**I BRIGADA AEREA
(FAA)**

**GRUPO 2
DE BOMBARDEO (FAA)**

**GRUPO 3
DE ATAQUE (FAA)**

**GRUPO 5
DE CAZA (FAA)**

**ESCUADRON
HELICOPTEROS (FAA)**

**GRUPO 4
DE CAZA (FAA)**

**V BRIGADA AEREA
(FAA)**

**VIII BRIGADA AEREA
(FAA)**

**GRUPO 6
DE CAZA (FAA)**

**VII BRIGADA AEREA
(FAA)**

**ESCUADRON C-130
(FAA)**

**BATALLON DE
AVIACION DE
COMBATE 601 (CAE)**

**1 ESCUADRILLA
DE ATAQUE (CANA)**

**2 ESCUADRILLA
DE CAZA Y ATAQUE (CANA)**

**3 ESCUADRILLA
DE CAZA Y ATAQUE (CANA)**

# UNIT BADGES OF THE FUERZA AEREA ARGENTINA, COMANDO AVIACION NAVAL ARGENTINA AND COMANDO AVIACION DEL EJERCITO

A-4Q Skyhawk 0657/3-A-304 of 3 Escuadrilla de Caza y Ataque is seen here at Espora during 11.82. The camouflage was adopted by CANA after the heavy losses on 21.5.82 when a flight of three 3 Escuadrilla aircraft was lost to Sea Harriers, the British successes being attributed to the navy grey colours being highly visible over the South Atlantic and Falklands' murk. The adoption of this revised scheme, however, is not thought to have taken place until after the end of the conflict. (Via A. Price)

A-4C Skyhawk C-321 of Grupo 4 de Caza is seen here at Mendoza during 11.82. C-321 was one of the survivors of the mission that took place on 30.5.82 and is marked with the dated silhouette of 'Invincible' which Grupo 4 believed was damaged in the combined Super Etendard/Skyhawk attack. Only the "last two" of the serial appears on the aircraft's tailpipe. A Grupo 4 F-86F Sabre can be seen in the background. (Via A. Price)

A-4B Skyhawk C-231 of Grupo 5 de Caza is seen here at Villa Reynolds during 11.82. The aircraft is marked with two ships' silhouettes which reflect its role in two successful missions. After the missions of 12.5.82 Grupo 5, unlike Grupo 4, stopped dating silhouettes which appear to reflect both damaged and sunken vessels. Most of the Group 5 A-4B's noted during late-1982 exhibited at least one ship silhouette.

*Grupo 6 de Caza Dagger C-414 is seen, probably at Tandil, in late-1982. The Dagger is marked with a single ship's silhouette which is believed to indicate its role in the attack against 'Plymouth' in Falkland Sound on 8.6.82. That mission was typical of many air attacks on British shipping when Dagger pilots over-estimated their success (although 'Plymouth' was indeed badly damaged) whilst Royal Navy gunners were adamant in their claims to have brought down aircraft; in fact all Daggers had returned safely to Rio Grande.*
*(via S. Mafé Huertas)*

*The tail unit of a Grupo 6 de Caza Dagger, which is possibly that of C-407 which was brought down on 21.5.82 (but see the main text) was later recovered from its crash site near Port Howard, West Falkland and subsequently shipped back to RAF Odiham. The port side paintwork shows standard Grupo 6 insignia but when the FAA paintwork was removed from the starboard side the badge of an unidentified Israeli unit emerged. Further evidence of the Dagger's Israeli origin was found in the wreckage, when a cockpit plate revealed the marking "05-4XFWY". Sadly the complete tail assembly no longer exists.* *(Simon Van Tromp)*

*An unidentified Mirage IIIEA of Grupo 8 de Caza leaves Rio Gallegos for an operational sortie during 5.82. The aircraft carries a Matra R530 AAM on its centreline pylon and two 1700 litre underwing tanks. These tanks were carried on all Mirage and Dagger sorties.* *(FAA)*

Against the open and featureless Patagonian landscape ground-crews make their final checks to Mirage IIIEA I-014 of Grupo 8 de Caza on one of the hastily-prepared dispersal pans at Rio Gallegos. In an effort to camouflage aircraft at Rio Gallegos some Mirages were parked beneath the awnings and overhangs of the airport terminal buildings, just visible in the distance. Note also the A-4B Skyhawk of Grupo 5 de Caza in the background. (FAA)

Of all the aircraft operated during the Falklands conflict perhaps the most feared by British Forces were the five Super Etendards of 2 Escuadrilla de Caza y Ataque. Two of the aircraft, 0751/3-A-201 and 0752/3-A-202, are seen here in a postwar view at Espora, during 9.82. 0752 took part in the attack against 'Sheffield' on 4.5.82 and undertook a further mission on 30.5.82 whilst 0751 was held in reserve as a valuable spares source throughout the conflict. (K. Ebata)

The Exocet attack against 'Sheffield' on 4.5.82 was effectively the swansong of the SP-2H Neptune in CANA use. 0707/2-P-111 and 0708/2-P-112 of the Escuadrilla de Exploracion were both involved in missions with the Super Etendards but had been withdrawn from use when photographed at BAN Espora in 9.82. (K. Ebata)

The S-2E Trackers of the Escuadrilla Antisubmarina played a significant role in early operations from the carrier '25 de Mayo' and an evaluation of their potential deployment as a successor to the SP-2H Neptune in the Super Etendard guidance role was later undertaken (although results were disappointing). Typical of those used was 0700/2-AS-21 seen here at BAN Espora during 9.82. (K. Ebata)

Seen here in happier times, Canberra B.62 B-108 of Grupo 2 de Bombardeo had the misfortune to become the last FAA aircraft to be lost during the War. It was brought down over Mount Kent shortly before midnight (local time) on 13.6.82 with the loss of one of its crew. In fact B-108 had probably logged several successful missions against British Forces before being caught at medium-high level by a Sea Dart fired from 'Exeter'.

(Aviacion LatinoAmericana)

MB-339A 0767/4-A-116 of 1 Escuadrilla de Ataque was one of three such aircraft that were surrendered to British Forces at Stanley Airport on 14.6.82. When found on the CANA hardstanding (at the edge of the runway) the aircraft was in sound condition and with only very minor damage evident. The hastily-applied yellow fuselage band had been added for identification purposes shortly after its arrival at Stanley.

(Ministry of Defence)

Perhaps one of the most daring of exploits during the Falklands War was the SAS raid on Pebble Island on 15.5.82. Amongst those aircraft immobilised during the attack were four 4 Escuadrilla de Ataque T-34C Mentors, one of which -- 0730/412 -- is seen here. The major damage was to the engine compartment, but the aircraft was nevertheless left in a clearly repairable state as this 7.82 photograph shows. Of course, no such repair facilities were available and twelve months later the hulk was removed to the "Rabbit Range" weapons range on East Falkland.

In spite of their general robustness and rugged construction, together with a remarkable short-field performance making them well suited for operations within the Falkland Islands, the two PNA Skyvans enjoyed relatively little success. Ultimately operations were defeated by the terrain and, in the case of PA-54, by shrapnel damage from Royal Navy gunfire during the night of 3/4.5.82. PA-54 remained, immobilised, on Stanley Racecourse until finally demolished by British artillery fire during the night of 12/13.6.82, as evidenced by this view taken on 24.7.82. Eventually small pieces of the wreck were removed and shipped back to the Fleet Air Arm Museum, Yeovilton.

(Simon Van Tromp)

The PNA Puma PA-12 lies abandoned at the side of Ross Road, near to the entrance of Government House, Port Stanley and in the exact spot where Royal Marines of NP8901 surrendered to Argentine "Buzo Tactico" marine commandos on 2.4.82. The Puma had already been extensively cannibalised, probably by CAB601 personnel, well before the Argentine surrender on 14.6.82. The crudely applied yellow identification bands can be clearly seen in this view, taken on 24.7.82.

(Simon Van Tromp)

Although dogged by engine trouble for much of the conflict, the CAB601 CH-47C Chinook AE-520 was found relatively intact behind the Governor's Residence when British forces entered Port Stanley. To 18 Squadron personnel the Chinook would have been a valuable prize had they been able to start the engines satisfactorily. In the event repairs could not be carried out locally and instead AE-520 was cannibalised for the benefit of "Bravo November" and other RAF Chinooks. It is seen here on 24.7.82 just one week before it was shipped out to the United Kingdom, on 1.8.82.

(Simon Van Tromp)

Shortly before the final surrender of Argentine forces, Grupo 7 COIN/Escuadron de Helicopteros Bell 212 H-83 was abandoned by the FAA on the Port Stanley Racecourse. With total disregard to the fact that it was still in working order, souvenir hunters rapidly set upon the helicopter and when photographed, during 7.82, it was already in a very poor state. H-83 was eventually burned-out while being cut up for scrap.

Subsequently displayed at the Fleet Air Arm Museum, Grupo 3 de Ataque Pucara A-522 is seen here at Comodoro Rivadavia before its ferry flight to the Falkland Islands. In this photograph, probably taken for publicity purposes, the aircraft is armed with 2.75 inch rocket pods and three napalm cannisters on the fuselage centreline rack. The Pucara's colour scheme is typical of that applied to those aircraft that arrived in the Falklands after the Pebble Island raid.

Later to fly in Britain as ZD485, Grupo 3 de Ataque Pucara A-515 is seen at Stanley Airport shortly after the surrender of Argentine forces. The dark camouflage pattern had been applied over an earlier lighter scheme upon realisation that the latter was inappropriate for the Falklands. In the repainting process the yellow identification stripe on the fin was obliterated, a fact which supports evidence that A-515 was one of the last Pucaras to reach the Islands.

In contrast Grupo 3 de Ataque Pucara A-556 was one of the original aircraft to arrive at Stanley Airport on 2.4.82, and retains the earlier (and standard) lighter camouflage pattern. However, the crudely applied yellow fuselage band was unique to A-556 and did not appear on other Pucaras. Immobilised by the SAS on 15.5.82, the damaged hulk stands forlornly in the Pebble Island snow in 7.82 before its removal to a West Falkland Weapons range.

Looking down upon the desolation outside the FIGAS Beaver floatplane hanger shortly after 14.6.82. VP-FAT was demolished during British bombardments on 11/12.6.82 whilst its sister-aircraft, VP-FAV (on the slipway), sustained substantial damage. Any thoughts of repairing the latter were dispelled on 28.7.82 when it was blown over onto its back during a gale and completely wrecked.
(Ministry of Defence)

In seemingly pristine condition on 26.8.82 at the Helicopter Refuelling Point, RAF Stanley, is the former CAB601 "Huey" AE-424 which had been partially renovated and repainted in FIGAS livery on 'Invincible'. Its beauty, however, was only skin deep as was proven during a subsequent detailed external and internal inspection which revealed evidence of a heavy landing while in Argentine service. VP-FBD was, as a consequence, withdrawn from use and stored pending eventual display in a planned Falkland Islands' museum. The registration letters, however, lived on when they were reallocated to a FIGAS BN-2B Islander during mid-1985.
(Simon Van Tromp)

This immediately post-conflict view shows a CAB601 UH-1H Iroquois AE-413 and 2 Escuadrilla de Helicopteros Sea King 0678/2-H-234 engaged in ferrying Argentine wounded from Port Stanley to the hospital ships 'Almirante Irizar' and 'Bahia Paraiso', on 16.6.82. This was, in fact, the last occasion on which CAB601 crews were permitted to fly AE-413, although it continued to operate under British control and in support of 5 Infantry Brigade.
(Ministry of Defence)

Also seen on 16.6.82 is the anonymous CASEVAC-configured CAB601 Puma, similarly engaged in ferrying Argentine wounded from RAF Stanley to its parent vessel 'Almirante Irizar'. Unlike the UH-1H AE-413, however, this Puma was subsequently able to return to normal CAE service on mainland Argentina.
(Ministry of Defence)

tion seats and within a few days the souvenir hunters had begun their inexorable process of demolition. Within a few weeks the MB-339A's were reduced to the status of airfield rubbish and treated accordingly.

The surviving aircraft continued to fly operational sorties from Rio Grande after the War but the Squadron, numerically much weakened, had suffered badly on the Falklands. With the single exception of Crippa's dramatic mission the unit had achieved little of either public or military significance and, despite the efforts of dedicated flight and ground crews, the deployment was little short of a disaster. No operational statistics are known to have been published. Following the loss on 28 October 1982 of another MB-326GB, the unit was restored to strength in July 1983 with the receipt of 11 EMB-326GB Xavantes, transferred to CANA from surplus Brazilian stocks.

---

*1 Escuadrilla de Ataque pilots deployed to Port Stanley included:*

*Capitan de Corbeta C.E.Molteni (commander); Teniente de Navio G.O.Crippa; Teniente de Navio H.Talarico; Teniente de Fragata C.A.Benitez (KIA); Teniente de Fragata D.E.Miguel (KIA); Teniente de Corbeta R.L.Lambert.*

---

# INDIVIDUAL AIRCRAFT DETAILS

Until March 1982 1 Escuadrilla's MB-339A fleet was painted in a bright red and white training colour scheme. The ARMADA title was applied to the rear fuselage and the individual aircraft serial and call-sign/code letters were worn on the tail, below the national flag. Fuselage roundels were not worn. The camouflage applied at the time of the landings on the Falklands was of the same kind as that applied to CANA T-34C Mentors and to PNA Skyvans, consisting of dark green and tan upper, and light grey lower, surfaces. The ARMADA title was reapplied in black letters in the original location on the rear fuselage, as was the aircraft call-sign on the fin. The CANA serial, however, reappeared only in tiny numerals on the rear fuselage. The national flag was also reapplied in the same place and at the original size and, as before, no roundels were applied to the fuselage or upper wing surfaces. As far as is known, that colour scheme was standard to all MB-339A's with only the slightest of changes being made in the field. One such change is described below in the aircraft details.

As explained in the text only six aircraft were deployed to Stanley Airport with 1 Escuadrilla, the balance being held at Rio Grande and Punta Indio. The subsequent histories are concerned only with those six aircraft — as far as is known the other four remained in service at Punta Indio during 1984.

---

**0761**

In 3.82 with 1 Escuadrilla as '4-A-110'. Deployed to Stanley Airport, probably from Rio Grande, by 14.5.82 and captured intact there on 14.6.82.

Progressively stripped and smashed, it was eventually broken-down into two fuselage sections. On 17.5.83 the forward section was put on board 'St Helena' in Stanley Harbour and on 19.5.83 the vessel sailed for the UK, arriving at Falmouth 11.6.83. Off-loaded 13/14.6.83 and left by road transport for Yeovilton, arriving there the following day. Reassembled using parts of 0767/4-A-116 and put on static display in the FAAM (still resident in 5.85). The rear fuselage section of 0761, together with its wings, was taken to a weapons range on the Falklands sometime after 9.83.

**0763**

In 3.82 with 1 Escuadrilla as '4-A-112'. Deployed to Stanley Airport, probably from Rio Grande, by 14.5.82 and captured intact there on 14.6.82. Progressively stripped and smashed, it was eventually broken-down into two fuselage sections. The cockpit section was still visible at RAF Stanley in 2.85 although, by then, other parts had been removed to a Falklands weapons range.

**0764**

In 3.82 with 1 Escuadrilla as '4-A-113'. Believed to have deployed to Stanley Airport from Rio Grande on 24.4.82. Crashed in bad visibility on 3.5.82 while on final approach to Stanley Airport, killing the pilot, Teniente de Fragata Benitez. Wreckage was still visible among the rocks between Christina Bay and Fish Rock in early 1985.

**0765**

In 3.82 with 1 Escuadrilla as '4-A-114'. Deployed to Stanley Airport, probably from Rio Grande, by 14.5.82. Shot down at Goose Green on 28.5.82 by a Blowpipe missile fired by Marine Strange of 3 Cdo Bde Air Defence Troop, crashing near the airfield perimeter and killing its pilot Teniente de Fragata Miguel. Much of the wreckage was buried near the crash site (UC 632577) in late 1982 but some small pieces were left on a nearby scrap dump.

**0766**

In 3.82 with 1 Escuadrilla as '4-A-115'. Deployed to Stanley Airport, probably from Rio Grande, by 14.5.82. Following Teniente de Navio Crippa's successful reconnaissance mission and attack on 'Argonaut' on 21.5.82, it was recovered to Rio Grande 30.5.82 where it survived the War.

**0767**

In 3.82 with 1 Escuadrilla as '4-A-116'. Believed to have deployed to Stanley Airport from Rio Grande on 24.4.82. On an unknown date (presumably after 1.5.82) it acquired a crudely painted yellow band round the rear fuselage for identification purposes. Captured on 14.6.82 with some shrapnel damage to the fuselage.

Progressively stripped and smashed, it was eventually broken-down into two fuselage sections. On 17.5.83 the rear section and wings were loaded onto 'St Helena' in Stanley Harbour and on 19.5.83 the vessel sailed for the UK, arriving at Falmouth on 11.6.83. The components were off-loaded 13/14.6.83 and left for Yeovilton by road on 14.6.83, arriving the following day. They were reassembled by the FAAM and combined with the forward fuselage section of 0761/4-A-110 for display in the museum (still resident in 5.85). 0767's original cockpit section was still visible at RAF Stanley in 2.85.

# SUPER ETENDARD

## 2 ESCUADRILLA DE CAZA Y ATAQUE

It was during 1979 that CANA ordered Super Etendards from France to replace its ageing fleet of A-4Q Skyhawks. They were to operate from the aircraft carrier '25 de Mayo' and, in order to accommodate them, the elderly warship required some modification. The changes, which included the strengthening of some deck areas, were not completed until after the Falklands War. A total of 14 aircraft was ordered and, in anticipation of their delivery, some 50 personnel from the reformed 2 Escuadrilla de Caza y Ataque were sent to France in September 1980 for basic training on the type. In addition to pilot training, the courses included tuition on the primary weapons system, the AM.39 Exocet missile. That training programme was undertaken at Rochefort, Landivisiau and on the French carrier 'Clemenceau', and was completed by July 1981 when the unit returned to Argentina. The first aircraft were expected to join the 2 Escuadrilla later in the year and it was the intention that the new Squadron would work-up at the Comandante Espora base at Bahia Blanca, Buenos Aires alongside 3 Escuadrilla, the Skyhawk Squadron. Both of these units were components of CANA's 3 Escuadra Aeronaval.

2 Escuadrilla accepted the first five "SUE's" at a ceremony at Espora on 17 November 1981. They were serialled 0751/3-A-201 to 0755/3-A-205 and with them had come just five Exocet missiles. For the next four months the Squadron progressively worked-up on the aircraft and familiarised itself with the new avionics and weapons. The training received in France had been fairly basic and much work was necessary before more aircraft could usefully be employed at Espora. Thus, as the remaining nine aircraft left the production line, they were temporarily stored at Bordeaux. During 1981 there was discontent amongst some CANA personnel who firmly believed that the French had been deliberately unhelpful to them by offering only the barest of operational data to aid their training. In spite of that and other technical grumbles, by the end of March 1982, each of the ten pilots at Espora had achieved about 80 flying hours on the type. The second batch of five aircraft was due for delivery at the end of April 1982.

The order to deploy the Super Etendard and Exocet system operationally — and in the shortest possible time — was received on 31 March. Rather than it being a prophetic warning of things to come, it was part of a general directive issued to all CANA units to bring themselves to a high state of readiness for Operacion "Rosario". Within a few days, however, it was obvious to all that the Squadron might indeed become involved in a real war and a crash programme of operational training was embarked upon. Despite the subsequent French arms embargo — an issue that embittered CANA which saw it as a simple breach of contract — the men of 2 Escuadrilla continued their task and, by mid-April, declared themselves operationally ready. That, of course, was no mean achievement for it had involved bringing the Exocet system to a ready-state without French assistance and the perfection of new mission profiles requiring long over-water flights in radio and electronic-silence and with in-flight refuelling.

For a few days it was hoped that the Super Etendard might be used from Stanley Airport in any action against the British Task Force, but a simulation of operations quickly revealed that although the aircraft could land safely on a dry runway, that would not be possible in the wet. Take-off, even in the best of conditions, would have been marginal and it was therefore decided to use Stanley Airport only in an emergency. Without the benefit of an operating base on the Falklands, it was thus decided that mainland-based attack profiles would require the aircraft to work in pairs, using in-flight refuelling to provide adequate fuel for the mission. In anticipation of the sophisticated SAM and ECM defences that would be met by the Super Etendards, 2 Escuadrilla planned all its missions to be undertaken at extremely low level and in radio and electronic-silence. During a period of intensive practice Argentina's own Type 42 destroyers were "attacked" by the Super Etendards in full-profile missions. The FAA KC-130H tankers enabled these attacks to take place at more than 300 miles from the mainland. Before the first combat mission was launched each of the ten operational pilots had increased his flight hours to about 100.

The first two aircraft were deployed from Espora to Rio Grande on 19 April, to be followed by a second pair the next day. The fifth machine, 0751/3-A-201, was left at Espora to be stripped of all useful parts to support the other four. All five Exocets were also taken to Rio Grande. More training sorties were undertaken, primarily to establish how great a problem the local weather would be to any mission. One such exercise was undertaken on 25 April with two Grupo 6 Daggers providing a fighter escort, it having been reasoned that their Shafrir AAM's would provide a useful element of protection for at least part of the mission. The exercise was, however, a dismal failure as one Dagger failed to take-off and the other returned prematurely to Rio Grande with a fuel leak. The experiment was not repeated.

The first mission against the British fleet was launched from Rio Grande on 2 May but was abandoned after an unspecified problem arose during the in-flight refuelling phase. The mission had been led by the unit's commander, Capitan de Fragata Jorge Colombo, and his wingman is thought to have been Teniente de Fragata Carlos Manchetanz. The men of 2 Escuadrilla appear to have agreed that they would fly the Exocet sorties in pre-arranged pairs and that once each pair had actually launched "for real" then they would not, in the event of an aborted attack, get a second opportunity until all five pairs had flown a mission. With each Super Etendard carrying one of the five missiles, a second opportunity was most unlikely and indeed Colombo was not to fly again. An aborted mission also meant that the Exocet had to be removed from the aircraft and its guidance system reprogrammed by sophisticated equipment before it could be used again. That equipment could not be moved from Espora and thus each "carried" missile had to be flown back there after an abandoned mission. With a round trip distance of 900 miles involved, that was a considerable operational hindrance.

It was at 1010Z on 4 May that the SP-2H Neptune 0708/2-P-112 warned Espora and Rio Grande that it had made radar contact south of the Falklands with what was thought to be a potentially vulnerable British warship. It was believed to have been a lone radar-picket vessel but within an hour or so it became apparent that other ships were in the general area which was about 85 miles south of Port Stanley. The two standby Super Etendard pilots were the unit's deputy commander, Capitan de Corbeta Augusto Bedacarratz, and Teniente de Fragata Armando Mayora and, soon after 1030Z, it became clear that their mission was "on" for as long as the Neptune could follow the contact. The alert aircraft were ready with all avionics and weaponry programmed and warmed. The Super Etendard's INS would ensure that even the poor morning weather would not prevent the attack. Indeed, the weather might provide an element of cover to shield the attack from the Sea Harriers. Once the aircraft had been brought to the flight-line from their nearby highway revetments the mission was soon under way (from the outset CANA feared the possibility of a British commando attack and it had thus taken exceptional measures to protect the Super Etendards). The two men took-off from Rio Grande at 1245Z, Bedacarratz in 0752/3-A-202 and Mayora in 0753/3-A-203, and by 1304Z had successfully completed their in-flight refuelling with the Grupo 1 KC-130H of Vicecomodoro Pessana. With 250 miles still to run they pressed on in silence and by 1330Z both men could hear the sounds of British ESM activity. With their cockpit

warning lights confirming the danger the two aircraft dropped to wave-top height to continue their run-in on the unseen ship.

At 1335Z, in conditions of showery rain and fogbanks, giving only 1,000yds of visibility, and a cloud ceiling of 500ft, the Neptune again updated the target's position and identified it as one large ship, with two others of medium size, at a distance of 115 miles. A third medium-sized ship was a further 30 miles away. Soon after that Bedacarratz decided that the target for both missiles would be the large ship and their attack units were so programmed. Shortly afterwards the two aircraft climbed to 500ft to check with their own radars that their target was still in the anticipated position but, to their dismay, they found nothing at all! The manoeuvre did, however, allow the British radars to confirm their presence and at 1350Z 801 Sqdn Sea Harriers were scrambled from 'Invincible' to intercept the high-speed, low-level radar "pop-ups". The British were in no doubt that there was an Exocet attack about to occur. The Super Etendards meanwhile had once more descended to sea-level and they continued on their original course for another 25 miles before rising to repeat their acquisition manoeuvre. On that occasion they were successful, although the ships' relative positions had changed. Then, at 1404Z, after another rapid correction to the attack unit, first Bedacarratz and then Mayora successfully launched their Exocets.

The missiles were directed at 'Sheffield' from a range of between 20 and 30 miles and they took approximately three minutes to run the distance. Only one of them hit her but the result was catastrophic, with an immediate explosion and fire ultimately destroying the ship. Of the other Exocet little is known, and it may indeed have passed harmlessly through the nearby group of warships, narrowly missing 'Yarmouth'. The Super Etendards returned safely to Rio Grande, initially at high speed and low level. In order to conserve fuel the pilots eventually elected to climb and were soon confident enough to decline an offer of assistance from the anxiously orbiting KC-130H. Finally, at 1510Z, first Bedacarratz and then Mayora landed safely on Rio Grande's 07 runway and taxied in to an ecstatic welcome. They had made military history and, even without the explicit knowledge of the destruction of 'Sheffield', all those present seemed to be aware of the fact.

The third pair of pilots designated to fly a mission were Capitan de Corbeta Roberto Agotegaray and Teniente de Navio Juan Rodriguez Mariani. They were obliged to wait almost three weeks for their opportunity and, while they waited, the nature of the next mission was repeatedly altered. The most significant change was precipitated by the sudden retirement on 15 May of the CANA Neptunes. They were simply worn-out, and their radars, ECM and other electronic equipment had become chronically unreliable. Missions had become increasingly frustrating and, despite the Neptune's invaluable role on 4 May, it was withdrawn. Unsuccessful trials took place using an S-2E Tracker in its stead and so, by late May, it was clear that other means of target identification would have to be adopted by CANA for Super Etendard sorties. By that time, however, CANA was satisfied that the naval controllers deployed to Port Stanley had at last optimised their ability to assess the tracks of the Sea Harriers to and from their aircraft carriers which were beyond the range of the Argentine radars. The technique was certainly crude but it enabled the controllers to provide the mainland commanders with a reasonably accurate position of at least one aircraft carrier as long as the Sea Harrier CAP's continued to be launched and flown towards the Falklands. It was thus possible to provide 2 Escuadrilla with adequate data to enable it to fly a mission against the carriers although the Super Etendards would only have their own radars to make a final judgement as to the suitability of their target.

The third Exocet mission was launched from Rio Grande on 23 May. Agotegaray and Mariani took-off in the early afternoon in search of a target known to be to the north of the Falklands. The refuelling passed off without incident but once in the target area the two aircraft were unable to find the anticipated warship. Despite repeated searches nothing was revealed and at about 2050Z the mission was abandoned. The Super Etendards turned south to return to Rio Grande, passing to the east of Port Stanley before turning south-west for home. When to the south of the Islands both aircraft received clear warning that they were being tracked by British fire-control radars and they immediately dropped to sea-level to escape. Flying flat out at sea-level in the pitch-dark of the South Atlantic was extremely hazardous and once the signals faded both aircraft rapidly climbed back to a safer altitude. After three frustrating hours in the air Agotegaray and Mariani finally returned safely.

Capitan de Corbeta Roberto Curilovic and Teniente de Navio Julio Barraza were the next nominated pair to fly a mission and their moment came on 25 May. At 1030Z, in the pre-dawn murk, they were briefed to attack a target that was thought to be some 110 miles to the north-east of Port Stanley. Their departure was planned for 1200Z. The target had been identified by the Port Stanley CIC and the Super Etendards would first have to travel north-east from Rio Grande to meet the KC-130H some 160 miles east of Puerto Deseado. They would then continue east before turning south to run-in on the target which was some 300 miles from the refuelling point. In order to ensure that the attack from the north came as a complete surprise, the Super Etendards would have to pass no nearer than 100 miles to the north of the Falklands.

Curilovic and Barraza were carrying out cockpit checks in anticipation of an "on schedule" departure when they were advised that the KC-130H would not be available until late afternoon. The mission was accordingly delayed. They eventually left Rio Grande at 1728Z in aircraft 0753/3-A-203 and 0754/3-A-204. The refuelling passed without any problems and, at about 150 miles from the target, both aircraft descended to fly at an altitude of about 30ft above the waves. To the surprise of both men their first radar sweep was positive and two large ships and one smaller one were found as predicted. The rest of their task was then easy and, having selected the largest of the three images, both Exocets were launched simultaneously. Curilovic and Barraza were travelling some 200yds apart and they fired from a distance of about 31 miles. According to CANA the two

missiles were launched at 1932Z.

The Task Force appears to have received about six minutes of warning that it was under attack and in that time all its established anti-Exocet measures were implemented. However, despite the rapid launching of several jamming helicopters and the firing of many chaff rockets, one of the missiles found 'Atlantic Conveyor' and at 1936Z she, like 'Sheffield', caught fire and later sank. The fate of 2 Escuadrilla's second Exocet remains something of a mystery, but one that has generated a substantial amount of British argument and speculation. When the Exocets were launched the three big ships in the area were fairly close together — 'Hermes' some two miles from 'Atlantic Conveyor' with 'Invincible' another eight miles distant — and it must be a reasonable assumption that the missile that hit 'Atlantic Conveyor' did indeed find its intended target — despite the British defences. However, the Task Force may have been more successful in dealing with the other Exocet although deflection, rather than destruction, was probably the means. A full two minutes after 'Atlantic Conveyor' was hit, 'Invincible' fired three salvoes of two Sea Dart missiles in rapid succession at a "low fast" target that had been seen on radar at a distance of 20 miles. It had subsequently closed to a range of about 14 miles before disappearing. If both missiles had indeed been simultaneously launched then clearly 'Invincible' had not been shooting at an Exocet, nor is it likely to have been a Super Etendard. They had both turned to the north-west some five minutes earlier and were on their way home!

The Super Etendards had planned to land at Puerto Deseado on their return but the FAA had unexpectedly left the KC-130H on station and, once the fighters were clear of the British fleet, contact was established and a second in-flight refuelling took place. That done, both aircraft were able to make a safe return to Rio Grande where they landed at 2138Z. They had been airborne for three hours and 50 minutes and had covered 1,620 miles to achieve what was ultimately to be the longest 2 Escuadrilla mission of the War.

With only one remaining missile, CANA was determined that it should be used to the greatest possible effect. The priority continued to be the pair of aircraft carriers from which the British had established what was virtually total air superiority over the Falkland Islands. In the belief that their attack of 25 May had at least damaged 'Hermes', the immediate target was thus seen as 'Invincible'. CANA was fairly confident that she was operating from a position due east of Port Stanley at a range of about 100 miles but it was equally aware that the Royal Navy was using picket ships and helicopters to provide her with a very strong defence screen. It was obvious that a degree of novelty would be necessary to ensure the success of the final mission.

A demanding profile was created, in which the missile-carrying Super Etendard of Capitan de Corbeta Alejandro Francisco would be accompanied by the unarmed aircraft of Teniente de Navio Luis Collavino. After departure the aircraft were to travel south-east and then east from Rio Grande to meet the KC-130H far to the south of the Falkland Islands. After the refuelling all three aircraft would travel east together until, after a second refuelling, the Super Etendards were to leave the tanker and run-in on their target from the south-east. It was assumed that an attack from that quarter would not be anticipated by the Task Force and that it was the key to the success of the mission. All personnel were accordingly briefed.

The mission was planned for 29 May and at 1500Z the 2 Escuadrilla pilots were only waiting for the usual call from the KC-130H to confirm that it was on station before they departed. At that moment the commanding officer, Capitan de Fragata Colombo, astounded all those present by announcing that in fifteen minutes time four FAA A-4C Skyhawks from Grupo 4 would land at Rio Grande and that they would accompany the Super Etendards on the mission! They would follow the same flight profile as the 2 Escuadrilla aircraft and would run-in on the target behind the Exocet. Taking advantage of the confusion caused by the missile, each Skyhawk would drop two 500lb bombs into the ship. The ensuing uproar at Rio Grande is easily imagined and, not surprisingly, Colombo was persuaded to tell the FAA that such a mission was impossible without a lengthy briefing and, even more fundamentally, without a second KC-130H! As some measure of calm returned it was decided that the original mission would go ahead without the Skyhawks (which had by then arrived) but, almost immediately, operations for the day were cancelled, ostensibly because the KC-130H could no longer hold its station. It was not long after that anticlimax that higher authority made it clear to 2 Escuadrilla that the mission would go ahead with the Skyhawks, irrespective of local views. Thus it was reinstated for the following day, 30 May, and two KC-130H tankers would be made available.

The morning of 30 May saw the six pilots engaged in an intensive briefing. It was agreed that all the CANA parameters that had hitherto been observed by 2 Escuadrilla would be adhered to by the FAA pilots. For the final phase of the attack each Super Etendard would lead in two Skyhawks until the missile was launched and then Grupo 4 would be on its own! It was agreed that if more than two Skyhawks aborted the mission, then FAA participation would be cancelled.

Shortly after 1530Z the Super Etendards of first Francisco and then Collavino took-off, followed some five minutes later by the Skyhawks. Francisco's armed aircraft was 0752/3-A-202 while Collavino had been given 0755/3-A-205. They flew at 12,000ft in two groups about a mile apart for the first 50 minutes and, in good weather, easily found the waiting tankers. The first refuelling was made at 20,000ft and the group flew together for 190 miles as each fighter was progressively "topped up". Once the final transfer was complete the six fighters formed-up into an arrowhead strike profile and descended to sea-level for the final stage of the attack. Unknown to them, however, the British had received their first warning of a possible attack at 1645Z and had gone to action stations. Once at low level though, the formation was not visible on the Task Force radars and the British were almost convinced that they had been the victims of yet another false alarm. The weather had worsened to conditions of low cloud and rain

by the time that the Super Etendards made two fast "pop-ups" to look for a suitable target. On the second occasion they found their "big ship" and its co-ordinates were entered into the Exocet's attack unit. At 1731Z, moments before the last missile was launched at them, the British picket ships realised that they were indeed under Exocet attack and, again, helicopters and aircraft were scrambled and the chaff rockets fired.

The Exocet was launched from a range of 24 miles and, as the Skyhawks followed the distant smoke trail towards the horizon, Francisco and Collavino turned sharply away to return to Rio Grande, their mission completed. However, for the Grupo 4 Skyhawks, the next few minutes were to be as traumatic as anything previously experienced. *[A full account of their attack can be found in the Grupo 4 section].*

For the third time the fate of an Exocet missile was to become the subject of great debate. The essence of the Argentine claim that it damaged 'Invincible' was that the two surviving Skyhawk pilots overflew (and attacked) a burning warship and identified it, positively, as an aircraft carrier. Their claim cannot be correct for there is abundant evidence that the ship that they attacked was the frigate 'Avenger', a picket ship operating at least 25 miles south of 'Invincible' and about 10 miles south-east of the destroyer 'Exeter'. If the isolated 'Avenger' was the Skyhawks' unplanned target, then it was probably 'Exeter' that the Exocet had been programmed to hit. In spite of all the Argentine theories and speculation about the missile, it is clear that it did not hit either 'Avenger' or 'Exeter', nor did it hit 'Invincible' which was more than 40 miles from the Exocet's launching point and well beyond its range.

The expenditure of the last Exocet missile effectively closed the wartime account of the Super Etendard and 2 Escuadrilla returned to Espora, taking with it four undamaged aircraft. The unit's contribution to the War was colossal and its cold-blooded professionalism must surely have been an object lesson to many others in the Argentine forces. Its successes shook the Royal Navy, forcing the carriers to operate further to the east of the Falklands and, ultimately, to fundamentally re-examine its methods of fleet protection. It was indeed fortunate for the British that only five AM.39 Exocets had been delivered to Argentina.

The French arms embargo was eventually lifted and, on 8 December 1982, five more aircraft (0757/3-A-207 to 0760/3-A-210 and 0771/3-A-211) and their missiles were finally delivered by sea to Bahia Blanca. They were followed at the end of the month by the last batch of four (0756/3-A-206 and 0772/3-A-212 to 0774/3-A-214, although confusion at Bordeaux had resulted in the serials "0761" to "0764" being applied to the aircraft with call-signs '3-A-211' to '3-A-214' and in May 1984 these incorrect serials were still worn). By April 1983 the modifications to the '25 de Mayo' had been completed at Puerto Belgrano and her sea trials commenced soon afterwards with the Super Etendards of 2 Escuadrilla operating alongside the surviving Skyhawks of 3 Escuadrilla. In July 1983 it was observed that six of the Super Etendards had been placed in long-term storage for later operational use.

The 2 Escuadrilla de Caza y Ataque pilots who deployed to Rio Grande and who flew missions were:

Capitan de Fragata J.Colombo (commander); Capitan de Corbeta R.Agotegaray; Capitan de Corbeta A.C.Bedacarratz; Capitan de Corbeta

continued

R.Curilovic; Capitan de Corbeta A.Francisco; Teniente de Navio J.Barraza; Teniente de Navio L.Collavino; Teniente de Navio J.R.Mariani; Teniente de Fragata C.Manchetanz; Teniente de Fragata A.Mayora.

Super Etendard 0751/3-A-201, seen here at Comandante Espora, was not deployed to Rio Grande with the other four aircraft on 19/20.5.82 but remained at home base, ostensibly as a source of spares. When this photograph was taken in 9.82, 2 Escuadrilla de Caza y Ataque was still the proud possessor of five beautifully presented aircraft but, presumably, no Exocet missiles. 0751 is armed with practice bombs.                    (K. Ebata)

# INDIVIDUAL AIRCRAFT DETAILS

The Super Etendards were delivered to CANA in an overall dark blue-grey colour scheme with white under surfaces. The rudder and fin top carried the Argentine national colours in the same style as those of the naval Skyhawks. The principal fuselage markings consisted of the ARMADA title at the rear, the call-sign on the centre section and the "last two" of the call-sign on the nose. All of these markings were in white. The CANA serial number was applied in small white digits in the centre of the fin. As with all CANA combat types, the only roundels applied were those on the lower wing surfaces. 2

Escuadrilla's pugnacious eagle motif was applied to the nose of each of the aircraft below the cockpit on the port side. The silhouettes of the ships attacked by the Super Etendards were stencilled in yellow on the port side of the nose adjacent to the unit badge. A small red cross was superimposed on each to indicate its destruction and a single diagonal to show damage.

Brief details of the five aircraft that were on CANA charge in March 1982 are included below.

**0751**

In 3.82 with 2 Escuadrilla as '3-A-201'. Used throughout the War as a source of spares at Espora and was intact there, but not confirmed as airworthy, in 9.82. Restored to flying condition by 1983 and noted as such in 5.84.

**0752**

In 3.82 with 2 Escuadrilla as '3-A-202'. Deployed to Rio Grande from Espora on 19 or 20.4.82. Used on the missions of 4.5.82 and 30.5.82 and subsequently marked with silhouettes to show the loss of 'Sheffield' and sup-

posed damage to 'Invincible'. In use at Espora in 11.82.

**0753**

In 3.82 with 2 Escuadrilla as '3-A-203'. Deployed to Rio Grande from Espora on 19 or 20.4.82. Used on the missions of 4.5.82 and 25.5.82 and subsequently marked with silhouettes to show the losses of 'Sheffield' and 'Atlantic Conveyor'. In use at Espora in 11.82.

**0754**

In 3.82 with 2 Escuadrilla as '3-A-204'. Deployed to Rio Grande from Espora on 19 or

20.4.82. Used on the mission of 25.5.82 and subsequently marked with a silhouette to show the loss of 'Atlantic Conveyor'. In use at Espora in 11.82.

**0755**

In 3.82 with 2 Escuadrilla as '3-A-205'. Deployed to Rio Grande from Espora on 19 or 20.4.82. Used on the mission of 30.5.82 and subsequently marked with a silhouette to show supposed damage to 'Invincible' (although it had not carried an Exocet). In use at Espora in 11.82.

# SKYHAWK

# 3 ESCUADRILLA DE CAZA Y ATAQUE

During 1971/72 CANA received 16 refurbished A-4B Skyhawks from the United States Navy. For their export to Argentina the DoD redesignated them as the A-4Q model and this revised mark was always used by CANA (the FAA ignored the A-4P designation given to their A-4B's and continued to identify them as "A-4B"). They re-equipped CANA's 2 Escuadrilla de Caza y Ataque, a component of the 3 Escuadra Aeronaval, at the Comandante Espora base, Bahia Blanca, Buenos Aires. It was shortly after their receipt that an organisational change renumbered the Skyhawk unit, which then became the 3 Escuadrilla. The change was "on paper only", however, for both personnel and aircraft remained at Espora with 3 Escuadra.

By March 1982 the Squadron had lost six of its aircraft in accidents, three of them occurring during the regular deployments on the aircraft carrier '25 de Mayo'. Two more Skyhawks had been withdrawn from the active inventory and thus only eight aircraft remained fully operational. By 1982, however, the A-4Q was an old and tired aircraft and, although it was in the process of being augmented by the new Super Etendard, CANA was actively investigating the ways and means of extending 3 Escuadrilla's operational life. The most attractive option was the acquisition of late-model Skyhawks but, far from making the event likely, the United States was actually inhibiting CANA's A-4Q operation. Although the Reagan Administration's attitude to the supply of arms to Argentina was showing signs of mellowing in early 1982, the embargo imposed by its predecessors had seriously affected Skyhawk operations at Espora.

3 Escuadrilla embarked eight aircraft on the '25 de Mayo', the flagship of Task Force 20, for the exercises of late March and for her historic voyage from Puerto Belgrano on 28 March. The role of Task Force 20 in Operacion "Rosario" was that of protection for the assault element, Task Force 40, when it made the landings on the Falklands on 2 April. However, although '25 de Mayo' featured prominently in the Argentine media of the period, no operational Skyhawk sorties were necessary for the capture of the Islands. Shortly after the successful operation one aircraft, 0658/3-A-305, made a brief visit to Stanley Airport, perhaps for a runway inspection and

some publicity.

Once the Falklands had been secured, all the Armada warships returned to their home ports and the Skyhawks of 3 Escuadrilla were soon back at Espora for routine operations and, eventually, another deployment on '25 de Mayo'. However, within days the situation changed and by mid-April the unit was once again on board the carrier, with the knowledge that a sea battle with the British Task Force, then ten days out from Portsmouth, was a real possibility. Task Force 79, of which '25 de Mayo' was a major unit, had put to sea between 15 and 17 April and for the next two weeks the fleet was engaged in full-scale exercises designed to have it war-ready by 30 April. It has not been possible to positively identify the eight embarked Skyhawks but the ten aircraft on unit strength, including those in storage, were:

| | | |
|---|---|---|
| 0654/3-A-301 | 0658/3-A-305 | 0662/3-A-309 |
| 0655/3-A-302 | 0659/3-A-306 | 0665/3-A-312 |
| 0657/3-A-304 | 0660/3-A-307 | 0667/3-A-314 |
| | 0661/3-A-308 | |

The carrier force was not involved in the fighting of 1 May but, by the early hours of 2 May, '25 de Mayo' had established that the British fleet was approximately 150 miles away to her south-east and Task Force 79 remained at action stations. Following the earlier launching of nine unproductive air defence sorties from '25 de Mayo' there had been much activity during the night by the two opposing carrier groups and CANA was prepared to take offensive action at first light on 2 May. The 3 Escuadrilla crews were called to a mission briefing at 0500Z (it took two hours to complete) and were told that all eight Skyhawks would be launched against the British fleet. Each was armed with iron bombs and the Skyhawks would have to fly without the benefit of accompanying missile-equipped aircraft. In anticipation of just such an attack the British fleet went to action stations at 1015Z. However, the attack was never launched and many sources have suggested that unusually light winds that morning prevented the Skyhawks launching at their maximum take-off weight.

The destructive power of the Exocet-equipped Super Etendards of 2 Escuadrilla de Caza y Ataque was convincingly demonstrated during 5.82. CANA subsequently published considerable detail of their missions and the original five aircraft were regularly displayed during the ensuing months. Seen here at Espora in 9.82, 0752/3-A-202 was marked to show the destruction of 'Sheffield' and supposed damage to 'Invincible'. The **Lower Right** inset (of 0754/3-A-204) shows markings reflecting the destruction of 'Atlantic Conveyor'. (K. Ebata)

Typical of the 3 Escuadrilla de Caza y Ataque A-4Q Skyhawks embarked in '25 de Mayo' in 3/4.82 and later deployed to Rio Grande, 0661/3-A-308 was photographed at its Comandante Espora base, Bahia Blanca, in 11.82. The sea-grey colour scheme remained unchanged throughout the War in spite of its obvious shortcomings when overflying the Falkland Islands or the dark waters of the South Atlantic. (via A. Price)

0662/3-A-309 was the 3 Escuadrilla de Caza y Ataque A-4Q Skyhawk from which Capitan de Corbeta Carlos Zubizarreta ejected, losing his life in the process, on 23.5.82. The aircraft sustained surprisingly slight damage in the incident at Rio Grande and, after repair, was returned to service in a new, unique two-tone brown splinter camouflage. It was photographed at Comandante Espora in 9.82. (K. Ebata)

Without their full fuel load the aircraft would not have had the range to reach the enemy without an unacceptable modification to their war-load. In fact, 3 Escuadrilla did not attack 'Invincible' or other British warships because, at about 0900Z, a searching S-2E Tracker finally acknowledged that it could no longer locate the British carrier group on its radar. Later in the day, at 1858Z, the Argentine cruiser 'General Belgrano' was torpedoed and '25 de Mayo', which had herself unwittingly lost a stalking submarine, was recalled to territorial waters. 3 Escuadrilla was thus not destined to fight the anticipated classic carrier battle. '25 de Mayo' returned to port on, or shortly after, 5 May and 3 Escuadrilla returned to Espora to prepare itself for the inevitable next phase of the War.

On 9 May the commander, Capitan de Corbeta Rodolfo Castro Fox, took the Squadron to the naval base at Rio Grande from where it was expected that the unit would soon see action alongside the already deployed FAA aircraft. 12 pilots and, initially, eight aircraft were deployed although efforts were well under way by then to restore the two "hangar queens" to an airworthy state (both aircraft were ultimately restored to operational service and at least one of them later saw combat use). For the next two weeks the Squadron flew operational training missions in anticipation of British landings on the Falklands when it was expected that the warships would come within range of attack from Rio Grande. At last, on the evening of 20 May, positive intelligence of unusual British activity was received and early the following day that was confirmed, by aerial reconnaissance, to be the long-awaited landing.

At 1315Z on 21 May 3 Escuadrilla launched two flights of three Skyhawks to attack a somewhat vaguely defined target in Falkland Sound. The two flight leaders were Castro Fox and Capitan de Corbeta Carlos Zubizaretta, the former taking wingmen Teniente de Navio Marcos Benitez and Teniente de Fragata Daniel Olmedo and the latter leading Teniente de Navio Carlos Oliveira and Teniente de Corbeta Felix Medici. In CANA's operational jargon they were known as "1 Seccion" and "2 Seccion" and together they constituted "1 Division". The mission was, however, launched prematurely without either reliable or adequate information concerning the strength and location of the British fleet. Their orders were changed en route and then, amid some confusion, all were recalled to Rio Grande before reaching their target. Once safely home, the six pilots were stood down and their Skyhawks were refuelled and rearmed for the men of "2 Division".

"2 Division's" first mission was led by Capitan de Corbeta Alberto Philippi and his two wingmen were Teniente de Navio Jose Arca and Teniente de Fragata Marcelo Marquez. Teniente de Navio Benito Rotolo was the second flight leader and his wingmen were Teniente de Navio Roberto Sylvester and Teniente de Fragata Carlos Lecour. Each Skyhawk was equipped with four 500lb Snakeye bombs carried on the centre-line ejection rail, while the wing hard-points carried the vital fuel drop tanks. CANA did not use the FAA's KC-130H tankers for in-flight refuelling on 21 May and in consequence there was little room for navigational errors or other en route delays. "2 Division's" target was specified as a frigate that was thought to be acting as a picket vessel in Falkland

Sound and which was apparently isolated to the south of the main body of the landing force.

Philippi's flight launched shortly before 1730Z, followed by Rotolo's aircraft at 1745Z. Should they not find their intended target, then any ship at all could be attacked. All pilots had been carefully briefed to keep well clear of the Sea Harrier CAP's which were known to be on station over West Falkland. The crossing to the Islands was made at 30,000ft and Philippi descended to low level for his final run-in from the south. The weather was foul, with the usual rain and low cloud to contend with, but the three Skyhawks were able to pass easily enough up Falkland Sound towards Grantham Sound. There they made a slight right turn and then swung west to attack a lonely frigate which was out in the Sound off North West Island. 'Ardent' had already suffered at the hands of the FAA that afternoon and was in little shape to withstand yet another sustained attack from Argentine fighter-bombers. Initially it had been Philippi's intention to use his 20mm cannon on the frigate but, as often happened, they jammed and he thus went straight in on his bomb run. Both he and Arca made successful runs from astern the frigate and both hit 'Ardent' with several bombs. Marquez appears to have been less successful but, in the event, it did not matter because 'Ardent' was already mortally damaged by the flight leader and the number two. The burning warship was soon abandoned by her crew and she eventually sank the following evening.

'Ardent' had in fact put up a considerable amount of small-arms fire at the Skyhawks and Arca's aircraft had sustained several hits. More ominously they had been seen some moments earlier by patrolling 801 Sqdn Sea Harrier pilots who had had little difficulty in spotting the clear bright sea-grey colours of the CANA Skyhawks against the generally dark surroundings of the late afternoon. The three Skyhawks had travelled about 10 miles south-west down Falkland Sound and were to the east of Swan Island when they were caught by the 800 Sqdn Sea Harriers of Lt Clive Morrell and Flt Lt John Leeming. Although Marquez saw them before they were attacked, and each had time to jettison the underwing fuel tanks, the three Skyhawks had little chance of escaping the rapidly closing Sea Harriers. Morrell's first AIM-9L, fired from his aircraft XZ457, detonated in the tail-pipe area of Philippi's Skyhawk, 0660/3-A-307, and, as the rear of the aircraft broke away from the cockpit section, Philippi ejected to safety. Morrell's second missile would not immediately launch and thus he resorted to a gun attack on Arca's Skyhawk, 0665/3-A-312. It was hit several times in the wings and Arca had a narrow escape (of which he remained ignorant) when Morrell's second Sidewinder suddenly launched of its own accord. Arca had major problems nevertheless, and seriously considered ejecting until he realised that his aircraft was still flyable and that the Sea Harrier had gone! Marquez, however, had not been so fortunate and he had been killed when Leeming, in XZ500, had made a successful gun attack on him from the rear. At very low level over Falkland Sound his Skyhawk, 0667/3-A-314, had exploded and disintegrated, killing him.

Arca struggled on to Port Stanley with the intention of landing there but, to his chagrin, he had great difficulty in communicating with the FAA controller. When, with the aid of an Ejercito UH-1H, he finally succeeded he was then informed that his port main undercarriage leg had gone and that he must eject! He eventually left the Skyhawk over the coast at the edge of the airfield, ultimately to be rescued from the water by the same CAB601 UH-1H that had helped him a few moments earlier. His battered aircraft resolutely refused to crash and it was eventually brought down by anti-aircraft gunfire, south of the airfield, on the shoreline. While Arca was being dragged from the water his flight leader was recovering from a similar soaking in Port King and, after giving himself up to some Islanders on 24 May, he was returned, unhurt, to Rio Grande on 30 May.

Philippi's flight had attacked 'Ardent' at about 1810Z and some fifteen minutes afterwards Rotolo's flight followed from the south on a similar track. They approached over Lafonia and crossed the coast on the southern side of Grantham Sound before turning west across Falkland Sound. There they attacked an unidentified frigate (which was probably 'Ardent') in the middle of the Sound but, although several bombs fell very near to the ship, no damage was thought to have been caused. After making a violent turn to the north to avoid gunfire from a nearby ship the flight crossed the coast of West Falkland north of Port Howard and continued westwards at low level. Although both Lecour's and Sylvester's aircraft had received some shrapnel damage in the attack all three Skyhawks were subsequently able to climb to 25,000ft and reach Rio Grande safely.

On the morning of 23 May 3 Escuadrilla had just four serviceable aircraft — one of the pair damaged on 21 May was still out of action — and therefore the next mission to San Carlos was planned round the four available aircraft. The commander, Capitan de Corbeta Castro Fox, would lead using one of the Squadron's two VLF Omega-equipped Skyhawks (the equipment had been used for the first time by Rotolo and Sylvester on 21 May). He was to lead Zubizarreta, Benitez and Oliveira in an attack on any suitable target in San Carlos Water. Hard lessons had been learned by both CANA and the FAA on 21 May and the KC-130H tankers would henceforth be used for all missions to San Carlos Water and beyond. In-flight refuelling would take place on the outward leg of the mission and the timing of future CANA sorties would be carefully integrated with those of CdoFAS. The flight's refuelling was thus scheduled for 1620Z at a point some 200 miles east of Rio Grande.

The flight took-off at 1535Z and the four Skyhawks encountered no difficulties in meeting the KC-130H at 12,000ft in a clear blue sky. The refuelling was not without incident though, and Oliveira was obliged to return home when his aircraft refused to transfer fuel into its drop tanks. The others approached at low level from the west over West Falkland, crossing the east coast just north of Mount Rosalie. They had been scheduled to follow a flight of Grupo 5 Skyhawks into the Falkland Sound area and it was that flight that had, some 15 minutes earlier, left two unexploded bombs in 'Antelope'. The three 3 Escuadrilla aircraft ran-in from the west and each pilot selected a warship for an individual attack. Despite making good, low runs at their targets no hits were achieved and Zubizarreta had his four bombs hang-up. The three

men were nevertheless fortunate, for all managed to escape undamaged by the heavy gunfire directed at them. Some minutes later they regrouped over West Falkland and it was at that moment that Castro Fox realised that one of his drop tanks was not transferring fuel into the wing tank. Using the recently fitted new navigation equipment he was, however, able to calculate his precise position and therefore the optimum fuel burn to get him back safely to Rio Grande. Fortunately he had adequate fuel available and the three men reached home base safely. Castro Fox landed after the others and when he touched down he was dismayed to see Zubizarreta's aircraft on the side of the runway where it had slewed off after the landing. Zubizarreta had heavy-landed with the bomb-load still in place and had lost control of the Skyhawk when a tyre burst. Realising that his aircraft was about to leave the runway and knowing full well that it was still carrying four 500lb bombs, he had ejected from the Skyhawk at the last possible moment. Unfortunately he had inadequate forward speed and no altitude and consequently his parachute had failed to deploy fully and he had come down heavily on the runway. Zubizarreta was killed in the incident although, ironically, his aircraft, 0662/3-A-309, was little damaged and was returned to service after repair.

The mission of 23 May achieved little and it is difficult even to identify the ships that were attacked by Castro Fox and his two colleagues that afternoon. Only two airworthy aircraft were available for operational use by that evening and the decision was taken to suspend combat flying until more aircraft were serviceable. The unit's worst fears concerning shortcomings in the fuel systems and ejection seats had proven themselves well-founded. Nevertheless their missions were eventually resumed and a flight of 3 Escuadrilla Skyhawks attacked suspected British positions on Broken Island on 8 June. A similar sortie was undertaken by Teniente de Navio Rotolo to the Darwin area on 12 June but, again, nothing tangible was achieved. On the latter occasion Rotolo jettisoned his bombs when he saw what he believed to be an approaching Sea Harrier.

In all, 3 Escuadrilla de Caza y Ataque flew 34 operational sorties between mid-April and 14 June. Its war was brief and somewhat bloody but by the autumn of 1982 the Squadron was once again operational at Espora, most of the aircraft having been brought back to airworthiness. Seven A-4Q Skyhawks remained on the inventory until 11 November 1982 when another was lost in a fatal crash at Espora. The six survivors apparently included both the rebuilt "hangar queens" as well as the aircraft damaged in the runway incident of 23 May. It would appear that one lesson from the events of 21 May was demonstrably well learned, for, by autumn 1982, the Skyhawks of 3 Escuadrilla began to receive a new, if somewhat garish, camouflage scheme.

In late 1983 the unit was still operational at Espora with the A-4Q model Skyhawk under the new command of the promoted Capitan de Fragata Alberto Philippi. The elderly Skyhawks, used to support marine forces, were still operationally deployed on '25 de Mayo', although by then complemented by the co-located Super Etendards of 2 Escuadrilla de Caza y Ataque. Despite the wishful thoughts of its crews, 3 Escuadrilla did not, at the time of writing in early 1985, appear likely to receive surplus USMC A-4M or Israeli A-4E/F model Skyhawks in the forseeable future.

The 3 Escuadrilla de Caza y Ataque pilots embarked with the Squadron on '25 de Mayo' and who deployed to Rio Grande were:

Capitan de Corbeta R.A.Castro Fox (commander); continued

continued —————————————————————
Capitan de Corbeta A.J.Philippi; Capitan de Corbeta C.M.Zubizarreta (KIA); Teniente de Navio J.C.Arca; Teniente de Navio M.A.Benitez; Teniente de Navio C.Oliveira; Teniente de Navio B.Rotolo; Teniente de Navio R.G.Sylvester; Teniente de Fragata C.Lecour; Teniente de Fragata M.G.Marquez (KIA); Teniente de Fragata D.Olmedo; Teniente de Corbeta F.Medici.

# INDIVIDUAL AIRCRAFT DETAILS

When the Skyhawks of 3 Escuadrilla were deployed to Rio Grande on 9 May 1982 all the aircraft were still in the grey colour that they had worn for all their CANA service lives. The rudder and fin top was decorated with a stylised blue and white national flag but all other markings were in black on the overall gull-grey paintwork. The AR-MADA title was worn on the rear fuselage, the call-sign on the engine intake and the "last two" digits of the call-sign on the nose. The aircraft serial number was inscribed in small digits in the centre of the fin, while the title 'A.R.A.25 DE MAYO' was written in tiny script at the fin-top. In equally small digits on the jet-pipe, immediately behind the ARMADA title was the original USN BuAer number. It is thought that by March 1982 CANA had removed the naval anchor markings from the upper wing surfaces but that they remained on the undersurfaces (no fuselage roundels were worn). All the aircraft that were deployed to Rio Grande are believed to have worn the 3 Escuadrilla crest below the cockpit on the port side of the fuselage. The drop tanks were either grey or white and some of them were marked with a black flash. The camouflage schemes that replaced the original grey colour scheme on some aircraft were not introduced before June 1982 and were almost certainly a post-war innovation.

CANA stated that eight Skyhawks were airworthy at the outbreak of the war and that a further two were later brought back to flying condition. Aircraft 0656/3-A-303 does not seem to have been in the CANA inventory in March 1982 despite its appearances in undated publicity photographs released during and after the War.

**0654**

In 3.82 with 3 Escuadrilla as '3-A-301'. Used by the Squadron commander, Capitan de Corbeta Castro Fox. Operated from '25 de Mayo' with Task Forces 20 and 79 between 28.3 and c5.5.82 and deployed to Rio Grande from Espora, probably on 9.5.82. In use at Espora in 11.82 and 5.84, still in the original grey colour scheme.

**0655**

No evidence of use until 11.82 when noted with 3 Escuadrilla at Espora as '3-A-302'. At that time it still wore the original grey paintwork but by early 1983 it had been camouflaged in a dark brown and green colour scheme.

**0657**

In 3.82 with 3 Escuadrilla as '3-A-304'. Presumed to have been used during the War. When seen in use at Espora in 11.82 it had been camouflaged in a dark brown and green colour scheme although, by 5.84, it was reportedly back in the grey scheme.

**0658**

In 3.82 with 3 Escuadrilla as '3-A-305'. Operated from '25 de Mayo' with Task Forces 20 and 79 between 28.3 and c5.5.82 and seen at Stanley Airport shortly after 2.4.82. Deployed to Rio Grande from Espora on or after 9.5.82. In use at Espora in 5.84.

**0659**

In 3.82 with 3 Escuadrilla as '3-A-306'. Probably operated from '25 de Mayo' with Task Forces 20 and 79 between 28.3 and c5.5.82 and certainly deployed to Rio Grande from Espora on or after 9.5.82. Camouflaged post-war in a dark brown and green colour scheme and was subsequently destroyed in a fatal crash at Espora on 11.11.82.

**0660**

In 3.82 with 3 Escuadrilla as '3-A-307'. Probably operated from '25 de Mayo' with Task Forces 20 and 79 between 28.3 and c5.5.82 and certainly deployed to Rio Grande from Espora on or after 9.5.82. On 21.5.82, after successfully bombing 'Ardent', it was shot down over Falkland Sound by an AIM-9L fired from the 800 Sqdn Sea Harrier XZ457 of Lt Morrell. The pilot, Capitan de Corbeta Philippi, ejected safely and was eventually returned to Argentina on 30.5.82. The aircraft crashed into the sea at the southern end of the Sound.

**0661**

No evidence of use until 9.82 when seen in service with 3 Escuadrilla at Espora as '3-A-308'. When last noted at Espora in 11.82 it was still in the original grey colour scheme.

**0662**

In 3.82 with 3 Escuadrilla as '3-A-309'. Prob-

ably operated from '25 de Mayo' with Task Forces 20 and 79 between 28.3 and c5.5.82 and certainly deployed to Rio Grande from Espora on or after 9.5.82. Damaged in a landing accident at Rio Grande on 23.5.82 in which the pilot, Capitan de Corbeta Zubizarreta, was killed. By 9.82 it had been rebuilt and was in use at Espora in a new splinter camouflage scheme. It was still in service in 5.84.

**0665**

In 3.82 with 3 Escuadrilla as '3-A-312'. Probably operated from '25 de Mayo' with Task Forces 20 and 79 between 28.3 and c5.5.82 and certainly deployed to Rio Grande from Espora on or after 9.5.82. On 21.5.82, after successfully bombing 'Ardent', it was struck over Falkland Sound by cannon fire from the 800 Sqdn Sea Harrier XZ457 of Lt Morrell. The pilot, Teniente de Navio Arca, eventually ejected safely from the damaged aircraft near Stanley Airport which was then brought down by Argentine gunfire. It crashed on the shoreline, 400yds south of the airfield perimeter.

**0667**

In 3.82 with 3 Escuadrilla as '3-A-314'. Operated from '25 de Mayo' with Task Forces 20 and 79 between 28.3 and c5.5.82 and deployed to Rio Grande on or after 9.5.82. On 21.5.82, after unsuccessfully bombing 'Ardent', it disintegrated over Falkland Sound during a cannon attack by the 800 Sqdn Sea Harrier XZ500 of Flt Lt Leeming. The pilot, Teniente de Fragata Marquez, was killed.

Although 'D' Sqdn 22SAS Regt had immobilised all eleven Argentine aircraft found at Pebble Island on 15.5.82, some were more convincingly demolished than others! The most severely damaged of the 4 Escuadrilla de Ataque T-34C Mentors was 0719/401 which was completely destroyed by explosion and fire. Seen here in the winter snow of 7.82, the wreckage was later buried on site during 1983.

Mentor 0729/411 suffered only M15 rifle-fire damage in the Pebble Island raid and was later earmarked by the local population for private preservation. Before its eventual transportation to the United Kingdom, however, the elements got to work on it and, as can be seen, by 2.83 the camouflage was beginning to weather and the original colour scheme beneath was becoming visible.                    (W. G. Calvert)

The PNA Skyvan PA-50 was another of those aircraft completely destroyed on 15.5.82 by 22SAS Regiment. The Skyvan's fate may well have been sealed several days earlier when the waterlogged Pebble Island airfield had prevented all aircraft departures. Seen here a few days after the Argentine surrender, the wreckage was eventually buried on the airfield's perimeter.
(Ministry of Defence)

# MENTOR

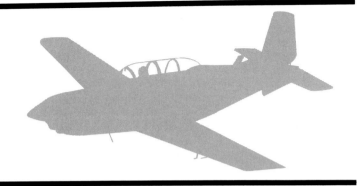

# 4 ESCUADRILLA DE ATAQUE

Since 1978 the Escuela de Aviacion Naval at Punta Indio, Buenos Aires had operated 15 T-34C-1 Mentors in the basic and intermediate training role. As a component of the 1 Escuadra Aeronaval the School had a notional combat role in the CANA order of battle and, accordingly, its aircraft had always used "Ataque" call-signs. All 15 aircraft are believed to have remained in use at Punta Indio in March 1982.

It is thought that the decision to deploy the Mentor to the Falkland Islands was not made until it was realised that the British might use force to repossess them. The Mentor's ability to fly from a grass strip with a mixed war-load of small bombs, rockets and 7.62mm machine-guns made it an attractive combat aircraft for certain missions. In the event of small-scale landings the Mentor would certainly have had the ability to harrass the enemy, although it would clearly be extremely vulnerable to air attack. Accordingly, in mid-April, preparations were made to ferry a group of the School's aircraft south to Rio Grande.

A decision was made to deploy four aircraft to the Falklands and it was anticipated that they would operate from Stanley Airport or, perhaps, from the newly established FAA airstrip at Goose Green. In spite of some reservations concerning the safety of the ferry flight (4 Escuadrilla was worried by the inadequacy of the Mentor's navigational aids and the fact that it did not possess an anti-icing system) the first two aircraft were prepared for the crossing on 24 April. They departed from Rio Grande at 1130Z in the hands of Teniente de Navio Jose Pereyra and Teniente de Fragata Miguel Uberti and were escorted to Port Stanley by a CANA Queen Air 80. The crossing was made smoothly and the second pair of aircraft quickly followed them. Thus, the four aircraft deployed to the Falklands were:

| 0719/401 | 0726/408 | 0729/411 | 0730/412 |
|----------|----------|----------|----------|

Their anticipated redeployment from the crowded and vulnerable Stanley Airport to Goose Green was delayed because of naval dissatisfaction with the state of the grass strip. BAM Condor might well have been considered suitable for the FAA's Pucaras but CANA did not like it at all! 4 Escuadrilla eventually went, on 29 April, to an even more remote grass strip located on Pebble Island on the northern coast of West Falkland. This small field, already identified as Grupo 3's alternate base should Goose Green be rendered unusable, had a 2,100ft landing strip of coarse grass. It was undulating and looked suspiciously liable to flooding. The modest little airfield was officially renamed the "Estacion Aeronaval Calderon", although to most Argentines it was simply "Borbon" (for Isla de Borbon, the Argentine name for Pebble Island).

All Argentine forces on the Falklands were uncertain of how Britain intended to attack the Islands and consequently by the last few days of April the outlying garrisons at Pebble Island, Darwin and on West Falkland were braced to expect a full-scale assault. During and immediately after the bombing of 1 May all the locally launched missions, particularly those of the FAA Pucaras, were thus "search-and-destroy" sorties intended to slow the advance of the British forces who, it was believed, had been flown ashore in helicopters. It was not until the late afternoon that it was finally appreciated that the air attacks had not heralded a full-scale invasion, although they had provided a diversion while small numbers of reconnaissance troops had been landed.

Shortly after 1545Z three 4 Escuadrilla Mentors took-off from Pebble Island on just such a mission. They were to investigate a reported helicopter landing in the area to the north of Berkeley Sound in East Falkland. The flight leader was Teniente de Navio Pereyra and his wingmen were Teniente de Fragata Daniel Manzella and Teniente de Fragata Uberti. Each Mentor was armed with three rocket pods, each with seven rockets, and the twin machine-guns. They were clear of Pebble Island by 1600Z and, after flying east for some while, they were roughly 10 miles to the north of Port Stanley when a British Sea King was sighted at low level and at a range of about 300yds. It was travelling west and was thought to have seen them because it looked to be taking evasive action. However, as the Mentors closed for the kill, they were themselves jumped by the 801 Sqdn Sea Harriers of Lt Cdr Nigel Ward and Lt Mike Watson. The latter pair had been vectored to the 4 Escuadrilla aircraft by 'Brilliant', which had presumably also been keeping an eye on the activities of the Sea King. In a brief but dramatic turning action Ward fired his guns at both Manzella and Pereya, hitting the former's aircraft in the rear cockpit area but otherwise causing no damage. The three CANA pilots saved themselves by a combination of good airmanship and good fortune; having jettisoned their rocket pods they sought safety in cloud and, although Ward all but collided with one of them in the cloud, their strategy was successful and the Sea Harriers gave up the search and returned to their CAP. The Mentors subsequently returned to Pebble Island at wave-top height and eventually landed safely.

Three more armed reconnaissance missions were carried out without further incident before, in the early hours of 15 May, the waterlogged Pebble Island airstrip was attacked by British Special Forces. The 0740Z pre-dawn attack effectively put all four Mentors (and seven other aircraft) out of action although the damage inflicted varied considerably. None of them was to fly again and their hulks remained on the airstrip until 1983.

4 Escuadrilla's war thus ended abruptly although its personnel on Pebble Island were obliged to suffer several Harrier and Sea Harrier attacks before they were rescued two weeks later. The last naval personnel were eventually, and somewhat dramatically, airlifted out on 31 May by two CANA Sea Kings.

It is difficult to judge the wisdom of the deployment but, although little was achieved and four aircraft were lost, CANA had no option but to utilise all suitable resources and to use whatever ingenuity it could to defend the Islands. But for 'Brilliant' and the 801 Sqdn Sea Harriers, the Mentors of 4 Escuadrilla might well have destroyed a Sea King!

In 1984 4 Escuadrilla de Ataque was operating its camouflaged Mentors at Punta Indio much as it had done before the War. Although negotiations were underway with the manufacturer in 1982 to replace the lost aircraft with new machines, that had not occurred by 1984.

---

*The 4 Escuadrilla de Ataque pilots who deployed to Port Stanley and Pebble Island were:*

*Teniente de Navio Batlori; Teniente de Navio J.Pereyra; Teniente de Fragata D.Manzella; Teniente de Fragata M.Uberti.*

---

# INDIVIDUAL AIRCRAFT DETAILS

The T-34C-1 Mentors of the Escuela de Aviacion Naval (4 Escuadrilla de Ataque) were delivered to CANA in 1978 in basic training colours. That was primarily an overall high-gloss white scheme with bright red rear fuselage bands. The national blue colours were worn on the rudder and elevators and the fuselage was marked with the aircraft serial, call-sign and ARMADA title in the usual CANA style. It is not known with absolute certainty when the aircraft were camouflaged — it might have been during 1981 — but by April 1982 all the aircraft are thought to have been resprayed. The lower surfaces were not changed and they remained white with the black CANA anchor marking retained beneath each wing. The green and tan camouflage was applied to all the upper surfaces and the bright red training band was reapplied to the rear fuselage (this remained in place on those aircraft deployed to the Falklands). The ARMADA title was also reapplied in black letters on the rear fuselage. The aircraft serial numbers were not externally restored and a small Argentine flag was painted directly over the original location on the tail. The call-sign/code was reapplied in a truncated format (eg '1-A-401' became '401'). No roundels of any kind were applied to the upper surfaces.

Four aircraft were deployed to Stanley Airport and then to Pebble Island. Their operational histories are detailed below.

---

**0719**

In 3.82 with 4 Escuadrilla and thought to have been already camouflaged and coded '401'. Flown by Teniente de Navio Pereya to Stanley Airport from Rio Grande on 24.4.82 and then to Pebble Island 29.4.82. During the 'D' Sqdn 22 SAS Regt raid on Pebble Island on 15.5.82 it was completely destroyed by explosive charges. The wreckage was finally cleared and buried on the site by autumn 1983.

**0726**

In 3.82 with 4 Escuadrilla and thought to have been already camouflaged and coded '408'. Flown to Stanley Airport from Rio Grande on 24.4.82 and then to Pebble Island on 29.4.82. During the 'D' Sqdn 22 SAS Regt raid on Pebble Island on 15.5.82 it was badly damaged by explosive charges detonated beneath the tail assembly and in the engine compartment. When inspected post-14.6.82 it was still standing on its undercarriage. On 21.7.83, while being airlifted as an underslung load beneath an

18 Sqdn Chinook to 'Sand Shore' in Elephant Bay, Pebble Island, it began to "fly" and had to be released. The Mentor fell into Elephant Bay and was not recovered.

**0729**

In 3.82 with 4 Escuadrilla and thought to have been already camouflaged and coded '411'. Flown to Stanley Airport from Rio Grande on 24.4.82 and then to Pebble Island 29.4.82. During the 'D' Sqdn 22 SAS Regt raid on Pebble Island on 15.5.82 it was sprayed with M15 rifle fire and disabled, although with little visible damage.

Protected from post-war vandalism by the Pebble Islanders, it being their intention to retain it as permanent reminder of the War. Removed by helicopter and loaded on board 'Sir Geraint' before sailing with her from Port Stanley on 10.6.83 for the UK. Arrived at Marchwood c4.7.83 where it was off-loaded and dismantled prior to leaving by MARTSU road transport on 7.7.83 for delivery that day to the FAAM at Yeovilton. After being reassembled it was put on static display in the Museum on 11.7.83 (still resident in 5.85). A plaque was set up near the aircraft acknowledging the Islanders' help in its preservation.

**0730**

In 3.82 with 4 Escuadrilla and thought to have been already camouflaged and coded '412'. Flown to Stanley Airport from Rio Grande on 24.4.82 and then to Pebble Island 29.4.82. Immobilised at Pebble Island in the 'D' 22 SAS Regt raid on 15.5.82, suffering blast damage to the engine compartment area. When inspected post-14.6.82 it was found to be in reasonable condition and still standing on its undercarriage. Airlifted by an 18 Sqdn Chinook to 'Sand Shore' in Elephant Bay, Pebble Island on 21.7.83. Overnight sailed with the ship, arriving in San Carlos Water on 22.7.83 where it was removed by Chinook to a weapons range on East Falkland. Noted in the "Rabbit Range" between Rabbit Mount and Mount Usborne (UC 770745) in 2.85.

# NEPTUNE

# ESCUADRILLA DE EXPLORACION

Between October 1958 and May 1959 CANA received eight Dutch-overhauled P2V-5 Neptune maritime reconnaissance aircraft. Prior to their overhaul, the Neptunes had served with RAF Coastal Command in the United Kingdom and approval from the United States was necessary for the transfer. The eight P2V-5's were later augmented by four SP-2E models, the first of which was received from the United States in 1966. They remained in use for many years until they were eventually superseded by the later SP-2H. CANA received four SP-2H's in 1977 and 1978 from the United States and by March 1982 these aircraft were the only Neptunes still available for operational use. The four aircraft were used by the Escuadrilla de Exploracion, a component of the 2 Escuadra Aeronaval, at the Comandante Espora base, Bahia Blanca. Their CANA serials and call-signs were 0706/2-P-110 to 0708/2-P-112 and 0718/2-P-114.

In reality there were only two aircraft that were available for operational use in early 1982 and it was only after considerable engineering effort that those two Neptunes, 0707/2-P-111 and 0708/2-P-112, were made airworthy and deployed from Espora to Rio Grande in April 1982 under the command of Capitan de Corbeta Julio Perez Roca. For the latter part of the month they were both extensively used for reconnaissance, fleet support and other special missions in anticipation of the arrival in the Falklands' waters of the British Task Force. Particular attention was paid to the search for British submarines. As the Task Force approached, training and exercise sorties gave way to operational missions and by 30 April searches for British shipping were making very considerable demands on both crews and airframes.

A pre-dawn mission was scheduled from Rio Grande for 1 May to search for British ships in the Falkland Islands area but the Neptune became unserviceable and could not be readied in time to meet its scheduled launch at 0850Z. It had been planned that an escort of two FAA Grupo 6 Daggers would be provided for the part of the flight which would take the aircraft to the east of Port Stanley on its trip round the Islands. However, after a lengthy wait, the Daggers took-off without the Neptune on a revised mission (and then they had the doubtful distinction of being overhead West Falkland coincident with the first Sea Harrier attack of the War).

The Neptunes were decidedly vulnerable to attack by the Sea Harriers and although both of the deployed aircraft had excellent newly-fitted VLF Omega navigational equipment, the inadequacies of their search radars forced them to within 100 miles of enemy warships in order to detect them. The Grupo 6 Daggers could offer some protection for such missions but, if caught over the open ocean by the carrier-based interceptors, the Neptunes would have had little chance of survival.

After an involvement with an aborted Super Etendard mission on 2 May and an unsuccessful submarine search the following day, 0708/2-P-112 was launched from Rio Grande at 0807Z on 4 May tasked to establish that a safe passage existed from the mainland to Port Stanley for three FAA C-130's. Capitan de Corbeta Ernesto Proni Leston and his crew were to seek early warning of the presence of British warships and, should any be found, the C-130's were to be warned off. The flight-plan called for the Neptune to fly due east from Rio Grande, passing to the south of the Falklands, before turning north and then west for home. Port Stanley was to be passed away to the west of the Neptune, making the flight a somewhat hazardous circumnavigation of the Islands. The range of the mission precluded a Dagger escort.

The Neptune's first contact of the morning, at 0850Z, was with the patrol vessel 'Comodoro Somellara', still engaged in the search for survivors from 'General Belgrano'. The operation continued as planned until, at about 1000Z, the C-130 mission was abandoned because Stanley Airport came under Sea Harrier attack but Proni, then still south-west of West Falkland, was ordered to stay on station and to await further orders. At 1050Z the Neptune crew was able to confirm to Rio Grande that a ship, first found on radar at 1010Z, was certainly a British warship and for nearly three hours Proni stayed in the area monitoring its position. After a while it became apparent that there were at least four warships in an area about 85 miles south of Port Stanley and, when first discovered, at a range of 90 miles from the Neptune. It was clear from the Neptune's RWR that its presence was known to the British but it continued to fly a series of orbits and zig-zags (in an attempt to simulate what the

British might assume to be an aircraft searching for survivors from the cruiser 'General Belgrano') and whenever it climbed to use its own search radar it was found that British ECM was in use against it. The nearest that Proni got to the warships was about 60 miles to the west of them.

While the crew of the aged Neptune struggled to keep the radar functioning and to remain in contact with the British fleet, CANA was preparing to launch two Exocet-equipped 2 Escuadrilla Super Etendards from Rio Grande to attack one of Proni's targets. He and his crew had guessed that to be the case and all were well aware of the importance of their task. Finally, at 1335Z, the Neptune climbed to 3,500ft and, in full radar and electronic view of the British ships, passed the positions of all four to the Super Etendards that, by then, were well on their way to the target. At 1504Z the Neptune, with its 12-man crew, landed at Rio Grande to await news of the Super Etendards and the unidentified Type 42 destroyer that they had found. Shortly afterwards they learned that it was 'Sheffield'.

The mission of 4 May proved to be the swansong of the Neptune in CANA service. While they were still capable of the demanded task, the aircraft were in poor condition and dreadfully unreliable. Their airframes and engines were worn out, as was much of the radar and avionics fit, but, perhaps above all else, the Neptune was obsolete and too vulnerable for a war in which modern electronics and weaponry would play a major part. Even in the absence of any suitable replacement, both Neptunes were withdrawn from operational use on 15 May 1982 and the aircraft were ferried back to Espora for storage.

Some Neptune missions were subsequently undertaken by the FAA C-130's while much of the coastal patrol work was passed to the Trackers of the Escuadrilla Antisubmarina and to other types, at least for the duration of the War. Two EMB-111A's were supplied to CANA by Brazil in May 1982 but they provided no true substitute for the long-range mission profile of the Neptune. First reported to be operating in the markings of 2 Escuadra, they were later both transferred to 6 Escuadra, Trelew.

The experiences of the War with Britain exposed the deficiencies of Argentina's maritime reconnaissance, AEW and ELINT capability. Within weeks of the termination of open hostilities the first of a small fleet of Lockheed Electra transports was obtained on the second-hand market. These Electras, which entered operational service in 1983, represented the best available compromise replacement for the Neptune.

---

*Escuadrilla de Exploracion pilots who were deployed to Rio Grande included:*

*Capitan de Corbeta J.Perez Roca (commander); Capitan de Corbeta E.Proni Leston.*

---

# INDIVIDUAL AIRCRAFT DETAILS

The two Escuadrilla de Exploracion SP-2H Neptunes deployed to Rio Grande wore their normal low-visibility colours comprising dark blue/grey upper surfaces with lighter sea grey lower surfaces. Argentina's national flag was worn on the tail above the black radio call-sign/code letters. The last three digits of the call-sign were worn on the nose but, except for a tiny serial number on the rear fuselage, no other fuselage titles or markings were carried.

Relatively little is known of the markings of the two former Brazilian EMB-111A's supplied to CANA during May 1982. Reports that year suggested that they had been allocated, and presumably wore, the call-signs '2-P-201' and '2-P-202' but later information indicated that they had been more recently based at Trelew (or perhaps Rio Grande) with the codes/call-signs '6-P-201' and '6-P-202'.

The notes below are the brief histories of the two airworthy SP-2H Neptunes that were deployed to Rio Grande in April 1982.

---

**0707**

In 3.82 with Escuadrilla de Exploracion as '2-P-111'. Deployed from Espora to Rio Grande in 4.82 and withdrawn from use there on 15.5.82. Subsequently returned to Espora by 9.82 and was last noted in storage there on 13.7.83.

**0708**

In 3.82 with Escuadrilla de Exploracion as '2-P-112'. Deployed from Espora to Rio Grande in 4.82 from where, on 4.5.82, it was involved in the radar identification of 'Sheffield' prior to her being attacked by Super Etendards of 2 Escuadrilla de Caza y Ataque. Withdrawn from use at Rio Grande on 15.5.82 and returned to Espora by 9.82 where it was last noted in storage on 13.7.83.

# TRACKER

# ESCUADRILLA ANTISUBMARINA

CANA received its first S-2A Trackers in 1962 when six refurbished aircraft were supplied from the United States for anti-submarine duties on the aircraft carrier 'Independencia' and, later, on her successor '25 de Mayo'. In 1967 a seventh aircraft was acquired. These seven Trackers were allocated the serial numbers 0510 to 0515 and 0542 and given the radio call-signs/codes '2-AS-1' to '2-AS-7'. Those that survived until 1977 were withdrawn from first-line duties to be replaced by six reconditioned S-2E models. The new machines re-equipped CANA's Escuadrilla Antisubmarina, a component of 2 Escuadra Aeronaval, based at the Comandante Espora base, Bahia Blanca. The new Trackers, serialled 0700 to 0705, were thus given the sequential radio call-signs '2-AS-21' to '2-AS-26'. In 1982 the four surviving S-2A's (thought to have been 0511 to 0514) were still in use with 6 Escuadra's Escuadrilla de Propositos Generales at the Vice Almirante Zar base, Trelew.

Commanded by Capitan de Corbeta Hector Skare, the Squadron deployed four Trackers from Espora to '25 de Mayo' on 29 March 1982 and, if the unit's account of the War is accurate, it was not until they had embarked that the pilots were briefed on the nature of their mission — the recapture of the Falkland Islands. Their role with Task Force 20 in Operacion "Rosario" was the maintenance of a continuous airborne watch to seek out any British surface or submarine presence that might interfere with the operation. None was found but the Trackers duly investigated a fleet of some 50 Russian and Polish fishing vessels to the north of the Islands. That flotilla remained in the area for some weeks, eventually dispersing only after Argentina and the United Kingdom began fighting for the Islands on 1 May.

Once the Falklands were secured by Task Force 40 two Trackers, one of which was 0701/2-AS-22, were deployed to Stanley Airport to undertake a reconnaissance of the Islands for the new military government. The first landed there from '25 de Mayo' at 1630Z on 3 April and both remained until 13 April, when they returned to Espora. During their stay they were credited with the "discovery" of the landing strip on Pebble Island that was later adopted by CANA as the "Estacion Aeronaval Calderon". It was during April that a priority modification

programme was undertaken to upgrade the avionics and sensors fitted to the Trackers. Particular attention was paid to the installation of new RWR equipment that would enhance their ability to assess the threats of the British search and fire-control radars. The equipment was commercially obtained, apparently from the United States.

The Squadron re-embarked '25 de Mayo' on, or soon after, 17 April and worked with the other elements of Task Force 79 to prepare the fleet for what might have been a full-scale naval battle. During the night of 30 April/1 May the northern elements of Task Force 79 reached a point on the north-western perimeter of the British TEZ and in the early hours of 1 May the Tracker of Capitan de Corbeta Skare took-off on a search mission to find the approaching British carrier group. Unknown to him at that time, 'Hermes', 'Invincible' and their support vessels had entered the TEZ at 0530Z from the north-east of the Falklands in readiness for their combined Sea Harrier attacks on Stanley Airport and Goose Green airfield later in the morning. Although Skare found nothing with his radar the newly fitted ESM equipment confirmed a nearby British naval presence. The Tracker sorties re-commenced at dawn but it was not until about 1500Z that Capitan de Corbeta Dabini (in 0702/2-AS-23) first found between 30 and 40 Russian fishing vessels (between the Argentine and British carrier groups) and then suddenly became aware that British search radars were in local use. The Tracker began to climb to an altitude to use its own radar but, before reaching it, the ESM illuminated, revealing several air search and surface search radars actively hunting the CANA aircraft. It was vital that the Argentine fleet should know the location and strength of the British fleet and thus the Tracker's search radar had to be briefly used. It revealed the British Task Force at a distance of 55 miles and, of course, the Tracker was well within the range of the Sea Harriers. Dabini immediately withdrew from the area following an erratic low-level track to protect the position of '25 de Mayo' but, as far as is known, he was not pursued and he returned safely to the aircraft carrier. There, he and his crew were debriefed and Task Force 79 considered the implications of their information. After a tense wait another Tracker sortie was launched at 0001Z on 2 May.

Capitan de Corbeta Emilio Goitia took his Tracker (0705/2-AS-26) eastwards at low level and eventually discovered four ships at a range of 60 miles beyond his position. As he returned to '25 de Mayo' at 0400Z, the aircraft carrier warned him that two unidentified aircraft were pursuing him and that he should descend to sea-level and draw them away from the ship. In fact the 801 Sqdn Sea Harriers, for that is what they were, had been scrambled at 0331Z in response to what the British believed to have been a searching C-130, detected some twenty minutes earlier. It seems probable that the "C-130" was actually Goitia's Tracker. The searching Sea Harriers withdrew rapidly, however, when they became aware of an Argentine Sea Dart control radar hunting for them from the destroyer 'Hercules', one of the '25 de Mayo' escorts. While Goitia had been taking evasive action, the Sea Harriers, still unaware of his presence, had got to within 60 miles of the Argentine carrier (and 25 miles from 'Hercules') before breaking off and returning towards 'Invincible'. Flt Lt Ian Mortimer was safely out of Sea Dart range and some 150 miles to the north-west of 'Invincible' when he turned towards the Argentine fleet and finally used his own search radar. Having quickly counted five surface contacts, he returned to 'Invincible'. Goitia, by then convinced that it was safe to return to '25 de Mayo', did so and landed soon afterwards.

At 0828Z another Tracker sortie was launched from '25 de Mayo' and its mission, as before, was to seek out and identify the British fleet. That aircraft was in the hands of Teniente de Navio Carlos Cal and he was well aware that, depending upon the nature of information that he might gather, '25 de Mayo' was ready to launch an eight-aircraft attack by the Skyhawks of 3 Escuadrilla de Caza against the British. However, Cal first experienced radar problems and then suddenly found himself overhead the Russian fishing fleet which had finally decided to vacate the TEZ! To the surprise of Cal and his three crewmen it appeared that a British warship was standing a radar picket in the very midst of the fleet (this has not been confirmed by any British source but such tactical devices were fairly routine in European waters). Eventually, after a long, cold and fruitless search, the Tracker returned to the carrier. At 1015Z, while Cal was probably still airborne, the British carrier group went to action stations fearing a dawn attack from '25 de Mayo', but that did not materialise. Post-war explanations have suggested that the calm conditions of the morning did not allow the fully-laden Skyhawks to take-off safely from '25 de Mayo' and that she was too far from the British fleet to launch the strike with anything less than maximum fuel in the aircraft but the reality was that Cal had simply "lost" the British fleet. His Tracker's radar malfunction at 0838Z and his subsequent digression with the fishing fleet meant that the "fix", established earlier by Goitia, was not re-confirmed and, without that, the Skyhawk attack was cancelled at about 0900Z. Cal's aircraft is thought to have remained airborne until after 1200Z, but without further radar contact with the enemy.

The northerly elements of Task Force 79 remained at sea until the loss of the cruiser 'General Belgrano' at 1858Z that afternoon caused the Armada to withdraw its warships to the safety of home waters. On 5 May a Tracker and a Sea King from '25 de Mayo' identified, but unsuccessfully attacked, a submarine some 45 miles from Bahia Camerone (44°10'S 64°00'W).

Once the Squadron was ashore, five Trackers were redeployed to the FAA base at Rio Gallegos from where they were to undertake anti-submarine and reconnaissance duties for the rest of the War. During mid-May trials were undertaken with one aircraft (thought to have been 0703/2-AS-24) to investigate the possibility of adopting the Tracker as a Neptune replacement for the Super Etendard/Exocet mission but they were unsuccessful and the experiment was abandoned.

The Escuadrilla Antisubmarina flew a total of 112 sorties during the entire operational period and, of those, 35 to 40 were adjudged to have made contact with British warships. After 14 June the unit returned to Espora and continued to undertake anti-submarine and reconnaissance operations from there with occasional routine deployments on '25 de Mayo'.

---

*Escuadrilla Antisubmarina aircrew who flew missions from '25 de Mayo' included:*

*Capitan de Corbeta H.Skare (commander); Capitan de Corbeta J.Covarrubias; Capitan de Corbeta Dabini; Capitan de Corbeta E.Goitia; Teniente de Navio C.Cal; Teniente de Fragata D.Marinsalta; Teniente de Fragata L.Sanguinetti; Teniente de Corbeta J.Razan; Suboficial J.Lencina; Suboficial R.Lencina; Cabo Principal J.Carrera; Cabo Principal N.Conde; Cabo Principal E.Paulinkas.*

---

# INDIVIDUAL AIRCRAFT DETAILS

The S-2E Trackers of the Escuadrilla Antisubmarina embarked '25 de Mayo' in their normal peace-time markings and no changes were subsequently made during the hostilities. Their low-visibility colours comprised dark grey upper surfaces and lighter sea grey lower surfaces. The national flag was applied to the tail and the standard ARMADA and 'A.R.A.25 DE MAYO' titles were painted in black characters on the tail and rear fuselage respec-tively. The call-signs and serials were also respectively applied to the fin and rear fuselage, the former in large black characters and the latter in tiny digits. The last two digits of the call-sign were worn on the nose-wheel door.

All six S-2E's are thought to have been in service with the Escuadrilla Antisubmarina in March 1982. Although at least five of the aircraft saw some operational use with

'25 de Mayo' on her two war cruises and from Rio Galle-gos, the histories below only note positively identified deployments.

**0700**

In 3.82 with Escuadrilla Antisubmarina as '2-AS-21'. Not confirmed as being in use during the War but was certainly operational at Espora in 9.82.

**0701**

In 3.82 with Escuadrilla Antisubmarina as '2-AS-22'. Embarked '25 de Mayo' 29.3.82 and was later deployed to Stanley Airport from 3.4.82 to 13.4.82. In operational use at Espora in 11.82.

**0702**

In 3.82 with Escuadrilla Antisubmarina as '2-AS-23'. Embarked '25 de Mayo' for her Task Force 79 deployment in 4.82.

**0703**

In 3.82 with Escuadrilla Antisubmarina as '2-AS-24'. Presumably embarked '25 de Mayo' with Task Forces 20 and 79 between 29.3 and c5.5.82 and thought to have been the aircraft used in mid-5.82 for Neptune replacement trials at Rio Grande with 2 Escuadrilla de Caza in connection with the latter's Super Etendard/Exocet mission. Noted in use at Espora in 5.84.

**0704**

In 3.82 with Escuadrilla Antisubmarina as '2-AS-25'. Not confirmed as being in use during the War period although Argentine publicity photographs illustrating this aircraft on '25 de Mayo' were issued with the statement that it showed carrier operations in 3.82. Noted in use at Espora in 5.84.

**0705**

In 3.82 with Escuadrilla Antisubmarina as '2-AS-26'. Embarked '25 de Mayo' for her Task Force 79 deployment in 4.82. Noted in service at Espora in 5.84.

*Operating from the carrier '25 de Mayo', the S-2E Trackers of the Escuadrilla Antisubmarina were the primary means by which the Armada's Task Force 79 sought to find, and engage, the British Task Force on 2.5.82. The search was ultimately unsuccessful although it was much a matter of chance that the British ships were not found. Had that happened, an Armada air strike against at least some elements of the Task Force would almost certainly have been undertaken. Within a few days, however, '25 de Mayo' had returned to Puerto Belgrano and her Trackers had disembarked to Comandante Espora. They then saw busy but undramatic service, operating from the FAA base at Rio Gallegos where all survived the War. 0700/2-AS-21 is seen here in the low visibility colour scheme at Espora in 9.82* (K. Ebata)

# FELLOWSHIP

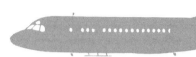

# ELECTRA

## 1 & 2 ESCUADRILLA DE SOSTEN LOGISTICO MOVIL

The Armada exhibited a considerable degree of independence from both the Ejercito and the FAA in most aspects of the War with Britain, indeed co-operation seems to have been limited to those occasions when it was absolutely unavoidable. The small fleet of transport aircraft available to CANA — those of 5 Escuadra Aeronaval — operated from their base at Ezeiza, Buenos Aires solely in support of naval and marine forces and, unlike virtually every other transport aircraft in Argentina, appear to have done so outside the FAA's otherwise all-embracing CdoAeTr. That autonomy did not, however, preclude the Armada from using FAA aircraft, particularly the Grupo 1 C-130's, for the carrying of outsize air cargo.

5 Escuadra's two Squadrons, the 1 and 2 Escuadrilla de Sosten Logistico Movil, operated three Electras and three F-28's respectively. The small force was primarily used to ferry men and material between the major mainland bases and from Rio Grande to Port Stanley. During the period from 2 to 30 April the six aircraft made 45 trips into Stanley Airport, carrying 1,500 personnel and 500 tons of naval equipment. Subsequently they continued to use the increasingly battered Airport although the operation progressively became more hazardous. After 1 May the FAA had closed it to all of their transports except the nocturnal C-130's but CANA, possessing no such rugged type, was obliged to continue as before or else abandon the operation completely. The task was demanding and only 14 flights were made in the six weeks before the surrender of 14 June. The final attempt to get an F-28 into Stanley Airport was made on 13 June but the aircraft returned to Rio Grande and it was thus an Electra that made the last run (by any Argentine aircraft) during the early hours of 14 June. The 14 flights carried 304 men and 70 tons of cargo to the Falklands but no details have been published of the number of personnel evacuated.

In addition to the 5 Escuadra aircraft, CANA also tasked the general purpose King Air 200's and Queen Air 80's of the operational wings with a small number of trips into Port Stanley during April and, conceivably, May. They were undertaken mainly (and perhaps entirely) as escorts for ferry flights from Rio Grande and involved small groups of Mentors and MB-339A's.

> *No details are known of 1 or 2 Escuadrilla de Sosten Logistico Movil crewmembers who took part in these operations.*

# INDIVIDUAL AIRCRAFT DETAILS

The serial and call-sign/code details of the 5 Escuadra transport aircraft (and those of the communications machines of the combat wings) are contained elsewhere in this book. With the exception of one or two isolated sightings (for example, Electra 0691/5-T-1 at Stanley Airport in early April) few specific details of their movements through Stanley Airport are known and thus no listing of these aircraft is possible. Limited photographic evidence indicates that no special markings were applied and that all the large aircraft retained their normal airline-style liveries throughout the War.

# LYNX

# ALOUETTE

# 1 ESCUADRILLA DE HELICOPTEROS

1 Escuadrilla de Helicopteros, a component of 3 Escuadra Aeronaval at the Comandante Espora base, Bahia Blanca was, in 1982, the unit tasked with the operation of all CANA helicopters other than the Sea Kings of 2 Escuadrilla. In March 1982 its fleet comprised two Lynx HAS.23's and about nine Alouette III's, the latter having been obtained in small batches over several years to various modification standards. The first of eight eagerly awaited new Lynx HAS.87's was in an advanced state of construction in the United Kingdom and several Armada destroyers and frigates were expected to re-equip with them.

Between 1969 and 1978 a total of 14 Alouettes had actually been received but attrition had limited the number on charge to no more than 10 at any time. The most recently received batch of four had brought the strength up to nine in March 1982 although only seven of them were available for operational use. Both Lynx HAS.23's, received in 1978 specifically for use on the Type 42 destroyers 'Hercules' and 'Santisima Trinidad', were in operational use in March 1982.

As the Armada assembled its forces in late March in preparation for Operacion "Rosario" some of the Alouettes and both the Lynx were embarked on the warships of Task Forces 20 and 40. Three Alouettes were deployed on '25 de Mayo', an unusual move which is thought to have been consequent to the temporary transfer of the carrier's normal Sea King complement to the ships of the assault force. The helicopters of 1 Escuadrilla received little attention in any Argentine accounts of the invasion and their activities appear to have been of a routine and unspectacular nature. The same cannot be said of the Alouette 0699/3-H-110 which was the duty helicopter embarked on the polar vessel 'Bahia Paraiso' for her autumn Antarctic cruise. The Alouette and the CAB601 Puma AE-504 (the latter having embarked 'Bahia Paraiso' at Ushuaia in late February for unrelated research purposes) were both tasked with support and reconnaissance operations off South Georgia when the political situation there deteriorated in late March, 'Bahia Paraiso' having reached Leith on 25 March. The Alouette was ordered to shadow 'Endurance' and report on the activities of her crew and Wasp helicopters. That demand-

ing task was undertaken with dogged determination, often in atrocious weather; indeed it was 0699's attentions that caused the crew of 'Endurance' to camouflage her Wasps during the night of 25/26 March. Finally, during the late hours of 31 March, 'Endurance' escaped from the radar of 'Bahia Paraiso' and she slipped away unnoticed.

During the morning of 2 April 'Bahia Paraiso' was told of the events on the Falkland Islands and that she would, with the frigate 'Guerrico', now constitute Task Force 60, the latter being on her way to South Georgia to ensure the surrender of the small British military presence at Grytviken. She arrived at 0900Z on 3 April and, having joined 'Bahia Paraiso', both helicopter crews were briefed for their role in the operation. In essence the Alouette was to provide reconnaissance ahead of the troop-carrying Puma, the latter making multiple journeys to put ashore the marines who, by 3 April, had embarked 'Bahia Paraiso' from Leith. Thus, at 1400Z that day, the Alouette left the research vessel for its first reconnaissance sortie to Grytviken.

The Alouette's pilot was, as usual, Teniente de Navio Remo Busson and his co-pilot was Teniente de Fragata Guillermo Guerra. An NCO, Sub Segundo Julio Gatti, accompanied them. The Alouette flew the seven miles round the coast to Grytviken at extremely low level and climbed to make its first reconnaissance pass. Busson saw nothing unusual and after several runs over the area and nearly an hour in the air he was told that the Puma was on its way in with 20 marines. Almost immediately 'Guerrico' entered the harbour at Grytviken and her crew warned Busson that troops could be seen, apparently taking up defensive positions among the buildings. Busson then left the area and, after a quick discussion with the Puma's crew, the marines were dropped into shallow water in a revised landing area. As the Alouette continued its reconnaissance the Puma left to collect a second batch of marines.

When AE-504 returned Busson directed it to land further along the beach in order that its marines would quickly combine with the first group that was slowly picking its way forward. As the Puma descended it was hit by heavy machine-gun and rifle fire that killed two of the marines and left several others wounded. The Puma was badly damaged and the crew was fortunate to be able to get it airborne and across the bay where it made a heavy landing and rolled onto its side. The Alouette was also hit in the rear fuselage area but was able to fly safely across to the Puma where it made a precautionary landing to inspect the damage to both helicopters. The Puma was in a sorry state but the Alouette had only taken hits to the emergency flotation gear and was otherwise in good order. Thus, while Gatti and the Puma's engineer picked up machine-guns and joined the uninjured marines, Busson began to ferry the wounded, two at a time, back to 'Bahia Paraiso'. On each return run he brought two more marines to reinforce the landing party and whenever he was unable to land because of British fire, they dropped into the sea and waded ashore. By the time 'Guerrico' had used her 100mm gun against the defending Naval Party 8901 to force its surrender, the Alouette had made nearly 20 round trips to 'Bahia Paraiso' and had been operating for some three hours. Without the Alouette's assistance the capture of South Georgia would probably have been arduous and more bloody than it was. Not surprisingly Busson, Guerra and Gatti were later decorated for their actions.

After the capture of the Falklands the Argentine fleet returned to port although not before some of the helicopters had paid visits to Stanley Airport. During the days following the landings the two Lynx helicopters were seen together in Port Stanley. Much of April was spent in preparation for the arrival of the British Task Force. As Task Force 79 was assembled to meet that threat the Alouettes were more conventionally deployed to their warships when the Sea Kings of 2 Escuadrilla were re-instated on '25 de Mayo'.

No significant incidents befell 1 Escuadrilla until 2 May when two helicopters were destroyed. An Alouette, 0649/3-H-105, was lost with the cruiser 'General Belgrano' when she was torpedoed at 1858Z that afternoon some 200 miles south-west of the Falklands while elsewhere, probably to the north of the Falklands, the Lynx 0735/3-H-142 collided with the hull of 'Santisima Trinidad' and was lost with its crew (in fact the wreck was later recovered). Following the loss of 'General Belgrano' all the large Armada surface vessels were withdrawn to the safety of home waters and their helicopters disembarked for land-based duties.

After her early adventures 'Bahia Paraiso' spent the period until 13 April ferrying CAB601 helicopters and other war materials from Puerto Deseado to Port Stanley. On 13 April she was found another task — that of ambulance ship. Her refit took place at Puerto Belgrano and she was at sea by 1 May equipped with an Alouette III and a CAB601 Puma. Her first duty was to join the search for survivors from 'General Belgrano' on 3 May but it was not until late in the month that she was ordered to the Falklands to evacuate wounded from the Islands. She was inspected by the Royal Navy and the International Red Cross on 31 May and was found to be carrying the Alouette and the Puma, both of which were in full Red Cross markings and ambulance configuration. No obvious external markings were visible to identify the

*The two Lynx HAS.23's of 1 Escuadrilla de Helicopteros were both deployed with the Armada's Task Force 40 for the invasion and were particularly active at Port Stanley during the first day or so of the Argentine occupation. Probably operating from 'Hercules' and 'Santisima Trinidad', 0734/3-H-141 and 0735/3-H-142 are seen here with rotors running during a brief stopover on the football field between Government House and the hospital. One month later, on 2.5.82, 0735 was destroyed in an accident involving 'Santisima Trinidad'.* (via 'Globe & Laurel')

Alouette but it is presumed that it was one of the 1 Escuadrilla helicopters.

Both 'Bahia Paraiso' and the polar vessel 'Almirante Irizar' were extensively used for hospital duties during June and both helicopters made visits to British ships and, later, land bases in the course of those duties. Argentine helicopters are known to have visited 'Uganda' on 4, 10 and 16 June and on subsequent occasions when 'Almirante Irizar' accepted casualties from 'Uganda'. Armada records indicate that 'Bahia Paraiso' made four visits to Port Stanley as well as to Fox Bay, Port Howard and Pebble Island. The Alouette and Puma were used in most of those evacuations.

In the immediate post-war period an Alouette was noted on 'Santisima Trinidad' at Puerto Madryn on 19 June (presumably having replaced her Lynx) but, in general, little of significance appears to have happened to 1

Escuadrilla de Helicopteros in the months after June 1982. The new Lynx HAS.87's were never received (their fates are considered elsewhere) and the wreck of 0735/3-H-142, although recovered, was never rebuilt. The fate of the surviving Lynx 0734/3-H-141 was still unclear in late 1984 (although CANA could probably continue to use it indefinitely with third party support). The Alouette strength was further reduced on 21 April 1983 when 0699/3-H-110 was destroyed in a fatal crash near Espora.

With the exceptions of Teniente de Navio Busson, Teniente de Fragata Guerra and Sub Segundo Gatti, mentioned in the text in connection with their 'Bahia Paraiso' deployment, no crew details are known of 1 Escuadrilla de Helicopteros for the War period.

# INDIVIDUAL AIRCRAFT DETAILS

As far as is known no changes were made to the markings of either the Alouette III's or the Lynx HAS.23's for the emergency period. For the former that meant that they wore a dark brown and green camouflage with the only light marking being a small national flag on the forward part of the boom. The serial was applied in tiny digits to the side door and the code was in larger script on the rear boom. The anonymous Alouette used for ambulance duties was painted white overall with large red crosses on the side doors and a small one on the nose. The two Lynx

remained in their basically white colours with grey undersides. The call-sign/code and the title ARMADA were worn on the boom and a large national flag was applied at the rear of the cabin beneath the engine exhaust.

The histories below include details of the two Lynx HAS.23's and all the Alouette III's thought to have been on 1 Escuadrilla de Helicopteros charge in 3.82. Such details that are known of the undelivered Lynx HAS.87's (which would have gone to 1 Escuadrilla) are included elsewhere in this book.

## ALOUETTE III

**0642**

In 3.82 with 1 Escuadrilla as '3-H-102'. Not confirmed as being used operationally during the War but thought to have been active in 1982.

**0649**

In 3.82 with 1 Escuadrilla as '3-H-105'. Sailed with Task Force 79 from Ushuaia on 'General Belgrano' 26.4.82 and was lost on 2.5.82 when the cruiser was torpedoed by 'Conqueror', 200 miles south-west of the Falklands.

**0651**

In 3.82 with 1 Escuadrilla as '3-H-107'. Not confirmed as being used operationally during the War but in service at Espora in 5.84.

**0681**

In 3.82 with 1 Escuadrilla as '3-H-109'. Not confirmed as used being operationally during the War but in service at Espora in 5.84.

**0699**

In 3.82 with 1 Escuadrilla as '3-H-110'. De-

ployed with 'Bahia Paraiso' on her Antarctic cruise 2.82 and was used during all phases of reconnaissance and capture of South Georgia from 25.3.82 to 3.4.82. Slightly damaged by gunfire at Grytviken on 3.4.82 but immediately repaired and returned to service. Further details of War service are unconfirmed. Destroyed in a fatal crash near Espora on 21.4.83.

**0736**

In 3.82 with 1 Escuadrilla as '3-H-111'. Not confirmed as being used operationally during the War but in service at Espora in 9.82.

**0737**

In 3.82 with 1 Escuadrilla as '3-H-112'. Not confirmed as being used operationally during the War but thought to have been active in 1982.

**0738**

In 3.82 with 1 Escuadrilla as '3-H-114'. Not confirmed as being used operationally during the War but thought to have been active in 1982.

**0739**

In 3.82 with 1 Escuadrilla as '3-H-115'. Not

confirmed as being used operationally during the War but thought to have been active in 1982.

## LYNX

**0734 HAS.23**

In 3.82 with 1 Escuadrilla as '3-H-141'. Deployed with Task Force 40 c28.3.82 for Operacion "Rosario" and noted near the Governor's Residence in Port Stanley early in 4.82. Presumably embarked 'Hercules' in 4.82 with Task Force 79 but no confirmation of further operational use after the loss of 0735 on 2.5.82. Some unofficial reports suggest that it was withdrawn from use in 1982 and stored pending disposal.

**0735 HAS.23**

In 3.82 with 1 Escuadrilla as '3-H-142'. Deployed with Task Force 40 c28.3.82 for Operacion "Rosario" and noted near the Governor's Residence in Port Stanley early in 4.82. Presumably embarked 'Santisima Trinidad' in 4.82 with Task Force 79 and lost in a fatal accident on the ship 2.5.82. The wreck was recovered but not rebuilt.

# SEA KING

# 2 ESCUADRILLA DE HELICOPTEROS

CANA acquired four new S-61D-4 Sea Kings in 1972 for anti-submarine duties on the aircraft carrier '25 de Mayo'. Serialled 0675 to 0678, they were used for many years by 2 Escuadrilla de Helicopteros as part of 3 Escuadra Aeronaval at the Comandante Espora naval base, Bahia Blanca. Shortly before the Falklands War an organisational change within CANA transferred 2 Escuadrilla from the helicopter wing to 2 Escuadra Aeronaval, the maritime reconnaissance and antisubmarine unit at the same base. The Sea Kings' call-signs were thus amended to '2-H-231' to '2-H-234'. In 1978 a fifth aircraft (serial 0696) had been purchased, ostensibly for anti-submarine duties, but unlike the original batch it was camouflaged and, at the time of the War, wore only the code '35'. This special duties Sea King was, nevertheless, on the establishment of 2 Escuadrilla. In March 1982 all five helicopters were in service with the Squadron at Espora.

Under the command of Capitan de Corbeta Norberto Barro, 2 Escuadrilla embarked with the fleet in late March for Operacion "Rosario". Its primary role was not that of ASW however, and, instead of operating from the aircraft carrier '25 de Mayo', the Sea Kings flew from the polar vessel 'Almirante Irizar' to carry ashore the marines of Task Group 40.1. The "large white helicopters" that were seen by the inhabitants of East Falkland to be bringing ashore Argentine troops in the early hours of 2 April were the Sea Kings of 2 Escuadrilla de Helicopteros. During the first few days of April the Squadron was extensively tasked to undertake reconnaissance patrols further afield and it was the 2 Escuadrilla Sea Kings that were the first helicopters to reach Darwin (4 April), Fox Bay and probably Port Howard.

Because they were CANA's only medium-sized helicopters, the Sea Kings were active on a variety of duties throughout early and mid-April while the fleet was in port but, when '25 de Mayo' put to sea with Task Force 79, 2 Escuadrilla was back on board the carrier. On that cruise there was a considerable sense of urgency and much attention was given to the ASW role. Some serious doubts had been expressed for some time concerning the effectiveness of the Sea Kings' ASW equipment fit and efforts had been made to improve it during April. Some new gear had been

obtained on the commercial market and had been quickly fitted, but the situation was generally depressing for it was feared that the obsolescent sonar would leave the fleet inadequately protected from the British nuclear submarines.

Throughout the tense hours of 30 April and 1 and 2 May the three embarked Sea Kings were almost constantly airborne, operating with the Trackers of the Escuadrilla Antisubmarina, but it was the cruiser 'General Belgrano' and not the '25 de Mayo' that succumbed on 2 May to the feared torpedo attack. Operating well to the south of the main elements of Task Force 79, Task Group 79.3 had been without ASW cover and had paid a dreadful price. The Royal Navy's preoccupation with '25 de Mayo' is still publicly unrevealed at the time of writing (although there is little doubt that the aircraft carrier was, at various times, followed by at least one submarine) but two CANA Sea Kings did attack an underwater contact, believed to have been a British submarine, some 45 miles off the Argentine coast abeam the Bahia Camerones on 5 May. By then most of the Argentine fleet had withdrawn to home waters and it is not clear what might have been the subject of the submarine's attentions. In any event the CANA depth-charge attack was unsuccessful and '25 de Mayo' and her Squadrons returned to port.

2 Escuadrilla was immediately redeployed to Rio Grande; indeed at least one Sea King was flying from there by 4 May on ASW and SAR duties. Later in the month at least two Sea Kings were sent to Viedma, a coastal town south of Bahia Blanca, tasked to provide an anti-submarine watch and to ensure that no enemy landings on Argentina should pass undetected! On 28 May, however, 2 Escuadrilla received a most unexpected order and all routine work at Rio Grande immediately stopped. It had been decided that a group of 10 naval personnel who had been isolated on Pebble Island for some days needed immediate evacuation to the mainland. The FAA was actually in the throes of undertaking a similar mission using a Grupo 9 Twin Otter to recover some of their men and it seems clear that the Armada felt obliged to do likewise. The mission (of surely questionable value, for the men were in little danger) was highly dangerous for, by then, the Sea Harrier CAP's had complete command of

the skies over Pebble Island. For two days two Sea Kings were stripped of all non-vital equipment and lightened in every conceivable way. Not for the first time was VLF Omega equipment quickly fitted in a CANA aircraft (only one of the two Sea Kings was so modified). Both helicopters were also to carry auxiliary fuel in five drums and the contents were to be hand-pumped into the main tanks on the outward journey. All tanks and drums would be replenished on Pebble Island from the local fuel stocks.

The mission was launched at 1730Z on 31 May using aircraft 0677/2-H-233 and 0678/2-H-234 and, as they set out from Rio Grande on the 350 miles journey, they were accompanied by a Prefectura Naval Puma that was to stay with them for 120 miles to calibrate their Omega and to generally escort them. A third 2 Escuadrilla Sea King was positioned to Rio Gallegos for rescue purposes. The two operational crews were those of Capitan de Corbeta Norberto Barro and Teniente de Navio Osvaldo Iglesias. Barro's crew comprised Teniente de Navio Guillermo Iglesias and Suboficial Beltran Giqueaux while Osvaldo Iglesias took Teniente de Fragata Oscar Branderburgo and Suboficial Roberto Montani. The weather was good and, aside from a valve malfunction in the fuel system of the Iglesias Sea King, the flight passed without incident. It took more than three hours and was performed at very low level and in extreme cold. The Sea Kings landed at 2036Z, collected the one remaining 4 Escuadrilla Mentor pilot and nine NCO mechanics, and left shortly after 2115Z. The engines had been left running throughout the turn-round in order to obviate any start-up problems. The return trip was undertaken in darkness using night-flying goggles and without the benefit of the Omega which had failed immediately after the landing on Pebble Island. The two helicopters flew in radio-silence but maintained visual contact with one another.

Barro "hedgehopped" along the island chain and, by using the open side windows to visually avoid the mountains after fog was encountered, he successfully cleared West Falkland. Iglesias, unhappy with his night goggles, elected instead to climb to mountain-top height (about 1,000ft) to clear the Islands. There he was safe from a high ground crash but was exposed to the British radar. However, in spite of all these hazards and the strain on the airframes caused by flying at 500lbs above the maximum AUW at maximum speed (120 knots), the two Sea Kings returned safely to Rio Grande at 0055Z on 1 June. Contrary to Argentine legend there was no Sea Harrier

attack on Pebble Island shortly after their departure, nor was there a helicopter-launched commando attack! The 2 Escuadrilla pilots might have been amused, however, to learn that when intelligence of the two Sea Kings reached the British fleet it was considered possible that they were Exocet-equipped — supplied from Peru — and that, if found, they should be destroyed. A Sea Harrier reconnaissance mission was duly flown over Pebble Island by Lt Cdr Frederiksen and Flt Lt Morgan of 800 Sqdn at 1855Z on 1 June and at 1923Z the airfield was duly attacked by Lt Cdrs Braithwaite and Craig of 801 Sqdn and then by Lt Cdr Thomas and Lt McHarg of 800 Sqdn.

The 2 Escuadrilla Sea Kings returned to the Falklands briefly after the surrender of 14 June when at least two were deployed on 'Almirante Irizar' for ambulance duties. 0675/2-H-231 and 0678/2-H-234 were used to ferry casualties from Port Stanley to the hospital ships and for such purposes they operated in normal anti-submarine markings alongside the ambulance-configured Puma, Alouette III and UH-1H's.

Post-war intelligence confirmed that all five Sea Kings remained in use after the War but has suggested that only three were used operationally during the conflict, accumulating some 300 flight hours. Presumably the activities of 0696/35 have been excluded from this Argentine summary, for the camouflaged Sea King was most certainly active during the War and is known to have been used from Rio Grande.

In spite of continuing post-war maintenance difficulties, a desire to replace the elderly AQS-13 sonar and to add a new acoustic processor, there were, in 1984, no immediate plans to replace the CANA Sea Kings with a more modern type of helicopter. Four new AS-61D Sea Kings were ordered soon after the War, however, and the first two, 0794/2-H-236 and 0795/2-H-237, were ready for delivery from Italy early in 1984.

---

*2 Escuadrilla de Helicopteros crewmembers deployed to Rio Grande included:*

*Capitan de Corbeta N.Barro (commander); Teniente de Navio G.Iglesias; Teniente de Navio O.Iglesias; Teniente de Fragata O.Branderburgo; Suboficial B.Giqueaux; Suboficial R.Montani.*

---

# INDIVIDUAL AIRCRAFT DETAILS

The anti-submarine Sea Kings used by 2 Escuadrilla de Helicopteros during the War flew throughout in their normal peace-time colours. In essence they were painted with white upper sides and sea grey lower surfaces with large black fuselage flashes in the engine exhaust areas. A yellow rotor warning stripe was worn and, in the mid-boom area, a large national flag was applied. The call-sign was applied in large black characters aft of the main side door but the serial and 'A.R.A.25 DE MAYO' titles were carried only in tiny characters on the rear fuselage. AR-

MADA titles were not applied. The unit badge appears to have been applied above the cockpit between the engine intakes. The one Sea King not positively identified as used operationally during the War, 0676/2-H-232, was seen in 1984 in an amended scheme in which the principal changes were the addition of the title ARMADA to the rear fuselage in large characters (and beneath the cab window in smaller letters), a smaller, truncated side code ('2-H-32') with the last three digits on the nose and the Argentine flag displaced to the main side door.

The special duties Sea King, 0696, retained its dark green and light brown camouflaged upper surfaces and light grey undersurfaces with its only markings believed to have been the last two digits of the call-sign, painted in black on the rear fuselage. By 1984 those markings appeared to have been slightly changed with a full code, albeit in small characters, now applied to the fuselage and the last three digits applied in grey to the nose. The unit badge was applied as on the anti-submarine Sea Kings.

As indicated earlier, at least four of the five aircraft on the strength of the 2 Escuadrilla de Helicopteros are thought to have taken an active part in the War.

**0675**

In 3.82 with 2 Escuadrilla as '2-H-231'. Deployed with Task Force 40 c28.3.82 and used by 'Almirante Irizar' on 2.4.82 to land troops on East Falkland. Noted at Port Stanley early in 4.82. Presumably embarked on '25 de Mayo' in mid-4.82 until c5.5.82 and then to Rio Grande, via Espora. Used for ambulance shuttle duties between 'Almirante Irizar' and Port Stanley after 14.6.82. Noted in post-war use at Espora.

**0676**

In 3.82 with 2 Escuadrilla as '2-H-232'. Not confirmed as used operationally during the War but in service at Espora in 5.84.

**0677**

In 3.82 with 2 Escuadrilla as '2-H-233'. Presumed to have embarked with Task Force 40 c28.3.82 and then Task Force 79 until c5.5.82, later deploying to Rio Grande via Espora. Used on the Pebble Island rescue mission of 31.5.82. Reported in post-war use at Espora.

**0678**

In 3.82 with 2 Escuadrilla as '2-H-234'. Deployed on 'Almirante Irizar' c28.3.82 with Task Force 40 and used in the landings on East Falkland on 2.4.82. Noted at Port Stanley early in 4.82. Presumably deployed with Task Force 79 and then to Rio Grande, via Espora, in early 5.82. Used on the Pebble Island mission of 31.5.82 and for ambulance shuttle duties between 'Almirante Irizar' and Port Stanley after 14.6.82. Reported in post-war use at Espora.

**0696**

In 3.82 with 2 Escuadrilla as '35'. This special duties Sea King is not known to have been embarked with the anti-submarine helicopters on either the Task Force 40 or Task Force 79 missions although it could have played a part in the former. Later deployed to Rio Grande and present there c1.6.82. In use at Espora in 5.84.

*The Sea King 0678/2-H-234 of 2 Escuadrilla de Helicopteros was one of the first Armada helicopters to land on East Falkland when it brought ashore the invading marines of Task Group 40.1 on 2.4.82. Following an active war it was allowed back on East Falkland to assist with the evacuation of Argentine wounded to their hospital ships. It is seen here, in Red Cross markings, operating from the Sportsfield at Port Stanley on 16.6.82. The airlift appears to have been largely organised and undertaken by Argentine personnel.*
*(V. Steen)*

# SKYVAN

# PUMA

# PREFECTURA NAVAL ARGENTINA

In early 1982 the air component of the Argentine coastguard service, the Prefectura Naval, was essentially a Buenos Aires-based force whose aircraft were deployed away from the northern regions to the more remote coastal areas only for specific missions. In March of that year it operated six Hughes 500C's, three SA.330L Pumas and five Skyvan transports, the helicopters being based at Puerto Nuevo Heliport, Buenos Aires and the Skyvans at Jorge Newbery Airport (Aeroparque), Buenos Aires. The Hughes 500C's were used mainly for patrol work in such areas as the Parana and Uruguay river regions and in the Rio de La Plata estuary area while the larger Pumas were used for SAR and maritime surveillance duties. The multi-functional Skyvans were used as personnel and cargo transports but were occasionally tasked with SAR, surveillance and paradrop missions.

As a completely military-staffed naval department, commanded by an Armada admiral, the Prefectura's involvement in the post-invasion consolidation on the Falklands was predictable and routine. Two Skyvans (PA-50 and PA-54) and a Puma (PA-12) were deployed with two patrol vessels to Port Stanley in early April to provide a full coastguard service for the new territory. The aircraft, under the command of Prefecto Aviador Pedro Gomez, were further tasked to undertake extensive communications duties in support of the naval forces. The short-field performance of the Skyvan made it, at least in theory, particularly well suited to the task but even its ruggedness was ultimately defeated by the terrain and other inadequacies of the Falklands' tiny airstrips. On the mainland other Prefectura Skyvans and Pumas were deployed south to locations such as Rio Grande for local communications and patrol duties.

The aircraft at Port Stanley operated mainly from the Racecourse but use of the Skyvans appears to have been limited to a handful of visits to Goose Green during April and a few to Pebble Island after the CANA base was established there late in the month. It was a Skyvan that took the first CANA personnel to Pebble Island on 24 April and, from somewhat limited evidence, it seems that once the Calderon base was established, a Skyvan was positioned there from Port Stanley for local use. The Puma was extensively used throughout April for a variety of purposes, frequently as a staff transport, but also on SAR and observation tasks. When noted at Fox Bay West on 27 April it was being used to carry forced evacuees there from Port Stanley.

Unfortunately, the three aircraft on the Falklands were all early casualties of the fighting and thus played little part in the War. The demise of the Skyvan PA-54 and the Puma PA-12 was rapid with both falling victim to early Royal Navy warship bombardments. The circumstances have not been precisely explained but it appears that a bombardment during the night of 3/4 May caused the incapacitation, by blast damage, of the Skyvan on the Racecourse although its eventual destruction was probably the result of 105mm artillery fire during the shelling of Port Stanley on 12/13 June. The Puma was also badly damaged by naval gunfire and one official Argentine account states that that occurred during the same night, the 3/4 May. The Puma was subsequently robbed of several items, including the rotor-blades, and was eventually found by British forces as an abandoned hulk on the roadside by the Governor's Residence.

The Skyvan PA-50 survived a little longer, becoming bogged-down at Pebble Island for some days before it was destroyed there in the early hours of 15 May. It was blown-up by British Special Forces in the course of their commando raid on the base and was left burned-out.

The Prefectura did not make good its losses on the Falklands and, although the mainland-based Pumas and Skyvans were extensively utilised for the remainder of the War, no other aircraft were involved in a combat situation.

The Prefectura Naval continued to operate the three surviving Skyvans and the two remaining Pumas alongside the six Hughes 500C's after June 1982. However, despite an obvious need to replace lost equipment, funds were not forthcoming and, by late 1984, the five new helicopters that the Prefectura had publicly stated that it needed had not materialised.

*With the exception of Prefecto Aviador Pedro Gomez mentioned earlier, no PNA aircrew names are known for the Falklands deployment.*

When found by British forces in Port Stanley, the PNA Puma PA-12 had already been unserviceable for several weeks and components had been removed, probably by CAB601 personnel. However, in common with other captured aircraft, PA-12 suffered further and unnecessary damage at the hands of British troops and what would normally have been a simple restoration to flying status became something far more complex. Nevertheless the Puma was brought to RNAY Fleetlands for inspection and in 1.85 it was finally delivered to Westland Helicopters for rebuild as ZE449. PA-12 is seen at the Portsmouth Navy Days, 28–30.8.82.

(Peter J. Cooper)

The 4 Escuadrilla de Ataque Mentor 0729/411 eventually arrived at Marchwood in 7.83, having been brought to the United Kingdom specifically for exhibition in the Fleet Air Arm Museum, Yeovilton. Thanks to the efforts of the Pebble Islanders, who had identified it as the least damaged Mentor (and had anticipated retaining it), post-war damage was minimal and the aircraft was easily reassembled at Yeovilton. In this view 0729 is seen outside the Museum prior to going on display within.

(Ministry of Defence)

It was unfortunate that no-one at Port Stanley displayed the enterprise of the Pebble Islanders and sought to preserve an MB-339A before the three aircraft were wrecked by the British forces. At the eleventh hour the Royal Navy recovered enough pieces to assemble a composite aircraft and those pieces, mainly of 0761 and 0767, were brought to Yeovilton in 6.83. The reassembled machine is seen here on exhibition at the Fleet Air Arm Museum. (Ministry of Defence)

# INDIVIDUAL AIRCRAFT DETAILS

The two Skyvans deployed to Stanley Airport in April 1982 were both camouflaged, as were those used on the mainland, but it is thought that the new colour scheme was applied some while before the Argentine invasion of the Falklands (possibly as early as 1979). The original and basically white colour scheme was completely replaced by the same new camouflage that was later applied to the CANA Mentors and MB-339A's (post-war inspection of the wrecks revealed that a brown and yellow mottle had been added to the basically green camouflage). The PREFECTURA NAVAL ARGENTINA title is thought to have been retained on the rear fuselage and the serial number remained at the base of each fin. A small national flag above the serial replaced the earlier and much larger flag. After 1 May a broad vertical yellow identification band was painted around the rear fuselage.

The Puma PA-12 retained its peace-time colours when deployed to Port Stanley. Essentially they comprised a white fuselage and boom/tail with dark blue upper surfaces, lower fuselage and undercarriage housings. The PREFECTURA NAVAL ARGENTINA title and serial number was applied to the boom in black letters and the national flag was painted on the tail unit. After 1 May a broad vertical yellow identification stripe was applied to the forward part of the boom and a similar (and very crude) yellow stripe was horizontally applied to pass through the window line and along the boom.

The three histories below reflect only the known details of those aircraft deployed to the Falkland Islands. No specific details are available for those aircraft used from Rio Grande and elsewhere on the mainland.

## PUMA

### PA-12 SA.330L

In 3.82 with the "Agrupacion Albatros". Presumed to have been shipped to Port Stanley early in 4.82 although its first positive sighting was on 27.4.82 at Fox Bay West. Argentine accounts state that it was damaged by Royal Navy gunfire at Port Stanley during the night of 3/4.5.82 and that it did not fly again. Cannibalised and later abandoned on the roadside near the Governor's Residence, it was found there by British troops on 14.6.82. Its internal blast damage may have been caused at that time. Airlifted by 18 Sqdn Chinook ZA718 to 'Tor Caledonia' in Port William for carriage to the UK.

Sailed with the vessel on 1.8.82. Airlifted off by 18 Sqdn Chinook ZA709 on 19.8.82 while the ship was off Portsmouth (before it docked at Felixstowe on 20.8.82) and carried by the helicopter to RNAY Fleetlands for inspection and possible rebuild. Displayed on the quayside at the Portsmouth Navy Days 28-30.8.82. Transferred by road to St Athan on 16.9.82 for the BoB display on 18.9.82 and returned to Fleetlands shortly afterwards for a detailed survey. The damage was found to be moderate with small arms/shrapnel punctures and the effects of a grenade explosion in the cockpit area. Anticipating restoration, it was allocated the serial ZE449 during 1984 and departed by road for Weston-Super-Mare on 16.1.85 (arriving that day) to be rebuilt to flying condition.

## SKYVAN

### PA-50

In 3.82 with the Prefectura Naval at Jorge Newbery Airport (Aeroparque), BA. Ferried to Port Stanley during 4.82. Used from Stanley Airport and the Racecourse until early 5.82 when it is thought to have been deployed to Pebble Island. Destroyed there on 15.5.82 during the commando raid by 'D' Sqdn 22 SAS Regt, with only the outer wings and tail area not consumed by fire. The wreckage was finally removed to the perimeter of the airfield in late 1983. The larger pieces were reportedly buried in a shell crater but in 2.85 some remains were still visible.

### PA-54

In 3.82 with the Prefectura Naval at Jorge Newbery Airport (Aeroparque), BA. Ferried to Port Stanley during 4.82. Used from Stanley Airport and the Racecourse until the night of 3/4.5.82 when it was damaged by British naval gunfire. Understood not to have flown again and was later destroyed on the Racecourse by shellfire during the final British bombardments of 12/13.6.82.

The wreckage was moved to the Beaver Hangar area by 10.83 although some small pieces, including one engine, were brought to the UK on 'St Helena', arriving at Falmouth 11.6.83. They were taken to the FAAM at Yeovilton on 14.6.83 for display. Pieces of wing and the tailplane were noted dumped near the edge of the Racecourse at Port Stanley in 9.84.

*Within a few days of the cease-fire some very strange stories concerning the PNA Puma PA-12 were circulating among certain elements of the British forces. Wild rumours of last-miniute efforts to extricate senior intelligence officers abounded and theories were on offer to explain how the unfortunate helicopter had come to meet its (presumed) end in Ross Road. Such accounts were, of course, all nonsense as this photograph, taken on 15.6.82, shows. The Puma had long been grounded and many components removed. Presumably the PNA, in the fullness of time, had hoped to return it to flying status.*

*(Paul R. G. Haley, 'SOLDIER')*

**Above** *On 18.6.82 the airworthy CAB601 UH-1H AE-413 was appropriated for 5 Infantry Brigade's use by Sqdn Ldr Rob Tierney. Here it is seen at the Sportsfield in the emergency aeromedical colours that had been applied by CAB601 some ten days earlier and which were only slightly modified for British operations. Because of the fear that the red crosses contravened the Geneva Convention once 5 Infantry Brigade had begun to carry fully fit and armed troops, they were deleted within a few days. During its brief operational life with the Brigade, "Sheto Hatti" (Gurkhali for "White Elephant") undertook 40 deck landings on 14 different ships.* **Above Right** *The inset view shows AE-413 departing from 'Intrepid' after the red crosses had been deleted. (via Lt S. A. George, RN/Ministry of Defence).*

**Below** *Another CAB601 UH-1H, AE-422, had been appropriated by Lt Cdr Keith Dudley of 820 Squadron but it was in the hands of 825 Squadron that it flew most of its 30 hours before being shipped to the United Kingdom. It is seen here in Dudley's hands on the Port Stanley Racecourse undergoing ground runs before its departure to San Carlos settlement on 16.6.82. The machine-gun mounting post is visible by the cabin door; the cockpit door was removed by CAB601. The "Huey's" markings are standard to CAB601, the yellow identification stripe having been applied after 1.5.82 in order to minimise the chances of it being fired upon in error by Argentine infantry. The* **Inset** *view shows AE-422's arrival at San Carlos settlement late that afternoon.*
*(via Lt S. A. George, RN)*

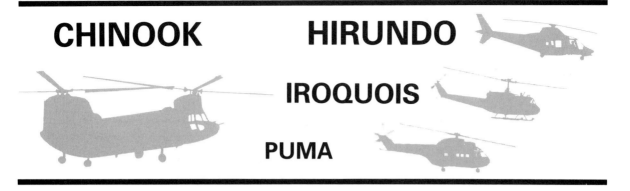

# CHINOOK    HIRUNDO

## IROQUOIS

## PUMA

# BATALLON DE AVIACION DE COMBATE 601

Argentina's army, the Ejercito, was, in 1982, organised in such a way that its aviation element, the Comando de Aviacion del Ejercito (CAE), was part of the Infantry. The CAE comprised two headquarters organisations; the Batallon de Aviacion de Combate 601 (CAB601) and the Compania de Aviacion de Apoyo General 601 (CAAG601), both of which were based at Campo de Mayo, Buenos Aires. CAB601 was composed solely of helicopters and constituted the CAE's combat force while CAAG601 was essentially a fixed-wing support unit tasked with several diverse duties. Within CAB601 were the flight companies; one attack company and two assault companies. The former, the Compania de Helicopteros de Ataque, was, in March 1982, equipped with the A-109A Hirundo and the SA.315B Lama; the Compania de Helicopteros de Asalto 'A' flew the SA.330L Puma and the CH-47C Chinook and the Compania de Helicopteros de Asalto 'B' flew the UH-1H Iroquois (the ubiquitous "Huey" was widely known as "UH" in CAE use).

The combat strength of CAB601 on 1 April 1982 was nine A-109A's, six Lamas, eight Pumas, two Chinooks and about 20 UH-1H's. Of those, one A-109A (AE-332) had been in major maintenance for 18 months and another (AE-333) for six months. A Lama (AE-388) had also been in maintenance for 18 months. A ninth Puma (AE-502) had recently been destroyed in an accident. In spite of problems caused by the United States arms embargo and the domestic financial constraints, CAB601 appears to have been a reasonably efficient and well-equipped organisation. Its helicopters were modern and among the best available on the world market and, by Latin American standards, the unit was numerically strong.

The Ejercito's role in Operacion "Rosario" was limited and just a handful of specialist troops went ashore on East Falkland on 2 April with the marines of Task Group 40.1. The only CAB601 helicopter to accompany them, a Puma, was disembarked from 'Almirante Irizar' on 3 April with slight damage, incurred in the heavy seas of 29 March, but was soon airworthy.

A month before "Rosario" CAB601 had detached a single Puma, AE-504, to Tierra del Fuego for routine Ejercito purposes. It was flown by Primer Teniente Juan Villagra and although it retained the normal dark camou-

flage the Puma was equipped with skis for snow operations. In late February it was embarked with a CANA Alouette III, 0699/3-H-110, on 'Bahia Paraiso' at Ushuaia for carriage to the South Orkney Islands where both were to be involved in the support of independent research programmes. Their presence on 'Bahia Paraiso' was of routine significance until mid-March when the ship became involved with the "scrap metal merchants" on South Georgia. Then, as the crisis deepened, the polar vessel's mission was changed. Throughout the last week of March her two helicopters were involved in a "cat and mouse" reconnaissance operation in which 'Bahia Paraiso' and 'Endurance' shadowed one another. Finally, at 2200Z on 31 March, 'Endurance' evaded 'Bahia Paraiso' to leave the latter waiting for 'Guerrico' to join her off South Georgia. It was 'Guerrico' that collected from Leith the marines who were tasked to capture the British naval force at Grytviken, Naval Party 8901. Together, the two ships comprised the hastily constituted Task Force 60.

'Guerrico' reached 'Bahia Paraiso' at about 0900Z on 3 April and it was quickly agreed that while the Alouette would provide reconnaissance information, the Puma could be used to carry ashore marines from 'Guerrico'. The Alouette would lead the Puma to a suitable landing site and it would thereafter keep an airborne watch for British troop activity. The mission began soon after 1400Z and AE-504 made its first trip with a crew of three and twenty marines. The Alouette had been airborne for an hour without seeing any sign of life but shortly before the Puma was due to land observers on 'Guerrico' spotted some movement near the hospital at Grytviken. A rapid change of plan resulted in the two helicopters approaching Grytviken from behind Mount Hodges but the Puma then found itself unable to land and the 20 marines were obliged to jump into the shallow water. As they waded ashore the Puma returned to 'Bahia Paraiso' for reinforcements. When it returned to the beach with the second group of marines it was fired upon by Naval Party 8901. At 1505Z AE-504 was struck by more than 50 rounds of GPMG and small-arms fire that killed two marines and wounded several others. Despite serious damage to the engine and hydraulic systems, Villagra and his co-pilot Primer Teniente Eduardo Leguizamon managed to keep the Puma flying and it staggered across the bay to the opposite shore before it heavy-landed and rolled onto its port side. The Alouette had also been hit by the same fusillade but its landing near the Puma was only precautionary and it continued to ferry out the wounded and bring in more marines until the eventual British surrender. The captain of 'Bahia Paraiso' allowed the crew forty minutes to recover all that they could from the Puma and, by the time they withdrew, an engine and several instruments had been salvaged. The hulk of AE-504 was never recovered by Argentina and in 1983 it remained where it had fallen, the first helicopter lost in action by CAB601.

Within a day or so of the loss of AE-504 the officers and men of CAB601 began to receive orders to prepare themselves and their helicopters for movement from Campo de Mayo to the Falklands. The orders came as something of a surprise to the majority of the unit's personnel for whom the success of "Rosario" had been a national triumph but one that they had learned of from the media! It was not until the prospect of British military retaliation became a serious threat that any plans were made to take more CAE helicopters to the Islands. Thus, as the British fleet sailed on 5 April, CAB601 was anxiously planning to move its first wave of reinforcements south to join the solitary Puma at Port Stanley.

The first helicopters to leave Campo de Mayo were three Pumas and two A-109A's. The first two Pumas and an escorting A-109A left the base at dawn on 6 April and made the long flight to Comodoro Rivadavia via the Comandante Espora naval base at Bahia Blanca. From Comodoro Rivadavia they flew onto 'Bahia Paraiso' which was at sea some 50 miles off Puerto Deseado. Once embarked they were hangared and the ship sailed for Port Stanley. All three helicopters were flown off early the following morning when the vessel was still over 100 miles from the Islands and made their way to Port Stanley across much of West and then East Falkland. Another Puma and a second A-109A quickly made a similar crossing and by 9 April CAB601 had four Pumas and two A-109A's operational at its new base at Moody Brook, the former Royal Marine barracks.

The first UH-1H's were ordered to make their departure from Campo de Mayo on 7 April and they accordingly left in two groups for the FAA base at Tandil, Buenos Aires. After a brief stop they continued to Espora which they reached at midday. There they remained until 9 April when AE-409 was flown by Teniente Molina to San Antonio West where it embarked on 'Bahia Paraiso' later in the day. As before, 'Bahia Paraiso' carried her CAE cargo to the Falklands overnight and AE-409 thus became the first Huey to reach Port Stanley. It was immediately put to work and on the first day, 10 April, it flew for more than six hours. AE-409 had been accompanied by another A-109A and thus, by then, eight helicopters were available; four Pumas, three A-109A's and the UH-1H.

The other Hueys experienced something of a hiatus after AE-409 had left for the Falklands. They remained at Espora until 11 April when they left for Comodoro Rivadavia via a refuelling stop at San Antonio West and a short stop at the naval base at Trelew. On reaching Como-

doro Rivadavia, their journey then fell foul of the British Maritime Exclusion Zone (MEZ) which was to become effective at 0400Z 12 April. The MEZ was viewed seriously by Argentina and it was decided that they should continue their journey as airfreight, rather than deck cargo. Accordingly, plans were made to prepare them for onward carriage by FAA C-130 transports. The planning of the exercise was simple enough but the locating of the special tools and equipment necessary to dismantle and stow the UH-1H's for airfreighting was very time-consuming and it was not until 18 April that the first of them, AE-410, was airlifted to Stanley Airport. Once reassembled they, too, were flown to the nearby Moody Brook base.

By 18 April the first of the Chinooks had been ferried to the Falklands where it joined the two FAA examples that were by then operational at Goose Green with the Grupo 7 detachment. CAB601 strength at Moody Brook was further increased to 11 with the simultaneous arrival of the fifth, and final, Puma. The UH-1H's continued to arrive as airfreight and further deliveries were made on 21 April, 22 April, 23 April (when four arrived) and 29 April. The second Chinook was delivered on 30 April and thus, as everyone tensely awaited the British Task Force's next move, CAB601 reached its full strength. 19 helicopters were in place; two Chinooks, five Pumas, three A-109A's and nine UH-1H's:

| Chinook | AE-520 | AE-521 | |
|---|---|---|---|
| Puma | AE-500 | AE-503 | AE-508 |
| | AE-501 | AE-505 | |
| A-109A | AE-331 | AE-334 | AE-337 |
| UH-1H | AE-406 | AE-412 | AE-418 |
| | AE-409 | AE-413 | AE-422 |
| | AE-410 | AE-417 | AE-424 |

For their duties on the Falklands the Pumas flew with their normal crew of two and an NCO loadmaster but the UH-1H co-pilots were replaced by engineers, normally NCO's, and a side gunner was added to the complement. The Pumas were used to make the initial troop deployments and to reinforce and resupply the more distant garrisons, particularly those on West Falkland. Major troop movements included the garrisoning of Fox Bay with RgtInf8 by Pumas on 12 April, a similar operation for both the Ejercito and FAA to Darwin from 16 April and the airlift of RgtInf5 and other units by Puma and UH-1H to Port Howard between 26 and 29 April. Throughout the month the UH-1H's conducted an endless shuttle of men and equipment from Port Stanley to its outer defences and the distant observation posts on East Falkland. The A-109A's flew escort sorties and general cargo missions. For these missions each type used an identifying call-sign. The A-109A's were "Tortas" (Cakes), the UH-1H's were "Panes" (Bread), the Chinooks were "Chanchas" (Pods) and the Pumas were "Flores" (Flowers).

In mid-April one of the two Pumas that was to have remained on the mainland was made available to 'Bahia Paraiso' for use in the ambulance role. The anonymous white Puma, marked only with red crosses, was embarked before 1 May and was still in use in late June when it was last seen on the Falklands evacuating Argentine injured.

As the unit braced itself for the anticipated attack, news was received of a mainland accident involving a UH-1H. AE-419 had crashed on 30 April at Caleta Olivia, killing the pilot, two NCO crewmen and eight others. It was depressing news that could only lower morale at a tense time.

The air and naval attacks by the British on 1 May marked a clear watershed for the helicopter operations on the Falklands. Until then flying had been relatively easy with only poor weather and the occasional low fuel state to cause worries. After 1 May the dreaded "Harriers" (as both the Naval and RAF versions were known) ruled the skies and their appearances spelled disaster for the helicopters. Long flights were undertaken only at dawn or dusk and by means of circuitous "safe" routes that made much use of the natural features of the rocky terrain. The helicopters were flown at very low level and it became routine to abandon the machine and to run for cover if caught by Sea Harriers. Not all problems were expected to come from the air, however, and the A-109A's regularly flew protection missions with the Pumas and UH-1H's on long flights against the possibility of attack from commando forces.

Although the air and naval bombardment of 1 May did not damage any of the helicopters parked at Moody Brook it was decided that they should immediately be moved to a safe area to the north of Mount Kent, about 15 minutes flight time away. CAB601's maintenance facilities — primarily the FIGAS "Beaver Hangar" situated near the Racecourse — would remain in use. The UH-1H's and the A-109A's were moved en masse at about 1400Z and with great caution for fear that they might be mistaken for the enemy and fired on. To minimise that possibility a yellow identification stripe was applied to the booms of all the helicopters. Only one UH-1H, possibly AE-418, failed to make the trip at that time because of a transmission oil problem.

Flying continued into the first week of May without loss although there were many scares. The "red alert" was commonplace (and in the Darwin and Goose Green area it became almost a permanent feature) as naval bombardment and air attacks were increased. The first Falklands loss eventually occurred on 9 May when the Puma AE-505 was tasked to search the sea area of Choiseul Sound in the general location of Sea Lion Island. It was to look for the impressed stern trawler 'Narwal' that had been attacked by 800 Sqdn Sea Harriers earlier in the day. At 1907Z it was seen on radar by 'Coventry', engaged at the time in a bombardment of the Port Stanley area, and the destroyer brought the Puma down from extreme range with a Sea Dart. At the time that was not realised by CAB601 and, for four days of truly atrocious weather, the unit was unable to mount a proper search for the missing Puma. Finally a BBC news bulletin confirmed their fears. The missing helicopter had carried a crew of three; the pilot Primer Teniente Roberto Fiorito, engineer Primer

Teniente Juan Buschiazzo and NCO Raul Dimotta. Neither they nor their Puma were ever found.

That same night, 9 May, another naval bombardment on Moody Brook damaged the picketed UH-1H AE-410. It suffered some splinter damage to the fuselage and engine and although it would have been rapidly repaired on the mainland it was a different matter at Moody Brook and the Huey remained unserviceable for the rest of the War. The Puma AE-508 was also damaged in the same attack but was soon repaired. As a direct result of the incident the CAB601 helicopters, which had recently returned to Moody Brook, were again moved and it was decided that their parking zone would be changed every two or three days. Even that measure provided little protection from the elements and more minor storm damage was inflicted on 11 May.

Although maintenance was difficult under the circumstances strict schedules were adhered to for as long as possible. Typical of the UH-1H's was AE-409 which received a 25-hour "Malvinas check" on 13 April, a 50-hour check on 30 April and a 75-hour check on 26 May. Those inspections were undertaken in very testing circumstances and by early May some critical spares shortages were evident. It was on 2 May that the Chinook AE-520 was grounded near the Governor's Residence, Port Stanley, with continuing engine problems.

The helicopters continued to fly every day unless prevented by the weather. Despite many alarms (including such horrors as artillery barrages from "friendly" forces) no more of them were lost until late May. On 16 May the unit returned to the Port Stanley area but within a few days it had moved on to the Two Sisters area and soon after that it returned to the northern slopes of Mount Kent. As each move was made all the personnel and support equipment went with the helicopters and the CAB601 "tent city" moved from site to site. At about 1245Z on 19 May 801 Sqdn unsuccessfully attempted to bomb the Mount Kent site through cloud from high altitude using VT bombs. No damage was sustained.

The long-awaited British landings took place on 21 May and the air attacks from both the RAF Harriers and naval Sea Harriers increased in intensity. At dawn that day, with many CAB601 men still asleep in their tents, the 1(F) Sqdn Harriers of Sqdn Ldr Jerry Pook (XZ988) and Flt Lt Mark Hare (XZ963) appeared over the helicopter park situated to the north of Mount Kent and, after a reconnaissance pass, they attacked the helicopters with CBU's. Their first run was unsuccessful but in a second attack Hare's cannon fire hit the Chinook AE-521 which caught fire and burned-out. A Puma, AE-501, which was tied down some 300yds to the east was also hit by gunfire during this and subsequent passes and was substantially damaged although not destroyed. The nearby UH-1H of Primer Teniente Sanchez Marino (thought to have been AE-417) had been parked with its engine running at the time of the attack and, in between the firing passes, he and his crew had managed to shut it down although not before the rotor-blades had been damaged by the 30mm cannon fire. The Harriers had actually caused little harm to the Huey and after a change of blades it was flown out of the area. However, CAE strength returns removed a UH-1H from the "available" list on 21 May and in the absence of any other known incident it may be presumed that other damage was inflicted which was not immediately repairable. The Puma, totally incapacitated, was picketed where it had been hit and left for later recovery although, as will become apparent, that was not to happen. The Mount Kent site was not protected by anti aircraft batteries and although a great deal of small-arms fire had been put up it had been generally ineffective. Once the "dust" had settled the helicopters were evacuated once more to Port Stanley and to the comparative safety of its air defences. The unit ended the day in better spirits, however, after a UH-1H flown by Capitan Jorge Svensen, the commander of the Huey company, rescued the 3 Escuadrilla pilot Teniente de Navio Jose Arca from the sea after he had ejected from his Skyhawk near Stanley Airport. On 22 May the UH-1H's were again involved in a rescue mission, airlifting two wounded sailors, one of whom later died, from the PNA patrol boat 'Rio Iguazu' after it had been attacked by 800 Sqdn Sea Harriers in Choiseul Sound.

While the UH-1H's continued to shuttle troops in the Port Stanley area the work of the Pumas was daily becoming more hazardous. Any carelessness could prove disastrous, for their crews by then had to watch for enemy forces on the ground as well as overhead. On 22 May a flight of three Pumas and an escorting A-109A left Port Stanley on an ammunition flight to Port Howard. The convoy was led by the Puma AE-508, carrying the company commander, with AE-500 and AE-503 following. The A-109A, AE-337, was flown by the deputy commander of CAB601. It was an important and dangerous mission because their cargo included a large quantity of urgently required Blowpipe missiles and mortar shells. As was routine for such a flight, a circuitous route was selected to take maximum advantage of the rugged terrain.

The four helicopters left Port Stanley in mid-afternoon and reached Darwin in the gathering gloom to find that a "red alert" was in progress with Sea Harriers reported to be in the vicinity. After some discussion the crews elected to push on to Port Howard immediately, making the dangerous crossing of Falkland Sound abeam Darwin and then using natural features for protection as they flew north up the coast to Port Howard. They made the short water crossing and all went well until the formation unexpectedly found a ship in its path. The hazy conditions made identification impossible and the helicopter crews decided that discretion would be the better part of valour and all returned to Darwin. There they were casually informed that the ship was the 'Rio Carcarana', aground and beached in Port King after an attack by 800 Sqdn Sea Harriers on 16 May!

The formation set out once more early the next day, 23 May, and followed the same course for Port Howard. It passed the remains of the 'Rio Carcarana' and made landfall over West Falkland in the vicinity of Shag House Cove shortly after 1330Z. The helicopters then turned to the right for the final short run to Port Howard. Almost immediately AE-503 was seen by Flt Lt Dave Morgan of 800 Sqdn who was flying a CAP pattern in Sea Harrier ZA192 8,000ft above. He saw it passing over a small area of water and so he descended at high speed to visually identify it as hostile before opening fire. As ZA192 approached the Puma it was seen by the crew of AE-500 who called a warning to the formation and for a few seconds there was pandemonium as Morgan and his wingman, Flt Lt John Leeming in ZA191, set about the scattering helicopters. Initially only AE-503 had been sighted and in an effort to avoid the fast closing Sea Harrier the pilot lost control and the Puma hit the ground hard. Morgan had been too near even for a cannon attack and it is probable that his close overflight contributed to the Puma's crash. The shaken crew kicked their way out of the Puma's emergency exit moments before AE-503 caught fire and exploded. It had been carrying three tons of 120mm mortar shells and was totally destroyed.

AE-508 found some cover several hundred yards to the north and AE-500 similarly went to ground in the same general area. The A-109A sought the protection of a small ravine about 2,000yds to the south-west but, as Morgan overflew the burning remains of AE-503, Leeming found AE-337 and opened fire with his cannon. It was then attacked by both Sea Harriers and on Morgan's second or third pass it exploded and burned. Its crew had, however, already escaped and they watched the A-109A's destruction from a safe distance. In the meantime the other crews were frantically trying to off-load their cargoes before the Sea Harriers came looking for them. They had armed themselves with machine-guns and were ready to fight if it proved necessary. It was perhaps foolish of the crew of AE-500 to fly to the wreck of AE-503 before they were absolutely certain that the Sea Harriers had left but they did so and were duly seen by the orbiting fighters. Morgan used his final rounds of 30mm shells on AE-500 and left the helicopter disabled in a position some 200yds from the gutted AE-503. Presumably ignorant of the attack, AE-508 took-off soon afterwards to search the area for survivors and it was the crew's good fortune that when they were spotted, the departing Sea Harriers had expended their ammunition! The damaged AE-500 was totally destroyed within about 15 minutes in a follow-up Sea Harrier attack by the 801 Sqdn aircraft of Lt Cdrs Dave Braithwaite (ZA190) and Tim Gedge (XZ494). Argentine accounts of the incident suggest that after Morgan had damaged AE-500 its crew, all of whom were safe, had assessed the Puma as repairable but only if it could be airlifted out by a Chinook. That they knew to be unrealistic and so, after more cargo had been salvaged, it was deliberately destroyed — either before or after the 801 Sqdn attack *(it should be said that the 801 Sqdn pilots consider that to be unlikely).*

AE-508 finally left the area for Port Howard at 2030Z carrying all 12 crew and passengers from the four helicopters. The worst injury sustained had been a broken collar-bone! It also carried some of the more valuable cargo including a quantity of Blowpipes for RgtInf5. The flight to Port Howard, although only of seven miles, was made at extremely low level because of fears of attack by "friendly" troops. Those fears were well-founded and it was a very relieved contingent that finally arrived at Port Howard. AE-508 eventually left for Port Stanley shortly after 0900Z on 26 May carrying all the CAB601 crews, Capitan Donadille of Grupo 6 (whose Dagger had been shot down near Port Howard on 23 May) and a number of Ejercito commandos. After a dramatic journey via Darwin, during which they became briefly lost, the 30 occupants arrived safely at Moody Brook Barracks a little after 0945Z.

**Above** *The bullet-ridden hulk of the CAB601 Puma AE-504 lies where it fell at Grytviken, South Georgia on 3.4.82. The first of all Argentine air losses, its cold-blooded destruction by Lt Keith Mills and his Royal Marines detachment is yet further testimony to the vulnerability of large, troop-carrying helicopters when used in an assault role. The rarely-fitted skis that AE-504 wore for its Antarctic duties can be clearly seen. The Puma sports a standard CAB601 colour scheme and, most unusually for a helicopter operating in such terrain, no Dayglo or other high-visibility markings appear to have been used.*
*(Ministry of Defence)*

*As a result of an explosion that followed its crash near Shag House Cove, West Falkland on 23.5.82, the tail rotor assembly was one of the few immediately recognisable pieces of the CAE Puma AE-503. The interception of the four helicopters by 800 Squadron Sea Harriers flown by Flt Lts John Leeming and Dave Morgan was the kind of attack long feared by CAB601 and the devastating results had been gloomily predicted by most of the crews. Amazingly, nobody was seriously injured in this attack.*
*(Flt Lt D. H. S. Morgan, RAF)*

*Although heavily armed and highly manoeuvrable, the CAB601 A-109A's were never used in combat against British forces. AE-331 was one of two found intact on Stanley Racecourse on 14.6.82 and within two days both had been appropriated by 846 Squadron and transferred to 'Fearless'. Seen here on the Racecourse on 16.6.82, the Hirundo is in standard CAE colours and markings and is carrying 2.75in rocket pods and 7.62mm Miniguns.*
*(via Lt S. A. George, RN)*

After the disasters of 21 and 23 May the CAB601 strength had reduced to 10 serviceable helicopters; one Puma, two A-109A's and seven UH-1H's. Two more UH-1H's and a Chinook were still more or less intact but required spare parts and repair equipment that were unavailable on the Falklands. Activity had been intense since the British landings on 21 May and the UH-1H's were utilised extensively for several days afterwards carrying commando forces to forward positions and then recovering them as their situation became progressively less tenable. Several missions were flown to Mount Simmons and Chata Hill as well as to Port Stanley's nearer defences. One typical rescue mission was a four-helicopter flight dispatched to recover a group of commandos from Horse Paddock, near Douglas, on 26 May after they had been trapped behind British lines for some days.

At 1830Z on 26 May 1(F) Sqdn's Harriers returned to Mount Kent and Jerry Pook (XZ989) and Martin Hare (XZ988) found the abandoned hulk of the Puma AE-501, still picketed on the spot where they had earlier attacked it (although that was not then appreciated by the British pilots). On this occasion Pook completely demolished it with CBU's and AE-501 was reduced to a fiery tangle of metal. On 27 May CAB601 reviewed its depleted resources and, in spite of the round-the-clock missions now demanded of its crews, concluded that the losses (particularly those of the Pumas) had resulted in a surfeit of pilots. Accordingly, several of them and a number of the other ranks were returned to the mainland.

By 28 May the Argentine situation at Darwin and Goose Green had become critical and so two maximum-effort missions were tasked in an attempt to help matters. During the morning six UH-1H's, the one Puma and two escorting A-109A's were called to carry reinforcements from the crack RgtInf25 to Goose Green. No sooner had they been set down than part of the formation was called upon to evacuate some of the wounded from Darwin. Eventually all the helicopters returned safely to Port Stanley but that afternoon the same aircraft were ordered to carry more men, from RgtInf12, forward from Mount Kent to Goose Green. For that mission they were joined by a Grupo 7 FAA Chinook and, because of speed differentials, the Puma and the Chinook flew ahead of the six UH-1H's. Each group was given an A-109A gunship escort. Again the mission was successfully executed although the second flight (which left Port Stanley at 1945Z) had an unpleasant moment en route when a Grupo 3 Pucara, apparently in distress, flew, unannounced, through their formation! The troops were landed at 2030Z about one mile from Darwin and, as the UH-1H's cleared the area, the first British artillery fire struck their recently vacated positions. The UH-1H's continued to deploy and recover commandos and other special forces as May gave way to June but the general situation was deteriorating rapidly with the British ground forces advancing slowly but certainly towards Port Stanley. In response to the increasingly desperate situation the crews of CAB601 found themselves undertaking missions unheard of in peace-time manoeuvres. The UH-1H was most definitely not equipped for nocturnal adventures in mountainous, enemy-held territory!

The CAE's last surviving Puma on the Falklands, AE-508, was finally destroyed during the morning of 30 May with the loss of six lives, although Argentine accounts of the incident are vague and the circumstances not explained with any precision. It was carrying several members of the small Gendarmeria Nacional force deployed to the Islands (Escuadron FEEE601GN) when, according to the CAE, it was brought down by a "British missile". At least four Argentine helicopters were operating on the slopes of Mount Kent in support of retreating troops when the Puma came down to the north-west of Murrell Bridge between 1200Z and 1300Z but, although the British were in the area, no unit has made any claim for AE-508. Harrier attacks in support of British ground forces played no part in the incident and it is thought conceivable that the Puma was brought down in error by Argentine forces. Interestingly, its crew, which included the detachment commander Primer Teniente Perez Cometto, survived the War but, while passing comment on the loss of their much liked AE-508, they have not been forthcoming about the incident itself.

Coincident with the return to the mainland of the two Grupo 7 Chinooks on 9 June, AE-520 returned to airworthiness (at least on paper) and remained so until 12 June. The A-109A's AE-331 and AE-334 continued to provide reliable service as gunships-cum-transports until the surrender but it was the UH-1H company that battled on as the only truly effective helicopter unit. Seven Hueys remained in use until 12 June — indeed two fresh crews were flown in to join the unit on 7 June — and it was on 7 June that the first of two Hueys received a crude whitewash colour scheme to clearly identify it as an ambulance helicopter. Notwithstanding, it was fired upon by both sides during an evacuation mission for RgtInf7 on 9 June! The damage was minor and after rapid repairs it was back in use the following day. Ultimately both AE-409 and the unique Nitesun floodlight-equipped AE-413 were put into the all-white colour scheme. By 10 June all the UH-1H activity was being undertaken from the Sportsfield and Racecourse areas of Port Stanley with most sorties being of a CASEVAC nature. Both AE-406 and AE-409 flew ambulance missions to and from 'Almirante Irizar' that day. By 11 June the Moody Brook barracks had been destroyed by the repeated British shelling and at 1400Z that day AE-418 was damaged beyond immediate repair in a naval bombardment. AE-409 was also hit but was quickly returned to flying condition. The last CAE "count" on 12 June identified six airworthy Hueys, thought to have been AE-406, AE-409, AE-412, AE-413, AE-422 and AE-424.

After two more days of unending ambulance missions surrender overtook CAB601's operations and, with the ceasefire on 14 June, all their flyable helicopters were moved from the Port Stanley Sportsfield to the Racecourse. The move was made in anticipation of the formal surrender and was intended to make room on the Sportsfield for British helicopter operations. The CAB601 commanders were refused permission to destroy the helicopters because it was thought that it might prove possible to retain them under the terms of a negotiated ceasefire. That, of course, proved not to be the case. The two white ambulance Hueys, AE-409 and AE-413, remained at the hospital in Port Stanley and were used that night to ferry wounded to 'Almirante Irizar'. Those helicopters that

# AE-409
## LOG-BOOK EXTRACTS

AE 409

EJERCITO ARGENTINO

COMANDO DE AVIACION

**LIBRETA HISTORIAL N° 2**

DE LA AERONAVE

Helicoptero Bell UH-1H

72-21506

### IDENTIFICACION

Avión: *Helicoptero Bell UH-1H*
N°. DE SERVICIO / MATRICULA: *AE 409*    N° de fabricación: *72-21506 Bell 13.214*
Construido por: *Bell Helicopter Co*   Fecha de fabric.:   Librado al servicio: *21 MAY 73*
Convertido por:   Fecha de reconversión:   Librado al servicio:

### CARACTERISTICAS

Avión tipo *HELICOPTERO.*
Empleo *TRANSPORTE.*
Envergadura ................. m. Longitud .............. mts. Altura en pos. de vuelo ............... m.
Superficie alar ............. m² Peso máx. admitido ......... kg. Peso vacio ............. kg.

NOTA: Las características, especificaciones técnicas, reglajes, ensayos e instrucciones de servicio serán anotados por personal técnico autorizado, quien fechará y firmará al pie de la hoja correspondiente.

One page from the No. 2 log-book of the UH-1H AE-409 makes interesting reading. Having flown on three occasions in the previous three weeks, AE-409 began its journey to Port Stanley in the hands of Teniente Molina on 7.4.82. The trip from Campo de Mayo to Espora, via Tandil, took 3hr 40min and it remained there until 9.4.82 when a 2hr 10min flight took it to San Antonio West and then onto 'Bahia Paraiso'. Molina flew the "Huey" from the ship to Port Stanley the next day and, as can be seen, it was used extensively, recording 6hr 10min in the air. His was the first UH-1H to arrive on the Falklands and the only one not to be airfreighted in. After a service on 13.4.82 (probably the cause of the clerical error on this page) AE-409 continued to fly in Molina's hands and it survived the War, eventually being brought to the United Kingdom. Both the other CAE pilots recorded on the page have interesting credentials; Captain Jorge Svensen, believed to have been the UH-1H detachment commander at Moody Brook, was the pilot who rescued Teniente de Navio Arca from the sea on 21.5.82 (although the UH-1H is not equipped for such operations) and was the man whom Capt Rowe of 3 Commando Brigade accused of being "drunk and aggressive" when the two were ordered to negotiate the surrender of isolated Argentine troops on 15.6.82. Primer Teniente Guillermo Anaya, also deployed to the Falklands and eventually captured by the British, had an unusual claim to fame. His father was, arguably, responsible for the entire War! Anaya senior, Almirante Jorge Isaac Anaya, was, until 1.10.82, commander-in-chief of the Armada and had been one of the invasion's instigators.

## ACTIVIDAD

| FECHA | | | PILOTO | Duración | | D. U. R. | | TOT. GEN. | | ATERRIZAJES | | | OBSERVACIONES |
|---|---|---|---|---|---|---|---|---|---|---|---|---|---|
| D | M | A | | Horas | Mín. | Horas | Mín. | Horas | Mín. | Cant. | DUR | Total | |
| TRANSPORTE | | | DEL | HISTORIAL | | | | | | N° | 1 | | |
| 19 | 03 | 82 | — | — | — | 99 | 40 | 1299 | 40 | — | — | 4155 | |
| 23 | 03 | 82 | Anaya | 05 | 25 | 105 | 05 | 1305 | 05 | 26 | - | 4181 | |
| 30 | 03 | 82 | Svensen | 03 | 00 | 108 | 05 | 1308 | 05 | 8 | - | 4184 | |
| Suma | Mar 82 | | | 08 | 25 | 108 | 05 | 208 | 05 | 32 | | 4184 | |
| 05 | 4 | 82 | Molina | 01 | 25 | 109 | 30 | 1309 | 30 | 2 | - | 4186 | |
| 07 | 4 | 82 | MOLINA | 03 | 40 | 113 | 10 | 1313 | 10 | 2 | - | 4188 | |
| 09 | 04 | 82 | Molina | 02 | 10 | 115 | 20 | 1315 | 20 | 1 | | 4189 | |
| 10 | 04 | 82 | Molina | 06 | 10 | 121 | 30 | 321 | 30 | 4 | - | 4193 | |
| 11 | 04 | 82 | Molina | 01 | 40 | 123 | 10 | 1323 | 10 | 3 | - | 4196 | |
| 13 | 04 | 82 | Molina | 02 | 15 | 125 | 25 | 1325 | 25 | 5 | - | 4201 | |
| 19 | 04 | 82 | Molina | 02 | 05 | 125 | 30 | 32f | 30 | 8 | | 4209 | |
| 21 | 04 | 82 | Molina | 03 | 50 | 128 | 20 | 1331 | 20 | 9 | | 4218 | ERROSE- |
| 22 | 04 | 82 | Molina | 00 | 00 | 130 | 05 | 1332 | 05 | 2 | | 4220 | |
| 23 | 04 | 82 | Molina | 02 | 05 | 1.33 | 10 | 1335 | 10 | 4 | | 4224 | |

were later found on the Racecourse were the A-109A's AE-331 and AE-334 and the UH-1H's AE-406, AE-412, AE-417, AE-422 and AE-424. The three unserviceable helicopters, UH-1H's AE-410 and AE-418 and the Chinook AE-520, the latter adjacent to the Governor's Residence in Port Stanley, remained where they had been abandoned.

On 15 June two senior CAB601 pilots used one of the UH-1H's (with British agreement) to search for Argentine dead and injured in some of the less accessible areas near Port Stanley but the task was soon abandoned because of high winds. Later in the day the same helicopter took a British intelligence officer, Capt Rowe of 3 Commando Brigade, to persuade a belligerent group of 11 RgtInf7 soldiers to surrender. It took the combined efforts of the crew and their British passenger to convince them that there was really no sensible alternative to surrender! The final UH-1H sorties in the hands of CAB601 crews were made on 16 and 17 June as more of the wounded were flown to 'Bahia Paraiso' (her own Alouette III and Puma had, by then, been joined by a 2 Escuadrilla Sea King to speed the operation).

With several Argentine helicopters still in airworthy condition and the British desperately short of airlift capacity there was a fairly obvious option available to the more adventurous of their pilots. Accordingly, the CASEVAC aircraft AE-409 and AE-413 were investigated for booby traps (none was found) and were pressed into British service. AE-409 was first flown by Major C.S.Sibun of 656 Sqdn on 18 June and, before its last flight on 13 July to San Carlos Water for transportation to the United Kingdom, it achieved 28 flight hours in British hands. During its time with 656 Sqdn a bold '656' was painted on the boom because its serial, AE-409, clashed awkwardly with that of 656 Sqdn's Gazelle XX409 and a new identity had to be created. '656' was an ideal solution and it still wore this "serial" when it later departed for the United Kingdom.

Like AE-409, AE-413 also made its first flight in British hands from the Sportsfield on 18 June and it was used in support of 5 Infantry Brigade until 12 July. It achieved 16 flight hours in the hands of Sqdn Ldr R.Tierney during that period and was distinctively marked with a large and crudely applied 'UK' marking. AE-413 was eventually positioned to Port Stanley on 12 July for shipment to the United Kingdom. AE-422 was similarly utilised, initially by Lt Cdr K.Dudley of 820 Sqdn and then by 825 Sqdn, and it flew some 30 hours in British hands between 16 June and 13 July before it was shipped with AE-413 to the United Kingdom in 'Atlantic Causeway'.

AE-424 was later selected (as the newest and lowest-houred Huey) for potential reclamation by FIGAS. FIGAS put in much work on the helicopter and, with the assistance of engineering personnel from 'Invincible', it was eventually able to make a short ferry flight to the carrier in San Carlos Water for a strip, inspection and

respray. It was returned to Port Stanley on 26 August as VP-FBD wearing the deck-letter 'N' (for 'Invincible') to make its initial flights in the hands of 657 Sqdn pilots. Unfortunately the Huey was later found to have signs of an earlier heavy landing and, with repairs, overhaul and its future commercial operation viewed as an uneconomic venture, VP-FBD was soon permanently grounded.

Of the other Hueys, AE-406 was returned to the United Kingdom in December 1982 but the remaining four (AE-410, AE-412, AE-417 and AE-418) were dumped near the Beaver Hangar and then progressively stripped by souvenir hunters. In May 1983 their hulks were removed to a dump at Moody Brook. Only AE-418 remained in November 1983 after two had been removed to the new weapons ranges and another (AE-410) had been reclaimed for display at the RAF Chinook facility at Kelly's Garden, near San Carlos settlement.

The two A-109A's were found intact at the Racecourse on 14 June by 3 CBAS personnel and it was decided that, subject to a short test-flight to confirm their airworthiness, both would be appropriated and brought to the United Kingdom. Fearing vandalism, the pair were briefly flown on 15 June by 846 Sqdn pilots and then put under overnight guard at the Racecourse until the next day when AE-331 made a long and circuitous journey (to avoid any over-eager British gunners) to 'Fearless' in San Carlos Water. AE-334 was flown to 'Fearless' on 17 June, by which time she had sailed from San Carlos Water to Port William. Neither helicopter was flown again until 6 July by which time both had been inspected and cleaned-up with the 846 Sqdn codes 'VC' (AE-331) and 'VV' (AE-334) applied. Each flight was only of some five minutes duration and no more were undertaken before 'Fearless' reached Plymouth and both the A-109A's were flown off to Yeovilton on 13 July. By then AE-331 had received ROYAL MARINES titles in lieu of its ROYAL NAVY markings and had an appropriate new 3 CBAS code, 'CC'.

CAB601's only other aircraft at Port Stanley was the Chinook AE-520 and both 18 Sqdn and the RAF aircrew attached to 5 Brigade investigated its condition. It was not flown again but after some cannibalising for the 18 Sqdn Chinooks and some vandalism, it too was eventually brought to the United Kingdom.

The men of CAB601 had been thrown, like all others, into totally unexpected combat in April 1982 and for them the conflict was one hard slog from first to last. It was, however, undertaken with great fortitude and much professionalism against a better equipped and trained enemy. Fortunately for them, in spite of the violent and wholesale destruction of their equipment, very few lost their lives or were even seriously injured. However, the unit did not easily recover and it was not until mid-1984 that the first of the new AS.332B Pumas was ready for delivery from France. In the light of bitter experience on the Falklands the CAE simultaneously announced a reorganisation of its combat helicopter forces.

# INDIVIDUAL AIRCRAFT DETAILS

All the CAB601 helicopters that were deployed to the Falklands and South Georgia were in a uniform olive drab colour scheme without, as far as is known, any variation. All helicopters wore the EJERCITO title and serial number in black and the Argentine national flag on the fin, the size being appropriate to the type. Many of them wore the small circular CAB601 crest, in the case of the UH-1H's it being worn on both cab doors. The yellow identification stripes, adopted by all the services for a brief period after 1 May, were applied to the CAB601 helicopters with some care, appearing as broad bands on either the front or the rear of the boom (or, in the case of the Chinooks, the rear fuselage).

The anonymous Puma that was used as an ambulance helicopter on 'Bahia Paraiso' was repainted in an overall white colour scheme with no markings other than red crosses on the nose and fuselage doors. The UH-1H's which were pressed into emergency use as ambulance vehicles were similarly repainted although much more crudely.

The individual aircraft histories should be read in close conjunction with the unit history.

---

### HIRUNDO

**AE-331** A-109A

On 5.4.82 with CAB601/Compania de Ataque; total hours until then 251.15. Flown to Port Stanley via 'Bahia Paraiso' by 10.4.82 and based in that area. Used throughout the War before being captured intact on the Racecourse by 3 CBAS personnel on 14.6.82.

Briefly flown by two 846 Sqdn pilots (Lt Cdr Thornewill and Lt Rainey) on 15.6.82 and ferried from the Racecourse to 'Fearless' in San Carlos Water on 16.6.82. 'Fearless' eventually sailed from Port William for Ascension Island on 25.6.82 and during the voyage AE-331 was inspected and underwent minor maintenance. Before its next flight on 6.7.82 (five minutes while off Ascension Island) it was spruced up and the 846 Sqdn code letters 'VC' and ROYAL NAVY titles applied. At the same time the roundels were modified to the British Red/Blue. While en route Plymouth, 846 Sqdn was imposed upon by 3 CBAS and the new markings were amended to 'CC' and ROYAL MARINES. Flown off with AE-334 to Yeovilton on 13.7.82 when 'Fearless' was anchored off Plymouth.

Transported to the AAC Centre, Middle Wal-

lop on 21.7.82 for the AAC 25th Anniversary and statically displayed there 23-25.7.82 before returning by road to Yeovilton 26.7.82. Exhibited statically at Yeovilton Air Day on 31.7.82, by which time it had lost the ROYAL MARINES titles and the Red/Blue roundels. Transported to Abingdon on 9.9.82 (arriving 10.9.82) for the BoB Day there on 18.9.82. Remained at Abingdon until 11.10.82 when it left for storage at Wroughton pending a decision to return it to airworthiness. Returned to the FAAM at Yeovilton on 4.5.83 for display but left again 16.5.83 for Middle Wallop and attention by 70 Aircraft Workshops. Departed on 17.5.83 for Lee-on-Solent and went on to Fairoaks 18.5.83 for a full survey by Alan Mann Helicopters Ltd. Returned to the FAAM at Yeovilton c24.6.83 (noted outside FAAM that day) and then back to Fairoaks on 9.1.84 for overhaul and the implementation of modifications for AAC service. The British serial ZE411 was allocated in early 1984 and the first flight with this identity (in a yellow/white colour scheme) was made at Fairoaks on 15.2.85. Delivered by air to 7 Regt HQ, Netheravon on 12.3.85.

**AE-334** A-109A

On 5.4.82 with CAB601/Compania de Ataque; total hours until then 218.50. Flown to Port Stanley via 'Bahia Paraiso' by 10.4.82

and based in that area. Used throughout the War before being captured intact on the Racecourse by 3 CBAS personnel on 14.6.82.

Briefly flown by two 846 Sqdn pilots (Lt Cdr Thornewill and Lt Rainey) on 15.6.82 (a hover check and then ten minutes flying). Not flown again until 17.6.82 when it was ferried from the Racecourse to 'Fearless' in Port William (some role flying was undertaken during that flight). 'Fearless' sailed from there for Ascension Island on 25.6.82 and during the voyage AE-334 was inspected and underwent minor maintenance. Before its next flight on 6.7.82 (five minutes while off Ascension Island) it was spruced up and the 846 Sqdn code letters 'VV' and ROYAL NAVY titles applied. At the same time the roundels were modified to the British Red/Blue. On 13.7.82 'Fearless' anchored off Plymouth and AE-334 flew off with AE-331 to Yeovilton.

Placed on display in the FAAM on 20.7.82 and noted there on 22.7.82 with the Argentine roundels, national flag and EJERCITO titles restored (the 846 Sqdn titles on the nose were removed shortly afterwards). Departed the FAAM by road on 26.11.82 for the AAC Centre, Middle Wallop for storage with 70 Aircraft Workshops. Stored in the D&T hangar until 20.5.83 when it was taken to Lee-on-Solent and then to Alan Mann Helicopters

The CAB601 UH-1H AE-406 had suffered badly at the hands of British souvenir hunters before it arrived at Devonport aboard 'Astronomer' on 3.12.82. The yellow identification stripe on the boom had been overpainted on the starboard side with REME colours but more serious vandalism had been inflicted on the airframe. By the time that this photograph was taken at RNAY Fleetlands on 13.6.83 it was still fundamentally intact but by mid-1985 its only useful purpose had been to supply Sqdn Ldr Rob Tierney with components for AE-413 (G-HUEY) and Fleetlands was actively seeking its disposal. (Geoffrey Elliott)

Used by CAB601 for CASEVAC duties during the final week of the War, UH-1H AE-409 passed into the hands of 656 Squadron and was flown extensively by them until 13.7.82 when it was shipped to the United Kingdom. It is photographed here at Nether-avon on 24.8.82, soon after its arrival. As can be seen from the inset view, the colour scheme was unchanged from that used by 656 Squadron on the Falk-lands. Prior to British use only the Argentine national markings had been removed (and "656" added) and the helicopter is very much in the colours adopted by CAB601 for their ambulance duties. After a series of moves it was, in mid-1985, on display at the Museum of Army Flying, Middle Wallop.
(Peter J. Cooper; (Inset) Flt Sgt D. W. Knights, RAF)

Seen here at Abingdon on 18.9.82, UH-1H AE-413 is wearing the CASEVAC markings used by CAB601 but modified by Sqdn Ldr Tierney for use on the Falklands in support of 5 Infantry Brigade. Damage suffered en route to Abingdon and other certification problems considerably delayed its restoration to flying status (as G-HUEY) but, by mid-1985, progress was good and hopes were high for an early first flight. (David J. Allen)

The third of the CAB601 UH-1H's flown by British forces, AE-422 remained in the full olive drab colour scheme while in use with 825 Squadron at San Carlos settlement. Seen here at Yeovilton on 30.7.82, it was subsequently exhibited at Plymouth and Culdrose before passing to the Fleet Air Arm Museum in 9.82 for display. The identification stripe had, by then, been removed. (Peter J. Cooper)

Ltd, Fairoaks on 23.5.83 (on 12.5.83 the aircraft was physically compared with the civilian A-109A G-OAMH that was flown to Middle Wallop from Hereford for the purpose). There it underwent a full survey, overhaul and the incorporation of modifications for AAC service. The British serial ZE410 was allocated in early 1984 and the first flight with this identity (in a yellow/white colour scheme) was made at Fairoaks on 20.6.84. Delivered by air to 7 Regt HQ, Netheravon on 23.7.84.

## AE-337 A-109A

On 5.4.82 with CAB601/Compania de Ataque; total hours until then 193.50. Flown to Port Stanley via 'Bahia Paraiso' by 10.4.82 and based in that area. Destroyed by cannon fire from the 800 Sqdn Sea Harriers ZA192 of Flt Lt Morgan and ZA191 of Flt Lt Leeming near Shag House Cove, West Falkland on 23.5.82 (no casualties). Small pieces were later put on display at the FAAM, Yeovilton.

---

## IROQUOIS

---

## AE-406 UH-1H

In 3.82 with CAB601/Compania de Asalto 'B'. Dismantled at Comodoro Rivadavia on 17.4.82 for airfreighting by C-130 to Stanley Airport (total hours to then 1550.00). Arrived by 29.4.82 and based in the Port Stanley area and used until at least 10.6.82. Captured in good condition on the Racecourse on 14.6.82. Almost certainly one of the Argentine helicopters airlifted by an 820 Sqdn Sea King on 16.8.82 from the Racecourse to the nearby FIGAS Beaver Hangar. Used for spares recovery until 8.11.82 when put on 'Astronomer', off Port Stanley, for transit to the UK.

Sailed with 'Astronomer' c14.11.82, arriving at Devonport on 3.12.82 where it was off-loaded overnight 3/4.12.82 for temporary storage in a compound by the dockyard's Granby Gate. Taken by road to RNAY Fleetlands on 9.12.82 for storage, arriving the following day. Still there on 13.6.85 awaiting a final decision on its future. External damage was initially limited to the unit badges hacked out of the doors.

*Prior to arrival in the UK, the identification band on the boom was overpainted on the starboard side in British Army REME colours (reason unknown) and these markings were still worn on 13.6.85. Dayglo red letters 'FRB' (significance unknown and since removed) were also applied by British troops to the cabin sides before arrival in the UK.*

## AE-409 UH-1H

In 3.82 with CAB601/Compania de Asalto 'B'. Departed Campo de Mayo for Espora (via Tandil) on 7.4.82. Continued to San Antonio West on 9.4.82 and embarked 'Bahia Paraiso' later that day for the Falklands (total hours to 9.4.82 1315.20). Flown off to Port Stanley 10.4.82 and based in that area. Used throughout the War (last recorded hours 1372.50 18.5.82). After 7.6.82 repainted in a crude whitewash and marked for ambulance duties. It was operating from the Sportsfield when British forces took control of the area on 14.6.82.

First flight in 656 Sqdn hands (Major Sibun) was made on 18.6.82 and 28.55 hrs were flown by the unit until 13.7.82 when it was flown onto a Mexeflote at the stern of 'Atlantic Causeway' in San Carlos Water before being loaded for transit to the UK. While with 656 Sqdn the crude marking '656' was applied to both sides of the boom for identification purposes.

Sailed with the ship on 13.7.82, arriving at Devonport 27.7.82. It was off-loaded on 28.7.82 to a compound at Camel's Head (near HMS Drake, Plymouth) and then statically displayed at HMS Drake. On 1.8.82 it was taken by road to Yeovilton (where it was seen the following day) en route Netheravon where it arrived by 9.8.82. Transferred to the AAC Centre, Middle Wallop on 11.10.82 and remained there until 6.6.83 when it was taken to the Imperial War Museum aircraft collection at Duxford for temporary display. On 31.5.84 it was delivered back to Middle Wallop for Museum of Army Flying. Still resident there in 5.85.

## AE-410 UH-1H

In 3.82 with CAB601/Compania de Asalto 'B'. Airfreighted by C-130 to Stanley Airport from Comodoro Rivadavia on 18.4.82 and based in the Port Stanley area. Used until the night of 9/10.5.82 when it was damaged at Moody Brook by naval bombardment. Not repaired and abandoned near the Racecourse where it was found by British forces on 14.6.82.

Almost certainly one of the Argentine helicopters airlifted by an 820 Sqdn Sea King on 16.8.82 from the Racecourse to the nearby FIGAS Beaver Hangar. After being progressively stripped and vandalised it was removed to a dump at Moody Brook between 12 & 18.5.83 but was reclaimed in 1983 (sometime after 20.7.83) and put on display at the RAF Chinook facility at Kelly's Garden, near San Carlos settlement. On 15.11.84 obtained by a Mr Harrison (Grampian Helicopters International Ltd) and sailed from San Carlos Water on 'St Angus' 13.1.85 for Port Stanley, arriving there c16.1.85. Unloaded and stored pending shipment to the UK. Still at Port Stanley in 3.85.

## AE-412 UH-1H

In 3.82 with CAB601/Compania de Asalto 'B'. Airfreighted by C-130 to Stanley Airport from Comodoro Rivadavia by 29.4.82 and based in the Port Stanley area. Used throughout the War and found by British forces on the Racecourse on 14.6.82. Utilised for spares reclamation and was almost certainly one of the Argentine helicopters airlifted by an 820 Sqdn Sea King on 16.8.82 to the nearby FIGAS Beaver Hangar. After being progressively stripped and vandalised the hulk was removed sometime between 12 & 18.5.83 to a dump at Moody Brook. Airlifted to a Falklands weapons range sometime after 20.7.83 (but before 2.11.83).

## AE-413 UH-1H

In 3.82 with CAB601/Compania de Asalto 'B'. Dismantled at Comodoro Rivadavia on 14.4.82 for airfreighting by C-130 to Stanley

Airport (total hours to then 1365.00). Arrived by 29.4.82 and based in the Port Stanley throughout the War. After 7.6.82 it was repainted in a crude whitewash with red crosses for local ambulance duties (the yellow identification stripe, applied after 1.5.82, was retained). It was operating from the Sportsfield when British forces took control on 14.6.82. The last recorded flight by an Argentine pilot was on 16.6.82.

Appropriated by the Air Tasking Officer 5 Brigade (Sqdn Ldr Tierney) on 18.6.82 and flown in support of 5 Brigade from Fitzroy from then until 1.7.82 (15.25 hrs). Open stored at Port Stanley until 12.7.82 when it flew for 45 minutes before being flown to a trailer on a Mexeflote at the stern of 'Tor Caledonia' in Port William and then wheeled aboard for transit to the UK.

Sailed with the ship on 1.8.82, arriving at Felixstowe on 20.8.82. Prior to its flight to 'Tor Caledonia' some instruments had been stolen and thus it was not deemed airworthy when it arrived in the UK. Transported by MARTSU c21.8.82 to Lee-on-Solent for storage, arriving c23.8.82. Departed for Finningley c27.8.82 for static display at the BoB Day on 4.9.82. Left on MARTSU transport for Abingdon on 13.9.82, arriving 15.9.82. It suffered damage in transit between these two points when the rotor blades struck a bridge. Displayed statically at the Abingdon BoB Day on 18.9.82 and then taken by road to Odiham on 18.10.82 for restoration by Sqdn Ldr Tierney to flying condition as G-HUEY. Statically displayed at the "Air Show South" at Hurn 18/19.8.84 and again at the Fleetlands Open Day 8.6.85 (arrived by road 7.6.85, departed 8.6.85). Exhibited as 'G-HUEY' at the International Air Tattoo, Fairford on 13/14.7.85 (arrived 8.7.85, departed to Odiham 15.7.85).

## AE-417 UH-1H

In 3.82 with CAB601/Compania de Asalto 'B'. Airfreighted by C-130 to Stanley Airport from Comodoro Rivadavia by 29.4.82. Based in the Port Stanley area until 21.5.82 when it is believed to have been the UH-1H that suffered slight rotor-blade and probably other damage when parked near Mount Kent. It had been attacked by the 1(F) Sqdn Harriers of Sqdn Ldr Pook (XZ988) and Flt Lt Hare (XZ963) but, following temporary repairs, was ferried back to Port Stanley. Found in generally good condition on the Racecourse by British forces on 14.6.82 and utilised for spares reclamation. Almost certainly one of the Argentine helicopters airlifted by an 820 Sqdn Sea King on 16.8.82 from the Racecourse to the nearby FIGAS Beaver Hangar. After being progressively stripped and vandalised was removed sometime between 12 & 18.5.83 to a dump at Moody Brook. It was airlifted to a Falklands weapons range in 1983 (after 20.7.83 but before 2.11.83).

## AE-418 UH-1H

In 3.82 with CAB601/Compania de Asalto 'B'. Airfreighted by C-130 to Stanley Airport from Comodoro Rivadavia by 29.4.82 and based in the Port Stanley area. Used throughout the War but damaged by naval gunfire on 11.6.82 and not flown again. Found by British forces on the Racecourse on 14.6.82. Almost

Although never used in action against British forces on the Falklands, the CAB601 Hirundos were potentially most aggressive helicopters and the capture, intact, of AE-331 and AE-334 caused considerable interest among the British helicopter crews. In view of the subsequent vandalism of other captured aircraft, it was indeed a wise decision to move both from Stanley Racecourse to 'Fearless' and their eventual appearance in British military service owes much to this prompt action.

AE-331 **(Upper)** is seen on display at Abingdon on 18.9.82 (having arrived by road) while AE-334 **(Lower)** is seen on the ramp at Yeovilton on 13.7.82 after flying in from 'Fearless', at the time anchored off Plymouth. In these photographs AE-331 wears the code "CC" (of 3 CBAS) and AE-334 wears "VV" (of 846 Squadron). Indecision, inspection, modification and certification subsequently grounded the helicopters for two years before both were eventually delivered to HQ 7 Regiment AAC at Netheravon.

(Peter J. Cooper/ Royal Navy)

Although fresh from overhaul at Campo de Mayo, the CAB601 CH-47C Chinook AE-520 was plagued by technical problems while on the Falklands but was structurally sound when found by the British. Some components were removed to service the 18 Squadron Chinooks but the airframe was considered to be recoverable and it was thus brought to the United Kingdom for inspection and potential rebuild. After three years at RNAY Fleetlands (except for a brief period at JATE Brize Norton) its future was still very much in doubt in mid-1985. In this view it is seen on display at the Portsmouth Navy Days, 28–30.8.82.

(Peter J. Cooper)

certainly one of the Argentine helicopters air-lifted by an 820 Sqdn Sea King on 16.8.82 from the Racecourse to the nearby FIGAS Beaver Hangar. After being progressively stripped and vandalised the hulk was removed sometime between 12 & 18.5.83 to a dump at Moody Brook. Noted there on 30.6.85.

### AE-419 UH-1H

In 3.82 with CAB601/Compania de Asalto 'B'. Not deployed to the Falkland Islands but destroyed in a mainland crash at Caleta Olivia on 30.4.82 with the loss of 11 lives.

### AE-422 UH-1H

In 3.82 with CAB601/Compania de Asalto 'B'. Airfreighted by C-130 to Stanley Airport from Comodoro Rivadavia by 29.4.82 and based in the Port Stanley area. Used throughout the War and found in good condition on the Racecourse by British forces on 14.6.82.

Flight-tested by Lt Cdr Dudley of 820 Sqdn on 16.6.82 and flown by him that day to the 820 Sqdn FOB at San Carlos settlement. Passed on to 825 Sqdn there on 17.6.82 because 820 Sqdn was about to depart on 'Invincible'. Accumulated nearly 30 flight hours with 825 Sqdn before being flown on 13.7.82 to a Mexeflote at the stern of 'Atlantic Causeway' in San Carlos Water for onload and transit to the UK.

Departed with the ship on 13.7.82, arriving at Devonport 27.7.82 where it was off-loaded and taken to a compound at Camel's Head (near HMS Drake, Plymouth). Arrived by road at Yeovilton on 29.7.82 for static display at the Air Day on 31.7.82 and then stored there. Placed on public display at Plymouth Navy Days 28-30.8.82. Left Yeovilton again on 7.9.82 for Culdrose (arriving 8.9.82) where it was briefly flown (seen airborne on 20.9.82). Departed by road for Yeovilton on 24.9.82 for display in the FAAM from 1.10.82. Still resident in 5.85.

### AE-424 UH-1H

In 3.82 with CAB601/Compania de Asalto 'B'. Airfreighted by C-130 to Stanley Airport from Comodoro Rivadavia by 29.4.82 and based in the Port Stanley area (total hours to 21.4.82, when at Comodoro Rivadavia, 630.00). Used throughout the War and found in good condition on the Racecourse by British forces on 14.6.82 (last recorded hours were 678.15 to 3.6.82).

Restored to a ferry-flight condition at the Beaver Hangar by FIGAS and 820 Sqdn personnel during 7/8.82 and flown to 'Invincible' in San Carlos Water on 18.8.82 by Lt Cdr Dudley of 820 Sqdn for a strip, check and a respray. Returned to the Beaver Hangar at Port Stanley 26.8.82 as VP-FBD 'N' in the bright red FIGAS colour scheme. Flown only twice on behalf of FIGAS by 657 Sqdn pilots before the MoD ordered the helicopter's grounding pending a full inspection and re-work. Eventually inspected by a Bristow Helicopters representative who found that it had suffered damage to the port rear skid consistent with a heavy landing. As the main rotor gearbox and rotor head required major overhaul it was decided to bring the UH-1H to the UK for complete overhaul by Bristow. Positioned by RAF

Chinook onto a ship (unidentified) for UK passage when the Civil Commissioner decided that it should remain in the Falklands as a museum piece. Picketed, rotorless, near the Beaver Hangar until 31.5.84 when it was moved by Chinook to Moody Brook. On 9.8.84 it was moved into the Hovercraft Hangar for internal storage and renovation prior to eventual display in a museum near Port Stanley. Still at Moody Brook in 2.85.

---

## PUMA

### AE-500 SA.330L

In 3.82 with CAB601/Compania de Asalto 'A'. Ferried to Port Stanley by 18.4.82 and based in that area until 23.5.82 when it was destroyed near Shag Cove House, West Falkland by cannon fire from the 800 Sqn Sea Harrier ZA192 of Flt Lt Morgan and the 801 Sqdn aircraft (ZA190) of Lt Cdr Braithwaite. There were no casualties.

### AE-501 SA.330L

In 3.82 with CAB601/Compania de Asalto 'A'. Ferried to Port Stanley by 18.4.82 and based in that area until 21.5.82 when it was damaged by cannon fire from the 1(F) Sqdn Harrier XZ963 of Flt Lt Hare near Mount Kent, East Falkland. Later destroyed in a CBU attack on 26.5.82 (at the same location) by the 1(F) Sqdn Harrier XZ989 of Sqdn Ldr Pook. The remains were still there in 2.85.

### AE-503 SA.330L

In 3.82 with CAB601/Compania de Asalto 'A'. Ferried to Port Stanley by 18.4.82 and based in that area until 23.5.82 when it was destroyed in an incident near Shag House Cove, West Falkland. It crashed after control was lost at low altitude while attempting to avoid the low flying 800 Sqdn Sea Harrier ZA192 of Flt Lt Morgan. There were no casualties. Small pieces of the helicopter were later displayed in the FAAM at Yeovilton.

### AE-504 SA.330L

In 3.82 with CAB601/Compania de Asalto 'A'. Embarked 'Bahia Paraiso' at Ushuaia late in 2.82 for a mission unconnected with Operacion "Rosario". Used in the South Orkney Islands and elsewhere in Antarctica in 3.82 until 'Bahia Paraiso' became involved in the Argentine "scrap metal merchants" incident on South Georgia on 25.3.82. Destroyed by Royal Marine gunfire at Grytviken, South Georgia on 3.4.82. The crew was unhurt but two Argentine marine passengers were killed and others wounded. The wreck remained on its port side at Grytviken in mid-1983.

### AE-505 SA.330L

In 3.82 with CAB601/Compania de Asalto 'A'. Ferried to Port Stanley by 18.4.82 and based in that area. On 9.5.82, while searching for 'Narwal' at the mouth of Choiseul Sound, it was destroyed by a Sea Dart fired from extreme range by 'Coventry'. Neither the wreckage nor the crew of three, Primer Teniente Fiorito (pilot), Primer Teniente Buschiazzo (engineer) and NCO Dimotta, were found.

### AE-5?? SA.330L

In 3.82 with CAB601/Compania de Asalto 'A'. This unidentified Puma (AE-506 or AE-507) was used for ambulance duties on 'Bahia Paraiso', embarking between mid-4.82 and 1.5.82. The helicopter wore an overall white colour scheme with red crosses on the nose and fuselage sides. Still in CASEVAC use for some days after 14.6.82.

### AE-508 SA.330L

In 3.82 with CAB601/Compania de Asalto 'A'. Ferried to Port Stanley by 18.4.82 (probably arriving 7.4.82) and based in that area. Damaged by naval gunfire at or near Moody Brook during the night of 9/10.5.82. Repaired and used until destroyed in confused circumstances on 30.5.82 (see text). The crew survived the incident but six Escuadron FEEE601GN passengers were killed. The helicopter crashed north-west of Murrell Bridge, East Falkland about two miles north-east of the summit of Mount Kent (51°39.9'S 58°03.7'W). The wreck was still there in 9.84, some 2,000yds east north-east of the remains of AE-501 and the Chinook, AE-521.

---

## CHINOOK

### AE-520 CH-47C

In 3.82 with CAB601/Compania de Asalto 'A' (total hours to 7.4.82 272.35 when a 75-hour inspection was completed at Campo de Mayo). Ferried to Port Stanley by 30.4.82 (probably arriving 18.4.82) and based in that area. It suffered engine problems throughout the campaign and is thought to have been grounded for the period 2.5 to 9.6.82. Found intact by British forces behind the Governor's Residence on 14.6.82 but an attempted start-up by 18 Sqdn was abandoned.

Stripped of some immediately useful parts by 18 Sqdn but several items, including the rotorblades, were removed and stored. Other items were taken by souvenir hunters before it was airlifted by 18 Sqdn Chinook ZA718 to 'Tor Caledonia' in Port William for carriage to the UK.

Sailed with the vessel 1.8.82 and removed to RNAY Fleetlands as an underslung load by 18 Sqdn Chinook ZA709 on 19.8.82 while the ship was off Portsmouth en route Felixstowe (where it docked the following day). Displayed at the Portsmouth Navy Days 28-30.8.82 but otherwise stayed at Fleetlands until 26.4.84 when it was taken by road to JATE at Brize Norton for installation and loading trials. Departed JATE by road on 27.2.85 for Fleetlands (via Lee-on-Solent on 28.2.85 and still there 8.3.85) to await a final decision on its future. Still resident at Fleetlands on 13.6.85.

### AE-521 CH-47C

In 3.82 with CAB601/Compania de Asalto 'A'. Ferried to Port Stanley by 30.4.82 (probably arriving that day). Destroyed on the ground near Mount Kent, East Falkland on 21.5.82 by cannon fire from the 1(F) Sqdn Harrier XZ963 of Flt Lt Hare. The burnt-out remains were still visible in 2.85.

# HERCULES

# GRUPO 1 DE TRANSPORTE AEREO ESCUADRON I

If the claim can be made that the Sea Harrier above all other aircraft enabled Britain to win the Falklands War then it should be said, with equal conviction, that it was the FAA's C-130 Hercules fleet that enabled Argentina to make a fight of it! In the roles of tactical transport, air-refuelling and oceanic reconnaissance the C-130, or "Chancha" (Mother Sow) as the Hercules was affectionately known, provided Argentine forces with priceless support throughout the War. It was involved from first to last.

The FAA received its first three Ç-130E's in 1968 and they were later augmented by five C-130H's, three of which arrived in 1972 and two in 1975. Two KC-130H tankers were subsequently received in 1979. In March 1982 this fleet was based at El Palomar, Buenos Aires where it was one of the components of I Brigada Aerea, equipping Escuadron I of Grupo 1 de Transporte Aereo (G1TA). One of the C-130E's, TC-62, had been destroyed by sabotage in 1975 but the rest of the fleet was in full working order and was already deeply involved in the build-up to Operacion "Rosario".

In addition to stepping up routine resupply activity to the bases at Comodoro Rivadavia and Rio Gallegos, several long-range reconnaissance missions were made to the Falklands and South Georgia (these islands were already routinely overflown by the Grupo 1 C-130's en route to the Marambio base in Antarctica). The last such preinvasion overflight of Port Stanley occurred (according to the local residents) at about 2300Z on 29 March. However, the C-130's of Grupo 1 had been fairly familiar sights at Stanley Airport as they had visited several times over the years, usually to augment the regular LADE service but occasionally on other missions. In recent times Port Stanley had become popular with FAA crews who had benefitted from the relatively cheap local shopping facilities. The unexpected visit of the KC-130H TC-69 on 6 March, given great significance by subsequent events, may well have been such a "mission" although the Flight Engineer was thought to have attended to a fractured fuel line during the brief sojourn. Perhaps greater attention should have been paid to its very presence in the area! It is ap-

posite to reflect at this juncture that in March 1982 there was virtually nothing that the FAA did not already know about Stanley Airport, its facilities or the local weather conditions.

The FAA airlift in support of the Armada's amphibious landings on the Falklands was named "Aries 82" and exclusively involved the aircraft of Grupo 1, with the C-130's of Escuadron I and the F-28 Fellowships of Escuadron II (qv) taking leading roles. During the evening of 1 April, three C-130's and two F-28's were ferried from El Palomar to Comodoro Rivadavia in preparation for the "air assault" phase of the operation due to take place the following morning. A fourth C-130 arrived at 0400Z, followed soon after by a KC-130H and, eventually, three more F-28's. This force was supported by a Guarani II and an F-27, the latter providing SAR facilities, respectively drawn from Grupo 1's Escuadrones III and IV.

"Aries 82" commenced, after a brief delay, at 0850Z on 2 April when C-130H TC-68 ("Litro 1") took-off for Port Stanley with 108 Ejercito and FAA command personnel and their equipment. These forces would later take control of Stanley Airport and establish other Island command functions. At 0920Z C-130E TC-63 ("Litro 2") followed, carrying a similar number of Ejercito staff, and at 0955Z C-130H TC-64 ("Litro 3") became airborne with a further 100 Ejercito personnel and a command vehicle. The departure of the next C-130H, TC-65 ("Litro 4"), carrying the mobile radar of G2VYCA, was delayed by technical problems but at about 1050Z the first of the F-28's, TC-53 ("Litro 5"), left on schedule with more key personnel.

Although the direct flight time for the 517 miles journey to Port Stanley normally took less than two hours for the C-130, it was not until about 1130Z that TC-68 finally landed at the recently captured Airport. Its arrival there heralded a brief procession of flights into Port Stanley which, by 1500Z on 2 April, saw the completion of the air assault phase of "Aries 82" (although it was not until 1900Z that afternoon that TC-65 finally arrived carrying the important AN/TPS-43F radar of G2VYCA).

The final element of "Aries 82", the support phase,

commenced on 3 April when the Grupo 1 transports began to ferry further supplies from the mainland to Stanley Airport. On the morning of 5 April the first Grupo 7 Bell 212 was brought in and the pattern continued for several days as bulky, high priority items continued to arrive from Comodoro Rivadavia and Rio Gallegos. Stanley Airport's limited and rather unsophisticated facilities were immediately put under pressure and although some extra ramp space was created by the FAA engineers, parking space was always a problem. The ramp area could theoretically handle five cargo aircraft simultaneously (on occasions the FAA also used taxiway and even runway areas to augment the ramp) but they were sometimes parked dangerously close together and a local eyewitness is convinced that a departing C-130 on 3 April narrowly avoided the folded wings of two parked CANA S-2E's as it took-off.

The occupation was scarcely more than a day old when British retaliation became a possibility and within a week all Argentine forces were taking emergency measures to consolidate their hold on the Islands. Argentine air transport was put under the control of the newly created CdoAeTr and that had the immediate effect of transferring all of Grupo 1's resources to the new command. Simultaneously, CdoAeEstr was formed to organise and co-ordinate all FAA strategic planning for any eventual war. The significance of that for Grupo 1 was that the concomitant formation of a new "operational" unit, GrAeExplRec1, on 4 April meant that its C-130's would be seconded, with other suitable aircraft, to that unit for reconnaissance and other special tasks. In practice, few significant changes occurred until about 11 April when the "Puente Aereo" (Air Bridge) from the mainland to the Falklands was created.

The announcement by Britain of an "exclusion zone" (MEZ), effective from 0400Z on 12 April, caused Argentina an immediate logistical crisis when it was realised that the cargo vessel 'Cuidad de Cordoba' would be liable to torpedo attack. By then she was at Puerto Deseado, fully laden with Ejercito armour, heavy guns, ammunition and other vital supplies as well as several hundred troops. The risk of loss was unacceptable and, although her cargo was assessed as being the equivalent of 100 C-130 flights, the decision was made to unload her and to carry the cargo by road to Comodoro Rivadavia for airfreighting to Port Stanley.

Thus, between 19 and 25 April 205 flights were made to Stanley Airport from Comodoro Rivadavia (91 by Grupo 1 C-130's, 74 by Grupo 1 F-28's, 36 by Aerolineas Argentinas Boeing 737's and four by Austral BAC 1-11's) carrying 1,544 tons of freight and 2,844 passengers. Five C-130's were allocated to Comodoro Rivadavia to operate the cargo shuttle to Port Stanley. These and other flights served all elements of the Argentine armed forces but were primarily geared to the needs of the Ejercito and the FAA. On 18 April the first Ejercito helicopters were carried by C-130 from Comodoro Rivadavia to Port Stanley.

In mid-April the first of the medium-range reconnaissance missions was flown by GrAeExplRec1 from Comodoro Rivadavia, probably using a C-130 drawn from those held there for cargo duties. At about the same time one of the KC-130H tankers was deployed to the

naval base at Comandante Espora to support the CANA Super Etendards of 2 Escuadrilla, whose sensitive, anti-shipping operations were then in an advanced state of training. Once CANA had discounted the possibility of using Stanley Airport as an operational base for these aircraft, air-refuelling had become vital to their mission and Grupo 1 operated the only "non-buddy" type tankers in the Argentine forces. After the successful conclusion of the trials the Super Etendards deployed to Rio Grande on 19 April while the KC-130H's went to nearby Rio Gallegos.

Throughout late April high priority cargo continued to be shuttled into Port Stanley and a typical afternoon's schedule, that of 23 April, included C-130's arriving at 1600Z and 1605Z, each carrying a CAE UH-1H and more than a ton of 7.62mm ammunition. Another at 1935Z brought in a UNIMOG vehicle and eight tons of ammunition and a fourth C-130 at 2000Z carried in a Roland missile launch vehicle. On another typical day, 25 April, a total of 34 flights was scheduled by the FAA to operate into Stanley Airport from Comodoro Rivadavia (13 Grupo 1 C-130's, 13 Grupo 1 F-28's and eight Boeing 737's) but eight of them were unable to land because of poor weather. In spite of a typical turn-round time of 15 minutes, some flights were off-loaded on the taxiways and on the runway.

At that time all fixed and temporary navaids were in use at Stanley Airport to minimise the dangers of the short runway and inclement weather. However, once British forces reached the Falklands waters the situation changed radically and Grupo 1 missions became altogether much more difficult. (Operating minima for the C-130 at Stanley permitted a maximum cross-wind component of 35 knots, a cloud ceiling of 80 metres and runway visibility of 4 kilometres. In practice the minima were regularly disregarded, particularly after 21 May.) Throughout the War the C-130's always carried a maximum fuel load into Stanley Airport where any surplus JP-1 was de-fuelled into pillow tanks and storage drums for local use.

By 28 April aerial reconnaissance and other intelligence data had convinced Argentina that British landings on the Falklands were likely within the next few days and, accordingly, the FAA made its final preparations to defend the Islands against what it believed might be a full-scale assault. CdoAeEst was stood down on 30 April and was replaced by CdoFAS at Comodoro Rivadavia. GrAeExplRec1, still with its Grupo 1 C-130's on call, was simultaneously transferred to the new command whose brief was to conduct the imminent air war. In a final effort on 29 April, six C-130 and eight F-28 flights successfully carried in 125 tons of cargo and 126 passengers between 1130Z and 2000Z. At 2000Z an air raid warning was called and the "Puente Aereo" had ended. By then the aircraft of Grupo 1 and the civilian carriers had carried 5,008 tons of cargo and 9,215 passengers into Stanley Airport. In the process, 1,929 flying hours and 452 landings were recorded.

At Rio Gallegos, the KC-130H's were readied for their first missions with the Super Etendards. By 29 April all the FAA combat squadrons assigned to CdoFAS on the southern bases were poised to counter-attack the British and for two days they waited for an amphibious assault on the Falklands.

**Upper Left** *After 21.5.82 the two KC-130H "Chancha" tankers of Grupo 1 de Transporte Aereo were used extensively in support of the Skyhawks and Super Etendards and frequently operated as a pair. In-flight refuelling was routine on outbound sectors but invariably occurred only in emergency situations on homeward runs. Such was the success of providing an aerial refuelling facility that no Skyhawk was lost after reaching a "Chancha" on the way home. The two A-4B's seen here are from Grupo 5 de Caza and are in standard markings without yellow identification flashes.* **Upper Right** *Photographed during an in-flight refuelling, probably before 1.5.82, this Grupo 4 de Caza A-4C is still wearing its serial number at both front and rear. Grupo 4 de Caza suffered relatively heavy losses during the conflict and, with only seven airworthy aircraft available, post-war re-equipment became inevitable. By 1985 Mirage IIICJ's were due to have replaced the Skyhawks at Mendoza.*

*(via S. Mafé Huertas)*

*In typically inclement weather at Rio Gallegos, C-130H TC-64 of Grupo 1 de Transporte Aereo wears the twin badges of Escuadron I (alias the "Escuadron C-130") and Grupo 1. For much of the War TC-64's operations were conducted from Comodoro Rivadavia, it having been one of the aircraft used in "Aries 82" on 2.4.82 and subsequently on many more resupply runs to Stanley Airport.* *(via S. Mafé Huertas)*

*Photographed in late 1982 at Villa Reynolds, C-225 is a typically marked A-4B Skyhawk of Grupo 5 de Caza. The two yellow stencils appear to show Type 42 destroyers, while the Grupo 5 badge can be seen just beyond the engineer's left leg. It is not known which British warships these stencils represented but the unit's achievements included the destruction of 'Antelope', 'Coventry' and 'Sir Galahad' and damage to 'Argonaut', 'Glasgow' and 'Sir Tristram'.*

When the British finally did attack on 1 May it was not on the anticipated scale. However, this was not immediately appreciated by CdoFAS and a large number of anti-shipping sorties were launched, although on 1 May none of the Grupo 4 and Grupo 5 Skyhawk sorties were air-refuelled. However, the C-130 operations to Port Stanley were significantly affected by the British attacks of 1 May and what had been a fairly routine task then became a far more dangerous undertaking. The single 1,000lb bomb that had hit the runway on 1 May had cratered it with one edge close to the centreline, about 1,500ft from the threshold in the 08 direction, on its southern side. The C-130's were thus obliged to operate on the northern half of the runway (a strip about 45ft wide).

No further C-130 operations were undertaken to Stanley Airport until 6 May, however, because of generally poor weather and considerable early worries about the proximity of the British Sea Harriers. The first aircraft to get in, C-130H TC-65 ("Tigre"), left Comodoro Rivadavia at 1500Z that day and, after a long and cautious flight, it touched down safely at 1850Z with 14 tons of cargo. When it departed at 1920Z it evacuated 23 men, wounded in the attacks of 1 May and in subsequent incidents. The mission proved that the runway could still be used, albeit with great caution, but, as far as the FAA was concerned, only by the C-130 (CANA had other ideas and they continued to use their Electras on occasions). Nevertheless, the crater was a major problem and its in-filling did not, by any means, restore the runway to normal status. The crater caused one potentially nasty incident late in the War when a C-130, obliged to make a night departure with a deflated tyre, hit its edge as it rotated and, with marginally adequate lift, only just staggered into the air and safety.

The daylight operation of 6 May demonstrated that the Sea Harriers were not always in a position to enforce the British blockade and that, with some thought and good communications, the C-130's might be able to get into Stanley for an indefinite period. The airfield was, however, regularly subjected to naval bombardment and air attack and was under observation from British Special Forces. It was thus considered prudent that whenever possible all flights should be made during the hours of darkness.

While Stanley Airport was recovering from the first air attacks the KC-130H's flew their initial operational sorties from Rio Gallegos. Although apparently not called into action on 1 May, at least one was airborne the following day when 2 Escuadrilla made its first unsuccessful attempt to use an Exocet against a British radar picket ship operating to the south of the Falklands. The mission failed because of an unspecified problem which occurred during the in-flight refuelling phase. That inauspicious first attempt was quickly forgotten, however, when at 1304Z on 4 May two Super Etendards separated from the KC-130H of Vicecomodoro Pessana and his crew and sped off towards 'Sheffield' and a place in military history.

During May, CdoFAS planned a total of 58 C-130 flights from the mainland, invariably from Comodoro Rivadavia, to Port Stanley. Of these, 47 were actually dispatched but only 27 of them landed at Stanley Airport. Of the 20 flights that were unable to land, seven aborted for reasons of poor weather and 13 for "tactical" reasons.

It would appear that the word "tactical" was used euphemistically to mean that the CIC had detected Sea Harrier activity! By the end of the month the C-130's had landed 354 tons of supplies and 241 passengers at Stanley Airport and had evacuated 151 wounded. Although roughly averaging two successful trips every three days, on some occasions two or even three flights would arrive within the space of a few hours when weather and the enemy permitted. Some cargo required two or three false starts before being successfully landed. Landings were undertaken without lights until the last possible moment and engines were never shut down. It was perhaps little short of miraculous that no accidents occurred during these frantic turn-rounds at Stanley.

A mission to Port Stanley on 7 May was not investigated by Sea Harriers because of poor visibility but on 9 May the British Task Force made its first serious attempt to bring down a C-130 which was inbound to Stanley Airport. 'Coventry' and 'Broadsword' had detached from the main group of British warships to a position off Port Stanley from where they were able to launch SAM's at any aircraft using the airfield or simply use gunfire against any selected shore target. At 1417Z 'Coventry' fired three Sea Darts at an inbound C-130 but all missed and other aircraft seen on British radar returned to the mainland. The following day the two ships were relieved by 'Glasgow' and 'Brilliant', but after 'Glasgow' was bombed by Grupo 5 Skyhawks on 12 May the trap was withdrawn. A typically successful night's operation was that of 15/16 May when one C-130 landed safely at 2330Z and was airborne again at 2359Z, to be followed by another which landed at 0030Z and departed at 0115Z. The extra 15 minutes taken on the second turn-round might, in part, be blamed on a VT bomb from a Sea Harrier that exploded nearby at 0040Z!

By mid-May the problem of resupplying the outlying garrisons such as Fox Bay, Port Howard and Darwin was becoming urgent. Small boats and light helicopters lacked capacity and were vulnerable to air attack, so it was decided that time and effort might be saved by air-dropping containers to those garrisons from C-130's. Such a plan had the added attraction that it avoided transhipments through Port Stanley with all the attendant hazards that that entailed. Two such missions were actually undertaken and each is worth detailing.

The first, on 19 May, was to Darwin and the operation was intently watched by the local inhabitants. Conceived by CdoFAS, the mission was dispatched from Comodoro Rivadavia at 1621Z under the command of Mayor Ruben Palazzi. C-130H TC-68 ("Tronco") routed over Santa Cruz and from there flew at an altitude of 100ft until it achieved landfall over the west coast of West Falkland. As normal the weather was foul with low cloud, drizzle and fog patches for the C-130 to thread its way through en route to Darwin. The drop was made at 1914Z from 600ft in fairly good visibility and passed off perfectly, although one of the loadmasters nearly fell out with the eight A22 containers. The FAA subsequently revealed that this mission delivered eight tons of supplies to Darwin, primarily for the Ejercito's RgtInf25.

A second drop was made the following day, 20 May, to Fox Bay East by C-130H TC-64. "Pato" flight carried 10 containers (9.5 tons) for the RgtInf8 garrison forces and, as before, the drop was guided by FAA personnel who had been flown in to Fox Bay by a Grupo 7 Bell 212. The drop was made successfully but TC-64 nearly came to grief when several Argentine guns opened fire in an attempt to bring it down. An eyewitness recalled a violent turn and a C-130 disappearing at high speed from whence it had come!

21 May was a significant date for all of the C-130 crews, particularly those assigned to the KC-130H's at Rio Gallegos. From then until the end of hostilities both aircraft were airborne virtually every day, flying two or three sorties each on peak days in support of the Skyhawks and Super Etendards. Lessons learned on 1 May and on subsequent missions dictated that all FAA Skyhawk sorties should be refuelled on the outbound sector by the KC-130H's, some 15 minutes after departure. The tankers would then hold station until the Skyhawks returned in order to administer whatever aid might be necessary. Usually that was a simple topping up operation but sometimes it was far more complicated with damaged and lost aircraft needing help. On several occasions damaged FAA and CANA Skyhawks could not have survived the journey home without the aid of the KC-130H's. Interestingly, the CANA Skyhawk sorties of 21 May were undertaken without air-refuelling, but within two days 3 Escuadrilla was using the tankers in the same way as the FAA Skyhawks.

In practice, Skyhawk missions further than 400 miles from the mainland were not practical without air-refuelling and, as the war progressed, the KC-130H's of Grupo 1 were obliged to venture further eastwards, both in support of planned combat operations and, occasionally, to seek lost Skyhawks. Such aircraft would invariably be damaged and low on fuel but were sometimes further troubled by communications problems or, in extreme cases, flown by a pilot whose behaviour was less than rational. It took all of the skill and authority of the Grupo 1 senior commanders to talk some distressed Skyhawk pilots to the tankers and then to help them compose themselves to take on fuel. Many of the known major missions and incidents involving the KC-130H's are detailed elsewhere but it is abundantly clear that senior pilots like Vicecomodores Pessana, Cano, Litrenta and Noe were held in the highest esteem by the fighter-bomber pilots, some of whom owed their lives to them.

While the KC-130H's were operating in support of the fighter-bombers, CdoFAS continued to use the other aircraft in a variety of roles, many of which were becoming more hazardous with each passing day. As the resupply flights to Port Stanley continued to breach the British blockade, so the Royal Navy devised new means of stopping them. On 22 May a C-130 had a fortunate escape when, at 0645Z, it was picked up on radar by 'Coventry' and 'Broadsword', operating a missile trap to the north of Pebble Island. At the moment of missile launch the 'Coventry' Sea Dart system malfunctioned and the C-130 passed safely by at a distance of eight miles. An 801 Sqdn Sea Harrier CAP was also launched but the Port Stanley CIC warned the C-130 of the latter's presence and the transport turned round and returned to Argentina. Such tactical retreats were fairly common, as a typical story from an Ejercito commando relates. His unit was given places on a C-130 flight from Comodoro Rivadavia on 26

May and his aircraft had been airborne for three hours when it was ordered back because of Sea Harrier activity in the area of East Falkland. He eventually arrived in Port Stanley the following evening.

Throughout May an acrimonious exchange took place between the FAA and CANA over who should be providing maritime reconnaissance data to CdoFAS. The FAA had no means to task its fighter-bombers to strike successfully at British warships unless it could update their original briefing data with real-time information after they were airborne. Clearly, without such information the CdoFAS aircraft were chasing warships which might have moved position some hours earlier. Traditionally, CANA's SP-2H Neptunes were the suppliers of such data but, by 21 May, they had been permanently withdrawn from use and a replacement was vital. With some bitterness, the mission was accepted by Grupo 1, well aware that its C-130's were far from ideal and that the crews were unskilled in the task. Their aircraft had range and radar but were large, cumbersome, had no ECM/ESM fit and could not defend themselves.

By the time that the first mission was flown in late May a rudimentary RWR fit was installed but it did little to allay crew fears. The task assigned by CdoFAS was highly dangerous, requiring a C-130 to be flown from Comodoro Rivadavia to arrive at dawn at a point 16 miles north of San Carlos Water on the 59°00′W meridian. The C-130, at sea-level until the last possible moment, would at that point climb rapidly to nearly 10,000ft and, once level, would conduct a rapid radar search of the surrounding sea area for British warships. When satisfied of the whereabouts of any such ships (or otherwise) the C-130 would return to sea-level and, by means of a "sawtooth" flightplan, would continue northwards on the meridian repeating the original search at 34 mile intervals. After the fifth search the C-130 would break off and return home. When conducting the radar search the C-130 would only hold station for a maximum of 90 seconds, for it was reasoned that to remain there longer would render the aircraft vulnerable to British Sea Dart missiles.

The pilot selected for the first flight was Vicecomodoro Alfredo Cano and his flight crew were Capitan Rubich (co-pilot) and Vicecomodoro Servatico (navigator). The officer in charge of the reconnaissance element of the mission was Mayor Oreffice, while its creator, Comodoro Ernesto Ferri, commander of GrAeExplRec1, was also carried as an observer. Fortunately for all concerned it was successful, although those on board the C-130 were badly shaken by an incident which could have easily led to the aircraft's destruction.

The first climb and search was apparently undetected, although no British ships were located despite the four-directional radar sweep. The C-130 descended and moved north to the second search point but as it climbed through 6,000ft the ESM illuminated, indicating the presence of an enemy search radar. The aircraft was immediately levelled and a quick scan with its radar revealed a warship some 42 miles away to the south-east. Having rapidly calculated its position and passed that to both CdoFAS and a flight of airborne fighter-bombers, Cano elected to make a second check of the warship's co-ordinates, from a distance of 50 miles to the south. That was done, but, to Cano's horror, it was realised that because of a navigational error the ship was only 25 miles away and that the C-130 had passed well within Sea Dart range. Argentine accounts of this incident unfortunately do not identify either the date or the warship but it is quite conceivable that it was 25 May, that the ship was 'Coventry' and that the early morning fighter-bombers were the A-4B Skyhawks of Grupo 5, led by Capitan Hugo del Valle Palaver.

A similar mission on 28 May vectored Skyhawks to the hospital ship 'Uganda' and yet another on 1 June ended in almost predictable disaster. For that day's mission Capitan Ruben Mertel, Capitan Carlos Krause and Vicecomodoro Hugo Meisner constituted the flight crew while the rest of TC-63's complement comprised Suboficial Principal Julio Lastra, Suboficial Ayudante Manuel Albelos, Cabo Principal Miguel Cardone and Cabo Principal Carlos Cantenzano.

Their C-130E departed Comodoro Rivadavia that morning at about the same time (0935Z) that a C-130H (TC-66) left Port Stanley for a long homeward run. The two aircraft were in occasional radio contact until about 1340Z, by which time TC-63 had been detected to the north of Pebble Island by search radars on the British frigate 'Minerva' in San Carlos Water. The 801 Sqdn Sea Harriers of Lt Cdr Nigel Ward and Lt Steve Thomas were diverted from the return leg of a routine CAP and they eventually found the C-130 below cloud, travelling low and fast towards the mainland. At 1346Z Ward, in Sea Harrier XZ451, fired both AIM-9L's, the first of which fell short before the second struck the right wing. Ward continued with a gun attack on the tail area and the burning Hercules suddenly dropped the right wing and dived into the sea. There were no survivors and the mission appears to have been the last of its kind.

On 29 May what was presumably a Grupo 1 C-130 featured in an unusual and unsuccessful attack on the isolated British Task Force supply tanker 'British Wye'. The vessel was at 47°54′S 39°19′W, north of South Georgia, when the C-130 first made a low reconnaissance pass and then, 15 minutes later, returned to bomb her. Grupo 1 had not, at the time of writing, acknowledged the sortie but the description of the incident from crewmen on the tanker leaves little doubt that the mission was one of long-range reconnaissance with some attack capability. The C-130 made its second run at an altitude of about 150ft and eight "500lb bombs" were dropped from the open ramp. Four of them fell into the sea without exploding; three exploded to port causing minor damage and one bounced off the foredeck without exploding. The C-130 climbed into cloud and left the area.

By early June the British grip on Port Stanley was tightening and, with more poor local weather, even fewer flights were able to get into the Airport. During the first week of the month only eight C-130 sorties were planned and even fewer, six, actually took-off for the Falklands, bad weather preventing the others from departing. Of the six that were dispatched, only three landed at Stanley Airport, the others having to return being thwarted by bad weather.

By then, most of the C-130 flights reaching Port Stanley were evacuating the wounded on their return runs and it was fortunate that none of them was intercepted by Sea Harriers. Senior Grupo 1 flight crew such as Comodores Beltramone, Bolzi and Mela; Mayores Bruno, Maldonado and Veliz; Capitanes Borchert and Daguerre and others still managed to land at Port Stanley in spite of some determined and ingenious British efforts to bring them down. One strategy, used late in the War, was typical. On 11 June two pairs of 801 Sqdn CAP Sea Harriers were launched to fly medium altitude patterns off the Falklands. Once on station one pair descended to low level over Queen Charlotte Bay, West Falkland to wait, hopefully unseen, for the anticipated C-130. On that occasion there was no contact and the pair on CAP returned to 'Invincible' while the other pair eventually refuelled at the FOB at Port San Carlos before later returning to their carrier. Ironically, a C-130 landed successfully at Port Stanley at 2115Z that evening.

In view of these and the earlier described attempts to shoot down C-130's, it is interesting to discover that the only occasion on which the Grupo 1 crews actually believed that they were under missile attack was on the night of 7 June. That night, two C-130's were unable to get into Stanley Airport and one of the crews reported a missile attack that they "evaded" at a point some 21 miles from the airfield. Limited evidence suggests that this may have been a malfunctioning Sea Dart, fired from 'Cardiff'.

The KC-130H operations continued until 13 June when the final Skyhawk combat sorties were launched. By then the end was near and British troops were poised for a final assault on Port Stanley. Although the situation was hopeless CdoFAS continued to push C-130 flights into the battered airfield, carrying urgently needed ammunition and weapons. Only the most vital of military hardware was shipped and in the previous days SA-7 SAM's, shells and small-arms ammunition had been brought in. The land-launched Exocet fire unit, later to seriously damage 'Glamorgan', was brought in by C-130 in late May but by 11 June the priority cargo was the 155mm CITEFA howitzers and their shells. C-130 movements through Port Stanley during the final hours included an arrival at 0815Z on 12 June, two more at about 0900Z on 13 June, another seen there at 1100Z (thought to be have been the aircraft that departed at 1155Z, shortly before Sea Harriers reached the area) and, finally, two more during the night of 13/14 June. Scheduled into Stanley Airport at 2200Z and 2300Z, the first of them was brought in by Mayor Bolzi carrying 155mm shells and other urgently required ammunition. During its turn-round the area was illuminated by starshells from a nearby British warship which then opened fire on the airfield as the C-130 departed. Shortly afterwards the final blockade-running C-130H, TC-65 ("Cobre"), was brought in by Comodoro Mela, Capitanes Victor Borchert and Capitan Hernan Daguerre and the non-commissioned officers Carabajal, Paolone and Sosa. It carried a complete 155mm howitzer and 80 shells and as the crew struggled to off-load the gun the flares began to fall again. Worse still, shortly before 2300Z, an 800 Sqdn Sea Harrier CAP was reported to be heading for Port Stanley from the British carrier group to the east. With the big gun still wedged in the Hercules the crew had little choice but to shut down the engines and seek cover from the expected attack. Somewhat surprisingly, this did not materialise and after a tense forty minutes the CAP finally left its nearby orbit and returned to the carrier, allowing TC-65 to unload its cargo and depart safely for the mainland at 2335Z. This last flight to safety evacuated 72 sick and wounded and, fortunately for all concerned, it reached home safely.

Despite many scares, not one of the C-130's on a Port Stanley resupply "run" was successfully intercepted by the enemy. The aircraft lost on 1 June was not involved in the resupply operation, a task which was a complete success. Throughout that undertaking 427 flight hours were accumulated and over 400 tons of cargo were carried with another 17 tons air-dropped. Between 1 May and 13 June 74 such C-130 sorties were planned and 61 were eventually dispatched to the Falklands. Of these, 31 landed successfully at Stanley Airport and another two were the air-drops to Darwin and Fox Bay. Of the 28 "failures", 21 approached to within 60 miles of Port Stanley and several of them returned to the mainland from positions overhead the airfield. 10 flights aborted because of unacceptable terminal weather conditions and 18 others did so for tactical reasons. The 13 sorties that failed to leave the mainland were blamed on tactical reasons (eight), weather (three) and technical problems (two). During the 44 days of warfare the 31 successful flights brought in 514 personnel to Port Stanley and evacuated another 264, most of whom were casualties.

When used as tankers, the two KC-130H's flew 29 missions and refuelled 93 flights of FAA fighter-bombers as well as a further 20 CANA sorties. The achievements of the two tankers speak for themselves. CANA's spectacular Exocet victories were only achieved with the assistance of the tankers, as indeed were many of the FAA triumphs in San Carlos Water, Falkland Sound and Port Pleasant.

However, the KC-130H's achieved most in the eyes of many pilots by simply being in the right place at the right time! In other roles the C-130's performed well but with mixed fortunes. The loss of TC-63 was arguably unnecessary and its mission probably achieved nothing.

There have been few publicised post-war developments affecting Escuadron I of Grupo 1 de Transporte Aereo, although a new model L-100-30 Hercules was received by Argentina in December 1982 in commercial markings. The limitations of a tanker fleet of only two aircraft cannot have failed to have concerned the FAA, however, and plans for further acquisitions or for tanker conversions may have been rapidly formulated in the light of experience gained.

> *Pilots and navigators known to have flown missions with Escuadron I during the war included:*
>
> *Comodoro Beltramone; Comodoro R.F.Mela; Vicecomodoro A.A.Cano; Vicecomodoro Dominguez; Vicecomodoro Litrenta; Vicecomodoro H.C.Meisner (KIA); Vicecomodoro Moro; Vicecomodoro R.Noe; Vicecomodoro Pessana; Vicecomodoro Servatico; Mayor Bolzi; Mayor R.Briend; Mayor Bruno; Mayor Maldonado; Mayor Mensi; Mayor R.O.Palazzi; Mayor Veliz; Capitan Bilmezis; Capitan V.Borchert; Capitan H.Daguerre; Capitan Destefanis; Capitan C.E.Krause (KIA); Capitan R.H.Mertel (KIA); Capitan Rubich.*

# INDIVIDUAL AIRCRAFT DETAILS

As far as is known, the entire FAA fleet of C-130 aircraft was used during the War from a variety of bases. The two C-130E's, TC-61 and TC-63, with the C-130H's TC-64 to TC-68 were primarily used from Comodoro Rivadavia while the KC-130H's TC-69 and TC-70 flew most sorties from Rio Gallegos.

Throughout the War the fleet continued to wear its normal peace-time dark camouflage of green and brown with light blue undersides although at least one aircraft

(TC-66) actually wore the wholly inappropriate yellow "identification" fin flash after 1 May. Most, and maybe all, aircraft wore the crests of I Brigada Aerea and the 'Escuadron Hercules' on the forward fuselage below and behind the cockpit windows.

*In the individual aircraft details the standard FAA abbreviation 'G1TA' has been used for Grupo 1 de Transporte Aereo.*

**TC-61** C-130E

In 3.82 with G1TA. Primarily used from Comodoro Rivadavia during the War.

**TC-63** C-130E

In 3.82 with G1TA. Primarily used from Comodoro Rivadavia until 1.6.82 when it was brought down north of Pebble Island by an AIM-9L and gunfire from the 801 Sqdn Sea Harrier XZ451 of Lt Cdr Ward. Seven men, Vicecomodoro Meisner, Capitan Mertel, Capitan Krause, Suboficial Principal Lastra, Suboficial Ayudante Albelos, Cabo Principal Cardone and Cabo Principal Cantenzano, were killed. The aircraft crashed into the sea some 50 miles north of Pebble Island. Unconfirmed reports suggest that some items of wreckage including a wheel were later washed ashore on Pebble Island.

**TC-64** C-130H

In 3.82 with G1TA. Primarily used from Comodoro Rivadavia during the War.

**TC-65** C-130H

In 3.82 with G1TA. Primarily used from Comodoro Rivadavia during the War. It had the distinction of making the last C-130 visit to Stanley Airport on 13.6.82.

**TC-66** C-130H

In 3.82 with G1TA. Primarily used from Comodoro Rivadavia during the War.

**TC-67** C-130H

In 3.82 with G1TA. Primarily used from Comodoro Rivadavia during the War.

**TC-68** C-130H

In 3.82 with G1TA. Primarily used from Comodoro Rivadavia during the War.

**TC-69** KC-130H

In 3.82 with G1TA. It made an unexpected visit to Stanley Airport on 6.3.82. Primarily used from Rio Gallegos during the War.

**TC-70** KC-130H

In 3.82 with G1TA. Primarily used from Rio Gallegos during the War.

# BOEING 707

# GRUPO 1 DE TRANSPORTE AEREO ESCUADRON II

At the time of writing, the last visit of an Argentine military aircraft to the United Kingdom was that of an FAA Boeing 707. In retrospect it seems barely credible that TC-93 of Grupo 1 de Transporte Aereo could have been seen at Stansted on 24 and 25 March 1982 surrounded by Royal Navy vehicles while loading military stores! It was the last of several such visits and one can but wonder whether its crew was more aware of the mission's significance than was the Royal Navy.

In March 1982 the FAA possessed three Boeing 707's (TC-91 to TC-93), all configured for long-range military freighting. Following their progressive introduction into FAA military colours they had been assigned to the I Brigada Aerea at El Palomar, Buenos Aires where they were operated by Grupo 1 de Transporte Aereo (G1TA). The three aircraft and their crews were assigned to Grupo 1's Escuadron II where they operated alongside a fleet of F-28 Fellowships (whose contributions to the War are considered elsewhere).

In the United Kingdom much of the post-war discussion that has considered the spontaneity, or otherwise, of Argentina's invasion of the Falkland Islands seems to ignore the evidence of Grupo 1's European activities early in 1982. It must be of some significance to such debate that for two months prior to the landings Argentina sought and acquired large quantities of military equipment from Britain, France, Israel, Italy, Spain and elsewhere, including many critically important spares items for her weapons and defence systems. Missile stocks were also reinforced.

A procession of resupply flights through Stansted commenced with the stay of TC-91 from 27 to 29 January, it having come from and returned to Gando, Las Palmas. It arrived with a "general cargo" (as, indeed, did all the flights through Stansted) and departed carrying "explosives". TC-93 arrived on 2 March from Orly, Paris and left for Gando the following day with a "hazardous" cargo, later returning to Stansted from Brindisi on 8 March. TC-93 departed again for Gando two days later, this time carrying more general items (all the subsequent departures carried a "general cargo"). TC-91 arrived from

Gando the same day, 10 March, and left for Getafe, Madrid on 12 March. Finally, TC-93 arrived from Charles de Gaulle, Paris on 24 March and left for Chateauroux-Deols in central France the following day. Yet another flight, due in from Ben Gurion, Tel Aviv on 5 April (and due out to Gando on 7 April) did not materialise! The Royal Navy was next to meet a Grupo 1 Boeing 707 a month after these events in circumstances that could not have been more different.

For much of April 1982 the 707's, in common with other FAA transport aircraft, were busily involved in the airlift of personnel and material from northern and central Argentina to Patagonia and the Falkland Islands. Unlike all other Grupo 1 aircraft, however, the 707's could not land on Stanley Airport's short runway and their role was thus restricted to mainland and international operations.

On 20 April the commander of Escuadron II was briefed by CdoAeEstr for a mission that had been requested of the FAA by the Armada. The Squadron was to undertake a reconnaissance flight in an attempt to locate the British Task Force, by then thought to have left Ascension Island on its way south. The 707's possessed no special equipment for such a task but, in the absence of specialist reconnaissance aircraft with the necessary range, Grupo 1 had been obliged to accept the mission. The first search was scheduled to take place the next day, 21 April, and it was expected that further flights would follow, at least until the Task Force was found.

With little more intelligence available than educated guesswork, it was decided to construct an imaginary triangle with Ascension Island the apex and a line between the Falklands and South Georgia forming the base. A flight-plan, limited only by the range of the 707, was created, in which the aircraft would fly east from Buenos Aires until the left-hand edge of the triangle was reached. The 707 would then turn north and fly towards Ascension Island until a predetermined point ("Alpha") was achieved. Once there, the aircraft would turn east once more until the right-hand edge of the triangle was reached

Argentina prepares for war – in Essex! Photographed at Stansted on 12.3.82, Boeing 707 TC-91 of Escuadrón II, Grupo 1 de Transporte Aereo, El Palomar, is seen shortly before departing to Getafe, Madrid on its way home to Argentina. On this occasion its "general cargo" is believed to have included urgently required spare parts as well as new equipment and weapons. Previous flights had certainly carried weapons and ammunition. The visit was typical of several made to Europe during early 1982. Some forty days later the same aircraft undertook a new role....
(C. Pocock)

.... when it performed the first of a series of reconnaissance sorties to determine the progress of the British Task Force. The first of these flights was undertaken on 21.4.82 and TC-91 was intercepted high over the South Atlantic by the 800 Squadron Sea Harrier XZ460 of Lt Simon Hargreaves. Both he and Vicecomodoro Jorge Ricardini, the 707's captain, were under strict instructions from their respective commanders to observe the opposition and to do nothing that would unnecessarily inflame an already tense situation. However, Hargreaves and the Armada photographer on board TC-91 did take these photographs of each other while the Sea Harrier was investigating the 707. XZ460's armed AIM-9L's would most certainly have been clearly visible to Ricardini and his crew and the 707's obvious vulnerability must have caused the FAA to ponder the wisdom of dispatching further unarmed aircraft to watch the British fleet. Nevertheless the risk was deemed acceptable (and certainly necessary) and several more 707 missions were launched before British forces recaptured South Georgia and the conflict entered a new phase.
(FAA/Ministry of Defence)

(the "Bravo" point). From the "Bravo" point the 707 would fly south towards South Georgia until it reached a position consistent with safe fuel reserves, after which it would turn to the west and return to Argentina. This rudimentary search pattern would require basic navigation and fuel management and the crew would have to rely on the 707's standard commercial weather radar for the sea search.

The mission was given to Vicecomodoro Jorge Ricardini, Escuadron II's most experienced 707 pilot, and, because of the nature and anticipated duration of the flight, he selected three pilots and a navigator to accompany him. Two engineers and a loadmaster would also travel. His four flight crew were all senior officers, but were chosen primarily because they had had the longest period of rest since their previous 707 missions. They were Vicecomodores Arguelles, Conte, Genolet and Lopez.

In order to carry the maximum possible fuel load it was decided that the chosen aircraft, TC-91, should be ferried to Ezeiza Airport where it would be able to make use of a longer runway than was available at its home base. The 707 left El Palomar at 0600Z on 21 April for the short trip to Ezeiza and, after fuelling and uplifting three naval passengers (a pilot adviser/co-ordinator, an intelligence specialist and a photographer), it was soon airborne again. The total mission was expected to last for up to 15 hours.

For fuel economy reasons the flight was made at an altitude above 40,000ft and, after four hours, the "Alpha" point was reached. The 707 crew was authorised to continue on the same track in view of better than expected fuel figures and it was soon after then that the radar image of a single ship was found. After a tense descent through the clouds to an altitude of 2,000ft, it was identified as a merchant vessel that had no connection with the British expedition! The 707 then turned south-east towards the "Bravo" point and, as it climbed towards 20,000ft, the crew suddenly saw the vague radar images of surface contacts away to the aircraft's right.

Shortly before 1200Z these radar contacts were visually identified as being six British warships, including the carriers 'Hermes' and 'Invincible'. They were found at 19°29'S 21°00'W, a point over the South Atlantic, some 1,400 miles east north-east of Rio de Janeiro. It was whilst TC-91 was banking to the north of this group in an attempt to improve the photographic angle, that it became apparent to the FAA crew that there might be aircraft activity below them. In fact, TC-91 had been detected at more than 150 miles distance by the Task Force and at 1145Z the 800 Sqdn Sea Harrier XZ460 of Lt Simon Hargreaves had been launched to investigate. By the time he had reached the 707 and had realised that he had not intercepted a wayward commercial aircraft, TC-91's crew had, already, passed its vital intelligence back to Argentina. Hargreaves, of course, was under clear instructions not to attack the 707 but Vicecomodoro Ricardini had already decided not to overfly the ships (in fact there had been a clear instruction to go no nearer than 22 miles to any British ships) and TC-91 was making a run for home when caught by the Sea Harrier. TC-91 was reached at an altitude of about 35,000ft and Hargreaves remained with the 707 for several minutes, moving from wing-tip to wing-tip and taking photographs, but, unlike the FAA crew, making no effort to communicate with the other aircraft. Eventually the Sea Harrier broke away and TC-91 returned to Ezeiza where it landed, without incident, some five hours later. The mission had been a clear, if fortunate, success although the aircraft and its crew had always been at the mercy of the Sidewinder-equipped Sea Harrier.

Encouraged by the nature of the first meeting and feeling that the British were reluctant to fire on its aircraft, the FAA immediately embarked on a series of investigatory 707 flights designed to keep the Task Force under close surveillance. These missions are presumed to have been conducted under the operational control of GrAeExplRec1, the special reconnaissance element of CdoAeEstr that had been created on 4 April with the express purpose of providing that command with early reconnaissance warning of the approach of the Task Force and of its subsequent activities.

At 0230Z on 22 April, the "alert" Sea Harrier in 'Invincible' was scrambled by Lt Brian Haigh to find an inbound 707 which he met some 60 miles from the carrier. At 1830Z the same day another 707 was met at 120 miles distance but on that occasion 'Invincible' put up three Sea Harriers. Flown by Lt Cdr John Eyton-Jones, Lt Cdr Mike Broadwater and Flt Lt Paul Barton, the three aircraft boxed the 707 in an exercise designed to impress the Grupo 1 pilot of his vulnerability. These 707 missions, typically intercepted at 35,000ft, were most disconcerting to the Task Force. The carriers had only been three days out from Ascension Island when first found by Grupo 1 and they were not to pass the strategically significant 35°00'S latitude until 25 April. Each 707 found them with unerring accuracy and, although the unwanted visitor was jokingly referred to as the "Burglar" by the British, the Task Force commanders were anything but amused by Grupo 1's presence. Conventional peace-time rules of interception were hardly thought applicable under the circumstances but the option of firing on the 707 over the international waters of the South Atlantic was politically unacceptable to the British government. Britain was of the opinion that a Boeing 707 would be emotionally identified by the rest of the world as a soft target (and might even be construed as a civilian aircraft, although clearly it was not). Besides, Britain had no wish to be seen, at that stage, to fire the shots that would escalate the tense situation. Nevertheless, the 707's posed a real threat to the Task Force which was greatly concerned at that moment about guidance given to the Argentine submarines. Argentina was naturally well aware of Britain's dilemma and correctly assumed that her aircraft would remain safe until she received a clear warning to the contrary.

Sea Harriers from 'Invincible' were again scrambled at 1100Z on 23 April to meet a 707 at 120 miles distance and again at 1500Z to the same aircraft. After the latter interception the 707 passed as close as five miles to the north of 'Invincible'. The final meeting of 707 and Sea Harrier occurred at 1550Z on 24 April when 'Hermes' aircraft intercepted a Grupo 1 aircraft 80 miles to the east of the ship. That same morning yet another 707 reconnaissance mission overflew 'Endurance' as she prepared to play her role in the recovery of South Georgia the next day. It was then that Argentina was advised through diplomatic channels that her Boeing 707's would be fired upon with immediate effect (the message, referring to aircraft and shipping, was delivered to Swiss intermediaries on 23 April). The blunt warning was heeded and it was to be a full month before a 707 reconnaissance mission again ventured near to British warships *[but see the Grupo 2 de Bombardeo notes concerning an incident that occurred on 26 April]*.

When CdoAeEstr was stood down on 30 April GrAeExplRec1 was transferred to CdoFAS and the unit's reconnaissance mission was formalised to encompass oceanic reconnaissance between 39°00′S and 56°00′S to a distance of 350 miles from the mainland. The brief suggests that either little use was made of the 707 (its potential range being far greater than that required) or that long-range reconnaissance was continued with the 707 outside the GrAeExplRec1 organisation. In any event little is known of the activities of the Grupo 1 707's during May 1982 and it may be that much of their time was simply devoted to domestic and international airfreighting.

On 19 May a 707 was detected some 180 miles to the north-east of the Task Force and two 1(F) Sqdn Harriers made an unsuccessful attempt to reach it. The Harriers, those of Wg Cdr Peter Squire and Flt Lt Jeff Glover, were armed with AIM-9G Sidewinders and were diverted from a working-up exercise with 'Hermes'. Three days later, on 22 May, a Grupo 1 707 again investigated British warships southbound from Ascension Island. As had happened a month before, the aircraft found a reinforcing group about three days sailing south of Ascension but north of 35°00′S. 'Bristol' and 'Cardiff' both reacted without any diplomatic constraint, each launching two Sea Darts at the Grupo 1 aircraft. The 707 took violent evasive action to avoid the missiles (having somewhat belatedly identi-

fied them) and successfully did so by diving almost to sea-level. Even after that scare the 707's continued to investigate the procession of British ships travelling south and on 7 June one actually passed overhead the damaged 'Argonaut' which was making slow progress home, having left the safety of the TRALA (the Royal Navy's ocean repair centre situated east of the Falklands and some 400 miles to the south of 'Argonaut').

The incident on 7 June appears to have been the final encounter between the FAA Boeing 707's and any British forces. Escuadron II survived the War without loss of either men or aircraft and in the process demonstrated the very substantial versatility of the 707. The aircraft had been an invaluable asset to Argentina and had proved its worth in a way that would have been unimaginable when the type entered service with the FAA. Its importance was further recognised when, coincident with the acquisition of a fourth aircraft (TC-94) in December 1982, the 707's were reorganised into Escuadron V, a discrete new unit within Grupo 1 at El Palomar. Soon after that, a pair of civilian registered aircraft was taken on strength for passenger duties and by early 1984 they were fully assimilated into military use with Escuadron V as T-95 and T-96.

---

*Boeing 707 pilots and navigators known to have flown missions with Escuadron II/Grupo 1 de Transporte Aereo during the War included:*

*Vicecomodoro Arguelles; Vicecomodoro Conte; Vicecomodoro Genolet; Vicecomodoro Lopez; Vicecomodoro J.E.Ricardini.*

---

# INDIVIDUAL AIRCRAFT DETAILS

---

The three aircraft TC-91 to TC-93 (respectively 707 series 389B, 372C and 387C) retained their normal peacetime colours throughout the conflict. They were basically in airline livery with grey undersides and white tops separated by a broad blue cheat line running the length of the fuselage through the window line. The national flag was worn on the lower nose area and tail with the FAA roundel on the rear fuselage. FAA titles were inscribed on the

forward fuselage above the cheat line. Aircraft serial numbers were applied in black to the lower fuselage both fore and aft of the wing.

*In the individual aircraft details the standard FAA abbreviation 'G1TA' has been used for Grupo 1 de Transporte Aereo.*

---

| TC-91 | TC-92 | TC-93 |
|---|---|---|
| In 3.82 with G1TA. Arrived at Stansted from Gando, Las Palmas on 10.3.82 and departed 12.3.82 for Getafe, Madrid. On 21.4.82 it had the distinction of being the first FAA aircraft to be intercepted by an aircraft of the British Task Force (800 Sqdn Sea Harrier XZ460 piloted by Lt Hargreaves). Not positively identified with any subsequent wartime activity but certainly involved. In use with Escuadron V in early 1985. | In 3.82 with G1TA. Not positively identified with any particular wartime activity, but certainly involved. In use with Escuadron V in early 1985. | In 3.82 with G1TA. Arrived at Stansted from Orly, Paris on 2.3.82 and departed 3.3.82 for Gando, Las Palmas. Returned to Stansted from Brindisi, Italy 8.3.82 and left for Gando on 10.3.82. Its final visit to Stansted was on 24.3.82 when it arrived from Charles de Gaulle, Paris and departed for Chateauroux-Deols, France 25.3.82. Not positively identifed with any particular wartime activity but certainly involved. In use with Escuadron V in early 1985. |

# LEARJET

# GRUPO 1 DE AEROFOTOGRAFICO

At the outbreak of the Falklands War the FAA possessed six Learjet 35A's, the first pair of which (T-21 and T-22) had been accepted from the manufacturer in January 1978. They had been delivered to II Brigada Aerea at Parana, Entre Rios where they augmented the survivors of six photo-reconnaissance/cartographic Guarani II's equipping Grupo 1 de Aerofotografico (G1A). Grupo 1's squadron was officially entitled Escuadron I Aerofotografico but was more commonly referred to as "Escuadron Fotografico" or "Escuadron Learjet". A second pair of aircraft (T-23 and T-24) was received late in 1980 to complete the nominal complement of four aircraft which was the unit's actual strength in March 1982. Two other Learjets (VR-17 and VR-18) were delivered to the FAA's Escuadron Verificacion Radioayudos in 1981 and 1982 for calibration duties.

T-23 caused a considerable stir on 19 March 1982 when it landed at Stanley Airport with "undercarriage problems". It was the first Learjet to land at Stanley and the only previous visit of the type had been in mid-February 1982 when one of the Escuadron Verificacion aircraft had undertaken the routine VOR check which, until then, had been the function of visiting Guarani II's. That Learjet had not landed, however, but made a series of low passes over the town. When enquiries were later made of the local LADE officials it was explained that it had not landed because the runway was too short!

Following the invasion and consolidation of Argentine forces on the Falkland Islands, all the FAA Learjets were pressed into urgent use in a variety of roles. The FAA aircraft were later to be used operationally of course, but as part of the general mobilisation in Argentina another 12 commercially registered Learjets were conscripted into the newly established "Escuadron Fenix" and their somewhat exaggerated contribution is considered elsewhere. While the civilian aircraft spent much time ferrying staff and urgent light cargo between mainland FAA bases, the Grupo 1 aircraft became fully occupied with preparations for the War in which they were destined to play a significant role. Their primary duties were those of reconnaissance and, later, pathfinding. For organisational purposes the four aircraft were transferred to the control of the specially formed GrAeExplRec1 at Comodoro

Rivadavia although their base may have been at Trelew (it is probable that many missions were flown from "in theatre" airfields such as Rio Gallegos and Rio Grande).

Before the arrival of the British Task Force the Learjets were used for photo-mapping the Falklands and generally "tidying up" any other outstanding cartographic matters. Once the British warships were within close range of the Islands then the Grupo 1 aircraft were used for pure reconnaissance work. Fast and high flying, equipped with Omega and INS, the Learjets were ideal for the tasks demanded of them and they flew by day and night on their intelligence missions.

After 21 May the Learjets also undertook a pathfinding role leading some fighter-bombers to the coast of West Falkland before they broke for home leaving the Daggers and Skyhawks to press on with the attacks. 14 such missions were launched in support of Grupo 6 alone, including that of 8 June when five Daggers bombed 'Plymouth' in Falkland Sound. That particular sortie, probably using T-23, was flown by Capitan Narciso Juri.

Such activities were undoubtedly hazardous but, with British warships rarely venturing further west than 59°00′W and the Sea Harrier CAP's ordered not to chase targets too far west across West Falkland, there has perhaps been some exaggeration of the dangers incurred by the Learjets. Nevertheless, their mission profiles were such that on British radars they were always a potential target should they have strayed too far east. Although British sources provide no clarification, Grupo 1 believed that its aircraft were twice fired on.

Following earlier successful high-altitude reconnaissance sorties on both 25 and 27 May, a photographic mission was launched at dawn on 7 June to Falkland Sound and the San Carlos area. Four Learjets were put up by Grupo 1 with the unit commander, Vicecomodoro Rodolfo de la Colina, leading the mission. They were tasked to make a high run over the Sound, in line-abreast formation spread across several miles, to provide CdoFAS with complete photographic reconnaissance of the area. By 7 June the British were well entrenched at San Carlos and details of their installations and strength were urgently sought.

At an altitude of 40,000ft it is presumed that Grupo 1

*Guards of Honour (Argentine and British), pomp, ceremony and a hint of tension marked the opening of the temporary airstrip at Hookers Point on 15.11.72. In attendance were two LADE-operated Friendships, T-43 and TC-76. From that date a regular weekly air service was established between Port Stanley and Comodoro Rivadavia.*

*(J. S. Wright)*

*Guarani II's were infrequent visitors to Hookers Point airstrip and, later, to Stanley Airport. T-122 (Left), marked "Comando General" (Commanding General) at Hookers Point on an unknown date post-11.72, had flown in senior FAA officers in connection with LADE operations. VR-16 (Right) at Stanley Airport, prior to 4.82, was operated by the Escuadron Verificacion Radioayudos and was visiting the Airport to calibrate the local FAA-owned and operated VOR.*

*(W. Felton)*

*The arrival of the Learjet T-23 at Stanley Airport on 19.3.82 was totally unexpected and the reasons for its landing were never satisfactorily explained by local LADE officials, who spoke of "undercarriage problems". Operated by Escuadron I Aerofotografico, Grupo 1 de Aerofotografico, Parana, the real purpose of the reconnaissance-configured Learjet's visit became more obvious several weeks later. T-23 subsequently saw considerable operational use during the War, principally in the photo-reconnaissance and pathfinding roles.* *(V. Steen)*

felt safe from British SAM's and, for that matter, must have trusted the Port Stanley CIC to warn them of local Sea Harrier activity. However, at 1203Z, in broad daylight and clear weather, 'Exeter', in Falkland Sound, identified the approaching aircraft as Canberras and in full view of other warships and troops ashore she fired two Sea Darts at the leading aircraft. As one missile fell away harmlessly the other climbed inexorably upward until, at extreme range, it impacted the tail area of T-24, de la Colina's aircraft. According to another of the airborne Grupo 1 pilots, Capitan Carlos Pane, it blew the tail off but left the pressure hull intact. The doomed Learjet remained substantially complete as it spiralled down, the coherent crew unable to escape. T-24 came down on Pebble Island, close to the airstrip, killing all on board. The five men lost in what seems to have been a badly misjudged mission were de la Colina, Mayor Juan Falconier, Capitan Marcelo Lutufo, Suboficial Ayudante Francisco Luna and Suboficial Auxiliar Guido Marizza.

With the single exception of the disastrous mission of 7 June the men of Grupo 1 performed their missions with considerable style, skill and good fortune. Their Learjets flew 129 sorties during the 76 days of the conflict and were airborne for a total of 342 hours. In 1982 the surviving aircraft proudly wore a small blue silhouette of the "Malvinas" in recognition of their achievements. Postwar, changes have been few and the lost Learjet does not appear to have been replaced.

*Grupo 1 de Aerofotografico pilots and navigators known to have flown operational sorties included:*

*Vicecomodoro R.de la Colina (commander) (KIA); Mayor J.J.Falconier (KIA); Capitan N.Juri; Capitan M.P.Lutufo (KIA); Capitan C.Pane.*

*The Grupo 1 de Aerofotografico Learjet T-24 was shot out of a clear sky on the morning of 7.6.82. The launch of two Sea Darts from 'Exeter' was witnessed by many servicemen in the Falkland Sound and San Carlos areas and the impact was clearly visible. The wreckage of the Learjet came down adjacent to Pebble Island airfield, killing the crew of five.* (815 Sqdn 'Exeter' Flight/ W. G. Calvert)

# INDIVIDUAL AIRCRAFT DETAILS

All four Grupo 1 Learjet 35A's were used during the War and, as far as can be ascertained, all retained their normal trim "executive aircraft" appearance. In essence the Learjets were white overall with a dark blue cheatline running the length of the fuselage with the FAA roundels and national flag on the engine nacelles and the tail respectively. FAA and unit titles remained on the forward fuselage above the cabin window line. As mentioned above, the three surviving aircraft now wear a small blue "Malvinas" silhouette on the port side of the fuselage.

*In the individual aircraft details the standard FAA abbreviation 'G1A' has been used for Grupo 1 de Aerofotografico.*

**T-21**

In 3.82 with G1A and used throughout the War.

**T-22**

In 3.82 with G1A and used throughout the War.

**T-23**

In 3.82 with G1A. Visited Stanley Airport on 19.3.82. Used throughout the War.

**T-24**

In 3.82 with G1A. Used throughout the War until brought down over Pebble Island, West Falkland on 7.6.82 by a Sea Dart fired from 'Exeter' in Falkland Sound. The crew of Vicecomodoro de la Colina, Mayor Falconier, Capitan Lutufo, Suboficial Ayudante Luna and Suboficial Auxiliar Marizza was killed. The aircraft crashed on the edge of Pebble Island airstrip and the remains were still there in 2.85.

# CANBERRA

## GRUPO 2 DE BOMBARDEO

During 1971 Argentina received 10 refurbished Canberra B.62's and two T.64's from Britain and for the following decade these reliable, if ageing, light bombers provided the FAA with the means to strike any local aggressor moderately hard. From the outset of their FAA service lives they were based at Parana, Entre Rios where they equipped II Brigada Aerea's Grupo 2 de Bombardeo (G2B). As was customary within the FAA, an official squadron identity, Escuadron I de Bombardeo, was allocated to Grupo 2 but other titles such as "Escuadron Canberra" were more commonly used by FAA personnel.

Grupo 2 had a good safety record with the Canberra and in its first ten years of use only two B.62's were lost. B-103 was destroyed in 1971 soon after delivery and a second aircraft, thought to have been B-106, was later lost in unclear circumstances. In 1981, work commenced in Britain on the refurbishing of two more Canberras, a B.62 and a T.64, for delivery to the FAA in mid-1982. At the time of the Falklands invasion Grupo 2 thus had a maximum strength of 10 aircraft, including both T.64's, reduced by any machines in major maintenance, storage or undergoing modification. It is believed that B-107 was unserviceable in March 1982 with some unspecified, long-term engineering problems and no evidence appeared to confirm its use in the subsequent fighting.

Grupo 2 initially deployed six B.62's and both T.64's to its temporary operating base, the naval field at Trelew, Chubut Province during late April where it was retitled the "Escuadron Canberra Trelew". The unit immediately began intensive working-up exercises which initially concentrated on anti-shipping sorties. Despite the considerable distance to the Falklands from Trelew (593 miles), it was considered that the Canberra's range would easily permit it to fly a "hi-lo-hi" mission against the British fleet. The sophisticated weaponry carried by the British warships was a particularly worrying factor and the FAA carried no illusions about the Canberra's vulnerability if caught over the open sea at medium or even high level. The Canberra's dark peace-time camouflage colours were considered adequate for the anticipated operations and no modifications were undertaken.

The Grupo 2 crews were brought to a state of readiness in anticipation of British amphibious landings which were initially expected to occur as soon as the Task Force reached the Falklands. The Canberras, in common with all FAA aircraft, had thus been at a high state of alert at Trelew for at least 48 hours when the Vulcan and Sea Harrier attacks were launched against Stanley Airport and Goose Green airfield on 1 May. *(Unconfirmed reports have suggested that the first Grupo 2 mission of the War took place on 26 April when three Canberras left Rio Grande for South Georgia to attack British shipping known to have been in that area. One aircraft aborted when south of the Falklands but the others, escorted by a Grupo 1 de Transporte Aereo Boeing 707, continued until poor weather in the target area caused the mission's cancellation. A second attempt the following day was cancelled because of the Argentine surrender of South Georgia. It should be noted, however, that the Argentine forces at Grytviken capitulated to the British on the afternoon of 25 April and those at Leith did so the following morning.)*

All the sorties launched by the FAA on 1 May were reactionary to the mistaken belief that the British fleet was relatively close inshore to the Falklands, supporting major landings. Although the reality of the situation gradually dawned on CdoFAS many missions were wasted, searching for targets that did not exist. The few warships that did venture close to East Falkland for various purposes further added to the Argentine confusion. It was against that scenario that Grupo 2 was tasked to launch two three-aircraft missions to seek British warships in the waters close to the Falklands and, simply, to sink them. The first flight (B-102 and B-105 were two of the three) took-off from Trelew during the late afternoon but it appears to have had an uneventful and fruitless mission, making no contact with the enemy. Their target had probably been identified from earlier naval intelligence — possibly obtained by CANA SP-2H Neptunes — but, not for the last time, the FAA aircraft were unable to find the enemy in the predicted area. The lack of good reconnaissance and intelligence data was to plague the FAA throughout the War.

The second Canberra flight, led by Capitan Alberto Baigorri (each Canberra had a two-man crew, a pilot and a navigator/bombardier), took-off soon afterwards and, at a point about 100 miles north-west of the main British Task Force, which was itself situated nearly 100 miles north-east of Port Stanley, it descended to a lower level to begin the run-in to its target. At that moment the flight was positively identified by the fighter controller in 'Invincible' who vectored two 801 Sqdn Sea Harriers towards the three Canberras. The Grupo 2 aircraft were approximately 50 miles from 'Invincible' when, at 2047Z, they were intercepted by Lt Alan Curtis (in XZ451) and Lt Cdr Mike Broadwater (in ZA175). Post-war remarks by Baigorri have indicated that at that time he was still 150 miles from his planned target which seems to suggest that he was on his way to Port Stanley rather than the carrier group which had just found him. The Sea Harriers caught the Canberras at less than 100ft below cloud cover and the first that Baigorri knew of the interception was when his number three called that a missile had been fired. In fact the AIM-9L launched by Alan Curtis was not bound for the flight leader but the number two, Canberra B-110 of Teniente Eduardo de Ibanez and his navigator Primer Teniente Mario Gonzalez, and it detonated adjacent to one of the engines. The damaged Canberra, its engine and wing burning, briefly continued to fly straight and level before it began a gradual descent towards the sea. Just before both men ejected, Curtis launched his second Sidewinder at B-110 but it failed to impact because the Canberra hit the sea before being caught by the missile.

In the meantime, Mike Broadwater had watched Curtis fire his first missile and had manoeuvered ZA175 into a position to fire at one of the surviving Canberras, but neither of his missiles caused any serious damage and both aircraft escaped. de Ibanez and Gonzalez were both thought to have made good ejections and once the two Sea Harriers had left the area Baiggori returned to search for them. Unfortunately, despite initial optimism, no trace could be found of either man by Baiggori or the extensive sea search subsequently mounted by Argentine naval forces.

The experience of 1 May was salutory and, while CdoFAS analysed the general war situation, Grupo 2 closely reassessed its own tactics. The daylight attack profile had been hopelessly naive and the unit was perhaps fortunate to have escaped relatively lightly in the circumstances. British radar defences were at least as good as had been anticipated and it was clear that only attacks at extremely high or low level could have any hope of success. Moreover, the Canberra's rudimentary ECM/ESM fit was obviously inadequate for the task ahead. For Grupo 2, May was to seem a long and tense month as the small unit prepared itself for the inevitable British landings on the Falklands and its next combat mission.

Grupo 2 flew relatively little during May and, unlike the FAA Daggers and Skyhawks, the Canberras had no involvement in the anti-shipping operations in the Falkland Sound area after the British landings on 21 May. However, by 29 May the Canberras were again in action flying night sorties at high and low level against British troop positions ashore. These missions were initially sent to the San Carlos area and the Canberras bombed over predetermined co-ordinates, usually dropping four 1,000lb bombs. The first such sortie, apparently of at least two aircraft, attacked the Port San Carlos area at about

0500Z on 29 May but the bombs, dropped from very high altitude, did not cause any damage or casualties to the British forces. A subsequent similar attack at 0530Z on 31 May dropped four 1,000lb bombs into the 846 Sqdn area at Fern Valley Creek, near San Carlos settlement, causing no serious injuries or damage although the bombing created a good deal of alarm. Following that attack some of the British helicopters in the San Carlos and Port San Carlos areas were further dispersed.

After these raids the Canberras transferred their attentions to the more easterly British positions and most subsequent missions were dispatched to the general locality of Mount Kent. Generally speaking, little damage was inflicted by these nocturnal sorties but they were viewed by the British as having morale-sapping qualities. From the Grupo 2 point of view, however, the missions were tiring and hazardous, typically requiring a deployment from Trelew to Rio Gallegos before being briefed for an operation later in the night.

Another early mission was that of "Huinca" flight, led by Capitan Garcia Puebla, in the pre-dawn hours of 1 June against troops in the vicinity of Mount Kent. Puebla and his navigator, Primer Teniente Jorge Segat, led the two-aircraft flight out of Rio Gallegos at 0700Z and their flight-plan took them, in radio-silence at 25,000ft, to a point south of the Falklands for a low-level run-in over Mount Kent. They were to bomb from an altitude of 160ft and would escape by flying due north over the coast of East Falkland. At 0739Z the 800 Sqdn Sea Harrier ZA177 of Lt Andy McHarg was scrambled from 'Hermes' to intercept what was identified on radar as an incoming flight of four aircraft approaching East Falkland from the south-west. McHarg was unable to intercept the Canberras before they had made their run over the target (during which they had narrowly avoided a collision with the summit of Mount Kent which had suddenly loomed, snow covered, out of the night and directly in their path). As both crews regained their composure, the Port Stanley CIC warned them of the approaching Sea Harrier and both Canberras immediately jettisoned their empty wing tanks and dropped chaff to confuse the Sea Harrier's radar. By then McHarg was at extreme range from 'Hermes' and although he got to within four miles of the nearer Canberra his fuel state dictated an immediate return to the carrier. Unaware of that, "Huinca" flight accelerated to maximum speed (exceeding airframe limitations in the process) in an effort to escape, but both crews were certain that there would be an inevitable Sidewinder impact. Of course, it never came and "Huinca 1" and "Huinca 2" both reached the safety of the mainland at 1030Z.

Mount Kent proved to be a particularly nasty obstacle to the Canberra crews on these nocturnal sorties and more than one aircraft came very close to the 1,504ft peak when it pulled up from a low-level run. Another typical mission a few nights after the "Huinca" sortie was one led by Mayor Jorge Chevalier. On that occasion four Canberras were ferried from Trelew to Rio Gallegos at 0215Z for a later three-aircraft mission to the Mount Kent area. The fourth aircraft was a spare against unserviceability at Rio Gallegos. The attack was planned for 0815Z, following a 0700Z departure from Rio Gallegos. The outbound leg was to be flown at 27,000ft and the usual radio-silence would be observed. "Negro" flight left on schedule with each aircraft armed with four 1,000lb bombs. Navigation was the responsibility of Chevalier's "Negro 1" (B-105) with the others required to hold formation and to watch for the pre-arranged light signals that would warn of course corrections and the bombing run. The descent to about 2,000ft was made in good time and the mission proceeded well until "Negro 3" returned home with a failed fuel regulator when the flight was south of Falkland Sound. "Negro 1" and "Negro 2" turned north near the Sea Lion Islands and, descending to below 1,000ft, they accelerated to 350kts towards Mount Kent. At two miles from the target, and when travelling at 400kts, they experienced the first anti-aircraft fire but no hits were sustained and the bomb run was successful. Both Canberras continued to fly fast and low until the northern coast of East Falkland had disappeared behind them and they could make their way home safely.

The nocturnal raids continued through early June and the Royal Navy eventually began to make greater efforts to anticipate the Grupo 2 visits. As the missions continued, however, the Argentine crews became more adept at avoiding the Sea Harrier CAP's. The Canberra's immunity was essentially due to the FAA's AN/TPS-43F and other radar in the Port Stanley area which continued to provide the CIC with the means to warn incoming aircraft that a CAP was airborne. The Canberras simply held off or aborted the mission and, despite one or two close encounters, the Sea Harriers were never able to repeat their success of 1 May. The British tried hard though and one such attempt was made at dusk on 4 June when 'Invincible' detached from the carrier group and made for a position south of Falkland Sound to enable her to mount a CAP to the west of the Falklands. The manoeuvre was as much for the benefit of the nocturnal FAA C-130's as it was for the Canberras, but either way the British suffered a frustrating night because just as 'Invincible' left the main group at about 2030Z two Grupo 2 Canberras arrived early to bomb targets on East Falkland. 'Invincible', completely fog-bound, was unable to launch her Sea Harriers and the two Canberras escaped unmolested.

Grupo 2 again bombed in the early hours of 6 June and following that attack the British conceived another strategy (known locally as Operation "Canbelow") to stop the Canberra incursions. At dusk on 6 June 'Invincible' and 'Brilliant' detached from the main battle group and moved to within 160 miles of the Falklands to wait for either Canberra or Hercules movements. The Royal Navy thought that a CAP and an alert Sea Harrier might combine to confuse the FAA but no Canberra mission was detected that night and so the tactic was repeated the following night. The warships detached from the main group at 1930Z and at 2300Z 'Cardiff', on picket duty, directed the CAP to a contact, thought to have been a Canberra, which was approaching from the west. On that occasion it was only low fuel states that prevented the Sea Harriers from catching the aircraft as it escaped towards the mainland.

On 8 June two Canberras attacked the Liberian registered tanker 'Hercules' when she was well to the north of the Falkland Islands and at least 400 miles north-east of the main body of the British Task Force. Although none of the eight 1,000lb bombs detonated on impact, one lodged in the ship's structure and the vessel was eventually scuttled as an unwanted hazard! Despite Argentine insistence that 'Hercules' had ignored clear warnings to stop, it seems that the ship was attacked in the mistaken belief that it was part of the British supply chain. The presence of a C-130 in the area has led to some confusion and the belief in certain quarters that the C-130 was the aircraft that actually dropped the bombs on the supertanker.

Grupo 2's night attacks continued into the second week of June, to the great satisfaction of its crews who felt that they were at last striking directly at the enemy. At 0435Z on the morning of 12 June a force of "five" Canberras was recorded by the British as having bombed in the Mount Kent area but the actual number of aircraft involved may have included escorting Grupo 8 Mirage IIIEA's which, very late in the War, offered Grupo 2 some assistance on the night missions. Again, all aircraft returned safely.

On the penultimate night of the War it was "business as usual" for the Grupo 2 Canberra crews and a two-aircraft mission was prepared for yet another run to Mount Kent. On that occasion Capitan Juan Nogueira, a flight leader and seasoned veteran, was unable to lead his flight and thus it was Capitan Puebla and Primer Teniente Segat who were to lead the sortie, with Capitan Martinez Villada and Primer Teniente Pagano in the second Canberra. They departed from Rio Gallegos at 0200Z on 13 June and, after experiencing some difficulty forming up in the low cloud in radio-silence, the pair flew south-east and then north towards the Falklands. The weather was typically bad with cloud and icing to contend with but the Canberras pushed on and, despite another close encounter with Mount Kent, an alarm involving St Elmo's Fire and a visitation from a Sea Harrier CAP which could not quite reach them, successfully bombed their target at 0320Z. Interestingly, the Royal Navy regarded their CAP that night as successful and no damage was reported by the British land forces. After another tiring night Puebla and Villada landed safely at 0500Z.

As the War entered its final hours and with imminent defeat obvious to CdoFAS, Grupo 2 was again tasked to go into the Mount Kent area to bomb British positions. For what would be the last combat mission of the air war two Canberras, "Baco 1" and "Baco 2", would be escorted by Grupo 8 Mirages to the target area. "Baco 1" was crewed by Capitan Roberto Pastran and Capitan Fernando Casado and "Baco 2" by Primer Teniente Rivolier and Primer Teniente Anino. "Baco" flight launched from Rio Gallegos with a flight-plan that was by then very familiar, although on that occasion their run from south to north over Mount Kent was to be at 40,000ft, hopefully too high to provoke a Sea Harrier attack and beyond the range of most British SAM's. With the Mirage escort following, the Canberras ran-in towards the target area but briefly checked when a Sea Harrier flown by Lt Cdr Mike Blissett of 800 Sqdn took-off from 'Hermes' at 0132Z to investigate them. The Canberras held for some minutes before continuing their run over the brightly lit landscape to the west of Port Stanley. For the Grupo 2 crews it was a sad but awe-inspiring sight as the British artillery continued to pound the Argentine positions far below them. Having successfully released their bombs both aircraft turned through 180° to return southwards on their inbound track, out over the coast and to safety. However, the British anti-aircraft systems were also active and both 'Cardiff' and 'Exeter' launched salvoes of Sea Darts at the high flying Canberras and their escorting Mirages.

As the Canberras passed over the coast the Mirages called a warning to "Baco 2" that there was a SAM tracking him and Rivolier was able to drop both chaff and flares before diving sharply to avoid the missile travelling upwards towards him. "Baco 1" (B-108) was not so fortunate and at 0155Z it was hit in the lower front fuselage area by a Sea Dart, almost certainly one launched from 'Exeter'. With the aircraft burning and obviously doomed, Pastran endeavoured to slow its descent by flaming-out both engines and extending the air brakes. In order to eject safely he knew that the aircraft had to be held in a fairly stable attitude down to a safer altitude. At 15,000ft Pastran ordered the navigator to eject but, to his dismay, Casado told him that it was impossible — the seat had refused to fire. At 11,000ft the Canberra began to spin and, with Casado apparently unconscious, Pastran realised that he had to abandon the aircraft. He eventually ejected at about 7,000ft and immediately blacked-out although he recovered consciousness shortly before landing safely in the sea south of Fitzroy. Fortuitously, an onshore wind took his dinghy close enough to the coast for him to scramble ashore long before dawn and, although cold and wet, he was well enough to spend much of the day walking inland. Eventually he reached the southern shore of Port Pleasant and spent the last hour or so of daylight watching British helicopter operations at Fitzroy. After dark he was quickly found by one of the helicopters, his SARBE signal having at last been identified and located by the British who had been unaware of the Canberra's loss. By that time the Argentine forces had capitulated and Pastran was destined to spend a few weeks in British hands before being repatriated. His navigator, Capitan Fernando Juan Casado, went down with the Canberra and was never found.

During Grupo 2 de Bombardeo's incarnation as the Escuadron Canberra Trelew, 54 combat sorties were formally planned by CdoFAS. According to unit sources only 35 of these were actually undertaken from Trelew and Rio Gallegos and 25 of them were night missions during the latter part of the War. About 100,000lbs of bombs were dropped, mainly against British troops dug-in in forward positions in the Fitzroy and Mount Kent area. Having lost two aircraft and three crew, Grupo 2 returned to peace-time operations sadly aware of the limitations of their much loved but elderly Canberras.

A post-war support programme was forthcoming from Peru and Israel with the former providing a means to circumvent the British embargo on spare parts and the latter involved in a modification programme designed to enhance the Canberra's ECM and avionics (the standard pre-war ECM fit was basic with a simple chaff/flare dispenser and an underwing ECM pod). The two replacement aircraft from Britain were, of course, not delivered. The unit suffered another blow on 13 August 1982 when another of the B.62's was destroyed in a fatal crash in Argentina. On the credit side, B-107 was reportedly airworthy again by May 1983 but, with only up to five B.62's and two T.64's available and a continuing British embargo on all direct support, the Canberra's days of FAA service looked limited.

> *Grupo 2 de Bombardeo pilots and navigators deployed to Trelew and known to have flown combat missions included:*
>
> *Mayor J.A.Chevalier; Capitan A.Baigorri; Capitan F.J.Casado (KIA); Capitan J.Nogueira; Capitan R.Pastran; Capitan G.Puebla; Capitan M.Villada; Primer Teniente Anino; Primer Teniente M.H.Gonzalez (KIA); Primer Teniente Pagano; Primer Teniente Rivolier; Primer Teniente J.Segat; Primer Teniente E.J.R.de Ibanez (KIA).*

The normal weapons load of the Grupo 2 de Bombardeo Canberra B.62's for their anti-personnel and equipment strikes against British troops was four 1,000lb HE bombs. Here two such weapons are seen cradled alongside sundry servicing and handling items at Trelew in 5.82. This Canberra T.64, B-111, has had its wing-tip tanks removed.

The adoption of the CANA airfield at Trelew for the use of the Grupo 2 de Bombardeo Canberras in the CdoFAS battle order seems a little strange. The consequent round trip required of the Canberras to reach the Falklands was considerable, although well within their range, and it is thought that, but for airfield congestion, they would have been deployed to Rio Gallegos or Rio Grande. In the event, all Canberra missions to the Falklands after 21.5.82 are thought to have been launched from Rio Gallegos. Here B-112, another T.64, is seen at home base Parana, Entre Rios, after the conflict.

# INDIVIDUAL AIRCRAFT DETAILS

As far as is known no changes were made to the Canberras' colour schemes during the War period. The normal peace-time camouflage of dark green and grey with grey undersurfaces was viewed as satisfactory for both the day and night roles that were undertaken by the Grupo 2 aircraft and, as far as can be ascertained, no machines wore the yellow "identification" stripes. No aircraft are known to have worn any "zaps" or mission markings, indeed the "Pelicano" markings of B-101 may be of post-war origin.

There is no definitive list available of those aircraft deployed to Trelew and Rio Gallegos but it is known that both Canberra T.64's, B-111 and B-112, and most of the B.62's were used.

*In the individual aircraft details the standard FAA abbreviation 'G2B' has been used for Grupo 2 de Bombardeo.*

**B-101** B.62

In 3.82 with G2B. Deployed to Trelew, presumably in late 4.82, with later operational detachments to Rio Gallegos. Noted in post-war use at Parana in 11.82 with the name "Pelicano 1" inscribed on nose.

**B-102** B.62

In 3.82 with G2B. Deployed to Trelew in late 4.82, with later operational detachments to Rio Gallegos. It survived the War.

**B-104** B.62

In 3.82 with G2B. Deployed to Trelew, presumably in late 4.82, with later operational detachments to Rio Gallegos. It survived the War.

**B-105** B.62

In 3.82 with G2B. Deployed to Trelew in late 4.82, with later operational detachments to Rio Gallegos. It survived the War.

**B-107** B.62

In 3.82 with G2B although believed to have been unserviceable and thus not used during the fighting. Subsequently reported at Rio Gallegos in 5.83.

**B-108** B.62

In 3.82 with G2B. Deployed to Trelew, presumably in late 4.82, with later operational detachments to Rio Gallegos. Brought down south of Mount Kent by a Sea Dart fired from 'Exeter' at 0150Z on 14.6.82, crashing in the sea to the south of Fitzroy. The navigator, Capitan Casado did not eject and was killed but the pilot, Capitan Pastran, ejected successfully and was recovered by British forces.

**B-109** B.62

In 3.82 with G2B. Not confirmed as deployed to Trelew but noted in post-war use at Parana in 11.82.

**B-110** B.62

In 3.82 with G2B. Deployed to Trelew in late 4.82. It was brought down over the South Atlantic approximately 150 miles north north-west of Port Stanley on 1.5.82 by an AIM-9L fired from 801 Sqdn Sea Harrier XZ451 of Lt Curtis. Pilot, Teniente de Ibanez, and navigator, Primer Teniente Gonzalez, were both seen to eject but neither man was subsequently found.

**B-111** T.64

In 3.82 with G2B. Deployed to Trelew, presumably in late 4.82. Noted in post-war use at Parana in 11.82.

**B-112** T.64

In 3.82 with G2B. Deployed to Trelew, presumably in late 4.82. Survived the War although not subsequently noted.

# PUCARA

## GRUPO 3 DE ATAQUE

By late March 1982 some 60 IA.58A Pucaras had been built at the FMA plant at Cordoba (aircraft A-564 and A-565 were occupying the flight test hangar during part of the month) and production was in full swing against domestic and export orders. Of those delivered, six had been diverted from the production line in 1981 to meet an order from Uruguay and the balance had been accepted by the FAA. In late March, 35 Pucaras were in active use or under overhaul on the charge of Grupo 3 de Ataque (G3A), the flight component of III Brigada Aerea, at Reconquista and a handful more had recently been delivered to the newly created Grupo 4 de Ataque (G4A) which was working up on the type at Comodoro Rivadavia with IX Brigada Aerea. Of the balance, a few had been lost in accidents, several were in the hands of FMA, the Centro de Ensayos en Vuelo (CEV) and other test facilities. Others awaited FAA acceptance at Cordoba. Grupo 3 was itself still receiving new deliveries in March 1982 as its third squadron slowly moved towards full equipment strength. On 22 March the 35 Pucaras on strength were:

| | | | | | | |
|---|---|---|---|---|---|---|
| A-501 | A-510 | A-515 | A-522 | A-528 | A-534 | A-550 |
| A-502 | A-511 | A-516 | A-523 | A-529 | A-536 | A-552 |
| A-505 | A-512 | A-517 | A-524 | A-531 | A-537 | A-553 |
| A-506 | A-513 | A-518 | A-526 | A-532 | A-538 | A-555 |
| A-509 | A-514 | A-520 | A-527 | A-533 | A-549 | A-556 |

A-553 had suffered an accident on 25 February and A-531 and A-538 were both in major overhaul. The high-time aircraft was A-514 with 1,150 flight hours and that with least was A-555 with 32 hours.

It was never envisaged that the Pucara would be used in support of the Argentine landings on the Falkland Islands but, as part of a small FAA presence on the Islands, four aircraft were deployed to Port Stanley on 2 April. The date is significant for it is indicative that the Pucara's early presence was part of the original occupation plan and not simply a part of the later emergency redeployment programme. The four Grupo 3 aircraft were:

| | | | |
|---|---|---|---|
| A-523 | A-529 | A-552 | A-556 |

The four were flown to Stanley Airport on 2 April, probably from Rio Gallegos. By then, their temporary new home had been renamed BAM Malvinas (BAMMLV). During their first days on the Islands flights were made in pairs and were concerned with crew familiarisation as much as with operational reconnaissance activity. Most of the principal settlements were overflown during the early days of the occupation but no landings were made away from Port Stanley. However, the situation changed dramatically within a few days once it became apparent that a British military reaction was possible, and the FAA was quick to appreciate its dilemma if required to provide air defence over the Falklands. It was Grupo 3's fortune to fly the only combat aircraft in the inventory that could actually undertake operational missions from Stanley Airport, let alone from any of the smaller airstrips!

Grupo 3's preparations for war were extensive and as radical as those of British units similarly preoccupied eight thousand miles away. At Port Stanley the unit strength was increased to 12 aircraft by 9 April and the new squadron was officially christened "Escuadron Pucara Malvinas" under the command of Mayor Navarro, a senior Grupo 3 pilot. The eight new arrivals were:

| | | | |
|---|---|---|---|
| A-502 | A-509 | A-517 | A-527 |
| A-506 | A-513 | A-520 | A-528 |

When later inspected by British forces, none of them was found to be wearing the yellow identification bands adopted after 1 May for the benefit of Argentine AAA on the Falklands (the publicity photographs of most of the Pucaras with yellow tail and fuselage markings were taken on the mainland at Comodoro Rivadavia after 1 May — the markings were not "invasion" stripes). As the Squadron strength at Port Stanley was being increased the FAA had rapidly surveyed all the obvious sites on the Islands

**Upper Left** *Pucara A-506 of Grupo 3 de Ataque was damaged in the 800 Squadron attack against Goose Green on 1.5.82. The FAA was unable to restore it to immediate airworthiness and the aircraft became an obvious target for subsequent British air and commando attacks. When these photographs were taken c4.6.82 the hulk was already considerably damaged, both by weapons and by souvenir hunters.* **Upper Right** *The name "Satan Tripa" (Satan's Guts) can be read on the forward fuselage.* (Flt Sgt D. W. Knights, RAF)

*Although it was never to fly again, Pucara A-529 of Grupo 3 de Ataque sustained only slight damage during the SAS attack on Pebble Island airfield on 15.5.82. A-529 is seen here in the snow of 7.82 showing obvious signs of damage to the engines, but the airframe was in generally sound condition. During 7.83 it was taken to RAF Stanley to serve as a "gate guardian".*

*The third of the Grupo 3 de Ataque Pucaras abandoned at Goose Green after receiving damage on 1.5.82, A-517 was successfully used as a decoy until the garrison surrendered to 2 PARA on 29.5.82. After lying in the open for more than two years it was eventually given, by the Ministry of Defence, to the local citizens in 10.84. However, on 30.1.85 it was shipped to Port Stanley to await transportation to the United Kingdom, it having been registered as G-BLRP! The photograph shows the Pucara as it was in c7.82.* (R. McLeod)

for other operating locations and the reluctant conclusion had been reached that the spartan grass strip at Goose Green was the best of several poor options! It was appreciated that once any fighting commenced, Stanley Airport would come under immediate attack and any aircraft left there would be vulnerable to air raids. Coincidentally, ramp and air-traffic congestion had rapidly reached unacceptable levels and thus CdoFAS instructed Mayor Navarro and other FAA officers at Port Stanley that, by 14 April, they should be ready to redeploy the bulk of the Squadron to Goose Green.

Under the command of Vicecomodoro Wilson Pedrozo, Goose Green was readied, anti-aircraft defences installed, the original Ejercito garrison (part of the Darwin occupation forces) reinforced and a large detachment of FAA personnel brought in from the mainland. Many of the latter were cadets from the EAM who were flown in to act as observers in remote areas (particularly those where the Port Stanley radars were ineffective) and as scouts in the Goose Green area when the War commenced. The latter arrangement seems to have something to do with a certain lack of Ejercito enthusiasm to involve itself with all but the most vital of airfield air defence tasks at Goose Green. As described elsewhere, Goose Green eventually became operational as BAM Condor on 15 April with the arrival of the first of the helicopters of the Escuadron Helicopteros Malvinas.

On the mainland Grupo 3 moved to a forward operating location at the airfield of Santa Cruz which served the dual purpose of a jumping-off point for further Pucara deployments to the Falklands and, later, as an operating base for a limited number of surveillance missions seeking British activity close inshore or actually on mainland Argentina (Alferez Mario Valko of Grupo 4 was killed after crashing in A-540, date unknown, undertaking one such sortie from Comodoro Rivadavia). Limited evidence suggests that only a skeletal Grupo 3 organisation remained at Reconquista during that period although a third mainland element was established at Cordoba. It is thought that the Cordoba unit was an acceptance group for new aircraft which were assimilated into the FAA during the emergency period. It is known that a batch of Pucaras was rapidly completed during May and June (A-575 was reportedly delivered on 12 June) although none of them reached the Falklands.

During the latter part of April Pucara missions were still only launched from Port Stanley and the first visit of a Pucara to Goose Green was not until 24 April when the local population was treated to a firepower display with cannon and rockets being used against a small island target in the harbour in front of the settlement. It was during that period that other sites on the Islands were more seriously considered for Pucara use. However, although locations such as Pebble Island and Sea Lion Island were closely investigated, they were viewed as being far from ideal and were considered unacceptable except as emergency alternates.

By late April it was apparent that the British aircraft carrier force would, within a few days, be in a position to launch an air attack on Stanley Airport and so, on 29 April, the 12 aircraft of the Escuadron Pucara redeployed to Goose Green. FAA accounts of the move are precise and consistent that 12 aircraft made the short journey and

local eyewitnesses have independently confirmed that 12 arrived at Goose Green that day. All the indications are that no Pucaras were left at Stanley Airport, although in their place the FAA drew up the few requisitioned civilian aircraft. With some hastily prepared mock-ups and the unfortunate CANA MB-339A's (which could not be evacuated) the Airport was thus "populated" for the anticipated onslaught. On 29 and 30 April the Escuadron Pucara launched several sorties from Goose Green, gingerly getting the feel of its new home.

The airfield was potentially very dangerous for Pucara operations and strict attention — as had also been the case at Port Stanley — was paid to all aspects of safety. The longest available strip of grass at Goose Green that was considered acceptable for a laden Pucara was only 450yds in length and possessed a nasty undulation which was to cause problems during later operations. Not least of the local dangers was the weather, which could seriously impair all aspects of any sortie.

At 0746Z on 1 May Stanley Airport was attacked by an RAF Vulcan and at 0800Z Mayor Navarro was contacted by Brigadier Castellano, FAA commander at Port Stanley, and ordered to be ready to launch sorties from first light to seek out and destroy any British troops who had been carried by helicopter onto the Islands during the night. Navarro was further warned by Castellano to expect Sea Harriers to attack Goose Green at any time and that he should be prepared to evacuate the Escuadron Pucara to the recently established naval airstrip at Pebble Island (which by then had been formally identified as Goose Green's alternate). Accordingly, Navarro briefed his staff.

The first flight of the day, scheduled to take-off at 1015Z, would be led by Capitan Ricardo Grunert and his numbers two, three and four would be Tenientes Calderon, Russo and Cimbaro. Grunert and Calderon were briefed to fly an armed reconnaissance mission to the south of Goose Green while the second section would investigate a reported helicopter landing in the Port Stanley area. A technical problem briefly delayed Grunert's section and although he reached the narrow runway fairly rapidly, the second pair was cleared to depart first. One of them, thought to have been Russo, rotated prematurely when his undercarriage struck an unnoticed undulation and after a few seconds in the air the Pucara came down heavily to continue its take-off roll. With great difficulty a hedge at the end of the runway was cleared but not before the nose-wheel leg had struck a landing light. The second section was even less fortunate and what is thought to have been Calderon's machine failed to get airborne at all after its nose-wheel stuck in the mud in a flooded area. The forward oleo collapsed and the Pucara stood on its nose with the tail in the air. Although not seriously damaged, the aircraft completely blocked the runway (it took twenty minutes to clear) and the second flight of the morning, two of whose pilots would have been Tenientes Hernandez and Jukic, was unable to take-off on schedule. Meanwhile the three airborne Pucaras combined their missions and spent the next three hours engaged in a fruitless search for British helicopters and Special Forces.

Soon after 1100Z Sea Harriers of 800 Sqdn first attacked Stanley Airport and then, at about 1125Z, Goose

Green airfield. Stanley was hit by formations of four and five aircraft carrying 15 1,000lb bombs of various kinds and 12 CBU's while Goose Green received three 1,000lb bombs and six CBU's from three aircraft. Stanley Airport was liberally sprinkled with ordnance but, while there is clear evidence of damage to some of the locally registered Cessnas and the Islander, British claims to have destroyed Pucaras in the attack seem to be unfounded because there would appear to have been none there that morning (although by late afternoon at least one aircraft had visited the Airport and others had overflown).

At Goose Green the story was very different, despite the early warning from Castellano, for the arrival of the three Sea Harriers was completely unexpected. They appeared overhead as the second flight was at last preparing to leave the parking area. While officers and men dived for cover, the luckless Teniente Antonio "Daniel" Jukic, his Pucara's engines running, received a direct hit from a CBU. His aircraft, A-527, was blown apart and, besides Jukic, seven nearby airmen were killed with another 14 seriously wounded by that and other explosions. The Sea Harriers left the airfield in chaos with several fires burning out of control and an ammunition dump in danger of exploding.

Serious aircraft damage was limited to the destruction of A-527 and to what was considered repairable damage to two other Pucaras. Minor attention was needed by one or two more. In fact the two damaged aircraft were never to be repaired and are thought to have been A-506 and A-517. A-506, named "Satan Tripa" (Satan's Guts), was initially left on the edge of the airfield with its tail high in the air and could well have been Calderon's Pucara which had failed to get airborne before the Sea Harrier attack. It and A-517 were both later used as decoys at Goose Green and, with the wreck of A-527, were the only three Pucaras found on the airfield when it was captured four weeks later. Of those with minor damage only A-502, which required a cockpit canopy change, has been identifed and within a few days of the attack it had been removed to the safety of Pebble Island. Later British photographic reconnaissance revealed five damaged Pucaras at Goose Green although local eyewitnesses counted at least seven aircraft still on the field during the evening of 1 May. Subsequent British air attacks in the following few days failed to inflict damage on any other aircraft.

Oblivious to the mayhem at Goose Green, Grunert had terminated his search for British helicopters at about 1230Z and requested landing permission. That was peremptorily refused and, in spite of an extremely low fuel state, he was obliged to take his flight of three aircraft to the naval base at Pebble Island where, despite Russo's damaged nose-wheel leg and a runway in worse shape than that at Goose Green, all three landed safely. In the aftermath of the attack Goose Green airfield was temporarily closed while order was restored. Grunert's flight at Pebble Island was joined on 3 May by three more arrivals from Goose Green and on the following day at least one more arrived when Teniente Cruzado terminated an armed reconnaissance mission over Lafonia and landed at the naval field. According to CANA sources, EAN Calderon (as Pebble Island was known to the Armada) then had seven Pucaras on strength. After 4 May, however, Pebble Island became waterlogged and for several days

the airfield was closed to fixed-wing traffic (Cruzado, however, was nevertheless able to make a solo flight to Port Stanley on 7 May). After then there was little flying from the 700yds long main strip although it was presumably during that period that a Pucara came to grief when its nose-wheel collapsed on landing at Pebble Island (the FAA was later to state that two Pucaras suffered broken nose-wheel legs during the War, although the inference is that both incidents happened at Goose Green). Pebble Island's operational life was abruptly ended in the early hours of 15 May when 'D' Sqdn 22 SAS Regt raided the base. Six Pucaras were destroyed or immobilised, together with a Prefectura Naval Skyvan and four CANA T-34C's. Subsequent examination of the debris revealed the hulks of A-520, A-523, A-529, A-552, A-556 and the totally demolished remains of A-502.

By mid-May the Escuadron Pucara had suffered something of a battering but had little to show in return. Of its original 12 aircraft, nine had been permanently put out of action at Goose Green and Pebble Island and a tenth was unserviceable at Port Stanley. In the aftermath of the Pebble Island disaster it was decided that a further four Pucaras should be immediately flown to the Islands as attrition replacements to bring the total operational strength back up to six aircraft and, accordingly, four aircraft were flown in to Goose Green during the afternoon of 15 May. They have not been positively identified by serial but may well have included A-511, A-531 and A-533. The flight brought in a new air operations adviser, Vicecomodoro Costa, to assist Wilson Pedrozo.

It was felt by the local FAA commanders that six Pucaras were adequate for all anticipated duties and a force that small could be dispersed at Goose Green in such a way that the British might not consider it a worthwhile target in view of their earlier losses there (Argentine forces believed that more than the one Sea Harrier had been lost in earlier attacks on Goose Green). However, the destruction of the aircraft at Pebble Island finally convinced Navarro and his senior officers that Goose Green was too vulnerable to commando attack to continue to house all the surviving Pucaras and so four aircraft were soon ferried back to the relative safety of Stanley Airport (it was under a "red alert" air raid warning when they landed). One of the pilots, Alferez Pontecorvo, was later to recount how he and a colleague, Teniente Alsogaray, were destined in the ensuing weeks to watch the progressive destruction of their Pucaras at Port Stanley by air attack and naval bombardment.

By 20 May the three Argentine airfields had been attacked many times by Sea Harriers and naval gunfire. At Goose Green the FAA and Ejercito forces had braced themselves for the British landings, which were considered to be imminent. The Escuadron Pucara's strength there was about six serviceable aircraft with perhaps a further three at Port Stanley thought to be unserviceable (another three Pucaras are thought to have been ferried to the Falklands as a group after 15 May to bring the then deployed total of aircraft to 19). As one of a series of diversionary attacks in the early hours of 21 May British commando forces claimed the destruction of a Pucara at Goose Green but it seems probable that one of the decoys (possibly A-517) was the aircraft in question.

At first light on 21 May six Pucaras were drawn up on the Goose Green flight-line for the morning's missions. With British landings underway, two sections were briefed to search for helicopters putting troops ashore in the Port San Carlos area. "Tigre" flight would, as usual, operate in two pairs with Capitan Jorge Benitez and Teniente Brest leaving first at about 1130Z to be followed shortly after by Primer Teniente Juan Micheloud and Mayor Carlos Tomba. As the first section endeavoured to get airborne the frigate 'Ardent' began to shell the airfield and prevented Teniente Brest following Benitez into the air, although the second pair got airborne without incident soon afterwards. Benitez, flying A-531, continued his solo mission searching for British forces in the area of Bombilla Hill. For over an hour he found nothing at all but then, having moved west, he saw the British warships in San Carlos Water and became aware of troops moving up the hills from the beach. As he sought a suitable target for his first attack he was fired at by a missile and then by a second one which hit his aircraft causing the failure of the starboard engine. He had been caught by an FIM-92A Stinger launched by a senior NCO of 'D' Sqdn 22 SAS Regt who was in a forward patrol position. Benitez rapidly lost control of the Pucara which climbed and then began to spin. As it descended he struggled to eject and successfully escaped at a height of about 300ft. The Pucara came to ground nearby at a point about one mile west of Flat Shanty settlement. Benitez was unhurt and was quickly able to strike out to the east away from the forward British positions. Although he was overflown several times by friendly aircraft and helicopters during the afternoon it was not until about 2200Z that he reached Argentine lines and safety.

Micheloud and Tomba had been given a similar mission to that of Benitez and had also sought British helicopters in the Bombilla Hill area without any success. After some time they, too, turned west in search of targets of opportunity in the Port San Carlos area but, as they approached the coast, they were shot at by machine-gun fire and at least two missiles which passed close by them. By that time, about 1430Z, both men were aware that Benitez had been brought down but they continued with their mission, looking for the source of the missiles fired at them. The search was short-lived, for Goose Green control again redirected them to attack a British observation post which was guiding naval gunfire onto the airfield with increasing accuracy. The Pucaras made a successful rocket attack on the identified position near the airfield and were on their way south-west to a second observation position when the Sea Harriers of Lt Cdr Nigel Ward, Lt Cdr Alisdair Craig and Lt Steve Thomas of 801 Sqdn were vectored to their position by 'Brilliant'.

The two Pucaras were caught some seven miles southwest of Goose Green but, after a brief turning manoeuvre, Micheloud was able to escape by flying low through a valley. Tomba, in A-511, was less fortunate and although flying at extremely low level was unable to escape from Ward's Sea Harrier (XZ451). Ward made three firing passes at the Pucara which at times was at less than 40ft above the ground. The first cannon burst damaged the flaps, the second struck the canopy and upper fuselage and the final burst damaged an engine and the propeller. Although having displayed great determination to save his

aircraft, Carlos Tomba was finally obliged to leave it and he ejected at extremely low level. He landed unhurt alongside the wreckage and was eventually recovered by an Argentine helicopter at about 2030Z. His Pucara had crashed to the north-west of Drone Hill. In the meantime fortune had smiled on Micheloud when low fuel states forced the Sea Harriers to abandon their search for him, allowing his safe return to Goose Green.

The loss of A-531 and A-511 and the deteriorating situation at Goose Green, which by 21 May had severely restricted air operations, brought about the inevitable decision to evacuate all airworthy FAA Pucaras and helicopters to Port Stanley. Accordingly, two Pucaras were ferried out by Tenientes Cruzado and Gimenez at dusk that same day. A passing post-war remark made by Cruzado is revealing — he mentioned that their arrival at Port Stanley increased the holding of airworthy Pucaras to three and that two of them were destroyed within three days by air attacks and naval gunfire. On the basis of known Pucara movements there were thus about eight at Port Stanley by 24 May, of which only one, according to Teniente Cruzado, seems to have been airworthy.

As British troops advanced overland from Port San Carlos towards Darwin, Argentine forces realised that a fixed battle seemed inevitable and thus frantic efforts were made to reinforce the Ejercito garrison at Darwin and Goose Green. The loss of the 'Rio Iguazu' in Choiseul Sound to Sea Harriers on 22 May was a serious blow because the vessel had been carrying vital artillery pieces and ammunition as well as aircraft spares for Darwin and Goose Green. Prodigious efforts were made to salvage as much as possible of the cargo and indeed many items were recovered and used. On the eve of the British offensive at Darwin Pucara reinforcements were readied at Santa Cruz for what was by then a very hazardous ferry flight to Port Stanley. Two aircraft were brought in at dusk on 27 May, led by Teniente Arganaraz and escorted to within sight of West Falkland by a civilian Mitsubishi MU-2. The MU-2, assigned to the Escuadron Fenix, flew at an altitude of 10,000ft as the Pucaras wave-hopped below, although soon after making landfall the latter became lost, eventually being guided home by the Port Stanley radar and landing safely at about 1945Z.

From the British point of view the battle for Darwin and Goose Green was seen as an epic victory achieved under adverse circumstances against a numerically superior enemy. The Argentine view is broadly that the British were better trained and equipped and that, under the circumstances, the mixed garrison of Ejercito troops and FAA cadets, privates and NCO's gave 2 PARA a good run for their money. The pilots of Grupo 3 de Ataque have particular cause to remember 28 May as the day that they were tasked to fly several support sorties in atrocious weather conditions in an effort to slow the British advance. Both they and the naval pilots of 1 Escuadrilla paid a high price for those missions. In fact, only a handful of sorties were actually launched that day but the weather and the British firepower combined to make each one something of a nightmare.

The first Pucara attack of the morning is thought to have been a three-aircraft mission to the Darwin/Camilla Creek area where they arrived over the target at about

# IA.58A PUCARA A-511 GRUPO 3 DE ATAQUE

Flown by Mayor Tomba on 21 May 1982 when shot down by Lt Cdr Ward of 801 Naval Air Squadron in Sea Harrier FRS.1 XZ451.

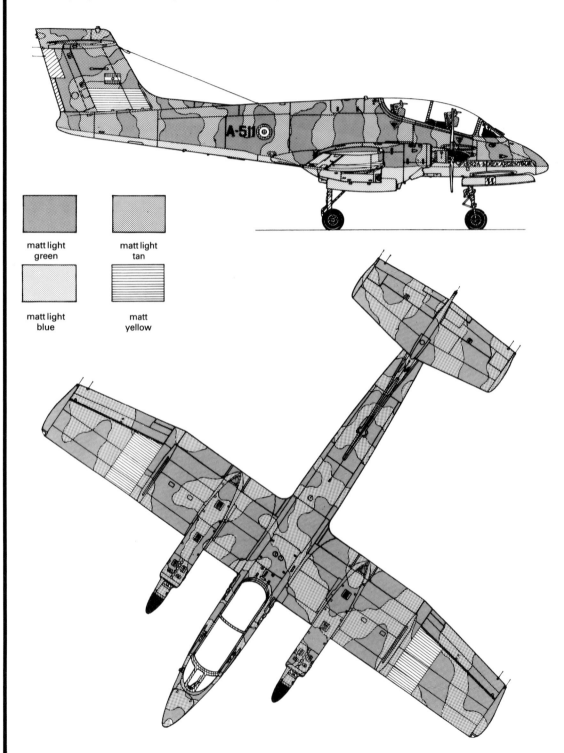

matt light
green

matt light
tan

matt light
blue

matt
yellow

Caution: all colour shades are approximate as they have not been physically checked against any British, American or other accepted paint standards.

# IA.58A PUCARA A-511 GRUPO 3 DE ATAQUE

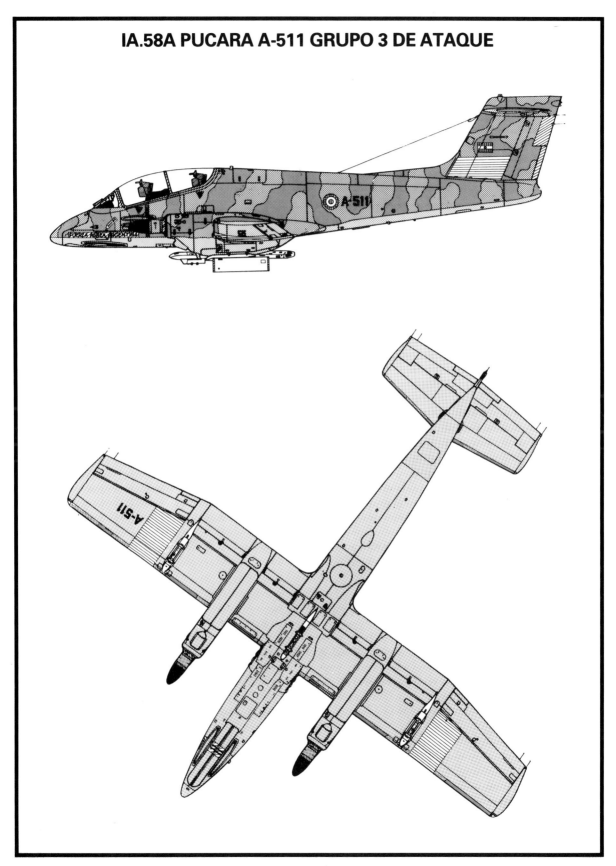

1200Z. It was led by Capitan Roberto Villa, his numbers two and three being respectively Teniente Cimbaro and the recently arrived Teniente Arganaraz. Both Villa and Arganaraz made ineffective attacks with 2.75in rockets on British positions but it was Cimbaro at whom the first SAM (probably a Blowpipe) was fired. As Cimbaro narrowly evaded the missile another was launched at Arganaraz and that time there was a fierce detonation immediately in front of and below the Pucara. The aircraft was flung upwards, inverting as it rose, and it was only the knowledge that a downward ejection would be fatal that kept Arganaraz with his aircraft. To his amazement it righted itself and was still flyable — just. Closely watched by the other two, both of whom had earlier thought him lost, Arganaraz limped home safely to Port Stanley.

The second mission was a two-aircraft sortie directed at forward British positions on the battlefield and any other chance targets of opportunity. The section was led by Teniente Miguel Gimenez with Teniente Cimbaro, flying his second mission of the day, on his wing. The pair reached the Camilla Creek House area at about 1455Z and almost immediately saw two Scout helicopters of 3 CBAS engaged on CASEVAC duties (to the Pucara pilots they were naturally only seen as two enemy helicopters). Gimenez and Cimbaro each took one of the Scouts for a cannon attack but the British helicopters saw them and took evasive action. As they turned away from one another and attempted to land Gimenez was able to catch XT629 with a burst of cannon fire which killed the pilot Lt R.J.Nunn and seriously injured the observer Sgt A.R.Belcher. Cimbaro, somewhat over-optimistically, believed that he had hit the second helicopter, causing it to force-land and the two Pucara pilots left the area believing that their mission had been a complete success. Soon afterwards, and in circumstances which are far from clear, the two aircraft became separated in low cloud and both Cimbaro and the Port Stanley CIC lost radio contact with Gimenez. He was never seen again and no trace was found of his aircraft A-537. In Argentina several theories were later advanced to explain his disappearance, some of which were a little fanciful, but the most likely cause of his loss was a high-ground crash in poor visibility.

The weather at Port Stanley on 28 May was foul with high winds and low cloud restricting air operations throughout the day. Aircraft technical problems also inhibited the CIC's efforts to get more air support to Goose Green and it was not until 1600Z that two CANA MB-339A's were finally launched. Their mission was identical to that of the earlier Pucara sorties — attack and demoralise the British troops. Unfortunately for the defending Goose Green forces the strike aborted from a position that was virtually overhead the battlefield. With cloud cover to ground level, the FAA controller at Goose Green instructed the CANA pilots not to hazard themselves unnecessarily and to return to Port Stanley. They did so and, once home, the aircraft were rapidly refuelled and prepared for a second attempted strike planned for an 1830Z launch. However, at 1830Z, dangerous cross-winds prevented an immediate departure and both the CANA and FAA crews were forced to wait in the gathering gloom for an improvement in the weather.

During the afternoon three more Pucaras had been ferried to Stanley Airport from the mainland and, with the urgently needed additional strength, another sortie had been planned — subject, of course, to the weather! Primer Teniente Micheloud was tasked to lead a two aircraft section against British mortar positions and for that mission he would carry napalm. His wingman was to be Teniente Cruzado whose Pucara would be configured to carry rockets and incendiary bombs. The weather improved sufficiently to enable the two Pucaras to launch at about 1930Z and they were followed immediately by the two MB-339A's. The faster naval jets reached Goose Green first at about 2000Z and, as they pressed home their attack in the Darwin School area, one was brought down by a Blowpipe missile. It dived into the ground, killing its pilot instantly.

The two Pucaras followed in at low level at 2009Z and successfully delivered their ordnance although, fortunately for the British, causing no casualties. In the process they attracted massive retaliatory ground fire and Cruzado's aircraft, A-555, was hit many times by small-arms fire which caused the loss of flight control. From extremely low altitude Cruzado immediately ejected and, having landed safely, was captured by the British and spent the rest of the War as a prisoner. His aircraft had come down in a nearby paddock known as "Peter's Park". Micheloud's aircraft was also damaged and as he started the long run home in the evening murk he was far from sure that he would reach Port Stanley. Obliged to fly at low level because of fears of marauding Sea Harriers that were reported to be in the area, Micheloud flew with engine warning lights glowing and the conviction that sooner or later he would have to eject from his damaged aircraft. However, his fears were unfounded and with some moral support from crossing Ejercito helicopters, themselves en route to Goose Green, he was able to nurse the Pucara home to the safety of Port Stanley.

As the Sea Harriers and warships of the Royal Navy continued to bombard Stanley Airport the local FAA commanders took stock of the situation in their theatre. No more Pucaras would be committed to the Islands after 28 May — it was recognised that to do so would be to lose them — and those few that survived at Stanley Airport would be protected by dispersing them to roadside bases between the airfield and the town. When required for a mission they were ferried the short distance to the airfield for full fuelling and arming but after each sortie they were flown back to their hiding places. That strategy appears to have worked fairly well although by the surrender on 14 June all airworthy aircraft were back at Stanley Airport.

The 12 aircraft that had thus been ferried to the Islands on and after 15 May were:

| A-511 | A-515 | A-522 | A-532 | A-536 | A-549 |
| A-514 | A-516 | A-531 | A-533 | A-537 | A-555 |

After 28 May up to seven aircraft could be made airworthy although it seems that they were never simultaneously available. They would have been drawn from A-509, A-513 to A-516, A-522, A-528, A-532, A-533, A-536 and A-549, the 11 Pucaras eventually found at Stanley Airport on 14 June. Very little major repair work

**Upper Left** *Fox Bay West was one of the settlements on West Falkland that was garrisoned by the Ejercito but which remained virtually unscathed by subsequent land and air combat. Here a Grupo 7 de Helicopteros Chinook passes over the School House in the evening of 11.4.82 bringing in elements of RgtInf8; many more flights were to arrive the following day.* **Upper Right** *Six weeks later, and just prior to the British landings at San Carlos, one of the final visitors to the settlement was this CAB601 Puma which overnighted 19/20.5.82. Within 10 days the last of all five Pumas deployed to the Falklands by the CAE had been destroyed.*
(Graeme Hyde)

*The broken wreckage of the Grupo 3 de Ataque Pucara A-511 lies where it fell near Drone Hill, East Falkland on 21.5.82. Having been caught and shot-up by the 801 Squadron Sea Harrier XZ451 of Lt Cdr "Sharkey" Ward, the Pucara's pilot, Mayor Carlos Tomba, owed his life to the efficiency of his Martin-Baker ejection seat. His escape, made seconds before the Pucara hit the ground, clearly demonstrated the "zero-zero" qualities of the seat. The Pucara's yellow wing and fin flashes can be seen in this photograph, taken in late 1982.*
(Ministry of Defence)

*Teniente "Daniel" Jukic of Grupo 3 de Ataque was killed on the morning of 1.5.82 at Goose Green when his Pucara was destroyed by Sea Harriers of 800 Squadron. A-527 was blown apart by a CBU as Jukic prepared to taxy towards the grass runway; the unfortunate pilot died instantly. Shortly afterwards the Argentine government issued a ludicrous account of Jukic heroically attacking and damaging 'Hermes' before losing his life to a guided missile. Jukic's unit was acutely embarrassed by the nonsensical invention.*
(R. McLeod)

was possible at Port Stanley and engine and cannon changes were about the most demanding engineering tasks that were undertaken in the field. Some Pucaras were literally flown with holes in them because there were no battle-damage repair facilities available. Naturally much ingenuity was displayed but Grupo 3's engineering support facilities were inadequate for the circumstances and, by late May, vital spares and tools were in short supply. The wet Falklands weather penetrated everything — men, aircraft, ground equipment, ordnance — and all suffered universally. Electrical systems were affected by the damp with demoralising, if not actually disastrous, effects. Once completely useless, the Pucaras were distributed across Stanley Airport as decoys.

One of the final strikes by the aircraft of the Escuadron Pucara Malvinas was a three-aircraft mission against British positions at dawn on 10 June. Artillery fire from the slopes of Mount Kent had been causing considerable discomfort and Primer Teniente Micheloud was briefed to destroy some of the guns. He was accompanied by Teniente Morales and Primer Teniente Ayerdi but although all three returned safely little was achieved. In response to the attack 800 Sqdn delivered a four-aircraft Sea Harrier strike at 1130Z against Stanley Airport, specifically directed at the surviving Pucaras. The mission was partially successful and although all the airworthy aircraft had been dispersed away from the airfield, one unserviceable Pucara was officially acknowledged as destroyed in the attack. The Pucaras were, however, able to launch a second mission against the same artillery positions at dusk on 11 June. Again all aircraft returned safely. The final sorties were flown without loss on 13 June and when Argentine forces surrendered the following day it was generally reckoned that three or perhaps four Pucaras were airworthy. British assessment concurred with that view and A-515, A-536 and A-549 were probably the three in question.

The Escuadron Pucara Malvinas flew 186 sorties from its bases on the Falklands between 2 April and 13 June. The vast majority were launched from Port Stanley and Goose Green with relatively few from Pebble Island. Despite many accounts to the contrary no other bases were used, indeed it is difficult to find much evidence of even exploratory landings elsewhere. A further six operational sorties were launched from mainland bases to search for reported landings of British commando forces but these may have been flown by either Grupo 3 or Grupo 4 crews.

Post-war consolidation at Reconquista and Comodoro Rivadavia was immediately hindered by a shortage of aircraft and, with many components in short supply, production remained slow for some time. On a positive note, both Grupo 3 and Grupo 4 gained considerably in experience from the War and, with few local fatalities, morale remained high. Pucaras in service with Grupo 3 in November 1982 included A-501, A-505, A-518, A-538 and new machines A-563, A-564, A-567 to A-569, A-572 and A-573. During the same period A-550, A-570 and A-574 were seen at FMA Cordoba, A-575 having been delivered to the FAA there on 12 June. The newest recognisable Pucaras on the production line at Cordoba in November 1982 were A-584 and A-585. Aircraft A-561 and the newly manufactured A-591 were publicly displayed in Chile in March 1984, while in August of that year A-585 and A-590 were amongst those on display at the Cordoba "Air Force Day". A-596 to A-598 were seen to be on the FMA production line that day in an advanced state of construction.

Post-war Pucara accidents at Reconquista include one circa October 1982, one on 6 January 1983 and a third on 21 September 1983.

---

*Grupo 3 de Ataque pilots deployed to the Falkland Islands included:*

*Mayor Navarro (Escuadron commander); Mayor C.A.Tomba; Capitan J.Benitez; Capitan R.Grunert; Capitan R.Villa; Primer Teniente Ayerdi; Primer Teniente J.Micheloud; Teniente Alsogaray; Teniente Arganaraz; Teniente Brest; Teniente Calderon; Teniente Cimbaro; Teniente Cruzado; Teniente M.A.Gimenez (KIA); Teniente Hernandez; Teniente A.D.Jukic (KIA); Teniente Morales; Teniente Russo; Alferez Pontecorvo; Alferez Sassone. Alferez M.L.Valko of Grupo 4 de Ataque was also KIA while flying from Comodoro Rivadavia.*

---

# INDIVIDUAL AIRCRAFT DETAILS

---

With the exception of a few aircraft that had at various times been painted in experimental camouflage schemes, no Grupo 3 de Ataque Pucaras were operationally camouflaged before April 1982. The hastily applied wash that was then adopted was not put on with any consistency although virtually all aircraft received light tan and green upper fuselage camouflage with light blue or grey undersides. In some instances the paintwork was so rushed that the FAA titles on the forward fuselage, the side roundels, serial numbers and occasionally even the national flag on the fin were partially or completely obliterated.

The first 12 aircraft ferried to Stanley Airport prior to 1 May were thus received in the above "standard" camouflage scheme without the yellow fin and wing markings and indeed the early destruction of most of them ensured that none were to retrospectively receive these highly visible stripes. The second 12 Pucaras were received on the Falklands progressively from 15 May and their markings reflected the rapid changes of philosophy that occurred during the latter half of the month. Most of the early deliveries (of the second 12), and perhaps all but the last few, came in "standard" camouflage but with the bright yellow fin and wing stripes. Thus A-511 and A-531, both destroyed on 21 May, were still wearing these stripes when lost. A-533 was similarly marked and was still in these colours when found at Stanley Airport on 14 June. It is thus presumed that A-533 was "grounded" before the end of May and before the identification stripes were painted out on other Pucaras. Of the others, A-514, A-516, A-522, A-532 and A-549, when found, all displayed evidence that their yellow stripes had been painted out but it is not known whether this happened before their departure from Santa Cruz (A-549 arrived in a noticeably lighter camouflage scheme than the others). Of the remaining four, nothing is known of A-537's colours but A-515, A-536 and A-555 were repainted in a dark brown and green camouflage. These colours, also presumably applied at Santa Cruz, were crudely painted on top of the lighter "standard" camouflage (and they may well also have worn yellow stripes), indeed the repaint did not totally cover the fin area, the upper part of which remained in the earlier and lighter camouflage.

The FAA's adoption of darker camouflage colours is thought to have resulted from the late realisation that lighter colours were inappropriate for the Falklands terrain. The FAA philosophy concerning aircraft camouflage was to relate it to the normal operating area and thus it was not inconsistent that the light camouflage colours were retained on post-war Grupo 3 Pucaras at their home base at Reconquista. The somewhat curious uncamouflaged area at the top of the fins of some of the Grupo 3 Falklands' Pucaras is believed to reflect the haste in which the aircraft were repainted.

*In the individual aircraft details the standard FAA abbreviation 'G3A' has been used for Grupo 3 de Ataque and 'G4A' for Grupo 4 de Ataque.*

*The "total hours" figures quoted for each Pucara are the total recorded airframe hours as at 22 March 1982.*

---

### A-502

On 22.3.82 with G3A; total hours 86.30. Flown to Stanley Airport by 9.4.82 and then to Goose Green on 29.4.82. Received minor damage there on 1.5.82 in the 800 Sqdn Sea Harrier attack. Repaired within a few days and flown to Pebble Island where it was destroyed in the 'D' Sqdn 22 SAS Regt raid on 15.5.82. Last noted there in late 1982 but by 1.83 the remains had been blown up and buried on site.

*Light camouflage scheme without yellow flashes. Fuselage markings (if any) not known.*

### A-506

On 22.3.82 with G3A; total hours 1,114.35. Flown to Stanley Airport by 9.4.82 and then to Goose Green on 29.4.82. Received terminal damage there (almost certainly on 1.5.82 in the 800 Sqdn Sea Harrier attack) and subsequently used as a decoy. An airframe inspection by the British post-28.5.82 revealed nose-wheel leg and propeller damage which was indicative of a take-off accident. This aircraft may well have been that of Teniente Calderon which failed to get airborne on 1.5.82. Hulk last noted there (on its back) in 7.83. By 2.84 it had been carried by Chinook to a Falklands weapons range. During the manoeuvre the fuselage bent and the tail section fell from an altitude of about 100ft. In 7.85 that section remained at Goose Green, south of the airstrip.

*Light camouflage scheme without yellow flashes. The name "Satan Tripa" (Satan's Guts) worn on the nose below the cockpit (port side only).*

### A-509

On 22.3.82 with G3A; total hours 1,027.50. Flown to Stanley Airport by 9.4.82 and then to Goose Green on 29.4.82. Returned to Stanley Airport (sometime after 1.5.82) where it was badly damaged (date and circumstances unknown). Post-14.6.82 its crumpled remains were found dumped near a hangar. It appeared to have suffered blast damage and

undercarriage collapse. The propellers had gone and the rudder was torn loose from the fin. Noted derelict at RAF Stanley in 2.85 when one of only two Pucara wrecks remaining (see A-514).

*Light camouflage scheme without yellow flashes.*

### A-511

On 22.3.82 with G3A; total hours 884.35. One of the 12 aircraft flown to the Falklands on or after 15.5.82 (possibly on 15.5.82 to Goose Green) and used from Goose Green. Shot down by cannon fire from the 801 Sqdn Sea Harrier XZ451 of Lt Cdr Ward near Drone Hill, Lafonia, East Falkland on 21.5.82. The pilot, Mayor Tomba, ejected safely and was later recovered by Argentine helicopter to Goose Green. Wreckage still visible at the crash site (UC 4349) in 2.85.

*Light camouflage scheme with yellow flashes.*

### A-512

On 22.3.82 with G3A; total hours 898.35. No record of this aircraft having been used on the Falklands. Period Argentine photographs (5.82) record the aircraft in a *light camouflage scheme with yellow fin and wing identification flashes* but the aircraft is believed to have been photographed at Comodoro Rivadavia and not at Stanley Airport as some captions have suggested.

### A-513

On 22.3.82 with G3A; total hours 1,033.10. Flown to Stanley Airport by 9.4.82 and then to Goose Green on 29.4.82. Sometime after 1.5.82 it returned to Stanley Airport where it was badly damaged (date and circumstances unknown). When inspected there post-14.6.82 it was supported under the nose by an oil-drum, having suffered nose area damage. The fuselage was intact with the engines and propellers undamaged. Categorised as in poor condition. Last noted at RAF Stanley in 5.83 but removed to a Falklands weapons range by 7.83.

*Light camouflage scheme without yellow flashes.*

### A-514

On 22.3.82 with G3A; total hours 1,150.50. One of the 12 aircraft flown to the Falklands on or after 15.5.82. Badly damaged at Stanley Airport (date and circumstances unknown). When inspected post-14.6.82 it had obviously suffered blast damage to the starboard wing and nose area. The nose-leg, port propeller and engine cowling were missing. Noted derelict at RAF Stanley in 2.85 when one of only two Pucara wrecks remaining (see A-509).

*Light camouflage scheme without yellow flashes.*

### A-515

On 22.3.82 with G3A; total hours 762.05. One of the 12 aircraft flown to the Falklands on or after 15.5.82. Its *dark camouflage scheme (without yellow flashes)* and excellent condition when inspected post-14.6.82 at Stanley Airport (airworthy with rocket pods in place) almost certainly identifies it as one of five flown to Stanley Airport from Santa Cruz on 27/28.5.82.

Airlifted on 10.7.82 by 18 Sqdn Chinook (ZA707) to 'Atlantic Causeway' in Port William and sailed with the ship 12.7.82 (via San Carlos Water 13.7.82) for the UK, arriving at Devonport 27.7.82. It was due to be lifted off by Chinook on 28.7.82 but this was cancelled (see A-549 for reason). Instead it was off-loaded, stripped down and removed by road on 1.8.82 to A&AEE Boscombe Down, arriving there the same day. Shortly after that a British serial (ZD485) was allocated by the MoD. Following a protracted survey and replacement of some damaged and missing parts it was brought back to flight status. Taxying trials took place on 22.2.83 and the first flight was on 28.4.83, by which time Red/Blue roundels and fin-flashes had been applied to the "nearly original" Argentine colour scheme. Flown by 'A' Sqdn project pilot Sqdn Ldr Peart, the aircraft was fully evaluated in a programme which included operations from grass. It performed very well,

Within a few days of the cease-fire British forces made safe all of the surviving Grupo 3 de Ataque Pucaras at Stanley Airport and grouped eight of them beside the runway pending a decision on their future. Eventually four of these aircraft were shipped to the United Kingdom for evaluation or static display. The diversity of their camouflage and other markings can be clearly seen on (left to right) A-533, A-528, A-536, A-513, A-522, A-549, A-532 and A-514.

(Lt Cdr R. C. Nichol, RN)

**Above** The LADE/Grupo 9 de Transporte Aereo Twin Otter T-82 was marked with an inscription to commemorate a hazardous overnight mission to Isla Borbon (Pebble Island) on 28/29.5.82 when a group of isolated FAA personnel were airlifted out to the mainland. The group included at least two pilots who had been recovered to Pebble Island after ejecting nearby and a number of other personnel who were in need of medical attention. (via S. Mafé Huertas).

**Right** On 6.9.82 Grupo 3 de Ataque Pucara A-522 was airlifted from RAF Stanley to 'Contender Bezant' by the 18 Squadron Chinook ZA720. A-528 "Toto Juan" (Little Juan) followed in a similar manner later that day and both arrived in the United Kingdom on 23.9.82 for use as exhibition aircraft. (Simon Van Tromp)

particularly off the grass, and was flown in simulated combat against many types including the Sea Harrier. One Falklands' veteran considered that it provided a splendid image for AIM-9L acquisition. A-515 was found to be a robust and capable aircraft although no useful function for such a type in the RAF could be envisaged (its most obvious shortcoming was felt to be the lack of air-conditioning!). Flown to Greenham Common on 21.7.83 for the International Air Tattoo on 23/24.7.83, returning to Boscombe Down on 25.7.83. On completion of the assessment programme it was flown from Boscombe Down to the Cosford Aerospace Museum on 9.9.83 for preservation and possible eventual exhibition in the RAF Museum, Hendon or the FAAM, Yeovilton.

## A-516

On 22.3.82 with G3A; total hours 868.35. One of the 12 aircraft flown to the Falklands on or after 15.5.82. Destroyed at Stanley Airport (date and circumstances unknown). When inspected post-14.6.82 it was found to be a total wreck, with the appearance of having taken a direct bomb or shell hit. The hulk was later buried at RAF Stanley (pieces still visible in 5.83).

*Light camouflage scheme without yellow flashes.*

## A-517

On 22.3.82 with G3A; total hours 787.55. Flown to Stanley Aiport by 9.4.82 and then to Goose Green on 29.4.82. Received terminal damage there, almost certainly in the 800 Sqdn Sea Harrier attack on 1.5.82. When inspected by the British post-28.5.82 it was found to be badly damaged with a collapsed nose-wheel leg, shrapnel cuts and without propellers. Like A-506 it had been used as a decoy and had probably been attacked several times.

*Light camouflage scheme without yellow flashes.*

On 5.10.84 the MoD handed over the semi-derelict aircraft to the residents of Goose Green to be disposed of as they wished. The same day it was sold to a Mr Harrison (Grampian Helicopters International Ltd) to be shipped to the UK. Registered G-BLRP (not worn) in 12.84, it was dismantled and put on a trailer prior to leaving Goose Green on the 'Monsunen' on 30.1.85 for Port Stanley where it arrived later that day. Off-loaded on 31.1.85, then put in a container and stored pending shipment to the UK in a civilian vessel. Still at Port Stanley in 3.85.

## A-520

On 22.3.82 with G3A; total hours 507.40. Flown to Stanley Airport by 9.4.82 and then to Goose Green on 29.4.82. Ferried to Pebble Island on or after 1.5.82 and badly damaged there in the 'D' Sqdn 22 SAS Regt raid on 15.5.82. Inspection of the wreck post-14.6.82 found evidence of explosive charges in the engine and wing-root areas. In spite of that, the aircraft was still standing on its undercarriage. It was last noted in late 1982 and by 1.83 the hulk had been removed to a weapons range near Chartres settlement on West Falkland.

*Light camouflage scheme without yellow flashes.*

## A-522

On 22.3.82 with G3A; total hours 761.10. One of the 12 aircraft flown to the Falklands on or after 15.5.82. Located at Stanley Airport on 14.6.82 and when inspected was assessed as being in a fair, but non-flyable, condition with no significant external signs of damage.

*Light camouflage scheme without yellow flashes.*

Airlifted on 6.9.82 by 18 Sqdn Chinook ZA720 to 'Contender Bezant' in Port William and sailed with the ship that day for the UK, arriving Southampton on 23.9.82. Off-loaded onto the quay and removed by road on 25.9.82, arriving at Abingdon the following day. The RAF maintenance serial 8768M was allocated on 27.9.82 in anticipation of it becoming part of the RAF Museum Regional Collection at St Athan. To St Athan by road 25.10.82 where it remained until transported to the FAAM at Yeovilton on 7.12.82 (replacing A-549 which was transferred that day to A&AEE as a spares source for A-515). Robbed for spares by the A&AEE and, in 6.85, remained on display at Yeovilton, the maintenance serial never having been applied.

## A-523

On 22.3.82 with G3A; total hours 800.45. One of the original four aircraft flown to Stanley Airport on 2.4.82 and then to Goose Green on 29.4.82. To Pebble Island on or after 1.5.82 and immobilised there in the 'D' Sqdn 22 SAS Regt raid on 15.5.82. Inspection of the aircraft post-14.6.82 revealed that it had suffered blast and shrapnel damage but its collapsed nose-wheel leg and propeller damage may have been the legacy of an earlier landing accident (see text). Airlifted by an 18 Sqdn Chinook to 'Sand Shore' in Elephant Bay on 21.7.83. Sailed overnight with the ship, arriving in San Carlos Water on 22.7.83 where it was removed by Chinook to a weapons range on East Falkland.

*Light camouflage scheme without yellow flashes.*

## A-527

On 22.3.82 with G3A; total hours 724.30. Flown to Stanley Airport by 9.4.82 and then to Goose Green on 29.4.82. Destroyed at Goose Green on 1.5.82 by a direct CBU hit from an 800 Sqdn Sea Harrier, killing the pilot, Teniente Jukic, and several other FAA personnel in the immediate area. Wreckage still at Goose Green 2.84 but removed by 9.84, leaving only charred pieces on the airfield and the tail on the local rubbish tip.

*Light camouflage scheme without yellow flashes.*

## A-528

On 22.3.82 with G3A; total hours 522.45. Flown to Stanley Airport by 9.4.82 and then to Goose Green on 29.4.82. Sometime after 1.5.82 it returned to Stanley Airport. When inspected there post-14.6.82 it was found to be in poor condition. Although still standing on

its undercarriage it had broken propeller blades, nose damage and shrapnel cuts below the cockpit area.

*Light camouflage scheme without yellow flashes. The name "Toto Juan" (Little Juan) worn on the nose below the cockpit (port side only).*

Airlifted on 6.9.82 by 18 Sqdn Chinook ZA720 to 'Contender Bezant' in Port William and sailed with the ship that day for the UK, arriving Southampton on 23.9.82 where it was off-loaded on to the quay. Allocated the maintenance serial 8769M on 27.9.82 by the RAF (not worn) and removed by road to Abingdon 30.9.82 (arriving there the same day) and then on to the Cosford Aerospace Museum, its intended home, on 18.10.82. On 19.11.82 returned to Abingdon and departed again on 13.12.82 for exhibition at the London "Boat Show" in 1.83 after which it was returned to Cosford for display. Transferred to the Museum of Army Flying at Middle Wallop, arriving by road on 16.5.85. Still resident (with A-533) in late 7.85.

## A-529

On 22.3.82 with G3A; total hours 682.45. One of the original four aircraft flown to Port Stanley on 2.4.82 and then to Goose Green on 29.4.82. To Pebble Island on or after 1.5.82 and immobilised there in the 'D' Sqdn 22 SAS Regt raid on 15.5.82. Inspection post-14.6.82 revealed that the damage was limited and caused by small detonations in the engine and wing-root areas. Airlifted by an 18 Sqdn Chinook to the 'Sand Shore' in Elephant Bay, Pebble Island on 21.7.83. Sailed overnight with the ship, arriving in San Carlos Water on 22.7.83. Still on board the ship in Stanley Harbour on 24.7.83. Removed by 18 Sqdn Chinook to RAF Stanley to become the "gate guardian". Still resident as such in 6.85 but by then passed to the Falklands Islands Govt for eventual display in a museum at Port Stanley.

*Light camouflage scheme without yellow flashes.*

## A-531

On 22.3.82 with G3A; total hours 696.30. One of the 12 aircraft flown to the Falklands on or after 15.5.82 (possibly on 15.5.82 to Goose Green) and used from Goose Green. Shot down by a Stinger missile fired by a senior NCO of 'D' Sqdn 22 SAS Regt near Flat Shanty settlement, East Falkland on 21.5.82. The pilot, Capitan Benitez, ejected successfully. Wreckage still visible in 2.85.

*Light camouflage scheme with yellow flashes.*

## A-532

On 22.3.82 with G3A; total hours 639.40. One of the 12 aircraft flown to the Falklands on or after 15.5.82. Located at Stanley Airport on 14.6.82 and when inspected it was assessed as being in poor condition, having lost the nose-wheel leg and both propellers. Last noted at RAF Stanley in 5.83. The hulk was removed to a Falklands weapons range by 7.83.

*Light camouflage scheme without yellow flashes although an Argentine photograph, probably taken on the mainland, clearly shows*

Five Grupo 3 de Ataque Pucaras were brought to the United Kingdom during 1982 for evaluation and display purposes. The final pair to arrive were A-522 and A-528, intended only for exhibition purposes. Both are seen here on 23.9.82 being off-loaded from 'Contender Bezant' at Southampton Docks. A-522 and A-528 (seen on the sling) were allocated the maintenance serials 8768M and 8769M four days later. (Michael I. Draper)

One of the three Pucaras intended for use in an evaluation programme, A-533 (ZD486) was never, in fact, flown in the United Kingdom. Instead, it appeared on public exhibition at the Finningley and Abingdon Battle of Britain displays during 9.82 and is seen here at Abingdon. The original light camouflage and unnecessary identification stripe are shown to good effect, as is the polythene cover over the damaged cockpit canopy. In mid-1985 A-533 was on display outside the Museum of Army Flying, Middle Wallop, having arrived there on 15.2.84.
(Peter J. Cooper)

A-549 was another of the Grupo 3 de Ataque Pucaras brought to the United Kingdom for evaluation by the A&AEE and, but for damage sustained while being carried by Chinook from Devonport to Yeovilton on 28.7.82, might well have been flown as ZD487. In the event it was used at Boscombe Down only as a spares source for ZD485 (A-515). A-549 is seen here, fitted with 2.75in rocket pods and a centre-line minigun, at Yeovilton on 30.7.82 awaiting positioning for exhibition at the "Air Day" the following day. After several moves in 1982 and 1983 it passed to the Imperial War Museum collection at Duxford where it remained in mid-1985.
(Peter J. Cooper)

*the aircraft with yellow tail and wing flashes.*

## A-533

On 22.3.82 with G3A; total hours 594.55. One of 12 aircraft flown to the Falklands on or after 15.5.82 (possibly on 15.5.82 to Goose Green). Located at Stanley Airport on 14.6.82 and when inspected it was assessed as being in fair condition with no external signs of damage.

*Light camouflage scheme with yellow flashes.*

Airlifted by 18 Sqdn Chinook ZA718 to the 'Tor Caledonia' in Port William and sailed with the ship on 1.8.82 for the UK, arriving at Felixstowe on 20.8.82. Taken by road to Finningley 23.8.82 for the BoB display on 4.9.82 and then transported to Abingdon (seen there 15.9.82) for a further BoB display on 18.9.82. British serial ZD486 was allocated (but not worn) against possible flight use and the aircraft was removed by road to A&AEE Boscombe Down on 23.9.82. Not flown but served as a spares source for A-515/ZD485. Dumped outside by mid-9.83 but delivered to the Museum of Army Flying at Middle Wallop on 15.2.84 for display. Still resident in 7.85.

## A-536

On 22.3.82 with G3A; total hours 595.35. One of the 12 aircraft flown to the Falklands on or after 15.5.82. Its *dark camouflage scheme without yellow flashes* and excellent condition (probably airworthy) when inspected at Stanley Airport post-14.6.82 almost certainly identifies it as one of five Pucaras flown to Port Stanley from Santa Cruz on 27/28.5.82. Although only missing an upper nose panel it was, in common with other captured Argentine aircraft, rapidly vandalised and its battered hulk was eventually carried by an 18 Sqdn Chinook to a Falklands weapons range on 14.5.83.

## A-537

On 22.3.82 with G3A; total hours 698.30. One of the 12 aircraft flown to the Falklands on or after 15.5.82 (possibly on 15.5.82 to Goose Green). Not found post-war but known to have been lost during the campaign and is believed to have been the aircraft of Teniente Gimenez, missing after a mission from Stanley Airport to Goose Green on 28.5.82. The pur-

pose of the sortie had been to attack 2 PARA positions in the Darwin and Goose Green areas and, if A-537 was so involved, it was also the aircraft that shot down the 3 CBAS Scout XT629 near Darwin that day. The Scout's pilot, Sgt Nunn, was killed and his aircrewman, Sgt Belcher, seriously injured.

## A-540

On 22.3.82 with G4A. The aircraft was lost on an unknown date in the course of a reconnaissance mission from Comodoro Rivadavia. It crashed into the sea killing the pilot Alferez Valko.

## A-549

On 22.3.82 with G3A; total hours 106.20. One of the 12 aircraft flown to the Falklands on or after 15.5.82. Located at Stanley Airport on 14.6.82 and when inspected was found to be in excellent condition.

*Very light camouflage scheme without yellow flashes.*

Airlifted on 10.7.82 by 18 Sqdn Chinook (ZA707) to 'Atlantic Causeway' in Port William and sailed with the ship 12.7.82 (via San Carlos Water 13.7.82) for the UK, arriving Devonport 27.7.82. Lifted off the vessel on 28.7.82 by 240 OCU Chinook (ZA676) and taken that day as an underslung load to Yeovilton for display at the "Air Day" on 31.7.82. Unfortunately, damage was done to the mainplane during transit and plans to remove A-515 (also on 'Atlantic Causeway') in the same way were abandoned. Airlifted again by 18 Sqdn Chinook (ZA709) on 9.8.82 from Yeovilton to A&AEE Boscombe Down ostensibly to participate in the flying evaluation programme. A British serial, ZD487, was allocated (not applied) but due to the earlier airframe damage was used only as a spares source for A-515/ZD485. Released by A&AEE for public viewing and taken to St Athan 14.9.82 for the BoB display on 18.9.82. Remained there until 28.10.82 when it was removed by road to Yeovilton for display in the FAAM. Departed for Boscombe Down on 8.12.82 (arrived 9.12.82) when the FAAM received A-522 in its stead. By mid-9.83 A-549 had been dumped in the open at Boscombe Down. Taken by road to the Imperial War Museum aircraft collection at Duxford on 2.11.83 for eventual display. Still resident in 6.85.

## A-552

On 22.3.82 with G3A; total hours 137.35. One of the original four aircraft flown to Stanley Airport on 2.4.82 and then to Goose Green on 29.4.82. To Pebble Island on or after 1.5.82 and ostensibly destroyed there in the 'D' Sqdn 22 SAS Regt raid on 15.5.82. In fact, when inspected post-14.6.82, it was found to have very little damage and would probably have been easily repaired in other circumstances. Airlifted by an 18 Sqdn Chinook to the 'Sand Shore' in Elephant Bay, Pebble Island on 21.7.83. Sailed overnight with the ship, arriving in San Carlos Water on 22.7.83 where it was removed by Chinook to a weapons range on East Falkland.

*Light camouflage scheme without yellow flashes.*

## A-555

On 22.3.82 with G3A; total hours 32.00. One of the 12 aircraft flown to the Falklands on or after 15.5.82. Its noticeably *dark camouflage scheme without yellow flashes* probably identifies it as one of the five aircraft flown to Stanley Airport from Santa Cruz on 27/28.5.82. It was shot down close to Goose Green on 28.5.82 by small-arms fire from 2 PARA. The pilot, Teniente Cruzado, ejected safely. By late 1982 its wreckage had been "tidied up" but was still visible near Peter's Park in 2.84.

## A-556

On 22.3.82 with G3A; total hours 119.15. One of the original four aircraft flown to Stanley Airport on 2.4.82 and then to Goose Green on 29.4.82. To Pebble Island on or after 1.5.82 and immobilised there in the 'D' Sqdn 22 SAS Regt raid on 15.5.82. Inspection post-14.6.82 revealed that explosive charges had been detonated in the engine and wing-root areas. In spite of that it was still standing on its undercarriage. Last noted in late 1982 but by 1.83 it had been removed to a weapons range near Chartres settlement on West Falkland.

*It was in the "standard" light camouflage scheme but uniquely decorated with a crudely painted yellow band round the rear fuselage.*

*Journey's end – almost. With a police escort and on two "Queen Mary" trailers, Pucara A-528 proceeds slowly northwards along the M271 Motorway on 30.9.82, en route from Southampton Docks to Abingdon. The task of dismantling the Pucara on the quayside without the aid of manuals or expert guidance was complex and many difficulties were experienced, much delaying its departure. In late 1985 A-528 was on exhibition at the Museum of Army Flying, Middle Wallop.*

*(Michael I. Draper)*

# SKYHAWK

# GRUPO 4 DE CAZA

25 refurbished A-4C Skyhawks were delivered to Argentina in 1976 from surplus United States Navy stocks and entered FAA service that year at Los Tamarindos, El Plumerillo, Mendoza — the home of the IV Brigada Aerea. In March 1982 all of the surviving aircraft equipped one squadron of IV BA's Grupo 4 de Caza (Bombardeo). Within Grupo 4 (G4C) the Skyhawk squadron was loosely referred to as 'Escuadron A-4C' or 'Escuadron Skyhawk' and, rarely, as 'Escuadron III de Caza Bombardeo' which is thought to have been its formal identity. Of the 25 aircraft originally received probably fewer than 19 remained in use by March 1982, indeed four had been lost in accidents during the previous sixteen months. Of those on strength, several were not in an airworthy state, awaiting spare parts delayed by the United States arms embargo. By March, that embargo had been lifted and the situation was expected to improve fairly rapidly. Nevertheless, when Argentine forces landed on East Falkland, several A-4C's were in storage and gathering dust at Mendoza and at the Rio Cuarto maintenance facility in Cordoba.

In common with all other FAA combat units, Grupo 4 de Caza was instructed to bring to war readiness as many aircraft and pilots as possible for deployment to one of the southern bases. For Grupo 4 that was to be the erstwhile civilian airport of San Julian in Santa Cruz province and would be shared with one of the Dagger Escuadrones of Grupo 6 de Caza, normally based at Tandil, BA. The transfer of the first Skyhawks took place on 11 April, only two days after the first Grupo 4 inspection personnel had reached San Julian. 12 aircraft were initially deployed and, at that time, only three Skyhawks remained at Mendoza, probably for training purposes, with the rest under maintenance at Rio Cuarto. During the War other aircraft were ferried south, making good attrition, as and when they became available. The aircraft taken to San Julian formed a special Squadron which was officially entitled the "Escuadron A-4C San Julian".

San Julian was a small and remote airport and its rudimentary construction and facilities were far from ideal for the anticipated combat missions of Skyhawks and Daggers. Major problems included inadequate hard-standing and covered areas and the complete absence of taxiways

to the runway thresholds. The latter difficulty was solved by the emergency provision of aluminium planking. Once the first aircraft were in place on the airfield it became apparent that there were also serious communications problems that had to be overcome. By late April, these and many other difficulties had been resolved to an acceptable degree.

The new unit spent the final days of April simulating combat missions which, at that time, were identified as likely to be anti-shipping sorties over the open sea. Such sorties would have to culminate in extreme low-level attacks on the British warships in the hope of avoiding radar detection and acquisition by the Royal Navy's SAM's which were regarded with justifiable apprehension by the FAA. As the British Task Force approached the Falkland Islands, progress was closely monitored and, by 30 April, all FAA units were on full alert, anxiously awaiting Britain's next military move. At that time it was still thought that air raids against mainland targets were a possibility — the "pre-emptive strike" — and emergency evacuations of San Julian's aircraft had been practised. Ironically, the last such evacuation occurred at just about the same time that an RAF Vulcan left Ascension Island to bomb Stanley Airport for the first time. At 2200Z on 30 April all the Skyhawks and Daggers were ordered to leave for their alternate base (possibly Puerto Deseado) when an unidentified radar image was detected, apparently on course for San Julian. The warning was a false one — or rather it was not a Vulcan — but all aircraft were successfully scrambled between 2233Z and 2300Z. Interestingly, many aircraft had been bombed-up waiting for a mission and had to be rapidly disarmed before the evacuation.

The FAA's reaction to the bombing of Stanley Airport and Goose Green airfield on 1 May was, in effect, simply the long anticipated execution of a contingency plan. It involved all the combat units, with each of them tasked to launch a number of sorties seeking naval targets of opportunity in the waters off East Falkland. There was, of course, a fundamental flaw in the plan and that was the Argentine misconception that the Vulcan and Sea Harrier strikes heralded a full-scale amphibious landing by the

British and that many ships would be close inshore. All FAA sorties were to be guided to targets by operations controllers in Port Stanley (the CIC) and all Skyhawk and Dagger strike missions would receive top-cover from the Mirage IIIEA and Dagger interceptors. Grupo 4 was tasked to fly 16 sorties on 1 May in four flights of four aircraft.

For those first missions each flight comprised an Escuadrilla formed by four pilots who flew together as a matter of routine during peace-time and it is significant that the casual reference to the 'Escuadron' in FAA terminology was for that reason. The FAA "Grupo" was composed of a number of flights or "Escuadrillas", each of which was formally recognised and had a flight leader. The "Escuadron", or Squadron, was formed by a variable number of Escuadrillas, either for special purposes or when the Grupo had enough aircraft (or a diversity of equipment) to warrant permanently established Escuadrones.

The first Grupo 4 flight took-off from San Julian at 1320Z and for that mission each Skyhawk is thought to have carried two 500lb bombs. The only other armament was the much-disliked pair of 20mm cannon which were prone to jamming and, even when operative, were regarded as inadequate weapons. In common with all Skyhawk sorties on 1 May, the mission was not air-refuelled and was therefore range-limited. To the disappointment of all concerned the flight found nothing to attack and soon after 1450Z the four aircraft returned safely to San Julian. That inauspicious start heralded a dismal day for the Skyhawk units. Many aircraft failed to find any targets at all and the constant Sea Harrier presence over East Falkland obliged others to return to base even though the Port Stanley CIC had identifed potential targets. One such Grupo 4 sortie was that of "Lana" flight led by Capitan Jorge Garcia, which was warned off by the Port Stanley controllers when a Sea Harrier CAP approached them. The day ended quietly for Grupo 4 with much frustration, no combat but no losses. However, lessons had been learned and further opportunities were soon to occur for the unit to prove itself in combat.

The next week was rather an anti-climax. Poor flying weather and a dearth of suitable enemy targets meant that no operational sorties could be launched against the British fleet (although elsewhere the CANA Super Etendards were achieving spectacular success). Eventually, on 9 May, CdoFAS was able to order a series of strikes against British warships that had been sighted close to East Falkland. Unfortunately for the FAA the weather rapidly deteriorated and virtually all missions were aborted or cancelled. In an effort to get to a target in the Port Stanley area one Grupo 4 flight (thought to have been Garcia's) elected to continue on at low level in the worsening weather. The result was catastrophic and two Skyhawks, those of Teniente Jorge Farias and Teniente Jorge Casco, failed to return from a mission which did not make any contact with the enemy. Casco's Skyhawk, C-313, was destroyed when it hit the north-west face of the cliffs of South Jason Island, situated to the north-west of West Falkland. When the Skyhawk was eventually found by the Royal Navy some months later, the bomb-load was still intact and the pilot was found in the wreckage. Farias and his aircraft, C-303, were never found and he, too, is pre-

sumed to have crashed in poor visibility. The British warships 'Broadsword' and 'Coventry' were off Port Stanley at the time of the mission and were probably the Skyhawks' intended target. The two ships engaged an unseen enemy formation at 1417Z, believing it to be a C-130 with Mirage escorts, but the three Sea Darts fired from 'Coventry' all missed their target. However, the incident took place some considerable distance from South Jason Island.

Grupo 4's next action was not until 21 May when it was thrown into combat against British shipping in San Carlos Water. By then CdoFAS had modified the mission profiles and all Skyhawk sorties were air-refuelled shortly after their departure and, whenever possible, the Grupo 1 KC-130H would remain on station to cover any emergency situations when the aircraft returned. Isolated sorties were temporarily abandoned and groups of fighter-bombers, often from multiple mainland bases, were scheduled to arrive over the target within a short space of time in order to create maximum confusion to British defences. On 21 May this strategy generally worked well and much British warship damage was sustained before a solid air defence umbrella was created. Attacks were undertaken by Grupo 4 and Grupo 5 Skyhawks, Grupo 6 Daggers and CANA Skyhawks but, again, Grupo 4's Skyhawks did not have a good day. It can be said with some certainty that no major damage was attributable to Grupo 4 attacks on 21 May but, again, the unit sustained losses.

Shortly after the successful Grupo 5 Skyhawk attack on 'Ardent' at 1555Z, a flight of four Grupo 4 aircraft was inbound at low level to Falkland Sound when it had the misfortune to be visually spotted by two 800 Sqdn Sea Harrier pilots who were vainly searching for the aircraft that had attacked 'Ardent'. The Skyhawks were travelling north-east in the vicinity of Chartres Settlement, West Falkland and once the Grupo 4 crews realised that there was an approaching CAP they took evasive action. Bombs and auxiliary fuel tanks were jettisoned and the flight broke to the south to escape at speed and low level. At 1605Z the two pursuing Sea Harriers independently fired AIM-9L's at two of the four aircraft which were, by then, in a wide echelon, about one mile across, heading west towards the coast of West Falkland. The first Sidewinder to impact was that fired by Lt Cdr Mike Blissett in the leading Sea Harrier, XZ496. It struck one of the aircraft in the centre of the formation and the rear of the Skyhawk was blown off in a bright fireball. The aircraft immediately nosed down and plunged into the ground trailing white smoke. It was followed by a second Skyhawk which had been hit in much the same fashion by the Sidewinder fired by the flight leader, Lt Cdr Neill Thomas in XZ492. The two Grupo 4 aircraft crashed almost simultaneously, several hundred yards apart, in an area south of Christmas Harbour, West Falkland. Neither pilot, Teniente Nestor Lopez in C-309 nor Primer Teniente Daniel Manzotti in C-325, survived the attack although Lopez was able to eject before his Skyhawk hit the ground. From very circumstantial evidence, it seems possible that it was Blissett who brought down Manzotti and that Thomas brought down Lopez but neither Sea Harrier pilot was aware of an ejection from either aircraft. A third Skyhawk in the formation was subsequently attacked by Blissett with cannon fire and, although it sustained some hits, the anonymous aircraft escaped and eventually reached San Julian safely. Thus Grupo 4 lost two aircraft with their pilots on 21 May.

No missions were flown to the Falklands on 22 May and poor weather the following day prevented any aircraft reaching the Falkland Sound area until after 1600Z. Earlier sorties had even failed to find their KC-130H tankers! Although Grupo 4 suffered no more losses on 23 May they again failed to achieve any successes against British shipping (indeed there is scant evidence of them penetrating the San Carlos Water area at all). By 24 May the British land and sea based air defence missiles and anti-aircraft guns were solidly in place in and around the beach-head at San Carlos Water and the surrounding area. Missions into the area were not simply hazardous — they were hair-raisingly dangerous! Both Grupo 4 and Grupo 5 had, by then, made subtle changes to their battle formations and it had become fairly standard procedure to launch six aircraft at a time in two waves of three, a few minutes apart (the Escuadrilla having effectively been reduced from four to three aircraft).

On some missions they were accompanied by a spare aircraft which would follow until the in-flight refuelling was successfully concluded. The change of style not only reflected a belief that two or three aircraft provided an air attack of optimum effectiveness, but must also have reflected aircraft and pilot availability problems.

Typical of those missions were the flights of Teniente Ricardo Lucero and Primer Teniente Jose Vazquez, launched during the afternoon of 24 May against ships in San Carlos Water. Lucero's flight of three attacked first and was fortunate to escape intact after an attempt at interception by a Sea Harrier CAP. Their warning calls were heard by Vazquez and his own "Jaguar" flight as they descended to low level over West Falkland for their run-in across the Falkland Sound. It is thought that theirs were the attacks that left unexploded 500lb bombs on both 'Sir Lancelot' and 'Sir Galahad' at about 1615Z, but for these first "successes" Grupo 4 again paid the ultimate price.

"Jaguar" flight met intense anti-aircraft fire over San Carlos Water and all three Skyhawks were hit by gunfire and shrapnel. The flight leader, Vazquez, and his number two, Alferez Martinez, were both losing fuel as they overflew West Falkland on their way home, but the most seriously damaged Skyhawk was that of the number three, Teniente Jorge Bono. All successfully cleared West Falkland and were at 21,000ft when it became clear that Bono would not be able to reach the waiting tanker. With radio communication difficulties further complicating the situation, Vazquez and Martinez watched helplessly as Bono's Skyhawk, C-305, progressively lost altitude and finally crashed into King George Bay. Although both Vazquez and Martinez had been frantically calling on Bono to eject he had not been seen to do so and, with their own critical fuel condition, neither man could remain in the area to search for the number three. With both men believing that he had not escaped, they alerted the SAR services and moved towards their tanker rendezvous. Both their aircraft had been damaged to the extent that the KC-130H was obliged to escort them to San Julian where they were safely recovered. No trace was found of Jorge Bono.

Argentina's national day, 25 May, dawned with Grupo 4 preparing for more strikes into San Carlos Water. Although the unit had been confident enough of success the previous day to mark at least one Skyhawk with a ship silhouette and the date "24.5.82", their achievements thus far had been minimal. Despite many determined efforts and the loss of five pilots, none of the sunken or severely damaged British warships had succumbed to Grupo 4 air attacks. Shortly before midday another mission took-off, led by the experienced Capitan Garcia. Garcia's "Toro" flight comprised five aircraft which, conceivably, may have been all the immediately available airworthy Skyhawks at San Julian. Their mission was again contained in one of the thoroughly disliked "Fragmentary Orders" which required them to launch against a target on the basis of recently acquired intelligence. Only essential flight planning data was normally available at the briefing and the pilots had to rely on the Port Stanley CIC for updated information. Target information was invariably inaccurate, incomplete or out of date.

"Toro" flight took-off safely but one Skyhawk soon aborted the mission with smoke in the cockpit to leave Garcia, Teniente Lucero (two), Teniente Paredi (three) and Alferez Gerardo Isaac (four) to continue in customary radio-silence. In clear weather "Toro" flight attacked British shipping in San Carlos Water in a rough line-astern pattern. By 25 May the British anti-aircraft systems were able to throw up an awesome barrage of gunfire and SAM's and, again, Grupo 4 could not escape unscathed. Lucero's Skyhawk, C-319, went first at about 1530Z when it disintegrated at low level, having been hit by multiple weapons, probably cannon and machine-gun fire, and conceivably by a Rapier blast. Lucero was extremely fortunate under the circumstances, for he successfully ejected from his Skyhawk and was rapidly recovered from the sea by sailors from nearby 'Fearless'. Wet and in pain from a damaged knee, he was recovered to the 'Fearless' half-deck in front of the waiting medical team and television cameras! The other three aircraft completed their run but both Garcia's and Isaac's Skyhawks were damaged in the process.

Garcia's aircraft, C-304, had experienced a weapons' hang-up during the bomb run but, as the three surviving Skyhawks made good an escape to the north-west, he was not in great difficulty and was able to talk to the others. Unbeknown to them, however, his aircraft was suddenly struck by a Sea Dart, fired from 'Coventry' at her picket position north-east of Pebble Island, and it broke up. He ejected from the crippled aircraft, which is presumed to have fallen in the sea where he also landed. It seems that neither side was aware of his survival and his body was eventually found, washed ashore in a dinghy on Golding Island, West Falkland, over a year later.

Isaac's aircraft was hit by 20mm cannon fire in the attack and he had lost much fuel by the time he and Paredi cleared West Falkland. He elected to press on to the tanker rendezvous rather than eject over either West Falkland or the open sea and it was with a critically low fuel state that he eventually met the KC-130H. The tanker then remained linked to his Skyhawk for the remainder of the flight to San Julian, for it was losing almost as much fuel as it was receiving from the "Chancha". However, on that occasion fortune smiled on Grupo 4 and eventually Isaac landed safely, with Paredi in close attendance. Isaac's Skyhawk, C-312, was duly decorated with the silhouette of a Type 22 frigate and the date "25.5.82" (which was a little odd because Isaac himself believed that he had damaged a Type 42 destroyer). However, in reality the mission had failed and no damage had been inflicted on any British ships by "Toro" flight.

Of all the missions undertaken by Argentine aircraft during the Falklands War, one of the most bitterly debated in Argentina is the one of 30 May in which a combined FAA and CANA strike was made against the British carrier group, far to the east of the Islands. Essentially the mission was a naval one, conceived to make the best possible use of the one remaining air-launched Exocet missile. It was originally to have been of the same nature as the successful mission of 25 May in which 'Atlantic Conveyor' had been destroyed by one of a pair of precisely launched Exocets after two Super Etendards had made a long over-water flight to get behind the British radars. The final Exocet mission was thus planned for 29 May, with the departure from Rio Grande scheduled for soon after 1500Z. As before, FAA KC-130H tanker support was to be fundamental to the mission.

It is clear from both FAA and, particularly, CANA records that the decision to add four A-4C Skyhawks to the mission was made at very short notice and that it was imposed on CANA. Without the FAA tankers there could be no mission at all and that was made abundantly clear to the naval headquarters at Espora by CdoFAS. It was reasoned that if CdoFAS must assist CANA then so should CANA assist CdoFAS. The revised plan was simple enough in theory although it must have been clear to CdoFAS that what was to have been a "safe" mission profile for the Super Etendards on their own, would now be highly hazardous, particularly for the FAA Skyhawks. The plan required four Grupo 4 Skyhawks to accompany the Super Etendards from Rio Grande, via a lengthy air-refuelling, to a point south and east of the Falklands from where they would run-in towards the British fleet from the south. The INS-equipped Super Etendards would undertake all navigation until the Exocet was launched, after which they would return home, leaving the Skyhawks to run-in behind the missile. Each Skyhawk would carry two 500lb bombs and would drop them on the damaged aircraft carrier. Radio and electronic-silence would only be broken when tactically necessary.

The plan was revealed to the Grupo 4 flight commanders at San Julian at about 1330Z on 29 May and the mission profile was explained to them. Their A-4C's would be used because they were air-refuellable and because they had a greater Liquid Oxygen capacity than the A-4B's of Grupo 5. Two flight commanders, Primer Teniente Ernesto Ureta and Primer Teniente Vazquez, reluctantly volunteered to lead the mission — they were experienced enough to appreciate the dangers involved. They were invited to select their wingmen but, amazingly, those chosen, Primer Teniente Omar Castillo and Alferez Isaac, were not told of the mission. They were simply informed that they would be two of a diversionary flight for a Super Etendard mission and that they would initially deploy to an alternate base. Thus five Grupo 4 Skyhawks left San Julian for Rio Grande shortly before 1545Z. The

fifth machine, that of Teniente Paredi, was to be a spare for the mission although the pilot was completely unaware of the fact. As recounted elsewhere, the news of the FAA participation was broken to the 2 Escuadrilla crews shortly before the five Skyhawks landed at Rio Grande. Castillo and Isaac were briefed on the ramp at Rio Grande soon after landing at about 1610Z.

The situation at Rio Grande was, therefore, less than satisfactory for both the FAA and CANA crews. While two shocked young Grupo 4 pilots and their troubled flight leaders attempted to assimilate their briefing in time for a 1730Z departure, the CANA pilots were trying to prevent their involvement in the mission! The pilots of 2 Escuadrilla were persuading their senior officers that the revised mission was impossible, if not absolutely, then certainly so in the demanded time-scale. As the KC-130H from Rio Gallegos moved southwards onto station, the Escuadron A-4C commander arrived by Learjet from San Julian with final fuel figures for the Skyhawks. However, in the meantime, and presumably unknown to the Skyhawk crews, CANA had been impressed by the 2 Escuadrilla protests that the planned mission was impossible without a longer briefing and, vitally, a second KC-130H on station. Thus CANA agreed to reconstitute the mission as originally planned — without the Grupo 4 Skyhawks! However, soon after that decision was taken the KC-130H commander announced that he could no longer hold station and the mission was cancelled. Phoenix-like, it was reinstated for the following day when it would comprise two Super Etendards, four Skyhawks and two KC-130H tankers. In the event, two of the Skyhawks were obliged to return to San Julian that evening for urgent repairs.

The mission was launched soon after 1530Z on 30 May with the Super Etendards using the radio call-sign "Ala" and the Skyhawks "Zonda". The four Skyhawks took-off five minutes after the CANA pair and all aircraft climbed to 20,000ft on a south-easterly heading to meet the KC-130H's. A complicated refuelling exercise then took place in which all the fighters repeatedly took on fuel from the tankers as the formation moved steadily east and then north-east to the separation point. Until that point was reached the navigation was undertaken by the KC-130H's and the fighters were led for some 190 miles to a point south-east of the last estimated position of the British carrier group operating in an area to the north-east of East Falkland. When the tankers left them the fighters descended to less than 100ft above the ocean and, in conditions of heavy cloud and rain, they continued on their course of 350° at a speed of 413kts. The leading Super Etendards made their customary "pop-ups" for target acquisition and course correction purposes and at last, at 1732Z, "Ala 1" broke radio-silence to announce that he had found the target and that he was launching his missile. Immediately the two Super Etendards made a sharp turn to the left and headed for home.

The Exocet had been launched from a range of between 20 and 24 miles — accounts differ — and at that distance the Grupo 4 pilots could not see any target, indeed the accelerating missile was soon out of sight, in spite of an increase in their speed to 489kts. Their formation was led by Vazquez with his wingman Ureta (three) close on his right side and to his rear. Castillo (two) was further away to the left of Vazquez and to the rear of the leading pair, while Isaac (four) was similarly placed on the right-hand side of the formation. "Zonda" flight was travelling at that moment flat out, at less than 100ft, over open ocean towards an invisible target. Suddenly, a single warship appeared on the horizon with smoke apparently coming from her hull, but much too distant for positive identification.

The formation headed on, intent on delivering further wounds to 'Invincible'. Unfortunately for "Zonda" flight it was not 'Invincible' but 'Avenger' that it was bearing down upon, and at that moment there was considerable activity on the frigate as her crew attempted to protect the ship from what had been correctly identified as an Exocet attack. It is now reasonably clear that the "large target" acquired by the Super Etendards' fire control radars was not the aircraft carrier 'Invincible' but probably the smaller warship 'Exeter' (or even 'Avenger'). At the moment of missile launch, 'Exeter' was to the north-west of the Super Etendards and, having been recently warned of their presence, she and all other ships in the main group 20 miles further north were turning stern-on to the attack and were firing chaff rockets in an effort to confuse the missile. It is also evident that 'Exeter' was about 20 miles from the launch point and that 'Invincible' was a further 20 miles to the north, well beyond the published range of the Exocet missile. 'Avenger' was some 10 miles south-east of 'Exeter' on picket duty and she would have been the first ship seen by the incoming Skyhawks. 'Exeter' launched her first Sea Dart at the incoming Exocet — but believed it to have missed — as 'Avenger' opened fire with her 4.5in gun at the incoming group, which she believed to be a force of two or three Exocet-equipped Super Etendards.

"Zonda" flight had sighted 'Avenger' at a range of about 10 miles but, within a few seconds and at a range of about nine miles from the intended target, the Skyhawk of Jose Vazquez was hit by the second Sea Dart launched from the unseen 'Exeter'. C-301's left wing separated from the fuselage and the fuel tank exploded. Vazquez had no chance to escape and was probably killed immediately. Horrified by what had happened, the others pressed on and prepared to run-in for a cannon and bomb attack on the "smoking" vessel in front of them. Suddenly, at about two miles and only a few seconds from the target, the Skyhawk C-310 of Omar Castillo disintegrated, almost certainly hit by a third Sea Dart from 'Exeter'. The explosion buffeted Isaac's aircraft and caused him to deviate slightly from his intended track but the two surviving Skyhawks passed over the frigate's stern at extremely low level and both dropped two 500lb bombs as they overflew. All missed, but the two pilots left the area at high speed absolutely convinced that 'Invincible' had been severely damaged.

Argentina's case that the carrier was so damaged rests entirely on the identification of the warship by Isaac and Ureta — all other evidence is circumstantial and owed much to wishful thinking. 'Avenger', in smoke and making violent course corrections to avoid the Skyhawks, was undamaged by the attack. What became of the Exocet is far from clear, but no British ship was hit on 30 May. The optimistic claim by 'Avenger' to have destroyed an Exocet with its 4.5in gun during the attack is probably explained by the range at which the "kill" was supposedly achieved.

"Eight miles out" looks suspiciously like the distance at which Vazquez was lost. Perhaps it was her gun that brought him down and not the Sea Dart, but that also seems unlikely.

The surviving Skyhawks successfully met the two KC-130H's at the appointed location at an altitude of 16,500ft. Their refuelling was difficult, with both pilots initially unable to get their probes into the tankers' drogues — the stress of their mission had begun to have a physical effect on Ureta and Isaac. However, "Zonda 3" and "Zonda 4" were ultimately safely recovered at Rio Grande after 3 hours and 47 minutes in the air and their pilots later returned to a heroes welcome at San Julian. At least one of the Skyhawks involved, C-321, was subsequently marked with a large red 'Invincible' silhouette and the date "30.5.82".

FAA operations were somewhat muted during the first week of June, the result of several factors. Attrition and the need to review tactics in the light of British successes were obviously significant, but continuing poor weather and the domination of the Falklands' skies by the Sea Harrier CAP's also had a generally inhibiting influence. Finally, on 8 June CdoFAS launched a series of missions designed to sink or damage British shipping known to be putting troops ashore in the Fitzroy area of East Falkland. Grupo 4's role was part of a carefully orchestrated series of attacks involving most of the available FAA combat aircraft. Following successful early attacks by Grupo 5 Skyhawks on the auxiliaries 'Sir Galahad' and 'Sir Tristram' in Port Pleasant and Grupo 6's Dagger attack on 'Plymouth' in Falkland Sound, CdoFAS ordered two late evening strikes on the still-burning auxiliaries and local troop dispositions. Grupo 4 was briefed to hit any British troop concentrations found around Port Pleasant or close inshore. In its determination to slow down the British advance, CdoFAS made the unwise decision to send aircraft into an area which was now heavily defended and thoroughly alerted to the FAA's intentions after the day's earlier disasters. The Grupo 5 flight of four A-4B Skyhawks ("Mazo" flight), briefed to attack before the Grupo 4 flight, paid a high price for that misjudgement and it was with sheer luck that the Grupo 4 Skyhawks survived their evening mission.

By the time that the order to launch the final strike was received at San Julian at 1840Z, the "alert" flight of Capitan Mario Cafaratti, Teniente Zattara, Teniente Paredi and Alferez Codrington had already decided that there would be no further missions that night. It was obviously too late and too dark. CdoFAS had other ideas, however, and at about 1900Z "Yunque" flight (some sources refer to it as "Tigre" flight) was airborne, armed with "anti-personnel" bombs and on its way to meet the KC-130H tanker. The journey was uneventful although, occasionally, the setting sun burst through the cloud cover to dazzle them. Once over Choiseul Sound, the brightly burning 'Sir Galahad' made navigation simple.

Their attack was made line-astern to the accompaniment of a "firework display" from tracer ammunition and SAM exhausts and all the Skyhawks received hits from shrapnel and small-arms fire. Cafaratti, believing that he had been badly damaged, turned to the south to escape over the sea where he felt that he could eject safely but,

# A-4C SKYHAWK C-321 GRUPO 4 DE CAZA

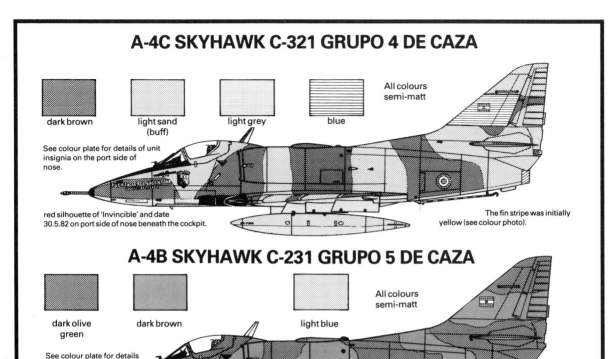

dark brown

light sand (buff)

light grey

blue

All colours semi-matt

See colour plate for details of unit insignia on the port side of nose.

red silhouette of 'Invincible' and date 30.5.82 on port side of nose beneath the cockpit.

The fin stripe was initially yellow (see colour photo).

# A-4B SKYHAWK C-231 GRUPO 5 DE CAZA

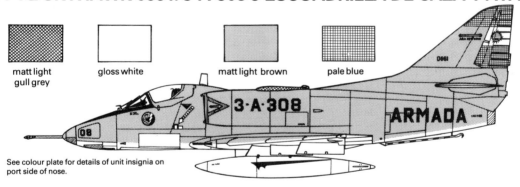

dark olive green

dark brown

light blue

All colours semi-matt

See colour plate for details of unit insignia on the port side of nose.

Two yellow ship silhouettes on the nose (port side only) beneath the serial.

# A-4Q SKYHAWK 0661/3-A-308 3 ESCUADRILLA DE CAZA Y ATAQUE

matt light gull grey

gloss white

matt light brown

pale blue

See colour plate for details of unit insignia on port side of nose.

# SUPER ETENDARD 0753/3-A-203 2 ESCUADRILLA DE CAZA Y ATAQUE

gloss dark blue-grey

gloss white

gloss pale blue

See colour plate for details of unit insignia on the port side of nose. Yellow ship silhouette on the nose (port side only) representing attacks on 'Sheffield' and 'Atlantic Conveyor'. Small red crosses superimposed on the silhouettes indicate destruction of the vessels.

Caution: with the exception of the Super Etendard, all colours are approximate as they have not been physically checked against any British, American or other accepted paint standards.

once at 6,000ft he realised that his Skyhawk was responding normally and he turned for home. Zattara and Paredi also turned south, passing near the burning ships, to escape from anti-aircraft fire while Codrington broke north to escape over Mount Kent. There he encountered fierce ground fire and his aircraft was extremely fortunate to escape without serious damage. The flight was totally fragmented and Cafaratti was certain that both Paredi and Codrington had been lost because he only had communications with Zattara. Whilst worrying about that, Cafaratti then realised that he had an oxygen starvation problem and he was obliged to make the rest of his sortie below 20,000ft. Paredi and Codrington's aircraft had fuel tanks punctured by ground-fire and their fuel states were critical when they were met by the KC-130H's (which had earlier spent a dramatic few minutes recovering the sole survivor of the Grupo 5 "Mazo" flight). Both Skyhawks were leaking badly and were "carried" to San Julian by the tankers. They disengaged shortly before reaching the runway threshold but one was in such a bad state that it actually flamed-out with dry tanks after taxying onto the Grupo 4 ramp. Thus all aircraft returned home safely from a mission described locally as "chaotic". It is perhaps understandable that many British soldiers are firmly convinced that that evening they brought down Skyhawks from "Yunque" flight.

No more significant combat missions appear to have been tasked to Grupo 4 after 8 June and it may be that that was their last day of action. Circumstantial evidence suggests that with at least three of "Yunque" flight requiring repairs on 9 June, the Escuadron A-4C San Julian may have then been reduced to fewer than four airworthy aircraft. Their six weeks of war had seen 106 combat missions planned for the Grupo 4 aircraft but probably fewer than 65 had actually reached the intended targets. Nine aircraft were lost in combat with eight of their pilots killed.

The War is thought to have left the FAA with only seven airworthy A-4C Skyhawks and although Grupo 4 managed to make Mendoza look very active when the base was occasionally visited by foreigners in 1982, there were clearly too few aircraft for a viable first-line combat unit. It thus came as no surprise when it was announced in December 1983 that the surviving A-4C's would be consolidated with the remaining A-4B's at Villa Reynolds with Grupo 5. Grupo 4 was, by 1984, due to have undergone a re-equipment programme which should have seen it reconstituted at Mendoza with Mirage IIICJ's but, at the time of writing in early 1985, this had not been confirmed.

---

*Grupo 4 de Caza pilots deployed to San Julian and known to have flown combat missions included:*

*Capitan M.J.Cafaratti; Capitan J.O.Garcia (KIA); Primer Teniente O.J.Castillo (KIA); Primer Teniente D.F.Manzotti (KIA); Primer Teniente E.R.Ureta; Primer Teniente J.D.Vazquez (KIA); Teniente J.A.Bono (KIA); Teniente J.E.Casco (KIA); Teniente J.R.Farias (KIA); Teniente N.E.Lopez (KIA); Teniente R.Lucero; Teniente Paredi; Teniente Zattara; Alferez Codrington; Alferez G.G.Isaac; Alferez Martinez.*

---

# GRUPO 5 DE CAZA

Between 1966 and 1970 50 refurbished A-4B Skyhawks were supplied to the FAA by the United States for service with Grupo 5 de Caza, the flying element of V Brigada Aerea, based at Villa Reynolds, San Luis. These venerable little aircraft, identified as A-4P models for export to Argentina, were, for many years, the backbone of the FAA but by, March 1982, attrition had taken its toll and their numbers had been much reduced. Although at least one source has claimed that a total of 36 aircraft survived to 1982, that figure seems high and in reality the total was probably in the order of 30. Other sources have suggested a total of only 26 but that figure may well have taken no account of a handful of Skyhawks believed to have been withdrawn from active service. Efforts to augment the survivors with more aircraft from the United States in the late seventies were frustrated by the embargo on new deliveries and spare parts, although by late 1981 hopes were high that 29 surplus USN A-4B's, stored in the USA and earmarked for Argentina, would be released to the FAA in 1982. Of equal concern was the supply of 32 similarly held J65 engines which were desperately needed to keep the remaining Grupo 5 aircraft airworthy. All hopes of the FAA receiving these items were finally dashed during April 1982 when the United States announced its intention to support the British cause.

Grupo 5 de Caza (G5C) had been the strongest element of the FAA's combat forces for many years and, until the arrival in service of the Dagger with Grupo 6 de Caza, it had been the largest first-line unit. In March 1982 "Los Halcones" (The Hawks) was still technically a two squadron Grupo (with the IV and V Escuadrones de Caza Bombardeo) but, for operational purposes, its organisation was heavily dependent on a "flight" (Escuadrilla) concept. Within Grupo 5 there were several permanently constituted Escuadrillas, each of which comprised four men who flew as a unit. When Grupo 5 ultimately went to war this concept was used with some success although losses and fatigue inevitably changed their composition.

When it became apparent in early April that the FAA might need to use Grupo 5 in combat, it has been suggested that only 12 A-4B's were immediately ready, although another 14 were in various states of unserviceability and storage at Villa Reynolds and Rio Cuarto. A few more A-4B's required major rework before they could be considered combat-ready. That virtually all of the unserviceable machines were later made airworthy can largely be credited to FAA ingenuity and determination, but does suggest that there was third-party help with the supply of spare parts. Some aircraft were ultimately pressed into combat without items of avionics (including IFF) and thus these "austere" Skyhawks were always flown as wingmen to fully equipped flight leaders. In the later stages of the War, the increased incidence of communication equipment failures combined with the basic shortages to produce several dangerous incidents.

The initial deployment of Grupo 5 took place on 14 April when the first of 12 aircraft were flown to Rio Gallegos where they became known as the "Escuadron A-4B Rio Gallegos". All aircraft deployed at that time retained Grupo 5's standard peace-time dark camouflage colours with light blue undersides. By 30 April the unit was at full war readiness and, with the British fleet within close striking distance of the Falklands, action was expected at very short notice. The integrated plan conceived by CdoFAS as a response to the anticipated attack required Grupo 5 to launch 12 sorties in three flights of four against targets which would be identified by the Port Stanley CIC. Ships operating close inshore would be attacked by the Skyhawks and other FAA fighter-bombers under CIC control with final instructions being passed to the aircraft as they approached the Falklands. Such a series of attacks could be launched at any time during daylight once the anticipated British landings had commenced. It was on 1 May that the first air and sea attacks were made by Britain but, although some special forces were put ashore, Argentina made the mistake of assuming that full-scale landings had been initiated. That error directly influenced Grupo 5's missions, and indeed those of the other units that day, for the Skyhawks were dispatched to seek out ships wrongly assumed to be in the close proximity of Port Stanley. There were, of course, one or two in the area but the Skyhawks failed to find them and Grupo 5's day was consequently one of confusion and frustration.

That only 12 Grupo 5 sorties were planned by CdoFAS for 1 May is probably indicative of an inability to find many more than 12 serviceable A-4B's (there was no pilot shortage), while still launching the customary battle formation of the four-aircraft Escuadrilla. Each flight was to be led by an experienced leader and, for the anti-shipping mission, each Skyhawk was limited to two 500lb bombs. Each flight was to be provided with top-cover escort from Grupo 8 Mirages or Grupo 6 Daggers. The Skyhawks would rely on their own fuel, in-flight refuelling being considered unnecessary (and perhaps would not have been available anyway) because the sortie distance was not considered critical.

The first mission of the morning was given to the highly experienced Capitan Hugo del Valle Palaver and his "Topo" flight comprised Teniente Galvez, Primer Teniente Luciano Guadagnini and Alferez Hugo Gomez, his usual numbers two, three and four. "Topo" flight took-off after the first Sea Harrier attacks on Port Stanley and Goose Green and for its mission it was provided with top-cover from the Mirage section of Capitan Gustavo Garcia Cuerva and Primer Teniente Carlos Perona ("Dardo" flight).

Palaver led his flight towards the Islands and was eventually informed by the Port Stanley CIC controller that a target had been identified and that it was to the north-east of the town. "Topo" flight was duly directed towards a point some 30 miles distant but then the controller horrified Palaver by telling him that the target was at 20,000ft! In the confusion of the moment the controller had vectored the Skyhawks to intercept a pair of Sea Harriers (almost certainly the 801 Sqdn aircraft of Lt Cdr Eyton-Jones and Flt Lt Barton), inbound to East Falkland from the British carrier group. The listening "Dardo" flight was low on fuel but, realising that the Grupo 5 aircraft were in grave danger even if they broke away immediately, turned and accelerated to put themselves between the Skyhawks and the Sea Harrier CAP. Palaver had already ordered his flight to dive sharply to get below acquisition height of the British ship-borne radars but, perhaps naively, he did not call for jettisoning of the underwing tanks or even bombs, reasoning that they would be needed later. However, the Sea Harriers did not engage the six FAA aircraft (apparently they thought that they were all Mirages) and all the Skyhawks and Mirages were safely recovered at Rio Gallegos with virtually dry tanks. The pilots and local FAA commanders were immediately involved in an investigation to ascertain how the mission had been so badly executed and how such a near disaster could be avoided in the future. However, before that was concluded a second and ultimately equally inglorious mission was getting under way.

"Trueno" flight was led by Capitan Pablo Carballo and he, too, was able to take his usual wingmen, Teniente Carlos Rinke, Primer Teniente Cachon and Alferez Leonardo Carmona, on their first combat mission. Carmona's sortie was a short one, however, for he was forced to return early to Rio Gallegos with unspecified technical problems, leaving the others to press on in search of British shipping to the north-east of East Falkland. While en route, Carballo listened to (and subsequently became involved in) exchanges between the Port Stanley controller and Grupo 4's "Lana" flight flying from San Julian. As a result of Carballo's intervention, the four San Julian Skyhawks were able to avoid another approaching Sea Harrier CAP. Carballo eventually found his target, a ship at sea to the north of Port Stanley, and he was able to make a cannon attack before dropping both bombs over the vessel. Both Rinke and Cachon followed suit but it was realised that all three Skyhawks had missed with their bombs and, after a second cannon attack, Carballo led "Trueno" flight safely home. The following morning a party of senior FAA officers arrived at Rio Gallegos and informed Carballo that his target, which he had fortunately failed to damage, had been an Argentine ship!

1 May was a bad day for the FAA in virtually all respects with none of the combat units having achieved any significant success but suffering losses and, in certain cases, some considerable embarrassment. Grupo 5 (whose third mission had achieved as little as the others) survived without damage but with much hurt pride and a resolution to do better next time. Unfortunately, the next few days were frustrating, for the poor weather prevented Grupo 5 launching any further sorties against the British warships that were soon bombarding the Port Stanley area on a regular basis. However, the dangers of over enthusiasm were brought home sharply on 9 May when

two Grupo 4 Skyhawks were lost in poor weather over the Falklands.

Eventually, on 12 May, short-notice orders were received by Grupo 5 to launch aircraft against two British ships engaged in daylight bombardment off Port Stanley. The Grupo 5 crews had been on standing "alerts" as complete flights and thus the two available Escuadrillas were those ordered into action. It was "Cuna" flight that was launched first, led by Primer Teniente Oscar Bustos with wingmen Teniente Jorge Ibarlucea, Teniente Mario Nivoli and Alferez Jorge Vazquez. They were airborne shortly before 1600Z and were followed out of Rio Gallegos thirty minutes later by "Oro" flight comprising Capitan Zelaya, Teniente Juan Arraras, Primer Teniente Fausto Gavazzi and Alferez Dellepiane. Skyhawk sorties to East Falkland were still being undertaken without the benefit of in-flight refuelling and a mission to the Port Stanley area left little margin for error in fuel management. That, in turn, put pressure on the attack itself because there was little time available to make a second pass in the event of an aborted first strike. "Cuna" flight, however, had no difficulty in finding the two warships and Bustos elected to attack in two pairs, each taking one of the vessels.

Their arrival had been long detected by the British, however, and the Seawolf equipped 'Brilliant' had prepared herself to meet the incoming fighters while 'Glasgow' had interrupted her bombardment. At 1644Z the Skyhawks attacked at speed and at low level but, over open water, the Seawolf system performed perfectly and both Bustos and Ibarlucea were killed when their aircraft, C-246 and C-208 respectively, were destroyed by the missiles. Nivoli, following in C-206, also lost his life when his aircraft crashed into the sea as he desperately sought to avoid another missile. Only the shaken Vazquez survived the run and, although able to drop both his 500lb bombs, he caused no damage to either ship.

As Vazquez made his way home, Zelaya prepared to make the second attack on the ships at 1715Z. "Oro" flight had approached Port Stanley by way of Goose Green and Fitzroy and, like "Cuna", had no difficulty finding the targets. Thus, in mid-afternoon, the four Skyhawks ran-in on the two warships. Because of a misunderstanding within the flight, Zelaya, Gavazzi and Dellepiane all made for 'Glasgow', leaving Arraras to attack 'Brilliant' on his own. Fortunately, luck was on their side that afternoon, for the Seawolf system on 'Brilliant' malfunctioned at the worst possible moment for the British ships, leaving them without their air defence missile cover. Although both warships put up considerable gunfire they caused no damage to the Skyhawks which were then able to bomb both of them with some ease. 'Brilliant' experienced the nearest of misses as Arraras released his two 500lb bombs, only to see them bounce off the water's surface, clear the ship and then fall harmlessly into the sea. 'Glasgow' was less fortunate. Gavazzi saw one of his bombs strike her amidships near the water-line and as he climbed away beyond the ship he was aware of an explosion. In fact his bomb had passed through the ship and out the other side before detonating. Although the bomb's passage through an engine room had not damaged any critical structures or fittings, the holes made were large and close to the water-line. Despite rapid and ingenious repairs, 'Glasgow' had effectively been dam-

aged to an unacceptable degree and, although she was subsequently to spend several days ostensibly operational with the Task Force, she was returned to Britain at the earliest opportunity.

Jubilant at the success, "Oro" flight made its way home to Rio Gallegos but, in his moment of triumph, Fausto Gavazzi lost his life in the most unfortunate circumstances. For reasons that are not clear — as his aircraft was not thought to have been damaged — Gavazzi passed dangerously low over the Darwin area and was brought down by the radar-controlled Argentine anti-aircraft guns sited round the airfield. The aircraft hit the ground hard and flat on a promontory about one and one half miles south of Goose Green settlement and exploded on impact, the wreckage being spread over several hundred yards. Gavazzi is thought to have ejected from the Skyhawk before it impacted but he did not survive. The largest part of C-248 was still present in 1984 where it came down, in a field known as "Goats Rincon".

Arraras and Dellepiane searched briefly for their colleague but, still ignorant of what had happened, they returned home. The final stages of their flight were particularly difficult because of salt encrustations on their windscreens that had accumulated during the low-level run over the sea and had dried, considerably restricting visibility. The landing at Rio Gallegos was thus extremely hazardous, indeed Vazquez had earlier careered off the runway with the same problem (fortunately without injury to himself), but "Oro" flight got down safely and reached the apron area without further incident.

12 May had been a day of great significance for the Rio Gallegos Skyhawks, with Grupo 5 the first FAA unit to have effectively "taken out" a British warship. It must be said, however, that CdoFAS was hopelessly confused about precisely what had been achieved. Grupo 5 believed that 'Brilliant' had been sunk in the attack and, accordingly, at least one aircraft, C-239, was so marked and dated. The loss of four aircraft with their pilots was a serious and sad loss but some important tactical lessons had been learned by CdoFAS and, perhaps, some of Grupo 5's later successes were built on the experience of 12 May.

For the next week the unit continued to be on standby at Rio Gallegos but, while there existed the prospect of short-notice strikes against the British fleet, most minds were on the long anticipated landings that were only days away. When that happened Grupo 5 would fly anti shipping missions, but they would be planned with far greater sophistication than were those of 1 May. Among some significant changes was the planned use of KC-130H tankers for missions further east than Falkland Sound (although that was subsequently modified to include those sorties to the Sound itself). To avoid the dangers of bird-strikes, windscreen salting and striking the sea through basic pilot error, it was resolved to fly only the final run-in at the warship targets at extremely low level. The FAA squadrons appear to have decided before 21 May that such attacks would be made at right-angles to the vessels rather than from the oblique, stern-on "textbook" angles favoured and well practised by the CANA fighter-bomber units.

The morning of 21 May broke murky and cold at Rio

Gallegos and, although at command level there had been rumours of British naval operations close to the Islands during the night, Grupo 5 awoke to a routine situation. That rapidly changed when it was confirmed from Port Stanley that British warships were in Falkland Sound and that landings were apparently under way. In one respect that was welcome news to CdoFAS because a mission to the west coast of East Falkland was an easier undertaking than would have been the case had the landings been relatively near to Port Stanley. By the time Grupo 5 was ready to launch its first sorties that morning, the available intelligence data was still incomplete, but it was already clear that the British were in the San Carlos Water area in considerable strength.

As part of a carefully considered and co-ordinated strike, Grupo 5 was tasked to launch six aircraft which would ultimately run-in over a target a few minutes after eight Grupo 6 Daggers from San Julian and Rio Grande. In that way it was reasoned, correctly as events proved, that the British defences would be confused and perhaps even swamped by waves of attacking aircraft arriving on different headings within a very short space of time. Accordingly, "Leo" and "Orion" flights took-off from Rio Gallegos soon after 1200Z to follow the marginally earlier "Cuna", "Nandu" and "Perro" Grupo 6 Dagger flights from the other bases. "Leo" was led by Primer Teniente Filippini with wingmen Teniente Vicente Autiero and Alferez Vottero while "Orion" was led by Primer Teniente Mariano Velasco with wingmen Teniente Fernando Robledo and Teniente Mariano Osses. Each Skyhawk was armed with cannon and a single 1,000lb bomb, there having been something of a change of mind since 12 May about the optimum anti-shipping ordnance for Grupo 5's A-4B mission profile. The flight to the Falklands was made in generally clear weather but without the benefit of in-flight refuelling which had not been planned for the mission. No technical or navigational difficulties were encountered en route. The Daggers attacked on schedule at about 1325Z and both 'Antrim' and 'Broadsword' were damaged in the process.

At 1330Z "Leo" and "Orion" swept in from the north at low level at an unidentified frigate off Fanning Head which, in the few seconds available to them, impressed the Grupo 5 pilots as a suitable target. She was 'Argonaut', already slightly damaged by an earlier rocket attack from a lone CANA MB-339A from Stanley Airport, and Grupo 5's efficiently executed attack was to effectively put her out of action for all but static air defence purposes for the remainder of the War. The Skyhawks flew low and used the local hills for cover to defeat the British radar-guided SAM's. In spite of 40mm gunfire and the launch of at least one Seacat missile, the Grupo 5 aircraft put two bombs into 'Argonaut' and had others narrowly miss the ship. One bomb entered the boiler room and the other penetrated the forward magazine where two Seacat heads partly exploded. The damage was serious and, after dark, the disabled 'Argonaut' was towed into San Carlos Water where she was to remain, effective only as a gun platform, for some days until she departed for the TRALA and, eventually, the United Kingdom. "Leo" and "Orion" had achieved a significant, if not an immediately obvious, success and had done so without aircraft loss.

While 'Argonaut' was under attack by "Leo" and "Orion" flights Capitan Carballo was preparing to take his Escuadrilla up from Rio Gallegos as part of the next wave of sorties. They were scheduled to attack at about 1600Z in conjunction with an ill-fated Grupo 4 Skyhawk flight, each unit contributing four aircraft. Carballo's flight was given the call-sign "Mula" for the mission and his wingmen, as on previous occasions, were Teniente Rinke, Primer Teniente Cachon and Aleferez Carmona. It was to be an air-refuelled operation with the rendezvous taking place on the outbound sector. The flight was soon reduced to three, however, when Cachon's aircraft experienced fuel transfer problems and he was obliged to return home.

"Mula's" course took a northerly track with the flight due to cross West Falkland, passing between Mount Adam and Mount Maria, before running in on the British ships from the north. However, as the flight, by then at low level, approached West Falkland Rinke began to experience fuel transfer problems because his auxiliary tanks were not feeding the main tank smoothly. After a brief and somewhat clipped conversation with Carballo (the mission should have been in radio-silence) Rinke was ordered to return home. Carballo and Carmona pressed on but were dismayed to find that cloud extended to ground level in the Mount Maria area and there was no question of them continuing on their original track. They turned south towards a more broken cloud cover and eventually crossed the coast in the vicinity of Swan Island where they immediately came upon the unexpected sight of a cargo vessel in the Sound, close inshore to West Falkland. The two Skyhawks made a careful run-in on the ship and both opened fire with their cannon and, at high speed and low level, they prepared to release their bombs. At the last moment Carballo realised that something was amiss, there being no defensive fire, and he called for Carmona not to bomb. The call came too late, however, and Carmona's bomb dropped towards the 'Rio Carcarana'. Whether or not it hit is not known, but it would not have mattered a great deal for the Argentine freighter had been abandoned in Port King several days earlier after having been caught by a Sea Harrier attack. Naturally, that was not realised at the time and Carballo was left, on his own, over Falkland Sound with only one bomb available for the British fleet.

He continued to the north-east and quickly came upon the isolated silhouette of 'Ardent' in Grantham Sound, where she was still engaged in the periodic bombardment of the Goose Green airfield area. Carballo's attack was swift and direct and 'Ardent' was only able to throw up 20mm and GPMG gunfire at him as she began to turn. His bomb narrowly missed the frigate, passing over her, and, in ignorance of a Sea Harrier CAP on its way towards him, Carballo turned for safety and home. His solo attack on 'Ardent' had taken place at 1555Z. The pursuing 800 Sqdn Sea Harriers did not reach him, instead finding the inbound Grupo 4 flight (with devastating result), and Carballo eventually reached the safety of Rio Gallegos, without further incident, where he was welcomed by his three wingmen. It must be said, however, that Grupo 5 was much confused about what "Mula" had achieved. The loss of 'Ardent', later in the day, was clearly the achievement of the CANA Skyhawks in their attack at 1815Z but that was not known to Grupo 5 until some time after the event and the unit believed that the frigate had been sunk by Carballo. Similarly, the unidentified freighter was optimistically rumoured to have been a British support ship. Nevertheless, the day was clearly a successful one, with 'Argonaut' disabled and all aircraft safely recovered to Rio Gallegos with no worse damage than a birdstrike to Vottero's Skyhawk.

Poor weather on 22 May prevented further operations but it had improved by the following day although, by then, the British defences had been much strengthened and the chance of actually stopping the landings by air attack had really disappeared. CdoFAS planned 46 sorties for the day, fewer than on 21 May, but in the event the weather did not clear properly until mid-afternoon and it was not until 1650Z that the first FAA aircraft appeared over San Carlos Water. They were Grupo 5 Skyhawks and they achieved the ultimate success sought — a warship sunk.

A two-flight, six-aircraft mission had been planned with Capitan Carballo, Teniente Rinke and Primer Teniente Cachon combining with Capitan Palaver, Primer Teniente Guadagnini and Alferez Gomez, but, finally, only four aircraft were actually launched as "Nene" flight. Cachon was injured in a freak accident when he slipped and fell from his Skyhawk's wing and, although saved from serious injury by the gymnastics of the ground crew, he damaged an arm on the cannon and was unfit to fly the mission. Palaver's aircraft developed trouble before departure and he was obliged to return to the ramp, leaving Carballo to take the two groups out as a consolidated flight. The weather was "sad and grey" (to quote the flight leader) and, because of an unnoticed flight planning error, the air-refuelling took place in cloud well to the east of its intended position, very close to the west coast of West Falkland. "Nene" flight subsequently approached San Carlos from the south-west and, as the Skyhawks passed over Grantham Sound, they overflew 'Antelope' Flight's Lynx (XZ723), travelling north-east back to the ship. The Skyhawks ignored the helicopter and continued towards San Carlos Water, passing north across the mouth of the anchorage. Using all their recently acquired knowledge of the area, the Grupo 5 men went north before turning to run-in on San Carlos Water from behind the Verde Mountains and, after briefly reconnoitring the bay, Carballo and Gomez ran-in fast and low at 'Antelope'.

Argentine and British accounts of the subsequent events are inconsistent and both are confusing, but it seems clear that both Carballo and Gomez survived the first pass and that their strike put the first of the unexploded 1,000lb bombs into the aft part of the ship on the starboard side. Carballo's Skyhawk was, however, badly damaged in the attack by small-arms and cannon fire as well as a proximity blast from a SAM that he believed was fired from an adjacent warship. It exploded beneath his left wing after he had passed over 'Antelope' and, for some moments, he was prepared to eject as it appeared that he must crash into the sea. The Skyhawk somehow stayed airborne and as Carballo considered his situation, and indeed was narrowly missed again by a second missile, he heard Guadagnini and Rinke announcing their intention of attacking what they (mistakenly) believed to be

'Canberra'. Cdr Tobin, Captain of 'Antelope', has described how a second pair of Skyhawks, presumably those of Carballo and Gomez who were still in the area, made a distant second pass but were driven off by 4.5in gunfire and a Seacat. That account appears to be consistent with Carballo's description of his second narrow escape after which he headed north and then west at high speed and low level.

The next attack on 'Antelope', which put another unexploded bomb in the forward part of the ship, followed moments later and looks certain to have come from Guadagnini and Rinke. Guadagnini, in C-242, did not survive the mission and although accounts of his death are confused, it seems that he was lost to a SAM during the course of, or immediately after, the attack on 'Antelope'. Both Rapier and a 'Broadsword' Seawolf have been credited with a Skyhawk's destruction in that attack but it should not be overlooked that most British accounts of the incident firmly believe that Carballo's aircraft was lost in the first pass and that some vivid accounts of SAM hits are entangled with the myth of that particular claim. Carballo was able to nurse his damaged Skyhawk home and, after a safe landing, the post-flight inspection revealed a bent fin on an underwing tank caused by shrapnel or, consistent with British accounts, perhaps by impact with the frigate's mast top. Rinke and Gomez also reached Rio Gallegos safely and the day closed with Grupo 5 mourning the loss of another senior pilot, their first over San Carlos Water. Guadagnini was revenged, so to speak, for overnight 'Antelope' exploded and, early on 24 May, she sank close to the spot where Grupo 5 had attacked her.

On 23 May only some 20 or so FAA aircraft reached the San Carlos area and on the following day even fewer, just 12, were able to get past the Sea Harrier CAP's to reach the British bridgehead. Grupo 5's contribution to the effort of 24 May consisted of two flights of three aircraft of which five ultimately reached their targets. "Chispa" and "Nene" flights left Rio Gallegos at 1400Z and 1402Z but they were unexpectedly reduced to five when the "Chispa" flight leader, thought to have been Primer Teniente Danilo Bolzan, accidently armed and jettisoned his bombs shortly after the in-flight refuelling. His wingmen, Teniente Luis Cervera and Alferez Marcelo Moroni, thus joined "Nene" to form a five-aircraft flight. Bolzan's embarrassment must have been acute for "Nene" was led by the veteran commander of Grupo 5, Vicecomodoro Mariel, undertaking his first combat mission of the War. His wingmen were Primer Teniente Hector Sanchez and Teniente Roca.

The flight took a track to the south of West Falkland and then turned north-east abeam Darwin up Falkland Sound. In fairly good weather the flight could glimpse Port Stanley away to the east. Sightseeing was brief, however, for the flight quickly descended to low level for the run-in from the south and, at about 1500Z, they made what appears to have been the first attack of the day on the British warships and auxiliaries in San Carlos Water. It caught many of them unawares and in the following moments of pandemonium on board the ships, 'Fort Austin' and others experienced near misses from the Skyhawks' bombs. However, by 24 May, the British Rapier batteries were well established and well practised and four missiles (possibly including ship-launched Blowpipes) passed very close to the aircraft of Mariel and Roca. Moroni's Skyhawk was actually hit by gunfire but remained in the air, as did those of Sanchez and Cervera. Despite the very considerable anti-aircraft fire, all five Skyhawks survived the attack (contrary to the widespread belief of the British) and, ultimately, all reformated for a safe flight home at 40,000ft. The post-flight debriefing suggests that Mariel, Sanchez and Roca attacked an unidentified "frigate", causing no significant damage, while Cervera and Moroni had attacked an auxiliary (probably 'Fort Austin').

25 May, Argentina's national day, was to be one of high drama, marked for the British by the loss of two important ships, each in controversial circumstances. The involvement of Grupo 5 in one of these incidents was considerable and began, unusually, with a pre-dawn mission from Rio Gallegos. CdoFAS was aware that two warships, 'Coventry' and 'Broadsword', were providing the British forces with excellent radar intelligence from a picket position to the north of Pebble Island. Capitan Palaver's flight was thus briefed to seek out and attack those ships, its early departure perhaps catching them unawares. It is believed that the Skyhawks were aided by a reconnaissance C-130 flight *[described in detail in the Grupo 1 de Transporte Aereo/Escuadron I section]* whose purpose was to relay a more precise position of the ships to Palaver as he approached Pebble Island. The mission, which also involved an unusual night refuelling from a KC-130H, was stopped short at about 1230Z when Palaver's Skyhawk, C-244, was destroyed at long range by a Sea Dart launched from 'Coventry'. Palaver was killed and the attack was abandoned, leaving 'Coventry' to continue as radar picket and missile platform. Later in the day Grupo 5 again tried to reach her.

It was the intention of CdoFAS to launch two flights of three Grupo 5 Skyhawks to attack 'Coventry' and her "goalkeeper" 'Broadsword' at about 1800Z and preparations to that end commenced at Rio Gallegos during the morning. The two ships (some 15 miles to the north of Pebble Island) were under constant Argentine observation and the relative closeness of the vessels meant that the mission would not require outbound air-refuelling. Moreover, each Skyhawk would carry three 1,000lb bombs, a bomb load that was not normally possible. "Vulcan" flight launched first led by the doughty Capitan Carballo, but only Teniente Rinke took-off with him because Alferez Carmona's aircraft was declared unserviceable at the last moment. "Zeus" flight was likewise affected and Primer Teniente Velasco and Alferez Jorge Barrionuevo were obliged to continue without Teniente Osses who was forced to return to Rio Gallegos soon after departure. The mission was aided by a support aircraft, thought to have been a C-130, which provided information on the position of the two warships, while the Port Stanley CIC continued to feed it details of any Sea Harrier activity in the area.

Carballo's flight plan took him on a central track to approach Pebble Island from the west but, by the time he reached King George Bay, windscreen salting was causing him some difficulty. "Zeus" flight took a more northerly track, passing over the Passage Islands en route Pebble Island. As both flights descended, the CIC warned them of local Sea Harrier activity but the 800 Sqdn CAP was never to trouble them. Unknown to the Grupo 5 pilots as they caught their first distant glimpse of their targets, the 'Broadsword' Seawolf system had locked on to "Vulcan" flight, and the Sea Harriers, regarded as superfluous and in danger of hazarding themselves, were directed away from the area. Carballo's luck (and luck it certainly was) remained with him, for as he and Rinke ran-in on 'Broadsword', the more westerly of the two warships, her missile control radar tripped-out and broke the Seawolf lock on the Skyhawks. With only light gunfire to contend with, the two aircraft were able to make a precise attack and 'Broadsword' was indeed fortunate not to be severely damaged. Most of the Skyhawks' bombs missed the helpless warship but one bounced off the sea to strike her aft on the starboard side. It passed upwards through the flight-deck, demolishing all in its path including the nose of the Lynx XZ729, before falling harmlessly in the sea, failing to explode.

As Carballo and Rinke pulled away safely, Velasco and Barrionuevo began their run-in on 'Coventry' from a distance of about ten miles. Simultaneously 'Coventry' turned towards 'Broadsword' and again the Sea Harrier CAP offered its assistance. Again 'Broadsword' thought that she had the situation in hand and declined the offer. 'Coventry' then launched a Sea Dart at the approaching Skyhawks but, on that occasion, the head-on launch in clear weather was seen, and both pilots carefully followed the missile's run as they descended to wave-top height. Then, with the aid of a carefully judged course change, both men watched the missile pass harmlessly by them, some distance away. In an effort to confuse the Skyhawks, 'Coventry' had begun to make evasive turns in the water with her 4.5in gun firing. However, it was only when she passed across the frigate's bows that her fate was sealed. As she moved between aircraft and "goalkeeper" she broke the Seawolf missile lock and the results were catastrophic. Even though Barrionuevo's bombs hung-up, Velasco, in C-207, was able to put all three of his into the destroyer's port side where they exploded causing fire and flooding. The attack had taken place at 1821Z and at 1848Z 'Coventry' was abandoned. At 1922Z she capsized with the damaged 'Broadsword' still in close attendance. Velasco, Barrionuevo, Carballo and Rinke all returned safely to Rio Gallegos and a tremendous reception while at nearby Rio Grande CANA were celebrating the destruction, in an Exocet attack, of what they later learned was 'Atlantic Conveyor'. In spite of the sadness for Palaver the day had been a great success for Grupo 5 and Argentina.

Many appraisals of the Falklands War regard the night of 25 May as a significant turning point of events, but it was not because of the loss of 'Coventry' and 'Atlantic Conveyor'. The evening of 25 May effectively marked the end of the air war for supremacy over the San Carlos beach-head and, with that battle lost, CdoFAS was obliged to discover other ways to slow or stop the British advance to Port Stanley. At the same time it needed to limit its own losses. Accordingly, FAA air activity was sharply reduced on 26 May and no significant operations were recorded for any unit.

On 27 May Grupo 5 was tasked with what appears to have been the first mission from the mainland against

British forces ashore. For these anti-personnel sorties each Skyhawk was armed with 400kg parachute-retarded bombs and the crews given specific briefings from recent reconnaissance data acquired by the Grupo 1 Aerofotografico Learjets. Two flights of three Skyhawks were prepared for the mission but, as usual, technical shortcomings reduced their ultimate number to four. Capitan Carballo, Teniente Rinke and a third unidentified pilot (soon to return to Rio Gallegos) comprised "Truco" flight while Primer Teniente Velasco and Teniente Osses were the surviving pair that took-off as "Poker" flight. They were airborne at 1900Z, much later than normal, for an attack on troop dispositions on the west bank of San Carlos Water at a site known as Ajax Bay. Their crossing to West Falkland was routine although Carballo's aircraft suffered from radio difficulties, a problem increasingly troubling the Grupo 5 Skyhawks (avionics malfunctions of all kinds were leading to the cannibalising of aircraft at Rio Gallegos and the difficulties looked like becoming worse as time passed).

"Truco" flight led the mission by a few minutes and the four aircraft all approached Grantham Sound from the south-west to make a final run-in over the Sussex Mountains and into San Carlos Water. The dusk sky at 1950Z was dark and grey as Carballo and Rinke dropped down towards Ajax Bay, their guns firing. They made for the 40 Commando camp area, leaving the old refrigeration plant buildings to the following "Poker" flight. Carballo caught everyone by surprise but the British response was rapid and he was fired at by several ships and many men on the ground. As he and Rinke cleared the hills to the north, Velasco and Osses began their run-in over the same ground. With all British guns firing at the Skyhawks and two SAM's only narrowly missing him, Velasco knew that his aircraft was damaged moments after he had released his bombs. As he cleared the target area, hydraulic pressure warning lights were warning him of serious problems with his Skyhawk C-215. The damage had been done by the 40mm guns of 'Fearless' and 'Intrepid' and, as Velasco turned onto a westerly heading over Falkland Sound, his wingman Osses warned him of a fire in the root of his left wing. It was potentially catastrophic, with the burning fluid perilously close to the liquid oxygen tank, and the listening Carballo was quick to instruct Velasco to abandon his damaged Skyhawk. Velasco needed little persuasion and he successfully ejected from the aircraft a few moments later near Port Howard on West Falkland, coming to ground near his Skyhawk suffering no more than a badly swollen ankle. After some confused efforts to find friendly forces and avoid the British, he was eventually found and returned to Argentine forces by some of the local Islanders. His reappearance at Port Howard took until 1 June, however, by which time Grupo 5 had considered him lost.

Carballo and Osses had both had their aircraft damaged in the attack and it seemed to the former that very little of anything was working well on the return leg. Communication between Carballo and Rinke was limited to hand signals and, after mistaking two passing Pucaras for Sea Harriers, it was a very relieved Carballo who eventually landed safely at Rio Gallegos. Post-flight inspection of his aircraft revealed a shell lodged in the left main wheel and a large hole in the left side of the Skyhawk's nose. Both the drop tanks on Osses' aircraft had also been punctured by gunfire. Their attack had caused several casualties and a fire in an ammunition dump, while other bombs had not detonated and required urgent attention by bomb disposal teams. However, such damage, although demoralising to the enemy, could not have justified the loss of one aircraft and serious damage to others. There thus appears to have been a conscious decision to abandon such attacks on targets in the San Carlos area except for those that could be safely bombed by the high-flying Canberras. The targets were simply too well defended.

For nearly two weeks Grupo 5 was to see very little operational activity, indeed CdoFAS launched few combat sorties of any kind during the first week of June. One Grupo 5 mission was launched on 28 May at the height of the battle for Goose Green and Darwin to investigate a warship in nearby Grantham Sound, but when the ship was identified as the hospital vessel 'Uganda' the attack was abandoned. The ship's log recorded the Skyhawks overhead at 1421Z. That "attack", like the one on 'Coventry' three days earlier, made use of an airborne Grupo 5 controller, Mayor Medina, who was apparently able to provide the incoming aircraft with the latest available target information. His aircraft, presumably operating from a safe distance, has not been identified but may, on that occasion, have been a Learjet or a C-130.

The poor weather and lack of suitable targets gave Grupo 5 the opportunity to continue with urgent aircraft repairs and to stand down, albeit temporarily, some of their pilots who by then were in need of a well-earned break away from Rio Gallegos. Grupo 5 had accredited itself well and had been by far and away the most successful FAA fighter-bomber unit in the anti-shipping role. Since the disastrous 12 May only three A-4B Skyhawks had been lost and on 1 June came the very welcome news that Mariano Velasco was safe. Incredibly, no Grupo 5 Skyhawks had been lost to the lethal Sea Harriers and even that threat was believed dissipated since it was thought that 'Invincible' had been damaged on 30 May (that was untrue, but both 'Hermes' and 'Invincible' had withdrawn to the east and fewer CAP's were in evidence over the Islands). Nevertheless, the Skyhawks had taken a real battering since 21 May and, with both battle damage and component failure to contend with, it was clear that Grupo 5, like the other units, could not continue such a war of attrition for many more days.

At last, on 8 June, CdoFAS found a suitable target for the fighter-bombers. The British had continued to advance overland towards Port Stanley for several days, but that morning Argentine intelligence discovered that a second anchorage had been created at Fitzroy, a settlement a few miles to the south-west of Port Stanley. A small group of transports was reported to be at anchor in nearby Port Pleasant, an open bay surrounded by flat coastal plain with no natural defences. If the Sea Harriers could be kept away, CdoFAS reasoned that there existed the opportunity to inflict real damage to the enemy. Thus, a mission was rapidly conceived and at 1300Z Grupo 5 was advised of its role in the planned attack. Two flights of four Skyhawks were bombed-up, each with three 500lb bombs fused for the anti-shipping role. The morning was

Argentine anti-aircraft guns were responsible for shooting down Grupo 5 de Caza A-4B Skyhawk C-248 on 12.5.82 and killing the pilot, Primer Teniente Fausto Gavazzi. Inexplicably, the pilot had flown low through the Goose Green defences after successfully attacking 'Glasgow'. The yellow wing stripes, applied to many aircraft after 1.5.82 to aid recognition and to prevent such incidents, are clearly visible.
(R. McLeod)

**Left** Dramatically photographed from 'Broadsword' during the afternoon of 25.5.82, two Grupo 5 de Caza A-4B Skyhawks of "Vulcan" flight are here seen just seconds before the frigate was bombed. The flight leader, Capitan Pablo Carballo, is in the left-hand aircraft; Teniente Carlos Rinke is his wingman. Splashes from the Skyhawks' cannon fire can be seen in the foreground. It was this attack that seriously damaged the 815 Squadron Lynx XZ729 when one of the bombs bounced from the sea and passed upwards through the flight-deck.
(Ministry of Defence)

bitterly cold and many of the Grupo 5 pilots viewed the mission with some resignation, being only two days away from their rotational leave back at Villa Reynolds.

"Dogo" flight took-off first at 1450Z and it was followed minutes later by "Mastin" flight. "Dogo" comprised Capitan Carballo, Teniente Rinke, Primer Teniente Cachon and Alferez Carmona, an Escuadrilla which had collectively survived several combat missions, and "Mastin" comprised Primer Teniente Filippini, Teniente Galvez, Teniente Autiero and Alferez Gomez. The two flights flew at 10,000ft towards the pair of KC-130H tankers that were waiting, as usual, half-way between the mainland and West Falkland, but it was during the refuelling phase that the mission hit serious trouble. As "Dogo" began its refuelling Filippini's Skyhawk developed an engine oil pressure problem and, as it showed no sign of resolution, he was obliged to abandon the sortie. Simultaneously both Carballo and Autiero ran into refuelling difficulties as their aircraft refused to take on fuel. It was later reasoned that their probes had somehow become frozen and, try as they might, no fuel could be accepted from the KC-130H's. Both men followed Filippini back to Rio Gallegos, leaving the remaining aircraft without an experienced flight leader.

Cachon took command of the integrated group of five aircraft which immediately adopted an arrow formation that he led as number one. His number two was Rinke and, to Cachon's left, Carmona formed up as number three. Galvez and Gomez followed as four and five respectively. The weather steadily deteriorated as they approached the Falklands and a heavy cloud cover built up as they passed Cape Meredith and Speedwell Island for a final approach from the south-west across Lafonia to Fitzroy. As they crossed low over Choiseul Sound they passed through the last of several short rain showers until finally, about two minutes short of the target, a British Sea King helicopter was seen in their path. The flight deviated from the direct track to avoid it and then, some 45 seconds away from Fitzroy, a low flying Scout was similarly avoided. The first run over Fitzroy revealed nothing except many British troops who opened fire, slightly damaging the Skyhawk of Teniente Galvez. Having overflown the area, the flight made a turn to the right and it was at that moment that Gomez saw 'Sir Galahad' and 'Sir Tristram' in Port Pleasant. The run-in from the east was unobstructed and, although a ground-launched SAM passed between Cachon and Rinke, the subsequent attack on the ships was virtually unopposed. The three leading aircraft went for 'Sir Galahad', the more northerly vessel, and Cachon put all three bombs into her stern area. In the seconds before their detonation an excited call from the third pilot, Carmona, distracted Rinke whose bombs were consequently never released. Carmona had managed to run-in ahead of Rinke and had seen his own stick of bombs skate off the water's surface and miss the ship, but his shout of frustration confused Rinke into believing that it was his bombs that had released and missed. It was a few minutes later, as he sought to escape, that Rinke became aware of unusual drag and the mistake was realised.

Within a few moments of Cachon's devastating attack that had left 'Sir Galahad' in flames that would take a week to subside, Galvez and Gomez made their run at the nearby 'Sir Tristram'. She was hit by a stick of bombs

from Galvez but those of Gomez fell short and 'Sir Tristram', although badly damaged, survived the attack. The five Grupo 5 Skyhawks escaped to the south and the open sea leaving behind them a scene of absolute chaos and carnage. They had taken the fullest possible advantage of a situation created by the enemy's carelessness. The FAA was still very much a force to be reckoned with, and with Grupo 5's crushing assault at 1650Z virtually coinciding with the Grupo 6 Dagger attack on 'Plymouth' in Falkland Sound, the Royal Navy had been sharply reminded of the fact. As the five jubilant Skyhawk pilots cruised home safely at 35,000ft, they had the confidence to decline assistance from the waiting tankers.

It would have been as well for Grupo 5 had CdoFAS regarded 8 June as a day of total success there and then. Unfortunately that was not the case and a decision was taken at Comodoro Rivadavia to press home further attacks on what were presumed to be the demoralised and confused British troops at Fitzroy. Two further sorties were thus planned for that afternoon; one to come from Grupo 5 at Rio Gallegos and the other from Grupo 4 at San Julian. "Mazo" flight took-off from Rio Gallegos at about 1830Z armed for an anti-shipping strike (the even later Grupo 4 sortie was armed for an anti-personnel attack) and comprised Primer Teniente Bolzan, Primer Teniente Sanchez, Teniente Arraras and Alferez Vazquez, all combat veterans. They successfully refuelled from the tanker and followed the routing of the earlier attack to Fitzroy, arriving safely from the south-west. Their target was to be any shipping found in the Port Fitzroy area but as the flight overflew Fitzroy en route, it was met by a barrage of ground fire from the many British troops below. 20mm, GPMG, small-arms fire, Blowpipe and Rapier were all used against the flight, but miraculously no-one received serious damage and the Skyhawks cleared the area and turned to the south, still seeking any British shipping in the deteriorating visibility.

Suddenly, at the mouth of Choiseul Sound, a landing-craft was sighted. It was 'Foxtrot 4' of 'Fearless', en route to Fitzroy from Goose Green, and, once seen by Bolzan, it became an immediate target for he and his number two, Vazquez, and both dived down to attack. Bolzan lacked the time and airspace to line-up his aircraft properly and thus did not release any bombs on his pass but Vazquez, with more time available, caught the landing-craft with a direct hit and, within minutes, it had sunk.

When the attack commenced, the Skyhawks had been seen by a pair of 800 Sqdn Sea Harriers, orbiting high above at 10,000ft. They dived at high speed towards the Skyhawks and, from a range of about 1,000yds, Flt Lt Dave Morgan in ZA177 launched a Sidewinder at Arraras. It impacted C-226 seconds later, at 1945Z, and the Skyhawk fireballed and fell in the Sound near Philimore Island, killing the pilot. Moments earlier, Sanchez had realised what was happening but his shout had come too late for Arraras. The others broke, Bolzan to the north, Vazquez and Sanchez to the south, but they could not escape the missiles. Vazquez, in C-228, in spite of a desperate jink by his Skyhawk, was hit in the rear fuselage by Morgan's second Sidewinder and the tail separated from the rest of the aircraft. As the Skyhawk disintegrated Vazquez ejected. His aircraft crashed some two miles north of Middle Island but Vazquez, whose parachute was reported to have been on fire, was never found.

Bolzan, in C-204, was then subjected to a cannon attack from Morgan's Sea Harrier before he became the target of another Sidewinder, this time from Lt Dave Smith in XZ499. The missile was fired at low level from a range of two to three miles but as Bolzan held his low, fast course he hit the coastal sand dunes at Rain Cove near Island Creek on the northern shore of Lafonia. It is a matter of perhaps academic conjecture whether the AIM-9L actually impacted before the crash, for Bolzan was killed and the aircraft destroyed. In the meantime, Sanchez had jettisoned his bombs and underwing tanks and had made his own desperate high speed, low-level, jinking run to the south, absolutely convinced that at any moment he, too, would be destroyed by a Sidewinder. He had been considerably shaken, but when he began to realise that he was safe, he also realised that he would soon be very low on fuel and that he must climb to a more economical cruise height. Having reached Falkland Sound, he thus began the climb but then realised that his fuel state was critical and that he would only reach a point some 200 miles east of Rio Gallegos before having to eject. He was saved by a KC-130H but the refuelling was itself hazardous and deserves a detailed account in its own right.

Although Sanchez and the tanker talked easily enough on VHF radio as the Skyhawk crossed West Falkland, there existed no simple way for them to find one another. The A-4B did not have either an Omega or IFF fit and without these important locating items the Grupo 1 tanker crew was obliged to use radar and dead reckoning to find him. That particular Skyhawk had been one of those pressed into use without vital avionics and Sanchez had doubtlessly relied upon the aircraft of Bolzan and, perhaps, Arraras for the in-flight refuelling rendezvous. Having lost his companions, Sanchez was in severe difficulties. The KC-130H crew was quick to appreciate the situation and flew east towards West Falkland, in the process entering the potentially dangerous Sea Harrier CAP territory, and, as it descended through the clearer upper flight levels, it began to leave a thick, highly visible condensation trail. To have left such a trail in normal circumstances would have invited disaster, it being so close to the Falklands, but, on that occasion it was seen by Sanchez who immediately made for the Hercules and safety. The fuel transfer commenced when the Skyhawk was down to its last few minutes of flying time, but, even then, all was not plain sailing and the agitated and literally shaking Sanchez needed to be carefully coaxed into the tanker's drogue before the process could begin.

Grupo 4's "Tigre" flight somehow escaped from the Fitzroy area, without loss, shortly after "Mazo" flight's disaster, but the launching of the two evening Skyhawk missions was, nevertheless, a gross error of judgement by CdoFAS. Grupo 8 Mirages, apparently provided for escort purposes, had remained at 35,000ft above East Falkland while the Sea Harriers destroyed the Skyhawks at sea-level. In the circumstances the missions were little short of suicidal and, despite outstanding earlier successes, Grupo 5 was left that evening to mourn the unnecessary loss of three more pilots.

The final significant sorties for Grupo 5 took place on 13 June and, with the vicissitudes of war being what they are, they might have been spectacularly successful. British victory was imminent when CdoFAS tasked its most successful fighter-bomber unit to launch eight Skyhawks against troop positions in the Mount Kent area. Armed with parachute retarded bombs, two flights of four, "Nene" and "Chispa", were simultaneously launched from Rio Gallegos during the late morning. "Nene" was soon reduced to three when its leader, Capitan Zelaya, was obliged to return to base with an overheating engine, but the seven others completed the in-flight refuelling and continued on in radio-silence. The three aircraft of "Nene" combined with "Chispa" in one large formation led by Capitan Varela. His wingmen were Teniente Roca, Teniente Mayor and Alferez Moroni while the three "Nene" survivors were Teniente Gelardi, Teniente Cervera and Alferez Dellepiane. Varela's target, for what was by then a formation of rather inexperienced pilots, was specified as troop positions to the north-east of Two Sisters, but it is not clear whether "Nene" flight had been given an identical brief or was tasked to hit a nearby target. In any event, the seven aircraft, formating in the rainy conditions on Varela's uniquely grey-painted C-222 (it was nicknamed "El Tordillo"), passed over the north-west tip of East Falkland, ignoring a Sea King below them, as they flew on at low level towards Mount Kent. At 1513Z, with two minutes to run to Two Sisters, the Port Stanley CIC warned the Skyhawks of four Sea Harrier CAP's airborne in the area of East Falkland and then attempted to reassure Varela by telling him that he was so low he would not be seen!

As the formation passed over the western slopes of Mount Kent it came upon the headquarters of the 3rd Commando Brigade and, with it, the British commander, General Moore, and many of his senior officers. The bombs that were dropped, but which missed any vital targets, appear to have been those of "Nene" flight. The leading four Skyhawks of "Chispa" flight continued east towards their planned target. The attack on their headquarters had come as a surprise to the British but their response was rapid and the Skyhawks were immediately fired upon by many guns and missiles. In the following moments a SAM detonated between Varela and Mayor, noticeably jolting the leader's aircraft. Varela, having ignored another Sea King that had appeared in his path (he believed that it had fired at him), was on the point of making a cannon attack on yet another that had appeared in front of him when he realised that the SAM had indeed caused significant damage. His engine was overheating and making unusual noises so, with flight control becoming difficult, he decided to jettison his external stores. Although that was accomplished easily enough, his inexperienced flight misinterpreted the action as the signal to bomb and thus all three pilots wasted their weapons in what was seen by the British as an unsuccessful attack on paratroop positions to the west of Mount Longdon.

As "Nene" flight pulled away from Mount Kent it turned north and, immediately, Dellepiane found himself faced by an 846 Sqdn Sea King, ZA298, flown by Lt Cdr Simon Thornewill. Dellepiane's cannon attack left the Sea King with a damaged rotor-blade and he could have considered himself unfortunate not to have been claiming Grupo 5's first air-to-air "kill". Nearby, two more SAM's exploded dangerously close to Cervera and "Nene" flight departed the area in some confusion. Elsewhere, "Chispa" flight was travelling west across East Falkland in similar disarray and, following close behind Roca, Varela was ready to eject from his aircraft should the Skyhawk's condition deteriorate any more. They passed over Falkland Sound safely and Varela's preoccupation with his own serious problems was temporarily forgotten when Dellepiane became distressed with his situation. He, too, had jettisoned the auxiliary tanks and believed that he would have to eject very soon. In fact, neither Varela nor Dellepiane did eject and their damaged Skyhawks successfully met the KC-130H's over the open sea. Dellepiane's situation was, nevertheless, critical and the young pilot's Skyhawk was ultimately accompanied by one of the tankers to Rio Gallegos where he made a safe landing with his six colleagues.

The War ended the following day and Grupo 5's achievements during the conflict had been most impressive. The Skyhawks had participated in what the FAA regarded as seven major missions and they had been directly responsible for the loss of 'Antelope', 'Coventry' and 'Sir Galahad'; the crippling damage to 'Argonaut' and 'Sir Tristram' and moderate damage to 'Glasgow' and several other warships. Their attack on the installations at Ajax Bay had been one of the rare occasions that CdoFAS had managed to inflict serious damage on the British land forces. Those successes had been achieved at the cost of nine lives and 10 aircraft destroyed, but, by any measure of performance, Grupo 5 de Caza was the most successful of all the FAA combat units. It is not known exactly how many of the 149 planned sorties were actually achieved by the aircraft of the Escuadron A-4B Rio Gallegos, but it was probably in excess of 100.

It has been reported that some 14 A-4B's remained serviceable at the end of the War and, during 1983, Grupo 5 was reinforced by the transfer of the surviving Grupo 4 A-4C's. At the time of writing (1985) it remains a matter of speculation whether refurbished aircraft will ever be received, either from the United States or elsewhere, but, since June 1982, existing stocks have continued to dwindle as a result of peace-time attrition. At least four more Grupo 5 A-4B Skyhawks were lost in post-war accidents on 12 November 1982, 13 July 1983, 31 October 1984 and 19 November 1984.

---

*Grupo 5 de Caza pilots deployed to Rio Gallegos and believed to have flown combat missions included:*

*Vicecomodoro Mariel (G5C commander); Vicecomodoro E.Dubourg (Escuadron commander); Vicecomodoro R.Zini (Escuadron commander); Capitan P.M.Carballo; Capitan H.A.del V.Palaver (KIA); Capitan Varela; Capitan Zelaya; Primer Teniente D.R.Bolzan (KIA); Primer Teniente O.M.Bustos (KIA); Primer Teniente Cachon; Primer Teniente Filippini; Primer Teniente F.Gavazzi (KIA); Primer Teniente L.Guadagnini (KIA); Primer Teniente H.H.Sanchez; Primer Teniente M.A.Velasco; Teniente J.J.Arraras (KIA); Teniente V.L.Autiero; Teniente J.Carlos; Teniente L.A.Cervera; Teniente Galvez; Teniente Gelardi; Teniente J.R.Ibarlucea (KIA); Teniente Mayor; Teniente M.V.Nivoli (KIA); Teniente M.Osses; Teniente C.Rinke; Teniente F.Robledo; Teniente Roca; Alferez J.N.Barrionuevo; Alferez L.Carmona; Alferez Dellepiane; Alferez H.E.Gomez; Alferez M.Moroni; Alferez J.A.Vazquez (KIA); Alferez Vottero.*

---

# INDIVIDUAL AIRCRAFT DETAILS

Throughout the War the Grupo 4 A-4C Skyhawks retained their light sand and brown camouflage which differed noticeably from the darker colours of the Grupo 5 A-4B Skyhawks. The A-4C scheme had been specially designed to suit the arid Mendoza terrain and it is thought that when the FAA asked the combat units to apply identification markings after 1 May, the camouflage rendered pointless continued use of yellow painted stripes and so the wing and tail stripes were uniquely overpainted bright blue by Grupo 4. No other major changes were made at San Julian to the normal markings except in respect of the aircraft serial numbers. These were removed from their position on the fuselage sides below the cockpit area where they had been displayed above the large white FUERZA AEREA ARGENTINA and IV BRIGADA AEREA titles (which remained). They were reinstated only as two tiny white digits at the base of the tail (immediately above the jet-pipe) as a "last two". It is presumed that the change was made for security reasons.

When the surviving aircraft were inspected at Mendoza late in 1982 some were wearing a small blue "Malvinas" silhouette of the Islands aft of the IV Brigada Aerea badge on the port side just beneath the cockpit. Those aircraft with ship "kill" markings wore them in the form of a large red silhouette on the port side immediately beneath the windscreen.

A definitive list of A-4C's deployed to San Julian is not available but the following histories include those of all aircraft lost in combat, other aircraft that are known to have been used during the War and aircraft which, although not confirmed as involved, have been subsequently noted in use.

With the single known exception of C-222 (which was grey overall), all the Grupo 5 A-4B Skyhawks that deployed to Rio Gallegos retained their normal peace-time camouflage of dark green and brown upper surfaces with light blue undersides. Unlike most of the FAA combat units, Grupo 5 did not wear the FUERZA AEREA ARGENTINA titles on its aircraft. Aircraft serial numbers were painted in black beneath the cockpit and on the extreme rear fuselage. Only the last two digits of the serial appeared on the nose-wheel door. In contrast to Grupo 4, Grupo 5 made no effort to delete these serials during the war period. The brightly coloured crest of Grupo 5 was worn on virtually all aircraft on the port side of the nose. After 1 May 1982 bright yellow identification stripes were applied to the wings of some aircraft but the practice seems to have been short-lived and may well have been abandoned after the loss of C-248 on 12 May. A few Skyhawks (C-214 was one) also had a vertical yellow flash applied to the fin. "Kill" markings were worn by several Grupo 5 Skyhawks in the form of yellow ship silhouettes applied to the port side of the fuselage beneath the cockpit. In the early stages of the air war dates were applied beneath each silhouette, but that practice also seems to

have been discontinued after 12 May.

It is not known which Skyhawks were originally deployed from Villa Reynolds to Rio Gallegos with the Escuadron A-4B Rio Gallegos. During the course of the War several aircraft were withdrawn from storage and long-term maintenance and these aircraft were used to make good the eventual losses and to increase the original establishment of 12 to an estimated peak strength of 20. The following aircraft histories include details of all those known to have been used operationally as well as those recorded in post-war use. The list of combat losses can be considered definitive.

*In the individual aircraft details the standard FAA abbreviations 'G4C' and 'G5C' have been used for Grupo 4 de Caza and Grupo 5 de Caza.*

**C-204** A-4B

In 3.82 with G5C. Deployed to Rio Gallegos on or after 14.4.82. Brought down over Choiseul Sound on 8.6.82 by an AIM-9L fired from the 800 Sqdn Sea Harrier XZ499 of Lt Smith. The pilot, Primer Teniente Bolzan, did not eject and his body was found in the wreckage at Rain Cove, Island Creek.

**C-206** A-4B

In 3.82 with G5C. Deployed to Rio Gallegos on or after 14.4.82. Crashed into the sea off Port Stanley on 12.5.82 while attacking 'Glasgow' and 'Brilliant' off the east coast of East Falkland. The pilot, Teniente Nivoli, was killed.

**C-207** A-4B

In 3.82 with G5C. Deployed to Rio Gallegos on or after 14.4.82. Survived the War and was noted decorated with two ship silhouettes, one of which represents 'Coventry' sunk north of Pebble Island by this aircraft on 25.5.82. The other silhouette (of a Type 22 frigate) appears to represent 'Brilliant', presumably for the attack of 12.5.82. Last noted with these stencils in 11.82 but earlier, perhaps during 7.82, it was temporarily decorated with five ship silhouettes, thought to represent the major war achievements of G5C.

**C-208** A-4B

In 3.82 with G5C. Deployed to Rio Gallegos on or after 14.4.82. Brought down by a Seawolf fired from 'Brilliant', off the east coast of East Falkland, on 12.5.82. The pilot, Teniente Ibarlucea, was killed when it crashed into the sea off Port Stanley.

**C-212** A-4B

In 3.82 with G5C. Deployed to Rio Gallegos on or after 14.4.82. Survived the War and was noted at Villa Reynolds in 11.82 decorated with two ship silhouettes.

**C-214** A-4B

In 3.82 with G5C. Deployed to Rio Gallegos on or after 14.4.82. Survived the War and was noted at Villa Reynolds in 11.82 decorated with two ship silhouettes.

**C-215** A-4B

In 3.82 with G5C. Deployed to Rio Gallegos on or after 14.4.82. Brought down by 40mm gunfire from 'Fearless' after attacking British positions at Ajax Bay on 27.5.82. The pilot, Teniente Velasco, successfully ejected over West Falkland and was recovered to Port Howard on 1.6.82. Wreckage was found near Port Howard, West Falkland (UC 209868) and pieces, including a fuselage section decorated with one ship silhouette, were recovered and taken to the FAAM at Yeovilton for display.

**C-222** A-4B

In 3.82 with G5C, conceivably in storage or maintenance at Villa Reynolds or Rio Cuarto. Deployed to Rio Gallegos on or after 14.4.82 in a unique grey overall colour scheme. No ship silhouettes visible in undated photograph taken during the War. Believed to have survived the conflict although not noted in post-war use.

**C-224** A-4B

In 3.82 with G5C. Believed to have been used during the War from Rio Gallegos and was subsequently noted in use at Villa Reynolds in 11.82. No ship silhouettes were worn at that time.

**C-225** A-4B

In 3.82 with G5C. Deployed to Rio Gallegos on or after 14.4.82. In an undated 1982 photograph it can be seen to be wearing only one ship silhouette but in a (presumably) later picture it wears two silhouettes. The stencils are identical and appear to show Type 42 destroyers. Noted in use at Villa Reynolds in 11.82.

**C-226** A-4B

In 3.82 with G5C. Deployed to Rio Gallegos on or after 14.4.82. Brought down over Choiseul Sound on 8.6.82 by an AIM-9L fired from the 800 Sqdn Sea Harrier ZA177 of Flt Lt Morgan. It fell into the sea off Philimore Island, killing the pilot Teniente Arraras.

**C-227** A-4B

In 3.82 with G5C. Deployed to Rio Gallegos

on or after 14.4.82. A period photograph shows it to be wearing two ship silhouettes. Not noted in post-war use.

**C-228** A-4B

In 3.82 with G5C. Deployed to Rio Gallegos on or after 14.4.82. Bombed and sank landing-craft 'Foxtrot 4' of 'Fearless' in Choiseul Sound on 8.6.82. However, almost immediately after that attack it was brought down by an AIM-9L fired from the 800 Sqdn Sea Harrier ZA177 of Flt Lt Morgan and fell into the sea about two miles north of Middle Island. The pilot, Alferez Vazquez, unsuccessfully ejected and was killed.

**C-231** A-4B

In 3.82 with G5C. Deployed to Rio Gallegos on or after 14.4.82. Survived the War and was noted at Villa Reynolds in 11.82 decorated with two ship silhouettes.

**C-233** A-4B

In 3.82 with G5C. Deployment to Rio Gallegos unconfirmed but noted in use at Villa Reynolds in 11.82. No ship silhouettes worn at that time.

**C-234** A-4B

In 3.82 with G5C. Deployment to Rio Gallegos unconfirmed but the aircraft was subsequently destroyed in a post-war crash on 31.10.84 at Vicuna Mackenna, Cordoba.

**C-235** A-4B

In 3.82 with G5C. Deployment to Rio Gallegos unconfirmed but the aircraft was subsequently destroyed in a post-war crash on 13.7.83 at 9° de Julio, Buenos Aires.

**C-236** A-4B

In 3.82 with G5C. Deployment to Rio Gallegos unconfirmed but an undated, post-war photograph shows the aircraft decorated with five ship silhouettes. The circumstances of the photograph suggest that these markings may have been applied for ceremonial purposes. Noted in use at Villa Reynolds in 11.82.

**C-237** A-4B

In 3.82 with G5C. Deployed to Rio Gallegos

on or after 14.4.82. Used by Primer Teniente Bolzan in one of the missions of 1.5.82. Not subsequently noted.

**C-239** A-4B

In 3.82 with G5C. Deployed to Rio Gallegos on or after 14.4.82. A widely published photograph shows it decorated with a single ship silhouette and the date "12.5.82". This is thought to represent 'Brilliant', initially believed to have been sunk by G5C on that date. The pilot, seated in the cockpit for this press-release picture, is Capitan Carballo, a non-participant in the mission of 12.5.82! Noted in post-war use at Villa Reynolds in late 1982.

**C-240** A-4B

In 3.82 with G5C. Deployed to Rio Gallegos on or after 14.4.82 (but prior to 12.5.82). When noted in post-war use at Villa Reynolds in 11.82 it was decorated with a single ship silhouette, identical to that on C-239 and one similar to that depicted on C-207 (presumably representing a Type 22 frigate).

**C-242** A-4B

In 3.82 with G5C. Deployed to Rio Gallegos on or after 14.4.82. Brought down by an un-identified British SAM in the San Carlos Water area on 23.5.82 while 'Antelope' was under attack by G5C. The pilot, Primer Teniente Guadagnini, was killed when the aircraft crashed into the sea.

**C-244** A-4B

In 3.82 with G5C. Deployed to Rio Gallegos on or after 14.4.82. Brought down by a Sea Dart fired from 'Coventry', off Pebble Island, on 25.5.82. The pilot, Capitan Palaver, was killed when the aircraft crashed into the open sea, north of Pebble Island.

**C-246** A-4B

In 3.82 with G5C. Deployed to Rio Gallegos on or after 14.4.82. Brought down by a Seawolf fired from 'Brilliant', off the east coast of East Falkland, on 12.5.82. The pilot, Primer Teniente Bustos, was killed when the aircraft crashed into the sea off Port Stanley.

**C-248** A-4B

In 3.82 with G5C. Deployed to Rio Gallegos on or after 14.4.82. Brought down by Ar-gentine 35mm anti-aircraft fire when overfly-ing Goose Green after attacking 'Glasgow' off the east coast of East Falkland on 12.5.82. It crashed into a field known as "Goats Rincon", killing the pilot Primer Teniente Gavazzi. Wreckage, spread over several hundred yards, was still present in early 1984.

**C-250** A-4B

In 3.82 with G5C. Deployed to Rio Gallegos on or after 14.4.82. Survived the War and was noted at Villa Reynolds in 11.82 decorated with one ship silhouette.

**C-301** A-4C

In 3.82 with G4C. Deployed to San Julian on

or after 11.4.82. Temporarily operating from Rio Grande on 30.5.82 (in conjunction with two Super Etendards of 2 Escuadrilla). It was destroyed that day (whilst about to attack 'Avenger') by a Sea Dart fired from 'Exeter', operating to the east of East Falkland. The pilot, Primer Teniente Vazquez, was killed when the aircraft crashed into the South At-lantic, east of the Falklands.

**C-303** A-4C

In 3.82 with G4C. Deployed to San Julian on or after 11.4.82. Lost in unexplained circum-stances on 9.5.82 when it was one of a flight of four seeking British warships in the Port Stanley area. Thought to have crashed into the sea in poor visibility to the north-west of West Falkland with the pilot, Teniente Farias, miss-ing presumed killed (see C-313).

**C-304** A-4C

In 3.82 with G4C. Deployed to San Julian on or after 11.4.82. While returning from a mis-sion to San Carlos Water on 25.5.82 it was hit by a Sea Dart fired from 'Coventry', po-sitioned to the north-east of Pebble Island. The aircraft probably crashed into the sea but not before its pilot, Capitan Garcia, ejected. He is believed to have survived the ejection but was not recovered and his body was washed ashore in a dinghy at Golding Island, West Falkland, in 1983.

**C-305** A-4C

In 3.82 with G4C. Deployed to San Julian on or after 11.4.82. Destroyed on 24.5.82 when the aircraft crashed in King George Bay, West Falkland. It had been damaged by gunfire and shrapnel over San Carlos Water. The pilot, Teniente Bono, was not seen to eject and was presumed killed in the crash.

**C-309** A-4C

In 3.82 with G4C. Deployed to San Julian on or after 11.4.82. Brought down over West Falkland on 21.5.82 by an AIM-9L fired from the 800 Sqdn Sea Harrier XZ492 of Lt Cdr Thomas or XZ496 of Lt Cdr Blissett (see C-325). The pilot, Teniente Lopez, unsuccess-fully ejected and was killed. The aircraft crashed south of Christmas Harbour near Chartres settlement. The ejection seat was put on display at the FAAM Yeovilton.

**C-310** A-4C

In 3.82 with G4C. Deployed to San Julian on or after 11.4.82. Temporarily operating from Rio Grande on 30.5.82 (in conjunction with two Super Etendards of 2 Escuadrilla). It was destroyed that day (whilst about to attack 'Avenger') by a Sea Dart fired from 'Exeter', operating to the east of East Falkland. The pilot, Primer Teniente Castillo, was killed when the aircraft crashed into the South At-lantic, east of the Falklands.

**C-312** A-4C

In 3.82 with G4C. Deployed to San Julian on or after 11.4.82. Used by Alferez Isaac on the mission of 25.5.82 to San Carlos Water (where the aircraft was hit by British cannon fire) and was marked accordingly (see text). It survived

the War and was in use at Mendoza in 1983.

**C-313** A-4C

In 3.82 with G4C. Deployed to San Julian on or after 11.4.82. Destroyed on 9.5.82 when it crashed into high ground on the north-west side of South Jason Island. The aircraft was still bombed-up and had not been abandoned by its pilot, Teniente Casco, whose body was found in the wreckage. Examination of the aircraft revealed its former BuAer number, 150595.

**C-314** A-4C

In 3.82 with G4C. Not confirmed as having been deployed to San Julian but noted in post-war use at Mendoza in 11.82.

**C-318** A-4C

In 3.82 with G4C. Deployed to San Julian on or after 11.4.82. It survived the War and in 5.83 was in use as a test vehicle for a Matra Belouga installation. Remained in IV BA markings for those trials wearing an unidenti-fied ship silhouette, presumably applied in 1982.

**C-319** A-4C

In 3.82 with G4C. Deployed to San Julian on or after 11.4.82. The aircraft disintegrated over San Carlos Water on 25.5.82 after suffer-ing hits from multiple weapons, perhaps including Rapier. The pilot, Teniente Lucero, successfully ejected and was recovered to 'Fearless'. He was later repatriated to Argentina.

**C-321** A-4C

In 3.82 with G4C. Deployed to San Julian on or after 11.4.82. Temporarily operating from Rio Grande on 30.5.82 (in conjunction with two Super Etendards of 2 Escuadrilla), it un-successfully attacked 'Avenger', east of East Falkland, that day. The aircraft survived the War and when seen at Mendoza in 11.82 it was marked with a poor silhouette of 'Invincible' and the date "30.5.82". "Malvinas" logo was also worn. In 5.83 used for Magic AAM in-stallation trials, probably at CEV Cordoba.

**C-322** A-4C

In 3.82 with G4C. Not confirmed as having been deployed to San Julian but noted in post-war use at Mendoza in 11.82. No ship silhou-ette or "Malvinas" markings applied.

**C-324** A-4C

In 3.82 with G4C. Not confirmed as having been deployed to San Julian but noted in post-war use at Mendoza in 11.82.

**C-325** A-4C

In 3.82 with G4C. Deployed to San Julian on or after 11.4.82. Brought down over West Falkland on 21.5.82 by an AIM-9L fired from the 800 Sqdn Sea Harrier XZ492 of Lt Cdr Thomas or XZ496 of Lt Cdr Blissett (see C-309). Its pilot, Primer Teniente Manzotti, did not eject and was killed when the aircraft crashed south of Christmas Harbour near Chartres settlement.

# DAGGER

## GRUPO 6 DE CAZA

The FAA received the first of 39 Israeli-built Mirage 5's in November 1978 to replace its ageing F-86F Sabres in the twin roles of fighter-interceptor and fighter-bomber. Known in IDFAF use as the 'Nesher', the IAI constructed, Atar 9C-engined Mirage was named 'Dagger' by the FAA (although often referred to by the FAA as "Mirage V" for operational purposes) and, by December 1980, a total of 26 refurbished machines had been received. 24 of them were single-seat aircraft known as 'Dagger A' and two were dual-seat machines known as 'Dagger B'. Between May 1981 and February 1982 a further 11 Dagger A's and two more Dagger B's were received. Of the total of 39 aircraft, two, one of each model, were lost in accidents that occurred before March 1982. All the Daggers were delivered to VI Brigada Aerea at Tandil, Buenos Aires where they entered service with two squadrons of Grupo 6 de Caza (G6C), primarily for use in the air defence role. When the unit was warned to prepare itself for deployment south in April 1982 and to anticipate combat, the assimilation of the second batch of aircraft had barely been completed and there were several pilots on strength with little experience of the new aircraft.

The FAA had, in the Dagger, a modern and operationally established combat aircraft which, unlike some of the other tactical aircraft, was not subject to the problems of embargoed spare parts and shortages of operational equipment. The aircraft were in technically excellent condition and, by Latin American standards, Grupo 6 was a powerful force in either the air defence or tactical role. By world standards, however, the Dagger was austerely equipped and its relatively early withdrawal from first-line Israeli use reflected its pedigree — a development design towards their definitive Kfir. Specifically, the Dagger lacked air-refuelling capability, ECM, ESM and INS. Its elderly Shafrir AAM's, later to be described by a senior Grupo 6 pilot as "useless", required visual/manual firing procedures which subsequently put the Dagger at a considerable disadvantage in combat against more sophisticated systems. The twin 30mm DEFA cannon packed a good punch but, as with all such guns, only a brief burst or two was possible. More positively, the aircraft was extremely tough and its Martin Baker ejection seat provided a reliable escape system!

Grupo 6 de Caza was commanded by Comodoro Thomas Rodriguez and, in March 1982, his squadron commanders were Mayor Juan Sapolski (Escuadron II) and Mayor Carlos Napoleon Martinez (Escuadron III). Although many of their pilots were still fairly new to the type they nevertheless included several veterans with considerable experience of other combat aircraft. Sapolski and Martinez were each charged with working-up a squadron of about 12 aircraft to combat readiness and to take them to bases in the CdoFAS region by late April. With plenty of aircraft available, the engineering and logistical aspects were relatively straightforward but the training programme was hectic and Grupo 6 probably needed to achieve more in the short time available than did any other FAA unit. Escuadron II, later to gain the nickname "Las Avutardas Salvajes" (The Wild Bustards), was deployed first to the small civilian airport at San Julian, Santa Cruz on 25 April where it was formally named "Escuadron Dagger San Julian". Later that day Escuadron III deployed to the naval base at Rio Grande, Tierra del Fuego where it was titled "Escuadron Dagger Rio Grande".

Both Escuadrones were deemed operational at their new bases on 25 April and various trials and exercises were then undertaken in anticipation of forthcoming combat. In their fighter-interceptor role their primary duty seems to have been planned as escort to the Skyhawks of Grupo 4, co-located at San Julian, and to various naval sorties from Rio Grande. Inter-service relationships at the latter base appear to have been a little strained, however, and although top-cover was provided for SP-2H Neptune missions, the failure of a simulated Super Etendard/Exocet sortie on 25 April was blamed on the Daggers and all subsequent CANA jet missions were planned without Grupo 6 escort.

The first mainland-launched FAA combat sortie of the War was planned on the night of 30 April as a simple escort mission for two of the Rio Grande Daggers. At 0930Z the following morning, 1 May, they were to launch to rendezvous with a CANA Neptune in the general area of Port Stanley and, while the latter aircraft searched for the British fleet, the Daggers would provide an element of cover. Overnight, however, the British struck the first blow and, by 0930Z on 1 May, everyone at Rio Grande was aware that a Vulcan attack on Stanley Airport had taken place earlier that morning. Capitan Moreno and Teniente Hector Volponi were also aware that the Neptune had failed to take-off at the planned time of 0850Z and were thus a little disconcerted to learn at 0930Z that they were still to launch at 0945Z for an air-cover sortie over the Falklands. In fact their mission was launched a little after that, and at about 1125Z the two of them, "Toro" flight, were some 50 miles west of Port Stanley when the local CIC controller warned them of the presence of a large number of Sea Harriers which had recently attacked the airfield. Each Dagger was carrying three 1,300 litre underwing fuel tanks and two Shafrirs as well as their internal cannon. That battle configuration was a standard fit for long-range escort work and it provided the Daggers with a maximised fuel load.

The Port Stanley CIC quickly identified two Sea Harriers as potential interceptors of "Toro" flight and warned the Daggers of their presence. In fact they were the 801 Sqdn aircraft of Lt Cdr Robin Kent and Lt Brian Haigh on their second CAP of the morning. From a distance of 120 miles, the four aircraft closed on each other until, at nine miles range, both Daggers blew off their outer drop tanks. As the pairs crossed, "Toro" flight ejected the centre-line tanks and both pilots desperately tried to see the Sea Harriers which, according to the CIC, were some 5,000ft below them at about 18,000ft. For a few moments the two pairs of interceptors turned in circles, each seeking the others, but with the Dagger pilots acutely aware of the Sea Harrier's AIM-9L head-on missile capability and their own dwindling fuel states. Finally, and with afterburners in use, they left the area and ran for home at high speed. Once the Sea Harriers had broken away, the Daggers climbed to their most economical cruise height of 37,000ft for the return journey which was accomplished safely. Despite visibility of little more than a mile and a 300ft cloud base, the ILS-assisted landing at Rio Grande was made safely.

Ironically, both pairs of aircraft had left the engagement erroneously believing that the others had launched AAM's against them. The 801 Sqdn pilots believed that two missiles were fired at them head-on from a distance of about four miles, and Volponi thought that he saw a missile pass between he and his section leader while both aircraft were turning and searching for the Sea Harriers. In fact no-one had acquired a target and neither pair had launched a missile, Shafrir or Sidewinder! The British claim is difficult to explain, however, as it would have been pointless for the Daggers to have fired the Shafrir in such a fashion, and there must be at least a suspicion that the explosive release of the drop-tanks was misconstrued as a missile launch.

CdoFAS had held its Skyhawks and Canberras in a state of readiness for several days for the moment of open hostility when they would be launched against units of the British Task Force and, on 1 May, that moment had arrived. Shortly after the recovery of "Toro" section, the first flights of Skyhawks took-off from Rio Gallegos and San Julian seeking targets of opportunity in the waters surrounding East Falkland. From post-war FAA accounts, it is apparent that seven four-aircraft Skyhawk and two three-aircraft Canberra sorties were planned for 1 May, although, as is discussed elsewhere, all of the early missions were unsuccessful. Each flight appears to have been allocated a pair of covering interceptors to provide protection against the Sea Harriers, and, with the British radars being normally unable to differentiate escorts from bombers, it thus appeared to the Sea Harrier pilots that large formations of "Mirages" were seeking them out for combat. The reality was rather different with most FAA pilots desperately aware of the dangers of meeting the Sea Harrier. CdoFAS launched both Daggers and Mirage IIIEA's in identical top-cover escort roles on 1 May and, from available post-war evidence, it seems that 12 of the former and 10 of the latter were planned (the role of the Mirage in the battles of 1 May is considered elsewhere). Of the 12 planned Dagger sorties from Rio Grande and San Julian, at least 11 were flown in the escort and tactical roles.

The first pair of escorting Daggers left Rio Grande at about 1300Z to provide cover for one of the day's early Skyhawk missions. The aircraft of Capitan Mir Gonzalez and Teniente Juan Bernhardt were configured identically to those of the earlier "Toro" section and, again, the mission would be controlled by the CIC at Port Stanley. Using the CIC's long-range radar, the Daggers were to be vectored towards any hostile aircraft perceived as a threat to the attacking Skyhawks. The pattern established by the subsequent engagement with four Sea Harriers was to become classical for the day. As the Sea Harriers approached East Falkland from the north-east at their optimum fighting altitude of about 18,000ft, the CIC directed the two Daggers towards them from an orbit at 28,000ft. Although low on fuel, the Daggers jettisoned their external tanks and accelerated towards the Sea Harriers and the two groups of aircraft found themselves in cloud, turning and searching for each another. Bernhardt briefly gave chase to an aircraft that he glimpsed below him but there was no true contact and, with low fuel states, the Dagger crews soon abandoned the search. Frustrated that the Sea Harriers had not come up to their optimum combat altitude where they had been waiting in clean-configuration, Gonzalez and Bernhardt returned to Rio Grande at a cruise height of 39,000ft and subsequently landed safely, albeit with very little fuel left. Again, no AAM's had been launched by the Daggers or Sea Harriers and both sides viewed the engagement with some frustration.

As morning gave way to afternoon CdoFAS continued to launch periodic Skyhawk missions, although most were escorted by Mirages operating from Rio Gallegos. The Grupo 6 aircraft were again thrown into action, and most dramatically, late in the afternoon when the San Julian squadron was tasked with its first anti-shipping sortie of the War. Three Daggers were ordered to make a late afternoon attack on four British warships which had been reported in the Berkeley Sound area, north of Port Stanley. Each would carry two 500lb bombs, with three 1,300 litre drop tanks, as well as the DEFA cannon which would be used offensively in the attack. The flight was to be escorted by another pair of Daggers armed with twin Shafrirs and cannon. "Torno" flight took-off from San Julian at 1900Z, with a planned attack time of 1945Z, led by Capitan Dimeglio in Dagger C-432. His wingmen were Teniente Aguirre Faget and Primer Teniente Cesar Roman, respectively flying C-407 and C-412. The escort section, "Fortin" flight, that followed them into the air a few minutes later at 1905Z, was led by Capitan Guillermo Donadille with Primer Teniente Jorge Senn flying as his wingman.

"Torno" flight had an uneventful crossing to the Falklands, passing north of Saunders Island at 1935Z and the west coast of East Falkland five minutes later. Although Roman thought that he glimpsed a Sea Harrier, no contact was made with any of the British CAP's and the three Daggers ran-in over Berkeley Sound fast and low seeking the ships. They were nowhere to be seen and a decision was quickly made to search elsewhere, despite their dwindling fuel reserves. The three Grupo 6 Daggers turned south to round Cape Pembroke and there before them, withdrawing from a bombardment in the Port Stanley area, were 'Alacrity', 'Arrow' and 'Glamorgan'.

The British warships were not anticipating an attack and each Dagger had time to select a target and make a carefully judged run-in before dropping its bombs. As would happen many times in the days to follow, the Royal Navy ships came within a whisker of catastrophe. 'Glamorgan' was straddled by two bombs which caused some slight underwater damage, 'Alacrity' was similarly damaged and took on water and 'Arrow' was more visibly affected by cannon shells that stitched a line of holes across her funnel and adjacent structure. "Torno" flight had inflicted the first, albeit minor, damage on the British Task Force. Nevertheless, their return to San Julian was still a tense business for, being low on fuel, the Daggers could not hold the extreme low-level profile that would avoid radar detection. Obliged to climb, the three aircraft maintained separated flight levels at 45,000ft, 23,000ft and 33,000ft to complicate any attempted interception by Sea Harriers. A CAP did, in fact, get to within five miles of the number two but it broke off when its own fuel state became critical and the escorting "Fortin" section itself closed on the Sea Harrier. Once again the Dagger interceptor pilots felt thwarted, but it was nevertheless a most relieved Aguirre Faget who heard the CIC controller tell him of the Sea Harrier's departure. He had been within missile range and had been acutely aware of the fact!

At about the same time that "Torno" flight had been crossing East Falkland en route to the the warships, two of the Rio Grande Daggers were locked in a desperate struggle with two more Sea Harriers. Their escort mission to East Falkland had followed the same pattern as previous sorties and the Daggers had been vectored towards Sea Harriers approaching from 'Hermes', away to the north-east. The Daggers were at about 33,000ft with the Sea Harriers at 20,000ft and, as they closed on one another, an AAM, presumably a Shafrir, was launched at the aircraft of Lt Martin Hale of 800 Sqdn. It is clear from Hale's own account, although not from any FAA source, that the missile did indeed lock-on to his aircraft and followed him down to 5,000ft until it fell away, either deflected by his chaff or simply at the end of its travel. Either way, the missile passed frighteningly close to his aircraft. Meanwhile, the Dagger that had fired the missile, C-433 of Primer Teniente Jose Ardiles, began to climb rapidly towards a safe altitude but fell victim to a Side-

winder launched from the other Sea Harrier, XZ455 of Flt Lt Bertie Penfold. The missile had been launched from a range of nearly three miles and had been helped on its way by the bright glow of the Dagger's afterburner. C-433, the first Grupo 6 aircraft to be lost in combat, exploded at about 1941Z and pieces were later found as far south as Lively Island. No trace was found of the Dagger's unfortunate pilot.

1 May was not a good day for the FAA and its first all out assault on the ships and aircraft of the British fleet had resulted only in missed chances, confusion and tactical mistakes. Naivety had contributed to the loss of four aircraft and five crew in air battles and a rapid reassessment of tactics was obviously necessary if CdoFAS was to have any chance of winning an air war. For Grupo 6 the outlook was particularly grim. The events of 1 May had demonstrated that the Daggers simply did not have the fuel capacity to loiter over East Falkland in an escort role for more than a few minutes and, without air-refuelling, there was no room for any error of judgement or fuel loss from battle damage. Both Grupo 6 and the Mirage-equipped Grupo 8 also realised that their well disciplined enemy would not allow the Sea Harriers to be drawn into combat except when it suited them. Grupo 6 also knew that its Shafrir missiles would probably prove inadequate in any dogfight with the Sea Harriers. Thus, during the ensuing three weeks of generally inclement weather, new plans were made to repulse the inevitable British landings.

No long-range Grupo 6 missions were launched during early May, mainly because British warships took care not to venture close inshore to Port Stanley in good weather and invite retaliation from CdoFAS. Coastal bombardments were rarely undertaken during daylight hours and on the few occasions that FAA Skyhawks were launched against ships there were Argentine losses. Nevertheless, during that period, Grupo 6 supplied escort sorties for several naval and air activities away from the immediate area of the Falklands. One small success was achieved on 4 May when Capitan Robles and Capitan Cimatti of the Escuadron Dagger Rio Grande provided top-cover for the Grupo 1 KC-130H which refuelled the two CANA Super Etendards that destroyed 'Sheffield'.

As had been the situation on 30 April, the evening of 20 May saw the CdoFAS squadrons tense and irritated at waiting for combat which was known to be imminent. The long-anticipated British amphibious landings were rumoured to be close, but their location, scale and style were only being guessed at by FAA intelligence. It was, however, clear that an all out assault on the landing forces would be necessary if they were to be repulsed and all the dangers inherent in such missions were, by then, very well appreciated. Anti-shipping Skyhawk missions on 9 May and 12 May had clearly demonstrated the damage that British missiles and inclement weather could inflict on the FAA fighter-bombers.

The morning of 21 May dawned cold, grey and misty. The first sorties launched from the mainland against the British warships in Falkland Sound were dispatched against early and, at that time, unconfirmed sightings from land-based observation posts. The aerial reconnaissance data from the CANA MB-339A and the Grupo 3 Pucaras was not received until nearly midday and there

## MIRAGE IIIEA I-014 GRUPO 8 DE CAZA

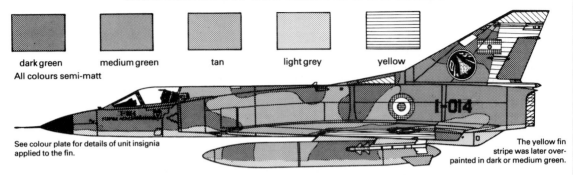

dark green   medium green   tan   light grey   yellow

All colours semi-matt

See colour plate for details of unit insignia applied to the fin.

The yellow fin stripe was later over-painted in dark or medium green.

## DAGGER 'A' C-413 GRUPO 6 DE CAZA

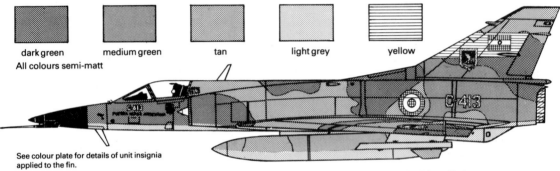

dark green   medium green   tan   light grey   yellow

All colours semi-matt

See colour plate for details of unit insignia applied to the fin.

Serial colours: port and starboard nose and port rear fuselage – tan; starboard rear fuselage – dark green; nosewheel door – black.

## MB-339A 0767/4-A-116 1 ESQUADRILLA DE ATAQUE

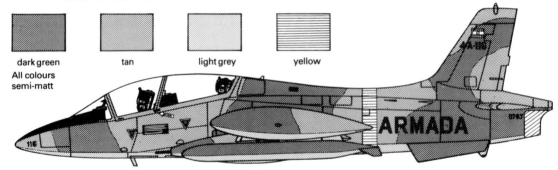

dark green   tan   light grey   yellow

All colours semi-matt

## CANBERRA T.64 B-112 GRUPO 2 DE BOMBARDEO

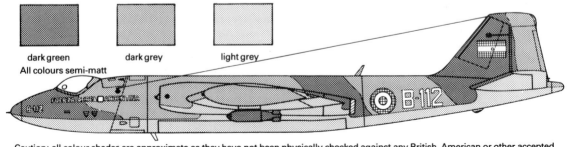

dark green   dark grey   light grey

All colours semi-matt

Caution: all colour shades are approximate as they have not been physically checked against any British, American or other accepted paint standards.

was therefore something of a "hit or miss" nature to some of the early sorties. The first pair of Grupo 6 Daggers to depart that morning were those of Capitan Dimeglio and Teniente Carlos Castillo, "Cuna" flight, of the Escuadron San Julian. They took-off at about 1230Z (the quoted FAA time is imprecise) as part of a larger formation, or rather an assembly of flights, which was designed to arrive over the target in waves of attacks within a short period of time. The intention was to create the maximum possible confusion to the ship-borne defences, while minimising their own difficulties when running-in on their targets. Each Dagger was armed with two 500lb bombs and carried three 1,300 litre tanks, a configuration intended to get the aircraft home safely while giving it as great a weapon load as possible. The bombs were fitted with delay fuses designed to enable an aircraft to clear the ship beneath it before the weapon detonated. The DEFA cannon were also to be used on the run-in although it was realised that their value might be as much psychological as anything else.

The weather had improved considerably by the time that "Cuna" flight made landfall over West Falkland. Its track had been a northerly one and consequently the run-in over Falkland Sound was from the north-west of the British picket ships. Dimeglio and Castillo found eight ships in the Sound and chose one particularly isolated warship which was three-quarters stern-on to their attack. Both Daggers approached her in a rough line-astern attack pattern and the pilots were subsequently confident that they had hit her superstructure with cannon fire although they were less sure of any achieved bomb damage. In fact 'Antrim' was little damaged in that first attack at 1325Z, although she was caught off-guard and offered very little anti-aircraft and no missile fire back at the Daggers. They passed safely overhead to begin their long run home to San Julian. The next few minutes, though, would see her badly damaged as further Dagger strikes were pressed home.

Less than an hour earlier, shortly after "Cuna" flight had left San Julian, the Escuadron Dagger Rio Grande had dispatched its first anti-shipping sortie of the War. Two flights of three aircraft took-off within a few minutes of one another with orders to seek out and destroy British shipping, assault ships and transports wherever possible, in Falkland Sound. They were scheduled to arrive in the area more or less together a few minutes after the "Cuna" attack. The first flight was "Nandu" and it was led by the commander, Mayor Martinez, with wingmen Capitan Carlos Rohde and Teniente Pedro Bean. "Perro" flight comprised Capitan Moreno, Teniente Volponi and Capitan Janett. The two flights closed up to within 1,000yds of each another on the over-water leg of the journey, with "Napo" Martinez leading the formation in on a northerly route over Mount Rosalie towards Falkland Sound. Like Dimeglio a few minutes before, he was soon confronted by a few ships in the Sound and several others in the distance within San Carlos Water. He rapidly decided to attack the three obvious warships out in the Sound and he headed for the vessel to the left of the group which he identified as a Type 42 Destroyer. In reality, it seems that the subject of his cannon and bomb attack was 'Broadsword', although damage to the frigate was limited to 30mm shellfire from the DEFA's. Rohde and Bean

both attacked the ship in the centre of the group and that has been identified by British sources as 'Argonaut', the frigate which had earlier suffered slight damage in an MB-339A rocket attack. Again 'Argonaut' escaped, suffering no serious damage. In the course of the attack, however, Teniente Pedro Bean was caught by a ship-launched missile as he ran-in on the target and his aircraft, C-428, broke up and hit the water, killing him. Some of his colleagues thought that they saw an ejection but that seems unlikely and his body was never recovered.

Post-war FAA analysis of the incident identified the missile concerned as a Seacat launched from either 'Argonaut' or 'Plymouth', but a more likely candidate would be a Seawolf fired from 'Broadsword'. Although shocked by the sight of Bean's disintegrating Dagger, Moreno's flight followed in behind "Nandu" and all three Daggers bombed 'Antrim' at 1331Z. It was that attack which left the destroyer with an unexploded 1,000lb bomb in one of the "heads" after it had entered the stern area and had passed through various compartments, including the Seaslug magazine. The attack effectively put 'Antrim' out of action and she was obliged to seek the relative safety of San Carlos Water for urgent repairs and defusing of the bomb. "Perro" flight escaped safely (despite the earlier attentions of a Seaslug from 'Antrim') and once they had passed southwards down Falkland Sound, they turned west for home. It was at that moment that one of the Daggers had a very fortunate escape when an AIM-9L was fired at it from extreme range by Lt Martin Hale in an 800 Sqdn Sea Harrier. He and his flight leader had been vectored to intercept the Daggers but they had arrived too late to have had a reasonable chance of bringing them down. Both Sea Harriers gave brief chase over West Falkland, but failed to catch the faster Daggers and, eventually, broke away as their fuel became short.

Grupo 6's first missions to the British anchorages in Falkland Sound set a clear pattern for those of future days in terms of achievement and cost. Of eight Daggers dispatched in the three flights, one had been lost and its young pilot killed. Although one warship had suffered some serious damage, none of the bombs dropped (apparently a mixture of 500lb and 1,000lb) detonated on impact with any vessel and the Daggers' cannon fire had caused only minor damage. By early afternoon CdoFAS was certain that the landings could not be diversionary and that the British invasion had indeed begun. Argentine land forces were unable to interfere to any significant extent and it was clear that only the FAA could slow the advance by inflicting unacceptably high losses on the Royal Naval ships offshore. With the benefits of continuing good weather, improving intelligence from the Islands and the experiences of the morning, the afternoon's missions were planned.

In essence, Grupo 6's role for the afternoon of 21 May was to provide one maximum-effort mission which would put a dozen or so Daggers into the Falkland Sound area in successive waves, a few minutes apart. The basic strategy had worked well during the morning and it was hoped that the Sea Harrier CAP's might be unable to cope with an increased number of aircraft attacking on different headings. Six Daggers were planned to depart from San Julian in two flights shortly after 1645Z and another group would leave Rio Grande approximately ten minutes later. "Laucha" flight would be first off from San Julian followed by "Raton" a minute later, while "Cueca" and "Libra" would leave Rio Grande at about 1655Z, although all times were considered flexible. In practice, the Rio Grande aircraft took-off first in anticipation of reaching the target at 1730Z. "Cueca" flight was led by Capitan Gonzalez and his wingmen for the mission were Teniente Bernhardt and Primer Teniente Hector Luna. "Libra" flight, following immediately after, had difficulties and only two aircraft, those of Capitan Cimatti and Capitan Robles, actually got airborne. Gonzalez had been briefed to attack a single British ship which had been reported lying off Port Howard in Falkland Sound, and thus his flight would cross West Falkland and pass over the Hornby Mountains before reaching the Sound. The mission suffered a second setback en route when Cimatti's Dagger began to lose oil and, trailing black smoke, he aborted and returned home to Rio Grande where he landed safely. Robles moved up to join "Cueca" flight and the four Daggers pressed on in radio-silence. Before they descended from cruise height to the vital low-level profile necessary to avoid detection they had, however, already been identified by the British radars, in particular those of 'Brilliant', and an 800 Sqdn Sea Harrier CAP was on the way to meet them.

The Daggers passed over Jason Island and at King George Bay they turned on to a heading of 060° to pass through the gap between Mount Robinson and Mount Maria. When north of Chartres Settlement, they were seen by the Sea Harriers and Robles and Luna, the left-hand element of the group, were pursued by Lt Cdr Rod Frederiksen (in XZ455) who fired a Sidewinder at the nearer Dagger. Moments before Luna's aircraft (C-409) was hit by the missile, he caught a glimpse of S/Lt Andy George's Sea Harrier above him but his attempt to warn the others was thwarted by a radio malfunction. The missile severely damaged the control surfaces, causing the Dagger to roll violently. Luna had no option but to abandon his aircraft as quickly as possible and, at about 1735Z, he made a successful, low-level ejection near Teal River Inlet. The remains of his Dagger fell nearby. His injuries were minor and he was recovered the following day, eventually to be returned to Argentina on 25 May.

Unaware of the attack on Luna, Robles was equally oblivious to subsequent gun attacks on his aircraft by Frederiksen. A similarly unsuccessful attack by George on Gonzalez and Bernhardt also passed unnoticed! The Grupo 6 pilots were preoccupied with finding a way through the mountains below the cloud which had descended across their planned track. Eventually a small ravine was spotted and the Daggers passed through, line-astern. At that moment Robles broke radio-silence to report that Luna was no longer with them and it was concluded that he had struck a mountain during the previous few minutes. More immediate matters required attention, however, for, as the three Daggers passed over the coast of West Falkland, in front of them, close inshore in Grantham Sound, was 'Ardent'. Gonzalez led in the trio, and, as they approached through her light gunfire, he released his single 1,000lb bomb. As he passed low over the ship he saw the bomb fall short, striking the water and raising a great plume of spray, before bouncing up and embedding itself near the stern. Next it was Bernhardt, the

number two, whose bomb actually detonated on impact with the frigate, demolishing Lynx XZ251, its hangar, the Seacat launcher and several other fittings. Several crew were also killed or injured in the attack. As Robles ran-in on the ship, pieces of 'Ardent' were still twisting and turning in the air from the blast. His bomb did no further damage however, and, shortly before 1740Z, the three Daggers turned south to escape down Falkland Sound and ultimately returned safely to Rio Grande. 'Ardent', damaged but far from finished, moved north-west to the protection of other warships grouped near the entrance to San Carlos Water.

The six San Julian Daggers had taken-off soon after 1645Z, with the intention of being in the target area in two groups at 1750Z and 1751Z. "Laucha" flight was led by Primer Teniente Roman with his numbers two and three respectively Mayor Luis Puga and Primer Teniente Mario Callejo. "Raton" flight was led by Capitan Donadille and his two and three were Mayor Justo Piuma and Primer Teniente Senn (although senior men, Puga and Piuma gave way to more experienced junior pilots on combat missions). "Laucha" flight crossed the central part of West Falkland without incident, although visibility was indifferent with some heavy cloud with low ceiling and intermittent rain showers, and, at about 1745Z, the three Daggers crossed the coast of West Falkland and passed over the Sound towards a group of British warships which were appearing ever larger on the eastern horizon. Roman and Puga made a direct attack on 'Brilliant' which, at that moment, was in the neck of the San Carlos anchorage, but no bomb damage was sustained and their cannon caused only slight damage and few casualties. Meanwhile, Callejo attacked a nearby "frigate" and was most fortunate to escape unscathed when a shrapnel splinter crazed part of his windscreen during the run-in. He pressed on, remorselessly, with his cannon attack but, like his colleagues, his bombs caused no damage and he left the area pursued by a firework display of SAM's and gunfire. Fortune smiled on "Laucha" flight, however, and all three pilots were able to climb to a safe, economical cruise level at 35,000ft and they returned home without further incident.

"Raton" was due to follow "Laucha" flight over Falkland Sound from the Port Howard area, within a minute or so of the latter's strike on 'Brilliant', but its descent to low level over West Falkland had been seen on radar by, of all ships, 'Brilliant' herself. As "Laucha" flight turned south to escape, the controller in her damaged operations room was already vectoring two 801 Sqdn Sea Harriers from a CAP orbit, north-west of Mount Maria, towards the incoming "Raton" flight. As they passed low over the ground to the north of Mount Maria, still a minute or so away from their target, Donadille and Piuma were seen by Lt Steve Thomas in ZA190 and Lt Cdr Nigel Ward in ZA175 who were flying above and behind them. Ironically, it was the bright yellow wing markings that had been introduced after 1 May to avoid further incidents with Argentine AAA batteries that had initially attracted Thomas' attention.

Senn, flying on the right of the formation, spotted the Sea Harriers approaching from his right and called a warning to the others. In a swift series of events Donadille and Piuma blew off their drop-tanks, jettisoned their bombs and turned to the right to meet Ward who was descending towards them. However, they did not notice Thomas who was moving behind them, seeking a missile-lock. Unseen by the Sea Harriers, and momentarily late in dropping his tanks and bombs, Senn continued east, passing above Donadille's track as the latter made a head-on run at Ward. Donadille fired two bursts of cannon fire, the first from a range of 700yds, but Ward escaped unscathed, passing beneath Donadille's Dagger. As Donadille subsequently climbed sharply (having passed uncomfortably close to the ground) he briefly checked to avoid the returning Senn who was crossing his path and, as he did so, he became Steve Thomas' second kill of the engagement.

Seconds earlier, Piuma's Dagger, C-404, had disintegrated when it was struck by a Sidewinder launched from ZA190. Thomas' second missile was fired almost immediately, and it followed Donadille's Dagger in a right-hand turn before detonating within a few feet of the wing root. As had been Hector Luna's experience a few minutes before, Donadille suffered a complete loss of control, with his aircraft first rearing and diving and then entering an uncontrollable spin. Fortunately for Donadille he was able to eject from the doomed C-403.

After a brief low-level chase, Jorge Senn, in C-407, was also shot down by a Sidewinder, his Dagger disintegrating before cartwheeling into the ground. He had been brought down by Nigel Ward, the pilot of the Sea Harrier that Senn had first glimpsed a few moments earlier. Amazingly, both Piuma and Senn were able to make successful ejections (although the latter suffered facial injuries) from their doomed aircraft and all three Grupo 6 pilots were eventually recovered safely to Port Howard. The brief and violent engagement had taken place over the Green Hill Bridge area, about three miles south-west of Mount Caroline, and the Daggers of Donadille and Piuma (C-403 and C-404) both came to ground near Green Hill Bridge itself. Senn's aircraft (C-407) fell four miles to the west, about two miles south of Mount Caroline. They had been destroyed at 1750Z, the precise time at which they had been scheduled to make their attack in Falkland Sound.

The day was traumatic for both the FAA and Grupo 6. There were undoubtedly successes for Argentina but in the evening of 21 May much of that was still unconfirmed. What was beyond doubt was the punishment sustained by the FAA in achieving those successes. 54 FAA sorties had ultimately been launched — CdoFAS failed to achieve its planned maximum effort of 63 — but seven aircraft had been lost and most of their pilots were dead or still missing. For Grupo 6 the situation was little short of catastrophic, with five Daggers destroyed, four of them in the space of 15 minutes. Unlike 1 May, the Sea Harriers had operated over West Falkland below the level at which the FAA Port Stanley radars could detect them and, without any warning of their presence, the Daggers and Skyhawks were completely helpless and had been caught absolutely "cold". A veritable arsenal of weapons was ranged against them at San Carlos Water and the barrage had increased in ferocity during the course of the day. Several of the Daggers that had reached the safety of San Julian and Rio Grande were already showing scars of battle by that evening. The prospect of a second such day was simply untenable.

While the British worked ceaselessly to disembark their forces at San Carlos, the FAA worked equally furiously to repair the battle damage sustained by the fighter-bombers. Although robust and durable enough for all to have returned safely to the mainland, several of the Daggers had sustained multiple shrapnel and cannon hits on 21 May and they required considerable overnight attention to make them airworthy for the following day. Inevitably, some were not readied in time and by dawn CdoFAS had already scaled down its planned operation. The weather, too, was awful with low cloud and rain over the Falklands and much of southern Patagonia and Tierra del Fuego. In the event, only two Skyhawk sorties appear to have been launched in the late afternoon of 22 May. By midday on 23 May the weather had improved enough to allow missions to recommence and, for the Daggers, their profiles were little changed. Having no air-refuelling capability the flight plan was a simple "hi-lo-hi" with drop-tanks and a single 1,000lb bomb carried. None of the Daggers carrying bombs were Shafrir armed, and they were totally reliant on the Port Stanley CIC and other aircraft to warn them of the presence of Sea Harrier CAP's. If warned early enough, they would simply return to Argentina. When launched in waves from the mainland, the faster Daggers would go first, leaving the following Skyhawks to air-refuel and then attack the ships when they were still recovering from the Dagger onslaught.

On 23 May the first Argentine attacks did not take place until about 1645Z and fewer than half of the planned 46 sorties were successful in reaching the target area and performing their mission. Neither the San Julian nor Rio Grande squadrons enjoyed any notable successes in their few sorties that afternoon but, late in the day, disaster struck again. Shortly before 1900Z a pair of Rio Grande Daggers (possibly two of four) were running in from the north of Falkland Sound when, presumably warned of the nearby presence of two Sea Harriers, they aborted the mission and returned along their outbound track. They were sighted over Pebble Island by the commander of 800 Sqdn, Lt Cdr Andy Auld, and his wingman Lt Martin Hale. The leading Dagger was travelling too fast to be caught but the aircraft of Teniente Hector Ricardo Volponi, C-437, was well over a mile behind and within missile range of Hale in Sea Harrier ZA194. Hale fired a Sidewinder from a distance of about 1,000yds behind the Dagger and, at the end of its inevitable run, the missile exploded as it hit in the jet-pipe area. The Dagger disintegrated at low level, killing Volponi, the wreckage coming to ground on the western side of Elephant Bay, some two miles north of Pebble Island settlement. It had been at least the third time that Volponi had brushed with Sea Harriers and the second time that Martin Hale had fired at his flight.

By 24 May the battle for the bridgehead had been virtually won by the British and it was becoming clear to CdoFAS that if air-power was still to win the day for Argentina then it would have to be by striking isolated, but highly damaging, blows at British shipping or troop concentrations. Nevertheless, as long as supplies were going ashore at San Carlos, the auxiliaries would still have to be attacked, but, by the 24 May, the British air defences there were truly awesome. Three days of grim fighting had ensured that the British had assembled a

**Upper Left** *As one Grupo 6 de Caza Dagger climbs away to the west a second continues its run northwards over the San Carlos Water anchorage on 24.5.82. Although not positively identified, it is thought probable that both aircraft were Rio Grande-based and led, that morning, by Captain Horacio Mir Gonzalez. The frigate in the foreground is 'Plymouth'. (Ministry of Defence).* **Upper Right** *Another photograph of the same flight of Grupo 6 de Caza aircraft, probably taken moments later, shows one of the Daggers passing behind 'Fearless'. Despite many British claims, the flight reached the safety of Rio Grande without loss although three of the Daggers had been damaged by shrapnel and small arms fire during their passage over San Carlos Water.*

*(Ministry of Defence)*

*A posed photograph, probably taken c5.82, of a Grupo 6 de Caza Dagger A at Tandil, the unit's home base. When deployed to Rio Grande and San Julian many of the Daggers received yellow tail and wing markings to identify them to friendly forces. Unfortunately, little has emerged of C-421's wartime career although it was certainly not amongst the casualties of the conflict.*

*C-403 was one of the ten Mirage 5P's supplied to the FAA from Peru in 6.82. These aircraft were allocated the serials of ten Daggers that had been lost during the conflict but none of the new arrivals saw combat. As can be seen from this photograph, taken at Mariano Moreno c8.82, the lighter Peruvian camouflage was retained with FAA markings simply superimposed on those of the FAP.*

sophisticated SAM net and the Rapier missiles were now a real menace to every FAA sortie. Every conceivable gun would now be brought to bear on the Daggers and Skyhawks that penetrated the outer defences of San Carlos Water.

During the late morning another four-aircraft mission was launched from San Julian and, again, it took a northern route into Falkland Sound. By 24 May the CIC had become more proficient at warning such flights of the presence of Sea Harriers but on that occasion the recent arrival on station north of Pebble Island of the 800 Sqdn aircraft of Lt Cdr Auld and Lt Dave Smith was either missed or not communicated. From 10,000ft the two Sea Harriers were vectored by 'Broadsword' towards the incoming Daggers which, by the time they had reached Pebble Island, were travelling very low and fast towards the Sound. At 1415Z Auld, in XZ457, rolled in behind the leading pair and fired his Sidewinders in rapid succession, destroying both Daggers in bright fireballs. Smith, in ZA193, gave chase to the second pair. They broke to the right and jettisoned their bombs and tanks but he successfully locked a missile onto the nearer of the two and, moments later, it exploded in a bright fireball as the Sidewinder found the hot tail-pipe. The burning debris hit the ground and the Dagger disintegrated in a fiery mass. Both Sea Harriers gave brief chase to the fourth Dagger but, with its greater speed, it remained beyond missile range and finally escaped.

The three downed aircraft were those of Mayor Puga (C-419) and Capitan Raul Diaz (C-430), both of whom successfully ejected, and Teniente Castillo (C-410) who was killed. Both of Auld's Daggers fell into the sea north of Pebble Island, while Smith's impacted on the western edge of Elephant Bay on the slopes of First Mount. Puga spent some hours in a dinghy before being rescued by CANA personnel and he appears to have been one of Auld's victims, while unconfirmed and rather circumstantial evidence suggests that Auld's other "kill" was Diaz, the second survivor. Castillo therefore appears to have been the pilot killed in the First Mount wreck.

At approximately the same time that disaster overtook the San Julian flight, Capitan Mir Gonzalez was leading another flight of four Rio Grande aircraft northwards up Falkland Sound to come into San Carlos Water over the Sussex Mountains. His flight held a loose line-abreast battle formation and attacked the first target of opportunity that they found which they later described as "a large ship". It is far from clear which vessel that actually was, but the inflicted damage, if any at all, was presumably light, there being no serious incidents reported by the British. The Daggers continued to fly low up San Carlos Water (and in the process provided the British photographers with many excellent "now you see me, now you don't" pictures that later received wide publication) and subsequently all made a safe return to Rio Grande. Significantly, only the leading Dagger of Gonzalez had been undamaged by anti-aircraft fire and his numbers two, three and four were each found to have been hit by between two and six rounds of ammunition during their run across San Carlos Water.

The FAA was later to admit that on 24 May only 12 aircraft actually reached targets in the San Carlos area (the other eight were Skyhawks) and effectively the air battle had been lost by Argentina. For Grupo 6 it had been a particularly bad day, with another flight decimated by the Sea Harriers. Indeed, nine of the their ten losses since 1 May had been to "La Muerta Negra" (The Black Death). Some comfort lay in the knowledge that six of their pilots, five of them of senior rank, had made good ejections but that was small consolation in strict military terms. Losses of the magnitude already experienced by Grupo 6 were unacceptable and could not be sustained. It is thought that it was after the losses of 24 May that Peru offered the FAA ten Mirage 5P's from the Fuerza Aerea Peruana. These essentially similar aircraft are believed to have originally been intended as direct replacements to make good the Dagger attrition but, although the offer was quickly accepted and the aircraft were rapidly delivered (allegedly to Rio Grande), they took no part in the War and were not assimilated into FAA service for some months.

Both sides have retrospectively agreed that the evening of 25 May marked the end of the battle for beach-head supremacy at San Carlos. In spite of heroic efforts by the FAA and CANA pilots which achieved some outstanding successes in the early stages, the British had successfully scrambled ashore and had consolidated their positions. On 25 May the FAA was only able to launch 22 sorties against British ships (some of which were well away from San Carlos Water) and only 17 of them were adjudged to have successfully reached their targets. The previous day's losses may well have kept the Daggers on the ground that day, for none was reported by British forces over the Islands, and the three FAA losses on 25 May were Grupo 4 and Grupo 5 Skyhawks. Between 26 May and 7 June CdoFAS scheduled 110 attack sorties from the mainland but in fact only 57 actually completed "successful" missions. The CIC and the FAA pilots did, however, become increasingly adept at terminating missions before the Sea Harrier CAP's could reach them. Some successes were claimed by the FAA when Sea Harriers were forced into pursuing "decoy" flights, indeed the tactic was claimed to have played a considerable role in the attacks on British shipping on 8 June.

Most CdoFAS missions launched during the last days of May were undertaken by the Skyhawks and, in particular, those of Grupo 5, which ultimately achieved greater successes against British warships than any other FAA unit. Nevertheless, Grupo 6 continued to mount spasmodic Dagger attacks and on 29 May another sortie was launched from Rio Grande to San Carlos Water. The fear of further Super Etendard attacks had, by then, taken the British aircraft carriers well to the east of the Falklands and in consequence it was less easy to maintain the blanket of CAP cover over West Falkland. On that occasion the Daggers got into the target area but, for the first time, one of them was brought down by a land-launched SAM. The circumstances surrounding the loss of Teniente Juan Bernhardt are not entirely clear but it appears that his Dagger, C-436, was brought down that afternoon as he passed over San Carlos Water. It was probably his misfortune to have been caught by a Rapier launched from a nearby coastal battery. His aircraft crashed into the sea, possibly into Falkland Sound, and Bernhardt was killed, although reportedly after an unsuccessful ejection. His body was not recovered.

Bernhardt's death, the fifth of a Grupo 6 pilot, marked the end of a bitter month for the unit. In 29 days it had lost 11 aircraft to a technically superior enemy and it had discovered that simple "stick and rudder" skills and determination were inadequate attributes to win the air war. Unless their tactics were radically changed, losses would inevitably continue until neither Escuadron would be able to launch a credible mission. Already the CANA Skyhawk Escuadrilla was in such a situation and Grupo 4's losses had considerably weakened its strength. Launching of missions against the so-called "Fragmentary Orders", whereby target updates were passed to the crews en route, would continue but most future sorties would be more fully and carefully considered before tasking, for careful husbandry of the remaining fighter-bombers was vital. The opening days of June, however, were full of typically nasty regional winter weather and virtually no FAA combat operations were undertaken for a full week.

On the morning of 8 June the situation changed dramatically with clear weather over East Falkland and intelligence reports of further British landings in the Port Pleasant area, some 15 miles south-west of Port Stanley. A pair of transports were in open water surrounded by flat coastal plain which, clearly, afforded no natural defence against air attack. Such an opportunity to slow the British advance was too tempting to ignore, but CdoFAS was only too well aware of the havoc that the Sea Harriers could cause among the fighter-bombers unless they could be temporarily distracted away from the Port Pleasant area (and in the event that was achieved, although in some measure the result of circumstances of which CdoFAS was totally unaware). The mission to Port Pleasant was fairly simple in conception and initially involved Grupo 5, Grupo 6 and the Mirages of Grupo 8 which would re-appear over the Falkland Islands for the first time in several weeks. The Mirages, simulating a fighter-bomber sortie, would make a decoy run towards the San Carlos area from the north, while eight Grupo 5 Skyhawks and six Grupo 6 Daggers would follow a southerly route to Port Pleasant a few minutes later. The anticipated time over the target for the Rio Grande Daggers was to be in the order of 1700Z and the diversionary Mirage run was planned to coincide with the slightly earlier Skyhawk attack.

The six Daggers, each carrying one 1,000lb bomb, comprised two flights, "Perro" and "Gato" and the mission was led by Capitan Rohde. He led "Perro" flight and his wingmen were Primer Teniente Ratti and Primer Teniente Gabari, while "Gato" was led by the experienced Capitan Cimatti. Surprisingly, his wingmen were the Escuadron commander, Mayor Martinez, and Primer Teniente Antonietti. The two flights took-off together at about 1600Z but almost immediately Antonietti aborted the mission after a bird-strike broke his windscreen. His emergency landing at Rio Grande was made safely. For the others there would be no navigational or communications difficulties, for a Learjet of Grupo 1 Aerofotografico had been assigned to them as a lead-ship. Accordingly, they were led to about 70 miles from the target area, a point on the west coast of West Falkland near Cape Meredith. From there, the five Daggers turned north-east towards Falkland Sound, with the intention of later turning east

across northern Lafonia to run-in on Port Pleasant from the west. It was at that moment, as the Daggers flew north-east up the Sound, that 'Plymouth' appeared in front of them in solitary splendour. She had left the safety of San Carlos Water for an NGS mission and was steadily steaming across the Sound when the Daggers saw her. Having lost the element of surprise for their attack in Port Pleasant, the Grupo 6 force immediately changed their plan and made 'Plymouth' the subject of their attention.

After overflying to the north they made a wide turn and ran-in on the frigate, which by then was making a rapid turn to the east and the safety of the defences of San Carlos Water. The Daggers attacked line-astern at 575kts and, despite the frigate's 20mm gunfire and a Seacat launch, they were able to bomb 'Plymouth' with considerable accuracy but little luck. She was hit by cannon fire and four of the Daggers actually hit the ship with bombs which either struck her cleanly or after ricocheting from the sea. Amazingly, none detonated but 'Plymouth' was left burning from a fire caused by an exploding depth charge. She was most fortunate to have survived the attack and Argentine intelligence might perhaps be forgiven for briefly believing that she had in fact been sunk. In reality, the burning warship was able to limp back to San Carlos Water and safety where her considerable fire damage was attended to so that she could ultimately return to Britain for major repairs. Despite optimistic claims by her gunners, none of the Daggers suffered serious damage from 'Plymouth', indeed only one was hit at all. In spite of a belated Sea Harrier chase, the five Daggers eventually reformed at 35,000ft over West Falkland and returned safely to Rio Grande. Although it was eventually realised that their unidentified target had been 'Plymouth' and that she had not been sunk, there was naturally considerable excitement at Rio Grande on their return and the aircraft used in the attack were duly marked to indicate their achievements. The silhouette worn by C-401 was certainly that of 'Plymouth', while that worn by C-414 may also have related to that attack.

In spite of the success of the mission of 8 June, it appears that no more Dagger sorties were flown over the Falklands before the surrender of the local Argentine forces some six days later. However, while Grupo 5's Skyhawks flew a handful of last-ditch sorties to East Falkland on 13 June, Grupo 6 seems to have made a final attempt to bring down one of the British ESM-equipped picket helicopters that the FAA knew had been carefully stationed north and south of the Islands. During that morning, two Daggers attacked 'Cardiff' Flight's Lynx (XZ233) at a position roughly 50 miles south of Falkland Sound. The two aircraft attacked with cannon fire but were unable to hit the turning helicopter and they were obliged to break off the engagement, presumably after exhausting their ammunition.

The FAA credits the Daggers of Grupo 6 with 145 wartime sorties, although unofficial sources claim 160. 11 aircraft were lost in combat and five pilots were killed in action. Despite its fuel-carrying limitations and the considerable volume of battle damage sustained by the aircraft, no Dagger that cleared the immediate combat zone failed to reach the mainland safely. Its limited combat achievements should perhaps be considered sympathetically, for the aircraft was clearly inadequately equipped for the task demanded.

Post-war developments at Tandil and elsewhere in Argentina have concentrated on reducing the Dagger's vulnerability to interception and particular emphasis has been placed on providing it with a modern ECM fit. Under Israeli guidance, such a modification programme was commenced in late 1982 and an in-flight refuelling capability was also being investigated. At the time of writing in 1985, no more Daggers had been received by the FAA and, in 1983, another Dagger A had been lost in an accident leaving Grupo 6 with a maximum of 22 aircraft in use. It should be mentioned that unconfirmed local rumours suggested that up to six of the Daggers used during the War received damage which was serious enough to have warranted major rework on them before their restoration to normal operational use.

*Grupo 6 de Caza pilots deployed to Rio Grande and San Julian who are known to have flown combat missions included:*

*Comodoro T.Rodriguez (Grupo 6 commander); Mayor C.N.Martinez (Escuadron III commander); Mayor J.Sapolski (Escuadron II commander); Mayor G.Justo Piuma; Mayor L.A.Puga; Capitan Cimatti; Capitan R.Diaz; Capitan Dimeglio; Capitan G.Donadille; Capitan Janett; Capitan H.Mir Gonzalez; Capitan Moreno; Capitan Robles; Capitan C.Rohde; Primer Teniente Antonietti; Primer Teniente J.R.Ardiles (KIA); Primer Teniente M.M.Callejo; Primer Teniente Gabari; Primer Teniente H.Luna; Primer Teniente Ratti; Primer Teniente C.Roman; Primer Teniente J.D.Senn; Teniente Aguirre Faget; Teniente P.I.Bean (KIA); Teniente J.D.Bernhardt (KIA); Teniente C.J.Castillo (KIA); Teniente H.R.Volponi (KIA).*

# INDIVIDUAL AIRCRAFT DETAILS

All the Grupo 6 Daggers remained in their normal green and tan camouflage, with most aircraft wearing the crest of VI Brigada Aerea on the fin. The standard presentation of aircraft serials was unchanged with one applied in large green (starboard side) and tan (port side) digits to the rear fuselage and repeated in small tan numerals beneath the windscreen area on the fuselage sides. The lower fuselage and wing areas were white and the serial number also appeared (in full) in black script on the nose-wheel door. The FUERZA AEREA ARGENTINA title was applied in black letters to both sides of the fuselage beneath the small serial. Yellow identification bands were applied to many aircraft after 1 May in the form of a vertical fin stripe through the centre of the Dagger's fin, together with similar stripes over the outer part of the wings. Ship "kill" markings, in the form of silhouettes, were applied in yellow or white beneath the cockpit area. A damaged ship would appear (typically) with the forward hull solidly painted and the aft hull in outline. Underwing drop-tanks, originally camouflaged, were used in large numbers and were eventually carried in white, yellow, white and yellow, natural metal, red primer and other colour schemes!

As far as is known only the Dagger A model was deployed from Tandil to Rio Grande and San Julian. It is not exhaustively known which aircraft were actually used in combat but the following aircraft histories include details of all the Dagger A's confirmed to have been involved (including all those lost in combat) as well as those confirmed in post-war use.

*In the individual aircraft details the standard FAA abbreviation 'G6C' has been used for Grupo 6 de Caza.*

**C-401**

In 3.82 with G6C. Deployed to Rio Grande on or after 25.4.82. Used in the attack on 'Plymouth' in Falkland Sound on 8.6.82 and accordingly marked with a solid white ship silhouette. The aircraft survived the War and was noted at Tandil in 11.82.

*This aircraft, possibly the unit commander's, was photographed several times during the War and illustrations show it both with and without yellow stripes and with and without the ship silhouette.*

**C-403**

In 3.82 with G6C. Deployed to San Julian on or after 25.4.82. Brought down over West Falkland on 21.5.82 by an AIM-9L fired from the 801 Sqdn Sea Harrier ZA190 of Lt Thomas. Capitan Donadille ejected safely and was later recovered to Port Howard. His aircraft crashed near Green Hill Bridge (UC 190886) but the fuselage remained essentially intact and was later retrieved and noted in the Chinook hangar at RAF Kelly's Garden, near San Carlos Settlement on 15.7.83 (but had gone by 18.9.84).

**C-404**

In 3.82 with G6C. Deployed to San Julian on or after 25.4.82. Brought down over West Falkland on 21.5.82 by an AIM-9L fired from the 801 Sqdn Sea Harrier ZA190 of Lt Thomas. Mayor Justo Piuma ejected successfully and was later recovered to Port Howard. His aircraft crashed near Green Hill Bridge (UC 188864).

**C-407**

In 3.82 with G6C. Deployed to San Julian on or after 25.4.82. Used in the attack on 'Alacrity', 'Arrow' and 'Glamorgan' near Port Stanley on 1.5.82 but no later evidence of "kill" markings. Brought down over West Falkland on 21.5.82 by an AIM-9L fired from the 801 Sqdn Sea Harrier ZA175 of Lt Cdr Ward. Primer Teniente Senn ejected successfully and was later recovered to Port Howard. His aircraft crashed south of Mount Caroline (UC 252869).

*Dagger wreckage from this area, but not absolutely confirmed as that of C-407 (it could have been from C-403 or C-404), was investigated in late 6.82 and a fin with the VI Brigada Aerea unit crest was recovered. Later, closer investigation revealed a former Israeli squadron marking beneath the FAA* paintwork. *A small radio call-sign plate recovered from the cockpit was inscribed '05-4XFWY'. The fin was eventually taken to Odiham but only the VI BA crest later survived.*

## C-408

In 3.82 with G6C. Not confirmed as having been deployed to Rio Grande or San Julian but was noted in post-war use at Tandil in 11.82.

## C-409

In 3.82 with G6C. Deployed to Rio Grande on or after 25.4.82. Brought down over West Falkland on 21.5.82 by an AIM-9L fired from the 800 Sqdn Sea Harrier XZ455 of Lt Cdr Frederiksen. The pilot, Primer Teniente Luna, ejected successfully and was later recovered to Port Howard. His aircraft crashed near Teal River Inlet.

## C-410

In 3.82 with G6C. Deployed to San Julian on or after 25.4.82. Brought down over Pebble Island, West Falkland on 24.5.82 by an AIM-9L, probably fired from the 800 Sqdn Sea Harrier ZA193 of Lt Smith. Teniente Castillo was killed in the explosion. The wreck site has not been positively identified but may be that found in the First Mount area (UD 170160).

## C-412

In 3.82 with G6C. Deployed to San Julian on or after 25.4.82. Used in the attack on 'Alacrity', 'Arrow' and 'Glamorgan' near Port Stanley on 1.5.82 and decorated with a ship silhouette to indicate a damaged vessel. The aircraft survived the War and was noted in use at Tandil in 11.82.

## C-413

In 3.82 with G6C. Deployed to Rio Grande or San Julian on or after 25.4.82. Used during the War although not noted in post-war service. Not a known casualty.

## C-414

In 3.82 with G6C. Believed deployed to Rio Grande on or after 25.4.82. When noted in post-war use at Tandil in 8.82 it was wearing a "kill" marking, thought to reflect its use in the attack on 'Plymouth' in Falkland Sound on 8.6.82.

## C-417

In 3.82 with G6C. Deployed to Rio Grande or San Julian on or after 25.4.82. Used during the War and was later noted in use at Tandil in 11.82.

## C-418

In 3.82 with G6C. Not confirmed as having been deployed to Rio Grande or San Julian but displayed at Tandil in 9.85. For the purposes of that ceremony it appeared to have been marked with four ship "kills" (although they were unlike those applied to other Daggers during the conflict), presumably to represent G6C's total wartime achievements.

## C-419

In 3.82 with G6C. Deployed to San Julian on or after 25.4.82. Brought down over Pebble Island, West Falkland on 24.5.82 by an AIM-9L almost certainly fired from the 800 Sqdn Sea Harrier XZ457 of Lt Cdr Auld. Mayor Puga ejected safely over the sea and was later recovered to Pebble Island. His aircraft is thought to have crashed in the sea north of Pebble Island.

## C-420

In 3.82 with G6C. Not confirmed as having been deployed to Rio Grande or San Julian but noted in post-war use at Tandil in 11.82.

## C-427

In 3.82 with G6C. Not confirmed as having been deployed to Rio Grande or San Julian but noted in post-war use at Tandil in 11.82.

## C-428

In 3.82 with G6C. Deployed to Rio Grande on or after 25.4.82. Brought down over San Carlos Water on 21.5.82 by a SAM (thought to have been a Seawolf from 'Broadsword'). The pilot, Teniente Bean, was killed, his aircraft crashing into the sea.

## C-430

In 3.82 with G6C. Deployed to San Julian on or after 25.4.82. Brought down over Pebble Island, West Falkland on 24.5.82 by an AIM-9L probably fired from the 800 Sqdn Sea Harrier XZ457 of Lt Cdr Auld. Capitan Diaz ejected successfully. His aircraft is thought to have crashed into the sea north of Pebble Island.

## C-432

In 3.82 with G6C. Deployed to San Julian on or after 25.4.82. Used in the attack on 'Alacrity', 'Arrow' and 'Glamorgan' near Port Stanley on 1.5.82 and decorated with a ship silhouette to indicate a damaged vessel. Not a known casualty, but unrecorded in post-war use.

## C-433

In 3.82 with G6C. Deployed to Rio Grande on or after 25.4.82. Brought down in the Lively Island area of East Falkland on 1.5.82 by an AIM-9L fired from the 800 Sqdn Sea Harrier XZ455 of Flt Lt Penfold. The pilot, Primer Teniente Ardiles, was killed. Pieces of the aircraft were found on Lively Island.

## C-436

In 3.82 with G6C. Deployed to Rio Grande on or after 25.4.82. Brought down by a SAM (believed to have been a Rapier) over San Carlos Water on 29.5.82. The pilot, Teniente Bernhardt, was killed, his aircraft crashing into the sea.

## C-437

In 3.82 with G6C. Deployed to Rio Grande on or after 25.4.82. Brought down over Pebble Island, West Falkland on 23.5.82 by an AIM-9L fired from the 800 Sqdn Sea Harrier ZA194 of Lt Hale. The pilot, Teniente Volponi, was killed, his aircraft crashing on the west side of Elephant Bay, Pebble Island (UC 186155).

*The core of the Argentine air defence network on the Falklands were the Westinghouse AN/TPS-43F three-dimensional radar of G2VYCA and its supporting Cardion AN/TPS-44 Alert IIA tactical surveillance radar. Both were fundamental to local defence and fighter-bomber control and, fortunately for the Argentine forces, they remained functional until the cease-fire. The AN/TPS-43F was found intact (although showing signs of attempted FAA sabotage) in Port Street, while the illustrated AN/TPS-44 was located in a garden several hundred yards away on the Airport road. Both radars had survived a number of air attacks including those of Vulcans using Shrike anti-radiation missiles.*

# BELL 212

# CHINOOK

# GRUPO 7 DE COIN
# ESCUADRON HELICOPTEROS

In March 1982 the FAA's modest helicopter force was headquartered at Moron, Buenos Aires within the structure of VII Brigada Aerea, although most equipment was dispersed to other major bases where it undertook a variety of functions. The primary flying unit at Moron was Grupo 7 COIN (G7COIN — "COIN" was an acronym for the term "counter-insurgency", but it is by no means certain that Grupo 7 was still officially known as such in 1982). Grupo 7's Escuadron Helicopteros (sometimes referred to as the "Escuadron Aereo") was the operator of a mixed force of UH-1H's, Bell 212's, Hughes 369's, S-61R's and SA.315B Lamas, as well as the FAA's small CH-47C Chinook fleet. Although within the structure of the Escuadron Helicopteros, the latter element operated its two helicopters semi-autonomously. Many of the Hughes 369's and Lamas were permanently detached to other bases where they combined the functions of local rescue and communications vehicles. In March 1982 the two surviving Grupo 7 Chinooks were engaged in routine Antarctic support duties with one actually on station at the Vicecomodoro Marambio base with the Escuadron Antartica (confusingly, the Chinook element of the Escuadron Helicopteros/Escuadron Aereo was also often referred to as the "Escuadron Chinook").

Grupo 7's early involvement in Operacion "Rosario" was low-key to the point of passing virtually unnoticed by most of the unit. In late March a vague order was received to the effect that one Bell 212 should be broken-down for airfreighting by FAA C-130 to "somewhere in Patagonia". With it was to travel one flight crew and a technical support team. In the event, the helicopter concerned was unable to reach Port Stanley before 5 April because, until then, other equipment was given greater priority for C-130 space. As was the case with most of the FAA's personnel, news of the invasion was broken to Grupo 7 by the media on 2 April and then the significance of the Bell 212's mysterious departure became obvious. The unit's general mobilisation followed soon after, when, on 5 April, new instructions were received from FAA headquarters.

Many of Grupo 7's dispersed crash-rescue light helicopters remained at their normal bases to continue with routine duties but, with the formation of the temporary SAR organisation known as the Seccion Operativa de Busqueda y Salvamento (SOBS) on 5 April, some of the light and medium helicopters were flown south to new operational bases where they eventually came under the direct control of CdoFAS. Together with a LADE F-27, a LADE Twin Otter and three impressed Mitsubishi MU-2's, the SOBS helicopters were allocated to Comodoro Rivadavia, Trelew, Puerto Deseado, San Julian, Santa Cruz, Rio Gallegos and to the Falkland Islands themselves. The equipment so used on the mainland for SAR purposes comprised four Grupo 7 Bell 212's and two Hughes 369's together with two impressed S-58T's and S-61NR's.

The Falkland Islands component of SOBS was established at four helicopters, two Grupo 7 Bell 212's and both Chinooks, and their immediate movement to Port Stanley commenced on 5 April when orders were received at 1300Z. The first Chinook readied was H-93 and for its new role several modifications were quickly completed. For greater range, four internal fuel tanks were added and provision was made for three 12.7mm GPMG's for self-defence. The work was done rapidly and by 1600Z that afternoon H-93 was airborne on its way south! It night-stopped at Comodoro Rivadavia and, while the crew slept, its glorious Dayglo red and grey Antarctic colours were overpainted with a new green and brown camouflage scheme. With the paint barely dry, H-93 continued its long journey the following morning and eventually reached Rio Gallegos in typically foul weather. It had improved somewhat by the following day, 7 April, but it was not until 1700Z that the Chinook with its crew of seven was able to commence the final overwater leg of the journey. It eventually landed at Port Stanley at 2015Z, coincident with a recorded gust of wind of 75mph!

The second Chinook, H-91, was ferried from Vicecomodoro Marambio to Rio Grande on 10 April and, in the process, became the first helicopter to make a solo crossing of the dangerous Drake Strait. At maximum permitted weight it was unable to climb through the ambient icing conditions and much of the 800 miles flight was made using only instruments at an altitude of little more than 300ft. While en route, the South Shetland Islands were overflown well below hilltop height. Not surprisingly, the flight was described by the crew as "exciting". The Chinook travelled on from Rio Grande to Port Stanley the following day where it arrived without further excitement. Ironically, H-91 had recently achieved some measure of fame when, on 10 January 1982, it had touched the flight-deck of 'Endurance' during operations in the vicinity of Seymour Island near Marambio. The Chinook had thus become the largest helicopter to "operate" from the deck of the British Antarctic vessel. The fourth and last Grupo 7 helicopter to reach Port Stanley was the second of the pair of deployed Bell 212's (H-83 and H-85) and it was airfreighted in by C-130H on 13 April.

The new unit established at Port Stanley was officially styled the "Escuadron de Helicopteros Malvinas" but the Squadron was not destined to remain long at BAM Malvinas. On 14 April it was transferred from Port Stanley to the newly adopted BAM Condor at Goose Green, from where all the subsequent operations were flown until the base became untenable some six weeks later. The helicopters were "maids-of-all-work" throughout the War and they flew missions in support of the FAA, Ejercito and the naval forces. The Chinooks were particularly valuable and had been pressed into service immediately after arriving on the Islands. Between dusk on 11 April and the evening of the following day, at least 14 round trips, presumably from Darwin, were made into Fox Bay West as the West Falklands settlement was occupied by the Ejercito. A few operations were also undertaken in support of the local civilian population, although it is not immediately obvious what such unsolicited help entailed.

Before the first British air attacks, many of the missions in support of the Ejercito were of a reconnaissance nature, carrying senior officers in the Bell 212's. In the absence of any worthwhile roads across East Falkland the Chinooks provided a vital link between Port Stanley and Darwin, carrying both internal and underslung loads. Regular links were also established to Port Howard, Fox Bay and Pebble Island and by the end of April the four helicopters had accumulated 270 flight hours on the Falklands.

Until the morning of 1 May, the helicopters were parked with the Pucaras in the open at Goose Green airstrip; however their vulnerability was obvious and all four were moved into the housing area of the nearby settlement shortly before the Sea Harrier attack which occurred at about 1125Z that day. In the aftermath of the attack one of the Chinooks was quickly employed to carry the wounded to Port Stanley. Later in the day the unit was heavily involved in supporting the transfer of several Pucaras to Pebble Island, while, at dusk, the first Bell 212 SAR mission was launched to search for the missing Grupo 6 pilot Primer Teniente Ardiles whose Dagger had been shot down over Lively Island. Unfortunately, the search was in vain.

As the month progressed and British air activity increased, so Grupo 7's missions became more hazardous. CdoFAS further heightened the Squadron's state of ten-

sion by tasking the unit on 3 May with a reconnaissance mission that was somewhat more demanding than usual. In the early hours of 4 May a Chinook was ordered to fly a low-level course of 168° from Port Stanley for a distance of 47 miles and then to climb to altitude and use its radar to search for British ships! No ships were found and the Chinook scrambled home safely with a Sea Harrier CAP in pursuit. Another less dramatic mission was the recovery of the Pucara crews from Pebble Island on 15 May after the British had destroyed their aircraft in the early hours of that morning.

After the British landings on 21 May, Goose Green became even more dangerous and the four helicopters, still undamaged, could not remain there for much longer. Finally, on 24 May, the Chinooks were withdrawn to Port Stanley to be followed by the two Bell 212's during the morning of 28 May. On 27 May a Chinook reinforced Darwin with 67 troops and returned to Port Stanley with a mixed group of FAA personnel, including some downed airmen and others who had earlier been evacuated from Pebble Island. When the Bell 212's were evacuated from Goose Green at dawn on 28 May, the battle there was already fierce and it was their crews' testimony which led to the assembly of the helicopter convoy that evening to bring reinforcing troops to Darwin. Although primarily an Ejercito operation, one Grupo 7 Chinook was involved, carrying troops and a 120mm mortar.

Subsequent incidents involving Grupo 7 helicopters included an unsuccessful British attack by what was thought to have been a Blowpipe missile on a Bell 212 which was recovering FAA scouts from forward positions in the Goose Green area, and the unsuccessful search by a Chinook for Flt Lt Ian Mortimer of 801 Sqdn after he had ejected from his Sea Harrier, five miles south of Port Stanley on 1 June. By the first week of June it was clear that Stanley would eventually fall and it was decided to extricate the two Chinooks to the safety of the mainland. That was not an easy undertaking for neither Chinook possessed the necessary long-range fuel tanks (they had been abandoned at Goose Green and were later utilised by 18 Sqdn's Chinooks at Port San Carlos) and one of them, mechanically the less reliable of the pair, required an engine change. The new engine was eventually brought in by C-130 and the crossing to the mainland was finally made using manual means to transfer internally carried fuel from fifteen 200 litre drums to the integral tanks.

Both Chinooks left Port Stanley at 0900Z on 9 June for Rio Grande but an emergency repair stop was made en route on Staten Island. Eventually the two helicopters reached the mainland and were subsequently ferried home to Moron via Comodoro Rivadavia. Unfortunately, the Bell 212's could not be found space in the C-130's and they were eventually ferried to the Port Stanley Racecourse where they received some minor shrapnel damage before being wrecked by British troops after the surrender. On 14 June both Bell 212's were probably still airworthy — at worst a few minor repairs would have made them so.

During its brief existence, the Escuadron de Helicopteros Malvinas recorded 455 flight hours and its achievements included the recovery of six Argentine pilots, one British pilot, six Prefectura Naval survivors from the 'Rio Iguazu' and many other Argentine personnel from behind British lines. Post-war, there were few changes of any significance affecting the organisation or equipment of Grupo 7 COIN and the unit continued to operate much as it did before March 1982. A new BV234ER Chinook is reported to have been acquired in 1984 for use in the Antarctic. A Hughes 369, H-29, was lost on 17 February 1984 in a crash at San Antonio de Pauda.

> *Escuadron Helicopteros pilots deployed to the Falkland Islands included:*
>
> *Mayor Posse; Capitan Giaigischia; Teniente Brea.*

# INDIVIDUAL AIRCRAFT DETAILS

The four helicopters deployed to the Falklands with Grupo 7 crews were the Bell 212's H-83 and H-85 and the CH-47C Chinooks H-91 and H-93. Both Chinooks were repainted before leaving Argentina from light grey and bright Dayglo red Antarctic colours into a dark green and brown camouflage with FAA titles on the upper fuselage. The unit badge, that of the 'Escuadron Chinook' worn by the aircraft in Antarctic colours, was masked during the respray and remained on the camouflaged Chinooks. The national markings were similarly retained. The Bell 212's received a similar camouflage scheme. At least one of the Chinooks is known to have worn a small "Malvinas" silhouette by the port cockpit door when at Goose Green. Yellow identification bands were applied to all four helicopters after 1 May 1982.

*In the individual aircraft details the standard FAA abbreviation 'G7COIN' has been used for Grupo 7 COIN.*

## BELL 212

**H-83**

In 3.82 with G7COIN (Escuadron de Helicopteros). Airfreighted to Port Stanley by C-130 on either 5.4.82 or 13.4.82 and transferred to Goose Green by 15.4.82, remaining based there until 28.5.82 when it returned to Port Stanley. Captured with slight shrapnel damage at Port Stanley Racecourse on 14.6.82. Post-war, progressively stripped of all possible souvenirs and by 5.83 in pieces on a local dump.

*Reportedly set on fire (date not known) when an oxy-acetylene burner being used to remove the tail boom ignited a fuel tank. The charred remains were buried on site.*

**H-85**

In 3.82 with G7COIN (Escuadron de Helicopteros). Airfreighted to Port Stanley by C-130 on either 5.4.82 or 13.4.82 and transferred to Goose Green by 15.4.82, remaining there until 28.5.82 when it was returned to Port Stanley. Captured with slight shrapnel damage at Port Stanley Racecourse on 14.6.82. Post-war, progressively stripped of all possible souvenirs and by 5.83 in pieces on a local dump. Last noted in derelict condition (without tail boom, engines and rotors) near the FIGAS Beaver Hangar at Port Stanley in 12.83. Moved to Moody Brook in early 1.84. Returned to the UK aboard the 'Slotergracht', arriving at Ridham on 20.6.84 (fuselage only — no boom). No further details known by 5.85.

## CHINOOK

**H-91** CH-47C

In 3.82 with G7COIN (Escuadron de Helicopteros/Antarctica). Ferried Vice-comodoro Marambio-Rio Grande on 10.4.82 and presumed camouflaged 10/11.4.82 before flying Rio Grande-Port Stanley on 11.4.82. Transferred to Goose Green by 15.4.82 and based there until 27.5.82 when it returned to Port Stanley. Recovered to Rio Grande on 9.6.82.

**H-93** CH-47C

In 3.82 with G7COIN (Escuadron de Helicopteros/Antarctica). Ferried Moron-Comodoro Rivadavia on 5.4.82. Repainted from Antarctic colours to camouflage on 5/6.4.82 before flying Comodoro Rivadavia-Rio Gallegos on 6.4.82 and then Rio Gallegos-Port Stanley on 7.4.82. Transferred to Goose Green by 15.4.82 and based there until 27.5.82 when it returned to Port Stanley. Recovered to Rio Grande on 9.6.82.

*Photographed on the Port Stanley Racecourse, probably in 4.82, this unidentified Grupo 7 Chinook still wears the badge of the 'Escuadron Chinook' on the forward fuselage. Although equipped with a winch (unlike the two CAB601 aircraft), the only known instance of an attempted rescue involving an FAA Chinook was the unsuccessful search for Flt Lt Ian Mortimer of 801 Squadron during the night of 1/2.6.82.*

# MIRAGE

## GRUPO 8 DE CAZA

The FAA received its first Mirage IIIEA's in June 1972 when the first of ten new aircraft were accepted from France. They were complemented by two dual-seat Mirage IIIDA's which were also delivered during 1972. All 12 aircraft entered service with VIII Brigada Aerea at Mariano Moreno, Buenos Aires from where they always provided air defence cover for Argentina's capital city. They equipped Grupo 8 de Caza (G8C) in a single squadron, I Escuadron de Caza, and during nearly ten years of operations only two aircraft, one of each model, were lost in accidents. After some years of funding difficulties, a second batch of seven Mirage IIIEA's was acquired in 1980 and, shortly before the Falklands War, a pair of refurbished dual-seat aircraft were ordered from France. The "new" machines, described as Mirage IIIDA's, are thought to have been former French Air Force Mirage IIIBE's. It is not known precisely when they were ordered but delivery was certainly post-war, taking place in December 1982.

In FAA service the Mirages were primarily tasked with all-weather interception duties although they could undertake all the usual tactical roles if so required. For their normal role, the earlier Mirages were set up to carry the MATRA R530 AAM (either in SARH or IR version) on the centre-line hard-point. The newer aircraft, acquired in 1980, also carried the R530 but were additionally wired to carry the R550 Magic. Both Mirage IIIEA versions were fitted with twin DEFA-553 30mm cannon.

When the FAA mobilised its resources in early April 1982 it was not immediately obvious to the FAA what the Mirage's role should be. Being the only all-weather interceptor it would have been unwise to have tasked the Mirage exclusively with a tactical fighter-bomber role, but to use it as an escort for other fighter-bombers would have left important strategic targets undefended. Because Britain's initial military intentions were not apparent to Argentina, the possiblity of a Vulcan attack on a key mainland target was taken very seriously in April 1982. Had the FAA elected to have left the mainland largely undefended (not that its small Mirage force could have guaranteed the point defence of more than one or two key targets anyway) and deployed the Grupo 8 aircraft exclusively to the Falklands Islands theatre, there would still

have been certain serious operational difficulties to have been overcome. Without an air-refuelling capability, Mirage sorties over the Islands would be difficult, with only brief loiter time available, and, to further complicate matters, the new Magic AAM's were only just entering service and Grupo 8 was still uncertain of a number of technical aspects of their operation. Naturally, in the event of air combat with the Sea Harriers, the FAA would have wished to match the more potent Magic-equipped Mirages against them, rather than those having only the R530 fit.

The decision was eventually made to deploy the bulk of the Mirage force south, leaving only a small alert group at Mariano Moreno. Of the 16 single-seat Mirages notionally available to the FAA in early April, only 11 are reported to have been combat-ready with Grupo 8 and eight of those were deployed away from Mariano Moreno. The initial move was made in April to the CdoFAS headquarters at Comodoro Rivadavia where a new temporary unit, the "Escuadron Mirage Comodoro Rivadavia" was established under the command of Comodoro Carlos Corino, Grupo 8's peace-time commander. Once there, some aircraft were further deployed to Rio Gallegos, from where the first combat missions were eventually flown.

There is a measure of inconsistency between some Argentine accounts of Mirage operations from Rio Gallegos on 1 May but it appears that 12 escort sorties were planned for the day and that they were to be launched as three pairs of flights during the morning and early and late afternoon. The first two sections were launched in the morning within minutes of each other, coincident with the launch of the first Grupo 5 Skyhawk sortie ("Topo" flight) from Rio Gallegos. The Grupo 5 mission was to seek out and attack enemy shipping but the FAA controller at Port Stanley became extremely confused and vectored the four Skyhawks towards a Sea Harrier CAP at 20,000ft over East Falkland. Fortunately the mistake was quickly appreciated and although one of the Mirage flights, "Dardo" flown by Capitan Gustavo Garcia Cuerva and Primer Teniente Carlos Perona, managed to get between the Skyhawks and the Sea Harriers, the latter broke away without engaging them in combat.

It is perhaps not surprising that the British pilots were

perplexed at what the FAA was doing on 1 May, for, unknown to them, CdoFAS believed that a full-scale British landing was underway and that therefore fighter-bomber sorties were being dispatched to seek out shipping close inshore to East Falkland. The confusion was increased when some of the Skyhawks adopted interceptor profiles on the Royal Navy's radars.

Garcia Cuerva and Perona returned safely to Rio Gallegos after the incident but with very little fuel left. The other flight, possibly led by Corino himself, also recovered safely after having failed to draw a Sea Harrier CAP up to the Mirages' optimum fighting height. As far as can be established, most of the sorties flown on 1 May by Grupo 8 were with the Mirages of the second batch, armed with two Magic AAM's on the outer wing pylons. In order to provide a 12 to 15 minutes loiter time over East Falkland, these aircraft also carried three 1,300 litre drop tanks of fuel. An alternative configuration — and it is far from clear when each was utilised on 1 May — used two 1,700 litre fuel tanks and added an R530 missile to the centre-line pylon. Those first batch Mirages that were deployed to Rio Gallegos flew with one R530 and two 1,700 litre tanks (the FAA later explained that the Mirage IIIEA flight manual did not recommend the fit of Magics on the outer pylons with the 1,700 litre tanks fitted, but that the advice was rejected and Mirages were safely operated in that configuration).

The second pair of flights appear to have been launched after 1500Z and it was probably two of those Mirages which offered assistance to three T-34C Mentors of 4 Escuadrilla de Ataque from Pebble Island at about 1610Z and which later confronted the Sea Harriers of Lt Cdr Nigel Ward and Lt Mike Watson of 801 Sqdn. According to the British pilots, the Mirages resisted a temptation to be drawn north to meet the Sea Harriers head-on, but eventually pursued them at medium altitude when the CAP feigned disinterest in any engagement. With only 15 miles between them, the Sea Harriers turned and closed rapidly from a head-on position. Again, from British reports, the Mirages, before breaking for home, fired AAM's from a head-on position but the missiles fell short and were of no danger to the Sea Harriers.

The incident was strange because, despite FAA denials that any of their pilots fired either R530's or Magics on 1 May, it is very difficult to imagine what was seen by the British pilots if they were not missiles. That said, clearly none of the missiles would have been capable of achieving a hit under such conditions and would surely not have been launched in more considered circumstances. Despite the denials, at least one R530 is known to have been fired by a Grupo 8 pilot at a Sea Harrier on 1 May and it is possible that it was launched in frustration at Lt Cdr Ward's aircraft during this particular engagement.

The final Mirage missions of the day were launched soon after 1800Z but, again, there is some confusion evident in the Argentine accounts of the sorties. Capitan Garcia Cuerva and Primer Teniente Perona both took-off for their second mission of the day but there is evidence that, because of Mirage unserviceabilities at Rio Gallegos, two Daggers were launched from Rio Grande in place of a second pair and that it was that mission which cost the life of the Grupo 6 Dagger pilot Primer Teniente Jose Ardiles.

Garcia Cuerva and Perona were eventually vectored by the Port Stanley controller towards a pair of Sea Harriers over East Falkland. They were 801 Sqdn aircraft XZ452, flown by Flt Lt Paul Barton, and XZ453, flown by Lt Steve Thomas. The Grupo 8 pilots approached them from a high, head-on position with the intention of getting one of the Mirages behind the Sea Harriers by means of a scissor movement. In fact they approached the Sea Harriers nearly a mile apart, allowing Thomas to hold course at them while Barton could move away to the north and west to approach them from the side. The Mirages were spotted by the Sea Harrier pilots at a range of about eight miles and, from five miles distance, Thomas saw what he thought was the failed launch of missiles from each Mirage. While that has not been specifically denied by the FAA, the chances are that Thomas saw underwing drop tanks being blown off. Garcia Cuerva was an experienced senior pilot and is unlikely to have wasted even an inadequate weapon in such a fashion. Perona's own account of the subsequent engagement makes no mention of a missile launch.

Shortly before 1910Z Thomas and Perona crossed very close to one another (probably within 300ft) but as Perona attempted to follow Thomas visually, his Mirage, I-015, was struck by an AIM-9L fired from Barton's aircraft. While the two Grupo 8 pilots had been turning gently, Barton had carefully locked a Sidewinder onto the rear aircraft and, from a range of about one mile and at a height of 12,000ft, he had claimed the first "kill" of the War. To Perona, the impact came as a complete surprise but he was unhurt and was able to eject safely from his uncontrollable and disintegrating aircraft. Moments later, XZ453 closed on Garcia Cuerva's Mirage and Thomas was able to successfully launch his first Sidewinder at the exhaust of I-019. Subsequent events are not fully accounted, but it is clear that before the missile detonated Garcia Cuerva was aware of its presence and was diving fast through cloud in an effort to evade it. As far as is known, the missile exploded close to the rear fuselage and virtually crippled the Mirage, rupturing the fuel tanks and damaging control runs. In an effort to save the aircraft, or perhaps simply to eject nearer home, Garcia Cuerva attempted to reach Port Stanley and in that respect he was successful, for he reached the outskirts safely. Unfortunately, he then had the misfortune to be brought down by Argentine anti-aircraft fire and his aircraft dived into the ground, killing him instantly. Perona, meanwhile, had been more fortunate and, as his aircraft had fallen into the sea, he had dropped into the shallows north of Pebble Island, some 80 miles from Port Stanley. He damaged both ankles as he struggled ashore but was quickly recovered by CANA personnel from the nearby airstrip and, within a day or so, he was back in Buenos Aires providing the media with unlikely accounts of how a Sea Harrier had collided with his Mirage.

The events of 1 May left Grupo 8 in a state of some confusion. Not only had a senior pilot been killed and two new aircraft lost, but it was clear that the Mirage was simply not the equal of the Sea Harrier/AIM-9L combination in the existing circumstances. British pilots were much later to speak of naive tactics by the Argentine, but, on 1 May, the feeling at Rio Gallegos was more one of frustration at being outgunned by an enemy who was able to dictate the terms on which he would fight. It is also evident that the manoeuverability of the Sea Harrier had been grossly underestimated by the FAA. Clearly, there could be no repetition of those disasters and CdoFAS took immediate steps to avoid such eventualities. The FAA was worried that the next Vulcan target might be rather more ambitious and it was thus decided to withdraw most of the Grupo 8 Mirages to Comodoro Rivadavia to protect the CdoFAS headquarters. No more long-range missions to the Falklands were flown for some weeks, although a few escort sorties were undertaken during early May, shadowing C-130's to within sight of the Islands. At Comodoro Rivadavia the Mirages stood constant alert and, in the subsequent weeks, regularly patrolled the Argentina-Chile border zone. Incidents such as the Sea King affair at Punta Arenas did nothing to reassure the FAA that an attack would not come from west of the Andes and, accordingly, Mirage activity was increased.

By early June the general situation had changed substantially and Argentina no longer feared a major attack on her mainland. The War was progressing badly in the Falklands, though, and eventually the Escuadron Mirage Comodoro Rivadavia repositioned some of its aircraft to Rio Gallegos. Their first operational use appears to have been in the role of decoy while other combat aircraft actually made the attacks and one such mission seems to have been part of the elaborate, and very successful, attack on British shipping in Port Pleasant on 8 June. Grupo 8's first role appears to have been to put four Mirages into the air, possibly in two pairs, in a simulated strike at the British bridgeheads in the San Carlos Water area. Flying a simulated Dagger attack profile, the Mirages ran-in across north-west West Falkland shortly before 1645Z, but broke off the "attack" as soon as the Sea Harrier CAP's showed interest in their presence. For several minutes the Sea Harriers were thus engaged and their attention was diverted from the Daggers and Skyhawks tasked with the real missions to Port Pleasant. Although it must be highly debatable whether the FAA attacks at "Bluff Cove" (as the British media incorrectly identified Fitzroy) would have been prevented had the Sea Harriers not been so preoccupied, CdoFAS regarded the Grupo 8 decoy mission as a great success. Later top-cover sorties to Fitzroy failed to prevent the loss of three Grupo 5 Skyhawks, and one mission, warily watched from below by the Sea Harriers, has been ignored in all FAA accounts of the day's operations.

As the War drew to its inevitable close, CdoFAS tasked the Canberras of Grupo 2 with a series of night strikes against British troops in the Mount Kent area of East Falkland. Canberras were usually launched in pairs but they had thus far achieved rather little, with the British forces regarding them only as something of a nuisance. On what was destined to be the last night of the War, a pair of Canberras was launched from Rio Gallegos late in the evening of 13 June. On that occasion they were provided with a Grupo 8 escort, "Pluton" flight, led by the veteran Mirage pilot Mayor Jorge Sanchez with Capitan Gonzalez flying as wingman.

The mission commenced well enough and they initially flew in radio-silence, approaching West Falkland from the south at an altitude of about 33,000ft. However, even before finding the Canberras on radar or making radio contact with the Port Stanley CIC, both pilots saw the glow of shellfire from Port Stanley, well over 100 miles away. Through broken cloud, the effects of naval and artillery bombardment could clearly be seen. The Canberras were found at about 40,000ft and at 0150Z they made their radar-guided attack on predetermined positions while the Mirages, still at 33,000ft, orbited to the west. Several SAM's were launched at the Canberras and, although the CIC had reassured "Pluton" flight to the contrary, a Sea Harrier CAP from 'Hermes' was also airborne looking for the bombers. As the Canberras came under SAM attack, so did the Mirages and one missile locked-on to Sanchez' aircraft. As it came up at him, glowing brightly, he spiralled down towards it in an attempt to break the lock but the missile suddenly exploded below him at the end of its run, leaving his Mirage undamaged. A second missile passed by him at 15,000ft shortly afterwards but without detonating. By then both Mirages were in the Goose Green area and the CIC instructed them to climb rapidly to get above the Sea Harrier and SAM danger levels. As they climbed they were told that the leading Canberra had been brought down by a SAM. The missiles launched at the Mirages had been Sea Darts from 'Cardiff' and those that had brought down the Canberra were from 'Exeter', both warships having been in the Choiseul Sound area of East Falkland.

With the safe recovery of "Pluton" flight at 0303Z on 14 June, the War was effectively over for Grupo 8 and its Escuadron Mirage Comodoro Rivadavia. For the FAA's elite Squadron the War had been a sobering experience and many hard lessons had been learned during the relatively few sorties flown. While it had never anticipated that its first combat missions would occur against any air force other than that of a neighbouring state, Grupo 8 had still considered itself good enough to take on the British Sea Harriers in a "one-to-one" situation. That belief had admittedly been qualified by statements about optimum combat altitudes and, subsequently, by comments about tail radars and other systems unavailable to the Mirage pilots, but it is clear that the Sea Harrier was simply underestimated. The manoeuverability of the aircraft, the lethality of its Sidewinders and the training of the Royal Navy pilots had combined to make dogfighting a one-sided contest and, on 1 May, Grupo 8 had learned that to its cost.

Official FAA statistics credit Grupo 8 with 45 operational sorties, although an unofficial count by the unit claims 90 of all kinds during the War period. In post-war service the 15 surviving aircraft were joined by the pair of refurbished Mirage IIIDA's in December 1982 and in 1984 Grupo 8 continued to provide Buenos Aires with its air defence (although another of the IIIEA's was lost in a crash at Rio Gallegos on 8 October 1983). As part of the FAA's wholesale aircraft modification programme, it was intended, at the time of writing in 1984, that the Grupo 8 Mirages would be equipped with in-flight refuelling systems if trials proved successful.

Grupo 8 de Caza pilots deployed to Comodoro Rivadavia and Rio Gallegos and believed to have flown combat missions included:

*continued*

*continued* ——————

Comodoro   C.E.Corino   (commander);   Mayor
J.Sanchez;   Capitan   G.Ballasteros;   Capitan
G.A.Garcia   Cuerva   **(KIA)**;   Capitan   Gonzalez;
Primer Teniente C.Perona; Primer Teniente Yebra.

# INDIVIDUAL AIRCRAFT DETAILS

The Mirage's normal peace-time green and tan camouflage was not altered in any way during the conflict and, as far as is known, the yellow identification stripes adopted by other combat types after 1 May were either not worn at all, or applied for only a short period, by Grupo 8. All aircraft are thought to have worn the normal circular VIII Brigada Aerea badge on the fin throughout the emergency period.

There is not a definitive list available of those Grupo 8

Mirages which were deployed in April 1982 to Comodoro Rivadavia and Rio Gallegos but the notes detail all aircraft extant in March 1982. All aircraft are Mirage IIIEA models with the exception of I-002, the then sole dual-seat Mirage IIIDA on FAA strength, which is fairly reliably reported to have been used operationally from Comodoro Rivadavia.

*In the individual aircraft details the FAA abbreviation 'G8C' has been used for Grupo 8 de Caza.*

**I-002 IIIDA**

In 3.82 with G8C. Unconfirmed reports suggest that this dual-seat aircraft was deployed to Comodoro Rivadavia in 4.82 and may have been used on one "mission". Noted in post-war use at Mariano Moreno in 9.82.

**I-003 IIIEA**

In 3.82 with G8C. Not confirmed as deployed to Comodoro Rivadavia or Rio Gallegos but noted in post-war use at Mariano Moreno in 11.82.

**I-004 IIIEA**

In 3.82 with G8C. Not confirmed as deployed to Comodoro Rivadavia or Rio Gallegos but noted in post-war use at Mariano Moreno in 9.82.

**I-005 IIIEA**

In 3.82 with G8C. Deployed to Rio Gallegos, probably in 4.82. Noted in post-war use at Mariano Moreno in 11.82.

**I-006 IIIEA**

In 3.82 with G8C. Not confirmed as deployed to Comodoro Rivadavia or Rio Gallegos but noted in post-war use at Mariano Moreno in 11.82.

**I-007 IIIEA**

In 3.82 with G8C. Not confirmed as deployed to Comodoro Rivadavia or Rio Gallegos but noted in post-war use at Mariano Moreno in 11.82.

**I-008 IIIEA**

In 3.82 with G8C. Deployed to Rio Gallegos, probably in 4.82 but noted in post-war use at Mariano Moreno in 9.82.

**I-010 IIIEA**

In 3.82 with G8C. Not confirmed as deployed to Comodoro Rivadavia or Rio Gallegos but noted in post-war use at Mariano Moreno in 11.82.

**I-011 IIIEA**

In 3.82 with G8C. Deployed to Rio Gallegos, probably in 4.82. Noted in post-war use at Mariano Moreno in 9.82.

**I-012 IIIEA**

In 3.82 with G8C. Not confirmed as deployed to Comodoro Rivadavia or Rio Gallegos in 4.82. Reported to be in use at Mariano Moreno in 1983.

**I-013 IIIEA**

In 3.82 with G8C. Not confirmed as deployed to Comodoro Rivadavia or Rio Gallegos but noted in post-war use at Mariano Moreno in 11.82.

**I-014 IIIEA**

In 3.82 with G8C. Deployed to Rio Gallegos, probably in 4.82. Noted in post-war use at Mariano Moreno in 11.82.

**I-015 IIIEA**

In 3.82 with G8C. Deployed to Rio Gallegos in 4.82. Brought down over Pebble Island, West Falkland on 1.5.82 by an AIM-9L fired from the 801 Sqdn Sea Harrier XZ452 of Flt Lt Barton. Primer Teniente Perona ejected successfully into shallow water north of Pebble Island and was recovered shortly afterwards. Perona reported that his aircraft crashed into the sea but pieces are believed to have come to ground in the North West Pass area of West Falkland.

**I-016 IIIEA**

In 3.82 with G8C. Not confirmed as deployed to Comodoro Rivadavia or Rio Gallegos but noted in post-war use at Mariano Moreno in 11.82. Later destroyed in a crash at Rio Gallegos on 8.10.83.

**I-017 IIIEA**

In 3.82 with G8C. Deployed to Rio Gallegos, probably in 4.82. Noted in post-war use at Mariano Moreno in 11.82.

**I-018 IIIEA**

In 3.82 with G8C. Deployed to Rio Gallegos, probably in 4.82. Noted in post-war use at Mariano Moreno in 11.82.

**I-019 IIIEA**

In 3.82 with G8C. Deployed to Rio Gallegos in 4.82. Damaged over West Falkland on 1.5.82 by an AIM-9L fired from 801 Sqdn Sea Harrier XZ453 of Lt Thomas. Capitan Garcia Cuerva flew the aircraft to the environs of Port Stanley where it was brought down by Argentine AAA. Garcia Cuerva was killed in the crash.

# TWIN OTTER
# FRIENDSHIP
# FELLOWSHIP

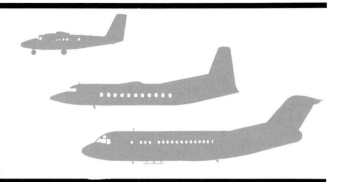

# AIR TRANSPORT AND THE "PUENTE AEREO"

For nearly a decade before the invasion of 2 April 1982, the present Stanley Airport, and before that its predecessor at Hookers Point, had been regularly served by an air service from the Argentine mainland. A weekly FAA flight was operated, usually from and to Comodoro Rivadavia, by LADE, Argentina's military airline responsible for providing air services to the more remote regions of the south. LADE services were operated by F-27's, F-28's and, on rare occasions, by other types such as C-130's and, as necessary, the schedule was changed to meet current requirements. The arrival had been handled in various ways over the years; sometimes the schedule required a simple turn-round of 30 minutes, while at other times LADE planned a night-stop. At the time of the invasion, the once weekly F-28 was scheduled to operate the LD350 service inbound from Comodoro Rivadavia at 1830Z on a Tuesday, and the LD351 outbound the following morning at 1100Z.

LADE's F-27's and F-28's were operated from Comodoro Rivadavia by the local Grupo 9 de Transporte Aereo although it did not "own" the aircraft in question. They were borrowed from Grupo 1 de Transporte Aereo, El Palomar, with their flight crews, on a "tour of duty" basis for LADE and were thus attached to IX Brigada Aerea at such times. The operation was routine, involving the F-28 crews of Grupo 1's Escuadron II and the F-27 crews of Escuadron IV (post-war, Grupo 9 was allocated its own F-27 resources and they joined the local Twin Otter fleet in a new unit, reported to be Escuadron VI). LADE cabin crew were civilians and were permanently stationed in the LADE region.

The FAA's invasion plan was given the name "Aries 82" and much of the "assault" phase involved the use of C-130's from Grupo 1 rather than LADE's resources. However, the F-28's of Escuadron II were used on 2 April and five aircraft brought many specialist and reinforcing troops to Port Stanley in the early stages of the operation. TC-53, using the call-sign "Litro 5", was the first of them, departing from Comodoro Rivadavia for Stanley Airport at about 1050Z that morning.

The limitations of Stanley's 4,100ft long asphalt runway were well appreciated by the FAA and throughout the planning of Operacion "Rosario" it was recognised that all large consignments of cargo (and indeed many of the smaller items) would go to the Falklands by sea. It was anticipated that, after the initial flurry of activity associated with the landings, the airfield would fairly soon settle back to its old style of operation, albeit with more LADE and sundry FAA flights than before.

The runway was stressed to take aircraft of Boeing 727 size and many of the FAA's transport aircraft had for long been routine visitors. However, limited hardstanding would prevent more than a few medium transports to be simultaneously on the ground. In the event, that situation was slightly improved after 2 April by FAA engineers who were able to increase the size of the ramp area. Nevertheless, taxiways and, on rare occasions, the runway, were pressed into use at peak periods to provide additional ramp space for the unloading of aircraft.

In the immediate aftermath of the landings a succession of C-130 and F-28 supply flights brought in vital equipment and key personnel. As is explained elsewhere, that "assault" phase of "Aries 82" was concluded on 2 April and the support phase of the operation commenced the next day. The bulk of the military equipment needed by the Ejercito on the Islands had been scheduled to travel by sea and, initially, air movements into Port Stanley were limited to FAA and CANA aircraft carrying vital items or important personnel. The British military reaction caused a considerable increase in air activity, however, and the creation of a "Puente Aereo" (Air Bridge) in early April was the direct result of the decision to dispatch a Task Force to repossess the Islands. The "Puente Aereo" was intended to achieve two major goals. The first was the urgent need to place several thousand troops onto the Falklands and the second was to get their equipment to them safely, once the British had imposed the maritime blockade that became effective on 12 April. The latter was achieved in an operation that made considerable use of the Grupo 1 C-130's, primarily flying from Comodoro Rivadavia, and their operations are discussed at length elsewhere in this book.

Argentina's newly created CdoAeTr was tasked with reorganising air transport within Argentina to meet the new circumstances and to utilise all aircraft, both military and commercial, to best national benefit. After 7 April that meant moving large numbers of troops from the north of the country through Comodoro Rivadavia and Rio Gallegos to Port Stanley and creating a logistics organisation capable of supporting the troops on the Falklands and at the southern bases for an indefinite period. Much of the movement of men to the bridgehead airfields was undertaken by commercial airliners, including the Boeing 707's and 747's of Aerolineas Argentinas, as well as by all of the available FAA transports. Although much of the freight carried into Stanley was uplifted by C-130's from Comodoro Rivadavia, most of the 9,000 or so personnel to reach the Falklands were unfortunate enough to have to pass through the cramped terminal facilities at Rio Gallegos. The bulk of the Ejercito troops were subsequently carried across to Port Stanley during mid and late April by FAA F-27's and F-28's, Austral BAC 1-11's, Aerolineas Argentinas Boeing 737's and, from Comodoro Rivadavia, by FAA C-130's. The independently operated CANA transports invariably departed for Port Stanley from Rio Grande. Removed from the immediate Falklands area, the major centres of the resupply network were the FAA base at El Palomar and the CANA base at Espora.

LADE services from the mainland continued during April and entries from the log at Stanley Airport indicate that the weekly departures to Comodoro Rivadavia were made on 7 April (an F-28 at 0910Z), 13 April (an F-28 at 1007Z), 20 April (a C-130 at 1020Z) and 27 April (an F-28 at 1030Z). Clearly, the schedules were somewhat disrupted! After the departure of 27 April circumstances changed and the LADE service was permanently suspended.

The "Puente Aereo" was terminated at 2000Z on 29 April when the danger of attack by British ships and aircraft was believed to be imminent at Port Stanley. The air and naval attacks of 1 May forced the FAA to restrict its subsequent flights into Stanley to those operated by the Grupo 1 C-130's, although the CANA F-28's and Electras continued to make their occasional and successful dashes in and out of the beleaguered Airport! No serious accidents occurred during these activities and between 2 and 30 April some 389 landings were made at Stanley Airport by the FAA and civilian transports. A little less than 2,000 flight hours were recorded during the operations, comprising 1,627 by the FAA, 293 by Aerolineas Argentineas and 16 by Austral. Of the 9,000 men carried into Stanley, 84% were Ejercito soldiers with FAA personnel and civilians making up the balance. 5,000 tons of cargo of all kinds were also airlifted in.

The performance of the FAA C-130's and CANA transports after 1 May is considered at length elsewhere, but it is worthwhile repeating here that 31 successful missions were undertaken to Stanley Airport by the former aircraft and 14 by the latter before the Argentine capitulation on 14 June. However, in addition to those flights into Stanley there was at least one fairly desperate rescue mission undertaken by a Grupo 9 Twin Otter from Rio Gallegos to Pebble Island. That took place overnight on 28/29 May and involved aircraft T-82 which made its dash apparently undetected by the British radars. It evacuated a handful of FAA wounded and one or two pilots who had successfully ejected from aircraft in the Pebble Island area during the previous few days.

CdoAeTr continued to function throughout the War in its controlling role and its achievements were summarised by the FAA in statistics published for the period 2 April to 28 June. During that time CdoAeTr aircraft flew 7,719 hours, of which 6,639 were by FAA aircraft, 986 were by Aerolineas Argentinas and 94 by Austral. 9,798 tons of cargo (51% Ejercito, 45% FAA and 4% Armada) and 49,165 personnel (72% Ejercito, 21% FAA and 7% Armada) were carried in the process.

*Very few of the many crews assigned to Grupo 9 de Transporte Aereo, LADE and other CdoAeTr-operated organisations have been individually identified. In view of this, no attempt has been made to tabulate them.*

# INDIVIDUAL AIRCRAFT DETAILS

The process of ferrying personnel and equipment from Comodoro Rivadavia and Rio Gallegos to Port Stanley involved FAA F-27's, F-28's, C-130's and the commercial airliners of Aerolineas Argentinas and Austral. Relatively few of those aircraft have been individually identifed as used although it is reasonable to assume that virtually all the F-27's and F-28's on FAA strength were so utilised (the C-130's are considered elsewhere). As far as is known no unusual markings were applied to any of those aircraft although some modifications were made to the markings of some Grupo 9 Twin Otters. Variations which have been identified are detailed below.

Because the Grupo 1/Grupo 9 transports and the commercial airliners operated in their normal peace-time colours, and there being no evidence of their use in specifically hazardous circumstances, they have been ignored for the purposes of these individual histories (their serial details are included elsewhere). The Grupo 9 Twin Otters did, however, see "action" during the post-1 May period and their details, such that are known, are included below.

*In the individual aircraft details the standard FAA abbreviation 'G9TA' has been used for Grupo 9 de Transporte Aereo.*

## T-81

In 3.82 with G9TA. No details of wartime use are known. Destroyed in a take-off accident at Rio Gallegos on 28.1.83.

## T-82

In 3.82 with G9TA. Used in the Pebble Island mission of 28/29.5.82. Thought to have had normal Orange Dayglo rear fuselage, nose and wingtip markings but it is not known whether an additional "identification" horizontal fin stripe was added.

*Post-war it wore a blue and white "Malvinas"*

silhouette on the left-hand side of the nose with the inscription: *"28-29 De Mayo De 1982 - Isla Borbon - Recuperacion Al Continente De Tripulantes Eyectados y Meridos En Combate".*

## T-83

In 3.82 with G9TA. In addition to the usual Orange Dayglo areas it wore a yellow/orange horizontal fin band (not across the rudder) which passed behind the national flag. This is thought to have been a wartime identification marking.

## T-85

In 3.82 with G9TA. No wartime details known.

## T-86

In 3.82 with G9TA. No wartime details known. Usual Orange Dayglo markings worn (without the horizontal fin stripe) when noted at Comodoro Rivadavia in 1983.

## T-87

In 3.82 with G9TA. No wartime details known.

*In 4.82 activity on the apron at Stanley Airport varied from the busy to the truly hectic. On peak days of the "Puente Aereo" (Air Bridge) late in the month the FAA was scheduling more than 30 arriving transport flights, all of which required rapid turn-rounds. In this photograph, taken soon after the invasion, a CANA Electra (0691/5-T-1) of 2 Escuadrilla de Sosten Logistico Movil is making its way towards the terminal building. The F-28 Fellowships of Grupo 1 de Transporte Aereo were regular visitors.*

*(via Flt Lt R. Robinson, RAF)*

*Photographed post-war at Comodoro Rivadavia, these Grupo 9 de Transporte Aereo Twin Otters (T-83 and T-86) wear an FAA colour scheme which incorporates high visibility Dayglo bands round the nose, wing-tips and rear fuselage. The aircraft in the foreground (T-83) appears to have a yellow wing stripe, outboard of the engine, as well as another on the rail. These are thought to have been wartime identification stripes.*

*(via S. Mafé Huertas)*

150

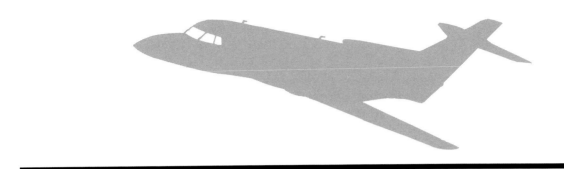

# ESCUADRON FENIX

Shortly before the British Task Force began its counter-offensive action on 1 May 1982 to recover the Falkland Islands, Argentina impressed all her civilian registered aircraft into the FAA and all commercial flight crews were given the status of junior officers for the duration of the emergency. Thus, all the civilian executive and corporate owned transports and a few other useful aircraft and helicopters effectively joined the airliners of Aerolineas Argentinas, Austral and other operators as potential FAA equipment for use in any appropriate theatre. In practice, many of them were indeed so used and they provided valuable service to the FAA, particularly in the CdoFAS region, where they served throughout the War in many communications and transport roles. Many of them, and perhaps all of them that were used in the CdoFAS region, served in a specially formed unit known as the "Escuadron Fenix" (Phoenix Squadron).

Escuadron Fenix was created to control the activities of about 35 impressed aircraft and helicopters from a headquarters at Comodoro Rivadavia. The function of the unit has, however, been somewhat overstated, particularly by the Argentine media and, while it is true that some aircraft were used in very demanding situations, it is something of a distortion of the truth to imply that it was a clandestine unit which was created for the sole purpose of deceiving the Royal Navy by electronic means!

The impressed aircraft are known to have included the HS.125-700B LV-ALW of Yacimientos Petroliferos Fiscales (the state oil concern YPF), six of about ten civilian registered Citations including the appropriately marked model 550 LQ-TFM of Fabricaciones Militares, five of seven known Learjet 24/25's (one of which was probably the model 24D LV-LRC of the Province of Tierra del Fuego), four Learjet 35A's (LV-ALF of Loma Negra SA was certainly one — the letters "ALF" were for Amalia Lacroze de Fortabat, a prominent national figure and supporter of the War — and presumably LV-OAS, LV-OFV and LV-ONN, the other three such aircraft on the Argentine register), the Learjet 36 LV-LOG, one Merlin III (probably LV-MRL), six Aero Commanders, seven Aerostar TS.601's, three Mitsubishi MU-2's, an A-109, a Bell 206 and four Bo.105S's.

Many of the aircraft were used simply for communica-

tions purposes, all on the mainland, and several, including the three MU-2's, were allocated to SAR duties. In the event, most of the operational SAR activity took place in the immediate vicinity of the Falkland Islands and thus the Escuadron Fenix aircraft were restricted to domestic patrol functions.

A few aircraft, and the HS.125 has been so identified, served as high-altitude radio relay stations between the mainland bases and combat aircraft engaged on low-level missions. That important task was undertaken largely unhindered because of the extreme distances between the British aircraft carriers and the holding patterns flown by the Escuadron Fenix aircraft. Argentine accounts of the HS.125 being chased by Sea Harriers appear to be total fiction. According to FAA statistics the Escuadron Fenix flew 27 communications relay sorties.

Other aircraft were used to escort ferry flights to the Falklands although none of the Escuadron Fenix aircraft so used actually landed at Stanley. As always, their value lay in their comparatively sophisticated avionics fits. One such mission, on 27 May, involved an MU-2 which escorted a pair of Grupo 3 Pucaras from Santa Cruz to Stanley (other similar missions were flown by military aircraft such as the CANA King Airs and Queen Airs that provided escort facilities for its T-34C and MB-339A ferry flights). No details of the number of such sorties flown have been released but they may be included in the 27 radio relay missions mentioned above.

The Escuadron Fenix is also credited with undertaking the extremely hazardous functions of fighter formation lead-ship and the radar simulation of fighter aircraft. It is known that FAA Learjets performed lead-ship duties and it is suspected that the Escuadron Fenix has been misidentified by Argentine sources as the unit responsible. Nevertheless, the FAA has stated that nine such missions were undertaken by the civilian aircraft, presumably the high performance Learjets and Citations. However, there is absolutely no evidence of them venturing within range of the Task Force's Sea Harriers or SAM's. Poor weather was probably the greatest hazard encountered by such missions.

The reality of fighter simulation is also questionable. Sea Harrier CAP's were maintained over West Falkland within very tight control parameters and, again, there is no evidence of them being vectored to intercept such Escuadron Fenix-type sorties. Sea Harriers were scrambled from their carriers many times during the later stages of the fighting to meet incoming aircraft but invariably they were clearly identified FAA combat aircraft or C-130's. The 123 decoy sorties attributed to the Escuadron Fenix are thought to have been missions dispatched with the intention of confusing the Task Force radars and causing unnecessary Sea Harrier launches, but very few of those missions are thought to have ventured as far east as West Falkland.

Other sorties were flown in support of the regular FAA and CANA coastal patrol operations and many missions were undertaken to search the remote coastline of southern Argentina for evidence of British landings or even Chilean military activity in the region.

As far as is known no impressed aircraft were lost in any operations during the War and, by early July 1982, normal commercial flying had been resumed in Argentina. The Escuadron Fenix was coincidentally stood down.

*None of the many crews assigned to Escuadron Fenix have been individually identified.*

At least ten commercially owned Argentine Learjets were impressed, with their crews, into the 'Escuadron Fenix' to provide the FAA with urgently required high-speed communications aircraft, primarily for use in the CdoFAS region. Some Learjets, with other impressed executive jets, were used for more hazardous missions but, contrary to Argentine mythology, there do not appear to have been any confrontations with the Task Force's Sea Harriers! Two of those used, LV-ALF and LF-OFV, are seen here post-war at the Aeroparque, Buenos Aires on 21.8.82 and 13.8.83 respectively: *(Aviacion Latino Americana)*

**Left** *Stanley Airport and the surrounding area was littered with Argentine equipment and weapons, both unused and spent. Items visible in this view include Tigercat missiles, boxed SA-7 launchers and a loose pile of 70mm/2.75in rockets. (Flt Sgt D. W. Knights, RAF)* **Centre** *The Grupo 3 de Ataque ammunition store at BAM Condor (Goose Green) was nothing more than a requisitioned shed. When inspected post-29.5.82 the contents included 2.75in rocket launchers, six-store centre-line weapons carriers and Napalm cannisters. All of these items would have been carried by the locally-based Pucaras.* **Lower Left** *The Skyguard was a sophisticated fire-control system used by the Ejercito in conjunction with the twin-barrelled 35mm Oerlikon anti-aircraft guns. This highly efficient combination was used in the defence of Stanley Airport and Goose Green airfield and, at Goose Green, it was a GADA601 gun that brought down the 800 Squadron Sea Harrier XZ450 of Lt Nick Taylor on 4.5.82.* **Lower Right** *Conceptually crude but devastatingly effective, a trailer-mounted MM.38 Exocet was eventually used successfully against 'Glamorgan' on 12.6.82. Concealed during daylight hours, the launch vehicle could only operate from paved surfaces because of its weight and the whole contraption required a lengthy setting-up period on each occasion that it was used. Here the trailer is parked in Davis Street, Port Stanley near the Ionospheric Station yard where it was kept after its arrival by air in late 5.82.*

**Part 1**
# appendices

# ARGENTINE AIR ARMS, ORDERS OF BATTLE & AIRFIELDS

## COMANDO AVIACION NAVAL ARGENTINA

The aviation element of the Armada, the Comando Aviacion Naval Argentina (CANA), was organised. into six air wings operating from four major bases. The Argentine coastguard, the Prefectura Naval Argentina (PNA), was an adjunct to the Armada and, in 1982, was fully staffed by naval personnel. It possessed a small air element and its organisation is included here (for the sake of convenience) as an appendix to the CANA structure.

CANA aircraft wore radio call-signs/codes and these prominently displayed markings identified wing, squadron and individual aircraft. Because of their significance the first (or only) code of each range is included in the organisational summary below.

### COMANDO AVIACION NAVAL ARGENTINA (CANA)

**1 Escuadra Aeronaval** (BAN Punta Indio)
Escuadrilla de Ataque (T-34C '1-A-401')
Escuadrilla Aerofotografico (Queen Air 80, King Air 200 '1-G-41'; '4-F-21' was the quoted current code of the Queen Air in March 1982).
(1 Escuadra Aeronaval maintained the dual roles of training and light attack and was also known as the Escuela de Aviacion Naval. Some Argentine literature referred to an "Escuadrilla de Reconocimiento" with King Air 200 and Queen Air 80 types and it is thought that was one and the same unit as the "Escuadrilla Aerofotografico".)

**2 Escuadra Aeronaval** (BAN Comandante Espora, Bahia Blanca)
Escuadrilla Antisubmarina (S-2E '2-AS-21')
Escuadrilla de Exploracion (SP-2H '2-P-110')
2 Escuadrilla de Helicopteros (Sea King '2-H-231')

**3 Escuadra Aeronaval** (BAN Comandante Espora, Bahia Blanca)
2 Escuadrilla de Caza y Ataque (Super Etendard '3-A-201')
3 Escuadrilla de Caza y Ataque (A-4Q '3-A-301')

1 Escuadrilla de Helicopteros (Alouette III '3-H-101' and Lynx HAS.23 '3-H-141')

**4 Escuadra Aeronaval** (BAN Punta Indio)
1 Escuadrilla de Ataque (MB-326GB '4-A-101', MB-339A '4-A-110')

**5 Escuadra Aeronaval** (BAN Ezeiza)
1 Escuadrilla de Sosten Logistico Movil (Electra '5-T-1')
2 Escuadrilla de Sosten Logistico Movil (F-28 '5-T-10', '5-T-20' and HS.125 '5-T-30')
(Some Argentine accounts referred to the CANA transport squadrons simply as "Escuadrillas de Transporte".)

**6 Escuadra Aeronaval** (BAN Vicealmirante Zar, Trelew)
Escuadrilla de Propositos Generales (Turbo Porter '6-G-1', S-2A '6-G-51', Queen Air 80 reportedly '6-G-81')
(The Turbo Porters were, in March 1982, based at BAN Rio Grande and, with the Escuadrilla Antarctica, at BAN Petrel, Antarctica.)

King Air 200 communications aircraft were based at Punta Indio and Espora in March 1982. Assigned to 2 and 4 Escuadra, they used the suffix range 'G-43' to 'G-48' with the prefix appropriate to the Escuadra.

### PREFECTURA NAVAL ARGENTINA (PNA)
### (Division de Aviacion)

**Agrupacion Albatros** (Puerto Nuevo, BA)
This small unit operated Puma and H-500 helicopters in March 1982.

**Agrupacion Skyvan** (Jorge Newbery Aeroparque, BA)
In March 1982 the fixed-wing element of the PNA comprised five Skyvan transports.

### EMERGENCY ORDER OF BATTLE: 10 MAY 1982

Unlike the FAA, CANA did not restructure its forces in the face of the emergency. There was, however, a considerable redeployment of units, particularly after the return of the aircraft carrier '25 de Mayo' to port in early May and the release of her squadrons to land bases. The movement of each unit is fully explained elsewhere and for simplicity the organisation outlined below represents CANA's redeployed forces as they were located after '25 de Mayo's' return. Most of the aircraft were transferred to Rio Grande.

## BAN RIO GRANDE
2 Escuadrilla de Caza y Ataque (Super Etendard)
3 Escuadrilla de Caza y Ataque (A-4Q)
Escuadrilla Antisubmarina (S-2E)
Escuadrilla de Exploracion (SP-2H)
1 Escuadrilla de Helicopteros (Alouette III)
2 Escuadrilla de Helicopteros (Sea King)
PNA (Skyvan and Puma)

Rio Grande was also the temporary base for sundry CANA communications aircraft, transports and small detachments of 1 Escuadrilla de Ataque MB-326GB's and MB-339A's. It is thought that the two EMB-111A's that were loaned to CANA by Brazil (initially as '2-P-201' and '2-P-202') probably operated from Rio Grande at least until the surrender on the Falklands. An FAA Dagger unit, the "Escuadron Dagger Rio Grande" was located on the base.

## BAN USHUAIA
Limited use was made of Ushuaia's facilities although its tiny runway considerably restricted those aircraft that could be safely operated. In general, movements were restricted to helicopters and light communications aircraft.

## EAN MALVINAS (Stanley Airport)
1 Escuadrilla de Ataque (MB-339A)
PNA (Skyvan and Puma)

Although Stanley Airport was much transitted by CANA aircraft, the only ones actually to be deployed were the small detachments of MB-339A's and T-34C's, the latter moving on immediately to Pebble Island. The small PNA detachment operated from the Airport and adjacent locations.

## EAN CALDERON (Pebble Island)
4 Escuadrilla de Ataque (T-34C)

## POST-WAR ORGANISATIONAL CHANGES

With relatively few aircraft lost and the national economy in poor shape, CANA re-equipment and reorganisation was of a generally low order in the years 1982 to 1984. A few vital changes were made and some new aircraft, including the balance of the Super Etendard order, were received. The organisational changes can be summarised thus:

### 2 Escuadra Aeronaval
Both the SP-2H's that were in working order at the commencement of the War were permanently withdrawn from service during May 1982 and were temporarily replaced by two EMB-111A's loaned by Brazil. These aircraft were reported to have been allocated the call-signs '2-P-201' and '2-P-202' but their allocation to 2 Escuadra appears to have been of limited duration and they were later transferred to 6 Escuadra. By 1984 at least one of the 6 Escuadra S-2A's had returned to Espora as '2-G-51'.

### 3 Escuadra Aeronaval
The cancellation of the Lynx HAS.87 order and the loss of one of the HAS.23's during the War resulted in the deletion of the type from the CANA inventory. The 1 Escuadrilla de Helicopteros call-sign range '3-H-141' was no longer in use in late 1984.

### 4 Escuadra Aeronaval
1 Escuadrilla de Ataque was strengthened in mid-1983 with the arrival of 11 reconditioned EMB-326GB's from Brazil. They were allocated the call-signs '4-A-130' to '4-A-140'.

### 6 Escuadra Aeronaval
Experience gained during the War appeared to cause CANA to look to Trelew and, particularly, Rio Grande as first-line maritime reconnaissance bases and this became apparent by the disposition of the new equipment. The urgently needed Electras were issued to a new unit, probably operating from Trelew with a detachment at Rio Grande, reportedly known as "1 Escuadrilla de Reconocimiento". Its initial aircraft were given the call-signs/codes '6-P-101' to '6-P-104'. The Squadron probably achieved limited operational status during 1983.

The two EMB-111A's were reported to have been recoded '6-P-201' and '6-P-202' late in 1982 but their subsequent status with CANA was unconfirmed in late 1984.

As indicated above, at least one of the S-2A's ('6-G-51') had been returned to 2 Escuadra by 1984.

# COMANDO DE AVIACION DEL EJERCITO

## THE ORDER OF BATTLE — 1 APRIL 1982

By March 1982 the aviation element of the Ejercito, the Comando de Aviacion del Ejercito (CAE), had been recently reorganised into two principal flying organisations that administered and flew all helicopters and fixed-wing aircraft. The Batallon de Aviacion de Combate 601 (CAB601) operated all the helicopters while all other types were administered by the Compania de Aviacion de Apoyo General 601 (CAAG601). Both entities were based at Campo de Mayo, Buenos Aires although some equipment, particularly elements of CAAG601, were operated from other locations.

## COMANDO DE AVIACION DEL EJERCITO (CAE)

**Batallon de Aviacion de Combate 601** (Campo de Mayo)
  Compania de Helicopteros de Asalto 'A' (CH-47C, Puma)
  Compania de Helicopteros de Asalto 'B' (UH-1H)
  Compania de Helicopteros de Ataque (A-109A, Lama)

**Compania de Aviacion de Apoyo General 601** (Campo de Mayo)
  CAAG601 was, in 1982, nominally responsible for at least 16 types and sub-types of fixed-wing aircraft ranging from medium transports and executive jets to basic trainers. They included the G-222, Cessna 500 and 550, Sabre 75A, King Air 100, Queen Air 80, Merlin III and IV, Twin Otter, Aero Commander 680, Cessna 320, Navajo, T-41D, U-17 and Cessna 207. The two VIP Bell 212's may also have been operated by CAAG601 rather than by one of the helicopter companies. A small number of aircraft were operated in CAE markings on behalf of the Instituto Geografica Militar.

### EMERGENCY ORDER OF BATTLE: 1 MAY 1982

As with the CANA, but unlike the FAA, the CAE made no attempt to create formal new organisations to meet the emergency situation. A total of 19 Puma, CH-47C, A-109A and UH-1H helicopters were progressively deployed to Port Stanley where CAB601 established a headquarters at Moody Brook. There, the UH-1H's appear to have operated in two discrete groups at the direction of the local Ejercito commanders while the Pumas and CH-47C's remained together for transportation duties. The A-109A's were used for escort and other special tasks. As will be read elsewhere in this book, the CAB601 mobile headquarters was moved several times between 1 May and 14 June although it always remained in the general area of Port Stanley.

### POST-WAR ORGANISATIONAL CHANGES

The CAB601 helicopter force deployed to the Falklands was totally lost and, with other losses incurred, the unit was virtually a "paper-only" force in July 1982. Although nearly all personnel survived, the CAE was unable to rebuild the unit with any speed because of financial constraints and the continuing refusal of the United States to make refurbished equipment available. Eventually, the new AS.332B Super Puma was purchased but in mid-1984 the first of these was still in France awaiting delivery. It was reported in 1984 that the CAE would be reorganised in the light of experience gained on the Falkland Islands.

# FUERZA AEREA ARGENTINA

### THE ORDER OF BATTLE — 1 APRIL 1982

Before the Falklands War the Argentine Air Force, the Fuerza Aerea Argentina (FAA), comprised five primary commands and a staff headquarters, all subordinate to a commander in chief. In March 1982 this position of Comando en Jefe was held by Brigadier General Basilio Lami Dozo. The primary commands and the staff headquarters were:

  Comando de Operaciones Aereas
  Comando Aereo de Defensa
  Comando de Instruccion
  Comando de Material
  Comando de Regiones Aereas
  Estado Mayor General

Comando de Operaciones Aereas (Air Operations Command) controlled all first-line flying units and associated installations with the exception of those concerned with air defence. The latter functions, which included interceptor aircraft, air defence radars and anti-aircraft weapons, were controlled by Comando Aereo de Defensa (Air Defence Command). All training functions were undertaken by Comando de Instruccion (Training Command) and maintenance and some manufacturing tasks by Comando de Material (Material Command). Regional FAA duties were controlled by Comando de Regiones Aereas (Air Regions Command) through four geographical areas.

In March 1982 the primary commands were structured thus:

### COMANDO DE OPERACIONES AEREAS

**I Brigada Aerea** (BAM El Palomar)
Grupo Base 1
Grupo Tecnico 1
Grupo 1 de Transporte Aereo (G1TA):
  Escuadron I (C-130E/H, KC-130H)
  Escuadron II (F-28, Boeing 707)
  Escuadron III (Guarani II)
  Escuadron IV (F-27)

**II Brigada Aerea** (BAM Parana, Gen Urquiza)
Grupo Base 2
Grupo Tecnico 2
Grupo de Comunicaciones 2
Grupo 1 Aerofotografico (G1A):
  Escuadron I (Learjet, Guarani II)
Grupo 2 de Bombardeo (G2B):
  Escuadron I (Canberra)

**III Brigada Aerea** (BAM Reconquista)
Grupo Base 3
Grupo Tecnico 3
Grupo 3 de Ataque (G3A):
   Escuadron I (Pucara)
   Escuadron II (Pucara)
   Escuadron III (Pucara)
Curso de Entrenamiento Para Aviadores de Combate

**IV Brigada Aerea** (BAM El Plumerillo, Mendoza)
Grupo Base 4
Grupo Tecnico 4
Grupo 4 de Caza (G4C):
   Escuadron III (A-4C)
   Escuadron "CB-1" (F-86F)
   Escuadron I ("CB-2") (Paris)
   Escuadron II ("CB-2") (Paris)

**V Brigada Aerea** (BAM Villa Reynolds, Cor Pringles)
Grupo Base 5
Grupo Tecnico 5
Grupo 5 de Caza (G5C):
   Escuadron IV (A-4B)
   Escuadron V (A-4B)

**VII Brigada Aerea** (BAM Moron)
Grupo Base 7
Grupo Tecnico 7
Grupo 7 COIN (G7COIN):
   Escuadron Helicopteros (UH-1H, Bell 212,
   H-369, H-500, Lama, S-61R)
   Escuadron Chinook (CH-47C)
   Escuadron Sanitario (Merlin IVA)
Grupo de Operaciones Especiales (GOE)
(The GOE was the FAA's "Blue Berets" special forces unit.)

**IX Brigada Aerea** (BAM Comodoro Rivadavia)
Grupo Base 9
Grupo Tecnico 9
Grupo 9 de Transporte Aereo (G9TA):
   LADE (F-27, F-28, Twin Otter, Guarani II)
Grupo 4 de Ataque (G4A):
   Escuadron IV (Pucara)

**X Brigada Aerea** (BAM Rio Gallegos)
Grupo Base 10

*Notes on the Brigada Aereas:*

Within each Brigada Aerea (Air Brigade) there existed three primary organisations — a base group, a technical group and aircraft operating group(s). The primary flying unit was the Grupo (Group) rather than the Escuadron (Squadron) although in several instances mixed equipment within the Grupo resulted in the routine use of some Escuadron titles. It was, however, unusual for any Escuadron to be identified by its numeric designation and it was commonplace to identify many units by a more obvious name. Thus FAA personnel would (officially) use "Escuadron Hercules" or "Escuadron C-130" but not "Escuadron I de Transporte". In some instances the numeric Escuadron designations were not used at all at base level.

*Notes on the Comando de Operaciones Aereas units:*

G1TA provided resources (F-27, F-28 and Guarani II) to IX Brigada Aerea with aircraft and pilots detached to Comodoro Rivadavia to operate LADE services as required. The bulk of the G1TA Guarani fleet was, however, dispersed and served various FAA commands, air brigades and other establishments as communications aircraft. When so used, some aircraft wore the appropriate title of the borrowing unit. BAM El Palomar was the home of a Sabre 75A used by the Comando en Jefe.

The "CB-1" and "CB-2" designations used by components of G4C were abbreviations based on the earlier titles "Grupo 1 de Caza Bombardeo" and "Grupo 2 de Caza Bombardeo". It is thought that by March 1982 the two Paris units were no longer officially referred to as Escuadron I and II, although two distinct flights (one training and one operational) still existed with small numbers of aircraft.

Several of the Escuadron Helicopteros H-369 and Lama helicopters were deployed to other bases where they served in the rescue and general duties roles. The latter function was shared with the G1TA Guarani II's, a few Aero Commanders and C-47's and smaller types such as the FMA Cessna 182. G7COIN helicopters were periodically loaned to the Escuadron Antarctica at BAM Marambio.

G9TA operated aircraft in southern Argentina on behalf of LADE, INAC and other agencies.

In early 1982 X Brigada Aerea, Rio Gallegos was under development to become the new permanent headquarters of Comando Fuerza Aerea Sur (CdoFAS — Southern Air Command). Once completed, the base was expected to provide the region (Region Aerea Sur) with a much needed modern communications and control centre.

Other functions and establishments controlled by Comando de Operaciones Aereas included the management of the FAA facilities at Aeroparque, BA; the Antarctic bases at Vicecomodoro Marambio and (the dormant) Teniente Matienzo and the rocket test centres CELPA I and CELPA II at Chamical, La Rioja and Laguna de Mar Chiquita, BA (CELPA was an acronym for Centro de Ensayo y Lanzamiento de Proyectiles Autopropulsados).

---

### COMANDO AEREO DE DEFENSA

---

**VI Brigada Aerea** (BAM Tandil)
Grupo Base 6
Grupo Tecnico 6
Grupo 6 de Caza (G6C):
   Escuadron II (Dagger)
   Escuadron III (Dagger)

**VIII Brigada Aerea** (BAM Dr Mariano Moreno)
Grupo Base 8
Grupo Tecnico 8

Grupo 8 de Caza (G8C):
  Escuadron I (Mirage IIIEA)

*Comando Aereo de Defensa also controlled a number of units that were not within the Brigada Aerea structure. Principal among them were:*

**Grupo 1 de Vigilancia Aerea** (G1VA) (Merlo, BA)
  (G1VA held network control of all the FAA fixed radar sites.)

**Grupo 2 de Vigilancia y Control** (G2VYCA) (Merlo)
  (G2VYCA operated all the FAA mobile radars. One such mobile station was permanently sited at X Brigada Aerea, Rio Gallegos.)

**Grupo 1 de Artilleria Antiaerea**
(G1AA) (BAM Mar del Plata, BA)
  Escuadron I
  Escuadron II
  (G1AA operated 20mm and 35mm anti-aircraft guns from both the central base, where a training establishment was situated, and the FAA airfields where they provided conventional air defence.)

## COMANDO DE INSTRUCCION

**Escuela Superior de Guerra Aerea** (Buenos Aires)

**Escuela de Suboficiales Cordoba**
(Guarnicion Aerea Cordoba)

**Escuela de Suboficiales Ezeiza** (Ezeiza, BA)

**Escuela de Aviacion Militar**
(EAM) (Guarnicion Aerea Cordoba)
  Grupo Base Escuela
  Grupo Tecnico Escuela
  Grupo Aereo Escuela (T-34A, Paris)

**Cuerpo de Cadetes**

Some T-34A's were used for reservist training at the civilian airfield of Jose C Paz (adjacent to BAM Dr Mariano Moreno, BA) with the Curso de Aspirantes a Officiales de Reserva. A sport and glider-towing "Escuadron" at Cordoba utilised several light aircraft including such types as the FMA Cessna 182, AB-180RVR, IAe46 Ranquel and a single FW-44J Stieglitz.

## COMANDO DE MATERIAL

**Area Material Rio Cuarto** (Rio Cuarto, Cordoba)

**Area Material Cordoba** (Guarnicion Area, Cordoba)

**Taller Regional Quilmes** (Quilmes, BA)

**Grupo Abastecimiento Palomar** (BAM El Palomar)

Both Area Material organisations operated C-47 and other general purposes types in early 1982.

## COMANDO DE REGIONES AEREAS

**Region Aerea Centro**

**Region Aerea Noreste**

**Region Aerea Noroeste**

**Region Aerea Sur**

## OTHER FAA ORGANISATIONS

**Instituto Nacional de Aviacion Civil** (INAC) (BAM Moron)
  Escuadron Tecnico INAC
  Escuadron Instruccion INAC
The national civil aviation institute provided training courses for civilian pilots and technicians as well as undertaking sundry local calibration and other facilities functions. INAC headquarters were at Moron but Comodoro Rivadavia and other airfields were also used. All equipment was provided by the FAA, many of the aircraft being categorised in the "Propositos Generales" class (General Purposes). Types in use in 1982 included C-47, Chincul Piper Arrow IV, Chincul Piper Seneca III, RACA Hughes 500 and FMA Cessna 182.

**Lineas Aereas Del Estado** (LADE) (BAM Comodoro Rivadavia)
  LADE operated F-27, F-28 and Twin Otter aircraft on scheduled services in the remote areas of southern Argentina and, until April 1982, the Falkland Islands. Technical support and flight crews were supplied by the FAA but cabin crew duties and other passenger handling functions were undertaken by civilians. As indicated earlier the F-27 and F-28 types were on the charge of Grupo 1 de Transporte Aereo and were transferred to Grupo 9 de Transporte Aereo for temporary duty with LADE.

**Escuadron Verificacion Radioayudos** (BAM Moron)
  Two Learjet 35A's were delivered in 1981/82 to augment and ultimately replace the pair of Guarani II's that were used for many years in the FAA navaid calibration function.

**Centro de Ensayos en Vuelo** (Guarnicion Aerea, Cordoba)
  The FAA flight test centre at Cordoba worked in close conjunction with the state aircraft manufacturing company Fabrica Militar de Aviones (FMA). The two organisations were co-located on the Cordoba airfield and both utilised FAA aircraft on an "as required" basis, some remaining on strength for long periods.

### EMERGENCY ORDER OF BATTLE: APRIL-JUNE 1982

In order to meet the demands of the situation that existed after 2 April 1982 a temporary restructuring of the

FAA was undertaken at several levels. This involved the creation of new commands and the reorganisation of combat and support units, much of it occurring progressively as the situation evolved during April. Initially, two new commands were created.

## COMANDO AEREO ESTRATEGICO (CdoAeEstr)
## COMANDO AEREO DE TRANSPORTE (CdoAeTr)

CdoAeEstr (Strategic Air Command) was made responsible for all FAA strategic planning to meet any eventualities. In practice this constituted the monitoring of the British fleet as it moved south, assessing Britain's general preparations for war and, finally, the creation of Argentine battle plans involving airpower. CdoAeTr (Air Transport Command) was created to organise and mobilise all air transport facilities within Argentina and to use them to the best effect. In achieving this CdoAeTr functioned throughout the War.

On 30 April CdoAeEstr was stood down, its task completed. In its stead a new command was created to control all FAA activity in the combat zone. It evolved naturally from CdoAeEstr and was titled Comando De La Fuerza Aerea Sur.

## COMANDO DE LA FUERZA AEREA SUR (CdoFAS)

CdoFAS (Southern Air Force Command) assumed active control from its headquarters at Comodoro Rivadavia of all regular and specially created FAA units on both the mainland and on the Falklands. CdoFAS did not control naval air operations although it did provide the means to co-ordinate CANA and FAA activity (eventually CANA combat operations could only be undertaken from the mainland with FAA tanker support and co-ordination became absolute). Control of air operations on the Falklands was achieved through a locally created, integrated organisation that was intended to meet the theatre demands of all the services while working in conjunction with CdoFAS.

The organisation outlined below explains the redeployment of the major combat and support elements of the FAA but it should be realised that many small and specialist detachments also made the journey south, each to play its own role in the CdoFAS structure. The major organisations controlled by CdoFAS were:

## BAM COMODORO RIVADAVIA

### Grupo Aereo de Exploracion y Reconocimiento 1

GrAeExplRec1 was created during April by CdoAeEstr and was transferred to CdoFAS on 30 April. It operated FAA Boeing 707's, C-130's, KC-130H's and Learjets for the duration of the War. These aircraft were transferred from their regular units solely for control purposes and were routinely further diverted for other tasks in keeping with their normal roles.

### Escuadron Fenix

Impressed civilian aircraft were organised into the "Phoenix Squadron", headquartered at Comodoro Rivadavia. They were dispersed and operated as required.

### Seccion Operativa de Busqueda y Salvamento

SOBS was created by CdoFAS on 5 April to provide SAR facilities at all the operational bases. It had sub-centres (Sub-Centros de Control de Busqueda y Salvamento — SCCBS) at Trelew, Puerto Deseado, San Julian, Santa Cruz, Rio Gallegos and on the Falkland Islands.

### Escuadron Mirage Comodoro Rivadavia

Grupo 8 de Caza Mirage III's were deployed to Comodoro Rivadavia in small numbers for air defence purposes. By 1 May however, most, if not all, had been redeployed to Rio Gallegos from where they flew several combat missions. After 1 May most returned to Comodoro Rivadavia for point defence duties although a few escort missions were later flown from Rio Gallegos.

### Grupo 2 de Vigilancia y Control

After 8 April one of the G2VYCA mobile radars was established at Comodoro Rivadavia.

### Locally based units

The resident LADE aircraft of Grupo 9 de Transporte Aereo and the recently received Pucaras of Grupo 4 de Ataque were also used by CdoFAS, the latter flying local missions only.

## BAN TRELEW

### Escuadron Canberra Trelew

The Grupo 2 de Bombardeo Canberras deployed to the naval base at Trelew from where they flew their first combat sorties on 1 May. Sorties were later flown from Rio Gallegos by aircraft that were positioned there from Trelew for each mission.

## PUERTO DESEADO AIRFIELD

Puerto Deseado served only as a diversion airfield and an SCCBS was maintained there for SAR duties.

## SAN JULIAN AIRFIELD

### Escuadron Dagger San Julian

Escuadron II of Grupo 6 de Caza was deployed to San Julian in late April and remained there for the duration of the War.

### Escuadron A-4C San Julian

Grupo 4 de Caza deployed to San Julian for the duration of the War. On at least one occasion (29 May) five A-4C's were further deployed to the Rio Grande naval base for a specific mission.

## SANTA CRUZ AIRFIELD

### Grupo 3 de Ataque

Although all of the combat missions flown by the Pucaras of G3A were undertaken from airfields on the Falkland Islands, mainland support for the major deployment from Reconquista was centred on Santa Cruz.

## BAM RIO GALLEGOS

### Escuadron A-4B Rio Gallegos

The Grupo 5 de Caza A-4B's were deployed to Rio Gallegos in late April and remained there for the duration of the War.

### Escuadron Mirage Rio Gallegos

Several Mirage III's of Grupo 8 de Caza were re-deployed from Comodoro Rivadavia to Rio Gallegos for operations on 1 May but were withdrawn soon afterwards. Some returned late in the War to fly a few escort sorties.

### Grupo Aereo de Exploracion y Reconocimiento 1

Although GrAeExplRec1's headquarters and main operating base was at Comodoro Rivadavia, many of its aircraft were flown from Rio Gallegos. Most, and maybe all, of the operational KC-130H tanker sorties were launched from Rio Gallegos.

### Grupo 2 de Vigilancia y Control

G2VYCA had operated a mobile radar at Rio Gallegos since 1980 in support of X Brigada Aerea and the combat units that were regularly deployed there. In early April 1982 this became part of the new Region Aerea Sur radar chain.

## BAN RIO GRANDE

### Escuadron Dagger Rio Grande

Escuadron III of Grupo 6 de Caza deployed to Rio Grande in late April and is believed to have remained there for the duration of the War.

### Grupo 2 de Vigilancia y Control

A G2VYCA mobile radar was deployed to Rio Grande in April.

### Locally based units

Rio Grande was the major established military base of the region in April 1982. Throughout the War it was the centre of naval air operations and CANA launched all of the Super Etendard and Skyhawk sorties from there. The locally based CANA helicopters obviated the need for an FAA SCCBS at Rio Grande.

## COMANDO DE LA FUERZA AEREA SUR
### (Islas de las Malvinas)

CdoFAS controlled all air activity on the Falklands although this control was delegated to the local unified de-fence command. The Islands' air defence was the responsibility of the **Seccion Operativa de Defence Aerea (SODA)**; local tactical air support was co-ordinated by the **Seccion Operativa de Apoyo Aereo Directo (SOAAD)** and forward air control was provided by **Oficiales de Control Aereo Adelanto (OCAA)**. Overall functional co-ordination was achieved through an executive liaison office — the **Oficiales Ejecutivos de Enlace de la FAA (OEEFAA)**. This rather cumbersome structure was considered necessary to combine the diverse locally deployed FAA, Ejercito and CANA units. Deployed units included:

## BAM MALVINAS (Stanley Airport)

### Escuadron Pucara Malvinas

The Pucaras of Grupo 3 de Ataque were first deployed to Stanley Airport in early April and, although dispersed to Goose Green in late April, they later returned and continued to operate from there until the surrender.

### G2VYCA Escuadron Malvinas

G2VYCA deployed to Port Stanley on 2 April and operated its AN/TPS-43F radar from sites in the area until the surrender.

### G1AA Malvinas

The 20mm and 35mm anti-aircraft guns of G1AA were deployed to sites on Stanley Airport and Goose Green airfield where they were integrated into anti-aircraft systems that combined Ejercito, Marina and FAA resources.

### CANA, PNA and Ejercito elements

BAM Malvinas hosted a number of flying units of the other services and although not part of the CdoFAS structure (but fully explained elsewhere) brief mention should be made of them here. The CANA element was deployed to a part of the Airport that was renamed the Estacion Aeronaval Malvinas and by late April MB-339A's of 1 Escuadrilla de Ataque and T-34C's of 4 Escuadrilla de Ataque were in place. The latter detachment departed to Pebble Island soon after arrival on the Falklands. Three PNA aircraft were initially deployed to Stanley Airport but were subsequently operated from the Racecourse, the Sportsfield and other remote sites.

The helicopters of the Ejercito's CAB601 were headquartered at nearby Moody Brook but were also operated from several locations in the Port Stanley area including the Airport. Other Ejercito units such as the anti-aircraft batteries of GADA101 and GADA601 were deployed to Port Stanley and Goose Green. Roland and the naval Tigercat SAM fire units were also deployed to the area around Stanley Airport.

## BAM CONDOR (Goose Green)

### Escuadron Pucara Malvinas

The Pucaras of Grupo 3 de Ataque were operated from Goose Green from late April until late May when the surviving aircraft were evacuated to Port Stanley.

### SCCBS Malvinas

The SCCBS on the Falklands was established at Goose Green on 14 April with two Grupo 7 CH-47C's and two Grupo 7 Bell 212's. They were withdrawn to Port Stanley in late May.

### EAN CALDERON (Pebble Island)

#### Escuadron Pucara Malvinas

The Grupo 3 de Ataque Pucaras operated from the naval airfield on Pebble Island for a brief period between 1 May and 15 May.

#### CANA units

The Estacion Aeronaval Calderon was initially established by CANA for the use of the T-34C's of 4 Escuadrilla de Ataque before the FAA accepted that it could be used as an alternate to Goose Green for Pucara operations. The T-34C's were deployed to Pebble Island in late April. Other light aircraft and helicopters were occasional visitors during Calderon's brief operational life.

*This sign was erected at Stanley Airport by FAA personnel in the early days of the occupation. A much valued prize, it was appropriated by 1(F) Squadron and, within a few weeks of the ceasefire, it had been placed on display with an accompanying Argentine flag at Wittering.* (P. A. Jackson)

### POST-WAR ORGANISATIONAL CHANGES

Following the effective military defeat in the Falklands the FAA consolidated its remaining resources and endeavoured to replace equipment lost in battle. Between 1982 and 1984 the FAA was frustrated in these efforts by Argentina's financial difficulties as well as the continuing arms embargoes of those nations that were sympathetic to the British cause. Nevertheless some equipment, much of it refurbished, was received. By early 1985 these acquisitions had resulted in some organisational changes.

### COMANDO DE OPERACIONES AEREAS

#### I Brigada Aerea

The acquisition of two more Boeing 707's resulted in the creation of a new squadron within G1TA in December

1982. This was Escuadron V and it left Escuadron II exclusively an F-28 unit.

#### II Brigada Aerea

No significant changes.

#### III Brigada Aerea

The loss of 24 G3A Pucaras in combat temporarily reduced the unit to a single Escuadron Grupo. Pucara production after June 1982 was slow and by late 1984 these losses had only just been made numerically good and the effect on the G3A structure was still unclear (it was reported in 1983 that the FAA had decided to abandon the "Escuadron" title completely for those units that possessed only one squadron within any Grupo structure).

#### IV Brigada Aerea

By July 1982 G4C (the "Escuadron A-4C" at San Julian during the War) possessed only seven flyable Skyhawks and on 15 December 1983 they were consolidated with the surviving A-4B's of G5C at Villa Reynolds. G4C was to be reconstituted at El Plumerillo with 14 of the Mirage IIICJ's that were received from Israel in December 1982. IV Brigada Aerea was also reported to be the new parent organisation for a planned Curso de Entrenamiento y Formacion de Pilotes (CEFPM), an advanced Mirage conversion unit, to be equipped with two Mirage IIIDA's, three Mirage IIIBJ's and two Dagger B's. By late 1984 these plans had not been confirmed. The F-86F's of "Escuadron CB-1" were still in use in August 1984.

#### V Brigada Aerea

As explained above G5C received the surviving A-4C Skyhawks from G4C in December 1983. It was reported that G5C's Squadrons were then renamed the "Escuadron A-4B" and the "Escuadron A-4C".

#### VII Brigada Aerea

There were no significant organisational changes in the immediate post-war period.

#### IX Brigada Aerea

The F-27's and Twin Otters of G9TA were organised into a locally based squadron with permanently allocated F-27 aircraft transferred from G1TA. Reports in 1984 identified the new squadron as Escuadron VI.

#### X Brigada Aerea

In the weeks following the Falklands War combat aircraft from all units remained at Rio Gallegos, Rio Grande and San Julian. The ten Mirage 5P's that were received from Peru in June 1982 appear to have remained at Rio Gallegos for at least the following 12 months, presumably crewed on a rotational basis by G6C or G8C pilots. A major refurbishment was, however, necessary to bring these Mirages to FAA standards.

On 19 March 1984 X Brigada Aerea was finally commissioned at Rio Gallegos with one operational element, Grupo 10 de Caza (G10C), which was initially equipped with five Mirage IIICJ's. Ultimately the refurbished Mirage 5P's were to join G10C, reportedly to form two squadrons within the Grupo.

In spite of the losses incurred during the War, particularly by G6C, there were no significant organisational changes implemented in its aftermath to affect VI Brigada Aerea, VIII Brigada Aerea or other major air defence elements.

# ARGENTINE AIRFIELDS

*Major airfields used by the* **FUERZA AEREA ARGENTINA** *were known as* **Base Aerea Militar** *(BAM) and each housed a major organisation, typically a Brigada Aerea or Aerea de Material. In March 1982 those in use on the Argentine mainland were:*

**BAM Reconquista** (Santa Fe, 29°11′S 59°40′W) was the home of III Brigada Aerea. It had a main runway of 6,400ft.

**BAM Cordoba** (Cordoba, 31°26′S 64°15′W) housed both the Escuela de Aviacion Militar and an Aerea de Material. The airfield was shared with the Fabricar Militar de Aviones (FMA) plant and the FAA's Centro de Ensayos en Vuelo. The length of the EAM runway was 6,100ft and that of the Area de Material runway was 5,700ft.

**BAM Parana (General Urquiza)** (Entre Rios, 31°47′S 60°29′W) was the home of II Brigada Aerea. It had a main runway of 6,900ft.

**BAM Mendoza (El Plumerillo)** (Mendoza, 32°50′S 68°47′W) was the home of IV Brigada Aerea. It had a main runway of 9,900ft.

**BAM Rio Cuarto** (Cordoba, 33°05′S 64°16′W) was the major FAA Aerea de Material. It had a main runway of 9,500ft.

**BAM Villa Reynolds (Coronel Pringles)** (San Luis, 33°44′S 65°23′W) was the home of V Brigada Aerea. It had a main runway of 7,500ft.

**BAM (Doctor) Mariano Moreno** (Buenos Aires, 34°34′S 58°47′W) was the home of VIII Brigada Aerea. It had a main runway of 7,900ft. The civilian airfield Jose C Paz was co-located.

**Aeroparque Jorge Newbery** (Buenos Aires, 34°34′S 58°25′W) was not a BAM but, as the downtown Buenos Aires airport, it was extensively used by many of the transport and executive types of all the armed forces. It had a main runway of 6,900ft.

**BAM El Palomar** (Buenos Aires, 34°36′S 58°36′W) was the home of I Brigada Aerea. It had a main runway of 6,900ft.

**BAM Moron** (Buenos Aires, 34°40′S 58°38′W) was the home of VII Brigada Aerea, INAC and the Escuadron Verificacion Radioayudos. It had a main runway of 7,900ft.

**BAM Tandil** (Buenos Aires, 37°14′S 59°15′W) was the home of VI Brigada Aerea. It had a main runway of 8,300ft.

**BAM Comodoro Rivadavia (General Enrique Mosconi)** (Santa Cruz, 45°47′S 67°28′W) was the home of IX Brigada Aerea, LADE and elements of INAC. It had a main runway of 7,700ft.

**BAM Rio Gallegos** (Santa Cruz, 51°37′S 69°17′W) was the intended home of X Brigada Aerea which was eventually commissioned on 19.3.84. It had a main runway of 11,600ft.

*During the emergency period of 1982 the FAA assumed control of all civilian aviation activity in Argentina. Three airfields were adopted for operational flying purposes. They were:*

**Puerto Deseado** (Santa Cruz, 47°44′S 65°55′W) was used as an emergency diversion base and for SAR duties although no combat aircraft were based there. It had a main runway of 4,900ft.

**San Julian** (Santa Cruz, 49°18′S 67°48′W) was used by the FAA as a combat base and aircraft from both IV and VI Brigada Aerea were deployed there. Some combat aircraft are thought to have remained in place at least until 1983. It had a main runway of 6,500ft.

**Santa Cruz** (Santa Cruz, 50°01′S 68°34′W) was used by the FAA as a forward depot for the Grupo 3 Pucaras that were deployed to the Falklands. It had a main runway of 6,500ft.

*Major airfields used by the* **COMANDO AVIACION NAVAL ARGENTINA** *were known as* **Base Aeronaval** *(BAN) and most were coastal installations adjacent to harbour facilities. In March 1982 those in use were:*

**BAN Ezeiza** (Buenos Aires, 34°49′S 58°32′W) was the main commercial airport of Buenos Aires and the home of 5 Escuadra. Ezeiza's longest runway was 10,800ft.

**BAN Punta Indio** (Buenos Aires, 35°21′S 57°17′W) was the home of 1 and 4 Escuadra. It had a main runway of 6,900ft.

**BAN Comandante Espora (Bahia Blanca)** (Buenos Aires, 38°43′S 62°09′W) was the home of 2 and 3 Escuadra. It had a main runway of 8,500ft.

**BAN Almirante Zar (Trelew)** (Chubut, 43°14′S 65°19′W) was the home of 6 Escuadra. It had a main runway of 8,400ft.

**BAN Almirante Quijada (Rio Grande)** (Tierra del Fuego, 53°47′S 67°43′W) was, in March 1982, the home of a few aircraft detached from 6 Escuadra, Trelew. It was extensively used by many CANA and FAA aircraft during the War with Britain. It was named in honour of Almirante Quijada on 17.5.83. It had a main runway of 6,500ft.

**BAN Ushuaia** (Tierra del Fuego, 54°50′S 68°17′W) was a small airfield adjacent to the Armada's port facilities. No aircraft were based there except for occasional detached communications purposes. The runway was 4,600ft and no combat operations were undertaken during the Falklands War.

*The* **PREFECTURA NAVAL ARGENTINA** *operated its small fleet of helicopters and aircraft from the Buenos Aires heliports of* **Puerto Nuevo** *and* **Darsena Norte** *and the* **Aeroparque Jorge Newberry.** *Other airfields were used as necessary.*

*The major* **COMANDO AVIACION EJERCITO** *base was* **Campo de Mayo** *(Buenos Aires, 34°32′S 58°40′W). The longest paved runway was 5,900ft.*

*During the period of occupation the following establishments were created on the* **FALKLAND ISLANDS:**

**BAM Malvinas** (Port Stanley Airport, East Falkland, 51°41′S 57°46′W) was created by the FAA for their purposes while a naval air establishment, created on the same site, was named **EAN Malvinas** (Estacion Aeronaval Malvinas). At the time of the invasion the runway was a 4,100ft asphalt strip.

**BAM Condor** (Goose Green airfield, East Falkland, 51°50′S 58°56′W) was adopted by the FAA.

**EAN Calderon** (Pebble Island airfield, West Falkland 51°19′S 59°35′W) was initially adopted by CANA but was later also used by the FAA.

165

# ARGENTINE MILITARY AIRCRAFT SERIAL ALLOCATIONS

## COMANDO AVIACION NAVAL ARGENTINA

Each CANA aircraft had a four digit serial number which was a permanent identity for its entire service life. Allocations were made in strict numerical sequence and not reissued when they fell vacant. The range commenced at 0001 and in 1984 the latest identified allocation was 0795, a new Agusta-Sikorsky ASH-3D helicopter.

Of greater operational significance than the serial numbers were the radio call-signs that were carried externally in the form of alpha-numeric combinations by all aircraft and helicopters. These infrequently changed call-signs identified Escuadra, Escuadrilla, role and the individual aircraft. The call-sign ranges are incorporated into the CANA Order of Battle elsewhere in this book and their allocation should be easily understood. The seven role letters incorporated in the codes in use in 1982 were 'A', 'AS', 'F', 'G', 'H', 'P' and 'T'. They signified 'Ataque' (Attack), 'Antisubmarina' (Anti-submarine), 'Fotografico' (Photographic), 'Generales' (General Purpose), 'Helicoptero' (Helicopter), 'Patrulla' (Patrol) and 'Transporte' (Transport).

The following list identifies all aircraft on CANA strength on 1 April 1982 and those known to have been subsequently received. It encompasses the complete serial ranges allocated to all the types then current, as well as those of types withdrawn, pending sale, at that time. Exceptions are the C-47, of which only the last two surviving examples are included, and the C-45, of which only the late models are listed. Early gaps in the serial list are those of types that had been withdrawn and disposed of by April 1982. Gaps after serial 0646 are explained in the text. If appropriate, previously unpublished relevant data concerning manufacturers' numbers (c/ns), previous identities and general information is included. For those aircraft involved in the conflict, these notes should be read in conjunction with the operational unit histories.

**0188:** One of the two surviving C-47's, '5-T-24' was withdrawn from use and made available for sale in 11.81.

**0510 to 0515:** Six reconditioned S-2A Trackers were received from USN stocks in 1962 and served in first-line use for many years until replaced by the S-2E's in 1977.

Only four of this batch, thought to have been 0511 to 0514, survived as '6-G-51' to '6-G-54' in 1982. By 1984 '6-G-51' (once USN 133249) had become '2-G-51'.

**0518 to 0532:** The last CANA C-45H was thought to have been withdrawn from use in 1979 and a few were available for sale in 11.81. Occasional reports suggested that 6 Escuadra might still have used them until 1982 ('6-G-16' had certainly been in late use) although it seems probable that all had been withdrawn by 1981.

**0541:** This serial was allocated in 1966 to the first SP-2E delivered to CANA. All the surviving SP-2E Neptunes, and 0541 was not one of them, were available for sale in 11.81.

**0542:** A single S-2A was acquired in 6.67 as an attrition replacement but was itself destroyed in 1973.

**0543 to 0546:** The last four C-45's received by CANA were two RC-45J's (0543 and 0544) and two UC-45J's (0545 and 0546). The remarks concerning the 0518 serial batch equally apply to these aircraft.

**0547 to 0591:** The first batch of 44 Sud Fennecs was delivered from France in mid-1966 but by 1981 all had been withdrawn from use. The last 12 or so were then in storage at Punta Indio and by the end of the year at least two, 0552/1-A-284 and 0553/1-A-261, were available for sale.

**0592 to 0609:** Aircraft serials were also applied to the Northrop MQM-36A drones used by CANA. The status of individual machines within this first batch is unknown!

**0613 to 0618:** The first batch of six MB-326GB's was ordered in 1966 and was quickly followed by a supplementary order for two more (0646 and 0647). These aircraft were in use in 1982 with 4 Escuadra although one unidentified aircraft had been lost before 4.82. A second, 0613/4-A-101, was lost in a crash on 28.10.82. The call-sign range in use in 1982 was still current in 1984: 0614/4-A-102 to 0618/4-A-106.

**0619 to 0638:** The second and final batch of 20 Fennecs was received from France in 10.67. All had been withdrawn from use by 1981.

**0641 to 0643:** The first three SE-3160 Alouette III's were delivered in 10.69. Both 0641 and 0643 were lost before 4.82 leaving only 0642/3-H-102 in use.

**0644:** This was the second SP-2E received by CANA, delivered in 1970. Withdrawn from use as '2-P-103', it was available for sale in 11.81.

**0646 and 0647:** The final two MB-326GB's were current in 1984 as 0646/4-A-107 and 0647/4-A-108 (see 0613 to 0618).

**0648 to 0651:** 0648 and 0649 were SE-3160 Alouette III's delivered to CANA in 5.70 and 0650 and 0651 were SA.316B models delivered in 9.70. 0648 and 0650 were both lost before 4.82 and 0649/3-H-105 was destroyed during the war with Britain. 0651/3-H-107 is thought to have survived until at least 1984.

**0652:** A VIP configured C-47A was transferred from Government registration to CANA in 1970 and, at the time of its withdrawal, was named "Stella Maris" with the call-sign '5-T-10'. It was available for sale in 11.81.

**0653:** A single HS.125-400B was acquired in 1970 for command use. After an extensive rebuild following an accident in 1977, it remained in use in 1982 as '5-T-30'.

**0654 to 0669:** 16 A-4B Skyhawks were acquired from surplus USN stocks as A-4Q's. Ordered in 1970, the aircraft were delivered to CANA in 1971/72. Their previous identities which, in 1982, were still worn on the rear fuselage, were 144872, 144882, 144895, 144915, 144929, 144963, 144983, 144988, 144989, 145001, 145004, 145010, 145025, 145050, 145053 and 145061 respectively. Six, thought to have been 0656, 0663, 0664, 0666, 0668 and 0669, were lost before 4.82 while three more, 0660, 0665 and 0667 were lost during the conflict with Britain. 0659 was lost in a post-war crash on 11.11.82. The survivors were still, in 1984, coded in the range 0654/3-A-301 to 0662/3-A-309.

**0670 to 0673:** These serials were allocated to a second batch of MQM-36A's.

**0674:** 0674 was a PC-6B-H2 that was received in 1.71 and subsequently lost in 1978.

**0675 to 0678:** Four S-61D-4 Sea Kings were received in 1972 and all were current in 1984. In 4.82 their call-signs were 0675/2-H-231 to 0678/2-H-234 and these were unchanged in 1984.

**0679:** A single Queen Air 80 was received in 11.71 and was in use in 1982 as '4-F-21'.

**0680 and 0681:** Another pair of SA.316B Alouette III helicopters was received in 11.71. 0680 was lost before 4.82 but 0681/3-H-109 was current in 1982.

**0682 and 0683:** The final pair of SP-2E's was received in 1972. Both were eventually withdrawn and were available for sale in 11.81 marked as 0682/2-P-104 and 0683/2-P-105.

**0684 to 0686:** Three PC-6B-H2's were received in 12.71 and they were current in 1984 with the call-signs '6-G-2' to '6-G-4'.

**0687 to 0690:** Four more Queen Air 80's were received between 11.71 and 2.72. Originally given the call-signs '1-G-81', '3-G-82', '3-G-83' and '1-G-84', all were passed to 6 Escuadra in c1982 when it is thought that they adopted call-signs '6-G-81' to '6-G-84'.

**0691 to 0693:** Three L-188A Electras were acquired on the second-hand market in 12.73 and they were refurbished by Lockheed AS to L-188PF standard before their delivery to Argentina in 1974. They were allocated call-signs and, in at least two instances, names, which in 1982 were respectively '5-T-1', '5-T-2' ("Ushuaia") and '5-T-3' ("Rio Grande"). A fourth unserialled airframe was also acquired for spares recovery in 1977 and its hulk was held, in 1983, at Taller Aeronaval Central in Buenos Aires.

**0694 and 0695:** These serials were allocated to two more MQM-36A's.

**0696:** A fifth S-61D-4 was ordered in 1974 and, in 1984, it remained in use with the code '35' (an abbreviation of the full call-sign '2-H-235').

**0697 and 0698:** Two King Air 200's were received in 3.75 and 9.75. They were initially used as '5-T-31' and '5-T-32' but in c1981 they were reissued to 1 Escuadra and received new call-signs '1-G-41' and '1-G-42'.

**0699:** Another SA.316B Alouette III attrition replacement, 0699 was ordered 12.74 and delivered in 6.75. It was destroyed in a post-war crash on 21.4.83 as '3-H-110'.

**0700 to 0705:** The S-2A's were finally replaced by six refurbished S-2E Trackers delivered from the USN in 1977/78. All are thought to have remained in service until at least 1984 as 0700/2-AS-21 to 0705/2-AS-26.

**0706 to 0709:** Four refurbished SP-2H Neptunes were also received from USN stocks in 1977/78 to replace the SP-2E in CANA service. They were given the call-signs '2-P-110' to '2-P-112' and '2-P-114' respectively. '0709' was delivered as such but, for reasons that have never become clear, was rapidly renumbered 0718.

**0710 to 0717:** These serials have not been identified and are thought to have probably been allocations to aircraft that were never received.

**0718:** This SP-2H '2-P-114' was the former 0709.

**0719 to 0733:** 15 T-34C-1 Turbo Mentors were received in 1978. Their c/ns were GM41 to GM44, GM49 to GM52 and GM65 to GM71. In 4.82 all were in service with the call-signs 0719/1-A-401 to 0733/1-A-415. Four aircraft,

0719, 0726, 0729 and 0730, were lost during the War.

**0734 and 0735:** Two Lynx HAS.23's were received in 8.78 and both were current in 4.82 as '3-H-141' and '3-H-142'. 0735 was destroyed during the War with Britain.

**0736 to 0739:** Four SA.319B Alouette III's were ordered in 1.78 and were received later that year. All remained in use in 4.82 as '3-H-111', '3-H-112', '3-H-114' and '3-H-115' respectively.

**0740 to 0742:** Three F-28-3000M Fellowships were received between 4.79 and 8.79. They were allocated the call-signs '5-T-10', '5-T-20' and '5-T-21'. All were thought to be current in 1984.

**0743:** This allocation has not been identified.

**0744 to 0749:** Six King Air 200's (c/ns BB460, BB471, BB488, BB543, BB546 and BB549) were received in two batches, with the first of them arriving in 1979. Their original call-signs were '4-G-43' to '4-G-48' but by 1982 0748 and 0749 had been reissued to 2 Escuadra as '2-G-47' and '2-G-48'.

**0750:** This allocation has not been identified.

**0751 to 0760:** The first batch of Super Etendards, ten aircraft with the call-signs '3-A-201' to '3-A-210', was ordered in 1979 and the first five were delivered to CANA for crew training in France in 3.81. These five were formally accepted in Argentina in 11.81. Delivery of the second five was anticipated in 5.82 but the French arms embargo delayed them until 12.82 when they and the final four aircraft, 0771 to 0774 (but see below), were delivered by sea to Argentina.

**0761 to 0770:** Ten MB-339A's were ordered by CANA in 1979 and all were received in 1980/81. In 4.82 they were current as '4-A-110' to '4-A-119' but five, 0761, 0763, 0764, 0765 and 0767, were later lost during the War with Britain. The c/ns of 0761, 0763 and 0767 were 6624, 6626 and 6630.

**0771 to 0774:** The final four Super Etendards, '3-A-211' to '3-A-214', were eventually received in 12.82. However, it appears that they were delivered with the serials 0761 to 0764 and it is presumed that this obvious compromise had gone unnoticed by CANA. In 5.84 they were noted in service still wearing their "incorrect" serials.

Serials allocated after 0774 are those of aircraft in the process of acquisition in March 1982 and those ordered post-war. Full details of those ranges were not known when these pages were prepared in early 1985 and thus the acquisitions are discussed by type rather than by serial.

**Lynx HAS.87:** An order for eight of these new helicopters was announced in 5.80 and at the outbreak of war they were under construction with Westland Helicopters at Yeovil. '3-H-143' (c/n 249), made its first flight on 29.3.82 with the flight test identity 'G-17-10'. The second one, '3-H-144' (256), was not completed before arms

deliveries to Argentina were suspended and then embargoed. Of the others, only small assemblies of '3-H-145' (264) had been produced by 3.82. The manufacturer was never provided with serial identities for any of these aircraft. '3-H-143' was subsequently registered in Britain as G-BKBL and was then serialled ZE388 for missile firing trials conducted in 7.83. In early 1985 customers for the first two aircraft were still being sought, with G-BKBL and "256" remaining in storage at Yeovil.

**EMB-111A:** Two of these Brazilian-built maritime reconnaissance aircraft were loaned to CANA c6.82, presumably as emergency replacements for the withdrawn SP-2H Neptunes. They were FAB machines P95 7058 (c/n 111-182) and P95 7060 (111-188) and for their loan period they were apparently given the call-signs '2-P-201' and '2-P-202'. Later reports have mentioned the 6 Escuadra call-signs '6-P-201' and '6-P-202' in connection with these aircraft but much is still unknown about their CANA use. They may not have been allocated serial numbers.

**EMB-326GB:** 11 Xavantes were ordered from Brazil soon after the war with Britain but it was not until mid-1983 that these surplus FAB aircraft were delivered. CANA allocated them the call-sign range '4-A-130' to '4-A-140' but no serial numbers were applied to the aircraft prior to delivery from the Embraer factory. Deliveries commenced on 15.6.83 and were completed by mid-7.83. Their former FAB serials were AT26 4545, 4561, 4573, 4574, 4576, 4588 (which became '4-A-132'), 4601, 4606, 4609, 4610 and 4612.

**L-188 Electra:** Seven commercial Electra aircraft were reportedly acquired on the second-hand market in late 1982. They were to be rebuilt into three naval configurations: (i) for passive intelligence collection (ELINT); (ii) with radars and ASM capability and the ability to guide combat aircraft; (iii) intelligence collection and maritime reconnaissance — ELINT and MR. Further details have not been forthcoming but it is known that four aircraft were quickly put into service and that a fifth airframe was broken-up as a spares source. The call-sign '6-P-101' was given to L-188PF c/n 1123 (the former N5538, received in 12.82); '6-P-102' to L-188C c/n 1067 (HR-TNN, received on 6.11.82), 0790/6-P-103 to L-188PF c/n 1070 (N5536) and 0793/6-P-104 to L-188PF c/n 1072 (N5534, seen in Miami, USA in 11.82 in CANA markings). L-188C c/n 1071 (N551PS, delivered 2.11.82) was used for spares reclamation.

**Agusta-Sikorsky ASH-3D:** Two new Sea Kings were ordered from Italy in 1983 and both were seen at the factory in 4.84 awaiting delivery. They were in full CANA markings with the serials/call-signs 0794/2-H-236 and 0795/2-H-237.

**McDonnell Douglas A-4E/A-4H:** In late 1984 it was revealed that 16 refurbished A-4E/A-4H Skyhawks had been ordered from Israel during 1982 (presumably when the Mirage IIICJ/IIIBJ deal was struck) but that they had not been received because of the enforced United States embargo on arms sales to Argentina. In early 1985 it was still unclear whether CANA would ever receive these Skyhawks.

# PREFECTURA NAVAL ARGENTINA

The Prefectura Naval Argentina numbered its small fleet of helicopters and fixed-wing aircraft in alpha numeric series that grouped each type in a range. This method of numbering closely paralleled the Prefectura's system of pennant numbering its ships. Aircraft serials were not normally reissued when they fell vacant.

---

**PA-11 to PA-13:** Three SA.330L Pumas were received in mid-1980 and all were current in 4.82. PA-12 was lost on the Falklands but the others remained in service in 1983.

**PA-30 to PA-35:** Six Hughes 500C's were received by the Prefectura and all are thought to have been in service in 1983.

**PA-50 to PA-54:** Five Skyvan 3M's were received in mid-1971. All five were current in 4.82 but two, PA-50 and PA-54, were lost on the Falklands.

# COMANDO DE AVIACION DEL EJERCITO

In 1982 all CAE aircraft and helicopters wore a three digit serial number prefixed by the letters 'AE' for Argentina Ejercito. Allocations were made in ranges to each aircraft type but a superficially simple system of numbering was complicated by the occasional renumbering of some of the fixed-wing types. In marked contrast, helicopter serial ranges were obvious and had changed little. Individual code letters were not worn.

The following list is that of all types that are thought to have been current in April 1982. The few known post-war Ejercito acquisitions have also been included. The somewhat eccentric allocation of serials to the fixed-wing types does not, we believe, disguise many unidentified aircraft! Where appropriate, details of previous Ejercito identities or other unpublished data is included.

### FIXED-WING AIRCRAFT

**AE-051 to AE-055:** The last five T-41D's (Cessna R172H) to be built were supplied to the CAE in about late 1974. Their c/ns were R1720613 to R1720617.

**AE-100:** A Twin Otter 200 (c/n 136) was delivered to the CAE in 8.68 with the serial AE-100. It was later renumbered AE-106 but was then reported to have been renumbered again to AE-257. In 11.82 a Twin Otter with the serial AE-106 was seen again but by 8.84 c/n 136 was again AE-100, attached to the Ejercito's III Cuerpo, Cordoba!

**AE-110:** At least one Cessna 320 was used by the CAE and may have been current in 1982.

**AE-128:** An Aero Commander twin with this serial was seen in 3.80 and in 5.80. It is thought that it was probably the model 680V of Fabricaciones Militares that had worn the serial AE-129 for several years until at least 1979. As will be seen below AE-129 was no longer an Aero Commander in 1982.

**AE-129:** A VIP Cessna 550 was received in 11.79 for the use of Fabricaciones Militares, but shortly before 4.82 it was given the government registration LQ-TFM.

**AE-175:** A Sabre 75A was, in 1982, used by the Comicion Especial de Adquisigiones, BA.

**AE-176 to AE-179:** Four new Merlin IIIA's were acquired in 1977 and three of them were current in mid-1982, AE-177 having by then been lost in an accident. Their c/ns were respectively T275, T277, T280 and T281.

**AE-180:** One Merlin IVA (c/n AT071E) was received in 1979.

**AE-185:** A Cessna 500 was delivered in 1.78 for the use of the Instituto Geografica Militar.

**AE-200 to AE-223:** This range of 24 serials was allocated by the CAE to Cessna utility aircraft. AE-200 and AE-201 were Cessna 180A's, both disposed of by 1971. AE-202 to AE-214 were U-17A's (commercial 185F) supplied by the USA under MDAP arrangements in the middle 'sixties. The survivors were still in service in 4.82 but what may have been the final six, AE-203, AE-207, AE-209 to AE-211 and AE-213 (FMS 66-8546), were disposed of to the civil market in 6.83. AE-214 was a locally built FMA model A182J, once used by the Instituto Geografico Militar, but its status in 1982 is unknown. AE-216 to AE-221 were Cessna 207's, the delivery of which commenced about 1978, and all are thought to have been current in 1983. AE-223 was, in 8.84, a T207A (c/n T207-00481), attached to III Cuerpo, Cordoba.

**AE-256 and AE-257:** Two Queen Air 80's are thought to have remained in use until at least 1983. AE-256 was delivered as AE-102 and was probably renumbered in 1969 while AE-257 was delivered as AE-109. The latter was thought to have been renumbered again when the Twin Otter AE-106 became AE-257 but, as will have been appreciated earlier, it is conceivable that the Queen Air 80

AE-257 may still have been current in 1983.

**AE-258 and AE-259:** This pair of Twin Otter 200's was received with AE-106 in 8.68. AE-258 was sold to the state oil company YPF on 28.9.82 and AE-259 was lost in an accident in 1.75.

**AE-260 to AE-262:** Three Aeritalia G.222's were received, the first two in 1977 and the third in 4.78. All are thought to have been current in 1983.

**AE-263:** A Twin Otter 300 was received in 7.78.

---

### HELICOPTERS

---

**AE-331 to AE-339:** A total of nine A-109A Hirundos was received during 1979/80. All were current in 4.82 although AE-332 had not flown for over a year, having spent the time under maintenance. AE-331, AE-334 and AE-337 were lost during the Falklands War.

**AE-359:** At least one of an unknown total of UH-12E's was noted at Campo de Mayo in 1981. It is thought that the type may have been withdrawn from use by then. At least four (c/ns 5133 and 5138 to 5140) are believed to have been used by the CAE.

**AE-385 to AE-390:** Six SA.315B Lamas were received in 11.75 and all were in use in 4.82. AE-388 was later damaged in an accident on 24.11.82.

**AE-400 to AE-424:** About 25 UH-1H's were delivered to the CAE between 1970 and 1978 as new equipment off US Army contracts. A few of their individual details have come to light as a result of the Falklands War and they are as follows: AE-403 (c/n 11884, FMS 69-15596), AE-406 (13190, 72-21491 built 3.73), AE-409 (13205, 72-21506), AE-410 (13220, 72-21521), AE-412 (13559, 73-22076 built 10.74), AE-413 (13560, 73-22077, delivered to CAE on 25.2.75), AE-415 (13567, 73-22084 built 12.74), AE-417 (13570, 73-22087), AE-418 (13571, 73-22088), AE-422

(13844, 74-22520 built 8.76), AE-423 (delivered with AE-424), AE-424 (13934, 77-22930 built 9.78). Oddly, Bell Textron appears to have made a clerical error with AE-413's FMS serial which appeared on all CAE paperwork as "73-21872". About five UH-1H's had been lost or withdrawn before 4.82 and one, AE-419, was lost on 30.4.82 in a mainland accident. Nine, AE-406, AE-409, AE-410, AE-412, AE-413, AE-417, AE-418, AE-422 and AE-424 were lost on the Falklands.

**AE-450 and AE-451:** Two Bell 212's were received in 1978 for VIP use. AE-450 was certainly in use in 4.82 but AE-451 is reported to have been destroyed before then. Their c/ns were 30767 and 30769.

**AE-500 to AE-508:** A total of nine SA.300L Pumas were delivered to the CAE in 1978/79. Their c/ns were 1539, 1540, 1544, 1550, 1551, 1554, 1556, 1559 and 1560 respectively. AE-502 was lost in an accident shortly before 5.82 and another six were lost on the Falklands and South Georgia. They were AE-500, AE-501, AE-503, AE-504, AE-505 and AE-508.

**AE-520 and AE-521:** Two new CH-47C Chinooks were ordered by the CAE in 1977 but both were embargoed by the United States before delivery. AE-520 was reported completed in 3.78 but was not delivered to Argentina until 24.8.79, by which time only 11.30 flight hours had been accumulated. (57.40 hours were recorded in 9.79, presumably during working-up activity. For the rest of its CAE life monthly utilisation averaged only 6.42 hours.) Both Chinooks were lost on the Falklands.

**AE-525 and AE-526:** In late 1982 the CAE announced its intention to procure 12 AS.332B Super Pumas. The first of them (c/n 2070) was due for delivery in early 1984 but AE-525 and AE-526 (stated to be the first two) were still with the manufacturer in France in 6.84 and 7.84 respectively. The c/ns of the second and third aircraft were quoted as 2072 and 2088. The total intended procurement was reported to be 24.

# FUERZA AEREA ARGENTINA

---

All FAA aircraft had alpha-numeric serial numbers allocated to them and their letter prefixes provided an identification of each type's basic duty. In certain instances serials were allocated to aircraft of the same basic type in more than one range to identify multiple roles. A few FAA aircraft current in 1982 had more than one serial during their service lives in recognition of changing roles, but this practice was generally restricted to the transport types. Some serials, and this applied particularly to the transports and helicopters, were reissued when they fell vacant. In some cases the reallocation was to aircraft of the same basic type.

The following tabulation of FAA serial numbers is presented in serial number sequence and it details all aircraft known to have been on strength on 1 April 1982 and those

subsequently added to the inventory (until about December 1984). Some basic historical data is included and this should be read in conjunction with the operational data contained in other sections of this book.

During the preparation of the book some previously unpublished data concerning details such as manufacturers' numbers (c/ns) and previous identities was discovered and, where appropriate, it is included here.

---

### ATAQUE (Attack)

---

*The prefix letter 'A' was used to indicate an 'Ataque'*

*(Attack) role. When used in conjunction with an 'X' ('AX') the role was modified to 'Ataque Experimento' (Attack/Experimental).*

**A-501 to A-602:** A-501 to A-575 was the first production batch of 75 IA.58A Pucaras delivered between early 1977 and 12.6.82 (A-501 actually made its first flight 8.11.74). By mid-1983 FMA had produced 90 of an apparent total of 102 IA.58A aircraft (said to constitute two prototypes and 100 production aircraft). Production of the aircraft was slowed during 1983 and 1984 and although A-579, A-582, A-584 and A-585 were seen under construction at Cordoba in 11.82, A-591 was publicly exhibited in 3.84 as a "recently built" machine. A-596 to A-598 were seen in production in 8.84.

Examination of numerous captured aircraft revealed that the manufacturer's numbers 001 to 052 appear to have been allocated to aircraft A-501 to A-552 in straight sequence and without obvious anomaly. There is, however, some confusion surrounding the identities of the six aircraft that were supplied to Uruguay in 10.81 as FAU-220 to FAU-225. They appear to have been aircraft 042 to 044 and 046 to 048 (ie the frustrated A-542 etc) but the FAU serials may be out of sequence with the c/ns. To the Authors' knowledge none of these aircraft had been noted in FAA markings (A-545, listed by some sources as supplied to the FAU, was seen at Cordoba before 5.82, precise date undetermined).

The use of the serial A-19 in 9.78 on an IA.58A displayed at Farnborough is not understood and it is thought that the aircraft might have been A-519, manufactured four months earlier. To our knowledge A-519 had never been noted but Argentine sources report that A-19 was last seen circa 1979/80, coincident with the appearance of AX-04.

Several late production IA.58A's (the first was apparently A-575) were modified when under construction to delete the rear seat and in 10.84 this change, with other modifications, resulted in the appearance of the IA.58C. The first aircraft rebuilt to this standard (serial unknown) was displayed at Cordoba at that time but, by early 1985, production plans for the type did not appear to have been finalised.

At least four aircraft, including A-503 and A-554, were lost prior to 1.4.82. 25 were lost during the War with Britain: A-502, A-506, A-509, A-511, A-513 to A-517, A-520, A-522, A-523, A-527 to A-529, A-531 to A-533, A-536, A-537, A-540, A-549, A-552, A-555 and A-556. At least three more had crashed by early 1985 (c10.82, 6.1.83 and 21.9.83).

**AX-01 to AX-06:** Six prototype and experimental Pucaras were allocated these serials (prototype AX-01 earlier wore the unofficial marking 'A-X2'). AX-04 is thought to have been the former A-19 (and was used from 5.82 for unsuccessful torpedo trials), AX-05 became the prototype IA.58B and AX-06 the prototype IA.66. (It is not clear from FMA publicity material exactly which aircraft were considered to be prototypes. Total production of the Astazou engined aircraft had, at the time of writing, been given as 108 comprising two prototypes, 100 production aircraft for the FAA and six for the FAU.)

## BOMBARDEO (Bomber)

*The prefix letter 'B' was used to indicate 'Bombardeo' (Bomber). 'BS' and 'BSH' were used for the unrelated 'Busqueda y Salvamento' (Search and Rescue) and, with the suffix letter 'H' for 'Helicoptero', 'SAR/Helicopter'.*

**B-101 to B-112:** B-101 to B-110 were ten surplus RAF Canberras refurbished by BAC in 1970/71 to B.62 standard. B-111 and B-112 were similarly reworked to T.64 configuration. As indicated elsewhere, B-103 and another B.62 (thought to have been B-106) were lost before 1.4.82 and B-108 and B-110 were lost during the conflict with Britain. An unidentified aircraft was destroyed in a post-war crash 13.8.82. A supplementary order for two aircraft was in work at BAe Samlesbury at the time of the Falklands invasion. An indefinite embargo was placed on their delivery and in 5.85 the uncompleted aircraft, B.2 WH914/G-27-373 and T.4 XH583/G-27-374, remained at Samlesbury.

## BUSQUEDA Y SALVAMENTO (Search and Rescue)

**BS-11:** The serial BS-11 was allocated to an Aero Commander twin used for SAR duties. Its status since 1982 is not known.

**BSH-72:** In 1982 the prefix letters 'BS' were added to the serial of an S-61NR, H-72. It is thought that H-71 may have received similar treatment.

## CAZA (Fighter)

*The prefix letter 'C' was used to indicate a 'Caza' (Hunter) duty which equated to a tactical fighter role.*

**C-101 to C-128:** 28 F-86F Sabres were delivered to the FAA from surplus USAF stocks from 1960. The FAA declared 12 available for disposal in 1976 but attempts to pass them to Uruguay were blocked by the United States and in 1984 they remained in second-line use in Argentina. Several aircraft were lost in accidents and at least one was lost after 6.82 (C-102 on 25.8.83).

**C-201 to C-250:** 50 surplus USN A-4B Skyhawks were acquired by the FAA from the United States from 1966 (C-201 made its first flight 31.12.65). Although officially designated A-4P this nomenclature was ignored by the FAA who referred to them as A-4B's (perversely, CANA always referred to its A-4B's as A-4Q's). The delivery of the first 25 aircraft commenced in 10.66 after pilot training had begun in the USA. C-226 to C-240 were later delivered in 11.69 and C-241 to C-250 followed in 4.70. Approximately 20 aircraft were lost before 4.82 but few identities are known (C-205 was lost in the USA 10.11.67). Another 10 were lost during the war with Britain: C-204, C-206, C-208, C-215, C-226, C-228, C-242, C-244, C-246 and C-248. At least four more were lost in post-war accidents on 12.11.82, 13.7.83 (C-235), 31.10.84

(C-234) and 19.11.84.

**C-301 to C-325:** 25 A-4C Skyhawks were received from surplus USN stocks in 1976 to replace the FAA's F-86F's. About six aircraft were lost in accidents before 4.82 and nine more were lost during the fighting with Britain. They were C-301, C-303 to C-305, C-309, C-310, C-313, C-319 and C-325.

**C-401 to C-439:** 24 IAI single-seat Neshers, (C-401 to C-424) and two dual-seat Neshers (C-425 and C-426) were delivered to the FAA between 26.11.78 and 23.12.80. For FAA service they were given the names Dagger A and Dagger B. A second batch of 11 Dagger A's (C-427 to C-437) and two Dagger B's (C-438 and C-439) was received between 29.5.81 and 2.82. Few details of any previous Israeli identities are known, but two of the Dagger A's are thought to have been the former IDF/AF 525 and 556. Two aircraft were lost in accidents before 4.82 (a Dagger A on 26.11.79 and a Dagger B, C-425, on 7.10.80). A further 11 were lost during the Falklands War: C-403, C-404, C-407, C-409, C-410, C-419, C-428, C-430, C-433, C-436 and C-437. At least one Dagger A was lost during 1983.

**C-403, C-404, C-407, C-409, C-410, C-419, C-428, C-430, C-433 and C-436:** Ten Mirage 5P's were received from Peru in 6.82 to make good FAA Dagger attrition and it is understood that these former FAP aircraft were allocated the serials of 10 Daggers destroyed in combat during 5.82. With the exceptions of C-403 and C-409, however, this sequence has not been confirmed. C-403 was seen at Mariano Moreno on 2.9.82 and again in early 11.82 where its purpose seemed to be that of a training/familiarisation airframe.

**C-701 to C-722:** 19 Mirage IIICJ's and three Mirage IIIBJ's were acquired from surplus Israeli stocks and the first of them arrived, by sea, at Buenos Aires on 18.12.82. Possibly the last of Israel's Mirages, all had been re-engined with the Atar 9C and, in contrast to the former FAP Mirage 5P's, were in excellent condition when received! The 19 Mirage IIICJ's were given the serials C-701 to C-719 and the IIIBJ's C-720 to C-722. C-711 was said to have the Dassault production number 'CJ34' while the IIIBJ's were quoted as having the original Dassault numbers 236, 237 and 239 (Israel is thought to have received 236 to 240). C-721 was further, and consistently, identified as having the production number 'BJ2' and being the former IDF/AF 639 (which requires confirmation). In 1983 C-701 was undergoing in-flight refuelling trials at Rio Cuarto. An unidentified Mirage III of Grupo 10 crashed near Rio Gallegos on 30.4.85.

---

### ESCUELA (Training)

*The prefix letter 'E' indicated the 'Escuela' (School) role which covered all basic training functions.*

**E-001 to E-090:** 90 Beech and locally assembled FMA T-34A Mentors were received by the FAA in the late 'fifties and about half survived in 1982 in various flying duties. Others had been relegated to ground instructional roles. At least one, E-075 on 24.3.83, was destroyed in a post-war accident.

**E-201 to E-248:** 48 MS-760 Paris were received from 1958 for training, communications and light attack purposes. 12 were built in France and then reassembled locally, the first nine of these being originally serialled A-01 to A-09. They were later renumbered E-201 to E-209. The balance of 36 were constructed by FMA. By 1973 only 32 were still in use and 20 of those were in service in the tactical role. The others undertook liaison, training and transport duties. By 1982 only enough aircraft to equip one tactical Escuadron remained in use although a few continued in the training role. One post-war accident occurred on 4.11.83 when an unidentified aircraft was lost in a mid-air collision.

**EX-01 and EX-02:** The prototype IA.63 Pampa (EX-01) made its first flight on 6.10.84. A total of 64 had been widely quoted as on order for the FAA but, in late 1984, it seemed likely that only an initial batch of 12 had been procured. By 1.85 EX-01 was in use with the CEV at Cordoba.

---

### FOTOGRAFICO (Photographic)

*The prefix letter 'F' was allocated to those aircraft used primarily in the 'Fotografico' (Photographic) role. Although the range was current in 1982, the latest photographic duties aircraft received by the FAA, the Learjet 35A, had been allocated serials in the 'Transporte' range.*

**F-31 to F-35:** Five reconnaissance equipped IA.50 Guarani II's were received in the late 'sixties. Although superseded by the new Learjets, at least two (F-32 and F-33), and possibly all five, were still current in late 1982.

---

### HELICOPTERO (Helicopter)

*The prefix letter 'H' was allocated to all FAA helicopters. Serial ranges were reissued and, as will be realised, several serials have been reallocated to new examples of the same type.*

**H-01 and H-02:** Two Carson-converted S-58T's were received as VIP transports. Both were former West German Army H-34A's.

**H-10 to H-13:** Four UH-1D's were received in the 'sixties and at least one (H-12 destroyed 16.8.82) was lost post-war.

**H-14 to H-16:** Three UH-1H's were reported to have been delivered in 1970.

**H-20 to H-33:** Two Hughes 369HE's (H-20 and H-21) and 12 Hughes 369HM's (H-22 to H-33) were received in 1969.

At least one was lost before 4.82, while H-29 was lost on 17.2.84.

**H-40 to H-43:** Three RACA-assembled Hughes 500D's (understood to have been H-41 to H-43) were received in 6.81 for use with INAC at Comodoro Rivadavia. H-40 was noted in 1984.

**H-61 to H-66:** Six SA.315B Lamas were received in 1972, four of which were later lost in accidents. Three of these four (H-62, H-63 and H-65) were subsequently replaced by three new examples which took up the serials of the earlier machines. Two of these (H-62 and H-63) were reported lost in subsequent accidents on 12.76 and 7.7.83 but a Lama serialled H-62 was seen in use 11.82! The fourth loss from the original batch was H-61 on 1.2.81.

**H-71 and H-72:** Two S-61NR's were received by the FAA for SAR duties. H-72 is known to have been given the new serial BSH-72.

**H-81 to H-89:** Eight Bell 212's were delivered to the FAA between 27.4.78 and 9.6.78 and all are thought to have been current on 1.4.82. A ninth helicopter (H-89) was in use by 1982. Their c/ns were respectively 30830, 30831, 30834, 30836 to 30840 and 31141. Two, H-83 and H-85, were lost on the Falklands.

**H-91 to H-93:** Three CH-47C Chinooks were received in 4.80. H-92 later crashed, and was presumably destroyed, in an accident in Antarctica in 1.82. It was replaced by a new BV234ER model that was reported to have been delivered in 1984.

---

### INTERCEPTAR (Interceptor)

---

*The prefix letter 'I' was used to indicate 'Interceptar' (Interceptor) duties and applied only to the Mirage IIIEA/IIIDA fleet whose function was essentially air defence.*

**I-001 to I-021:** The original batch of 12 Mirages was delivered to the FAA from 6.72 and comprised two Mirage IIIDA's (I-001 and I-002) and 10 IIIEA's (I-003 to I-012). They were augmented in 1980 by seven new IIIEA's (I-013 to I-019) and in 12.82 by two refurbished two-seat aircraft from France (I-020 and I-021). Two Mirages were lost pre-war (I-009 on 23.3.76 and I-001 on 30.3.79), two more (I-015 and I-019) were lost during the fighting and another (I-016) was destroyed in a post-war crash on 8.10.83.

---

### PROPOSITOS GENERALES (General Purposes)

---

*The letters 'PG' were allocated to aircraft with a 'Propositos Generales' (General Purposes) function. Such aircraft were used throughout Argentina for a variety of duties that included such diverse tasks as liaison, government agency work, glider towing, pilot training, sport flying and local patrol work. The first allocations in this category were made to accommodate the FMA built*

*Cessna 182 aircraft in the late 'sixties. The letters 'PGH' are similarly allocated to helicopters.*

**PG-311 to PG-313:** Two Chincul Piper PA-A-28RT-201 Arrow IV's were received by INAC in 12.81 and a third followed in 1982. The c/ns of PG-312 and PG-313 were AR28-8118054 and AR28-8118029 respectively.

**PG-321 to PG-323:** Two Chincul Piper PA-A-34-220T Seneca III's were received by INAC in 12.81. A third followed early in 1982. Their c/ns were AR34-8133039, AR34-8133033 and AR34-8133129 respectively.

**PG-330 to PG-340:** 10 MH1521C Broussards were reported to have been transferred to military markings in 1967. This serial range covered 11 allocations and all except PG-335 were seen in service. Although several were withdrawn by 1982 the type was certainly current in 12.82 when PG-340 was seen undertaking crop spraying.

**PG-341 to PG-380:** Between 1966 and 1980 FMA built 152 Cessna A182J/K/L/N models and at least 40 of them were delivered to the FAA and other military and governmental agencies (the first aircraft, an A182J c/n A182-0001, was delivered to the Secretaria de Aeronautica as LV-IPJ on 13.9.66). All of these aircraft were given civilian registrations until about 9.69 when many were transferred to this sequence of FAA serials. At that time serials from PG-341 to PG-373 were taken up by A182J and A182K models, the serials PG-374 to PG-380 being later allocations to A182N's. As with the earlier aircraft, the A182N's were given civilian registrations but they were not worn before the aircraft were transferred to the new military markings. In 1985 these aircraft continued to serve throughout Argentina in a variety of roles.

**PG-386 and PG-387:** Two Cessna 320's were used until 1982 when PG-387 was withdrawn (30.8.82). PG-386 (c/n 320-0032) was later disposed of as LV-HGF in 3.83.

**PG-391:** A single Cessna 336 was used by the FAA but was no longer current by 1983.

**PG-396 and PG-397:** Two PA-31P-425 Navajos were used by the FAA although only PG-397 (31P-7530136) was current in 1983. The history of PG-396 (31P-7300130) is unknown and the serial was later reallocated. PG-397, with CNIE in 1981, was originally serialled ER-106 and, later, TS-01. It assumed the serial PG-397 by at least 6.80.

**PG-396:** This FMA Focke Wulf FW-44J Stieglitz (c/n 172) had seen service with both CANA (where it was once coded '1-E-100') and probably with the FAA before being allocated this serial. In 1982 it was undertaking glider towing duties at Cordoba.

**PG-400:** This serial was reported in 1974 to be that of a Cessna 180 but may well have belonged to an indigenous design. Its status in 1982 was uncertain.

**PG-407:** This serial, perhaps one of a larger range, had been quoted as that of a Dinfia IAe.20 Boyero and a Super Cub. It was probably that of a Boyero, however, but its last sighting appears to have been in 1971.

**PG-416:** This Dinfia IA.51 Tehuelche was once LV-X26 and LV-IMF. Its status in 1982 is not known.

**PG-421 to PG-423 and PG-426:** PG-421 was an IAe.46 Ranquel while the others were Super Ranquels. PG-421 (c/n 01) was transferred from the civil register in 1970 and was current in late 1978. PG-422 and PG-423 (c/ns 0203 and 0216), also once civilians, were probably both current in 1982, PG-423 having been seen in 11.82.

**PG-431 and PG-432:** At least two Aero Boero AB-180RVR's were transferred from civilian markings to the FAA. PG-431 (c/n 008) was current in 10.81 and PG-432 was current in 1.84.

**PGH-01 to PGH-04:** Four RACA Hughes 500D's were obtained for general duties. The first pair was received in 6.81 and PGH-03 and PGH-04 were noted in use in 8.82, presumably soon after delivery.

## TRANSPORTE (Transport)

*The prefix letter 'T' was used to indicate a 'Transporte' (Transport) role but in many cases a qualifying suffix letter was added. 'C' indicated that the aircraft had been configured to carry 'Carga' (Cargo) but 'TC' serials were frequently worn by passenger carrying aircraft. An 'S' was used to indicate 'Sanitario' (Ambulance) duties. As explained earlier, allocations in these ranges had been re-issued several times since the early 'fifties and even some of the newer allocations were confusing as the FAA continued to shuffle serials to fill gaps. Where it is appropriate we have included explanatory data.*

**T-01 and T-02:** These serials were allocated to two VIP F-28-1000's and in 11.82 they were respectively held by aircraft c/n 11028 (received in 12.70 as T-01, later becoming T-02) and 11048 (received in 3.76 as LV-LZN, later T-03).

**T-10:** A Sabre 75A was used by the Comandante en Jefe de la Fuerza Aerea. Brigadier General Lami Dozo held this position in 4.82.

**TC-20 and TC-21:** More than 40 C-47's were received by the FAA over many years and at least 11 remained in FAA use in 1983. Their serials were once part of large batch allocations that have since been reallotted (in part or in whole) and this has left some of the surviving C-47's with compromised serials. In 10.84 TC-20 was current with V Brigada Aerea and in 1983 TC-21 was with the Rio IV overhaul unit.

**T-21 to T-24:** Two Learjet 35A's were received in 1.78 for photographic duties with II Brigada Aerea. Two more were received in 10.80 and 12.80. T-24 was lost during the conflict with Britain.

**TC-27 and TC-34 to TC-37:** Five more C-47's were still current in 1983. Their respective users then were INAC (although TC-27 was transferred from EAM in 12.82), II Brigada Aerea (and was still so in 9.84), II Brigada Aerea, III Brigada Aerea and INAC.

**T-41 to T-45:** These five F-27 Friendships were delivered to the FAA between 1969 and 1975. All were current in 1982 but had a history of serial renumbering. T-41 and T-42 (F-27-400's) were changed from T-80 and T-79 in 2.70, T-43 and T-44 (F-27-600's) were received as new aircraft in 12.71 and T-45 (F-27-400M) was renumbered from TC-79 in 12.76.

**TC-51 to TC-55:** Five F-28-1000C Fellowships were received in 1975 for use by LADE. All were current in 1982.

**TC-61 to TC-70:** Three C-130E's (TC-61 to TC-63) were received in 1968 and they were supplemented by five C-130H's delivered in two batches. TC-64 to TC-66 were received in 1972 and TC-67 and TC-68 followed in 1975. The two KC-130H's (TC-69 and TC-70) were delivered in 1979. TC-62 was lost pre-war and TC-63 was lost during the War with Britain. A new L-100-30, LV-APW (c/n 4891, the former N4170M) was received 12.82 although the aircraft was technically not on FAA charge.

**TC-71 to TC-79:** This serial batch comprised, in 1982, eight F-27 Friendship aircraft and one vacant serial (the once TC-77). Eight F-27-400M models were delivered for LADE use in 1969 and were serialled TC-71 to TC-78. TC-72 and TC-75 were lost in accidents in 3.75 and 6.70 and in 1981 they were replaced with new F-27-500's that took up the vacant serials. TC-77 was lost after an accident in Antarctica in 12.69 and, although struck off charge in 4.73, the allocation was not reused. A new F-27-400M was received in 1978 and was serialled TC-79. (None of these aircraft should be confused with those numbered T-41 to T-45!)

**T-81 to T-90:** Seven Twin Otters were delivered to LADE between 11.68 and 10.69 and one (T-84) was lost before 4.82. A second (T-81) was lost in a crash on 28.1.83. On 21.10.82 three civilian registered aircraft, LV-JMP (c/n 158), LV-JMR (178) and LV-JMS (179) were transferred to the FAA for use in southern Argentina. LV-JMR was subsequently confirmed to have been given the serial T-90.

**TC-91 to TC-94, T-95 and T-96:** Three Boeing 707's were in service with the FAA on 1.4.82. TC-91, a 707-389B, had formerly been the VIP T-01 while TC-92 and TC-93 were the former civil 707-372C LV-LGP and 707-387C LV-JGP, delivered to the FAA in mid-1980 and on 5.1.82 respectively. The 707-372C TC-94 (c/n 20076) was the former LV-LGO and was taken on FAA charge 17.12.82. Two more 707-387B's, LV-ISA and LV-ISD (c/ns 19238 and 19241) were transferred from Aerolineas Argentinas to the FAA in 1983 and by 1.3.84 they had become T-95 and T-96.

**T-101 to T-104:** Four C-47's were received by INAC on 31.7.81. All remained in use in 1983.

**TX-110 and T-111 to T-128:** This range of serials covered the main production batch of FMA IA.50 Guarani II's. Most of the aircraft remained in use in 1982 but it is thought that some had been transferred earlier to the markings F-31 to F-35 and VR-15 and VR-16. T-113 was damaged in an accident on 13.12.82 but was repairable. T-125 was destroyed in a crash on 10.10.83. T-123, alleged by some sources to have been lost pre-war, reappeared during 7.82 to repatriate Flt Lt Glover to Montevideo!

**T-130 to T-144:** 15 Aero Commander 500's were received by the FAA. T-130 was a model 500S in Presidential configuration while the others were 500U's in use with command functions, a few of the Brigadas Aereas and sundry other organisations. T-130 was the former LQ-MAY, delivered in 1956, while the others were received in 1968. At least one, T-140, was lost pre-war (in 1.78).

**T-151 and T-152:** Another pair of Aero Commanders was reported and T-152 was allegedly current in 1979.

**TS-01 and TS-02:** Two SA-226AT Merlin IVA's (c/ns AT063 and AT064) were delivered to Argentina in 1978 for ambulance duties. Both were current in 1982.

**TX-01 and TX-02:** These serials were allocated to the IA.50 Guarani II prototypes (TX-01 was formerly LV-X27 and had first flown on 23.4.63). TX-01 was still in use with the Cordoba Aerea de Material in 1975 and both could still have been current in 1982.

---

## VERIFICACION RADIOAYUDOS (Navaid Calibration)

*The letters 'VR' indicated 'Verificacion Radioayudos' (Navaid Calibration) duties and all aircraft undertaking this function were on the charge of the Escuadron Verificacion Radioayudos at Moron.*

**VR-14:** Last noted in 1974, this C-47 had probably been withdrawn from service by 1982.

**VR-15 and VR-16:** The two IA.50 Guarani II's that were acquired for the Escuadron Verificacion Radioayudos were still on INAC strength in 1982, their serials still reflecting their earlier purpose.

**VR-17 and VR-18:** Two Learjet 35A's were acquired in 1981 and 1982 for the Escuadron Verificacion Radioayudos.

# ARGENTINE SHIPPING

The first part of this appendix details those ships of the Armada Argentina thought to have been on strength in March 1982. Vessels known to have been under construction or on order at that time have also been included. With the exception of the pair of Z-28 patrol craft that were deployed to the Falklands theatre, the extensive fleet of the Prefectura Naval Argentina has been omitted.

Details of the operational use of these and other commercial vessels during the period of conflict are contained in the second part of the appendix.

# ARMADA

## AIRCRAFT CARRIER

Originally 'Colossus' Class HMS Venerable (commissioned 20.12.44); later HrMS Karel Doorman; sold to Argentina 15.10.68. Armed with 40mm/70 guns.

**V2   ARA 25 DE MAYO**          Commissioned 12.3.69

## SUBMARINES

'Guppy (1A)' Class; diesel fleet submarines. Armed with 21in torpedoes. ARA Santa Fe was formerly USS Catfish, commissioned 19.3.45, and ARA Santiago Del Estero was USS Chino, commissioned 28.4.45. Santiago Del Estero was paid off in 9.81 and disposed of in 1983.

**S21   ARA SANTA FE**                     Received 1.71
**S22   ARA SANTIAGO DEL ESTERO**          Received 1.71

'Salta' Class (Type 209/1); two diesel fleet submarines. Armed with 21in torpedoes.

**S31   ARA SALTA**          Commissioned  7.3.74
**S32   ARA SAN LUIS**       Commissioned 24.5.74

Type TR1700; two diesel fleet submarines, both under construction in 1982. Armed with 21in torpedoes and rocket launchers.

**S33   ARA SANTA CRUZ**     *Commissioned 2.84*
**S34   ARA SAN JUAN**       *Commissioned late 1984*

## CRUISER

Originally the 'Brooklyn' Class USS Phoenix (commissioned 18.3.39); sold to Argentina in 1951 as ARA 17 Octobre. Renamed ARA General Belgrano in 1956. Equipped to carry one light helicopter and armed with Seacat SAM, 6in, 5in, 47mm and 40mm guns.

**C4   ARA GENERAL BELGRANO**   Received 12.4.51

## DESTROYERS

Type 42; equipped to carry one Lynx HAS.23 helicopter. Armed with Exocet SSM and Sea Dart SAM systems, 4.5in and 20mm guns and ILAS-3 torpedoes.

**D1   ARA HERCULES**              Commissioned 12.7.76
**D2   ARA SANTISIMA TRINIDAD** Commissioned 7.81

Type 360; four under construction in 1982. Designed to carry two Lynx HAS.87's. Armed with Exocet SSM and Aspide SAM systems; 5in and 40mm/70 guns and ILAS-3 torpedoes.

**D10   ARA ALMIRANTE BROWN**
                                *Commissioned 2.2.83*
**D11   ARA LA ARGENTINA**   *Commissioned 11.5.83*
**D12   ARA HEROINA**        *Commissioned 7.11.83*
**D13   ARA SARANDI**        *Commissioned 26.4.84*

Originally the 'Fletcher' Class USS Braine (commissioned 11.5.43). Received by Argentina in 1971. Following a collision with ARA 25 de Mayo (5.80) she was repaired and recommissioned in 1981. Armed with 5in and 3in guns and 21in and Mk32 torpedoes. Almirante Domecq Garcia was used as a target for an MM.38 Exocet on 7.10.83.

### D23  ARA ALMIRANTE DOMECQ GARCIA
Received 1971

Three original 'Allen M Sumner' Class (all commissioned in 1944). USS Hank and USS Borie were delivered to Argentina in 1972 as ARA Segui and ARA Hipolito Bouchard; USS Collett delivered in 1974 for spares recovery (with USS Mansfield) but rebuilt and commissioned as ARA Piedra Buena. Hipolito Bouchard and Segui equipped to carry one Alouette III; all armed with Exocet SSM system and 5in guns (Segui also equipped with 3in guns) and ILAS-3 torpedoes. Segui was paid off in 1983.

| | | |
|---|---|---|
| D25 | ARA SEGUI | Commissioned 1972 |
| D26 | ARA HIPOLITO BOUCHARD | |
| | | Commissioned 1972 |
| D29 | ARA PIEDRA BUENA | Commissioned 1977 |

Originally 'Gearing' Class USS Perkins (commissioned 1945). Equipped to carry one Alouette III. Armed with Exocet SSM, 5in guns and ILAS-3 torpedoes.

| | | |
|---|---|---|
| D27 | ARA COMODORO PY | Commissioned 1973 |

## FRIGATES

Type A69; ARA Drummond and ARA Guerrico were laid-down in France in 1976 for South Africa as SAS Good Hope and SAS Transvaal but were embargoed and diverted to France as Lieutenant de Vaisseau de Henaff and Commandant L'Herminier. Armed with Exocet SSM, one 3.9in, 20mm and 40mm guns and Mk32 torpedoes.

| | | |
|---|---|---|
| P1 | ARA DRUMMOND | Received 2.11.78 |
| P2 | ARA GUERRICO | Received 2.11.78 |
| P3 | ARA GRANVILLE | Commissioned 22.6.81 |

Type 140; six under construction in 1982/83. Designed to carry one Lynx HAS.87. Armed with Exocet SSM system and 40mm and 76mm guns and ILAS-3 torpedoes.

| | | |
|---|---|---|
| P4 | ARA ESPORA | *Commissioned 1983* |
| P5 | ARA ROSALES | *Launched 4.3.83* |
| P6 | ARA SPIRO | *Launched 24.6.83* |
| P7 | ARA PARKER | *Launched 30.3.84* |
| P8 | ARA ROBINSON | *Under construction in 1983* |
| P9 | ARA SEAVER | *Under construction in 1983* |

## PATROL VESSELS

Originally 'Cherokee' Class USS Cahuilla and USS Luiseno (both commissioned 1945). Armed with 40mm/60 guns. (A third vessel of this class, A2 ARA Comandante General Zapiola, was lost after running aground on the Falkland Islands in 11.76).

| | | |
|---|---|---|
| A1 | ARA COMANDANTE GENERAL IRIGOYEN | |
| | | Recieved 1961 |
| A3 | ARA FRANCISCO DE GURRUCHAGA | |
| | | Received 1975 |

Originally 'Sotoyomo' Class USS Maricopa, USS Catawbe and USS Salish (commissioned in 1943, 1945 and 1944 respectively). Armed with 20mm and 40mm guns. (ARA Yamana was received as a tug but was re-rated in 1966).

| | | |
|---|---|---|
| A6 | ARA YAMANA | Received 1947 |
| A9 | ARA ALFEREZ SOBRAL | Received 2.72 |
| A10 | ARA COMODORO SOMELLARA | Received 2.72 |

'King' Class; two vessels used for cadet training.

| | | |
|---|---|---|
| P20 | ARA MURATURE | Commissioned 4.45 |
| P21 | ARA KING | Commissioned 11.46 |

## LANDING SHIP (TANK)

Argentine built, modified 'DeSoto County' Class. Armed with 40mm/60 guns. Equipped to carry one light helicopter and a variety of landing craft, including two LCU's, LCM's and LCVP's.

| | | |
|---|---|---|
| Q42 | ARA CABO SAN ANTONIO | |
| | | Commissioned 2.11.78 |

## FAST ATTACK CRAFT

Type TNC45. Armed with a 3in gun, 40mm/70 guns and 81mm rockets.

| | | |
|---|---|---|
| P85 | ARA INTREPIDA | Commissioned 20.7.74 |
| P86 | ARA INDOMITA | Commissioned 12.74 |

## COASTAL PATROL CRAFT

'Dabur' Class; built in Israel. Armed with 20mm guns and other light weapons.

| | | |
|---|---|---|
| P61 | ARA BARADERO | Commissioned 1978 |
| P62 | ARA BARRANGUERAS | Commissioned 1978 |
| P63 | ARA CLORINDA | Commissioned 1978 |
| P64 | ARA CONCEPCION DEL URUGUAY | |
| | | Commissioned 1978 |

## LARGE PATROL CRAFT

| | | |
|---|---|---|
| P55 | ARA SURUBI | Commissioned 1951 |

## FAST ATTACK CRAFT (TORPEDO)

Originally 'Higgins' Class. Armed with 40mm/60 guns and other light weapons. Obsolescent class, only two of nine were reported to have survived until 1982.

| | | |
|---|---|---|
| P82 | ARA ALAKUSH | Commissioned 1946 |
| P84 | ARA TOWWARA | Commissioned 1946 |

## COASTAL MINESWEEPERS AND MINEHUNTERS

Purchased in 1967, all were originally 'Ton' Class, respectively the former HMS Hickleton, HMS Tarlton, HMS Santon, HMS Bevington, HMS Rennington and HMS Ilmington. Each armed with 40mm/60 gun. ARA Chaco and ARA Formosa were Minehunters, converted in 1968 before delivery.

| | |
|---|---|
| M1 | ARA NEUQUEN |
| M2 | ARA RIO NEGRO |
| M3 | ARA CHUBUT |
| M4 | ARA TIERRA DEL FUEGO |
| M5 | ARA CHACO |
| M6 | ARA FORMOSA |

## SURVEY VESSELS

Two vessels of 'Puerto Deseado' Class.

| | | |
|---|---|---|
| Q8 | ARA PUERTO DESEADO | Commissioned 1979 |
| Q11 | ARA COMODORO RIVADAVIA | Commissioned 12.74 |

## SURVEY LAUNCHES

| | | |
|---|---|---|
| Q15 | ARA CORMORAN | Commissioned 2.64 |
| Q16 | ARA PETREL | Commissioned 1965 |

## TRANSPORTS, TANKERS, TRAINING AND POLAR VESSELS

'Costa Sur' Class transports.

| | | |
|---|---|---|
| B3 | ARA CANAL BEAGLE | Commissioned 29.4.78 |
| B4 | ARA BAHIA SAN BLAS | Commissioned 27.11.78 |
| B5 | ARA CABO DE HORNOS | Commissioned 28.6.79 |

Fleet transports.

| | | |
|---|---|---|
| B6 | ARA BAHIA BUEN SUCESO | Commissioned 6.50 |
| B8 | ARA ISLA DE LOS ESTADOS | Commissioned 1980 |

Fleet support tanker.

| | | |
|---|---|---|
| B12 | ARA PUNTA ALTA | Commissioned 1938 |

Fleet support vessel, originally 'Klickitat' Class.

| | | |
|---|---|---|
| B16 | ARA PUNTA DELGADO | Commissioned 1945 |

Fleet support tanker.

| | | |
|---|---|---|
| B18 | ARA PUNTA MEDANOS | Commissioned 10.10.50 |

Sail training vessel.

| | | |
|---|---|---|
| Q2 | ARA LIBERTAD | Commissioned 1962 |

Polar vessels.

| | | |
|---|---|---|
| Q5 | ARA ALMIRANTE IRIZAR | Commissioned 15.12.78 |
| Q6 | ARA BAHIA PARAISO | Commissioned 1978 |

Training vessel, originally MV Cuidad de Formosa.

| | | |
|---|---|---|
| Q31 | ARA PILOTE ALSINA | Commissioned 17.3.81 |

# PREFECTURA NAVAL ARGENTINA

## PATROL CRAFT

In 1982 the PNA possessed in excess of 40 patrol craft of various kinds. Two of these, both West German constructed Z-28 Type coastal vessels, were deployed to the Falkland Islands. Both were new vessels armed with 20mm guns.

| | | |
|---|---|---|
| GC82 | ISLAS MALVINAS | Commissioned 1981 |
| GC83 | RIO IGUAZU | Commissioned 1981 |

# INDIVIDUAL SHIP DETAILS

## ALFEREZ SOBRAL

Deployed in late 4.82 to a port on the Argentine mainland adjacent to the Falkland Islands for rescue duties. During the night of 1/2.5.82 dispatched to search for the crew of a Grupo 2 Canberra that had been brought down north of the Falklands. During an unsuccessful search she is reported to have fired on an 826 Sqdn Sea King soon after 0400Z on 3.5.82 and was herself then attacked by two 815 Sqdn Lynx from 'Coventry' (XZ242) and 'Glasgow' (XZ247). Each helicopter fired two Sea Skua missiles from a range of several miles and the vessel was severely damaged. Although eight of her crew were killed the damaged ship remained afloat and was escorted into Puerto Deseado by 'Comodoro Py' a few days later. She is believed to have been repaired.

## ALMIRANTE IRIZAR

Sailed for the Falkland Islands with Task Force 40 c28.3.82 as part of the landing group. As well as men and supplies she carried a CAB601 Puma (which arrived with storm damage) and at least three of the 2 Escuadrilla de Helicopteros Sea Kings, the latter to be used during the amphibious assault of 2.4.82. Anchored south of the San Felipe lighthouse near Port Stanley to play a key role in the landings. The Puma was off-loaded on 3.4.82 with other equipment and was returned to Argentina c5.4.82. There are no further reports of use until early 6.82, by which time she had been refitted as a hospital ship. Arrived off Port Stanley 10.6.82 and was used by the locally based CAB601 ambulance-designated UH-1H's which ferried wounded aboard. On 13.6.82 'Hydra' Flight's Wasp XT432 ferried on four IRCC personnel to inspect her. In the immediate post-war period again used by at least one 2 Escuadrilla de Helicopteros Sea King and other helicopters to ferry wounded from Port Stanley. Finally returned to Argentina 16.6.82.

## BAHIA BUEN SUCESO

On 19.3.82 arrived at Leith, South Georgia with 41 Argentine civilians who were to dismantle the derelict local whaling station. Departed 22.3.82, reportedly leaving behind some men and equipment, and returned to Argentina a few days later. Between 8.4.82 and 13.4.82 used to carry equipment to the Falkland Islands and, after the British announcement of the MEZ, for blockade-running. It was during such a voyage that she was caught at anchor in Fox Bay East, West Falkland on 16.5.82 by two 800 Sqdn Sea Harriers (XZ500 and ZA191) and attacked and damaged. On an unknown date (post-war) she broke loose from her moorings at Fox Bay

East during a gale and was blown aground. Towed to San Carlos Water by the tug 'Irishman' in late 6.82. Sunk by cannon and rocket fire from 809 Sqdn Sea Harriers on 21.10.82 after having been towed from San Carlos Water to a deep water position well to the east of Port Stanley.

## BAHIA PARAISO

On 23.3.82 diverted from a routine project in the Orcadas Islands and ordered to South Georgia to assist the Argentine civilians at Leith. She was carrying her CANA Alouette III, detached from 1 Escuadrilla de Helicopteros, and, fortuitously, a ski-equipped CAB601 Puma. The Puma had been used in a separate, non naval, project in the Orcadas Islands and arrived off Leith during the afternoon of 25.3.82 to find 'Endurance' in local waters actively reconnoitring the situation. On 26.3.82 'Bahia Paraiso' put ashore her combat marine force at Leith and on 27.3.82 left to take up station outside the territorial waters. Ordered to keep 'Endurance' and her Royal Marines force under constant surveillance, but, at 2200Z on 31.3.82, 'Endurance' escaped unnoticed (although she later returned to South Georgia on 3.4.82). 'Bahia Paraiso' eventually met 'Guerrico' on the morning of 3.4.82 (it is thought that the two vessels then constituted Task Force 60) and at midday the short battle for Grytviken commenced. 'Bahia Paraiso' is thought to have returned to the Argentine mainland immediately afterwards.

Between 8.4.82 and 13.4.82 used to ferry men and equipment from Mar del Plata to the Falklands and her deck was used to assist the ferry flights of several CAB601 helicopters from the mainland to Port Stanley. On 13.4.82 returned to Puerto Belgrano for conversion to the hospital ship role. Reconfigured by the end of the month, she was ordered to sea on 2.5.82 to search for survivors from 'General Belgrano'. Arrived in the area during the night of 3/4.5.82 and eventually took on board 74 survivors and 18 bodies from the sea. Returned to Ushuaia but not ordered to sea again until late 5.82. On 31.5.82, en route from Ushuaia to Port Stanley, she was boarded by personnel from 'Minerva' (in their 815 Sqdn Lynx XZ698) and her ambulance-configured CAB601 Puma and 1 Escuadrilla de Helicopteros Alouette III were both inspected. 'Bahia Paraiso' subsequently made four visits to Port Stanley and took sick and wounded from Fox Bay, Port Howard and Pebble Island. Again investigated on 4.6.82 by IRCC personnel flown on from 'Uganda' by 'Herald' Flight's Wasp XT794. At 2000Z on 10.6.82 she berthed at Port Stanley to take off injured but while there, at 1140Z on 11.6.82, was fortunately missed by an errant AS.12 missile, one of a pair launched from the 845 Sqdn 'A' Flight Wessex XT484 at the Town Hall, Port Stanley. She sailed, unscathed, at 1830Z that afternoon and on the following day her Alouette III carried two more IRCC delegates to 'Hydra'.

During the War 'Bahia Paraiso' carried 315

wounded and injured to the mainland and on her first post-war voyage she carried home 1,734 men. She subsequently made one more voyage to carry home 600 men to Puerto Belgrano before being stood down on 24.6.82. Finally returned to her homeport of Darsena Norte, Buenos Aires on 27.6.82.

## CABO SAN ANTONIO

Sailed with Task Force 40 c28.3.82 carrying 19 LVTP's to the Falkland Islands. As a component of the landing element, Task Group 40.1, she put ashore most of the 800-strong invading Marine force and LVTP's on York Beach, Port Stanley after 0915Z on 2.4.82. Returned to port c5.4.82. Between 8.4.82 and 13.4.82 used to carry equipment from the mainland to the Falklands.

## COMODORO PY

Sailed with Task Force 20 c29.3.82 as part of the carrier escort group and, after the completion of "Rosario", returned to port c5.4.82. Probably part of Task Force 79 in mid-4.82 and is believed to have deployed with the northern element (Task Groups 79.1 and 79.2) c27.4.82. On 3.5.82 diverted to assist 'Alferez Sobral' after the latter had been attacked by British helicopters, and then escorted the damaged ship to Puerto Deseado, arriving there c5.5.82. On 19.6.82 'Comodoro Py' escorted 'Canberra' into Puerto Madryn.

## COMODORO SOMELLARA

Deployed late 4.82 to a port on the Argentine mainland adjacent to the Falkland Islands for rescue duties. Last reported at sea at 0850Z on 4.5.82, east of Rio Grande, searching for survivors from 'General Belgrano' but is known to have survived the War undamaged.

## DRUMMOND

Sailed from Argentina 26.3.82 ostensibly for South Georgia but in reality as part of Task Force 40. Put ashore amphibious forces near Port Stanley on 2.4.82 during Operacion "Rosario" and subsequently returned to port c5.4.82. Probably at sea with Task Force 79 in mid-4.82. Diverted to become part of Task Group 79.4 on 1.5.82 but returned to port c4.5.82.

## FRANCISCO DE GURRUCHAGA

Configured as an ocean-going tug by 1982 and used as such in the search for survivors from 'General Belgrano'. 'Gurruchaga' recovered the last of the survivors, including the captain, 4.5.82 and returned them to Ushuaia on 5.5.82.

## GENERAL BELGRANO

Not deployed during Operacion "Rosario". Put to sea from Ushuaia 26.4.82 with Task Force 79 and, as part of the component Task Group 79.3, patrolled the area between the Isla de los Estados and the Burdwood Bank

Having been attacked and damaged by Royal Navy helicopters on 25.4.82, 'Santa Fe' struggled back to Grytviken where she was abandoned. With about nine tons of unstable explosives still aboard (including torpedoes), she remained in a semi-sunken state alongside the jetty until moved **(Upper Right)** on 15.7.82 with the assistance of 'Salvageman' to a location near the Hestesletten in the Cumberland Bays, clear of all personnel and buildings. Early in 1985 she was scuttled in the Cumberland Bays.

*(Ministry of Defence)*

The scene a few seconds after two 800 Squadron Sea Harrier FRS.1's (XZ500 '–/(1)30' and ZA191 '–/(7)18') strafed the transport 'Bahia Buen Suceso' at Fox Bay East on 16.5.82. Beyond the ship, and already burning furiously, are fuel storage tanks hit in the same attack. The vessel took no further role in the conflict. Immediately after this photograph was taken, the photographer was confronted by an irate Argentine soldier **(Inset)**. Incredibly, the film was not confiscated!

*(Graeme Hyde)*

'Rio Iguazu' was attacked by two 800 Squadron Sea Harriers in Choiseul Sound on 22.5.82. In a fierce exchange of cannon fire (during which 'Rio Iguazu' believed that she had brought down a Sea Harrier) one of her crew was killed and several injured. The virtually new patrol boat was beached in Button Bay but suffered further indignity on 13.6.82 when she was subjected to a Sea Skua attack by 'Penelope' Flight's 'Lynx'. Although the helicopter's crew believed that the vessel posed a genuine threat (despite her situation), their choice of target was unfortunate for 'Rio Iguazu' had already been earmarked by the Royal Navy for local operational use! *(Ministry of Defence)*

Photographed by the 801 Squadron Sea Harrier FRS.1 of Lt Cdr ''Sharkey'' Ward, the stern trawler 'Narwal' is seen here after being attacked and disabled by 800 Squadron Sea Harriers on 9.5.82. She sank under tow the following day. *(Royal Navy)*

from 29.4.82. At 1858Z on 2.5.82, when at 55°30′S 61°40′W, she was struck by two Mk8 (21in) torpedoes fired from 'Conqueror' and sank 15 minutes later with the loss of 321 lives. Her Alouette III 0649/3-H-105 was lost with the ship.

## GRANVILLE

Sailed from Argentina 26.3.82, ostensibly for South Georgia, but in fact as a component of Task Force 40. Used in support of the landings of Task Group 40.1, she returned to port after "Rosario" c5.4.82. Probably at sea with Task Force 79 in mid-4.82 but on 1.5.82 diverted to become part of Task Group 79.4. Returned to port c4.5.82.

## GUERRICO

Sailed for South Georgia on 1.4.82 when Task Force 60 was created and arrived at Leith in the early hours of 3.4.82. After taking aboard a small party of marines she joined 'Bahia Paraiso' (the other component of Task Force 60) later in the morning off Grytviken. During the ensuing battle she was struck by an anti-tank rocket and considerable small-arms fire from the British force, Naval Party 8901. It is believed that one rating was killed and two others injured. The damage was substantial enough to require three days of repair work in a naval dock. Probably at sea again with Task Force 79 by mid/late 4.82 and diverted to become part of Task Group 79.4 on 1.5.82. Returned to port c4.5.82.

## HERCULES

Having recently returned from Sea Dart missile firing trials off Aberporth, Wales, 'Hercules' sailed with Task Force 40 c28.3.82 in support of the landings on the Falkland Islands. Returned to port c5.4.82 and was used during mid/late 4.82 for exercises with both CANA and FAA aircraft in which she simulated British Type 42's. Allocated to escort duties with '25 de Mayo', she is thought to have sailed with Task Force 79 c15-17.4.82. She was on the point of launching a Sea Dart at an 801 Sqdn Sea Harrier on the edge of the TEZ while on picket ship duties at c0400Z on 2.5.82. The missile was not fired, however, and 'Hercules' returned to port c4.5.82. Later missions were restricted to coastal waters.

## HIPOLITO BOUCHARD

Sailed with Task Force 20 c29.3.82 as part of the carrier escort group, returning to port c5.4.82 after the completion of "Rosario". Probably part of Task Force 79 in mid-4.82 and deployed 26.4.82 with Task Group 79.3 in support of 'General Belgrano'. At 1858Z on 2.5.82 'Hipolito Bouchard' was hit by an over-running torpedo from the salvo that struck and sank 'General Belgrano' but there was no detonation. However, some damage resulted and she is reported to have spent several days under repair in a "sheltered bay" in Tierra del Fuego.

## ISLA DE LOS ESTADOS

Sailed with Task Force 40 for the Falkland Islands c28.3.82 carrying support equipment for the invasion. Returned to port c5.4.82 and spent the rest of the month carrying more sup-

plies to the Islands. In the early hours of 11.5.82 she was seen in Falkland Sound, apparently en route Port Howard, by 'Alacrity'. Illuminated by a starshell and then fired upon by the frigate's 4.5in gun, 'Isla de los Estados' was immediately hit and her cargo, much of which was fuel, exploded and she sank rapidly. Only two crew survived and they, with some of the cargo, were found 13.5.82 although Argentine search and rescue operations continued until 16.5.82.

## ISLAS MALVINAS

The aptly named 'Islas Malvinas' was deployed to the Apostadero Naval Malvinas, Port Stanley in early 4.82 and used for local transportation, pilot duties and coastal patrols. Damaged on 1.5.82 by a GPMG attack from 'Alacrity' Flight's Lynx XZ736 while sheltering near Kidney Island. Recovered to Port Stanley where she was eventually surrendered on 14.6.82. Subsequently used by a crew from 'Cardiff' and renamed "HMS Tiger Bay".

## PIEDRA BUENA

Sailed with Task Force 20 c29.3.82 as part of the carrier escort group. After the completion of "Rosario" returned to port c5.4.82. Probably part of Task Force 79 in mid-4.82 and deployed c26.4.82 with Task Group 79.3 in support of 'General Belgrano'. Presumed to have been the destroyer that pursued and unsuccessfully depth-charged 'Conqueror' after the latter's attack on 'General Belgrano' on 2.5.82. She later took part in the search for the cruiser's survivors.

## PUNTA MEDANOS

Sailed with Task Force 20 c28.3.82 in support of the carrier escort group and was presumably deployed again in mid-4.82 with Task Force 79.

## RIO IGUAZU

Deployed to the Apostadero Naval Malvinas, Port Stanley early in 4.82 and used locally for transportation, pilot duties and coastal patrols. Attacked and damaged by two 800 Sqdn Sea Harriers (XZ460 and XZ499) on 22.5.82 when in Choiseul Sound, some nine miles to the south-east of Darwin. The survivors were taken off by a Grupo 7 Bell 212 and the vessel was beached in Button Bay with the intention of salvaging her cargo. She had been carrying Pucara spares from Port Stanley to Goose Green and many items, as well as two 105mm guns, were subsequently recovered by Argentine divers. After the loss of Goose Green 'Rio Iguazu' fell into British hands but that did not prevent her being attacked again on 13.6.82 (while still in her beached position in Button Bay). On that occasion a Sea Skua attack was launched from 'Penelope' Flight's Lynx XZ691 and some minor damage was inflicted on the bridge. Post-war, some of the ship's components were used to keep 'Islas Malvinas' serviceable. In late 1982 she was pulled off by 'Salvageman' and towed to Goose Green where, with the assistance of the local vessel 'Penelope' and four tractors, she was dragged ashore. Still present in early 7.85 less her engines which were also removed for installation in 'Islas Malvinas'.

## SALTA

Reported to have been given a "free-fire" mission by the Armada, she deployed to an area north of the Falkland Islands in mid/late 4.82. Returned to port "early" (ie before 1.5.82) with mechanical problems, possibly engine and/or noise-related. Thought not to have been used again and noted at Mar del Plata in 12.82. (It should be noted that some sources have suggested that this submarine was in dockyard hands throughout the Falklands campaign.)

## SAN LUIS

Deployed to a "free-fire zone" to the north of the Falkland Islands in mid-4.82. Believed to have undertaken at least four torpedo attacks on elements of the British Task Force on 1.5, 4.5, 5.5 and 10.5.82, all of which were unsuccessful (USN sources have suggested that malfunctioning torpedo fire control panels were to blame for these failures). On each occasion British warships and helicopters responded to the attacks and on 1.5.82 'Brilliant', 'Yarmouth' and three 826 Sqdn Sea Kings pursued her for several hours in an area to the north-east of the Falklands. After a reported 36 days at sea returned safely to Mar del Plata where she was noted in 12.82.

## SANTA FE

Sailed from Argentina (probably Mar del Plata) c28.3.82 as a component of Task Force 40 and put ashore Special Forces at Port Stanley at 0500Z 2.4.82. Later used on a supply run to Grytviken, South Georgia where she arrived 23.4.82, docking in the evening of 24.4.82. At dawn on 25.4.82 she was caught on the surface while departing by several Royal Navy helicopters from 'Antrim', 'Brilliant', 'Endurance' and 'Plymouth'. 'Santa Fe' was attacked with depth-charges, ASM's, torpedoes and GPMG fire and, damaged and unable to dive, ran aground near the jetty at Grytviken. Post-war the hulk was moved twice in St Edward Cove, Grytviken before finally being towed out into Cumberland Bays and scuttled early in 1985.

## SANTIAGO DEL ESTERO

Although paid off in 9.81 she was still at Mar del Plata when the British Task Force sailed for the Falkland Islands. It has been reported that because she was unable to submerge and that her state of incapacitation would therefore have been obvious to satellite reconnaissance, she was taken on the surface to Bahia Blanca for concealment. 'Santiago del Estero' was finally disposed of in 1983.

## SANTISIMA TRINIDAD

Sailed as the Flagship of Task Force 40 c28.3.82 and, at 0015Z on 2.4.82, put ashore the first of the Argentine forces from a position off Port Harriet, East Falkland. Returned to port c5.4.82 and was used during mid/late 4.82 in exercises with CANA and FAA aircraft. Thought to have been tasked with escort duties with '25 de Mayo' when Task Force 79 was created 15-17.4.82. Her Lynx, 0735/3-H-142, was lost in an accident involving the ship 2.5.82. Thought to have returned to port c4.5.82 and noted at Puerto

Madryn in late 6.82.

## SEGUI

Sailed with Task Force 20 c29.3.82 as part of the carrier escort group and returned to port c5.4.82 after the completion of "Rosario". Probably a component of Task Force 79 in 4.82. On 22.5.82 deployed off the southern mainland coast as a radar picket but saw no action.

## 25 DE MAYO

Sailed from Puerto Belgrano c29.3.82 as the Flagship of Task Force 20 with aircraft of 3 Escuadrilla de Ataque, Escuadrilla Antisubmarina and 1 Escuadrilla de Helicopteros embarked. She provided cover and support for Task Force 40's landings on the Falkland Islands 2.4.82 before returning to port c4.4.82. Left port on exercises in mid-4.82 with her full air group (2 Escuadrilla de Helicopteros was restored) and worked-up in conjunction with mainland-based FAA aircraft. After a brief return to port she sailed again with a full air group c27.4.82 to maintain station with Task Force 79 on the edge of the British TEZ, to the north-west of the Falkland Islands. Went to action stations during the night of 1/2.5.82 and was prepared to launch her A-4Q Skyhawks against the British carrier group at dawn on 2.5.82. In the event '25 de Mayo' lost contact with the British group and the attack was not attempted. Returned to coastal waters 4.5.82 and soon afterwards her air group disembarked and the carrier returned to Puerto Belgrano.

## COMMERCIAL SHIPS DEPLOYED

### FORMOSA (1978) 12,762 GRT

A Spanish-built general purposes freighter owned by Empresa Lineas Maritimas Argentinas SA (ELMA). Used to carry military supplies to Port Stanley until 13.4.82 and then used as a blockade-runner.

### NARWAL (1962) 1,398 GRT

A stern trawler owned by Compania

Sudamerica de Pesca y Exportacion and requisitioned by the Armada at Mar del Plata 22.4.82 for intelligence gathering on the edge of the British TEZ. Warned c29.4.82 to keep clear of the Task Force, she was eventually attacked by four 800 Sqdn Sea Harriers (including XZ460 and ZA191) after unexpectedly being found some 60 miles south-east of Port Stanley on 9.5.82. She was hit by a 1,000lb bomb and cannon fire and immobilised. Later boarded by British Special Forces brought in by 846 Sqdn Sea Kings, her survivors were taken off and the vessel was made ready to tow. An attempt was made to take her as a prize but the following day she sank under tow.

*'Narwal' was marked with a broad yellow vertical stripe through the funnel and hull, presumably to identify her to Argentine forces as friendly.*

### RIO CARCARANA (1962) 8,482 GRT

A cargo vessel owned by Empresa Lineas Maritimas Argentinas SA (ELMA). Used to carry military supplies to Port Stanley until 13.4.82 and then put to use as a blockade-runner. Attacked by 800 Sqdn Sea Harriers (XZ459 and XZ494) in Port King on 16.5.82 and, although sustaining no casualties, was beached and abandoned with fires burning out of control. Her position in Falkland Sound made her a recognition feature for Argentine pilots travelling north towards San Carlos Water after 21.5.82 and on at least one occasion was bombed in error by the FAA. During the early hours of 22.5.82 she was shelled by a British warship and was again left burning. On 23.5.82 she was attacked once more, on that occasion by 'Antelope' Flight's Lynx XZ723 which hit her with two Sea Skua missiles, and she sank.

### RIO DE LA PLATA (1971) 10,409 GRT

A cargo vessel owned by Empresa Lineas Maritimas Argentinas SA (ELMA). Used to observe British shipping off Ascension Island until warned off c24.4.82.

### YEHUIN (1967) 494 GRT

Formerly the 'Millentor', this merchant oil rig

tender was owned by Geomatter SA of Buenos Aires. Requisitioned by the Armada soon after 23.4.82, she arrived at Port Stanley 1.5.82 for inter-island supply duties and other special tasks including minelaying. Eventually surrendered to the Royal Navy at Port Stanley on 15.6.82 and was initially used by a crew from 'Fearless'. Later renamed 'Falkland Sound'.

## IMPRESSED FALKLAND ISLANDS VESSELS

### FORREST (1967) 144 GRT

A motor cargo ship owned by the Falklands Islands Government. After brief use in the defence of Port Stanley 1/2.4.82 she was commandeered by Argentine forces 2.4.82 and used for local communications work, much as she had been used in peace-time. A routine visitor to Fox Bay, Port Howard and other such settlements, she was sheltering with the 'Islas Malvinas' near Kidney Island 1.5.82 when attacked by 'Alacrity' Flight's Lynx XZ736. Although 'Islas Malvinas' was hit by gunfire, 'Forrest' remained undamaged and was able to inflict some small-arms hits on the helicopter which then broke off from the engagement. Extensively used in Falkland Sound from 11.5.82 to 16.5.82 in the search for survivors from 'Isla de los Estados'. On 24.5.82 she towed the damaged 'Monsunen' to Darwin. Eventually surrendered to the British on 15.6.82 and used by them.

### MONSUNEN (1957) 230 GRT

A merchant cargo vessel owned by the Falklands Islands Company. Commandeered in early 4.82 by Argentine forces and used for local supply and communications tasks. In the early hours of 23.5.82, while en route from Darwin to Port Stanley, 'Brilliant' Flight's Lynx (XZ721) intercepted her in Choiseul Sound and the helicopter, operating with her ship and with 'Yarmouth', forced 'Monsunen' aground in Lively Sound. The following day, 24.5.82, she was towed into Darwin by 'Forrest' and was eventually adopted by British forces on 4.6.82, subsequently being used by them in support of 5 Brigade.

*Seen here in the Red Cross Box in 6.82, 'Bahia Paraiso' had an active and varied war. Tasked routinely as polar vessel and later as a troop and equipment transport, she assumed her hospital ship role on 2.5.82 when involved in the first search for survivors from 'General Belgrano'. Her ambulance-configured Alouette III can be seen on the flight-deck.*
*(Ministry of Defence)*

# Part 2
# UNITED KINGDOM

# UNITED KINGDOM'S WAR

## TASK FORCE

It was on 14 September 1981 that the Chiefs of Staff formally approved a paper examining Argentina's military options in the South Atlantic, it having been assumed that Argentina might one day use such means to resolve long-standing sovereignty claims to British territories in the region. The paper also identified the United Kingdom's possible responses to the perceived range of Argentine options. It recognised that, for several reasons, a British military response would have to be a naval one, with passage time to the area in the order of 20 days for surface ships. Assembly and storing time would increase this and significant penalties to other defence commitments would probably be incurred.

The most pessimistic scenario, the deterrence of a full-scale military invasion of the Falkland Islands, was seen to require a balanced force comprising an 'Invincible' Class carrier with four destroyers or frigates and possibly a nuclear-powered submarine. Supply ships and embarked troops, the latter to reinforce the garrison at Port Stanley, would also be required. Prophetically, the paper concluded that, if faced on arrival by occupying Argentine forces, such a British Task Group might not be strong enough to retake the Islands and that their recovery would demand further naval and land forces with substantial air support. The logistics of such an operation were recognised as being formidable.

Argentine activity on South Georgia in March 1982 was not perceived by the British Government as being preparatory to a full-scale invasion of the Falkland Islands and, although the Government was deeply concerned at the deteriorating political crisis, it was not until 29 March that warships were detached from routine activities in European waters to join the ice patrol vessel 'Endurance' in the South Atlantic. The fleet replenishment ship RFA 'Fort Austin' and submarine 'Spartan' sailed from Gibraltar on 29 March and 1 April respectively, while on 30 March a second submarine, 'Splendid', was ordered to deploy from Faslane. She did so on 1 April. It was on 29 March that the first steps were taken to prepare a larger group of ships for deployment to the South Atlantic, should the need arise.

The senior military officer responsible to the Govern-

ment was the Chief of Defence Staff, Admiral of the Fleet Sir Terence Lewin GCB MVO DSC, but it was his subordinate, Admiral Sir John Fieldhouse GCB, in whom the overall command of the subsequent military operation was vested in his capacity of Commander-in-Chief Fleet. It was Admiral Fieldhouse who, prior to his return to Northwood from Gibraltar on 29 March, ordered Flag Officer First Flotilla, Rear Admiral J.F.Woodward, to prepare a "suitable group" of ships at Gibraltar. On 31 March, by which time it was known that much of the Argentine fleet was at sea and reportedly exercising some 800-900 miles north of the Falkland Islands, Admiral Fieldhouse was instructed to make covert preparations for a Task Force for operations in the South Atlantic.

Argentine forces landed on East Falkland early on 2 April and by about 1300Z all local resistance had ceased. South Georgia fell the following day. These traumatic events were to herald a period of intense diplomatic and military activity, culminating in a short period of bitter fighting, before the Falkland Islands, South Georgia and Southern Thule were repossessed by the United Kingdom.

It is the purpose of this brief introduction to the activities of British airpower during that period to provide the reader with an appreciation of the Task Force's command structure and the more significant of the many events and incidents of those weeks. It outlines the major strategies of the operation (although it is assumed that the reader will already have acquired much general knowledge of such matters) and should provide a context within which the detailed individual unit histories of the subsequent pages can be read. Although some comment is made, in passing, on the roles and effectiveness of British airpower during the conflict, this introduction should not be seen as an attempted summary of British performance. The reader may make that judgement himself.

The operation to recover the Falkland Islands was named "Corporate" and ultimately, in military terms, was a complete success. It required, and received, the fullest co-operation of all elements of the British armed forces, the Merchant Navy, British industry and countless civilian organisations and individuals. While British diplomats and politicians unsuccessfully sought a satisfactory peaceful conclusion to the crisis, the Defence Chiefs, instructed to anticipate the failure of such efforts, prepared to fight. The events of 2 April caused widespread indignation and anger in the United Kingdom and the dispatch of a military Task Force would later be widely viewed as a regrettable but necessary measure. As Admiral Woodward sailed from Gibraltar for the South Atlantic on 2 April with ten warships from the recently concluded Exercise "Springtrain", a second and greater force, including the carriers 'Hermes' and 'Invincible', was assembled in the United Kingdom.

Fieldhouse assumed overall command of Operation "Corporate" as Commander Task Force 317 (all surface ships, land and air forces) and Commander Task Force 324 (submarine forces). His command was tri-service and was exercised from Northwood, Air Marshal Sir John Curtiss KCB (AOC 18 Group) becoming his Air Commander and, initially, Major General J.J.Moore CB OBE MC* (Major General Royal Marines Commando Forces) his Land Forces Deputy. General Moore later left for the South Atlantic on 20 May (eventually going ashore at San Carlos settlement on 29 May) to become Commander Land Forces, Falkland Islands and was replaced at Northwood by Lieutenant General Sir Richard Trant KCB on 21 May. Submarine forces were controlled by Vice Admiral P.G.M.Herbert OBE, while Vice Admiral D.J.Halifax became Fieldhouse's Chief of Staff responsible for planning and co-ordination functions. Admiral Woodward, having sailed from Gibraltar in 'Antrim', transferred his flag to 'Glamorgan' on 4 April and then on 15 April, as Commander of the Task Groups in the South Atlantic, to 'Hermes'.

The scale and complexity of the mobilisation of resources will become apparent from subsequent pages in which the preparations of the air elements of the Task Force are detailed *(this book, perforce, does not dwell on the mobilisation of naval and land forces, but the magnitude of those tasks will not be underestimated by the reader)*. While much of early April was spent in countless planning sessions and the garnering of stores of all kinds, the United Kingdom's military muscle was strengthened in other ways. The British could not hope to recover the Falkland Islands from a distance of 8,000 miles without the use of staging posts and other, more subtle, support. Diplomatic activity did not only seek to resolve the crisis by peaceful means but actively sought allies of all kinds who were prepared to provide tangible assistance to Operation "Corporate". Such assistance took many forms; perhaps most obvious were the use of staging posts, the urgent release of particular weapons and equipment from stockpiles and production lines, the embargoes on equipment sales to Argentina and much more besides. Other, less obvious, assistance was to prove of equal benefit. Such assistance was one of many factors, grossly misjudged by Argentina, which contributed to her ultimate defeat.

Most important to the United Kingdom was the use of Ascension Island, an isolated and vital forward base from which the Task Force was eventually dispatched on the final stage of its mission and from where direct air attacks were launched at Argentine forces. For a few weeks Wideawake became the world's busiest airfield.

Although, at the time, the United Kingdom had no means to fully enforce it, a Maritime Exclusion Zone effective from 0400Z on 12 April was announced on 7 April. This Zone, 200 miles in radius from the centre of the Falkland Islands, was created in order to prevent further reinforcement by sea of the occupying Argentine garrison. Initially enforced by submarines, the strategy was substantially successful and much Argentine equipment was considerably delayed on the mainland awaiting airfreight opportunities.

With both carriers and most of the first waves of warships en route to Ascension Island, the Chief of the Defence Staff instructed Fieldhouse on 7 April to plan the repossession of South Georgia. Operation "Paraquat", as it was eventually identified, was undertaken by elements of all the services between 20 and 26 April and its successful conclusion, albeit after some difficult moments, was a most important step on the road to the recovery of the Falkland Islands. The recapture of South Georgia provided the Royal Navy with an important anchorage in the Falklands region. It also demonstrated to Argentina the United Kingdom's resolve to fight, when necessary, at a time when considerable political pressure was being exerted on Buenos Aires to reach a peaceful settlement (although, perversely, the governing Junta ignored the ominous military implications of its loss) and, most importantly to an anxious Government, it generally reassured public opinion in the United Kingdom that "Corporate" was a viable operation. More soberly, the experiences of Task Group 317.9, commanded by Captain B.G.Young DSO in 'Antrim', provided some indication of the problems still to be faced by Woodward's Task Group 317.8.

By late April much of the preparation for the first stage of the recovery of the Falkland Islands had been completed. The bulk of the naval elements of the Task Force were at sea with the advanced units approaching the Islands. Woodward's Carrier Group had been intercepted as early as 21 April by long-range Argentine reconnaissance aircraft and on 23 April steps were taken to warn Argentina that any of her ships or aircraft, deemed by the United Kingdom to amount to a threat to interfere with her forces, would be liable to attack. The Maritime Exclusion Zone was extended to become a Total Exclusion Zone with effect from 30 April, the aim being to prevent resupply by air as well as by sea. By the end of the month RAF bomber, tanker and reconnaissance aircraft were in place on Ascension Island and long-range reconnaissance missions were well underway. Anticipating the need both for reinforcements to deal with the large Argentine presence on the Falkland Islands and to make good battle losses, a substantial resupply line had been established by the Royal Navy and, on 30 April, more than 70 vessels of all kinds were at sea.

# COMBAT

With no diplomatic solution appearing to be remotely possible and Argentina absolutely convinced that a full-scale British invasion of the Falkland Islands was imminent, the first blows were struck by the Task Force on the morning of 1 May. The air attacks on Stanley Airport and Goose Green airfield were designed to deny their use to combat aircraft and to destroy any aircraft found. Together with the first naval bombardment, which occurred that afternoon, they were also intended to create diversions of Argentine attention that would conceal the insertion of small groups of Special Forces on East and West Falkland. Without the subsequent intelligence provided by those skilled men, the amphibious landings, planned for later in the month, would have been extremely hazardous. Both Argentina and the United Kingdom were to learn much from the events of 1 May; a sudden and virtually unopposed attack on three close-in warships by Argentine fighter-bombers served due warning of the dangers of such naval operations without adequate early warning and consequent local air cover.

Throughout the night of 1/2 May a large Argentine carrier group to the north of the Falkland Islands sought to locate the British carrier force that it knew to be nearby. Once located by its searching aircraft, '25 de Mayo' was prepared to launch direct air attacks against 'Hermes' or 'Invincible'. These attacks were ultimately frustrated by factors beyond British control and they were never mounted, but the threat posed by the two Argentine capital ships, '25 de Mayo' and the elderly cruiser 'General Belgrano' (the latter at sea south-west of the Falkland Islands), was judged to be unacceptable and the cruiser was consequently sunk by torpedoes during the afternoon of 2 May. The attack, made by the submarine 'Conqueror', was consistent with the warning served on Argentina on 23 April. 'Conqueror' had earlier been instructed to take all necessary measures to prevent reinforcing Argentine warships from interfering with Operation "Paraquat", and for several days the British submarines had been prepared to make torpedo attacks on any menacing vessels. The loss of 'General Belgrano' dealt Argentine naval strategy a severe blow, serving to confirm the fears of those senior officers who recognised that the Armada possessed no realistic defence against British nuclear-powered submarines and that the United Kingdom would not hesitate to use them when the time came. Within a few days all large Argentine warships were withdrawn to coastal waters and on 7 May the United Kingdom informed Argentina that any of her warships or military aircraft found more than 12 miles from the mainland coast would be treated as hostile and the appropriate action taken. This warning was observed and no further forays were undertaken by large Argentine surface vessels.

Further efforts were made during early and mid-May to resolve matters before it became necessary for the British to undertake large-scale landings on the Islands. It was anticipated that there could be considerable bloodshed attendant to such an assault. Unfortunately, all such efforts failed and the planned amphibious assault on East Falkland became a necessity. The first three weeks of May were punctuated by a series of brief but violent encounters and both sides were made aware of the other's capabilities and, indeed, of their own weaknesses. If the Task Force possessed an "Achilles' Heel", then it was its lack of airborne early warning and the consequent problem of providing the warships with adequate air defence. Sophisticated and usually reliable that the British ship-launched anti-aircraft missiles were, the Royal Navy's frigates and destroyers were always vulnerable to sudden low-level air attacks. Most shocking of several incidents early in the month was the loss of 'Sheffield' on 4 May to an air-launched Exocet missile. That, and subsequent, superbly executed Exocet attacks forced the British Carrier Group well to the east of the Falkland Islands and thus further weakened the air defence cover available to the forward vessels and, later, the disembarked land forces. The loss of a British carrier would have been a catastrophe to the Task Force and would, at any stage, have jeopardised Operation "Corporate".

In mid-May British Special Forces effectively destroyed eleven Argentine aircraft in a well-executed raid on the small Pebble Island airstrip, situated to the north of West Falkland. The mission, which suffered only minor casualties, obliged Argentina to recognise that her forces were highly vulnerable to such attacks and that resources such as the Pucara aircraft could no longer be protected in quantity at such dispersed and isolated sites. From a British viewpoint, not only were eleven aircraft and an airfield rendered unusable, but the ability of the British soldier to achieve spectacular success was again demonstrated to the British public. With an amphibious assault on the Falkland Islands rumoured to be imminent, such a success was also welcome news to the embarked forces.

The selected location for the amphibious landing, San Carlos Water on East Falkland, provided the Task Force with a deep water anchorage that could be fairly easily protected by disembarked anti-aircraft weapons. It was far enough removed from the Argentine garrison at Darwin and the forces at Port Howard on West Falkland were considered unlikely to have the means to interfere with the landings. A helicopter-borne reinforcement of the area from Port Stanley might have been possible, but Combat Air Patrols would be able to suppress any such activity. It was hoped that the surrounding hills would provide some measure of protection against direct Argentine observation, aircraft radars and stand-off missiles such as Exocet. In summary, San Carlos Water, once the troops were off the beaches, looked a reasonable spot for such an adventure.

The landings, known as Operation "Sutton", commenced in the early hours of 21 May under the control of the Commander Amphibious Task Group, Commodore M.C.Clapp. Once ashore, the augmented forces of 3

Commando Brigade were commanded by Brigadier J.H.A.Thompson OBE ADC, Royal Marines, who remained senior officer ashore until General Moore's arrival on 29 May. The later reinforcing troops of the 5th Infantry Brigade were commanded by Brigadier M.J.A.Wilson OBE MC.

In spite of substantial Argentine air attacks on 21 and 23 May, the landings were successful. By 25 May the Sea Harriers flying from 'Hermes' and 'Invincible' and the Task Force's anti-aircraft defences had effectively nullified the threat of a successful counter-attack in the beach-head area. During the first five days, however, several warships in San Carlos Water and Falkland Sound had been damaged and two, 'Ardent' and 'Antelope', had been sunk. Elsewhere, Argentine aircraft remained a considerable threat and on 25 May 'Coventry' and the important support vessel 'Atlantic Conveyor' were both lost, the latter with her cargo of helicopters, aircraft spares, fuel and workshops.

The break-out from the San Carlos beach-head commenced during the night of 26/27 May. While 45 Commando and 3 PARA advanced towards Douglas settlement and Teal Inlet respectively, 2 PARA moved towards Darwin and the settlement at Goose Green. It was there that 2 PARA fought a bitter battle with defending forces on 28/29 May which cost the lives of the Commanding Officer and 17 other officers and men. The battle saw both sides use ground-attack aircraft in support of their troops, Argentina losing three in the process.

As the British troops pressed eastwards, the entrenched Argentine forces in Port Stanley and on the hilltop strongpoints to the west of the town were subjected to repeated attacks by Royal Navy and Royal Air Force aircraft and, most miserably for them, relentless shelling by warships. Eventually, British artillery was brought forward by helicopters and it was only the need to conserve ammunition stocks that limited the severity of the barrage then delivered to the forward Argentine positions.

By early June a British victory was in sight, although concern was increasing that fatigue was now discernable within some elements of the Task Force and that supplies of fuel and ammunition were running low in the forward areas. Nevertheless, a general mood of optimism prevailed as the British grip tightened on Port Stanley. Although intelligence suggested, correctly, that no more Exocet rounds remained in Argentina after 30 May, the fear of the weapon continued to dictate that the carriers be operated well to the east of East Falkland and, consequently, Sea Harrier Combat Air Patrols continued to spend less time over the Islands than was ideal. Expressed in another way, more aircraft were required to provide the previous level of cover. It was, however, rather more due to taking an unnecessarily casual attitude towards an enemy, perceived by some to be already beaten, than to a lack of air cover that the landing ships 'Sir Galahad' and 'Sir Tristram' were successfully attacked, with considerable loss of life, in Port Pleasant on 8 June. Argentine fighter-bombers took the maximum advantage of excellent recent intelligence, clear weather and poor defences to launch an attack which destroyed 'Sir Galahad' and severely damaged 'Sir Tristram'. However, this was to be the swansong of the Argentine fighter-bombers and they were to inflict no further significant damage to the British forces.

The final week of the War was one of bitter winter weather. Several of the heavily-defended hills to the west of Port Stanley were won by British troops in nocturnal and bloody struggles, and if the end came relatively suddenly on 14 June, it was primarily as a result of the Infantry's efforts during the three previous nights.

The formal surrender of all Argentine forces on the Falkland Islands became effective at 2359Z on 14 June. The surrender document was signed by General de Brigada Menendez, on behalf of all Argentine forces on the Falkland Islands, and General Moore. Six days later, on 20 June, when confronted by a Royal Navy Task Group led by Captain N.J.Barker in 'Endurance', the small Argentine military party on the island of Southern Thule in the South Sandwich Islands also surrendered.

Throughout the conflict and in all theatres the British made prodigious use of airpower. It was used both directly and in support of virtually every Task Force operation of any significance. Above all, it was used to great effect by skilled and enthusiastic men who performed, throughout, in a most professional fashion. Their individual achievements are described in the subsequent pages.

# UNITED KINGDOM'S AIRCRAFT LOSSES

## UNITED KINGDOM

To be read in conjunction with the appropriate Individual Aircraft Details and Unit Histories. Losses are listed by type in date and time order. The number in the left-hand column is cumulative, leading to the final total of United Kingdom aircraft losses.

### SEA HARRIER FRS.1 — Losses 6

| 1 | XZ450 | 800 Sqdn | 4.5.82 | c1612Z |
|---|-------|----------|--------|--------|
| 2 | XZ452 | 801 Sqdn | 6.5.82 | c1200Z |
| 3 | XZ453 | 801 Sqdn | 6.5.82 | c1200Z |
| 4 | ZA192 | 800 Sqdn | 23.5.82 | 2254Z |
| 5 | ZA174 | 801 Sqdn | 29.5.82 | 1849Z |
| 6 | XZ456 | 801 Sqdn | 1.6.82 | c1740Z |

### HARRIER GR.3 — Losses 4

| 7 | XZ972 | 1(F) Sqdn | 21.5.82 | c1235Z |
|---|-------|-----------|---------|--------|
| 8 | XZ988 | 1(F) Sqdn | 27.5.82 | c1635Z |
| 9 | XZ963 | 1(F) Sqdn | 30.5.82 | 1520Z |
| 10 | XZ989 | 1(F) Sqdn | 8.6.82 | c1500Z |

### CHINOOK HC.1 — Losses 3

| 11 | ZA706 | 18 Sqdn | 25.5.82 | 1936Z |
|----|-------|---------|---------|-------|
| 12 | ZA716 | 18 Sqdn | 25.5.82 | 1936Z |
| 13 | ZA719 | 18 Sqdn | 25.5.82 | 1936Z |

### SEA KING HC.4/HAS.5 — Losses 5

| 14 | ZA311 | 846 Sqdn | 23.4.82 | 2113Z |
|----|-------|----------|---------|-------|
| 15 | ZA132 | 826 Sqdn | 12.5.82 | 1735Z |
| 16 | XZ573 | 826 Sqdn | 18.5.82 | 0030Z |
| 17 | ZA290 | 846 Sqdn | 18/19.5.82 | unknown |
| 18 | ZA294 | 846 Sqdn | 19.5.82 | 2215Z |

### WESSEX HAS.3/HU.5 — Losses 9

| 19 | XT464 | 845 Sqdn 'C' Flight | 22.4.82 | c1520Z |
|----|-------|---------------------|---------|--------|
| 20 | XT473 | 845 Sqdn 'C' Flight | 22.4.82 | c1535Z |
| 21 | XS480 | 848 Sqdn 'D' Flight | 25.5.82 | 1936Z |
| 22 | XS495 | 848 Sqdn 'D' Flight | 25.5.82 | 1936Z |
| 23 | XS499 | 848 Sqdn 'D' Flight | 25.5.82 | 1936Z |
| 24 | XS512 | 848 Sqdn 'D' Flight | 25.5.82 | 1936Z |
| 25 | XT476 | 848 Sqdn 'D' Flight | 25.5.82 | 1936Z |
| 26 | XT483 | 848 Sqdn 'D' Flight | 25.5.82 | 1936Z |
| 27 | XM837 | 737 Sqdn 'Glamorgan' Flight | 12.6.82 | 0637Z |

### LYNX HAS.2 — Losses 3

| 28 | XZ251 | 815 Sqdn 'Ardent' Flight | 21.5.82 | 1740Z |
|----|-------|--------------------------|---------|-------|
| 29 | XZ242 | 815 Sqdn 'Coventry' Flight | 25.5.82 | 1821Z |
| 30 | XZ700 | 815 Sqdn 'Newcastle' Flight | 25.5.82 | 1936Z |

### SCOUT AH.1 — Loss 1

| 31 | XT629 | 3 CBAS 'B' Flight | 28.5.82 | c1455Z |
|----|-------|-------------------|---------|--------|

### GAZELLE AH.1 — Losses 3

| 32 | XX411 | 3 CBAS 'C' Flight | 21.5.82 | c1141Z |
|----|-------|-------------------|---------|--------|
| 33 | XX402 | 3 CBAS 'C' Flight | 21.5.82 | c1146Z |
| 34 | XX377 | 3 CBAS 'C' Flight | 6.6.82 | 0408Z |

# SEA HARRIER

"The Sea Harrier is the Swiss Watch of aircraft engineering". Thus spoke an unnamed Air Engineering Officer serving with the Task Force. Because of the quality of design which had given rise to that comment, maintenance personnel aboard 'Hermes' were able to provide at least 12 fully-serviceable Sea Harriers each day (from a maximum of 15 on board as from 18 May to a minimum of 14 after 23 May), even at the height of the campaign. About 20 aircraft would normally be needed to consistently achieve such a figure under wartime conditions. The Pegasus engine proved to be very reliable, as did the electronics; seldom was an aircraft launched with unserviceable or unreliable equipment. The Sea Harrier's robust but simple construction assisted quick and effective battle-damage repairs, the 1(F) Sqdn Harrier GR.3's in particular proving that the basic type could take a lot of punishment and still continue flying. AEO's, maintenance personnel and MARTSU battle damage repair technicians deployed on the two aircraft carriers were of outstanding ability — every pilot would vouch for that. It must also be borne in mind that with the loss of 'Atlantic Conveyor', the fleet was deprived of a most essential ship. She was to have been the base for in-depth aircraft structural repairs and maintenance. When she sank, her workshops, jigs, tools and other important machinery were lost to the Task Force, resulting in the onus for such work reverting to the carriers and other ships. 'Astronomer' was fitted out as her replacement, but did not arrive off the Falkland Islands until the end of June.

The reliability of the aircraft and the quality of the maintenance back-up gave the pilots the confidence to make full use of the type's potential as well as all aspects of their training. In some circles there had always been scepticism that the Sea Harrier was good only for performing at air displays, but the Falklands conflict dispelled any such British or Argentine thoughts! Armed with the AIM-9L Sidewinder, it entered the air-to-air combat fray on 1 May and fared so well that for the rest of the campaign, the Fuerza Aerea Argentina did not risk any of its dedicated interceptors in aerial combat. The failure of the Argentine Mirage III's to negate the Sea Harrier threat on 1 May, and the subsequent Argentine decision to use the interceptors purely for mainland airfield defence against possible Vulcan strikes, resulted in virtually all future missions over the Falkland Islands being unescorted. Henceforth, the Daggers and Skyhawks were left to their own devices. Once sighted by a Sea Harrier pilot, a Dagger pilot's best hope of escape was to use his aircraft's superior acceleration and speed, whilst a Skyhawk pilot in the same circumstances seldom escaped. Invariably, if a Skyhawk pilot saw a Sea Harrier before being himself seen, all underwing stores were jettisoned and the aircraft headed back towards the mainland as fast and low as possible. Without fighter cover the enemy pilots realised that it was prudent to recover to base and return later when, perhaps, there would be no CAP cover and therefore more chance of success in attacking a ship or shore target. That theory was proven on numerous occasions. Complementing the AIM-9L missile were the Sea Harrier's two 30mm Aden cannon which proved to be most useful for strafing ground targets, enemy shipping and aircraft.

A supreme effort by British industry ensured that the Sea Harrier, in addition to many other modifications, ultimately carried chaff and flare dispensers during the conflict. Both were put to good use, especially against SAM's. Alterations were made to on-board systems software so that, for example, toss-bombing could be carried out from the right profile. The aircraft was utilized in roles to which it was not normally accustomed. After the GR.3's had taken over the ground attack duties, Sea Harriers continued to be employed in toss-bombing during defence suppression sorties in support of the 1(F) Sqdn aircraft. Sea Harriers were used for armed photo-reconnaissance flights and in some quarters it was felt that more effort should have gone into that particular role. One of the type's greatest assets was its ability to operate in the worst weather conditions from carriers which did not have to turn into wind to launch or recover. The Argentines quickly learned that bad weather in or around the Falkland Islands did not necessarily mean that the area would be devoid of Sea Harriers! Furthermore, once the 850 ft metal airstrip at Port San Carlos had been established, the aircraft's combat patrol loiter time was significantly increased.

Thus it appeared that the aircraft was very well equipped to carry out all combat roles. That it had to be so was born out of necessity rather than forethought. Once the type had gained the upper hand by intercepting attacking aircraft and in air-to-air combat, it should have been able to effect complete mastery of the sky above the Falkland Islands. However, absolute control was never achieved and raids still penetrated the defence screen, although the numbers decreased as time passed. Complete aerial domination called for much more than just a good aircraft. Firstly, a much larger quantity of Sea Harriers was needed (they simply did not exist) while, secondly, an Airborne Early Warning aircraft would have helped to make better use of the limited number of fighters available. Good though it was, the Sea Harrier's Blue Fox radar did not possess a "look-down" capability. Aircraft were vectored towards the incoming raiders by ships' radars, but once in their vicinity the pilots would all too often have to resort to their own eyesight to locate the intruders, especially if the Argentine aircraft had descended to very low level. Over land, most ships' radars found it difficult to differentiate between low-level aircraft returns and ground clutter. Constant CAP's had to be maintained in order to ensure that interceptors were on the scene when something happened. Although Sea Harriers had a surprisingly meagre fuel consumption when loitering at low level, they did not always do so because of the need to maintain some height in order to keep a good look-out for any Argentine intruders. Medium and high-level CAP's left the Sea Harriers exposed to the enemy surveillance radars in and around Port Stanley. Such exposure, especially during transit to and from the COA, would entail giving away the general locations of the two aircraft carriers, if not their exact positions. Certain electronic and tactical measures were adopted to reduce that to a minimum, but as time went by, the enemy radar operators became very adept at tracking the Sea Harriers and advising their own aircraft at when to abort their missions or alter their inbound or outbound routes. That was why so much effort was put into destroying the Argentine Westinghouse TPS-43 and Cardion TPS-44 radars.

A good AEW aircraft would have transformed the aerial campaign. The Nimrod AEW.3 was not available, and although a couple of Gannet AEW.3's could have been mustered with a lot of effort, where could they have operated from? Certainly not the FOB at Port San Carlos! After the conflict, two Sea Kings which had been hastily converted to the AEW role by the addition of a modified Searchwater radar (as used by the maritime reconnaissance Nimrod fleet) were sent south on board 'Illustrious' to prove the concept.

As mentioned earlier, loiter and combat times available to the Sea Harriers were directly related to the distance of the carriers from the Islands. At times, the two ships were some 250 miles east of the Falkland Islands yet the aircraft still went out on CAP. Such distances absorbed many Sea Harriers; for every two on CAP another pair would be returning with a further pair on their way out. Three CAP stations were normally maintained, so with 18 aeroplanes required to patrol those areas, full CAP cover was only achieved because of the Sea Harrier's excellent serviceability record. It also illustrates why anything approaching complete mastery of the air was impossible until the FOB was established. Paradoxically, by the time that the strip close to Port San Carlos settlement was available, much of the pressure for such a facility had already been relieved. Even so, the odd Argentine raid still got through, notably on 8 June when the FOB was out of use due to a Harrier GR.3 accident and the two carriers were well east of the Islands.

In conclusion, it is fair to say that the Sea Harrier exceeded all expectations, outperforming every Argentine aircraft type and establishing effective air superiority. It was very reliable, nimble and a good weapons platform, while superb maintenance meant that virtually every Sea Harrier was serviceable all of the time. That was the equivalent of having an additional eight-aircraft squadron available! Attrition was well below that expected, thus negating the need to use Sidewinder-equipped GR.3's for air defence. It would have benefitted from greater endurance, four AAM's and a radar with "look-down" capability, but all of those deficiencies were recognised before and during the conflict. Shortly after the Argentine surrender, Sea Harriers were flying with four AIM-9L's and two larger 190 gallon underwing fuel tanks.

For the future, continued development of the type seems assured. 23 new-production Sea Harriers for the Fleet Air Arm (including the Falklands conflict attrition replacements) had been ordered by the summer of 1985. Modifications to later production machines and mid-life updates to earlier aircraft will see the introduction of a new radar (Blue Vixen), new missiles (4 AIM-120 AMRAAM/2 AIM-9L combination and the Sea Eagle ASM) plus new avionics and aerodynamic refinements (including leading-edge root extensions). If the Sea Harrier had not proved itself during the Falklands conflict, it is open to question whether many of the above mentioned improvements would have reached fruition.

# 800 NAVAL AIR SQUADRON

In the early hours of Friday 2 April, Lt Cdr A.D.Auld was instructed by FONAC/MoD to prepare his Squadron for immediate embarkation on 'Hermes'. Fortunately, the unit and its aircraft were fully operational, having only recently disembarked from the carrier. However, the ship was not ready to put to sea, being docked at Portsmouth and festooned in scaffolding in the midst of a maintenance period. Moreover, the Squadron personnel were to disperse on Easter leave in a few hours. Responsibility for the preparation of 'Hermes' rested with the ship's company and dockyard staff. The problems of cancelling leave, mustering personnel and gathering together equip-

ment were carried out very quickly and efficiently by the Squadron and by late afternoon on 2 April eight Sea Harriers had embarked the carrier at Portsmouth:

XZ492 'H/123'  XZ460 'H/126'  XZ500 'H/130'
XZ459 'H/125'  XZ496 'H/127'

XZ457 'VL/714'  XZ494 '-/716'  ZA191 '-/718'
[all three ex-899 Sqdn]

*A foreshortened view of 'Hermes', prior to her sailing from Portsmouth on 5.4.82, shows ten of the eleven 800 Squadron Sea Harrier FRS.1's on board. A twelfth joined the carrier in the English Channel. As can be seen from the variety of tail markings, the Squadron's increased complement was achieved by the transfer of 899 Squadron machines and drawing on reserve and development aircraft. In the background are Sea King HC.4's and HAS.5's of 846 and 826 Squadrons.*       *(Flt Lt D. H. S. Morgan, RAF)*

*Before reaching Ascension Island on 16.4.82 most, if not all, of the Sea King HAS.5's and Sea Harrier FRS.1's received low-visibility colour schemes. Each aircraft was hand-painted on an opportunity basis over a few days. Seen here is XZ450 '50' in the overall Extra Dark Sea Grey scheme with associated toned down markings. However, about to land is XZ492 '–/(1)23', still in full 800 Squadron regalia except for the deletion of the first digit of its code and the overpainting of the remaining two in Black. These two aircraft were to have mixed fortunes: XZ450 was shot down near Goose Green airfield on 4.5.82 with the loss of its pilot, Lt Nick Taylor, whereas XZ492 survived the conflict with one "kill" to its credit – an A-4C Skyhawk of Grupo 4 de Caza.*       *(Ministry of Defence)*

They comprised two-thirds of the Squadron's assigned wartime complement of 12 aircraft. Three others arrived aboard the ship on 4 April:

| | |
|---|---|
| ZA192, ZA193 | (both uncoded, ex-storage) |
| XZ450 '50' | (ex-MoD(PE) Sea Eagle ASM development aircraft) |

'Hermes' departed Portsmouth on 5 April to a tumultuous send-off. The twelfth (and last) Sea Harrier was flown aboard by Flt Lt R.Penfold while the carrier was underway down the English Channel, heading for the Bay of Biscay en route to Ascension Island:

| |
|---|
| XZ455 'VL/712'    (ex-899 Sqdn) |

The 12-aircraft complement had been achieved by the transfer of four Sea Harriers from 899 Sqdn and drawing on reserve and development aircraft. 899 was the Headquarters and Training Squadron based at Yeovilton. Its Commanding Officer, Lt Cdr N.W.Thomas, had been alerted at the same time as Lt Cdr Auld and he was tasked with providing additional aircraft and aircrew to be integrated into 800 and 801 Sqdns, thereby virtually eliminating 899 Sqdn's shore-based training capabilities. Lt Cdr Thomas was also Chief Tactical Instructor with 899 Sqdn and initially it was decided to retain him at Yeovilton. In the event, he too embarked 'Hermes' and ensured that 899 Sqdn retained its identity afloat as far as was possible, bearing in mind that it had no aircraft and its pilots were split between two squadrons on two carriers. In addition to the CO, other 899 Sqdn pilots drafted to 800 Sqdn aboard 'Hermes' were Lt Cdrs G.W.J.Batt and A.R.W.Ogilvy, S/Lt A.J.George and Flt Lts D.H.S.Morgan and R.Penfold. They supplemented the 800 Sqdn pilots, Lt Cdr Auld (CO), Lt Cdrs M.S.Blissett and R.V.Frederiksen, Lts M.Hale, S.N.Hargreaves, A.N.McHarg, C.R.W.Morrell, D.A.Smith and N.Taylor (fresh from 899 Sqdn) and Flt Lt E.H.Ball. Lt Cdr A.R.W.Ogilvy (the CO Designate of 801 Sqdn, scheduled to replace Lt Cdr N.D.Ward) happened to be on a refresher course with 899 Sqdn when the crisis arose. He went aboard 'Hermes', tasked as Air Warfare Instructor for the Sea Harrier squadrons. As a result of these machinations, a coherent policy of authority and planning evolved, with Andy Auld and "Sharkey" Ward as CO's of the two operational squadrons, the CO of 899 as CTI and the CO Designate of 801 as AWI; a strong team.

Typically inclement weather was encountered during the passage across the Bay of Biscay which delayed deck qualification for some of the newer pilots. Fortunately, by 8 April the weather had improved and a full-scale work-up commenced. Between 10 and 16 April most, if not all, of the Sea Harriers were painted in their wartime colours. A coat of Extra Dark Sea Grey was applied to the undersides and other White areas by means of brushes and, if rumours are to be believed, mops!

The reason for that somewhat crude method of application was really quite simple. Unlike 'Invincible', the hangar air-conditioning system in 'Hermes' could not cope with the amount of spray-painting required for each aircraft, so a manual method had to be adopted. However, there were advantages in that aircraft could be painted, on an opportunity basis, either in the hangar or on the flight-deck [see colour photo]. As a brush-painted application tended to achieve a thicker coat of paint than a spray-painted one, it proved to be the more durable of the two methods in the generally dreadful weather conditions later experienced in the South Atlantic.

Black ventral fin serials were retained, but all Squadron markings, ROYAL NAVY titles and deck letters were overpainted in Extra Dark Sea Grey and the White segments of the roundels painted Roundel Blue. No attempt was made to allocate 800 Sqdn side-codes to the additional Sea Harriers which had been integrated into the Squadron. Former 899 Sqdn and original 800 Sqdn machines had the first digit of their side-codes deleted with Extra Dark Sea Grey paint and the other two digits overpainted in Black or Roundel Blue (see table). MoD(PE) aircraft XZ450 and the two ex-storage Sea Harriers had the last two digits of their serials applied in Black or Roundel Blue to the engine air intake flanks. Summarising, all the aircraft wore two-digit codes which did not duplicate each other and were coloured as follows:

| | | | |
|---|---|---|---|
| XZ492 '-/(1)23' | (Black) | XZ457 '-/(7)14' | (Black) |
| XZ459 '-/(1)25' | (Black) | XZ494 '-/(7)16' | (Black) |
| XZ460 '-/(1)26' | (Black) | ZA191 '-/(7)18' | (Black) |
| XZ496 '-/(1)27' | (Black) | XZ450 '50' | (Black) |
| XZ500 '-/(1)30' | (Blue?) | ZA192 '92' | (Black) |
| XZ455 '-/(7)12' | (Black) | ZA193 '93' | (Blue?) |

*Notes:*

XZ459 *Returned to the UK aboard 'Hermes' on 21 July 1982, by which time the code was in Roundel Blue.*

XZ500 *Returned to the UK aboard 'Hermes' on 21*
ZA193 *July 1982 with Roundel Blue codes; the original colour has not been confirmed but is believed to have been Roundel Blue.*

It is interesting to note that if 801 Sqdn aboard 'Invincible' had also dispensed with the first digit of the aircraft side-code, there would still have been no duplication of numbering throughout the total Sea Harrier force. In fact, Sea Harrier squadrons had originally been allocated their side-code blocks with that in mind. Use of the last two digits of the serial was an idiosyncratic (but simple and effective) departure from the "norm".

From 12 to 16 April the Squadron carried out bombing and simulated ship-strike sorties in addition to practising ground attack and close support work (a fairly unfamiliar role). Additionally, all of the newer pilots were brought up to full operational standard, but it was not until a couple of days before 'Hermes' was due to arrive off Ascension Island that the reality of potential conflict was brought home. The Squadron was then informed that, for

**737 NAVAL AIR SQUADRON**
WESSEX HAS.3

**800 NAVAL AIR SQUADRON**
SEA HARRIER FRS.1

**801 NAVAL AIR SQUADRON**
SEA HARRIER FRS.1

**809 NAVAL AIR SQUADRON**
SEA HARRIER FRS.1

**815 NAVAL AIR SQUADRON**
LYNX HAS.2

**820 NAVAL AIR SQUADRON**
SEA KING HAS.5

**824 NAVAL AIR SQUADRON**
SEA KING HAS.2A

**825 NAVAL AIR SQUADRON**
SEA KING HAS.2/HAS.2A

**826 NAVAL AIR SQUADRON**
SEA KING HAS.5

**829 NAVAL AIR SQUADRON**
WASP HAS.1

**845 NAVAL AIR SQUADRON**
WESSEX HU.5

**846 NAVAL AIR SQUADRON**
SEA KING HC.4

**847 NAVAL AIR SQUADRON**
WESSEX HU.5

**848 NAVAL AIR SQUADRON**
WESSEX HU.5

**899 NAVAL AIR SQUADRON**
SEA HARRIER FRS.1

**3 COMMANDO BRIGADE
AIR SQUADRON RM**
GAZELLE AH.1
SCOUT AH.1

**656 SQUADRON AAC**
GAZELLE AH.1
SCOUT AH.1

All of the above Fleet Air Arm Squadrons were awarded the Battle Honour 'FALKLAND ISLANDS 1982'.
By tradition, units of the Royal Marines and the Army Air Corps are not awarded Battle Honours.

# BADGES OF *OPERATION CORPORATE* FLEET AIR ARM, ROYAL MARINES
# COMMANDO BRIGADE AND ARMY AIR CORPS SQUADRONS

**1(F) SQUADRON**
HARRIER GR.3

**10 SQUADRON**
VC-10 C.1

**18 SQUADRON**
CHINOOK HC.1

**24 SQUADRON**
HERCULES C.1/C.1P/C.3

**29(F) SQUADRON**
PHANTOM FGR.2

**30 SQUADRON**
HERCULES C.1/C.1P/C.3

**42(TB) SQUADRON**
NIMROD MR.1

**44 SQUADRON**
VULCAN B.2

**47 SQUADRON**
HERCULES C.1/C.1P/C.3

**50 SQUADRON**
VULCAN B.2

**51 SQUADRON**
NIMROD R.1

**55 SQUADRON**
VICTOR K.2

**57 SQUADRON**
VICTOR K.2

**70 SQUADRON**
HERCULES C.1/C.1P/C.3

**101 SQUADRON**
VULCAN B.2

**120 SQUADRON**
NIMROD MR.2/MR.2P

**201 SQUADRON**
NIMROD MR.2/MR.2P

**202 SQUADRON**
SEA KING HAR.3

**206 SQUADRON**
NIMROD MR.2/MR.2P

Of the above 1(F), 18, 42(TB), 44, 47, 50, 51, 55, 57, 70, 101, 120, 201 and 206 Squadrons were awarded the Battle Honour 'SOUTH ATLANTIC 1982'.

# BADGES OF *OPERATION CORPORATE* ROYAL AIR FORCE SQUADRONS

**Above** *Well south of Ascension Island in late-4.82, an 801 Squadron Sea Harrier FRS.1 in its immaculate, spray-painted, low-vis colour scheme is about to take-off on a sortie from 'Invincible'. The aircraft is XZ453 '--/009' which was lost when it almost certainly collided with another 801 Squadron Sea Harrier, XZ452 '--/007' (also lost), while investigating a low-level, unidentified contact in poor visibility to the south-east of the Falkland Islands on 6.5.82.*
*(Lt S. A. George, RN)*

**Left** *With the artistry of van Gogh wielding a three-inch paint brush, an 800 Squadron maintainer converts a three-colour Sea Harrier roundel to two. In the meantime, and with equal deftness, his shipmate applies a coat of Extra Dark Sea Grey paint to a normally White stores carrier. By 16.4.82 when 'Hermes' arrived off Ascension Island most, if not all, of the Squadron's Sea Harriers had been painstakingly hand-painted in the low-vis colour scheme.*
*(Flt Lt D. H. S. Morgan, RAF)*

*Parked at Wideawake, shortly after their arrival on 1.5.82, are four of six 809 Squadron Sea Harrier FRS.1's which were air-to-air refuelled during their flight from Yeovilton to Ascension Island via Banjul, The Gambia. In the centre of the photograph, and still fitted with its 'bolt-on', non-retractable IFR probe, is ZA174 which was lost on 29.5.82 when it slid sideways across the deck of 'Invincible' and over the side into the sea.*
*(Mel James)*

Always pictorially dramatic is a photograph of a Sea Harrier creating spray as it accelerates along a wet flight-deck towards the ski-jump. Flanked by two 1(F) Squadron Harrier GR.3's (including XZ133/10 in the foreground), XZ499 '99' of 800 Squadron is about to take-off on a CAP sortie from 'Hermes' sometime between 1.6.82 and the Argentine surrender on 14.6.82.

(Lt Cdr R. C. Nichol, RN)

Just visible in the background is the Cape Pembroke peninsula near Port Stanley; the date is 3.7.82 and the carrier is 'Hermes' with a packed flight-deck. In the foreground are 800 Squadron Sea Harrier FRS.1's, ZA193 '93' being manoeuvred by an aircraft tug and two former 809 Squadron aircraft (XZ499 '99' and ZA194 '94') sandwiching a 1(F) Squadron Harrier GR.3 XZ992/05. Early that afternoon 'Hermes' sailed for Portsmouth and on the following day the GR.3's disembarked to Port Stanley.

(Lt Cdr R. C. Nichol, RN)

Mirror-imaged in a pool of water created by the local fire service at Wideawake on 5.5.82 is one of 848 Squadron 'D' Flight's ill-fated Wessex HU.5's, XS512 '--/WT'. Twenty days later it, and five others, were victims of a successful 2 Escuadrilla Exocet attack on 'Atlantic Conveyor' to the north-east of the Falkland Islands. (Mel James)

In a zebra-like colour scheme XS539 (435), one of 829 Squadron 'Endurance' Flight's two Wasp HAS.1's, sits on a cleared area of concrete at the old whaling station, Grytviken, South Georgia on 28.5.82. In the background, and looming out of the mist, is 'Canberra' which departed later that day for San Carlos Water with men and equipment of 5 Infantry Brigade embarked. (Ministry of Defence)

'Canberra' anchored in San Carlos Water on 2/3.6.82 and during her stay 846 Squadron Sea King HC.4's airlifted 5 Infantry Brigade stores and equipment ashore. Seen here on 3.6.82 is ZA298 '--/VA' holding clear of the midship flight-deck while another HC.4 departs with a GPU as an underslung load.
(Ministry of Defence)

Silhouetted against the imposing snow and ice-covered mountains of South Georgia, 737 Squadron 'Antrim' Flight's Wessex HAS.3, XP142 (406) flies alongside 'Antrim' prior to landing on her, the precise date being unknown. Following an eventful war, "Humphrey" (as this Wessex was affectionately named) was statically displayed in the Fleet Air Arm Museum at Yeovilton.
(Ministry of Defence)

XZ314 Gazelle AH.1 of 656 Squadron aboard 'Nordic Ferry' during the voyage south begins a long and difficult journey from the lower deck, through the centre deck, and up to the flight-deck. All Gazelles were stowed below deck with main rotor blades pivoted back but this later made ground handling difficult on the upward journey due to the much increased weight at the tail.
(Cpl L. Beresford, AAC)

The idea of going to war with a large day-glo code letter must, with hindsight, seem a little strange. However, 656 Squadron Advanced Section did apply such codes to its Scout AH.1's on 23.4.82, the code being a derivation of the pilot's Tactical Call-sign. Captain John Greenhalgh's XR628 is seen coded 'C' whilst being prepared for flight aboard 'Europic Ferry' shortly after the ship departed the English Channel.
(Cpl S. Chollerton, AAC)

ZA728 Gazelle AH.1 led a much chequered (and charmed) life during Operation ''Corporate''. At the outset it was on the strength of 3 CBAS but not immediately shipped with the RM main party. By a change of boom it adopted ARMY titles for issue to 656 Squadron with whom it is seen here between tasking, midway through the campaign. Subsequently it readopted ROYAL MARINES titling for re-issue to 3 CBAS.
(Cpl L. Beresford, AAC)

Until the South Atlantic conflict PanAm staff at Wideawake had been used to just handling the occasional US Air Force transport aircraft in support of USAF and NASA facilities on Ascension Island. However, at one stage during Operation "Corporate" Wideawake's small ramp area accommodated up to 24 fixed-wing aircraft as well as 36 helicopters. This photograph, taken from the TACAN site on 18.5.82, highlights the parking problems faced by the British support crews. (Mel James)

Eight 1(F) Squadron Harrier GR.3's had reached Ascension Island from Wittering by late on 5.5.82, those visible in this shot including XW919/03, XZ129/29, XZ963/14 and XZ972/33. The aircraft all staged through St Mawgan, the long over-water leg south from the Cornish base being accomplished with the aid of Victor tankers from Marham. The 330-gallon ferry tanks used during the journey can be seen on the ground beside each aircraft. (Mel James)

Attempts to find a diplomatic solution to resolve the dispute between Britain and Argentina had yielded no sign of success at all by the end of 4.82. Thus the air war opened when Vulcan B.2 XM607 was launched from Wideawake late on 30.4.82 with a full armament of twenty-one 1,000 lb bombs for an attack on Stanley Airport early the next morning, under the codename "Black Buck 1". XM607 is seen at Wideawake on 1.5.82 immediately after its return from the first British offensive mission against Argentine forces on the Falkland Islands. (Mel James)

Supporting the Vulcan raid against Stanley Airport on 1.5.82 was a total of eleven Victor K.2's which, as part of a complicated series of air-refuelling operations, provided the Vulcan with sufficient fuel for the long flight south. A further seven Victor missions were launched from Wideawake to ensure the Vulcan's safe return to Ascension Island after the attack. One of those Victors deployed, XM717, is depicted at Wideawake on 1.5.82 immediately after supporting the Vulcan's return flight from Port Stanley.                    (Mel James)

One of the more noticeable conversions to emerge during the South Atlantic conflict was the fitting, by Marshall of Cambridge, of IFR probes to a number of RAF Hercules C.1 aircraft. When the urgent requirement for extended-range aircraft first arose, XV200 was undergoing an overhaul at Teversham and was thus selected as the first conversion. In its revised configuration XV200 first flew on 28.4.82 and after trials was deployed to Wideawake on 14.5.82 to carry out the first air-refuelled air-drop to the fleet two days later. It is seen here at Wideawake on 21.5.82

(Mel James)

Arguably one of the most famous of individual aircraft to have participated in Operation "Corporate" was 18 Squadron's Chinook HC.1 "Bravo November" which throughout the conflict was the Squadron's only available heavy-lift helicopter on the Falkland Islands. Three other Chinooks which had been shipped south with ZA718/BN aboard 'Atlantic Conveyor' were lost when the ship was hit by an Exocet missile on 25.5.82. Attrition replacements dispatched aboard 'Contender Bezant' arrived too late for effective use.

(Ministry of Defence)

the fighter role, the Sea Harriers would be armed with AIM-9L Sidewinder missiles and 200 rounds of 30mm High Explosive shells for the twin Aden cannon. In the strike configuration they would carry an assortment of weapons, ranging from 1,000lb bombs (in the form of DA, VT-fused or Retard) to 2 inch rocket pods or 600lb cluster bombs.

On 14 April the transitting ships had an unexpected visitor. A Soviet Tupolev Tu-20 "Bear D" made two low passes overhead the CVBG, almost certainly operating from Conakry in Guinea to assess the progress of the Fleet. Its curiosity satisfied, the aircraft returned whence it came.

As the ships approached Ascension Island at first light on 16 April, nine Sea Harriers carried out a demonstration of the effectiveness and lethality of some of their weaponry. Splash targets were bombed, while Martin Hale fired an AIM-9G at a LEPUS flare and achieved a hit. All of the ordnance appeared to work as required, which was encouraging if it was about to be used for real. Whilst off the Island, a plan to use Wideawake for a simulated attack on Stanley Airport was shelved due to the degree of aircraft activity at the airfield and elsewhere around the Island. The associated planning was not wasted, however, as was to be proved later on 1 May. 'Hermes' left Ascension Island at 1300Z on 18 April (slightly ahead of the departure time scheduled for that day) following a submarine alert during the morning which proved to be a false alarm. It was felt that the CVBG was unnecessarily vulnerable sitting offshore, especially as training, consolidation flying and VERTREP sorties had virtually been completed.

On 20 April, the Squadron was declared fully operational, with two Sidewinder-equipped aircraft being on deck alert both day and night while each pilot flew at least two sorties per day. The next day saw alertness turned into action at 1130Z when ship-borne radar picked up a contact some 160 miles south of the Fleet. Simon Hargreaves was airborne in XZ460 at 1145Z and the intruder intercepted at approximately 19°29′S 21°00′W. It turned out to be a reconnaissance Boeing 707 (TC-91) of the Fuerza Aerea Argentina (Grupo 1) flying at about 35,000ft. The Sea Harrier flew alongside the 707, to port, and photographed it, the 707 in turn "snapping" the Sea Harrier. A "wing-waggling" session by the latter left the 707 crew in no doubt that they were unwelcome and should clear the area. For the next few days the 707's arrived around dawn and dusk at various altitudes and ranges, each time being intercepted and sent on their way by either 800 or 801 Sqdn aircraft. The cat-and-mouse game came to a head at 1550Z on 24 April when 800 Sqdn intercepted a 707 80 miles east of 'Hermes'. The Argentine Government was informed through diplomatic channels that their aircraft would no longer be "welcome" and, indeed, would be "at risk". There were no further 707 incidents until the latter half of May *[see Grupo 1 and 1(F) Sqdn notes].* No doubt the Argentine military had understood the tone of the British warning and assessed the "risk" to be very real.

A Sea Harrier flown by Nick Taylor dropped a CBU for practice on 28 April as part of the final preparations leading to a possible attack on Stanley Airport and the weapon performed as required. That day, a statement by

the British Government created a significant increase in tension. The Falkland Islands "Total Exclusion Zone" (for ships and aircraft) replacing the previous "Maritime Exclusion Zone" (ships only) was announced, to be effective from 1100Z on 30 April. The Argentines followed suit with their own zone. 'Hermes', operating just outside the TEZ on 30 April, made final preparations for the next day's actions.

The "Black Buck" Vulcan raid on Stanley Airport at 0746Z on 1 May triggered off a series of incidents that day involving 800 Sqdn. By 1045Z 'Hermes' was about 95 miles east north-east of Port Stanley ready to launch all 12 of her Sea Harriers for attacks on Stanley Airport (nine aircraft) and Goose Green airfield (three aircraft). As the machines prepared for take-off, Sea Harriers from 801 Sqdn aboard 'Invincible' were already airborne to provide continuous CAP cover (to the east and north-east of Port Stanley) of at least four aircraft.

The Port Stanley attack group was first off the 'Hermes' ski-jump, led by Andy Auld in XZ494 who took off at 1048Z. Between then and 1055Z all nine were launched, in the following order:

| Aircraft | Pilot | Call-sign | Bombs |
|---|---|---|---|
| XZ494 | Lt Cdr Auld | "Black Ldr" | 3 CBU |
| ZA192 | Flt Lt Morgan | "Black 2" | 3 CBU |
| ZA193 | Lt Cdr Blissett | "Black 3" | 3 CBU |
| XZ450 | Flt Lt Ball | "Black 4" | 3 CBU |
| XZ459 | Lt Cdr Batt | "Red Ldr" | 3 VT |
| XZ500 | Lt Cdr Ogilvy | "Red 2" | 3 DA |
| XZ496 | Lt Cdr Thomas | "Red 3" | 3 VT |
| XZ492 | Lt Morrell | "Red 4" | 3 VT |
| XZ455 | Flt Lt Penfold | "Black 5" * | 3 DA |

*\* Delayed until last by a fault*

Once airborne they set course at low level for MacBride Head on the north-east coast of East Falkland (about 20 miles north of the Airport), arriving there about 1105Z. At that point "Gordy" Batt, Tony Ogilvy, Neill Thomas and Clive Morrell left the other five. Those four were the toss-bombers ("Red Section", led by Ogilvy and not Batt, whose NAVHARS had gone unserviceable shortly after he got airborne) and they initially headed south-west to attack the airfield from the north, ahead of the others. Three miles from the airfield they pulled up to toss their bombs, releasing them to explode on, and above, known Argentine AAA positions to the north-west and south-west of the Airport. These aircraft then broke away, departing to the south-east at low level. They had hopefully distracted the Argentine defences for long enough to allow Auld's "Black Section" to sweep in unnoticed for a follow-up attack on the airfield facilities, runway, parked aircraft and any other targets of opportunity that might present themselves. Bertie Penfold was to try and put his three DA retard bombs onto the runway to add to the damage already caused by the Vulcan raid. The others would attack all of the above-mentioned targets with CBU's. All five arrived at very low level from the direction of Mount Low, about 5 miles north-west of the airfield. Two of Penfold's bombs hit the runway, scabbing it, while CBU's fragmented all over the airfield. After the initial surprise of the attack was over, the sky positively glowed with Argentine AAA fire and missiles but, remarkably, the only damage inflicted on the Sea Harriers was to ZA192 flown by Dave Morgan when a 20mm HE round exploded as it passed through the fin. Smaller holes were made in the tailplane. A Tigercat missile also shot past him but was presumably aimed at another target. He also broke an AAA gun-laying radar lock-on by a combination of rapid manoeuvring and dumping chaff. Morgan returned safely to 'Hermes' at around 1130Z, as did the others. ZA192 was quickly returned to service after patch repairs by the BDR team.

The three aircraft which attacked Goose Green airfield took-off immediately following the Port Stanley raiders. Rod Frederiksen's aircraft was airborne first at 1056Z, followed by those of Martin Hale and Andy McHarg, both at 1057Z:

| Aircraft | Pilot | Call-sign | Bombs |
|----------|-------|-----------|-------|
| ZA191 | Lt Cdr Frederiksen | "Tartan Ldr" | 3 CBU |
| XZ460 | Lt Hale | "Tartan 2" | 3 CBU |
| XZ457 | Lt McHarg | "Tartan 3" | 3 DA |

The launch complete, the aircraft (flying at low level) turned towards MacBride Head. They continued west from there before turning south down Falkland Sound, sweeping in low and fast towards Darwin and Goose Green airfield on a south-easterly heading. During the latter stages of the run-in they were as low as 30ft, streaking over dykes and hedges. Blurred images of about nine fixed-wing aircraft (Pucaras of Grupo 3), but no helicopters, were seen as they passed over the airfield, their CBU's dropping and exploding behind them. One of McHarg's DA bombs detonated on the grass runway while the other two fell near its eastern end. The only reaction from the enemy had been some sporadic small-arms fire although they had been warned of a possible attack. The Sea Harriers were well on their way towards Cape Dolphin (the north-west tip of East Falkland) before the defenders recovered from the suddenness of the raid. By 1155Z "Tartan Section" had landed on 'Hermes' unscathed. The safe return of all Sea Harriers from both of those attacks gave rise to BBC Reporter Brian Hanrahan's oft-quoted phrase *"I counted them all out and I counted them all back"*.

An accurate assessment of the damage inflicted on Argentine installations and aircraft as a result of the bombing runs has been difficult to determine due to the additional damage sustained on the same targets by subsequent British attacks. In the case of Stanley Airport, the only aircraft believed to have been present on the field at the time of the raid were four 1 Escuadrilla MB-339A's (including 0764/4-A-113 and 0767/4-A-116), three privately-owned Falkland Islands registered Cessna 172's (VP-FAR, VP-FAS, VP-FBA) and the Argentine-impressed FIGAS BN-2A Islander VP-FAY. As far as can be

determined, there were no Grupo 3 Pucaras on the airfield as they had moved base to Goose Green on 29 April. From the available evidence, Dave Morgan's CBU's were almost certainly responsible for severing the aft end of the Islander. Some, if not all, of the Cessnas suffered shrapnel damage but the MB-339A's, at their remote location adjacent to the eastern threshold of the runway, received nothing worse than a dowsing of earth thrown up by a CBU which fell into soft ground some distance away.

On 1 May 12 Pucaras (the total force on the Islands at the time) were based at Goose Green airfield, but early that morning the resident two Chinooks and two Bell 212's from Grupo 7 had moved to "safe" locations in and around the civilian settlement, which explains why the Sea Harriers saw no helicopters during their run-in. About an hour before the "Tartan Section" attack, three Pucaras had taken-off on a reconnaissance patrol. A fourth aircraft which had failed to get airborne (thought to be A-506) was sitting tail-up and nose down in the mud at the end of the runway, delaying the next Flight's take-off and sealing the fate of an Argentine pilot and some of his colleagues. Just as the Pucaras finally got clearance to taxy out for take-off, the bombs from the Sea Harriers started exploding all over the airfield. Pucara A-527 received a direct hit from a CBU and blew up, killing the pilot (Teniente Daniel Jukic). Seven other FAA personnel were killed and 14 seriously injured in the wake of the detonating bombs. Other Pucaras were damaged to a greater or lesser extent including, it is thought, A-502 (repaired) and A-517 (not repaired). A-506 and A-517 were later propped up on oil drums and used as decoys. A Sea Harrier photo-reconnaissance flight later the same day revealed five damaged Pucaras on the airfield, while at least seven were seen there that evening by local residents, although their state of repair could not be determined with any great accuracy. *(Official Argentine records identify one aircraft destroyed and two seriously damaged at Goose Green on 1 May. This is consistent with the wrecks found on the airfield when it was later captured by British forces.)*

Overall, the two attacks could be considered as very successful; no losses on the British side, with enemy aircraft destroyed or damaged as were equipment and facilities. It is known from local reports at both Goose Green and Port Stanley that the Argentines were psychologically rattled by the ferocity of the raids. It was the shape of things to come — for both sides!

Many of the 800 Sqdn Sea Harriers, having returned safely to 'Hermes', were refuelled, rearmed with AIM-9L's and launched within 30 minutes of their arrival to provide CAP cover in the event of any retaliation. Argentine aircraft had been detected over West Falkland, but they had not ventured any further east. That picture was not long in changing, but mainly involved 801 Sqdn aircraft operating from 'Invincible'. However, 800 Sqdn did get drawn into combat again later in the day.

At about 1930Z Bertie Penfold (in XZ455) and Martin Hale were both scrambled from 'Hermes' to intercept two high-flying targets heading east north-east over East Falkland and it was not long before the two Sea Harriers were detected by the Argentine radars at Port Stanley. Both pairs of aircraft were then vectored towards each other by their respective radar controllers. A few minutes later the

Sea Harriers were engaged by two Grupo 6 Daggers, including C-433 flown by Primer Teniente Jose Ardiles (cousin of the famous footballer). Hale and Penfold were at 20,000ft with the Daggers some 13,000ft above them and five miles away when an AAM (almost certainly a Shafrir) was fired by one of the Argentine aircraft (believed to have been Ardiles' machine). The missile was aimed at Hale's aircraft and he avoided it by taking evasive action, dumping chaff and diving into cloud at around 5,000ft. Fortunately, just before he entered the cloud the missile dropped away, having either run out of fuel or been deflected by the chaff. It had missed its target, but not by far, and was certainly a frightening experience for Hale. In the meantime (about 1941Z) Penfold had swept in behind the enemy aircraft and, at a range of about three miles astern, fired an AIM-9L which hit Ardiles' Dagger. The fighter exploded, killing its pilot. Ardiles was not seen to eject, but pieces of the aircraft (but no pilot) were later found on Lively Island, a most unlikely location, being some 30 miles south-west of Port Stanley and well away from the combat area. The other Dagger broke away from the fray and headed for home, leaving the two Sea Harriers to return safely to 'Hermes'. That action concluded 800 Sqdn's close encounters with the Fuerza Aerea Argentina for the day, the unit being well pleased with its performance. The Sea Harrier/AIM-9L combination had proved lethal to the Argentines and caused them to hurriedly reassess their tactics to avoid further unneccessary losses.

Sunday 2 May was a day of expectancy, tension and high alert states in anticipation of further Argentine re-action. That was justified, as it turned out, by the historic events which took place that day. During the early hours of the morning a potential enemy aircraft was detected *[see Escuadrilla Antisubmarina notes]* and an investigating 801 Sqdn Sea Harrier picked up radar returns from five surface contacts about 150 miles north-west of the CVBG. Treated as potentially hostile, they in fact included the carrier '25 de Mayo', so a dawn strike by A-4Q Skyhawks of 3 Escuadrilla was a distinct possibility. A constant high alert state was maintained during the night for attack or defence, depending upon what was required. At first light (about 0930Z), 800 Sqdn resumed CAP operations. For reasons explained elsewhere in this book *[see 801 Sqdn and 3 Escuadrilla]*, the enemy carrier-borne attacks failed to materialise and, as the wind died down to an almost flat calm with thick fog, the threat receded. The day ended with the sobering news that the Argentine cruiser 'General Belgrano' had been torpedoed.

Fog, which reduced visibility to 100 metres, prevented 800 Sqdn operations on 3 May, but a full alert was maintained.

There was another "Black Buck" Vulcan raid on Stanley Airport in the early hours of 4 May. Dawn heralded a clear day and the Squadron initially carried out several missions which included armed reconnaissance of Fox Bay, Port Howard and Pebble Island. Another attack on Goose Green airstrip had been planned using three aircraft armed with CBU's and retard bombs. "Gordy" Batt was to lead the raid with Ted Ball and Nick Taylor. Batt and Taylor were to drop their CBU's on any parked aircraft or helicopters while Ball would follow-up, releasing his 1000lb retard bombs on the grass runways.

Lt Cdr Batt (in ZA192) was launched at 1546Z armed with three CBU's, followed two minutes later by Flt Lt Ball (in XZ460) with three retard bombs and Lt Taylor (in XZ450) at 1550Z with three CBU's. Batt and Taylor made a fast and low run-in on the strip from the south-east. Batt dropped his bombs, but at almost exactly the same moment Nick Taylor's Sea Harrier fireballed, exploded and hit the ground in a field called "The Calf Park", just short of the airfield. Its momentum carried it through a gate, across the Darwin road and through a fence before the disintegrating airframe finally came to rest in a field adjacent to the eastern perimeter of the airstrip. Lt Taylor was killed, his aircraft having almost certainly been tracked by a GADA601 Skyguard radar before being hit by 35mm shells from its associated Oerlikon guns. Ted Ball witnessed the event as his aircraft was running in from the south-west, but continued his attack to drop the retard bombs on the airfield before joining up with Batt for the return to 'Hermes', positioned about 100 miles east south-east of Port Stanley. Both aircraft recovered safely at 1636Z.

The results of the raid were not particularly impressive. Besides creating further disruption on and around the airfield, no more Pucaras had been destroyed, although those aircraft which had been damaged on 1 May and were subsequently set up as decoys may have received further hits. Of the serviceable Pucaras, however, only two at the most could have been present at Goose Green as the rest had already been evacuated to Pebble Island. Within 800 Sqdn, and throughout the aviation elements of the Task Force, there was sadness and shock at the loss of a fine pilot and a Sea Harrier, especially as it came so soon after the successful Argentine Exocet attack on 'Sheffield' earlier in the day. The loss of a pilot and an aircraft at Goose Green caused a fundamental change in operational policy. It was pointless risking limited and valuable resources (aircrew and aircraft) when other methods might achieve the same ends. Now that the initial heavy punches had shown the Argentines what the Sea Harrier was capable of, low-level bombing was discontinued except in the case of extreme necessity. Toss-bombing (as carried out on 1 May) and medium to high-level bombing (both within the capabilities of the Sea Harrier's weapons systems) were introduced instead, with varying degrees of accuracy.

Due to bad weather (visibility down to 350 metres or less at times, with a cloud base of 150 ft), 800 Sqdn only flew a total of four sorties between 5 and 8 May, although combat "Alert" status was maintained at all times.

CAP's were resumed on 9 May, along with the agreed tactical changes. The first mission of the day involved "Gordy" Batt and Dave Morgan, who were to carry out high-level bombing of the Airport at Port Stanley (both aircraft to carry a single bomb on the centreline pylon), beyond Roland missile range. However, due to cloud cover over the airfield, they decided to return to 'Hermes'. Whilst on their way back to the carrier, Morgan (in ZA191) picked up a return on his radar from a surface contact some 60 miles to the south-east. Batt (in XZ460) descended through the low cloud cover and identified the target as the Argentine stern trawler 'Narwal'. Permission to attack the vessel was given by their control ship ('Coventry') at 1250Z and both Sea

Harriers fired warning shots across her bows to bring the trawler to a halt. This she failed to do, so it was decided to bomb and strafe her, even though the bombs might present a problem as they were fused for high-level delivery and this was going to be a low-level attack at a shallow angle. The first bomb, dropped from Morgan's Sea Harrier, narrowly missed the ship, but Batt's bomb hit the fo'c'sle and lodged in the hull without exploding. Follow-up attacks with cannon fire damaged the ship along the waterline and elsewhere. Martin Hale and Andy George arrived on the scene at 1330Z and put another 400 rounds into the area amidships. The vessel was crippled by then and a boarding party was put aboard by Sea King. From documents found it was obvious that the ship had been intelligence gathering (as suspected). She sank under tow at 2015Z the next day, in bad weather, as a result of the battle damage.

Poor weather and low visibility prevailed again on 10/11 May. It had cleared sufficiently by about 1155Z on 12 May for 800 Sqdn aircraft to commence medium to high-level bombing of Stanley Airport. The overriding requirement to remain outside Argentine Roland missile range meant that pin-point accuracy was out of the question. On one such raid launched from 'Hermes' at 1545Z that day, four bombs were dropped from about 18,000ft, of which one did not detonate on impact, one was not seen, and the remaining two were observed to explode well away from the runway. Shortly before 1640Z, a further two 800 Sqdn Sea Harriers took-off from 'Hermes' for another Airport bombing sortie under the control of 'Brilliant' which was operating close to the shore with 'Glasgow' and shelling Argentine positions near Port Stanley. The bombing run was called off not long after launching when 'Brilliant' detected aircraft fast approaching her from the west at very low level *[see Grupo 5 notes for details of that and a subsequent raid]*.

Bad weather which curtailed Sea Harrier operations on 13/14 May had, by dawn on 15 May, started to improve. Medium to high-level bombing of Stanley Airport by 800 Sqdn recommenced that morning, but with little improvement in accuracy. However, reversion to toss-bombing during the afternoon proved more successful with an equal amount of risk. From then on, toss-bombing was adopted as a general practice although medium to high-level drops continued from Sea Harriers outbound on CAP (each carried a 1,000lb VT-fused bomb on the centreline pylon). The idea (and it proved to be a good one) was that random bombing might or might not do serious damage to Argentine installations, but it would certainly help to demoralise the ground forces or at least keep them constantly on edge (that was also a worry for the British in early June when Grupo 2 Canberras started night-bombing British positions).

Simon Hargreaves (in XZ494) and Dave Smith (in ZA191) took-off from 'Hermes' at 1223Z/1224Z on the morning of 16 May. Their mission was to carry out photographic and general reconnaissance of Fox Bay, Port King and the area south of Goose Green. The film and the information they brought back revealed desirable targets — two Argentine supply vessels. Anchored in Falkland Sound off Port King was the 'Rio Carcarana', while the 'Bahia Buen Suceso' was berthed alongside the pier at Fox Bay East. At 1603Z "Gordy" Batt (in XZ459) was

launched, followed one minute later by Andy McHarg (in XZ494), and both set course for Port King. Once there (at 1625Z), they bombed and strafed the 'Rio Carcarana' causing the crew to abandon ship when uncontrollable fires broke out (she was finally sunk on 23 May by Sea Skuas fired from Lynx HAS.2 XZ723 of 815 Sqdn 'Antelope' Flight). Both Sea Harriers recovered safely to 'Hermes'. Prior to their return, Andy Auld (in XZ500) and Simon Hargreaves (in ZA191) had taken-off at 1646Z/1647Z for a cannon attack on the 'Bahia Buen Suceso'. Due to the proximity of the ship to civilian habitation, she could not be bombed, but it was hoped that strafing would immobilise the ship and deny her future use to the Argentine forces. At 1720Z an eyewitness at Fox Bay West saw two fast-moving, low-level Sea Harriers make a south-west to north-east strafing attack on the 'Bahia Buen Suceso'. Shells from the Sea Harriers' cannon raked the bridge and set fire to a diesel fuel oil storage tank some 20 metres beyond the ship *[see photograph]*. Argentine guns opened fire at the departing aircraft but they escaped, apparently unscathed. Auld and Hargreaves recovered successfully to 'Hermes', although the latter's aircraft had been hit in the tail area by Argentine counter-fire during the attack. Fortunately, the damage was not serious, it being quickly repaired and the Sea Harrier restored to service. The damaged 'Bahia Buen Suceso' remained berthed at Fox Bay East until the end of the conflict *[see Argentine Shipping and 809 Sqdn notes for her eventual fate]*.

The Squadron carried out low-level photo-reconnaissance flights over various parts of East and West Falkland on 16 and 17 May as part of the intelligence build-up prior to the amphibious landings. 18 May was an important day for the Squadron as four 809 Sqdn Sea Harriers (XZ499, ZA176, ZA177 and ZA194) were flown to 'Hermes' from 'Atlantic Conveyor'. With them came four 809 Sqdn pilots, Lt Cdr H.G.B.Slade, Lt W.Covington and Flt Lts S.Brown and J.Leeming. The new aircraft, although ostensibly attrition replacements, in fact increased the overall Sea Harrier complement aboard 'Hermes' by three (XZ450 having been the only loss). Space on board was then at a premium as four 1(F) Sqdn Harrier GR.3's had also been transferred to the carrier on 18 May from 'Atlantic Conveyor', followed by two more on 19/20 May. In order to make room for the considerable increase in fixed-wing complement, a number of helicopters were found new homes on other ships. The GR.3's and their pilots were most welcome as they took much of the pressure off the Sea Harriers in the bombing and ground-attack roles, thus allowing them to return to their more natural function of air defence.

809 Sqdn's Sea Harriers and pilots were fully integrated into 800 Sqdn. All four machines had their ROYAL NAVY titles and "Phoenix" insignia overpainted in the nearest approximation to Medium Sea Grey available aboard ship, while the last two digits of the serial were applied in Black on the engine air intake flanks (in lieu of side-codes) as follows:

XZ499 '99'   ZA176 '76'   ZA177 '77'   ZA194 '94'

It was anticipated that Operation "Sutton" (the amphibious landings in Port San Carlos and San Carlos Water) on 21 May would bring about an inevitable counter-attack by Argentine aircraft. Consequently, CAP cover was continuously maintained over three essential areas: one at the northern end of Falkland Sound, one at the southern end and the third over central West Falkland. In addition, cover for the CVBG had also to be provided, along with any other tactical requirements. For 800 Sqdn, that meant up to ten aircraft were in the air at any one time. Care had to be taken to fly high over the landing areas to avoid missiles (both British and Argentine!). That in turn exposed the Sea Harriers to Argentine surveillance radars and measures had to be taken to avoid detection whenever possible. Both 800 and 801 Sqdns were in continuous action for much of 21 May. Their presence not only resulted in several air combats but also presented the Argentine aircraft with a "barrier" that had to be overcome before British ships or troop positions could be reached. Faced with the stark choice of risking a Sidewinder hit or an aborted mission, many Argentine pilots, acting under realistic orders, chose the latter.

800 Sqdn's first contact of the day with Argentine aircraft came around 1340Z. Six Grupo 6 Daggers had just attacked 'Antrim', 'Broadsword' and 'Argonaut' in Falkland Sound where the ships were covering the entrance to San Carlos Water. One of their number (C-428) had just been lost to a ship-launched missile while the remaining five were making off southwards in two groups at low level and high speed across Falkland Sound. A CAP consisting of Rod Frederiksen and Martin Hale was directed to them by 'Brilliant'. The Daggers, accelerating to full speed, were gradually outpacing the Sea Harriers, but Martin Hale managed to get a missile lock-on and fired a somewhat hopeful AIM-9L at one of the departing jets. The Sidewinder exploded harmlessly some distance behind its target but both Sea Harriers continued to give chase until a combination of increasing distance between the combatants and a shortage of fuel on the part of the Sea Harriers forced the pair to call off their pursuit and return to 'Hermes'.

About 1517Z, Neill Thomas (in XZ492) and Mike Blissett (in XZ496) took-off from 'Hermes' for CAP duties. They arrived in the vicinity of Falkland Sound at 1557Z to be vectored immediately by 'Brilliant' towards a departing A-4B Skyhawk of Grupo 5. The aircraft, flown by Capitan Pablo Carballo, had narrowly missed bombing 'Ardent' in her exposed position in Grantham Sound. The Sea Harriers dived towards Chartres Settlement on West Falkland but failed to make contact with the Skyhawk. Instead, they spotted no less than three out of four Grupo 4 A-4C Skyhawks at low level over West Falkland heading north-east towards San Carlos Water. The Argentine pilots saw the Sea Harriers and tried evasive manoeuvres, but to no avail. At 1605Z Neill Thomas and Mike Blissett both achieved good lock-ons and each fired an AIM-9L at a different Skyhawk. Blissett's missile struck its target and caused the aircraft to explode. Thomas' Sidewinder had in the meantime streaked past Blissett towards its intended target, which was by now making for the limited cloud cover available. The missile followed the Skyhawk into the cloud and obviously struck home, as the aircraft was seen to fall out of the cloud in

flames and explode on hitting the ground. Both Argentine machines crashed almost simultaneously a few hundred yards apart to the south of Christmas Harbour near Chartres Settlement. A third Skyhawk was fired at by Blissett using his Aden cannon and was seen to leave the area with black smoke trailing from its port side. However, that Skyhawk managed to return safely to base, as did Thomas and Blissett to 'Hermes' at 1621Z.

*Site investigation (after the War) to the south of Christmas Harbour revealed an ejector seat marked C-309, this being the serial of the aircraft flown by Teniente Nestor Lopez who was buried at nearby Little Chartres. Primer Teniente Daniel Manzotti was killed in C-325, the other Skyhawk involved. There is some very circumstantial evidence which points to Blissett having shot down Manzotti and Thomas having brought down Lopez. The latter Argentine pilot managed to eject before impact but his unsuccessful escape was not seen by either of the 800 Sqdn pilots.*

Rod Frederiksen (in XZ455) and Andy George (in ZA176) got airborne from 'Hermes' at 1645Z on 21 May to provide increased CAP cover near San Carlos Water in anticipation of intensified air attacks on the assembled shipping. Whilst on patrol at 1715Z, 'Brilliant' vectored them towards a flight of four Grupo 6 Daggers (led by Capitan Horacio Mir Gonzalez) which had just crossed the west coast of West Falkland at King George Bay and then turned north-east towards the north end of Falkland Sound. The Sea Harrier pilots spotted the formation flying at low level and high speed just to the north of Chartres Settlement in the valley between Mounts Robinson and Maria. George fell in behind XZ455 to give cover while Frederiksen lined up on one of the left-hand pair of Daggers and launched an AIM-9L. The Sidewinder impacted C-409, the aircraft of Primer Teniente Hector Luna, and the pilot ejected just before his uncontrollable aircraft hit the ground at about 1735Z near Teal River Inlet. He survived with a sprained knee and a dislocated arm. The rest of the Dagger flight pressed on towards their objective, aware that they had lost one of their number but believing him to have flown into high ground. In the meantime, Frederiksen and George had fired a number of cannon bursts at the other Daggers but achieved no hits. The two Sea Harrier pilots recovered to 'Hermes' at 1815Z.

Prior to the return to 'Hermes' of George and Frederiksen, Clive Morrell (in XZ457) and John Leeming (in XZ500) had been launched from the ship at 1737Z to provide CAP cover at the southern end of Falkland Sound in what turned out to be a very eventful patrol. At 1810Z, just as the pair were coming overhead Darwin en route to their assigned CAP position, three 3 Escuadrilla A-4Q Skyhawks put several bombs into 'Ardent' in Grantham Sound near North West Island. The flight was led by Capitan de Corbeta Alberto Philippi in A-4Q 0660/3-A-307, with Teniente de Navio Jose Arca in 0665/3-A-312 and Teniente de Fragata Marcelo Marquez in 0667/3-A-314. Arca's aircraft was damaged in the attack, one wing having been hit by machine-gun fire as he passed over the ship. All three aircraft turned south-west down the Sound to make good their escape. Meanwhile, Morrell and Leeming, who had been monitoring radio reports of the attack, also witnessed some of its aftermath. Anticipating

Even carriers roll in heavy seas! Six 800 Squadron Sea Harrier FRS.1's are seen here tied down on 'Hermes'. Those identifiable are XZ460 '–/(1)26', XZ459 '–/(1)25', XZ455 '–/(7)12' and XZ457 '–/(7)14'. Beyond them, parked precariously on the stern, is an 815 Squadron 'Newcastle' Flight Lynx HAS.2 (either XZ240 or XZ720), maintained at a constant alert state for ESM and Exocet decoy duties.

(Ministry of Defence)

Armed either with bombs or Sidewinders on the crowded 'Hermes' flight-deck are 800 Squadron Sea Harrier FRS.1's and 1(F) Squadron Harrier GR.3's. The Sea King HAS.5 belongs to 826 Squadron. Both identifiable Sea Harriers (ZA191 '–/(7)18' and XZ499 '99') took part in successful attacks on Argentine shipping. ZA191 was used against 'Narwal' off East Falkland on 9.5.82 and 'Bahia Buen Suceso' at Fox Bay East on 16.5.82. XZ499 strafed the 'Rio Iguazu' in Choiseul Sound on 22.5.82. (Ministry of Defence)

'Hermes', photographed on an unknown date after 18.5.82, with Sea Harriers and Harriers arrayed on the deck. Note the absence of Sea Kings and the lone Lynx on her stern. The fleet replenishment ship in the background is, reportedly, 'Fort Austin'. She has a Sea King on her flight-deck.

(Ministry of Defence)

the Skyhawks' south-westerly escape route, both pilots sighted the light grey aircraft through a gap in the clouds abeam Swan Island and dived at full speed in their Sea Harriers to attack them. Clive Morrell fired an AIM-9L at Philippi's Skyhawk which impacted, blasting the rear fuselage into debris and flames. Philippi ejected safely, coming down in the water at Port King. Morrell attempted to launch a second missile at Arca's aircraft but suffered a "hang-up" and had to resort to cannon fire. Not seeing any hits, he tried selecting the missile again and, that time, it responded of its own volition! The Sidewinder launched satisfactorily but was apparently a rogue round as it did not reach the target which was well within range. Arca had in fact been hit by some of Morrell's shells and the cumulative effect of these hits and those of the guns aboard 'Ardent' had damaged the aircraft sufficiently to cause fuel leaks. Returning to the mainland was out of the question, so Arca decided to make for Stanley Airport for an emergency landing. Arriving overhead, he lowered his undercarriage and eventually managed to contact the airfield controller — only to be told that his port main undercarriage leg was missing! He had no option but to eject and as he descended by parachute he noticed that his Skyhawk was still flying. It was finally brought down by Argentine AAA fire and crashed on the shoreline some 400 yards south of the airfield perimeter. Arca came down in the sea and was picked up by a CAB601 UH-1H helicopter.

While Clive Morrell was attempting to shoot down Arca, John Leeming was also experiencing difficulties with his AIM-9L's and was left with no option but to attack the third Skyhawk with his cannon. He dived on Marquez' aircraft from above and behind at high speed, firing at a point just aft of the cockpit. The Skyhawk disintegrated, killing Marquez, and the Sea Harrier pilot was forced to fly through the debris which fell into Falkland Sound. Morrell and Leeming recovered to 'Hermes' by 1845Z at the end of 800 Sqdn's last combat action of the day (flying ceased at 2130Z).

An appraisal of the day's events showed that the British warships in exposed positions covering the landings had suffered as a result of some determined flying by Argentine pilots. Ships in less vulnerable positions had been able to hold at bay the worst of the air attacks by both self and mutual protection. While losses and damage (in some cases severe) to warships had been sustained, the vital logistics ships had come through the day unscathed. The Sea Harrier/AIM-9L combination had also proved deadly in thwarting many of the enemy air attacks. The mere fact that the landing of personnel and equipment on the Islands had been successful showed that the combination of naval, ground and air tactics was starting to swing the balance of advantage in favour of the British.

The next day brought a little respite which allowed the British positions to be consolidated. Bad weather on the mainland resulted in only one air raid, two unidentified Skyhawks appearing late in the day to make an ineffective bomb run over the San Carlos landing area. Although there was little Argentine action in the air, both 800 Sqdn and 801 Sqdn remained at a high state of readiness and provided full CAP cover. Whilst no air-to-air combat took place, 800 Sqdn's first CAP of the day successfully attacked an Argentine patrol boat. Rod Frederiksen (in

XZ460) and Martin Hale (in XZ499) had taken-off from 'Hermes' at 1053Z to patrol the southern end of Falkland Sound. As they came over Choiseul Sound, the two pilots spotted the Prefectura patrol vessel 'Rio Iguazu' heading up the Sound towards Goose Green settlement with vital weapons, ammunition and aircraft spares for Darwin and Goose Green. Frederiksen provided overhead cover as Hale strafed the boat at about 1125Z, causing it to be beached and abandoned at Button Bay near Bluff Creek House. Both Sea Harriers returned safely to 'Hermes' at 1205Z. The unfortunate patrol boat was further damaged on 13 June *[see 815 Sqdn Penelope Flight notes]*.

23 May was a day of considerable aerial activity for the Squadron. Dave Morgan (in ZA192) and John Leeming (in ZA191) were launched from 'Hermes' at 1246Z for CAP. At about 1330Z, whilst on patrol at 8,000ft over West Falkland, Morgan saw a helicopter flying over water at very low altitude near Shag Cove House. He descended rapidly and made a head-on fast pass to positively identify the type as a Puma which, by definition, had to be Argentine as there were no British Pumas serving with the Task Force. Leeming then spotted two more Pumas and an A-109A Hirundo. All four belonged to CAB601 and were on their way from Port Stanley to Port Howard on West Falkland (via Darwin), carrying munitions, including Blowpipe missiles, for the Argentine forces there. Rather than be exposed over water for a lengthy period, they had crossed Falkland Sound at its narrowest point opposite Shag Cove House and were just turning northeast towards Port Howard when Dave Morgan saw the lead helicopter. The Pumas consisted of AE-503 in front followed by AE-500 and AE-508, with "gunship" A-109A AE-337 bringing up the rear. Morgan's first pass caused the pilot of AE-503 to take violent avoiding action and head for the relative safety of the nearby shore. Unfortunately, the pilot's desperate manoeuvres (possibly made worse by turbulent wake from the Sea Harrier) caused him to lose control of the helicopter, which then crash-landed on a hillside. Fortunately, the crew had just enough time to scramble clear before it caught fire and exploded. Aware of the Sea Harriers' presence, the other helicopters scattered, but they were progressively sighted by John Leeming. The A-109A had sought cover and was attempting to remain inconspicuous near a stream in a ravine some 2,000 yards to the south-west of the position where AE-503 crashed. Its crew had already abandoned the helicopter to its fate when it was seen by Leeming. He immediately attacked with Aden cannon fire and, after two or three strafing runs by both Leeming and Morgan, the heavily-armed AE-337 exploded.

The remaining two Pumas had gone to ground a few hundred yards north of AE-503 and remained inconspicuous. Both Morgan and Leeming stayed within visual distance of the wrecked Puma's position, each of them looking for the other two helicopters or some sign of movement. They were soon rewarded. An eagle-eyed Leeming caught sight of one of the missing Pumas (AE-500) very close to the remains of AE-503. *(The crew of AE-500 must have assumed that the Sea Harriers had departed as they had flown their helicopter across from its relatively safe hideaway to the downed Puma to search for survivors.)* Unfortunately, Leeming was unable to attack it because he had run out of ammunition. The Puma crew, by then realising that their helicopter had been seen, were not to know that and wisely evacuated AE-500 to maintain a low profile some distance away. Luckily, Morgan had a few rounds left which he fired into the Puma leaving it in a non-flyable condition.

Not only had the Sea Harriers exhausted their ammunition, but they were also running very low on fuel. That compelled Morgan and Leeming to break off the engagement and return to 'Hermes'. As they left the area the fourth Puma was seen, but there was nothing that they could do about it. Prior to their departure, an 801 Sqdn CAP consisting of Lt Cdrs T.J.H.Gedge (in XZ494) and D.D.Braithwaite (in ZA190) was ordered down to finish off AE-500 and, if seen, AE-508. They arrived on the scene about 20-25 minutes after Morgan's last strafing run and proceeded to attack AE-500 with cannon fire, destroying it completely. AE-508 was not found *[see CAB601 notes for details of that helicopter's subsequent actions]*. It should be noted that Argentine sources claim that AE-500 was destroyed by its crew before the 801 Sqdn attack, a view not shared by the Sea Harrier pilots.

Argentine air attacks that day were sporadic. Opportunities for raids were being more carefully assessed by the Argentines by making better use of ground observation reports, aerial reconnaissance data and Sea Harrier positional data plotted by Island-based radar units. Just before 1900Z, two Grupo 6 Daggers (possibly part of a flight of four) started a run-in over Pebble Island towards San Carlos Water then suddenly broke off their approach and turned back on to reciprocal headings, probably as a result of being warned by an Argentine radar controller that there were Sea Harriers in their area. Andy Auld (in ZA177) and Martin Hale (in ZA194) were on CAP over West Falkland when Hale noticed a Dagger at low level over Pebble Island. He tried to give chase but the Argentine aircraft was pulling away from him. However, all was not lost as, just at that moment, he saw another Dagger some way behind the first one. The Argentine pilot saw him almost simultaneously and began to accelerate, but Martin Hale was able to get in behind him, lock-on and fire an AIM-9L. The Sidewinder impacted the Dagger and it exploded killing the pilot, Teniente Hector Volponi. The remains of the aircraft (C-437) came down on the west side of Elephant Bay about two miles north of Pebble Island settlement.

During 23 May, reconnaissance reports had been received which indicated the presence of arrester gear on the runway at Port Stanley, suggesting that the Airport was being prepared to receive additional jet aircraft, perhaps even some Super Etendards. Whilst that was unlikely, action needed to be taken to prevent such a possibility. Four 800 Sqdn Sea Harriers were prepared for a night toss-bombing raid on the Airport, each carrying three 1,000lb radar air-burst VT bombs. The launch, originally scheduled for about 1900Z, was delayed until 2250Z. Neill Thomas (in XZ496), Mike Blissett (in XZ500) and Andy Auld (in XZ455) launched successfully, each delivering their three bombs on the airfield. The fourth aircraft, ZA192 flown by "Gordy" Batt, was seen to explode shortly after take-off, either just before or just after hitting the sea. Lt Cdr Batt, a most respected, experienced

and capable aviator, was killed. The cause of the accident, which occurred about 90 miles north-east of Port Stanley, was not established.

A follow-up attack to the previous night's raid took place on 24 May. Neill Thomas (in XZ496) and Mike Blissett (in ZA191) took-off from 'Hermes' at 1203Z/ 1204Z armed with 1,000lb radar air-burst VT bombs to provide defence suppression in support of four 1(F) Sqdn Harrier GR.3's. The Sea Harriers attacked from the north-east and toss-bombed, clear of the Argentine guns and missiles. They succeeded in distracting the defences for long enough to allow the first pair of GR.3's a clear run in from the north-west with Retard bombs. The other pair attacked from the west and although bombs were dropped on the runway it was not put out of action. All the Sea Harriers and Harriers had recovered safely to 'Hermes' by 1300Z.

800 Sqdn's next action of the day came shortly afterwards. Andy Auld (in XZ457) and Dave Smith (in ZA193) were launched for CAP at 1330Z, by which time 'Broadsword' and 'Coventry' had moved to a position north of Pebble Island in order to provide better radar cover to the north and north-west. Around 1415Z 'Broadsword' directed the two Sea Harriers towards an incoming flight of four Grupo 6 Daggers flying low and fast over Pebble Island, heading towards San Carlos Water. Both of the Sea Harriers dropped from 10,000ft to low level and when Auld saw three of the Daggers he swept in behind and fired both Sidewinders at two of the targets. Both missiles struck home and the two aircraft exploded, their remains tumbling into the sea. In the meantime, Smith engaged the third Dagger from an extremely awkward angle, but his AIM-9L locked-on and intercepted its target half-way round the trajectory and destroyed it. The wreck of that aircraft is thought to lie on the slopes of First Mount on the western edge of Elephant Bay near the Pebble Island settlement. The fourth intruder jettisoned its bombs and drop tanks and headed for home. Of the three downed pilots, Mayor Luis Puga (in C-419) and Capitan Raul Diaz (in C-430) ejected successfully, but Teniente Carlos Castillo (in C-410) was killed. Circumstantial and other unconfirmed evidence points to Auld having shot down Puga and Diaz, which would mean that Castillo was Smith's victim.

25 May, Argentina's National Day, was full of traumatic events from the British point of view. At about 1417Z, Neill Thomas (in XZ455) and Clive Morrell (in ZA191) got airborne from 'Hermes' to toss-bomb Stanley Airport prior to a run-in by four 1(F) Sqdn Harrier GR.3's. The aircraft all returned safely to the carrier about 1456Z. Later in the day, 'Broadsword' was damaged and 'Coventry' sunk by bombs from Grupo 5 Skyhawks, while 'Atlantic Conveyor' was mortally wounded in an Exocet attack carried out by a pair of 2 Escuadrilla Super Etendards.

800 Sqdn was involved only as a frustrated onlooker during the 'Broadsword' and 'Coventry' incidents. A raid was detected by both ships at around 1800Z and CAP cover was called for. Neill Thomas (in XZ496) and Dave Smith (in XZ459) were vectored towards the incoming aircraft which consisted of four A-4B Skyhawks from Grupo 5. The Skyhawk flight split into two separate attack elements, one pair flown by Capitan Carballo and Teniente

Carlos Rinke heading for 'Broadsword', while 'Coventry' became the target for the other pair which were being flown by Primer Teniente Mariano Velasco and Alferez Barrionuevo. Carballo and his wing-man were seen by Neill Thomas, who dived at the hostiles and got within three miles of them before being ordered to break off the interception. The Seawolf system on 'Broadsword' had locked-on to the two Skyhawks and the last thing that was wanted was for the missiles to achieve a lock-on to the Sea Harrier as well! All went well until the ship's missile control radar malfunctioned and contact was lost meaning that the Seawolf missiles could not be fired. The Skyhawks pressed home their attack and, of the four bombs dropped, three missed the ship while the fourth bounced off the sea and then entered the hull without exploding. Its momentum carried it up through the flight-deck, taking the nose of Lynx XZ729 with it, still without going off. The bomb's trajectory took it in an arc over the ship's side to disappear beneath the surface of the sea — still without detonating! 'Broadsword' had been extremely fortunate; 'Coventry' was less lucky. Whilst the 'Broadsword' incident was in progress, the other two Skyhawks were homing-in on the destroyer. The Sea Harrier CAP headed for that pair but was again ordered to clear the missile zone as 'Coventry' unsuccessfully attempted to shoot down at least one of the Grupo 5 aircraft with a Sea Dart. 'Broadsword' then locked-on to the targets and was just about to launch her Seawolf missiles when 'Coventry', in trying to present a smaller target to her attackers, turned between the Skyhawks and 'Broadsword' thus breaking the missile radar's lock-on and rendering both ships defenceless. A few minutes later 'Coventry' was sinking, three bombs having penetrated her hull, entered machinery spaces and exploded. The Skyhawks escaped unscathed and the Sea Harriers, which had been orbiting helplessly, recovered to 'Hermes' very short of fuel. Another 800 Sqdn CAP consisting of Andy Auld (in ZA177) and Ted Ball (in ZA176) arrived overhead 'Coventry' just before the ship finally capsized at 1922Z.

At 1927Z, within minutes of 'Coventry' capsizing, Clive Morrell (in ZA194) and Andy McHarg (in XZ460) took-off from 'Hermes' accompanied by a single 1(F) Sqdn Harrier GR.3 for a toss-bombing raid on Stanley Airport. Four minutes after they departed, two 2 Escuadrilla Super Etendards were detected heading towards the two Task Force carriers. By 1935Z ten of the Squadron's Sea Harriers were airborne and seeking the raiders, but to no avail because at 1936Z 'Atlantic Conveyor', positioned some 2 miles to starboard of 'Hermes', was hit by one of the two missiles fired by the Super Etendard pilots (Capitan de Corbeta Roberto Curilovic and Teniente de Navio Julio Barraza). Neither 800 nor 801 Sqdn Sea Harriers were able to intercept the Super Etendards, which had launched their missiles at low level from a position about 31 miles north of the two carriers before making off at high speed to the north-west.

Meanwhile, the toss-bombing trio which had set off for Port Stanley had not met with much success as their bombs had fallen short. That in itself was disappointing, but more worrying was the report that they brought back to 'Hermes' at 2041Z. Super Etendards, or something similar, had been sighted on the airfield. The dilemma

was, were they or were they not Super Etendards? It was possible (the presence of arrester gear had been noted on 23 May), but not probable, that they might have been the pair which attacked 'Atlantic Conveyor'. Mike Blissett, Clive Morrell and Andy McHarg were launched in their Sea Harriers from 'Hermes' at 2155Z for a toss-bombing raid on the Airport, their aircraft armed with VT-fused bombs, in the hope that the "Super Etendards" would be hit. They returned to 'Hermes' at 2255Z having carried out their task but unsure of their success, if any. *(The "Super Etendards" were in fact 1 Escuadrilla MB-339A's which, along with decoys, were mistaken for Super Etendards or "swept-wing fighters" on numerous occasions from that date until the end of the conflict.)*

By 26 May 'Hermes' had moved to a position about 200 miles east of the Falkland Islands. Attacks by Argentine aircraft were few and far between for the next few days. Full CAP was maintained and bombing raids carried out, the latter including the resumption of bombing Stanley Airport en route to CAP stations.

On 29 May a policy of bombing Stanley Airport from dawn to dusk using CAP aircraft (or other tasked sorties) was introduced. The idea was that irregular bombing throughout the day would interrupt airfield operations, deny or discourage any high performance aircraft from using the airfield and, hopefully, disrupt or even stop the Grupo 1 C-130 resupply flights. Typical of the pressure exerted on the Argentine forces at the Airport, and elsewhere, were the following examples of 800 Sqdn operations that day. A tasked sortie consisting of Mike Blissett (in XZ455) and Bill Covington (in XZ496) was launched from 'Hermes' at 1208Z to toss-bomb the Airport. Both aircraft returned at 1305Z and 30 minutes later Andy Auld (in XZ500) and Andy McHarg (in XZ460) took-off to drop bombs on the grass runways at the Pebble Island airstrip in order to deny their use to Pucaras and light transport aircraft which might still be using the airstrip to ferry freight or passengers between the mainland and the Islands. Prior to their return, Clive Morrell (in XZ455) and Neill Thomas (in XZ496) got airborne from 'Hermes' at 1430Z for another raid on Stanley Airport. Auld and McHarg recovered at 1437Z, having successfully bombed one runway at Pebble Island. Morrell and Thomas landed back aboard the carrier at 1525Z and 30 minutes later Blissett (in XZ500) and Covington (in XZ460) were launched again for yet another toss-bombing mission to the Airport. They witnessed six of their bombs exploding on the airfield prior to recovering to 'Hermes' at 1655Z. At 1737Z Auld (in XZ496) and McHarg (in XZ455) took-off to bomb the other runway at Pebble Island airfield. That they did and returned safely to the carrier. In addition to all those sorties (carried out in poor weather), there were other missions, CAP patrols and 1(F) Sqdn Harrier GR.3 taskings. The combination of random daylight bombing and night shelling from British warships must have made life fairly miserable for the Argentine forces dug-in at Stanley Airport.

Reports were received during the afternoon of 29 May that three Pucaras had been seen landing at Port Stanley Racecourse. There was little that could be done about it by 800 Sqdn Sea Harriers due to the enemy defences and the proximity of civilian dwellings which precluded bombing. The newly-established FOB strip just west of Port

San Carlos settlement was assessed that day for possible use by Harriers and Sea Harriers, but was unfortunately not yet considered suitable.

The poor weather of 29 May gave way to better weather on 30 May. As well as normal CAP operations, 800 Sqdn carried out the by then standard missions against Stanley Airport. Neill Thomas (in XZ500) and Ted Ball (in XZ496) were launched from 'Hermes' at 1717Z and set course to toss-bomb the airfield, on that occasion with poor results. About 1915Z Clive Morrell (in ZA176) and Rod Frederiksen (in XZ499) took-off for a photo-reconnaissance mission over East Falkland. Soon after their departure from the carrier the last Argentine Super Etendard/Exocet attack of the conflict took place which, although very well executed, achieved nothing in spite of Argentine claims to the contrary. The single missile fired by Capitan de Corbeta Alejandro Francisco (in 0752/3-A-202) passed through the fleet without hitting anything until, fuel exhausted, it fell into the sea. The Exocet appears to have either malfunctioned or been successfully deflected by British countermeasures. CAP Sea Harriers vectored towards the Super Etendards gave chase but with no hope of catching them, while a coincident attack by four Grupo 4 A-4C Skyhawks came to nothing for the loss of two of them (C-301 and C-310) to Sea Darts fired from 'Exeter'. By the time that Morrell and Frederiksen recovered to 'Hermes' at 2005Z the excitement was over!

At 1430Z on 31 May, a returning 801 Sqdn CAP Sea Harrier pilot saw and photographed what he thought were "swept-wing jets" at the eastern end of the Stanley Airport runway. Again, they were almost certainly the now immobilised 1 Escuadrilla MB-339A's but the potential threat could not be dismissed. A raid was hurriedly organised. At 1453Z Bill Covington (in XZ496) and Mike Blissett (in XZ500) were launched from 'Hermes' along with two 1(F) Sqdn Harrier GR.3's. The Sea Harriers were to provide defence suppression support (using toss-bombs) whilst the Harriers carried out a rocket attack. All the aircraft recovered to 'Hermes' about an hour later, the GR.3's having suffered battle damage during the raid. An MB-339A was reportedly damaged but that was never confirmed.

Later that day 800 Sqdn was involved in an interesting mission. Sea Harrier ZA191 was fitted with two LGB's with the idea of using a laser-designator equipped 1(F) Sqdn Harrier GR.3 to illuminate a target (or targets) for it. Clive Morrell was the chosen pilot and at 1647Z that day he took-off (in ZA191) along with the GR.3. Accompanying them were Rod Frederiksen (in XZ460) and Andy McHarg (in XZ455) whose Sea Harriers were armed with normal 1,000lb bombs. *[See 1(F) Sqdn notes for details of the operation.]* All the aircraft recovered safely to 'Hermes' at 1752Z.

Andy McHarg (in ZA177) was launched from the carrier at 0739Z on 1 June to be vectored towards a group of unidentified, high-flying aircraft (thought to be four in number) approaching East Falkland from the south-west. By the time McHarg came within striking distance of the intruders, he was at extreme range from 'Hermes' and the enemy aircraft were north of Mount Kent heading north. He got within 4 miles of one of them and identified it as a Canberra just before the Argentine pilot jettisoned his wing tanks, fired chaff and made for the mainland as fast as possible and by the shortest route. Due to his fuel state, McHarg was unable to give chase. Reluctantly, he turned away and recovered to 'Hermes' at 0855Z. The aircraft which he came so close to catching was in fact one of a pair of Grupo 2 Canberras which had taken-off from Rio Gallegos for a night bombing attack on Mount Kent *[See Grupo 2 notes for full details of the mission].*

Accompanied by a 1(F) Sqdn Harrier GR.3, Ted Ball (in XZ457) took-off from 'Hermes' at 1700Z that afternoon for a photo-reconnaissance sortie over the Islands and returned to the carrier at 1810Z. Prior to their recovery, John Leeming (in ZA177) had escorted two 1(F) Sqdn Harrier GR.3's over the last leg of their exhausting 8 hour 25 minutes flight from Ascension Island to 'Hermes', where they landed at 1732Z.

Of more immediate concern were intelligence reports concerning Argentine Sea King activities on or near the airfield at Pebble Island late the previous evening, the helicopters possibly armed with Exocet missiles. A reconnaissance sortie was quickly organised, resulting in Rod Frederiksen (in XZ500) and Dave Morgan (in ZA193) being launched at 1816Z to try to establish the accuracy of the reports. Half an hour later two 801 Sqdn Sea Harriers took-off from 'Invincible' to strafe the helicopters, if found. Nothing was sighted by either the 801 Sqdn pilots or Neill Thomas (in XZ492) and Andy McHarg (in ZA177) who had launched from 'Hermes' at 1936Z with the same objective. *(The Sea Kings did in fact exist; they belonged to 2 Escuadrilla de Helicopteros but were not Exocet-armed [refer to the 2 Escuadrilla de Helicopteros notes for details].)*

No unusual events involving 800 Sqdn occurred on 2 June and by the next day poor visibility, low cloud and fog had settled in. The fog lasted until 5 June, lifting at about 1100Z that day to allow the CAP to be launched. It closed in again shortly afterwards, causing Andy Auld (in XZ499) and Simon Hargreaves to become the first Task Force Harrier pilots to land at the FOB close to Port San Carlos settlement which had "opened for business" for the first time that day. The strip was 850ft long and constructed of 10ft by 2ft aluminium planking. There were also refuelling facilities, a vertical landing pad and two taxying loops at one end (one for refuelling and the other for parking). It had been built on a slight incline which aided take-offs but, of course, was nothing like as effective as a ski-jump. One of the taxy loops was later removed (after 8 June). In Naval circles the FOB soon became known as "HMS Sheathbill", whilst Air Force personnel referred to it as "Sid's Strip" after the FOB OC, Sqdn Ldr Sid Morris. Auld and Hargreaves flew four sorties from there before returning to 'Hermes' when the weather improved at about 1730Z. The advantage of the FOB was that it enabled the Sea Harriers to respond more quickly to attack and air defence taskings and increased the CAP on-station time by a factor of almost three.

Following intelligence reports of an enemy mobile land-launched MM38 Exocet system having arrived on the Islands, 800 Sqdn was tasked, in conjunction with 1(F) Sqdn, with seeking it out. To this end, at about 1850Z on 5 June, Clive Morrell (in XZ500) and Hugh Slade (in XZ457) got airborne along with two 1(F) Sqdn Harrier GR.3's and set off on an armed photo-reconnaissance sortie to the south and south-west of Port Stanley in search

# SEA HARRIER FRS.1 ZA177 '77' 800 NAVAL AIR SQUADRON

Flown by Flt Lt Morgan on 8 June 1982 when he shot down Grupo 5 de Caza A-4B Skyhawks C-226 and C-228.

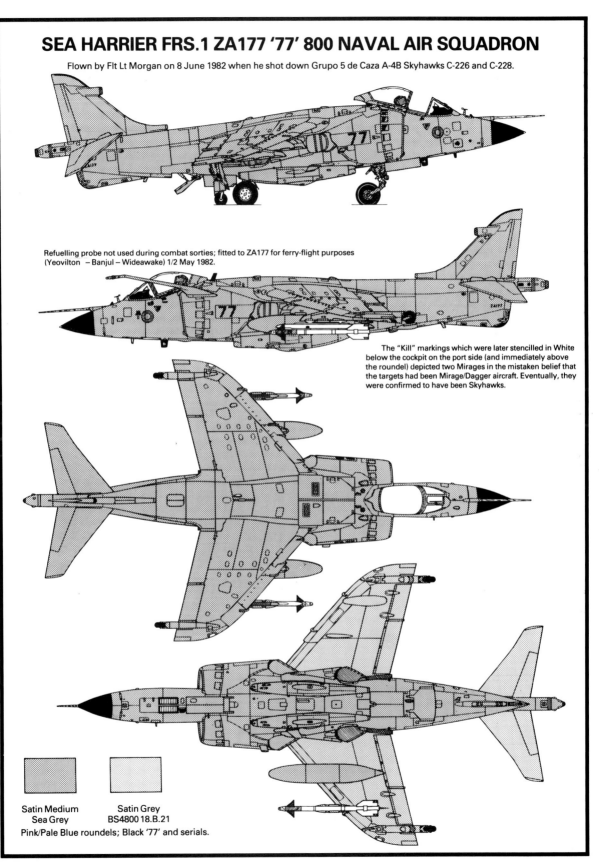

Refuelling probe not used during combat sorties; fitted to ZA177 for ferry-flight purposes
(Yeovilton – Banjul – Wideawake) 1/2 May 1982.

The "Kill" markings which were later stencilled in White
below the cockpit on the port side (and immediately above
the roundel) depicted two Mirages in the mistaken belief that
the targets had been Mirage/Dagger aircraft. Eventually, they
were confirmed to have been Skyhawks.

Satin Medium
Sea Grey

Satin Grey
BS4800 18.B.21

Pink/Pale Blue roundels; Black '77' and serials.

of the missile unit. They recovered at 2000Z having found nothing. It later transpired that the Exocets and launch tubes had been removed from an Argentine warship and brought to Stanley Airport in late May on one of the Grupo 1 C-130 resupply flights. Mounted on a trailer, the unit remained within the safe confines of Port Stanley *[see photograph]*, eventually being successfully used against 'Glamorgan' on 12 June.

On 6 June bad weather again hampered Sea Harrier patrol missions. A pair of 1(F) Sqdn Harrier GR.3's took-off from 'Hermes' (which was at that time some 240 miles east of Port Stanley) for a positioning flight to the FOB, where the poor weather limited operations to helicopters for most of the day. A two-aircraft CAP was launched from 'Hermes' at 1415Z but, that apart, little of note happened to 800 Sqdn that day.

7 June proved to be a fine, clear day and one on which the FOB came into full use. The first CAP of the day was launched from 'Hermes' earlier than usual in an attempt to intercept the regular early morning Grupo 1 C-130 re-supply flight, but no Hercules was detected on that occasion. Those aircraft had led a charmed life despite Operation "Canbelow" which had been mounted to intercept Canberras and Hercules *[see the 801 Sqdn, Grupo 1 and Grupo 2 notes for more details]*.

8 June was another fine day and, once again, it was intended that the air defence Sea Harriers and ground support GR.3's would make full use of the FOB. No enemy aerial activity was reported during the morning, but no chances could be taken and CAP was maintained. A detachment of GR.3's was sent to the FOB from 'Hermes' (positioned about 250 miles east of the Falkland Islands) to support British ground forces as and when needed. Upon arrival at Port San Carlos at about 1500Z, one of the Harriers (flown by OC 1(F) Sqdn) suffered a mechanical malfunction and crash-landed across the strip, effectively putting the FOB out of action for a few hours. Whether denial of access to the FOB during the afternoon was crucial or not to later events that day is purely conjecture, but it did mean that for a while all CAP cover by 800 and 801 Sqdns had to originate from the carriers with a corresponding reduction in continuous CAP cover and patrol loiter time.

At the time of the FOB accident, 'Sir Tristram' and 'Sir Galahad' were both anchored at Port Pleasant (near Fitzroy), off-loading troops and equipment. Their activities were witnessed by Argentine observers and an air strike from the mainland was asked for. The request initially resulted in eight A-4B Skyhawks from Grupo 5 and six Daggers from Grupo 6 taking-off from Rio Gallegos and Rio Grande to attack the ships. In the event, one of the Daggers was forced to return while the other five got embroiled with 'Plymouth' at about 1700Z in Falkland Sound. The ship was damaged and the Daggers escaped unscathed back to the mainland despite ferocious gun and missile fire from 'Plymouth' and a subsequent chase by CAP Sea Harriers. In the meantime, the five remaining Skyhawks (three having returned to base with technical problems) tracked to the south of the Islands then flew up the east coast of East Falkland to successfully bomb the two RFA's, with considerable loss of British life. The Skyhawks escaped back to the mainland as there was no CAP cover (it having been sent to the aid of 'Plymouth')

and little effective ground fire.

At 1850Z Dave Morgan (in ZA177) and Dave Smith (in XZ499) took off from the carrier on an armed "Duskers" (Naval parlance for dusk/night take-offs and landings) qualification and CAP sortie. Whilst flying at 10,000ft over Choiseul Sound about 1945Z, just as he was about to return to 'Hermes', Morgan noticed a landing-craft ('Foxtrot 4' from 'Fearless') heading towards Fitzroy from Goose Green. More importantly he realised that it was about to be attacked by a Skyhawk which was in fact one of a flight of four A-4B's from Grupo 5. Morgan dived his aircraft at full speed, followed by Smith. As they descended, they progressively spotted all four of the Skyhawks and watched a bomb exploding on the landing-craft. Morgan turned hard and fast behind the back marker and fired an AIM-9L from a range of 1,000 yards, hitting the Skyhawk which fireballed, its debris tumbling into the Sound near Philimore Island. He then pulled over and immediately fired his second AIM-9L at another aircraft, hitting it in the tail area causing the fuselage to break in two and fall into the sea some two miles north of Middle Island. Morgan then made a desperate attempt to bring down a third Skyhawk with his cannon. Unfortunately his HUD was ineffective but the splashes of his cannon shells on the surface of the water provided Smith with enough visual cues to fire a Sidewinder from two to three miles range. That missile hit the Skyhawk at extremely low level and the aircraft struck the ground on the northern shore of Lafonia, exploding on impact (it is possible that the Skyhawk hit the shoreline before the missile caught up with it). Teniente Hector Sanchez flying the fourth aircraft, realising what was happening, jettisoned his bombs and drop tanks and made off at high speed back towards the mainland. Morgan's first AIM-9L had in fact shot down Teniente Juan Arraras (in C-226) who was killed. His second missile brought down Teniente Alfredo Vazquez (in C-228) who managed to eject (Morgan's Sea Harrier very nearly snagged his parachute) but he did not survive. The wreck of the third Skyhawk was later found at Rain Cove near Island Creek and identified as C-204, its unfortunate pilot being Primer Teniente Danilo Bolzan.

Morgan and Smith recovered to 'Hermes' at 2016Z and 2018Z respectively. During the latter stages of the engagement a high-level 801 Sqdn CAP comprising Lt Cdr "Sharkey" Ward and Lt Steve Thomas arrived on the scene. They were about to chase the fourth Grupo 5 Skyhawk when warned of high-flying jets which turned out to be Mirages from Grupo 8, presumably providing high-altitude cover. As the two Sea Harriers approached they turned away back towards the mainland. It is worth noting that the "kill" markings eventually painted on ZA177 and XZ499 depicted Mirages (ie Daggers) and not Skyhawks; Dave Morgan apparently originally thought that they were Skyhawks but was subsequently "talked out of it"! The other significant event of the day was the arrival aboard 'Hermes' at 1700Z of another two Harrier GR.3's which had flown direct to the ship from Ascension Island. They were escorted during the latter stages of the flight by Ted Ball in ZA177.

The FOB was available for use again on 9 June which was welcome news to 800 Sqdn as 'Hermes' was then operating about 260 miles east of the Falkland Islands.

**Far Left** *Sea Harrier FRS.1 ZA192 '92' of 800 Squadron, patched after being struck by anti-aircraft gunfire during the "... I counted them all back" attack on Stanley Airport on 1.5.82.* **Left** *The same aircraft on 'Hermes' on 23.5.82 just a few hours before it exploded shortly after taking-off from the carrier killing its pilot, Lt Cdr "Gordy" Batt. In the background, keeping station with 'Hermes', is 'Broadsword'.*
*(Flt Lt D. H. S. Morgan, RAF)*

*The 850ft aluminium planking runway that was laid down close to Port San Carlos settlement was a valuable facility. For air defence purposes the elimination of long transit flights to and from the carriers now allowed the Sea Harriers more time on CAP. Identifiable on the taxy loop close to the refuelling pipeline is ZA194 '94' of 800 Squadron. The helicopters in the foreground are just "visiting".*
*(Ministry of Defence)*

*The temporary closure of the aluminium runway on 13.6.82 caused two CAP Sea Harrier FRS.1's of 800 Squadron to divert to 'Fearless' and 'Intrepid' in San Carlos Water. Safely down on the 'Fearless' flight-deck is XZ455 '–/(7)12' and* **(Inset)** *about to land on 'Intrepid' is ZA177 '77'. (Ministry of Defence)*

The Squadron made no contact with enemy aircraft that day in spite of a warning at about 1900Z of a potential attack approaching from the west. Ten 800 Sqdn Sea Harriers took up suitable CAP positions but the unidentified aircraft turned away, back towards the mainland.

Good weather prevailed from 9 to 11 June but the Squadron still had no contacts with Argentine aircraft. However, on 11 June, following reports of three Grupo 3 Pucaras attacking British troop positions on Mount Kent at dawn on 10 June *[see Grupo 3 notes for more details]*, an early morning raid on Stanley Airport (where the Pucaras were thought to be based) was organised. Four 800 Sqdn Sea Harriers were armed with a total of 12 1,000lb VT-fused radar air-burst bombs, to be tossed onto the airfield just after dawn. Andy Auld (in XZ455), Neill Thomas (in XZ496), Mike Blissett (in XZ494) and Clive Morrell (in XZ459) were launched from the carrier between 1058Z and 1100Z and set course for Port Stanley. As they approached the airfield the Argentine defenders let fly with everything they had, including SA-7's, Tigercats, Blowpipes and guns. It was like a repeat of 1 May and just as dangerous. The Sea Harriers closed to four miles, pulled up, released their bombs and escaped unscathed at low level back to 'Hermes', where they touched down between 1200Z and 1203Z. 11 of the bombs exploded as planned on or above the airfield and were seen to have started fires. The results of their efforts were not determined by reconnaissance due to cloud cover. *(Grupo 3 admits to an unserviceable aircraft being destroyed in the attack. However, it did not prevent the unit from mounting another Pucara raid against the same British positions at dusk that evening.)*

The first CAP of the day from 'Hermes' on 12 June made a reconnaissance run over West Falkland in an unsuccessful bid to locate an elusive Grupo 1 C-130, but was forced to return to the carrier as the FOB was unavailable due to fog and ice. A CAP from either 'Hermes' or 'Invincible' apparently failed to notice a 3 Escuadrilla A-4Q Skyhawk flown by Teniente de Navio Benito Rotolo about to attack troop positions near Goose Green. However, the Skyhawk pilot said he saw what he thought were two Sea Harriers and made off at high speed back to the mainland, having jettisoned his underwing stores.

Dawn on 13 June heralded another generally quiet day from the Squadron's point of view. Intelligence reports stated that at 1056Z a Grupo 1 C-130 was sitting on Stanley Airport with engines running. Despite some rapid planning, the aircraft managed to escape yet again at about 1155Z. In addition, a number of possible raids were driven back by the CAP or aborted as soon as the CAP arrived. After early morning fog, an unusual incident took place at Port San Carlos. Neill Thomas (in XZ455) and Simon Hargreaves (in ZA177) were about to land at the FOB to refuel when 18 Sqdn's sole Chinook HC.1 (ZA718/BN) lifted sections of the strip with its rotor downwash. XZ455 diverted to 'Fearless' and ZA177 to 'Intrepid'; their flight-decks had been offered for use on other occasions but that was the first time that the offer had been, somewhat gratefully, taken up. Once refuelled, they were ready to lift off and return to the, by then, repaired strip. Coincident with this, Argentine aircraft were detected, causing the rapid departure of the Sea Harriers from the two ships. No sooner were they airborne

than the threat was declared a false alarm and both aircraft recovered to the FOB. Another two Grupo 1 C-130's landed at Stanley Airport after dark that night and once again made good their escape.

The last significant action of the conflict for 800 Sqdn took place during the night of 13/14 June. A CAP was scrambled at 2335Z and again at 0132Z in response to potential raids from the south-west. On the first occasion the intruders turned away as the CAP approached. On the second occasion the raiders initially held off but finally flew north to the west of Port Stanley. The aircraft were a pair of Grupo 2 Canberras with an escort of two Grupo 8 Mirage III's. By 0155Z they were within range of the Sea Darts aboard 'Exeter' and 'Cardiff'. It was then that one of the CAP Sea Harrier pilots (Mike Blissett) witnessed the flash of an explosion as a Sea Dart from 'Exeter' hit, and destroyed, a Canberra (B-108). The pilot (Capitan Roberto Pastran) ejected safely but his navigator (Capitan Fernando Juan Casado) was unable to eject and was killed. 'Cardiff' had fired at the Mirages but, unlike 'Exeter', her Sea Darts fell short.

The surrender of all Argentine forces on the Islands became effective from 2359Z on 14 June. 800 Sqdn Sea Harriers operating from 'Hermes', the FOB and latterly Stanley Airport continued to provide CAP cover to discourage any Argentine post-surrender aggression. As tension eased over the next two weeks, it became apparent that the Argentine air arms were not going to make any further raids and therefore major elements of the British Task Force could return to the United Kingdom. MoD(Navy) had already decided that 'Invincible' would remain in the TEZ for a few more months and 'Hermes' would detach home, but before that could happen 'Invincible' and her Squadrons were to be allowed to withdraw from the area between 19 June and 1 July for crew rest and recuperation and essential ship and aircraft maintenance.

On 20 June the four 809 Sqdn pilots (Hugh Slade, Bill Covington, John Leeming and Steve Brown), who had been integrated into 800 Sqdn when they arrived on 'Hermes' from 'Atlantic Conveyor', were officially transferred to 800 Sqdn. Rod Frederiksen and Simon Hargreaves left the Squadron that day for home, some leave and then 809 Sqdn (which was working-up at Yeovilton for deployment aboard 'Illustrious').

Towards the end of June some statistics appeared, detailing 800 Sqdn operations during the period 2 April to 16 June:

*1,126 sorties flown*
*1,299 flying hours amassed*
*14 AIM-9L Sidewinders launched (including one which failed to guide and another fired out of range)*
*1 AIM-9G Sidewinder fired in practice*

'Invincible' returned to the TEZ on 1 July. Two 800 Sqdn Sea Harriers (XZ455 and XZ494, flown by Andy McHarg and Andy George) were flown across to her from 'Hermes' on 2 July to increase 801 Sqdn's complement of aircraft and pilots. The increase was necessary to cover air defence commitments within the TEZ and over the Falkland Islands during the coming months.

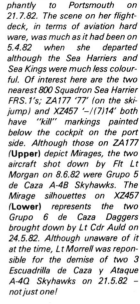

**Top** 'Hermes' returns triumphantly to Portsmouth on 21.7.82. The scene on her flight-deck, in terms of aviation hardware, was much as it had been on 5.4.82 when she departed although the Sea Harriers and Sea Kings were much less colourful. Of interest here are the two nearest 800 Squadron Sea Harrier FRS.1's; ZA177 '77' (on the ski-jump) and XZ457 '–/(7)14' both have "kill" markings painted below the cockpit on the port side. Although those on ZA177 **(Upper)** depict Mirages, the two aircraft shot down by Flt Lt Morgan on 8.6.82 were Grupo 5 de Caza A-4B Skyhawks. The Mirage silhouettes on XZ457 **(Lower)** represents the two Grupo 6 de Caza Daggers brought down by Lt Cdr Auld on 24.5.82. Although unaware of it at the time, Lt Morrell was reponsible for the demise of two 3 Escuadrilla de Caza y Ataque A-4Q Skyhawks on 21.5.82 – not just one!

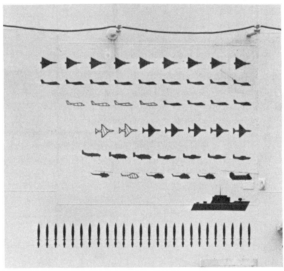

'Hermes' had stencilled on her island the tally of Argentine aircraft (and a ship) thought to have been destroyed or damaged as a result of attacks by the carrier's Sea Harriers or Special Forces inserted behind enemy lines by her helicopters. The daggers represent clandestine operations. Carefully removed before arriving at Portsmouth were the silhouettes of two whales, both "sunk" when suspected of being Argentine submarines! **(Top** J. Flack; **Others** Peter J. Cooper)

After the conflict Sidewinder-armed Sea Harrier FRS.1's and Harrier GR.3's were the only fighter aircraft that could be based at RAF Stanley until the runway was repaired and lengthened. Here, at immediate readiness and fitted with a 190 gallon drop tank and two Sidewinders beneath each wing, is 809 Squadron's ZA194 '–/251'. 29(F) Squadron, equipped with Phantom FGR.2's, assumed responsibility for the air defence of the Falklands shortly after the arrival of its first aircraft at Stanley on 17.10.82.

(Richard Gardner)

'Hermes' anchored in Port William Sound (north of Port Stanley) at 0800Z on 3 July and the Task Force Commander (Rear Admiral J.F.Woodward) disembarked to return to the United Kingdom. A 28-aircraft flypast (including 11 800 Sqdn Sea Harriers) was staged over Port Stanley to mark both his departure by Hercules to Ascension Island and that of 'Hermes' as well. The carrier weighed anchor at 1600Z and then proceeded east with her guardship 'Broadsword' for 120 miles to join other elements of the Task Force before sailing north to Ascension Island and Portsmouth. "Kill" markings are believed to have been applied to 800 Sqdn's Sea Harriers during the voyage.

Soviet "visitors" appeared on 10 July when two Tupolev Tu-20 "Bear D's" overflew the ship during a RAS with 'Tidespring'. Ascension Island was reached on 11 July, where Neill Thomas left the carrier to fly home, leaving Dave Morgan as the sole representative of 899 Sqdn aboard (both Tony Ogilvy and Bertie Penfold having left the Squadron sometime previously for the United Kingdom). North of the Island, a Kamov Ka-25 "Hormone B" helicopter from the 'Marshal Timoshenko' trailed 'Hermes' for some time on 15 July, coming very close the next day.

While the carrier was crossing the Bay of Biscay on 19 July, six Sea Harriers took off for a direct flight to Yeovilton. Tractors and tow-bars awaited their arrival so that they could be towed immediately into the hangars for survey, maintenance, repainting and (in some cases) re-issue to 809 Sqdn. The aircraft which arrived at Yeovilton on that day were:

| | | |
|---|---|---|
| XZ499 '99' | XZ500 '-/(1)30' | ZA193 '93' |
| ZA176 '76' | ZA191 '-/(7)18' | ZA194 '94' |

'Hermes' docked at Portsmouth on 21 July with Sea Harrier ZA177 sitting proudly at the head of the ski-jump. The welcome that the carrier and her ship's complement received was overwhelming and will be long remembered by all those present. The remaining Sea Harriers were flown off to Yeovilton the following day for the same treatment as those which had left earlier. They were:

| | |
|---|---|
| XZ457 '-/(7)14' | XZ460 '-/(1)26' |
| XZ492 '-/(1)23' | XZ496 '-/(1)27' |
| XZ459 '-/(1)25' | ZA177 '77' |

*800 Sqdn pilots in 'Hermes' during Operation "Corporate" and their awards: Lt Cdr A.D.Auld RN DSC; Lt Cdr M.S.Blissett RN MID; Lt Cdr R.V.Frederiksen RN MID; Lt D.A.Smith RN MID; Lt M.Hale RN; Lt S.N.Hargreaves RN; Lt A.N.McHarg RN MID; Lt C.R.W.Morrell RN MID; Lt N.Taylor RN MID (KIA); Flt Lt E.H.Ball RAF MID.*

*809 Sqdn pilots integrated into 800 Sqdn in 'Hermes' during Operation "Corporate": Lt Cdr H.G.B.Slade RN; Lt W.Covington RN; Flt Lt S.Brown RAF; Flt Lt J.Leeming RAF.*

*899 Sqdn pilots integrated into 800 Sqdn in 'Hermes' during Operation "Corporate" and their awards: Lt Cdr N.W.Thomas RN DSC; Lt Cdr G.W.J.Batt RN DSC (KIA); Lt Cdr A.R.W.Ogilvy RN; S/Lt A.J.George RN; Flt Lt D.H.S.Morgan RAF DSC; Flt Lt R.Penfold RAF.*

# 801 NAVAL AIR SQUADRON

Lt Cdr N.D.Ward, the Commanding Officer of 801 Sqdn, was contacted by FONAC/MoD in the early hours of 2 April and told to prepare his Squadron for immediate embarkation on 'Invincible', at that time berthed at Portsmouth. Unlike 800 Sqdn, Lt Cdr Ward's Squadron was actually on leave at the time, but otherwise the organisational problems were not dissimilar. Easter leave had to be cancelled and personnel recalled; aircraft had to be checked prior to "flying-on" and a multitude of stores associated with supporting modern combat aircraft loaded aboard the carrier. Those tasks were carried out in a smooth and efficient manner.

801 Sqdn's Sea Harrier FRS.1 complement was increased to its wartime total of eight, all of which embarked 'Invincible' on 4 April as follows:

| | | |
|---|---|---|
| XZ493 'N/001' | XZ498 'N/005' | XZ456 '-/713' |
| XZ495 'N/003' | XZ451 'VL/710' | XZ453 'VL/715' |
| ZA175 'N/004' | XZ452 'VL/711' | |

The total of eight was achieved by the transfer of four aircraft from 899 Sqdn, the Yeovilton-based Headquarters and Training Squadron. Those Sea Harriers replaced two temporarily unserviceable 801 Sqdn machines with the 899 Sqdn SHSU (XZ499 'N/000' and ZA174 'N/002') in addition to bringing the total up to the required complement. 899 Sqdn also supplied an additional five pilots: Lt Cdrs R.S.G.Kent, J.E.Eyton-Jones and G.J.M.W.Broadwater, Flt Lt P.S.Barton and, fresh off the 899 Sqdn "production line", Lt M.W.Watson. They complemented the then current 801 Sqdn pilots: Lt Cdrs "Sharkey" Ward (CO) and D.Hamilton, Lts C.M.Cantan,

W.A.Curtis, B.D.Haigh and S.R.Thomas and Flt Lt I.Mortimer. The 899 Sqdn Sea Harriers and pilots were immediately integrated into 801 Sqdn.

'Invincible' sailed from Portsmouth on 5 April to a magnificent send-off by the many thousands of people crowding the shoreline. By midday that day the first of the Squadron's aircraft was airborne, the intensive work-up period having started. An early priority was to get the five newly-arrived pilots deck-qualified and worked-up to front-line standard. It took only a minimum amount of time for this to be achieved, mainly due to the resolution of the individuals involved.

During the passage south to Ascension Island the aircraft were spray-painted in their wartime colour scheme. In that respect, the 801 Sqdn maintainers had a distinct advantage over their counterparts in 800 Sqdn. Unlike 'Hermes', 'Invincible' (being a more modern carrier) had an excellent air-conditioning system which allowed spray-painting to be carried out in the hangar. 801 Sqdn's Sea Harriers thus emerged from respray in pristine condition, whilst 800 Sqdn's machines had what was described as a "textured and more durable hand-painted finish"! Extra Dark Sea Grey was applied to the underside (covering the serials) and other White areas, while all ROYAL NAVY titles, deck letters and Squadron markings were oversprayed in the same colour. Black ventral fin serials were retained, the White segments of the roundels being overpainted in Roundel Blue. The original 801 Sqdn aircraft had their side-codes repainted Roundel Blue with the last digit being repeated in White on the starboard outrigger cover. The former 899 Sqdn machines were recoded (in Roundel Blue) within 801 Sqdn's side-code allocation and the unit's complement then appeared as follows:

| | |
|---|---|
| XZ493 '-/001' | XZ451 '-/006' |
| XZ495 '-/003' | XZ452 '-/007' |
| ZA175 '-/004' | XZ456 '-/008' |
| XZ498 '-/005' | XZ453 '-/009' |

The work-up during the latter stages of the voyage to Ascension Island involved practice interceptions and fighter combat tactics, plus some training in ground-attack and close-support work. To the Sea Harrier pilots, the latter had been designated a "third-level role" during peacetime and was something of which many of them had little or no experience. Tactical exercises took place utilising the Sea Harriers from both of the carriers, the escort ships acting as targets. 2 inch RP's were also fired, including a night RP attack illuminated by LEPUS flares. Toss-bombing with live 1,000lb bombs added a touch of reality to the operational preparations. A direct hit on a LEPUS flare was achieved on 10 April by an AIM-9G Sidewinder launched from a Sea Harrier. Coincident with that increase in expertise, a lot of effort was also put into efficient handling of the Sea Harrier's Blue Fox radar and the practice of multi-aircraft combat manoeuvres. By the time a Soviet Tupolev Tu-20 "Bear D" overflew the ships on 14 April there was an air of satisfaction with the work-up in general and, in particular, the reliability of the weapons used.

'Invincible' anchored off the north-east coast of Ascen-

sion Island at 1747Z on 16 April, 'Hermes' arriving there the same day. In conjunction with 800 Sqdn, it had been planned to use Wideawake for a simulated attack on the airport at Port Stanley. Unfortunately, it had to be cancelled due to the potential disruption of essential air traffic movements into, out of and around Wideawake. The planning, however, was not wasted as the events of 1 May were to prove.

During the morning of 18 April, following a submarine alert (which turned out to be a false alarm) whilst 'Invincible' was on a RAS with 'Olmeda' off the Island, it was felt that the Carrier Group sitting offshore was unnecessarily vulnerable. Helicopter VERTREP operations and Sea Harrier exercises were completed as quickly as possible and the carriers and their escorts made ready for an accelerated, but organised, departure that day. 'Hermes' weighed anchor at 1300Z and sailed south from the Island towards the Falkland Islands Maritime Exclusion Zone. 'Invincible' did not depart until 1745Z because, following the RAS, she had to return to anchor off Ascension Island to take on board 80 helicopter loads of stores and ammunition. The carrier and her escorts caught up overnight with 'Hermes' and the rest of the southbound fleet.

With effect from 20 April, two manned 801 Sqdn Sea Harriers, armed with live AIM-9L's, were put on "deck alert" night and day. All Sea Harrier pilots were carefully briefed on what to do if contact was made with any Argentine vessel or aircraft in international waters or airspace. 800 Sqdn on 'Hermes' was the first to be put to the test on 21 April, when a Fuerza Aerea Argentina Boeing 707 of Grupo 1 was intercepted and photographed. 801 Sqdn's opportunity came at 0230Z on 22 April when another Boeing 707 was detected at 60 miles range and a Sea Harrier flown by Brian Haigh was launched to intercept it. The "exercise" was repeated later that day at 1830Z, that time at a range of 120 miles. One of the difficulties associated with those interceptions was in sorting out the Argentine reconnaissance aircraft from a number of civilian airliners crossing the South Atlantic. Interceptions continued on 23 April at 1100Z (again at 120 miles range) and at 1500Z, but on the latter occasion the aircraft subsequently passed only five miles north of the fleet. On 24 April a Grupo 1 Boeing 707 appeared again at 1550Z some 80 miles east of the fleet and was intercepted by an 800 Sqdn Sea Harrier. The Argentine Government was advised through diplomatic channels that such flights were no longer "welcome" and would in the future be "at risk". The Argentine authorities understood the tone of the message, assessed the "risk" as real, and no more 707's ventured close to Royal Navy warships until 19 May [see Grupo 1 and 1(F) Sqdn notes for details].

On 28 April it was announced that a Falkland Islands TEZ, prohibiting Argentine ships and aircraft, was to become effective from 1100Z on 30 April. Argentina responded with a similar proclamation of her own. By that date 801 Sqdn was fully worked-up for both the strike and interception roles. The latter function was considered to be the Squadron's forte as during December 1981 it had undertaken a very successful operational Air Combat Manoeuvring (ACM) trial of the Sea Harrier's Blue Fox radar and weapon system on the Decimomannu ranges off Sardinia. It was therefore decided that the unit would provide cover on 1 May for a pre-dawn Vulcan bombing raid on Stanley Airport as well as follow-up attacks at first light on the Airport (and the airfield at Goose Green) by 800 Sqdn Sea Harriers.

At 0530Z on Saturday 1 May, 'Invincible' entered the TEZ to take up her position to the north-east of East Falkland. Bombs from the "Black Buck" Vulcan raid started exploding on the Airport about 0746Z. While no Argentine fighter reaction was expected (nor in fact appeared) so early in the morning, 801 Sqdn Sea Harriers were available to provide protection until the Vulcan was safely out of harm's way en route back to Ascension Island. In anticipation of retaliation as soon as news of the raid reached Argentina, the Squadron launched four of its eight Sea Harriers at 0900Z to take up CAP positions to the east and north-east of Port Stanley. They were flown by "Sharkey" Ward (in XZ495), Robin Kent (in ZA175), Brian Haigh (in XZ498) and Steve Thomas (in XZ452). An hour later they were relieved by Paul Barton (in XZ493), Charlie Cantan (in XZ451), John Eyton-Jones (in XZ456) and Ian Mortimer (in XZ453). That allowed the first group to return to the carrier, refuel and get airborne again to provide maximum continuous CAP cover prior to, during and immediately after the 800 Sqdn attacks on Stanley Airport and Goose Green airfield.

The first of the 800 Sqdn Sea Harriers took-off from 'Hermes' at 1048Z, but ten minutes earlier 'Invincible' went to "action stations" having detected enemy aircraft at high level to the west of her, over West Falkland. At 1120Z, whilst the Sea Harrier bombing raid on Stanley Airport was underway, two Grupo 6 Daggers flown by Capitan Moreno and Teniente Hector Volponi were about 50 miles north-west of Port Stanley heading east. They were being vectored by the Port Stanley radar controller towards two Sea Harriers on CAP to the north-east of the Islands. The Sea Harriers concerned were those of Robin Kent and Brian Haigh, on their second CAP of the day. The protagonists were steered towards each other by their respective controllers and by the time they made contact at a point to the north of the Islands, the Sea Harriers were at an altitude of about 15,000ft with the Daggers flying at least 5,000ft above them. As both pairs of aircraft circled and manoeuvred for the ideal combat position, they eventually came head-on to each other at a range of about 4 miles. Both Kent and Haigh were convinced that they then saw the Daggers launch two missiles which fell away long before reaching the Sea Harriers. Coincidentally, Volponi believed that a Sidewinder had been fired by one of the Sea Harriers and that it had passed harmlessly between the two Daggers. In fact neither side had launched AAM's although Kent and Haigh may have witnessed Moreno and Volponi jettisoning drop tanks prior to combat *[see Grupo 6 notes for details]*. Ever conscious of their fuel states, the Dagger pilots broke away immediately after the missile incident and made off at high speed back to Rio Grande. Kent and Haigh recovered to 'Invincible', still puzzled as to why Argentine AAM's had been fired from such a totally unsuitable position with no chance at all of hitting either Sea Harrier. They assessed it, at that time, as a lack of professionalism.

Following their successful raids on Stanley Airport and Goose Green airfield, the 800 Sqdn aircraft were quickly reconfigured to the interceptor role and by mid-morning they were supplementing the 801 Sqdn aircraft on CAP missions. As the morning progressed, Argentine aircraft were being detected in increasing numbers, mostly at high level over West Falkland. Few ventured further east and, from a British point of view, it was difficult to understand the Argentine tactics. In addition to pairs, groups of four and occasionally loose formations of six aircraft would be seen on the Royal Navy ships' radars. British observers naturally assumed that most, if not all, of those high-level intruders were Mirage-type fighters. That was not so, as was proved in a confrontation involving 801 Sqdn.

John Eyton-Jones and Paul Barton were on CAP when their ship-based radar controller advised them of three pairs of Argentine aircraft which were approaching from the west, height unknown, at a range of 120 miles. The two Sea Harriers, flying at their patrol altitude of about 15,000ft, were then vectored towards the intruders. The closing distance rapidly decreased until it was less than 10 miles. Try as they might, Eyton-Jones and Barton (covering each other) could still not see the Argentine aircraft, although they should by then have been well within visual distance. Meanwhile, the radar controller continued to relay the position of a group of four of the intruders relative to the Sea Harriers. According to the controller they were then within 2 miles of Eyton-Jones and Barton, so the latter concluded that the Argentine aircraft, although close to the Sea Harriers horizontally, had to be well separated vertically. To verify that, Barton accelerated his aircraft in a shallow dive before pulling up into a vertical climb, scanning the sky above with his Sea Harrier's Blue Fox radar. As anticipated, the radar picked up returns from aircraft some 20,000ft above him and obscured by a layer of cloud. Neither Eyton-Jones nor Barton had any intention of entering into high-level combat, especially with odds of three-to-one. It was also apparent that the Argentine aircraft were not going to descend to the Sea Harriers' level. After a short period of stalemate, both parties broke off, the Argentines to the west and the Sea Harriers to the east and 'Invincible'. John Eyton-Jones and Paul Barton were of the opinion that the Argentine aircraft were Mirages. Had they known, however, that four of the aircraft were almost certainly A-4B Skyhawks of Grupo 5 whose only means of self defence were cannon, then they might have been tempted to intercept them.

The four Skyhawks, led by Capitan Hugo Del Valle Palaver, had taken-off from Rio Gallegos shortly after the 800 Sqdn raid on Stanley Airport and Goose Green airfield to seek and attack British ships. Two Grupo 8 Mirages, flown by Capitan Gustavo Garcia Cuerva and Primer Teniente Carlos Perona, provided top cover. On arrival over the Islands the Port Stanley radar controller mistakenly thought that all six aircraft under his control were interceptors and thus had actually vectored them towards what are thought to have been the CAP Sea Harriers of Eyton-Jones and Barton! Fortunately, Garcia Cuerva and Perona realised what had happened and accelerated to position themselves at high altitude between the Skyhawks and Sea Harriers. Palaver's Skyhawks managed to break off, dive to a lower altitude (hopefully below British radar cover) and headed back towards Rio

Gallegos, closely followed by Garcia Cuerva and Perona who had successfully distracted the Sea Harrier pilots. The Skyhawks and Mirages had all escaped unharmed, but Garcia Cuerva and Perona were not to be so fortunate later in the day when they did become involved with Paul Barton (then accompanied by Steve Thomas).

In order to appreciate Argentine aerial tactics on 1 May, it is necessary to understand what their military commanders actually thought was happening. They believed that the Vulcan and Sea Harrier attacks were the prelude to a full-scale British counter-invasion of the Islands. That was one reason why increasing numbers of enemy aircraft detected over West Falkland and to the north of the Islands seldom ventured further east. They had no intention of being drawn into premature combat. Instead, they remained on hand to attack shipping or aircraft on an opportunity basis, especially if vessels came close inshore to land troops without Sea Harrier cover. Therefore, the Argentine aircraft detected by Royal Navy radars were not only Grupo 8 Mirages but also Grupo 4 and 5 Skyhawks and Grupo 6 Daggers ready to strike or intercept as appropriate.

Throughout the morning, Argentine military commanders on the Falkland Islands had received intelligence reports of Royal Navy helicopters being sighted on, over, or close to the Islands. Armed Pucara (and later Mentor) patrols were mounted to deal with such infiltrators, if found. British Special Forces were indeed being inserted but, contrary to Argentine conviction, no full-scale landings were planned. At 1500Z when 'Glamorgan', 'Alacrity' and 'Arrow' (operating close to East Falkland) started shelling military positions near to Port Stanley, the Argentine view that the long-awaited invasion was imminent was reinforced.

"Sharkey" Ward (in XZ495) and Mike Watson (in ZA175) were launched from 'Invincible' at 1515Z to protect a group of Royal Navy ships (including 'Brilliant') which was operating just north of East Falkland. At approximately 1545Z, Teniente de Navio Jose Pereya of 4 Escuadrilla took-off from Pebble Island airfield leading a flight of three Mentor light attack aircraft. Flying at low level and armed with rocket pods and machine guns, their mission was to seek out and attack a British helicopter which had been sighted to the north of Berkeley Sound (north of Port Stanley). At 1600Z, 'Glamorgan' (control ship for the Sea Harriers) detected three small slow-flying aircraft which appeared to be heading for the 'Brilliant' group of ships. Ward and Watson were about 20 miles from Port Stanley when they were vectored towards the trio. There was quite dense cloud cover below them when they arrived over the designated area but, fortunately, Watson had already picked up the aircraft on his Blue Fox radar. Both Sea Harriers descended rapidly through the cloud, and as they emerged the three Mentors came into view. The enemy aircraft had in turn just sighted their objective, a Royal Navy Sea King. Pereya and his wingmen saw Ward and Watson as soon as they broke cloud. The Mentors immediately climbed into the cloud, but not before Ward made a high-speed pass at them, firing his Aden cannon. He thought he had missed, but in fact one of his shells hit the rear cockpit canopy of Teniente de Fragata Daniel Manzella's aircraft, causing superficial damage. Ward followed the Mentors into the cloud and

unintentionally passed dangerously close to the starboard wing of one of them. As the Argentine aircraft broke cloud cover again, they were seen to jettison their underwing stores. Both Ward and Watson tried unsuccessfully to engage the Mentors as they popped in and out of cloud. Reluctantly, the Sea Harriers broke away as the 4 Escuadrilla machines scattered towards the nearby Port Stanley AAA defences and relative safety. The Sea King (believed to have been an 826 Sqdn HAS.5) also escaped unscathed, while Ward and Watson resumed their medium-level CAP to the north-east of East Falkland.

No sooner were they back on patrol than the 'Glamorgan' radar controller advised them of two high-level aircraft (Mirages of Grupo 8) about 40 miles south of their position and heading towards them. Ward and Watson were vectored towards the Mirages which then turned away, the Grupo 8 pilots possibly aware that the AIM-9L had a head-on capability. The two 801 Sqdn pilots decided to feign disinterest in the Mirages by turning onto a northerly heading, as if returning to the CAP area. Immediately, the Argentine fighters (under ground radar control) accelerated towards Ward and Watson until only 15 miles separated them. The Sea Harrier pilots quickly turned on to reciprocal headings and scanned the sky above them for the Mirages. Ward thought he saw three vapour trails and was about to lock-on to one of them with a Sidewinder when he realised that they in fact belonged to Argentine AAM's which had been fired at the two Sea Harriers from extreme range. All three missiles fell harmlessly away long before they came anywhere near Ward and Watson. Meanwhile, the Mirages had broken off the engagement to head for home. "Sharkey" Ward and Mike Watson recovered safely to 'Invincible' at 1635Z, somewhat irked at having achieved so little for so much effort.

It was not until 1910Z that 801 Sqdn managed to achieve its first "kills". Two CAP aircraft had been vectored by the 'Glamorgan' radar controller towards two high-level contacts over West Falkland. They were in fact Mirages of Grupo 8 flown by Capitan Gustavo Garcia Cuerva (in I-019) and Primer Teniente Carlos Perona (in I-015), both of whom were on their second sortie of the day (see earlier). Flying the two Sea Harriers were Paul Barton (in XZ452) and Steve Thomas (in XZ453). The Argentine radar controller at Port Stanley, who had already directed the Mirages towards Barton and Thomas, warned Garcia Cuerva and Perona that the Sea Harriers were also on an interception course. On receipt of that information, both Argentine pilots altered their headings but soon resumed their original track. Thomas was the first to acquire the Mirages on radar and observed that they were flying directly towards him about one mile apart on parallel headings. Barton broke off to the north before turning west to sweep in, if possible, alongside or behind the Argentine fighters. Thomas, flying at 14,000ft, continued towards them and at a range of 8 miles sighted both Mirages straight ahead and slightly above him. At a range of 5 miles he was convinced that he saw an AAM fired in close succession from each enemy fighter. The first missile appeared to be in trouble from the start as it fell away almost immediately, whilst the second seemed to go astray very quickly to pass harmlessly well to the port side of his aircraft *(Thomas may have witnessed the Mi-*

*rages jettisoning their drop tanks and not seen AAMs at all [refer to Grupo 8 notes]).* Thomas tried unsuccessfully to get a missile lock-on to the leading Mirage (flown by Garcia Cuerva). He then broke to starboard, passing above and very close to Perona's aircraft. Perona saw Thomas' Sea Harrier as it flashed overhead and he started a turn on to an interception course. However, unknown to Perona, Barton had cut in behind him (having fired his cannon at the Mirages seconds earlier as they passed in front of his Sea Harrier) and, from a range of about one mile and slightly below Perona, launched a Sidewinder at the unsuspecting pilot. It exploded on impact and I-015 began to disintegrate. Fortunately, Perona was able to eject, both he and the remains of his aircraft coming down in shallow water to the north of Pebble Island. Although he had injured both ankles, he was able to struggle ashore to safety.

Meanwhile Thomas, having witnessed Barton's successful attack (the first air-to-air "kill" of the conflict), came in behind Garcia Cuerva's aircraft, locked-on and fired an AIM-9L. Garcia Cuerva must have been aware of either the missile or the Sea Harrier behind him because he dived into cloud, closely followed by the Sidewinder. No hit was sighted but it later transpired that the missile had exploded close to I-019, rupturing some of its fuel tanks and damaging control runs. Garcia Cuerva then headed for Stanley Airport either to eject overhead into "friendly" territory or to make an emergency landing. Neither objective was achieved as he was killed when the Mirage was brought down by Argentine AAA near the town. Barton and Thomas recovered to 'Invincible' well pleased with their efforts, Barton more so than Thomas who remained unaware of the damage done to (and the subsequent fate of) I-019 until well after the conflict.

At 1942Z, just as 'Glamorgan', 'Alacrity' and 'Arrow' were withdrawing from the gunline off Cape Pembroke, the ships were attacked and damaged by three Grupo 6 Daggers led by Capitan Dimeglio. A CAP Sea Harrier gave chase as the Argentine aircraft headed for the mainland, but had to break off due to shortage of fuel when within 5 miles of one of Dimeglio's wingmen (Teniente Aguirre Faget in C-407).

It was not until 2047Z that 801 Sqdn achieved another "kill" in what turned out to be the last Argentine air attack of the day. A few minutes earlier, the Fighter Director aboard 'Invincible' had detected on his radar screen three returns some 60 miles west of the carrier (positioned about 100 miles north-east of Port Stanley). Two 801 Sqdn CAP Sea Harriers flown by Mike Broadwater (in ZA175) and Al Curtis (in XZ451) were vectored to the area and gained their own radar contact at a range of 26 miles, by which time the targets were some 50 miles from 'Invincible'. Broadwater and Curtis descended to low level and closed in on the enemy intruders, identifying them as three Canberras flying in loose formation about 100ft above the sea. The Grupo 2 bombers led by Capitan Alberto Baigorri were en route to the Port Stanley area (not the CVBG) to seek and destroy Royal Navy shipping.

Curtis fired an AIM-9L at one of the three Canberras (B-110) and the Sidewinder was seen to explode near one of the engines, setting it and the wing alight. As the Canberra appeared still to be flyable on its remaining engine, Curtis launched a second Sidewinder. As he did so the Canberra pilot, Teniente Eduardo de Ibanez, and his navigator, Primer Teniente Mario Gonzalez, ejected and the bomber hit the sea before it was reached by the missile. Broadwater fired both his AIM-9L's at another Canberra which he hit, as pieces were seen to fall from it. However, it was not seriously damaged and, after jettisoning its bombs, returned safely to its base at Trelew. Baigorri also disposed of his bomb load and departed the area as quickly as possible. By that time both Broadwater and Curtis were low on fuel and therefore could not give chase. They recovered to 'Invincible' at 2104Z in the knowledge that they had destroyed another enemy aircraft and prevented a potentially dangerous raid on British shipping. Shortly after the Sea Harriers left, Baigorri returned to the scene to look for his downed compatriots. Unfortunately, they were never found.

"Sharkey" Ward was well pleased with his Squadron's performance that day and all of the pilots were of the opinion that it must have been an enlightening experience for the Argentine aircrews. The Sea Harrier/AIM-9L combination plus the superior tactical skills of the British pilots had proved to be more than a match for the Argentine pilots, missiles and fighters. Aircraft endurance had obviously been a problem to both sides with perhaps a slight edge in favour of the British. However, the Argentines recognised that their greatest chance of success appeared to be surprise attacks on shipping, provided that the British missile defences could be penetrated.

As expected, 2 May was a day of high "Action States" in anticipation of further enemy reaction. The British Task Force Commander, Rear Admiral J.F.Woodward, was aware that major elements of the Armada Argentina were at sea, including the carrier '25 de Mayo' and the cruiser 'General Belgrano'. At 0300Z that morning, the British CVBG was at least 160 miles north north-east of the Islands, whilst the '25 de Mayo' and her escorts were near the north-west perimeter of the TEZ. 12 minutes later, 'Invincible' received early warning of radar emissions which were thought to emanate from a C-130 (possibly with a fighter escort) on a radar reconnaissance mission to the north-west of the carrier. Ian Mortimer was launched in Sea Harrier XZ451 at 0331Z to investigate the source using only his RWR (having been told to maintain strict radar-silence) and report back to the carrier. No C-130 was intercepted (it was in fact S-2E Tracker 0705/2-AS-26 of the Escuadrilla Antisubmarina from '25 de Mayo', herself seeking the British CVBG) but, about 150 miles north-west of 'Invincible', he picked up signals from a Sea Dart control radar scanning the sky. Knowing that there were no British ships in the area and that Sea Darts and their associated Type 909 tracking radars were fitted to the two Argentine Type 42 destroyers (Mortimer had detected the 'Hercules'), he turned on to a reciprocal heading to get out of range and then nosed back towards the source. He switched on his radar at 0358Z and noted five surface contacts 25 miles ahead of him. With that knowledge he was recalled to 'Invincible' and recovered at 0457Z.

Unknown to the British, the Escuadrilla Antisubmarina S-2E Tracker from '25 de Mayo' had already located a group of four British Task Force ships and at 0500Z preparations were underway on the Argentine carrier for a dawn attack by eight A-4Q Skyhawks of 3 Escuadrilla. A

# SEA HARRIER FRS.1 XZ451 '-/006' 801 NAVAL AIR SQUADRON

Flown by Lt Curtis on 1 May 1982 when he shot down Grupo 2 de Bombardeo Canberra B.62 B-110. Also flown by Lt Cdr Ward on 21 May 1982 when he shot down Grupo 3 de Ataque Pucara A-511 and again on 1 June 1982 when he brought down Grupo 1 de Transporte Aereo – Escuadron I C-130E TC-63.

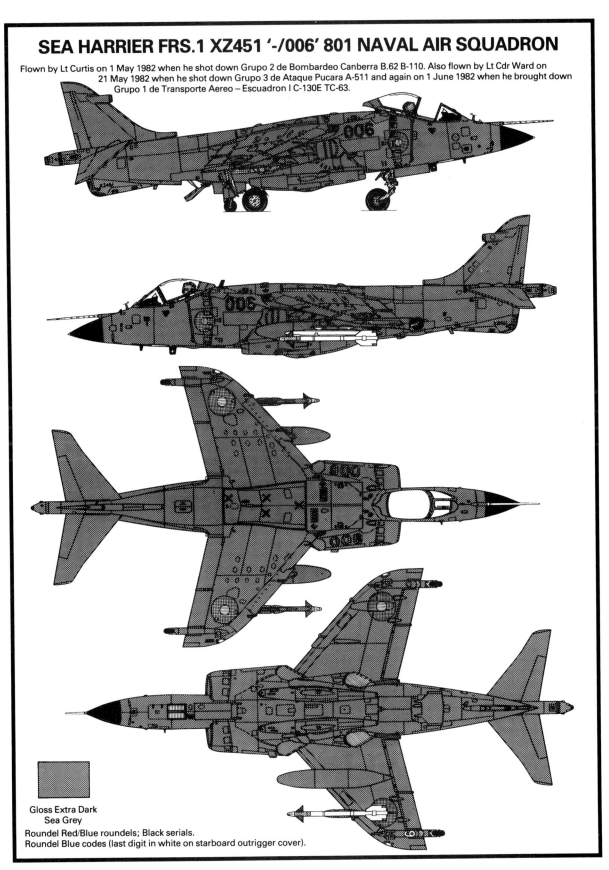

Gloss Extra Dark
Sea Grey

Roundel Red/Blue roundels; Black serials.
Roundel Blue codes (last digit in white on starboard outrigger cover).

second Tracker was launched from '25 de Mayo' at 0828Z to update the position of the CVBG as, without that explicit knowledge, the dawn Skyhawk attack would not take place. As fate would have it, the Tracker crew first encountered technical problems with the aircraft's radar and then were simply unable to find the British fleet. At about 0900Z the Skyhawk mission was finally abandoned, not because of light winds and range considerations (although both were significant factors) but primarily because the target could not be found!

After Ian Mortimer's "sighting", a constant alert was maintained on 'Invincible' and the other Task Force ships as a surprise dawn attack by the Skyhawks was considered very likely. Even though the limitations of '25 de Mayo' and her aircraft were known, they did not reduce the impending threat but only served to make the preparations more thorough. 'Invincible' went to "Action Stations" at 1015Z with full CAP cover. No attack came and the weather "improved" (as far as the British were concerned) from light winds to a flat calm and, finally, fog. As far as is known, no air attack on the Argentine ships was planned. Perhaps it was considered prudent to hold back and let other Task Force elements take appropriate action, as demonstrated later that day by the sinking of the 'General Belgrano'. The '25 de Mayo' returned to home waters by 5 May and thereafter posed no further threat to the Task Force, although her disembarked A-4Q Skyhawks did so later in the month. No other significant events involving 801 Sqdn took place on 2 May.

The fog continued into 3 May. The only noteworthy occurance that day was at 2100Z when what was thought to be an SP-2H Neptune patrol aircraft of the Escuadrilla de Exploracion was detected to the south-west of 'Invincible' (the carrier was east south-east of the Falkland Islands at the time). An investigating 801 Sqdn Sea Harrier found nothing. Dawn on 4 May brought a clear day. At 1350Z, some low-level, high-speed "pop-up" targets were detected coming into British radar cover before disappearing again. 801 Sqdn Sea Harriers were sent to investigate but nothing was seen. The radar returns reappeared at 1412Z and Task Force ships (including 'Invincible') came to "Action Stations". 'Sheffield' was reported hit by an Exocet missile while a second passed close to 'Yarmouth' before it was seen from 'Alacrity' to fall harmlessly into the sea when its propellant was exhausted. The "pop-up" targets investigated earlier by the Sea Harriers had been two Super Etendards (0752/3-A-202 and 0753/3-A-203) of 2 Escuadrilla climbing into the Task Force radar cover for Exocet target acquisition.

Squadron operations on 5 May were very restricted due to persistent low cloud and poor visibility. CAP was provided during the daylight hours, whilst at night "Alert" Sea Harriers were held ready for immediate take-off if required. 801 Sqdn provided CAP cover over the stricken 'Sheffield' from first light on 6 May. During the morning, a brief fast-moving, low-level contact was detected near 'Sheffield' by the Observer in a Sea King to the south of the fleet. Two 801 Sqdn CAP aircraft, operating some 20 miles apart, were vectored towards the area, XZ452 being flown by John Eyton-Jones and XZ453 by Al Curtis. In order to investigate the report, both had to descend through very low cloud and fog, virtually to sea-level. Nothing more was seen or heard of them; it had to be

presumed that they had either flown into the sea or (more likely) collided at, or near, position 53°00′S 57°00.7′W. While the loss of two Sea Harriers was a severe blow, much more important and sobering were the deaths of two greatly experienced and much respected airmen. Subsequent searches found nothing.

During the night of 6/7 May, the interception of a Grupo 1 C-130 departing from the Falkland Islands was not attempted due to zero visibility, one of the few occasions that a mission of any kind had to be aborted due to the weather. At about 1800Z on 7 May, a potential air raid from the north-west was investigated by 801 Sqdn CAP aircraft but nothing was found. A similar pattern developed during 8 May. At approximately 1530Z another potential air raid was detected, coming from the south-west, but as the 801 Sqdn CAP arrived in the vicinity the intruders turned back. The same thing happened at 1850Z when another possible attack was detected. Those raids may just have been probing flights to provoke British defences and find out more about Sea Harrier reaction time. Whatever the Argentine forces were trying to do, it kept everyone on the British side vigilant.

On 9 May "Sharkey" Ward in his Sea Harrier provided aerial cover while a boarding party was put aboard the damaged Argentine intelligence-gathering stern trawler 'Narwal'. Otherwise, the period from 9 to 13 May was noteworthy for its singular lack of activity by the 'Invincible' Sea Harriers (CAP flights excepted) due to the poor weather.

14 May saw 801 Sqdn implement a new plan to disrupt the Argentines on the Falkland Islands. Each Sea Harrier which went out on CAP carried a 1,000lb VT-fused bomb on its centreline pylon, to be dropped on unsuspecting Argentine positions. The idea, although not new, was a simple and often effective one. Bombs dropped in such a manner could cause damage to ground installations, creating consternation and a certain amount of demoralisation amongst the enemy's ground forces. There is ample Argentine evidence, both verbal and written, to show that that did indeed happen. Initially, such overflights were made at around 15,000ft, which was considered sufficiently high to avoid missiles and AAA gunfire. It was also about the right height to provoke AAA reaction, which served the dual purpose of identifying missile and gun emplacements and created some useful attrition of the Argentine ammunition.

'Invincible' was operating about 80 miles east of Port Stanley during the afternoon of 15 May and 801 Sqdn CAP aircraft continued to drop bombs on Argentine positions. By 16 May the CAP bombing height had been raised to 20,000ft as flying at the lower level had been found to be within range of AAA fire. That day the Squadron dropped six VT-fused bombs but the damage was not determined. At 1050Z on 17 May, 801 Sqdn aircraft had just been launched to drop bombs on Argentine troop positions en route to their CAP stations when a potential air attack was detected. The Sea Harriers were diverted towards the contacts but nothing was found.

"Sharkey" Ward (in XZ498) and Ian Mortimer (in XZ495) were launched from 'Invincible' at 0802Z/0803Z on 18 May to drop flares over the Islands as part of a series of diversionary tactics leading up to the forthcoming landings. They both recovered safely to the carrier about 0919Z. Later in the day, Squadron aircraft dropped six bombs on Stanley Airport. That evening, at 2042Z to be precise, Lt Cdr T.J.H.Gedge (Commanding Officer of the then recently-formed 809 Sqdn) landed Sea Harrier ZA190 on 'Invincible'. His was the first of four Sea Harriers to arrive aboard the carrier from 'Atlantic Conveyor' *[see 809 Sqdn notes for details]*.

A planned pre-dawn attack on 19 May by four 801 Sqdn aircraft on some CAB601 helicopters grouped near Mount Kent had to be postponed due to low cloud and uncertainty about the strength of the AAA defences. The original plan involved dropping 1,000lb Retard bombs on the area, but by the time the attack was eventually launched, the profile had been changed to a high-level drop using VT-fused bombs. "Sharkey" Ward (in ZA175), Ian Mortimer (in XZ498), Robin Kent (in XZ495) and Paul Barton (in XZ451) took-off from 'Invincible' at 1214Z/1215Z and set course for Mount Kent, to the west of Port Stanley. About half an hour later they dropped their bombs over the target area. Explosions were seen through gaps in the cloud cover but, unfortunately, no Ejercito helicopters were damaged or destroyed *[see CAB601 notes]*. All four Sea Harriers landed back on board the carrier around 1318Z. Between 1200Z and 1300Z that day Lt Cdr D.D.Braithwaite (in XZ458), Lt D.Austin (in XZ491) and Lt A.Craig (in ZA174) flew from 'Atlantic Conveyor' to 'Invincible' to replace the two lost machines (and aircrew) and further increase the Sea Harrier complement aboard. Both the aircraft and pilots were integrated into 801 Sqdn and the aircrew given deck familiarisation.

During the next five days the ROYAL NAVY titles and 809 Sqdn "Phoenix" motifs were oversprayed with the nearest equivalent paint mixture to Medium Sea Grey available on the ship. 801 Sqdn side-codes were allotted and applied in Pale Blue on the upper part of the engine intake flanks. The result was as follows:

| | | |
|---|---|---|
| ZA174 | '-/000' | (vacant code) |
| XZ491 | '-/002' | (vacant code) |
| XZ458 | '-/007' | (replaced XZ452) |
| ZA190 | '-/009' | (replaced XZ453) |

On 20 May 801 Sqdn Sea Harrier flying was limited to a total of six sorties. That was to prepare the aircraft for the British amphibious landing (Operation "Sutton") the next day and brief all personnel on the expected reaction from the Argentine air arms. Even so, Lt Cdrs Gedge (in XZ499) and Braithwaite managed to achieve a CAP within the sortie limitations.

Operation "Sutton" got underway with almost no immediate Argentine reaction. CAP cover was maintained by 800 and 801 Sqdns throughout the day over three essential areas, namely the northern and southern ends of Falkland Sound and over central West Falkland. "Sharkey" Ward (in XZ451) and Steve Thomas (in XZ456) were launched from 'Invincible' at 1131Z on what proved to be a CAP sortie without incident. They recovered to the carrier at 1246Z to rest and prepare for their next CAP, which proved to be more eventful.

Reports of Pucara, MB-339A and, later, fighter-bomber activity began to filter through to the Squadron during the morning, but it was not until 1510Z that the unit actually confronted Argentine aircraft. The incident involved three 801 Sqdn Sea Harriers and two Grupo 3 Pucaras. In company with Alisdair Craig (in XZ495) and Steve Thomas (in XZ456), "Sharkey" Ward (in XZ451) took-off from 'Invincible' at 1410Z for a CAP under the control of 'Brilliant' positioned at the northern end of Falkland Sound. It was Craig's first sortie from the carrier since he had arrived on board from 'Atlantic Conveyor'. At the time the Sea Harriers were taking-off from 'Invincible', the Pucaras of Mayor Carlos Tomba (in A-511) and Primer Teniente Juan Micheloud were already airborne from Goose Green on patrol to the east of Port San Carlos, searching for suitable infantry targets to attack. Shortly after 1430Z they were ordered back to Goose Green to seek out and destroy a British observation post which had been identified (the post was accurately directing 4.5 inch shells from 'Ardent' in Grantham Sound on to the airfield). The arrival of the Pucaras was witnessed from 'Ardent' and it was erroneously thought on board that she was about to be attacked. That prompted a barrage of 4.5 inch shells and a Seacat to be directed against the two Grupo 3 machines. In fact, the Pucara pilots had no brief to attack her, or any other shipping in the area. Tomba and Micheloud successfully rocketed the observation post, which was located close to the airfield, and were then ordered to carry out a similar mission against another observation post south-west of Goose Green. As they set course for their new target (at about 1505Z), the radar controller on 'Brilliant' saw two low and slow radar returns on his screen some seven miles to the south-west of Goose Green and vectored Ward's trio of Sea Harriers towards them. Thomas, flying at 15,000 ft, was the first to sight one of the low-flying Pucaras. Followed by Craig, he dived to intercept what was Tomba's aircraft. Realising the speed differential between the two types of aircraft, Thomas and Craig tried unsuccessfully to reduce their airspeed sufficiently to achieve a steady target before opening fire with their Aden cannon. The shells missed A-511 and it was left to Ward to try to shoot down the Pucara.

Whilst all the attention was centred on his companion, Micheloud manoeuvred clear of the combat area and escaped at very low level through a valley. Meanwhile, with Tomba in his sights, Ward made a passing cannon attack on A-511 and damaged its port aileron. Ward realised that his speed was too high, lowered his flaps and put the Sea Harrier into a hard left turn to curve in behind Tomba for another strafing run. His next shells hit Tomba's starboard engine. A third attack on the twisting and turning Pucara achieved hits on its canopy and upper fuselage, while at the same time smoke and flames emerged from the port engine. With his machine then out of control, Tomba had no option but to make an extremely low-level ejection. A-511 crashed to the north-west of Drone Hill, about 10 miles south-west of Goose Green. Tomba came down unhurt close to the smoking wreck of his Pucara and made his own way back to Goose Green. The three Sea Harriers were, by that time, low on fuel and so headed back towards the carrier (recovering at 1534Z) rather than search for Micheloud. Tomba became a PoW when Goose Green and Darwin were retaken by British

215

Bombed-up with three 1,000lb bombs and tethered to the flight-deck of 'Invincible' is 801 Squadron Sea Harrier FRS.1 ZA175 '–/004'. The bomb beneath the port wing is inscribed "From 848 'A'" – a Wessex HU.5 Flight based on the ammunition and stores ship 'Regent'. In addition to the bombs, the aircraft also carries two 100-gallon drop tanks and two podded 30mm Aden cannon. While flying this machine on 21.5.82 the Squadron's CO, Lt Cdr "Sharkey" Ward, brought down a Grupo 6 de Caza Dagger with an AIM-9L Sidewinder.                    (Royal Navy)

800 Squadron Sea Harrier FRS.1 XZ496 '–/(1)27', having just returned to 'Hermes' from a CAP over the Falkland Islands (date unknown), creates a fine spray as its pilot prepares to taxy backwards, clear of the landing spot. This aircraft returned to the United Kingdom on 21.7.82 only to head south again twelve days later on 'Illustrious' as '–/257' of 809 Squadron.
                                                                              (Ministry of Defence)

forces. *(His flying helmet ended up in the possession of Surgeon Cdr "Rick" Jolly who later donated it to the Fleet Air Arm Museum for display in its Falkland Islands Exhibition.)*

Later that day, a series of related events happened which involved 801 Sqdn. "Sharkey" Ward (in ZA175) and Steve Thomas (in ZA190) took-off from 'Invincible' at 1721Z for a low altitude CAP (remaining below Argentine radar cover) to the north and north-west of Mount Maria, West Falkland. Meanwhile, three Grupo 6 Daggers flown by Mayor Puga and Primer Tenientes Roman and Callejo were en route from their base at San Julian to attack shipping in the San Carlos area. They were part of a series of concentrated raids designed to stretch to the limit British gun, missile and Sea Harrier resources so that at least some Argentine aircraft would penetrate the defences. At 1745Z, just as the Sea Harriers started their patrol, Puga and Roman bombed and strafed 'Brilliant' near the entrance to San Carlos Water (Callejo went for another target). The bombs missed, but their cannon shells caused damage and casualties in the operations room, including injuring an arm of the Fighter Direction Officer. Puga, Roman and Callejo escaped to the south down Falkland Sound back to their mainland base.

Immediately following that attack the injured FDO saw incoming raiders over West Falkland on his radar screen and vectored Ward and Thomas towards them. Thomas was the first to sight the yellow wing and fin identification bands of two of the three Grupo 6 Daggers flown by Capitan Guillermo Donadille (in C-403), Mayor Gustavo Justo Piuma (in C-404) and Primer Teniente Jorge Senn (in C-407). The time was approaching 1750Z as Thomas dived in behind the rearmost of the two Daggers (Justo Piuma's machine), firing an AIM-9L at the Argentine aircraft as it started to make a turn to the right. C-404 disintegrated when the missile impacted but, remarkably, Justo Piuma managed to eject safely. Thomas then made for the second Dagger (Donadille's machine) which was by then in a tight climbing turn to the right. He fired his second Sidewinder which exploded when it hit the Dagger's port wing. Before Thomas launched his first missile, Ward had unknowingly been seen by Senn who was flying well to the right of his companions. The Dagger pilot had warned Donadille and Piuma of the Sea Harrier's presence (although none of the Argentine aircrew had seen Thomas' aircraft). They immediately jettisoned their underwing stores and broke to the right in a climbing turn to intercept Ward's Sea Harrier. It was just then that Thomas' initial missile hit Piuma's Dagger. Meanwhile, Donadille was by then head-on to Ward's rapidly descending aircraft and fired his cannon at the Sea Harrier (Ward was of the opinion that an AAM had been fired at him). Seconds later, Thomas' second missile hit the port wing of Donadille's Dagger close to the wing root and exploded. C-403 did not fireball or disintegrate, but instead went into an uncontrollable spin. Donadille ejected safely as his aircraft spun into the ground close to the wreck of Justo Piuma's aircraft near Green Hill Bridge, to the south-west of Mount Caroline on West Falkland.

Senn, who had originally been flying east at extremely low level when the aerial conflict began, altered course onto a westerly heading and cut across Donadille's path just before Thomas' second AAM hit his colleague's Dagger. Ward saw the third low-level Dagger streaking across in front of him at right angles. He pulled his Sea Harrier into a tight right turn and fired an AIM-9L at the departing aircraft. C-407 disintegrated as soon as the missile hit it, but Senn was able to eject safely before his aircraft completely broke up around him. The remains of that Dagger came down to earth somewhat closer to Mount Caroline than the other two Grupo 6 machines.

Ward and Thomas withdrew from the scene of the recent combat and formated prior to leaving the patrol area. When heading east at low level just after 1800Z, three "white" (actually a light sea grey) Skyhawks were sighted over Falkland Sound about to attack the already damaged 'Ardent' lying off North West Island at the northern end of Grantham Sound. Vectored by 'Brilliant', they set course in pursuit of the Skyhawks (A-4Q's of 3 Escuadrilla). Both Ward and Thomas soon realised that they were too far behind the Argentine aircraft to catch them. They decided to keep the Skyhawks in sight for as long as possible in the murky conditions until another, closer, CAP could be vectored towards them. An 800 Sqdn CAP comprising Lt C.R.W.Morrell and Flt Lt J.Leeming overheard some of the transmissions about 'Ardent' and successfully intercepted the Skyhawks as they exited south down Falkland Sound *[see 800 Sqdn notes for details]*.

While Ward was talking to 'Brilliant', he and Thomas were crossing the east coast of West Falkland close to Port Howard. Ward soon realised that he had lost sight of, and radio contact with, his wingman. Reluctantly, after a brief search for him, Ward informed 'Invincible' that he thought Thomas had been shot down. In fact he had been hit by AAA fire from Port Howard which had damaged his TACAN and put his radio out of action. By then very low on fuel, Ward recovered to the carrier at 1830Z where he found a recently arrived Steve Thomas safe and sound after his eventful afternoon. The battle damage to Thomas' aircraft (the first to be inflicted on an 'Invincible' Sea Harrier) was repaired within 24 hours.

Argentine air raids ceased at dusk, thus allowing 801 Sqdn time to assess the day's events. Whilst Ward and Thomas had had the lion's share of the action, both they and the other 801 Sqdn CAP pilots were more than satisfied that the Sea Harrier had earned the title "*La Muerta Negra*", bestowed on it by some Argentines ("*The Black Death*", a reference to the Extra Dark Sea Grey colour scheme worn by the Sea Harriers which the enemy pilots found very difficult to see over land or sea).

22 May was relatively quiet as both sides reassessed the previous day's actions and altered their tactics accordingly. At 0645Z that morning a Grupo 1 C-130 was detected on a track that would take it very close to 'Coventry'. Unfortunately, at the crucial moment, and at a mere eight miles range, the ship's Sea Dart system malfunctioned enabling the Hercules to fly past quite oblivious to what was going on. 801 Sqdn CAP Sea Harriers were launched, but the Argentine radar unit at Port Stanley is presumed to have informed the C-130 pilot of their presence and turned him back to Argentina before the fighters came within range.

While 23 May was a day of much activity overall, 801

217

Sqdn only came into direct contact with one Argentine aircraft that day. Tim Gedge (in XZ494) and Dave Braithwaite (in ZA190) were launched from 'Invincible' at 1328Z for a routine CAP. At about that time two 800 Sqdn pilots, Flt Lts D.H.S.Morgan and J.Leeming, were successfully attacking a formation of three CAB601 Pumas and an Agusta A-109A near Shag Cove House on West Falkland *[see 800 Sqdn notes for details]*. One of the Pumas and the A-109A were destroyed, while another Puma (AE-500) was slightly damaged before the 800 Sqdn pilots had exhausted their ammunition; the third Puma escaped unscathed. As Gedge and Braithwaite approached the area, they were called down to dispose of the damaged Puma. Braithwaite was the first to sight some smoking wreckage and the immobilised helicopter nearby. They totally destroyed AE-500 by strafing it with cannon fire, after which both of the Sea Harriers recovered to 'Invincible' at 1443Z.

24 May was an equally frustrating day for 801 Sqdn. In the four-day period up to and including that day, the Squadron had flown over 100 missions, almost all of which involved discouraging and turning back potential Argentine raids. By 25 May, Argentine air raids had become more sporadic. However, 25 May was Argentina's National Day and overnight 24/25 May the Task Force had made plans to deal with an expected upsurge in activity. 'Coventry' and 'Broadsword' took up positions to the north of Pebble Island to provide earlier and better radar and missile cover against Argentine air attacks. 'Invincible' and 'Hermes' located themselves some 90 miles north-east of Port Stanley thereby reducing Sea Harrier transit times to and from their CAP areas. That also ensured that there would be more 800 and 801 Sqdn aircraft on patrol at any given time.

As anticipated, there were a number of Argentine air attacks and initially the 'Broadsword' and 'Coventry' "missile trap" was very effective. 801 Sqdn provided continuous CAP cover over their appointed areas but did not come into contact with any Argentine aircraft. However, 'Broadsword' was damaged in the late afternoon and 'Coventry' sunk *[see 800 Sqdn and Grupo 5 notes for details]*. The final and most sobering blow that day came at 1936Z when 'Atlantic Conveyor', positioned some 90 miles north-east of Port Stanley and 8 miles away from 'Invincible', was hit and set on fire by one of two Exocets fired from two Super Etendards of 2 Escuadrilla (0753/3-A-203 and 0754/3-A-204). 'Invincible' and 801 Sqdn received warning of the impending attack about six minutes before the missile impacted. All but one of the remaining Sea Harriers aboard were scrambled to protect the Task Force and to deal with the raiders if possible. Two 801 Sqdn Sea Harriers returning from a CAP had to hold off in case they were hit by British missiles as the Task Force ships (including 'Invincible') prepared to fire at the incoming Argentine aircraft and Exocets. At 1938Z, two minutes after 'Atlantic Conveyor' was hit, a low and fast radar contact was detected 20 miles from the carrier. When it closed to 14 miles Sea Darts were launched at the target. The outcome of the onslaught was not determined but the target disappeared. "Sharkey" Ward witnessed the whole event at close quarters from his cockpit as it was his Sea Harrier which remained on board when the others were scrambled. The two Super Etendards escaped un-

scathed as their Exocets had been fired from a range of about 31 miles north of 'Atlantic Conveyor', well away from interception by Sea Harriers. Both of the 801 Sqdn machines which had been holding clear of 'Invincible' recovered safely to the carrier, although by the time they touched down they were critically short of fuel.

For the next few days, 'Invincible' and 'Hermes' withdrew to the eastern boundary of the TEZ. Argentine air attacks on British positions and ships diminished considerably with few raids penetrating the CAP cover and missile defences. Those that did so caused little damage. On 28 May the Squadron resumed the practice of dropping bombs on Stanley Airport en route to their CAP areas.

'Invincible' was still positioned at the eastern extremity of the TEZ on 29 May. Continuous CAP cover over the Falkland Islands was maintained all day in spite of the long transit distance to and from the carrier. No direct contacts with Argentine aircraft were made, but a returning 801 Sqdn CAP reported what appeared to be Super Etendards (actually 1 Escuadrilla MB-339A's) parked on Stanley Airport. Super Etendards or not, any type of attack aircraft presented a potential threat at a crucial stage in the British advance across East Falkland. It also confirmed that the runway, or a portion of it, was still usable. Two 801 Sqdn Sea Harriers were each armed with three 1,000lb VT-fused bombs for an attack on the airfield, but the results of the raid were inconclusive except that three of the bombs were thought to have exploded prematurely. Unconfirmed reports after the conflict indicated that an MB-339A may have received minor damage in that raid *[see 1 Escuadrilla notes for full details]*. At 1847Z that evening, there was a high sea state and strong winds. Mike Broadwater (in ZA174) was taxiing out for take-off just as 'Invincible' (operating due east of the Falkland Islands) was turning to starboard to come into wind. The carrier's list in the turn, combined with a slippery flight-deck, caused the aircraft to skid sideways and roll over the side into the sea. Mike Broadwater managed to eject at the last possible moment and was rescued from the sea by helicopter, only slightly injured. Unfortunately, his aircraft was lost at position 51°48.3′S 54°29.8′W.

30 May turned out to be the date of the final Super Etendard/Exocet raid of the conflict, the target being 'Invincible' to the east of the Falkland Islands. Advance electronic warning of the attack was received, but it was not until 1731Z that 'Ambuscade' could provide information. Two "pop-ups" appeared on her radar to the north-east of the ship (2 Escuadrilla Super Etendards 0752/2-A-202 and 0755/2-A-205) and at 1732Z 'Ambuscade' reported seeing what could only have been an Exocet release. 'Exeter' launched three Sea Darts and 'Avenger' fired her 4.5 inch gun, both ships claiming to have hit the missile (only one was fired). It is more likely that the Exocet was deflected off course by countermeasures until its propellant was consumed and it fell harmlessly into the sea. 801 Sqdn CAP Sea Harriers were sent after the Super Etendards without any real hope of catching them. Four Grupo 4 A-4C Skyhawks followed up the Exocet attack, hoping to capitalise on the confusion of gunfire, smoke and missiles. Theirs was a disastrous mission from the Argentine point of view. The Argentines claimed that 'Invincible' had been hit, but that was impossible as the carrier was outside the Exocet's range when the missile

was launched from about 40 miles south-east of her position [see 2 Escuadrilla, Grupo 4 and 815 Sqdn Exeter Flight notes for details].

Just before midnight on 30 May a Vulcan B.2 took-off from Wideawake for another "Black Buck" raid armed with a pair of Shrike anti-radar missiles. Prior to dawn on 31 May, 801 Sqdn Sea Harriers carried out two toss-bombing raids an hour apart on Stanley Airport. Each aircraft carried two impact-fused and one VT-fused bomb, but their real role was to keep the enemy radars transmitting long enough for the Vulcan's missiles to home-in on them; the ploy was successful but the results less so.

At about 1430Z an 801 Sqdn CAP Sea Harrier pilot returned to 'Invincible' having seen and photographed what appeared to be three swept-wing aircraft of unidentified type just off the eastern threshold of Stanley Airport's runway. It was realised that the aircraft might have been the 1 Escuadrilla MB-339A's attacked on 29 May, or replacements, or even dummies. Whatever they were, the three aeroplanes presented a potentially serious threat to British sea and ground forces at a crucial stage in the conflict. Details of the sighting were passed to 'Hermes', where the pilots of two 1(F) Sqdn Harrier GR.3's about to depart on a mission were hurriedly briefed on their new target. Meanwhile, two 801 Sqdn CAP Sea Harriers had been diverted off patrol to make a high-level reconnaissance run over the Airport to confirm the previous sighting. Confirmation received, the two Harrier GR.3's, accompanied by a pair of 800 Sqdn Sea Harriers for defence suppression, took-off at 1452Z for a rocket attack against the three enemy aircraft which, as a later photo-reconnaissance flight confirmed, were indeed MB-339A's.

At 1340Z on 1 June, "Sharkey" Ward (in XZ451) and Steve Thomas had just completed a low-level CAP near Port Howard under control from 'Minerva' in San Carlos Water. As they climbed to the south-east to recover to 'Invincible' some 200 miles east of the Falkland Islands, the radar controller on 'Minerva' advised them of a possible Argentine aircraft heading west north-west 20 miles north of the ship. Only three fleeting radar returns had been detected, but for long enough to plot the aircraft's current position and approximate direction of flight. Despite being low on fuel, both Ward and Thomas immediately turned to port, taking up a north-westerly heading to try and intercept the contact. As he rolled out of the turn, Ward's radar picked up a westbound target 38 miles north north-west of his Sea Harrier. Ward and Thomas accelerated towards the radar return until the distance between them and the contact had been reduced to 8 miles. By then, Ward had asked the 'Minerva' fighter controller to make arrangements for the two Sea Harriers to divert to 'Fearless' and 'Intrepid' in San Carlos Water should their fuel states become critical. With the target still showing on his radar, Ward descended through a layer of low cloud, leaving Thomas at 3,000ft to provide top cover. As he emerged from the cloud, he saw the target 6 miles away about 200ft above the waves, identifying it as a C-130E (TC-63 of Grupo 1). He told Thomas to join him, thus increasing the available fire-power against the Argentine aircraft. Mindful of their dwindling fuel reserves, Ward fired his first AIM-9L from extreme range, only to see it

fall away before reaching the C-130E. He closed the gap a little and launched his second missile which hit the transport aircraft between the engines on the starboard wing, setting it on fire. Ward followed up the missile attack with cannon fire to the tail area in order to destroy the control surfaces. It worked: the blazing Hercules dipped its starboard wing and, at 1346Z, nose-dived into the South Atlantic Ocean about 50 miles north of Pebble Island with the loss of all seven persons on board. Ward and Thomas calculated that they then had just enough fuel for a high-level flight back to 'Invincible'. The aircraft were recovered safely to the carrier although extremely short of fuel. Both pilots were elated at having at last shot down one of the elusive C-130's.

Later that afternoon (about 1740Z), 801 Sqdn lost a Sea Harrier to an Argentine SAM. The Squadron AWI, Ian Mortimer (in XZ456) had taken-off from 'Invincible' for an armed reconnaissance sortie to the south of Port Stanley. He was at a height of 10,000ft and 7 miles south of the Airport looking at what he thought was an aircraft moving on the airfield when he noticed the flash of a surface-to-air missile (a Roland) being fired and the smoke trail as it climbed inexorably towards him. Mortimer thought that he would easily outclimb or outrun the Roland but, a few seconds after it had disappeared from view beneath him, the rear fuselage of his Sea Harrier exploded when the SAM impacted. Fortunately, he ejected safely before the aircraft completely disintegrated around him, the pieces falling into the ocean. After what seemed to him like an eternity (actually about 10 minutes) he landed in the sea about 1750Z some 5 miles south of Port Stanley and took to his dinghy. He made two short voice transmissions on his SARBE in the hope that they would be heard by the British and not the Argentines. His broadcasts were received by CAP Sea Harriers and Sea King HAS.5's from 820 Sqdn aboard 'Invincible' started to home in on them. However, after the second brief transmission no more was heard from him, which was not surprising as he had switched off his SARBE (presumably to preserve its batteries).

In his initial transmission Mortimer had reported his approximate position. Shortly after that he saw an Argentine twin-engined aircraft (possibly a Pucara) and a Chinook (in fact a Grupo 7 machine) searching an area about 5 miles west of him where the remains of his Sea Harrier had come down. Both machines then headed east towards him and it was then that he made his second transmission stating the position of the Argentine aircraft in case a Sea Harrier CAP was near enough to attack them. The aeroplane and helicopter then overflew him, without apparently sighting his dinghy, before turning away back towards Port Stanley. All Mortimer could do then was wait and hope that he would be rescued by the British. It proved to be a long wait.

In response to intelligence reports which suggested that Argentine Sea Kings equipped with Exocets (possibly supplied by Peru) could be operating out of Pebble Island airfield, 800 and 801 Sqdns were both tasked to carry out armed reconnaissance and attack missions to locate and, if possible, destroy any such helicopters. A pair of 800 Sqdn Sea Harriers took-off from 'Hermes' on a reconnaissance sortie at 1816Z, followed at 1846Z by Dave Braithwaite (in XZ491) and Alisdair Craig (in XZ495) who departed 'Invincible' to attack any targets discovered by the two aircraft from 'Hermes'. The airfield was strafed, but no helicopters were found by either pair of Sea Harriers or another two 800 Sqdn machines which took off from 'Hermes' at 1936Z. Braithwaite and Craig recovered to 'Invincible' at 2001Z. The intelligence source had been correct about Sea Kings being at Pebble Island but was wrong about their purpose. Two Sea Kings of 2 Escuadrilla de Helicopteros (0677/2-H-233 and 0678/2-H-234) had touched down on the airfield at 2036Z on 31 May but their objective was not to seek out and destroy British ships with Exocet missiles. Their mission was in fact to evacuate back to the mainland ten CANA personnel who had been stranded (but were otherwise safe) on Pebble Island. Whilst on the ground, the Sea Kings' engines were kept running and at about 2115Z that night they left for Rio Grande with their passengers [refer to 2 Escuadrilla de Helicopteros notes for details].

At 0230Z on 2 June, after nearly nine hours in his dinghy, Ian Mortimer was found by an 820 Sqdn Sea King HAS.5 (XZ574). After many hours of fruitless searching, Lt Cdr K.Dudley and his crew had seen Mortimer's emergency strobe light and homed-in on it. Cold and exhausted, Mortimer was winched aboard the helicopter and flown the 120 miles back to the carrier. Within a week he had fully recovered from his ordeal and was flying again. The weather on 2 and 3 June consisted of low cloud and poor visibility which prevented fixed-wing flying from either the carriers or the newly-completed FOB which was less than half a mile north-west of Port San Carlos settlement.

Bad weather continued into 4 June, and at dusk that day (around 2030Z) 'Invincible' sailed under the cover of darkness to a position south of Falkland Sound. The plan was that from such a location 801 Sqdn Sea Harriers could be launched to patrol well to the east of the Falkland Islands in the hope of detecting or intercepting Grupo 2 Canberras or one of the elusive Grupo 1 C-130's flying to and from Stanley Airport. Just as 'Invincible' detached, 'Bristol' detected two radar returns, but it was not prudent to dispatch any Sea Harriers due to dense fog which was enveloping the carrier. The intruders were later identified as two Canberras on their way to East Falkland for a night bombing mission against the British positions.

At 0300Z on 5 June, the first of two pairs of CAP Sea Harriers took-off but no contact was made with enemy aircraft. However, the Sea Harriers must have been visible on Argentine radar screens and hopefully had a deterrent effect on any enemy raids or resupply flights planned for that night. Following those sorties, 'Invincible' set course back to the eastern perimeter of the TEZ. The weather conditions were still very poor at 0840Z when Charlie Cantan got airborne from 'Invincible' in his Sea Harrier to investigate a potential target which had been detected off Port Stanley by 'Exeter'. Unfortunately, nothing was found and Cantan returned to the carrier to find her completely fog-bound. On his first Carrier Controlled Approach, flares were dropped astern of the ship, but he saw nothing at all and went round again for another (and final) attempt as his aircraft was extremely low on fuel. He put his Sea Harrier into the hover at 200ft above the sea and moved cautiously forward until he sighted a vertically-aimed beam of light from a searchlight aboard the carrier. Retaining it in sight, Cantan descended through the swirling fog and "landed-on". Nobody on board had seen his Sea Harrier until it was over the deck. A subsequent fuel check revealed a mere 150lb (less than two minutes flying time) remaining in its tanks! The fog cleared sufficiently about 1100Z for CAP's to be resumed. Unfortunately, the fog returned shortly afterwards, causing a short cessation of CAP's, and did not clear again until 1730Z.

6 June was another day of low cloud and poor visibility. The FOB at Port San Carlos settlement was again available, but the weather precluded fixed-wing operations either afloat or ashore. More annoying was the fact that, overnight, Grupo 2 Canberras had again bombed British positions without being intercepted. As a result of that, Operation "Canbelow" was devised by the planners aboard 'Invincible' (sometimes referred to aboard the carrier as the "Think Tank Junta"!). The idea was that at dusk each evening 'Invincible' and 'Brilliant' would detach to within 100 miles of the East Falkland coastline and operate CAP and "alert" aircraft. At the very least, the very presence of Sea Harriers would have a deterrent effect. No intruders approached on the first night.

The ships detached again at 1930Z on 7 June for another attempt. At 2300Z 'Cardiff' picked up a radar contact heading east towards the Falkland Islands, so an 801 Sqdn CAP was launched to intercept it. Shortly afterwards the target turned west, no doubt warned off by Argentine radar. The Sea Harriers gave chase and began to catch the aircraft, but were forced to break off due to low fuel states.

8 June was another fine day, but once again 801 Sqdn Sea Harriers did not come into close contact with Argentine aircraft. However, the Squadron was involved to a certain extent in the events which followed the Grupo 4 and Grupo 5 Skyhawk attacks that day on 'Sir Tristram' and 'Sir Galahad' in Port Pleasant, East Falkland. "Sharkey" Ward (in ZA190) and Steve Thomas (in XZ458) were launched from 'Invincible' at 1905Z for a medium-level CAP at the southern end of Falkland Sound under the control of 'Cardiff'. At about 1945Z, Flt Lt Morgan and Lt Smith in their 800 Sqdn Sea Harriers were successfully attacking three out of four Grupo 5 A-4B Skyhawks over Choiseul Sound. Ward and Thomas were vectored north from their patrol area and, as they approached the Sound, they saw three Skyhawks ahead of them (but well below) explode in quick succession. They sighted the fourth aircraft escaping from the fray and set off in pursuit. As they did so, 'Cardiff' advised them of what appeared to be two pairs of high-level aircraft approaching from the west. Those radar contacts were thought to be Mirages, presumably providing top cover for the Grupo 5 Skyhawks. Ward and Thomas broke off the Skyhawk chase and were directed instead by the 'Cardiff' radar controller towards the incoming Mirages. It was not long before Ward and Thomas sighted their contrails about 30 miles away and some 15,000ft above them (the two Sea Harriers were flying at 20,000ft). The two 801 Sqdn pilots visualized a repeat of 1 May when each side tried to tempt the other into its optimum combat environment. However, when the Sea Harriers closed to 10 miles, the Mirages turned away back towards the mainland. The Sea Harriers recovered to 'Invincible' at 2036Z,

their pilots somewhat frustrated but also satisfied that their 800 Sqdn compatriots had at least partly avenged the attacks on the two LSL's.

After dark, Lt Cdr Gedge left the carrier by 820 Sqdn Sea King HAS.5 for 'Sir Bedivere' and then sailed overnight with the ship to San Carlos Water. There he joined a team aboard 'Fearless' charged with the organisation and tasking of Harrier GR.3 missions. He remained aboard the assault ship until after the Argentine surrender on 14 June and was then involved in establishing the Harrier/Sea Harrier base at Stanley Airport prior to rejoining 809 Sqdn at Yeovilton. Later that night 'Invincible' detached for yet another unrewarding Operation "Canbelow" patrol.

Good weather prevailed again on 9 June and it was on that day that 801 Sqdn aircraft operated for the first time from the FOB at Port San Carlos settlement *(known as "HMS Sheathbill" to the Royal Navy (named after an Antarctic and Falkland Islands seabird) and "Sid's Strip" to the Royal Air Force [see 800 Sqdn notes for the reason and other details about the FOB]).* The idea was that the Sea Harriers would make use of the FOB to increase CAP effectiveness, returning to the carrier at night or when required. Refuelling facilities at the FOB meant that, on average, Sea Harrier pilots could increase the length of their patrols by a factor of almost three. A possible Argentine attack about 1900Z caused an 801 Sqdn CAP to be launched from the carrier, but the approaching aircraft turned back as the Sea Harriers closed in.

10 June was another fine day, but with little aerial activity involving 801 Sqdn. On 11 June a new tactic using two pairs of Sea Harriers was devised in an effort to try and intercept the continuing C-130 runs into Stanley Airport. All four aircraft would deploy to their normal CAP positions, where one pair would break off, descend rapidly to low level and make for Queen Charlotte Bay on the west coast of West Falkland. The medium-level CAP would then return to 'Invincible' to refuel as normal, whilst the low-level pair loitered in the Queen Charlotte Bay area waiting for the C-130 to appear. When necessary, that pair would go to the FOB for fuel. It was hoped that the recovery of the medium-level Sea Harriers would be visible on the Argentine radars. A Hercules might then be tempted to take-off from or fly into Stanley Airport. The plan was a reasonable one, based on knowledge of previous C-130 movements. Unfortunately, none appeared when it was attempted on 11 June. The two low-level Sea Harriers went to the Port San Carlos FOB to refuel. While there they cut their tyres on the metal landing strip, but were later able to return to 'Invincible'. A Grupo 1 C-130 managed to land unmolested at the Airport at 2115Z that evening! 12 and 13 June were both very quiet days for 801 Sqdn. CAP's were launched in response to some potential air raids which all turned back before the arrival of the Sea Harriers.

The Squadron's final contact with the enemy came at 0130Z on 14 June when an incoming raid was detected approaching the Mount Kent area from the south-west. An 801 Sqdn CAP was launched but the intruders turned away as the two Sea Harriers approached. However, they returned at 0155Z and came within range of Sea Dart missiles aboard 'Cardiff' and 'Exeter'. The aircraft were two Canberras from Grupo 2 with an escort of two Grupo

8 Mirages. It was almost certainly a Sea Dart from 'Exeter' which brought down one of the Canberras (B-108). Although 801 Sqdn did not gain contact with the Canberra, they were satisfied that the Operation "Canbelow" tactics had, at last, been vindicated.

The surrender of all Argentine forces on the Falkland Islands became effective from 2359Z on 14 June, although CAP's continued in case of post-surrender Argentine reaction. On 15 June some Squadron statistics were published on board the carrier covering the period from 2 April until the surrender:

*599 combat missions flown (786 flying hours)*
*Each pilot averaged 57 sorties*
*56 1,000lb bombs dropped*
*3,061 30mm cannon shells fired*
*12 AIM-9L Sidewinders launched*

Events settled down during the next few days. The MoD(Navy) had decided that 'Hermes' would be the first carrier to return to the United Kingdom, whilst 'Invincible' would remain on station until she could be relieved by 'Illustrious'. However, before that could be achieved, 'Invincible' would withdraw from the TEZ for a period of crew rest and recuperation plus essential ship and aircraft maintenance.

At 2224Z on 18 June, 'Invincible' headed north accompanied by 'Andromeda'. "Fall out from flying stations" was "piped" at 2000Z on 19 June after a long and hectic 75 days at sea. On 20 June one of the 809 Sqdn pilots, Lt Dave Austin, left the carrier to return to Yeovilton and rejoin 809 Sqdn which was working up for deployment on 'Illustrious'.

A suitably refreshed 'Invincible' returned to the TEZ on 1 July to relieve 'Hermes'. On 2 July two 800 Sqdn Sea Harriers (XZ455 and XZ494) were flown across from 'Hermes' to 'Invincible' to bring 801 Sqdn's complement up to 10 aircraft. That was considered sufficient to give limited carrier and shore-based air defence cover within the TEZ and over the Falkland Islands. The two 800 Sqdn pilots joined 801 Sqdn on a temporary basis. Both Sea Harriers were resprayed and recoded within the 801 Sqdn side-code sequence as follows:

| | | |
|---|---|---|
| XZ455 '-/000' | (replaced ZA174) |
| XZ494 '-/008' | (replaced XZ456) |

'Hermes' finally left the COA for the United Kingdom with her guardship 'Broadsword' on 4 July, leaving 'Invincible' in charge. A "de facto cessation of hostilities" was announced by the British Foreign and Commonwealth Office on 12 July and ten days later a 150 miles radius protection zone (centred on Falkland Sound) was established around the Islands. It was known as the FIPZ and replaced the TEZ. The Squadron and ship's company received a pleasant fillip on 14 July when the British Government announced that 'Invincible' would be retained by the Royal Navy and not sold to Australia as had been planned.

Nigel Ward had been promoted to Commander on 30 June and returned to the United Kingdom in July. His successor, Lt Cdr A.R.W.Ogilvy, took command with ef-

The War two months over, 'Invincible' anchored in San Carlos Water on 18.8.82 primarily to allow her ship's company the opportunity to see for themselves the scene of so much earlier action. Few carriers have the ability to launch fixed-wing aircraft while at anchor, but with Sea Harriers aboard all things are possible! Just visible on deck is XZ725, 815 Squadron's Trials Flight Lynx HAS.2, which was based on 'Invincible' for ESM and Exocet decoy duties.
*(Royal Navy)*

*Seen here in the Medium Greys colour scheme, with the bleak Falkland Islands landscape as a backdrop, is Sea Harrier FRS.1 XZ458 '–/007' of 801 Squadron. On 26.8.82 it was transferred from 'Invincible' to 'Illustrious' where it joined 809 Squadron with the code '–/259'. All the Squadron's aircraft were named, XZ458 becoming "Ermantrude".*
*(Royal Navy)*

*Flying low over Stanley Harbour after the conflict is an 801 Squadron Sea Harrier FRS.1 (XZ493 '–/001) in the overall Extra Dark Sea Grey colour scheme. This proved to be the more effective of the two camouflage schemes used during the conflict and aircraft so painted were reportedly referred to as "La Muerta Negra" (The Black Death) by some Argentine pilots.*
*(Royal Navy)*

fect from 29 July. He had served with 800 Sqdn on 'Hermes' during the conflict until temporarily grounded with an ear infection. He returned to the United Kingdom on 30 May and did some refresher flying at Yeovilton before returning south to relieve "Sharkey" Ward.

801 Sqdn rotated its aircraft, pilots and maintainers every four days between the carrier, RAF Stanley (as the Airport was by then called) and, if required, the Port San Carlos FOB. That minimised the inevitable monotony of COA/FIPZ operations and allowed as many personnel as possible to have some time ashore.

'Illustrious' arrived in the South Atlantic towards the end of August. On 26 August, upon completion of an ADEX involving the two carriers, Tony Ogilvy and Robin Kent flew XZ458 and XZ491 across to 'Illustrious' to increase 809 Sqdn's complement to 10 aircraft. Dave Braithwaite, Mike Watson and Lt Andy George (promoted in mid-June) were also temporarily transferred to 809 Sqdn but later rejoined the homeward-bound 'Invincible' at Ascension Island. On 27 August 'Illustrious' entered the COA and formally relieved 'Invincible' on 28 August. The latter carrier sailed north that day out of the COA, en route to Ascension Island and Portsmouth where she arrived on 17 September to a spectacular and emotional welcome. 'Invincible' had travelled nearly 53,000 miles, had 58 RAS's and had been at sea for 167 days, while 801 Sqdn had recorded nearly 2,000 launches since the departure from Portsmouth on 5 April.

The Sea Harriers aboard were flown off to Yeovilton later that day. They were as follows:

| | | |
|---|---|---|
| XZ455'-/000' | ZA175'-/004' | XZ494'-/008' |
| XZ493'-/001' | XZ498'-/005' | ZA190'-/009' |
| XZ495'-/003' | XZ451'-/006' | |

*801 Sqdn pilots aboard 'Invincible' during Operation "Corporate" and their awards: Lt Cdr N.D.Ward AFC RN DSC; Lt Cdr D.Hamilton RN; Lt C.H.Cantan RN; Lt W.A.Curtis RN MID (KIA); Lt B.D.Haigh RN; Lt S.R.Thomas RN DSC; Flt Lt I.Mortimer RAF MID.*

*809 Sqdn pilots integrated into 801 Sqdn in 'Invincible' during Operation "Corporate": Lt Cdr T.J.H.Gedge RN; Lt Cdr D.D.Braithwaite RN; Lt Cdr A.Craig RN; Lt D.Austin RN.*

*899 Sqdn pilots integrated into 801 Sqdn in 'Invincible' during Operation "Corporate" and their awards: Lt Cdr G.J.M.W.Broadwater RN; Lt Cdr J.E.Eyton-Jones RN (KIA); Lt Cdr R.S.G.Kent RN MID; Lt M.W.Watson RN; Flt Lt P.C.Barton RAF.*

# 809 NAVAL AIR SQUADRON

A FONAC/MoD signal announcing the formation of 809 Sqdn and the appointment of Lt Cdr T.J.H.Gedge as its Commanding Officer was issued during the afternoon of 7 April. Lt Cdr Gedge, a former CO of 800 Sqdn and thus an experienced Sea Harrier pilot, had arrived at Yeovilton the previous day to set the wheels in motion prior to the official commissioning on 8 April. The unit's main role was to augment and, should the need arise, provide attrition replacement aircraft and pilots for 800 and 801 Sqdns on 'Hermes' and 'Invincible'. In addition, because 899 Sqdn was no longer viable at Yeovilton, responsibility for restarting pilot training was passed to 809 Sqdn.

As expected, the most immediate problems were providing the fledgling Squadron with experienced aircrew and serviceable aircraft. The eventual pool of eight pilots was drawn from exchange and Staff postings and the Royal Air Force. The CO (from a Staff post) and Lt D.A.Austin (from the Sea Harrier simulator unit at Yeovilton) were the first in situ, followed shortly afterwards by Lt W.Covington and Lt Cdr D.D.Braithwaite from exchange postings in the United States, Lt Cdr H.G.B.Slade from a similar post in Australia and Lt Cdr A.Craig who had been with 1(F) Sqdn flying Harrier GR.3's. Two experienced Harrier pilots from Royal Air Force Germany, Flt Lts S.Brown and J.Leeming, made up the complement. All ratings still with 899 Sqdn were transferred to the new Squadron.

The unit was to be allocated production Sea Harriers, any development aircraft being used for familiarisation and work-up with a secondary role of FIR should the need arise. That was logical as development aircraft tend to have numerous non-standard modifications which could well cause some unnecessary problems for maintenance personnel under wartime conditions. Initially, Tim Gedge had hoped to raise a ten-aircraft squadron, but he reluctantly had to accept that eight was the most that could be operationally available by the end of April without utilising development aeroplanes. Potential sources of Sea Harriers were the storage unit at St Athan (five), 899 SHSU Yeovilton (two) and British Aerospace (one under accelerated construction). All the aircraft at St Athan and Yeovilton were in various stages of maintenance or modification which would require a lot of effort to bring them up to service issue standard in the limited time available. Additionally, three out of four development aircraft could, if absolutely necessary, be made available for operational use. Naturally, MoD(PE) was reluctant to release them from the inevitable high-priority flight trials and equipment tests being, or about to be, undertaken for potential use by Sea Harriers in the South Atlantic.

Aircraft from St Athan, some of them without radar,

NAVHARS or HUD's, started arriving at the Yeovilton SHSU as early as 6 April to join others already being serviced. In under a week, as a result of co-operation and understanding between flying, maintenance, modification and repainting personnel, 809 Sqdn had acquired sufficient Sea Harriers to enable it to become a viable unit. To supplement those aircraft, full use was made of the resident dual-seat Harrier T.4's and Hunter T.8M [see 899 Sqdn notes].

Full Squadron work-up commenced on 12 April, the initial priority being given to converting Craig and the two Royal Air Force pilots to the Sea Harrier while the remainder refamiliarised themselves on the type. Steve Brown and John Leeming were two useful acquisitions as both had previous Lightning interceptor expertise which enabled them to adapt quickly to the Sea Harrier, its Blue Fox radar and associated AI tactics. Everyone received "ski-jump" take-off experience from Yeovilton's ramp, the angle of which could be adjusted to represent either 'Hermes' or 'Invincible'. ACM and weapons delivery were both practised, as was DACT against FRADU Hunters.

The intensive maintenance and preparation programme meant that the Squadron's aircraft spent more time hangared than flying. As an opportunity arose, each one was resprayed in the new Medium Greys air-combat livery. That scheme resulted from consultation with a weather and aircraft camouflage expert at RAE Farnborough (Mr P.J.Barley), a study of prevailing weather conditions around the Falkland Islands at the time Squadron aircraft were due to arrive in the South Atlantic, and an assessment of potential combat altitudes. In the final analysis, the camouflage adopted was not dissimilar to that being applied at the time to the Royal Air Force air defence fleet of Phantoms and Lightnings. The allocation and application of side-codes was not proceeded with as it was considered unnecessary. One aircraft (ZA177) was seen on 13 April masked-up as '252' but it finally emerged from the sprayshop uncoded.

By 21 April four aircraft had each acquired two 330 gallon underwing ferry tanks (borrowed from the Royal Air Force) and an IFR probe for practice "prodding" (Naval parlance for AAR) with Victor tankers that day and the next. Those link-ups were noteworthy as it was the first time that Sea Harriers had been air-to-air refuelled in service. The need for AAR capability resulted from tight work-up and deployment timescales which dictated that the aircraft would need to be flown out to Ascension Island at the end of April to embark the requisitioned (and aptly named) aircraft-ferry 'Atlantic Conveyor'. That plan also allowed the ship to leave the United Kingdom earlier than originally planned. Unfortunately, during limited flight trials the 330 gallon tanks proved too unreliable to risk using them on the long flight to Ascension Island. Tim Gedge decided to retain the Sea Harrier's normal, tried and proven, 100 gallon drop tanks and accept that more "prods" would be required en route to Wideawake.

Worthy of note was the opportunity taken on 22/23 April for three 809 Sqdn pilots to fly, in turn, in the rear seat of an Armee de l'Air two-seat Mirage IIIBE (261/2-ZF) which had flown to Coningsby for DACT with 1(F) Sqdn Harrier GR.3's. That at least gave some 809 Sqdn aircrew a chance to assess the combat capabilities of the type before they came face-to-face with it in the South Atlantic.

'Atlantic Conveyor' left Plymouth Sound on 25 April, but not before successful approach and touchdown trials had been conducted aboard her that day by Tim Gedge in XZ438. The Squadron work-up proceeded as planned with the last allocated Sea Harrier (ZA194) arriving from BAe Dunsfold on 28 April, having made its first flight a mere five days earlier! Between then and delivery it had been hurriedly brought up to service acceptance standard. 809 Sqdn then had its full complement of eight production Sea Harriers:

| | | | |
|---|---|---|---|
| XZ458 | XZ499 | ZA176 | ZA190 |
| XZ491 | ZA174 | ZA177 | ZA194 |

In addition, three development aircraft (XZ438, XZ439 and XZ497) had been delivered to Yeovilton, repainted in the Medium Greys scheme complete with 809 Sqdn Phoenix motifs on the fin and fitted with IFR probes in case any of the allotted aeroplanes went unserviceable at the last moment.

On 30 April six of the eight Sea Harriers departed Yeovilton to be air-to-air refuelled by Victor K.2 tankers en route to Ascension Island (via Banjul in The Gambia). The six, departing in two flights of three, were XZ458, XZ491, ZA174, ZA176, ZA190 and ZA194 flown by John Leeming, Bill Covington, Dave Braithwaite, Dave Austin, the CO and Steve Brown respectively. After a six-hour flight they arrived at Banjul, where they night-stopped before flying on to Wideawake next day. XZ499 and ZA177, flown by Alisdair Craig and Hugh Slade respectively, left Yeovilton on 1 May and, following the same route as the others, arrived safely at Wideawake on 2 May. Each aircraft had accrued more than nine hours flying and 14 link-ups with Victor tankers during the trouble-free deployment. Of the three work-up/FIR Sea Harriers left behind at Yeovilton, XZ438 was flown to A&AEE Boscombe Down on 30 April to continue development flying, whilst XZ439 and XZ497 were transferred to an embryo 899 Sqdn on 3 May.

At Wideawake the aircraft were parked on the airfield and protected as far as possible from the penetrating wind-driven sand and volcanic grit until 'Atlantic Conveyor' arrived off the Island on 5 May. The following day they were all washed down with fresh water and flown off for a short test-flight prior to landing vertically on the ship's forward pad (which had been flight-checked by Tim Gedge twelve days earlier). Once safely on board, the Sea Harriers were washed with fresh water yet again prior to being liberally sprayed with PX24 (a moisture dispersant). All but two were then cocooned in made-to-measure waterproof bags to prevent salt-water corrosion.

'Atlantic Conveyor' set course for the TEZ on 7 May with a crowded deck-cargo of Harriers, Sea Harriers, Wessex and Chinooks. Such a load was bound to be a tempting target for Argentine sea and air forces should the vessel ever come within range. Previous experience during the British carriers' passage to the South Atlantic had shown that shadowing Argentine Boeing 707's over

**Above Left** *'Atlantic Conveyor' off Ascension Island on 6.5.82 with her forward deck crammed with Sea Harriers, Harriers, Wessex and Chinooks.* **Above Right** *The majority of those aircraft were later "bagged" for corrosion protection during the journey to the TEZ.* **Below Left** *Fitted with an IFR probe, an armed and manned 809 Squadron Sea Harrier FRS.1 sits on the forward landing pad ready, if required, for a VTOL flight to intercept any hostile Argentine aircraft.* **Below Right** *An unidentified 809 Squadron aircraft lands on 'Invincible' after a short VTOL flight from 'Atlantic Conveyor' on 19.5.82.*
*(Ministry of Defence)*

much of the route to the TEZ were perfectly capable of, if so allowed, relaying ship positions back to base. In order to "Hack the Shad" (another self-explanatory Naval expression!), one of the non-cocooned Sea Harriers was kept fuelled and armed on permanent VTOL "alert" whilst the other remained in reserve. Tim Gedge and the Senior Pilot, Dave Braithwaite, were the designated "alert" pilots. Because of the fuel weight limitation associated with Sea Harrier vertical take-offs, an umbrella of Victor K.2 tankers was maintained until, and including, 13 May.

The journey south passed without incident and therefore no VTOL flights from 'Atlantic Conveyor' were necessary. By the morning of 18 May the ship was within VTOL range of 'Hermes' (although not 'Invincible' which was still some distance away). Between 1300-1500Z that day in perfect weather conditions, the following Sea Harriers were flown across to 'Hermes' by Steve Brown, Bill Covington, Hugh Slade and John Leeming respectively:

---

XZ499   ZA176   ZA177   ZA194

---

Later that day, around dusk, Tim Gedge flew ZA190 to 'Hermes' where he refuelled prior to a "ski-jump" launch at 2042Z for the 14-minute flight to 'Invincible' and his first non-simulator night landing for some considerable time!

Between 1200-1300Z the following day, the last three aircraft (flown by Dave Braithwaite, Dave Austin and Alisdair Craig) were cross-decked from 'Atlantic Conveyor' direct to 'Invincible'. Their arrival meant that the carrier then had her quota of 809 Sqdn Sea Harriers. They were:

---

XZ458   XZ491   ZA174   ZA190

---

Once aboard the carriers, the Squadron's aircrew, maintainers and aircraft were integrated into 800 and 801 Sqdns. Their exploits are dealt with under those two units.

Back in the United Kingdom, the training of further pilots for 809 Sqdn was already under way: Lt C.M.L.Gilbert and S/Lts A.R.McLaren and M.E.Robinson who commenced a Sea Harrier course in April joined the Squadron as "first-tour" pilots on 10 June. Two Sea Harrier conversion courses for the Royal Air Force provided a further four pilots during June, namely Sqdn Ldrs R.Thomas and J.A.West and Flt Lts P.J.Collins and D.R.Gibbons. With the exception of Thomas who left in July and Gibbons who departed in early October, the other five remained with the Squadron until it disbanded in December 1982. Lt Cdr T.H.Scott RNR, who had joined 809 Sqdn as AWI on 1 June, was the only Naval Reserve pilot to be called up during the conflict. He was normally employed by BAe and his flying skill allied to his knowledge of the radar and NAVHARS proved invaluable in bringing the new pilots up to operational standard. By mid-June the Yeovilton element of 809 Sqdn was becoming viable but what was needed before it could deploy was a carrier, some combat-experi-

enced pilots and, most important of all, aircraft!

Early in the conflict, the MoD had reviewed and dismissed the notion of returning 'Bulwark' to service. Instead, it was decided to accelerate the completion and commissioning of 'Illustrious' as a back-up to the other carriers. At the same time serious consideration was given to the idea of equipping her with Sidewinder-armed Harrier GR.3's. As events turned out the Argentine forces in the Falkland Islands had surrendered before the ship left Tyneside on 18 June to be commissioned at sea two days later en route to Portsmouth. The surrender meant that the carrier could then relieve either 'Hermes' or 'Invincible' and that returning Sea Harriers could be transferred to 809 Sqdn for redeployment on 'Illustrious'. The need to keep a carrier presence in the South Atlantic was two-fold. Firstly, after the Argentine capitulation, no declaration of cessation of hostilities was received from Argentina. Secondly, Stanley Airport would be unavailable to aircraft other than Harriers, Sea Harriers and helicopters whilst the runway was repaired and extended to accept RAF Phantoms. With those points in mind, and the fact that 'Illustrious' was not quite ready to deploy, the Royal Navy decided on the following course of action: 'Invincible' would withdraw well to the north of the COA for a short period of crew rest and recuperation and essential ship maintenance. On the return of 'Invincible' to the COA, 'Hermes' would set course for home where 'Illustrious' would be in her final work-up phase before sailing for the South Atlantic to relieve 'Invincible'.

'Hermes' was scheduled to dock at Portsmouth in late July. That would allow 809 Sqdn time to reach operational standard using the two 899 Sqdn Sea Harriers XZ439 and XZ497, the sole remaining MoD(PE) aircraft XZ440 (XZ438 having crashed on take-off from Yeovilton's "ski-jump" on 17 May) and any other available Harrier variants.

A core of combat-experienced pilots destined for the Squadron left the COA on 20 June. Lt Cdr R.V.Frederiksen and Lt M.Hale, both from 800 Sqdn, joined Tim Gedge (resuming his role as CO) and Dave Austin on the tanker 'British Wye' for the voyage to Ascension Island. On arrival, they transferred to a Hercules and endured the 15-hour flight to Lyneham and some well earned leave prior to reporting to Yeovilton. Meanwhile, back in the South Atlantic, the remaining two 809 Sqdn pilots who had been integrated into 801 Sqdn in May were officially transferred to that Squadron, while the four serving on 'Hermes' were formally posted to 800 Sqdn. Lt Cdr D.J.Thornton joined 809 Sqdn as Senior Pilot on 5 July and from that date almost daily training sorties were made to (and from) 'Illustrious' until, on 16 July, the two 899 Sqdn Sea Harriers (then totally dedicated to 809 Sqdn) embarked the carrier for an eleven-day final work-up. On 19 July, Tim Gedge and the other three Falkland Islands "veterans" reported to Yeovilton for refresher flying. That coincided with 'Hermes' being in the Bay of Biscay and within Sea Harrier range of Yeovilton. That day six aircraft (XZ499, XZ500, ZA176, ZA191, ZA193 and ZA194) flew off direct to the airfield for immediate attention by maintenance personnel. 'Hermes' arrived at Portsmouth on 21 July and the remaining Sea Harriers (XZ457, XZ459, XZ460, XZ492, XZ496 and ZA177) were flown off to Yeovilton the next day and towed straight into the workshops. By the time of the Yeovilton "Air Day" on 31 July, the best eight of the 12 had been overhauled, repainted and transferred to 809 Sqdn. All had been recoded in the '250' series, with at least one (ZA194) wearing Phoenix motifs in Pale Blue on both sides of the fin.

'Illustrious' sailed from Portsmouth dockyard on 2 August, seven Sea Harriers embarking that day in the English Channel while the eighth (XZ496) followed on 3 August. 809 Sqdn's complement was then as follows:

| | | | | | |
|---|---|---|---|---|---|
| ZA176 | '-/250' | ZA191 | '-/253' | XZ459 | '-/256' |
| ZA194 | '-/251' | ZA193 | '-/254' | XZ496 | '-/257' |
| XZ500 | '-/252' | XZ499 | '-/255' | | |

For the deployment the Squadron's aircraft had provision for a twin-Sidewinder installation under each wing and two of the new 190 gallon drop tanks. The new-size tanks were tried out by the Squadron for the first time on 3 August but, unfortunately, they induced a tendency for the aircraft to pitch-up during the launch. Because of that, four Sea Harriers were dispatched that day to Yeovilton to collect some standard 100 gallon tanks and return them to the carrier, which was by then south of Lizard Point in Cornwall heading for the Bay of Biscay. The 190 gallon tanks were not finally cleared for use until late September.

'Illustrious' continued south with two brief stops at Gibraltar and Ascension Island before she arrived in the COA off the Falkland Islands on 27 August. Two additional Sea Harriers had been flown aboard the previous day from 'Invincible' following in ADEX involving the two carriers. 'Illustrious' relieved 'Invincible' on 28 August, enabling the latter to sail north out of the COA that day en route to home waters and an ecstatic welcome at Portsmouth.

On 'Illustrious', 809 Sqdn's newly acquired aircraft were recoded as follows:

| | | |
|---|---|---|
| XZ491 | '-/258' | (ex-801 Sqdn '-/002') |
| XZ458 | '-/259' | (ex-801 Sqdn '-/007') |

The increase in complement enabled the Squadron to permanently detach two aircraft ashore to RAF Stanley (as the Airport was then named) and rotate aircrew and maintainers every few days. The arrangement had many advantages, helping to retain combat alertness amongst as many personnel as possible, helping to relieve the inevitable monotony of COA/FIPZ operations and helping to provide the basis for aircrew and groundcrew to spend some time on dry land and see something of the Islands, their inhabitants and the aftermath of the War.

Over the next two months there was a steady turnover in aircrew as leave-refreshed conflict "veterans" arrived to relieve other "veterans". The process actually started at the time of the two-aircraft transfer. Three pilots, Lt Cdr Dave Braithwaite (a former SP of 809 Sqdn) and Lts A.J.George and M.W.Watson were seconded to the Squadron until 5 September when their replacements, Lt D.A.Smith and Flt Lts John Leeming (a former 809 Sqdn

pilot) and D.H.S.Morgan arrived from the United Kingdom. The three 'Invincible' pilots rejoined their ship at Ascension Island, having flown there by Hercules from the repaired runway at RAF Stanley. Next to join was the recently-promoted Lt Cdr C.R.W.Morrell (formerly with 800 Sqdn on 'Hermes'), whose arrival on 15 September allowed a demobbed Lt Cdr Taylor Scott to return to BAe. Lt S.N.Hargreaves relieved Flt Lt Leeming on 27 September while Flt Lt Gibbons departed for home on 9 October.

Throughout that period of personnel changes, "alert" Sea Harriers (both ashore and afloat) were kept constantly available in addition to routine CAP cover. Work on RAF Stanley's runway extension was completed during the second week of October. One significant day, however, was 17 October when the first 29(F) Sqdn Phantom FGR.2 (XV468), escorted in by the Sea Harriers of Tim Gedge and Pete Collins, landed safely after an 8hr 45min flight from Wideawake which had involved seven AAR's. That event, the first ever arrival in the Falkland Islands of Royal Air Force fighter aircraft, signalled the transfer of responsibility for air defence of the Falkland Islands from the Fleet Air Arm to the Royal Air Force.

21 October was a memorable day: 809 Sqdn Sea Harriers bombed and sank the rat-infested hulk of the Argentine freighter 'Bahia Buen Suceso' which had been towed well east of Port Stanley. The vessel had previously lain in San Carlos Water since late June, having been towed there by the tug 'Irishman' after being blown aground when she broke loose from her moorings at Fox Bay East during a gale. Shortly after she sank, the Squadron's aircraft returned to strafe and rocket a smoke-float marking the spot where she went down. Ten Sea Harriers and eleven Sea Kings performed a final fly-past over Goose Green and Port Stanley before 'Illustrious' departed the FIPZ later that day for the United Kingdom, via the United States. Their services no longer required, Lts Hargreaves and Smith and Flt Lt Morgan left for home by air from RAF Stanley on 22 October. The Sea Harrier "alerts" ceased the following day.

'Illustrious' arrived in the Caribbean Sea on 4 November when four Sea Harriers were detached to NAS Roosevelt Roads in Puerto Rico. The carrier was berthed alongside at Roosevelt Roads from 5-11 November, moving to Fort Lauderdale in Florida on 12 November for a week. Her final port-of-call in the United States was Philadelphia from 22-29 November, the ship sailing for home on the latter date. On 6 December, two days prior to her arrival at Portsmouth, all ten 809 Sqdn Sea Harriers were flown off direct to Yeovilton.

809 Sqdn disbanded on 17 December and the well-known Phoenix emblem was laid to rest once more. The rising of the Phoenix between April and December 1982 is best summed up by this short poem penned by an unknown 809 Sqdn bard:

*Alas, too soon the day draws nigh*
*When the Phoenix squadron must cease to fly.*
*Though fire and flames are forced to dwindle,*
*The immortal spark awaits rekindle.*
*The snuffing out could hardly be faster,*
*But watch the BIRD at the next disaster!*

# 899 NAVAL AIR SQUADRON

From 2 April, all of 899 Sqdn's Sea Harriers and the majority of its personnel were dispersed between 'Hermes' and 'Invincible' and integrated into 800 and 801 Sqdns. Strictly speaking, the activities of its shore-based remnants are not within the context of this book. However, it is almost impossible to link together all the facets of the contribution made to Operation "Corporate" by the Sea Harriers and their aircrew without mentioning the activities of 899 Sqdn's Yeovilton element between April and August.

Throughout April the Squadron was bereft of Sea Harriers because those that remained after the departure of the two carriers were being worked on for issue to the newly-formed 809 Sqdn. The few maintainers left at Yeovilton were also absorbed into the new unit. Even the three MoD(PE) trials and development Sea Harriers (XZ438, XZ439 and XZ497) delivered to Yeovilton on temporary loan between 19 and 22 April did not join 899 Sqdn. As expected, they were used as work-up and FIR aircraft for 809 Sqdn prior to its deployment to the South Atlantic at the end of April.

809 Sqdn, equipped with eight production Sea Harriers, departed for Ascension Island over the two days 30 April and 1 May, leaving behind the three development aircraft. XZ438 returned to MoD(PE) at A&AEE Boscombe Down on 30 April but XZ439 and XZ497 were transferred to a grateful 899 Sqdn on 3 May. By 13 May, the Squadron's "winged fist" motif had been applied in Pale Blue outline form to the fins of both aircraft and each carried a small single-digit number (in the same colour) on either side of the nose underneath the cockpit.

---

XZ439 '2'    XZ497 '4'

---

What numbers '1' and '3' were remains unresolved, although logic would suggest that the four MoD(PE) aircraft (XZ438, XZ439, XZ440 and XZ497) had been allocated the digits '1' to '4' respectively for whatever reason.

A training course for three student Fleet Air Arm Sea Harrier pilots destined for 809 Sqdn began in April under joint 809/899 Sqdn responsibility. By the beginning of May, 899 Sqdn had acquired sufficient personnel to assume sole control of that and all subsequent training or conversion courses. Lt Cdr J.Gunning (formerly with the Naval Flying Standards Flight at Yeovilton) was appointed temporary CO (in lieu of Lt Cdr N.W.Thomas who was aboard 'Hermes') with a "called-up" RNR officer, Lt Cdr T.H.Scott from BAe, as Senior Pilot. 899 Sqdn's activities were, from the announcement of those appointments, almost exclusively linked to the creation of a pool of new, and converted, Sea Harrier pilots for 809 Sqdn.

899 Sqdn would have liked a third Sea Harrier on strength, but any such thoughts were dashed on 17 May

when Boscombe Down's XZ438 crashed on take-off from the "ski-jump" whilst on detachment to Yeovilton for a series of underwing tank trials. That left XZ440 as the only remaining development aircraft. The Squadron supplemented the shortage of Sea Harriers by making the fullest possible use of the detached 233 OCU Harrier T.4's maintained on its behalf by Airwork Ltd's FRADU at Yeovilton. Three T.4's were rotated through the station from the beginning of April to the end of July (XW927/Y XW934/W and XZ147/Z) with a maximum of two being available for most, if not all, of the time. At the end of May, training of the three new pilots for 809 Sqdn was reaching its peak and another single-seat Harrier was desperately required. A 233 OCU GR.3 (XV753/M) was delivered to FRADU from Wittering on 27 May, returning there on 4 June following the arrival at Yeovilton the previous day of Sea Harrier XZ440 on temporary loan to the Squadron. For "Blue Fox" radar training, 899 Sqdn used its Hunter T.8M (XL598 'VL/717') and, when available, a development example (XL602).

The scarcity of Sea Harriers for pilot combat training was partly offset by using the Yeovilton Sea Harrier simulator which had become available on 14 April. Being a very large piece of equipment, trainee pilots were provided with radar and visual displays of the Falkland Islands and realistic graphics of Pucaras, Skyhawks, Mirages and other types. Varying intensities of radar echoes for each type in relation to its altitude, attitude and range from the intercepting aircraft were programmable, as was the prevailing sea state (an important aspect which affects the discernable quality of an echo on a radar screen during an over-the-sea interception). Night landings and many other features of Sea Harrier flying could also be simulated.

On 1 June Lt Cdr Taylor Scott was transferred to 809 Sqdn as AWI. He was joined during the next fortnight by the three Fleet Air Arm pilots who had graduated from the 899 Sqdn training course and four Royal Air Force Harrier pilots from two Sea Harrier conversion courses *[see 809 Sqdn]*. During June those pilots consolidated their training using the two 899 Sqdn Sea Harriers and XZ440. Following the Argentine surrender on 14 June all the Squadron's efforts were channelled towards bringing 809 Sqdn up to full operational standard for deployment south aboard 'Illustrious' at the beginning of August. XZ440 (flown by Lt Cdr D.J.Ramsay RAN) made the first Sea Harrier landing aboard the new carrier on 24 June before returning to Yeovilton on 25 June. The aircraft continued to BAe Dunsfold that day upon reversion to MoD(PE) charge.

With only two Sea Harriers available until 'Hermes' returned from the South Atlantic in late July, additional aircraft had to be obtained from somewhere to complete the important final work-up phase of 'Illustrious', and 809 Sqdn, during July. To resolve that problem, 899 Sqdn hosted a detachment of eight 4(F) Sqdn Harrier GR.3's (XV740/A, XZ993/E, XW917/F, XZ968/K, XW763/N,

XZ138/Q, XZ132/R and XV787/T) which arrived at Yeovilton from Gutersloh on 9 July. After arrival, the Squadron was briefed on carrier operations and given some "ski-jump" practice before embarking 'Illustrious'. Sea Harriers XZ439 and XZ497 flew aboard the carrier on 17 July for operations until 25/26 July, being joined by up to six GR.3's at a time. During that short deployment, 'Hermes' had returned to Portsmouth (arriving on 21 July) where her final six Sea Harriers were flown off to the SHSU at Yeovilton (the previous six had flown off to Yeovilton on 19 July whilst the carrier was crossing the Bay of Biscay). The influx of Sea Harriers provided 809 Sqdn with its long-awaited aircraft and 899 Sqdn with enough machines to enable XZ439 and XZ497 to be returned to MoD(PE) on 2 August — the date that 'Illustrious' sailed for the South Atlantic to relieve 'Invincible'. Another sign of a return to normality was the arrival of 899 Sqdn's CO, Lt Cdr Neill Thomas. He had left 'Hermes' at Ascension Island, continuing his journey to the United Kingdom by air on 11 July for a short period of leave before rejoining the Squadron.

# INDIVIDUAL AIRCRAFT DETAILS

The basic low-vis scheme adopted by 800 Sqdn Sea Harriers aboard 'Hermes' during Operation "Corporate" (including those aircraft integrated from 899 Sqdn) consisted of Gloss Extra Dark Sea Grey overall, which was achieved by extending the normal topside colour to cover the standard White underside. Due to the lack of modern spray-painting facilities aboard the carrier, all colour scheme alterations were done by laborious brush-painting which gave rise to a crude but durable finish. ROYAL NAVY titles, underwing serials and Squadron marks were deleted by overpainting in Extra Dark Sea Grey. Black ventral fin serials were retained and Red/Blue roundels created by painting over the White portion in Roundel Blue.

Only the last two digits of the 800 and 899 Sqdn side-codes were retained, in Black or Roundel Blue, on the engine air intake flanks (original 800 Sqdn aircraft) or on the nose underneath the cockpit (former 899 Sqdn aircraft). Previously uncoded development or ex-storage aircraft were not allocated side-codes but instead carried the last two digits of their serial, in Roundel Blue or Black, on the engine air intake flanks.

On 'Invincible', the 801 and integrated 899 Sqdn Sea Harriers adopted the same low-vis scheme. In their case, however, the aircraft were spray-painted Extra Dark Sea Grey overall which gave a much smoother appearance. All former 899 Sqdn aeroplanes were allocated 801 Sqdn side-codes and, together with the original 801 Sqdn aircraft, wore the full three digits in Roundel Blue on the upper half of the engine air intake flanks. The last digit of the code was also carried in White on the cover of the starboard outrigger.

The formation of 809 Sqdn introduced another Sea Harrier colour scheme into the South Atlantic environment. In an effort to achieve the best air combat colours, RAE Farnborough expertise (allied to a knowledge of the general Falkland Islands weather conditions) gave rise to what became incorrectly known as the "Light Grey" scheme. A more correct title for the camouflage was the "Medium Greys" scheme, consisting as it did of Satin-Finish Medium Sea Grey overall except for the underside of the wing and tailplane which were painted in a Satin-Finish medium grey slightly lighter than Medium Sea Grey. The actual paint used was the nearest commercial equivalent to the colour more generally referred to as "Barley" Grey. Mr P.J.Barley was an RAE employee who had previously devised a similar colour scheme to that adopted for the Sea Harrier for use on Royal Air Force Phantom and Lightning interceptors.

Small-size Pink/Pale Blue roundels were worn on the nose only, below the cockpit. In addition, similarly coloured 809 Sqdn "Phoenix" motifs were applied to both sides of the fin, as were Pale Blue ROYAL NAVY titles. In general, the only position where the serial was carried was in Black on either side of the fuselage underneath the tailplane. There is evidence that 809 Sqdn side-codes were allotted [see ZA177], but that idea did not proceed beyond the masking-up of one aeroplane and all the Squadron's remaining aircraft stayed uncoded until integrated into 800 Sqdn and 801 Sqdn in the South Atlantic.

Those Sea Harriers absorbed into 800 Sqdn had their titles and "Phoenix" motifs overpainted in the nearest available equivalent to Satin-Finish Medium Sea Grey and the last two digits of the serial applied in Black to the engine air intake flanks. Those absorbed into 801 Sqdn aboard 'Invincible' also had their fin-markings deleted with an overspray of Satin-Finish Medium Sea Grey equivalent. 801 Sqdn side-codes were allocated and the three digits applied in Pale Blue to the upper half of the engine air intake flanks. The last digit of the code was also carried in White on the cover of the starboard outrigger.

For 809 Sqdn's second deployment to the South Atlantic during August 1982, the Medium Greys colour scheme was retained, as were the Pink/Pale Blue roundels on the nose (in a slightly higher location). The Black serials were repositioned on the ventral fin and three-digit 809 Sqdn side-codes applied in Black on the engine air intake flanks. In addition, the last digit of the side-code was worn, in Black, on the outrigger covers. Pink/Pale Blue Squadron "Phoenix" emblems were painted on the fin either prior to or after departure from Yeovilton. Black ROYAL NAVY titles were worn at the base of the fin immediately above the tailplane.

As expected, all the Squadrons mentioned had Sea Harriers in schemes and markings at variance (to a greater or lesser extent) with the accepted standards. Those anomalies are dealt with in the individual aircraft histories, as are the colour schemes and markings of the shore-based examples of 899 Sqdn and Sea Harriers involved in the inter-squadron transfers which took place post-14 June.

Prior to 801 Sqdn returning to the United Kingdom in September 1982, a review of the effectiveness of the two (very different) Sea Harrier camouflage schemes adopted during the Falklands conflict had been initiated. The Medium Greys scheme was found to have been less than ideal as most air combat had taken place not at medium to high levels, for which environment the scheme had been devised, but at low level over land or sea where the Extra Dark Sea grey painted aircraft proved to be much less conspicuous. By October 1982, a compromise had been arrived at whereby the Sea Harrier force would be progressively resprayed in Satin-Finish Dark Sea Grey overall with Red/Blue roundels and Black side-codes, serials and Squadron markings. The first aircraft so painted was ZA177, which emerged from the Yeovilton sprayshop on 11 October (the "winged fist" fin motif being applied two days later).

*Examples of abbreviations used for markings and their meanings:*

*'H/123' Deck-letter for 'Hermes' and side-code worn in full.*

*'N/004' Deck-letter for 'Invincible' and side-code worn in full.*

*'-/001' Deck-letter N for 'Invincible' not worn; side-code worn in full.*

*'-/(1)26' Deck-letter H for 'Hermes' not worn; first digit of side-code deleted.*

*'-/254' Deck-letter L for 'Illustrious' not worn; side-code worn in full.*

*'77' Last two digits of serial worn in lieu of a side-code.*

---

**XZ438** FRS.1    *Not deployed south*

On 29.3.82 with BAe Dunsfold on MoD(PE) loan wearing the last two digits of its serial in White on the fin. Transferred to 'A' Sqdn at A&AEE Boscombe Down on 8.4.82, returning to Dunsfold 13.4.82. Delivered to 899 Sqdn SHSU at Yeovilton on 19.4.82 for use as an 809 Sqdn training, work-up and FIR aircraft. An IFR probe and two 330 gallon underwing ferry tanks were fitted on/by 21.4.82 for practice AAR's with 55 and 57 Sqdn Victor K.2's on 21/22.4.82. Resprayed in the Medium Greys scheme on 23/24.4.82 complete with pale markings and 809 Sqdn "Phoenix" motifs on the fin. Carried out approach and touch-down trials on the deck of 'Atlantic Conveyor' in Plymouth Sound on 25.4.82 prior to refuelling at Roborough and returning to Yeovilton that day. Transferred back to MoD(PE) loan on 28.4.82 and left for Boscombe Down 30.4.82. Visited Yeovilton for the day on 6.5.82. Returned to Yeovilton 7.5.82 (on MoD(PE) charge but still wearing 809 Sqdn colours) for a series of ski-jump trials carrying 190 or 330 gallon underwing fuel tanks. On 17.5.82, whilst carrying two 330 gallon fuel tanks, it crashed on take-off from the ski-jump, the pilot (Lt Cdr Poole) ejecting safely. Wreckage removed by road 20.5.82, arriving at AIU Lee-on-Solent on 21.5.82. Officially Struck Off Charge on 12.4.83.

**XZ439** FRS.1    *Not deployed south*

On 29.3.82 with 'A' Sqdn at A&AEE Boscombe Down on MoD(PE) loan wearing the last two digits of its serial in White on the fin. Visited RAE West Freugh for the day 7.4.82 on trials. Detached to Valley on 8.4.82 for practice Sidewinder firings over the Cardigan Bay ranges, returning to Boscombe Down on 11.4.82. Allocated to 809 Sqdn on 20.4.82 and delivered to Yeovilton on 21.4.82 for use as a training, work-up and FIR aircraft. An IFR probe and two 330 gallon underwing ferry tanks were fitted on/by 21.4.82 for practice AAR's with 55 and 57 Sqdn Victor K.2's on 21/22.4.82. Resprayed in the Medium Greys scheme by 24.4.82, complete with pale markings and 809 Sqdn "Phoenix" motifs on the fin. Allotted to 899 Sqdn at Yeovilton 3.5.82. The Sqdn's "winged fist" outline (on the fin) and the small digit '2' (below the cockpit) were applied to both sides in Pale Blue on 11.5.82. Dark Red/Blue roundels (nose only) had replaced the pale variety by 17.6.82. Visited 'Illustrious' for the day on 2.7.82 and again

3.7.82. Embarked 'Illustrious' for trials/training on 17.7.82, returning to Yeovilton on 24.7.82. Reverted to MoD(PE) loan 2.8.82 and delivered that day to BAe Dunsfold. Transferred back to 899 Sqdn on 27.8.82 and flown from Dunsfold to Yeovilton that day (still coded '2' in 899 Sqdn markings). Departed Yeovilton on 27.9.82 for BAe Dunsfold upon reversion to MoD(PE) loan.

**XZ440** FRS.1    *Not deployed south*

On 29.3.82 undergoing maintenance (including an engine change) with 'A' Sqdn at A&AEE Boscombe Down on MoD(PE) loan wearing the last two digits of its serial in White on the fin. Overhaul completed, it was test-flown 12.4.82 then detached to RAE West Freugh 13.4.82 for trials, returning to Boscombe Down on 14.4.82. Delivered to 899 Sqdn SHSU at Yeovilton on 3.6.82 for 899 Sqdn. Still in the Extra Dark Sea Grey/White scheme, it embarked 'Illustrious' on 24.6.82 for trials/training. Returned to Yeovilton 25.6.82 and on to BAe Dunsfold the same day upon reversion to MoD(PE) loan. Delivered to 'A' Sqdn A&AEE Boscombe Down on 15.7.82 for trials (which commenced 16.7.82) with twin AIM-9L Sidewinder installations under each wing and two 190 gallon drop tanks. Ski-jump take-offs with those attachments were carried out at Yeovilton during day detachments on 4/18/26.8.82. Departed Boscombe Down on 2.9.82 upon transfer to BAe Dunsfold.

**XZ450** FRS.1

On 29.3.82 with BAe Dunsfold on MoD(PE) loan wearing the last two digits of its serial in White on the fin. Transferred to 899 Sqdn SHSU for 800 Sqdn on 2.4.82 and delivered to Yeovilton on 3.4.82. Embarked 'Hermes' at Portsmouth on 4.4.82 and sailed with the ship (sitting at the head of the ski-jump) on 5.4.82. As from c10.4.82 the brush-painted low-vis scheme was applied. The '50' on the fin was deleted and transferred in Black to the engine air intake flanks in lieu of a proper 800 Sqdn code.

On 4.5.82, during a cluster-bomb attack on Goose Green airstrip, it was hit by 35mm cannon shells from a GADA601 Oerlikon AA gun and crashed to the south-east of the airfield. The disintegrating airframe's momentum carried it through a gate, across the Darwin road

and through a fence before coming to a halt in a field (UC 641569) adjacent to the eastern perimeter of the airstrip. Lt Taylor was killed and the remains of his aircraft were later removed to a scrap area at Goose Green. Wreckage still present there on 11.8.85.

**XZ451** FRS.1

On 29.3.82 with 899 Sqdn at Yeovilton coded 'VL/710'. Transferred to 801 Sqdn 2.4.82 on an increase in complement and embarked 'Invincible' at Portsmouth on 4.4.82, still coded 'VL/710'. Sailed with the ship on 5.4.82 and during the passage south was resprayed in the low-vis scheme. At the same time the newly-allocated 801 Sqdn code '-/006' was applied.

During the afternoon of 1.5.82, while being flown by Lt Cdr Ward, one of a formation of three Mentors of 4 Escuadrilla was strafed to the north of Berkeley Sound, East Falkland. Although a cannon shell hit the rear cockpit area, the pilot (Teniente de Fragata Manzella) was uninjured. The aircraft (identity unknown) was only superficially damaged and returned safely to its base on Pebble Island.

During the evening of 1.5.82, while being flown by Lt Curtis, a low-flying Canberra (B-110 of Grupo 2) was attacked some 50 miles west of 'Invincible' (which was positioned north north-east of the Falklands). The first of two Sidewinders fired in quick succession hit the aircraft, which exploded and fell into the sea some 150 miles north north-west of Port Stanley. Crew members Primer Teniente Gonzalez and Teniente Ibanez both ejected but were never found.

On 21.5.82, while being flown by Lt Cdr Ward, a very low-flying Pucara (A-511 of Grupo 3) was attacked south-west of Goose Green. Using cannon, the first burst damaged the Pucara's port aileron, the second hit the starboard engine while the final burst damaged the canopy and upper fuselage. Its pilot, Mayor Tomba, ejected safely and the Pucara crashed to the north-west of Drone Hill, Lafonia.

On 1.6.82, again being flown by Lt Cdr Ward, a C-130E (TC-63 of Grupo 1) was intercepted some 50 miles north of Pebble Island. Two AIM-9L's were fired at it, the first of which fell short. The second hit the starboard wing setting it on fire. A follow-up burst of cannon fire to the tail area caused the Hercules to nose-dive into the sea, killing all seven persons on board.

Departed the FIPZ with 'Invincible' on 28.8.82 for the UK, arriving at Portsmouth on 17.9.82. Disembarked later in the day to Yeovilton on temporary transfer to 800 Sqdn.

*No "kill" markings - however, a Canberra was reportedly stencilled below the cockpit (on the port side) c2.5.82 but removed a few days later.*

### XZ452 FRS.1

On 29.3.82 with 899 Sqdn at Yeovilton coded 'VL/711'. Transferred to 801 Sqdn 2.4.82 on an increase in complement and embarked 'Invincible' at Portsmouth on 4.4.82 still coded 'VL/711'. Sailed with the ship on 5.4.82 and during the passage south was resprayed in the low-vis scheme. At the same time the newly-allocated 801 Sqdn code '-/007' was applied.

While being flown by Flt Lt Barton over West Falkland on 1.5.82, a Mirage IIIEA (I-015 of Grupo 8) was intercepted and shot down by an AIM-9L. The pilot, Primer Teniente Perona, ejected and survived. His Mirage reportedly crashed into the sea, but pieces of it are believed to have come down in the North West Pass area of West Falkland.

On 6.5.82 the aircraft was lost while being flown by Lt Cdr Eyton-Jones. He and Lt Curtis (in XZ453) were investigating a possible low-level fast-moving contact near the hulk of 'Sheffield' when they descended into very low cloud and/or fog and either collided or struck the sea. Both aircraft were lost at position 53°00'S 57°00.7'W.

*First air-to-air "kill" of the conflict but no kill markings applied.*

### XZ453 FRS.1

On 29.3.82 with 899 Sqdn at Yeovilton coded 'VL/715'. Transferred to 801 Sqdn 2.4.82 on an increase in complement and embarked 'Invincible' at Portsmouth on 4.4.82 still coded 'VL/715'. Sailed with the ship on 5.4.82 and during the passage south it was resprayed in the low-vis scheme. At the same time the newly-allocated 801 Sqdn code '-/009' was applied.

On 1.5.82, while being flown by Lt Thomas over West Falkland, a Mirage IIIEA (I-019 of Grupo 8) was engaged. The Mirage flew into cloud followed by an AIM-9L and it later transpired that the aircraft had been hit. The pilot, Capitan Garcia Cuerva, made for Stanley Airport to attempt an emergency landing but his Mirage was brought down by Argentine AAA fire and he was killed.

On 6.5.82 the aircraft was lost while being flown by Lt Curtis. He and Lt Cdr Eyton-Jones (in XZ452) were investigating a possible low-level fast-moving contact near the hulk of 'Sheffield' when they descended into very low cloud and/or fog and either collided or struck the sea. Both aircraft were lost at position 53°00'S 57°00.7'W.

*No "kill" markings applied.*

### XZ455 FRS.1

On 29.3.82 with 899 Sqdn at Yeovilton coded 'VL/712'. Transferred to 800 Sqdn 2.4.82 on an increase in complement and embarked 'Hermes' 5.4.82 while the carrier was underway in the English Channel following her departure from Portsmouth earlier that day. As from c10.4.82 the brush-painted low-vis scheme was applied. The last two digits of the 899 Sqdn code were retained and overpainted in Black, ie '-/(7)12'.

Flt Lt Penfold was flying the aircraft well north of Lively Island, East Falkland on 1.5.82 when he intercepted a Dagger (C-433 of Grupo 6) flown by Primer Teniente Ardiles. He fired an AIM-9L and the Dagger was seen to explode, presumably killing the pilot. Pieces of the aircraft were later identified on Lively Island but the pilot was never found. On 21.5.82, while being flown by Lt Cdr Frederiksen, a flight of four Daggers from Grupo 6 was attacked north-west of Port Howard. Frederiksen fired an AIM-9L and hit C-409 flown by Primer Teniente Luna, who managed to eject safely before his Dagger hit the ground near Teal River Inlet, West Falkland.

An interesting event took place on 13.6.82: Lt Cdr Thomas was about to land at the Port San Carlos FOB to refuel when 18 Sqdn Chinook HC.1 ZA718 lifted the strip with its downwash. The pilot diverted to 'Fearless' to refuel (ZA177, the other aircraft involved, diverted to 'Intrepid').

Flown from 'Hermes' to 'Invincible' on 2.7.82 upon transfer from 800 Sqdn to 801 Sqdn. Aboard 'Invincible' it was resprayed and recoded '-/000' (replacing ZA174) in Roundel Blue on the upper half of the engine intake flanks. Additionally, the last digit of the code was applied in White to the starboard outrigger cover. Departed the FIPZ with the carrier 28.8.82 on 17.9.82 from where it disembarked to Yeovilton later in the day upon transfer to 899 Sqdn.

*No known "kill" markings. If any were applied, they may have been removed when the aircraft was resprayed on Invincible.*

### XZ456 FRS.1

On 29.3.82 with 899 Sqdn at Yeovilton coded '-/713'. Transferred to 801 Sqdn 2.4.82 on an increase in complement and embarked 'Invincible' at Portsmouth on 4.4.82, still coded '-/713'. Sailed with the ship on 5.4.82 and during the passage south was resprayed in the low-vis scheme. At the same time the newly-allocated 801 Sqdn code '-/008' was applied.

On 1.6.82, while being flown by Flt Lt Mortimer on an armed reconnaissance mission south of Stanley Airport, it was hit by a Roland missile and extensively damaged. Flt Lt Mortimer ejected safely, both he and his aircraft coming down in the sea close to the coast south of Port Stanley. He was rescued over eight hours later (on 2.6.82) by an 820 Sqdn Sea King HAS.5 (XZ574) from 'Invincible'.

### XZ457 FRS.1

On 29.3.82 with 899 Sqdn at Yeovilton coded

'VL/714'. Transferred to 800 Sqdn 2.4.82 on an increase in complement and embarked 'Hermes' at Portsmouth the same day to sail with the ship on 5.4.82. From c10.4.82 the brush-painted low-vis scheme was applied. The last two digits of the 899 Sqdn code were retained and overpainted in Black, ie '-/(7)14'.

On 21.5.82 while being flown by Lt Morrell, a 3 Escuadrilla A-4Q Skyhawk (0660/3-A-307) was attacked as it headed south-west down Falkland Sound at about 5,000ft. An AIM-9L was fired at it, blowing the tail off, and the Skyhawk crashed into the water at the southern end of the Sound. Its pilot, Capitan de Corbeta Philippi, managed to eject successfully.

Lt Morrell then attacked another A-4Q from the same unit (0665/3-A-312) but he had a hang-up (and later a misfire) with his second Sidewinder and had to resort to cannon fire. The Skyhawk was damaged and made for Stanley Airport to effect an emergency landing, but the pilot (Teniente de Navio Arca) was told on arriving overhead that his port main undercarriage leg was missing. He ejected successfully and came down in the sea. His aircraft was then brought down by Argentine AAA fire and crashed on the shoreline some 400 yards south of the Airport perimeter.

While being flown by Lt Cdr Auld on 24.5.82, an incoming flight of four Grupo 6 Daggers was intercepted near Pebble Island. He fired two AIM-9L's at two of the aircraft. Each missile impacted and both Daggers exploded, one at least (possibly both) falling into the sea north of Pebble Island. Lt Smith in ZA193 brought down another of the above Daggers, the three "kills" being C-410 (Teniente Castillo), C-419 (Mayor Puga) and C-430 (Capitan Diaz). Of those, Auld almost certainly shot down C-419 and (probably) C-430, leaving C-410 as the aircraft destroyed by Smith *[see ZA193]*. Puga and Diaz ejected successfully while Castillo was killed when his aircraft exploded.

Sailed with 'Hermes' from Port William on 3.7.82 en route to the UK. Arrived at Portsmouth on 21.7.82 and disembarked to Yeovilton on 22.7.82. Resprayed in the Medium Greys scheme 25/26.7.82 for possible use by 809 Sqdn. Not adopted and transferred to 899 Sqdn instead.

*"Kill" markings consisted of two Daggers and one Skyhawk (the second was not confirmed until much later) stencilled in White below the cockpit on the port side. Removed post-22.7.82.*

### XZ458 FRS.1

On 29.3.82 located at St Athan marked as 'H/124' (ex-800 Sqdn). Delivered from St Athan to 899 Sqdn SHSU at Yeovilton on 7.4.82 (still coded 'H/124') for nominal issue to 809 Sqdn prior to transfer to 809 Sqdn. Officially transferred from 899 Sqdn to 809 Sqdn 15.4.82. Rubbed down 13-16.4.82 prior to respray on 17/18.4.82 in the Medium Greys scheme, but left devoid of all marks other than Pale Blue serials on the fuselage below the tailplane. By 21.4.82 it was flying with IFR probe and two 330 gallon underwing ferry tanks for practice AAR's with 55 and 57 Sqdn Victor K.2's on 21/22.4.82. ROYAL NAVY titles, roundels and the "Phoenix" motifs had been applied by 26.4.82. Departed Yeovilton on 30.4.82 for Banjul in The Gambia (air-to-air refuelled en route), arriving at Wideawake on 1.5.82. Embarked 'Atlantic Conveyor' off Ascension 6.5.82 and sailed with the ship for the TEZ on 7.5.82. Flown off to 'Invincible' on 19.5.82 where it was transferred to 801 Sqdn. The "Phoenix" motifs and ROYAL NAVY titles were sprayed out and the code '-/007' (replacing XZ452) applied. Flown from 'Invincible' to 'Illustrious' 26.8.82 upon transfer to 809 Sqdn, bringing that unit's complement up to 10 aircraft. Recoded '-/259' in Black on the engine air intake flanks with the last digit repeated in Black on both outrigger covers. The "Phoenix" and ROYAL NAVY titles were restored. By that date it had a Black serial under the tailplane on the starboard side and a White one on the port side. Departed the FIPZ with the carrier on 21.10.82 for the UK (via the USA), flying off to Yeovilton on 6.12.82 (upon transfer that day to 899 Sqdn) prior to the ship docking at Portsmouth on 8.12.82.

*Post-26.8.82 the name "Ermantrude" was inscribed in Black below the cockpit on the port side (removed pre-6.12.82).*

## XZ459 FRS.1

On 29.3.82 with 800 Sqdn at Yeovilton coded 'H/125'. Embarked 'Hermes' at Portsmouth on 2.4.82 and sailed with the ship 5.4.82. As from c10.4.82 the brush-painted low-vis scheme was applied (retaining Black underwing serials). The last two digits of the code were retained and overpainted Black, ie '-/(1)25'.

On 16.5.82, while flown by Lt Cdr Batt (in company with Lt McHarg in XZ494), the Argentine supply vessel 'Rio Carcarana' was bombed and strafed while at anchor in Falkland Sound near Port King. The crew abandoned ship after uncontrollable fires broke out, but the vessel was not finally sunk until 23.5.82 when she was hit by two Sea Skuas fired from Lynx XZ723 of 815 Sqdn 'Antelope' Flt.

Sailed with the carrier from Port William on 3.7.82 en route to the UK. Arrived at Portsmouth on 21.7.82 (the code '25' by then painted Roundel Blue) and officially transferred to 809 Sqdn that day, prior to being flown off to Yeovilton on 22.7.82. On 27.7.82 it was resprayed in the Medium Greys scheme and coded '-/256' by 28.7.82. Embarked 'Illustrious' on 2.8.82 after she had left Portsmouth that day to relieve 'Invincible' in the South Atlantic (the "Phoenix" motifs were applied en route). Departed the FIPZ with the carrier on 21.10.82 for the UK (via the USA), being flown off to Yeovilton on 6.12.82 (upon transfer to 899 Sqdn SHSU for 899 Sqdn) prior to the ship's arrival at Portsmouth on 8.12.82.

*Post-2.8.82 the name "Emanuelle" was inscribed in Black below the cockpit on the port side (removed pre-6.12.82).*

## XZ460 FRS.1

On 29.3.82 with 800 Sqdn at Yeovilton coded

'H/126'. Embarked 'Hermes' at Portsmouth 2.4.82 and sailed with the ship on 5.4.82. As from c10.4.82 the brush-painted low-vis scheme was applied. The last two digits of the code were retained and overpainted in Black, ie '-/(1)26'.

On 1.5.82 while being flown by Lt Hale during a bombing raid on Goose Green airfield (in company with Lt Cdr Frederiksen in ZA191), a CBU dropped from either XZ460 or ZA191 scored a direct hit on a Grupo 3 Pucara (A-527) which was about to taxy out for take-off. The pilot, Teniente Jukic, was killed and his aircraft totally destroyed.

On 9.5.82 Lt Cdr Batt was flying the aircraft when he strafed and bombed the Argentine intelligence gathering stern trawler 'Narwal' some 60 miles south-east of Port Stanley. His centreline bomb entered the fo'c'sle but did not explode. That, along with cannon fire from himself and Flt Lt Morgan in ZA191 (plus follow-up cannon attacks by Lt Hale and S/Lt George), so damaged the vessel that it was halted and later boarded. She sank under tow the following day, in bad weather, as a result of battle damage.

Sailed with the carrier from Port William on 3.7.82 en route for the UK. Arrived at Portsmouth 21.7.82 and officially transferred to 899 Sqdn that day prior to being flown off to Yeovilton on 22.7.82.

## XZ491 FRS.1

On 29.3.82 at St Athan marked 'N/004' (ex-801 Sqdn). Delivered by road from St Athan to 899 Sqdn SHSU at Yeovilton 14.4.82 (serials and codes covered over; no fin markings carried) for nominal issue to 899 Sqdn prior to transfer to 809 Sqdn which officially occurred on 23.4.82. Resprayed in the Medium Greys scheme 26.4.82 with all external markings applied. Departed Yeovilton for Banjul in The Gambia 30.4.82 (air-to-air refuelled en route), arriving at Wideawake on 1.5.82. Embarked 'Atlantic Conveyor' off Ascension on 6.5.82 and sailed with the vessel for the TEZ on 7.5.82. Flown off to 'Invincible' on 19.5.82 where it was transferred to 801 Sqdn. "Phoenix" and ROYAL NAVY titles were sprayed out and code '-/002' [vacant slot; see ZA174] applied. Flown from 'Invincible' to 'Illustrious' on 26.8.82 upon transfer to 809 Sqdn, bringing the unit's complement up to 10 aircraft. Recoded '-/258' in Black on the engine air intake flanks (last digit not applied to the outrigger covers) while the "Phoenix" and ROYAL NAVY titles were restored (on the port side only by the time the aircraft returned to the UK). Departed the FIPZ with the carrier on 21.10.82 for the UK (via the USA), flying off to Yeovilton on 6.12.82 (upon transfer that day to 801 Sqdn) prior to the carrier docking at Portsmouth on 8.12.82.

*Post-26.8.82 the name "Cindy Lou" was inscribed in Black below the cockpit on the port side (removed pre-6.12.82).*

## XZ492 FRS.1

On 29.3.82 with 800 Sqdn at Yeovilton coded 'H/123'. Embarked 'Hermes' at Portsmouth 2.4.82 and sailed with the ship on 5.4.82. As from c10.4.82 the brush-painted low-vis scheme was applied. The last two digits of the

code were retained and overpainted in Black, ie '-/(1)23' (appeared on the starboard side only by the time the aircraft returned to the UK).

On 21.5.82, while being flown by Lt Cdr Thomas, it intercepted one of four Grupo 4 A-4C Skyhawks inbound to San Carlos Water over West Falkland. He fired an AIM-9L and the missile struck the Skyhawk which exploded on hitting the ground. Lt Cdr Blissett in XZ496 brought down another of the Skyhawks. Teniente Lopez (flying C-309) ejected unsuccessfully and was killed. Primer Teniente Manzotti (in C-325) failed to eject and thus could have been killed before his aircraft struck the ground. Both Skyhawks crashed close together south of Christmas Harbour near Chartres Settlement.

Sailed with 'Hermes' from Port William on 3.7.82 en route to the UK. Arrived at Portsmouth on 21.7.82 and officially transferred to 899 Sqdn that day prior to being flown off to Yeovilton on 22.7.82.

*"Kill" marking consisted of a Skyhawk stencilled in White below the cockpit on the port side (removal date, post-22.7.82, not known).*

## XZ493 FRS.1

On 29.3.82 with 801 Sqdn at Yeovilton coded 'N/001'. Embarked 'Invincible' at Portsmouth on 4.4.82 and sailed with the ship on 5.4.82. During the passage south it was resprayed in the low-vis scheme and coded '-/001'. Sailed from the FIPZ with the carrier on 28.8.82 for the UK, arriving at Portsmouth on 17.9.82 where it disembarked to Yeovilton later in the day upon transfer to 800 Sqdn.

## XZ494 FRS.1

On 29.3.82 with 899 Sqdn at Yeovilton coded '-/716'. Transferred to 800 Sqdn 2.4.82 on an increase in complement and embarked 'Hermes' at Portsmouth that day, sailing with the ship on 5.4.82. As from c10.4.82 the brush-painted low-vis scheme was applied. The last two digits of the 899 Sqdn code were retained and overpainted in Black, ie '-/(7)16'.

On 16.5.82, while flown by Lt McHarg (in company with Lt Cdr Batt in XZ459), the Argentine supply vessel 'Rio Carcarana' was bombed and strafed while at anchor in Falkland Sound near Port King. The crew abandoned ship after uncontrollable fires broke out but the vessel was not finally sunk until 23.5.82 when she was hit by two Sea Skuas fired from Lynx XZ723 of 815 Sqdn 'Antelope' Flt.

While being flown by Lt Cdr Gedge on 23.5.82 (in company with Lt Cdr Braithwaite in ZA190), it carried out a strafing attack on Puma AE-500 of CAB601 which had been abandoned on the ground near Shag Cove House, West Falkland. The helicopter had been immobilised earlier that day by Flt Lt Morgan in ZA192. However, Morgan had run out of ammunition and it was left to Gedge and Braithwaite to finish it off with cannon fire. An Argentine account differed slightly in that the Puma crew was reported to have destroyed the grounded helicopter before Gedge and Braithwaite arrived, in order to prevent it falling into British hands.

Flown from 'Hermes' to 'Invincible' 2.7.82 upon transfer from 800 Sqdn to 801 Sqdn. Aboard 'Invincible' it was resprayed and re-coded '-/008' (replacing XZ456) in Roundel Blue on the upper half of the engine air intake flanks, the last digit of the code being repeated in White on the starboard outrigger cover. Departed the FIPZ with the carrier on 28.8.82 for the UK, arriving at Portsmouth on 17.9.82 where it disembarked to Yeovilton later in the day upon transfer to 899 Sqdn.

## XZ495 FRS.1

On 29.3.82 with 801 Sqdn at Yeovilton coded 'N/003'. Embarked 'Invincible' at Portsmouth on 4.4.82 and sailed with the ship 5.4.82. During the passage south it was resprayed in the low-vis scheme and coded '-/003'. Left the FIPZ with the carrier on 28.8.82 for the UK, arriving at Portsmouth on 17.9.82 where it disembarked to Yeovilton later in the day on temporary transfer to 800 Sqdn.

## XZ496 FRS.1

On 29.3.82 with 800 Sqdn at Yeovilton coded 'H/127'. Embarked 'Hermes' at Portsmouth on 2.4.82 and sailed with the ship 5.4.82. As from c10.4.82 the brush-painted low-vis scheme was applied. The last two digits of the code were retained and overpainted in Black, ie '-/(1)27'.

On 21.5.82, while being flown by Lt Cdr Blissett, one of four Grupo 4 A-4C Skyhawks was intercepted inbound to San Carlos Water over West Falkland. He fired an AIM-9L at it and the missile was seen to hit the Skyhawk which immediately blew up. Blissett then went on to attack another A-4C with cannon fire. That aircraft was seen to leave the area with black smoke trailing from its port side, although it did manage to return safely to the mainland. Lt Cdr Thomas in XZ492 brought down another of the Skyhawks. Teniente Lopez unsuccessfully ejected from C-309 and was killed, while Primer Teniente Manzotti (in C-325) failed to eject and thus could have been killed before his aircraft struck the ground. Both Skyhawks crashed close together to the south of Christmas Harbour near Chartres Settlement.

Sailed with 'Hermes' from Port William on 3.7.82 en route to the UK. Arrived at Portsmouth on 21.7.82 and was officially transferred to 809 Sqdn that day before being flown off to Yeovilton on 22.7.82. On 28.7.82 it was resprayed in the Medium Greys scheme and coded '-/257'. Embarked 'Illustrious' on 3.8.82, the ship having left Portsmouth on 2.8.82 to relieve 'Invincible' in the South Atlantic ("Phoenix" motifs were applied en route). Departed the FIPZ with the carrier on 21.10.82 for the UK (via the USA), being flown off to Yeovilton on 6.12.82 (upon transfer to 800 Sqdn) prior to the vessel's arrival at Portsmouth on 8.12.82.

*"Kill" marking consisted of one Skyhawk stencilled in White below the cockpit on the port side (removed post-22.7.82).*

*Post-3.8.82 the name "Mrs Robinson" was inscribed in Black below the cockpit on the port side (removed pre-6.12.82).*

## XZ497 FRS.1    *Not deployed south*

On 29.3.82 on MoD(PE) loan at BAe Dunsfold. Allocated to 809 Sqdn 22.4.82 and delivered that day from Dunsfold to Yeovilton already painted in the Medium Greys scheme with Black underwing and ventral fillet serials but devoid of roundels. Used in 809 Sqdn's final work-up phase to be available, if required, as an FIR aircraft. By 26.4.82 ROYAL NAVY titles, nose roundels and the "Phoenix" emblem had been applied. Transferred to 899 Sqdn on 3.5.82. The Sqdn's "winged fist" outline (replacing the fin "Phoenix") and the small digit '4' on both sides below the cockpit were applied in Pale Blue on 13.5.82. By 17.6.82 Dark Red/Blue roundels (nose only) had replaced the pale variety. Embarked 'Illustrious' on 17.7.82 for trials/training, returning to Yeovilton on 26.7.82. Departed Yeovilton on 2.8.82 for BAe Dunsfold upon reversion to MoD(PE) loan.

## XZ498 FRS.1

On 29.3.82 with 801 Sqdn at Yeovilton coded 'N/005'. Embarked 'Invincible' at Portsmouth on 4.4.82 and sailed with the ship on 5.4.82. During the passage south it was resprayed in the low-vis scheme and coded '-/005'. Sailed from the FIPZ with the carrier on 28.8.82 for the UK, arriving at Portsmouth on 17.9.82 and being flown off to Yeovilton later in the day upon transfer to 800 Sqdn.

## XZ499 FRS.1

On 29.3.82 with 801 Sqdn at Yeovilton coded 'N/000'. Transferred that day to 899 Sqdn SHSU and noted operating with the newly-formed 809 Sqdn 8.4.82 still coded 'N/000'. On 15.4.82 it was officially transferred from the SHSU to 809 Sqdn and resprayed in the Medium Greys scheme 21/22.4.82. By 26.4.82 it had received an IFR probe and all external markings. Departed Yeovilton for Banjul in The Gambia 1.5.82 (air-to-air refuelled en route), arriving at Wideawake on 2.5.82. Embarked 'Atlantic Conveyor' off Ascension 6.5.82 and sailed with the ship for the TEZ on 7.5.82. Flown off to 'Hermes' on 18.5.82 where it was transferred to 800 Sqdn. The "Phoenix" and ROYAL NAVY titles were painted out and the last two digits of the serial applied in lieu of an 800 Sqdn code, ie '99'.

On 22.5.82, while being flown by Lt Hale over Choiseul Sound, the Prefectura patrol vessel 'Rio Iguazu' was spotted heading for Goose Green settlement. With top cover provided by Lt Cdr Frederiksen (in XZ460), Hale strafed the boat and caused it to be beached and abandoned. The 'Rio Iguazu' was further damaged on 13.6.82 by a Sea Skua fired from Lynx XZ691 of 815 Sqdn 'Penelope' Flt.

On 8.6.82, while being flown by Lt Smith, an A-4B Skyhawk (C-204 of Grupo 5) was attacked at extremely low level over Choiseul Sound. An AIM-9L was fired, impacting the aircraft which struck the ground on the northern shore of Lafonia at Rain Cove (the Skyhawk may have hit the dunes before the missile caught it). The pilot, Primer Teniente Bolzan, was killed.

Sailed with 'Hermes' from Port William on 3.7.82 en route to the UK. Disembarked to Yeovilton 19.7.82 prior to the carrier docking at Portsmouth on 21.7.82. Reverted to 809 Sqdn that day and recoded '-/255' 26.7.82.

Embarked 'Illustrious' on 2.8.82 after she had left Portsmouth that day to relieve 'Invincible' in the South Atlantic ("Phoenix" motifs were applied en route). Departed the FIPZ with the carrier on 21.10.82 for the UK (via the USA), being flown off to Yeovilton on 6.12.82 (upon transfer to 801 Sqdn) prior to the carrier docking at Portsmouth on 8.12.82.

*"Kill" marking consisted of a Dagger stencilled in White under the cockpit on the port side; that was the type originally thought to have been hit before subsequent evidence revealed the aircraft to have been a Skyhawk (removed post-19.7.82).*

*Post-2.8.82 the name "Ethel" was inscribed in Black below the cockpit on the port side (removed post-6.12.82).*

## XZ500 FRS.1

On 29.3.82 with 800 Sqdn at Yeovilton coded 'H/130'. Embarked 'Hermes' at Portsmouth 2.4.82 and sailed with the ship 5.4.82. As from c10.4.82 the brush-painted low-vis scheme was applied. The last two digits of the code were retained and overpainted (almost certainly) in Roundel Blue, ie '-/(1)30'.

On 16.5.82, while being flown by Lt Cdr Auld (and accompanied by Lt Hargreaves in ZA191), the Argentine supply vessel 'Bahia Buen Suceso' was strafed as she lay alongside the pier at Fox Bay East. Damage was apparently slight but sufficient to prevent the ship putting to sea again.

On 21.5.82, while being flown by Flt Lt Leeming, an A-4Q Skyhawk of 3 Escuadrilla (0667/3-A-314) was attacked over Falkland Sound. Leeming experienced difficulties with his AIM-9L's and resorted to cannon fire. He dived at the Skyhawk from above and behind, firing at a point behind the cockpit area. The A-4Q disintegrated and he flew through the debris which fell into the Sound. Its pilot, Teniente de Fragata Marquez, was killed.

Sailed with 'Hermes' from Port William on 3.7.82 en route to the UK, disembarking to Yeovilton on 19.7.82 prior to the carrier docking at Portsmouth on 21.7.82 (the code '30' by then definitely in Roundel Blue). Transferred to 809 Sqdn on 21.7.82 and by 28.7.82 had been resprayed in the Medium Greys scheme and coded '-/252'. Embarked 'Illustrious' on 2.8.82 after she had left Portsmouth that day to relieve 'Invincible' in the South Atlantic ("Phoenix" motifs were applied en route). Departed the FIPZ with the carrier on 21.10.82 for the UK (via the USA), flying off to Yeovilton on 6.12.82 (upon transfer that day to 800 Sqdn) prior to the vessel docking at Portsmouth on 8.12.82.

*"Kill" marking consisted of a Skyhawk stencilled in White below the cockpit on the port side (removed post-19.7.82).*

*Post-2.8.82 the name "Myrtle" was inscribed in Black below the cockpit on the port side (removed pre-6.12.82).*

## ZA174 FRS.1

On 29.3.82 with 801 Sqdn at Yeovilton coded 'N/002'. Transferred to 899 Sqdn SHSU on 31.3.82 and noted there on 2.4.82. Seen flying with the newly-formed 809 Sqdn on 8.4.82 still coded 'N/002'. On 13.4.82 the code markings were rubbed down in preparation for a respray prior to its official transfer from the SHSU to 809 Sqdn on 15.4.82. Resprayed in the Medium Greys scheme 20/21.4.82 and by 26.4.82 had acquired an IFR probe and all external markings. Departed Yeovilton for Banjul in The Gambia on 30.4.82 (air-to-air refuelled en route), arriving at Wideawake on 1.5.82. Embarked 'Atlantic Conveyor' off Ascension on 6.5.82 and sailed with the ship for the TEZ on 7.5.82. Flown off to 'Invincible' on 19.5.82 where it was transferred to 801 Sqdn. The "Phoenix" and ROYAL NAVY titles were sprayed out and the code '-/000' (a vacant slot) applied.

On 29.5.82, while positioning for take-off, the ship rolled heavily in a very rough sea on turning into wind and the aircraft slid out of control across the deck, over the side and into the water. Its pilot, Lt Cdr Broadwater, managed to eject and was only slightly injured when rescued by helicopter, but the aircraft was lost at position 51°48.3′S 54°29.8′W.

**ZA175 FRS.1**

On 29.3.82 with 801 Sqdn at Yeovilton coded 'N/004'. Embarked 'Invincible' at Portsmouth on 4.4.82 and sailed with the ship on 5.4.82. During the passage south it was resprayed in the low-vis scheme and coded '-/004'.

On 21.5.82, while being flown by Lt Cdr Ward, a very low flying Dagger of Grupo 6 (one of three) was attacked to the west of Port Howard. Ward fired an AIM-9L as it crossed his path, the Dagger (C-407) exploding when the missile impacted. The pilot, Primer Teniente Senn, ejected safely prior to the aircraft hitting the ground about 2 miles south of Mount Caroline.

Departed the FIPZ with the carrier 28.8.82 for the UK, arriving at Portsmouth on 17.9.82 from where it disembarked to Yeovilton later in the day upon transfer to 800 Sqdn.

*No "kill" markings applied.*

**ZA176 FRS.1**

On 29.3.82 in storage (uncoded) at St Athan (the Fleet Reserve Storage Base). Transferred to 899 Sqdn SHSU (nominally for 899 Sqdn) on 6.4.82 and delivered to Yeovilton the same day. Noted flying with newly-formed 809 Sqdn 8.4.82. Officially transferred to 809 Sqdn 14.4.82 prior to being resprayed in the Medium Greys scheme on 22.4.82. By 26.4.82 it had acquired an IFR probe and all external markings. Departed Yeovilton for Banjul in The Gambia on 30.4.82 (air-to-air refuelled en route), arriving at Wideawake on 1.5.82. Embarked 'Atlantic Conveyor' off Ascension on 6.5.82 and sailed with the ship 7.5.82. Flown off to 'Hermes' on 18.5.82 and transferred to 800 Sqdn. The "Phoenix" and ROYAL NAVY titles were painted out and the last two digits of the serial applied in lieu of an 800 Sqdn code, ie '76'. Sailed with 'Hermes' from Port William on 3.7.82 en route to the UK, disembarking to Yeovilton on 19.7.82 prior to the carrier docking at Portsmouth on 21.7.82. Officially transferred to 809 Sqdn 21.7.82 and coded '-/250' on 22.7.82. Embarked

'Illustrious' on 2.8.82 after she had left Portsmouth that day to relieve 'Invincible' in the South Atlantic ("Phoenix" motifs were applied en route). Departed the FIPZ with the carrier on 21.10.82 for the UK (via the USA), flying off to Yeovilton on 6.12.82 (upon transfer that day to 801 Sqdn) prior to the carrier docking at Portsmouth on 8.12.82.

*Post-2.8.82 the name "Hot Lips" was inscribed in Black (along with a pair of lips in Red) below the cockpit on the port side (removed pre-6.12.82).*

**ZA177 FRS.1**

On 29.3.82 in storage (uncoded) at St Athan (the Fleet Reserve Storage Base). Delivered from there to the 899 Sqdn SHSU (nominally for 899 Sqdn) at Yeovilton on 7.4.82 and officially transferred to the unit 8.4.82. However, on that date it was seen flying with the newly-formed 809 Sqdn. On 13.4.82, whilst still in the Extra Dark Sea Grey/White scheme, the code '252' was masked-up on the nose ready for application but not proceeded with. Officially transferred from 899 Sqdn to 809 Sqdn on 15.4.82. Resprayed in the Medium Greys scheme on 17/18.4.82, devoid of roundels and serials. An IFR probe and two 330 gallon underwing ferry tanks were fitted by 21.4.82 for practice AAR's with 55 and 57 Sqdn Victor K.2's on 21/22.4.82. On/by 23.4.82 roundels and serials were applied, followed on 24.4.82 by ROYAL NAVY titles and "Phoenix" motifs. Departed Yeovilton for Banjul in The Gambia 1.5.82 (air-to-air refuelled en route), arriving at Wideawake on 2.5.82. Embarked 'Atlantic Conveyor' off Ascension 6.5.82 and sailed with the ship for the TEZ on 7.5.82. Flown off to 'Hermes' on 18.5.82 where it was transferred to 800 Sqdn. The "Phoenix" and ROYAL NAVY titles were painted over and the last two digits of the serial applied in lieu of an 800 Sqdn code, ie '77'.

On 8.6.82, while being flown by Flt Lt Morgan over Choiseul Sound, two A-4B Skyhawks of Grupo 5 were engaged at very low level. Two AIM-9L's were fired and one of the Skyhawks (C-226) fireballed and fell into the Sound near Philimore Island. The second (C-228) was hit in the tail area and disintegrated, falling into the sea about 2 miles north of Middle Island. Both pilots, Teniente Arraras (in C-226) and Teniente Vazquez (in C-228), were killed, although Vazquez was seen to eject from his aircraft.

An interesting event took place on 13.6.82: Lt Hargreaves was about to land at the Port San Carlos FOB to refuel, when 18 Sqdn Chinook HC.1 ZA718 lifted the strip with its downwash. The pilot diverted to 'Intrepid' to refuel (XZ455, the other aircraft involved, diverted to 'Fearless').

Sailed with 'Hermes' from Port William on 3.7.82 en route to the UK, arriving at Portsmouth on 21.7.82 (sitting at the head of the ski-jump). Disembarked to Yeovilton 22.7.82 for maintenance by 899 Sqdn SHSU prior to issue to 899 Sqdn c6.8.82.

*"Kill" markings consisted of two Daggers stencilled in White below the cockpit on the port side; that was the type originally thought (although not by Flt Lt Morgan) to have been*

*hit before other evidence confirmed them to have been Skyhawks. "Kill" markings removed post-18.8.82.*

**ZA190 FRS.1**

On 29.3.82 in storage (uncoded) at St Athan (Fleet Reserve Storage Base). Allocated to 899 Sqdn SHSU on 6.4.82 (nominally for 899 Sqdn) and delivered to Yeovilton 7.4.82. Seen flying with newly-formed 809 Sqdn on 8.4.82. Officially transferred from the SHSU to 809 Sqdn on 15.4.82 and resprayed in the Medium Greys scheme on 19.4.82. By 26.4.82 it had acquired an IFR probe and all external markings. Departed Yeovilton for Banjul in The Gambia on 30.4.82 (air-to-air refuelled en route), arriving at Wideawake on 1.5.82. Embarked 'Atlantic Conveyor' off Ascension on 6.5.82 and sailed with the ship for the TEZ on 7.5.82. Flown off initially to 'Hermes' on 18.5.82 and then on to 'Invincible' later the same day upon transfer to 801 Sqdn. The ROYAL NAVY titles and "Phoenix" motifs were sprayed out and code '-/009' (replacing XZ453) applied.

On 21.5.82, while being flown by Lt Thomas, two of three Daggers from Grupo 6 were engaged west of Port Howard and an AIM-9L fired at each of them. The first aircraft (C-404, flown by Mayor Justo Piuma) blew up but its pilot managed to eject safely prior to the Dagger crashing close to Green Hill Bridge. Thomas' second missile exploded beneath the port wing of the second Dagger (C-403, flown by Capitan Donadille). The latter also managed a safe ejection before his aircraft crashed (virtually intact) near Green Hill Bridge, West Falkland.

On 23.5.82, while being flown by Lt Cdr Braithwaite (accompanied by Lt Cdr Gedge in XZ494), it carried out a strafing attack on Puma AE-500 of CAB601 which had been abandoned on the ground near Shag Cove House, West Falkland. The helicopter had been immobilised earlier that day by Flt Lt Morgan in ZA192. However, Morgan had run out of ammunition and it was left to Braithwaite and Gedge to finish it off with cannon fire. An Argentine account differed slightly in that the Puma crew was reported to have destroyed the grounded helicopter before Braithwaite and Gedge arrived in order to prevent it falling into British hands.

Departed the FIPZ with the carrier 28.8.82 for the UK, arriving at Portsmouth 17.9.82 where it disembarked to Yeovilton later that day on temporary transfer to 800 Sqdn.

*No "kill" markings applied.*

**ZA191 FRS.1**

On 29.3.82 with 899 Sqdn at Yeovilton coded '-/718'. Transferred to 800 Sqdn on 2.4.82 on an increase in Sqdn complement embarked 'Hermes' at Portsmouth that day, sailing with the ship on 5.4.82. As from c10.4.82 the brush-painted low-vis scheme was applied. The last two digits of the 899 Sqdn code were retained and overpainted in Black, ie '-/(7)18'.

On 1.5.82, while being flown by Lt Cdr Frederiksen during a bombing raid on Goose Green airfield (in company with Lt Hale in XZ460), a CBU dropped from either ZA191 or XZ460 scored a direct hit on a Grupo 3 Pucara (A-527) which was about to taxy out for take-off. The pilot, Teniente Jukic, was killed and his aircraft totally destroyed.

During the morning of 9.5.82, Flt Lt Morgan (in company with Lt Cdr Batt in XZ460) was flying the aircraft when he attacked the Argentine intelligence-gathering stern trawler 'Narwal' some 60 miles south-east of Port Stanley. His centreline bomb missed the target (although Batt's hit and failed to explode), but subsequent cannon fire from both aircraft (plus a follow-up cannon attack by Lt Hale and S/Lt George) so damaged the vessel that she was halted and later boarded. She sank under tow the following day, in bad weather, as a result of battle damage.

On 16.5.82, while being flown by Lt Hargreaves (in company with Lt Cdr Auld in XZ500), the Argentine supply vessel 'Bahia Buen Suceso' was strafed as it lay alongside the pier at Fox Bay East. Damage was apparently slight but sufficient to prevent the ship putting to sea again. The aircraft was damaged in the tail area by Argentine gunfire during the attack but was quickly repaired and returned to service.

On 23.5.82, while being flown by Flt Lt Leeming (accompanied by Flt Lt Morgan in ZA192), an A-109A (AE-337) of CAB601 was attacked whilst taking cover in a small ravine near Shag Cove House, West Falkland. Both Leeming and Morgan strafed it with cannon fire until the helicopter exploded and burst into flames. The crew escaped unharmed.

Sailed with 'Hermes' from Port William on 3.7.82 en route to the UK, disembarking to Yeovilton on 19.7.82 (upon transfer to 809 Sqdn) prior to the carrier docking at Portsmouth on 21.7.82. Resprayed in the Medium Greys scheme 23/24.7.82 and first noted as '-/253' on 25.7.82. Embarked 'Illustrious' on 2.8.82 after she had left Portsmouth that day to relieve 'Invincible' in the South Atlantic ("Phoenix" motifs were applied en route). Departed the FIPZ with 'Illustrious' on 21.10.82 for the UK, being flown off to Yeovilton on 6.12.82 (upon transfer to 899 Sqdn) prior to the carrier docking at Portsmouth on 8.12.82.

*No "kill" markings applied.*

*Post-2.8.82 the name "Phyllis" was inscribed in Black below the cockpit on the port side (removed pre-6.12.82).*

### ZA192 FRS.1

On 29.3.82 in storage (uncoded) at St Athan (Fleet Reserve Storage Base). Delivered from St Athan to 899 Sqdn SHSU at Yeovilton on 4.4.82 for final preparation prior to joining 800 Sqdn. Embarked 'Hermes' at Portsmouth the same day (still uncoded), sailing with the carrier on 5.4.82. As from c10.4.82 the brush-painted low-vis scheme was applied. The last two digits of the serial were applied in Black in lieu of an 800 Sqdn code, ie '92'.

On 1.5.82, while being flown by Flt Lt Morgan during a bombing raid on Stanley Airport, a CBU dropped from the aircraft was almost certainly responsible for severing the aft end of the Argentine-impressed FIGAS

Islander (VP-FAY) parked near the runway. The Sea Harrier was hit on the fin by an Argentine 20mm shell but returned safely to 'Hermes' where it was quickly repaired and restored to service.

On 23.5.82, again being flown by Flt Lt Morgan (accompanied by Flt Lt Leeming in ZA191), a Puma (AE-503) from CAB601 was seen flying very low over water close to Shag Cove House, West Falkland. Morgan descended and carried out a head-on pass to positively identify the type, but that caused the Puma pilot to take evasive action which resulted in it crashing and exploding soon after impact. Leeming then saw an A-109A (AE-337) from the same unit taking cover in a small ravine. Both he and Morgan strafed the helicopter until it exploded and burst into flames. The crew escaped unharmed.

Immediately following that attack, a second Puma (AE-500) was sighted close to AE-503. Leeming's ammunition was exhausted, so Morgan strafed the helicopter with his few remaining rounds and immobilised it (the Puma was destroyed later that day during a follow-up attack by Lt Cdr Gedge in XZ494 and Lt Cdr Braithwaite in ZA190). As Morgan and Leeming departed the area, a third Puma (AE-508) was sighted but had to be left unharmed.

Later that evening, Lt Cdr Batt took off from 'Hermes' in the aircraft for a toss-bombing attack on Stanley Airport. Shortly after take-off, it was seen to explode, either just before or on hitting the sea close to position 50°35′S 56°15′W. Lt Cdr Batt was killed.

*No "kill" markings are believed to have been applied.*

### ZA193 FRS.1

On 29.3.82 in storage (uncoded) at St Athan (Fleet Reserve Storage Base). Delivered to 899 Sqdn SHSU at Yeovilton 3.4.82. Transferred to 800 Sqdn on 4.4.82 and embarked 'Hermes' at Portsmouth the same day (still uncoded). Sailed with the ship on 5.4.82. As from c10.4.82 the brush-painted low-vis scheme was applied (retaining underwing 'D' Class Red/White/Blue roundels). The last two digits of the serial were applied, almost certainly, in Roundel Blue in lieu of an 800 Sqdn code, ie '93'.

On 24.5.82, while being flown by Lt Smith near Pebble Island, a Dagger from Grupo 6 (one of four) was engaged at low level. An AIM-9L was fired, destroying the aircraft. Lt Cdr Auld in XZ457 brought down two more of the Daggers. The three "kills" were C-410 (Teniente Castillo), C-419 (Mayor Puga) and C-430 (Capitan Diaz). Of those, Auld almost certainly shot down C-419 and (probably) C-430. That would leave C-410 as the one destroyed by Smith and is believed to account for the unidentified Dagger wreckage found on the west side of Elephant Bay on the slopes of First Mount. Puga and Diaz both ejected successfully but Castillo was killed when his aircraft exploded.

Sailed with 'Hermes' from Port William on 3.7.82 en route to the UK, disembarking to Yeovilton on 19.7.82 (upon transfer to 809 Sqdn) prior to the carrier docking at Ports-

mouth on 21.7.82 (the code '93' was by then definitely in Roundel Blue). Resprayed in the Medium Greys scheme 24/25.7.82 and first noted as '-/254' on 25.7.82. Embarked 'Illustrious' on 2.8.82 after she had left Portsmouth that day to relieve 'Invincible' in the South Atlantic ("Phoenix" motifs were applied en route). Departed the FIPZ with the carrier on 21.10.82 for the UK (via the USA), flying off to Yeovilton on 6.12.82 (upon transfer that day to 801 Sqdn) prior to the vessel docking at Portsmouth on 8.12.82.

*"Kill" marking consisted of a Dagger stencilled in White below the cockpit on the port side (removed post-19.7.82).*

*Post-2.8.82 the name "Esmeralda" was inscribed in Black below the cockpit on the port side (removed pre-6.12.82).*

### ZA194 FRS.1

On 29.3.82 still under construction at BAe Dunsfold. Final assembly and testing were accelerated by two months, resulting in its first flight from Dunsfold on 23.4.82. Delivered to Yeovilton (upon transfer to 809 Sqdn) on 28.4.82, having already been sprayed in the Medium Greys scheme with Black underwing and ventral fin serials but minus roundels. On 29.4.82 ROYAL NAVY titles, roundels and the "Phoenix" motifs were applied (Black underwing serials were retained), and by that date it had also acquired an IFR probe. Departed Yeovilton for Banjul in The Gambia on 30.4.82 (air-to-air refuelled en route), arriving at Wid="Widomething"Wideawake on 1.5.82. Embarked 'Atlantic Conveyor' off Ascension on 6.5.82 and sailed with the ship for the TEZ on 7.5.82. Flown off to 'Hermes' 18.5.82 where it was transferred to 800 Sqdn. The "Phoenix" and ROYAL NAVY titles were painted over and the last two digits of the serial applied in lieu of an 800 Sqdn code, ie '94'.

On 23.5.82, while being flown by Lt Hale, a Dagger (C-437 from Grupo 6) was intercepted over Pebble Island. An AIM-9L was fired and it hit the aircraft which crashed on the west side of Elephant Bay about two miles north of Pebble Island settlement. The pilot, Teniente Volponi, was killed.

Sailed with 'Hermes' from Port William on 3.7.82 en route to the UK, disembarking to Yeovilton 19.7.82 prior to the carrier docking at Portsmouth on 21.7.82. On arrival it was transferred to 809 Sqdn and coded '-/251' on 22.7.82. By Yeovilton Air Day on 31.7.82 it had regained ROYAL NAVY titles and Pale Blue "Phoenix" motifs (they were Pale Blue/Pink by the time the aircraft returned to the UK). Embarked 'Illustrious' on 2.8.82 after she had left Portsmouth that day to relieve 'Invincible' in the South Atlantic. Departed the FIPZ with the carrier on 21.10.82 for the UK (via the USA), flying off to Yeovilton on 6.12.82 (upon transfer to 899 Sqdn SHSU) prior to the vessel docking at Portsmouth on 8.12.82.

*"Kill" marking consisted of a Dagger stencilled in White below the cockpit on the port side (removed post-19.7.82).*

*Post-2.8.82 the name "Rosie" was inscribed in Black below the cockpit on the port side (removed pre-6.12.82).*

South of Ascension Island en route to the MEZ in late 4.82 is Sea King HAS.5 ZA134 '–/(0)13' of 820 Squadron, being used in the utility role from 'Invincible'. The insatiable demand for load-lifting helicopters during the conflict meant that virtually every Royal Navy anti-submarine Sea King deployed to the South Atlantic was tasked with HDS or VER-TREP duties in addition to its normal function.     (Lt S. A. George, RN)

825 Squadron HAS.2A XV656 '–/703' parked, most appropriately, on Victory Green, Port Stanley, sometime after the cease-fire of 14.6.82 but before 13.7.82, the date on which the helicopter departed for the United Kingdom aboard 'Atlantic Causeway'.     (E. Wareing)

Spruced up for the arrival of 'Hermes' at Portsmouth on 21.7.82 were the Sea King HAS.5's of 826 Squadron. On the right of the photograph is XZ571 '–/(1)43' which returned to the South Atlantic at the end of 1982 for FIPZ duties.     (Peter J. Cooper)

Unfortunately too late for involvement in the Falklands War were the Sea Kings AEW.2A's XV704 '–/361' and XV650 '–/362' (illustrated here over southern England) of 824 Squadron 'D' Flight. Conversion of the two former HAS.2A's to the early-warning radar role commenced at Yeovil in late 5.82 and by 30.7.82 both were ready for deployment. Three days later they departed in 'Illustrious' for the South Atlantic. Had they been available during the conflict at least some of the British tragedies might have been prevented.     (Ministry of Defence)

# SEA KING

## 814 NAVAL AIR SQUADRON

814 Sqdn did not leave the United Kingdom for the South Atlantic until 2 August, sailing aboard 'Illustrious' from Portsmouth. The unit is not therefore eligible for inclusion in the main text of this book, but its deployment is important for the continued ASW capability which the Squadron provided between 28 August (when 'Illustrious' relieved 'Invincible') and the end of the year, when a more permanent Falkland Islands detachment of 826 Sqdn was established. 814 Sqdn deployed with the following Sea King HAS.5's:

| | | | | | |
|---|---|---|---|---|---|
| XV675 | '-/264' | ZA168 | '-/267' | XZ922 | '-/272' |
| XV655 | '-/265' | XV652 | '-/270' | ZA167 | '-/273' |
| XV651 | '-/266' | XZ919 | '-/271' | XV661 | '-/274' |

These aircraft returned aboard 'Illustrious' and 'Fort Austin' during December 1982, basic details of the Ship and Squadron movements being included in the Individual Ship and Aircraft Details sections of this publication.

## 820 NAVAL AIR SQUADRON

Under the command of Lt Cdr R.J.S.Wykes-Sneyd, 820 Sqdn's aircraft were already embarked on 'Invincible' from the unit's home base of Culdrose before the start of the conflict. The Squadron's primary role was that of ASW, for which it was equipped with nine Sea King HAS.5's. At that time the helicopters were all painted in the standard RAF Blue-Grey colour scheme with White serials, deck-letters, codes and titles plus 'D' class roundels. The nine helicopters were coded as follows:

| | | | | | |
|---|---|---|---|---|---|
| XZ920 | 'N/010' | ZA134 | 'N/013' | XZ574 | 'N/016' |
| ZA127 | 'N/011' | ZA128 | 'N/014' | XZ921 | 'N/017' |
| ZA126 | 'N/012' | ZA135 | 'N/015' | XZ918 | 'N/020' |

'Invincible' had returned to Portsmouth on 22 March from Exercise "Alloy Express" in Norway with XZ574, ZA127, ZA134 and ZA135 embarked, all stowed below deck. The remainder of the Squadron's Sea Kings arrived from Culdrose the following day in preparation for the ship's next deployment, while the aircrew were looking forward to a period of shore leave over the Easter weekend. Following the order to prepare for sailing to the South Atlantic, personnel from 820 Sqdn were recalled to embark at Portsmouth and it was fortuitous that the aircraft were already on board. A further two Sea Kings were added as FIR aircraft from 706 Sqdn at Culdrose on 2 April:

| | | |
|---|---|---|
| XZ573 'CU/593' | | XZ578 'CU/589' |

This pair embarked at Portsmouth on 4 April and the carrier sailed at 1015Z the following day with XZ573, XZ574, XZ578 and one other on deck at the stern.

Application of a low-visibility colour scheme to the helicopters commenced circa 11 April, but the task was not completed until some time after 'Invincible' had left Ascension Island. The aircraft had their ROYAL NAVY titles and deck-letters deleted with RAF Blue-Grey. White serials were retained but the two-digit fuselage side-codes were over-painted in Black and the full three-digit code deleted altogether from the port side of the nose. Roundels were amended to Red/Blue by over-painting the White portion. The two 706 Sqdn Sea Kings were painted in a similar fashion and recoded within the 820 Sqdn sequence, the Squadron's complement then appearing as follows:

| | |
|---|---|
| XZ920 '-/(0)10' | XZ574 '-/(0)16' |
| ZA127 '-/(0)11' | XZ921 '-/(0)17' |
| ZA126 '-/(0)12' | XZ918 '-/(0)20' |
| ZA134 '-/(0)13' | XZ578 '-/(0)21' |
| ZA128 '-/(0)14' | XZ573 '-/(0)22' |
| ZA135 '-/(0)15' | |

Before Ascension Island was reached on 16 April, the Squadron conducted an intensive work-up period of training, trials and refresher flying. This included OTHT, HIFR, surface search and fighter evasion techniques. Live weapon drops began on 8 April using Mk.11 depth charges, while on 12 April Lt M.R.W.Lanyon and the Air Engineering Department designed, built, fitted and tested their own GPMG mounting for the Sea King within 24 hours of the requirement being placed. Two days spent at Ascension Island provided a change of task as the aircraft joined in the massive HDS operation to lift personnel, equipment and stores aboard the ships of the assembling Task Force as they arrived off the Island. ASW operations began in earnest when 'Invincible' sailed on 18 April and, as the ship approached the TEZ, surface search sorties were added to the flying programmes with one aircraft always airborne on the screen.

On 23 April the Squadron was involved in SAR operations in connection with ditched 846 Sqdn Sea King HC.4 ZA311 from 'Hermes'. At 2130Z the pilot (Flt Lt R.Grundy) was picked up by Sea King HAS.5 XZ574 (crewed by S/Lt C.P.Heweth, S/Lt HRH The Prince Andrew, Lt I.McAlister and LACMN T.Arnull) but, despite an intensive search, the aircrewman (POACMN K.S.Casey) was never found. The carrier arrived in the TEZ at 0530Z on 1 May, the Squadron being tasked with countering the threat posed by enemy submarines. The ship went to "Action Stations" at 1030Z after reports of an incoming air raid, tasking being increased to three aircraft on ASW screen and one on surface search, while the others were engaged in chaff-laying throughout the day. Following reports of enemy submarine activity, five aircraft maintained the ASW screen on 4 May but no contact was gained. Unconfirmed reports suggest that one such submarine (the 'San Luis') was detected and attacked on 5 May. There were even some reports of an enemy torpedo being launched at (and avoided by) 'Invincible' and the other ships. 5 May saw two aircraft on the screen and one on surface search duties, while a fourth aircraft flew to the wreck of 'Sheffield' to assess the damage and transfer a salvage team aboard. ASW operations continued during the next week, one Sea King flying a repair team to the damaged 'Glasgow' on 12 May. 826 Sqdn aboard 'Hermes' lost Sea King HAS.5 ZA132 on 12 May when it ditched and XZ578 was transferred from 820 Sqdn to replace it, flying from 'Invincible' to 'Hermes' on 14 May. On 15 May the second FIR HAS.5 (XZ573) was also transferred to 'Hermes', but its stay aboard the carrier was short-lived as it was lost on 18 May.

On 20 May the Squadron was involved in load-lifting between the ships of the Task Force in preparation for the landings the following day. Screening then continued, with three aircraft on ASW and one on surface search,

and on 25 May the Squadron was involved in the SAR operations for 'Atlantic Conveyor' (this task continuing until 0100Z the following day). One aircraft flew each day on 26/27 May to make a salvage assessment of the stricken container ship. A two-helicopter detachment (XZ920 and XZ921) transferred to 'Tidepool' on 29 May for ASW cover as the ship went into Falkland Sound to refuel other vessels inside the AOA, both returning to 'Invincible' at 1645Z on 30 May. Two days later, the Squadron was again involved in SAR operations when Flt Lt Mortimer of 801 Sqdn ejected from Sea Harrier FRS.1 XZ456 at 1740Z after being hit by a Roland missile while on a reconnaissance sortie near Stanley Airport. He was finally located by his small helmet light after an intense search, having switched off his SARBE transmitter after two short voice transmissions. Mortimer was eventually picked up at 0230Z on 2 June by Sea King HAS.5 XZ574 crewed by Lt Cdr K.Dudley, S/Lts J.A.Carr and M.Finucane and LACMN J.D.Trotman (he was delighted to see his old friend Mark Finucane on the end of the winch). Ian Mortimer had spent over eight hours in the sea very close to the enemy-held coast line and, when rescued, was some 120 miles from 'Invincible'.

'Invincible' detached to the south of the Falkland Islands in company with 'Brilliant' at dusk on 4 June to try and intercept enemy resupply flights to the Islands. The Squadron provided ASW cover while the 801 Sqdn Sea Harriers flew CAP missions during the hours of darkness, the ships returning to the CVBG early the next morning. A break in the ASW missions occurred again on 5 June, the Squadron claiming a "first" when one of its Sea Kings was dispatched to 'Fort Austin' in order to airlift a Pegasus engine to 'Invincible', the first time that such a transfer had been carried out between ships at sea. On 6 June Operation "Canbelow" was devised to try and intercept (or dissuade) not only the resupply flights but also the night bombing raids by Grupo 2 Canberras. 820 Sqdn continued to provide ASW cover during "Canbelow" detachments on the nights of 6/7 and 7/8 June.

As preparations were being made for the final assault on Port Stanley, XZ921 and ZA127 were detached to COMAW at San Carlos on 10 June in order to fly night surface search sorties to the west of the Falkland Islands, trying to locate enemy ships engaged on resupply missions. Two of the crews concerned were Lt Cdr K.Dudley, S/Lts J.A.Carr, M.Finucane, LACMN J.D.Trotman and Lt Cdr R.C.Green, Lt S.W.Marlow, S/Lt D.I.Hayes, LACMN M.Kenney. The detachment remained ashore (co-located with 825 Sqdn) under the command of Keith Dudley. After four days XZ921 was flown back to 'Invincible' and replaced by XZ920; by rotating the aircraft it was intended to maintain high serviceability in what was anticipated could be a prolonged time ashore. However, in the late evening of 14 June Keith Dudley was called from his tent and instructed to get his aircraft and crew onto 'Fearless'. He duly did so in XZ920 and was informed there that a ceasefire had been arranged. He was to fly to Fitzroy and collect Major General J.Moore (Commander Land Forces Falkland Islands) and take him to Port Stanley to accept the Argentine surrender. Dudley was briefed that at that stage the ceasefire was somewhat precarious, guaranteed to hold in Stanley but not over the Airport; his landing point was to be the football pitch, approaching from the north and remaining clear of known enemy troop concentrations to minimise any temptations to break the ceasefire. It had been intended to use a PNG-equipped 846 Sqdn Sea King HC.4 for the mission, but it was subsequently decided that an Observer-manned, radar-equipped HAS.5 would be better able to contend with the gale force winds and heavy snow showers. The flight to Fitzroy was uneventful and, having collected Maj Gen Moore, Keith Dudley proceeded to Port Stanley. Despite increasing snow storms and low cloud, he landed successfully at the Sportsfield which was illuminated by jeep lights. Maj Gen Moore disembarked and proceeded to the surrender talks. The terms of surrender of all Argentine forces on the Falkland Islands were finally agreed to and the document signed by both General de Brigada Menendez and Maj Gen Moore (witnessed by Col B.T.Pennicott RA) at 2359Z on 14 June, to take effect immediately.

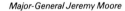

Headquarters, Land Forces
Falkland Islands

INSTRUMENT OF SURRENDER

I, the undersigned, Commander of all the Argentine land, sea and air forces in the Falkland Islands ~~unconditionally~~ surrender to Major General J. J. MOORE CB OBE MC* as representative of Her Britannic Majesty's Government.

Under the terms of this surrender all Argentinian personnel in the Falkland Islands are to muster at assembly points which will be nominated by General Moore and hand over their arms, ammunition, and all other weapons and warlike equipment as directed by General Moore or appropriate British officers acting on his behalf.

Following the surrender all personnel of the Argentinian Forces will be treated with honour in accordance with the conditions set out in the Geneva Convention of 1949.  They will obey any directions concerning movement and in connection with accommodation.

This surrender is to be effective from 2359 hours ZULU on 14 June (2059 hours local) and includes those Argentine Forces presently deployed in and around Port Stanley, those others on East Falkland, ~~M3M~~ West Falkland and all the outlying islands.

*[signature]* Commander Argentine Forces

.............................. J. J. MOORE
Major General

.............................. Witness

.............................. Hours    June 1982

*General de Brigada Mario Menendez*

*Major-General Jeremy Moore*

On 16 June, two days after the surrender, Keith Dudley test-flew the captured CAB601 UH-1H AE-422 at Stanley Racecourse (having been trained on the UH-1D during an exchange tour with the West German Heeresflieger). The Racecourse was dotted with UH-1H's which had been abandoned on many of the prime landing spots so Dudley volunteered (with a team of engineers) to move them away from the area. During 16 June two were moved to the edge of the Racecourse and it was decided that the serviceable examples should be flown to a safe area (the souvenir hunters being out and about already!). Having test-flown AE-422, Keith Dudley took it to San Carlos that evening and returned to Stanley on 17 June, intending to remove the remaining UH-1H's. However, his detachment was recalled to 'Invincible', XZ920 and ZA127 re-embarking that day to leave AE-422 with 825 Sqdn (who "impressed" it into service). Meanwhile, the remainder of 820 Sqdn's aircraft had also flown to Port Stanley on 15 June for use by the Land Forces on load and troop-lifting sorties before they also re-embarked the carrier two days later.

An additional Sea King embarked from 824 Sqdn 'A' Flight aboard 'Olmeda' on 16 June was HAS.2A XV660. The helicopter remained on 'Invincible' while 'Olmeda' was dispatched for Operation "Keyhole" (the retaking of Southern Thule), returning to its parent vessel on 27 June. In the meantime, the carrier detached north from the

Falkland Islands on 18 June for a period of crew rest and recuperation and essential maintenance, a necessary break as it had been decided that 'Invincible' would relieve 'Hermes' in early July to allow the latter to return home. At 2000Z on 19 June, 820 Sqdn was stood down from flying stations after 75 days of intense operations. 'Invincible' returned to the TEZ on 1 July, thus allowing 'Hermes' to depart northward three days later. During July, two or three of the Squadron's helicopters were engaged in daily HDS sorties to Port Stanley and other areas of the Falkland Islands, one of them load-lifting 656 Sqdn Scout AH.1 XV130 from Port Stanley to 'Tor Caledonia' in Port William circa 29 July. The Squadron also carried out night exercises with ships newly arrived in the TEZ, while on 11 July one aircraft went to assist an 824 Sqdn 'A' Flight crew whose Sea King HAS.2A (XV698) had ditched. Two of 820 Sqdn's aircrew found new tasks during the month taking over the command of captured vessels, Lt Steve Jermy going to 'HMS Tiger Bay' and Lt Mike Shrives to 'Falkland Sound' *[see United Kingdom and Argentine Shipping sections]*.

The HDS sorties continued during August, despite frequent bad weather. On 11 August one of the Squadron's Sea Kings was in collision with an LTW Hercules as it taxied out of the crowded dispersal at Stanley Airport. The main rotors struck the wing of the Hercules, damaging three of the blades. A Chinook HC.1 from 18 Sqdn flew in five new blades on 13 August and the repaired Sea King duly re-embarked 'Invincible' later that day. On 16 August an 820 Sqdn aircraft flew to the Stanley Racecourse and airlifted five damaged CAB601 UH-1H's from there to the AAC HQ at the nearby FIGAS Beaver Hangar. Two days later, while 'Invincible' was in San Carlos Water, one of these "Hueys" (AE-424, nicknamed "Hernandez") was made sufficiently serviceable by cannibalising parts from the other four machines to enable Keith Dudley to fly it to the carrier for more detailed attention and a respray. 'Invincible' anchored in Port William for the first time on 24 August and the Squadron commenced the transfer aboard of stores and equipment from the shore.

On 26 August the reworked and resprayed UH-1H (then registered VP-FBD) was flown to Port Stanley (by Keith Dudley and an Army Air Corps pilot, Major R.E.Connel CAF, on exchange with 657 Sqdn) and handed over to the Falkland Islands Government Air Service at their Beaver Hangar. The UH-1H's flying life with FIGAS was short-lived, however, as the helicopter was soon grounded for both technical and administrative reasons. Some people thought, quite naturally, that it had become the victim of bureaucracy, but this was unfair criticism as there were legitimate reasons for the action being taken *[see AE-424 and VP-FBD aircraft details]*. The sad part was that so many people aboard 'Invincible' and within FIGAS had put in such a lot of time and effort renovating "Hernandez" so that the Islanders could have a helicopter service of their own. In retrospect, even if another "Huey" had been available, it would have been a very expensive machine to operate on a commercial basis within such a small community.

By 26 August the time had at last come for 'Invincible'

to leave for home. She was relieved by 'Illustrious' and sailed for the United Kingdom two days later. During the passage the ROYAL NAVY titles and deck letters were re-applied in Black (as were Red/Blue Squadron motifs on either side of the nose below the cockpit) to all of the helicopters as part of a general "sprucing up" of the aircraft on board. The carrier arrived at Portsmouth on 17 September with all nine Sea Kings of 820 Sqdn's original complement on the flight deck, the Squadron having suffered no aircraft losses during the conflict. They were involved in de-storing duties between the carrier and Lee-on-Solent the following day before flying home to Culdrose.

In retrospect, the extent of the Squadron's intense anti-submarine and utility operations is demonstrated by the following statistics: 4,700 hours flown (average of 321 per pilot, 336 per observer and 522 per aircraft); 1,650 sorties flown; 1,172 loads flown; 1,200 tons lifted; 6 torpedoes and 10 depth charges used.

---

*820 Sqdn aircrew aboard 'Invincible' during Operation "Corporate" and their awards:*

### Pilots

*Lt Cdr R.J.S.Wykes-Sneyd RN (CO) AFC; Lt Cdr K.Dudley RN (Senior Pilot) CINCFC; Lt Cdr R.C.Green RN; Lt G.E.Beats RN; Lt D.M.Craig RN; Lt M.P.Jennings RN; Lt M.R.Johnston RN; Lt B.A.Jones RN; Lt M.R.W.Lanyon RN; Lt M.L.McDougall RN; Lt E.A.McNair RN; Lt M.R.Osman RN; Lt M.J.Pamphilon RN; Lt M.P.Shrives RN; Lt J.S.Wilson RN; Lt J.A.Yearsley RN; S/Lt HRH The Prince Andrew RN; S/Lt S.C.B.Burch RN; S/Lt J.A.Carr RN; S/Lt R.J.Churchley RN; S/Lt K.Doherty RN; S/Lt N.Foss RN; S/Lt C.R.Hanney RN; S/Lt D.I.A.Hayes RN; S/Lt I.J.Hendry RN; S/Lt C.P.Heweth RN; S/Lt M.R.Kelham RN; S/Lt P.R.Stone RN; S/Lt P.J.Thornton RN; S/Lt D.Whitehead RN.*

### Observers/Aircrewmen

*Lt Cdr P.Galloway RN (Senior Observer) CINCFC; Lt Cdr I.F.McAllister RN; Lt A.R.C.Bell RN; Lt W.Gibson RN; Lt S.C.Jermy RN; Lt S.R.Kirby RN; Lt J.C.Smith RN; Lt J.S.Wallace RN; S/Lt M.Finucane RN; S/Lt N.R.Gaunt RN; S/Lt M.J.Green RN; S/Lt K.A.F.Jones RN; S/Lt D.L.Lee RN; S/Lt S.W.Marlow RN; S/Lt C.J.Martin RN; FCACMN A.J.Charnley; POACMN W.R.Collins; POACMN R.G.Irwin; POACMN J.P.Wade; POACMN R.J.Walters; LACMN T.Arnull; LACMN A.J.Butcher; LACMN A.C.Davies; LACMN D.C.Hollier; LACMN P.D.Johnson; LACMN M.Kennie; LACMN J.W.Pease; LACMN A.C.Pocock; LACMN M.P.Scott; LACMN J.D.Trotman; LACMN S.G.Wood.*

# 824 NAVAL AIR SQUADRON

At the start of the conflict, 824 Sqdn was based at Culdrose under the command of Lt Cdr I.Thorpe and equipped with six Sea King HAS.2A's. The Squadron was divided into three Flights which were normally deployed aboard the 'Ol' Class RFA tankers 'Olmeda', 'Olna' and 'Olwen'. The colour scheme of its aircraft was standard RAF Blue-Grey overall with White serials, deck-letters, codes and titles plus 'D' Class roundels. The Squadron complement was as follows:

| 'A' Flight | XV660 'OD/350' | XV698 'OD/351' |
|------------|----------------|----------------|
| 'B' Flight | XV666 'CU/352' | XV657 'CU/353' |
| 'C' Flight | XV697 'CU/354' | XV649 'CU/355' |

'A' Flight was temporarily based at Prestwick (HMS Gannet) during March whilst operating on support duties. For these operations, all markings except the serials (but including the roundels) had been overpainted with washable dark grey paint. 'B' Flight had disembarked from 'Olna' at Gibraltar (the ship sailing on for Gulf Patrol duties) and was due to embark 'Fort Austin' for Exercise "Springtrain". 'C' Flight was operating from Culdrose while 'Olwen' was away on refit at Gibraltar. On 5 May, implementing a scheduled appointment, Lt Cdr D.J.Ackland took over command of the Squadron from Lt Cdr Thorpe.

The conflict itself saw the deployment of 'A' and 'C' Flights to the South Atlantic, while the need for shipborne Airborne Early Warning aircraft, which was evident both prior to and during the war, led to the subsequent reformation of 'D' Flight equipped with two specially modified Sea Kings.

Following a post-conflict FONAC/MoD decision to deploy five 826 Sqdn Sea King HAS.5's at the end of 1982 as a Falkland Islands detachment, 824 Sqdn's 'A' and 'C' Flights were transferred to 826 Sqdn on 1 February 1983.

# 'A' FLIGHT

The Flight left Prestwick on 30 March with its two unmarked aircraft (XV660, XV698) flying back to Culdrose, where they arrived the following day. XV698 required maintenance, so the Flight gained XV649 'CU/355' from 'C' Flight on 1 April. The dark grey paint applied to XV660 was easily washed off, both XV649 and XV660 subsequently having low-visibility markings applied. All White markings were overpainted in Black, except for the deck letters which were deleted, and the roundels were modified to Red/Blue. The two helicopters were coded as follows:

| XV660 '-/350' | XV649 '-/355' |
|---------------|---------------|

On 2 April the Flight, under the command of Lt Cdr I.S.McKenzie, was placed at four hours notice to move and both Sea Kings were flown aboard 'Olmeda' alongside at Devonport on 4 April. The ship sailed for the South Atlantic on 5 April, the Flight commencing ASW operations interspersed with HDS and VERTREP sorties as 'Olmeda' refuelled other Task Force ships during the passage south. On 1 May the vessel joined the CVBG stationed to the east of the Falkland Islands, 'Olmeda' being amongst the first group of ships to enter the TEZ that day, and the Flight's ASW, HDS and VERTREP tasking became intense over the next five weeks.

On 3 June, with only five hours notice, the Flight was detached to the FOB at Port San Carlos settlement to assist in the unloading of ships in San Carlos Water. It was intended that 'A' Flight would only remain ashore overnight, but in the event it flew these missions almost continuously for three days, unloading stores, ammunition and equipment until re-embarking 'Olmeda' on 6 June. Operations were then continued as before, although XV649 became unserviceable on 11 June.

Following the Argentine surrender on 14 June, 'Olmeda' was ordered to sail to Southern Thule for Operation "Keyhole" (the retaking of the Island) with 'Yarmouth' and 'Endurance'. For the duration of that operation the Flight was to transfer one of its Sea Kings to 'Invincible' for a prolonged stay from 15 June while the second was to transfer to 'Regent' in exchange for the two Wessex HU.5's of 848 Sqdn 'A' Flight. In the event, the two 848 Sqdn aircraft did not embark as one had already sailed aboard 'Endurance' some 36 hours earlier and the other required an engine change. However, XV660 did embark 'Invincible' on 16 June and that date saw 'Olmeda' sail for Operation "Keyhole". Upon reaching South Georgia on 18 June XV649 was serviceable once again, with its SONAR equipment removed, for use in the utility role. The Flight assisted with the embarkation of 'M' Coy 42 Cdo before the ship sailed to Southern Thule. On 20 June the assault on the Island saw the operation successfully concluded with the surrender of the Argentine forces there. 'Olmeda' arrived back at South Georgia on 21 June to disembark the Marines and PoW's before detaching to the CVBG later that day. The order to return to the United Kingdom was received on 21 June and the ship carried out a rendezvous with 'Invincible' on 27 June after the carrier had sailed north for a period of rest and recuperation. XV660 rejoined the Flight from 'Invincible' that day and 'Olmeda' continued her homeward passage (via Ascension Island on 30 June/1 July). 'A' Flight disembarked to Culdrose on 10 July, two days prior to the vessel's arrival at Devonport.

During the conflict, the Flight had maintained an excellent serviceability rate on its anti-submarine, surface search and load-lifting tasks, and at one stage carried out an HDS sortie which lasted 9hrs 30mins.

---

*824 Sqdn 'A' Flight aircrew aboard 'Olmeda' during Operation "Corporate" and their awards:*

### Pilots

*Lt Cdr I.S.McKenzie RN (Flt Cdr) MBE; Lt D.J.Issitt RN; Lt I.D.Moffatt RN; Lt D.P.Murphy*

*———————————— continued*

---

*continued ————————————*

*RN; Lt T.D.Riviere RN; S/Lt D.R.Taylor RN.*

### Observers/Aircrewmen

*Lt P.Blackman RN; S/Lt P.R.Smith RN; S/Lt D.V.Stanton RN; POACMN R.J.Hartfield; LACMN K.J.Allison; LACMN M.Cook.*

---

XV657 '-/350' (replaced XV660) and XV649 '-/355' embarked 'Fort Austin' on 26 August and transferred to 'Olmeda' in the South Atlantic on 21 September. Both helicopters were temporarily detached to Lively Island, East Falkland from 20-22 November before returning with 'Olmeda' to the United Kingdom. They disembarked to Culdrose on 19 December prior to the vessel docking the same day at Devonport. On 1 February 1983 the Flight was transferred to 826 Sqdn.

# 'B' FLIGHT

Basic details of this Flight are included in the book because Gibraltar was a very important staging post and replenishment base for ships and aircraft en route to and from the United Kingdom, Ascension Island and the South Atlantic. The Flight was equipped with two Sea King HAS.2A's:

---

XV666 'CU/352'     XV657 'CU/353'

---

They had embarked 'Olna' on 19 February for the passage to Gibraltar, where they were flown off to RAF North Front on 26 February. 'Olna' sailed on to join the Gulf Patrol, taking 772 Sqdn 'C' Flt Wessex HU.5 XS507 'ON/314', while the two Sea Kings were due to deploy aboard 'Fort Austin' for Exercise "Springtrain". In the event, the ship was dispatched to the South Atlantic on 29 March for a rendezvous with 'Endurance' on 12 April (the latter had been monitoring events on South Georgia and

then sailed north to be replenished). 'B' Flight remained at RAF North Front.

Following the Argentine invasion, the two helicopters provided essential medium-lift capacity for the transfer of stores and equipment to those ships deploying south from the Mediterranean. The parade ground at Lathbury Barracks, some 300ft above sea-level at the southern end of the Rock, acted as a landing site. During westerly winds, the helicopters had to approach the site below the level of the cliff top, pulling up and over the edge at the last minute, much to the surprise of those below! With the arrival of 'Uganda' on 16 April, the Flight provided a personnel transfer service to the stern during her conversion to a hospital ship. When she sailed south on 19 April, XV666 was used as a photographic mount to record the occasion. Meanwhile, the refit of 'Olwen' at Gibraltar was hastily completed and 'B' Flight embarked on 7 June when she sailed for Devonport, the Sea Kings flying off to Culdrose on 10 June before the ship docked later that day.

# 'C' FLIGHT

In order for 'A' Flight to embark 'Olmeda' as soon as possible, 'C' Flight lost Sea King HAS.2A XV649 on 1 April in exchange for the unserviceable XV698. At that stage the Flight was not scheduled to deploy south and both aircraft were transferred to 706 Sqdn on 5 April. However, they were then quickly reassigned to 824 Sqdn two days later and had low-visibility markings applied, XV698 being serviceable again by this time. On 29 April the Flight received an additional aircraft with the transfer

from 706 Sqdn of Sea King HAS.2A XV672 '-/145', already in a low-visibility scheme and still wearing its former 826 Sqdn markings. 'C' Flight embarked 'Fort Grange' on 7 May under the command of Lt Cdr R.G.Harrison with the following three helicopters:

---

XV698 '-/351'  XV697 '-/354'  XV672 '-/145'

---

'Fort Grange' had recently completed a refit and, after a short period of sea trials, sailed from Devonport on 14 May with the Flight still embarked. On 3 June she arrived in the TEZ to begin her replenishment duties, 25 vessels being resupplied over the next eight days before she moved to San Carlos Water as a "24 hour filling station" for helicopters. The Flight was heavily engaged in HDS and VERTREP tasks around the Task Force which continued well after the Argentine surrender on 14 June. Unfortunately, HAS.2A XV698 was lost on 11 July during a sortie to replenish 'Leeds Castle'. The helicopter suffered a single engine failure and was forced to ditch; it later sank but all of its crew were rescued. Sea King HAS.2 XZ579 '-/271', an FIR aircraft with Naval Party 2050 aboard 'Contender Bezant' (which was due to return to the United Kingdom), was transferred to 'C' Flight on 13 July as its replacement.

'Fort Grange' sailed for the United Kingdom on 17 September, the Flight's three helicopters disembarking to Culdrose on 2 October prior to the vessel's arrival at Devonport the following day. During the deployment, the Flight had lifted over 2,000 tons of stores in 650 hours of transfer operations.

---

*824 Sqdn 'C' Flight aircrew on 'Fort Grange' during Operation "Corporate":*

### Pilots

*Lt Cdr R.G.Harrison RN (Flt Cdr); Lt Cdr P.H.Symonds RN; Lt J.T.Betteridge RN; Lt D.I.Cunnah RN; Lt F.R.E.Edwards RN; Lt J.J.Shaw RN; S/Lt G.M.Hickey RN; S/Lt G.R.Smith RN; S/Lt H.A.Stacey RN.*

### Observers/Aircrewmen

*Lt J.N.B.Leask RN; Lt C.A.Sutton RN; Lt W.J.H.Western RN; S/Lt A.H.Beach RN; S/Lt A.R.Lilly RN; S/Lt J.O'H.Tobin RN; FCACMN G.Redfern; POACMN R.Henshaw; LACMN S.Dodd; LACMN J.Fileman; LACMN P.Leonard.*

---

# 'D' FLIGHT

---

Strictly speaking, as 824 Sqdn 'D' Flight did not deploy to the South Atlantic until after 14 June, it does not merit detailed coverage within the context of this book. However, the obvious requirement for Airborne Early Warning cover over the Falkland Islands and the rapid development and deployment of a viable carrier-based aircraft is highly important. The AEW element must therefore be included so that the reader is made aware of the background and decisions which led to the formation of the Flight.

The Royal Navy had been without a carrier-borne AEW aircraft since the four 849 Sqdn 'B' Flt Gannet AEW.3's were catapulted off 'Ark Royal' for the last time on 28 November 1978 and the Squadron disbanded on 15 December that year. With the Task Force deploying some 8,000 miles from the United Kingdom, the requirement for "local" AEW cover became more and more evident. Use of 8 Sqdn's fleet of venerable Shackleton AEW.2's was completely out of the question. Patrols from Ascension Island by Nimrod MR.2P's provided useful assistance but these aircraft were operating at extreme range with a constant round of air-to-air refuellings from the ageing fleet of Victor tankers. On 4 May a DNAW review of all potential AEW systems was initiated. A serious investigation into the status of the few remaining Gannet AEW.3's found that a total of five aircraft could have been made airworthy from the six potentially available:

| | |
|---|---|
| XL449 | Preserved at Cardiff Airport. |
| XL482 | Airworthy in the USA as N1350X. |
| XL497 | Gate-guardian at HMS Gannet, Prestwick. |
| XL500 | In excellent condition at Culdrose. |
| XL503 | Preserved under cover at Yeovilton. |
| XP226 | Reasonable condition at Lee-on-Solent. |

In addition, the following airframes could have been cannibalised for spares:

| | |
|---|---|
| XL450 | BDR airframe at Bruggen. |
| XL471 | Semi-derelict at Farnborough. |
| XL472 | Semi-derelict at Boscombe Down. |
| XL494 | Semi-derelict at Gibraltar. |
| XR432 | Poor condition, dumped at Lossiemouth. |

Sufficient Gannet engines and radars for the task were traced, but cost and the lack of experienced manpower made completion in the time available impracticable. Apart from the hardware, there was the seemingly insurmountable problem of finding an operational base. They certainly could not take-off from 'Hermes' or 'Invincible' because of their "ski-jumps". The best that could be hoped for was a suitably reinforced strip ashore similar to (but much longer than) the one which was eventually established close to Port San Carlos settlement. Once the Falkland Islands had been recaptured, it might have been feasible to base Gannet aircraft at Stanley Airport to provide temporary cover whilst proper land-based radars were established. All in all, the proposal became less practical the more it was investigated.

At the time of the Argentine invasion, plans were already in hand to upgrade AEW capability by conversion of 11 Royal Air Force Nimrods to AEW.3 standard, but service entry was still some time away. The Thorn-EMI Searchwater radar fitted to the updated Nimrod MR.2 was available, however, and it was decided to install this in a carrier-borne aircraft. Westland Helicopters had already carried out design studies for an AEW variant of the Sea King and this was to influence the final choice of type. On 23 May the MoD gave approval for the fitting of Searchwater radar to two Sea King HAS.2A's and work started on the conversions only a week after the feasibility study had been completed.

The first aircraft chosen was HAS.2A XV650 which was transferred from 706 Sqdn to MoD(PE) loan on 24 May and flown from Culdrose to Westland Helicopters at Yeovil on 27 May, still painted as 'CU/588' with White markings. The second aircraft was HAS.2A XV704, already on MoD(PE) charge with Westland's trials fleet. It had returned from MAD trials at A&AEE Boscombe Down on 26 April and was uncoded but otherwise retained White markings. It joined XV650 for AEW conversion and trials work on 26 May, the Searchwater radar aerial being fitted to the starboard rear fuselage on a swivelling arm. This enabled the unit to be positioned facing the rear while the helicopter was on the ground and point downwards while in operation. The aircraft had to be lifted by crane during ground tests so that the scanner could be lowered into a flight position. Its appearance was ungainly and clearly had some effect on the Sea King's aerodynamic and handling qualities. In addition, I-Band jammers were also fitted for use in the anti-Exocet missile role. Confidence in the programme was displayed by the reformation of 824 Sqdn 'D' Flight at Culdrose on 14 June with eight pilots, eight observers (four of whom had previously served with 849 Sqdn) and 33 ratings under the command of Lt Cdr Peter Flutter (an ex-Gannet Observer).

In the event, the Argentine surrender had been secured before the aircraft could be deployed to the South Atlantic in their new guise. XV704 first flew after conversion on 23 July, followed by XV650 on 30 July, on which date the aircraft was cleared for service entry. Both helicopters were flown from Yeovil to Portland on 2 August using the very appropriate call-signs "Cyclops 1" (XV650, still coded 'CU/588') and "Cyclops 2" (XV704). They embarked 'Illustrious' the same day as she passed down the English Channel en route to the South Atlantic. All White markings were repainted Black during the deployment and the two aircraft were recoded as follows:

| | |
|---|---|
| XV704 '-/361' | XV650 '-/362' |

During the deployment, the aircraft and radar were well able to carry out the primary role of AEW and fighter control, as well as their secondary roles of surface search and tactical direction, the performance often being better than expected. At the end of this deployment, the Flight returned to Culdrose on 7 December, 'Illustrious' arriving at Portsmouth the following day.

That first deployment of the AEW Sea King had been successful and proved the suitability of the helicopter as an AEW platform. Development of the radar continued and more Sea Kings were converted, leading to the reformation of 849 Sqdn at Culdrose on 1 November 1984.

# 825 NAVAL AIR SQUADRON

On 3 May the Commanding Officer of 706 Sqdn at Culdrose, Lt Cdr H.S.Clark, was ordered to reform 825 Sqdn with Sea King helicopters. The Squadron was to operate in the utility role, using its aircraft in support of ground forces in the Falkland Islands, and was to commission and be ready for deployment within one week. Ten Sea Kings were transferred to the new Squadron, all of them being HAS.2 or HAS.2A machines drawn from 706 Sqdn (the Operational Flying Training Unit) and 814 Sqdn at Culdrose, along with one HAS.2A from 819 Sqdn at Prestwick. They were all transferred to the new unit on 3 May (the 819 Sqdn aircraft arriving from Prestwick that day) and work began immediately to remove the ASW SONAR equipment while extra radios for communications with Army units were installed. The cabins were fitted out with troop seats but, unfortunately, no GPMG's were fitted due to lack of time. With the aircraft thus converted from "pingers" (ASW role) to "junglies" (utility role), it was inevitable that these Sea Kings should become known as "pinglies"!

The aircraft remained RAF Blue-Grey overall with the 'D' Class roundels altered to Red/Blue. No new side-codes were allocated to the aircraft, their former allocations being retained. Together with the ROYAL NAVY titles, these were overpainted in Black and all deck-letters deleted. Prior to their departure, all of the Sea Kings were given a coating of PX28 wax-oil preservative which gave them some measure of protection from salt-water corro-

sion during the journey south. The effect of this coating was to give the impression that the helicopters had been resprayed in Matt Olive Drab (ie similar to 846 Sqdn's Sea King HC.4's).

825 Sqdn was commissioned at Culdrose on 7 May with 36 aircrew, 100 maintenance personnel and the following Sea Kings:

| | | |
|---|---|---|
| **HAS.2** | XZ580 '-/272' | (ex-814 Sqdn) |
| **HAS.2A** | XV700 '-/264' | (ex-814 Sqdn) |
| | XV696 '-/268' | (ex-814 Sqdn) |
| | XV663 '-/581' | (ex-706 Sqdn) |
| | XV659 '-/584' | (ex-706 Sqdn) |
| | XV654 '-/585' | (ex-706 Sqdn) |
| | XV714 '-/586' | (ex-706 Sqdn) |
| | XV677 '-/595' | (ex-706 Sqdn) |
| | XV648 '-/597' | (ex-706 Sqdn) |
| | XV656 '-/703' | (ex-819 Sqdn) |
| *Note:* | | *825 Sqdn was allocated the codes '500' to '510' at Culdrose. Although used as call-signs when the Sea Kings embarked 'Queen Elizabeth 2' and 'Atlantic Causeway' (see Individual Aircraft Details), the codes were never painted on the aircraft.* |

Tethered on her stern flight-deck are the two 825 Squadron Sea King HAS.2A's (XV677 '–/595' and XV648 '–/597') which embarked 'Queen Elizabeth 2' in The Solent on 12.5.82. They provided the requisitioned liner with her own medium-lift helicopter capability until transferred to 'Canberra' at Grytviken, South Georgia, on 28.5.82 for passage to the Falkland Islands.

(Ministry of Defence)

Behind 825 Squadron Sea King HAS.2A XV654 '–/585' undergoing field maintenance at San Carlos settlement FOB is another Squadron machine, XV696 '–/268'. Following a landing accident on 4.6.82, in which its main rotor-blades were damaged, XV696 was airlifted to the FOB on 7.6.82 by 18 Squadron's Chinook "Bravo November". There, the tail pylon was removed to restore a damaged 846 Squadron Sea King HC.4 (ZA310 '–/VS') being repaired at the nearby Fern Valley Creek FOB. Indicative of the marrying process is the hybrid tail "Danger" marking clearly visible (Inset) on ZA310 at Yeovilton shortly after its return from the Falklands on 13.7.82.

(Ministry of Defence; (Inset)
Peter J. Cooper)

825 Squadron Sea King HAS.2A XV700 '–/264' flown by the unit's CO, Lt Cdr Hugh Clark, hovers in acrid and blinding smoke at the stern of 'Sir Galahad' while a survivor from the LSL is winched on board. Carefully directed downwash from rescue helicopters helped to move the life-rafts away from the ship towards the safety of the nearby shore. Four 825 Squadron Sea Kings were involved in 'Sir Galahad' and 'Sir Tristram' rescue missions on that disastrous day – 8.6.82 – at Port Pleasant, East Falkland.

(Ministry of Defence)

On 12 May the first two aircraft (XV648 and XV677) flew on board 'Queen Elizabeth 2' in The Solent following the liner's departure from Southampton. The remainder of the Squadron embarked 'Atlantic Causeway' in Plymouth Sound on 13 May, the vessel sailing for the South Atlantic the following day. Prior to this, about 30 of the Squadron personnel had sailed with 'Engadine' on 10 May, although they were not to reach the Falkland Islands until after the main body of 825 Sqdn. These hurried preparations for departure prompted the following Squadron Ode:

*Support and utility was our role*
*The recapture of the Falklands our ultimate goal*
*For most Atlantic Causeway, but for the lucky two*
*A life of luxury in the QE2*
*Will be home soon, Mum, please don't worry*
*Must rush now, in a tearing hurry!*

Flying on to the vessels was a new experience for some of the Squadron pilots as the crews were made up of instructors and students formerly with 706 Sqdn. Despite the weeks of intensive flying which were to come, the students still had to return to Culdrose to complete their training after the conflict! Aboard 'Atlantic Causeway', the helicopters were positioned on the foredeck aft of the hangar, with the forward landing spot left free. During the passage south, flying training was undertaken with the associated drills of lashing, unlashing and refuelling the aircraft. On 22 May, some 25 miles off Ascension Island, 'Atlantic Causeway' carried out a rendezvous with 'Queen Elizabeth 2'. On the following day the two crews aboard the latter ship (including Lt Cdrs H.S.Clark, R.H.S.Everall and S/Lt D.L.Nelson) were swopped with two crews from the former (including Lt Cdr J.R.Skinner with Lts P.J.Sheldon and H.R.Ridgeway). After Ascension Island, the helicopters were stowed and lashed against the rougher seas of the South Atlantic. 'Queen Elizabeth 2' sailed for South Georgia as she was to be kept out of the range of enemy air activity and her troops were to be transferred to other vessels for transport to the war zone. She arrived at Grytviken on 27 May and the two Sea Kings provided essential medium-lift support for the cross-decking operation from the liner to 'Canberra' and 'Norland'. The latter two vessels received the men of the 5th Infantry Brigade, 1st Btn Welsh Guards, 2nd Btn Scots Guards and 1st/7th Gurkha Rifles together with personnel from 656 Sqdn Army Air Corps. On completion of this transfer operation, both Sea Kings embarked 'Canberra' on 28 May and the vessel sailed for the Falkland Islands in company with 'Norland'. 'Atlantic Causeway' entered the TEZ on 29 May and an advance party of four aircraft from the Squadron (XV659, XV696, XV700 and XV656 or XV714) flew ashore to set up the FOB at San Carlos settlement. The flight took four hours in total, routing via 'Hermes' and 'Invincible' to refuel, and the helicopters arrived as dusk was falling. Initially operating as individual units at San Carlos, the four moved to Port San Carlos settlement on 31 May. The 'Canberra' pair flew aboard 'Atlantic Causeway' on 31 May to assist with the disembarkation of the Gurkhas the next day when the vessel arrived in San Carlos Water. The four Sea Kings remaining aboard 'Atlantic Causeway' (XV654, XV663, XZ580 and XV656 or XV714) dis-

embarked to Port San Carlos settlement on 1 June, while XV648 and XV677 returned to 'Canberra' on 2 June when the ship arrived in San Carlos Water. They helped to transfer troops ashore, collecting PoW's in return, before joining the others at Port San Carlos later in the day.

The Squadron then set about joining the overworked 846 Sqdn Sea King HC.4's in resupply and administration tasks around the anchorage as well as moving some 800 prisoners from Darwin and Goose Green to 'Sir Percivale' in San Carlos Water. Having initially operated from a field at Port San Carlos, the unit moved back to San Carlos settlement on 3 June where there were fewer helicopters and thus less congestion. It remained based there for the duration of the campaign. Crews were not accustomed to the "junglie alfresco" style of living with plenty of running water — all down the sides of the trenches and tents! Squadron ground crews and maintainers deserved special credit; having shipped 10 helicopters 8,000 miles on open decks, they kept them flying each day in the Falkland Islands in dismal conditions.

Initial operations were in support of the 5th Infantry Brigade, but the Squadron subsequently supported any of the units ashore as the advance on Port Stanley progressed, pushing from Teal in the north and Fitzroy in the south. All types of support and utility tasks were performed; artillery and troop movements, food and ammunition supplies, flying-in survey parties, movement between ships and San Carlos, casualty evacuation and carrying members of the Press. Normally 16 fully-equipped troops could be transported, but on occasions up to 20 SAS troops with all of their equipment were carried (literally strap-hanging!). The helicopters would fly over nine hours each day before being dispersed ashore for the night.

Elements of the Squadron went forward to assist 846 Sqdn with the battery lifts to Teal Inlet, in the process claiming to be the first unit to see Two Sisters mountain but encountering some enemy fire at the same time. During the course of operations on 4 June, Lt P.J.Sheldon (in XV696) was moving Rapier units around the hills above San Carlos when he landed the helicopter on what was thought to be firm ground near the summit of Lookout Hill. However, the starboard wheel broke through the peat crust, causing all five main-rotor tips to strike the ground during an attempt at correcting the role. Although the aircraft only suffered CAT.1 damage, the lack of on-site spares meant that XV696 had to be left in situ temporarily and it was used as a source of spares. The helicopter was airlifted out by 18 Sqdn Chinook HC.1 ZA718 on 7 June and taken to the FOB at San Carlos settlement, where the tail section was removed to be fitted to 846 Sqdn Sea King HC.4 ZA310 in order that the latter could be made airworthy again.

On 8 June Lt Cdr Hugh Clark and crew (S/Lt Brian Evans and CPOACMN David Jackson) landed a surveying party at Fitzroy settlement in XV700 shortly before the enemy air attacks on 'Sir Tristram' and 'Sir Galahad' in Port Pleasant, off Fitzroy. Hearing the attack and the bombs dropping, Hugh Clark took cover then quickly got airborne and went to the rescue. He was joined by three more 825 Sqdn Sea Kings flown by Lt Phil Sheldon (XV654), Lt John Boughton (XV663) and Lt Steve Isacke (XZ580) in recovering to safety troops and crew-members from both ships. Many of the survivors were in shock or injured and Hugh Clark rescued several from the confined area of the burning foredeck on 'Sir Galahad'. Casualties were ferried to the field hospital at Ajax Bay and one aircraft continued flying well into the hours of darkness.

'Engadine' arrived in San Carlos Water on 9 June, bringing with her the remaining party of 825 Sqdn personnel. Resupply and troop transfer operations continued until the Argentine surrender on 14 June, by which time the unit had achieved in excess of 1,700 hours flying in two weeks. This was equivalent to six months flying in peacetime! In fact, 14 June was the Squadron's busiest day with the nine available aircraft amassing a total of 80 hours flying. The unit then joined in the massive PoW transfer operation, moving prisoners to ships for their eventual repatriation by sea to Argentina. 825 Sqdn was heavily involved in the equally large operation to transfer British troops and equipment aboard ships for return to the United Kingdom. After the surrender, the Squadron "acquired" the captured CAB601 UH-1H AE-422. It had been flown from Stanley Racecourse to San Carlos by Lt Cdr Keith Dudley of 820 Sqdn on 16 June, but the 820 Sqdn detachment at the San Carlos settlement FOB returned to 'Invincible' on 17 June and AE-422 was "passed on" to 825 Sqdn. Following a familiarisation flight on 20 June, the "Huey" was usefully employed as a runabout by 825 Sqdn as well as assessing the suitability of Eddie Anderson (a FIGAS pilot) as a potential helicopter pilot. It accumulated nearly 30 flying hours before being flown by Hugh Clark onto a Mexeflote at the stern of 'Atlantic Causeway' on 13 July and pushed on board via the aft ramp for the journey to the United Kingdom. In the meantime, a trio of 825 Sqdn aircraft lifted three unserviceable Army Air Corps helicopters from San Carlos to Fitzroy on 19 June, while four days later Squadron personnel were able to move from their tents to the relative luxury of outbuildings at San Carlos.

The hulk of XV696 (minus engines, rotors and rear fuselage) was airlifted on board 'Engadine' in San Carlos Water by an 18 Sqdn Chinook HC.1 and sailed with the ship from there on 7 July en route to Devonport. 'Atlantic Causeway' sailed from Port Stanley on 12 July, having embarked the unserviceable or surplus Wessex HU.5's of 845, 847 and 848 Sqdn's, and it arrived in San Carlos Water in the late evening of that day to embark the Sea Kings of 825 Sqdn for their return home to the United

Kingdom. Embarkation was completed on 13 July after a "last fling" flypast. The vessel sailed north for home at 1920Z that evening with the majority of the maintainers, while the aircrew were flown home from Port Stanley. On the morning of 27 July, while the 'Atlantic Causeway' was anchored about two miles out in Mount's Bay, Cornwall, Squadron aircrew came back aboard and ferried nine Sea Kings to Culdrose. The vessel herself arrived at Devonport at 1030Z. 30 July saw the arrival of 'Engadine' at Devonport and the hulk of XV696 was later taken by road to NASU Culdrose for survey, repair and (as it turned out) conversion to HAS.5. 825 Sqdn finally disbanded on 17 September, their slogan "Stay alive with 825" holding good as they had suffered no casualties at all. In fact, the unit had flown 1,756 hours in 394 sorties involving 1,051 deck landings during Operation "Corporate".

---

*825 Sqdn aircrew during Operation "Corporate" and their awards:*

### Pilots

Lt Cdr H.S.Clark RN (Commanding Officer) DSC; Lt Cdr M.J.D.Brougham RN (AEO) MBE; Lt Cdr R.H.S.Everall RN; Lt Cdr M.P.Rayner RN; Lt Cdr J.R.Skinner RN; Lt J.K.Boughton RN QGM; Lt G.J.Boyce RN; Lt E.J.Buckett RN; Lt J.R.Harvey RN; Lt S.J.Isacke RN; Lt H.R.Ridgeway RN; Lt P.J.Sheldon RN QGM; Lt G.Smith RN; Lt M.C.P.Snow RN; Lt P.E.B.Taylor RN; S/Lt P.Eldridge RN; S/Lt P.Evans RN; S/Lt C.J.Greaves RN; S/Lt P.Lyall RN; S/Lt D.L.Nelson RN; S/Lt D.P.Wolstenholme RN.

### Observers/Aircrewmen

Lt C.T.Bean RN; Lt M.G.Cribley RN; Lt S.Mather RN; CPOACMN J.T.Freemantle; CPOACMN D.J.Jackson; CPOACMN M.A.Rowsell; CPOACMN P.Withell; POACMN A.J.Dunsmore; POACMN P.N.A.Gibbs; POACMN L.Hoyland; POACMN J.R.Humfryes; POACMN R.P.Wilson; LACMN R.Eggleston; LACMN R.G.Harris; LACMN T.G.Steele.

---

# 826 NAVAL AIR SQUADRON

The order to embark saw the rapid recall of 826 Sqdn personnel from Easter leave in order to prepare its complement of nine Sea King HAS.5's at Culdrose for deployment to the South Atlantic. This was achieved within 36 hours, and on the morning of 3 April the Squadron embarked 'Hermes' alongside at Portsmouth with a complement of 224 personnel (including 15 crews) under the command of Lt Cdr D.J.S.Squier. Only two of the 826 Sqdn helicopters were not deployed, these being XZ919 'H/141' (which was unserviceable) and the unit's sole HAS.2A XV672 'H/145'. The Squadron took two former

706 Sqdn passive SONAR equipped HAS.5's in their place. 'Hermes' sailed at 1045Z on 5 April with all nine 826 Sqdn Sea Kings positioned on deck for the occasion, marked as follows:

| | | |
|---|---|---|
| ZA130 'H/132' | ZA133 'H/135' | XZ571 'H/143' |
| ZA131 'H/133' | ZA136 'H/140' | ZA129 'CU/582' |
| ZA132 'H/134' | XZ577 'H/142' | ZA137 'CU/596' |

Four of the Sea Kings (ZA130, ZA131, ZA132, ZA133) were fitted with Magnetic Anomaly Detection (MAD) gear, trials with the helicopters thus modified having been completed in January 1982.

Low-visibility markings were applied to the aircraft during the initial passage to Ascension Island (around 10 April), the White segments of the roundels being overpainted Red/Blue, the White titles and codes overpainted in Black and the deck letters completely deleted. The former 706 Sqdn aircraft were dealt with in similar fashion except that they initially retained the last two digits of their 706 Sqdn codes in Black. ZA137 received an 826 Sqdn code during the passage south, while ZA129 for some unknown reason did not receive its allocated code until the return trip to the United Kingdom! The aircraft were thus coded as follows:

| | |
|---|---|
| ZA130 '-/(1)32' | ZA136 '-/(1)40' |
| ZA131 '-/(1)33' | XZ577 '-/(1)42' |
| ZA132 '-/(1)34' | XZ571 '-/(1)43' |
| ZA133 '-/(1)35' | |

ZA129 '-/(5)82' changed to '-/(1)44' post-3.7.82
ZA137 '-/(5)96' changed to '-/(1)46' pre-1.5.82

In preparation for the Squadron's role, which was the protection of Task Force vessels from submarine attack, the voyage to Ascension Island was used as a shakedown and work-up period. After Ascension Island had been passed (16-18 April), operations began in earnest, the pace of ASW flying increasing to the point where most crews would be achieving over 100 flying hours per month. Three of the Squadron's aircraft were maintaining an almost continuous ASW screen up to 12 miles ahead of the CVBG, while a fourth carried out surface search operations up to a range of 200 miles. With the establishment of the TEZ, 826 Sqdn's first action occurred on 1 May with a three-aircraft ASW detachment operating alongside 'Brilliant' and 'Yarmouth' against an enemy submarine, believed to be the 'San Luis'. The submarine was thought to be off the north coast of the Falkland Islands so in the late morning Lt Cdr A.J.M.Hogg led three Sea Kings with the specific mission of locating it. Each aircraft carried a spare four-man crew which was disembarked to the frigates before commencing the search in an area north-east of Port Stanley, 180 miles from 'Hermes'. During the operation, the method developed for refuelling helicopters in flight (HIFR) was used in action for the first time, the Sea Kings hovering over the ship's stern, lowering a hook and picking up the fuel line. The fuel transfer took about 15 minutes, during which the ship performed normal ASW manoeuvres with the aircraft maintaining the correct refuelling position relative to the vessel.

The search for the enemy submarine continued throughout the night of 1/2 May although the three Sea Kings returned to 'Hermes' after dark, having dropped six Mk.11 depth charges and launched two Mk.46 torpedoes during the operation. Throughout that period they had refuelled a total of 10 times from the two frigates, with a crew-change in the hover half-way through the 10 hours of flying. In fact, one of the Sea Kings (XZ577) spent

10hrs 20mins in the air to establish what was, at that time, a new world record for the longest period that a helicopter had remained airborne on an operational mission. Argentine claims that the 'San Luis' had closed to within 1,400yds of one of the frigates and launched a torpedo attack were treated with some scepticism as no hits were scored and no torpedoes were detected by either frigate.

During the Argentine air raids on 1 May, a Grupo 2 Canberra B.62 (B-110) was shot down by Lt Curtis (801 Sqdn) and its crew of two had ejected before the aircraft came down 50 miles north-west of the CVBG. The patrol boat 'Alferez Sobral' sailed from the mainland on 2 May to search for the crew but without success. Shortly after midnight on 2/3 May, Lt Cdr J.S.M.Chandler and crew (S/Lts C.C.MacBean and A.J.Moss and LACMN P.W.Coombes), on patrol in ZA129 some 70 miles north of the CVBG, detected a small surface contact on radar north of the Falkland Islands and closed in to investigate and identify using night vision aids. As the Sea King approached, the ship extinguished its lights. Upon moving in closer, the helicopter came under fire from the vessel's automatic weapons. The pilot pulled back out of range to call in support and the Sea King escaped unscathed. What was thought to have been a second ship was then detected, but it was in fact the original vessel which had moved position. The destroyers 'Coventry' and 'Glasgow' launched their Lynx HAS.2's for an attack with Sea Skua missiles [see 815 Sqdn] and the 'Alferez Sobral' suffered serious damage. The Canberra crew was never found.

The anti-submarine patrols continued for the next few days, especially on 4 May when reports from 'Yarmouth' and other vessels indicated submarine activity. 'Sheffield' was struck by an Exocet missile that day which, despite failing to explode, caused serious fires that spread out of control. In the SAR operation that followed, S/Lt P.G.R.Dibb and his 826 Sqdn crew in XZ577 were first on the scene, having been engaged in an ASW patrol of the area (some 20 miles west of the CVBG). Unable to make radio contact with the stricken vessel, S/Lt Dibb winched a crewman down to the fo'c'sle where the injured and shaken ship's crew informed him of the damage caused and assistance required. The crewman was winched back up and S/Lt Dibb climbed XZ577 to 200ft to report back to 'Hermes'; this was the first news that the carrier had received of the attack. Despite the efforts of a constant stream of helicopters delivering fire-fighting equipment and taking off survivors, the ship was abandoned and left to burn herself out.

The Squadron suffered its first loss on 12 May when ZA132 was forced to ditch following an engine failure while in the hover. An attempted transition from the hover to forward flight, seconds prior to ditching, was unsuccessful due to the prevailing seas. After successfully settling on the water, the heaving sea hit the tail rotor causing the helicopter to swing to starboard, roll over to port, then quickly sink. Lt Cdr Chandler and his crew (S/Lt Moss, S/Lt Sutton and LACMN Coombes) were rescued safely after about 20 minutes in the sea. To replace it, FIR Sea King HAS.5 XZ578 '-/(0)21' was transferred from 820 Sqdn aboard 'Invincible' and flown to 'Hermes' on 14 May. The 820 Sqdn side-code was retained for the rest of the conflict and the journey home. It was joined by the second FIR Sea King, XZ573 '-/(0)22', on 15 May and the 820 Sqdn side-code was retained by that aircraft as well. With the need for more deck space aboard 'Hermes' to accommodate the Harrier GR.3's and Sea Harrier FRS.1's expected from 'Atlantic Conveyor', the Squadron detached four aircraft and six crews to 'Fort Austin' on 17 May under the command of Lt Cdr J.R.B.Bullock. This detachment was to carry out ASW operations in Falkland Sound during the landings and involved XZ577, ZA130, ZA133 and ZA137. 17 May also saw the Squadron's aircraft come under attack from enemy aircraft and land-based missiles but without loss. Unfortunately, XZ573 hit the sea and ditched some two miles from 'Hermes' following a radio altimeter malfunction during a SONAR hover at 0030Z on 18 May. Once again the crew (Lts Tonkin, Barber and Swain and LACMN Haycock) were safely rescued by another 826 Sqdn aircraft. Attempts to recover XZ573 (which remained afloat and upright) were abandoned because of the potential submarine threat to ships loitering in the area. In addition, there was a danger that Mk.11 depth charges in the helicopter might explode if it sank close to a recovery ship. The Sea King was sunk by naval gunfire and, as predicted, the depth charges detonated as it sank! On 19 May, aircraft from 'Hermes' were involved in the SAR operation for ditched 846 Sqdn Sea King HC.4 ZA294, but 21 crew and troops of the 30 aboard were unfortunately lost.

At 0200Z on 21 May, as 'Antrim' and 'Ardent' detached to begin shore bombardment in support of the landings at San Carlos, two Sea Kings from the 'Fort Austin' detachment were launched to position themselves at the northern end of Falkland Sound to conduct SONAR searches for possible enemy submarines. During the enemy air raids that day, the crew of a 'Fort Austin'-based Sea King (Lt Robertson, S/Lts Lancaster and Porter and LACMN Wright) was convinced that their helicopter had been unsuccessfully attacked by two "Mirages" (meaning Grupo 6 Daggers). Another "Mirage" over Falkland Sound reportedly strafed an 826 Sqdn Sea King (crewed by S/Lts Dibb, Dawson and Lapthorne and LACMN Taber) during a sortie to follow-up a SARBE signal. Once again the cannon attack was unsuccessful and the helicopter continued its search over West Falkland, but found nothing. On returning for fuel, the helicopter was fired at in the vicinity of Port Howard, that time by a Blowpipe which was spotted by S/Lt Lapthorne, but the pilot managed to avoid the missile by taking evasive action. Lt Robertson and crew were attacked by another "Mirage" on 23 May but once again the enemy aircraft was unsuccessful. *(There were numerous reports of British helicopters being strafed by Argentine aircraft. Research has shown that only on rare occasions did Daggers and Skyhawks deliberately attack British helicopters; opportunities did arise during attacks on British shipping but most were resisted.)* ASW operations continued until 25 May, on which date the four helicopters were scrambled to help evacuate survivors from the stricken 'Coventry'; 55 personnel were taken to 'Uganda', 'Fort Austin' and 'Broadsword'. 'Atlantic Conveyor' was also hit on 25 May and three Sea Kings from 'Hermes' rescued 13 survivors from the vessel's burning deck.

ASW operations continued, but on 30 May the Squadron carried out yet another SAR mission after Sqdn Ldr

Jeremy Pook had ejected from 1(F) Sqdn Harrier GR.3 XZ963 and came down in the sea 31 miles from 'Hermes'. XZ571 was vectored to him by 'Exeter' Flight's Lynx and, after only 10 minutes in the water, he was winched up to the Sea King which was being flown by S/Lt K.B.Sutton. On 3 June the four 'Fort Austin' aircraft (by then under the command of Lt Cdr P.N.Dickinson) deployed ashore to the FOB at Port San Carlos settlement due to the shortage of utility helicopters following the loss of 'Atlantic Conveyor' and her cargo of Wessex HU.5's and Chinook HC.1's. These load-lifting tasks continued until 6 June when the detachment was recalled to 'Hermes', allowing 'Fort Austin' to detach and sail for the United Kingdom. On the same day, XZ578, ZA129 and three crews under the command of Lt Cdr Hogg embarked 'Atlantic Causeway' to make room for two 1(F) Sqdn Harrier GR.3's arriving non-stop from Ascension Island. The ship entered San Carlos Water on 8 June and the two Sea Kings carried out ASW, ASV and utility tasking during the unloading. The vessel was to leave the following day and the pair were prepared to move to 'Engadine' so that they could go ashore on 10 June, but XZ578 became unserviceable and remained on 'Atlantic Causeway' when she sailed from the AOA. She was some 200 miles east of Port Stanley by the time the Sea King had been repaired on 10 June and commenced its flight back to the Falkland Islands via 'Hermes'. However, its journey ended on 'Hermes' that day following a decision to give the shore tasking to 820 Sqdn. On 11 June ZA129 from 'Engadine' returned to 'Hermes', having embarked 'Fort Grange' the previous day for passage out of the AOA.

Following the Argentine surrender on 14 June, a further two-aircraft (three aircrew) detachment involving XZ578 and ZA133 went ashore to the San Carlos settlement on 17 June to carry out more utility tasks and ASV missions on West Falkland, relieving 820 Sqdn. The remainder of the Squadron commenced HDS tasks to Port Stanley, initially to the Racecourse and Sportsfield and then to the Airport. On 23 June the San Carlos detachment re-embarked 'Hermes' and the Squadron carried out a CASEX operation with the submarine 'Courageous'. However, two Sea Kings went ashore once more on 25 June, one of them flying Rear Admiral Woodward to Stanley Airport to greet the returning Civil Commissioner, Rex Hunt. The other aircraft acted as a communications link for a much less pleasant task, namely the torpedoing and sinking of 'Sir Galahad' as a war grave. The carrier sailed from Port William at 1600Z on 3 July with 826 Sqdn embarked, rejoining the CVBG some 120 miles east of the Falkland Islands. The following day the ship set course for the United Kingdom and arrived at Portsmouth on 21 July with all nine of the unit's aircraft ranged on deck. The Squadron disembarked to Culdrose on 22 July.

It is worth reflecting that, from the time 'Hermes' had left Ascension Island on 18 April, the Squadron had maintained a minimum of three Sea Kings in the air around the clock for the following two months. There was always the threat of enemy submarines, real and imaginary, creating the need for vigilance. The number of hours accumulated by each aircraft between April and June bears witness to this continuous state of alertness:

| Serial | April | May | June | |
|--------|-------|-----|------|--|
| XZ571 | 83 | 186 | 166 | |
| XZ573 | - | 6 | - | Received 15.5.82<br>Ditched 18.5.82 |
| XZ577 | 51 | 147 | 160 | |
| XZ578 | - | 105 | 85 | Received 14.5.82 |
| ZA129 | 103 | 180 | 164 | |
| ZA130 | 55 | 136 | 142 | |
| ZA131 | 67 | 256 | 142 | |
| ZA132 | - | 72 | - | Ditched 12.5.82 |
| ZA133 | 105 | 157 | 47 | |
| ZA136 | 87 | 135 | 92 | |
| ZA137 | 71 | 91 | 197 | |

*826 Sqdn aircrew embarked in 'Hermes' for "Operation Corporate" and their awards:*

### Pilots

Lt Cdr A.J.M.Hogg AFC RN; Lt P.R.Ayers RN; Lt P.A.Barber RN; Lt P.Crudgington RN; Lt D.Duthie RN; Lt E.R.Hardman RN; Lt J.M.Rayner RN; Lt F.W.Robertson RN **MID**; Lt P.StC.Steel RN; Lt J.D.Stratton RN; Lt N.P.M.Tonkin RN; Lt M.D.Wells RN; S/Lt P.G.R.Dibb RN; S/Lt C.R.Eaton RN; S/Lt S.R.J.Gibson RN; S/Lt A.P.Greenall RN; S/Lt A.P.Hands RN; S/Lt N.J.Hughes RN; S/Lt A.J.Hunt RN; S/Lt M.P.Lancaster RN; S/Lt S.G.Lapthorne RN; S/Lt C.C.MacBean RN; S/Lt R.G.S.Mitchell RN; S/Lt A.J.Moss RN; S/Lt R.J.Noble RN; S/Lt S.T.Pegg RN; S/Lt M.B.Sambrook RN; S/Lt D.E.Sealy RN; S/Lt K.B.Sutton RN; S/Lt L.Taylor RN; S/Lt J.M.C.Wells RN.

— continued

continued —

### Observers/Aircrewmen

Lt Cdr D.J.S.Squier RN (CO) **AFC**; Lt Cdr J.R.B.Bullock RN; Lt Cdr J.S.M.Chandler RN **MID**; Lt R.W.R.Cox RN; Lt N.J.P.Dedman RN; Lt P.N.Dickinson RN; Lt T.R.Forrester RN; Lt D.W.Hall RN; Lt C.J.Hamp RN; Lt D.A.Lunt RN; Lt N.M.Mansell RN; Lt D.H.Swain RN; Lt M.J.Whitehouse RN; S/Lt C.Dawson RN; S/Lt P.G.Freemantle RN; S/Lt N.N.Porter RN; CPOACMN N.Darby; CPOACMN R.P.Godley; POACMN V.C.Gover; LACMN M.D.Andrews; LACMN P.B.P.Blackburn; LACMN D.A.Cokayne; LACMN P.W.Coombes; LACMN P.H.Daubney; LACMN M.P.Dodd; LACMN A.S.Eakins; LACMN D.R.Galway; LACMN C.C.Haycock; LACMN L.Lovitt; LACMN J.W.Paterson; LACMN P.J.Penny; LACMN T.M.Stapleton; LACMN G.Taber; LACMN S.W.Wright **MID**.

With the return of the main body of 814 Sqdn aboard 'Illustrious' and the detachment aboard 'Fort Austin' to the United Kingdom in December, it was deemed necessary to maintain an effective anti-submarine capability in the South Atlantic, especially for ships operating in the FIPZ. Five 826 Sqdn Sea Kings were therefore detached south aboard 'Fort Grange' (XZ571, XZ577, ZA136, ZA137) and 'Tidespring' (ZA129), all the helicopters embarking as the vessels passed down the English Channel. 'Tidespring' had completed her refit at Gibraltar and returned to Devonport on 17 October, departing again on 25 October for sea trials from which she sailed direct to the South Atlantic on 8 November, the date the Sea King embarked. 'Fort Grange' sailed from Devonport on 19 November and her four helicopters embarked two days later. The five Sea Kings became a Falkland Islands detachment which was eventually designated 826 Sqdn 'A' Flight.

XZ578 'CU/589' Sea King HAS.5 of 820 Squadron on 'Invincible', whilst just north of Ascension Island c14.4.82, still wears its former 706 Squadron markings. Although recoded '–/(0)21' shortly after this photograph was taken and transferred to 826 Squadron on 14.5.82 to replace the ditched HAS.5 ZA132, it retained its 820 Squadron code throughout the conflict but never returned to that Squadron.

(Lt S. A. George, RN)

# 846 NAVAL AIR SQUADRON

Under the command of Lt Cdr S.C.Thornewill, 846 Sqdn had returned to Yeovilton in March 1982 following the unit's participation in Exercise "Alloy Express" in northern Norway. The majority of its personnel had gone on leave, while the few remaining at Yeovilton were looking forward to the Easter break. At 0500Z on 2 April, the signal went out recalling Squadron personnel to Yeovilton for immediate embarkation. At that time, the unit had a complement of 12 Sea King HC.4's all painted Matt Olive Drab overall with Black titles, codes and serials plus Red/Blue roundels. It was initially decided to deploy the aircraft in two groups, so early on 3 April nine Sea Kings and 152 personnel (under the command of Simon Thornewill) embarked 'Hermes' berthed at Portsmouth. The aircraft were as follows:

| | | | | | |
|---|---|---|---|---|---|
| ZA298 | '-/VA' | ZA299 | '-/VE' | ZA295 | '-/VM' |
| ZA291 | '-/VB' | ZA292 | '-/VH' | ZA311 | '-/VP' |
| ZA290 | '-/VC' | ZA293 | '-/VK' | ZA294 | '-/VT' |

All nine were positioned on deck when the carrier sailed (to a memorable send-off) at 1045Z on 5 April. The following day the remaining three Sea Kings (under the command of the senior pilot, Lt Cdr W.A.Pollock) flew to Portland, uplifted contingents of the Special Forces, and then embarked 'Fearless' the same day while she was in the Portland area. The three helicopters were:

| | | | | | |
|---|---|---|---|---|---|
| ZA296 | '-/VF' | ZA297 | '-/VG' | ZA310 | '-/VS' |

Both ships set course for Ascension Island, trials and training for the operations ahead commencing on 12 April. Preparations to put the Squadron on a war footing included giving the extra pilots and aircrew conversion or refresher training on the Sea King HC.4, as appropriate. Aboard 'Fearless', training included DLP's, VERTREP's by day and by night, SCA's and cabin gunnery practice. As the ships approached Ascension Island, the VERTREP and HDS tasking became heavier. In the meantime, ZA312 (a recently-built HC.4) had been taken from temporary storage at NASU Culdrose and flown to Yeovilton on 5 April on issue to 846 Sqdn. By 7 April it had been coded '-/VW' in the low-vis scheme. That day it was loaded aboard Heavylift Belfast G-BFYU for air transportation to Wideawake where it arrived on 8 April. Under the command of Lt P.Spens-Black, this one-aircraft detachment joined Naval Party 1222 on 11 April to assist in the setting up of the forward logistics base at Wideawake, helping the movement of stores and equipment.

'Hermes' arrived off Ascension Island on 16 April and the nine Squadron aircraft on board immediately went to work transferring stores, equipment and personnel around the various ships. This included a large quantity of stores arriving by air at Wideawake airfield and everything had to be positioned on the correct ship in the right order for unloading and use in the operations to come. 'Fearless' anchored off the Island on 17 April and her detachment immediately joined in the massive re-storing task. On the following day 'Hermes' departed hastily after a sonar contact was reported in the vicinity of the Task Force. Four of her helicopters (ZA291, ZA295, ZA298 and ZA299) went ashore to join the detachment under the command of the Squadron CO, while Lt N.J.North took command of the five aircraft which remained aboard 'Hermes'. The 'Fearless' aircraft also went ashore on 17 April, giving the detachment a complement of eight Sea Kings.

Following her hasty departure, the 'Hermes' aircraft had little opportunity for any rehearsal. The first chance for 846 Sqdn pilots to evaluate the Passive Night Goggles (PNG's) had been on 17 April before 'Hermes' weighed anchor the following day, and they were tested again along with the TANS on a long-range HDS sortie to Ascension Island on the evening of 18 April. Sea King HC.4 ZA311 was unfortunately lost at 2113Z on 23 April when it crashed into the sea in poor weather during the return from a night VERTREP mission. Its pilot (Flt Lt R.Grundy) was rescued by 820 Sqdn Sea King HAS.5 XZ574, but tragically the aircrewman (POACMN K.S. "Ben" Casey) was never found. Weather and aircraft serviceability permitting, PNG training continued each night until 28 April. By day, tasking on VERTREP and HDS sorties continued around the ever-expanding CVBG.

Back in the United Kingdom, ZA313 (another new aircraft) was being prepared for shipment. It joined 706 Sqdn from NASU Culdrose for aircrew training on 21 April and then transferred to 846 Sqdn on 26 April, embarking 'Intrepid' that day direct from Culdrose as the ship passed down the English Channel. The Sea King had been allocated 846 Sqdn side letters (VZ) but these were neither applied by its departure date nor worn during the conflict (as photographic evidence has proven). 'Intrepid' arrived off Ascension Island on 5 May to join 'Fearless' with 'Canberra' and 'Elk' which had arrived on 20 April. The detachment of Sea King HC.4's on the Island (now nine aircraft with the arrival of ZA313 aboard 'Intrepid') had begun operations from 'Canberra' and 'Elk' on 21 April, carrying out amphibious assault rehearsals. With the imminent departure from Ascension Island of the assembling Amphibious Group, the Squadron redistributed its aircraft between the various ships before departing as follows:

| | | |
|---|---|---|
| 'Canberra' | 6 May | ZA299 |
| 'Elk' | 6 May | ZA291 ZA295 ZA312 |
| 'Fearless' | 8 May | ZA296 ZA298 ZA310 |
| 'Intrepid' | 8 May | ZA297 ZA313 |

The 'Elk' contingent had embarked on 28 April with Peter Spens-Black in charge of the Flight.

'Hermes' arrived in the TEZ on 1 May and from then until the landings on 21 May, her detachment was engaged in covert operations to land Special Forces ashore while the carrier remained between 80 and 140 miles east of the Falkland Islands. The first of these missions occurred during the evening of 1 May and involved Nigel North in ZA292; 'Hermes' moved closer to the Islands and the first intelligence-gathering patrol from 'G' Sqdn 22 SAS Regt was flown ashore. In all, some 25 such operational sorties at night saw the insertion, resupply and extraction of reconnaissance parties plus the insertion of SAS units for direct action against enemy positions. All of the PNG tasks were completed without loss, demanding exceptional levels of skill and concentration from the crews in low-level flying and night navigation over rugged terrain. Despite frequently appalling weather and low visibility, only three missions failed to reach their objectives. The day tasking during this period consisted of trooping, VERTREP, HDS and MEDEVAC flights between the Task Force ships, continually hampered by days of fog, gales and rough seas. The attack on 'Sheffield' (4 May) saw all four 'Hermes' aircraft involved in SAR and CASEVAC operations to rescue survivors from the burning vessel. Before 'Sheffield' was taken in tow by 'Yarmouth' on 9 May, the Squadron transferred salvage parties aboard and recovered much vital equipment ('Sheffield' sank under tow on 10 May). 800 Sqdn Sea Harriers attacked the Argentine trawler 'Narwal' on 9 May and two 846 Sqdn Sea Kings (in company with a HAS.5 from 826 Sqdn) were tasked with apprehending the vessel, which was believed to have been spying on the Task Force. An SBS unit was roped down to board the 'Narwal' and the Sea Kings picked up the prisoners (which included some casualties). On the return trip, Lt Cdr Bill Pollock (in ZA292) had to alight on 'Glasgow' to refuel as the CVBG was at some distance from the operation.

On the night of 11/12 May an eight-man troop from 'D' Sqdn 22 SAS Regt had gone ashore on West Falkland to reconnoitre the Argentine forces on Pebble Island. They found ammunition and aviation fuel stored at this location, along with 11 aircraft. Having established details of the enemy presence there, the night of 14/15 May saw the now famous SAS raid on Pebble Island which involved 846 Sqdn in its most complex and risky operation to date. The raid was carried out by two of the PNG aircraft and, despite a delayed take-off, they landed 45 men of 'D' Sqdn with the poor weather providing good cover. The attack went according to plan, the ammunition dump and all 11 aircraft present being immobilised or destroyed.

Two of the HC.4's (ZA290 and ZA292) were transferred from 'Hermes' to 'Invincible' during the night of 17 May for a special long-range reconnaissance mission which later achieved notoriety when one of the aircraft was destroyed. 'Invincible' detached westward with 'Broadsword' and the ships steamed at 25 knots, one mile apart, in total darkness and radar-silence. Lt R.Hutchings RM and crew set out from 'Invincible' in ZA290 at 0315Z on 18 May, reportedly with a contingent of SAS personnel aboard, and the two ships reversed course back to the

CVBG, still at 25 knots. While there is no official explanation for their tasking, it is generally suggested that the mission was to insert Special Forces on the South American mainland close to the Super Etendard base at Rio Grande. In any event, ZA290 was put down by Richard Hutchings that evening on a beach at Agua Fresca, some 11 miles from Punta Arenas in southern Chile. The Sea King was then deliberately set on fire by its crew (Lt Hutchings plus Lt A.R.C.Bennett and LACMN P.B.Imrie) who surrendered to the Chilean authorities some days later and were subsequently repatriated to the United Kingdom. The second aircraft (ZA292, which had remained aboard 'Invincible' as a reserve machine for ZA290) returned to 'Hermes' on 18 May.

The Amphibious Group joined the CVBG on 19 May, and at fairly short notice the detachment aboard 'Hermes' was ordered to prepare its three remaining helicopters for transfer to 'Intrepid'. Space on 'Hermes' was at a premium following the arrival on 18 May of four 809 Sqdn Sea Harrier FRS.1's and four 1(F) Sqdn Harrier GR.3's from 'Atlantic Conveyor', with two more Harrier GR.3's expected. The 'Hermes' trio (ZA292, ZA293, ZA294) spent 19 May transferring men and equipment across to 'Intrepid', but the carrier's intensive flying programme made an otherwise routine transfer operation a hectic affair. Sadly, Sea King HC.4 ZA294 was lost near 'Hermes' at 2215Z on 19 May, while transferring SAS troops to 'Intrepid'. It was on a long, high final approach to the Assault Ship when both pilots heard a loud thump above their heads followed by an immediate loss of power. The helicopter hit the sea, rolled over and floated inverted for a short period before sinking. Of the 30 men aboard, only nine were recovered, including the two pilots (Lt R.Horton and S/Lt P.Humphreys), while the aircrewman (Cpl ACMN M.D.Love RM) was amongst those lost (he was awarded the DSM). ZA294 sank without trace, leaving the reason for its crash open to conjecture. Possible causes were collision with, or engine ingestion of, a large seabird such as an albatross (pieces of a similar-sized bird were found near the scene but sometime after the accident), or an engine or systems failure.

While the 'Hermes' detachment embarked, 'Intrepid' disembarked ZA291 (which had joined the ship from 'Elk' on 14 May for maintenance) to 'Canberra' on 19 May to join ZA299. 'Elk' was not due to participate in the landings, so on 19 May ZA295 was flown to 'Norland' while ZA312 went to 'Fearless' to make up her complement of four aircraft. The following day saw ZA313 dispatched from 'Intrepid' to 'Norland' in exchange for ZA295, a PNG aircraft (replacing the unfortunate ZA294). Pre-assault preparations now became a priority task, including the carriage of senior officers and orders to and from 'Fearless' along with the final movement of embarked forces and equipment to their pre-assault positions. The LSL Group had been joined by the 'Fearless' and 'Intrepid' Group to complete the amphibious force and the problems of HDS and VERTREP flying around such a fleet in poor visibility increased. One of the Sea Kings suffered a single engine failure during transit to the AOA, but serviceability of the aircraft remained generally high. The line-up for the assault was as follows:

**Top** *On 3.4.82 only one 826 Squadron Sea King HAS.5 from the unit's Culdrose base reached 'Hermes', alongside at Portsmouth, before fog forced the others to divert to nearby Lee-on-Solent. The same fog affected the Yeovilton-based Sea King HC.4's of 846 Squadron, also bound for the carrier. Later in the day the weather improved and seen here is HC.4 ZA298 '–/VA' taking-off for 'Hermes' accompanied by an unidentified example. (Ministry of Defence).*

**Centre Left** *At San Carlos Water, sometime after the 21.5.82 landings, an unidentified 846 Squadron Sea King HC.4 is manoeuvred into position above the flight-deck of either 'Fearless' or 'Intrepid' so that a fuel "Bollock" (APFC) can be hooked onto its sling and carried ashore. (Ministry of Defence).*

**Centre Right** *At Wideawake on 1.5.82 one of a batch of 3 PARA's Wombat 120mm anti-tank weapons is about to be taken as an underslung load to 'Canberra' by 846 Squadron Sea King HC.4 ZA299 '–/VE'. Note that ZA299 is still wearing its Squadron badge aft of the cockpit. (Mel James).*

**Bottom** *846 Squadron's PNG-modified Sea King HC.4's were involved in many clandestine intelligence-gathering operations during the conflict. Such missions included depositing Special Forces at numerous locations on the Falklands. Here, an SBS specialist in camouflage emerges from cover to obtain a better view of Argentine military movements close to Port Stanley. (Ministry of Defence)*

| 'Fearless' | ZA296 ZA298 ZA310 ZA312 |
|---|---|
| 'Intrepid' | ZA292 ZA293 ZA295 ZA297 |
| 'Canberra' | ZA291 ZA299 |
| 'Norland' | ZA313 |

'Intrepid' was to be base for the Special Forces, and at dusk on 20 May the four PNG aircraft were launched to land troops north of Darwin and Goose Green and south of the Sussex Mountains. They were to carry out diversionary operations (code-named Operation "Tornado"), all of the helicopters recovering without incident.

At dawn on 21 May (1100Z), the Squadron's aircraft from 'Fearless', 'Canberra' and 'Norland' commenced operations in support of the landings, moving the 105mm guns of 29 Cdo Regt RA and the Rapier batteries to positions ashore. Little resistance was encountered while ferrying stores, weapons and ammunition, although Lt R.Harper (in ZA296) became involved in an incident which proved to be disastrous, not for the Sea King but for a Gazelle. Shortly before 1141Z that day, ZA296 in company with a "protecting" 3 CBAS Gazelle AH.1 (XX411) was heading east with an underslung load flying over Hospital Point towards Port San Carlos settlement when it was shot at by Argentine ground fire. Realising that he had overflown the leading elements of the 3 PARA landing (and was therefore too far east), Ray Harper immediately turned the Sea King onto a reciprocal heading out of harm's way. As he cleared the area he warned the accompanying Gazelle of the enemy presence but, in spite of this, XX411 was shot down and minutes later so was another 3 CBAS Gazelle AH.1, XX402 *[see 3 CBAS notes for full details]*. At the end of the day, the majority of the Squadron's aircraft were involved in CASEVAC flights and ferrying survivors from 'Ardent' to 'Canberra' following the enemy air attacks on the escort vessels in Falkland Sound. The detachment aboard 'Intrepid' joined in the CASEVAC operations late that afternoon before completing two further Special Forces tasks during the night. ZA291 was transferred from 'Canberra' to 'Norland' late the same day to release the landing pad for an 845 Sqdn 'E' Flt Wessex HU.5 (XT449) on a CASEVAC mission. 'Norland' departed San Carlos Water that evening followed by 'Canberra' at 0142Z on 22 May, both ships taking their aircraft with them having completed their part in the landings. In all, the day had seen the Squadron's 11 aircraft fly some nine and a half hours each, with the seven "day" aircraft moving some 912,000lbs of stores and equipment plus approximately 520 troops during the landings.

On 22 May the PNG aircraft disembarked from 'Intrepid' for dispersal to "Eagle Bases" ashore for protection against the daytime air attacks, returning to the ship each night. Each "Eagle Base" accommodated one Sea King and aircrew and groundcrew in a self-contained well-camouflaged unit sited in the field. The detachment aboard 'Fearless' spent the day transferring stores to 2 PARA in the Sussex Mountains and consolidating the position at San Carlos. These operations were frequently interrupted by air raid warnings, with the danger of being shot down or even hit by the barrage of answering missiles and artillery/small-arms fire. The crew of Sea King

ZA296, tasking from 'Fearless' at dusk, had a close call when 'Intrepid' reported them to be an enemy aircraft! Nevertheless, this pattern of operations was to continue until a FOB had been set up ashore. In the meantime, those aircraft aboard 'Canberra' and 'Norland' were engaged in de-storing to 'Stromness' whilst still in the CVBG so that the two ships could sail for South Georgia and a rendezvous with 'Queen Elizabeth 2'.

Before that took place, 'Norland' returned briefly to San Carlos Water on 23 May and her detachment (ZA291 and ZA313) disembarked that day to set up "Eagle Bases" ashore, joining the 'Fearless' aircraft in consolidating the positions around the bridgehead. The bases were established at a FOB at Old House Creek, some 2.5 miles north of San Carlos settlement on the east bank of San Carlos Water. During the day, ZA310 from 'Fearless' (flown by Lt D.A.Lord) suffered an accident which was to ground it until the end of the conflict. It had been tasked to pick up some casualties from a patrol to the north of Fanning Head, but its tail rotor hit the ground rendering it unserviceable (fortunately, none of the crew was hurt). A second 'Fearless' aircraft (ZA312) went ashore to the Old House Creek FOB on 23 May, this time for repairs to an auxiliary hydraulics problem. One of the PNG aircraft was based ashore all day for CASEVAC duties at the Ajax Bay field dressing station, while two of them airlifted one company of 2 PARA to Camilla Creek House during that night as part of the assault. The day also saw the Squadron's involvement in SAR missions after the loss of 'Antelope'.

Another clear day on 24 May heralded further enemy air attacks on the anchorage, but 846 Sqdn managed to complete a hard day of stores transfer and consolidation. A night mission for the PNG detachment to reinforce the 2 PARA position at Camilla Creek had to be cancelled because of low cloud on the Sussex Mountains.

Tasking continued on 25 May as more vessels arrived with stores and equipment. These included 'Europic Ferry' (the smallest ship to take part in the landings), ZA299 embarking her from 'Canberra' at a position some 170 miles north-east of Port Stanley on 25 May before entering San Carlos Water the following day to de-store. Once this task had been completed, ZA299 disembarked to the Old House Creek FOB on 26 May and 'Europic Ferry' sailed for the TRALA the next day. Meanwhile the unfortunate ZA310 was robbed of all useful parts by a maintenance crew. 25 May was also Argentina's National Day and clear weather meant that air raids were to be expected. In the event, 'Broadsword' and 'Coventry' received most of the attention while out on radar picket duty in the "missile trap" some 12 miles north of Pebble Island. All of 846 Sqdn's aircraft (including the PNG machines) were scrambled for SAR duty to pick up survivors after 'Coventry' capsized, winching them up for transfer either to 'Broadsword' and 'Fort Austin', or to the hospital ship 'Uganda' and the Ajax Bay station if injured. CPOACMN "Alf" Tupper was lowered down to a liferaft from ZA298 (flown by Lt Cdr Simon Thornewill), unhooked himself and swam from raft to raft, aiding the injured and guiding in the rescue helicopters. Although not wearing a survival suit, he was credited with actively assisting the saving of between 40 and 50 lives, for which he was awarded the DSM. The planned insertion of Special Forces by the PNG aircraft into the Mount Kent and Mount Challenger areas that night was cancelled as a result of the attack on 'Coventry' and the subsequent SAR tasking. Later that day came news that 'Atlantic Conveyor' had been hit by an Exocet missile. Of the 11 transport helicopters aboard, only one (Chinook HC.1 ZA718) survived to reach the FOB at Old House Creek on 26 May. The Squadron's workload was to remain very heavy as a result of these losses.

The cancelled Special Forces task for the PNG aircraft was rescheduled for 26 May. Difficult terrain, poor weather and navigational problems combined to make this mission unsuccessful, so early the next morning two aircraft attempted to reposition the troops on Mount Kent but were forced to take them off due to bad weather. The detachment aboard 'Fearless' (ZA296, ZA298, ZA312) moved ashore on 27 May to the new FOB at Fern Valley Creek about 1.5 miles south of the Old House Creek site on the east bank of San Carlos Water, joining ZA291, ZA299 and ZA313. 'Fearless' then sailed for a rendezvous with 'Antrim' in order to collect Major General Jeremy Moore (Commander Land Forces) and Brigadier M.J.A.Wilson (5th Inf Bde) together with their respective staffs. Resupply operations at the bridgehead and CASEVAC missions from Ajax Bay to 'Uganda' continued with further casualties arising from air attacks on the surgical unit at Ajax Bay and the Brigade HQ at San Carlos. Later that night an Argentine unit was intercepted to the south-east of the FOB site. The night also proved more successful for the PNG aircraft despite the poor weather, as Nigel North in ZA292 completed a three and a half hour operation to move half a battery and ammunition to Camilla Creek House while troops were inserted into the Mount Kent and Mount Challenger areas.

The morning of 28 May saw 2 PARA start their push for the Darwin and Goose Green settlements. The Squadron was tasked with moving ammunition to their guns, but an early halt to flying was made necessary by a shortage of aviation fuel after the departure of 'Fearless'. The Royal Engineers were completing a refuelling site at the San Carlos airstrip and ZA298 acted as a "guinea pig" for the fuel handling equipment, visiting the new site when tasked with the night move of a Cymbeline (artillery mortar-locating radar) trailer and Land Rover down to Camilla Creek. The night also saw the completion of a Special Forces insertion on Mounts Kent and Challenger by the PNG aircraft. Nigel North (flying ZA292) came under fire when tasked with picking up casualties from Darwin. Despite the belief that a local surrender had been secured, the Sea King was fired at by a ground-based 7.62mm gun and one round hit the fuselage near the gearbox mainframe, just missing the hydraulic run. Fortunately, no one was hurt and the damage was only superficial. The three remaining PNG aircraft moved 800 Bergens (back packs) to 45 Cdo at Douglas settlement without incident.

At 1450Z on 29 May the Argentine forces at Goose Green surrendered to 2 PARA, some 1,100 prisoners being taken *(Argentine sources say 1,083)*. In the meantime, 3 PARA and 45 Cdo continued through Douglas settlement and on to Teal Inlet. The Squadron was heavily engaged in moving men and stores to all these locations until, at the end of the day, the first stripped-out Sea King

HAS.2A's belonging to 825 Sqdn disembarked from 'Atlantic Causeway' to a FOB at San Carlos settlement. The detachment of PNG HC.4's aboard 'Intrepid' now moved ashore to a FOB site at UC 555885 (in a river gully about 1.5 miles north of the Ajax Bay Refrigeration Plant on the west bank of San Carlos Water, becoming known as "Pollock's Passage" after Lt Cdr Pollock) tasked with moving 42 Cdo from Port San Carlos to Mount Kent. Heavy snow showers defeated several attempts to complete this mission. With the front line now some 30 miles away, the 825 Sqdn aircraft were a welcome addition, taking over resupply operations around the anchorage. Good weather on 30 May saw 846 Sqdn flying troops to the forward positions, but reports of enemy soldiers south of Evelyn Hill meant an arduous route to the front via Douglas settlement. With one aircraft unserviceable, the three remaining PNG machines completed the move of 42 Cdo and 105mm ammunition onto Mount Kent, the operation lasting well into the early hours of 31 May.

'Fearless' had returned on 30 May, embarking four aircraft for an overnight stay which proved to be a fortunate move. At 0530Z on 31 May, one "Eagle Base" tent was demolished and the telephone exchange rendered unserviceable by splinters during a bombing raid by a Grupo 2 Canberra. None of the Sea Kings was damaged when the four bombs exploded. Unfortunately, Lt Cdr R.C.Harden (the Squadron AEO) suffered facial injuries as a result of the attack and had to be flown first to Ajax Bay and then to 'Uganda' for treatment. With no further attacks from enemy air or ground forces, 846 Sqdn continued ferrying men, stores and batteries up to Teal Inlet. Having all four of its helicopters serviceable once again, the PNG contingent spent another long night supporting the build-up on Mount Kent. ZA291 was the Sea King used on 31 May to deposit 19 men from the RM Mountain and Arctic Warfare Cadre close to Top Malo House (near Mount Simon, East Falkland). In the house were 17 members of the recently formed (on 22 May) Argentine Special Forces unit, CC602 (Compania de Comandos 602). All of them were either killed, wounded or captured in the subsequent fighting that day.

On 1 June, the remainder of 825 Sqdn plus the majority of 847 Sqdn's Wessex HU.5 fleet disembarked from 'Atlantic Causeway' to set up base at Port San Carlos settlement. The next tasks were to lift gun batteries to Teal Inlet and, once again, to fly Special Forces into the area of Mounts Kent and Challenger. There were no enemy air or ground attacks, so three PNG aircraft set off at dusk to fly Special Forces onto Mount Vernet, near Estancia House, before joining the fourth aircraft on the final night resupply mission to Mount Kent.

Bad weather restricted operations for the next three days, giving the maintenance crews an opportunity to work on the aircraft between sorties. Progress was made in consolidating the positions, with more equipment flown to Teal Inlet and guns moved forward to Estancia House. Further night flying in support of the Special Forces was planned for 4 June but had to be cancelled due to bad weather at the landing site. The weather improved on 5 June to allow two battery uplifts and the deployment of Rapiers to Teal Inlet, while the previous night's cancelled PNG mission was accomplished despite low cloud and fog. The weather closed in once more on 6 June

"Penguin" FOB (Port Stanley Racecourse), sometime between 18.6 and 3.7.82, with a group of abandoned CAB601 UH-1H "Hueys" in the background. Taking-off from the rubbish-strewn surface is 826 Squadron Sea King HAS.5 XZ578 '–/(0)21' while on the ground, with its main rotor-blades tethered to the fuselage stubs, is Sea King HC.4 ZA291 '–/VB' of 846 Squadron. During the period mentioned both units were involved in transporting men and equipment to and from the many ships at anchor in Stanley Harbour and Port William. (Ministry of Defence).

'Fearless', homeward bound near Ascension Island in early 7.82, with her four 846 Squadron Sea King HC.4's (ZA298 '–/VA', ZA299 '–/VE', ZA296 '–/VF' and ZA313 '–/VZ') lined up on the flight-deck. Flanking them, and wearing 846 Squadron side-codes, are the two captured CAB601 A-109A Hirundos AE-334 '–/VV' (left) and AE-331 '–/VC'. All six helicopters were flown off to Yeovilton on 13.7.82, but not before AE-331's code had been amended to 'CC' in deference to a 3 CBAS "request"! (Ministry of Defence).

Sqdn Ldr Jerry Pook of 1(F) Squadron is winched aboard Sea King HAS.5 XZ571 '–/(1)43' of 826 Squadron. He had spent less than ten minutes in the water, some 30 miles from 'Hermes', after ejecting from his battle-damaged and fuel-exhausted Harrier GR.3 (XZ963/14) in the early afternoon of 30.5.82.

(815 Sqdn 'Exeter' Flight)

when, in heavy showers, the Squadron was briefed to search for Gazelle AH.1 XX377 of 656 Sqdn which had disappeared in the vicinity of Mount Pleasant. The wreck was found but the four occupants were dead *[see 656 Sqdn notes for details]*. Once again, a successful PNG mission was carried out that night by two Sea Kings in support of Special Forces. On 7 June, ZA313 was detached to 'Sir Galahad', tasked with the deployment of Rapiers ashore at first light the following day. In the meantime, the sole Chinook HC.1 (ZA718) at last lifted ZA310 from its landing position down to the FOB area at Fern Valley Creek, followed by 825 Sqdn's crashed Sea King HAS.2A XV696 to that Squadron's FOB at San Carlos settlement. The latter's rear tail-pylon was removed and fitted to ZA310 in order to make the HC.4 airworthy once again.

As the night tasks began to diminish, the 'Intrepid' aircraft carried out more daytime tasking and on 8 June moved from the west bank to the east bank FOB at Fern Valley Creek. During that day's operations, an enemy air raid on the shipping at Port Pleasant saw the bombing of 'Sir Galahad' and 'Sir Tristram', both left burning and abandoned. Rescue operations to Ajax Bay and to 'Fearless' continued well into the night using the PNG aircraft. ZA313 (crewed by Lt J.A.G.Miller and POACMN A.Ashdown) had been off-loading Rapiers from 'Sir Galahad' and was some 200 yards away towards the shore when the five A-4B Skyhawks of Grupo 5 attacked. Lt Miller cleared the area and hovered behind some high ground until it was safe to fly out to the LSL and rescue survivors, four or five at a time, from the foredeck and fly them ashore. Whilst close to the ship, John Miller had to manoeuvre ZA313 in billowing smoke no more than 20ft above the water. Throughout the rescue ammunition was exploding on both LSL's. The same aircraft and crew were involved in the rescue of survivors from 'Foxtrot 4' (a 'Fearless' LCU) which was attacked and sunk later in the day.

The following day saw the Squadron continue tasking for the forward units, while suspected Argentine reinforcement and resupply to West Falkland was investigated that night with PNG sorties on Special Forces operations.

By 10 June most of the Squadron was operating from Teal Inlet, with one aircraft lifting spares to the Rapier batteries at San Carlos, Teal and Fitzroy while another inserted an SAS patrol on West Falkland to search for two of their number with whom radio contact had been lost. Although carried out in daylight, the mission succeeded without incident, as did a further one-aircraft PNG sortie that night. A fine day on 11 June did not bring forth any enemy air raids and intensive flying activity by the Squadron was split between 3 Cdo Bde and 5 Inf Bde, with six aircraft moving 2 PARA from Fitzroy to Bluff Peak. A refuelling base was established at Fitzroy and the 18 Sqdn Chinook (ZA718) flew fuel up from San Carlos to the forward locations. A further PNG task for the Special Forces was carried out that night. On 12 June the Squadron once again flew batteries and ammunition forward, by now within range of the enemy artillery on the other side of Two Sisters mountain. No enemy air raids materialised and further PNG tasking saw the Special Forces progress to Beagle Ridge despite the diffi-

culties of night refuelling in the forward areas.

The next day followed a similar pattern until 1515Z when an Argentine air raid consisting of seven Grupo 5 A-4B Skyhawks materialised, heading east towards Mount Kent. Three of the aircraft dropped their bombs on the western slopes of Mount Kent and then turned immediately northwards towards Estancia House. About 1.5 miles south of that position (at VC 190750) the A-4B Skyhawk flown by Alferez Dellepiane suddenly came upon Sea King ZA298 being piloted by Lt Cdr Thornewill. Simon Thornewill and his crew (Lt D.A.Lord, CPOACMN M.J.Tupper and POACMN J.Sheldon) had just delivered a load of 105mm shells from Teal Inlet to Mount Kent and as the helicopter came out of Impassable Valley near Mount Challenger, CPO Tupper at the GPMG position by the starboard rear door and PO Sheldon looking out of the observation bubble on the port side saw the Skyhawk flying towards them and warned Lt Cdr Thornewill. Using standard helicopter fighter evasion tactics, Simon Thornewill turned to face his potential attackers, keeping out of the line of fire as the leading aircraft overflew him. The remaining Skyhawk, flown by Alferez Dellepiane, opened fire on the Sea King purely because it was in his sights as he rapidly exited the area *[see Grupo 5 notes]*. There was a loud bang as a cannon shell passed through the spar of one of the main rotor blades without exploding. The Sea King did not handle any differently and Lt Cdr Thornewill managed to take cover in a ravine until the danger had passed. He landed the helicopter safely in Impassable Valley (VC 173738) at about 1530Z and the crew disembarked to examine the damage, the 20mm round having punched a hole through the blade 8ft from its tip. They radioed for a new blade to be flown over and it duly arrived in ZA291; the blade was manhandled into place and ZA298 was flying back to San Carlos within a couple of hours. Subsequent examination of the damaged blade showed that the shell had "armed" as it went through the main spar and probably exploded as it exited!

Overnight, two PNG aircraft were allocated to CASEVAC duties at Teal and Fitzroy, but were not used. Weather and tasking on 14 June followed the previous day's pattern as the 105mm guns continued their insatiable demand for ammunition. Fuel for the aircraft now became a problem as the Chinook could not keep up with the supplies needed at Teal and Fitzroy. A solution to this was to become unnecessary, for at 1550Z the Argentines surrendered at Port Stanley. The Squadron began moving troops forward to Moody Brook immediately, while the night tasking was cancelled. One of the Sea Kings (ZA298) had white panels painted on the nose and fuselage sides so that the Argentines would hopefully recognise it as a non-combatant aircraft when it was used for the planned mission to take Maj Gen Moore into Port Stanley to accept the surrender. However, appalling weather meant that the Squadron had to forego this honour, the task falling to an Observer-manned, radar-equipped 820 Sqdn Sea King HAS.5, XZ920. Despite the blizzard conditions, ZA298 (crewed by Lt Cdr Thornewill, Lt P.I.M.Rainey, CPOACMN Tupper and POACMN Sheldon) did fly General de Brigada Menendez and four of his senior officers from the western end of Port Stanley Racecourse back to 'Fearless' in San Carlos Water on 15 June (the white markings were removed the following day).

The newly-repaired ZA310 made its first flight on 15 June and embarked 'Intrepid' in San Carlos Water that day. Three further Sea Kings (ZA292, ZA293 and ZA297) embarked 'Intrepid' in San Carlos Water on 16 June and the four aircraft detachment was tasked with the transfer of PoW's from Fox Bay, Port Howard and Pebble Island. After that, the detachment joined the MACC programme from 17 to 23 June. 'Fearless' also re-embarked four aircraft on 16 June (ZA296, ZA298, ZA299 and ZA313) before moving from San Carlos Water to Port Stanley overnight. The detachment aboard 'Fearless' operated with the other three aircraft ashore in collecting guns and ammunition from the mountain areas. A FOB site (known as "Penguin") was established at Stanley Racecourse, the three aircraft ashore (ZA291, ZA295 and ZA312) moving in on 18 June from their Fern Valley Creek base.

By 18 June a pair of CAB601 Agusta A-109A's (AE-331 and AE-334), which had been abandoned by the Argentine forces at the Racecourse, were safely stowed aboard 'Fearless' thanks to 846 Sqdn. The helicopters had originally been "found" by 3 CBAS personnel on 15 June. Both appeared to be in good condition but unfortunately no one within 3 CBAS could fly them due to lack of twin-engined helicopter experience or ratings. Lt Cdr Thornewill and Lt Rainey of 846 Sqdn had the necessary qualifications and thus "impressed" them into their Squadron! Their main concern was to ensure that neither aircraft was vandalised before being test-flown and removed to a safer location.

Simon Thornewill and Peter Rainey test-flew both aircraft from the Racecourse on 15 June (after short hover checks). Both helicopters were guarded overnight and on

16 June Lt Cdr Thornewill flew AE-331 to 'Fearless' in San Carlos Water. He took a circuitous route via Estancia House, Teal Inlet and Bombilla Hill to avoid the attention of over-eager British troops who might have thought it was still in Argentine hands. Just to make sure that all went well, a Sea King HC.4 flew alongside as escort. On 17 June 'Fearless' was anchored in Port William, Lt Rainey flying AE-334 aboard later that day on a short flight from the Racecourse. Once embarked, both helicopters (still in their original CAB601 markings) were stowed below in the tank deck.

'Intrepid' deployed to Port William on 23 June to embark elements of 29 Cdo Regt RA by helicopter. ZA312 embarked 'Canberra' that day in Port William to sail with her for the United Kingdom on 25 June, while the rest of the Squadron was subsequently involved in the re-embarkation of 3 Cdo Bde and 5 Inf Bde, the rebuilding of Stanley Airport and assistance with the equipment for clearing minefields. 'Fearless' then sailed for the United Kingdom with her detachment on 24 June, followed by 'Intrepid' and her four aircraft two days later. The last two aircraft (ZA291 and ZA295) embarked 'Hermes' for the return voyage on 3 July.

During the passage of 'Fearless' to Ascension Island the Sea Kings were generally spruced up, including the application (in Black) to ZA313 of ROYAL NAVY titles and the side-letters '-/VZ'. The two A-109A's were also surveyed and any faults rectified. By the time the ship arrived off the Island on 3 July, their original paint scheme had been modified so that they then wore Black ROYAL NAVY titles on the booms (in place of the EJERCITO ones) with Red/Blue roundels and Black 846 Sqdn side-letters on the nose and fuselage sides (AE-331

*An unidentified 846 Squadron Sea King HC.4 alights on the flight-deck of 'Uganda' near Ascension Island sometime between 28.4 and 1.5.82. The vessel had been converted to a hospital ship at Gibraltar during mid-4.82, accounting for the acronym "NOSH" on her flight-deck.*

'-/VC' and AE334 '-/VV'). They were given five-minute test-flights on 6 July and found to be satisfactory.

Following a gentle, good-humoured reminder by Major C.P.Cameron (OC 3 CBAS) as to which unit had originally "found" the aircraft, the colour scheme of AE-331 was altered in deference to 3 CBAS: ROYAL MARINES replaced the ROYAL NAVY titles and the side-letters were modified to 'CC'. Honour had thus been satisfied! 'Fearless' and 'Intrepid' arrived off Plymouth on 13 July and the two A-109A's led the eight 846 Sqdn Sea Kings in a formation flypast at Yeovilton that day prior to landing there. The two ships finally docked at Portsmouth on 14 July.

Of the remaining Squadron Sea King HC.4's, ZA312 had already disembarked 'Canberra' on 10 July before the ship arrived at Southampton, while ZA291 and ZA295 arrived at Portsmouth aboard 'Hermes' on 21 July and disembarked the following day.

846 Sqdn's statistics covering the Operation "Corporate" period during April, May and June 1982 clearly show how extensively the helicopters were used:

| | |
|---|---|
| *Total aircraft flying hours* | 3,107 |
| *Total number of sorties* | 1,818 |
| *Total deck landings* | 3,343 |
| *Pilots' flying hours* | 4,563 |
| *(includes 736 at night)* | |
| *Average hours per pilot* | 228 |

It is worth noting that much of the flying was achieved without the benefit of a co-pilot as the Sea King HC.4 is cleared for single-pilot operations with the aircrewman trained to land the helicopter in an emergency. The aircraft flew constantly at very low-level maintaining speeds of 100-110 knots. While some 40 or 50 modifications were incorporated into the aircraft during the War, 100% reliability was considered normal and the only real faults were blade erosion due to flying in rain and snow, and bent ventral aerials caused by so many landings on soft ground. A single GPMG was found to be insufficient, so four window-mounted sets were made for the aircraft. Finally, the Squadron suggested further amendments to the colour scheme by painting out the Red and White blade tips, making the red of the roundel darker and using green instead of white aerials. These were adopted and became standard.

---

*Aircrew with 846 Sqdn during Operation "Corporate" and their awards:*

*Lt Cdr S.C.Thornewill RN (CO) DSC; Lt Cdr C.Ives RN; Lt Cdr W.A.Pollock RN (Senior Pilot); Lt Cdr C.Wrighton RN; Lt A.R.C.Bennett RN DSC; Lt R.L.Crawford RM MID; Lt W.J.T.Fewtrell RN MID; Lt R.Harper RN; Lt I.Horton RN MID; Lt R.Hutchings RM DSC; Lt D.A.Lord RN MID; Lt J.Middleton RN; Lt J.A.G.Miller RN MID; Lt N.J.North RN DSC; Lt P.I.M.Rainey RN MID; Lt S.Robinson RN; Lt P.Spens-Black RN; Flt Lt R.W.Grundy RAF; S/Lt M.Eales RN; S/Lt D.Hickey RN; S/Lt P.J.Humphreys RN MID; S/Lt T.Jackson RN; CPOACMN W.Hammond; CPOACMN T.Kelly; CPOACMN T.Short; CPOACMN M.J.Tupper DSM; POACMN A.Ashdown MID; POACMN S.Branley; POACMN J.Brennan; POACMN R.Burnett MID; POACMN K.S.Casey (KIA); POACMN P.Jackson; POACMN I.McRoberts; POACMN C.Rankin; POACMN J.Sheldon; POACMN C.W.Tattersall MID; POACMN S.Wooley; CplACMN M.D.Love RM DSM (KIA); LACMN P.B.Imrie DSM; LACMN I.Robertson MID; LACMN P.Turner; Cpl C.Lelittka.*

# INDIVIDUAL AIRCRAFT DETAILS

The low-vis scheme applied to the Sea Kings of 814, 824 (all Flights), 825 and 826 Sqdns consisted of standard RAF Blue-Grey overall (deleting any deck-letters previously carried), Red/Blue roundels, the ROYAL NAVY titles, serials and codes being in Black.

In the case of 820 Sqdn, the only differences were that the ROYAL NAVY titles were deleted with RAF Blue-Grey and the serials were retained in White.

The 846 Sqdn aircraft were already in the standard Sea King HC.4 low-vis scheme prior to Operation "Corporate". This consisted of Matt Olive Drab overall with Red/Blue roundels and the ROYAL NAVY titles, serials and Squadron/individual aircraft letters were applied in Black (no deck-letters carried).

Any exceptions or subsequent modifications to the colour scheme or markings are explained under each individual aircraft history.

*Examples of abbreviations used for markings and their meanings:*

'N/014'   *Deck-letter for 'Invincible' and side-code worn in full.*

'N/(0)14'   *Deck-letter for 'Invincible' worn but first digit of side-code deleted.*

'-/350'   *Deck-letters 'OD' for 'Olmeda' not worn but side-code worn in full.*

'-/(1)32'   *Deck-letter 'H' for 'Hermes' not worn and first digit of side-code deleted.*

'-/VA'   *Deck-letters not allocated; Squadron letter and individual aircraft letter worn in full.*

(VZ)   *Deck-letters not allocated and neither Squadron nor individual aircraft letter worn.*

**XV648** HAS.2A

On 29.3.82 with 706 Sqdn at Culdrose, coded 'CU/597'. Transferred to 825 Sqdn 3.5.82 and adopted the low-vis scheme, retaining code '-/597'. Departed Culdrose 12.5.82 *[using call-sign (500) or (505) - see XV677]*, embarking 'Queen Elizabeth 2' that day in The Solent shortly after the liner had sailed from Southampton for South Georgia. Arrived at Grytviken on 27.5.82 where it was transferred to 'Canberra' on 28.5.82, sailing with the ship that day en route to San Carlos Water. The liner arrived there on 2.6.82 and the aircraft disembarked to the FOB at Port San Carlos settlement the same day. Moved FOB with the rest of the Sqdn to San Carlos settlement on 3.6.82. Remained based there until it embarked 'Atlantic Causeway' in San Carlos Water 13.7.82, sailing with the ship that day for the UK. Flown off to Culdrose on 27.7.82 whilst the vessel was anchored in Mount's Bay, Cornwall prior to docking at Devonport later the same day. Although 825 Sqdn disbanded on 17.9.82, the aircraft remained on nominal 825 Sqdn/NASU charge (for restoration to previous ASW configuration) until transferred to 706 Sqdn at Culdrose on 2.11.82.

**XV649** HAS.2A

On 29.3.82 with 824 Sqdn 'C' Flt at Culdrose coded 'CU/355'. Transferred to 824 Sqdn 'A' Flt 1.4.82 for service aboard 'Olmeda' (replacing XV698 'CU/351') and adopted the low-vis scheme, retaining 'C' Flight code '-/355'. Departed Culdrose on 4.4.82, embarking 'Olmeda' that day at Devonport prior to her departure for the South Atlantic on 5.4.82. Flown off to the FOB at Port San Carlos settlement on 3.6.82 for utility duties, returning to the ship on 6.6.82. Sailed with the vessel on 16.6.82 for South Georgia and Operation "Keyhole" (the retaking of Southern Thule), the Island being repossessed 20.6.82. Sailed with the ship for the UK on 21.6.82 (via South Georgia) and flown off to Culdrose 10.7.82 prior to the vessel's arrival at Devonport on 12.7.82.

Still coded '-/355', it redeployed with 'A' Flight to the South Atlantic, embarking 'Fort Austin' on 26.8.82. Transferred to 'Olmeda' in the South Atlantic on 21.9.82, remaining with the ship until she returned to the UK. Flown off to Culdrose on 19.12.82 prior to the vessel docking that day at Devonport.

**XV650** AEW.2A          *Deployed post-14.6.82*

On 29.3.82 with 706 Sqdn at Culdrose as a HAS.2A coded 'CU/588'. Embarked 'Engadine' on 8.4.82 for a training detachment, disembarking to Culdrose 22.4.82. Transferred to MoD(PE) loan 24.5.82 for AEW conversion by WHL and delivered to Yeovil on 27.5.82, still coded 'CU/588'. First flight as an AEW.2A from Yeovil on 30.7.82. Delivered to Portland 2.8.82 using call-sign "Cyclops 1" (still retaining its old code 'CU/588') prior to embarking 'Illustrious' in the English Channel that day upon allocation to 824 Sqdn 'D' Flight (which had formed at Culdrose on 14.6.82). ['Illustrious' had departed Portsmouth on 2.8.82 to relieve 'Invincible' in the South Atlantic.] During the deployment it was repainted in the low-vis scheme with the 824 Sqdn code '-/362' allo-

cated and applied in Black. Departed the FIPZ with the carrier on 21.10.82 for the UK (via the USA) and was flown off to Culdrose on 7.12.82 prior to the vessel's arrival at Portsmouth on 8.12.82.

**XV651** HAS.5          *Deployed post-14.6.82*

On 15.6.82 with 814 Sqdn at Culdrose coded '-/266' in the low-vis scheme. Embarked 'Illustrious' in the English Channel from Culdrose on 2.8.82 (the carrier having left Portsmouth earlier in the day), sailing with her to relieve 'Invincible' in the South Atlantic. Departed the FIPZ with the ship on 21.10.82 for the UK (via the USA), flying off to Culdrose 7.12.82 prior to the vessel's arrival at Portsmouth on 8.12.82.

**XV652** HAS.5          *Deployed post-14.6.82*

On 15.6.82 with 814 Sqdn at Culdrose coded '-/270' in the low-vis scheme. Embarked 'Illustrious' in the English Channel from Culdrose on 2.8.82 (the carrier having left Portsmouth earlier in the day), sailing with her to relieve 'Invincible' in the South Atlantic. Departed the FIPZ with the ship on 21.10.82 for the UK (via the USA), being flown off to Culdrose 7.12.82 prior to the vessel's arrival at Portsmouth on 8.12.82.

**XV654** HAS.2A

On 29.3.82 with 706 Sqdn at Culdrose, coded 'CU/585'. Transferred to 825 Sqdn 3.5.82 and adopted the low-vis scheme, retaining code '-/585'. Departed Culdrose 13.5.82 [using call-sign (501)], embarking 'Atlantic Causeway' that day in Plymouth Sound before sailing with her for the South Atlantic on 14.5.82. Flown off to the FOB at Port San Carlos settlement on 1.6.82. Moved FOB with the rest of the Sqdn to San Carlos settlement on 3.6.82.

On 8.6.82 it was being flown by Lt Sheldon on a survey of the Fitzroy area which coincided with the attacks on 'Sir Tristram' and 'Sir Galahad' at Port Pleasant by five Grupo 5 A-4B Skyhawks. Lt Sheldon and his crew carried out several dangerous but successful rescue sorties (in particular to 'Sir Galahad').

Remained based at San Carlos settlement FOB until it re-embarked 'Atlantic Causeway' 13.7.82 in San Carlos Water, sailing with the ship for the UK that day. Flown off to Culdrose on 27.7.82 whilst the vessel was anchored in Mount's Bay, Cornwall prior to docking at Devonport later in the day. Although the Sqdn disbanded on 17.9.82, the aircraft remained on nominal 825 Sqdn/NASU charge (for restoration to ASW configuration) until transferred to 706 Sqdn at Culdrose on 11.10.82.

**XV655** HAS.5          *Deployed post-14.6.82*

On 15.6.82 with 814 Sqdn at Culdrose coded '-/265' in the low-vis scheme. Embarked 'Illustrious' in the English Channel from Culdrose on 2.8.82 (the carrier having left Portsmouth earlier in the day), sailing with her to relieve 'Invincible' in the South Atlantic. Departed the FIPZ with the ship on 21.10.82 for the UK (via the USA), being flown off to Culdrose 7.12.82 prior to the vessel's arrival at Portsmouth on 8.12.82.

**XV656** HAS.2A

On 29.3.82 with 819 Sqdn at Prestwick coded 'PW/703'. Transferred to 825 Sqdn 3.5.82 and flown from Prestwick to Culdrose that day. Once there it adopted the low-vis scheme, retaining code '-/703'. Departed Culdrose 13.5.82 [using call-sign (503)], embarking 'Atlantic Causeway' that day in Plymouth Sound before sailing with her for the South Atlantic 14.5.82. Flown off to the FOB at San Carlos settlement on 29.5.82 (or Port San Carlos settlement on 1.6.82). Moved FOB with the Sqdn to San Carlos settlement on 3.6.82. Remained based there until it re-embarked 'Atlantic Causeway' in San Carlos Water on 13.7.82, sailing with the ship that day for the UK. Flown off to Culdrose on 27.7.82 whilst she was anchored in Mount's Bay, Cornwall prior to docking at Devonport later in the day. Although the Sqdn disbanded on 17.9.82, the aircraft remained on nominal 825 Sqdn/NASU charge (for restoration to ASW configuration) until transferred to 819 Sqdn at Prestwick on 10.11.82, arriving there 11.11.82.

**XV657** HAS.2A          *Deployed post-14.6.82*

On 29.3.82 with 824 Sqdn 'B' Flt coded 'CU/353', disembarked at RAF North Front, Gibraltar *[see 824 Sqdn 'B' Flt notes]*. Remained at Gibraltar on VERTREP and HDS duties until 7.6.82 when it embarked 'Olwen' at the end of her refit for return to the UK. Flown off to Culdrose 10.6.82 prior to the ship docking at Devonport later that day. By 24.682 it had joined 706 Sqdn at Culdrose (still coded 'CU/353') and then to NASU by 28.7.82. On 16.8.82 transferred to 824 Sqdn 'A' Flt. at Culdrose and coded '-/350' (replacing XV660).

Deployed with 'A' Flight to the South Atlantic, embarking 'Fort Austin' on 26.8.82. Transferred to 'Olmeda' in the South Atlantic on 21.9.82, remaining with the ship until she returned to the UK. Flown off to Culdrose on 19.12.82 prior to the vessel docking that day at Devonport.

**XV659** HAS.2A

On 29.3.82 with 706 Sqdn at Culdrose, coded 'CU/584'. Transferred to 825 Sqdn 3.5.82 and adopted the low-vis scheme, retaining code '-/584'. Departed Culdrose 13.5.82 [using call-sign (502)], embarking 'Atlantic Causeway' that day in Plymouth Sound before sailing with her for the South Atlantic on 14.5.82. Flown off via 'Hermes' and 'Invincible' to the FOB at San Carlos settlement 29.5.82. Moved FOB to Port San Carlos settlement on 31.5.82 prior to returning with the Sqdn to the San Carlos settlement FOB on 3.6.82. Remained based there until it re-embarked 'Atlantic Causeway' in San Carlos Water on 13.7.82, sailing with the ship that day for the UK. Flown off to Culdrose on 27.7.82 whilst she was anchored in Mount's Bay, Cornwall prior to docking at Devonport later in the day. Although the Sqdn disbanded on 17.9.82, it remained on nominal 825 Sqdn/NASU charge (for restoration to ASW configuration) until transferred to 706 Sqdn at Culdrose on 22.12.82.

**XV660 HAS.2A**

On 29.3.82 with 824 Sqdn 'A' Flt, coded 'OD/350' (having recently served aboard 'Olmeda'), temporarily based at Prestwick for support duties. Whilst there, all markings (except the serial, but including the roundels) were overpainted in a washable dark grey. Returned to Culdrose on 31.3.82 where the "wash" was removed and a proper low-vis scheme applied, retaining the code '-/350'. Departed Culdrose 4.4.82 to embark 'Olmeda' the same day at Devonport, sailing with her for the South Atlantic on 5.4.82. Flown off to the FOB at Port San Carlos settlement on 3.6.82, returning to the ship 6.6.82. Transferred temporarily to 'Invincible' on 16.6.82 while 'Olmeda' detached to South Georgia prior to Operation "Keyhole". Returned to 'Olmeda' 27.6.82 while the ship was en route to the UK from South Georgia, being flown off to Culdrose on 10.7.82 before the vessel's arrival at Devonport on 12.7.82.

**XV661 HAS.5**     *Deployed post-14.6.82*

On 15.6.82 uncoded with NASU Culdrose. Transferred 23.6.82 from NASU to 814 Sqdn in the low-vis scheme, coded '-/274'. Embarked 'Illustrious' on 17.7.82 for a short series of trials/training, returning to Culdrose c21.7.82. Re-embarked the carrier in the English Channel on 2.8.82 ('Illustrious' having left Portsmouth earlier in the day), sailing with her to relieve 'Invincible' in the South Atlantic. Detached to 'Fort Austin' in the FIPZ c21.10.82 and remained with her until she returned to the UK. Flown off to Culdrose 16.12.82 prior to the vessel anchoring in Plymouth Sound on 17.12.82.

**XV663 HAS.2A**

On 29.3.82 with 706 Sqdn at Culdrose, coded 'CU/581'. Transferred to 825 Sqdn 3.5.82 and adopted the low-vis scheme, retaining code '-/581'. Departed Culdrose 13.5.82 [using call-sign (504)], embarking 'Atlantic Causeway' that day in Plymouth Sound before sailing with her for the South Atlantic on 14.5.82. Flown off to the FOB at Port San Carlos settlement on 1.6.82. Moved FOB with the Sqdn to San Carlos settlement on 3.6.82.

On 8.6.82 it was being flown by Lt Boughton on a survey of the Fitzroy area which coincided with the attack on 'Sir Tristram' and 'Sir Galahad' at Port Pleasant by five Grupo 5 A-4B Skyhawks. Lt Boughton and his crew carried out several dangerous but successful rescue sorties (in particular to 'Sir Galahad').

Remained based at San Carlos settlement FOB until it re-embarked 'Atlantic Causeway' in San Carlos Water 13.7.82, sailing with the ship that day for the UK. Flown off to Culdrose on 27.7.82 whilst the vessel was anchored in Mount's Bay, Cornwall prior to docking at Devonport later in the day. Although the Sqdn disbanded 17.9.82, the aircraft remained on nominal 825 Sqdn/NASU charge (for restoration to previous ASW configuration) until transferred to 706 Sqdn at Culdrose on 4.10.82.

**XV666 HAS.2A**     *Not deployed south*

On 29.3.82 with 824 Sqdn 'B' Flt, coded 'CU/352', disembarked at RAF North Front, Gibraltar [see 824 Sqdn 'B' Flt notes]. Remained at Gibraltar on VERTREP and HDS duties until 7.6.82 when it embarked 'Olwen' at the end of her refit prior to the UK. Flew off to Culdrose 10.6.82 prior to the ship docking at Devonport later that day.

**XV672 HAS.2A**

On 29.3.82 with 826 Sqdn at Culdrose, coded 'H/145'. Transferred to 814 Sqdn on 5.4.82 and to 706 Sqdn on 6.4.82. The low-vis scheme was applied while with 706 Sqdn, but code '-/145' was retained. Maintained this code upon transfer to 824 Sqdn on 29.4.82. Allotted to 'C' Flight, it embarked 'Fort Grange' from Culdrose 7.5.82 for a work-up period. Remained aboard and sailed with the ship from Devonport 14.5.82 for the South Atlantic. Departed the FIPZ with the ship on 17.9.82 for the UK, being flown off to Culdrose 2.10.82 prior to the vessel's arrival at Devonport on 3.10.82.

**XV675 HAS.5**     *Deployed post-14.6.82*

On 15.6.82 with 814 Sqdn at Culdrose coded '-/264' in the low-vis scheme. Embarked 'Illustrious' in the English Channel from Culdrose on 2.8.82 (the carrier having left Portsmouth earlier in the day), sailing with her to relieve 'Invincible' in the South Atlantic. Departed the FIPZ with the ship on 21.10.82 for the UK (via the USA), being flown off to Culdrose 7.12.82 prior to the vessel's arrival at Portsmouth on 8.12.82.

**XV677 HAS.2A**

On 29.3.82 with 706 Sqdn at Culdrose, coded 'CU/595'. Transferred to 825 Sqdn 3.5.82 and adopted the low-vis scheme, retaining code '-/595'. Departed Culdrose 12.5.82 [using call-sign (500) or (505) - see XV648], embarking 'Queen Elizabeth 2' that day in The Solent shortly after the liner had sailed from Southampton for South Georgia. Arrived at Grytviken on 27.5.82 where it was transferred to 'Canberra' on 28.5.82, sailing with the ship that day en route to San Carlos Water. The liner arrived there on 2.6.82 and the aircraft disembarked to the FOB at Port San Carlos settlement the same day. Moved FOB with the rest of the Sqdn to San Carlos settlement on 3.6.82. Remained based there until it embarked 'Atlantic Causeway' in San Carlos Water 13.7.82, sailing with the ship that day for the UK. Flown off to Culdrose 27.7.82 whilst the vessel was anchored in Mount's Bay, Cornwall prior to docking at Devonport later in the day. Although the Sqdn disbanded 17.9.82, it remained on nominal 825 Sqdn/NASU charge (for restoration to its previous ASW configuration) until transferred to 706 Sqdn at Culdrose on 4.10.82.

**XV696 HAS.2A**

On 29.3.82 with 814 Sqdn at Culdrose, coded '-/268'. Embarked 'Engadine' 23.4.82 for a Sqdn training detachment, disembarking to Culdrose on 30.4.82. Transferred to 825 Sqdn on 3.5.82 and adopted the low-vis scheme, retaining code '-/268'. Departed Culdrose 13.5.82 [using call-sign (506)], embarking 'Atlantic Causeway' that day in Plymouth Sound before sailing with her for the South Atlantic on 14.5.82. Flown off via 'Hermes' and

'Invincible' to the FOB at San Carlos settlement on 29.5.82. Moved FOB to Port San Carlos settlement 31.5.82 prior to returning with the Sqdn to the San Carlos settlement FOB on 3.6.82.

Whilst involved in moving Rapier batteries around the hills behind San Carlos 4.6.82, it landed on what was thought to be firm ground near the summit of Lookout Hill. However, the starboard wheel broke through the peat crust and the aircraft started to sink to one side. The pilot (Lt Sheldon) tried to correct the helicopter's attitude but unfortunately all five main rotor blade tips clipped the ground in the process and suffered CAT.1 damage. Due to the lack of on-site spares, it was left in situ and used as a spares source until lifted out to the FOB at San Carlos settlement on 7.6.82 by 18 Sqdn Chinook ZA718. There the tail unit was removed to restore 846 Sqdn Sea King HC.4 ZA310 to airworthy condition.

Minus engines and tail unit, it was airlifted aboard 'Engadine' in San Carlos Water by an 18 Sqdn Chinook HC.1 on 7.7.82 and sailed with her that day for the UK. The ship docked at Devonport on 30.7.82 and the aircraft was off-loaded, leaving by road for Culdrose that day (arriving there 31.7.82) upon transfer to NASU for survey, repair and subsequent conversion to HAS.5.

**XV697 HAS.2A**

On 29.3.82 with 824 Sqdn 'C' Flt at Culdrose coded 'CU/354'. Transferred to 706 Sqdn on 5.4.82, returning to 824 Sqdn charge at Culdrose 7.4.82 and adopted the low-vis scheme, retaining code '-/354'. Allotted to 'C' Flight, it embarked 'Fort Grange' from Culdrose 7.5.82 for a work-up period. Remained aboard, sailing with the ship from Devonport 14.5.82 for the South Atlantic. Departed the FIPZ with the ship 17.9.82 for the UK, flying off to Culdrose on 2.10.82 prior to the vessel's arrival at Devonport on 3.10.82.

**XV698 HAS.2A**

On 29.3.82 with 824 Sqdn 'A' Flt, coded 'OD/351' (having recently served aboard 'Olmeda'), temporarily based at Prestwick for support duties. Whilst there, all markings (except the serials, but including the roundels) were overpainted in a washable dark grey. Returned to Culdrose 31.3.82 and was transferred to 706 Sqdn on 5.4.82 (replaced by XV644). Reallocated to 824 Sqdn on 7.4.82 and by 27.4.82 the low-vis scheme had been applied, retaining the 'A' Flight code '-/351'. Allotted to 'C' Flight, it embarked 'Fort Grange' from Culdrose on 7.5.82 for a work-up period. Remained on board, sailing with the ship from Devonport on 14.5.82 for the South Atlantic.

Whilst engaged on a VERTREP mission to 'Leeds Castle' on 11.7.82, it ditched close to the port bow of the ship. The aircraft sank in a heavy swell, after the crew had been picked up safely by a boat from 'Leeds Castle' (HAS.2 XZ579 from the 'Contender Bezant' replaced XV698 on 13.7.82).

**XV700 HAS.2A**

On 29.3.82 with 814 Sqdn, coded '-/264', on a Sqdn training detachment aboard 'Engadine', disembarking to its base at Culdrose on 6.4.82. Embarked 'Engadine' 23.4.82 for a further training detachment, flying off to Culdrose on 30.4.82. Transferred to 825 Sqdn on 3.5.82 and adopted the low-vis scheme, retaining code '-/264'. Departed Culdrose on 13.5.82 [using call-sign (507)], embarking 'Atlantic Causeway' that day in Plymouth Sound before sailing with the ship on 14.5.82 for the South Atlantic. Flown off, via 'Hermes' and 'Invincible', to the FOB at San Carlos settlement on 29.5.82. Moved FOB to Port San Carlos settlement on 31.5.82 prior to returning with the Sqdn to the San Carlos settlement FOB on 3.6.82.

On 8.6.82 it was being flown by Lt Cdr Clark on a survey of the Fitzroy area which coincided with the attack by five Grupo 5 A-4B Skyhawks on 'Sir Tristram' and 'Sir Galahad' at Port Pleasant. Lt Cdr Clark and his crew carried out several dangerous but successful rescue sorties (notably to 'Sir Galahad').

Remained based at San Carlos settlement FOB until it re-embarked 'Atlantic Causeway' in San Carlos Water on 13.7.82, sailing with ship that day for the UK. Flown off to Culdrose 27.7.82 whilst she was anchored in Mount's Bay, Cornwall prior to docking at Devonport later in the day. Although the Sqdn disbanded on 17.9.82, the aircraft remained on nominal 825 Sqdn/NASU charge (for restoration to previous ASW configuration) until transferred to 706 Sqdn at Culdrose on 2.12.82.

**XV704** AEW.2A    *Deployed post-14.6.82*

On 29.3.82 with the WHL Trials Fleet as a HAS.2A and undergoing MAD trials at A&AEE Boscombe Down. Returned to WHL at Yeovil from A&AEE on 26.4.82 and dedicated to AEW conversion and development trials 26.5.82. First flew as an AEW.2A at Yeovil 23.7.82. Delivered to Portland on 2.8.82 using the call-sign "Cyclops 2" before embarking 'Illustrious' in the English Channel that day upon allocation to 824 Sqdn 'D' Flt (which had reformed at Culdrose on 14.6.82). ['Illustrious' had departed Portsmouth on 2.8.82 to relieve 'Invincible' in the South Atlantic.] During the deployment it was repainted in the low-vis scheme with the 824 Sqdn code '-/361' being allocated and applied in Black. Departed the FIPZ with the carrier 21.10.82 for the UK (via the USA), flying off to Culdrose 7.12.82 prior to the vessel's arrival at Portsmouth on 8.12.82.

**XV714** HAS.2A

On 29.3.82 with 706 Sqdn at Culdrose, coded 'CU/586'. Embarked 'Engadine' 8.4.82 for a Sqdn training detachment, disembarking to Culdrose on 22.4.82. Transferred to 825 Sqdn 3.5.82 and adopted the low-vis scheme, retaining code '-/586'. Left Culdrose on 13.5.82 [using call-sign (508)], embarking 'Atlantic Causeway' in Plymouth Sound the same day before sailing with her for the South Atlantic on 14.5.82. Flown off to the FOB at San Carlos settlement on 29.5.82 (or Port San Carlos settlement on 1.6.82). Moved FOB with the Sqdn to San Carlos settlement on 3.6.82. Remained based there until it re-embarked 'Atlantic Causeway' in San Carlos Water on 13.7.82, sailing with the ship that day for the UK. Flown off to Culdrose on 27.7.82 whilst

she was anchored in Mount's Bay, Cornwall prior to docking at Devonport later in the day. Although the Sqdn disbanded 17.9.82, the aircraft remained on nominal 825 Sqdn/NASU charge (for restoration to previous ASW configuration) until transferred to 824 Sqdn 'C' Flt at Culdrose on 15.12.82.

**XZ571** HAS.5

On 29.3.82 with 826 Sqdn at Culdrose, coded 'H/143'. Detached to Prestwick on 30.3.82, returning to Culdrose (via Valley) 31.3.82. Embarked 'Hermes' at Portsmouth (via Lee-on-Solent) 3.4.82 and sailed south with the ship on 5.4.82. Low-vis markings were applied c10.4.82, retaining modified code '-/(1)43'.

On 30.5.82, whilst being flown by S/Lt Sutton, it was vectored by 'Exeter' Flt's Lynx to pick up Sqdn Ldr Pook of 1(F) Sqdn who had ejected from Harrier GR.3 XZ963 some 30 miles from 'Hermes'. The pilot spent less than 10 minutes in the sea before being rescued.

Departed with the carrier from Port William on 3.7.82 en route for the UK. Arrived with the ship at Portsmouth on 21.7.82 and was flown off to Culdrose on 22.7.82.

Remained on 826 Sqdn charge, the applied code reverting to '-/143' by mid-11.82. Embarked 'Fort Grange' off Culdrose on 21.11.82 (the ship having sailed from Devonport 19.11.82) for deployment to the South Atlantic as part of a FIPZ-based Flight (designated as 826 Sqdn 'A' Flt early in 1983). Returned to the UK aboard 'Fort Austin', flying off to Culdrose on 9.12.83 (still coded '-/143') prior to the ship's arrival in Plymouth Sound that day.

**XZ573** HAS.5

On 29.3.82 with 706 Sqdn at Culdrose, coded 'CU/593'. Transferred to 820 Sqdn as an FIR aircraft 2.4.82, embarking 'Invincible' at Portsmouth (via Lee-on-Solent) 4.4.82, still coded 'CU/593'. Sailed with the ship 5.4.82 and during the passage south low-vis markings were adopted. A modified 820 Sqdn code '-/(0)22' was allocated and applied. Flown to 'Hermes' on 15.5.82 upon transfer to 826 Sqdn and retained code '-/(0)22'.

At 0030Z on 18.5.82, when about to enter a SONAR hover 2 miles to starboard of the carrier, it hit the sea (reportedly due to a RADALT problem) and ditched, the crew (Lts Tonkin, Barber, Swain and LACMN Haycock) being rescued. The helicopter remained afloat but salvage attempts were abandoned *[see text]* and it was eventually sunk by naval gunfire.

**XZ574** HAS.5

On 29.3.82 with 820 Sqdn, hangared on 'Invincible' at Portsmouth dockyard and coded 'N/016'. Sailed with the ship on 5.4.82 and low-vis markings were applied during the passage south, retaining the modified code '-/(0)16'.

On 23.4.82 (whilst crewed by S/Lts Heweth and HRH The Prince Andrew, Lt McAllister and LACMN Arnull) it went to the aid of ditched 846 Sqdn Sea King HC.4 ZA311 at

approximate position 26°S 24°W. The pilot, Flt Lt Grundy, was rescued but POACMN Casey was never found and became the first British casualty of the conflict.

At 0230Z on 2.6.82 (whilst crewed by Lt Cdr Dudley, S/Lts Carr and Finucane and LACMN Trotman) it rescued Flt Lt Mortimer who had spent over eight hours in the water. His 801 Sqdn Sea Harrier (XZ456) had been shot down by a Roland missile on 1.6.82 and he had ejected, landing in the sea south of Port Stanley close to the coast.

Sailed with the carrier from the FIPZ on 28.8.82 for the UK. At some stage during the homeward passage the ROYAL NAVY titles and deck-letter were reapplied in Black (ie 'N/(0)16'). The White serials were retained and Red/Blue Sqdn motifs painted on both sides of the nose below the cockpit. Arrived at Portsmouth with the ship on 17.9.82 and flown off to Culdrose on 18.9.82.

**XZ577** HAS.5

On 29.3.82 with 826 Sqdn at Culdrose, coded 'H/142'. Embarked 'Hermes' at Portsmouth (via Lee-on-Solent) 3.4.82 and sailed south with the ship on 5.4.82. Low-vis markings were applied c10.4.82, retaining modified code '-/(1)42'. On 17.5.82 it was detached to 'Fort Austin' with three others (ZA130, ZA133 and ZA137) for ASW duties in Falkland Sound and San Carlos Water. Remained with the ship until 3.6.82 when it was flown to the FOB at Port San Carlos settlement to provide additional utility capacity ashore. Returned to 'Hermes' on 6.6.82. Departed with the carrier from Port William 3.7.82 en route for the UK. Arrived at Portsmouth with the ship 21.7.82, being flown off to Culdrose on 22.7.82.

Remained on 826 Sqdn charge, the applied code reverting to '-/142' by mid-11.82. Embarked 'Fort Grange' off Culdrose on 21.11.82 (the ship having sailed from Devonport 19.11.82) for deployment to the South Atlantic as part of a FIPZ-based Flight (designated as 826 Sqdn 'A' Flt early in 1983). Returned to the UK aboard 'Fort Austin', being flown off to Culdrose on 9.12.83 (still coded '-/142') prior to the ship's arrival in Plymouth Sound that day.

**XZ578** HAS.5

On 29.3.82 with 706 Sqdn at Culdrose, coded 'CU/589'. Transferred to 820 Sqdn as an FIR aircraft on 2.4.82, embarking 'Invincible' at Portsmouth (via Lee-on-Solent) 4.4.82, still coded 'CU/589'. Sailed with the ship 5.4.82 and during the passage south low-vis markings were adopted. The modified 820 Sqdn code '-/(0)21' was allocated and applied. Flown to 'Hermes' on 14.5.82 upon transfer to 826 Sqdn (replacing ditched ZA132) but retained code '-/(0)21'. On 6.6.82 it was detached with ZA129 to 'Atlantic Causeway' in order to provide the ship with an ASW, ASV and limited utility capability, and to relieve flightdeck congestion on 'Hermes'. A planned transfer to 'Engadine' (both ships were in San Carlos Water) on 9.6.82 was cancelled due to aircraft unserviceability and it sailed the same day with 'Atlantic Causeway' for a position east of the TEZ. Repaired, it rejoined 'Hermes' on 10.6.82. Detached again 17.6.82 (with

ZA133), this time to the FOB at San Carlos settlement (to relieve an 820 Sqdn detachment) for utility and ASV tasks on West Falkland. Returned to 'Hermes' on 23.6.82, sailing with the carrier from Port William en route for the UK on 3.7.82. Arrived at Portsmouth with the ship 21.7.82 (by now with serials and ROYAL NAVY titles in Black), flying off to Culdrose 22.7.82.

## XZ579 HAS.2

On 29.3.82 with 814 Sqdn coded '-/271', embarked on 'Engadine' for a Sqdn training detachment. Disembarked to its base at Culdrose on 6.4.82. Transferred to 706 Sqdn 3.5.82, retaining the 814 Sqdn code. Officially transferred to Naval Party 2050 on 20.5.82 for deployment aboard 'Contender Bezant' as an FIR aircraft. Prior to this the low-vis scheme had been applied (standard RAF Blue-Grey overall with Red/Blue roundels; White ROYAL NAVY titles, serial and code '-/271' over-painted Black). Departed Culdrose on 20.5.82, embarking 'Contender Bezant' in Plymouth Sound prior to sailing with her from Start Bay 21.5.82 for the South Atlantic. The ship arrived at Port William on 17.6.82 and the aircraft was used in the HDS role. Transferred to 824 Sqdn 'C' Flt aboard 'Fort Grange' on 13.7.82 (as a replacement for XV698) prior to 'Contender Bezant' setting course from Port William for the UK later the same day. Departed the FIPZ aboard 'Fort Grange' on 17.9.82 for the UK, flying off to Culdrose 2.10.82 (still coded '-/271') prior to the vessel's arrival at Devonport on 3.10.82.

## XZ580 HAS.2

On 29.3.82 with 814 Sqdn at Culdrose, coded '-/272'. Embarked 'Engadine' 23.4.82 for a Sqdn training detachment, disembarking to Culdrose on 30.4.82. Transferred to 825 Sqdn 3.5.82 and adopted the low-vis scheme, retaining code '-/272'. Departed Culdrose 13.5.82 [using call-sign (509)], embarking 'Atlantic Causeway' in Plymouth Sound that day before sailing with her for the South Atlantic on 14.5.82. Flown off to the FOB at Port San Carlos settlement on 1.6.82 and moved FOB with the Sqdn to San Carlos settlement on 3.6.82.

On 8.6.82 it was being flown by Lt Isacke on a survey of the Fitzroy area which coincided with the attacks by five Grupo 5 A-4B Skyhawks on 'Sir Tristram' and 'Sir Galahad' at Port Pleasant. Lt Isacke and his crew carried out several dangerous but successful rescue sorties (in particular from 'Sir Galahad').

Remained based at the San Carlos settlement FOB until it re-embarked 'Atlantic Causeway' in San Carlos Water on 13.7.82, sailing with the ship that day for the UK. Flown off to Culdrose on 27.7.82 whilst she was anchored in Mount's Bay, Cornwall prior to docking at Devonport later in the day. Although the Sqdn disbanded 17.9.82, the aircraft remained on nominal 825 Sqdn/NASU charge (for restoration to previous ASW configuration) until transferred to 706 Sqdn at Culdrose on 18.10.82.

## XZ918 HAS.5

On 29.3.82 with 820 Sqdn, hangared in 'Invincible' at Portsmouth dockyard and

coded 'N/020'. Sailed with the ship 5.4.82 and low-vis markings were applied during the passage south, retaining the modified code '-/(0)20'. Sailed with the carrier from the FIPZ on 28.8.82 for the UK. At some stage during the homeward passage the ROYAL NAVY titles and deck-letter were reapplied in Black (ie 'N/(0)20') but White serials were retained. Red/Blue Sqdn motifs were painted on both sides of the nose below the cockpit. Arrived at Portsmouth with the carrier on 17.9.82 and flown off to Culdrose on 18.9.82.

## XZ919 HAS.5                 *Deployed post-14.6.82*

On 15.6.82 with 814 Sqdn at Culdrose coded '-/271' in the low-vis scheme. Embarked 'Illustrious' in the English Channel from Culdrose on 2.8.82 (the carrier having left Portsmouth earlier in the day), sailing with her to relieve 'Invincible' in the South Atlantic. Departed the FIPZ with the ship on 21.10.82 for the UK (via the USA), flying off to Culdrose on 7.12.82 prior to the vessel's arrival at Portsmouth 8.12.82.

## XZ920 HAS.5

On 29.3.82 with 820 Sqdn, hangared in 'Invincible' at Portsmouth dockyard and coded 'N/010'. Sailed with the ship 5.4.82 and low-vis markings were applied during the passage south, retaining the modified code '-/(0)10'. Detached to 'Tidepool' on 29.5.82 (along with XZ921), returning to 'Invincible' the next day. Disembarked to the San Carlos settlement FOB on 14.6.82 to relieve XZ921.

During the late evening of 14.6.82, whilst being flown by Lt Cdr Dudley, it collected Maj Gen Moore from Fitzroy and flew him to Port Stanley in very bad weather conditions to accept the surrender of the Argentine forces on the Islands.

Returned to 'Invincible' from shore detachment on 17.6.82 and finally sailed with the carrier from the FIPZ 28.8.82 for the UK. At some stage during the homeward passage the deck-letter and ROYAL NAVY titles were applied in Black (ie 'N/(0)10') but White serials were retained. Red/Blue Sqdn motifs were applied to both sides of the nose below the cockpit. Arrived with the ship at Portsmouth on 17.9.82 and flown off to Culdrose 18.9.82.

## XZ921 HAS.5

On 29.3.82 with 820 Sqdn, hangared in 'Invincible' at Portsmouth dockyard and coded 'N/017'. Sailed with the ship on 5.4.82 and low-vis markings were applied during the passage south, retaining modified code '-/(0)17'. Detached to 'Tidepool' (along with XZ920) on 29.5.82, but returned to 'Invincible' the next day. Disembarked to the San Carlos settlement FOB on 10.6.82 along with ZA127 (replacing a cancelled 826 Sqdn detachment), returning to 'Invincible' on 14.6.82 (relieved by XZ920). Sailed with the carrier from the FIPZ on 28.8.82 for the UK. At some stage during the homeward passage the ROYAL NAVY titles and deck-letter were reapplied in Black (ie 'N/(0)17') but White serials were retained. Red/Blue Sqdn motifs were applied on both sides of the nose below the cockpit. Arrived at Portsmouth with the carrier on 17.9.82 and flown off to Culdrose 18.9.82.

## XZ922 HAS.5                 *Deployed post-14.6.82*

On 15.6.82 with 814 Sqdn at Culdrose coded '-/272' in the low-vis scheme. Embarked 'Illustrious' in the English Channel on 17.7.82 for a short series of trials and training, returning to Culdrose c21.7.82. Re-embarked the carrier in the English Channel 2.8.82 ('Illustrious' having left Portsmouth earlier in the day), sailing with her to relieve 'Invincible' in the South Atlantic. Departed the FIPZ with the ship on 21.10.82 for the UK (via the USA) and flown off to Culdrose on 7.12.82 prior to the vessel's arrival at Portsmouth on 8.12.82.

## ZA126 HAS.5

On 29.3.82 with 820 Sqdn, hangared in 'Invincible' at Portsmouth dockyard and coded 'N/012'. Sailed with the ship 5.4.82 and low-vis markings were applied during the passage south, retaining modified code '-/(0)12'. Sailed with the carrier from the FIPZ on 28.8.82 for the UK. At some stage during the homeward passage the ROYAL NAVY titles and deck-letter were re-applied in Black (ie 'N/(0)12') but White serials were retained. Red/Blue Sqdn motifs were painted on both sides of the nose below the cockpit. Arrived at Portsmouth with the carrier 17.9.82 and flown off to Culdrose on 18.9.82.

## ZA127 HAS.5

On 29.3.82 with 820 Sqdn, hangared in 'Invincible' at Portsmouth dockyard and coded 'N/011'. Sailed with the ship 5.4.82 and low-vis markings were applied during the passage south, retaining modified code '-/(0)11'. Disembarked to the San Carlos settlement FOB on 10.6.82 along with XZ921 (replacing a cancelled 826 Sqdn detachment) and returned to 'Invincible' on 17.6.82. Sailed with the carrier from the FIPZ on 28.8.82 for the UK. At some stage during the homeward passage the ROYAL NAVY titles and deck-letter were re-applied in Black (ie 'N/(0)11') but White serials were retained. Red/Blue Sqdn motifs were painted on both sides of the nose below the cockpit. Arrived at Portsmouth with the carrier 17.9.82 and flown off to Culdrose on 18.9.82.

## ZA128 HAS.5

On 29.3.82 with 820 Sqdn, hangared in 'Invincible' at Portsmouth dockyard and coded 'N/014'. Sailed with the ship 5.4.82 and low-vis markings were applied during the passage south, retaining modified code '-/(0)14'. Sailed with the carrier from the FIPZ on 28.8.82 for the UK. At some stage during the homeward passage the ROYAL NAVY titles and deck-letter were reapplied in Black (ie 'N/(0)14') but White serials were retained. Red/Blue Sqdn motifs were painted on both sides of the nose below the cockpit. Arrived at Portsmouth with the carrier 17.9.82 and flown off to Culdrose on 18.9.82.

## ZA129 HAS.5

On 29.3.82 with 706 Sqdn at Culdrose, coded 'CU/582'. Transferred to 826 Sqdn 2.4.82 and embarked 'Hermes' at Portsmouth (via Lee-on-Solent) 3.4.82, still coded 'CU/582', sailing south with the carrier 5.4.82. Low-vis markings were applied c10.4.82, retaining modified 706 Sqdn code '-/(5)82'. On 6.6.82 it was detached with XZ578 to 'Atlantic Causeway' in order to provide the vessel with an ASW, ASV and limited utility capability, and to relieve congestion aboard 'Hermes'. Transferred to 'Engadine' from 'Atlantic Causeway' on 9.6.82 (both ships were in San Carlos Water) to deploy ashore the next day for general utility duties. The deployment cancelled, it left San Carlos Water on 10.6.82 aboard 'Fort Grange' to rejoin 'Hermes' on 11.6.82. Departed Port William with the carrier on 3.7.82 en route for the UK. At some stage during the homeward passage, the 826 Sqdn code '-/(1)44' was allocated and applied in Black. Arrived at Portsmouth with the vessel on 21.7.82 (devoid of serials), flying off to Culdrose the following day.

Remained on 826 Sqdn charge, the applied code becoming '-/144' by mid-11.82. Embarked 'Tidespring' at sea on 8.11.82 from Culdrose for a deployment to the South Atlantic as part of a FIPZ-based Flight (designated 826 Sqdn 'A' Flt early in 1983). Returned to the UK aboard 'Fort Austin', flying off to Culdrose on 9.12.83 (still coded '-/144') prior to the ship's arrival in Plymouth Sound that day.

## ZA130 HAS.5

On 29.3.82 with 826 Sqdn at Culdrose coded 'H/132' and detached to Prestwick that day. Returned to Culdrose (via Valley) on 31.3.82. Embarked 'Hermes' at Portsmouth (via Lee-on-Solent) 3.4.82 and sailed south with the ship on 5.4.82. Low-vis markings were applied c10.4.82, retaining modified code '-/(1)32'. On 17.5.82 it was detached to 'Fort Austin' with three others (XZ577, ZA133 and ZA137) for ASW duties in Falkland Sound and San Carlos Water. Remained with the ship until 3.6.82 when it was flown to the FOB at Port San Carlos settlement to provide additional utility capacity ashore. Returned to 'Hermes' on 6.6.82. Departed with the carrier from Port William 3.7.82 en route for the UK. Arrived at Portsmouth with the ship on 21.7.82, flying off to Culdrose on 22.7.82.

## ZA131 HAS.5

On 29.3.82 with 826 Sqdn at Culdrose, coded 'H/133'. Embarked 'Hermes' at Portsmouth (via Lee-on-Solent) 3.4.82 and sailed south with the ship 5.4.82. Low-vis markings were applied c10.4.82, retaining modified code '-/(1)33'. Departed with the carrier from Port William 3.7.82 en route for the UK. Arrived at Portsmouth with the ship 21.7.82, flying off to Culdrose 22.7.82.

## ZA132 HAS.5

On 29.3.82 with 826 Sqdn coded 'H/134' on detachment at Prestwick. Returned to its base at Culdrose (via Valley) on 31.5.82. Embarked 'Hermes' at Portsmouth (via Lee-on-Solent) 3.4.82 and sailed south with the ship on 5.4.82. Low-vis markings were applied c10.4.82, retaining modified code '-/(1)34'.

On 12.5.82, following an engine failure in the hover east of the Falklands (some 5 miles south of 'Hermes'), it ditched in spite of a determined effort to remain airborne. Heavy seas then hit the tail rotor and the helicopter

pivoted to the right, rolled over to port and quickly sank. The crew members (Lt Cdr Chandler, S/Lts Sutton and Moss and LACMN Coombes) were rescued uninjured.

## ZA133 HAS.5

On 29.3.82 with 826 Sqdn at Culdrose coded 'H/135' and detached to Prestwick that day. Returned to Culdrose (via Valley) on 31.3.82. Embarked 'Hermes' at Portsmouth (via Lee-on-Solent) 3.4.82 and sailed south with the ship on 5.4.82. Low-vis markings were applied c10.4.82, retaining modified code '-/(1)35'. On 17.5.82 it was detached to 'Fort Austin' with three others (XZ577, ZA130 and ZA137) for ASW duties in Falkland Sound and San Carlos Water. Remained with the ship until 3.6.82 when it was flown to the FOB at Port San Carlos settlement to provide additional utility capacity ashore. Returned to 'Hermes' on 6.6.82. Detached to the FOB at San Carlos settlement 17.6.82 with XZ578 (to relieve an 820 Sqdn detachment) for utility and ASV tasks on West Falkland, returning to the carrier on 23.6.82. Departed with 'Hermes' from the UK from Port William on 3.7.82. Arrived at Portsmouth with the ship on 21.7.82, flying off to Culdrose on 22.7.82.

## ZA134 HAS.5

On 29.3.82 with 820 Sqdn, hangared in 'Invincible' at Portsmouth dockyard and coded 'N/013'. Sailed with the ship 5.4.82 and low-vis markings were applied during the passage south, retaining modified code '-/(0)13'. Sailed with the carrier from the FIPZ on 28.8.82 for the UK. At some stage during the homeward passage the ROYAL NAVY titles and deck-letter were re-applied in Black (ie 'N/(0)13') but White serials were retained. Red/Blue Sqdn motifs were painted on both sides of the nose above the cockpit. Arrived at Portsmouth with the carrier 17.9.82 and flown off to Culdrose on 18.9.82.

## ZA135 HAS.5

On 29.3.82 with 820 Sqdn, hangared in 'Invincible' at Portsmouth dockyard and coded 'N/015'. Sailed with the ship 5.4.82 and low-vis markings were applied during the passage south, retaining modified code '-/(0)15'. Sailed with the carrier from the FIPZ on 28.8.82 for the UK. At some stage during the homeward passage the ROYAL NAVY titles and deck-letter were re-applied in Black (ie 'N/(0)13') but White serials were retained. Red/Blue Sqdn motifs were painted on each side of the nose below the cockpit. Arrived at Portsmouth with the carrier 17.9.82 and flown off to Culdrose on 18.9.82.

## ZA136 HAS.5

On 29.3.82 with 826 Sqdn coded 'H/140' on detachment at Prestwick. Returned to its base at Culdrose (via Valley) on 31.5.82. Embarked 'Hermes' at Portsmouth (via Lee-on-Solent) 3.4.82 and sailed south with the ship on 5.4.82. Low-vis markings were applied c10.4.82, retaining modified code '-/(1)40'. Departed with the carrier from Port William on 3.7.82 en route for the UK. Arrived at Portsmouth with the carrier on 21.7.82, being flown off to Culdrose on 22.7.82.

Remained on 826 Sqdn charge, the applied

code reverting to '-/140' by mid-11.82. Embarked 'Fort Grange' off Culdrose on 21.11.82 (the ship having sailed from Devonport 19.11.82) for deployment to the South Atlantic as part of a FIPZ-based Flight (designated as 826 Sqdn 'A' Flt early in 1983). Returned to the UK from the FIPZ on 'Fort Grange' and disembarked to Culdrose 24.3.84, still coded '-/140'.

## ZA137 HAS.5

On 29.3.82 with 706 Sqdn at Culdrose, coded 'CU/596'. Transferred to 826 Sqdn 2.4.82 and embarked 'Hermes' at Portsmouth (via Lee-on-Solent) 3.4.82 still coded 'CU/596', sailing south with the carrier on 5.4.82. Low-vis markings were applied c10.4.82, retaining modified 706 Sqdn code '-/(5)96'. At some stage prior to 'Hermes' entering the TEZ on 1.5.82, 826 Sqdn code '-/(1)46 was allocated and applied in Black. On 17.5.82 it was detached to 'Fort Austin' with three others (XZ577, ZA130 and ZA133) for ASW duties in Falkland Sound and San Carlos Water. Remained with the ship until 3.6.82 when it was flown to the FOB at Port San Carlos settlement to provide additional utility capacity ashore. Returned to 'Hermes' on 6.6.82. Departed the carrier from Port William on 3.7.82 en route for the UK. Arrived at Portsmouth with the ship 21.7.82 and flown off to Culdrose on 22.7.82.

Remained on 826 Sqdn charge, the applied code becoming '-/146' by mid-11.82. It embarked 'Fort Grange' off Culdrose on 21.11.82 (the ship having sailed from Devonport 19.11.82) for deployment to the South Atlantic as part of a FIPZ-based Flight (designated as 826 Sqdn 'A' Flt early in 1983). Returned to the UK from the FIPZ on 'Fort Grange' and disembarked to Culdrose 24.3.84, still coded '-/146'.

## ZA167 HAS.5 *Deployed post-14.6.82*

On 15.6.82 with NASU Culdrose prior to joining 814 Sqdn 18.6.82 coded '-/273' in the low-vis scheme. Embarked 'Illustrious' in the English Channel from Culdrose on 2.8.82 (the carrier having left Portsmouth earlier in the day), sailing with her to relieve 'Invincible' in the South Atlantic. Detached to 'Fort Austin' in the FIPZ c21.10.82 and remained with her until she returned to the UK, flying off to Culdrose 16.12.82 prior to the ship anchoring in Plymouth Sound on 17.12.82.

## ZA168 HAS.5 *Deployed post-14.6.82*

First flew with WHL at Yeovil on 2.6.82 and delivered to NASU Culdrose (via Yeovilton) on 2.7.82. Joined 814 Sqdn 15.7.82 in the low-vis scheme and coded '-/267'. Embarked 'Illustrious' in the English Channel on 17.7.82 for a short series of trials and training, returning to Culdrose c21.7.82. Re-embarked 'Illustrious' 2.8.82 (the ship having left Portsmouth earlier in the day), sailing with her to relieve 'Invincible' in the South Atlantic. Departed the FIPZ with the carrier on 21.10.82 for the UK (via the USA), flying off to Culdrose 7.12.82 prior to the vessel's arrival at Portsmouth on 8.12.82.

## ZA290 HC.4

On 29.3.82 with 846 Sqdn at Yeovilton coded

'-/VC'. Embarked 'Hermes' at Portsmouth (via Lee-on-Solent) 3.4.82 and sailed with the carrier on 5.4.82 for Ascension Island, arriving there on 16.4.82. Departed south (as a PNG-modified aircraft) with the ship 18.4.82, entering the TEZ on 1.5.82.

Flown from 'Hermes' to 'Invincible' 17.5.82 *[see also ZA292]* and detached with the ship that evening for an unknown position west of the Falklands. In the early hours of 18.5.82, piloted by Lt Hutchings, it took off with (reportedly) a contingent of SAS troops and headed towards the South American mainland for a covert operation. No more information confirming its activities has been confirmed until the late evening of 18.5.82 when it was put down on a beach at Agua Fresca, some 11 miles south of Punta Arenas in Chile. The three-man crew made a deliberate attempt to destroy the helicopter before they disappeared into the hinterland *(Lts Hutchings, Bennett and LACMN Imrie gave themselves up to Chilean authorities a few days later)*. Its remains were discovered and inspected on 19.5.82 by journalists (amongst others). Although the aircraft was almost burnt out, the serial was just visible on a surviving section of the rear fuselage, thus identifying it to the world as a British helicopter. The debris was buried on site by the Chileans.

## ZA291 HC.4

On 29.3.82 with 846 Sqdn at Yeovilton coded '-/VB'. Embarked 'Hermes' at Portsmouth (via Lee-on-Solent) 3.4.82 and sailed with the carrier on 5.4.82 for Ascension Island, arriving there on 16.4.82. Did not depart with 'Hermes' on 18.4.82 but instead was detached to Wideawake to be based ashore on HDS and VERTREP duties. Flown to 'Elk' off Ascension on 28.4.82, sailing with her for the TEZ 6.5.82. Transferred from 'Elk' to 'Intrepid' 14.5.82 for maintenance, moving to 'Canberra' on 19.5.82. Arrived in San Carlos Water with the liner on 21.5.82 but was transferred to 'Norland' (also in San Carlos Water) later in the day. Departed with her that evening for a position east north-east of the Islands and returned with the ship to San Carlos Water on 23.5.82. Disembarked later that day to the Old House Creek FOB (on the east bank of San Carlos Water about 2.5 miles north of San Carlos settlement). Moved FOB on 27.5.82 to Fern Valley Creek (about 1.5 miles to the south-east). Flown to a FOB at Port Stanley Racecourse on 18.6.82 and remained based there on utility tasks until 3.7.82 when flown to 'Hermes' in Port William, sailing with her that day for the UK. Arrived at Portsmouth with the carrier 21.7.82, being flown off to Yeovilton on 22.7.82.

## ZA292 HC.4

On 29.3.82 with 846 Sqdn at Yeovilton coded '-/VH'. Embarked 'Hermes' at Portsmouth (via Lee-on-Solent) 3.4.82 and sailed with the ship 5.4.82 for Ascension Island, arriving there on 16.4.82. Departed south with the carrier 18.4.82, entering the TEZ on 1.5.82. Flown to 'Invincible' 17.5.82 (as a reserve for ZA290) and remained with her until late on 18.5.82 when it returned to 'Hermes'. Being a PNG-modified aircraft it was transferred to 'Intrepid' on 19.5.82 for Special Forces operations preparatory to, and after, the landings

on 21.5.82 for Operation "Sutton".

Whilst being flown by Lt North on CASEVAC duties on 28.5.82 in the Darwin area near Goose Green, it was fired at by ground-based Argentine 7.62mm small arms fire. A round hit the fuselage near the gearbox mainframe (immediately behind the winch) just missing the hydraulics run. No one was injured and the damage was superficial.

Remained based on 'Intrepid' in San Carlos Water until 29.5.82 when it was detached to the FOB about 1.5 miles north of the Ajax Bay Refrigeration Plant on the west bank of San Carlos Water. On 8.6.82 it moved to a new FOB near Fern Valley Creek (less than 1 mile north of San Carlos Water on the east bank of San Carlos Water). Re-embarked 'Intrepid' in San Carlos Water on 16.6.82 for various post-surrender tasks. Moved to Port William with the ship on 23.6.82 and sailed with her from there 26.6.82 for the UK. Arrived with the vessel off Plymouth 13.7.82, flying off to Yeovilton that day prior to 'Intrepid' docking at Portsmouth on 14.7.82.

## ZA293 HC.4

On 29.3.82 with 846 Sqdn at Yeovilton coded '-/VK'. Embarked 'Hermes' at Portsmouth (via Lee-on-Solent) 3.4.82 and sailed with the ship on 5.4.82 for Ascension Island, arriving there on 16.4.82. Departed south with the carrier 18.4.82, entering the TEZ on 1.5.82. Being a PNG-modified aircraft, transferred to 'Intrepid' on 19.5.82 for Special Forces operations preparatory to, and after, the landings on 21.5.82 for Operation "Sutton". Remained based on the ship in San Carlos Water until 29.5.82 when it was detached to the FOB some 1.5 miles north of the Ajax Bay Refrigeration Plant on the west bank of San Carlos Water. On 8.6.82 it moved to a FOB near Fern Valley Creek on the east bank of San Carlos Water (less than 1 mile north of San Carlos settlement). Re-embarked 'Intrepid' in San Carlos Water on 16.6.82 for various post-surrender tasks prior to moving to Port William with the ship 23.6.82. Sailed with the vessel from there on 26.6.82 for the UK. Arrived with 'Intrepid' off Plymouth 13.7.82, flying off to Yeovilton that day prior to the ship docking at Portsmouth on 14.7.82.

## ZA294 HC.4

On 29.3.82 with 846 Sqdn at Yeovilton coded '-/VT'. Embarked 'Hermes' at Portsmouth (via Lee-on-Solent) 3.4.82 and sailed with the ship on 5.4.82 for Ascension Island, arriving there on 16.4.82. Departed south with the carrier 18.4.82, entering the TEZ on 1.5.82.

During the evening of 19.5.82 it was the last of three PNG-modified aircraft to leave 'Hermes' on transfer to the nearby 'Intrepid'. The helicopter was carrying SAS troops and, during a long, high, final approach to the ship, there was a loud thump followed by a loss of power. It crashed into the sea, rolled over and floated inverted for a short period before sinking. Of 30 people on board only nine were rescued, including the pilots (Lt Horton and S/Lt Humphreys). The aircrewman (Cpl Love) was one of the 21 men lost. The crash occurred about 200 miles north-east of Port Stanley. The reason for the power loss was not ascertained but one of the

most probable causes appeared to be collision with, or engine ingestion of, a large seabird, possibly an albatross (several pieces of a similar-sized bird were found after the accident).

## ZA295 HC.4

On 29.3.82 with 846 Sqdn at Yeovilton coded '-/VM'. Embarked 'Hermes' at Portsmouth (via Lee-on-Solent) 3.4.82 and sailed with the ship on 5.4.82 for Ascension Island, arriving there on 16.4.82. Did not depart with 'Hermes' on 18.4.82 but instead detached to Wideawake to be based ashore on HDS and VERTREP duties. Embarked 'Elk' off Ascension on 28.4.82, departing south with her 6.5.82 for the TEZ. Transferred across to 'Norland' on 19.5.82 prior to moving to 'Intrepid' 20.5.82 (replacing ZA294). As a PNG-modified aircraft, it remained with the ship for Special Forces tasks preparatory to, and after, the landings on 21.5.82 for Operation "Sutton". Based on 'Intrepid' in San Carlos Water until 29.5.82 when it was detached to the FOB some 1.5 miles north of the Ajax Bay Refrigeration Plant on the west bank of San Carlos Water. It moved on 8.6.82 to a FOB near Fern Valley Creek on the east bank of San Carlos Water (less than 1 mile north of San Carlos settlement) and flew to a new FOB located at Port Stanley Racecourse on 18.6.82, remaining there on utility duties until 3.7.82 when it embarked 'Hermes' lying in Port William and sailed with the ship that day en route for the UK. Arrived with her at Portsmouth 21.7.82, flying off to Yeovilton 22.7.82.

## ZA296 HC.4

On 29.3.82 with 846 Sqdn at Yeovilton coded '-/VF'. Departed Yeovilton on 6.4.82 for Portland prior to embarking 'Fearless' that day in the English Channel (off Portland) and sailing with her for Ascension Island. Arrived with the vessel off the Island on 17.4.82 and commenced a period of VERTREP and HDS duties ashore and afloat before departing again with the ship on 8.5.82 for the TEZ. Remained 'Fearless'-based after she anchored in San Carlos Water 21.5.82. Disembarked on 27.5.82 to the FOB at Fern Valley Creek (less than 1 mile north of San Carlos settlement on the east bank of San Carlos Water). Re-embarked 'Fearless' in San Carlos Water on 16.6.82 and moved with her to Port William overnight 16/17.6.82. Sailed with the ship from there on 24.6.82 for the UK. Arrived with 'Fearless' at Plymouth on 13.7.82, flying off that day to Yeovilton prior to the vessel docking at Portsmouth on 14.7.82.

## ZA297 HC.4

On 29.3.82 with 846 Sqdn at Yeovilton coded '-/VG'. Departed Yeovilton on 6.4.82 for Portland prior to embarking 'Fearless' that day in the English Channel (off Portland) and sailing with her for Ascension Island. Arrived with the vessel off the Island on 17.4.82 and commenced a period of VERTREP and HDS duties ashore and afloat. Departed Ascension with 'Intrepid' on 8.5.82 for the TEZ. As a PNG-modified aircraft it stayed with the ship for Special Forces operations preparatory to, and after, the landings on 21.5.82 for Operation "Sutton". On 29.5.82 it detached from 'Intrepid' in San Carlos Water to the FOB some 1.5 miles to the north of the Ajax Bay Refrigeration Plant situated on the west bank of San Carlos Water. Moved on 8.6.82 to a new FOB near Fern Valley Creek (less than 1 mile north of San Carlos settlement on the east bank of San Carlos Water). Re-embarked 'Intrepid' in San Carlos Water on 16.6.82 for various post-surrender tasks. Moved with the ship to Port William on 23.6.82 and sailed with her from there 26.6.82 for the UK. Arrived with the vessel off Plymouth on 13.7.82, flying off to Yeovilton that day prior to 'Intrepid' docking at Portsmouth 14.7.82.

## ZA298 HC.4

On 29.3.82 with 846 Sqdn at Yeovilton coded '-/VA'. Embarked 'Hermes' at Portsmouth (via Lee-on-Solent) 3.4.82 and sailed with the carrier on 5.4.82 for Ascension Island, arriving there on 16.4.82. Did not depart on 'Hermes' on 18.4.82 but was instead detached to Wideawake to be based ashore on HDS and VERTREP tasks. Departed the Island 8.5.82 for the TEZ embarked on 'Fearless'. Remained based aboard (after she anchored in San Carlos Water 21.5.82) until 27.5.82 when it detached to the FOB at Fern Valley Creek on the east bank of San Carlos Water (less than 1 mile to the north of San Carlos settlement).

On 25.5.82, whilst being flown by Lt Cdr Thornewill, it was used to rescue survivors from the stricken 'Coventry' about 10 miles north of Pebble Island. The aircrewman, CPO Tupper, was credited with actively assisting in the saving of between 40 and 50 lives.

Whilst being flown by Lt Cdr Thornewill on 13.6.82 1.5 miles south of Estancia House (just west of Mount Kent), it was attacked by an A-4B Skyhawk of Grupo 5. A cannon shell from the Skyhawk (being flown by Alferez Dellepiane) went through a main rotor blade before exploding. The helicopter (its crew uninjured) landed safely in Impassable Valley near Mount Challenger and was airworthy again in under two hours after a new blade brought in by ZA291 had been fitted.

On 15.6.82 (crewed by Lt Cdr Thornewill, Lt Rainey, CPOACMN Tupper and POACMN Sheldon) it was used to ferry General de Brigada Menendez and four of his senior officers from Port Stanley Racecourse to 'Fearless' in San Carlos Water.

Re-embarked 'Fearless' in San Carlos Water on 16.6.82 and moved with the ship to Port William overnight 16/17.6.82. Sailed with the vessel from there on 24.6.82 for the UK. Arrived with her off Plymouth 13.7.82 and flew off to Yeovilton that day prior to the ship docking at Portsouth on 14.7.82.

*Large White panels were painted on the nose and fuselage sides on 14.6.82 to signify that it was a "non-combatant" helicopter. These markings were removed on 16.6.82.*

## ZA299 HC.4

On 29.3.82 with 846 Sqdn at Yeovilton coded '-/VE'. Embarked 'Hermes' at Portsmouth (via Lee-on-Solent) 3.4.82 and sailed with the ship on 5.4.82 for Ascension Island, arriving there on 16.4.82. Did not depart with 'Hermes' on 18.4.82 but was instead detached to Wideawake to be based ashore on HDS and VERTREP tasks. Flown to 'Canberra' off

Ascension on 6.5.82, sailing south with the liner that day for the TEZ. Arrived in San Carlos Water with the ship 21.5.82 and departed with her from there in the early hours of 22.5.82 for a position some 170 miles north-east of Port Stanley. There it was transferred to 'Europic Ferry' on 25.5.82. The ship anchored in San Carlos Water on 26.5.82 and the aircraft disembarked that day to the FOB at Old House Creek (about 2.5 miles north of San Carlos settlement on the east bank of San Carlos Water) prior to moving to a new FOB at Fern Valley Creek on 27.5.82 (about 1.5 miles to the south-east). Embarked 'Fearless' in San Carlos Water 16.6.82 and moved to Port William with the ship overnight 16/17.6.82 before sailing with her from there on 24.6.82 for the UK. Arrived off Plymouth with the vessel on 13.7.82, flying off to Yeovilton that day prior to 'Fearless' docking at Portsmouth 14.7.82.

## ZA310 HC.4

On 29.3.82 with 846 Sqdn at Yeovilton coded '-/VS'. Departed Yeovilton on 6.4.82 for Portland prior to embarking 'Fearless' that day in the English Channel (off Portland) and sailing with her for Ascension Island. Arrived with the vessel off the Island on 17.4.82 and commenced a period of VERTREP and HDS duties ashore and afloat before departing again with the ship on 8.5.82 for the TEZ. Remained based on 'Fearless' when she anchored in San Carlos Water 21.5.82.

On 23.5.82 it was tasked to pick up casualties at a position to the north of Fanning Head. As it touched down, the tail rotor hit the ground rendering the aircraft unserviceable. Remained there until 7.6.82 when 18 Sqdn Chinook HC.1 ZA718 lifted it back to the 846 Sqdn FOB at Fern Valley Creek (less than 1 mile north of San Carlos settlement) for repair. Returned to flying condition by fitting the tail unit from 825 Sqdn Sea King HAS.2A XV696 which had also been involved in a landing accident.

It first flew following repair on 15.6.82 and embarked 'Intrepid' in San Carlos Water the same day for various post-surrender tasks. Moved to Port William with the ship 23.6.82 and sailed with her from there on 26.6.82 for the UK. Arrived off Plymouth with the vessel on 13.7.82, flying off the same day to Yeovilton prior to 'Intrepid' docking at Portsmouth on 14.7.82.

## ZA311 HC.4

On 29.3.82 with 846 Sqdn at Yeovilton coded '-/VP'. Embarked 'Hermes' at Portsmouth (via Lee-on-Solent) 3.4.82 and sailed with the ship on 5.4.82 for Ascension Island, arriving there on 16.4.82. Departed south with the carrier on 18.4.82 for the MEZ.

Whilst returning to 'Hermes' from a night VERTREP mission on 23.4.82, it crashed into the sea in bad weather and sank soon after impact (approximate position 26°S 24°W). The pilot, Flt Lt Grundy, was rescued by 820 Sqdn Sea King HAS.5 XZ574 but, unfortunately, aircrewman POACMN Casey was lost.

## ZA312 HC.4

On 29.3.82 uncoded at NASU Culdrose with

White serials and titles. Transferred to 846 Sqdn on 5.4.82 and flown to Yeovilton that day. By 7.4.82 it had been repainted in the low-vis scheme and coded '-/VW'. Partially dismantled, it departed on 7.4.82 aboard Heavylift Belfast G-BFYU bound for Ascension Island. Arrived at Wideawake on 8.4.82 where it was reassembled by Naval Party 1222 and used at Ascension for HDS and VERTREP duties from 11-28.4.82. Flown to 'Elk' 28.4.82 and sailed with her on 6.5.82 for the TEZ. Transferred to 'Fearless' on 19.5.82 and remained based on her when she anchored on 21.5.82 in San Carlos Water. Flown ashore on 23.5.82 (for repairs to an auxiliary power unit) to a FOB at Old House Creek (about 2.5 miles north of San Carlos settlement on the east bank of San Carlos Water). Remained ashore and moved on 27.5.82 to a new FOB near Fern Valley Creek (about 1.5 miles southeast). On 18.6.82 it detached to a new FOB at Port Stanley Racecourse and remained there on utility duties until it embarked 'Canberra' in Port William on 23.6.82. Sailed with her from there on 25.6.82 for the UK. Flew off to Yeovilton (via Culdrose) on 10.7.82 prior to the liner docking at Southampton on 11.7.82.

## ZA313 HC.4

On 29.3.82 uncoded with NASU Culdrose. Noted test-flying with NASU on 8.4.82 still uncoded but using an 846 Sqdn code (VZ) as a call-sign. Issued to 707 Sqdn at Culdrose on 21.4.82 prior to being transferred to 846 Sqdn 26.4.82. Departed Culdrose that day (the code (VZ) still allocated but not worn) to embark 'Intrepid' in the English Channel en route to Ascension Island. Arrived there with the ship 5.5.82 prior to continuing south with her for the TEZ on 8.5.82. Transferred to 'Norland' in exchange for ZA295 on 20.5.82 (noted on board still uncoded and the ROYAL NAVY titles deleted with Matt Olive Drab) and arrived with her in San Carlos Water on 21.5.82. Sailed late that evening with 'Norland' for a position east north-east of the Islands and returned with the ship to San Carlos Water 23.5.82. Disembarked later that day to the FOB at Old House Creek (about 2.5 miles north of San Carlos settlement on the east bank of San Carlos Water) prior to moving to a new FOB at Fern Valley Creek (about 1.5 miles to the south-east) on 27.5.82. Detached to 'Sir Galahad' on 7.6.82 in order to deploy Rapiers on 8.6.82 in the Fitzroy/Bluff Cove area.

On 8.6.82 (crewed by Lt Miller and POACMN Ashdown) it rescued survivors from 'Sir Galahad' in Port Pleasant and later from the 'Fearless' landing-craft 'Foxtrot 4'. The small vessel had been near the mouth of Choiseul Sound when it was bombed by a Grupo 5 A-4B Skyhawk.

Embarked 'Fearless' in San Carlos Water 16.6.82 and moved to Port William with the ship overnight 16/17.6.82. Noted lifting a 3 CBAS Gazelle AH.1 onto 'Elk' off Port Stanley c23/24.6.82. Departed Port William with 'Fearless' on 24.6.82 for the UK. During the passage home (in the vicinity of Ascension Island c3.7.82) the code '-/VZ' and ROYAL NAVY titles were applied in Black. Arrived with the ship off Plymouth 13.7.82, flying off to Yeovilton that day prior to her docking at Portsmouth 14.7.82.

# WESSEX

# 737 NAVAL AIR SQUADRON

At the start of the conflict, 737 Sqdn was based at Portland under the command of Lt Cdr M.S.Tennant and equipped with the ageing Wessex HAS.3 anti-submarine helicopter, its role being to train aircrew in the skills of ASW before progressing to the Lynx or Sea King. The Wessex HAS.3 was in the process of being phased out of service in favour of the Sea King and several had already been placed in storage at Wroughton. In fact, two 814 Sqdn Sea King HAS.2A's (XV671 '-/267' and XV705 '-/265') were already operating with the unit at Portland during March 1982. The Squadron was expected to disband on 30 July, but involvement in Operation "Corporate" was to delay that event by six months. Although it was a second-line unit operating in the training role, 737 Sqdn also maintained those Ships' Flights which equipped the last of the County Class destroyers, 'Antrim' and 'Glamorgan' ('Fife' Flight being out of commission during the vessel's refit). With one exception, all of the Squadron's helicopters were painted in RAF Blue-Grey overall with Yellow upper surfaces, White titles, serials, codes and deck letters plus 'D' Class (Red/White/Blue) roundels. The exception was XP150 which was Olive Drab overall with Black serials and no titles from its service with the security forces in Northern Ireland. 737 Sqdn's total complement of Wessex HAS.3's on 29 March was as follows:

With the departure of aircraft and crews from 771 Sqdn at Culdrose to form 847 Sqdn, 737 Sqdn took over aircrewman training duties at the beginning of May.

The two Ships' Flights had already embarked their respective vessels for participation in Exercise "Springtrain" when the Argentine invasion took place. Both ships were ordered to the South Atlantic in early April and it is worth noting that between then and the end of June the Flights flew a total of 334 hours on 213 sorties, carrying out 522 deck landings. After the conflict the Squadron resumed its training role on 19 October, having gained three former 825 Sqdn Sea Kings and 30 maintainers from 814 Sqdn. A final flypast of 737 Sqdn's remaining Wessex HAS.3's took place at Portland on 6 December, prior to the Squadron's long overdue disbandment on 4 February 1983. With effect from 15 February, its role was taken over by the reformed 810 Sqdn flying Sea Kings from Culdrose.

### HQ Squadron

| | | |
|---|---|---|
| XS862 'PO/650' | XP140 'PO/654' | XP137 'PO/665' |
| XM836 'PO/651' | XP110 'PO/655' | XM916 'PO/666' |
| XM870 'PO/652' | XS149 'PO/661' | XP150 '-/-' |
| XM328 'PO/653' | XS153 'PO/662' | |

# 'ANTRIM' (100) FLIGHT

'Antrim' was ordered to detach from Exercise "Springtrain" for the South Atlantic on 2 April, immediately embarking extra stores and ammunition from 'Ariadne' before heading south for Ascension Island. Rear Admiral John "Sandy" Woodward, Flag Officer First Flotilla (FOF1) for "Springtrain", was on board the vessel. Following the order to detach, he became Commander Task Group 317.8 with 'Antrim' as flagship, leading the first vessels south. Under the command of Lt Cdr I.Stanley, 'Antrim' Flight was embarked with Wessex HAS.3 XP142, affectionately known as "Humphrey". During the passage south the Wessex was repainted with low-visibility markings, becoming RAF Blue-Grey overall (covering the deck letters) with very dull Dark Red/Dark Blue (almost Black) roundels and Black serials and titles; the code (406) was deleted but remained allocated. The journey southwards to Ascension Island was one of continual training and preparation for war. On 7 April 'Antrim' was ordered to detach to South Georgia with 'Plymouth' and 'Tidespring' for Operation "Paraquat" (the retaking of the Island). Rear Admiral Woodward had transferred to 'Glamorgan' on 4 April before his final move to 'Hermes' on 15 April when Capt B.G.Young aboard 'Antrim' became Commander of the South Georgia Task Group (TG317.9). The vessels arrived at Ascension Island on 10 April, 'M' Coy 42 Cdo embarking 'Tidespring' for the operation. The Group departed on 12 April, 'Antrim' Flight joining the Wessex HU.5's of 845 Sqdn 'C' Flight aboard 'Tidespring' in flying training and HDS sorties. On 14 April the ships carried out a rendezvous with 'Endurance' and continued south together.

The Task Group arrived off South Georgia on the morning of 21 April. Initial plans called for the insertion of a Special Forces reconnaissance party on the Fortuna Glacier to observe Argentine positions at Leith and Stromness, with a second party to observe the enemy position at Grytviken. At first light on 21 April (0930Z), Lt Cdr Stanley flew XP142 on a preliminary reconnaissance of the glacier and conditions appeared suitable for the operation although there was some driving rain and wind. It was decided that 'Antrim' Flight's Observer-manned radar-equipped Wessex HAS.3 would lead the way onto the glacier, followed by the two Wessex HU.5's of 845 Sqdn 'C' Flight aboard 'Tidespring'. "Humphrey" returned to 'Antrim' to collect four troops and the Wessex HU.5's landed alternately on the vessel to embark further members of the Special Forces. All three then set off towards the Island, but by the time they reached Possession Bay the operation had to be abandoned due to thick low cloud plus driving rain and snowstorms. The weather later improved a little and at 1315Z the formation set off once again, penetrating Possession Bay to cross Antarctic Bay and climb onto the Glacier amidst swirling low cloud. Visibility problems were frequently worsened by driving snow squalls, creating "white-out" conditions, and by sudden gusts of wind of up to 60 knots. The operation was completed successfully, however, with the troops and their equipment being unloaded in the required landing zone and the aircraft all returning safely to the ships.

Conditions that night proved remarkable for their ferocity; the barometer fell from 995mbs to 960mbs in eight hours with Storm Force 10 winds gusting up to 70 knots. Not surprisingly, the troops on the Glacier radioed the next morning to say that they might not survive the next 12 hours and it was decided that the three helicopters would have to go back and retrieve them. Their passage to the Glacier was hampered by the gusting winds and snow storms, Ian Stanley in the HAS.3 making three attempts to land while the two HU.5's circled over Antarctic Bay

before landing on a spit of land to conserve fuel. In the end, all three helicopters had to return to their ships to refuel. The next attempt (by then on 22 April) was more successful, the troops having ignited smoke flares to guide the helicopters in to a successful landing on the Glacier. However, the weather closed in once more creating "white-out" conditions. With its quota of troops embarked, one of the HU.5's (XT464) was the first to take-off during a slight improvement in the weather but, shortly after becoming airborne, it was enveloped in a "white-out" and crashed. Fortunately only one person was slightly injured. The other two helicopters landed nearby and, between them, took on board all the personnel from XT464. After successful take-offs, both aircraft set off back to 'Antrim'. Unfortunately, the second HU.5 (XT473) encountered further "white-out" conditions, hit a small ridge and rolled onto its starboard side. Once again, there was only one minor injury — to the person hurt in the first crash! Already overloaded, the HAS.3 returned to 'Antrim' to unload before making two attempts to rescue the survivors of the second accident. It was not until 1635Z that the third attempt met with success. Later that same night a further insertion of Special Forces troops was made by Gemini boats as 'Antrim' crept into Stromness Bay. The following morning (23 April) two of the five boats involved were reported missing, having suffered engine failures, so XP142 was launched to try and find them. After an hour-long search, one of the drifting boats was located by radio beacon and its occupants recovered by winch from a position close to the Cumberland Bays and almost in sight of Argentine observation posts. The Special Forces troops from the other disabled Gemini were found at Cape Saunders (the last landfall before Antarctica) and rescued on 27 April.

During the course of 23 April the ships were overflown by a Grupo 1 Hercules. That afternoon intelligence was received that the Argentine submarine 'Santa Fe' was in the area. The Task Group was ordered north while the situation was reassessed, the ships going to ASW stations. Later reports indicated that the submarine might attempt to enter Grytviken harbour during the night of 24/25 April (which it did) so 'Antrim' closed to 50 miles in order to launch her Wessex for an ASW/surface search mission at first light on 25 April. In addition to the HAS.3 which was armed with Mk.11 depth charges, two Lynx HAS.2's from 'Brilliant' Flight were to join the surface search (the ship having joined the Task Group on 24 April), while the 'Plymouth' Flight Wasp was placed on standby armed with AS.12 missiles. "Humphrey" took-off at 0810Z and flew towards the mouth of the Cumberland Bays in radio-silence. At 0855Z the crew detected a faint echo which they went to investigate. At a range of 0.75 miles the 'Santa Fe' was identified on the surface, close to Barff Point, having departed from Grytviken. At 0900Z the Wessex attacked the submarine with depth charges which exploded close to the port side. 'Brilliant' Flight joined in the attack at 0905Z with a Mk.46 torpedo and GPMG fire, while the 'Endurance' Flight Wasps pressed home the assault, firing several AS.12's which damaged the fin. The submarine remained on the surface due to damage from the depth charges and a Mk.46 torpedo circling underneath it, but reversed course back to Grytviken. 'Plymouth' Flight joined in at 1015Z with a further AS.12

attack and by 1100Z the damaged 'Santa Fe' was being abandoned alongside the BAS pier at King Edward Point.

The Task Group Commander, Capt Young, decided that the final assault on South Georgia should go ahead, so at 1445Z Ian Stanley and Lt Chris Parry in XP142 led the two 'Brilliant' Flight Lynx HAS.2's ashore to land troops opposite Grytviken, following an impressive display of the effect of naval bombardment by 'Antrim' and 'Plymouth'. Later in the day 'Antrim' Flight was involved in two more sorties in support of the operation, the first as an airborne communications link and the second to put ashore the vessel's Medical Officer to assist the only Argentine casualty. With Battle Ensigns flying, 'Antrim' entered the Cumberland Bays and at 1700Z the 'Endurance' Flight crew of Wasp HAS.1 XS527 spotted a white flag.

The ship sailed from South Georgia on 2 May to escort 'Tidespring' and her cargo of 200 PoW's back to Ascension en route to repatriation. On 6 May the vessel was ordered to hand over the escort role to 'Antelope' before proceeding south once again as an escort for the LSL's, joining the main Amphibious Group heading towards the Falklands on 16 May. Three days later a Wessex HU.5 (XT449 from 845 Sqdn 'E' Flight aboard 'Tidepool') was embarked for special operations, both XP142 and the 'E' Flight machine landing Special Forces on Fanning Head on 20 May before 'Antrim' escorted the Amphibious Group into Falkland Sound for the landings on 21 May. The ship then detached to a position off Fanning Head to carry out shore bombardments. At around 1325Z and again at 1331Z, 'Antrim' was attacked by Grupo 6 Daggers. The result of this onslaught was that the ship was hit by a 1000lb bomb which fortunately failed to explode. It badly damaged the Seaslug launcher, finally coming to rest in the after "heads" surrounded by shattered porcelain! Two of the ship's crew were injured, while XP142 suffered splinter damage (including punctured fuel-tanks). A bomb disposal team flew aboard in the 'Yarmouth' Flight Wasp and at 2350Z the bomb was lowered gently into the sea as 'Antrim' departed Falkland Sound, the ship rejoining the CVBG to the east the following day. The 845 Sqdn 'E' Flight Wessex had left 'Antrim' by that time and embarked 'Canberra' as a CASEVAC aircraft.

'Antrim' went alongside 'Stena Seaspread' for repairs on 25 May then detached later the same day for a rendezvous with 'Queen Elizabeth 2' near South Georgia. XP142 was serviceable again by 26 May. The rendezvous took place on 27 May and 'Antrim' took aboard the Commander Land Forces Falkland Islands, Major General Jeremy Moore, together with the Staff of the 5th Infantry Brigade. 'Antrim' returned west and Major General Moore embarked 'Fearless' on 29 May. Two days later she sailed once again for South Georgia to take up duties as Air Defence Ship, anchoring in Husvik Bay on 2 June where she joined 'Endurance', 'Resource' and several STUFT vessels. While at South Georgia, the ship carried out off-shore patrols and the Flight was engaged in ASW sorties and load-lifting. At last, on 14 June, news came of the Argentine surrender and on 26 June 'Antrim' left South Georgia for the last time on passage to the Falkland Islands, joining the CVBG two days later. The ship and her helicopter were ordered back to the United Kingdom on 28 June and sailed from Port Howard on West Falkland the following day. Having made a brief call at Ascension Island on 7 July, 'Antrim' docked at Portsmouth on 17 July with XP142 aboard, adorned with various "zaps" which indicated the Flight's actions [see the aircraft history]. The Wessex was flown off to Portland the next day and on 26 July was transferred to the Fleet Air Arm Museum for its Falkland Islands Exhibition. "Humphrey" arrived at Yeovilton by road later the same day and had been placed on display in the Museum by the time of the Yeovilton Air Day (31 July 1982).

*737 Sqdn aircrew with 'Antrim' Flight during Operation "Corporate" and their awards: Lt Cdr I.Stanley RN (Flt Cdr) DSO; Lt C.J.Parry RN (Observer) MID; S/Lt S.G.Cooper RN (2nd Pilot) MID; POACMN D.B.Fitzgerald MID.*

'Antrim' made a second deployment to the Falkland Islands during 1982. She left Portsmouth on 8 November with replacement Wessex HAS.3 XM328 embarked. It was during that deployment that 737 Sqdn disbanded, 772 Sqdn becoming the "parent" to 'Antrim' Flight. The ship returned to Portsmouth on 25 March 1983 and the Wessex disembarked to Portland.

# 'GLAMORGAN' (103) FLIGHT

As with 'Antrim' Flight, 'Glamorgan' Flight and its Wessex HAS.3 XM837 nicknamed "Willie" were embarked on the parent vessel and operating out of Gibraltar for Exercise "Springtrain" when the order to detach directly to the South Atlantic was received on 2 April. By 11 April low visibility markings had been applied to the Wessex, its White markings and Yellow upper surfaces giving way to overall RAF Blue-Grey with the serials and ROYAL NAVY titles overpainted in Black and the roundels modified to Red/Blue, while the code (400) is believed to have been deleted although it remained allocated. Under the command of Lt Cdr G.C.Hunt, the

Flight carried out some consolidation flying between 5-14 April. Having arrived at Ascension Island on 11 April, the ship detached northwards three days later to rendezvous with the CVBG which then reached the Island on 16 April. In the meantime, XM837 had been flown ashore to Wideawake to be fitted with a new set of main rotor blades on 13 April and a GPMG two days later.

The Group sailed south on 18 April and the Flight began ASW sorties in earnest five days later before arriving in the TEZ on 1 May. 'Glamorgan' then commenced naval bombardment duties against Argentine positions around Port Stanley, for which an armed Wessex HU.5

269

**Above** *"Humphrey" (XP142 (406)), 737 Squadron 'Antrim' Flight's seemingly pristine, but actually battle-scarred, Wessex HAS.3, is seen here on the ship's flight-deck after its arrival at Portsmouth on 17.7.82. (R. A. Walker).* **Above Right** *XP142's eventful war was symbolised on the cabin door: the attack on 'Santa Fe' on 25.4.82 (submarine); two CASEVAC missions (crosses); Special Forces insertions on Fortuna Glacier, South Georgia on 21.4.82 and Fanning Head, East Falkland on 20/21.5.82 (daggers); the rescue of SAS troopers and aircrew from the two Wessex HU.5's which crashed on the Fortuna Glacier on 22.4.82 (R13 later altered at the FAAM to the correct total, R20); the rescue of Special Forces personnel from a Gemini boat off South Georgia on 23.4.82 (R3); the rescue of two crewmembers swept from the hull of a British submarine off South Georgia (R2).*

(R. A. Walker)

**Left** *"Willie" (XM837 (400)), 737 Squadron 'Glamorgan' Flight's Wessex HAS.3, makes its last-ever flight from the ship on 11.6.82. The following morning XM837 was burned out in a fire which erupted in the destroyer's hangar after the vessel had been hit by an Argentine land-launched Exocet missile.* **Right** *Just visible in the blackened and twisted shell of the hangar is XT429 (445), 829 Squadron 'Plymouth' Flight's Wasp HAS.1, which was temporarily accommodated on 'Glamorgan' from 27–29.6.82 while both warships were in passage to Ascension Island and the United Kingdom.*

(A. B. Walsh)

**Left** *SAS troopers on the Fortuna Glacier, South Georgia on 22.4.82 warily approach an 845 Squadron 'C' Flight Wessex HU.5 (XT464 '–/(Y)F') which had crashed in "white-out" conditions and rolled onto its port side a few minutes previously. In the background is the Flight's other HU.5 (XT473 '–/(Y)A') which came to grief in essentially similar circumstances shortly after this photograph was taken.*

(Ministry of Defence)

(XS483 from 845 Sqdn 'A' Flight aboard 'Resource') had embarked on 30 April to provide protection for the NGS spotter carried on board 'Alacrity' Flight's Lynx HAS.2 (XZ736). 1 May saw the Wessex HU.5 fired at by shore-based guns and almost certainly one (possibly even two) land-based Tigercat missiles, but no damage was suffered. In fact, the Wessex had to take fairly violent evasive action to avoid the missile which fortunately fell in the sea some 200 yards from "Willie", its fuel exhausted.

On 6 May 'Glamorgan' detached with 'Alacrity' and 'Arrow' as a Surface Action Group tasked with investigating a possible surface contact close to the hulk of 'Sheffield'. This turned out to be a false alarm, later being identified as a friendly helicopter. While 'Glamorgan' continued the bombardment operations, her Flight maintained continuous ASW patrols until 13 May when the ship detached, along with 'Hermes' and 'Broadsword', for the Pebble Island operation. However, for various reasons, the raid was delayed 24 hours, during which time 'Glasgow' replaced 'Glamorgan'. Between 16 and 21 May, the ship was engaged in Operation "Tornado" which was a plan to deceive the enemy into thinking that the landings would be to the south of Port Stanley. Engaged in shore bombardment duties, she also launched five Seaslug missiles from ship to shore. Any damage which they may have inflicted is not known, but the firings were a great morale booster. The Flight carried out ASW sorties and XM837 was fired upon by machine guns to the north of Lively Island on 17 May during the operation. On 22 May she joined other Task Force vessels in Falkland Sound but continued to detach each night for bombardment duty on the Stanley gunline. The ship departed for the TRALA (some 200 miles east of the Falkland Islands) on 30 May for some repairs alongside 'Stena Seaspread'. Unfortunately the Wessex had become unserviceable the previous day with an oil leak. Following the completion of repairs, 'Glamorgan' took up duties as the TRALA "manager" on 3 June although XM837 remained unavailable until 10 June. To assist in the heavy round of VERTREP and HDS flying, an unknown Wessex HU.5 was embarked from 3 to 8 June, during which period it collected a number of airdrops from Hercules C.1P's flying from Wideawake.

At 1700Z on 11 June, 'Glamorgan' detached for more bombardment operations, this time in support of 45 Cdo on Two Sisters mountain, handing over the role of TRALA "manager" to 'Tidepool'. The operation was completed at 0615Z on 12 June and, as the ship headed back from the gunline at 0636Z, an Exocet missile was detected. Despite violent avoiding action by 'Glamorgan', turning her stern towards the threat and firing a Seacat which narrowly missed the Exocet, the enemy missile hit the ship at 0637Z, struck the flight-deck and "bounced" into the hangar. It failed to explode, but in the fire which ensued from the missile's unspent fuel the hangar was burnt out and "Willie" totally destroyed, the remains being dumped overboard. A hole 15ft by 10ft was left in the ship's port waist. Damage was inflicted to the galley and Seaslug launcher, while the port Seacat system was demolished. The attack claimed the lives of 13 of the ship's company (including POACMN C.P.Vickers) while a further 14 received injuries. With the fires extinguished and floods pumped out, 'Glamorgan' finally sailed at 1000Z at a speed in excess of 20 knots, coming alongside 'Stena Seaspread' for repairs on 13 June to take up the role of TRALA "manager" once again. The following day saw the Argentine surrender secured and Wessex HU.5 XT486 of 848 Sqdn 'D' Flight was embarked from 'Tidepool' for airdrop pick-ups in the TRALA. However, that aircraft suffered CAT.4 damage during a storm on 15 June [see 848 Sqdn 'D' Flight]. With her stop-gap repairs completed, 'Glamorgan' detached to San Carlos Water at 2330Z on 16 June in company with 'Active' and 'Stena Seaspread'. She spent the next few days there completing more effective repairs, while the damaged Wessex was lifted ashore to the Port San Carlos FOB by 18 Sqdn Chinook ZA705 on 19 June. 'Glamorgan' sailed from San Carlos Water at 2200Z that day to visit Port William on 20 June, then rejoined the CVBG prior to sailing for home at 1345Z on 21 June (firing a full salute on passing 'Hermes'). The ship arrived at Portsmouth on 10 July, having steamed over 30,000 miles since 2 April. Her guns had fired some 1,243 shells during the war, more than any other vessel. On 13 August the Flight formally disbanded at Portland, although the decision had already been made that an 815 Sqdn Lynx Flight would form to embark the ship when her hangar had been rebuilt.

> 737 Sqdn aircrew with 'Glamorgan' Flight during Operation "Corporate": Lt Cdr G.C.Hunt RN (Flt Cdr); Lt G.Stephenson RN; S/Lt D.E.Winton RN; POACMN C.P.Vickers (KIA).

# 845 NAVAL AIR SQUADRON

When the order to prepare for deployment to the South Atlantic was received on 1 April, 845 Sqdn (under the command of Lt Cdr R.J.Warden) had at its disposal a complement of 22 Wessex HU.5's. 18 of them were at Yeovilton, while a further four were on detachment to the British Forces in Northern Ireland. Several Flights were rapidly formed for deployment aboard vessels of the Task Force, some helicopters being prepared for air transportation to Ascension Island from where they would embark ships deploying directly south from Exercise "Springtrain" in the Mediterranean. The Squadron normally supported the Royal Marines in the assault role, for which purpose its aircraft were painted in the low-visibility scheme of Matt Olive Drab overall with Red/Blue roundels, while the serials, ROYAL NAVY titles and single-letter codes were applied in Black. In most, if not all, cases the ROYAL NAVY titles had already been removed altogether, and with the onset of the conflict those aircraft still carrying the titles also had them deleted. The aircraft codes were theoretically prefixed by the letter 'Y' in order to differentiate 845 Sqdn's machines from those of the other units, but that letter was not carried (nor were any deck letters). The Squadron's complement on 1 April was as follows:

| | | |
|---|---|---|
| XT473 '-/(Y)A' | XT484 '-/(Y)H' | XS516 '-/(Y)Q' |
| XT459 '-/(Y)B' | XT451 '-/(Y)J' | XT455 '-/(Y)R' |
| XT449 '-/(Y)C' | XT460 '-/(Y)K' | XT765 '-/(Y)S' |
| XT468 '-/(Y)D' | XS514 '-/(Y)L' | XS483 '-/(Y)T' |
| XT481 '-/(Y)E' | XT472 '-/(Y)M' | XS506 '-/(Y)U' |
| XT464 '-/(Y)F' | XS515 '-/(Y)N' | XT450 '-/(Y)V' |
| XT453 '-/(Y)G' | XT458 '-/(Y)P' | XT461 '-/(Y)W' |

Unmarked XT470, previously '-/(Y)A', was still on unit strength although earmarked for storage at Wroughton. Official transfer took place on 1 April, the helicopter arriving there the following day.

'A' Flight formed on 1 April (allocated XS483 and XT484) and was ordered to prepare for immediate embarkation aboard 'Resource' at Rosyth. The same day 'B' Flight was ordered to detach from Yeovilton and embark 'Fort Austin' at Ascension Island with XT468 and XT765, so the two aircraft were duly stripped down on 3 April and loaded that night aboard Heavylift Belfast G-BEPE which left for Wideawake the following day. Next came 'C' Flight which was allocated XT464 and XT473 on 10 April and then ordered south to Ascension Island for embarkation aboard 'Tidespring', the two aircraft having been stripped down at Yeovilton on 4 April for departure the following day aboard Heavylift Belfast G-BFYU. With the anticipated requirement for HDS operations on Ascension Island, 'D' Flight was to be based at Wideawake for assistance with the dispersal to Task Force ships of the troops, equipment and stores which were being flown in to the airfield. XT451 and XT460 departed Yeovilton for Wideawake aboard Heavylift Belfast G-BEPE on 8 April for use by the Flight. Finally, 'Intrepid' (due for refit just prior to the conflict) was rapidly returned to operational status and left Portsmouth on 15 April for sea trials, embarking 'E' Flight with XT449 and XT461 on 20 April. The Flight worked up with the ship and then returned to Yeovilton on 22 April to await a sailing date.

On 4 May the Northern Ireland detachment aircrew were withdrawn to Yeovilton in order to join the reformed 847 Sqdn. The Royal Air Force had requested approval for its own aircrew to fly the four 845 Sqdn Wessex HU.5's in Ulster and this was duly received. However, on 9 May it was decided to withdraw the helicopters in order to make more available for deployment to the South Atlantic, so XS506, XS514, XS515 and XT455 were returned to Yeovilton the next day. The first three were transferred to 847 Sqdn on 11 May along with XS516 and XT472, while XT455 was transferred to NASU. In the meantime, the increasing workload at Ascension Island raised a requirement for more helicopters so, on 6 May, the Squadron was directed to prepare two additional machines for air transportation to the Island. Heavylift Belfast G-BEPS left Yeovilton the same day with XT450 and XT459 aboard, arriving at Wideawake on 7 May. In the event, these two replaced the original 'D' Flight helicopters which had embarked 'Intrepid' as FIR aircraft

('E' Flight having moved from 'Intrepid' to 'Tidepool' with its pair). Therefore the need for more aircraft still stood, so XS491 and XT761 (both uncoded, although XT761 was unusual in still having Black ROYAL NAVY titles) were transferred from 847 Sqdn on 7 May and stripped down for air transportation to Wideawake inside Heavylift Belfast G-BEPS, joining 'D' Flight. The initial aircraft allocation to the Squadron's five Flights was therefore as follows:

| | | | |
|---|---|---|---|
| **'A' Flight** | 'Resource' | | XT484 '-/(Y)H' |
| | | | XS483 '-/(Y)T' |
| **'B' Flight** | 'Fort Austin' | | XT468 '-/(Y)D' |
| | | | XT765 '-/(Y)S' |
| **'C' Flight** | 'Tidespring' | | XT473 '-/(Y)A' |
| | | | XT464 '-/(Y)F' |
| **'D' Flight** | Wideawake | *(1)* | XT451 '-/(Y)J' |
| | | *(1)* | XT460 '-/(Y)K' |
| | | *(2)* | XT459 '-/(Y)B' |
| | | *(2)* | XT450 '-/(Y)V' |
| | | | XS491 uncoded |
| | | | XT761 uncoded |
| **'E' Flight** | 'Intrepid' | *(3)* | XT449 '-/(Y)C' |
| | | *(3)* | XT461 '-/(Y)W' |

| Notes: | |
|---|---|
| *(1)* | *Later embarked 'Intrepid' as FIR aircraft.* |
| *(2)* | *Temporary allocation; actually replacements for XT473 and XT464 of 'C' Flight lost in South Georgia.* |
| *(3)* | *Later moved to 'Tidepool'.* |

As can be seen from the table, 845 Sqdn became very fragmented which must have made it rather difficult to operate as a co-ordinated Commando support unit, at least until the majority of its Flights disembarked onto the Falkland Islands. To further complicate matters, the CO became Lt Cdr (Flying) at Ascension Island and the Senior Pilot (Lt Cdr M.Booth) took charge of 845 Sqdn.

The Squadron's three remaining aircraft were passed to other units. Two of them joined 707 Sqdn, being XT481 (on 19 May) and XT453 (on 13 July). XT458 was transferred to 772 Sqdn at Portland on 27 May for that unit's 'A' Flight due to the impending departure of 'Illustrious', but in the event did not deploy south with the ship. One additional Wessex HU.5 joined 845 Sqdn, being XS484 on MoD(PE) loan to the British Hovercraft Corporation at Cowes. Allotted to the Squadron on 31 May, it arrived at Yeovilton on 3 June still in the very old "sand and spinach" camouflage scheme. Following the Argentine surrender, XS484 was transferred to 771 Sqdn on 2 August as part of that unit's re-equipment programme and was delivered to Culdrose on 6 August. The Squadron's aircraft flew 2,259 hours in over 600 sorties during Operation "Corporate".

Although the details which follow relate to individual 845 Sqdn Flights, it is important to note that as soon as any of the Flights disembarked to the Falkland Islands, Flight status ceased. Once ashore, all aircraft and personnel were pooled for operation by 845 Squadron. In fact, when the FOB at Port San Carlos settlement was well established, Wessex helicopters tended to be used by 845, 847 or 848 Sqdn aircrew as and when required (regardless of which Squadron they were "on charge" to).

# 'A' FLIGHT

The Flight embarked 'Resource' at Rosyth, taking XS483 aboard on 2 April followed by XT484 the next day. She sailed for Ascension Island at 0145Z on 6 April and, during her passage down the English Channel the following day, XS483 was flown off to Yeovilton (via Lee-on-Solent) to collect some last-minute supplies, returning later in the day via Portland. XT484 was also flown to Yeovilton on 7 April, on that occasion for night alignment modifications, and returned to the ship the same day via Culdrose. Last-minute supplies were brought on board the ship off Cornwall by VERTREP, involving Chinook, Sea King and Wessex helicopters operating from Culdrose. The Flight was expected to operate ashore in the Falkland Islands in the support role and during the passage south to Ascension Island both aircraft were fitted with weapons platforms. Flying training included GPMG cabin-gun sorties, 2in RP firings and AS.12 attack profiles, culminating in four live AS.12 missile launches on 15 April. Subsequent events on 11 June proved that to have been a useful exercise. The ship arrived off Ascension Island on 17 April, continuing south the following day.

On 30 April XS483 was detached to 'Glamorgan' to act as an armed escort to 'Alacrity' Flight's Lynx HAS.2 (XZ736) which was to fly NGS spotting duties when 'Alacrity' and 'Glamorgan' began naval bombardment on 1 May. On that date the Wessex HU.5 was fired on by two Tigercat missiles but escaped unscathed and duly returned to 'Glamorgan' prior to transfer back to 'Resource' on 2 May. On 4 May the Flight joined in the search for survivors from the stricken 'Sheffield'. In the two weeks that followed it was engaged in VERTREP and personnel transfer sorties within the CVBG before 'Resource' anchored in San Carlos Water on 21 May to give support to operations ashore. The ship then detached eastwards to make a rendezvous with 'Canberra' in the TRALA on 23 May, some 170 miles north-east of Port Stanley. All of the stores and ammunition aboard 'Canberra' which were destined for the beach-head were cross-decked to 'Resource' and both of the Flight's helicopters were heavily engaged in VERTREP sorties. Unloading took place the following day when the Flight disembarked to be co-located with some 846 Sqdn Sea King HC.4's at the Old House Creek FOB on the east bank of San Carlos Water, some two miles north of San Carlos Settlement. It was there that Lt Cdr H.J.Lomas set about establishing the Squadron ashore. His determined efforts, forthright attitude and exceptional leadership later earned him the DSC. 'A' Flight was supplemented two days later by 'E' Flight (and one 'B' Flight aircraft) before the Squadron moved its FOB to the Port San Carlos Settlement on 30 May, being joined there by 847 Sqdn two days day. In

early June the Flight was heavily engaged in troop movements and reconnaissance flights, especially in the Teal Inlet area where a joint 845/847 Sqdn FOB was established on 4 June, followed by another at Fitzroy from 11 June.

10 June saw a rehearsal for one of the more unusual operations of the campaign. Predictably enough it stemmed from the Special Forces, an SBS patrol in the area of Port Stanley having reported that a conference of senior Argentine officers took place in the Town Hall each morning, the road outside being crowded with parked vehicles. The SBS believed that General de Brigada Menendez, General de Brigada Jofre and other senior staff attended regularly, so the temptation to further demoralise the enemy forces by "taking out" their command structure was irresistible. The SBS felt that to carry out the action themselves might produce reprisals on the local civilian population. A missile-carrying helicopter with an expert crew seemed to offer the best solution to the problem. The choice of weapons platform was a Wessex HU.5 armed with AS.12 missiles. An SBS Officer is reputed to have put the idea to Lt Cdr Lomas, who approved enthusiastically. Having endorsed the operation, he obtained approval from higher authority. XT484 was the helicopter selected, to be crewed by Lt P.C.Manley who was originally from 848 Sqdn 'D' Flight aboard 'Atlantic Conveyor' (that Flight's Helicopter Warfare Instructor, given the job because of his expertise) and a skilful 'A' Flight missile aimer, POACMN J.A.Balls BEM. XT484 was one of a four-Wessex detachment operating from the Teal Inlet FOB. Following a Special Forces briefing, the helicopter was armed with two live AS.12's and the practice got under way. Target for the rehearsal was Bob's Island just over seven miles to the north-west of Teal Inlet settlement. Lt Manley positioned the aircraft in the hover at a range of 3.5 miles from the Island; POACMN Balls launched the first missile and guided it towards the target. The second missile was launched at the closer range of 3 miles, once again from the hover. Satisfied with the results, they returned to the FOB to ready themselves for the following morning's mission.

Just before dawn (1100Z) on 11 June, XT484 was airborne and heading east at very low level, following the contours towards the selected launch point just south of Beagle Ridge, some 3 miles to the north-west of the Town Hall. Whilst en route Peter Manley was informed over the radio by an SAS observer that an Argentine helicopter, possibly a gunship, was in the vicinity. As a result, the planned firing position was slightly overshot. Once XT484 was steady in the hover in the dawn light, POACMN Balls fired the first missile which missed the Town Hall by a few yards and impacted instead in the upper floor and roof area of the Police Station next door. XT484 had by then been in an exposed position for some two to three minutes with no return of fire. A secondary target was not attacked, the remaining AS.12 being aimed once more at the Town Hall. On that occasion the control wire snagged (possibly on the ridge over which the missile was aimed) and the AS.12 hit the water in Port Stanley harbour some distance short of the Argentine hospital ship 'Bahia Paraiso' which was moored alongside a jetty. Seconds later, enemy anti-aircraft fire opened up from an emplacement in the vicinity of Cortley Hill on the north side of Port Stanley Harbour. Peter Manley made an "expeditious withdrawal", XT484 departing west back towards Teal Inlet just as shells from 105mm guns near Sapper Hill began to fall and explode behind him. The Wessex and its crew arrived safe and sound at the FOB around 1200Z.

Naturally, they were a little disappointed that the prime objective had been missed by a few, but vital, yards. However, it transpired that the Police Station was itself a very satisfactory target as it was being used as an "Intelligence Headquarters". Argentine reports on the attack make no mention of any loss of life or the status of the target, other than identifying it as the "Political Officer's house", but they do emphasise that a missile only missed the hospital ship by some 25 metres. However, other sources reveal that the operation certainly shook the morale of both senior and junior Argentine officers alike. As to the secondary target mentioned above, that was to have been any visible Argentine Chinooks or Pumas. None was seen, so the second missile was turned on the Town Hall.

*(What Peter Manley and Arthur Balls did not realise was that by 11 June all of the CAB601 Pumas on the Falkland Islands had either crashed or been shot down, while the Prefectura example had been damaged. Of the four Chinooks which had been based on the Islands, one CAB601 machine had been reduced to ashes on Mount Kent while the other was lying (almost certainly) unserviceable in Port Stanley. The two Grupo 7 Chinooks had been flown back to the mainland on 9 June upon completion of their tasking when it became obvious that defeat was inevitable.)*

Following the Argentine surrender, the Squadron utilised a supplementary FOB established at the Port Stanley Racecourse on 15 June for the movement of troops and their kit preparatory to the return home of the Task Force (although Port San Carlos settlement continued to be the unit's main base). 'Resource' anchored off Port Stanley on 17 June, XS483 and XT484 re-embarking on 24 June to sail with the ship for South Georgia two days later and finally leaving there for the United Kingdom on 29 June. The Flight disembarked to Yeovilton (via Culdrose) on 19 July prior to the ship's arrival at Devonport.

*845 Sqdn 'A' Flight aircrew during Operation "Corporate" and their awards:*
*Lt Cdr H.J.Lomas RN (Flt Cdr) DSC; Lt S.P.Judd RN; Lt D.F.Knight RN; S/Lt R.Morton RN; POACMN J.A.Balls BEM MID; POACMN S.McNaughton.*

# 'B' FLIGHT

The Flight arrived at Ascension Island on 5 April, its Wessex HU.5's (XT468 and XT765) being off-loaded from Belfast G-BEPE to be reassembled by Naval Party 1222. 'Fort Austin' arrived from Gibraltar the following day, while both aircraft were test-flown on 7 April having been equipped for the gunship role with GPMG, 2in RP and AS.12 missiles. XT468 embarked the vessel that day, followed by XT765 on 8 April, the ship sailing south on 9 April to rendezvous with, and replenish, 'Endurance'. That took place on 12 April when troops, stores and equipment were cross-decked, 'Endurance' then sailing for South Georgia and Operation "Paraquat". Meanwhile, 'Fort Austin' set course back to Ascension Island on 13 April, arriving there on 20 April to disembark 815 Sqdn 'Minerva' Flight and to be re-stored and replenished herself before sailing south again on 23 April, entering the TEZ on 3 May. XT765 was slightly damaged the following day while engaged in transferring survivors from the stricken 'Sheffield' to 'Fort Austin', but the helicopter was serviceable again by 9 May when flown aboard 'Invincible' to make room for a fourth Lynx HAS.2 aboard 'Fort Austin' *[see 815 Sqdn 'Newcastle' Flight]*. On 12 May XT468 was kept busy with the transfer of survivors from 'Sheffield' to other ships for repatriation to the United Kingdom. However, it had become unserviceable by 14 May, which was a disappointment as the Flight was to have taken part in the raid on Pebble Island.

17 May saw the dispersal of one 'Fort Austin' Lynx to 'Invincible' and the remaining three, plus XT468, to 'Hermes'. That allowed 'Fort Austin' to accept a detachment of four 826 Sqdn Sea King HAS.5's which in turn created more deck space on 'Hermes' for Harriers and additional Sea Harriers due from 'Atlantic Conveyor' over the next few days. Once the transfer of the latter had been completed, congestion on the carrier's flight-deck became acute. XT468 was therefore flown off to 'Atlantic Conveyor' on 20 May for "garaging". 'Invincible' was also having space problems caused by the influx of additional aircraft so XT765 was transferred to 'Atlantic Conveyor' on 19 May prior to embarking 'Stromness' on 21 May, primarily for use in the support role. Additionally, it could provide a limited load-lifting capability whilst the ship was unloading in San Carlos Water, if so required. The Wessex disembarked ashore to "Red Beach" at Ajax Bay (alongside the refrigeration plant) on 22 May to support 45 Cdo over the next few days. XT765 then moved on 26 May to the 845 Sqdn FOB at Old House Creek on the east bank of San Carlos Water. It embarked 'Fearless' in San Carlos Water on 27 May and sailed with her to rendezvous with 'Antrim' to the east of the TEZ.

After collecting Major General Moore from 'Antrim' on 29 May, XT765 returned to San Carlos Water aboard 'Fearless' on 30 May where it disembarked ashore that day to be based at the Port San Carlos Settlement FOB. In the meantime, the Flight's other aircraft (XT468 aboard 'Atlantic Conveyor') had a lucky escape on 25 May when the ship was hit by an Exocet missile. It happened to be airborne on a test-flight at the time the vessel was being attacked. Sadly, two of the Flight's maintainers were killed (LAEM D.L.Pryce and AEM A.S.Anslow). After picking up survivors from the burning ship, it recovered to 'Hermes' to operate in the HDS role along with an element of 848 Sqdn 'D' Flight, seconded from 845 Sqdn on 28 May but retaining the code '-/(Y)D'.

Unfortunately, being fitted out for the gunship role meant that the lifting capacity of the Wessex was limited. It was therefore exchanged for XT471 (of 847 Sqdn) on 3 June, one of eight HU.5's being held on 'Atlantic Causeway' at that stage (XT471 was in turn seconded to 848 Sqdn 'D' Flight although it remained on 847 Sqdn charge). XT468 appears to have remained aboard 'Atlantic Causeway', certainly until at least 8/9 June when the ship was anchored in San Carlos Water for the second time. There it is presumed to have either remained aboard or disembarked to the Port San Carlos FOB to join XT765. The next confirmed sighting was on 11 July when it was airlifted by 18 Sqdn Chinook HC.1 onto a Mexeflote at the stern of 'Atlantic Causeway' in Port Stanley harbour. The helicopter was then taken aboard the ship, sailing with her to San Carlos Water the following day prior to departing from there on 13 July for the United Kingdom. She arrived at Devonport on 27 July, where XT468 was off-loaded the next day to a compound at Camel's Head (near HMS Drake, Plymouth). It was taken by road to Yeovilton on 2 August, arriving there the same day and remaining on 845 Sqdn charge.

Throughout June XT765 remained ashore based at the Port San Carlos FOB to assist with the resupply operations to forward positions. A supplementary 845 Sqdn FOB was established at Port Stanley Racecourse on 15 June and the Wessex is believed to have operated from there until 3 July when it embarked 'Hermes' in Port William (joining XT450 of 'C' Flight). The carrier sailed later that day en route for the United Kingdom, arriving at Portsmouth on 21 July. XT765 was flown off to Yeovilton the next day, although the majority of the Flight's personnel were taken to Ascension Island by 'British Tay' and returned by air to Brize Norton on 7 July. It has been estimated that the Flight flew some 210 hours during Operation "Corporate", but official records were all lost with the sinking of 'Atlantic Conveyor'.

*845 Sqdn 'B' Flight aircrew during Operation "Corporate": Lt G.R.N.Foster RN (Flt Cdr); Lt K.D.J.Slowe RN; S/Lt I.S.Brown RN; S/Lt G.Fox RN; C/Sgt D.Greet; Cpl I.Tyrell.*

# 'C' FLIGHT

The Flight's two Wessex HU.5's (XT464, XT473) arrived at Wideawake aboard Belfast G-BFYU on 6 April. Like 'B' Flight's aircraft, they were equipped as GPMG, 2in RP and AS.12 missile platforms to operate in the gunship role. Both were reassembled and test-flown by Naval Party 1222, and then awaited the arrival of 'Tidespring' which had been ordered south from Exercise "Springtrain" on 2 April. She arrived at Ascension Island on 10 April, the Flight embarking the following day prior to the vessel's departure for South Georgia in company with 'Antrim' and 'Plymouth'. The group carried out a rendezvous with 'Endurance' on 14 April and then commenced Operation "Paraquat". The four ships arrived off South Georgia on 21 April, the two Wessex HU.5's joining with 'Antrim' Flight's radar-equipped Wessex HAS.3 XP142 to successfully land men of 'D' Sqdn 22 SAS Regt on the Fortuna Glacier despite the prevailing 60 knot winds. The 18-man patrol was incapacitated during the night by Storm Force 10 winds and driving snow, with the result that a rescue operation became necessary. The three helicopters went back to the Glacier early on 22 April when the conditions had marginally improved. Having embarked six troopers, XT464 (crewed by Lt M.J.Tidd and LACMN R.Wilson) lifted off before the other two and moved forward but, within a mile, Mike Tidd experienced sudden and total "white-out" conditions. As the Wessex was already on its icing limits he could not climb clear of the weather and the surrounding high mountains.

Tidd therefore decided to turn back in order to try and regain some visual references, but no sooner had he done so than the RADALT was seen to be indicating 40ft, decreasing. Realising that impact was inevitable, he flared the helicopter which then struck the ground tail first, rolled onto its port side and skidded to a halt. Of the eight people on board only one, an SAS trooper, was slightly injured. All of the personnel from XT464 were taken aboard the other two aircraft, one of which (XT473) had to dump fuel due to the increased load. XP142 then took-off, closely followed by XT473 (crewed by Lt I.A.Georgeson and LACMN A.Lomas). Within a few minutes both pilots encountered "white-out" conditions but Georgeson, relying on the radar-equipped (and manned) HAS.3 to find a safe route through the weather, managed to keep XP142 in sight. Suddenly, though, he saw the HAS.3 climb and then, just as quickly, descend and disappear from view (it had climbed over a ridge and then dropped down over a fjord). Ian Georgeson, his RADALT indicating 80ft and descending, assumed there was high ground ahead of him and reduced XT473's airspeed to zero ready to land. As he did so, the helicopter hit a ridge, slid sideways and then rolled over onto its starboard side. Again, only one person was injured — the same trooper as before! Already overloaded, the 'Antrim' Flight helicopter returned to its parent ship before going back to successfully rescue the personnel from the second HU.5 accident. Both of the crashed aircraft were abandoned on the Glacier.

With the Argentine surrender on South Georgia secured on 26 April, 'Tidespring' sailed north once again for Ascension Island (with 186 PoW's), where replacement helicopters were in the process of being delivered. Heavylift Belfast G-BEPS landed at Wideawake on 7 May with Wessex HU.5's XT450 and XT459 aboard, the two helicopters being reassembled by Naval Party 1222 and test-flown on 9 May, ostensibly for 'D' Flight. 'Tidespring' arrived within helicopter range of the Island three days later and 'C' Flight was duly re-equipped on 13 May, the two Wessex HU.5's embarking the following day after re-storing the vessel. With her Flight fully operational once more, 'Tidespring' sailed on 16 May, entering the TEZ 11 days later to take up tanker duties in the TRALA. The Flight carried out HDS, VERTREP and communications duties as required until 9 June when helicopter support was needed ashore. 'C' Flight embarked 'Fort Grange' for passage to San Carlos Water and at dawn on 10 June disembarked to the Port San Carlos FOB to join the rest of 845 Sqdn in resupply operations until the surrender on 14 June.

On 21 June one of the Flight's helicopters was flown to Pebble Island where the aircrew were involved in cataloguing captured enemy aircraft and stores. Both Wessex were then detached, as and when required, to the Port Stanley Racecourse where, on 24 June, XT459 (crewed by Lt P.C.Manley and LACMN F.S.McKie) unfortunately suffered CAT.4/5 damage. A woven nylon sack, blown up by the slipstream, got caught on one of the main rotor blades of the Wessex just after it landed, causing the blade to be ripped back through its "drag hinge"

and creating severe ground resonance. The affected blade then dropped so far below its normal rotation height that it cut the tail rotor drive shaft in half. By that stage all of the blades were rotating at too low a height resulting in the tailcone being virtually sliced away from the rest of the fuselage. The helicopter was shut down and, fortunately, nobody was injured. The Wessex was airlifted to 'Atlantic Causeway' off Port Stanley by 18 Sqdn Chinook on/by 11 July for return to the United Kingdom and arrived at Devonport on 27 July in two sections. It was offloaded the following day to a compound at Camel's Head (near HMS Drake, Plymouth), then taken by road to Yeovilton on 29 July on transfer that day to NASU.

While 'Tidespring' continued with her tanker duties, 'C' Flight took XT450 aboard 'Hermes' on 3 July for the return journey to Ascension Island. There it was to await the arrival of 'Tidespring', but by the time the vessel reached the Island she had lost her aircraft support facilities so the Flight remained aboard the carrier (along with XT765 of 'B' Flight) for the journey home. She arrived at Portsmouth on 21 July and XT450 was flown off to Yeovilton the next day, remaining on 845 Sqdn charge. A total of 427 flying hours and 1,084 deck landings were accrued by the Flight during Operation "Corporate".

> 845 Sqdn 'C' Flight aircrew during Operation "Corporate": Lt M.J.Tidd RN (Flt Cdr); Lt I.A.Georgeson RN; Flt Lt A.Pulford RAF; S/Lt A.C.Berryman RN; LACMN A.Lomas; LACMN R.Wilson.

# 'D' FLIGHT

Heavylift Belfast G-BEPE arrived at Wideawake on 9 April with Wessex HU.5's XT451 and XT460 for 'D' Flight (the Ascension Island Base Flight). Naval Party 1222 had already been established as a "mini-NASU", tasked with preparing the airlifted helicopters for flight and subsequent embarkation aboard Task Force ships, and the two 'D' Flight HU.5's duly underwent the treatment. Having test-flown XT460 on 11 April and XT451 the next day, HDS and VERTREP tasks began immediately as stores, equipment and personnel arrived at the airfield for transfer to Task Force ships. As the fleet assembled, everything had to be positioned on the right ship and in the correct order for unloading at their destinations. The operations were interrupted only once, on 22 April, when XT460 flew a sick seaman from 'Elk' to 'Canberra' for treatment.

On 6 May two more helicopters were prepared at Yeovilton for air transportation. Heavylift Belfast G-BEPS arrived at Wideawake the following day with XT450 and XT459 aboard. They were reassembled and test-flown on 9 May and then used by 'D' Flight prior to handover to 'C' Flight aboard 'Tidespring' when the ship returned to Ascension Island from South Georgia three later. While controlling and organising the helicopter site during this major ship storing operation, Lt George

Croston successfully sat his 'A' Level Law examination!

In the meantime, XT451 and XT460 had embarked 'Intrepid' on 7 May to be transported south as FIR aircraft, sailing with the ship on 8 May. They are believed to have disembarked, when a suitable opportunity arose around 30 May, to the Port San Carlos Settlement FOB alongside the rest of 845 Sqdn ('A', 'B' and 'E' Flights) to be used in the utility role following the loss of the aircraft on board 'Atlantic Conveyor' on 25 May. Both joined 847 Sqdn as replacement aircraft (possibly on, or shortly after, 1 June), eventually moving to Navy Point opposite Port Stanley on 25 June.

The next two to arrive at Wideawake were XS491 and XT761 (both uncoded), delivered aboard Heavylift Belfast G-BEPS on 12 May to be reassembled and test-flown by Naval Party 1222. This pair remained with 'D' Flight and undertook HDS and VERTREP tasking as the various Task Force ships came and went. The stay of XT450 and XT459 was short-lived as they embarked 'Tidespring' on 14 May to replace the two 'C' Flight aircraft lost on South Georgia. 'Engadine' arrived on 25 May with 847 Sqdn 'A' Flight, of which Wessex HU.5 XT764 '-/XM' was partly unserviceable. The aircraft was flown ashore in exchange for XS491 and the ship sailed again on 26 May.

'D' Flight continued to operate at Ascension Island,

*A returning reconnaissance patrol is offloaded at Port San Carlos settlement from XT450 '–/(Y)V', a Wessex HU.5 of 845 Squadron 'C' Flight. This HU.5 was a replacement for one of the Flight's two helicopters lost on the Fortuna Glacier, South Georgia, and it did not arrive on the Falklands until 10.6.82, dating the photograph between then and the Argentine surrender on 14.6.82.* (Ministry of Defence)

*This 848 Squadron 'D' Flight Wessex HU.5 (XS512 '–/ WT') had just completed engine runs on 25.5.82 when 'Atlantic Conveyor' was hit by an Exocet missile. Flames, heat and smoke from the ensuing fire prevented a flight crew reaching the Wessex and, with five others belonging to the Flight, it was left to perish.* (Ministry of Defence)

XT764 still carrying the code '-/XM' on 16 June although it had been removed by 11 August. Both XT761 and XT764 were still uncoded on 17 September when 'D' Flight added a third Wessex to its complement with the arrival of XS521 aboard 'Olmeda', still wearing its former 772 Sqdn code 'PO/621' and ROYAL NAVY titles in White with 'D' Class roundels. By late October the trio were unique within 845 Sqdn, having been repainted where necessary and coded with the prefix letter 'Y' actually carried on the airframe:

XS521 '-/YB'    XT764 '-/YG'    XT761 '-/YP'

Between 11 April and 28 July, 'D' Flight aircraft flew a total of 503.20 hours by day plus 40.30 hours by night, uplifted 3.5 million pounds of stores and transferred 2,500 personnel to and from ships off Ascension.

*845 Sqdn 'D' Flight aircrew during Operation "Corporate" and their awards: Lt Cdr R.J.Warden RN (CO of 845 Sqdn, Lt Cdr (Flying) AI); Lt A.S.Roelich RN (Flt Cdr); Lt G.R.Croston RN; Lt M.A.Ellis RM; S/Lt R.R.Cuthbert RN CINCFC; S/Lt C.Dick RN; S/Lt J.N.D.Ridge RN; FCACMN D.H.Carter; CPOACMN D.E.Brown.*

# 'E' FLIGHT

The Flight had embarked 'Intrepid' on 20 April with Wessex HU.5's XT449 and XT461 for two days of sea trials off Portland before returning to Yeovilton on 22 April to await a sailing date. That occurred on 26 April when the Flight re-embarked the ship in Weymouth Bay after she had left Portland for the South Atlantic. She arrived at Ascension Island on 5 May, 'E' Flight moving ashore to Wideawake to assist 'D' Flight with its HDS and VERTREP tasks. However, 'E' Flight was transferred to 'Tidepool' on 5 May and sailed south with the ship the following day, while the two original 'D' Flight Wessex HU.5's (XT451 and XT460) were flown aboard 'Intrepid' on 7 May as FIR aircraft, the vessel sailing the following day. 'E' Flight set about working up the aircraft facilities aboard 'Tidepool' prior to operations in the South Atlantic.

Between 9 May and 18 May armour plating was fitted to the aircraft and all white markings were painted out. XT449 was detached to 'Antrim' on 19 May to assist her Wessex HAS.3 in an operation to land Special Forces on Fanning Head. That took place around 2315Z on 20 May, just prior to the invasion proper the following morning. Instead of returning to 'Tidepool', XT449 was transferred to 'Canberra' on 21 May for CASEVAC work. Lt M.S.Crabtree (pilot), S/Lt P.J.J.Heathcote (observer) and Cpl K.G.Gleeson (aircrewman) were joined by Surgeon Cdr Rick Jolly in a particularly difficult rescue of two survivors from the bomb attack on 'Ardent'. The first was having great difficulty in grasping the strop which had been lowered for him. Cdr Jolly realised that the man was drowning and volunteered to be lowered (without any immersion clothing) to assist him. Mike Crabtree, by means of voice control from his aircrewman, skilfully manoeuvred the Wessex into position and Rick Jolly, because of adroit handling of the winch by Cpl Gleeson, managed to grasp and then clutch the exhausted man to his body. They were then both hauled up to safety. Although numb with cold, the Surgeon Cdr was lowered once more for the second survivor and managed to attach the winch hook to the front of the desperate man's lifejacket. In theory the snatch pull of the winch should have ripped the jacket apart but it did not and both of them were raised to the helicopter and into its cabin.

In the meantime, 'Tidepool' had begun the seemingly endless task of refuelling the ships of the Task Force, during which she was involved in a collision with 'Ambuscade', although neither vessel suffered serious damage. XT449 returned to the ship from 'Canberra' on 24 May when both vessels were some 170 miles north-east of Port Stanley. On 25 May the Flight disembarked from 'Tidepool' to a temporary landing site at Ajax Bay, moving the next day to the FOB at Old House Creek on the east bank of San Carlos Water, some two miles north of San Carlos Settlement. There the Flight's aircraft teamed up with those of 'A' Flight (and one from 'B' Flight) to carry out resupply and HDS tasks to forward positions following the loss of the helicopters on board the 'Atlantic Conveyor' on 25 May. The Squadron moved its FOB to the Port San Carlos settlement on 30 May, being joined there by the Wessex HU.5's of 847 Sqdn two days later. Further FOB's were established at Teal Inlet (on 4 June) and Fitzroy (from 11 June). Intense utility work continued as the British forces pushed further forward until the surrender on 14 June. Following that, men and equipment had to be transferred to the ships which were returning home and operations continued ashore until the helicopters and their maintainers were loaded aboard 'Atlantic Causeway' at Port Stanley on 12 July, sailing for home with the ship from San Carlos Water the following day (the Flight's aircrew returned home by air from Port Stanley). Having arrived at Devonport with the ship on 27 July, XT449 and XT461 were flown off to Yeovilton the following day, remaining on 845 Sqdn charge. The two helicopters flew 459 hours in 140 sorties (involving 467 deck landings) during Operation "Corporate".

*845 Sqdn 'E' Flight aircrew during Operation "Corporate": Lt M.S.Crabtree RN (Flt Cdr); Lt R.M.Evans RN; S/Lt R.D.Harden RN; S/Lt P.J.J.Heathcote RN; LACMN A.Smiles; Cpl K.G.Gleeson.*

*Additional 845 Sqdn aircrew aboard 'Fearless' during Operation "Corporate": Lt Cdr D.C.Pulleyn RN; Lt E.C.E.Brown RN.*

# FALKLAND ISLANDS DETACHMENT

On 24 September 1982 847 Sqdn was effectively disbanded with the transfer of the unit's final 11 Wessex HU.5's to the 845 Sqdn Falkland Islands Detachment. 845 Sqdn actually took over operation of the aircraft earlier (on 14 September) although the formal handover by the CO of 847 Sqdn, Lt Cdr Booth, was completed at Ascension Island on the later date. As if to complicate matters further, official transfer of the helicopters was effective from 27 September (such is the aftermath of war!). Under the command of Lt Cdr H.J.Lomas (from 'A' Flight), the Detachment continued to be based at Navy Point (on the north bank of Port Stanley Harbour and known locally as "The Camber") with the following aircraft:

| | | |
|---|---|---|
| XS491 '-/XM' | XT456 '-/XZ' | XT481 '-/XF' |
| XS506 '-/XE' | XT460 '-/(Y)K' | XT482 '-/XL' |
| XS523 '-/XJ' | XT466 '-/XV' | XT759 '-/XY' |
| XT451 '-/XN' | XT475 '-/XG' | |

Of those, two were unserviceable, and of the nine airworthy machines six were kept available for tasking. That number was reduced by one per week as the commitment decreased, and in early October a MARTSU team arrived to survey and repair two aircraft at a time aboard 'Astronomer'. The 847 Sqdn side letters were retained as there was no need (or desire) to change them, bearing in mind the short period of time that the Detachment would be required in the Islands.

Supported by 'Astronomer', operations by the Detachment continued until 6 November when the helicopters were loaded aboard the ship for return to the United Kingdom. The vessel sailed circa 14 November and arrived at Devonport on 3 December. Her aircraft were all off-loaded overnight on 3/4 December and transported to a compound at the Granby Gate entrance to the docks for dispersal by road. XS491, XS506 and XT456 all arrived at Wroughton on 6 December upon transfer to the RNAY for storage, being followed two days later by XT466 and XT759 (the latter for survey pending possible reissue). Four aircraft were transferred to NASU Yeovilton, being XT475 (on 3 December, arriving there the following day) and XS523, XT451, XT481 (all on 5 December, arriving there the same day). 4 December saw the arrival at Yeovilton of XT482 (upon transfer to 707 Sqdn) plus XT460, the last of the Squadron's original complement to return home, discounting the short period when it was allocated to 847 Sqdn. The latter remained on 845 Sqdn charge.

# 'ILLUSTRIOUS' FLIGHT

On 16 October 1982 848 Sqdn 'C' Flight effectively ceased operations with the official transfer of its two aircraft (XS520 '-/WZ' and XT760 '-/WV') from 'Fort Austin' to a detachment of 845 Sqdn aboard 'Illustrious'. They embarked the carrier on 19 October and operated in the HDS role until disembarked to Yeovilton on 7 December (still wearing 848 Sqdn codes) prior to 'Illustrious' docking at Portsmouth the following day.

# 847 NAVAL AIR SQUADRON

Lt Cdr M.D.Booth (formerly the Senior Pilot with 845 Sqdn) was ordered to reform 847 Sqdn at Yeovilton on 4 May and preparations immediately began to equip the Squadron with 24 Wessex HU.5's, divided into 'A' and 'B' Flights. The unit was commissioned only three days later and ordered to be on course for the South Atlantic within a week, having been earmarked to become the Garrison Squadron following the retaking of the Falkland Islands. It was formed and commissioned in such a short space of time that an ode (which alluded to the Captain's commissioning speech) was penned. One verse will suffice to show how well known the new Squadron was!

*He said you're 847*
*A Commando Squadron true*
*And as the words had left his lips*
*We all whispered — "84 Who??"*

The Squadron's helicopters were drawn from several sources, principally the second-line units whose Wessex HU.5's at that time had White titles, deck-letters and codes. As they began to arrive at Yeovilton the task of preparing them for Squadron use commenced, including respray in Matt Olive Drab overall with Black serials and codes plus Red/Blue roundels, but without ROYAL NAVY titles in the majority of cases. That had been completed by 13 May when the last aircraft embarked, only nine days after the Squadron had reformed.

The first Wessex to arrive for the Squadron was XS523, which was coded '-/XJ' on 5 May in the commando colour scheme and officially joined the unit the following day. That gave the first insight into the code range adopted by the unit, and over the next seven days the remaining aircraft slotted into the code range '-/XA' to '-/XZ'. In all, 27 Wessex HU.5's were received by 847 Sqdn in the following week. Their identities and transfer dates were as follows (previous units are given in parenthesis):

| 5 May | |
|---|---|
| (772 Sqdn, Portland) | XS507 XT766 XT773 |
| (771 Sqdn, Culdrose) | XT466 XT471 XT759 |
| (SAR Flt, Lee-on-Solent) | XS491 |

| 6 May | |
|---|---|
| (772 Sqdn, Portland) | XS518 XT469 XT480 XT486 |
| (771 Sqdn, Culdrose) | XT755 XT761 |
| (707 Sqdn, Yeovilton) | XS488 XS523 |
| (RNPT/707 Sqdn, Yeovilton) | XT764 |
| (NASU, Yeovilton) | XT456 |
| (848 Sqdn, Yeovilton) | XT482 |

| 7 May | |
|---|---|
| (707 Sqdn, Yeovilton) | XT757 |

| 11 May | |
|---|---|
| (845 Sqdn, Yeovilton) | XS506 XS514 XS515 XS516 XT472 |
| (707 Sqdn, Yeovilton) | XS479 |
| (NASU, Yeovilton) | XT475 |

| 13 May | |
|---|---|
| (NASU, Yeovilton) | XT479 |

Those from 771 Sqdn had their previous marks removed at their former base, although they were unique in that they retained ROYAL NAVY titling, albeit in Black. Three of the aircraft only had a short stay with 847 Sqdn, XS491 and XT761 being transferred to 845 Sqdn on 7 May to replace the pair from 845 Sqdn 'D' Flight which had sailed from Ascension Island aboard 'Intrepid' as FIR aircraft, while XT479 joined 707 Sqdn on 14 May. Thus the complement of Wessex HU.5's had been achieved. By 11 May all had received the frontline colour scheme and were coded as follows:

| | | |
|---|---|---|
| XS514 '-/XA' | XS523 '-/XJ' | XT766 '-/XS' |
| XS515 '-/XB' | XS488 '-/XK' | XT773 '-/XT' |
| XT472 '-/XC' | XT482 '-/XL' | XS507 '-/XU' |
| XS516 '-/XD' | XT764 '-/XM' | XT466 '-/XV' |
| XS506 '-/XE' | XT469 '-/XN' | XT471 '-/XW' |
| XS479 '-/XF' | XS518 '-/XP' | XT755 '-/XX' |
| XT475 '-/XG' | XT480 '-/XQ' | XT759 '-/XY' |
| XT757 '-/XH' | XT486 '-/XR' | XT456 '-/XZ' |

Under the command of the Squadron CO, 'A' Flight embarked 'Engadine' at Devonport on 9 May with XS523,

XT456, XT482 and XT764, sailing south the following day as part of the 'Bristol' Group. The remainder of the Squadron formed 'B' Flight under Lt Cdr P.Hails and left Yeovilton for HMS Raleigh (Torpoint) on 13 May. They embarked the 'Atlantic Causeway' in Plymouth Sound the same day. Aboard the vessel the HU.5's were given priority over the Sea Kings of 825 Sqdn and were stowed in the forward hangar, but two landed on the after deck (where the superstructure gave some protection against the elements) in order to fulfil the SAR role and carry out general communications duties. The ship sailed on 14 May and during the passage south to Freetown, Sierra Leone the Squadron practised flying and flight deck drills (the latter including the lashing, unlashing and refuelling of its aircraft). By the time that the ship arrived off Ascension Island on 22 May, those operations had all become routine. From that date onwards the helicopters were stowed and lashed down. The forward hangar offered less protection than had been expected from the rougher seas and poorer weather conditions experienced south of Ascension Island, so hasty modifications using plywood and canvas were carried out before the war zone was reached.

'Engadine' arrived at Gibraltar on 15 May with one of the 'A' Flight Wessex HU.5's (XT764) partly unserviceable. When she reached Ascension Island on 25 May, the aircraft was flown ashore in exchange for XS491 from 845 Sqdn 'D' Flight (at that time uncoded) which took up the vacated code '-/XM'. The vessel sailed from Ascension Island the next day, some four days behind 'Atlantic Causeway' which entered the TEZ on 29 May and anchored in San Carlos Water on 1 June. 12 of her Wessex HU.5's were disembarked during the day to the FOB at Port San Carlos Settlement where they joined elements of 845 Sqdn. 'Atlantic Causeway' sailed on 2 June to position well to the east of the Falkland Islands, taking with her the remaining eight Wessex HU.5's along with a NASU. Those helicopters were all available for use as support or replacement aircraft, if and when required.

Meanwhile, 'B' Flight immediately began operations ashore in support of the push forward by the land forces, ferrying ammunition, equipment and stores to the forward areas. This had been necessitated by the loss of the 848 Sqdn Wessex HU.5's and 18 Sqdn Chinook HC.1's aboard 'Atlantic Conveyor' on 25 May, the Squadron being called on to assist the overworked 846 Sqdn Sea King HC.4's, 845 Sqdn Wessex HU.5's and lone 18 Sqdn Chinook HC.1 (ZA718) in the utility role. The successful north-east thrust of the ground forces warranted the establishment of a joint 845/847 Sqdn FOB at Teal Inlet settlement on 4 June. Aircraft and aircrew were detached to the FOB on a 24-hour rotational basis. The southerly push to Fitzroy was highlighted on 8 June, from a Squadron point of view, when XT480 (flown by Lt T.Hughes with CPO W.R.Tuttey as his aircrewman) was involved in the dramatic rescue and evacuation of personnel from the blazing 'Sir Galahad' at Port Pleasant, at one stage blowing a dinghy away from the ship with its rotor downwash. The following day saw another joint 845/847 Sqdn FOB firmly established at Fitzroy settlement under the command of Lt Cdr Booth, initially with XT449 (from 845 Sqdn) and XT755, although the number of Wessex HU.5's detached there increased considerably over the next three days.

The parade ground at HMS Raleigh, Torpoint, Devon on 13.5.82 hosts 847 Squadron 'B' Flight's Wessex HU.5's prior to their embarkation in 'Atlantic Causeway' in Plymouth Sound later that day. Visible here are sixteen of the twenty HU.5's which sailed with the ship the following day for the South Atlantic.
(Ministry of Defence)

Although wearing an 847 Squadron code, '–/XW', Wessex HU.5 XT471 was based on 'Hermes' while seconded to 848 Squadron 'D' Flight when this photograph was taken on 26.6.82. The Wessex is on a VERTREP sortie to 'Astronomer' from 'Hermes', both vessels being in the TRALA at the time. Just visible in the rudimentary hangar are two 18 Squadron Chinook HC.1's, ZA720/BG and ZA717/BK, which were flown off to the Port San Carlos settlement FOB on 27 and 29.6.82.
(via T. & J. Harrison Ltd)

Tucked into a narrow valley and parked close to farmhouses and outbuildings near the Port San Carlos settlement FOB are twelve Wessex HU.5's. Most, if not all, belong to 847 Squadron which established itself at the FOB on 1.6.82. (Ministry of Defence)

'Engadine' entered the TEZ on 6 June and arrived in San Carlos Water on 9 June, on which date 'A' Flight disembarked to Port San Carlos settlement in order to complete the FOB element there, consisting of 845 and 847 Sqdn's and the lone 18 Sqdn Chinook HC.1. Of the Wessex HU.5's still aboard 'Atlantic Causeway', XT471 was seconded to an element of 848 Sqdn 'D' Flight on 3 June, by then operating from 'Hermes' on HDS duties. It replaced XT468 which, in turn, had been seconded from 845 Sqdn 'B' Flight but proved to be unsuitable for the HDS role as it had been fitted out as a gunship. XT468 was brought aboard 'Atlantic Causeway'. On 10 June XT486 was seconded to the 848 Sqdn 'D' Flight element on board 'Tidepool' (remaining on 847 Sqdn charge), 845 Sqdn 'E' Flight having long since moved ashore to join the rest of its Squadron by that time. The aircraft was dispatched from 'Atlantic Causeway' via 'Fort Grange' and embarked 'Tidepool' on 11 June.

Whilst on task near Bluff Cove on 11 June, XT480 sustained slight damage when a mortar bomb exploded close to the helicopter. The Squadron's aircraft were fortunate to escape further damage during an air raid near Estancia House by three Grupo 5 A-4B Skyhawks on 13 June. Utility tasking continued until the Argentine surrender on 14 June, following which six of the Squadron's aircraft took part in the celebratory flypast over Port Stanley on 15 June. XS507 was collected from 'Atlantic Causeway' on 16 June by the 848 Sqdn 'D' Flight crew from 'Tidepool', that aircraft being the replacement for XT486 which had suffered CAT.4 storm damage on 15 June while embarked aboard 'Glamorgan' for HDS duties in the TRALA (XS507 remained on 847 Sqdn charge, however). XT486 was lifted ashore to the Port San Carlos FOB by 18 Sqdn Chinook HC.1 ZA705 on 19 June whilst 'Glamorgan' was in San Carlos Water for repairs.

Of the Squadron's aircraft positioned ashore on 19 June, 16 were dispersed as follows:

| | | |
|---|---|---|
| **Division HQ** | Stanley Sportsfield | 3 |
| **3 Cdo Bde** | Stanley Racecourse | 3 |
| **5 Inf Bde** | Fitzroy Settlement | 3 |
| **40 Cdo Bde** | West Falkland | 2 |
| **Rapier resupply** | Stanley and San Carlos | 2 |
| **AQ Logistics** | Red Beach, Ajax Bay | 2 |
| **CASEVAC** | | 1 |

Towards the end of June, the 12 best aircraft were surveyed by a MARTSU team at the Port San Carlos settlement FOB and any necessary work on them was carried out aboard the Helicopter Support Ship 'Engadine' in San Carlos Water. That was to ensure that 847 Sqdn, as Garrison Squadron, would have fully serviceable aircraft on strength when it moved to Navy Point. The Squadron moved to that location, just north of Port Stanley and known locally as "The Camber", on 25 June. With the unit went XT451 '-/(Y)J' and XT460 '-/(Y)K', two FIR aircraft which had been transferred to 847 Sqdn at the Port San Carlos FOB on, or shortly after, 1 June *[see 845 Sqdn 'D' Flight for details]*. XT451 was later recoded '-/XN' as a replacement for XT469.

'Astronomer' arrived in Port William on 27 June with six Wessex HU.5's of 848 Sqdn 'D' Flight aboard as attrition replacements for those lost aboard 'Atlantic Conveyor'. The vessel began her duties supporting all Wessex operations in early July (taking over from 'Engadine') and around 1 July XT481 disembarked to Navy Point where it replaced XS479 as '-/XF' upon transfer from 848 Sqdn to 847 Sqdn. On 3 July the two helicopters seconded to 848 Sqdn 'D' Flight's element aboard 'Hermes' (XS507 and XT471) sailed with the carrier from Port William on their way back to the United Kingdom. XS516 and XT755 had been transferred to 'Engadine' at Port William on 5 July and sailed with the ship for the United Kingdom on 7 July (via San Carlos Water). She arrived at Devonport on 30 July where the two helicopters were flown off to Yeovilton the same day upon transfer to NASU.

At Port Stanley 'Atlantic Causeway' began loading aircraft around 10-12 July for the return passage. Damaged and unserviceable Wessex HU.5's were lowered by Chinook onto a Mexeflote at the stern and then towed onto the trailer deck. The following day two Mexeflotes were joined together to make a large floating landing platform at her stern and the operational HU.5's were flown onto it. Their blades folded, the helicopters were then towed inside the hull. The vessel moved to San Carlos Water late on 12 July to collect the Sea Kings of 825 Sqdn before sailing for the United Kingdom on 13 July. The 847 Sqdn aircraft aboard were:

| | | |
|---|---|---|
| XS514 '-/XA' | XT757 '-/XH' | XT480 '-/XQ' |
| XS515 '-/XB' | XS488 '-/XK' | XT486 '-/XR' |
| XT472 '-/XC' | XT469 '-/XN' | XT766 '-/XS' |
| XS479 '-/XF' | XS518 '-/XP' | |

'Atlantic Causeway' arrived at Devonport on 27 July, XS515 and XS518 flying off to Yeovilton the following day upon transfer to 845 and 707 Sqdn's respectively. The remaining helicopters were unloaded on 28 July and moved to a compound at Camel's Head (near HMS Drake) from where they were transferred to other units and departed by road as follows: XS488, XT469, XT480, XT486, XT766 (all transferred to 771 Sqdn on 1 August) had arrived at Culdrose by that date for survey, service issue or spares retrieval; XS479 (transferred to 707 Sqdn on 31 July) arrived at Yeovilton on 1 August; XS514 (transferred to 845 Sqdn on 28 July) arrived at Yeovilton on 1 August; XT472 (transferred to 845 Sqdn on 28 July) arrived at Yeovilton on 30 July; XT757 (transferred to NASU Yeovilton on 28 July) arrived there on 2 August.

Supported by 'Astronomer', the rest of the Squadron continued operations in the Falkland Islands where they were particularly involved in the transfer of stores, equipment and personnel aboard those ships of the Task Force which were returning home. XT773 was flown aboard 'Contender Bezant' on 2 September, sailing with her from Port William four days later to arrive at Southampton on 23 September. It had been off-loaded by 24 September (still coded '-/XT') and arrived by road at Yeovilton on 27 September on transfer to NASU.

By early September it would appear that some 847 Sqdn personnel began to wonder whether or not they had been forgotten by "their Lordships in the Admiralty". In fact, the Squadron was due to be relieved very shortly but that did not prevent other verses being added to the ode mentioned earlier, including the following:

> Now the warlords have had their meeting
> And decided what to do
> "You're certainly not forgotten,
> We know you're 84 Who?"

The Squadron was effectively disbanded on 24 September when Lt Cdr Mike Booth completed the formal handover (at Ascension Island) to 845 Sqdn Falkland Islands Detachment. 845 Sqdn had in fact taken over the operation of the aircraft, still based at Navy Point, on 14 September although the helicopters themselves were not officially transferred to its charge until 27 September. The Wessex HU.5's handed over were as follows:

| | | |
|---|---|---|
| XS491 '-/XM' | XT456 '-/XZ' | XT481 '-/XF' |
| XS506 '-/XE' | XT460 '-/(Y)K' | XT482 '-/XL' |
| XS523 '-/XJ' | XT466 '-/XV' | XT759 '-/XY' |
| XT451 '-/XN' | XT475 '-/XG' | |

During the conflict 847 Sqdn flew over 1,000 operational sorties. Mike Booth was awarded the DSC for his leadership and selfless effort in support of the ground forces. More importantly, it represented recognition for the unstinting effort given by all Squadron personnel in such difficult, dangerous and inhospitable terrain.

---

*847 Sqdn aircrew during Operation "Corporate" and their awards:*

### 'A' Flight

Lt Cdr M.D.Booth RN (CO) DSC; Lt Cdr N.R.Anstis RN; Lt Cdr R.P.Eitzen RN; Lt Cdr R.Flexman RN; Lt Cdr C.Sams RN; Lt Cdr M.Spencer RN; Lt R.Colborne RN; Lt N.A.Lees RN; Lt P.W. Skinner RN; Lt D.Smith RN; Lt J.H.Thomas RN; Lt G.W.A.Wallace RN; S/Lt C.H.R.Benson RN; S/Lt D.J.Kelly RN; S/Lt J.A.J.Spence RN; Maj A.G.E.Short RM; Capt R.P.D.Gilderson RM; CPOACMN R.Sharland; POACMN S.Bull; POACMN C.Eke; POACMN P.Mesney; POACMN R.Saunders; POACMN I.Weston; POACMN D.Worth; LACMN N.Cummins; LACMN A.Doughty; LACMN E.Grey; LACMN S.Larsen; LACMN I.McKie; LACMN J.Smyth; Cpl M.Brickell.

### 'B' Flight

Lt Cdr P.W.Hails RN (Flt Cdr); Lt W.P.Harrower RN; Lt T.J.Hughes RN; Lt P.McIntosh RN; CPOACMN W.R.Tuttey; POACMN Clamp.

---

# 848 NAVAL AIR SQUADRON

Commanded by Lt Cdr D.E.P.Baston, 848 Sqdn was reformed at Yeovilton on 19 April, essentially upgrading 707 Sqdn to front line status. 12 Wessex HU.5's were transferred from 707 Sqdn to the new unit, all in the overall Matt Olive Drab colour-scheme but with White serials, codes, deck-letters and ROYAL NAVY titles along with Red/Blue roundels. Work began immediately to apply wartime markings, deleting the deck letters and titling in Olive Drab while the serials and codes were overpainted in Black. All 12 aircraft had appeared in toned-down markings by 23 April as follows:

| | | |
|---|---|---|
| XT756 '-/WM' | XT771 '-/WR' | XS517 '-/WV' |
| XS499 '-/WN' | XT476 '-/WS' | XS486 '-/WW' |
| XS495 '-/WP' | XS512 '-/WT' | XS489 '-/WY' |
| XS480 '-/WQ' | XT483 '-/WU' | XT463 '-/WZ' |

XT482 '-/WL' joined 707 Sqdn on 27 April but was passed on to the newly-formed 847 Sqdn on 6 May. Two changes to the above complement also occurred in mid-May, XS520 '-/WZ' joining the unit on 17 May followed by XT760 on 21 May (the latter being coded '-/WV' two days later). They replaced XT463 and XS517 respectively, both of which returned to 707 Sqdn on 18 May.

848 Squadron was divided into four Flights for deployment on four Task Force ships. The Flights embarked their respective vessels with the following helicopters:

| | | |
|---|---|---|
| 'A' Flight 'Regent' | XT756 '-/WM' | XS486 '-/WW' |
| 'B' Flight 'Olna' | XT771 '-/WR' | XS489 '-/WY' |
| 'C' Flight 'Olwen' | XT760 '-/WV' | XS520 '-/WZ' |
| 'D' Flight 'Atlantic Conveyor' | XS499 '-/WN' XT476 '-/WS' XS495 '-/WP' XS512 '-/WT' XS480 '-/WQ' XT483 '-/WU' | |

*Note: XS512 & XT483 were last-minute replacements for XT463 & XT771*

# 'A' FLIGHT

The Flight was formed on 17 April (while still under the auspices of 707 Sqdn), embarking 'Regent' in Plymouth Sound on 19 April with Wessex HU.5's XS486 and XT756 prior to the ship sailing later that day for Ascension Island and the South Atlantic. As she sailed south, the Flight began a work-up period which lasted from 19 April to 30 April (the day after 'Regent' reached Ascension Island) and included practice GPMG firing on 28 April. On 1 May both helicopters were noted on HDS duties at Wideawake before sailing south with the ship the next day. On 4 May the opportunity to practice 2in RP firings was taken, using XT756. 'Regent' entered the TEZ on 12 May and began Fleet Replenishment duties around the Task Force prior to joining the Amphibious Force which was assembling and stocking up for the future landings. The Flight commenced intense HDS and VERTREP operations, ferrying stores, ammunition and weapons to the many vessels in the CVBG.

Those operations continued until 8 June when 'Regent' was dispatched to South Georgia, arriving three days later for a rendezvous with 'Olmeda'. On 15 June 'A' Flight was required to transfer from 'Regent' to 'Olmeda' with the two Wessex HU.5's in exchange for one of the 824 Sqdn 'A' Flight Sea Kings. 'Olmeda' was then to sail with 'Endurance' and 'Yarmouth' for Southern Thule and Operation "Keyhole". Unfortunately, XT756 needed an engine change and remained on board 'Regent', while XS486 embarked 'Endurance' on 17 June and was armed with 2in RP's for the operation. Trial landings had been made aboard 'Endurance' in the Cumberland Bays, South Georgia and it was found that a Wessex could not only land on her deck but could also be stowed in the hangar along with both of her Wasp HAS.1's. During that Op-

eration XS486 had its code letters crudely "washed" out. It was flown to Southern Thule on 19 June to insert a reconnaissance party, then took part in the mock landings on Cook Island later in the day. On 20 June the aircraft (crewed by Lt Cdr Blight, Lt Mason and POACMN Hogan) was used to insert troops on Southern Thule, this time to recapture the Island by force if necessary. In the event, the Island's ten Argentine occupants surrendered without a shot being fired. 'Endurance' returned to South Georgia from the successful operation on 24 June and the Wessex re-embarked 'Regent'. Two days later it was flown on a reconnaissance sortie over Leith harbour before 'Regent' sailed on 28 June to rejoin the CVBG on 1 July. The Flight was then engaged in HDS and VERTREP sorties, while the ship anchored off Port Stanley from 6-13 July. On 10 July XS486 moved to 'Atlantic Causeway' (also lying off Port Stanley) for the passage home. It sailed with the ship on 12 July (via San Carlos Water on 13 July), arriving at Devonport on 27 July. XS486 was flown off to Yeovilton the next day, being transferred to 707 Sqdn upon arrival. 'Regent' remained on station with the Flight (and XT756) until 24 August, when she sailed for the United Kingdom. The helicopter was flown off to Yeovilton on 12 September upon transfer to NASU, 'Regent' arriving at Rosyth three days later. In all, the Flight carried out over 2,000 VERTREP missions in 450 hours of flying.

---

*848 Sqdn 'A' Flight aircrew during Operation "Corporate": Lt Cdr C.J.Blight RN (Flt Cdr); Lt T.Mason RN; Lt P.Thame RN; POACMN M.D.Hogan; POACMN P.R.Mansell.*

---

# 'B' FLIGHT

The Flight was formed on 19 April (allocated Wessex HU.5 XS489) with a projected embarkation date aboard 'Olna' of 22 April. However, as the vessel made its way back from Gulf Patrol in the Middle East, the embarkation date was twice put back. On 20 April the date was changed to 27 April, while on 23 April it was further delayed until 10 May. Meanwhile, 'Olna' had arrived at Portland on 22 April to be replenished and re-stored, 'B' Flight making a visit to the ship that day followed by special training operations from Yeovilton on 23 April. The ship left Portland on 26 April and arrived at Portsmouth the following day to complete re-storing. Allocated XT771 on 29 April, the Flight operated from Lee-on-Solent on 7 May to VERTREP last-minute stores to 'Olna', the ship then moving to the Spithead buoy two days later. On 10 May the Flight embarked from Yeovilton with XS489 landing on at 1030Z followed by XT771 at 1100Z. The vessel sailed for Ascension Island at 1115Z the same day and joined the 'Bristol' Group on 13

May.

The Flight commenced its work-up and, after passing Ascension Island on 19 May, carried out practice SS.11 and AS.12 missile firings at a splash target on 21 May, scoring five hits out of eight missiles fired from XT771. 2in RP firings were practised from XS489 on the following day, while on 23 May the Flight recovered four loads from Hercules air-drops. 'Olna' joined the Task Force on 28 May but immediately detached to the east for minor engine repairs. She rejoined the CVBG on 30 May and commenced her tanker duties and they continued until 2200Z on 7 June when she detached to San Carlos Water, arriving at 1200Z the following day. It soon became apparent that the majority of the Flight's tasking would be HDS and VERTREP sorties, therefore the SS.11/AS.12 and 2in RP equipment was progressively stripped from the two aircraft to give them more payload. While 'Olna' was anchored in San Carlos Water, the aircrew also provided some air defence for the ship by man-

**Above** *Hovering over the flight-deck of 'Endurance' (reportedly on 19.6.82 off Southern Thule) and near the tug 'Salvageman' is Wessex HU.5 XS486 '–/WW' of 848 Squadron 'A' Flight. XS486 was temporarily detached from its parent ship, 'Regent', to the ice patrol vessel from 17–24.6.82 to take part in the retaking of Southern Thule in the South Sandwich Islands (the island had been illegally occupied by Argentina since late 1976). The Union Flag* **(Inset)** *flies over Southern Thule following the surrender on 20.6.82 of the ten Argentine occupants (nine of whom were military personnel) led by Teniente de Corbeta Martinez. (Ministry of Defence).*

**Left** *On the northern shore of Stanley Harbour lies a fuel storage area at Navy Point (known locally as The Camber). It was here that 847 Squadron established itself on 25.6.82 as the Falkland Islands Garrison Squadron. In 9.82 occupation was ceded to the Wessex HU.5's (mostly ex 847 Squadron) of 845 Squadron FI Detachment and the Sea King HAR.3's of 202 Squadron. This photograph, believed taken in late 7.82, shows nine HU.5's parked by the shoreline and further inland.*

*(Ministry of Defence)*

ning four GPMG's mounted above the hangar and the bridge. HDS and VERTREP duties were carried out but the Flight did not detach ashore. 'Olna' sailed for the TRALA on 10 June to refuel from the STUFT tankers before returning to San Carlos Water on 13 June.

Following the Argentine surrender, 'Olna' continued her tanker duties around the CVBG and the anchorages, with the Flight still engaged in HDS and VERTREP sorties. On 21 August the ship detached 800 miles north of the Falkland Islands for a rendezvous with 'Illustrious' three days later, then waited for 'Invincible'. The latter rendezvous took place on 31 August, after which 'Olna' began her return journey to the United Kingdom. 'B'

Flight disembarked to Yeovilton with its two Wessex HU.5's on 16 September prior to the ship arriving at Portsmouth the following day. During Operation "Corporate" XS489 flew 167.00 hrs and XT771 flew 223.20 hrs.

---

*848 Sqdn 'B' Flight aircrew during Operation "Corporate": Lt M.D.Salter RN (Flt Cdr); Lt P.Bowden RN; S/Lt D.Coles RN; POACMN J.P.Grinney; POACMN R.Tarrant.*

---

# 'C' FLIGHT

The Flight was formed on 19 April and designated for service aboard 'Olwen', but at that time the ship was on refit at Gibraltar so embarkation was planned provisionally for mid-June. She sailed on 7 June, arrived at Devonport on 10 June and left for the South Atlantic on 16 June, on which date the Flight embarked from Yeovilton (via HMS Drake, Plymouth) with Wessex HU.5's XS520 and XT760. The Argentine surrender had been received two days earlier, and on 18 June (after operations in the Portland area) 'Olwen' joined the "Task Force Two" vessels 'Apollo', 'Birmingham' and 'Southampton'.

The Group arrived at Ascension Island on 28 June and 'C' Flight went ashore from 1-4 July to assist 845 Sqdn 'D' Flight at Wideawake and then remained there until 9 July moving troops from ship to shore. 'Olwen' sailed south from the Island on 9 July in company with 'Norland' and began her tanker duties, refuelling other ships in transit to and from the Falkland Islands while the Flight practised GPMG, AS.12 and 2in RP firings. 'Olwen' embarked the change-over garrison for South Georgia whilst off Port Stanley on 21 July, sailing on 22 July to arrive at Grytviken on 24 July. She departed for Port Stanley the same day, arriving there on 26 July to off-load troops and stores before detaching to the CVBG later in the day. The Flight carried out HDS and VERTREP sorties within the CVBG from 27 July to 6 August. When 'Olwen' anchored in San Carlos Water on 7 August the two helicopters spent three days on tasking with 847 Sqdn at Navy Point. The ship rejoined the CVBG on 10 August, the load-lifting sorties continuing until she anchored in Berkeley Sound on 18 August, whereupon the Flight went ashore once again for further tasking with 847 Sqdn. Additional tasking within the

CVBG was carried out from 21-30 August, 2-6 September and 17-25 September, while the Flight operated ashore on 1 September and from 9-16 September.

When 'Olwen' sailed for the United Kingdom, 'C' Flight transferred to 'Fort Austin' on 27 September (the ship then being on her second deployment to the South Atlantic). She anchored in Berkeley Sound three days later for the Flight to carry out VERTREP tasks ashore before joining the CVBG on 1 October. Load-lifting tasks continued as the ship transferred stores from the Falkland Islands to vessels in the CVBG. 'Fort Austin' was anchored at Port San Carlos from 4-6 October and in Port William Sound on 8 October and from 10-12 October. The remaining time was spent in the CVBG until, on 13 October, the Flight was instructed to embark 'Illustrious'. Following a full day's VERTREP operations to the carrier, the two helicopters moved aboard on 16 October, on which date 'C' Flight effectively disbanded with the transfer of its aircraft to a detachment of 845 Sqdn. 848 Sqdn 'C' Flight personnel left RAF Stanley by air for Ascension Island on 21 October, returning to Brize Norton the following day. The Flight had accumulated 391 hours on the two Wessex HU.5's during the deployment, lifting 1,230 underslung loads, transporting 1,716 passengers and carrying out 772 deck landings.

---

*848 Sqdn 'C' Flight aircrew scheduled for Operation "Corporate" but deployed post-14 June 1982: Lt N.R.Metcalfe RN (Flt Cdr); Lt A.J.Jeffrey RN; Lt A.P.Hooker RN; CPOACMN W.Charlton; POACMN M.I.Johnson.*

---

# 'D' FLIGHT

The Flight was formed on 20 April as a Battle Casualty Replacement Flight, to embark 'Atlantic Conveyor' with six Wessex HU.5's. XS480, XS495, XS499, XT463, XT476 and XT771 duly left Yeovilton on 24 April for the Royal Marines landing area at Longroom, Plymouth,

from where they were to be ferried out to the ship in Plymouth Sound the next day. Unfortunately, XT771 needed minor repairs and was flown back to Yeovilton that evening to be replaced by XS512. In addition, XT463 suffered FOD and XT483 was flown to Longroom on 25

April in its place (XT463 returned to Yeovilton the following evening). The complement restored, all six helicopters were flown out to 'Atlantic Conveyor' on 25 April and sailed with the ship for Ascension Island and the South Atlantic that day. Five of the six aircraft were placed in temporary storage while the sixth remained on flying duties for HDS and communications tasks. XT483 was noted on HDS duties at Wideawake on 2 May, as was XS512 on 5 May, before the ship departed Ascension Island on 7 May to join the CVBG 11 days later.

'Fort Austin' was scheduled to embark four 826 Sqdn Sea King HAS.5's from 'Hermes' on 17 May, releasing space aboard the carrier for the planned arrival on 18 May of the Sea Harriers and Harriers from 'Atlantic Conveyor'. In exchange, Wessex XT468 '-/(Y)D' of 845 Sqdn 'B' Flight was to be transferred from 'Fort Austin' to 'Hermes'. This duly occurred as planned on 17 May but congestion on the 'Hermes' flight-deck meant that the Wessex had to be moved to 'Atlantic Conveyor' on 20 May for secondment to 848 Sqdn and "garaging". There it joined XT765, also an 845 Sqdn 'B' Flight aircraft which had embarked from 'Invincible' on 19 May for temporary storage, but that Wessex was flown to 'Stromness' on 21 May by Lt P.C.Manley of 848 Sqdn 'D' Flight.

The Flight was scheduled to go ashore on the evening of 25 May, but that did not take place as 'Atlantic Conveyor' was hit by an Exocet missile at 1936Z that day 90 miles north-east of Port Stanley as she headed towards Falkland Sound. All six 'D' Flight Wessex HU.5's were destroyed in the ensuing fire, although XT468 was fortunately airborne on a test flight when the missile struck. After picking up survivors, it recovered to 'Hermes'. XS512 was unfortunate not to have been saved as, shortly before the ship was hit, it had completed an engine run. However, due to the heat from the fire, a flight crew was unable to reach the helicopter and fly it to another ship. At the carrier's request, a 'D' Flight element (under the command of Lt I. Bryant) was transferred aboard 'Hermes' on 28 May and on that date XT468 was seconded from 845 Sqdn 'B' Flight, retaining the code '-/(Y)D'. However, that particular Wessex was not entirely suited to the required HDS role as it was fitted out as a gunship, so on 3 June it was exchanged for XT471 '-/XW' from 847 Sqdn aboard 'Atlantic Causeway'. XT471 was also seconded, remaining on 847 Sqdn charge and retaining the code '-/XW'. Following the attack on the 'Atlantic Conveyor' there was a redistribution of Flight aircrew. Peter Manley remained ashore flying XT765 and other 845 Sqdn helicopters, later carrying out the daring attack on Stanley Town Hall [see 845 Sqdn 'A' Flight]. The remaining aircrew embarked the tanker 'British Tay' on 27 May for passage to Ascension Island, arriving at Brize Norton by air on 7 June. A second element of 'D' Flight (Lt R.Miles and S/Lt J.Thomas) embarked 'Tidepool' for HDS duties on 10 June, allocated Wessex HU.5 XT486 '-/XR' of 847 Sqdn from 'Atlantic Causeway'. The aircraft went to 'Fort Grange' before embarking 'Tidepool' the next day. 845 Sqdn 'E' Flight aboard the latter vessel had disembarked earlier in the conflict to operate ashore.

'Tidepool' operated in the TRALA from 11-14 June, with XT486 heavily engaged in HDS operations around the various vessels and in airdrop pick-ups. On 14 June the helicopter was detached to 'Glamorgan' (TRALA "manager" at that time) for air-drop pick-ups as her Wessex HAS.3 had been destroyed in an Exocet attack two days earlier. XT486 attempted to return to 'Tidepool' the same day, but due to the rapidly deteriorating weather it was forced to remain aboard 'Glamorgan' and had to be left on deck as the vessel's hangar had been very badly damaged in the attack. During a particularly severe storm on 15 June when the wind reached Gale Force 9, the Wessex suffered CAT.4 damage with two broken main rotors plus a damaged rotor head and a collapsed mainwheel tyre. When 'Glamorgan' arrived in San Carlos Water on 18 June XT486 was airlifted ashore by 18 Sqdn Chinook HC.1 ZA705 the following day and later joined the other surplus 847 Sqdn aircraft for passage home aboard 'Atlantic Causeway'.

In order to replace XT486 the 'D' Flight crew transferred by Gemini boat from 'Glamorgan' to 'Atlantic Causeway' on 16 June to collect XS507 '-/XU' from 847 Sqdn. The Wessex was flown to 'Tidepool' the same day and operations continued from the ship until 1 July, although XS507 remained on 847 Sqdn charge. On 27 June it was decided that the 'Tidepool' aircraft would move to 'Hermes' for the homeward journey, so on 1 July the Wessex embarked the carrier to join XT471, thereby centralising 'D' Flight's operations aboard the vessel under the command of Lt R.Miles. By that time the Flight had been nicknamed "The Nomads" due to its constant travelling from ship to ship. In the meantime 'Tidepool' (having lost her aircraft) left the area to complete her handover to the Chilean Navy, to whom she had been en route when the conflict began. By way of a parting gesture, the two Wessex HU.5's joined the 'Hermes'-based aircraft on their "Goodbye" flypast over Port Stanley on 3 July. The carrier sailed from Port William for the United Kingdom later that day, arriving at Portsmouth on 21 July. XS507 and XT471 were flown off to Yeovilton the following day upon transfer from 847 Sqdn to 707 Sqdn.

With the loss of the six 'D' Flight Wessex HU.5's aboard 'Atlantic Conveyor' on 25 May, it was decided to deploy an attrition replacement batch of six aircraft to the South Atlantic for use by 'D' Flight. On 28 May the Ministry of Defence made enquiries about the schedule of 'Astronomer', which was in fact due in Felixstowe that evening from the Caribbean. The ship was duly requisitioned as a replacement for 'Atlantic Conveyor' and after unloading moved to Devonport, arriving on 31 May for her conversion to a mini-NASU. The objective was to install sufficient workshop machinery for the vessel to cope with everything from routine helicopter maintenance to in-depth structural repairs.

Reserve Wessex HU.5's had already been drawn from storage at Wroughton for allocation to the depleted second-line units. XS481 and XT467 were delivered by road to NASU Culdrose on 10/11 May to be made airworthy again for 771 Sqdn (still coded 'CU/522' and 'CU/525' respectively from earlier service with the unit). On 14 May XS498 'VL/WQ' (ex-707 Sqdn) and XS522 marked '-/-/5' (ex-772 Sqdn 'PO/635') arrived by road at NASU Yeovilton where both had the low-visibility markings applied before delivery to 772 Sqdn at Portland on 28 and 27 May respectively. Their time at Portland was very short-lived, however.

XS481 (still coded 'CU/522') and XT467 (code (525) not worn but used as a call-sign) were flown to Yeovilton from Culdrose on 2 June. Both of them were transferred to 848 Sqdn 'D' Flight that day along with XT481 '-/ZE' from 707 Sqdn which was already in the low-visibility scheme. On 4 June XS498 and XS522 were allotted to 'D' Flight and flown from Portland to Yeovilton the next day, still uncoded but using call-signs (623) and (625) respectively. Full complement was reached on 5 June with the transfer of XT463 '-/ZB' from 707 Sqdn (again in the low-visibility scheme). By the time that the six aircraft departed Yeovilton for HMS Raleigh (Torpoint) on 6 June, XT467 had also been repainted with low-visibility markings but XS481 still retained its old code 'CU/522'. The Flight embarked 'Astronomer' in Plymouth Sound on 7 June and sailed with the ship the following day for Ascension Island and the South Atlantic.

During the passage south the Argentine forces on the Falkland Islands surrendered. By the time that the ship arrived in Port William on 27 June her role had been changed, relieving 'Engadine' as the Helicopter Support Ship South Atlantic. Over the following few months her well-equipped workshops earned the vessel the nickname "HMS Incredible". 'D' Flight's need for additional helicopters had dissipated following the surrender, a pool of aircraft then being available for use by 848 and other Wessex squadrons on the Islands. XS522 and XT463 appear to have remained on board the ship, whilst the other four aircraft are believed to have flown off around 1 July to Navy Point. XT481 immediately joined 847 Sqdn and was recoded '-/XF' to replace XS479, while XS498 had only a short stay as it was loaded aboard 'Atlantic Causeway' off Port Stanley around 11 July together with XS522 and XT463. The ship sailed from San Carlos Water on 13 July and arrived at Devonport on 27 July, by which time all three helicopters were uncoded. XS498 was flown off to Yeovilton on 28 July upon transfer to 707 Sqdn, while on the same day XS522 and XT463 were off-

loaded and moved to a compound at Camel's Head, near HMS Drake. Both aircraft were transferred to 707 Sqdn on 30 July and arrived by road at Yeovilton the same day.

The remaining pair continued operations from Navy Point until 2 September when both XS481 and XT467 were airlifted aboard 'Contender Bezant' off Port William by an 18 Sqdn Chinook HC.1. The ship sailed for the United Kingdom on 6 September, arriving at Southampton on 23 September where both helicopters were unloaded the following day (by then uncoded). The pair arrived at Yeovilton by road upon transfer from 848 Sqdn to NASU (XT467 on 27 September and XS481 on 28 September).

---

*848 Sqdn 'D' Flight aircrew during Operation "Corporate" and their awards:*

### Main party

*Lt Cdr D.E.P.Baston RN (Flt Cdr); Lt I.Chapman RN; Lt N.Kidd RN; Lt P.C.Manley RN MID; Lt P.Schwartz RN; Lt S.Henley RN; Lt B.Reynoldson RN; CPOACMN R.A.Duriez; POACMN I.K.Harris; Cpl K.Sturgess.*

### Support personnel

*Aircrew embarked in 'Norland' and subsequently detached during Operation "Corporate": Lt I.Bryant RN (to 'Hermes'); Lt R.Miles RN (to 'Tidepool'); S/Lt D.Ockleton RN (to 'Hermes'); S/Lt J.Thomas RN (to 'Tidepool'); POACMN S.P.Woolley (to 'Tidepool'); POACMN J.Burns (to 'Hermes'); LACMN M.F.Moreby (to 'Tidepool').*

---

*In wartime unofficial markings are sometimes applied to aircraft. They range from a few crudely applied words to sophisticated and colourful artwork. This is the artwork applied to two of the Wessex HU.5's flown in the Falklands conflict.*

**Left** *"848 NOMADS" was painted in White just below the cockpit on the starboard side of XT471, an 847 Squadron aircraft which was seconded to 848 Squadron during the War. A dictionary definition of "nomad" is "a member of a tribe wandering from place to place". An apt decription of 848 Squadron, its Flights, aircraft and personnel.*

*(Peter J. Cooper)*

**Right** *XT759, which served with 847 Squadron, had these markings painted on the starboard side cabin door. The Red and Yellow bird clutching the vibrator is "Buzby", a creature who appeared in telephone advertisements on British television. The connotation becomes obvious when reading the inscription. It also helps to know that a "buzz" in Royal Navy parlance means a "rumour".*

*(Michael I. Draper)*

# INDIVIDUAL AIRCRAFT DETAILS

The low-vis scheme applied to each Wessex HAS.3 is explained under the individual aircraft history.

The low-vis scheme applied to the Wessex HU.5's consisted of Matt Olive Drab overall with Red/Blue roundels, devoid of ROYAL NAVY titles and with the serials and codes applied in Black. Exceptions to this (if any) are explained under each individual aircraft history.

*Examples of abbreviations used for markings and their meanings:*

'ON/314'  *Deck-letters for 'Olna' and side-code worn in full.*

'-/WM'  *Deck-letters not allocated; Squadron letter and individual aircraft letter worn in full.*

'-/(Y)T'  *Deck-letters not allocated; Squadron letter not worn; individual aircraft letter worn.*

(406)  *Neither deck letters 'AN' for 'Antrim' nor side-code worn.*

---

**XM328** HAS.3          *Deployed post-14.6.82*

On 15.6.82 with 737 Sqdn at Portland coded 'PO/653'. Allocated to 'Antrim' Flight 9.8.82 (replacing XP142) and recoded 'AN/406' in the low-vis scheme (RAF Blue-Grey overall with Red/Blue roundels; ROYAL NAVY titles believed deleted; serials, code and deck letters all Black). Sailed with 'Antrim' from Portsmouth 8.11.82 en route for the South Atlantic. Transferred to 772 Sqdn 'Antrim' Flt 4.2.83 with the disbandment of 737 Sqdn. Returned to Portsmouth with the ship 25.3.83 and disembarked to Portland.

**XM837** HAS.3

On 29.3.82 with 737 Sqdn 'Glamorgan' Flt, coded 'GL/400' and named "Willie", operating out of Gibraltar on Exercise "Springtrain". Detached directly from the Exercise to the South Atlantic with the ship 2.4.82. Prior to arrival at Ascension on 11.4.82 it had been repainted in a low-vis scheme (RAF Blue-Grey overall with Red/Blue roundels; ROYAL NAVY titles and serials overpainted Black; deck letters deleted). The code is believed to have been removed, but remained allocated (400).

Hangared aboard 'Glamorgan' (operating not more than 23 miles east of Port Stanley) on 12.6.82 when a land-launched Exocet missile hit the ship, striking the flight-deck but failing to explode. Instead, it bounced into the hangar where its unspent fuel continued to burn, setting fire to the hangar and totally destroying the aircraft. Its remains were ditched overboard.

**XP142** HAS.3

On 29.3.82 with 737 Sqdn 'Antrim' Flt coded 'AN/406' and named "Humphrey", operating out of Gibraltar on Exercise "Springtrain". Detached directly from the Exercise to the South Atlantic with the ship 2.4.82. Prior to arrival at Ascension on 10.4.82 it had been repainted in a low-vis scheme (RAF Blue-Grey overall with very dull Red/Dark Blue [almost

black] roundels; deck letters deleted; ROYAL NAVY titles, serials and the name "Humphrey" on the nose all overpainted Black). The code was removed but remained allocated (406).

In appalling weather conditions on 22.4.82, during the evacuation of Special Forces off the Fortuna Glacier (South Georgia), one of two accompanying 845 Sqdn 'C' Flt Wessex HU.5's (XT464) crashed, followed shortly afterwards by the other (XT473). "Humphrey" (piloted by Lt Cdr Stanley) ferried some survivors from XT464 back to 'Antrim', returning later for the remainder plus the additional survivors from XT473. On 23.4.82 "Humphrey" was involved in another rescue mission, winching up four survivors and equipment from a Special Forces Gemini boat adrift off the Cumberland Bays, South Georgia.

On 25.4.82, whilst being flown by Lt Cdr Stanley and crew, the Argentine submarine 'Santa Fe' was depth-charged shortly after she had departed from Grytviken, South Georgia. The charges exploded close to the port side. That and subsequent attacks by other Ships' Flights forced the damaged submarine to return to Grytviken.

Suffered splinter damage which ruptured the fuel tanks when 'Antrim' was attacked by three Daggers from Grupo 6 on 21.5.82 when near the entrance to San Carlos Water. Airworthy again by 26.5.82 following repairs.

Sailed with 'Antrim' from Port Howard, West Falkland on 29.6.82 for return to the UK, arriving at Portsmouth on 17.7.82. Flown off to Portland 18.7.82, from where it was transferred (and delivered by road) to the Fleet Air Arm Museum 26.7.82 for the Falkland Islands Exhibition. On display in the Museum by 30.7.82 and still resident in 7.85.

*Dayglo Red rescue and mission symbols were applied to the starboard main cabin door [see photograph], together with a Dayglo submarine annotated "Santa Fe". A Dayglo mouse on a playing card was stuck on the nose under the name "Humphrey".*

**XS479** HU.5

On 29.3.82 in storage at Wroughton coded 'PO/623' (ex-772 Sqdn Portland). Transferred to NASU Yeovilton on 23.4.82 and arrived there by road 27.4.82 still coded 'PO/623'. Officially transferred to 707 Sqdn on 7.5.82 prior to issue to 847 Sqdn on 11.5.82. By that date, it had been painted in the low-vis scheme and coded '-/XF'. Allocated to 'B' Flight, it was flown from Yeovilton to HMS Raleigh (Torpoint) on 13.5.82 and embarked 'Atlantic Causeway' the same day in Plymouth Sound, sailing with her for the South Atlantic on 14.5.82. Disembarked to the FOB at Port San Carlos settlement on 1.6.82 and later operated from Teal Inlet, Fitzroy and elsewhere, prior to moving to Navy Point on 25.6.82. Replaced as '-/XF' c1.7.82 by XT481 which had arrived at Port William on 27.6.82 aboard 'Astronomer'. Loaded aboard the 'Atlantic Causeway' off Port Stanley c12.7.82 and sailed with the ship from San Carlos Water 13.7.82, arriving at Devonport 27.7.82. Offloaded 28.7.82 to a compound at Camel's Head (near HMS Drake) still coded '-/XF'. Officially transferred to 707 Sqdn from 847 Sqdn on 31.7.82 and removed by road to Yeovilton on 1.8.82, arriving there the same day.

**XS480** HU.5

On 29.3.82 with NASU Yeovilton coded '-/VT' (ex-846 Sqdn Yeovilton). Transferred from NASU to 707 Sqdn 18.4.82 and on to the newly-formed 848 Sqdn 19/20.4.82. Painted in the low-vis scheme by 20.4.82 and coded '-/WQ'. Allocated to 'D' Flt, it departed Yeovilton for Longroom, Plymouth on 24.4.82 and embarked 'Atlantic Conveyor' 25.4.82 in Plymouth Sound prior to sailing with the ship that day for Ascension and the South Atlantic.

On 25.5.82, whilst the ship was some 90 miles north-east of Port Stanley (at 50°37'S 56°10'W) en route to Falkland Sound, 'Atlantic Conveyor' was hit by an Exocet missile (one of two launched from a pair of 2 Escuadrilla Super Etendards) and caught fire. The Wessex was consumed by the fire, its remains sinking with the ship on 30.5.82.

**XS481** HU.5

Delivered by air from Culdrose to Wroughton for storage 30.3.82 coded 'CU/522' (ex-771 Sqdn Culdrose). Transferred by road from Wroughton to NASU Culdrose on 10/11.5.82 (upon allocation to 771 Sqdn) to be made airworthy. Flown from Culdrose to Yeovilton on 2.6.82 upon transfer from 771 Sqdn to 848 Sqdn 'D' Flt that day as an attrition replacement for those aircraft lost aboard 'Atlantic Conveyor'. Still coded 'CU/522', it left Yeovilton 6.6.82 for HMS Raleigh (Torpoint) and embarked 'Astronomer' in Plymouth Sound 7.6.82 prior to the ship's departure on 8.6.82 for the South Atlantic. Arrived at Port William on board the vessel on 27.6.82, from where it is believed to have been off-loaded to Navy Point c1.7.82. Airlifted aboard 'Contender Bezant' (reportedly from 'Astronomer') off Port William by Chinook 2.9.82 and departed with the ship for the UK on 6.9.82. Arrived with the vessel at Southampton on 23.9.82 (by then uncoded in the low-vis scheme) and was off-loaded by 24.9.82, being taken to Yeovilton by road that day (via Lee-on-Solent) where it arrived on 27.9.82. Officially transferred from 848 Sqdn to NASU on 28.9.82.

**XS483** HU.5

On 29.3.82 with 845 Sqdn at Yeovilton in the low-vis scheme coded '-/(Y)T'. Allocated to 'A' Flight and left Yeovilton for Rosyth on 2.4.82 to embark 'Resource' prior to the vessel's departure 6.4.82 for Ascension and the South Atlantic. During the ship's passage down the English Channel on 7.4.82, it was flown to Yeovilton (via Lee-on-Solent) for supplies, returning to 'Resource' the same day via Portland. Temporarily detached to 'Glamorgan' on 30.4.82 as an armed escort for 'Alacrity' Flt's Lynx XZ736 during NGS spotting duties on 1.5.82.

Two Argentine land-based Tigercat missiles were reportedly fired at it on 1.5.82 but missed. Both aircraft returned unscathed to their respective ships.

Returned to 'Resource' 2.5.82. Disembarked to the FOB at Old House Creek, San Carlos 24.5.82 before moving to the Port San Carlos settlement FOB on 30.5.82. Based at Port Stanley Racecourse from 15.6.82 until re-embarking 'Resource' off Port Stanley on 24.6.82 for return to the UK via South Georgia. It disembarked to Yeovilton (via Culdrose) 19.7.82 prior to the ship's arrival at Devonport later that day.

**XS486** HU.5

On 29.3.82 with 707 Sqdn at Yeovilton coded 'VL/WW'. Transferred to 848 Sqdn 'A' Flt 19.4.82 and repainted that day in low-vis markings and coded '-/WW'. Left Yeovilton on 19.4.82 to embark 'Regent' in Plymouth Sound, sailing with the ship later in the day for Ascension and the South Atlantic. Noted at Wideawake 1.5.82 on HDS duties prior to

sailing south with the ship the following day. Departed the TEZ with the vessel on 8.6.82 for South Georgia, arriving there on 11.6.82. Temporarily transferred to 'Endurance' from 17-24.6.82 for Operation "Keyhole", the re-taking of Southern Thule. For that Operation the code letters were temporarily painted out with an Olive Drab "wash". After returning to 'Regent', it remained with the vessel until 10.7.82 when transferred to 'Atlantic Causeway' off Port Stanley for return to the UK. Arrived with the ship at Devonport 27.7.82 (still coded '-/WW') and flown off to Yeovilton 28.7.82 for transfer upon arrival to 707 Sqdn.

**XS488** HU.5

Delivered from Portland to Wroughton for storage 31.3.82 coded 'PO/625' (ex-772 Sqdn Portland). Transferred to NASU Yeovilton on 23.4.82 and delivered there by road 27/28.4.82, still coded 'PO/625'. On 5.5.82 it was painted in the low-vis scheme and coded '-/XK'. Officially transferred to 707 Sqdn on 5.5.82 for issue to the newly-formed 847 Sqdn on 6.5.82. Allocated to 'B' Flight, it departed Yeovilton for HMS Raleigh (Torpoint) on 13.5.82, embarking 'Atlantic Causeway' that day in Plymouth Sound prior to departing with the ship for the South Atlantic on 14.5.82. Disembarked to the FOB at Port San Carlos settlement on 1.6.82 and later operated from Teal Inlet, Fitzroy and elsewhere prior to moving to Navy Point on 25.6.82. Loaded on 'Atlantic Causeway' off Port Stanley c12.7.82 and departed with the vessel from San Carlos Water on 13.7.82, arriving at Devonport on 27.7.82. Still coded '-/XK', it was off-loaded on 28.7.82 and taken to a compound at Camel's Head (near HMS Drake). Removed by road on 31.7.82 to Culdrose, arriving the same day. Officially transferred from 847 Sqdn to 771 Sqdn at Culdrose on 1.8.82.

**XS489** HU.5

On 29.3.82 with 707 Sqdn at Yeovilton coded 'VL/WY'. Transferred to 848 Sqdn at Yeovilton on 19.4.82 and the low-vis scheme had been applied by 21.4.82 (coded '-/WY'). Allocated to 'B' Flight (wef 19.4.82), it embarked 'Olna' at Spithead from Yeovilton on 10.5.82 and sailed with her the same day for the South Atlantic. Remained with the ship until 'Olna' returned to the UK, disembarking to Yeovilton 16.9.82 prior to the vessel's arrival at Portsmouth on 17.9.82.

**XS491** HU.5

On 29.3.82 with Lee-on-Solent SAR Flight coded 'LS/812'. Transferred to 847 Sqdn on 5.5.82 and delivered by air the same day from Lee-on-Solent to Yeovilton, where it immediately went into the spray-shop to receive the low-vis scheme. Transferred (uncoded) to 845 Sqdn 7.5.82 and prepared for air transportation to Ascension upon allocation to 'D' Flight (the Ascension Island Base Flight). Departed uncoded on 9.5.82 aboard Heavylift Belfast G-BEPS, arriving at

Wideawake 12.5.82 where it was assembled and test flown by Naval Party 1222. No known code allocated whilst with 845 Sqdn 'D' Flt. Transferred to 847 Sqdn 'A' Flt aboard 'Engadine' (lying off the Island) on 25.5.82 in exchange for XT764 '-/XM'. Coded '-/XM' and sailed with the ship for the TEZ on 26.5.82. Disembarked to the FOB at Port San Carlos settlement on 9.6.82 and operated from Teal Inlet, Fitzroy and elsewhere prior to moving to Navy Point on 25.6.82. Remained there on transfer to 845 Sqdn Falkland Islands Detachment on 27.9.82. Embarked 'Astronomer' off Port Stanley by 6.11.82, sailing with the ship for the UK c14.11.82. Arrived at Devonport with the vessel on 3.12.82 (still coded '-/XM') and off-loaded overnight 3/4.12.82 to a compound at the Granby Gate entrance to the dockyard. Removed by road to Wroughton on 5.12.82, arriving there on 6.12.82. Officially transferred that day from 845 Sqdn to the RNAY for storage.

**XS495** HU.5

On 29.3.82 with NASU Yeovilton coded 'C' (ex-2 FTS Shawbury). Transferred from NASU to 707 Sqdn at Yeovilton on 18.4.82, then on to the newly-formed 848 Sqdn 19/20.4.82. Resprayed in the low-vis scheme by 22.4.82 and coded '-/WP'. Allocated to 'D' Flight, it left Yeovilton on 24.4.82 for Longroom, Plymouth and embarked 'Atlantic Conveyor' in Plymouth Sound 25.4.82 prior to sailing with the ship that day for Ascension and the South Atlantic.

On 25.5.82, whilst the ship was some 90 miles north-east of Port Stanley (at 50°37'S 56°10'W) en route to Falkland Sound, 'Atlantic Conveyor' was hit by an Exocet missile (one of two launched from a pair of 2 Escuadrilla Super Etendards) and caught fire. The Wessex was consumed by the fire, its remains sinking with the ship on 30.5.82.

**XS498** HU.5

On 29.3.82 in storage at Wroughton coded 'VL/WQ' (ex-707 Sqdn at Yeovilton). Delivered by road from Wroughton to NASU Yeovilton, arriving there on 14.5.82 still coded 'VL/WQ'. Delivered from NASU to 772 Sqdn at Portland 28.5.82, by which time it had been resprayed in the low-vis scheme. Code (623) was allocated but not carried. Allotted to 848 Sqdn 'D' Flt on 4.6.82 as an attrition replacement for those aircraft lost aboard 'Atlantic Conveyor' and was flown to Yeovilton on 5.6.82. Departed (still uncoded) on 6.6.82 for HMS Raleigh (Torpoint) and embarked 'Astronomer' in Plymouth Sound on 7.6.82, sailing with her for the South Atlantic on 8.6.82. After the vessel's arrival at Port William on 27.6.82, it is believed to have been off-loaded to Navy Point c1.7.82 for a short period ashore. It embarked 'Atlantic Causeway' c12.7.82 off Port Stanley and departed with the ship from San Carlos Water on 13.7.82, arriving at Devonport on 27.7.82 (still uncoded). Flown off to Yeovilton on 28.7.82 upon transfer from 848 Sqdn to 707 Sqdn.

**XS499** HU.5

On 29.3.82 with NASU at Yeovilton coded 'VL/WV' (ex-temporary loan to 707 Sqdn at Yeovilton). Transferred from NASU to 707 Sqdn on 18.4.82 and on to the newly-formed 848 Sqdn on 19/20.4.82. Resprayed in the low-vis scheme by 23.4.82 and coded '-/WN'. Allocated to 'D' Flight, it left Yeovilton on 24.4.82 for Longroom, Plymouth and embarked 'Atlantic Conveyor' in Plymouth Sound on 25.4.82 prior to sailing with her that day for Ascension and the South Atlantic.

On 25.5.82, whilst the ship was some 90 miles north-east of Port Stanley (at 50°37′S 56°10′W) en route to Falkland Sound, 'Atlantic Conveyor' was hit by an Exocet missile (one of two launched from a pair of 2 Escuadrilla Super Etendards) and caught fire. The Wessex was consumed by the fire, its remains sinking with the ship on 30.5.82.

**XS506** HU.5

On 29.3.82 with the 845 Sqdn detachment in Northern Ireland in the low-vis scheme and coded '-/(Y)U'. Returned to Yeovilton on 10.5.82 and transferred to 847 Sqdn on 11.5.82, being recoded '-/XE' that day. Allocated to 'B' Flight, it left for HMS Raleigh (Torpoint) on 13.5.82 and embarked 'Atlantic Causeway' that day in Plymouth Sound prior to the vessel's departure for the South Atlantic on 14.5.82. Disembarked to the FOB at Port San Carlos settlement on 1.6.82, later operating from Teal Inlet, Fitzroy and elsewhere prior to moving to Navy Point on 25.6.82. Following a period of storage/maintenance (post 27.6.82) aboard 'Astronomer', it was flown to Navy Point 10.7.82 and remained based there until officially transferred to 845 Sqdn Falkland Islands Detachment on 27.9.82. Embarked 'Astronomer' off Port Stanley by 6.11.82, sailing with the ship for the UK c14.11.82. Arrived at Devonport on 3.12.82 (still coded '-/XE') and off-loaded overnight 3/4.12.82 to a compound at the Granby Gate entrance to the dockyard. Removed by road to Wroughton on 6.12.82, being transferred from 845 Sqdn to the RNAY for storage upon arrival there the same day.

**XS507** HU.5

On 29.3.82 with 772 Sqdn 'C' Flt, coded 'ON/314' and named "Busby II", embarked on 'Olna' on Gulf Patrol in the Middle East. Departed Mombasa, Kenya with the ship on 5.4.82 to arrive at Portland naval base 22.4.82. Flown off the same day to nearby RNAS Portland. Whilst passing Gibraltar en route to Portland on 19.4.82, it had carried out the first deck-landing on 'Uganda' following her conversion to a hospital ship at Gibraltar. Flown from Portland to Yeovilton on 5.5.82 (still coded 'ON/314', wearing Red/Blue roundels) upon transfer to 847 Sqdn. Resprayed in the low-vis scheme 6.5.82, the code '-/XU' being applied on 7.5.82. Allocated to 'B' Flight, it left Yeovilton for HMS Raleigh (Torpoint) on 13.5.82, embarking 'Atlantic Causeway' the same day in Plymouth Sound prior to the vessel's departure for

the South Atlantic on 14.5.82. Believed to have remained on the ship post 1.6.82 when the majority of the Flight disembarked to the FOB at Port San Carlos settlement. Flown from 'Atlantic Causeway' to 'Tidepool' 16.6.82 as a replacement for XT486 which had been damaged during a storm whilst on detachment to 'Glamorgan'. Although operated by 848 Sqdn 'D' Flt on board 'Tidepool', it remained on 847 Sqdn charge and retained code '-/XU'. Transferred to 'Hermes' on 1.7.82 (due to 'Tidepool' being prepared for her long-overdue handover to Chile), joining another element of 848 Sqdn 'D' Flt already aboard the carrier (utilising XT471 '-/XW' of 847 Sqdn). Sailed with 'Hermes' from Port William on 3.7.82 en route to the UK, arriving at Portsmouth on 21.7.82 (still coded '-/XU'). It was flown off to Yeovilton on 22.7.82 upon transfer from 847 Sqdn to 707 Sqdn.

**XS512** HU.5

On 29.3.82 with 707 Sqdn at Yeovilton coded 'VL/WT'. Transferred to 848 Sqdn 19.4.82 and by 21.4.82 had been resprayed in the low-vis scheme and coded '-/WT'. Allocated to 'D' Flight, it left Yeovilton on 24.4.82 for Longroom, Plymouth *[see XT771]* and embarked 'Atlantic Conveyor' on 25.4.82 in Plymouth Sound prior to sailing with the ship that day for Ascension and the South Atlantic. Noted at Wideawake 5.5.82 on HDS duties.

On 25.5.82, whilst the ship was some 90 miles north-east of Port Stanley (at 50°37′S 56°10′W) en route to Falkland Sound, 'Atlantic Conveyor' was hit by an Exocet missile (one of two launched from a pair of 2 Escuadrilla Super Etendards) and caught fire. It had just completed engine runs at the time the ship was hit but unfortunately a flight crew could not reach it because of the heat. Consumed by the fire, its remains sank with the vessel on 30.5.82.

**XS514** HU.5

On 29.3.82 with the 845 Sqdn detachment in Northern Ireland in the low-vis scheme and coded '-/(Y)U'. It returned to Yeovilton on 10.5.82 and was transferred to 847 Sqdn on 11.5.82, being recoded '-/XA' that day. Allocated to 'B' Flight, it left for HMS Raleigh (Torpoint) 13.5.82 and embarked 'Atlantic Causeway' the same day in Plymouth Sound, sailing with her for the South Atlantic on 14.5.82. Disembarked to the FOB at Port San Carlos settlement on 1.6.82 and later operated from Teal Inlet, Fitzroy and elsewhere before moving to Navy Point on 25.6.82. Re-embarked 'Atlantic Causeway' off Port Stanley c12.7.82 and departed with the ship from San Carlos Water on 13.7.82 to arrive at Devonport on 27.7.82. Still coded '-/XA', it was off-loaded and taken to a compound at Camel's Head (near HMS Drake). Officially transferred from 847 Sqdn to 845 Sqdn on 28.7.82 and removed by road to Yeovilton on 1.8.82, arriving there the same day.

**XS515** HU.5

On 29.3.82 with the 845 Sqdn detachment in

Northern Ireland in low-vis scheme coded '-/(Y)N'. Returned to Yeovilton on 10.5.82 and transferred to 847 Sqdn on 11.5.82, being recoded '-/XB' that day. Allocated to 'B' Flight, it was flown to HMS Raleigh (Torpoint) on 13.5.82 and embarked 'Atlantic Causeway' that day in Plymouth Sound, sailing with the ship for the South Atlantic on 14.5.82. Disembarked to the FOB at Port San Carlos settlement on 1.6.82 and later operated from Teal Inlet, Fitzroy and elsewhere before moving to Navy Point on 25.6.82. Re-embarked 'Atlantic Causeway' off Port Stanley c12.7.82 and departed with the ship from San Carlos Water on 13.7.82, arriving at Devonport on 27.7.82. Still coded '-/XB', it was flown off to Yeovilton on 28.7.82 upon transfer to 845 Sqdn.

**XS516** HU.5

On 29.3.82 with 845 Sqdn at Yeovilton in the low-vis scheme and coded '-/(Y)Q'. Transferred to 847 Sqdn on 11.5.82 and recoded '-/XD' that day. Allocated to 'B' Flight, it was flown from Yeovilton to HMS Raleigh (Torpoint) on 13.5.82 and embarked 'Atlantic Causeway' that day in Plymouth Sound, sailing with the ship for the South Atlantic on 14.5.82. Disembarked to the FOB at Port San Carlos settlement on 1.6.82 and later operated from Teal Inlet, Fitzroy and elsewhere prior to moving to Navy Point on 25.6.82. Transferred to 'Engadine' 5.7.82 before the ship left Port William on 7.7.82 (calling briefly that day at San Carlos Water) for the UK, arriving at Devonport on 30.7.82. Still coded '-/XD', it was flown off later that day to NASU Yeovilton upon transfer from 847 Sqdn.

**XS518** HU.5

On 29.3.82 with 772 Sqdn at Portland coded 'PO/626'. Flown to Yeovilton on 5.5.82 for 847 Sqdn with Red/Blue roundels already applied. Painted in full low-vis scheme and coded '-/XP' later the same day. Officially allocated to 847 Sqdn on 6.5.82. Allotted to 'B' Flight, it was flown from Yeovilton to HMS Raleigh (Torpoint) on 13.5.82, embarking 'Atlantic Causeway' the same day in Plymouth Sound and sailing with the ship for the South Atlantic 14.5.82. Disembarked to the FOB at Port San Carlos settlement on 1.6.82 and later operated from Teal Inlet, Fitzroy and elsewhere before moving to Navy Point on 25.6.82. Re-embarked 'Atlantic Causeway' off Port Stanley c12.7.82 and departed with the ship from San Carlos Water on 13.7.82, arriving at Devonport 27.7.82. Still coded '-/XP', it was flown off to Yeovilton on 28.7.82 upon transfer from 847 Sqdn to 707 Sqdn.

**XS520** HU.5          *Deployed post-14.6.82*

On 29.3.82 on overhaul at Fleetlands (uncoded). Delivered by air to Yeovilton on 17.5.82 in the low-vis scheme upon transfer to 848 Sqdn (replacing XT463) and was coded '-/WZ' the same day. Allocated to 'C' Flight for service aboard 'Olwen' (the Flight had actually formed 19.4.82) although the ship was undergoing refit at Gibraltar and did not arrive back at Devonport until 10.6.82. Finally flown from Yeovilton to HMS Drake (Plymouth) on 16.6.82, embarking 'Olwen' the same day just after she had sailed from Devonport for operations in the Portland area prior to departing for the South Atlantic on 18.6.82. Shore-based at Wideawake 1-9.7.82, assisting the hard-pressed 845 Sqdn 'D' Flt and ferrying troops from ship to shore. Detached ashore in the Falklands on a number of occasions during 8/9.82 prior to moving with 'C' Flight to 'Fort Austin' on 27.9.82 as 'Olwen' was returning home. The Flight was effectively disbanded 16.10.82 with the transfer that day of its aircraft to a detachment of 845 Sqdn aboard 'Illustrious'. Sailed from the FIPZ with the carrier on 21.10.82 for the UK (via the USA) and flown off to Yeovilton on 7.12.82 (still coded '-/WZ') prior to the ship docking at Portsmouth on 8.12.82. Remained with 845 Sqdn.

**XS521** HU.5     *Deployed post-14.6.82*

Delivered from Portland to Wroughton for storage 31.3.82 coded 'PO/621' (ex-772 Sqdn at Portland). On 6.5.82 it was transferred to Fleetlands for overhaul. Delivered out to 772 Sqdn at Portland on 23.7.82 still coded 'PO/621' (noted as such at the Yeovilton Air Day on 31.7.82). Embarked 'Olmeda' at Devonport and sailed with the ship for Ascension 6.9.82. Transferred to 845 Sqdn 'D' Flt at Wideawake 17.9.82 retaining the code 'PO/621', but had been recoded '-/YB' by 10.82. Noted at Wideawake during 9.83 wearing small size ROYAL NAVY titles in Black with the serial in White and code in Black. Embarked 'Fort Grange' at Ascension on 1.9.84 for return to the UK, disembarking to Yeovilton 20.9.84 (still coded '-/YB') on transfer to NASU.

**XS522** HU.5

On 29.3.82 in storage at Wroughton coded '-/--5' (ex-'PO/635' of 772 Sqdn Portland). Delivered by road to NASU Yeovilton on 14.5.82 still coded '-/--5'. Departed NASU for 772 Sqdn at Portland on 27.5.82, uncoded in the low-vis scheme, the code (625) being allocated but not worn. Allotted to 848 Sqdn 'D' Flight on 4.6.82 as an attrition replacement for those aircraft lost aboard 'Atlantic Conveyor' and flown to Yeovilton 5.6.82. Departed on 6.6.82 for HMS Raleigh (Torpoint) and embarked 'Astronomer' in Plymouth Sound on 7.6.82 (still uncoded), sailing with her for the South Atlantic on 8.6.82. Believed to have remained aboard 'Astronomer' after the ship arrived at Port William 27.6.82. Transferred to 'Atlantic Causeway' c12.7.82 off Port Stanley and sailed with the ship from San Carlos Water 13.7.82, arriving at Devonport on 27.7.82. Still uncoded, it was off-loaded 28.7.82 and taken to a compound at Camel's Head (near HMS Drake). Removed by road to Yeovilton on 30.7.82 (arriving there the same day) and officially transferred that day from 848 Sqdn to 707 Sqdn.

**XS523** HU.5

On 29.3.82 with NASU Yeovilton uncoded in the SAR colour scheme. Transferred from NASU to 707 Sqdn at Yeovilton on 27.4.82, still in the SAR scheme but partially coded '-/X-' (in White) forward of the roundel. On 5.5.82 it was repainted in the low-vis scheme and coded '-/XJ' prior to being officially

transferred to 847 Sqdn 6.5.82. Allotted to 'A' Flight and flown aboard 'Engadine' at Devonport from Yeovilton on 9.5.82 before sailing with the ship for Ascension and the South Atlantic 10.5.82. Disembarked to the FOB at Port San Carlos settlement on 9.6.82, later operating from Teal Inlet, Fitzroy and elsewhere before moving to Navy Point on 25.6.82. Remained there on transfer to 845 Sqdn Falkland Islands Detachment 27.9.82. Embarked 'Astronomer' off Port Stanley by 6.11.82, sailing with the ship for the UK c14.11.82. Arrived with the vessel at Devonport 3.12.82 (still coded '-/XJ') and was off-loaded overnight 3/4.12.82 to a compound at the Granby Gate entrance to the dockyard. Removed by road to Yeovilton on 5.12.82 (arriving there the same day) upon transfer that day from 845 Sqdn to NASU.

**XT449** HU.5

On 29.3.82 with 845 Sqdn at Yeovilton in the low-vis scheme coded '-/(Y)C'. Allotted to 'E' Flight, it embarked 'Intrepid' on 20.4.82 for a short period of sea trials off Portland before returning to Yeovilton on 22.4.82. Re-embarked 'Intrepid' in Weymouth Bay on 26.4.82 and departed with her that day for Ascension and the South Atlantic. Transferred to 'Tidepool' (with the Flight) at Ascension on 5.5.82, sailing south on 6.5.82. Detached to 'Antrim' 19.5.82 for insertion of Special Forces on Fanning Head. Flown from 'Antrim' to 'Canberra' for CASEVAC duties on 21.5.82.

On 21.5.82, whilst crewed by by Lt Crabtree, S/Lt Heathcote and Cpl Gleeson, a particularly difficult rescue mission was successfully carried out. Two survivors from 'Ardent' were saved from almost certain death. Surgeon Cdr Jolly was also involved in that mission.

Returned to 'Tidepool' on 24.5.82. Disembarked to Ajax Bay 25.5.82 before moving to the FOB at Old House Creek, San Carlos on 26.5.82 then on to the Port San Carlos settlement FOB on 30.5.82. Detached to the supplementary FOB at Fitzroy settlement from at least 11-14.6.82. Remained ashore until 12.7.82 when it embarked 'Atlantic Causeway' off Port Stanley, sailing with the ship the next day from San Carlos Water. Arrived at Devonport with the vessel on 27.7.82 (still coded '-/(Y)C') and flown off to Yeovilton 28.7.82, remaining on 845 Sqdn charge.

**XT450** HU.5

On 29.3.82 with 845 Sqdn at Yeovilton in the low-vis scheme coded '-/(Y)V'. Left Yeovilton 6.5.82 inside Heavylift Belfast G-BEPS on delivery to Ascension, arriving at Wideawake on 7.5.82 where it was reassembled by Naval Party 1222 and test-flown on 9.5.82. Temporarily utilised by 'D' Flight (the Ascension Island Base Flight) until officially transferred to 'C' Flight at Wideawake on 13.5.82 (one of two replacements for XT464 and XT473 which had been abandoned on South Georgia). Embarked 'Tidespring' 14.5.82 and sailed with the ship for the TEZ 16.5.82. Embarked 'Fort Grange' 9.6.82 for passage to San Carlos Water and disembarked to the FOB at Port San Carlos settlement on 10.6.82 to operate ashore with the other elements of 845 Sqdn. After the surrender on 14.6.82 it

remained ashore, operating from Port San Carlos and Port Stanley racecourse until 3.7.82 when it flew from the Port San Carlos base (via Port Stanley) to 'Hermes' at Port William for passage to Ascension to rejoin 'Tidespring'. In the event, 'Tidespring' no longer had any helicopter support facilities available, so it remained aboard 'Hermes' (along with XT765 of 'B' Flight) until the carrier arrived at Portsmouth on 21.7.82. Still coded '-/(Y)V', it was flown to Yeovilton on 22.7.82 and remained on 845 Sqdn charge.

**XT451** HU.5

On 29.3.82 with 845 Sqdn at Yeovilton in the low-vis scheme coded '-/(Y)J'. Left Yeovilton 8.4.82 inside Heavylift Belfast G-BEPE on delivery to 'D' Flight (the Ascension Island Base Flight), arriving at Wideawake on 9.4.82. Reassembled by Naval Party 1222, test-flown 12.4.82 and remained on Base Flight duties at Wideawake until 7.5.82 when it embarked 'Intrepid' off the Island as an FIR aircraft. Believed to have been off-loaded c30.5.82 to the FOB at Port San Carlos settlement. Transferred to 847 Sqdn (possibly c1.6.82 at Port San Carlos) and recoded '-/XN' (replacing XT469). Operated out of Navy Point as from 25.6.82. Officially transferred to 845 Sqdn Falkland Islands Detachment 27.9.82 and remained based at Navy Point. Embarked 'Astronomer' off Port Stanley by 6.11.82, sailing with the ship for the UK c14.11.82. Arrived with the vessel at Devonport on 3.12.82 (still coded '-/XN') and was off-loaded overnight on 3/4.12.82 to a compound at the Granby Gate entrance to the dockyard. Removed by road to Yeovilton on 5.12.82 (arriving there the same day) upon transfer that day from 845 Sqdn to NASU.

**XT456** HU.5

On 29.3.82 with NASU Yeovilton (ex '-/VA' of 846 Sqdn at Yeovilton). Transferred to 847 Sqdn from NASU on 6.5.82 in the low-vis scheme. Code '-/XZ' was applied on 7.5.82. Allocated to 'A' Flight, it left Yeovilton 9.5.82, embarking 'Engadine' the same day at Devonport before sailing with her for Ascension and the South Atlantic 10.5.82. Disembarked to the FOB at Port San Carlos settlement on 9.6.82, later operating from Teal Inlet, Fitzroy and elsewhere before moving to Navy Point 25.6.82. Transferred to the 845 Sqdn Falkland Islands Detachment 27.9.82 and remained based at Navy Point. Embarked 'Astronomer' off Port Stanley by 6.11.82, sailing with the ship for the UK c14.11.82. Arrived with the vessel at Devonport on 3.12.82 (still coded '-/XZ') and off-loaded overnight 3/4.12.82 to a compound at the Granby Gate entrance to the dockyard. Removed by road to Wroughton on 5.12.82, arriving there on 6.12.82 upon transfer that day from 845 Sqdn to the RNAY for storage.

**XT459** HU.5

On 29.3.82 with 845 Sqdn at Yeovilton in the low-vis scheme coded '-/(Y)B'. Left Yeovilton 6.5.82 inside Heavylift Belfast G-BEPS on delivery to Ascension, arriving at Wideawake on 7.5.82 where it was reassembled by Naval Party 1222 and test-flown on 9.5.82. Temporarily utilised by 'D' Flight (the Ascension Island Base Flight) until officially transferred to 'C' Flight at Wideawake on 13.5.82 (one of two replacements for XT464 and XT473 which had been abandoned on South Georgia). Embarked 'Tidespring' 14.5.82 and sailed with her for the TEZ on 16.5.82. Embarked 'Fort Grange' 9.6.82 for passage to San Carlos Water and disembarked to the FOB at Port San Carlos settlement 10.6.82 to operate ashore with other elements of 845 Sqdn. Following the surrender on 14.6.82, it remained ashore operating from Port San Carlos and the Port Stanley racecourse.

As the Wessex (flown by Lt Manley) landed at the Racecourse on 24.6.82 a woven nylon sack, blown up by the slipstream, became caught on one of the main rotor blades. The blade dropped below its normal rotation height and severed the tail rotor drive shaft. As the other blades dropped they virtually sliced the tailcone off from the rest of the fuselage. Damage to the helicopter was assessed as CAT.4/5.

Airlifted by 18 Sqdn Chinook to 'Atlantic Causeway' off Port Stanley on/by 12.7.82 and sailed with the ship for the UK from San Carlos Water on 13.7.82, arriving at Devonport on 27.7.82. Still coded '-/(Y)B' (but in two sections) it was off-loaded on 28.7.82 and moved to a compound at Camel's Head (near HMS Drake). Removed by road to Yeovilton on 29.7.82 (arriving the same day) where it was officially transferred that day from 845 Sqdn to NASU.

## XT460 HU.5

On 29.3.82 with 845 Sqdn at Yeovilton in the low-vis scheme coded '-/(Y)K'. Left Yeovilton 8.4.82 inside Heavylift Belfast G-BEPE on delivery to 'D' Flight (the Ascension Island Base Flight), arriving at Wideawake 9.4.82. Assembled by Naval Party 1222 and test-flown on 11.4.82. Remained on Base Flight duties until 7.5.82 when it embarked 'Intrepid' off the Island as an FIR aircraft. Believed to have been off-loaded c30.5.82 to the FOB at Port San Carlos settlement. Transferred to 847 Sqdn (possibly c1.6.82 at Port San Carlos) but retained the code '-/(Y)K'. Operated out of Navy Point from 25.6.82, remaining there on transfer 27.9.82 back to the 845 Sqdn Falkland Islands Detachment. Embarked 'Astronomer' off Port Stanley by 6.11.82, sailing with the ship for the UK c14.11.82. Arrived with the vessel at Devonport on 3.12.82 (still coded '-/(Y)K') and off-loaded overnight on 3/4.12.82 to a compound at the Granby Gate entrance to the dockyard. Removed by road on 4.12.82 for Yeovilton, arriving there the same day. Retained by 845 Sqdn.

## XT461 HU.5

On 29.3.82 with 845 Sqdn at Yeovilton in the low-vis scheme and coded '-/(Y)W'. Allocated to 'E' Flight, it embarked 'Intrepid' on 20.4.82 for a short period of sea trials off Portland, returning to Yeovilton 22.4.82. Re-embarked 'Intrepid' in Weymouth Bay on 26.4.82 and sailed with her that day for Ascension and the South Atlantic. Transferred to 'Tidepool' (with the Flight) at Ascension on 5.5.82, sailing south on 6.5.82. Disembarked to Ajax Bay on 25.5.82 before moving to the FOB at Old House Creek, San Carlos on 26.5.82 and then on to the Port San Carlos

settlement FOB 30.5.82 to operate ashore with other elements of 845 Sqdn. Remained ashore until 12.7.82 when embarked on 'Atlantic Causeway' off Port Stanley, sailing homeward with the ship from San Carlos Water 13.7.82 to arrive at Devonport on 27.7.82. Still coded '-/(Y)W', it was flown to Yeovilton 28.7.82, remaining on 845 Sqdn charge.

## XT463 HU.5

On 29.3.82 with 707 Sqdn at Yeovilton coded 'VL/WZ'. Transferred to 848 Sqdn at Yeovilton 19.4.82 and by 21.4.82 had been painted in the low-vis scheme and coded '-/WZ'. Allotted to 'D' Flight, it left Yeovilton 24.4.82 for Longroom, Plymouth to embark 'Atlantic Conveyor', but after suffering FOD it returned to Yeovilton from Longroom on 26.4.82 (having been replaced the previous day by XT483). After repairs it was transferred to 707 Sqdn on 18.5.82 (being replaced within 848 Sqdn by XS520) and re-coded '-/ZB'. Reallocated to 848 Sqdn 'D' Flt on 5.6.82 as an attrition replacement aircraft for those lost aboard 'Atlantic Conveyor'. Still coded '-/ZB', it left Yeovilton 6.6.82 for HMS Raleigh (Torpoint) and embarked 'Astronomer' in Plymouth Sound on 7.6.82 prior to sailing with the ship for the South Atlantic on 8.6.82. Believed to have remained aboard 'Astronomer' after the ship arrived at Port William 27.6.82. Transferred to 'Atlantic Causeway' off Port Stanley c12.7.82 and departed with the vessel from San Carlos Water on 13.7.82, arriving at Devonport (uncoded) on 27.7.82. Off-loaded 28.7.82 and taken by road to a compound at Camel's Head (near HMS Drake). Removed by road on 30.7.82 to Yeovilton (arriving there the same day) upon official transfer that day from 848 Sqdn to 707 Sqdn.

## XT464 HU.5

On 29.3.82 with 845 Sqdn at Yeovilton in the low-vis scheme coded '-/(Y)F'. Stripped down ready for air transportation on 4.4.82 and departed for Ascension 5.4.82 aboard Heavylift Belfast G-BFYU. Arrived at Wideawake 6.4.82, reassembled by Naval Party 1222 on 8.4.82 and then test-flown. Allocated to 'C' Flight on 10.4.82, it was flown aboard 'Tidespring' off the Island on 11.4.82 and sailed with her the same day for South Georgia.

Embarked Special Forces aboard 'Antrim' on 21.4.82 and airlifted them onto the Fortuna Glacier, South Georgia in company with the other 'C' Flight Wessex (XT473) and 'Antrim' Flight's HAS.3 (XP142). During the night the weather deteriorated and it became necessary to evacuate the troops on 22.4.82 using the same three helicopters. Unfortunately XT464 (flown by Lt Tidd) crashed in "white-out" conditions almost immediately after take-off from the Glacier and ended up on its side with no fatalities. The crew and passengers were transferred to XT473 and XP142, both of which took off successfully, but XT473 hit a small ridge while flying in "white-out" conditions and ended up on its side on the Glacier, luckily with no loss of life. XP142 returned to 'Antrim' and, after an improvement in the weather, went back to pick up the remaining personnel and ferried them to 'Antrim'. XT464 was left abandoned on the Glacier, as was XT473.

## XT466 HU.5

On 29.3.82 with 771 Sqdn at Culdrose coded 'CU/528'. Transferred to 847 Sqdn 5.5.82 and delivered by air to Yeovilton on 6.5.82 uncoded in the low-vis scheme (but with the ROYAL NAVY titles applied in Black). By 7.5.82 it had been coded '-/XV'. Allocated to 'B' Flight, it was flown from Yeovilton to HMS Raleigh (Torpoint) on 13.5.82 and embarked 'Atlantic Causeway' that day in Plymouth Sound, sailing with the ship for the South Atlantic on 14.5.82. Disembarked to the FOB at Port San Carlos settlement on 1.6.82 and later operated from Teal Inlet, Fitzroy and elsewhere prior to moving to Navy Point 25.6.82. Remained there on transfer to 845 Sqdn Falkland Islands Detachment 27.9.82. Embarked 'Astronomer' off Port Stanley by 6.11.82, sailing with the ship for the UK c14.11.82. Arrived with the vessel at Devonport on 3.12.82 (still coded '-/XV') and off-loaded overnight on 3/4.12.82 to a compound at the Granby Gate entrance to the dockyard. Removed by road to Wroughton on 8.12.82 (arriving there the same day) where it was transferred that day from 845 Sqdn to the RNAY for survey prior to possible reissue.

## XT467 HU.5

Delivered by air from Culdrose to Wroughton for long-term storage on 30.3.82 (coded 'CU/525', ex-771 Sqdn at Culdrose). It was restored to 771 Sqdn and delivered by road to NASU Culdrose (still coded) 10/11.5.82 to be made airworthy once again. Flown from Culdrose to Yeovilton on 2.6.82 (code 525) not carried, but being used as a call-sign) upon transfer that day from 771 Sqdn to 848 Sqdn 'D' Flt as an attrition replacement for those aircraft lost on the 'Atlantic Conveyor'. By 6.6.82 it had been resprayed in low-vis scheme. Flown from Yeovilton to HMS Raleigh (Torpoint) the same day, still uncoded. Embarked 'Astronomer' in Plymouth Sound on 7.6.82 and sailed with the ship for the South Atlantic on 8.6.82. Arrived with the ship at Port William on 27.6.82 and believed to have been off-loaded to Navy Point c1.7.82. Airlifted by Chinook aboard the 'Contender Bezant' 2.9.82 off Port William (reportedly from 'Astronomer') and sailed with the ship for the UK 6.9.82, arriving at Southampton 23.9.82. Still uncoded, it was off-loaded by 24.9.82 and removed by road the same day to Yeovilton (via Lee-on-Solent) where it arrived on 27.9.82. Officially transferred that day from 848 Sqdn to NASU.

## XT468 HU.5

On 29.3.82 with 845 Sqdn at Yeovilton in the low-vis scheme and coded '-/(Y)D'. Allocated to 'B' Flight, it was stripped down 3.4.82 ready for air transportation. Departed for Ascension on 4.4.82 aboard Heavylift Belfast G-BEPE, arriving at Wideawake on 5.4.82. Reassembled by Naval Party 1222 and test-flown on 7.4.82 prior to embarking 'Fort Austin' that day. It sailed south with the ship on 9.4.82 to rendezvous with 'Endurance'. Returned to Ascension with the vessel on 20.4.82 prior to sailing south with her again on 23.4.82 for the TEZ. Transferred to 'Hermes' 17.5.82 to make room for four 826 Sqdn Sea King HAS.5's. Owing to lack of room on 'Hermes' (due to the arrival of Harriers and additional Sea Harriers on 18-20.5.82), it flew to 'Atlantic Conveyor' on 20.5.82. Whilst airborne on a test flight from 'Atlantic Conveyor' on 25.5.82, the ship was hit by an Exocet. Carried out some rescue missions before recovering to 'Hermes'. Seconded to 848 Sqdn 'D' Flt aboard 'Hermes' on 28.5.82, mainly for use in the HDS role, but was not entirely suited to that task as it had been fitted out as a gunship. It was therefore transferred to 'Atlantic Causeway' on 3.6.82 in exchange for XT471, an 847 Sqdn 'B' Flight aircraft. Nothing further known until 11.7.82 when it was airlifted aboard 'Atlantic Causeway' off Port Stanley by an 18 Sqdn Chinook. Sailed with the ship for the UK from San Carlos Water 13.7.82, arriving at Devonport on 27.7.82. Still coded '-/(Y)D', it was off-loaded 28.7.82 and taken by road to a compound at Camel's Head (near HMS Drake). Removed by road to Yeovilton on 2.8.82 (arriving there the same day). Retained by 845 Sqdn.

**XT469** HU.5

On 29.3.82 with 772 Sqdn at Portland coded 'PO/624'. Noted uncoded at Portland on 4.5.82. Delivered to Yeovilton on 5.5.82 for 847 Sqdn with Red/Blue roundels already applied but retaining the 772 Sqdn crest. Officially transferred to 847 Sqdn on 6.5.82. By 7.5.82 it was in the full low-vis scheme and coded '-/XN' (the crest having been painted over). Allocated to 'B' Flight, it was flown from Yeovilton to HMS Raleigh (Torpoint) 13.5.82 and embarked 'Atlantic Causeway' in Plymouth Sound the same day, sailing with the ship on 14.5.82 for the South Atlantic. Disembarked to the FOB at Port San Carlos settlement on 1.6.82 and later operated from Teal Inlet, Fitzroy and elsewhere. Replaced by XT451 (possibly c10.6.82 at Port San Carlos) and probably moved with the other San Carlos aircraft to Navy Point on 25.6.82. Believed to have been loaded aboard 'Atlantic Causeway' off Port Stanley c12.7.82, sailing with the ship from San Carlos Water on 13.7.82 to arrive at Devonport 27.7.82. Still coded '-/XN' (with the 772 Sqdn crest mentioned earlier now visible), it was off-loaded 28.7.82 to a compound at Camel's Head (near HMS Drake). Removed by road to Culdrose on 31.7.82, arriving there the same day. Officially transferred from 847 Sqdn to 771 Sqdn at Culdrose on 1.8.82.

**XT471** HU.5

On 29.3.82 with 771 Sqdn at Culdrose coded 'CU/524'. Transferred to 847 Sqdn on 5.5.82 and flown from Culdrose to Yeovilton on 6.5.82, uncoded in the low-vis scheme but with Black ROYAL NAVY titling. By 7.5.82 it had been coded '-/XW'. Allocated to 'B' Flight and flown from Yeovilton to HMS Raleigh (Torpoint) on 13.5.82, embarking 'Atlantic Causeway' in Plymouth Sound the same day and sailing with her for the South Atlantic on 14.5.82. Transferred from 'Atlantic Causeway' to 'Hermes' on 3.6.82 for use in the HDS role (retaining code '-/XW') on secondment to 848 Sqdn 'D' Flt, replacing XT468. Remained with the carrier, sailing with her for the UK from Port William on 3.7.82. Arrived with the ship at Portsmouth on 21.7.82 and flown off to Yeovilton 22.7.82 upon transfer from 847 Sqdn to 707 Sqdn.

*Noted in the Falklands and on return to the*

---

*UK aboard 'Hermes' wearing the legend "848 NOMADS" in White below the starboard cockpit above the door.*

**XT472** HU.5

On 29.3.82 with 845 Sqdn at Yeovilton in the low-vis scheme coded '-/(Y)M'. Transferred to 847 Sqdn on 11.5.82 and recoded '-/XC'. Allocated to 'B' Flight and flown from Yeovilton to HMS Raleigh (Torpoint) on 13.5.82, embarking 'Atlantic Causeway' in Plymouth Sound that day and sailing with the ship on 14.5.82 for the South Atlantic. Disembarked to the FOB at Port San Carlos settlement on 1.6.82 and later operated from Teal Inlet, Fitzroy and elsewhere prior to moving to Navy Point on 25.6.82. Re-embarked 'Atlantic Causeway' off Port Stanley c12.7.82 and sailed with the ship from San Carlos Water on 13.7.82, arriving at Devonport 27.7.82. Still coded '-/XC', it was off-loaded on 28.7.82 and taken to a compound at Camel's Head (near HMS Drake). Officially transferred from 847 Sqdn to 845 Sqdn 28.7.82 and removed by road to Yeovilton on 30.7.82, arriving there the same day.

**XT473** HU.5

On 29.3.82 with 845 Sqdn at Yeovilton in the low-vis scheme coded '-/(Y)A'. Stripped down 4.4.82 ready for air transportation and left for Ascension 5.4.82 inside Heavylift Belfast G-BFYU, arriving at Wideawake 6.4.82 where it was assembled by Naval Party 1222 and then test flown. Allocated to 'C' Flight on 10.4.82 and flown to 'Tidespring' off Georgia the same day.

Embarked Special Forces aboard 'Antrim' on 21.4.82 and airlifted them onto the Fortuna Glacier, South Georgia in company with other 'C' Flt Wessex (XT464) and 'Antrim' Flt's HAS.3 (XP142). During the night the weather deteriorated and it became necessary to evacuate the troops on 22.4.82 using the same three helicopters. Unfortunately, XT464 crashed in "white-out" conditions almost immediately after take-off from the Glacier, luckily with no fatalities. The crew and passengers were transferred to XT473 and XP142, both of which took off successfully, but XT473 (flown by Lt Georgeson) hit a small ridge while flying in "white-out" conditions and ended up on its side on the Glacier, luckily with no loss of life. XP142 returned to 'Antrim' and, after an improvement in the weather, went back to pick up the remaining personnel and ferried them to 'Antrim'. XT473 was left abandoned on the Glacier, as was XT464.

**XT475** HU.5

On 29.3.82 in storage at Wroughton (coded 'VL/WN', ex-707 Sqdn at Yeovilton). Transferred to NASU Yeovilton 23.4.82, arriving there on 29.4.82. Allotted to 847 Sqdn on 11.5.82 and by that date had been painted in the low-vis scheme and coded '-/XG'. Allocated to 'B' Flight and flown from Yeovilton to HMS Raleigh (Torpoint) on 13.5.82, embarking 'Atlantic Causeway' that day in Plymouth Sound prior to sailing with her on 14.5.82 for the South Atlantic. Disembarked to the FOB at Port San Carlos settlement on

---

1.6.82 and later operated from Teal Inlet, Fitzroy and elsewhere, prior to moving to Navy Point on 25.6.82. Remained at Navy Point on transfer from 847 Sqdn to 845 Sqdn Falkland Islands Detachment on 27.9.82. Embarked 'Astronomer' off Port Stanley by 6.11.82, sailing with the ship for the UK c14.11.82. Arrived with the vessel at Devonport on 3.12.82 (still coded '-/XG') and off-loaded overnight 3/4.12.82 to a compound at the Granby Gate entrance to the dockyard. Although officially transferred from 845 Sqdn to NASU Yeovilton charge on 3.12.82, it was not removed by road until 4.12.82 (arriving at Yeovilton the same day).

**XT476** HU.5

On 29.3.82 with 707 Sqdn Yeovilton coded 'VL/WS'. Transferred to 848 Sqdn 19.4.82, the letters 'WS' being overpainted in Black that day. By 21.4.82 it had been resprayed in full low-vis scheme with code '-/WS'. Allocated to 'D' Flight and flown from Yeovilton to Longroom, Plymouth on 24.4.82, embarking 'Atlantic Conveyor' in Plymouth Sound on 25.4.82 to sail with the ship that day for Ascension and the South Atlantic.

On 25.5.82, whilst the ship was some 90 miles north-east of Port Stanley (at 50°37'S 56°10'W) en route to Falkland Sound, 'Atlantic Conveyor' was hit by an Exocet missile (one of two launched from a pair of 2 Escuadrilla Super Etendards) and caught fire. The Wessex was consumed by the fire, its remains sinking with the ship on 30.5.82.

**XT480** HU.5

On 29.3.82 with 772 Sqdn at Portland coded 'PO/621' and noted there as such on 4.5.82. Delivered to Yeovilton 5.5.82 (with Red/Blue roundels already applied) prior to its official transfer to 847 Sqdn 6.5.82. In the full low-vis scheme by 7.5.82, coded '-/XQ'. Allocated to 'B' Flight and flown from Yeovilton to HMS Raleigh (Torpoint) 13.5.82, embarking 'Atlantic Causeway' the same day in Plymouth Sound prior to sailing with the ship on 14.5.82 for the South Atlantic. Disembarked to the FOB at Port San Carlos settlement 1.6.82, later operating from Teal Inlet and Fitzroy.

Crewed by Lt Hughes and CPOACMN Tuttey, it was directly involved in the rescue and evacuation of personnel from the blazing 'Sir Galahad' at Port Pleasant on 8.6.82.

Whilst on task near Bluff Cove on 11.6.82 it suffered slight shrapnel damage from a mortar bomb which exploded close by. The aircraft remained serviceable.

Moved with the Squadron to Navy Point on 25.6.82 prior to being loaded aboard the 'Atlantic Causeway' off Port Stanley c12.7.82. Departed with the ship from San Carlos Water 13.7.82, arriving at Devonport on 27.7.82. Still coded '-/XQ', it was off-loaded on 28.7.82 to a compound at Camel's Head (near HMS Drake). Removed by road to Culdrose on 29.7.82, arriving there the same day. Officially transferred from 847 Sqdn to 771 Sqdn at Culdrose on 1.8.82.

**XT481** HU.5

On 29.3.82 with 845 Sqdn at Yeovilton in the

low-vis scheme coded '-/(Y)E'. Transferred to 707 Sqdn 19.5.82 and by 21.5.82 had been re-coded '-/ZE'. Reallocated to 848 Sqdn 'D' Flt 2.6.82 as an attrition replacement for those aircraft lost aboard the 'Atlantic Conveyor'. Flown from Yeovilton to HMS Raleigh (Torpoint) 6.6.82 and embarked 'Astronomer' in Plymouth Sound 7.6.82 prior to sailing with the ship for the South Atlantic on 8.6.82 (still coded '-/ZE'). Arrived at Port William with the vessel on 27.6.82 and is believed to have disembarked to Navy Point c1.7.82 upon transfer to 847 Sqdn, replacing XS479 as '-/XF'. Noted as such at RAF Stanley 15/21.8.82. Remained at Navy Point when transferred to 845 Sqdn Falkland Islands Detachment on 27.9.82. Embarked 'Astronomer' off Port Stanley by 6.11.82, sailing with the ship for the UK c14.11.82. Arrived with the vessel at Devonport on 3.12.82 (still coded '-/XF') and off-loaded overnight 3/4.12.82 to a compound at the Granby Gate entrance to the dockyard. Removed by road to Yeovilton on 5.12.82 (arriving there the same day) where it was transferred that day from 845 Sqdn to NASU.

**XT482** HU.5

On 29.3.82 with NASU Yeovilton (ex-'CU/527' of 771 Sqdn at Culdrose). Transferred to 707 Sqdn at Yeovilton on 26.4.82 prior to joining the newly-formed 848 Sqdn 27.4.82. Finished in the low-vis scheme on that date and coded '-/WL'. That allocation was short-lived because on 6.5.82 it was transferred to 847 Sqdn and recoded '-/XL' the next day. Allotted to 'A' Flight and departed Yeovilton on 9.5.82 to embark 'Engadine' at Devonport the same day, sailing with the ship for Ascension and the South Atlantic on 10.5.82. Disembarked to the FOB at Port San Carlos settlement on 9.6.82 and later operated from Teal Inlet, Fitzroy and elsewhere prior to moving to Navy Point 25.6.82. Remained there upon transfer to 845 Sqdn Falkland Islands Detachment on 27.9.82. Embarked 'Astronomer' off Port Stanley by 6.11.82, sailing with the ship for the UK c14.11.82. Arrived with the vessel at Devonport on 3.12.82 (still coded '-/XL') and off-loaded overnight 3/4.12.82 to a compound at the Granby Gate entrance to the dockyard. Taken by road to Yeovilton 4.12.82 (arriving there the same day) upon transfer that day from 845 Sqdn to 707 Sqdn.

**XT483** HU.5

On 29.3.82 with 707 Sqdn at Yeovilton coded 'VL/WU'. Transferred to 848 Sqdn 19.4.82 in the low-vis scheme coded '-/(W)U' in Black. By 23.4.82 it had been recoded '-/WU'. Allocated to 'D' Flight and flown from Yeovilton to Longroom, Plymouth on 25.4.82 (see XT463). Embarked 'Atlantic Conveyor' in Plymouth Sound on 25.4.82 before sailing with the ship that day for Ascension and the South Atlantic. Noted on HDS duties at Wideawake on 2.5.82.

On 25.5.82, whilst the ship was some 90 miles north-east of Port Stanley (at 50°37′S 56°10′W) en route to Falkland Sound, 'Atlantic Conveyor' was hit by an Exocet missile (one of two launched from a pair of 2 Escuadrilla Super Etendards) and caught fire. The Wessex was consumed by the fire, its remains sinking with the ship on 30.5.82.

**XT484** HU.5

On 29.3.82 with 845 Sqdn at Yeovilton in the low-vis scheme and coded '-/(Y)H'. Allocated to 'A' Flight and left Yeovilton on 3.4.82 for Rosyth, embarking 'Resource' prior to sailing with her for Ascension and the South Atlantic 6.4.82. Flown off to Yeovilton for modifications during the ship's passage down the English Channel 7.4.82, returning to the vessel the same day via Culdrose. Disembarked to the FOB at Old House Creek, San Carlos 24.5.82 before moving to the FOB at Port San Carlos settlement on 30.5.82.

Just prior to dawn on 11.6.82, it took-off from the FOB at Teal Inlet armed with two AS.12 missiles, its target being Port Stanley Town Hall where senior Argentine officers were believed to be in conference. The pilot (Lt Manley) positioned the Wessex on the south side of Beagle Ridge some 3 miles northwest of the Town Hall. Whilst in the hover at 200ft, the missile aimer (POACMN Balls) fired the first AS.12 which just missed its target, hitting the nearby Police Station and demolishing its roof. The second missile's control wire snagged and it impacted in the water some distance short of the Argentine Hospital Ship 'Bahia Paraiso' moored alongside a jetty. The Wessex returned safely to Teal Inlet in spite of AAA fire.

Operated from Port San Carlos settlement and a new FOB at Port Stanley Racecourse until re-embarked on 'Resource' off Port Stanley on 24.6.82 for return to the UK via South Georgia. Still coded '-/(Y)H', it disembarked to Yeovilton (via Culdrose) on 19.7.82 prior to the ship's arrival at Devonport later that day.

**XT486** HU.5

On 29.3.82 with 772 Sqdn at Portland coded 'PO/623'. Visited Northolt 4.5.82, uncoded but using call-sign (623). Delivered out to Yeovilton on 5.5.82 (with Red/Blue roundels already applied) prior to its official transfer to 847 Sqdn 6.5.82. The respray was completed at Yeovilton and by 7.5.82 it was in full low-vis scheme coded '-/XR'. Allotted to 'B' Flight and flown from Yeovilton to HMS Raleigh (Torpoint) on 13.5.82, embarking 'Atlantic Causeway' in Plymouth Sound the same day prior to sailing with her for the South Atlantic on 14.5.82. Retained on 'Atlantic Causeway' after the majority of 'B' Flight aircraft had disembarked to the FOB at Port San Carlos settlement on 1.6.82. Allotted to 'Tidepool' on 10.6.82 to be operated by 848 Sqdn 'D' Flt on HDS duties in the TRALA. Left that day and routed via 'Fort Grange', finally arriving aboard 'Tidepool' on 11.6.82 (code '-/XR' retained). Carried out TRALA HDS duties 11-14.6.82. Detached to 'Glamorgan' on 14.6.82 for air-drop pick-ups as 'Glamorgan' Flight's own Wessex HAS.3 (XM837) had been destroyed on 12.6.82.

On 14.6.82 it attempted the return flight to 'Tidepool', but diverted back to 'Glamorgan' due to bad weather. It had to be left on deck as the ship's damaged hangar was still unusable. That resulted in CAT.4 damage being sustained during a very bad storm on 15.6.82 (two broken main rotor blades, a damaged rotor head and a collapsed mainwheel tyre). Remained aboard the ship which arrived in San Carlos Water on 18.6.82. Airlifted ashore to

the Port San Carlos settlement FOB on 19.6.82 by 18 Sqdn Chinook HC.1 ZA705.

Departed with 'Atlantic Causeway' for the UK (from either Port Stanley on 12.7.82 or San Carlos Water on 13.7.82), arriving at Devonport on 27.7.82. Still coded '-/XR', it was off-loaded on 28.7.82 and taken to a compound at Camel's Head (near HMS Drake). Removed by road to Culdrose on 1.8.82 (and arrived there the same day) where it was officially transferred that day from 847 Sqdn to 771 Sqdn.

**XT755** HU.5

On 29.3.82 with 771 Sqdn at Culdrose coded 'CU/523'. Transferred to 847 Sqdn 6.5.82 and delivered to Yeovilton the same day, uncoded in the low-vis scheme (retaining Black ROYAL NAVY titles). By 7.5.82 it had been coded '-/XX'. Allotted to 'B' Flight and flown from Yeovilton to HMS Raleigh (Torpoint) on 13.5.82, embarking 'Atlantic Causeway' the same day in Plymouth Sound prior to sailing with her for the South Atlantic on 14.5.82. Disembarked to the FOB at Port San Carlos settlement on 1.6.82 and later operated from Teal Inlet, Fitzroy (from at least 11-14.6.82) and elsewhere before moving to Navy Point on 25.6.82. Transferred to 'Engadine' on 5.7.82 before the ship left Port William 7.7.82 en route for the UK (calling briefly at San Carlos Water the same day) to arrive at Devonport on 30.7.82. Still coded '-/XX', it was flown off that day to NASU Yeovilton upon transfer from 847 Sqdn.

**XT756** HU.5

On 29.3.82 with 707 Sqdn at Yeovilton coded 'VL/WM'. Transferred to 848 Sqdn 'A' Flt 19.4.82 in the low-vis scheme and coded '-/WM'. Departed that day to embark 'Regent' in Plymouth Sound prior to the ship setting course later in the day for Ascension and the South Atlantic. Noted at Wideawake 1.5.82 on HDS duty, sailing south with the ship the following day. Remained embarked on 'Regent' during and after the conflict. Departed the FIPZ for the UK with the vessel 24.8.82 and was flown off to Yeovilton on 12.9.82 (still coded '-/WM') upon transfer from 848 Sqdn to NASU. 'Regent' continued to Rosyth and arrived there on 15.9.82.

**XT757** HU.5

On 29.3.82 with NATIU at Lee-on-Solent (uncoded). Transferred to 707 Sqdn on 30.4.82 and flown to Yeovilton on 7.5.82 where it immediately joined 847 Sqdn. In the low-vis scheme and coded '-/XH' by 11.5.82. Allocated to 'B' Flight and flown from Yeovilton to HMS Raleigh (Torpoint) on 13.5.82, embarking 'Atlantic Causeway' the same day in Plymouth Sound prior to sailing with the ship for the South Atlantic on 14.5.82. Disembarked on 1.6.82 to the FOB at Port San Carlos settlement and later operated from Teal Inlet, Fitzroy and elsewhere before moving to Navy Point on 25.6.82. Loaded aboard 'Atlantic Causeway' off Port Stanley c12.7.82 and sailed with the ship from San Carlos Water on 13.7.82, arriving at Devonport 27.7.82. Still coded '-/XH', it was off-loaded 28.7.82 and taken to a compound at Camel's Head (near HMS Drake). Officially transferred from 847 Sqdn to NASU Yeovilton on 28.7.82 and removed by road on 2.8.82, arriving there the same day.

**XT759 HU.5**

On 29.3.82 with 771 Sqdn at Culdrose coded 'CU/529'. Transferred to 847 Sqdn 5.5.82 and delivered to Yeovilton the next day, uncoded in the low-vis scheme (retaining Black ROYAL NAVY titles). By 7.5.82 it had been coded '-/XY'. Allotted to 'B' Flight and flown from Yeovilton to HMS Raleigh (Torpoint) 13.5.82, embarking 'Atlantic Causeway' that day in Plymouth Sound prior to sailing with the ship for the South Atlantic on 14.5.82. Disembarked on 1.6.82 to the FOB at Port San Carlos settlement and later operated from Teal Inlet, Fitzroy and elsewhere before moving to Navy Point on 25.6.82. Remained at Navy Point upon transfer to 845 Sqdn Falkland Islands Detachment on 27.9.82. Embarked 'Astronomer' off Port Stanley by 6.11.82, sailing with the ship for the UK c14.11.82. Arrived with the vessel at Devonport on 3.12.82 (still coded '-/XY') and off-loaded overnight 3/4.12.82 to a compound at the Granby Gate entrance to the dockyard. Removed by road to Wroughton 8.12.82 (arriving there the same day) where it was transferred that day from 845 Sqdn to the RNAY for survey pending possible reissue.

*Noted in storage at Wroughton on 2.2.84 with a cartoon-type motif applied to the starboard fuselage door near the cockpit. It consisted of a Red/Yellow "Buzby" bird clutching a vibrator, with the legend "Heard any good Buzzes?" ("Buzz" in Royal Navy parlance means a rumour). Alongside, the perpetrators had left the inscription "848 'C' FLT. ZAP!".*

**XT760 HU.5**          *Deployed post-14.6.82*

On 29.3.82 at Fleetlands (uncoded) on overhaul. Allocated to 707 Sqdn on 3.5.82 and flown to Yeovilton on 19.5.82, uncoded in the low-vis scheme. Transferred to 848 Sqdn 21.5.82 and coded '-/WV' on 23.5.82 (replacing XS517). Allotted to 'C' Flight for service aboard 'Olwen'. The Flight had formed on 19.4.82, although the ship was then undergoing a refit at Gibraltar and did not return to Devonport until 10.6.82. It finally left Yeovilton for HMS Drake (Plymouth) on 16.6.82, embarking 'Olwen' the same day just after she had sailed from Devonport for operations in the Portland area prior to setting course for Ascension and the South Atlantic on 18.6.82. Shore-based at Wideawake 1-9.7.82 assisting the hard-pressed 845 Sqdn 'D' Flt and ferrying troops from ship to shore. Detached ashore in the Falklands on several occasions during 8/9.82, prior to transferring to 'Fort Austin' with 848 Sqdn 'C' Flt on 27.9.82 as 'Olwen' was returning to the UK. The Flight effectively disbanded on 16.10.82 with the transfer of the aircraft that day to a detachment of 845 Sqdn on 'Illustrious'. Departed the FIPZ with the carrier on 21.10.82 en route for the UK (via the USA), being flown off to Yeovilton on 7.12.82 (still coded '-/WV') prior to the vessel docking at Portsmouth on 8.12.82. Remained with 845 Sqdn.

**XT761 HU.5**

On 29.3.82 with 771 Sqdn at Culdrose coded 'CU/521'. Transferred to 847 Sqdn 6.5.82 and

delivered that day to Yeovilton uncoded in the low-vis scheme (but retaining Black ROYAL NAVY titles). Transferred to 845 Sqdn on 7.5.82 and prepared for air transportation south to Ascension on allocation to 'D' Flight (the Ascension Island Base Flight). Departed Yeovilton 9.5.82 inside Heavylift Belfast G-BEPS and arrived at Wideawake on 12.5.82 where it was assembled by Naval Party 1222 and test-flown. Still uncoded with the Flight on 18.9.82, but had become '-/YP' (in Black) by 16.12.82. Seen during 9.83 wearing small size ROYAL NAVY titles in White (still coded '-/YP') and minus serial on the port side at least. Returned to Yeovilton on 19.12.83 inside Heavylift Belfast G-BEPE.

**XT764 HU.5**

On 29.3.82 with the 707 Sqdn Royal Navy Schools Presentation Team at Yeovilton wearing code '-/RN'. Resprayed in the low-vis scheme on 4.5.82 and by 5.5.82 had been coded '-/XM' prior to its transfer to 847 Sqdn 6.5.82. Allocated to 'A' Flight and departed Yeovilton 9.5.82 to embark 'Engadine' the same day at Devonport prior to sailing with the ship on 10.5.82. The vessel arrived at Gibraltar on 15.5.82 with the Wessex partly unserviceable. Flown ashore to Ascension on 25.5.82 upon transfer to 845 Sqdn 'D' Flt (in exchange for that Flight's XS491). Noted at Ascension 16.6.82, still coded '-/XM'. However, noted uncoded on 11.8.82 and 18.9.82. By 16.12.82 it was reportedly without serials but had been coded '-/YG' (in Black) and was current as such during 1.84. Noted again on 1.9.84 coded '-/(Y)G' and still devoid of serials. Embarked 'Sir Percivale' at Ascension on 18.5.85 for return to the UK, disembarking to Yeovilton from Marchwood (Southampton) c11.6.85.

**XT765 HU.5**

On 29.3.82 with 845 Sqdn at Yeovilton in the low-vis scheme and coded '-/(Y)S'. Allocated to 'B' Flight, it was prepared for air transportation 3.4.82 and left for Ascension 4.4.82 inside Heavylift Belfast G-BEPE, arriving at Wideawake on 5.4.82. Reassembled by Naval Party 1222 and test-flown 7.4.82 prior to embarking 'Fort Austin' on 8.4.82 and sailing south with the vessel 9.4.82 for a rendezvous with 'Endurance'. Returned to Ascension with the ship 20.4.82 prior to sailing with her again on 23.4.82 for the TEZ. Detached to 'Invincible' on 9.5.82 to make room for another Lynx. Transferred to 'Atlantic Conveyor' for temporary storage on 19.5.82 (releasing space on the carrier for the additional Sea Harriers). On 21.5.82 it was detached to 'Stromness' in the armed role, being flown ashore to Ajax Bay on the ship on 22.5.82 in support of 45 Cdo. Moved on 26.5.82 to the 845 Sqdn FOB at Old House Creek on the east bank of San Carlos Water. Embarked 'Fearless' on 27.5.82 to rendezvous with 'Antrim' to the east (outside the TEZ). Returned to San Carlos Water with 'Fearless' on 30.5.82 and disembarked that day to the Port San Carlos settlement FOB. Believed detached to the Port Stanley racecourse FOB from 15.6.82 until it embarked 'Hermes' on 3.7.82 (joining XT450 of 'C' Flight). Sailed from Port William aboard the carrier that day en route for the UK, arriving at Portsmouth 21.7.82. Flown off to Yeovilton 22.7.82 (still coded '-/(Y)S') and remained with 845 Sqdn.

**XT766 HU.5**

On 29.3.82 with 772 Sqdn at Portland coded 'PO/622'. Noted uncoded at Portland on 4.5.82. Delivered to Yeovilton 5.5.82 on transfer to 847 Sqdn (Red/Blue roundels already applied at Portland), painting in the low-vis scheme being completed there later that day and code '-/XS' applied. Allocated to 'B' Flight and flown from Yeovilton to HMS Raleigh (Torpoint) 13.5.82, embarking 'Atlantic Causeway' the same day in Plymouth Sound prior to sailing with the ship on 14.5.82 for the South Atlantic. Disembarked to the FOB at Port San Carlos settlement on 1.6.82 and later operated from Teal Inlet, Fitzroy and elsewhere before moving to Navy Point on 25.6.82. Loaded aboard the 'Atlantic Causeway' off Port Stanley c12.7.82 and sailed with the ship from San Carlos Water on 13.7.82, arriving at Devonport 27.7.82. Still coded '-/XS', it was off-loaded on 28.7.82 and transported to a compound at Camel's Head (near HMS Drake). Removed by road to Culdrose on 31.7.82, arriving there that day. Officially transferred from 847 Sqdn to 771 Sqdn at Culdrose on 1.8.82.

**XT771 HU.5**

On 29.3.82 with 707 Sqdn at Yeovilton coded 'VL/WR'. Transferred to 848 Sqdn 19.4.82 and by 21.4.82 had been painted in the low-vis scheme and coded '-/WR'. Allocated to 'D' Flight and flown from Yeovilton to Longroom, Plymouth on 24.4.82 to embark the 'Atlantic Conveyor'. Due to the need for minor repairs it returned to Yeovilton from Longroom that day. Its replacement (XS512) was dispatched the same day to Longroom. After repairs, XT771 was reallocated to 'B' Flight (as from 29.4.82) and embarked 'Olna' at Spithead from Yeovilton on 10.5.82, sailing with the ship the same day for the South Atlantic. Remained with 'Olna' until she returned to the UK, disembarking to Yeovilton 16.9.82 prior to the ship's arrival at Portsmouth 17.9.82. Flown to Portland from Yeovilton on 17.9.82 upon transfer to 772 Sqdn (still coded '-/WR').

**XT773 HU.5**

On 29.3.82 with 772 Sqdn at Portland coded 'PO/620'. Noted uncoded there on 4.5.82. Delivered to Yeovilton on 5.5.82 upon transfer to 847 Sqdn (Red/Blue roundels already applied at Portland). Painting in the full low-vis scheme with code '-/XT' was completed on 6.5.82. Allocated to 'B' Flight and flown from Yeovilton to HMS Raleigh (Torpoint) on 13.5.82, embarking 'Atlantic Causeway' in Plymouth Sound the same day prior to sailing with the ship for the South Atlantic on 14.5.82. Disembarked on 1.6.82 to the Port San Carlos settlement FOB and later operated from Teal Inlet, Fitzroy and elsewhere before moving to Navy Point on 25.6.82. Reportedly flown aboard 'Contender Bezant' off Port William 2.9.82 (supposedly from 'Astronomer') and sailed with her for the UK on 6.9.82, arriving at Southampton 23.9.82. Still coded '-/XT', it had been off-loaded by 24.9.82 and was removed by road that day to Yeovilton (via Lee-on-Solent) where it arrived on 27.9.82. Officially transferred that day from 847 Sqdn to NASU.

# LYNX

## 815 NAVAL AIR SQUADRON

Equipped with the Lynx HAS.2, 815 Sqdn was parent unit to an increasing number of individual Ships' Flights which deployed aboard the frigates and destroyers of the Royal Navy. As production of the Lynx continued, the type was replacing the earlier Wasp HAS.1's of 829 Sqdn with the Ship's Flights, each operating one helicopter. 815 Sqdn also operated a Headquarters Flight, Trials Flight and Joint Services Trials Unit. At the time of the Argentine invasion the various Ships' Flights were spread far and wide from the Squadron's base at Yeovilton, supporting Royal Navy vessels which were deployed as far apart as the Far East and the West Indies carrying out their various peacetime roles. However, as it turned out, that was to the advantage of Operation "Corporate" as several Royal Navy ships were operating from Gibraltar for the annual Exercise "Springtrain" and were able to deploy almost immediately to the South Atlantic.

The ships involved in "Springtrain" whose Flights were parented by 815 Sqdn included the destroyers 'Coventry', 'Glasgow' and 'Sheffield' plus frigates 'Arrow', 'Battleaxe', 'Brilliant' and 'Broadsword'. The destroyer 'Cardiff' and frigate 'Amazon' were deployed to the Middle East on Gulf Patrol, from which the frigate 'Ambuscade' had recently returned to the United Kingdom. The frigates 'Andromeda' and 'Danae' were deployed to North America/Bahamas and the Standing Naval Force Atlantic respectively, while at home the frigates 'Alacrity' and 'Antelope' were both engaged in sea trials and work-up from Portland. The destroyers 'Birmingham' and 'Newcastle' (both at Portsmouth) plus frigates 'Ardent', 'Charybdis', 'Cleopatra', 'Sirius' (at Devonport) and 'Phoebe' (at Chatham) were all undergoing refits. The Ships' Flights of the last four were in fact out of commission at the time with no helicopters assigned to them. Of the remaining frigates, 'Argonaut' and 'Penelope' were involved in sea trials (the latter's Exocet missile conversion having only recently been completed), 'Avenger' was on maintenance at Devonport (its Lynx having embarked 'Brilliant' for Exercise "Springtrain"), while 'Minerva' was due to arrive at Devonport on 2 April for a refit followed four days later by 'Battleaxe'. Completing the overall picture, the destroyer 'Southampton' was undergoing sea trials (shortly to be joined by sister-ship 'Liverpool'), while the Royal

Navy was also due to take imminent delivery of 'Brazen', its newest frigate.

Under the command of Lt Cdr R.I.Money, 815 Sqdn had the following Lynx HAS.2's assigned to its various Flights on 29 March:

| HQ Flight | | |
|---|---|---|
| XZ731 '-/300' | XZ229 '-/302' | XZ246 '-/304' |
| XZ230 '-/301' | XZ727 '-/303' | XZ250 '-/305' |
| 217 (29 JSTU) Flight | | XZ227 '-/478' |
| 230 (Trials) Flight | | XZ719 '-/479' |

### Ships' Flights

*A Flight consisted of personnel and usually one helicopter. For both administrative and operational reasons each Flight was allocated a three-digit number (beginning with '2') which was normally associated with a particular ship.*

| 'Alacrity' | 206 Flight | XZ720 'AL/327' |
|---|---|---|
| 'Amazon' | 208 Flight | XZ735 'AZ/320' |
| 'Ambuscade' | 219 Flight | XZ721 'AB/323' |
| 'Andromeda' | 222 Flight | XZ722 'AM/472' |
| 'Antelope' | 216 Flight | XZ691 'AO/321' |
| 'Ardent' | 207 Flight | XZ244 'AD/340' |
| 'Argonaut' | 211 Flight | XZ233 'AT/466' |
| 'Arrow' | 204 Flight | XZ241 'AW/326' |
| 'Avenger' | 205 Flight | XZ692 'AG/341' |
| 'Battleaxe' | 201 Flight | XZ728 'BX/403' |
| 'Birmingham' | 200 Flight | XZ247 (333) |
| 'Brilliant' | 220 Flight | XZ729 'BT/342' |
| 'Broadsword' | 221 Flight | XZ736 'BW/346' |
| 'Cardiff' | 214 Flight | XZ254 'CF/335' |
| 'Coventry' | 212 Flight | XZ700 'CV/336' |
| 'Danae' | 218 Flight | XZ699 'DN/464' |
| 'Exeter' | 239 Flight | XZ733 'EX/420' |
| 'Glasgow' | 215 Flight | XZ732 'GW/344' |
| 'Minerva' | 210 Flight | XZ248 'MV/424' |
| 'Newcastle' | 203 Flight | XZ242 'NC/345' |
| 'Penelope' | 209 Flight | XZ730 'PN/454' |
| 'Sheffield' | 213 Flight | XZ725 'SD/337' |
| 'Southampton' | 202 Flight | XZ238 'SN/334' |

At that stage, all aircraft were in the standard Oxford Blue scheme with White serials, codes, deck letters and titles, plus 'D' Class roundels. In addition, several Flights had applied a nickname to their helicopter (for example, the 'Newcastle' Flight Lynx was named "Wee Geordie"), while others had the name of the parent vessel applied. Some were marked to reflect the status of the vessel within the various ships' squadrons (for example, the 'Argonaut' Flight Lynx was marked "Captain F7" to denote the commanding ship of the 7th Frigate Squadron). All such additional marks were applied in White to the nose. The conflict was to see the end of that colour-scheme, with a general order to tone down all markings and to adopt the wartime scheme generally referred to as low visibility (or "low-vis").

As a rule, all codes, deck-letters and nose markings were overpainted in Oxford Blue, the White portion of the roundel was overpainted in either Red or Blue, while the serials and titles were overpainted in Black. The tail-rotors were left in the existing colour scheme although the Red and White transfers were removed. It was generally considered practical to leave the Red and White danger markings unchanged but with Black lettering instead of White. In point of fact the orders did not specify the exact colour-scheme to be adopted, and there were exceptions to the basic outline given above which did produce some highly individual results. There was still confusion as to the exact details of the wartime colour-scheme when the 'Bristol' Group left on 10 May and it was subsequently recommended that a standard wartime scheme be formulated and retained in peacetime as well. It is interesting to note that none of the Lynx HAS.2's involved in the conflict received the revised overall Dark Sea Grey scheme which was frequently (and incorrectly) referred to as "South Atlantic Grey". The later arrivals in this scheme were found to be considerably less conspicuous. Efforts to remove all White markings from the Lynx were invalidated when standard white-painted Sea Skuas were carried, so it was recommended that the missiles should adopt a suitable scheme as well.

With the deployment of much of the fleet to the South Atlantic, many changes occurred between the aircraft assigned to individual Ships' Flights in order to ensure that those with the most up-to-date weapons and equipment were embarked on those ships already deployed or about to deploy. Other aircraft became involved in a hurried modification programme with the installation of ECM, ESM, MAD and TICM equipment, much of which was carried out by NATIU Lee-on-Solent. The TICM (Thermal Imaging Common Modules) provided a new generation of day/night surveillance capability, making use of the inherent Infra-Red radiation of a scene totally independent of the level of visible light or any artificial illumination which effectively allowed the aircrew to "see in the dark". The advantages over conventional night vision devices are that TICM imagers are able to penetrate smoke, haze, mist or camouflage, permitting 24-hour viewing, and being a passive system it is not detectable in use. In terms of weaponry, the new Sea Skua missile was technically still on its acceptance trials but made its operational debut in the South Atlantic. While the Lynx did have to slow down in order to fire the missile (presenting the enemy with a more difficult and not, strange though it

may seem, an easier target), it was still a dangerous opponent. The speed and comparatively wide turning circle of a jet aircraft meant that it would take longer to acquire the very manoeuvrable Lynx in its firing parameters. In addition, the new Stingray torpedo received the "go-ahead" for use on the Lynx from 21 April.

In a manner typical of the conflict, ingenuity and improvisation were quickly applied to devising a GPMG mounting for the Lynx in order to fulfil the anticipated role of gunship. Work commenced on an interim design for this purpose on board 'Brilliant' while she was on her way south. A basic frame able to be mounted on either of the aircraft's door carriers was constructed from the base of a swivel-chair, upturned and mounted on two lengths of angle-iron, and topped by a brass valve rod gearing joint to which the GPMG could be attached! With safety stops constructed from a webbing strop and a wire strap, the gun could be moved in both elevation and azimuth, while the mounting could easily be fitted to either door carrier without interfering with the Sea Skuas, torpedoes or use of the winch, and the whole unit could be stored internally. Without such a cheap and extremely effective "interim" fit, the GPMG could not practically have been used aboard the helicopter. By comparison, when the "official" mounting finally arrived, it was found to be very cumbersome and restricted the aircraft's other roles, so use of the "interim" mounting continued throughout the conflict.

Reflecting the requirement for Lynx HAS.2's equipped with Sea Skua, three Flights ('Minerva', 'Newcastle' and the Trials Flight) were flown out to Ascension Island from Yeovilton by LTW Hercules C.1's on 3 April for onward delivery to 'Fort Austin'. They were followed by 'Ambuscade' Flight's Lynx on 10 April and TICM-equipped XZ240 from NASU on 16 April. Meanwhile, when 'Battleaxe' returned from Gibraltar, her Flight disembarked to Yeovilton on 6 April and XZ728 was passed straight to NATIU for updating to Sea Skua standard before being airlifted out to Wideawake on 12 April. The conflict itself saw numerous changes of aircraft between the Flights involved in order to fulfil the various different tasks assigned to different vessels. It is also worth noting that the frigates 'Brilliant' and 'Broadsword' made full use of their capacity to embark a two-aircraft Flight. The movements and operations are described under the various Flights involved, the majority of which were to return to a new base at the end of the conflict as 815 Sqdn moved to Portland on 19 July. It is worth noting that during Operation "Corporate", those Flights which were involved flew 1,728 sorties totalling 2,567 hours, accomplishing 3,796 deck landings.

# 'ALACRITY' (206) FLIGHT

'Alacrity' was ordered to deploy to the South Atlantic for Operation "Corporate" on 2 April and immediately began loading stores at Portland before moving to Devonport over the weekend of 3/4 April. At that time the Flight was embarked on the ship with Lynx HAS.2 XZ720 (not Sea Skua equipped) coded 'AL/327' and named "Phoenix", having joined the vessel on 24 March for trials in the Portland sea areas. 'Alacrity' sailed for the South Atlantic on 5 April along with 'Antelope'. During the passage the low-vis scheme was applied to XZ720 with the code (327) remaining allocated but not carried. This also applied to replacement aircraft received during the conflict. The Flight began a programme of consolidating ESM and OTHT procedures, a considerable amount of this being done in unison with 'Antelope' Flight. The stopover at Ascension Island from 16 to 18 April saw the Flight practising NGS spotting duties, while once south of the Island it was engaged in chasing spurious submarine contacts and practising night landings without lights or radar.

In order to equip the Flight with a Sea Skua armed Lynx, a three-way aircraft exchange occurred on 24 April. XZ736 was received from 'Broadsword' Flight, while XZ720 transferred to 'Invincible' from which 'Broadsword' had received XZ240. XZ736 required an immediate engine change which was completed within 24 hours, to be followed by half a day of training aboard 'Broadsword'. On 29 April the Flight received its GPMG and 'Alacrity' sailed into the TEZ. The frigate was detached along with 'Arrow' and 'Glamorgan' on 1 May for the first daylight NGS operation which was to take place off Stanley. The tensions of the wartime situation became clear when the Flight was launched, armed with two Sea Skuas, to investigate a radar contact thought to be a fast patrol boat which turned out to be an uncharted rock just off the coast (it later became known as "FPB Rock"!). After that, XZ736 was launched at 1800Z for the NGS spotting mission. The helicopter approached Kidney Island, some 4 miles north-east of Port Stanley, at an exceedingly low altitude, having flown in a wide arc to approach from the north (thereby avoiding detection). As the Lynx gained height to seaward of the Island in order to take up position for its spotting task, the enemy Z28 patrol boat 'Islas Malvinas' was sighted in company with the impressed Falkland Islands vessel 'Forrest', both sheltering between the Island and the coast of East Falkland. The ensuing action resulted in the 'Islas Malvinas' returning to Port Stanley with casualties caused by fire from the Flight's GPMG, while XZ736 itself was hit by six bullets fired from the other vessel. The Lynx circled to engage the 'Forrest' as well, but unfortunately the GPMG trigger mechanism jammed so the action had to be called off. The NGS task was then proceeded with, the heli-copter landing near Mount Low after reconnoitring the area for any enemy presence. Upon landing, the NGS spotter from 148 Battery RA made an "unscheduled exit" from the Lynx, which in the event proved rather fortunate as he noticed a severe fuel leak. That, together with a signal which had been received delaying the planned NGS bombardment by one hour, prompted an immediate return to 'Alacrity'.

XZ736 was transferred to 'Fort Austin' on 3 May for battle-damage repairs, the Flight gaining non-Sea Skua equipped XZ700 from 'Newcastle' Flight in return. The reverse exchange took place on 8 May when a duly repaired XZ736 was returned to 'Alacrity'. Action came the following day when the Flight took-off to investigate a sonar contact and a Mk.46 torpedo was launched. The torpedo was heard to run but no explosion followed — the only sighting being a very suspicious-looking lump of seaweed! Two days later on 11 May, 'Alacrity' herself made night passage through Falkland Sound during which she encountered the Argentine transport ship 'Islas de los Estados' heading for Port Howard. The vessel was sunk using the 4.5 inch gun aboard 'Alacrity' as her Flight's Lynx was airborne at the time, probing the defences of Fox Bay and other harbours and thereby missing all of the action. The three days from 13 May found XZ736 suffering serviceability problems; two main rotor blades were damaged when the helicopter slid into the side of the hangar in rough seas, after which the radar scanner jammed. Another Sea Skua capable radar unit had to be transferred from 'Broadsword'. However, the Lynx was serviceable once again on 17 May when the Flight dropped two flares over Port Howard as a diversion to the landing of NGS spotting teams in the build-up to the main landings four days later.

During and after the landings on 21 May, the majority of airborne time was spent on ESM barrier operations, with the odd diversion which included Hercules air-drop pick-ups, landing on 'Exeter' while 'Alacrity' rescued 74 survivors from the stricken 'Atlantic Conveyor' on 25 May, and more NGS spotting around Port Stanley. 'Alacrity' left the TEZ on 2 June for repairs alongside 'Stena Seaspread' and, following work on her main engines, she was ordered to sail homeward on 6 June. XZ736 took-off as the vessel entered Plymouth Sound, prior to docking at Devonport on 24 June, and proceeded to Yeovilton.

*815 Sqdn aircrew with 'Alacrity' Flight during Operation "Corporate" and their awards: Lt Cdr R.G.Burrows RN (Flt Cdr) MID; Lt R.E.Sleeman RN MID.*

# 'AMBUSCADE' (219) FLIGHT

After five months on Gulf Patrol, 'Ambuscade' arrived at Devonport at the end of February and the Flight disembarked to Yeovilton with its Lynx HAS.2 XZ721, coded 'AB/323' and named "Gonzo". As the helicopter was equipped with both Sea Skua and Stingray, it was exchanged for XZ696 on 9 April while the ship entered a short maintenance period. XZ721 was flown out to Ascension Island the next day inside LTW Hercules C.1 XV292 for onward delivery to 'Brilliant' Flight. 'Ambuscade' was only due for deployment on Gibraltar guardship duties and XZ696 (formerly with 702 Sqdn) was not Sea Skua equipped. The Flight embarked on 9 April and the ship left Devonport that day to arrive at Gibraltar on 13 April. In the event the deployment was cut short as 'Ambuscade' was ordered to the South Atlantic on 28 April. She docked at Gibraltar to make last-minute preparations, then sailed for Ascension Island on 3 May. While the Flight began practising wartime flying operations, XZ696 had the low-vis markings applied; the code (323) was adopted but not carried by this or subsequent replacement aircraft.

The ship arrived in the TEZ on 22 May and three days later a Sea Skua equipped Lynx became available when 'Glasgow' was ordered to proceed east from the main force for essential repairs to be carried out. XZ696 was passed on to 'Glasgow' Flight in exchange for XZ247. Operations for 'Ambuscade' Flight were mainly ESM duties and NGS spotting missions as the ship took part in the bombardment around Port Stanley in support of the advancing British land forces. As a break from those operations, the Flight took XZ247 aboard 'Avenger' for a 12-hour loan on 29 May while her own Lynx (XZ249) was temporarily unserviceable and one was needed to complete the insertion of SBS forces off Volunteer Bay. Following the Argentine surrender on 14 June, 'Ambuscade' remained on station until 5 July when she departed the TEZ and returned to the United Kingdom. The ship arrived in Plymouth Sound on 24 July, XZ247 flying off to its new base at Portland having flown 167 hours during the South Atlantic deployment. 'Ambuscade' docked at Devonport later that day.

> *815 Sqdn aircrew with 'Ambuscade' Flight during Operation "Corporate": Lt P.Henry RN (Flt Cdr); Lt A.Bucknell RN.*

# 'ANDROMEDA' (222) FLIGHT

At the time of the Argentine invasion of the Falkland Islands, the Flight was embarked aboard 'Andromeda' for a deployment to North America and the Bahamas with Lynx HAS.2 XZ722 coded 'AM/472' and named "Arfa". The ship was ordered to return to the United Kingdom and arrived at Devonport on 23 April, the Flight disembarking to Yeovilton the same day. While the ship was re-stored and the Flight personnel went on leave, XZ722 had low-vis markings applied with the code (472) remaining allocated but not carried. The Lynx was flown to Lee-on-Solent for Sea Skua and Stingray equipment fits and returned to Yeovilton on 5 May, on which date the aircrew returned from leave. Two days later the Flight took XZ722 to Lee-on-Solent once again, this time to be fitted with MAD equipment, before moving on to the ranges at Aberporth in Wales for trials on 9 May. 'Andromeda' had sailed on 7 May to join in the MAD equipment trials over the weekend of 8/9 May before returning to Devonport. There the Flight re-embarked on 10 May and sailed with the ship that day for the South Atlantic as part of the 'Bristol' Group.

The Flight busied itself with practising ESM procedures and night-flying techniques without the aid of radar or ship's lights. There was little time to practise NGS spotting as the Group passed Ascension Island on 19 May. As they progressed further south, spurious submarine contacts were investigated but these often turned out to be members of the South Atlantic whale population. 'Andromeda' entered the TEZ during the night of 25/26 May and joined the CVBG as an escort vessel, principally for 'Invincible'. The Flight engaged itself in ESM barrier operations, communications and utility work. Unlike the majority of Flights, it retained the same aircraft for the duration of the conflict.

After the Argentine surrender the vessel anchored in San Carlos Water on 15 June before detaching with 'Cardiff' the following day to escort 'Canberra' into Port William. 'Andromeda' remained on station until August. She visited South Georgia 15-22 August during which time the Flight took XZ722 aboard 'Invincible' for continuation training. The Lynx re-embarked when 'Andromeda' returned to the CVBG before sailing north for the United Kingdom. On passing the breakwater in Plymouth Sound on 10 September accompanied by 'Avenger' and 'Penelope', all three Flights took to the air to perform a flypast before departing to Portland as the ships docked at Devonport.

> *815 Sqdn aircrew with 'Andromeda' Flight during Operation "Corporate": Lt Cdr R.A.McKellar RN (Flt Cdr); Lt L.M.Jeram Croft RN.*

# 'ANTELOPE' (216) FLIGHT

'Antelope' was ordered to deploy to the South Atlantic for Operation "Corporate" on 2 April, at which time she was operating from Portland on sea trials. Her Flight was assigned Lynx HAS.2 XZ691 coded 'AO/321' and named "Norman". The helicopter was flown ashore to Yeovilton on 4 April while the ship had moved to Devonport to complete storing over the weekend of 3/4 April. XZ691 (not Sea Skua equipped) was exchanged for Sea Skua and ECM equipped Lynx HAS.2 XZ723 previously held by NASU. The aircraft was flown aboard 'Antelope' at Devonport late on 4 April and sailed south with the ship the next day.

The Flight began a programme of consolidating OTHT and ESM procedures in company with 'Alacrity' Flight. 'Antelope' detached from the CVBG on 9 April to join the 'Fearless' Group and escort it to Ascension Island which was reached on 21 April. The low-vis markings were applied to XZ723 between that date and 30 April, the code (321) remaining allocated but not carried. The ship stayed at Ascension Island as the Amphibious Group assembled and the Lynx joined in the intense HDS and VERTREP activity between engagements on spurious submarine contacts. 'Antelope' departed south on 29 April along with the LSL's, detaching on 1 May for a rendezvous with the South Georgia vessels and to escort 'Tidespring' with its Argentine PoW's from Grytviken to Leith. She embarked Annie Price and Cindy Buxton (two British Naturalists) together with Capitan de Corbeta Alfredo Astiz (Commander of the Argentine forces at Leith on South Georgia) then sailed for Ascension Island once again on 7 May, arriving on 12 May to disembark her passengers. 'Antelope' left the Island once more three days later with 'Ambuscade' and entered the TEZ on 22 May.

The Flight first saw action on 23 May, when 'Argonaut' Flight had been tasked with an attack on the Argentine supply vessel 'Rio Carcarana' which, despite having been bombed and strafed by 800 Sqdn Sea Harriers on 16 May,

had been reported sailing from Port King. In the event, 'Argonaut' Flight's two Sea Skua missiles failed to lock-on to the target and the mission passed to 'Antelope' Flight. XZ723 was launched at 1600Z for the attack and engaged the enemy vessel with two Sea Skua missiles. Both scored direct hits and set the ship ablaze. The Flight returned later to make a damage assessment and the ship was seen to be settling in the water, still on fire. It was also to be an unlucky day for the Flight's parent ship. During air attacks by two pairs of Grupo 5 A-4B Skyhawks (one of the second pair clipping her mast), she was hit by two 1000lb bombs on the starboard side, neither of which exploded but caused fires on board. XZ723, which was returning from its reconnaissance mission to the 'Rio Carcarana' at the time of the attacks, had in fact been overflown (but ignored) by the incoming Skyhawks. The helicopter held off during the raid but landed back on board following the departure of the A-4B's. The Flight took XZ723 ashore to Ajax Bay in the evening, then embarked 'Fearless' for an overnight stop while bomb disposal experts tackled the unwanted cargo aboard 'Antelope'. Tragically, one of the bombs exploded while being examined by the disposal team, killing two and causing further fires. The ship blew up during the night and sank on 24 May in San Carlos Water.

On 24 May the Flight moved ashore to the FOB at San Carlos and spent the day flying in support of 3 Cdo before recovering to 'Fearless' again for the night. With the loss of the ship, the Flight personnel were transferred to 'Norland' for return to the United Kingdom while XZ723 was left aboard 'Fearless', later being passed on to 'Brilliant' Flight.

---

*815 Sqdn aircrew with 'Antelope' Flight during Operation "Corporate": Lt T.J.McMahon RN (Flt Cdr); Lt D.G.Hunt RN.*

---

# 'ARDENT' (207) FLIGHT

While 'Ardent' was undergoing a short refit at Devonport, her Flight was ashore at Yeovilton with non-Sea Skua equipped Lynx HAS.2 XZ244 coded 'AD/340'. Following the invasion of the Falkland Islands, the refit was cut short and the vessel quickly prepared to sail. Her Flight, meanwhile, had passed XZ244 to 702 Sqdn on 7 April, receiving Sea Skua equipped XZ251 from NASU in its place. The aircraft was duly coded 'AD/340' and received the name "Avon" on 16 April, despite the prevalence of low-vis markings being applied to Lynx HAS.2's on their way south at this stage. On 19 April the Flight embarked 'Ardent' at Devonport prior to sailing with her at 1033Z the same day. The marks carried by XZ251 were

short-lived, as the low-vis scheme was applied during the passage south. The code (340) remained allocated but was not carried. The Flight began to practise flying the expected roles of ESM barrier patrols and ASW, particularly at night. 'Ardent' reached Ascension Island on 29 April and the Flight, when not engaged in practice NGS spotting, helped with the heavy HDS programme between Wideawake and the vessels at anchor.

'Ardent' sailed from Ascension Island on 6 May accompanied by 'Argonaut', acting as escort to 'Canberra', 'Elk' and 'Tidepool' before joining the CVBG during the night of 18/19 May. On 21 May the ship acted as an escort to the Amphibious Group for the landings and commenced bombardment duties in Grantham Sound in support of the SAS at Goose Green. The landings produced the expected Argentine reaction, the first attack by a lone 1 Escuadrilla MB-339A taking place shortly after 1300Z followed by further raids from Grupo 6 Daggers, Grupo 5 A-4B Skyhawks and, finally, 3 Escuadrilla A-4Q Skyhawks. 'Ardent' was attacked by a single Grupo 5 Skyhawk at 1555Z, but it was during the Grupo 6 Dagger attack at about 1740Z that she was hit by a bomb which destroyed the Lynx and demolished the hangar roof, while a second (unexploded) bomb was lodged in the stern. With the resulting fires all under control, she was ordered to the north-west from Grantham Sound in order to join the other ships in Falkland Sound for protection.

During the air raids, the aircrew (Lt Cdr J.Sephton and Lt B.Murphy) bolted machine guns to the stern railings and "let loose" at the raiders. In the final attacks by 3 Escuadrilla A-4Q Skyhawks at 1810Z the ship suffered two more hits at the stern and, tragically, both John Sephton and Brian Murphy, last seen "blasting away" at the aircraft, were among the 22 ship's company killed (another 30 were injured). 'Ardent' dropped anchor, having lost her steering, and serious flooding caused her to list heavily. The survivors were taken off by 'Yarmouth' which later took the stricken vessel in tow, but during the evening of 22 May 'Ardent' sank off North West Island in Falkland Sound taking the remains of the Lynx with her.

> *815 Sqdn aircrew with 'Ardent' Flight during Operation "Corporate": Lt Cdr J.M.Sephton RN (Flt Cdr) DSC (KIA); Lt B.Murphy RN (KIA).*

# 'ARGONAUT' (211) FLIGHT

'Argonaut' had completed a refit just prior to the Argentine invasion of the Falkland Islands and was engaged in sea trials prior to her next deployment. The Flight embarked on 5 April for the trials with Lynx HAS.2 XZ233 coded 'AT/466' and named "Jason". They were quickly completed following receipt of the order to deploy south, the Flight disembarking to Yeovilton on 14 April. That enabled XZ233 to receive the Sea Skua fit before re-embarking on 19 April, by which time the Lynx had received low-vis markings (but retaining White titles, reportedly due to a shortage of Oxford Blue paint but more likely due to confusion over the exact scheme to be adopted). Code (466) remained allocated but was not carried by XZ233 or its subsequent replacements. The Lynx was flown aboard at 1500Z, just after 'Argonaut' had sailed from Devonport.

In common with the other Flights, a programme of training and consolidation of wartime flying operations took place before 'Argonaut' reached Ascension Island on 28 April. Whilst there the Lynx joined in the intense activity to prepare the Amphibious Group, then sailed aboard 'Argonaut' on 6 May in company with 'Ardent', 'Tidepool', 'Elk' and 'Canberra'. The vessels made passage to the east of the TEZ to rendezvous with the 'Fearless' Group, completing the build-up of the amphibious forces. 'Argonaut' Flight carried out the usual round of ESM and surface search sorties against the ever present threat from Argentine submarines and all of the crew's flying skills were tested to the limit in the deteriorating weather conditions encountered that far south.

'Argonaut' entered Falkland Sound on 20 May as escort to the Amphibious Group for the landings on 21 May, before taking up position north-west of the beachhead to act as a radar picket in company with 'Broadsword' and 'Coventry'. During the air raids on 21 May 'Argonaut' was attacked soon after 1300Z by Teniente de Navio Crippa in a 1 Escuadrilla MB–339A (0766/4-A-115) using cannon and rockets, causing damage to her Seacat system and injuries to three of the ship's company. Following an ineffective passing attack by two Grupo 6 Daggers, 'Argonaut' was attacked again soon after 1330Z by six Grupo 5 A-4B Skyhawks and the vessel was hit by two 1000lb bombs which fortunately failed to explode. However, her engines were rendered unserviceable and the steering was lost, while the ensuing fires caused severe damage before being brought under control. Two of the ship's company were killed and three others injured in this attack. Her Lynx managed to escape any damage in the attacks and 'Argonaut' was later towed to a safe anchorage by 'Plymouth'. While anchored to the north of Falkland Sound and with the two unexploded bombs still aboard, her Flight continued operations. On 23 May the Lynx was tasked to carry out an attack on the Argentine merchant vessel 'Rio Carcarana' which was spotted leaving Port King. Much to the crew's dismay the two Sea Skua missiles failed to lock-on and the mission passed to 'Antelope' Flight.

Following proficient repairs by the ship's company to keep 'Argonaut' afloat and make her mobile again, she was declared operational on 26 May and resumed anti-aircraft duties in San Carlos Water. That was short-lived, however, as 'Minerva' arrived to take the ship's place overnight on 29/30 May and 'Argonaut' sailed east for a rendezvous with the repair ship 'Stena Seaspread'. A detailed inspection revealed that the damage was too severe for the vessel to continue operations and she was ordered back to the United Kingdom on 5 June. Her Sea Skua equipped Lynx thus became available for another Flight, and was passed to 'Cardiff' on 5 June in exchange for XZ254. 'Argonaut' arrived back at Devonport on 26 June, on which date XZ254 disembarked to Yeovilton via Longroom (Plymouth).

> *815 Sqdn aircrew with 'Argonaut' Flight during Operation "Corporate": Lt Cdr A.J.Walker RN (Flt Cdr); S/Lt J.H.Davies RN; S/Lt J.F.Hopkins RN.*

# 'ARROW' (204) FLIGHT

'Arrow' sailed from Gibraltar on 26 March to participate in Exercise "Springtrain" with her Flight embarked. At that stage Lynx HAS.2 XZ241 was in use, a non-Sea Skua equipped aircraft coded 'AW/326'. The vessel was ordered directly to the South Atlantic on 2 April and became one of the first ships in the Advanced Group. The Flight consolidated ESM procedures while en route and practised NGS spotting while at Ascension Island (11-14 April), the Lynx receiving low-vis markings during that period. The code (326) remained allocated but was not carried by XZ241 or its subsequent replacement. The requirement for a Sea Skua equipped Lynx was met on 17 April when 'Arrow' carried out a rendezvous with 'Fort Austin', then on her way back north to Ascension Island. The Flight exchanged XZ241 for XZ730, which was also ESM-equipped and formerly with 'Minerva' Flight.

'Arrow' entered the TEZ on 1 May and detached later that day with 'Alacrity' and 'Glamorgan' to a position south of Port Stanley in order to carry out NGS on the airfield. 'Alacrity' Flight's Lynx was launched for spotting duties, but came under fire from two enemy vessels sheltering near Kidney Island and suffered a fuel leak. 'Arrow' Flight was launched to take over the NGS mission, taking Capt "Willie" McCracken (148 Battery RA) along as spotter. Positioned to the east of the runway, the crew watched the first daylight bombardment begin at 1500Z as 'Arrow' fired her first round. The Flight's position attracted little attention at first, but then a barrage of anti-aircraft fire was seen coming from the vicinity of Moody Brook and three Grupo 6 Daggers were seen flying around Cape Pembroke (just over two miles away) with a fourth to the south of Port Stanley. The Flight Commander, Lt P.J.Barber, decided to become inconspicuous as soon as possible by climbing into cloud. 'Arrow' herself suffered some cannon damage in the ensuing attack and the Flight was recalled to the ship in order to beat a hasty retreat from the gunline. NGS spotting missions then continued during the hours of darkness and, despite enemy radars fixing the Flight's position, the resultant barrage of anti-aircraft fire was fortunately out of range.

2 May proved to be a much quieter day, during which a sailor injured in the air raids was flown to 'Hermes', while 4 May saw urgently-needed fire-fighting equipment being flown to the stricken 'Sheffield', followed by further CASEVAC flights with her survivors. The Flight was then recalled from those operations to help investigate a submarine contact but, despite several attacks with Mk.46 torpedoes, no signs of wreckage were found. All was quiet the following day, but on 6 May XZ730 took-off to investigate a contact to the south-west accompanied by the Lynx from 'Coventry' Flight. Two 801 Sqdn Sea Harriers had already been lost investigating the same (or a similar) contact, so the helicopters were both armed with two Sea Skuas apiece. They picked up the target on their own radars but a thick layer of fog made identification difficult at first. On closing in, however, the hulk of 'Sheffield' drifted out of the fog towards them looking (in the words of Lt Barber) "like the Marie Celeste". Nothing else was found.

The next eight days saw the Flight employed in surface search and ESM sorties around the CVBG. At sunset on 15 May 'Arrow' detached to the north coast of the Falklands where, early the following day, the Flight inserted three groups of Special Forces troops as an advance reconnaissance party. The ship then returned to the CVBG and the Flight continued surface search and ESM operations in the build-up to the landings on 21 May. Even though 'Arrow' escaped unscathed from the enemy air raids on 21 and 23 May, she was suffering from cracks in her superstructure which had been caused by the severe sea conditions and was ordered into San Carlos Water for an indefinite period. While the ship stayed under the protective umbrella of her own AA defences and the the Rapier missile units ashore, the Flight was mainly employed as an AEW post to the north of Falkland Sound along with observation duties on known enemy positions. At one stage a large Argentine tented encampment was spotted at Port Howard and this was subsequently bombed by Harrier GR.3's.

On 31 May 'Arrow' and 'Minerva' Flights were tasked with locating the Argentine hospital ship 'Bahia Paraiso', which was suspected of assisting the war effort. The vessel was soon found and while 'Arrow' Flight's Lynx acted as a gunship and radio link, 'Minerva' Flight's helicopter landed aboard to investigate. However, nothing untoward was found. 'Arrow' moved to Fox Bay on 2 June and the Flight carried out NGS spotting duties once again, while the following day saw the Lynx involved in a coastal reconnaissance of the Stanley area. On 4 June XZ730 required a tail-rotor hub change, for which it was disembarked to the FOB at Port San Carlos, but the foggy weather put paid to any repairs being carried out. Three days later 'Arrow' rejoined the CVBG, having survived two weeks in "Bomb Alley", and her Flight returned to routine ESM barrier patrols during the week leading up to the surrender. As if to celebrate that event, the port windscreen on XZ730 cracked during a flight on 14 June! 'Arrow' left for the United Kingdom on 18 June, sailing north via Ascension Island where the Lynx was flown ashore on 26 June for a CASEVAC mission and to collect the mail. The Flight disembarked to Yeovilton on 7 July prior to the ship docking at Devonport later that day.

---

*815 Sqdn aircrew with 'Arrow' Flight during Operation "Corporate" and their awards: Lt P.J.Barber RN (Flt Cdr) MID; Lt C.L.Palmer RN MID.*

# 'AVENGER' (240) FLIGHT

In March 'Avenger' Flight had embarked 'Brilliant' for Exercise "Springtrain" with Lynx HAS.2 XZ692, a non-Sea Skua equipped aircraft coded 'AG/341' and named "Purdy". That was the original 'Avenger' (205) Flight with Lt Cdr B.W.Bryant and Lt N.A.Butler as aircrew. They both remained aboard 'Brilliant' with XZ692 when the ship deployed to the South Atlantic. At that time 'Avenger' was at Devonport undergoing a short maintenance period which was rapidly completed when she too was directed to deploy south. That resulted in a new 'Avenger' (240) Flight being formed on 19 April at Yeovilton with aircrew Lt M.A.McBride and Lt N.T.Sibbit plus Lynx HAS.2 XZ249 acquired from NASU Yeovilton. The aircraft was still coded '-/327' at that stage from former service with 'Alacrity' Flight, but was then allocated the code (307) although it was not carried.

The new Flight embarked 'Avenger' on 26 April for a ten-day period of sea trials, the Lynx being flown off to Yeovilton for an engine change on 5 May. This was completed between 6-9 May, during which time a Sea Skua HIE was also fitted. The Flight re-embarked 'Avenger' on 10 May as she passed the Plymouth breakwater at the start of her journey south with the 'Bristol' Group. Low-vis markings were applied to the helicopter during the passage, while flying involved training in ESM procedures and night sorties without the use of the ship's lights. While at Ascension Island on 18 May, an intense round of VERTREP operations brought aboard last-minute stores. Before the ship entered the TEZ on 25 May, the Flight also recovered two parachute drops from LTW Hercules aircraft.

After 25 May the Flight was engaged in ESM barrier patrols, Special Forces insertion, NGS spotting and surface spotting, interspersed with the ever-present need for HDS and VERTREP sorties. On 29 May XZ249 was suffering from engine problems once again, so XZ247 was borrowed from 'Ambuscade' Flight for 12 hours to complete the insertion of SBS forces off Volunteer Bay, while on 30 May the planned ESM barrier sortie was carried out by 'Exeter' Flight's Lynx. The latter date was to prove quite eventful for the ship. At about 1700Z warning of a possible air raid was received and it eventually materialised from the south at 1731Z when 'Ambuscade'

reported having detected a Super Etendard. What happened next is not absolutely clear, but after one of the two 2 Escuadrilla aircraft had launched the last Argentine Exocet, four Grupo 4 A-4C Skyhawks followed it in and ran into the missile screen. *[See the 'Exeter' Flight, Grupo 4 Skyhawk and 2 Escuadrilla Super Etendard notes for further details of this raid.]*

With XZ249 serviceable once again, the Flight resumed ESM barrier patrols and the ship entered San Carlos Water for the first time on 31 May. On 6 June another SBS party was inserted ashore, this time on Sea Lion Island, while on 8 June 'Avenger' detached for a three-day mission which involved holding close to West Falkland during the daytime and patrolling the area by night, searching for enemy ships and aircraft involved in re-supply missions. NGS spotting took place on 11 June as the ship gave gunfire support to 3 PARA, while two days later XZ249 was tasked as an Exocet deflector to decoy suspected land-based MM.38 missiles away from shipping.

Following the Argentine surrender on 14 June, 'Avenger' went to Fox Bay on West Falkland where the Flight took ashore the First Lieutenant, one officer and four ratings to accept the surrender of the Argentine garrison, a total of some 950 men! The Flight was engaged in area searches of West Falkland between 15-23 June, looking for any continued enemy presence. 'Avenger' assumed the role of guardship at Port Stanley on 24 June which involved some periods with the CVBG, while the Flight carried out HDS and VERTREP tasks and was involved in three separate SAR incidents. The ship finally departed for the United Kingdom on 23 August. On reaching Ascension Island her original two aircrew (Lts Barry Bryant and Nick Butler) embarked to resume their duties with the Flight. As 'Avenger' passed the Plymouth breakwater on 10 September with 'Andromeda' and 'Penelope', all three Flights took-off and performed a flypast over the ships as they entered Devonport before flying off to the Squadron's new home at Portland.

> 815 Sqdn aircrew with 'Avenger' Flight during Operation "Corporate": Lt M.A.McBride RN (Flt Cdr); Lt N.T.Sibbitt RN.

# 'AVENGER' (205) & 'BRILLIANT' (220) FLIGHTS

'Brilliant' sailed from Gibraltar on 26 March for participation in Exercise "Springtrain" and was making full use of the Type 22's ability to embark a two-aircraft Flight. Deployed with her had been her own Flight with Lynx HAS.2 XZ729, a MAD equipped aircraft coded 'BT/342', plus XZ692 (from 'Avenger' Flight) coded

'AG/341' and named "Purdy". The Flights' aircrew were Lt Cdr M.J.Kay and Lt P.A.McKay (XZ729) plus Lt Cdr B.W.Bryant and Lt N.A.Butler (XZ692). Lt Cdr Bryant was overall Flight Commander of both helicopters. Following the order to deploy direct to the South Atlantic on 2 April, 'Brilliant' took on board stores and ammunition from sister-ship 'Battleaxe' (earmarked for return to the United Kingdom) which involved both aircraft in an intensive round of VERTREP flying. During the passage south to Ascension Island, work was carried out on the construction of an interim GPMG mounting for the Lynx as described earlier. 'Brilliant' arrived at the Island on 11 April and three days later XZ692 was exchanged for Sea Skua and Stingray equipped XZ721 which was at that time coded 'A(B)/323' from previous service with 'Ambuscade' Flight. It had been flown out from Yeovilton aboard LTW Hercules C.1 XV292 on 10 April and reassembled by Naval Party 1222, while XZ692 made the reverse journey back to Yeovilton (via Lyneham) where it arrived on 24 April. The ship sailed from Ascension Island on 14 April and the low-vis markings were applied to XZ721 during the passage south. The code (341) remained allocated but was not carried by XZ721 or its subsequent replacements. XZ729 had been similarly treated and retained its code allocation (342). The ship made a rendezvous with 'Fort Austin' on 17 April which allowed Lt Cdr J.N.Clark to embark, replacing Lt Cdr Kay who had left the ship at Ascension Island.

On 22 April 'Brilliant' detached to join the South Georgia Group for Operation "Paraquat". For that operation XZ721 was exchanged for XZ725 (a non-Sea Skua equipped aircraft previously with 'Sheffield' Flight) as its role was only expected to involve basic radar, ESM barrier patrol and trooping sorties. The rendezvous with 'Antrim', 'Endurance', 'Plymouth' and 'Tidespring' took place on 24 April off South Georgia. 'Antrim' Flight (Wessex HAS.3 XP142) sighted the Argentine submarine 'Santa Fe' leaving Grytviken harbour the following morning and attacked the vessel with depth charges. At 0905Z Barry Bryant and Nick Butler took off in XZ725 to attack the submarine with a Mk.46 torpedo and GPMG. The fleeing vessel headed back to the harbour and was forced to stay on the surface as the torpedo circled underneath it. Wasp HAS.1's from 'Endurance' and 'Plymouth' Flights joined in the attack using AS.12 missiles while John Clark and Paul McKay followed up by taking-off from 'Brilliant' at 0930Z in XZ729 to make a GPMG attack on the 'Santa Fe' (joined once again by Bryant and Butler in XZ725). By 1100Z the submarine was alongside in the harbour at Grytviken damaged and leaking oil, and appeared to be settling in the water as the crew escaped. The two Lynx HAS.2's duly returned to 'Brilliant'.

In preparation for the landings on South Georgia XZ725 carried out some coastal searches looking for fast patrol boats before she recovered to the ship at 1300Z. Shortly before that, XZ729 (now re-roled for trooping) departed to 'Antrim' for the assault briefing. At 1430Z both aircraft were launched to make high-speed landings of SAS and Royal Marines personnel for the retaking of Grytviken, led in by the 'Antrim' Flight Wessex. The surrender of Argentine forces on South Georgia was declared at 1715Z, following which both Lynx HAS.2's continued to perform VERTREP and trooping sorties ashore. Later that night XZ729 took-off once again to carry out surface searches but only found icebergs and returned to the ship in very poor visibility. In consolidation of the operation, the two helicopters continued trooping and VERTREP duties on 27/28 April, while PoW's were flown to 'Tidespring' on 27 April. On that

date one of the Flight's aircraft made what was believed to have been the first landing of a Lynx aboard a Type 12 Frigate, in this case 'Plymouth'.

On 28 April 'Brilliant' sailed in company with 'Plymouth' to join the CVBG, arriving the next day to become the escort for 'Invincible'. Accompanied by 'Yarmouth', she was detached for ASW action to the north-east of the Falkland Islands on 1 May in a search for the Argentine submarine 'San Luis' which was suspected of being in the area. In the event, no submarine was found but the operation saw the unfortunate demise of some members of the local whale population!

As a direct consequence of the 4 May Exocet attack on 'Sheffield', the role of XZ729 was changed to electronic surveillance, a task which became more common following the loss of that ship. Luckily, 'Sheffield' Flight's Lynx HAS.2 XZ721 (a Sea Skua and Stingray equipped helicopter which had already seen service aboard 'Brilliant' — see earlier) had escaped the attack unscathed and landed on board 'Hermes'. This Lynx rejoined 'Brilliant' Flight once again on 7 May in exchange for non-Sea Skua equipped XZ725 which transferred to 'Newcastle' Flight aboard 'Fort Austin' the following day.

On 8 May Lt Cdr Bryant and Lt Butler took XZ729 aboard 'Glasgow' while the latter Ship's Flight aircrew (Lt Cdr Lister and Lt Ormshaw) embarked 'Brilliant' with XZ247 to give the Flight two Sea Skua equipped helicopters. 'Brilliant' was detached to the north of Falkland Sound that night and the 'Glasgow' Flight Lynx joined XZ721 (Clark/McKay) in an ESM search for enemy shipping before harassing the enemy troops at Port Howard with a combination of GPMG fire and flare drops. XZ247 returned to its parent ship on 9 May, when XZ729 returned to 'Brilliant'. The two aircrews had not as yet had an opportunity to use the Sea Skua. On 10 May 'Brilliant' and 'Glasgow' relieved 'Broadsword' and 'Coventry' in the bombardment of installations around Port Stanley, both Lynx crews taking turns to fly NGS spotting missions. From a position close to the shore they frequently came under enemy artillery attack but suffered no damage. On 12 May, while operating some 25 miles east of Port Stanley, the two vessels were attacked by Grupo 5 A-4B Skyhawks. Of the first flight of four aircraft, two (C-246 and C-208) fell victim to Seawolf missiles from 'Brilliant' at 1644Z while a third (C-206) crashed into the sea as it took avoiding action. The fourth Skyhawk dropped two 500lb bombs but neither ship was damaged. As the second flight attacked at 1715Z, the Seawolf system malfunctioned and one Skyhawk dropped two 500lb bombs which fortunately bounced off the sea, cleared the ship and fell harmlessly into the water. The other three Skyhawks attacked 'Glasgow' which was less fortunate [see 'Glasgow' Flight and Grupo 5 notes].

During the night of 15/16 May both Lynx took part in an attack on the 'Bahia Buen Suceso', an Argentine transport vessel moored at Fox Bay East. A "home-made" bomb with a short-delay fuse was to be dropped onto the ship by XZ729 (Clark/McKay), while XZ721 (Bryant/Butler) carried Sea Skua missiles in case the ship moved into open waters away from the settlement. The harbour was well defended however, and XZ729 encountered heavy (but inaccurate) anti-aircraft fire which forced the crew to abandon the mission. The vessel was successfully immobilised by 800 Sqdn Sea Harriers the following day. 'Brilliant' rejoined the CVBG on 16 May and the Flight resumed ESM and surface search tasking.

Having arrived in the area, the Amphibious Group was committed on 20 May to the landings at San Carlos with 'Brilliant' forming part of the escort into the AOA which was reached under the cover of darkness. Soon after 1300Z on 21 May (the day of the landings), the first enemy air raid occurred and attacks by Grupo 6 Daggers, Grupo 5 A-4B Skyhawks and 3 Escuadrilla A-4Q Skyhawks continued until sunset. At about 1745Z the ship suffered damage to the forward Seawolf system and one Exocet launcher during a cannon attack by two Grupo 6 Daggers. In the evening XZ729 was loaned to 'Broadsword' as both her helicopters were unserviceable, but the Lynx was not to return as on 25 May it was wrecked by a bomb which bounced off the sea, came up through the ship's flight deck and removed the aircraft's nose.

On the evening of 22 May both 'Brilliant' and 'Yarmouth' were tasked with locating the Falkland Islands-based coastal freighter 'Monsunen', known to be en route from the Sound to Port Stanley having been taken over by the Argentines. During the early hours of 23 May XZ721 was launched to locate the ship and enable SBS personnel to capture it, but in the event the helicopter came under heavy fire as it approached. However, pursued by the two frigates, the 'Monsunen' was driven aground in Lively Sound.

'Brilliant' was detached on 27 May for a period of maintenance alongside 'Stena Seaspread' to the east of the Falkland Islands during which time Lynx HAS.2 XZ721 was exchanged for non-Sea Skua equipped XZ254 from 'Cardiff' Flight. On 30 May the two helicopters returned to their original ships upon completion of the maintenance. Following the loss of XZ729 aboard 'Broadsword',

'Brilliant' embarked XZ723 (a Sea Skua and ECM equipped Lynx) from 'Fearless', to which ship the helicopter had recovered after the loss of 'Antelope'. XZ723 joined XZ721 on ESM barrier patrols until 9 June while 'Brilliant' escorted ships into and out of the AOA (as well as acting as "guardship" to 'Invincible').

On 9 June the ship detached to the east for a rendezvous with 'Contender Bezant' as the two Lynx were to accompany her cargo of 18 Sqdn Chinook HC.1's to the CVBG. Various delays occurred due to the weather, deployment ashore of the Chinooks not being completed before the Argentine surrender on 14 June. 'Brilliant' rejoined 'Hermes' on 17 June and expected orders to return home to the United Kingdom. She was relieved by 'Broadsword' on 22 June, on which date XZ721 departed once more, this time going to 'Cardiff' Flight in exchange for XZ233. On the following day XZ723 was swopped for XZ732 from 'Broadsword' Flight. Both new arrivals were battle-scarred and XZ732 was in fact marked as "XZ729" (in Black), having been fitted with the boom from that Lynx whilst aboard 'Broadsword'! 'Brilliant' sailed for home on 23 June, calling at Ascension Island where Lt Cdr Bryant and Lt Butler were disembarked to resume their duties aboard 'Avenger'. 'Brilliant' Flight disembarked on 13 July, XZ732 (still marked as "XZ729" but carrying the legend 'HMS Brilliant' on its nose) flying off to Yeovilton followed by XZ233, both before the ship docked at Devonport at 1000Z.

*815 Sqdn aircrew with 'Brilliant' Flight during Operation "Corporate" and their awards: Lt Cdr J.N.Clark RN ('Brilliant' Flt Cdr) MID; Lt P.A.McKay RN; Lt Cdr B.W.Bryant RN ('Avenger' Flt Cdr) MID; Lt N.A.Butler RN MID.*

# 'BROADSWORD' (221) FLIGHT

'Broadsword' had sailed from Gibraltar on 26 March to participate in Exercise "Springtrain", taking her Flight which was operating Sea Skua equipped Lynx HAS.2 XZ736 coded 'BW/346'. The ship was recalled to prepare for Far East deployment and sailed again from Gibraltar on 5 April, heading for Naples. However, she was recalled to Gibraltar yet again and arrived there on 6 April to prepare for the South Atlantic, sailing on 8 April to join the CVBG. Her Flight carried out training in wartime flying procedures whilst en route to Ascension Island. In common with the other Flights, low-vis markings were applied to XZ736 while the code (346) remained allocated but not carried. Following the example of 'Brilliant' (see earlier), 'Broadsword' made full use of her ability to accommodate a two-aircraft Flight and a second Lynx was embarked at Ascension Island on 18 April. This was MAD, ESM and Sea Skua equipped XZ728 'BX/403' (formerly with 'Battleaxe' Flight) which had left Yeovilton on 13 April aboard LTW Hercules C.1 XV298. Reassembled by Naval Party 1222 at Wideawake, it officially joined the Flight on 16 April and was test-flown

the following day. The code (347) was allocated but not carried, as by then the aircraft was in the low-vis markings.

Meanwhile, Lt Cdr R.B.Jones (the 'Broadsword' Flight Commander) had gone ashore to collect Lynx HAS.2 XZ240 from Wideawake, a TICM, ESM and Sea Skua equipped aircraft, flying it to 'Invincible' on 18 April for eventual use by 'Broadsword' Flight. In fact the Flight borrowed this helicopter from 'Invincible' for the day on 20 April, while on 24 April a three-way exchange took place in which XZ240 was gained from 'Invincible' on a more permanent basis and allocated code (348), although this was not carried. In the meantime XZ736 was transferred to 'Alacrity' Flight whose own Lynx (XZ720) was sent to 'Invincible'. Accompanied by 'Sheffield', 'Broadsword' took over radar picket duty off Port Stanley in early May and the two assigned aircraft were engaged on ESM patrols. On 5 May XZ240 was transferred to the Trials Flight on board 'Fort Austin' in exchange for non-Sea Skua equipped Lynx XZ732 which was allocated the code (349) although this was not carried.

*LYNX HAS.2 XZ730 (326) of 815 Squadron 'Arrow' Flight is airborne,while on the ground near San Carlos settlement is XZ733 (420) of 'Exeter' Flight. Both helicopters are carrying glossy-white Sea Skua missiles which rather negate their otherwise effective low-visibility colour schemes.*
*(Royal Navy and 815 Sqdn 'Exeter' Flight)*

*On 25.5.82 a bomb dropped by a Grupo 5 de Caza A-4B Skyhawk bounced from the sea, struck the hull of 'Broadsword' and exited via her flight-deck, causing the damage shown, before falling into the sea – without detonating! The victim was 815 Squadron 'Brilliant' Flight's Lynx HAS.2 XZ729 (342), on loan to 'Broadsword' Flight. Had the bomb exploded the damage to both frigate and helicopter could have been catastrophic. The Lynx was later restored to pristine condition in the Dark Sea Grey colour scheme at RNAY Fleetlands.*
*(Royal Navy)*

*Many variations of the basic Lynx low-visibility colour scheme were applied to 815 Squadron HAS.2's during the conflict. Here, on 'Hermes' at Portsmouth on 21.7.82, is 'Newcastle' Flight's XZ720, devoid of markings (except for the Red centre spots of the roundels) including the serial. This particular Lynx was based on 'Hermes' for ESM AND Exocet decoy duties.* *(Peter J. Cooper)*

Relieved of radar picket duties by 'Brilliant' on 10 May, the ship took up duties as an escort to 'Glasgow' for the bombardment of shore positions around Port Stanley on 12 May. At 1800Z the following day, she was detached with 'Hermes' and 'Glamorgan' for a raid on Pebble Island but three hours later the three vessels were on their way back as the operation had been delayed for 24 hours. 'Broadsword' detached once again on 14 May, this time with 'Hermes' and 'Glasgow', to insert Special Forces personnel for the Pebble Island operation in which 11 aircraft were wrecked or immobilised. In addition, a fuel dump and an ammunition store were destroyed. The ship returned to the CVBG on 15 May, but XZ728 suffered slight damage aboard on that date due to rough seas. Its Sea Skua equipment was removed on 19 May to be fitted to XZ732, but during an enemy air attack at 1325Z on 21 May (the day of the landings), XZ732 was itself the victim of some splinter damage when 'Broadsword' was hit by cannon fire from a Grupo 6 Dagger whilst the helicopter was on deck. Having two unserviceable aircraft, the Flight then temporarily borrowed MAD equipped Lynx HAS.2 XZ729 from 'Brilliant' Flight. This aircraft did not return to 'Brilliant', however, as it suffered serious damage at 1800Z on 25 May during an Argentine air raid while the ship was operating with 'Coventry' to the north of Pebble Island. A pair of Grupo 5 A-4B Skyhawks dropped four bombs, three of which fell harmlessly into the sea, but the fourth bounced off the surface of the water, passed up through the side of the hull and exited via the flight deck, taking the nose of XZ729 with it. The bomb fell harmlessly into the sea on the other side of 'Broadsword' without exploding. As a result of this action, the vessel found herself with three unserviceable helicopters aboard and was ordered to rejoin the CVBG to the east of the Falkland Islands. While repairs to the ship were carried out, the Flight succeeded in making XZ728 serviceable once more by 1 June, so ESM operations for the CVBG were commenced. Two days later work started on repairing the

cannon damage to XZ732, during which it was fitted with the boom from the wrecked XZ729. XZ728 was transferred to 'Hermes' for the day on 8 June (permitting XZ732, still incorrectly marked as "XZ729", to be test flown) and again on 9 June (to facilitate ground runs by XZ732 on the 'Broadsword' flight deck). The hulk of XZ729, by now robbed of all usable spare parts, was transferred to 'Atlantic Causeway' by Sea King on 11 June for return to the United Kingdom.

Following the Argentine surrender on 14 June, 'Broadsword' underwent a brief period of repairs inshore, after which she took over as escort for 'Hermes' on 22 June to allow 'Brilliant' to return home. On 23 June Lynx XZ732 embarked 'Brilliant', while 'Broadsword' Flight gained XZ723 in exchange (ECM and Sea Skua equipped). It was not allocated a sequential code as had happened with the earlier replacement Lynx, the code (349) being assigned but not carried. The ship's own turn to sail for home came on 3 July when she departed Port William in company with 'Hermes' to join the main Group some 120 miles to the east before heading north the following day. With the order to sail, XZ723 was passed to 'Penelope' Flight on 2 July in exchange for Sea Skua equipped XZ691 which was suffering from vibration problems. 'Broadsword' arrived at Devonport on 23 July and XZ691 disembarked at the Plymouth breakwater half an hour before the ship docked at Devonport. XZ728 remained aboard until lifted off by crane on 24 July. The journey to Portland was made by road on 24/25 July as the helicopter had a mechanical fault.

---

*815 Sqdn aircrew with 'Broadsword' Flight during Operation "Corporate": Lt Cdr R.B.Jones RN (Flt Cdr); Lt C.E.Thornton RN; Lt M.T.Chirnside RN; S/Lt R.Middleton RN.*

---

# 'CARDIFF' (214) FLIGHT

'Cardiff' had deployed during February for a five-month period of Gulf Patrol with her Flight embarked, using Lynx HAS.2 XZ254, a non-Sea Skua equipped aircraft coded 'CF/335'. The vessel was ordered to join the Task Force and departed from Mombasa, Kenya, on 20 April en route to Gibraltar. The Flight practised OTHT procedures and low-level night flying during the passage, but XZ254 became unserviceable at Suez following which the aircrew could only brush up on their recognition of enemy ships and aircraft and assimilate the news from the South Atlantic. On 7 May the ship arrived at Gibraltar and began taking on stores, but the Lynx was still awaiting a vital part when 'Cardiff' sailed on 12 May to join the 'Bristol' Group the next day. The missing spare part (a gauge) was collected from Ascension Island on 19 May (in fact two of them had arrived!) and the Flight returned to preparing in earnest for the operations to come. Night flying without lights or radar was carried out as well as one airdrop pick-up. On the night of 25 May the Lynx was

flown to 'Glasgow' (then on her way to the TRALA) to collect a brief of the war situation for the Captain aboard 'Cardiff'. The following day the ship joined the CVBG to the east of the Falkland Islands and by that time the aircraft was in low-vis marks. The code (335) was still allocated but was not carried by XZ254 or its subsequent replacements.

On 27 May XZ254 and its aircrew were swopped with 'Brilliant' Flight, 'Cardiff' receiving XZ721 (Sea Skua and Stingray equipped) in exchange. During the following 36 hours aboard 'Brilliant', the 'Cardiff' Flight crew received a detailed briefing on Sea Skua operations. When they returned to 'Cardiff' they retained XZ721 while 'Brilliant' spent the weekend out of the TEZ for repairs. XZ721 duly returned to 'Brilliant' on 30 May while 'Cardiff' Flight regained XZ254. While the hours flown by the Flight during May were not high by "Corporate" standards, some 80% of them took place in the last five days of the month.

The Flight was tasked daily by 'Hermes' and normally maintained ESM barrier patrols some 60 to 80 miles from the CVBG as well as carrying out HDS requirements. A Sea Skua equipped aircraft became available again when 'Argonaut' was detached from the TEZ for repairs (subsequently returning to the United Kingdom), and on 5 June XZ254 was exchanged for XZ233. This aircraft was also in the low-vis scheme but had surprisingly retained its White ROYAL NAVY titles. However, the Sea Skua HIE equipment was unserviceable until repaired with the aid of a new "black box" and the assistance of the Group AEO, Lt Ackerman. The problem was further complicated by the fact that the two Sea Skua missiles which had been received were also unserviceable. Later on 5 June, during a sortie into the AOA in preparation for night bombardment duties, the helicopter suffered an oil loss from the main rotor gearbox and had to divert to 'Arrow'. Several friendly fire control radars locked onto the Lynx during the process, giving its crew a few harrowing moments! Duly repaired, XZ233 was able to return to its parent vessel.

'Cardiff' relieved 'Exeter' as the AAWC in San Carlos Water on 13 June, a day that was to prove memorable for her Flight. While returning from a surface search some 50 miles to the south of Falkland Sound armed with one Sea Skua missile, the crew heard a loud ripple of noise. Their initial reaction was to think that there was something drastically wrong mechanically, but a rapid instrument scan indicated that everything appeared normal. However, a quick glance to port out of the cockpit provided the view of a Grupo 6 Dagger's silhouette turning in steeply! Just at that moment another Dagger flew by close to the starboard side having just completed an unsuccessful strafing run from behind XZ233. The helicopter pilot (Lt C.H.Clayton) immediately banked steeply to port and dived to sea-level as the second Dagger turned in, now almost dead ahead. Chris Clayton attempted to keep on the inside of the Dagger's turn, thus denying it a straight attack run, and as the turn tightened his speed was reduced, allowing him to keep the Dagger in front and in sight. The enemy aircraft eventually fired at the Lynx whilst still in the turn, but the fire splashed some 100 yards wide. Having exhausted its supply of ammunition, the Dagger climbed away and the Lynx crew scanned the sky for the second aircraft. It was spotted on their starboard side in a shallow dive flying straight towards the Lynx. Chris Clayton banked steeply, turned towards the attacker and levelled out, then accelerated at maximum torque towards the Dagger. The head-on situation continued until the two aircraft were only some 100 yards apart,

when the Dagger broke to starboard and climbed away. The fall of its cannon fire was not seen by the Lynx crew, but is believed to have passed over the top of the helicopter. The two Argentine Daggers did not attempt to repeat the attack and climbed away towards the mainland. By excellent handling, the Flight crew survived to tell the tale, and after holding off for a while in case the attackers came back, the Lynx returned to 'Cardiff'. One would have thought that the two Daggers could easily have brought down the unarmed helicopter but their unsuccessful tactics allowed Chris Clayton to take the appropriate avoiding action.

The Flight was launched again that evening to reconnoitre enemy positions using thermal imaging equipment, providing intelligence prior to an SAS night insertion for which the Flight also provided SAR cover. The news of the Argentine surrender came through on the evening of 14 June and on the following morning the Flight took the CO of 40 Cdo Bde to Port Howard to accept the surrender of the troops there. It was a strange experience for the seven officers involved, taking the surrender of some 1000 armed enemy troops, but no problems were encountered. Supporting the ground forces became the Flight's priority task for the remainder of June. On 22 June XZ233 was transferred across to 'Brilliant' Flight for return home to the United Kingdom due to serviceability problems, while XZ721 was received once again in exchange along with its armament of Stingray torpedoes and Sea Skua missiles. The Lynx required an engine change almost immediately and the Flight also had to sort out some outstanding avionics problems.

'Cardiff' remained as "manager" at Port San Carlos until 30 June when she was relieved by 'Exeter' and sailed to rejoin the CVBG. The next week was spent on anti-aircraft picket duties, while at one stage the helicopter suffered damage to a main rotor blade caused by a freak wave breaking over the flight deck. On 7 July 'Cardiff' handed over to the newly arrived 'Birmingham' and sailed for the United Kingdom in company with 'Exeter' and 'Yarmouth'. Patrol and HDS sorties continued as far north as Ascension Island, which was reached on 18 July. The ship arrived at Portsmouth during the morning of 28 July and the Flight disembarked to Portland that afternoon.

*815 Sqdn aircrew with 'Cardiff' Flight during Operation "Corporate" and their awards: Lt C.H.Clayton RN (Flt Cdr) MID; Lt P.K.Hullett RN.*

# 'COVENTRY' (212) FLIGHT

'Coventry' had sailed from Gibraltar on 26 March to take part in Exercise "Springtrain" with her Flight embarked, using Lynx HAS.2 XZ700 coded 'CV/336' and named "Lady G". The ship was ordered direct to the South Atlantic on 2 April, the Lynx having low-vis markings applied on 12/13 April during the passage to Ascension Island. The code allocation (336) was retained but

not carried by the aircraft or its replacement. Having passed Ascension Island the ship made a rendezvous with 'Fort Austin' on 17 April and exchanged XZ700 for Sea Skua equipped Lynx XZ242 from 'Newcastle' Flight. For the next two weeks nothing untoward happened concerning the Flight, but that situation changed during the early hours of 3 May.

About 0400Z that morning, while some 70 miles north of the Falkland Islands, the crew of 826 Sqdn Sea King HAS.5 ZA129 were attempting to identify a small ship when it opened fire on the approaching helicopter with automatic weapons *[see 826 Sqdn notes for details]*. Before the vessel could be identified in the darkness as anything other than an unknown patrol boat (but obviously Argentine!), the Sea King withdrew to a safe distance and called for assistance.

Both 'Coventry' and 'Glasgow' Flights were scrambled for the attack, each Lynx being equipped with a pair of Sea Skua missiles. 'Glasgow' Flight's aircraft suffered a UHF radio failure soon after departure from the ship and held off while the 'Coventry' Flight Lynx was directed in on radar by the Sea King's Observer. Having achieved a lock-on to the patrol boat, the Flight closed to 8 miles and fired its two missiles in quick succession. Both of them scored direct hits and detonated. Explosions were seen and the ship seemed to disappear without trace (believed sunk).

Meanwhile, 'Glasgow' Flight's aircraft had regained the use of its radio and both helicopters circled the area in the dark to look for any survivors and drop life-rafts. As they searched in vain for personnel and wreckage, what was believed to have been a second patrol boat was detected on radar some distance from the search area. That contact was successfully attacked by 'Glasgow' Flight at 0435Z.

'Coventry' Flight thought that they had sunk the 'Comodoro Somellera' but, in fact, both Flights had attacked and damaged the same patrol boat — the 'Alferez Sobral' *[see Glasgow Flight notes for details]*. The 'Comodoro Somellera' was nowhere near her sister-ship that night and at 0850Z on 4 May is known to have been south-west of the Falkland Islands searching for survivors from the 'General Belgrano'.

Following the 'Alferez Sobral' events of 3 May 'Coventry' Flight resumed its normal ESM patrols, but on 6 May was dispatched once again (in company with 'Arrow' Flight) to investigate a surface contact some 90 miles south-west of the CVBG. Each Lynx was armed with two Sea Skua missiles as unfortunately two Sea Harriers had already been lost in the thick surface fog while investigating the same contact, which turned out to be the hulk of 'Sheffield' *[see Arrow Flight notes]*. After flying over the wreck, both aircraft returned to their respective ships.

On 9 May 'Coventry' was to fire her Sea Dart missiles in anger when a Grupo 1 Hercules was detected at extreme range attempting a resupply mission. The vessel fired three Sea Darts at 1417Z but they failed to reach the target and the Hercules turned away towards the mainland. On the following day 'Coventry' was relieved from picket duty off Port Stanley by 'Glasgow' and the ship rejoined the CVBG where the Flight continued ESM patrols. On 14 May XZ242 was flown to 'Broadsword' to have its radar checked. In company with 'Broadsword', 'Coventry' was tasked on 22 May to operate in the "missile trap" role, basically lying in wait to ambush any enemy aircraft engaged in resupply missions. When in position north of Pebble Island another Grupo 1 Hercules was detected at 0645Z, but the ship's Sea Dart system failed at the critical moment and the aircraft passed by at a range of eight miles, its crew oblivious to the fact that they had lead a charmed life! The operation continued over the next few days. On 25 May an early Grupo 5 A-4B Skyhawk attack was thwarted at 1230Z when 'Coventry' brought down C-244 with a Sea Dart fired from long-range. Soon after 1540Z another of her Sea Darts brought down the Grupo 4 A-4C Skyhawk C-304 although the aircraft was actually returning from an unsuccessful sortie to San Carlos Water and was not attacking the ship. In a second direct raid at 1821Z the ship was not so fortunate, being attacked by two Grupo 5 Skyhawks. 'Coventry' was hit by three bombs dropped from A-4B C-207 (flown by Primer Teniente Velasco) and her port side ruptured; the vessel quickly rolled to port and later capsized. The order to abandon ship was given at 1848Z with 19 of her company dead and 25 injured. The ship sank at 1922Z 10 miles north of Pebble Island taking Lynx XZ242 with her. The aircrew returned to the United Kingdom aboard the 'Queen Elizabeth 2'.

---

*815 Sqdn aircrew with 'Coventry' Flight during Operation "Corporate" and their awards: Lt Cdr A.Rich RN (Flt Cdr)* **MID**; *Lt H.T.Ledingham RN* **MID**.

---

# 'EXETER' (239) FLIGHT

'Exeter' sailed from Portsmouth on 16 March for deployment to the West Indies on guard-ship duties. Her Flight had embarked with Lynx HAS.2 XZ733 coded 'EX/420', the first Lynx HAS.2 to be operationally equipped with the Sea Skua missile. Following the loss of 'Sheffield' on 4 May, her programme was cut short. On 7 May 'Exeter' put into St.Johns, Antigua to prepare for deployment to the South Atlantic and sailed that evening, despite an Argentine claim on 29 April that she was ablaze off the Falkland Islands after hitting a mine! On the morning of 10 May the Flight spent three hours in VERTREP operations transferring stores from 'Green Rover', following which the Lynx was re-roled to the Sea Skua fit that afternoon (even though the Flight had no missiles at that stage). For the next week the Flight worked up and practised wartime procedures, while the Lynx was given low-vis markings. The code (420) remained allocated but was not carried.

'Exeter' entered the TEZ on 21 May and took up station as an AAW picket 20 miles west of the CVBG on 22 May. The Flight was tasked with ESM barrier patrols 80 miles west of the CVBG and also flew some HDS sorties. It was during an ESM sortie on 25 May that the Flight heard that a Super Etendard had been detected to the north-west of the CVBG and that two missiles were closing, probably aimed at 'Ambuscade' which had fired off chaff immediately. The missiles were thought to have been successfully decoyed but unfortunately at least one of them had locked on to the 'Atlantic Conveyor' which was lost as a result.

By 25 May the Flight had acquired its Sea Skua missiles. ESM barrier patrols continued to the west and south-west of the CVBG, the sortie programme being directed from 'Hermes'. On 30 May 'Exeter' Flight flew an ESM sortie which was originally scheduled for 'Avenger' Flight (whose Lynx XZ249 had become unserviceable), as well as carrying out an HDS sortie to 'Hermes'. Later the same day, whilst returning from an ESM patrol at about 1400Z, the Flight successfully located the pilot of 1(F) Sqdn Harrier GR.3 XZ963 (Sqdn Ldr Pook) whose aircraft had suffered damage during attacks near Port Stanley, forcing him to eject. So expeditious was the rescue that the helicopter arrived on the scene to find that the pilot had not even reached the water, even though his ejection seat transmitter was blaring away! He was picked up by 820 Sqdn Sea King XZ571 only ten minutes later.

At about 1700Z on 30 May, 'Exeter' received warning of a possible raid on the CVBG, and the attack was detected at 1731Z from the south-east, the ship being stationed about 100 miles to the north-east of the Falkland Islands at that time. Within seconds, the ship was being manoeuvred and chaff had been fired, indicating to all aboard that the attack was being performed by a Super Etendard with Exocet missiles. Flight personnel were scrambled to take up their positions on the flight deck and man the LMG's. The attack in fact comprised two 2 Escuadrilla Super Etendards (one armed with the last Argentine AM.39 Exocet) and four Grupo 4 A-4C Skyhawks. The raiders were detected at just over 40 miles range and 'Exeter' turned her stern towards the threat, firing off chaff. Three contacts were seen on radar; the first Sea Dart fired at this group missed, while the second Sea Dart brought down A-4C C-301, but by this time the Exocet had been launched and its radar had locked onto 'Exeter'. A third Sea Dart was fired at this contact and at a range of nine miles from the ship both of the missiles stopped dead and disappeared from the radar display. To those on the flight deck it appeared that a second enemy missile had been fired at either 'Avenger' (stationed some ten miles south-east) or 'Exeter' as a very low, fast-moving object was observed passing astern where it splashed and stopped. However, a second A-4C (C-310) was also brought down by a Sea Dart and that may have been what was seen. In any event, both vessels escaped unscathed, as did 'Invincible' despite Argentine claims that the carrier had been bombed in the raid.

During May the Flight had achieved 84 flying hours with no serviceability problems. Another rescue mission on 1 June proved less successful for the Flight than the one on the previous day. Flt Lt Mortimer had ejected from 801 Sqdn Sea Harrier XZ456 and by the time the Flight arrived in the expected area it was dark and, as it happened, the search between 2200Z and 0025Z was conducted in the wrong area because Mortimer had inadvertently switched off his SARBE transmitter. Fortunately, the pilot was eventually recovered the following day by an 820 Sqdn Sea King HAS.5. On 3 June Lynx HAS.2 XZ733, affectionately known as "Trigger", celebrated one year and 401.05 flying hours with the Flight. The following day saw the Lynx in action as an Exocet decoy, having been fitted with radar reflectors to simulate the response from a ship in order to seek out a reported land-based MM.38 Exocet launcher in the vicinity of Stanley. Although the helicopter was tracked by various enemy fire control radars, no Exocet missiles materialised. That night 'Exeter' detached to a position just north of Falkland Sound in order to intercept the high-level bombing sorties which had been adopted by Grupo 2 Canberra B.62's. The following day was spent in San Carlos Water while the Flight carried out shore patrols. The night of 5 June found the ship on interdiction duties again in anticipation of further Argentine Canberra attacks, but none materialised. On 7 June the Flight searched the southern half of East Falkland for enemy radar sites and succeeded in locating a party of SBS men on Sea Lion Island who duly produced cups of much-needed Special Forces coffee! That day 'Exeter' successfully shot down a Learjet 35A of Grupo 1 Aerofotografico (T-24) with a Sea Dart missile. The ship was to continue her night interdiction tasks up to 10 June.

On 10 June XZ733 was equipped to take thermal imaging equipment and carried out a search along the north side of Wickham Heights and then Mount Pleasant. On the following evening 'Exeter' and 'Minerva' Flights were launched on a deception mission to fire chaff and to mislead the enemy into thinking that a major helicopter assault on the beaches adjacent to Port Stanley was about to take place (the mission was a great success — see 'Minerva' Flight). While the ship was ordered back to the CVBG on 13 June, the Flight was to carry out a covert mission near Mount Rosalie on West Falkland. Having embarked 'Sir Lancelot' for the briefing, the Flight then successfully located an enemy observation post before returning to its parent ship via 'Fearless' and 'Intrepid'.

By the evening of 13 June XZ733 was once again fitted with Sea Skua missiles and returned to the ESM barrier patrol role. Later that night (at 0155Z) the ship's Sea Darts claimed another victim by bringing down Grupo 2 Canberra B.62 B-108 over East Falkland. The Flight continued ESM sorties following the Argentine surrender as the Task Force did not allow itself the luxury of relaxing. However, on 16 June the aircraft became unserviceable, first requiring an engine change (completed overnight), then suffering failures in two of its hydraulic systems. Having acquired the necessary spares from XZ729 aboard 'Atlantic Causeway' on 20 June, a third hydraulic pump failed and XZ729 was again looked to for a spare. A new unit finally arrived from Ascension Island on 1 July and was fitted, after which the Lynx was test-flown to Swan Island in Falkland Sound (to the north-east of Fox Bay) and proved to be serviceable once again. Meanwhile, 'Exeter' had commenced duties as the Port Stanley guard-ship on 30 June. The Flight carried out a reconnaissance patrol over the Islands on 2 July, a transfer of casualties to 'Uganda' on 3 July and a long-range search for a reported enemy warship to the west of the Islands on 4 July. Two Sea Skuas were carried on the last mission and the Flight routed out via 'Penelope', but nothing was found. On 5 July the crash site on Pebble

Island of the Learjet 35A shot down by a Sea Dart from 'Exeter' was visited, followed by HDS sorties, while the next day was spent at Port Stanley Airport as 'Exeter' was in the harbour there. The ship sailed for the United Kingdom on 7 July and arrived at Portsmouth on 28 July, the Flight disembarking to Portland the following day.

# 'GLASGOW' (215) FLIGHT

At the time of the Argentine invasion of the Falkland Islands, 'Glasgow' Flight was assigned Lynx HAS.2 XZ732 coded 'GW/344'. The helicopter, which was not Sea Skua equipped, had embarked the ship for participation in Exercise "Springtrain", sailing from Portsmouth on 8 March and departing Gibraltar for the Exercise on 23 March. 'Glasgow' was ordered direct to the South Atlantic on 2 April and the Flight began practising ESM and night flying techniques before reaching Ascension Island on 11 April. VERTREP sorties were flown to store the ship and the opportunity was taken to practise NGS spotting duties before she sailed on 14 April. A rendezvous with 'Fort Austin' three days later allowed XZ732 to be exchanged for Sea Skua equipped XZ247 (formerly with the Trials Flight), although at that time its Sea Skua fit was unserviceable. It was rectified on 28 April by which time XZ247 (with low-vis scheme applied) had adopted the code (344) although it was not carried by the helicopter or its subsequent replacements.

'Glasgow' entered the TEZ on 1 May. Two days later the Flight saw action when it was scrambled, in company with 'Coventry' Flight, to attack an unidentified Argentine patrol boat which had fired on an 826 Sqdn Sea King some 70 miles north of the CVBG. XZ247 lost the use of its UHF radio soon after take-off, holding off as 'Coventry' Flight attacked the Argentine vessel. With its radio serviceable once again, the Flight joined in the search for survivors, but what was thought to have been another patrol boat was detected some 5 to 10 miles away. 'Glasgow' Flight attacked it with two Sea Skua missiles, the Lynx coming under fire itself, and two detonations were seen at 0435Z. No damage assessment could be made due to shortage of fuel, but two days later the vessel (the 'Alferez Sobral') limped into the mainland port of Puerto Deseado escorted by the 'Comodoro Py', her bridge blown away and the Captain and seven crewmen dead. 'Coventry' Flight thought they had sunk the 'Comodoro Somellera' (sister-ship to the 'Alferez Sobral') but, in fact, both Flights had attacked and damaged the same patrol boat *[see 'Coventry' Flight notes]*.

Surface search sorties continued until 8 May, when the Flight took XZ247 aboard 'Brilliant' for an operation which required two Sea Skua equipped Lynx, 'Brilliant'

Flight's MAD-equipped Lynx XZ729 moving to 'Glasgow'. 'Brilliant' detached that night to the north of Falkland Sound where the two Flights joined in an ESM search for enemy shipping before harassing the enemy troops at Port Howard with GPMG fire and flare drops — a rude awakening! The Flight returned to 'Glasgow' with XZ247 on 9 May and XZ729 was flown back to 'Brilliant'. On 10 May 'Glasgow' relieved 'Coventry' on shore bombardment duties, shelling the enemy positions around Port Stanley. Two days later, while operating some 25 miles east of Port Stanley, she was attacked by two flights of Grupo 5 A-4B Skyhawks and hit just above the waterline by a 500lb bomb. It passed through the engine room, over the main propulsion units and out the other side of the ship without exploding, but left a 3ft diameter hole in each side. Temporary repairs were effected and on 14 May 'Glasgow' was detached with 'Hermes' and 'Broadsword' to insert Special Forces personnel for the now famous Pebble Island operation. The ship returned the following day to continue her bombardment duties, but that role was handed over to 'Cardiff' on 25 May and XZ247 was transferred to 'Ambuscade' Flight in exchange for XZ696 (a non-Sea Skua equipped Lynx). 'Glasgow' went alongside the 'Stena Seaspread' for repairs in the TRALA on 26 May, sailing for the United Kingdom the following day. The Flight disembarked to Yeovilton on 19 June, where XZ696 was seen to be marked with a white ship broken in two on the port side of the nose; 'Glasgow' docked at Portsmouth later that day.

The ship made a second deployment to the Falkland Islands during 1982, leaving Portsmouth on 6 September with replacement Lynx HAS.2 XZ694 aboard. She returned to Portsmouth on 20 December and the Lynx disembarked to Portland.

# 'MINERVA' (210) FLIGHT

When 'Minerva' docked at Devonport on 2 April she was due for a refit. As a result, her (210) Flight equipped with non-Sea Skua Lynx HAS.2 XZ248 'MV/424', dis-

embarked to Yeovilton that day and was due to become 'Liverpool' Flight on 6 April. In the event, the transfer did not take place and the Flight was allocated Sea Skua equipped Lynx HAS.2 XZ730 on 3 April, still coded 'PN/454' from its previous service with 'Penelope' Flight (XZ248 being transferred to NASU on 6 April). XZ730 departed Yeovilton on 3 April aboard Hercules C.1 XV299, arriving at Wideawake (at 0230Z on 5 April) where it was reassembled. It embarked 'Fort Austin' on 6 April along with 'Newcastle' Flight and the Trials Flight, sailing south with the ship on 9 April. 'Fort Austin' carried out a rendezvous with 'Endurance' three days later in order to transfer troops and stores prior to Operation "Paraquat". The vessel then set course back towards Ascension Island on 13 April, making an en route rendezvous with 'Arrow', 'Coventry' and 'Glasgow' on 17 April when the three Sea Skua equipped Lynx HAS.2's were exchanged for those aboard the other three ships. 'Minerva' Flight's Lynx (XZ730) was transferred to 'Arrow' Flight in exchange for XZ241, which was neither Sea Skua nor ESM equipped but was already in low-vis marks. On 17 April it was decided that the Flight should return to the United Kingdom so that XZ241 could undergo modification and the aircraft disembarked 'Fort Austin' at Ascension Island on 22 April. It was airlifted back to Yeovilton, arriving there the next day along with the Flight's personnel.

In the meantime, 'Minerva' had her refit cut short so that she could be deployed to the South Atlantic and a new (224) Flight had been formed for that purpose. It was allotted Lynx HAS.2 XZ698 on 16 April, a Sea Skua equipped aircraft which had previously been held by NASU. The Lynx was allocated, and carried, the marks '-/306' (an 815 Sqdn HQ Flight code) but with the return to Yeovilton of the original 'Minerva' Flight on 23 April a dual identity problem arose. This was resolved by transferring the new 'Minerva' (224) Flight to 'Liverpool' while the old 'Minerva' (210) Flight took over XZ698 to replace XZ241. XZ698 was then allocated code (424) although it was not carried. The Flight embarked 'Minerva' at Devonport on 10 May with the same personnel from the earlier 'Fort Austin' deployment, sailing that day for the South Atlantic with the 'Bristol' Group. Wartime flying techniques were practised en route, with only a short stop at Ascension Island on 19 May before the vessel entered the TEZ on 26 May to join the main force that night.

The Flight commenced ESM barrier patrols and surface spotting sorties for the CVBG until the ship was detached on 29 May to relieve the bomb-damaged 'Argonaut' as AAWC in San Carlos Water. On 31 May 'Minerva' and 'Arrow' Flights were tasked to find the Argentine hospital ship 'Bahia Paraiso', suspected of assisting the war effort. She was soon found to the south of Falkland Sound and the 'Minerva' Flight helicopter landed aboard to investigate, while 'Arrow' Flight's Lynx acted as gunship and radio link. Nothing untoward was found, but the ship's hangar was seen to contain a CAB601 Puma and a 1 Escuadrilla de Helicopteros Alouette III, both painted White overall with the requisite Red Cross markings applied. 'Minerva' remained in San Carlos Water and the Flight was engaged in patrols of the coast and known enemy positions. It was usual for the Flights to remain airborne while the ships got on with their daily tasks. On 3 June, whilst flying some two miles south-east of Cape Pembroke, the Flight came under fire from an unidenti-

fied Argentine missile, but fortunately escaped unscathed. The missile was reportedly a Roland, but is more likely to have been a Tigercat or Blowpipe.

'Minerva' sailed to rejoin the CVBG on 3 June in order to carry out ESM work, but during the night of 8/9 June she returned to San Carlos Water as an escort for 'Engadine' and three of the MCM trawlers. Her next action came on 11 June when, in company with 'Exeter' Flight, the Lynx was launched for a deception mission to fire chaff and mislead the enemy into thinking that there was to be a major helicopter assault on the beaches close to Port Stanley. All went smoothly until enemy air defence radars started to attempt a lock-on to the two aircraft within about four miles of Stanley Airport. Guidance radar for the Roland missile was identified and the 'Minerva' Flight crew were particularly concerned, having had one possible close encounter with a missile already. It was learnt on 14 June that the Argentine forces had reported the repelling of a massed helicopter attack during the night of 11 June and Commodore Clapp (the Commander, Amphibious Warfare aboard 'Fearless') remarked on the success of the mission which had drawn attention away during the push forward by the land forces.

After the surrender, 'Minerva' moved round to Port William on 17 June and remained on station until relieved by 'Penelope' on 14 July. During that period, XZ698 was detached to 'Birmingham' Flight for two days on loan while the ship's own Lynx (XZ693) was unserviceable. 'Minerva' finally sailed from the TEZ on 15 July and the Flight disembarked to the Squadron's new home at Portland before the ship docked at Portsmouth on 3 August.

815 Sqdn aircrew with 'Minerva' Flight during Operation "Corporate": Lt Cdr G.R.Moodie RN (Flt Cdr); Lt S.K.O'Collard RN.

'Minerva' made a second deployment to the Falkland Islands during 1982. She should have sailed on 8 November but was delayed for six days by technical problems, followed by work-up at Portland where the ship was involved in a minor collision with 'Yarmouth' on 22 November. After repairs, she finally left Devonport on 29 November with Lynx HAS.2 XZ698 '-/424' (by then in the Dark Sea Grey scheme) which had embarked from Portland on 15 November. The vessel returned to Devonport on 24 March 1983 and the helicopter disembarked to Portland the next day.

# 'NEWCASTLE' (203) FLIGHT

'Newcastle' had commenced a 12-month refit at Portsmouth during February and did not deploy to the South Atlantic until later in the year. The Flight remained in commission, however, and was operating Lynx HAS.2 XZ242 'NC/345' named "Wee Geordie" (Sea Skua equipped). On 2 April the Lynx was prepared for air transportation to Ascension Island, leaving Yeovilton the following day aboard Hercules C.1 XV293. Upon arrival at Wideawake on 4 April the helicopter was reassembled and test-flown before embarking 'Fort Austin' on 6 April, accompanied by 'Minerva' Flight and the Trials Flight. 'Newcastle' Flight's aircrew (see later) were joined by Lt A.Harper (formerly with the HQ Flight) and Lt Cdr R.K.O'Neill (formerly HQ Flight Senior Observer) who was overall commander of the detachment.

'Fort Austin' sailed on 9 April to rendezvous with and replenish 'Endurance' prior to Operation "Paraquat", before returning north on 13 April to meet the Advanced Group and transfer the three Sea Skua equipped helicopters to the ships heading south. This latter rendezvous took place on 17 April when 'Coventry' Flight received XZ242 and passed non-Sea Skua equipped XZ700 across to 'Fort Austin' for 'Newcastle' Flight, although XZ700 did not adopt the code (345) as at that stage aircraft codes were dispensed with by the Flights aboard 'Fort Austin'. The ship reached Ascension Island once again on 20 April, disembarking 'Minerva' Flight on 22 April. The ship sailed south on the following day and entered the TEZ on 3 May.

'Fort Austin' immediately began operations as a "Floating NASU". 'Alacrity' Flight Lynx XZ736 was received on 3 May for battle damage repairs in exchange for XZ700, the reverse swop taking place on 8 May once repairs had been effected. On 4 May 'Newcastle' Flight personnel were transferred to 'Invincible' to recover XZ720, a non-Sea Skua Lynx previously with 'Alacrity' Flight which had been "sitting it out" since 24 April. The helicopter came aboard 'Fort Austin' that evening. A third Lynx HAS.2 joined 'Newcastle' Flight aboard 'Fort Austin' on 8 May when XZ725 was embarked from 'Brilliant'. A non-Sea Skua equipped aircraft, it had originally been with 'Sheffield' Flight, then passed to 'Brilliant' on 22 April in exchange for XZ721 to take part in Operation "Paraquat". When 'Sheffield' was hit on 3

May, XZ721 recovered to 'Hermes' before returning to 'Brilliant' on 7 May.

On 17 May 'Fort Austin' was required to take on board four Sea King HAS.5's of 826 Sqdn from 'Hermes' to make room aboard the carrier for more Sea Harrier FRS.1's and the Harrier GR.3's which were expected from 'Atlantic Conveyor' the next day. As a result, the Trials Flight (with XZ725) was transferred to 'Invincible' on 17 May, while 'Newcastle' Flight embarked 'Hermes' with XZ240 (from the Trials Flight), XZ700 and XZ720. Still further flight-deck congestion aboard 'Hermes' necessitated the transfer of XZ700 (which had received battle-damaged components from XZ736; see above) to 'Atlantic Conveyor' for storage on 20 May. This helicopter was unfortunately lost when the ship was hit by an Exocet missile on 25 May. Following the loss of 'Atlantic Conveyor', it was decided that 'Hermes' would operate one Lynx at a time in the ESM and Exocet deflection roles. The Trials Flight aboard 'Invincible' borrowed XZ720 on 10 June as XZ725 required a main gear-box change. 'Newcastle' Flight continued to use XZ240, while XZ720 did not return to 'Hermes' until 17 June, three days after the Argentines had surrendered. 'Hermes' remained on station until sailing from Port William on 3 July en route for the United Kingdom. The carrier arrived at Portsmouth on 21 July with XZ240 and XZ720 on deck, both flying off to Yeovilton the following day.

> *815 Sqdn aircrew with 'Newcastle' Flt during Operation "Corporate": Lt Cdr R.K.O'Neill RN (Det Cdr, Observer); Lt A.Harper RN (Pilot); Lt Cdr R.H.Sear RN (Flt Cdr, Pilot); Lt D.A.Murphy RN (Observer).*

'Newcastle' deployed to the Falkland Islands later in 1982, her refit taking only seven months to complete. She sailed from Portsmouth on 6 September, having embarked replacement Lynx HAS.2 XZ256. This helicopter was subsequently damaged in the South Atlantic during the deployment and transferred to 'Southampton' Flight on 23 September in exchange for XZ731. 'Newcastle' returned to Portsmouth on 20 December and the Lynx disembarked to Portland.

# 'PENELOPE' (209) FLIGHT

'Penelope' was at Devonport on 29 March, her Exocet SSM conversion almost complete. Sea trials were carried out between 12-15 April and from 19 April to 5 May. Her Flight was operating Lynx HAS.2 XZ730 coded 'PN/454', which was both Sea Skua and ECM equipped, but with the need for Sea Skua aircraft in the South Atlantic it was passed to 'Minerva' Flight on 3 April.

'Penelope' Flight received Sea Skua equipped XZ691 (wearing low-vis marks) from NASU on 26 April. The code (454) was allocated but not worn by XZ691 or its subsequent replacement. XZ691 was flown from Yeovilton to Lee-on-Solent on 6 May where NATIU fitted an I-Band transponder, the Lynx returning to Yeovilton the next day. The Flight embarked 'Penelope' on 10 May after the ship had sailed from Devonport for the South Atlantic that day with the 'Bristol' Group. The crew immediately began practising ESM barrier, surface spotting and night flying techniques, but there was little time to practice NGS spotting during the short stopover at Ascension Island on 19 May.

'Penelope' joined the Task Force overnight on 25/26 May and for the next three weeks was engaged primarily on escort duties within the AOA, her Flight carrying out ESM barrier and surface search tasks. An unidentified missile was fired at the helicopter from Pebble Island on 7 June (probably a Blowpipe), but the Lynx escaped unscathed. An opportunity to return the fire occurred six days later. On 13 June 'Penelope' Flight was tasked with a low-level patrol of Choiseul Sound in search of enemy shipping but the beached Argentine Prefectura coastal craft 'Rio Iguazu' was the only vessel found. It had been damaged during a much earlier Sea Harrier strafing attack on 22 May and was lying on the north coast of the Sound near Button Bay with a supply tent located just inland. One Sea Skua was fired at the vessel, striking the foredeck and exploding. There was no sign of a second vessel which was reportedly close to Becher Islands.

In the latter half of June, XZ691 began to develop vibration problems, so on 2 July it was transferred to 'Broadsword' which was about to sail home. XZ723 was received in exchange, a Sea Skua and ECM equipped aircraft which arrived via 'Fort Grange' and 'Regent'. On 4 July 'Penelope' played host to 'Exeter' Flight which arrived at 0815Z for refuelling and a rotors-running breakfast en route to investigate a radar contact west of the Falkland Islands.

The ship remained on station until 23 August, during which period the Flight carried out a short detachment to 'Birmingham' between 23 and 25 July while XZ693 was unserviceable. 'Penelope' arrived home on 10 September in company with 'Andromeda' and 'Avenger', and as the three ships passed the Plymouth breakwater all three Flights took off for a celebration flypast over Devonport, as the ships docked, before flying off to Portland.

> 815 Sqdn aircrew with 'Penelope' Flight during Operation "Corporate": Lt C.E.Mervik RN (Flt Cdr); Lt N.J.Last RN.

# 'SHEFFIELD' (213) FLIGHT

'Sheffield' sailed from Gibraltar on 26 March for participation in Exercise "Springtrain", for which her Flight was embarked with non-Sea Skua equipped Lynx HAS.2 XZ725 coded 'SD/337'. The ship was ordered direct to the South Atlantic on 2 April and, in common with all of the other Flights, its Lynx received low-vis markings. The code (337) remained allocated but not carried by XZ725 or its subsequent replacement. The crew began a period of consolidation of wartime flying techniques. The ship arrived at Ascension Island on 11 April and for the next three days the Flight was able to practise NGS spotting in between HDS sorties before 'Sheffield' sailed once again, in company with 'Brilliant', as part of the Advanced Group. On 22 April 'Brilliant' detached from the Group for South Georgia and Operation "Paraquat", leaving 'Sheffield' in command of the Group. For that operation, 'Brilliant' did not need a Sea Skua equipped Lynx for its intended basic radar and trooping roles, so XZ725 was transferred from 'Sheffield' in exchange for Sea Skua and Stingray equipped XZ721.

'Sheffield' was already on station when the TEZ was established on 1 May and took up duties as a forward radar picket some 20 miles west of the CVBG while the Flight commenced ESM barrier patrols and surface spotting tasks. She moved closer to the Falkland Islands on 4 May to take over the duties of 'Coventry' (which was experiencing problems with her radar). Unfortunately, the ship's operations were short-lived as at 1419Z on 4 May, while carrying out picket duties some 70 miles south south-east of Port Stanley, 'Sheffield' was attacked by two 2 Escuadrilla Super Etendards. The first Exocet missile is believed to have been deflected by chaff as a low

altitude radar contact closing from the west disappeared shortly afterwards. Lt B.S.Layshon (the Flight Commander) and Lt P.Walpole (of the ship's crew) were on the bridge at the time and looking over the starboard bow they spotted a smoke trail close to the sea, a second Exocet closing rapidly. Only five seconds later the missile struck 'Sheffield' amidships, six feet above the waterline, between the operations room and the forward machinery room. The missile did not appear to explode but the resulting fires from its unspent rocket fuel soon spread out of control. Damage-control teams immediately went to work but the ship's water main had been fractured in the initial impact. The fires spread rapidly, as did the resulting acrid smoke, and the Captain had no option but to order "Abandon Ship". The helicopter survived the attack and recovered to 'Hermes' later that day, before being returned to 'Brilliant' Flight on 7 May. 'Sheffield' was taken in tow by 'Yarmouth' on 9 May for safe harbour at South Georgia, but at 0435Z on 10 May she sank in stormy seas south-east of the Falkland Islands.

> 815 Sqdn aircrew with 'Sheffield' Flt during Operation "Corporate": Lt B.S.Layshon RN (Flt Cdr); S/Lt A.W.Clark RN.

# TRIALS (230) FLIGHT

At the beginning of the conflict, the Trials Flight was operating from Yeovilton with Lynx HAS.2 XZ719 coded '-/479' and marked with a White lightning flash on the fin in place of the deck letters. On 2 April the Flight prepared to deploy to the South Atlantic and XZ719 was exchanged for Sea Skua equipped XZ247 which had been operating with 'Birmingham' Flight. It had been allocated code (333) but this was not carried, although the title "HMS BIRMINGHAM" appeared in White on the nose. Upon transfer to the Trials Flight, these markings were removed and the code (306) was allocated but again not carried. The helicopter was prepared for air transportation to Ascension Island and departed Yeovilton on 3 April inside LTW Hercules C.1 XV306. It arrived at Wideawake the following day and was reassembled and test-flown prior to embarking 'Fort Austin' on 6 April, together with 'Newcastle' and 'Minerva' Flights. The ship sailed on 9 April to rendezvous with and replenish 'Endurance' prior to the latter taking part in Operation "Paraquat".

This rendezvous took place on 12 April and 'Fort Austin' sailed north once more the following day to return to Ascension Island. En route she carried out a rendezvous with the ships of the Advanced Group heading south, during which their non-Sea Skua aircraft were exchanged for the Sea Skua equipped Lynx HAS.2's aboard 'Fort Austin'. That occurred on 17 April when the Trials Flight exchanged XZ247 for XZ732 from 'Glasgow' Flight. XZ732 did not adopt a side code as the three Flights aboard 'Fort Austin' had dispensed with using them by that stage. The ship continued her journey north to Ascension Island, where 'Minerva' Flight was disembarked on 22 April for return to the United Kingdom. She sailed south once more the next day, entering the TEZ on 3 May. Two days later the Trials Flight sent XZ732 to 'Broadsword' Flight in exchange for XZ240, a TICM, ESM and Sea Skua equipped aircraft.

With the expected arrival aboard 'Hermes' of additional Sea Harrier FRS.1's and the Harrier GR.3's from 'Atlantic Conveyor' on 18 May, 'Fort Austin' was required as a platform for four 826 Sqdn Sea King HAS.5's in order to relieve flight-deck congestion aboard the carrier. The Trials Flight exchanged XZ240 for non-Sea Skua equipped XZ725 from 'Newcastle' Flight (also aboard 'Fort Austin') in preparation for a transfer, the Flight embarking 'Invincible' on 17 May for anti-Exocet jamming tasks. XZ725 promptly went unserviceable and a double engine change commenced, the aircraft being in the air again by 21 May. Jamming sorties continued until it went unserviceable again on 10 June when the main rotor gearbox needed changing. In place of the required spare parts, the Flight gained a second Lynx on 10 June with the arrival of XZ720 from 'Newcastle' Flight aboard 'Hermes'.

The Flight continued operations up to and following the Argentine surrender on 14 June. The gearbox change on XZ725 was completed on 16 June and XZ720 was returned to 'Newcastle' Flight aboard 'Hermes' the following day. Communications and HDS tasks were continued using XZ725, although the aircraft underwent further engine changes on 30 July and 16 August (when a tail-rotor gearbox change was also carried out). 'Invincible' sailed for the United Kingdom on 28 August and the Flight disembarked to Portland on 16 September, using the code (479) as a call-sign, prior to the carrier's arrival at Portsmouth the following day.

---

*815 Sqdn aircrew with the Trials Flight during Operation "Corporate": Lt M.W.Butcher RN (Flt Cdr); Lt M.D.Llewellyn-Jones RN.*

---

*Further 815 Sqdn aircrew involved in Operation "Corporate": Lt Cdr R.A.Edwards RN (formerly 'Argonaut' Flight CO); Lt Cdr D.H.Yates RN (formerly CO of 815 Sqdn); Lt P.Finan RN (from 702 Sqdn); Lt P.A.Harrall RN (815 Sqdn Warfare Instructor).*

---

# POST-SURRENDER DEPLOYMENTS

As the following ships and their Flights did not leave the United Kingdom until after the Argentine surrender they are not eligible for inclusion in the main text of this book. However, basic details of the ship and Flight movements are included in the Individual Ship and Aircraft Histories sections.

### 'AMAZON' (208) FLIGHT

The ship and her Flight (Lynx HAS.2 XZ735 (320)) did not depart the United Kingdom for the South Atlantic until 2 August.

### 'BATTLEAXE' (201) FLIGHT

The ship and her Flight (Lynx HAS.2 XZ727 (403)) did not depart the United Kingdom for the South Atlantic until 2 August.

## 'BIRMINGHAM' (235) FLIGHT

The ship and her Flight (Lynx HAS.2 XZ693 (333)) did not depart the United Kingdom for the South Atlantic until 18 June.

## 'BRAZEN' (235) FLIGHT

The ship and her Flight (Lynx HAS.2 XZ690 (330)) did not depart the United Kingdom for the South Atlantic until 6 October.

## 'CHARYBDIS' (228) FLIGHT

The ship and her Flight (Lynx HAS.2 XZ734 (431)) did not depart the United Kingdom for the South Atlantic until 8 November.

## 'DANAE' (218) FLIGHT

The ship and her Flight (Lynx HAS.2 XZ726 (464)) did not depart the United Kingdom for the South Atlantic until 18/19 June.

## 'LIVERPOOL' (224) FLIGHT

The ship and her Flight (Lynx HAS.2 XZ245 '-/332') did not depart the United Kingdom for the South Atlantic until 8 November.

## 'PHOEBE' (242) FLIGHT

The ship and her Flight (Lynx HAS.2 XZ724 (471)) did not depart the United Kingdom for the South Atlantic until 6 September.

## 'SIRIUS' (243) FLIGHT

The ship and her Flight (Lynx HAS.2 XZ255 (450)) did not depart the United Kingdom for the South Atlantic until 6 September.

## 'SOUTHAMPTON' (202) FLIGHT

The ship and her Flight (Lynx HAS.2 XZ731 (345)) did not depart the United Kingdom for the South Atlantic until 18 June.

# INDIVIDUAL AIRCRAFT DETAILS

The low-vis scheme applied to each Lynx HAS.2 is explained under the individual aircraft history.

*Examples of abbreviations used for markings and their meanings:*

'CV/336'  *Deck-letters for 'Coventry' and side-code worn in full.*

'-/424'  *Deck-letters for 'Minerva' not worn; side-code worn in full.*

(420)  *Neither the deck-letters 'EX' for 'Exeter' nor the side-code worn.*

**XZ233** HAS.2

On 29.3.82 with 815 Sqdn 'Argonaut' Flight at Yeovilton coded 'AT/466', named "Jason". Embarked 'Argonaut' from Yeovilton on 5.4.82 to work-up with the ship following her refit. Disembarked to Yeovilton 14.4.82 (for Sea Skua modification) and finally re-embarked 'Argonaut' 19.4.82 (just after she had departed Devonport), sailing with her that day for Ascension Island and the South Atlantic. By the embarkation date it had received low-vis markings which consisted of standard Oxford Blue overall (covering the deck-letters), Red/Blue roundels (in the standard proportions) plus Black serials. For some unknown reason, White ROYAL NAVY titles were retained. Code (466) remained allocated but was not worn. On 5.6.82 'Argonaut' was ordered to return to the UK. The aircraft was transferred that day to 'Cardiff' Flight (in exchange for non-Sea Skua equipped XZ254), code (335) being allocated but not worn.

On 13.6.82 whilst being flown by Lt Clayton some 50 miles south of the southern entrance to Falkland Sound, it was attacked by cannon fire from two Grupo 6 Daggers. In spite of repeated attacks it escaped unscathed.

Due to technical problems, it was transferred to 'Brilliant' Flt on 22.6.82 in exchange for the more serviceable XZ721 (Sea Skua/Stingray equipped), code (341) being allocated but not worn. Sailed with the ship from the TEZ on 23.6.82 for the UK and flown off to Yeovilton 13.7.82 prior to her arrival at Devonport the same day.

*On the date of arrival back at Yeovilton it was still wearing White ROYAL NAVY titles.*

**XZ240** HAS.2

On 29.3.82 at NASU Yeovilton coded 'VL/-'. Transferred to 815 Sqdn at Yeovilton on 10.4.82 (Sea Skua, ESM and TICM equipped). Prepared for airfreighting 14.4.82 (still coded 'VL/-') and departed on 16.4.82 for Ascension Island aboard Hercules C.1

XV185. On arrival it was assembled by Naval Party 1222 and although allotted to 'Broadsword' Flt, was flown to 'Invincible' on 18.4.82 for transportation south (as 'Broadsword' already had a two-Lynx complement aboard). Utilized for the day by 'Broadsword' on 20.4.82, then finally transferred to the ship from 'Invincible' 24.4.82 on a more permanent basis as part of a three-way swop between 'Invincible', 'Broadsword' and 'Alacrity' *[see also XZ720 and XZ736]*. At some stage during that period a low-vis scheme was applied (exact details unknown, see below). While with 'Broadsword' Flight the code (348) was allocated but not worn. Remained with the ship until 5.5.82 when it was passed to Trials Flight charge aboard 'Fort Austin' in exchange for XZ732, a non-Sea Skua Lynx. No side-code was allotted as the Flights aboard 'Fort Austin' had dispensed with their use. Transferred to 'Newcastle' Flt on 17.5.82 (also aboard 'Fort Austin') in exchange for XZ725, and was flown to 'Hermes' with the Flight that day to be based aboard the carrier for ESM/Exocet decoy duties, making

317

room aboard 'Fort Austin' for a detachment of four 826 Sqdn Sea Kings; no code was allocated. On 'Hermes' its low-vis scheme consisted of standard Oxford Blue overall, obliterated roundels and ROYAL NAVY titles, but serials retained in Black. Remained with the carrier, departing with her from Port William 3.7.82 en route for the UK. Arrived at Portsmouth aboard 'Hermes' on 21.7.82, flying off to Yeovilton on 22.7.82.

## XZ241 HAS.2

On 29.3.82 with 815 Sqdn 'Arrow' Flight coded 'AW/326' (non-Sea Skua aircraft) operating out of Gibraltar on Exercise "Springtrain". Ordered directly south with the ship on 2.4.82, arriving at Ascension Island on 11.4.82. Between that date and 14.4.82 (when the ship left for the South Atlantic) it was painted in a low-vis scheme consisting of standard Oxford Blue overall (deleting the ROYAL NAVY titles and deck letters). White serials were retained, Red/Blue roundels were adopted and the code (326) remained allocated but not worn. 'Arrow' made a rendezvous with 'Fort Austin' (which was heading north to Ascension Island) on 17.4.82 and the Lynx was transferred to her that day for use by 'Minerva' Flight in exchange for Sea Skua equipped XZ730. The 'Minerva' Flight code (424) was not adopted as by that time all of the Flights aboard 'Fort Austin' had dispensed with their use. Flown to Wideawake on 22.4.82, dismantled by Naval Party 1222 for airlift back to the UK on transfer to NASU Yeovilton, arriving there aboard Hercules C.1 XV297 on 26.4.82.

## XZ242 HAS.2

On 29.3.82 with 815 Sqdn 'Newcastle' Flight coded 'NC/345', named "Wee Geordie" (Sea Skua aircraft). At the time it was shore-based at Yeovilton whilst the ship was undergoing a refit. On 2.4.82 Flight personnel and the Lynx were prepared for deployment to Ascension Island prior to allotment to a Task Force ship. Dismantled (but still coded 'NC/345'), it was flown out to Wideawake 3.4.82 aboard Hercules C.1 XV293, arriving on 4.4.82. It had been reassembled by 5.4.82 and, following a test-flight, was flown to 'Fort Austin' on 6.4.82 (still allocated to 'Newcastle' Flight). Departed Ascension Island with the ship 9.4.82, remaining aboard until 17.4.82 when 'Fort Austin' made a rendezvous with 'Coventry'. Transferred that day from 'Newcastle' Flt to 'Coventry' in exchange for non-Sea Skua equipped XZ700. It was repainted in a low-vis scheme by that date (or very shortly afterwards), exact details not known. Code (336) was allocated but not worn.

On 3.5.82, crewed by Lt Cdr Rich and Lt Ledingham, it attacked the Argentine patrol boat 'Alferez Sobral' with two Sea Skuas. That attack, and a later one by XZ247 of 'Glasgow' Flight, achieved hits on the bridge area killing eight personnel. The damaged ship managed to return to Puerto Deseado in Argentina on 5.5.82.

'Coventry' was attacked by two Grupo 5 A-4B Skyhawks on 25.5.82 and hit on the port side by three bombs dropped by Primer Teniente Velasco (in C-207). The aircraft was on the flight deck at the time and sank with the ship that day 10 miles north of Pebble Island

(51°05 'S 59°45 'W).

## XZ245 HAS.2 *Deployed post-14.6.82*

On 15.6.82 with NASU Yeovilton prior to departing 17.6.82 to WHL Yeovil for the installation of MAD equipment. Delivered back to NASU Yeovilton 12.7.82 and noted there on 18.8.82 in a Medium (not Dark) Sea Grey scheme with Red/Blue roundels, Black serials and devoid of ROYAL NAVY titles. Transferred to 815 Sqdn 'Liverpool' Flight on 6.9.82 and flown to Portland the same day. Code (332) was allocated but not worn. Embarked the ship at Devonport on 8.11.82, reportedly coded '-/332' in Black, and sailed with her that day on deployment to the South Atlantic. Visited Culdrose on 27.3.83 then disembarked to Portland (via Yeovilton) on 28.3.83 prior to 'Liverpool' docking at Devonport that day.

## XZ247 HAS.2

On 29.3.82 with 815 Sqdn Birmingham Flight at Yeovilton wearing "HMS BIRMINGHAM" on the nose (Sea Skua aircraft); code (333) allocated but not worn. Transferred to 815 Sqdn Trials Flight at Yeovilton on 2.4.82 (less nose marking), the code (306) being allocated but not worn. Flight personnel and the aircraft were prepared that day for deployment to Ascension Island prior to allotment to a Task Force ship. The dismantled Lynx was flown out to Wideawake via Gibraltar on 3.4.82 aboard Hercules C.1 XV306, arriving the next day. Reassembled and test-flown prior to embarking 'Fort Austin' on 6.4.82 (still allocated to the Trials Flight). Sailed south with the ship on 9.4.82 and remained aboard until 17.4.82 when 'Fort Austin' carried out a rendezvous with 'Glasgow'. Transferred that day to 'Glasgow' Flight in exchange for non-Sea Skua equipped XZ732. By that time, or soon after the transfer, it was painted in a low-vis scheme consisting of standard Oxford Blue overall with Black ROYAL NAVY titles. The serials were obliterated with Black rectangles and the White segments of the roundels overpainted in Black. Code (344) was allocated but not worn.

On 3.5.82, crewed by Lt Cdr Lister and Lt Ormshaw, the Lynx attacked the Argentine patrol boat 'Alferez Sobral' with two Sea Skuas. That attack, and an earlier one by XZ242 of 'Coventry' Flight, achieved hits on the bridge area killing eight personnel. The damaged ship managed to return to Puerto Deseado in Argentina on 5.5.82.

"Borrowed" for 24hrs on 8.5.82 by 'Brilliant' for a mission which required two Sea Skua equipped Lynx. 'Brilliant' Flight's XZ729 operated temporarily from 'Glasgow', both aircraft reverting to their respective ships on 9.5.82. 'Glasgow' set course to the TRALA on 25.5.82 for repairs to bomb damage (suffered on 12.5.82) prior to returning to the UK. The Lynx was transferred to 'Ambuscade' Flight that day (in exchange for non-Sea Skua equipped XZ696), code (323) being allocated but not worn. Loaned to 'Avenger' on 29.5.82 for 12 hours whilst her Lynx (XZ249) was unserviceable. Sailed from the TEZ with 'Ambuscade' on 5.7.82 for return to the UK. Flown off to Portland on 24.7.82 prior to the vessel's arrival at Devonport later that day.

## XZ249 HAS.2

On 29.3.82 with NASU Yeovilton wearing its old 'Alacrity' Flight code '-/327'. To 815 Sqdn at Yeovilton 19.4.82 on the formation of a second 'Avenger' Flight (240 Flt) *[see XZ692 for details of 205 'Avenger' Flt]*. Code (307) was allocated but not worn. It embarked 'Avenger' on 26.4.82 for a 10-day COST in the Portland area until flown off to Yeovilton on 5.5.82 (still carrying the marks '-/327'). As it needed an engine change, the opportunity was taken to fit Sea Skua HIE as well (completed by 9.5.82). Embarked 'Avenger' once again off Plymouth 10.5.82 just after she had left Devonport en route to the South Atlantic. During the passage south to Ascension Island a low-vis scheme was applied (exact details unknown) but the code (307) remained allocated. XZ249 departed the Falkland Islands aboard 'Avenger' on 23.8.82 for return to the UK. As the ship entered Plymouth Sound on 10.9.82, it took off to formate with XZ722 and XZ723 of 'Andromeda' and 'Penelope' Flights for a flypast over the three ships as they docked at Devonport. Following the flypast, all three helicopters flew on to Portland.

## XZ251 HAS.2

On 29.3.82 with NASU Yeovilton (a Sea Skua equipped aircraft), still wearing its old 702 Sqdn code '-/746'. Test-flown (still coded) on 3.4.82 prior to its transfer to 815 Sqdn 'Ardent' Flt at Yeovilton 7.4.82 (replacing non-Sea Skua equipped XZ244). Coded 'AD/340' on 14.4.82 and named "Avon". Embarked 'Ardent' at Devonport on 19.4.82 and sailed with her that day for Ascension Island and the South Atlantic. During the passage south a low-vis scheme was applied (exact details not known), the code (340) remaining allocated but not worn.

On 21.5.82 whilst 'Ardent' was in Grantham Sound, a bomb from a Grupo 6 Dagger hit the ship close to the hangar. The explosion destroyed the Lynx, its remains sinking with the ship off North West Island (51°35 'S 59°13 'W) on 22.5.82.

## XZ254 HAS.2

On 29.3.82 with 815 Sqdn 'Cardiff' Flight on Gulf Patrol, a non-Sea Skua equipped aircraft coded 'CF/335'. Departed Mombasa, Kenya with the vessel on 20.4.82, arriving at Gibraltar on 7.5.82. Sailed with the ship for Ascension Island and the South Atlantic on 12.5.82. During the passage south a low-vis scheme was applied which consisted of standard Oxford Blue overall with the deck letters, ROYAL NAVY titles and serials deleted. Red/Blue roundels were adopted while the code (335) remained allocated but was not worn. Temporarily based on 'Brilliant' from 27-30.5.82. Transferred to 'Argonaut' Flight on 5.6.82 (in exchange for Sea Skua equipped XZ233), code (466) being allocated but not worn. Departed the TEZ aboard 'Argonaut' on 5.6.82 for return to the UK. Flown off to Yeovilton (via Longroom) on 26.6.82 prior to the vessel's arrival at Devonport later that day.

## XZ255 HAS.2 *Deployed post-14.6.82*

On 15.6.82 with WHL Yeovil for installation of MAD equipment. Delivered on 22.6.82 to

NASU Yeovilton and by 25.6.82 had been re-painted in the overall Dark Sea Grey scheme with Black serials, Red/Blue roundels and devoid of ROYAL NAVY titles. Transferred to 815 Sqdn 'Sirius' Flight at Yeovilton on 5.7.82, the code (450) being allocated but not worn. Flown to 815 Sqdn's new parent base at Portland on 19.7.82. Sailed with the ship from Devonport 6.9.82 on deployment to the South Atlantic. Believed to have disembarked to Portland just prior to the vessel docking at Devonport on 19.12.82.

### XZ256 HAS.2     *Deployed post-14.6.82*

On 15.6.82 with WHL Yeovil for installation of MAD equipment. Delivered to NASU Yeovilton 16.6.82 and on 17/18.6.82 was re-painted in overall Dark Sea Grey scheme with Black serials, Red/Blue roundels and devoid of ROYAL NAVY titles. Transferred to 815 Sqdn 'Newcastle' Flight at Yeovilton 28.6.82, code (345) being allocated but not worn. Flown to 815 Sqdn's new parent base at Portland on 19.7.82. Deployed to the South Atlantic with the ship from Portsmouth on 6.9.82. Damaged by a wave during the passage south while on the flight deck with its rotors turning. Removed by crane to 'Astronomer' in Berkeley Sound (north of Port Stanley), prior to being transferred to 'Southampton' which was about to detach for return to the UK. Officially joined 'Southampton' Flight on 23.9.82 (her own Lynx XZ731 being transferred to 'Newcastle' Flight); code (334) was allocated but not worn. Returned to Portsmouth with the ship 17.10.82 and off-loaded by crane 19.10.82. Removed by road to Yeovilton the same day upon transfer to NASU for repair.

### XZ690 HAS.2     *Deployed post-14.6.82*

On 15.6.82 with NASU Yeovilton. Delivered to WHL Yeovil 16.6.82 for installation of MAD equipment. Returned on 1.7.82 to NASU Yeovilton and on 5.7.82 was repainted in the overall Dark Sea Grey scheme with Black serials, Red/Blue roundels and devoid of ROYAL NAVY titles. Transferred to 815 Sqdn 'Brazen' Flt 16.7.82, code (330) allocated but not worn. Sailed with the ship from Devonport 6.10.82 on deployment to the South Atlantic. Believed to have disembarked to Portland just prior to the vessel docking at Devonport on 6.1.83.

### XZ691 HAS.2

On 29.3.82 with 815 Sqdn 'Antelope' Flight coded 'AO/321', named "Norman" (non-Sea Skua aircraft). Disembarked 'Antelope' 4.4.82 on transfer to NASU Yeovilton (in exchange for Sea Skua/ECM equipped XZ723). On 24.4.82, after modification to Sea Skua standard, it was transferred to 'Penelope' Flight at Yeovilton (replacing XZ730 which had been transferred to 'Minerva' Flight on 3.4.82). Noted there on 5.5.82 in the standard Lynx scheme but wearing incorrectly proportioned Red/Blue roundels (the White segment having been overpainted Blue). Neither the deck letters nor the allocated code (454) were worn. Flown to NATIU Lee-on-Solent 6.5.82 to be fitted with an I-Band transponder, returning to Yeovilton on 7.5.82. Embarked 'Penelope' on 10.5.82 following her departure from Devonport that day for Ascension Island and the South Atlantic. During the passage

south, the ROYAL NAVY titles were removed and the serials overpainted in Black.

On 13.6.82, crewed by Lt Mervik and Lt Last, it carried out an attack on the already beached Argentine Prefectura patrol boat 'Rio Iguazu' in Choiseul Sound with a Sea Skua. The resultant explosion caused further damage to that already inflicted by an earlier 800 Sqdn Sea Harrier strafing attack on 22.5.82.

Due to vibration problems it was transferred to 'Broadsword' Flight on 2.7.82 (in exchange for Sea Skua/ECM equipped XZ723); code (349) was allocated but not worn. Sailed with the ship from Port William on 3.7.82 en route to Devonport. Flown off 'Broadsword' to Portland on 23.7.82 just prior to the ship docking that day at Devonport.

### XZ692 HAS.2

On 29.3.82 with 815 Sqdn 'Avenger' Flight coded 'AG/341', named "Purdy" (non-Sea Skua) aircraft) embarked on 'Brilliant' as part of its two-Lynx complement and operating from Gibraltar on Exercise "Springtrain". Remained aboard when the ship was ordered directly to the South Atlantic from the Exercise on 2.4.82, arriving at Ascension Island on 11.4.82. A low-vis scheme was applied during the passage south consisting of standard Oxford Blue overall with the deck letters and ROYAL NAVY titles deleted, although White serials were retained. Red/Blue roundels were adopted, the code (341) remaining allocated but not worn. Disembarked to Wideawake 14.4.82, being replaced aboard that day by XZ721 (Sea Skua and Stingray equipped). XZ692 was prepared by Naval Party 1222 at Wideawake for airlift back to the UK upon transfer to NASU Yeovilton. Delivered to Lyneham by LTW Hercules, from where it was removed by road 23.4.82 to arrive at NASU Yeovilton the next day.

### XZ693 HAS.2     *Deployed post-14.6.82*

On 15.6.82 with 815 Sqdn 'Birmingham' Flight at Yeovilton in the overall Dark Sea Grey scheme wearing Black serials, Red/Blue roundels and devoid of ROYAL NAVY titles; code (333) allocated but not worn. Departed for Lee-on-Solent that day, embarking 'Birmingham' 17.6.82 and deploying with her for the South Atlantic from Portsmouth on 18.6.82. Disembarked to Portland 17.10.82 just before the ship docked at Portsmouth that day.

### XZ694 HAS.2     *Deployed post-14.6.82*

On 16.6.82 with 702 Sqdn at Yeovilton, code (746) being allocated but believed not worn at that time. Transferred to 815 Sqdn 'Glasgow' Flight at Yeovilton (replacing XZ696) on 7.7.82. Repainted in the overall Dark Sea Grey scheme by 15.7.82 with Black serials, Red/Blue roundels and devoid of ROYAL NAVY titles, code (344) being allocated but not worn. Flown to 815 Sqdn's new parent base at Portland on 19.7.82. Deployed with 'Glasgow' to the South Atlantic from Portsmouth on 6.9.82. Disembarked to Portland with the return of the ship to Portsmouth on 20.12.82.

### XZ696 HAS.2

On 29.3.82 with 702 Sqdn at Yeovilton coded 'VL/744' (non-Sea Skua aircraft). Transferred to 815 Sqdn 'Ambuscade' Flight at Yeovilton on 9.4.82 (replacing Sea Skua/Stingray equipped XZ721) and embarked the ship that day at Devonport. Believed to have still been wearing the marks 'VL/744' at that time, although by then allocated the code (323). The ship sailed on 9.4.82 for guardship duties at Gibraltar, arriving there on 13.4.82. Both ship and Flight were ordered south 28.4.82, leaving Gibraltar 3.5.82 for Ascension Island and the South Atlantic. During the passage south a low-vis scheme was applied, consisting of standard Oxford Blue overall which deleted the ROYAL NAVY titles and any remnants of the old deck letters and code. Red/Blue roundels were adopted, while the serials were overpainted Black; code (323) remained allocated but not carried. On 25.5.82 'Glasgow' detached to the TRALA for repairs and the opportunity was taken to give 'Ambuscade' Flt a Sea Skua equipped Lynx. XZ696 transferred to 'Glasgow' Flt that day (in exchange for XZ247), adopting the code (344) although it was not worn. Departed the TRALA for the ship on 27.5.82 for return to the UK and was flown off to Yeovilton 19.6.82 just prior to the vessel docking that day at Portsmouth.

*Noted at Yeovilton on 19.6.82 wearing a motif on the port side of the nose. It consisted of a white ship broken in two and almost certainly alluded to 'Glasgow' Flight's Sea Skua attack (in XZ247) on the 'Alferez Sobral' on 3.5.82.*

### XZ698 HAS.2

On 29.3.82 uncoded with NASU Yeovilton (Sea Skua equipped). Transferred to 815 Sqdn at Yeovilton 16.4.82 on the formation of a second 'Minerva' Flt (224 Flight; see XZ241/XZ730 for details of 210 'Minerva' Flight). By 21.4.82 it was wearing the code '-/306' (within the HQ Flight range), but that was removed on 23.4.82 when the aircraft was painted in a low-vis scheme consisting of standard Oxford Blue overall, deleting the ROYAL NAVY titles. Red/Blue roundels were adopted but the colour of the serials is not known. All that coincided with the arrival back at Yeovilton of 210 'Minerva' Flight from Ascension Island. 224 Flight was re-allotted as 'Liverpool' Flight and allocated a new aircraft (XZ239). XZ698 was transferred to 210 'Minerva' Flight, code (424) being allocated but not worn. Departed Yeovilton on 10.5.82 to embark 'Minerva' at Devonport, sailing with her that day for Ascension Island and the South Atlantic.

On 31.5.82 it landed aboard the Argentine hospital ship 'Bahia Paraiso' to check for suspected arms and war supplies (nothing found).

On 3.6.82, crewed by Lt Cdr Moodie and Lt O'Collard, it successfully avoided an Argentine land-launched missile (possibly a Roland) while on an operational sortie some two miles south-east of Cape Pembroke.

Transferred to 'Birmingham' Flight for two days commencing 8.7.82 (the latter Flight's XZ693 being unserviceable). Sailed from the TEZ aboard 'Minerva' 15.7.82 for return to the UK. Flown off to Portland on 3.8.82 prior to the ship's arrival at Devonport that day.

Sometime post-21.9.82 (when noted at Portland, still uncoded in low-vis scheme) it was repainted in the overall Dark Sea Grey scheme with Black serials, Red/Blue roundels and devoid of ROYAL NAVY titles; code (424) remained allocated but not worn. Embarked 'Minerva' at Devonport from Portland on 15.11.82, deploying once again to the South Atlantic with the ship (from Devonport) on 29.11.82 by which time it had been coded '-/424' in Black (seen wearing those marks at RAF Stanley on 22.12.82). Returned to Devonport with the ship on 24.3.83 coded 'MV/424' (visiting Culdrose that day) and then flown off to Portland on 25.3.83.

## XZ700 HAS.2

On 29.3.82 with 815 Sqdn 'Coventry' Flight coded 'CV/336', named "Lady G" (non-Sea Skua aircraft), operating from Gibraltar on Exercise "Springtrain". Ordered directly south from the Exercise to Ascension Island with the ship on 2.4.82. On 12/13.4.82 a low-vis scheme was applied (exact details unknown), the code (336) remaining allocated but not worn. 'Coventry' carried out a rendezvous with 'Fort Austin' on 17.4.82 and the helicopter was transferred to 'Newcastle' Flight on 'Fort Austin' (in exchange for Sea Skua equipped XZ242). No code was allocated by 'Newcastle' Flight as by that time those Flights aboard 'Fort Austin' had dispensed with their use. Loaned to 'Alacrity' Flt 3-8.5.82 whilst their Lynx (XZ736) was aboard 'Fort Austin' for BDR, code (327) being allocated but not worn. Flown to 'Hermes' 17.5.82 (still with 'Newcastle' Flight) to be based aboard the carrier and at the same time to make room on 'Fort Austin' for a detachment of four 826 Sqdn Sea Kings. However, due to lack of space on 'Hermes' after the arrival of additional Sea Harriers and Harriers, it was flown to 'Atlantic Conveyor' 20.5.82 for storage.

On 25.5.82, whilst the ship was some 90 miles north-east of Port Stanley (at 50°37′S 56°10′W) en route to Falkland Sound, 'Atlantic Conveyor' was hit by an Exocet missile (one of two launched from a pair of 2 Escuadrilla Super Etendards) and caught fire. The Lynx was consumed by the fire, its remains sinking with the ship on 30.5.82.

## XZ720 HAS.2

On 29.3.82 with 815 Sqdn 'Alacrity' Flight coded 'AL/327', named "Phoenix" (non-Sea Skua aircraft). At that time it was embarked on 'Alacrity' whilst the ship was operating from Portland naval base on sea trials. Returned with her to the naval base where storing commenced on 2.4.82. The vessel moved to Devonport then left for Ascension Island and the South Atlantic on 5.4.82 with the Flight still embarked. During the passage south, a low-vis scheme was applied (exact details unknown), the code (327) remaining allocated although not worn. In order to give 'Alacrity' Flight a Sea Skua equipped Lynx, a three-way shuffle between 'Broadsword', 'Invincible' and 'Alacrity' took place on 24.4.82 which resulted in XZ720 being flown aboard 'Invincible' for temporary storage (see also XZ240 and XZ736). On 4.5.82 a crew from 'Newcastle' Flight aboard 'Fort Austin'

ferried XZ720 back to their parent ship from 'Invincible'. Allotted to 'Newcastle' Flight but had no code allocated as by that time all Flights on 'Fort Austin' had dispensed with their use. Flown aboard 'Hermes' (still with 'Newcastle' Flt) on 17.5.82 to be based on the carrier for ESM/Exocet decoy duties (no code allocated), making room on 'Fort Austin' for a detachment of four 826 Sqdn Sea Kings. Its low-vis scheme while on board 'Hermes' consisted of standard Oxford Blue overall, obliterating ROYAL NAVY titles and serials with only the Red centre spots of the roundels retained. Loaned to the Trials Flight aboard 'Invincible' from 10-17.6.82 whilst their own Lynx (XZ725) was unserviceable. Departed with 'Hermes' from Port William on 3.7.82 en route to the UK, arriving at Portsmouth with the carrier 21.7.82. Flown off to Yeovilton 22.7.82 (still allotted to 'Newcastle' Flight).

## XZ721 HAS.2

On 29.3.82 with 815 Sqdn 'Ambuscade' Flight at Yeovilton coded 'AB/323', named "Gonzo" (Sea Skua/Stingray equipped). Replaced by XZ696 (a non-Sea Skua aircraft) with the Flight at Yeovilton on 9.4.82. XZ721 left for Ascension Island aboard Hercules C.1 XV292 on 10.4.82, coded 'A(B)/323'. On arrival at Wideawake it was assembled by Naval Party 1222 and transferred 14.4.82 to 'Brilliant' Flight (replacing non-Sea Skua equipped XZ692 of 'Avenger' Flight which was operating from 'Brilliant'). Painted in a low-vis scheme while with the Flight, believed to have comprised standard Oxford Blue overall which deleted the ROYAL NAVY titles, the old 'Ambuscade' deck letters and code. The colour of the serials is not known, but Red/Blue roundels were applied and the code (341) was allocated but not worn. On 22.4.82 'Brilliant' detached for participation in Operation "Paraquat" (the retaking of South Georgia), XZ721 being transferred that day to 'Sheffield' Flight (in exchange for XZ725) as a Sea Skua equipped aircraft was not required for the Operation. The code (337) was allocated but not worn.

On 4.5.82, whilst on radar picket duty 70 miles south south-east of Port Stanley (at 52°46′S 57°07′W), 'Sheffield' was hit by one of two Exocets launched from a pair of 2 Escuadrilla Super Etendards. The Lynx was aboard at the time but escaped unscathed to 'Hermes' after the attack.

Returned from 'Sheffield' Flight aboard 'Hermes' to 'Brilliant' Flight on 7.5.82 (replacing XZ725; see earlier). Code (341) was allocated but not worn.

Involved in harassing the Falkland Islands' coastal freighter 'Monsunen' in Lively Sound on 23.5.82 (the vessel having been impressed into Argentine service), causing it to be run aground and abandoned.

Temporarily borrowed by 'Cardiff' Flight for Sea Skua familiarisation 27-30.5.82 in exchange for non-Sea Skua equipped XZ254. As 'Brilliant' was due to leave for the UK on 23.6.82, the Lynx was transferred to 'Cardiff' Flight (exchanged for the less serviceable Sea Skua equipped XZ233). Code (335) was allotted but not worn. Departed the TEZ aboard 'Cardiff' on 7.7.82 for return to the UK, remaining on the ship until she docked at

Portsmouth on 28.7.82. Disembarked to Portland later that day.

## XZ722 HAS.2

On 29.3.82 with 815 Sqdn 'Andromeda' Flight coded 'AM/472', named "Arfa", on deployment to the Bahamas and North America. The ship returned to Devonport on 23.4.82 and the Lynx disembarked to Yeovilton that day. Seen at Yeovilton 27.4.82 being painted in low-vis scheme which consisted of standard Oxford Blue overall obliterating the ROYAL NAVY titles and deck letters (serial colour not known). Red/Blue roundels were adopted and the code (472) remained allocated but not worn. Flown to NATIU Lee-on-Solent for fitting of Sea Skua and Stingray equipment, returning to Yeovilton 5.5.82. Back to Lee-on-Solent again 7.5.82 for the fitting of MAD equipment. Trials were carried out at Aberporth 9/10.5.82 before it embarked 'Andromeda' at Devonport 10.5.82, sailing with the vessel that day for the South Atlantic. Remained aboard 'Andromeda' until c13.8.82 when it embarked 'Invincible' while 'Andromeda' sailed to spend a week at South Georgia. Returned to 'Andromeda' c24.8.82 before she departed north for the UK. As the ship entered Plymouth Sound on 10.9.82, XZ722 took off to formate with XZ249 and XZ723 of 'Avenger' and 'Penelope' Flights, overflying all three vessels as they docked at Devonport. Following the flypast the three helicopters flew on to Portland.

## XZ723 HAS.2

On 29.3.82 uncoded with NASU Yeovilton (a Sea Skua/ECM aircraft). Transferred to 815 Sqdn 'Antelope' Flight on 4.4.82 to replace non-Sea Skua equipped XZ691. Embarked the ship at Devonport the same day (believed still uncoded) prior to sailing with her for Ascension Island and the South Atlantic on 5.4.82. Repainted in a low-vis scheme sometime between 23-30.4.82, believed to have consisted of standard Oxford Blue overall obliterating the ROYAL NAVY titles (serial colour unknown). Red/Blue roundels were adopted, with the code (321) allocated but not worn.

On 23.5.82, crewed by Lt McMahon and Lt Hunt, it was tasked with an attack on the 'Rio Carcarana', an Argentine supply ship which was thought to be attempting to leave Port King, despite substantial damage inflicted on her by 800 Sqdn Sea Harriers on 16.5.82. Two Sea Skuas were launched, both scoring direct hits. The ship caught fire and settled in the water.

Soon after, at about 1650Z, 'Antelope' was bombed by four Grupo 5 A-4B Skyhawks while she was positioned in Falkland Sound, covering the entrance to San Carlos Water. The Lynx (which was returning from a recce run over the stricken 'Rio Carcarana') held off, but the ship was hit by two bombs which lodged inside her without exploding. 'Antelope' limped into San Carlos Water; the Lynx did fly aboard but disembarked to Ajax Bay late on 23.5.82 prior to the attempted defusing of the bombs. It embarked 'Fearless' overnight on 23/24.5.82. The defusing attempt aboard 'Antelope' failed and the vessel exploded, eventually sinking on 24.5.82.

The aircraft left 'Fearless' on 24.5.82 and flew

to San Carlos to support 3 Cdo Bde, recovering once again to 'Fearless' that evening. The Flight personnel were drafted back to the UK, leaving the Lynx with the Assault Ship until 30.5.82. On that date it was transferred to 'Brilliant' Flight (replacing MAD equipped XZ729 which had been loaned to 'Broadsword' since 21.5.82), code (342) being allocated but not carried. As 'Brilliant' was scheduled to leave for the UK on 23.6.82, the aircraft was transferred to 'Broadsword' Flt on 22.6.82 (in exchange for the recently repaired XZ732). The code (349) was allocated but not worn. 'Broadsword' herself was due to detach for the UK on 3.7.82 so the aircraft was transferred to 'Penelope' Flight on 2.7.82 (in exchange for the Sea Skua equipped and vibration-prone XZ691). The code (454) was allocated but not carried. Loaned to 'Birmingham' Flight 23-25.7.82 whilst their own Lynx XZ693 was unserviceable. On 23.8.82 it detached with 'Penelope' for return to the UK. As the vessel entered Plymouth Sound on 10.9.82, XZ723 took-off to formate with XZ249 and XZ722 of 'Avenger' and 'Andromeda' Flights, overflying the three ships as they docked at Devonport. Following the flypast, all three helicopters flew on to Portland.

**XZ724 HAS.2**          *Deployed post-14.6.82*

On 15.6.82 with WHL Yeovil for installation of MAD equipment still wearing its previous 702 flight code '-/740'. Delivered to NASU Yeovilton on 17.6.82 and between 18-21.6.82 it was repainted in the overall Dark Sea Grey scheme with Black serials, Red/Blue roundels and devoid of ROYAL NAVY titles. Transferred to 815 Sqdn 'Phoebe' Flight at Yeovilton on 7.7.82, the code (471) being allocated but not worn. Flew to 815 Sqdn's new parent base at Portland on 19.7.82. Embarked 'Phoebe' from Portland on 6.9.82 after the ship had sailed from Devonport the same day on deployment to the South Atlantic. Believed disembarked to Portland 19.12.82 prior to the vessel's arrival at Devonport that day.

**XZ725 HAS.2**

On 29.3.82 with 815 Sqdn 'Sheffield' Flight coded 'SD/337' (a non-Sea Skua aircraft), operating with the ship from Gibraltar on Exercise "Springtrain". Ordered directly south with the ship from the Exercise on 2.4.82, arriving at Ascension Island on 11.4.82 and sailing for the South Atlantic on 14.4.82. By that date a low-vis scheme had been applied. Exact details are not known but Red/Blue roundels and the deck letters deleted, the code (337) remaining allocated but not carried. Transferred to 'Brilliant' Flight 22.4.82 (in exchange for Sea Skua/Stingray equipped XZ721) as 'Brilliant' was detaching to take part in Operation "Paraquat" (the retaking of South Georgia) and had no anticipated need for a Sea Skua equipped Lynx. Code (341) was allocated but not worn.

On 25.4.82, crewed by Lt Cdr Bryant and Lt Butler, the aircraft carried out a Mk.46 torpedo attack on the surfaced Argentine submarine 'Santa Fe' (from Grytviken, South Georgia) which had just been depth-charged by 'Antrim' Flight's Wessex HAS.3. No hit was achieved, but the circling torpedo forced the submarine to remain surfaced. The torpedo attack was followed up by GPMG fire from the Lynx. 'Santa Fe' was subjected to further attacks by 'Brilliant' and other Ships' Flights, forcing it to return damaged to Grytviken.

Transferred to 'Newcastle' Flight on board 'Fort Austin' 8.5.82, having been replaced with 'Brilliant' Flight on 7.5.82 by XZ721 from 'Hermes' (the latter had recovered to the carrier following the Exocet attack on 'Sheffield' — see earlier). No code was allocated while with 'Newcastle' Flight, as by that time the Flights embarked on 'Fort Austin' had dispensed with their use. It was transferred to the Trials Flight aboard 'Fort Austin' 17.5.82 (in exchange for XZ240), then flown to 'Invincible' that day to be based on the carrier for ESM/Exocet decoy duties, making room on 'Fort Austin' for a detachment of four 826 Sqdn Sea Kings. No code was allotted while with the Trials Flight aboard 'Invincible' (but see later). Due to it being unserviceable from 10-17.6.82 one of the 'Newcastle' Flight aircraft embarked on 'Hermes' (XZ720) was borrowed for that period. 'Invincible' left the FIPZ on 28.8.82 with the Lynx still embarked for return to UK. Flown off to Portland on 16.9.82 using the Trials Flight call-sign (479) prior to the carrier's arrival at Portsmouth on 17.9.82.

*On 21.9.82 it was noted at Portland wearing Dayglo Red letters "SSTF" (Small Ships Trials Flight) on the fin.*

**XZ726 HAS.2**          *Deployed post-14.6.82*

On 15.6.82 with 815 Sqdn 'Danae' Flt at Yeovilton wearing the overall Dark Sea Grey scheme devoid of ROYAL NAVY titles, with Black serials and Red/Blue roundels. Code (464) was allocated but not worn. Embarked 'Danae' from Yeovilton on 19.6.82, the day after the ship had sailed from Devonport. Returned to Devonport 17.10.82 with the vessel and was flown off to Portland later that day.

**XZ727 HAS.2**          *Deployed post-14.6.82*

On 15.6.82 with 815 Sqdn 'Battleaxe' Flight at Yeovilton in the overall Dark Sea Grey scheme devoid of ROYAL NAVY titles, with Black serials and Red/Blue roundels. Code (403) was allocated but not worn. Flown to 815 Sqdn's new parent base at Portland on 19.7.82. Embarked 'Battleaxe' 2.8.82 from Portland after the ship had sailed that day from Devonport on deployment to the South Atlantic. Disembarked to Portland 19.11.82 prior to the vessel docking the same day at Devonport.

**XZ728 HAS.2**

On 29.3.82 with 815 Sqdn 'Battleaxe' Flight coded 'BX/403', named "Asterix", operating out of Gibraltar on Exercise "Springtrain". On 2.4.82 (due to mechanical problems with the ship) it was detached back to the UK aboard 'Battleaxe'. The vessel docked at Devonport on 6.4.82 and the Lynx flew off later that day to Yeovilton, where it was modified and updated by NASU and NATIU Lee-on-Solent to become a MAD/ESM/Sea Skua aircraft. Airfreighted out to Ascension Island from Yeovilton on 12.4.82 aboard Hercules C.1 XV298 (believed still to have been wearing 'Battleaxe' Flt markings). On arrival at Wideawake it was assembled by Naval Party 1222 and officially transferred from

'Battleaxe' to 'Broadsword' Flight on 16.4.82. (With its arrival the Flight became a two-aircraft unit, XZ736 being the other Lynx at that time). Left Ascension Island aboard the ship on 18.4.82 and was test-flown by the Flight on 19.4.82. By then a low-vis scheme had been applied which consisted of standard Oxford Blue overall, deleting the ROYAL NAVY titles and (if still carried) its former code and deck letters. The serials were in Black, Red/Blue roundels were adopted and code (347) was allocated but not worn. On 15.5.82 it was slightly damaged on board during rough seas and on 19.5.82 its Sea Skua equipment was removed to be fitted to the Flight's other Lynx (at that time being non-Sea Skua equipped XZ732). The damage was repaired and the aircraft made serviceable again by 1.6.82. Flown to 'Hermes' on 8.6.82 and again on 9.6.82 to free the flight deck for a flight test and then a ground run of XZ732 *[see XZ729 and XZ732 for what happened aboard 'Broadsword' 21.5.82 to 8.6.82]*. Detached with 'Broadsword' from Port William on 3.7.82 en route for the UK. During the return journey it developed a mechanical problem, docking with the ship at Devonport on 23.7.82. Lifted off by crane on 24.7.82 and left by road the same day for Portland, where it arrived on 25.7.82 for a survey prior to repairs. Transported by road from Portland to Yeovilton 6.8.82, upon transfer from 'Broadsword' Flight to NASU for overhaul.

**XZ729 HAS.2**

On 29.3.82 with 815 Sqdn 'Brilliant' Flight coded 'BT/342' (MAD aircraft) operating out of Gibraltar on Exercise "Springtrain". Ordered directly south with the ship from the Exercise 2.4.82, arriving at Ascension Island on 11.4.82. Sailed from the Island with the ship on 14.4.82 and during the passage south a low-vis scheme was applied. It consisted of standard Oxford Blue overall, deleting the ROYAL NAVY titles and deck letters. Red/Blue roundels were adopted and the serials overpainted Black, the code (342) remaining allocated but not worn.

On 25.4.82, crewed by Lt Cdr Clark and Lt McKay off Grytviken in South Georgia, the Argentine submarine 'Santa Fe' was strafed with GPMG fire as part of a concentrated attack by both 'Brilliant' Flight aircraft *[see XZ725]*, and other Ships' Flights, which damaged the submarine and forced it to return to Grytviken.

'Brilliant' Flight required a second Sea Skua equipped Lynx (in addition to XZ721) on 8.5.82 for a night mission in North Falkland Sound and the area of Port Howard. XZ729 was temporarily transferred with the Flight aircrew to 'Glasgow' that day, while 'Glasgow' Flight's Sea Skua equipped XZ247 (plus aircrew) came over to 'Brilliant'. Both reverted to their respective ships on 9.5.82. Temporarily borrowed by 'Broadsword' Flight on 21.5.82 *[see XZ728 and XZ732 for reason]*. However, on 25.5.82 'Broadsword' was attacked by two Grupo 5 A-4B Skyhawks. Of the four bombs dropped, three of them missed while the fourth bounced off the sea, penetrated the hull and carried on up through the flight deck, taking the nose of XZ729 with it. The bomb's trajectory took it over the ship's side and into the sea....still without exploding!

The noseless aircraft eventually had its tail boom and other parts removed to repair XZ732, 'Broadsword' Flt's other Lynx which had suffered shrapnel-damage on 21.5.82. The serial "XZ729" remained on the boom after its transfer to XZ732. The hulk of XZ729 was airlifted aboard 'Atlantic Causeway' by Sea King on 11.6.82 (nominally still on 'Brilliant' Flight charge), to be cannibalised as and when required. Left San Carlos Water with the ship on 13.7.82 for return to the UK, arriving at Devonport on 27.7.82. Off-loaded on 28.7.82 to a compound at Camel's Head (near HMS Drake). Removed by road to RNAY Fleetlands (upon transfer from 'Brilliant' Flight) on 1.8.82 and arrived there 3.8.82 for major rebuild.

## XZ730 HAS.2

On 29.3.82 with 815 Sqdn 'Penelope' Flight at Yeovilton coded 'PN/454' (Sea Skua/ECM aircraft). Transferred to 'Minerva' Flight at Yeovilton on 3.4.82 (replacing non-Sea Skua equipped Lynx XZ248). At that time 'Minerva' was at Devonport about to start a refit *[later cancelled: see XZ698]* and the Flight was scheduled for reallotment to 'Liverpool'. That was cancelled following the Argentine invasion of the Falklands. Instead, the Flight personnel and aircraft were hurriedly prepared for deployment to Ascension Island prior to being allocated to a Task Force ship. The aircraft, still coded 'PN/454', departed Yeovilton for Wideawake on 3.4.82 aboard Hercules C.1 XV299. On arrival there 5.4.82 it was reassembled and test flown before delivery to 'Fort Austin' on 6.4.82. Although still marked 'PN/454', the 'Minerva' code (424) had been allocated to the aircraft. Transferred to 'Arrow' Flight on 17.4.82 in exchange for non-Sea Skua equipped XZ241. By that time the aircraft was in a low-vis scheme which consisted of standard Oxford Blue overall, deleting the deck letters and the old 'Penelope' code. The ROYAL NAVY titles and serials were overpainted Black, while Red/Blue roundels (in the correct proportions) were adopted; code (326) was allocated but not worn. Detached from the TEZ with the ship on 18.6.82 for return to the UK, flying off to Yeovilton 7.7.82 prior to the ship docking at Devonport later that day.

*Noted after arrival at Yeovilton with "HMS ARROW" in White on the nose.*

## XZ731 HAS.2     *Deployed post-14.6.82*

On 15.6.82 with 815 Sqdn 'Southampton' Flight at Yeovilton in the overall Dark Sea Grey scheme devoid of ROYAL NAVY titles, with Black serials and Red/Blue roundels; code (334) was allocated but not worn. Embarked on 17.6.82 and sailed with the ship from Portsmouth for the South Atlantic on 18.6.82. Transferred to 'Newcastle' Flight in the FIPZ on 23.9.82 (in exchange for the damaged XZ256), code (345) being allocated but not worn. Disembarked to Portland with the return of the ship to Portsmouth on 20.12.82.

## XZ732 HAS.2

On 29.3.82 with 815 Sqdn 'Glasgow' Flight coded 'GW/344' (a non-Sea Skua aircraft) operating out of Gibraltar on Exercise "Springtrain". Ordered directly south with the ship from the Exercise on 2.4.82, arriving at Ascension Island on 11.4.82. Sailed with the ship on 14.4.82 for a rendezvous with 'Fort Austin' on 17.4.82. Transferred to the Trials Flight aboard 'Fort Austin' on that date (in exchange for the Sea Skua equipped XZ247). At some stage during that period a low-vis scheme was applied which consisted of standard Oxford Blue overall, deleting ROYAL NAVY titles and its former code and deck letters; Red/Blue roundels were adopted with Black serials. No code was allocated while with the Trials Flight as by that time those Flights aboard 'Fort Austin' had dispensed with their use. Transferred to 'Broadsword' Flight 5.5.82 (in exchange for Sea Skua/ESM/TICM equipped XZ240), code (349) being allocated but not worn. On 19.5.82 work commenced on the installation of Sea Skua equipment removed from the Flight's other, damaged, Lynx (see XZ728 for reason). Unfortunately the work was interrupted on 21.5.82 when it suffered splinter damage from a strafing attack on the ship by a Grupo 6 Dagger. Repair work on XZ732 commenced 3.6.82, utilising the boom from damaged XZ729. Test-flown on 8.6.82 still wearing the serial "XZ729". Transferred to 'Brilliant' Flight on 23.6.82 (in exchange for the more serviceable Sea Skua/ECM equipped XZ723) and detached with the ship from the TEZ that day en route for the UK. Code (342) was allocated but not worn. Just prior to the ship docking at Devonport on 13.7.82, it flew off to Yeovilton (still carrying the serial "XZ729") on transfer to NASU for overhaul. Noted there 21.7.82 wearing its correct serial in White.

## XZ733 HAS.2

On 29.3.82 with 815 Sqdn 'Exeter' Flight coded 'EX/420' (a Sea Skua aircraft), deployed with the ship on guardship duties in the West Indies. Sailed with the vessel from St Johns, Antigua on 7.5.82 en-route to Ascension Island and the South Atlantic, arriving in the TEZ on 21.5.82. During the passage south a low-vis scheme was applied, consisting of standard Oxford Blue overall, deleting the ROYAL NAVY titles and deck letters. Red/Blue roundels were adopted, but the serial colour remains unconfirmed (believed Black). The code (420) remained allocated but not worn. Detached with the ship from Port Stanley 7.7.82 for return to the UK, docking at Portsmouth with her on 28.7.82. Flown off to Portland on 29.7.82.

## XZ734 HAS.2     *Deployed post-14.6.82*

On 15.6.82 with A&AEE Boscombe Down engaged on Stingray torpedo trials. Delivered to NASU Yeovilton on 20.7.82 and repainted in the overall Dark Sea Grey scheme with Black serials, Red/Blue roundels and devoid of ROYAL NAVY titles. Flown out to Portland 17.8.82 on transfer to 815 Sqdn 'Charybdis' Flight, the code (431) being allocated but not worn. Embarked 'Charybdis' on 8.11.82 from Portland after the ship had sailed from Devonport the same day on deployment to the South Atlantic. Reported to have visited Culdrose 24.3.83 marked as '-/431' and been flown from there to Portland the next day. 'Charybdis' docked at Devonport on 25.3.83.

## XZ735 HAS.2     *Deployed post-14.6.82*

On 15.6.82 with 815 Sqdn 'Amazon' Flight at Yeovilton coded 'AZ/320'. Noted there on 6.7.82 wearing the name "Erica". Repainted on 9.7.82 in the overall Dark Sea grey scheme with Red/Blue roundels, Black serials and devoid of ROYAL NAVY titles. The code (320) remained allocated but not worn. Flown to 815 Sqdn's new parent base at Portland 19.7.82. Embarked 'Amazon' from Portland on 2.8.82 after the ship had left Devonport the same day on deployment to the South Atlantic. Flown off to Portland on 18.11.82 prior to the vessel docking at Devonport on 19.11.82.

## XZ736 HAS.2

On 29.3.82 with 815 Sqdn 'Broadsword' Flight coded 'BW/346' (a Sea Skua aircraft) which was operating out of Gibraltar on Exercise "Springtrain". Departed with 'Broadsword' from Gibraltar for Naples on 5.4.82 at the start of a Far East deployment. However, the ship was recalled to Gibraltar and arrived there on 6.4.82. It sailed again on 8.4.82 for the South Atlantic, arriving off Ascension Island on 16.4.82. A low-vis scheme had been applied to XZ736 during the journey south which consisted of standard Oxford Blue overall, obliterating the ROYAL NAVY titles and deck letters. Red/Blue roundels were adopted with Black serials, the code (346) remaining allocated but not worn. Sailed from the Island with the ship on 18.4.82 and by that date was scheduled to be transferred, as its replacement (XZ240) was on board 'Invincible' awaiting the opportunity to fly over to 'Broadsword'. That happened on 24.4.82 as part of a three-way shuffle between 'Broadsword', 'Invincible' and 'Alacrity' *[see also XZ240 and XZ720]* designed to provide 'Alacrity' Flight with a Sea Skua equipped Lynx (XZ736). The code (327) was allocated but not worn.

On 1.5.82, crewed by Lt Cdr Burrows, Lt Sleeman and an RA "spotter", it was tasked with carrying out low-level NGS spotting duties close to Port Stanley. As it neared Kidney Island (some four miles north-east of Port Stanley) the Argentine patrol boat 'Islas Malvinas' and the impressed Falklands' boat 'Forrest' were sighted between the Island and the coast of East Falkland. The Lynx attacked the patrol boat with its GPMG, causing slight damage and some casualties. The GPMG then jammed and the aircraft was hit by six rounds fired by the 'Forrest', but managed to return safely to 'Alacrity'.

Flown to 'Fort Austin' for BDR 3.5.82 ('Newcastle' Flight's XZ700 based on 'Fort Austin' being received as a temporary replacement). On 8.5.82 it returned to 'Alacrity', XZ700 being flown back to 'Fort Austin'. Detached with the ship from the TEZ on 6.6.82 for return to the UK. Disembarked to Yeovilton as the ship entered Plymouth Sound on 24.6.82 prior to docking at Devonport. On 5.7.82 it was transferred to NASU Yeovilton for overhaul and repairs.

*By the time it arrived at Yeovilton on 24.6.82 it was wearing "HMS ALACRITY" in White on the nose.*

# WASP

# 829 NAVAL AIR SQUADRON

At the time of the Argentine invasion of the Falkland Islands 829 Sqdn, under the command of Lt Cdr M.J.Mullane, was still operating a sizeable number of Ships' Flights from the unit's base at Portland. The late 1970's and early 1980's had seen the gradual withdrawal of the Wasp HAS.1 in favour of the Lynx HAS.2 and by March 1982 only two Royal Navy frigate squadrons retained the Wasp in service with their 829 Sqdn Flights. They were the older Ikara-equipped 'Leander' Class vessels of the 1st Frigate Sqdn and the Type 21 'Rothesay' Class vessels of the 6th Frigate Sqdn. Almost all of the 'Leander' Broadbeam Class vessels were undergoing conversion to Seawolf/Exocet armament and their Flights were re-equipping with the Lynx HAS.2's of 815 Sqdn. One other frigate, Type 21 'Active' of the 4th Frigate Sqdn, was the only one of its class not to have a Lynx-equipped Flight, while five other vessels also continued to have Wasp-equipped Flights. These were the four survey ships and the ice patrol ship 'Endurance', the latter engaged on what was to have been her last voyage to the South Atlantic. The Squadron also operated a sizeable Headquarters Flight.

However, as with 815 Sqdn, the 829 Sqdn Wasp HAS.1 Flights in commission at the beginning of the conflict were deployed far and wide in the various peacetime operations undertaken by the Royal Navy. Seven frigates had deployed during March for Exercise "Springtrain", being 'Ariadne', 'Aurora', 'Dido', 'Euryalus', 'Plymouth', 'Rhyl' and 'Yarmouth'. They had been joined by 'Active' which was returning from Gulf Patrol in the Middle East. 'Achilles' and 'Ajax' were both involved in Exercise "Caribtrain 82" while 'Bacchante' and 'Diomede' had been taking part in Exercise "Alloy Express" off Norway. 'Bacchante' was in fact due to go to the Royal New Zealand Navy later in the year. Other frigates operating in home waters were 'Apollo', 'Arethusa', 'Leander', 'Naiad' and 'Rothesay', while 'Galatea' Flight was due to recommission when the ship completed her refit at Gibraltar during May. Of the four survey vessels, 'Hecla' and 'Herald' were both deployed on survey work from which 'Hydra' had recently returned, while 'Hecate' was undergoing a refit.

At that stage, the standard colour scheme applied to the

Wasp was RAF Blue-Grey overall with White titles, deck-letters and codes, plus Class 'D' roundels. The only exceptions to this were the two 'Endurance' Flight aircraft which both had Roundel Red applied to the front fuselage, fin and flotation gear in order to make them more visible in the Antarctic snow conditions. However, they had been repainted in a camouflage scheme (minus codes) even before 29 March *[further details can be found in the 'Endurance' Flight notes]*.

Wasp HAS.1's assigned to the Squadron on 29 March were as follows:

| HQ Flight | | | | | |
|---|---|---|---|---|---|
| XT784 | '-/600' | XT783 | '-/604' | XT793 | '-/610' |
| XV626 | '-/601' | XT795 | '-/605' | XT430 | '-/611' |
| XT427 | '-/602' | XS529 | '-/606' | XT423 | '-/612' |
| XT790 | '-/603' | XV636 | '-/607' | | |

XT432 'HT/414' (ex-'Hecate' Flight)
XT420 uncoded (reserve)

### Ships' Flights

*A Flight consisted of personnel and usually one helicopter. For both administrative and operational reasons each Flight was allocated a three-digit number (beginning with '0') which was normally associated with a particular ship.*

| 'Achilles' | 043 Flight | XV638 | 'AC/430' |
|---|---|---|---|
| 'Active' | 035 Flight | XT779 | '-/322' |
| 'Ajax' | 020 Flight | XT791 | '-/421' |
| 'Apollo' | 041 Flight | XS567 | 'AP/470' |
| 'Arethusa' | 022 Flight | XT437 | '-/426' |
| 'Ariadne' | 023 Flight | XT426 | 'AE/455' |
| 'Aurora' | 030 Flight | XT443 | 'AU/422' |
| 'Bacchante' | 052 Flight | XS538 | '-/425' |
| 'Dido' | 055 Flight | XT786 | '-/473' |
| 'Diomede' | 021 Flight | XV634 | '-/423' |
| 'Endurance' | 001 Flight | XS527 | (434) |
| | | XS539 | (435) |

*continued*

continued

| 'Euryalus' | 044 Flight | XT421 | 'EU/433' |
|---|---|---|---|
| 'Herald' | 010 Flight | XT794 | '-/325' |
| 'Hydra' | 011 Flight | XS568 | '-/415' |
| 'Leander' | 034 Flight | XT415 | '-/476' |
| 'Naiad' | 045 Flight | XT782 | '-/324' |
| 'Plymouth' | 027 Flight | XT429 | '-/445' |
| 'Rhyl' | 026 Flight | XT439 | '-/446' |
| 'Rothesay' | 024 Flight | XT785 | 'RO/462' |
| 'Yarmouth' | 032 Flight | XV624 | '-/456' |

For those Flights deployed to the South Atlantic, the order to "tone down" markings at the beginning of the conflict resulted in all White markings being overpainted in RAF Blue-Grey or Matt Black with the roundels changed to low-vis Red/Blue and the codes applied in Black (in some cases). Some Flights applied heat resistant Black paint to the engine exhausts, but not all of the ships carried such paint so many of the exhausts remained silver.

In the event, only three Type 21 frigates and three of the survey ships were to join 'Endurance' in the South Atlantic. With the departure of the Task Force it became clear that the older frigates would be held on standby or would deploy to take over the peacetime roles vacated by other ships heading for the South Atlantic. Indeed, as a result of the conflict, 829 Sqdn was to see six Flights reform after a long absence as ships were brought out of reserve. The frigates 'Berwick', 'Falmouth', 'Gurkha', 'Tartar' and 'Zulu' were all recommissioned while 'Lowestoft' ceased operations as a trials ship, regaining her Flight once again. In order to increase the Squadron's

complement of Wasp HAS.1's, XS541 '-/(8)95' was withdrawn from the BRNC Flight at Dartmouth and transferred to the HQ Flight at Portland on 14 May.

The Wasp-equipped frigates which deployed to the South Atlantic were 'Active', 'Plymouth' and 'Yarmouth'. They were subsequently followed by the survey ships 'Hecla', 'Herald' and 'Hydra' after their conversion to ambulance vessels, their respective Wasp HAS.1's having been given Red Cross markings and fitted with blue anti-collision lights (instead of red) in accordance with the rules of the Geneva Convention. The Red Cross markings on a White background were applied to the nose, fuselage sides, underside and the top of the stabiliser. No side codes were carried, although they did remain allocated, while 'Herald' Flight's Wasp (at least) inevitably received the inscription "MASH" on the nose.

During May three additional Flights were formed by 829 Sqdn to equip merchant ships sailing south. Two Wasps were assigned to 'Contender Bezant' (029 and 031 Flights) and one to 'St Helena' (033 Flight), the latter deploying during June as an MCM support vessel. Although perhaps overshadowed by the Lynx helicopters of 815 Sqdn in terms of numbers involved and actions undertaken, the activities of 829 Sqdn's Wasps were memorable nonetheless, particularly for the part played by the helicopters aboard 'Endurance' and 'Plymouth' during the attack on the Argentine submarine 'Santa Fe'. To illustrate the level of 829 Sqdn's activities during April, May and June, the Flights involved in Operation "Corporate" flew a total of 451 hours in 727 sorties with 3,333 deck landings.

# 'ACTIVE' (027) FLIGHT

At the start of the conflict, 'Active' was taking part in Exercise "Springtrain" during her return from Gulf Patrol in the Middle East. The ship was operating from Gibraltar for the Exercise and her Flight was embarked with Wasp HAS.1 XT779 coded '-/322'. The Flight helped with the hectic stores transfer operations on 2 April, delivering supplies to those vessels departing south, while 'Active' herself was to return home to the United Kingdom for repairs (involving a clutch change). The ship arrived at Devonport on 6 April, on which date the Wasp was flown off to Portland. While the repairs were carried out and the ship was re-stored for deployment to the South Atlantic, low-vis markings were applied to XT779 (RAF Blue-Grey overall with Red/Blue roundels; no ROYAL NAVY titles and the serial, and code '-/322' being applied in Black). That had been completed by 6 May and the Flight embarked on 10 May following the departure of 'Active' from Devonport earlier that day to join the 'Bristol' Group. Training in wartime flying techniques took place during the journey south, but there was little time to practise NGS spotting with only a short stopover at Ascension on 18/19 May.

'Active' joined the CVBG on the night of 25/26 May,

although her first real "action stations" had occurred on 22 May when the Group was overflown by a Grupo 1 Boeing 707. On 28 May the ship sailed east to the TRALA for repairs, the Flight being engaged in HDS duties around the ships in the TRALA two days later. 'Active' sailed for San Carlos Water, arriving on 31 May with essential stores for 'Arrow', while the following night she took part in her first NGS mission. During the next two weeks, the ship was involved in screening operations for the CVBG by day, while by night she detached closer to the coastline for bombardment duties and the protection of convoys resupplying the beachhead. An NGS mission on 2 June had to be cancelled after intelligence was received warning of a threat from land-based Exocet missiles, while on 3 June 'Active' acted as escort for a convoy going to Teal Inlet. NGS spotting missions by the Flight took place on 6/10/12/13 June, although the ship suffered engine problems on 10 June but still managed to return to the screen by daylight.

Bombardment of the Moody Brook and Tumbledown areas during the night of 13/14 June saw 'Active' providing a significant contribution to the enemy surrender which occurred the following day. The Flight was airborne at the time and returned to find the inscription "Stanley Surrenders" chalked on the deck! The ship detached to Port San Carlos for repairs at 2330Z on 17 June in company with 'Glamorgan' and 'Stena Seaspread'. On 19 June XT779 suffered hydraulic problems but had been made serviceable by the following day. The aircraft became unserviceable again on 23 June and repairs were not completed until 4 July. In the meantime, 'Active' commenced a week's duty as the Port William guard-ship on 1 July then rejoined the CVBG on 8 July. The need for final repairs to the vessel saw her in San Carlos Water again on 14 July and she finally sailed north for the United Kingdom at 0830Z the following day in company with 'Minerva'. The two ships passed Ascension Island on 23/24 July and 'Active' arrived at Devonport on 3 August, her Flight disembarking to Portland the following day.

> *829 Sqdn aircrew with 'Active' Flight during Operation "Corporate": Lt G.J.Tilsley RN (Flt Cdr); LACMN S.P.Roberts.*

# 'CONTENDER BEZANT' (029 & 031) FLIGHTS

On 13 May two Wasp HAS.1's were transferred to 029 and 031 Flights in order to provide an HDS and defence capability aboard the chartered Ro-Ro merchant ship 'Contender Bezant'. The two aircraft concerned were XS562 '-/360' (in the low-vis scheme of RAF Blue-Grey overall with Red/Blue roundels, Black serials and codes, devoid of ROYAL NAVY titles) formerly with 'Galatea' Flight, and XT427 '-/602' which had been operating with 'Rhyl' Flight for a short while. The latter was also given low-vis markings and the two helicopters were recoded '-/371' and '-/372' respectively in Black. XS562 carried the phrase "One Eye" on the fuselage while XT427 went one better sporting "One Eye The Wasp" (see the aircraft histories for the background to these markings). Both helicopters embarked 'Contender Bezant' in Plymouth Sound on 20 May prior to her departure the following day from Start Bay, Devon (after a practice RAS) for Freetown (Sierra Leone), Ascension Island and the South Atlantic. Armed sorties were flown during the passage south, using each aircraft alternately to give the two crews practice at firing the AS.12 missiles.

The vessel arrived on station to the east of the Falkland Islands on 10 June and carried out a rendezvous with 'Brilliant' on 12 June. After the surrender, she moved to Port William on 17 June to unload her cargo of equipment and vehicles, taking up the role of helicopter support ship. The two Wasp HAS.1's flew to HQ CLFFI in Port Stanley each morning where their daily taskings were collected; ad hoc sorties were then flown on demand, the pair returning to the ship each evening usually after seven hours flying. Apart from HDS and personnel transfer sorties, Lt P.D.Clarke flew investigators to the crash sites of Argentine aircraft.

The Flights sailed north with the ship on 13 July en route for the United Kingdom, returning to Southampton on 1 August when XS562 disembarked to Portland later the same day followed by XT427 on 2 August. XS562 remained on nominal Flight charge (as it required maintenance) until 21 October, on which date it was transferred to the HQ Flight, but XT427 was allocated to the HQ Flight on 6 August. 'Contender Bezant' Flights did not deploy on 7 August when the vessel departed again for the South Atlantic.

> *829 Sqdn aircrew with 'Contender Bezant' Flights during Operation "Corporate": Lt P.D.Clarke RN (Flts Cdr); Lt D.R.Russell RN; POACMN M.W.Waters; LACMN M.C.Brown.*

# 'ENDURANCE' (001) FLIGHT

'Endurance' was already on station in the South Atlantic at the beginning of the conflict with her two Wasp HAS.1's XS527 'E/434' and XS539 'E/435'. The Flight was disembarked at Green Patch (East Falkland) on 19 March when news was received that the 'Bahia Buen Suceso' had landed civilian and military personnel at Leith on South Georgia. The Flight re-embarked 'Endurance' in Berkeley Sound on 21 March and sailed with her for South Georgia, inserting an observation post there on 24 March. On the following day one aircraft flew relief personnel to the observation post and while on the ground was overflown by 1 Escuadrilla de Helicopteros Alouette III 0699/3-H-110 from the 'Bahia Paraiso'. The Wasp HAS.1's distinctive red markings had been easily spotted so, during that night, both helicopters were resprayed in a camouflage scheme which consisted of random pattern Matt Black/Light Admiralty Grey/Olive Drab overall, to which were added patches of washable White as and when required; toned-down Red/Blue roundels; Light Admiralty Grey serials and small ROYAL NAVY titles behind the cockpit. The codes (434) and (435) remained allocated but were not carried.

On 31 March the observation post was removed, the detachment of Royal Marines aboard 'Endurance' disembarking to Grytviken in order to supplement the British forces there. The ship then sailed for Port Stanley. How-

Seen here on the flight-deck of 'Endurance' off Southern Thule on 19.6.82 is Wasp HAS.1 XS539 (435) of 829 Squadron 'Endurance' Flight. This suitably camouflaged, AS.12-equipped Wasp escorted a Wessex HU.5 **(Below)** which was used that day to insert a reconnaissance troop of 'M' Coy 42 Cdo onto the snow and ice-covered island. The following day the Argentine occupying force surrendered.
(Ministry of Defence)

Three into one will go! In addition to the ship's normal complement of two Wasps, the 'Endurance' hangar accommodated (with less difficulty than anticipated) XS486 '–/WW', a Wessex HU.5 of 848 Squadron 'A' Flight. Temporarily detached from 'Regent' to the ice patrol vessel from 17–24.6.82, the Wessex assisted in the recapture of Southern Thule, South Sandwich Islands. The Wasp on the extreme left is XS527 (434); XS539, with the White patches, is the other. (Ministry of Defence)

'Active' and her 829 Squadron Wasp HAS.1 XT779 '–/322' did not leave the United Kingdom for the Falkland Islands until 10.5.82. XT779, seen here on the Falklands on an unknown date, was used on numerous NGS spotting missions for 'Active' especially during the latter stages of the conflict.
(E. Wareing)

829 Squadron Wasp HAS.1 XT794 (325) was based on the hospital ship 'Herald' during the conflict. It was one of three ambulance-configured Wasps deployed to the South Atlantic. All were common sights, buzzing about the Red Cross Box to the north of the Falklands carrying casualties and medical supplies.
(Ministry of Defence)

ever, following the initial enemy assault at Mullet Creek on 2 April (0730Z), 'Endurance' reversed course back to South Georgia (at 0915Z). Grytviken was captured by the Argentine forces on 3 April, on which date the Flight carried out an armed reconnaissance sortie at maximum range to report on the situation there. The mission was undertaken by Lt Cdr J.A.Ellerbeck and Lt D.A.H.Wells in XS527, landing in the hills behind Grytviken where the camouflaged Wasp blended in well with the surroundings. They then found a vantage point from which to observe the movements of the 'Bahia Paraiso', the damaged 'Guerrico' and the LCVP's. For the crew it must have been somewhat depressing to see the two enemy ships not a mile away — ideal AS.12 missile targets. There was no sign of the Royal Marines, however, so the crew made their way back to the Wasp and returned to 'Endurance' to report their findings.

The ship sailed on 5 April under cover of darkness, firstly to rendezvous with 'Fort Austin' at 22°S on 12 April for replenishment, and then to regroup with 'Antrim', 'Plymouth' and 'Tidespring' at 25°S on 14 April. The four vessels arrived off South Georgia on 21 April for Operation "Paraquat" (the retaking of the Island). On that date one Wasp and a Gemini boat were used to insert two SBS units at Hounds Bay while XS527 went to St Andrews Bay to warn the local inhabitants there not to give away the position of 'Endurance' by radio. 'Endurance' Flight flew ASW sorties on 23 April

(an enemy submarine having been reported in the area) while the SBS units were recovered on 24 April, on which date a Grupo 1 Boeing 707 made a low-level reconnaissance of the area and spotted 'Endurance'.

Tony Ellerbeck and David Wells took-off in XS527 at 0910Z on 25 April, armed with two AS.12 missiles for surface search duties. Almost immediately they learnt that 'Antrim' Flight's Wessex HAS.3 had sighted and attacked the enemy submarine 'Santa Fe' using Mk.11 depth charges. Following that, a Lynx HAS.2 from 'Brilliant' (which had by then joined the Group) attacked with Mk.46 torpedoes; that was sufficient to keep the submarine on the surface as a torpedo circled beneath it. The two 'Endurance' Flight aircrew aboard XS527 spotted the submarine 2 miles north-west of Barff Point and attacked it with two AS.12's, achieving one hit on the conning tower which damaged pumps and sensors while the other missile fell some 30 yards short. At that stage, both of the 'Brilliant' Flight Lynx HAS.2's overflew the target and were joined by 'Plymouth' Flight's Wasp HAS.1. Lt Cdr Ellerbeck quickly returned to 'Endurance' to rearm and attacked again with two AS.12's, one of which hit the glass reinforced fin but because of the nature of the material went straight through it and exploded on hitting the sea. 'Plymouth' Flight attacked next, its only missile falling yards short. XS527 departed as the two 'Brilliant' Flight helicopters came in on strafing runs.

In the meantime, Lt T.Finding and LACMN

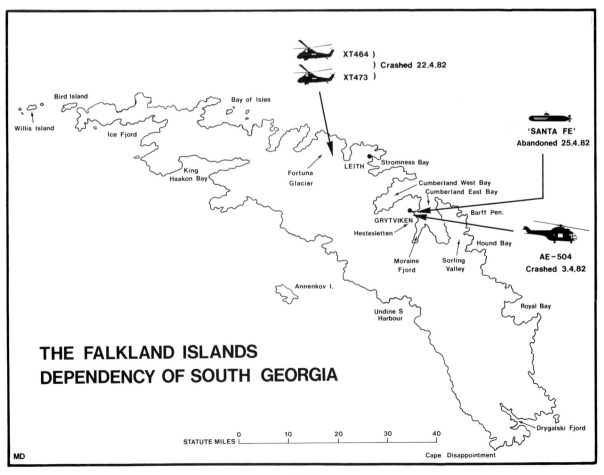

XT464 )
) Crashed 22.4.82
XT473 )

'SANTA FE'
Abandoned 25.4.82

Bird Island
Bay of Isles
Willis Island
Ice Fjord
King
Haakon Bay
Fortuna
Glacier
LEITH
Stromness Bay
Cumberland West Bay
Cumberland East Bay
Barff Pen.
GRYTVIKEN
Hestesletten
Hound Bay
Moraine
Fjord
Sorling
Valley
Annenkov I.
Undine S
Harbour
Royal Bay

AE-504
Crashed 3.4.82

THE FALKLAND ISLANDS
DEPENDENCY OF SOUTH GEORGIA

Drygalski Fjord

0        10        20        30        40
STATUTE MILES

MD                                                Cape Disappointment

R.B.Nadin took-off in XS539 armed with two AS.12 missiles. They sighted and attacked the submarine as it turned into King Edward Point, achieving one hit on the conning tower, but the missile failed to explode. XS527 was re-armed and launched again, attacking once more with two AS.12's from 200 feet over Dartmouth Point. Another hit on the conning tower was scored, destroying pumps, most of the aerials and the periscopes. This final attack accounted for the only casualty of the engagement when one Argentine crew member who was manning a machine gun subsequently lost a leg. The attacks on the 'Santa Fe' had been pressed home bravely through heavy machine-gun fire from the Argentine forces ashore.

The following table summarises the Flight's attacks on the submarine, giving firing altitude and range data for each missile expended:

| Missiles fired: LACMN Bob Nadin | | | |
|---|---|---|---|
| No 1 | 400ft | 4 miles | Missed by 50 yards |
| No 2 | 400ft | 3 miles | Hit conning tower, no explosion |

| Missiles fired: Lt David Wells | | | |
|---|---|---|---|
| No 1 | 1000ft | 3.5-4 miles | Hit conning tower |
| No 2 | 1000ft | 2.5-3 miles | Missed by 30 yards |
| No 3 | 100ft | 3 miles | Rogue, went left |
| No 4 | 100ft | 2-2.5 miles | Hit conning tower, no explosion |
| No 5 | 200ft | 3 miles | Two hang-ups so it was jettisoned |
| No 6 | 150ft | 2 miles | Hit conning tower, large explosion |

Following the removal of the enemy submarine threat, the operation to land the embarked forces by helicopter from 'Antrim' and 'Brilliant' commenced. 'Antrim' and 'Plymouth' put on a display of the power of naval bombardment, gunfire controllers from 148 Battery RA directing operations from the two 'Endurance' Flight Wasps to ensure that the fire-power was both accurate and effective. At 1700Z on 25 April, the crew of XS527 spotted an Argentine white flag and only minutes later the surrender was broadcast. At that point, XS527 landed with Captain Browne (who had been directing naval gunfire), picked up Major Sheridan RM who was commander of the land forces involved in Operation "Paraquat" and flew him to King Edward Point to accept the surrender.

'Endurance' remained on station off South Georgia for the remainder of the conflict, her Flight carrying out sur-face search duties against the ever-present submarine threat. The Flight recovered British Antarctic Survey personnel from Schleiper Bay and Bird Island on 1 May. Engineers from the 'Stena Seaspread' were put ashore by the Flight between 16-19 May to evaluate the local derelict whaling stations as a source of supply for steel. Sheet steel of good quality was found and utilised. On 18 May one aircraft carried out a surface search to verify a submarine sighting, but without result. The typically inclement South Atlantic weather at that time of year saw XS539 stuck on the Island in fog on 29 May, but it recovered to 'Leeds Castle' which duly returned the helicopter to 'Endurance' at Grytviken. XS527 developed a minor fault on 28 May but was airborne again the following day.

On 17 June, the Flight carried out practice SS.11 firings in the Cumberland Bays area and 'Endurance' embarked Wessex HU.5 XS486 of 848 Sqdn 'A' Flight from 'Regent', all in preparation for Operation "Keyhole" (the recapture of Southern Thule); the Wessex was to be accompanied by an AS.12-armed Wasp during troop insertion missions. 'Endurance' sailed for Southern Thule on 17 June, joining 'Yarmouth', 'Olmeda' and the tug 'Salvageman' two days later. During the passage it was found that the Wessex and both Wasps could be stowed inside the hangar. Reconnaissance and troop insertion sorties were flown in support of the retaking of the Island, which was accomplished on 20 June when the Argentine base surrendered.

The Flight carried out VERTREP sorties to 'Olmeda' and 'Yarmouth' on 21 June. 'Endurance' returned to South Georgia three days later at 1230Z, whereupon the Wessex re-embarked 'Regent'. The ship remained on station until 16 July when she sailed to spend a week in the Falkland Islands before departing north for the United Kingdom. 'Endurance' handed over to 'Hecate' off Ascension Island on 5 August and arrived in Weymouth Bay at 0200Z on 19 August. The Flight remained on board until the ship entered the Medway en route to Chatham the following day, when both helicopters took-off for a celebratory flypast accompanied by two other 829 Sqdn Wasps (XT439 '-/605' and XS541 '-/(8)95') which had arrived from Portland. The Flight finally disembarked to Portland the same day after the ship had docked. Hours flown by the Flight's two Wasps during "Corporate" were as follows: 78hrs 20mins by XS527 and 84hrs 55mins by XS539.

*829 Sqdn aircrew with 'Endurance' Flight for Operation "Corporate" and their awards: Lt Cdr J.A.Ellerbeck RN (Flt Cdr) DSC; Lt T.Finding RN (Senior Pilot); Lt D.A.H.Wells RN (Senior Observer) MID; S/Lt R.J.F.Buckland RN (Observer); LACMN R.B.Nadin.*

# 'HECLA' (012) FLIGHT

During March, 'Hecla' was engaged in a deep water survey in the North Atlantic Ocean. She had sailed on 2 March following work-up at Portland, having completed a refit at the end of 1981, but had no aircraft embarked as her Flight had been out of commission for over two years. While the vessel was en route to Gibraltar for a two-week maintenance period (arriving there on 8 April), plans were being made to fill the requirement for hospital ships in the Task Force, along with support vessels for the transport of casualties to neutral ports. 'Hecla' was ordered to prepare for deployment in the latter role as an ambulance ship (along with 'Herald' and 'Hydra'), to be ready by 20 April. On 16 April uncoded Wasp HAS.1 XT420 was transferred to the newly-reformed 'Hecla' Flight from 829 Sqdn's reserve and taken by road to Yeovilton the same day, leaving aboard Hercules C.3 XV221 on 19 April for delivery to Gibraltar. Lt C.T.deV.Hunt, who had just left 'Rothesay' as Flight Commander, was on leave when ordered to fly out and take charge of 'Hecla' Flight. Having test-flown XT420 on the morning of 20 April, the Flight embarked and 'Hecla' sailed from Gibraltar that afternoon. At that stage Red Cross markings were applied to the Wasp. The standard overall RAF Blue-Grey colourscheme with White markings was retained, as were the 'D' Class roundels. The side code (416) was allocated but not carried.

During the passage south the aircrew were trained in nursing procedures and flew practice casualty movement exercises until a rendezvous with the hospital ship 'Uganda' in the Red Cross Box (RCB) on 14 May. The RCB was a designated area north of the Falkland Islands where medical supplies and casualties were transferred to their respective country's hospital ships. Following the landings on 21 May, the Flight was fully engaged in casualty transfers between vessels arriving from the Falkland

Islands and 'Uganda'. 'Hecla' was joined by 'Hydra' on 19 May, but the delayed 'Herald' did not arrive until 25 May. 'Herald' Flight's aircraft had suffered a major fault on 13 May and was unserviceable, so before 'Hecla' departed to Montevideo in Uruguay on 29 May with casualties for repatriation, her Wasp donated spare parts to XT794 of 'Herald' Flight to make it serviceable while 'Herald' remained within the Red Cross Box. 'Hecla' arrived at Montevideo on 2 June to unload, collecting spare parts for XT420 before departing later in the day with her Wasp serviceable once again.

Returning to the Red Cross Box on 6 June, her Wasp joined 'Herald' Flight's aircraft in moving stores and personnel to 'Uganda' the next day. A second trip to Montevideo was made and 'Hecla' remained on station until the last of the British and Argentine casualties had left for home. She sailed for the United Kingdom during the evening of 29 June from a position 4-5 miles north of Falkland Sound, having sheltered for most of that day from a 75 knot wind which had caused 35 degrees of roll! The ship docked at Devonport on 29 July and the Flight disembarked to Portland later the same day.

---

829 Sqdn aircrew with 'Hecla' Flight during Operation "Corporate": Lt C.T.deV.Hunt RN (Flt Cdr); LACMN T.G.Monks.

# 'HERALD' (010) FLIGHT

'Herald' was returning to the United Kingdom from a seven-month survey deployment to the Middle East when Argentina invaded the Falkland Islands. The ship arrived at Portsmouth on 7 April, her Flight disembarking to Portland with Wasp HAS.1 XT794 '-/325' earlier in the day. 'Herald' was tasked with the ambulance ship role on 15 April and, following conversion, sailed from Portsmouth on 24 April (accompanied by 'Hydra') with the Flight embarking as the ship passed the Isle of Wight. The Wasp retained the standard RAF Blue-Grey overall colour scheme with White markings and 'D' Class roundels. The side code (325) remained allocated but not carried and XT794 had by then acquired Red Cross markings.

During the passage south the Flight exercised casualty evacuation procedures, while additional HDS sorties to embark stores and mail were carried out as 'Herald' passed Ascension Island on 8 May. The aircrew joined the ship's crew for training in all aspects of nursing, from the administration of drugs to bed changing! This training continued while XT794 was unserviceable, the Wasp having developed a serious defect on 13 May when its tail-rotor drive-shaft steady bearing was found to be breaking up due to overheating. One of the ship's crewmen suffered an accident the following day which required major surgery, so 'Herald' called at Rio de Janeiro in Brazil on 18 May to put him ashore. Severe gales delayed the vessel's subsequent arrival in the Red Cross Box until 25 May, her Wasp still being unserviceable on that date.

Casualty transfers were undertaken using the 'Hecla' and 'Hydra' Flight Wasps until 'Hecla' departed to Montevideo in Uruguay on 29 May to repatriate casualties, but not before the opportunity had been taken to rob 'Hecla' Flight's Wasp XT420 of the parts required by XT794 as 'Herald' continued its duties within the Red Cross Box.

The Flight continued with casualty transfer and HDS sorties as follows: 29/30 May medical stores to 'Uganda'; 1 June CASEVAC from 'Uganda' to 'Hydra'; 5 June HDS sorties to 'Uganda'; 7 June HDS sorties to 'Uganda' and to 'Hecla'; 8 June CASEVAC from 'Uganda' to 'Herald'. The Flight was also involved on 2/3 June in a search for the crew and other occupants of missing Grupo 1 C-130E TC-63 which had been shot down by an 801 Sqdn Sea Harrier on 1 June. On 4 June, the Flight took a party of International Red Cross officials from 'Uganda' to the 'Bahia Paraiso', an Argentine ship which was being used in the same role.

'Herald' embarked British casualties from 'Uganda' on 7 June (her Wasp being assisted by 'Hecla' Flight's aircraft during the transfer operation), sailing on 8 June for Montevideo where she arrived on 13 June. On 19 June the ship was alongside 'Uganda' once again for more casualty transfers in Grantham Sound before sailing once more for Montevideo to arrive there on 25 June. A further rendezvous with 'Uganda' took place on 29 June to deliver stores and embark personnel, completed after 3hrs 30mins of flying in appalling weather conditions.

'Herald' Flight transferred a total of 95 patients from 'Uganda' and delivered some 15 tons of medical supplies and provisions in return. Most of this was achieved in only 18 hours flying during June, but involved three hour sorties and some 220 deck landings. Following the final transfer to 'Uganda', 'Herald' departed for the United Kingdom, calling at Ascension Island on 5 July. The vessel returned to Portsmouth on 21 July, her Flight having disembarked to Portland that day just prior to the ship's arrival.

*829 Sqdn aircrew with 'Herald' Flight during Operation "Corporate": Lt S.P.Edding RN (Flt Cdr); LACMN S.D.Spear.*

# 'HYDRA' (011) FLIGHT

The Flight had disembarked to Portland on 4 March when 'Hydra' returned to Portsmouth from a six-month survey deployment to the Caribbean area. While Wasp HAS.1 XS568 '-/415' underwent a period of maintenance, the Flight acquired XT432 coded 'HT/414' from the HQ Flight on 1 April. This Wasp was formerly with 'Hecate' Flight, whose parent ship was undergoing a refit. 'Hydra' was expected to deploy again on 22 April for more survey work, but on 15 April she was re-tasked as an ambulance ship for use on Operation "Corporate". When the conversion work and other preparations had been completed, the Flight embarked at Portsmouth on 23 April, XT432 having acquired Red Cross markings but retaining the standard RAF Blue-Grey overall colour scheme with White markings and 'D' Class roundels. The deck letters from its service on board 'Hecate' were retained on the tail while the code (415) was allocated but not carried. 'Hydra' sailed along with 'Herald' on 24 April. During the passage south casualty transfer operations and nursing procedures were practised by the Flight until 19 May when the ship joined 'Uganda' on the edge of the TEZ, entering the Red Cross Box some 30 miles north of the Falkland Islands on 22 May.

The hectic round of CASEVAC flights commenced when Argentine casualties from the 'Narwal' were transferred from 'Hecla' to 'Uganda' on 20 May. 'Hydra' detached to the east on 25 May to receive casualties flown aboard from 'Canberra', returning to the Red Cross Box on 26 May to transfer them to 'Uganda'. Further casualty transfer sorties by the Flight were carried out on 28 May ('Uganda' to 'Hecla') and on 1/2 June ('Uganda' to 'Hydra'). The ship detached to Montevideo in Uruguay on 2 June, arriving there four days later to disembark the wounded servicemen. 'Hydra' was diverted to stand by close to the Liberian tanker 'Hercules' on 8 June after it had been bombed by two Grupo 2 Canberras. After completing this task she entered Grantham Sound with 'Uganda' on 11 June and the Flight was involved in the transfer of medical supplies which had been collected in Montevideo. The following day a 1 Escuadrilla de Helicopteros Alouette III from the Argentine hospital ship 'Bahia Paraiso' brought aboard a party of International Red Cross delegates, 'Hydra' Flight in turn taking them to the 'Almirante Irizar' on 13 June. On 14 June (the day of the surrender), 'Hydra' embarked 80 casualties from alongside 'Uganda' in Grantham Sound and then sailed for Montevideo again, arriving there on 18 June. Two further trips to repatriate more casualties saw her return to the Uruguayan port on 29 June and 13 July. Having arrived at Port Stanley on 18 July, the ship then made two passages around the Falkland Islands (from 26 July to 5 August and from 11 to 19 August) during which XT432 visited many of the more remote settlements. 'Hydra' finally sailed from Stanley Harbour on 27 August en route to the United Kingdom and arrived at Portsmouth on 24 September with Wasp XT432 aboard still wearing Red Cross markings, the Flight disembarking to Portland on 27 September.

*829 Sqdn aircrew with 'Hydra' Flight during Operation "Corporate": Lt Cdr R.F.Bryant RN (Flt Cdr); CPOACMN S.Huxley.*

# 'PLYMOUTH' (027) FLIGHT

At the beginning of April the Flight was embarked on 'Plymouth' whilst the vessel was operating from Gibraltar on Exercise "Springtrain" with Wasp HAS.1 XT429 '-/445' assigned. The ship was ordered to sail direct to the South Atlantic on 2 April and then specifically to South Georgia in company with 'Antrim' and 'Tidespring' on 7 April, proceeding via Ascension Island (10-12 April). XT429 had low-vis markings applied by 16 April. These consisted of standard RAF Blue-Grey overall with Red/Blue roundels, the serials being overpainted in Black while the ROYAL NAVY titles and codes are believed to have been deleted using Black rectangles. Code (445) was still allocated but not carried. Lt Cdr J.R.Dransfield relieved Lt Cdr J.P.K.Cooke as the Flight Commander of 'Plymouth' Flight at Ascension Island on 12 April, a scheduled appointment. Having made a rendezvous with 'Endurance' on 14 April, the four vessels arrived off South Georgia on 21 April to await the frigate 'Brilliant' prior to the commencement of Operation "Paraquat".

At 0855Z on the morning of 25 April, 'Antrim' Flight's Wessex HAS.3 sighted and attacked the Argentine submarine 'Santa Fe'. That was followed by further attacks from helicopters of both 'Endurance' and 'Brilliant' Flights which resulted in the submarine turning quickly for the harbour at Grytviken. Lt Cdr Dransfield and LACMN J.A.Harper arrived in time to see the third and fourth missiles fired by XS527 of 'Endurance' Flight. 'Plymouth' Flight's Wasp joined in the attack at 1015Z,

**Top Left** *'Contender Bezant' carried two 829 Squadron Wasp HAS.1's, XS562 '–/371' and XT427 '–/372', the latter seen here after the ship's return to Southampton on 1.8.82 from the Falkland Islands.* **Centre** *Improvisation was the name of the Falkland Islands conflict game – even to the extent of fitting out a freight container with a table and chairs and calling it "home"! "Bumps" and "bruises" were commonplace happenings to helicopters during the conflict and, here, patch repairs to XT427 have been annotated "Oops"! and "Ouch"! An attempt to explain the "One-Eye" logo applied to XT427 (and XS562) is contained in their Individual Aircraft Details* (Michael I. Draper)

**Bottom** *Clamped to the flight-deck of 'St Helena' during an engine run on 6.9.82 is her 829 Squadron Wasp HAS.1, XT795 '–/373'. The strange contraption attached to the fuselage is believed to be associated with the deflection of sea-skimming missiles such as Exocet.*

(via A. Bell,
Curnow Shipping Co Ltd)

331

John Dransfield approaching from the south-west over the Island and, as the submarine entered King Edward Cove, Joe Harper fired one AS.12 from a range of 5,000 yards at an altitude of 100 feet. The missile appeared to hit the target at the waterline on the starboard quarter, but no damage assessment was made (apparently it fell only a few yards short). 'Plymouth' then joined 'Antrim' in bombarding Grytviken before the forces were landed to retake the Island. The following day, the surrender of all Argentine forces on South Georgia was signed aboard 'Plymouth' by Capitan de Corbeta Alfredo Astiz. The vessel sailed on 28 April in company with 'Brilliant' to join the CVBG the following day.

The Flight picked up a long-range parachute drop from LTW Hercules C.1 XV196 on 8 May, on which date the ship joined the LSL's as an escort. The 'Fearless/Canberra' Group was reached on on 16 May and 'Plymouth' prepared to screen the landings in San Carlos Water on 21 May. From 21 to 29 May, while the ship carried out escort and bombardment duties, her Flight was engaged in NGS spotting and ASW sorties in San Carlos Water, and on 22 May inserted SBS units on West Falkland. On 30 May 'Plymouth' rejoined the CVBG, but two days later the ship took up air defence duties in San Carlos Water by day and patrolling by night, until she was detached for a bombardment mission on 8 June. At 1700Z the vessel entered the widest part of Falkland Sound and came under concerted attack from five Grupo 6 Daggers. She was hit by two bombs and some 20 cannon shells which passed straight through the funnel. The bombs hit the mortar area and exited through the side of the ship without exploding, but one caused a mortar projectile to explode resulting in a six foot hole in the starboard flight deck and ship's side. Fire broke out but was eventually extinguished after the vessel had limped back to the safety of San Carlos Water. Five of the ship's company received injuries, but XT429 only suffered from splinter damage and was quickly repaired (with the addition of a new tail rotor).

As a result of the attack 'Plymouth' detached to the east on 9 June and joined 'Stena Seaspread' for repairs the next day. They were completed on 13 June and the following day the ship closed on Port Stanley for bombardment duties, subsequently cancelled following the Argentine surrender that day. She joined the CVBG on 15 June but detached to Port William the next day and on 17 June became the first warship to enter Port Stanley harbour following the surrender. The Flight was gainfully employed on HDS, VERTREP and photographic sorties while 'Plymouth' transitted to San Carlos Water on 18 June before rejoining the CVBG again two days later. She left for home on 21 June, XT429 being transferred to 'Glamorgan' six days later for stowage in her burnt-out hangar (thereby clearing the deck on 'Plymouth' for victory celebrations by the ships' companies). The Wasp was retrieved upon arrival at Ascension Island on 29 June and the transit northwards continued that evening after refuelling. The Flight disembarked to Portland on 12 July prior to the ship's arrival at Rosyth on 14 July.

> *829 Sqdn aircrew with 'Plymouth' Flight during Operation "Corporate" and their awards: Lt Cdr J.R.Dransfield RN (Flt Cdr); LACMN J.A.Harper MID.*

# 'ST HELENA' (033) FLIGHT

The passenger and general cargo ship 'St Helena' was requisitioned on 22 May for duty in the South Atlantic as a support vessel to the minesweepers 'Brecon' and 'Ledbury'. She arrived at Portsmouth on 24 May for conversion, which included the construction of a helicopter deck because on 20 May, during the survey carried out just prior to her formal requisition, it had been decided that the ship would be equipped with a helicopter. Prior to that, Flight 033 had been formed at Portland on 12 May and was assigned to Naval Party 2100 ten days later along with Wasp HAS.1 XT795 (transferred from 'Galatea' Flight). The ship sailed on 9 June and arrived at Portland the following day for a short work-up, during which the Flight embarked on 11 June with XT795 coded '-/373'. The Wasp was in the low-vis scheme which consisted of RAF Blue-Grey overall with Red/Blue roundels, the serials and codes in Black, but devoid of ROYAL NAVY titles. A dozen AS.12 missiles were also taken aboard and the ship departed for the South Atlantic on 13 June along with the minesweepers 'Brecon' and 'Ledbury', arriving off Port Stanley on 10 July.

'St Helena' acted as "mother" ship to the minesweepers as they cleared safety lanes through actual and suspected mined areas. Her Ship's Flight was used to set up and maintain a Trisponder system as a source of accurate maritime navigational information. The system consisted of a chain of sets of three portable transmitters placed at various locations around the Islands by the Flight's Wasp to enable the minesweepers to chart the swept safety lanes. The information was made available to all relevant ships so that they could cross-check their positions relative to any given safety lane by plotting bearings obtained from the Trisponder chain. The use of the Wasp was extremely successful as the only alternative would have been to transport equipment overland across the hostile terrain of the Islands. As a result, the expected time needed to set up the system was cut by half, taking only four weeks. The Flight also carried out supply work in the weeks spent operating around the Falkland Islands.

'St Helena' departed for the United Kingdom on 13 August and returned to Rosyth on 16 September, her Flight having already disembarked to Portland on 13 September. The helicopter remained on nominal Flight charge until 6 October, when it was transferred to 829 Sqdn HQ Flight as an FIR aircraft.

> *829 Sqdn aircrew with 'St Helena' Flight during Operation "Corporate": Lt Cdr D.N.Heelas RN (Flt Cdr); POACMN J.G.Taylor.*

# 'YARMOUTH' (032) FLIGHT

'Yarmouth' was operating out of Gibraltar on Exercise "Springtrain" with her Wasp HAS.1 XV624 '-/456' embarked when the Falkland Islands were invaded. She was then due to deploy to the Far East with 'Broadsword' but, having departed for Naples at 0900Z on 5 April, the two vessels were ordered back to Gibraltar at 2100Z and arrived there the following day. 'Yarmouth' sailed for the South Atlantic on 8 April with her Flight embarked, making a rendezvous with the 'Fearless' Group on 9 April and then detaching to join 'Hermes' on 11 April. XV624 received the low-vis scheme during the journey south, and by the time of the ship's arrival at Ascension Island on 16 April the Wasp was standard RAF Blue-Grey overall with Red/Blue roundels, the serials in Black and the ROYAL NAVY titles deleted (believed overpainted with Black rectangles). The code (456) remained allocated but was not carried.

Upon joining the Task Force on 23 April, the Flight was prepared for its war role of ASW operations, but almost immediately became involved in searching for ditched 846 Sqdn Sea King HC.4 ZA311 during the night of 23/24 April. ASW operations did subsequently commence and on 1 May 'Yarmouth' detached to the northeast of the Falkland Islands with 'Brilliant' to search for a submarine which had been reported in that area. This was believed to have been the 'San Luis', but no trace of it was found and 'Yarmouth' rejoined the CVBG on 2 May. On 4 May the Flight was involved in CASEVAC operations, extracting survivors from the stricken 'Sheffield'. After four days of foggy weather, 'Yarmouth' was assigned the task of towing the abandoned 'Sheffield' clear of the TEZ, but the ship rolled over and sank on 10 May while under tow (at approximate position 53°04'S 56°56'W). 'Yarmouth' rejoined the CVBG the next day.

Following a week of storms, 'Yarmouth' was detached on 19 May to act as an escort vessel for the Amphibious Group. On 21 May (the day of the landings) the ship entered Falkland Sound at 0400Z and the Flight was later kept busy taking bomb disposal equipment to 'Ardent' and transferring casualties from both 'Argonaut' and 'Ardent'. 'Yarmouth' took up AAW station in San Carlos Water until 1 June, when she sailed for essential maintenance to be carried out alongside 'Stena Seaspread'. Rejoining the Task Force on 6 June, the vessel was then tasked with bombardment operations until hostilities ceased. The Flight was engaged in spotting operations and on 12 June took medical aid and fire-fighting equipment to 'Glamorgan' following her encounter with a land-launched Exocet missile.

After the Argentine surrender, 'Yarmouth' left for the South Sandwich Islands to rendezvous with 'Endurance', arriving off Southern Thule on 20 June for Operation "Keyhole" during which XV624 landed an NGS team on nearby Cook Island. The Argentine surrender was secured later in the day and the Flight was tasked with the transfer of personnel to 'Endurance' for the surrender ceremony. The ship sailed on 21 June for Port Stanley where she arrived on 25 June to transfer 10 PoW's. 'Yarmouth' sailed north for the United Kingdom on 7 July, the Flight disembarking to Portland on 27 July prior to the ship's arrival at Rosyth the following day.

> *829 Sqdn aircrew with 'Yarmouth' Flight during Operation "Corporate" and their awards: Lt P.G.Miller RN (Flt Cdr) MID; LACMN J.A.D'Souza.*

# POST-SURRENDER DEPLOYMENTS

As the following ships and their Flights did not leave the United Kingdom (or Gibraltar) until after the Argentine surrender they are not eligible for inclusion in the main text of this book. However, basic details of the ship and Flight movements are included in the Individual Ship and Aircraft Histories sections.

### 'APOLLO' (041) FLIGHT

The ship and her Flight (XS567 '-/470') did not sail from the United Kingdom for the South Atlantic until 18 June.

### 'ARIADNE' (023) FLIGHT

The ship and her Flight (XT426 '-/455') did not sail from the United Kingdom for the South Atlantic until 8 November.

### 'BACCHANTE' (052) FLIGHT

The ship and her Flight (XS538 '-/425') did not sail from Gibraltar for the South Atlantic until 20 June.

### 'DIOMEDE' (021) FLIGHT

The ship and her Flight (XV634 '-/423') did not sail from the United Kingdom for the South Atlantic until 22 June.

### 'HECATE' (013) FLIGHT

The ship and her Flight (XV626 '-/414') did not sail from the United Kingdom for the South Atlantic until 23 July.

# INDIVIDUAL AIRCRAFT DETAILS

Details of the low-vis scheme variations applied to the Wasp are explained under each individual aircraft history.

*Examples of abbreviations used for markings and their meanings:*

'-/322'  *Deck-letters 'AV' for 'Active' not worn; side-code worn in full.*

(434)  *Neither deck-letter 'E' for 'Endurance' nor side-code worn.*

---

**XS527 HAS.1**

On 29.3.82 with 829 Sqdn 'Endurance' Flight coded (434), engaged on coastal patrol and observation duties off South Georgia. It had been camouflaged overnight 25/26.3.82 (along with XS539) after an 'Endurance' Flt helicopter was spotted earlier in the day by a 1 Escuadrilla de Helicopteros Alouette from the 'Bahia Paraiso'. The camouflage consisted of a random-pattern Matt Black/Light Admiralty Grey/Olive Drab scheme (covering the codes and tail-boom ROYAL NAVY titles) to which was added patches of washable White as and when required. Mini-ROYAL NAVY titles (on the fuselage underneath the gearbox) and the starboard serial (at least) were retained but overpainted in Light Admiralty Grey. Red/Blue roundels were adopted.

Crewed by Lt Cdr Ellerbeck and Lt Wells, it attacked the surfaced enemy submarine 'Santa Fe' on three separate occasions off the entrance to the Cumberland Bays, South Georgia on 25.4.82 using AS.12 missiles. Three hits were achieved on the conning tower. As a result of damage inflicted by this and other Ships' Flights, the vessel limped back to Grytviken.

Sailed with the ship from Grytviken, South Georgia 16.7.82 for return to the UK (via the Falklands and Ascension), arriving in Weymouth Bay 19.8.82. It did not disembark at that stage, remaining aboard 'Endurance' until she arrived off Chatham on 20.8.82. Accompanied by XS539 and two more 829 Sqdn Wasps from Portland (XS541 '-/(8)95' and XT439 '-/605'), it escorted the ship into harbour and departed later that day (in company with the other three) to Portland.

*'Endurance' Flight's penguin motif was retained on the stretcher bulges on the rear cabin doors.*

**XS538 HAS.1**   *Deployed post-14.6.82*

On 15.6.82 with 829 Sqdn 'Bacchante' Flight coded '-/425' and based with the ship at Gibraltar. Noted that day in the low-vis scheme (RAF Blue-Grey overall with Red/Blue roundels; no ROYAL NAVY titles; serials and codes in Black). Sailed with the ship for the South Atlantic on 20.6.82. Remained with 'Bacchante' until she returned to the UK, disembarking to Portland on 30.8.82 before the vessel docked at Portsmouth the same day.

**XS539 HAS.1**

On 29.3.82 with 829 Sqdn 'Endurance' Flight coded (435), engaged on coastal patrol and observation duties off South Georgia. It had

been camouflaged overnight 25/26.3.82 (along with XS527) after an 'Endurance' Flt helicopter was spotted earlier in the day by a 1 Escuadrilla de Helicopteros Alouette from the 'Bahia Paraiso'. The camouflage consisted of a random-pattern Matt Black/Light Admiralty Grey/Olive Drab scheme (covering the codes and tail-boom ROYAL NAVY titles) to which was added patches of washable White as and when required. Mini-ROYAL NAVY titles (on the fuselage underneath the gearbox) and the starboard serial (at least) were retained but overpainted in Light Admiralty Grey. Red/Blue roundels were adopted.

Crewed by Lt Finding and LACMN Nadin, it attacked the surfaced Argentine submarine 'Santa Fe' outside the entrance to the Cumberland Bays, South Georgia on 25.4.82 using AS.12 missiles, achieving one hit on the conning tower. As a result of damage inflicted by this and other Ships' Flights, the vessel limped back to Grytviken.

Sailed with the ship from Grytviken, South Georgia 16.7.82 for return to the UK (via the Falklands and Ascension), arriving in Weymouth Bay 19.8.82. It did not disembark at this stage, remaining aboard 'Endurance' until she arrived off Chatham on 20.8.82. Accompanied by XS527 and two more 829 Sqdn Wasps from Portland (XS541 '-/(8)95' and XT439 '-/605'), it escorted the ship into harbour then flew off later that day (in company with the other three) to Portland.

*'Endurance' Flight's penguin motif was retained on the stretcher bulges on the rear cabin doors.*

**XS562 HAS.1**

On 29.3.82 with 829 Sqdn, in reserve at Portland (uncoded). Allocated to 829 Sqdn 'Galatea' Flt 23.4.82, the name "One Eye" being applied to the airframe 3.5.82 (see explanation below and XT427). In low-vis scheme coded '-/360' by 6.5.82 (RAF Blue-Grey overall devoid of ROYAL NAVY titles; Black serials and codes plus Red/Blue roundels). Transferred to 'Contender Bezant' Flight 13.5.82 and coded '-/371', still in low-vis scheme. Embarked the ship in Plymouth Sound on 20.5.82, sailing with her from Start Bay on 21.5.82 en route Ascension and the South Atlantic. Departed Port William with the ship 13.7.82 for the UK. Trailing a White Ensign (along with XT427 trailing a Red Ensign), it escorted the vessel into Southampton Docks 1.8.82. Flown off the ship to Portland later that day, where it remained in storage (still nominally allocated to 'Contender Bezant' Flight) until 21.10.82 when officially transferred to 829 Sqdn HQ Flight.

*"One Eye" reportedly refers to the unsuccessful relationship between Cyclops and Galatea in Greek mythology. The motif was retained during the aircraft's time aboard 'Contender Bezant'.*

**XS567 HAS.1**   *Deployed post-14.6.82*

On 15.6.82 with 829 Sqdn 'Apollo' Flight coded '-/470' in the low-vis scheme (RAF Blue-Grey overall with Red/Blue roundels; ROYAL NAVY titles, serials and codes in Black). Embarked 'Apollo' on 18.6.82 prior to her departure from Devonport for the South Atlantic that day. Remained with the ship until she returned to the UK, arriving in Plymouth Sound on 17.10.82 from where it disembarked to Portland before the vessel's arrival at Devonport later in the day.

**XT420 HAS.1**

On 29.3.82 with 829 Sqdn in reserve at Portland (uncoded). Allocated to 829 Sqdn 'Hecla' Flight 16.4.82 and delivered that day by road to Yeovilton still uncoded but carrying a 703 Sqdn crest (a legacy from the past) on the port side and an 829 Sqdn crest on the starboard side. It departed Yeovilton for Gibraltar 19.4.82 aboard LTW Hercules C.3 XV221. On 20.4.82 it was test flown, embarking 'Hecla' at Gibraltar prior to sailing with the ship that day for the South Atlantic. About that time Red Crosses on a White background were applied to the nose, fuselage sides/underside and top of the stabiliser. The aircraft remained in standard RAF Blue-Grey scheme with White titles and serials plus 'D' Class roundels. No code was worn although (416) remained allocated. Stayed with the ship throughout its deployment and sailed with her from just north of Falkland Sound for the UK on 29.6.82, returning to Devonport on 29.7.82. Flown off to Portland later in the day and transferred to 829 Sqdn HQ Flt on 13.8.82.

**XT426 HAS.1**   *Deployed post-14.6.82*

On 15.6.82 with 829 Sqdn 'Ariadne' Flight coded '-/455'. Remained as such and noted aboard the ship at Devonport on 28.10.82, sailing with her for the South Atlantic on 8.11.82. By that time it was in the low-vis scheme (RAF Blue-Grey overall with Red/Blue roundels; ROYAL NAVY titles, serials and codes in Black). Remained with 'Ariadne' until the vessel returned to the UK, disembarking to Portland on 25.3.83 before her arrival at Devonport later the same day.

**XT427 HAS.1**

On 29.3.82 coded '-/602' with 829 Sqdn HQ Flight at Portland. Transferred to 'Rhyl'

Flight at Portland on 26.4.82 (replacing XT439 '-/446'). Reallocated to 'Contender Bezant' Flight on 13.5.82 in the low-vis scheme (RAF Blue-Grey overall, devoid of ROYAL NAVY titles; serials and codes '-/372' in Black plus Red/Blue roundels). Embarked the ship in Plymouth Sound 20.5.82, sailing with her from Start Bay on 21.5.82 for Ascension and the South Atlantic. At some point the legend "One Eye The Wasp" was applied to the fuselage (see explanation below and XS562). Sailed from Port William with the ship for the UK on 13.7.82. Trailing a Red Ensign (along with XS562 trailing a White Ensign), it escorted the vessel into Southampton Docks on 1.8.82. Flown off the ship to Portland 2.8.82 prior to being transferred to 829 Sqdn HQ Flight 6.8.82 coded '-/606' with ROYAL NAVY titles (both in Black). Ditched off Portland 6.9.83 and taken to AIU Lee-on-Solent on 9.9.83. Delivered by road from AIU to the Fleet Air Arm Museum at Yeovilton on 28.3.84 for the Falkland Islands Exhibition (still resident in 7.85).

*"One Eye the Wasp" reportedly refers to the unsuccessful relationship between Cyclops and Galatea in Greek mythology. XT427 had no known connection with 'Galatea', so the reason for application of the motif remains a mystery (unless merely to complement the inscription "One Eye" on XS562). See also Gazelle AH.1 XX444.*

**XT429 HAS.1**

On 29.3.82 with 829 Sqdn 'Plymouth' Flight coded '-/445', operating out of Gibraltar on Exercise "Springtrain". Detached south with the ship on 2.4.82 directly from the Exercise. By 16.4.82 it had been repainted in the low-vis scheme (RAF Blue-Grey overall with Red/Blue roundels; the ROYAL NAVY titles deleted, believed by overpainting with Black rectangles; serials in Black). The code (445) was removed but remained allocated.

Crewed by Lt Cdr Dransfield & LACMN Harper, it attacked the surfaced enemy submarine 'Santa Fe' on 25.4.82 off the entrance to the Cumberland Bays, South Georgia. An AS.12 missile was fired which either just missed the hull or failed to explode (the vessel had already been damaged as a result of attacks by other Ships' Flights).

Suffered splinter damage on 8.6.82 during an air attack on 'Plymouth' in Falkland Sound by five Grupo 6 Daggers but was repaired very quickly and returned to service.

Departed the TEZ with the ship on 21.6.82 for return to the UK. On 27.6.82 it was flown to 'Glamorgan' for temporary storage in her burnt-out hangar, returning to 'Plymouth' at Ascension Island on 29.6.82. Disembarked to Portland on 12.7.82 prior to the vessel's arrival at Rosyth on 14.7.82.

*Noted at Portland 21.9.82 with four Dayglo Red CASEVAC crosses, a submarine "zap" (the 'Santa Fe') and an SAS mission dagger motif applied to the port side of the fuselage underneath the gearbox platform.*

**XT432 HAS.1**

On 29.3.82 being held by 829 Sqdn HQ Flight

at Portland coded 'HT/414' (ex-'Hecate' Flt) prior to reallotment. Transferred to 829 Sqdn 'Hydra' Flt on 1.4.82 (replacing XS568). Embarked 'Hydra' at Portsmouth 23.4.82 and departed with the ship on 24.4.82 enroute to the South Atlantic wearing Red Crosses and marked 'HT/-'. The Red Crosses (on a White background) were worn on the nose, fuselage sides/underside and top of the horizontal stabiliser. The remainder of the airframe was standard RAF Blue-Grey overall with White titles and serials plus 'D' Class roundels. The code (415) was not carried although it remained allocated, while the 'HT/-' was removed sometime during the deployment. Sailed from Port Stanley Harbour with the ship 27.8.82 en route to the UK, arriving at Portsmouth 24.9.82. It was flown off to Portland on 27.9.82.

**XT779 HAS.1**

On 29.3.82 with 829 Sqdn 'Active' Flight coded '-/322' and operating with the ship out of Gibraltar on Exercise "Springtrain". Departed with 'Active' from the Exercise area c2.4.82 for the UK, disembarking to Portland on 6.4.82 reportedly prior to the vessel docking that day at Devonport. Noted at the RN Barracks, HMS Drake, Plymouth on 6.5.82 in the low-vis scheme of overall RAF Blue-Grey with Red/Blue roundels (but devoid of ROYAL NAVY titles); serials and code '-/322' in Black. Embarked 'Active' from Portland on 10.5.82 (shortly after she had departed Devonport), sailing with her that day for Ascension and the South Atlantic. Left San Carlos Water with the ship on 15.7.82 en route for the UK and arrived at Devonport on 3.8.82. It was flown off to Portland on 4.8.82.

**XT794 HAS.1**

On 29.3.82 with 829 Sqdn 'Herald' Flight coded '-/325', the ship being on her way back to Portsmouth at that time following a Middle East survey deployment. It flew off to Portland 7.4.82 prior to the vessel docking at Portsmouth later that day. On 24.4.82 'Herald' left Portsmouth for Ascension, the aircraft embarking as she passed the Isle of Wight. Red Crosses (on a White background) had been applied to the nose, fuselage sides/underside and topside of the horizontal stabiliser. The remainder of the aircraft was in the standard RAF Blue-Grey scheme overall with White titles and serials plus 'D' Class roundels. The code (325) remained allocated but not carried. It was unserviceable from 13-29.5.82 while awaiting low-priority spares, but was finally made serviceable c29.5.82 with the aid of parts robbed from 'Hecla' Flight's XT420. Sailed from Montevideo, Uruguay with the ship on 25.6.82 for the UK (via Ascension Island), disembarking to Portland on 21.7.82 prior to the vessel's arrival at Portsmouth later that day.

*During the deployment it was noted carrying the name "MASH I" in front of the UHF aerials and "BANDIT" just in front of the starboard forward cockpit door.*

**XT795 HAS.1**

On 29.3.82 with 829 Sqdn HQ Flt at Portland coded '-/605'. Transferred to 'Galatea' Flt (replacing XS562, see earlier) 17.5.82 and probably allocated code '-/360'. That move

was short-lived because on 22.5.82 it was re-allotted to 'St Helena' Flight and coded '-/373' in the low-vis scheme (RAF Blue-Grey overall, devoid of ROYAL NAVY titles; serials and codes in Black; Red/Blue roundels). Embarked the ship at Portland Dockyard on 11.6.82, sailing with her for the South Atlantic on 13.6.82. Remained with the ship until it left Port Stanley on 13.8.82 en route for the UK, disembarking to Portland 13.9.82 prior to the vessel's arrival at Rosyth on 16.9.82. Stayed on nominal 'St Helena' Flight charge until 6.10.82 when transferred to 829 Sqdn as an FIR aircraft.

*Carried the St Helena Shipping Co Ltd "Sea Lion" motif on the stretcher bulges on the rear cabin doors (both facing forwards). The company motif is taken from the coat of arms of the New East India Company which originally colonised St Helena.*

**XV624 HAS.1**

On 29.3.82 with 829 Sqdn 'Yarmouth' Flight coded '-/456', operating from Gibraltar on Exercise "Springtrain". The ship departed Gibraltar for Naples 5.4.82 with the aircraft embarked but turned back the same day to arrive at Gibraltar on 6.4.82. Departed with the vessel for Ascension and the South Atlantic 8.4.82. By 16.4.82 it had gained the low-vis scheme (RAF Blue-Grey overall with Red/Blue roundels and Black serials; ROYAL NAVY titles removed, believed overpainted with Black rectangles). The code (456) was deleted but remained allocated. Detached with 'Yarmouth' from the TEZ c16.6.82 for Southern Thule (via South Georgia) to take part in Operation "Keyhole" (the retaking of the Island). Upon arrival there on 20.6.82 the aircraft put an NGS party ashore on nearby Cook Island prior to the Argentine surrender later that day. Departed Southern Thule with the ship on 21.6.82 for Port Stanley, arriving there on 25.6.82. On 7.7.82 it left the TEZ with the ship bound for the UK, disembarking to Portland 27.7.82 prior to the vessel's arrival at Rosyth on 28.7.82.

**XV626 HAS.1**          *Deployed post-14.6.82*

On 15.6.82 with 829 Sqdn 'Hecate' Flight at Portland coded '-/414' in the low-vis scheme (RAF Blue-Grey overall with Red/Blue roundels; ROYAL NAVY titles, serials and codes in Black). Sailed from Portland dockyard with the ship on 20.7.82 for a short work-up before continuing south on 23.7.82 to Ascension, where 'Hecate' relieved 'Endurance' as Ice Patrol Ship on 5.8.82 and proceeded to the South Atlantic. Remained with the ship until she returned to the UK, disembarking to Portland 18.2.83 prior to the vessel's arrival at Portsmouth later the same day.

**XV634 HAS.1**          *Deployed post-14.6.82*

On 15.6.82 with 829 Sqdn 'Diomede' Flight coded '-/423'. Embarked the ship 22.6.82 from Portland just after she had sailed from Portsmouth that day on deployment to the South Atlantic. It was in the low-vis scheme of RAF Blue-Grey overall with Red/Blue roundels, the ROYAL NAVY titles, codes and serials all being in Black. Remained with 'Diomede' until she returned to the UK, flying off to Portland 17.10.82 before the vessel docked at Portsmouth later the same day.

The three Scout AH.1's of 656 Squadron Advanced Section aboard 'Europic Ferry' just hours before sailing ex-Southampton on 22.4.82. From left to right XT649, XT637 and XR628 share the flight-deck with over 200 45-gallon drums of Avgas which, as it turned out, was sufficient stock to last until the battle for Darwin and Goose Green. 'Europic Ferry' had no internal ramps for vehicular access to the hold and so apart from a brief period of covered storage aboard 'Elk' these three Scouts remained on deck until 26.5.82.

(Michael I. Draper)

In contrast a 656 Squadron Gazelle AH.1 (believed to be XZ290) is virtually lost on the spacious flight-deck of 'Nordic Ferry'. Note the ship's conversion for Operation "Corporate" involved two heli-pads (the Gazelle being on the aft spot) while to the left can be seen the ramp down to the middle deck and the start of a long journey to the lower hangar deck. For a brief period flights from this ship were not authorised as a result of mis-laying Gazelle flotation equipment.        (Cpl L. Beresford, AAC)

Three Scout AH.1's of 3 CBAS/'B' Flight seen at Ascension 28.4.82. The centre Scout is XW616 and clearly displays the "toned-down" nose code letter 'P' together with the erased ROYAL MARINES titling on the boom. Identities of the other two Scouts remain unclear but are believed to be XV140 and XW615 both of which had joined 3 CBAS from 657 Squadron just prior to departure from the UK. Note the wire attached to the port skid (on the nearest example) used to avoid fouling of the SS11 wire-guidance system.

(via Major A. Eames, RM)

# GAZELLE

# SCOUT

The contribution made by 3 CBAS and 656 Sqdn to Operation "Corporate" was unquestionably one of immense value, although a lack of publicity surrounding their exploits seems to have resulted in a lack of appreciation of the extent of their role. The Scout performed admirably as a missile platform, even though the Argentines did not deploy tanks to the Falkland Islands, and it provided an invaluable CASEVAC facility, often at night and in extremely difficult conditions. It also played a vital role ferrying supplies to the front-line at a time when heavy-lift helicopters were hard-pressed to meet demands. Towards the latter stages of the campaign weight limits were frequently ignored, supporting a long-held belief amongst its pilots that the Scout was "designed and built by a blacksmith"! No greater mark of success, however, can be attributed to this helicopter than by recalling that, of the 12 deployed on Operation "Corporate", no less than a third won DFC's for their pilots.

The Gazelle appears to have performed well as a Battlefield Observation helicopter but its large perspex cockpit area proved susceptible to blast damage. While it was armed with SNEB rockets, the Gazelle never fired any in anger but did instead sometimes supplement the Scout on CASEVAC tasks with the result that both types evacuated some 400 injured soldiers to safety. Both Gazelles and Scouts operated from ships' decks with no apparent difficulty and without the aid of a specially designed undercarriage deemed so necessary for the Lynx and Wasp.

# 3 COMMANDO BRIGADE AIR SQUADRON RM

3 CBAS became involved in the crisis at its earliest stage. In response to signals reaching London from the South Atlantic, two Gazelle AH.1's of 'A' Flight were placed at four hours "Notice To Move" at midday on 1 April. When news of the Argentine invasion broke, the entire Brigade Air Squadron was brought to 72 hours "Notice to Move" at 0315Z on 2 April. Personnel were recalled and work began immediately on last-minute servicing and preparation of helicopters for shipment to the Falkland Islands. Commanded by Major C.P.Cameron RM, the role of 3 CBAS was to provide light helicopter support to the 3rd Commando Brigade HQ with Flights allocated to 40, 42 and 45 Commando RM. The Squadron's helicopter establishment normally stood at 12 unarmed Gazelle AH.1's (nine based at SHQ Bickleigh Barracks, Plymouth, and three with 'M' Flight at Arbroath to support 45 Commando), four ATGW Scout AH.1's equipped with SS.11 anti-tank missiles, plus two unarmed Utility Scout AH.1's. On 29 March 3 CBAS had the following helicopters on strength:

| Gazelle AH.1 | | |
|---|---|---|
| XX376 '(C)K' | XX399 '(C)E' | XX413 '(C)Z' |
| XX377 '(C)L' | XX402 '(C)G' | ZA728 '(C)A' |
| XX380 '(C)M' | XX411 '(C)X' | ZA730 '(C)F' |
| XX392 '(C)B' | XX412 '(C)Y' | ZA776 '(C)H' |

| Scout AH.1 (ATGW) | |
|---|---|
| XP902 '(D)T' | XT629 '(D)R' |
| XR627 '(D)Q' | XW616 '(D)P' |

| Scout AH.1 (Utility) | |
|---|---|
| XP893 '(D)S' | XP907 '(D)U' |

*Note:* *XP907 had previously operated in the ATGW role with full SS.11 mods, but had progressively lost its weapon fit until relegated to the Utility role.*

Although officially located at Bickleigh Barracks, construction work close to the landing area had necessitated temporary transfer of the Plymouth-based 3 CBAS aircraft to nearby Coypool.

In actual fact, there was a shortfall in Gazelle strength as XX377 was midway through a major modification programme at Fleetlands while XX399 was "grossly unserviceable" after suffering accident damage (the latter subsequently being cannibalised for spares, including gearbox and radio equipment, etc). An immediate request was passed to Director Army Air Corps for replacement aircraft, 3 CBAS urging the need for Gazelles with fixed fittings to accommodate flotation packs. As it happened, the ARWS at Middle Wallop held the three ex-Belize aircraft (XX409/AA, XZ326/W and XZ338/X), all with the required modifications fitted. Thus on 3 April, two of those Gazelles (XZ326 and XZ338) were flown from Middle Wallop to Plymouth in order to restore 3 CBAS to its full strength — although the fact that XZ326 was also one of a number of Gazelles fitted with the uprated Astazou IIIN2 engine was overlooked! Of the Scout AH.1's, XP902 was flown to Middle Wallop on 3 April for an ECU and AF120 Sight change at 70 Aircraft Workshops whilst the remainder were flown to Yeovilton on 4 April for modifications by MARTSU. They included the fitting of armour plating and exhaust heat deflector shields, all of which had been collected from Northern Ireland and flown in from Aldergrove by LTW Hercules. At the same time it was decided to replace the pair of Utility Scouts with two ATGW versions, so XV140 and XW615 of 657 Sqdn were flown from Oakington to Yeovilton on 4 April in exchange for XP893 and XP907. Both Utility machines were flown to Middle Wallop, where XP907 was fully restored to ATGW standard by replacing the entire cabin with that from XR630 (ex-AETW). XP893 remained at Middle Wallop for a period with the Demonstration and Trials (D&T) Squadron until ferried to Wroughton for storage on 16 July.

On 5 April the helicopters began to disperse to embarkation points. The three Gazelle AH.1's of 'C' Flight (XX402, XX411, XX412) were flown to Devonport where they landed aboard 'Sir Galahad' between 0815Z and 0845Z, whilst the 'A' Flight aircraft (XZ326, ZA730, ZA776) followed to land aboard 'Sir Geraint' between 0830Z and 0900Z. 'M' Flight (XX376, XX380, XX413) flew to Marchwood on the same date with half of 'B' Flight's Scouts (XV140, XW615, XW616) for loading on board 'Sir Percivale' and 'Sir Lancelot' respectively. The Squadron's Echelon, Advanced Maintenance Group and Forward Repair Team embarked 'Sir Geraint' at Devonport on 5 April. Final embarkations took place on the following day when the remaining three 'B' Flight Scouts (XP902, XR627, XT629) and the Squadron HQ were flown aboard 'Fearless' after the ship had left Portsmouth. Despite subsequent reports that 3 CBAS only intended to take nine Gazelle AH.1's, some credence must be attached to claims by the LSL Loadmasters that lack of space precluded the shipment of all 12 aircraft. It seems that the LSL's were simply loaded to such an extent that three of the Gazelles (XX392, XZ338 and ZA728) were denied shipping space along with various other vehicles and stores, etc. It also appears that a subsequent request to offload XZ326 in favour of XX392 or ZA728 was also denied by the Loadmasters due to lack of time. Thus the uprated (and non-standard to 3 CBAS) XZ326 was shipped south. Of those left behind, XZ338 was flown back to the ARWS on 7 April in company with XX392 (to replace XZ326), while ZA728 remained in temporary storage at Plymouth until it was delivered to 656 Sqdn on 19 April.

Because only nine Gazelles were deployed, but with as many aircrew as possible, so the pilot-to-Gazelle ratio was 2:1 with an aircrewman ratio just in excess of 1:1. 'B' Flight had seven crews for its six Scout AH.1's. Flight training (DLP's and VERTREP practice) was carried out almost daily during the transit from the United Kingdom

to Ascension Island, while the AMG performed some last-minute servicing under difficult conditions. On 16 April, for example, the torsion bar seals began leaking on Gazelle XZ326 after a replacement had been fitted just a couple of days earlier. Only complete replacement of the main rotorhead promised a cure to the problem, an operation which involved man-handling the new head from the vehicle deck up to the flight deck. As the LSL's began to arrive off Ascension Island on 19 April so the Gazelles began to fly off to Wideawake airfield for two major modifications, the fitment of I-Band Transponders and pylon-mounted SNEB 68mm rocket packs.

The lack of any suitable protective weapons fit on the Gazelle had been realised prior to departure from the United Kingdom, so immediately after the LSL's sailed the MoD embarked on a formidable programme of selection, acquisition and test of a weapon system against a schedule which necessitated its fitment when the LSL's arrived off Ascension Island. That that was achieved at all became one of the many successes to emerge from Operation "Corporate". With the knowledge that single SNEB rockets had been fired from an experimental launcher on a Scout back in 1970, and the fact that the SNEB system was part of the Harrier GR.3's armament pack, the Army Air Corps selected the MATRA/SNEB 68mm rocket pack for the Gazelle. D&T Sqdn Gazelle AH.1 XW847 was flown to Yeovil on 7 April for the fitting of a stores boom and a system based upon a Westland design study. At the same time, efforts were made to estimate the current availability of a six-tube rocket pod. Early on 8 April, chartered BAe125 G-TACE flew from Hurn to Paris with (amongst others) Westland technicians to begin negotiations with MATRA for the supply of enough equipment and technical details for trials to commence in the United Kingdom. *(Although universally referred to by the Army as "SNEB" Launchers the 68mm rocket pods were made by both MATRA and Brandt Armements, indeed when negotiations in Paris briefly faltered it was suggested by the British that they might contact Brandt. The MATRA pods subsequently acquired were always referred to as "SNEB" (the Brandt product). All 68mm ammunition was supplied to the Army from RAF stocks.)* The relevant data was successfully acquired and, back at Yeovil on 9 April, Westland staff began to analyse the data obtained in Paris while a 24-hour shift was introduced on the shop floor with a view to constructing and fitting a trial installation of booms and firing sequencers to XW847. By midday on 10 April, two pods had been delivered to Yeovil and flight trials commenced the following morning. Easter Monday (12 April) saw XW847 conducting single and ripple firing trials at Larkhill while operating from A&AEE Boscombe Down. During these a target the size of a platoon location was successfully engaged with 12 rockets from about 5,500 feet. Trials completed, XW847 returned to Yeovil and a production contract for further pods and rockets was confirmed with MATRA on 12 April. Andover C.1 XS606 of the ETPS flew to Avignon via Orly on 13 April to collect more pods, returning to Lyneham early the following day. From there the pods were conveyed to Yeovilton for onward shipment to Ascension Island by Heavylift Belfast. In the meantime, XW847 had flown back to Boscombe Down on 13 April for a rapid clearance of the SNEB fit for shipboard opera-

**Above** *Against a backdrop of Pyramid Point, Ascension Island, Scout AH.1 XR627/DQ of 'B' Flight/3 CBAS lifts off from 'Canberra's' forward heli-pad during a routine Helicopter Delivery Service task. 'Canberra' had had two heli-pads fitted for Operation "Corporate" but because of the high demand for HDS sorties a third landing spot was constructed on the flat roof of the air conditioning compartment just forward of the funnels. This photograph, probably taken on 30.4.82, clearly shows the fittings for an Infra Red Shield over the engine exhaust area. (Dr P. E. Mayner, P. & O.).* **Right** *During Operation "Corporate" the Scout AH.1's authorised Maximum Take-off/Landing Weight was increased from 5350lb to 5500lb which allowed a greater effectiveness in the use of Scout for Underslung Load sorties, especially when transferring stores and ammunition between ships just before the San Carlos landings. Naturally such operations severely limited the Scout's endurance and are reported to have caused several instances of tail-rotor root cracking. In this view an unidentified 3 CBAS Scout is seen approaching 'Norland' c18.5.82* (via R. Hill)

*Whilst making a return journey from Widewake Airfield to 'Sir Geraint' on 29.4.82 Gazelle AH.1 XZ326/(C)W of 'A' Flight/3 CBAS suffered a total engine failure. Travelling seaward and having just crossed the shoreline at 300 feet Pilot Sgt S. Congdon repositioned the aircraft to make an engine-off landing on a small area of beach. Surprisingly, and much to the amazement of the onlookers, '326 suffered only minor damage. This view clearly shows the 'toned-down' ARWS code and the erasure of ARMY titling. The stores boom is also clearly visible as is the I-Band Transponder just behind the rear port skid support.*

*(via Col D. E. Canterbury, AAC)*

tions. A second Gazelle (XX450/F of ARWS) was flown from Middle Wallop to Yeovil on the same day to act as a reserve trials platform, but in the event was not used. With the SNEB fit cleared for operations, the pods were removed from XW847 and taken to Yeovilton for airfreighting with the initial five sets. Further sets arrived from France on 18 April and those, together with spares and relevant documentation, were dispatched south to Ascension Island in time to meet the 3 CBAS Gazelles as they arrived aboard the LSL's. The two trials aircraft (XW847, XX450) returned to Middle Wallop on 15 April.

The first test-firing of SNEB rockets by 3 CBAS was carried out by 'A' Flt on 23 April, and the 70 Aircraft Workshops Detachment had completed all of the necessary work (I-Band Transponders and SNEB fits) within five days, in time for the next stage of the Squadron's journey south. Only an enforced engine-off landing by XZ326 on 29 April (caused by an earlier refuelling at too great a pressure which forced the fuel float to stick and which in turn gave an inaccurate gauge reading) interrupted a trouble-free stopover by 3 CBAS on Ascension Island. The arrival off the Island of 'Sir Tristram' from Belize enabled the Section of 'B' Flt aboard 'Fearless' (Scout AH.1's XP902, XR627 and XT629) to transfer ship on 28 April. However, as the Brigade HQ was to remain aboard 'Fearless' and as the LSL's were to depart for the Falkland Islands ahead of the assault ship, the positioning of two Scouts as liaison aircraft on board 'Fearless' was deemed necessary, so XR627 and XT629 returned the following day. All of the Gazelles returned to their respective LSL's in time for the departure south from Ascension Island during the night of 29/30 April in company with 'Pearleaf' and 'Antelope'. 'Fearless' remained at Ascension Island for a further week to await the arrival of shipping still en route from the UK, in particular the 'Europic Ferry' with an Advanced Section of 656 Sqdn embarked (Scout AH.1's XR628, XT637, XT649) and 'Norland' with 2 PARA embarked. Both ships arrived off the Island just after dawn on 7 May, whereupon the 656 Sqdn Section was formally transferred to the Royal Marines and retitled 5 Flight (656) 3 CBAS. (NB: This would suggest that the four existing 3 CBAS flights were renumbered as 1 to 4 Flights, but no evidence has been found to support this.) At the same time the Dayglo Red code letters on the three 656 Sqdn Scouts were removed and they were given new ones within the 3 CBAS sequence: XR628 'DO', XT637 'DV' and XT649 'DN'. (Although 3 CBAS Scout AH.1 strength had now been increased to nine aircraft, fuller details of the three 656 Sqdn aircraft can be found under that Squadron's heading).

The 'Fearless' Group ('Fearless', 'Norland', 'Europic Ferry' and 'Atlantic Conveyor') began to depart Ascension at 2130Z on 7 May. From 10 May the Group began to rendezvous with other Task Force ships. On that date it was joined by 'Canberra', 'Elk', 'Ardent' and 'Intrepid', and on 11 May by 'Argonaut' and 'Tidepool'. Flying training continued on the second stage of the journey south, albeit on a reduced scale as the need to conserve airframe hours became more important. Each of the Scout crews carried out Ship-Controlled Approaches to 'Fearless' (8 May), VERTREP practice on 'Europic

Ferry' (10 May) and night-flying practice from 'Fearless' (also on 10 May). The three 656 Sqdn Scouts and one of the 'Fearless' aircraft (XT629) were flown aboard 'Elk' on 11 May for below-deck storage until 17 May due to signs of salt-water corrosion. The remaining Scout aboard 'Fearless' (XR627) was then flown to 'Europic Ferry' for continued training and HDS operations and in fact stayed with the 656 Sqdn Detachment until after the "D-Day" landings.

At 1800Z on 16 May, the 'Fearless' Group made a rendezvous with the LSL's on the edge of the TEZ so that 3 CBAS was once again concentrated into one Group and positioned for the projected San Carlos landings. On 17 May the four Scouts stored aboard 'Elk' were flown to 'Europic Ferry' and during the afternoon of 19 May each of the Scouts fired one SS.11 at sea as a final preparation for the landings. On 20 May (D-1), several transfers took place as positioning for the landings was finalised. Two Scouts (XP902, XT629) transferred to 'Stromness' in support of 45 Cdo, while the three Gazelles of 'A' Flight (XZ326, ZA730, ZA776) transferred from 'Sir Geraint' to 'Sir Tristram'. The Scouts aboard 'Sir Lancelot' remained where they were, as did the Gazelles on 'Sir Galahad' and 'Sir Percivale'. "D-Day" tasking had then been finalised and all of the helicopters were in position. The 3 CBAS order of battle was issued as follows:

---

### 'A' Flight (OC Capt A.Newcombe)

(1) 1 Gazelle (SNEB) in direct support of Cdo Bde HQ from first light.
(2) 1 Gazelle (SNEB) in direct support of 29 Cdo Regt for fire/support direction and co-ordination. To be available at 15 mins notice to move from last light on D-1.
(3) 1 Gazelle (SNEB) in direct support of 29 Cdo Regt for general purpose recce from first light on D-Day.

---

### 'B' Flight (OC Capt J.P.Niblett)

(1) 1 Scout (Recce) in direct support of Bde Cmd
(2) 2 Scouts (ATGW) in direct support of 40 Cdo
(3) 2 Scouts (ATGW) in direct support of 45 Cdo

---

### 'C' Flight (OC Lt Cdr G.Coryton)

Under orders from first light D-Day to provide two Gazelles (SNEB) in direct support of 846 Sqdn on escort/protection duties. In addition to provide an observation helicopter for clearing of landing sites for anti-aircraft post positions.

---

### 'M' Flight (OC Capt N.Pounds)

To provide two Gazelles (SNEB) in direct support of 42 Cdo from first light D-Day. One Gazelle in reserve.

---

### '5' Flight (656) (OC Capt J.G.Greenhalgh)

(1) 2 Scouts (ATGW) in direct support of 2 PARA
(2) 2 Scouts (ATGW) in direct support of 3 PARA

---

Just prior to dawn on 21 May the entire Squadron sailed into Falkland Sound aboard ships of the Amphibious Group. Two 'A' Flight Gazelles immediately took-off to support an SBS attack on Fanning Head whilst, as dawn broke, two Gazelles of 'C' Flight (each with a waist-mounted GPMG in the rear port doorway for protection) took-off from 'Sir Galahad' at 1100Z to confirm positively the absence of enemy troops at certain locations which had been earmarked for Rapier battery sites and which Operation "Sutton" planners knew ground forces would be unable to reach. XX402 and XX411 cleared two proposed Rapier locations as a pair using a high-speed "penetration run" technique. The Gazelles then split up to begin the second phase of 'C' Flight's tasking, that of offering escort and protection to 846 Sqdn Sea Kings which by that time had begun to disembark stores from ships in San Carlos Water. Gazelle XX411 (Sgt A.P.Evans/Sgt E.R.Candlish) made a rendezvous with 846 Sqdn Sea King HC.4 ZA296 as the latter pulled away from 'Canberra' with an underslung cargo of mortar ammunition. The Sea King headed on past Hospital Point towards Port San Carlos settlement, overflying the leading elements of the 3 PARA landing force. Both helicopters continued on to Camerons Point where the Sea King crew began to realise their error in being too far forward and turned through 180° to head west. XX411 also turned, but as the manoeuvre to port was completed (at about 1141Z, at 80 knots and 40 feet above sea-level), it was hit in the tail-rotor and engine/gearbox by six rounds of small-arms fire. This gunfire came from an Ejercito unit, Compania 'C' of RgtInf25. The Gazelle pitched and yawed violently, then began to lose height. Within ten seconds Andrew Evans had successfully ditched the aircraft despite having been hit in the chest and stomach. XX411 sank rapidly as its flotation gear had been removed to make payload available for the GPMG fit. Both men managed to clear the helicopter and Edward Candlish then assisted his badly injured colleague in swimming ashore. Unfortunately, Andrew Evans died shortly afterwards.

Minutes after that loss, XX402 (Lt K.Francis/LCpl B.Griffin) was dispatched ahead of another Sea King to obtain more information on Argentine positions. The Gazelle overflew Camerons Point and made a left turn at 70 feet above ground level just short of The Knob when (at about 1146Z) it too was hit from starboard and below by small-arms fire from the same Ejercito unit that had shot down XX411. XX402 crashed into a hillside close to Clam Creek (UC 637922), killing both crew instantly. Gazelle XX412 (Capt R.J.Makeig-Jones/Cpl R.Fleming) of 'C' Flight also sustained a number of hits from small-arms fire during the early part of the day, but managed to fly back to 'Sir Galahad'. The Gazelle was serviceable again two hours later following repairs which included a new fenestron. At the end of the day, all of the remaining Gazelles were flown back to their parent LSL's for overnight parking, while the Scouts stayed ashore at a location just north of the Ajax Bay Refrigeration Plant (UC 559857). They included XR627 which had rejoined 'B' Flight after operating from 'Europic Ferry'. Thus 3 CBAS became the first aviation unit to be based ashore in the Falkland Islands. The three 656 Sqdn Scouts returned to 'Europic Ferry', which was subsequently ordered out of

San Carlos Water during the night in anticipation of dawn air attacks.

HQ 3 Commando Brigade moved ashore to San Carlos by landing-craft at first light on 22 May and during the day the three Gazelle Flights also flew ashore for dispersal and protection against Argentine air attacks. 'A' Flight joined 40 Cdo at the base of the Verde Mountains, San Carlos (UC 604840), 'C' Flight moved to a position opposite Bonners Bay (UC 575825), 'M' Flight took up residence just north of Ajax Bay (UC 550867) while the Squadron HQ and AMG were located at UC 590843. The sites selected by 3 CBAS subsequently proved to be well-founded, for during the period 22 May to 25 May a large number of Argentine aircraft overflew the positions but none of them carried out direct attacks on 3 CBAS locations. In fact, the only damage sustained by 3 CBAS during the initial period ashore occurred on 27 May when shrapnel from an ammunition fire at Ajax Bay (Red Beach) struck Scout XR627 while it was undergoing a main rotor gearbox change. Repairs had been completed by 31 May, however, without too much difficulty. A change in Flight establishment occurred on 22 May when Gazelle XX376 was transferred from 'M' Flight to 'C' Flight to compensate for the "D-Day" losses.

When the advance by 2 PARA towards Darwin began on 27 May, the two Gazelles of 'M' Flight (XX380 and XX413) under the command of Nick Pounds were placed in direct support, as were two Scouts of 'B' Flight (XP902, XT629) under the command of Jeff Niblett. At first light on 28 May the four helicopters moved to the Squadron Echelon position on the Sussex Mountains and then, when weather permitted, they moved forward to Camilla Creek. From there they began to ferry ammunition to front-line areas until news broke at 1445Z that the CO of 2 PARA (Lt Col H.Jones) and others in the Battalion Tactical HQ had been "severely wounded". The two Gazelles had already shut down, while small arms ammunition which had been loaded aboard the two Scouts was removed "in seconds" and stretchers were thrown into their rear cabins, to be secured by the air gunners. The pair then took-off to retrieve the casualties. Whilst flying forward, XP902 (Capt J.P.Niblett/Sgt J.W.Glaze) and XT629 (Lt R.J.Nunn/Sgt A.R.Belcher) came under attack from two Grupo 3 Pucaras. The two Scouts managed to successfully evade the first attack, the pilots being guided by their respective air gunners. One of the Pucaras (flown by Teniente Giminez, almost certainly A-537) made a second attack during which Sgt Belcher was hit in the right leg by 20mm cannon fire and in the left shin by 7.62mm shells, whilst Richard Nunn received a direct hit and was killed instantly. In the ensuing crash, less than one mile south-east of Camilla Creek House, Sgt Belcher was thrown clear and despite horrific injuries managed to inject himself with a painkiller. Meanwhile, XP902 was flown back to Camilla Creek and Gazelle XX413 (Capt N.Pounds/Cpl J.C.Wood) immediately flew forward to locate the wrecked Scout. XP902 then flew forward again for Sgt Belcher had been located and found to be alive. The Scout evacuated him to the Field Hospital at Ajax Bay. As Jeff Niblett approached Ajax Bay, he was able to radio a SITREP on the 2 PARA battle, at which point it was decided to send in the two 656 Sqdn Scouts (XT637 and XT649) for CASEVAC tasking. XP902 was then refuelled at 656 Sqdn's position before returning to Camilla Creek, followed by the 656 Sqdn helicopters and by two SS.11-equipped 3 CBAS Scouts flown by Sgt J.P.Menghini (XW615) and WO 2 A.S.Robinson (XW616).

As the result of a successful pincer attack, the assault against Goose Green regained momentum. It was therefore decided that the SS.11 Scouts were no longer required so they returned to Ajax Bay. The remaining Scouts spent the day carrying out heavy CASEVAC tasking. In recognition of the exceptional courage that Richard Nunn displayed in flying forward at the height of the battle, he was awarded a posthumous DFC. No less recognition was made of Jeff Niblett's leadership as 'B' Flight Commander. For his exceptional skill and teamwork with his aircrewman in avoiding the Pucara attack, as well as a later incident when he evacuated a seriously wounded Royal Marine from Mount Challenger in dark and misty conditions, he too was awarded the DFC.

Immediately after the capitulation of Darwin and Goose Green, 3 CBAS tasking included the resupply of water, CIVGAS and general rations, followed by the removal of important Argentine prisoners to San Carlos for questioning. One task allotted to 'M' Flight on 30 May came as a result of intelligence received from the liberated civilians at Goose Green. Several inhabitants had seen the pilot of a Harrier GR.3 (XZ988) eject successfully several miles west of the Settlement. Gazelle XX380 (Lt W.L.Scott/Sgt K.Priest) flew out to investigate each house in the outlying area in the hope that the pilot (Sqdn Ldr R.D.Iveson) was "holed up" and hiding. The search eventually proved fruitful and Iveson was coaxed out of hiding at Paragon House, about seven miles west of Goose Green, and flown back to San Carlos. With the arrival at San Carlos of the 5th Infantry Brigade, the three-Scout Section of 656 Sqdn which had operated with 3 CBAS since 7 May reverted to 656 Sqdn HQ control on 1 June. In the meantime, 3 CBAS aircraft had begun to support 3rd Commando Brigade units in the breakout from the San Carlos beach-head. By 30 May 45 Cdo and 3 PARA had moved overland to Teal Inlet, the march by the former from Douglas to Teal being supported by all of the available 3 CBAS aircraft. Tasking included the ferrying forward of equipment and the CASEVAC of twisted ankle cases and the like. 'M' Flight (XX380 and XX413) moved forward to Teal on 30 May and in order to assist the build-up there, two 'B' Flight Scouts (XP902 and XW616) moved forward on 31 May with HQ 3 Cdo Bde.

During the first three days of June, bad weather restricted the use of Wessex and Sea King helicopters in forward areas, so the Gazelles and Scouts were employed in ferrying both personnel and kit forward. At the same time 'Sir Percivale' was positioned offshore at Teal to act as a very welcome refuelling facility. The three Scouts which had remained at Ajax Bay (XR627, XV140 and XW615) moved to Estancia House on 4 June, where they were joined by XP902 and XW616 from Teal. Thus 'B' Flight was once again concentrated at one forward base (it in fact remained at Estancia House until after the surrender on 14 June). 'C' Flight (XX376 and XX412), which had operated in support of 3 PARA for their move to Teal, moved up from the San Carlos area to Teal Inlet on 5 June. Two days later 'A' Flight (XZ326, ZA730 and

ZA776) transferred to the forward base at Estancia House. In order to effect better communications, a number of Relay-Broadcast (REBRO) Stations were set up in forward areas and during the night of 8/9 June a Sea King HC.4 of 846 Sqdn inserted such a Station onto Mount Kent. Unfortunately, a mistake by the pilot and junior NCO in charge of the REBRO led to it being wrongly sited and in an exposed position. It came under heavy Argentine artillery fire later that night, and although the party of three men did manage to escape, one of them suffered minor injuries. Scout XP902 (Niblett/Glaze) performed a night CASEVAC during a respite in the shelling to retrieve the injured soldier.

Over the two days 9/10 June, most helicopters were involved in aiding the build-up of supplies to the forward units (42 Cdo, 45 Cdo and 3 PARA). Those units had taken their respective objectives of Mount Harriet, Two Sisters and Mount Longdon by 12 June and, apart from 'A' Flight moving some important prisoners for questioning, all tasking involved CASEVAC and resupply duties. Sadly, 'M' Flight was tasked with CASEVAC flights on 11 June following a friendly/friendly incident involving 45 Cdo. That day also saw the arrival at Estancia House of 656 Sqdn Scouts XT637 (Sgt R.Kalinski) and XT649 (Capt J.G.Greenhalgh) upon temporary attachment to 'B' Flight in support of 3 CBAS tasking, although Greenhalgh later exchanged XT649 for XW282. Early morning CASEVAC tasking by 'A' Flight on 14 June required in excess of five hours non-stop flying. The casualties were due to 42 Cdo becoming heavily bogged down in an Argentine minefield, and from first light all Flights became involved in CASEVAC duties. Later that morning, 'B' Flight Scouts XV140 (Sgt C.J.Watkins/Cpl H.Whale) and another flown by Lt V.B.Shaugnessy and Cpl G.Carvell (almost certainly XW616) joined the two 656 Sqdn Scouts to carry out a HELARM attack against bunkers and fleeing Argentine troops on the south-west outskirts of Port Stanley. Of the ten SS.11's fired, nine hit their predetermined targets whilst the remaining missile suffered a wire-break. One of the bunkers was later found to have been a strong 105mm gun position. For the remainder of the day, 3 CBAS flew non-stop CASEVAC and resupply flights until the announcement of the ceasefire at 1630Z. Gazelle XX412 (Lt Cdr Coryton, OC 'C' Flight) flew into Port Stanley with a white flag underneath and with the CO of 22 SAS aboard to begin the surrender negotiations. Scout XP902 (Niblett) also flew in to Stanley and remained there overnight.

With the surrender signed, HQ 3 Cdo Bde moved into Stanley on 15 June, while 'B' Flight moved to the Stanley Sportsfield. On 16 June HQ 3 CBAS moved into Stanley, while 'A' Flight moved forward to the Racecourse. 'C' and 'M' Flights remained at Teal Inlet until the morning of 23 June when personnel moved forward aboard 'Sir Percivale' in order to embark 'Canberra'. Two Battle Casualty Replacement Gazelles (XW893 and XX444) arrived in Port William on 18 June aboard 'Contender Bezant' and both were allotted to 'A' Flight. However, the 3 CBAS tour was virtually concluded and most of the Squadron's aircraft were loaded aboard 'Elk' on 23/24 June for passage back to the United Kingdom. ZA730 (for which no space aboard could be found) plus the two new arrivals were handed over to 656 Sqdn and flown to

*Scout AH.1 XW616/DP of 3 CBAS 'B' Flight is seen at the Forward Arming and Refuelling Point (FARP) at Teal during a routine rotors-running refuelling stop, on 31.5.82. Fuel, in 45-gallon drums, had been ferried forward earlier by Wessex helicopters and, as seen here, is delivered into the Scout's fuel tank by a Zenith pump. In the background the 'B' Flight Commander, Captain J. P. Niblett, awaits his turn in Scout AH.1 XP902/DT during the period when both helicopters were supporting the move forward by 45 Commando RM from San Carlos to Teal.*
*(P.O. P. Holdgate, RM)*

*Gazelle AH.1 XX402/(C)G of 3 CBAS 'C' Flight lies wrecked after sustaining enemy small-arms fire damage causing it to crash into a hillside near Clam Creek on 21.5.82 during an early "D-Day" tasking to determine the strength and location of Argentine positions. Both crew, Pilot Lt K. Francis and Aircrewman, L/Cpl B. Griffin were killed instantly as evidenced by the complete destruction of the forward fuselage area. The SNEB 68mm rocket pod is clearly visible in this view, taken a few days afterwards. (Simon Falla)*

Fitzroy on 23 June. 'Elk' arrived at Devonport on 12 July whereupon the Scouts and Gazelles were collected by MARTSU on 14 July for conveyance to temporary storage at Netheravon while Middle Wallop staged "Army Air '82". Apart from XZ326 (dispatched direct to Middle Wallop), all of the helicopters were taken by road to Netheravon on 14/15 July aboard either MARTSU or REME low-loaders, depending on vehicle availability *[see Individual Aircraft Details]*. Following "Army Air '82", the 3 CBAS fleet was taken in by 70 Aircraft Workshops for major overhaul or (in a few cases) an extensive rebuild.

Airframe flying hours by Scouts and Gazelles of 3 CBAS can be summarised as follows:

| Gazelle AH.1 | 5.4-20.5 | 21.5-24.6 | Total |
|---|---|---|---|
| XX376 | 46.5 hrs | 162.0 hrs | 208.5 hrs |
| XX380 | 47.9 | 141.1 | 189.0 |
| XX402 | 30.0 | 0.4 | 30.4 |
| XX411 | 34.1 | 0.4 | 34.5 |
| XX412 | 20.3 | 168.3 | 188.6 |
| XX413 | 45.3 | 149.6 | 194.9 |
| XZ326 | 18.1 | 121.8 | 139.9 |
| ZA730 | 31.2 | 152.9 | 184.1 |
| ZA776 | 25.8 | 127.1 | 152.9 |
| | 299.2 hrs | 1023.6 hrs | 1322.8 hrs |
| **Scout AH.1** | **5.4-20.5** | **21.5-24.6** | **Total** |
| XP902 | 33.7 hrs | 120.1 hrs | 153.8 hrs |
| XR627 | 60.2 | 65.0 | 125.2 |
| XT629 | 30.6 | 21.1 | 51.7 |
| XV140 | 39.8 | 132.3 | 172.1 |
| XW615 | 38.3 | 129.2 | 167.5 |
| XW616 | 13.5 | 104.0 | 117.5 |
| | 216.1 hrs | 571.7 hrs | 787.8 hrs |

Several publications have made mention of the operation by 3 CBAS of a captured CAB 601 Agusta A-109A in the Falkland Islands during the period immediately following the surrender. In fact, while 3 CBAS personnel (and Major Cameron in particular) "laid claim to" the two A-109A's found on Port Stanley Racecourse, nobody from the unit had the necessary twin-engine experience to fly them. They were instead "impressed" into service with 846 Sqdn, both being flown aboard 'Fearless' on 16/17 June for return to the United Kingdom. As the ship approached Ascension Island on 3 July, they were repainted and initially both were coded as 846 Sqdn aircraft (AE-

331 '-/VC' and AE-334 '-/VV'). However, in deference to 3 CBAS, the colour-scheme applied to AE-331 was modified during the final leg of the passage home and it gained their code 'CC' (a vacant slot). Sightings in those marks after its arrival in the United Kingdom created the false impression that the aircraft had been captured and used by 3 CBAS.

---

*Aircrew with 3 CBAS for Operation "Corporate" and their awards:*

### Pilots

*Major C.P.Cameron RM (OC)MC.* **'A' Flt:** *Capt A.B.Newcombe RM MID; Lt C.H.G.Baulf RCT; Lt G.W.Hall RM; CSgt D.R.Pulford RM; Sgt S.Congdon AAC; Sgt D.J.White RM.* **'B' Flt:** *Capt J.P.Niblett RM DFC; Lt R.J.Nunn RM DFC (KIA); Lt V.B.Shaugnessy RM; WO2 A.S.Robinson RM MID; Sgt R.A.Brocklehurst RM; Sgt J.P.Menghini RM; Sgt C.J.Watkins RM.* **'C' Flt:** *Lt Cdr G.R.A.Coryton RN MID; Lt K.Francis RM (KIA); Capt C.Gill RA; Capt R.J.Makeig-Jones RA MID; Sgt P.N.Beeston RM; Sgt J.A.Chappelle RM; Sgt A.P.Evans RM MID (KIA).* **'M' Flt:** *Capt N.E.Pounds RM MID; Lt W.L.Scott RM; Sgt A.Horswill GG; Sgt W.C.OBrien RM DFM; Sgt D.T.Waldron RM.*

*In addition to the above awards, Lt Scott later received a C-in-C Fleet Commendation. It should also be noted that the awards for Lt Nunn and Sgt Evans were given posthumously.*

### Aircrewmen

**'A' Flt** *(Observers): Sgt P.A.Cranch RM; Cpl A.G.Hamilton RM; Cpl C.J.Maguire RM; Cpl M.D.McDaniel RM; Cpl M.J.Roughton RM; Cpl G.A.Saxton RM.* **'B' Flt** *(Anti-Tank Gunners): Sgt A.C.Belcher RM; Sgt J.W.Glaze RM; Sgt J.Pitman RM; Cpl R.L.Campbell RM; Cpl G.Carvell RM; Cpl H.Whale RM; LCpl G.E.Blackstone RM.* **'C' Flt** *(Observers): Sgt E.Candlish RM MID; Cpl A.T.Blowers RM; Cpl R.Fleming RM; Cpl A.L.Hoggan RM; LCpl B.Griffin RM (KIA).* **'M' Flt** *(Observers): Sgt K.Priest RM; Cpl R.Davenport RM; Cpl J.C.Wood RM; Mne Drumond RM.*

*Sgt Glaze and Cpl Roughton were both awarded a C-in-C Fleet Commendation.*

---

# 656 SQUADRON AAC

The inclusion of 656 Squadron within the Operation "Corporate" infrastructure was in itself something of an anomaly. It followed a series of tasking changes made as a direct result of intelligence estimates as to the size of the Argentine forces on the Falkland Islands. Initial reaction by Whitehall upon learning of the Argentine invasion had been the dispatch of a Naval CVBG to enforce what was to become the TEZ, followed closely by a Royal Marines

Amphibious Landing Group, should the need for a sea-borne assault become the only method by which control of the Islands could be regained. The 3rd Commando Brigade sailed aboard 'Canberra' on 9 April (accompanied by 3 PARA which had been transferred from the 5th Infantry Brigade in order to bolster the strength of the Marines). When military intelligence later put the Argentine occupation force at an estimated 10,000 troops, 2 PARA received orders to deploy south (also as part of the 3rd Commando Brigade), while at the same time the 5th Infantry Brigade was itself ordered to "prepare for sailing", having been designated as the Falkland Islands Garrison Force. Prior to Operation "Corporate" (as at 29 March), the 5th Infantry Brigade consisted of the following three Battalions:

*1st Battalion 7th Duke of Edinburgh's*
*Own Gurkha Rifles*      *(1/7 GR)*
*2nd Battalion The Parachute Regiment*   *(2 PARA)*
*3rd Battalion The Parachute Regiment*   *(3 PARA)*

Under normal circumstances, light helicopter support (the Brigade Air Squadron) for the 5 Inf Bde was tasked to 658 Sqdn at Netheravon, who also provided a three-Scout detachment to support the SAS at Hereford. However, when it was announced on 16 April that an AAC Detachment would accompany the 2 PARA Group, 658 Sqdn was well below its normal establishment. In addition, some anxiety must have been expressed at the fact that 5 Inf Bde had only formed in January 1982, which clearly meant that 658 Sqdn and the Parachute Regiments had not yet established a close and effective working relationship (unlike, for example, that built up between 2 PARA and 656 Sqdn when the latter was based at Farnborough). In any case, when 2 PARA discovered that an AAC Detachment was to accompany them, they specifically requested 656 Sqdn (which as at 29 March was the Brigade Air Squadron within the 1st Infantry Brigade) and in particular those pilots with whom the Regiment had exercised in East Africa during 1981. Thus the Detachment was drawn from 656 Sqdn (by then on "standby status") with 657 Sqdn in reserve.

Commanded by Major C.B.Sibun AAC, 656 Sqdn had the following aircraft on charge as at 29 March:

| Scout AH.1 | Gazelle AH.1 |
|---|---|
| XR628 XT642 XV130 | XW912 XZ332 XZ346 |
| XT626 XT649 XV139 | XZ329  XZ340 |

The Squadron's helicopter establishment normally stood at six ATGW Scout AH.1's and six unarmed Gazelle AH.1's, but it was in fact short by one Scout. Unlike the hurried departure of 3 CBAS, 656 Sqdn's deployment plans allowed just enough time to ensure full suitability of its equipment. Reports suggest that one Gazelle and one Scout were flown to Portland on 10 April for the fitment of I-Band Transponders which had been removed from Royal Navy Wasp HAS.1's. Two of the Squadron's Scouts (XT626 and XT642) had yet to be fitted with ARC340 radio equipment and both of them were earmarked for eventual replacement. "Corporate" simply

accelerated those plans, XT637 and XW282 being flown from Wroughton to Netheravon on 16 April as replacements while XT626 and XT642 were flown in the opposite direction on 19 April. In complete contrast to the Scout situation, all of 656 Sqdn's Gazelles were at a low modification state and were therefore replaced by aircraft which had completed the "Phase II Mod Programme" at Fleetlands. XX409, XZ290, XZ314 and XZ321 were transferred from the ARWS at Middle Wallop during April, XX409 being the second of the ex-Belize Gazelles which had "Mod 60" embodied (fixed fittings for flotation equipment). The first aircraft so fitted (XZ326) had already joined 3 CBAS. ZA728 ('A' 3 CBAS), which had not been shipped with the main 3 CBAS departure (reportedly due to lack of space) was flown from Coypool to Netheravon on 19 April. Finally, to bring Gazelle strength up to its full establishment, XX377 (ex-3 CBAS) was issued to 656 Sqdn. That helicopter had been undergoing a modification programme at Fleetlands (including the fitment of a Radar Altimeter) when 3 CBAS departed, but was in any case earmarked for duty with the Northern Ireland Regiment. In fact, XX377 is believed to have been delivered to the Province on 26 April, but was then immediately reallocated to 656 Sqdn and is known to have arrived at Netheravon on 29 April. (XZ320/T of the ARWS was subsequently flown to Ulster to replace XX377.) All five of the original 656 Sqdn Gazelles (XW912, XZ329, XZ332, XZ340 and XZ346) were issued and flown to the ARWS at Middle Wallop. The aircraft prepared for deployment with 656 Sqdn to the South Atlantic can therefore be summarised as follows:

| Scout AH.1 | Gazelle AH.1 |
|---|---|
| XR628 XT649 XV139 | XX377 XZ290 XZ321 |
| XT637 XV130 XW282 | XX409 XZ314 ZA728 |

### 656 SQDN ADVANCED DETACHMENT

Respecting the wishes of 2 PARA, 656 Sqdn allotted command of its Advanced Section to Capt J.G.Greenhalgh. Two of the Squadron pilots went south with him, Sgt R.Kalinski and Sgt R.J.Walker. Three Scout AH.1's (XR628, XT637 and XT649) were flown to Southampton docks on 21 April for loading aboard 'Europic Ferry'. The ship sailed from Southampton on 22 April, although after a practice RAS with 'Grey Rover' and a brief opportunity for 656 to carry out DLP's, she sailed into Portland for a short stopover. That allowed Rich Walker to fly back to Middle Wallop on 23 April in Scout XT637 to change the SS.11 simulator (discovered to be faulty) and on to Netheravon to pick up last-minute items. While he was away, the rest of the aircrew went ashore and, on finding the steepest hill on Portland Bill, undertook some rigorous physical training! 'Europic Ferry' sailed from the Portland area on 25 April bound for Freetown, Sierra Leone, accompanied by 'Atlantic Conveyor' following a rendezvous off Plymouth. It was later joined by 'Norland' with 2 PARA embarked. On 23 April, John Greenhalgh decided that codes should be applied to the three Scouts for identification purposes and

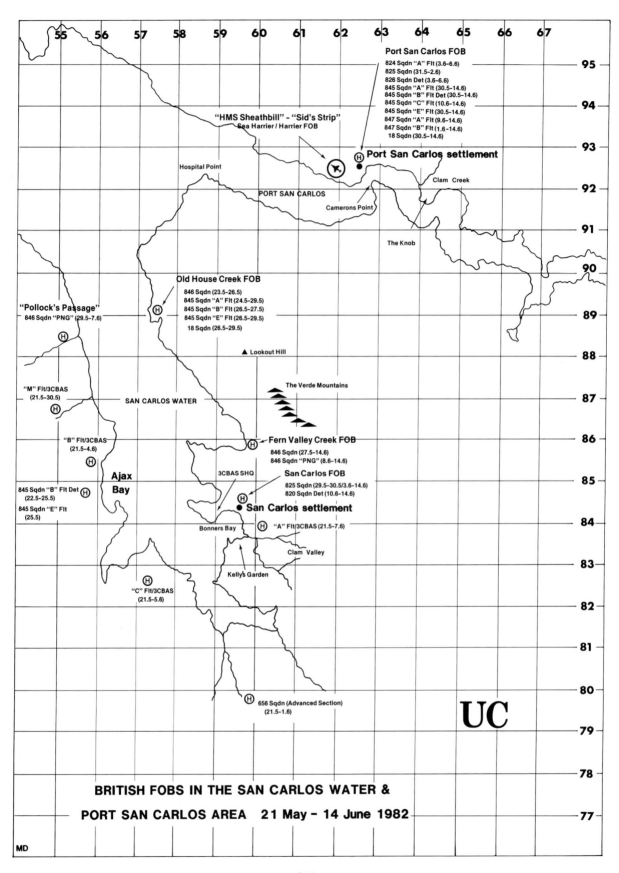

**Port San Carlos FOB**

824 Sqdn "A" Flt (3.6–6.6)
825 Sqdn (31.5–2.6)
826 Sqdn Det (3.6–6.6)
845 Sqdn "A" Flt (30.5–14.6)
845 Sqdn "B" Flt Det (30.5–14.6)
845 Sqdn "C" Flt (10.6–14.6)
845 Sqdn "E" Flt (30.5–14.6)
847 Sqdn "A" Flt (9.6–14.6)
847 Sqdn "B" Flt (1.6–14.6)
18 Sqdn (30.5–14.6)

**"HMS Sheathbill" – "Sid's Strip"**
Sea Harrier / Harrier FOB

Hospital Point

(H) **Port San Carlos settlement**

PORT SAN CARLOS

Clam Creek

Camerons Point

The Knob

**Old House Creek FOB**

846 Sqdn (23.5–26.5)
845 Sqdn "A" Flt (24.5–29.5)
845 Sqdn "B" Flt (26.5–27.5)
845 Sqdn "E" Flt (26.5–29.5)
18 Sqdn (26.5–29.5)

**"Pollock's Passage"**
846 Sqdn "PNG" (29.5–7.6)

▲ Lookout Hill

**"M" Flt/3CBAS**
(21.5–30.5)

SAN CARLOS WATER

The Verde Mountains

**"B" Flt/3CBAS**
(21.5–4.6)

**Fern Valley Creek FOB**

846 Sqdn (27.5–14.6)
846 Sqdn "PNG" (8.6–14.6)

**Ajax Bay**

3CBAS SHQ

**San Carlos FOB**

825 Sqdn (29.5–30.5/3.6–14.6)
820 Sqdn Det (10.6–14.6)

**845 Sqdn "B" Flt Det**
(22.5–25.5)

**845 Sqdn "E" Flt**
(25.5)

● **San Carlos settlement**

Bonners Bay

(H) **"A" Flt/3CBAS** (21.5–7.6)

Clam Valley

Kelly's Garden

(H) **"C" Flt/3CBAS**
(21.5–5.6)

(H) 656 Sqdn (Advanced Section)
(21.5–1.6)

**UC**

## BRITISH FOBS IN THE SAN CARLOS WATER &
## PORT SAN CARLOS AREA   21 May – 14 June 1982

MD

did so by utilising the final letter of each pilot's tactical radio call-sign. Thus XR628 became 'C' (Kalinski), XT637 'F' (Walker) and XT649 'A' (Greenhalgh). Those codes were applied in Dayglo Red on each Scout's nose panels. Daily training, mostly DLP's and VERTREP's, was conducted en route, including a NAVEX on 27 April when the Detachment Commander successfully proved a locally-devised system for being able to fly to a distant point then return to the ship (a moving starting point). That was a manoeuvre outside the normal confines of AAC operations and was believed not to have been previously attempted by the AAC. On 30 April XT637 was flown to 'Atlantic Conveyor' for waterproofing modifications, after which it returned to 'Europic Ferry' where the other two Scouts were similarly treated.

A brief stop at Freetown between 2 May and 4 May enabled the ship to replenish before departing in company with 'Norland'. Ascension Island was reached on 7 May, at which stage the Advanced Section became fully integrated within 3 CBAS and was officially retitled 5 Flight (656) 3 CBAS. As an immediate consequence, HQ 3 CBAS ordered the removal of the Dayglo Red codes and application of two-letter call-signs within the 3 CBAS sequence. XR628 became 'DO' with the letters painted in Matt Black just beneath the starboard windscreen panel, whilst XT637 became 'DV' and XT649 became 'DN'. Later on 7 May, 'Europic Ferry' sailed south from Ascension Island along with 'Fearless', 'Norland', 'Stromness' and 'Atlantic Conveyor'. Free air movement was then virtually restricted to a thrice daily HDS between the other ships of the Group although 656 Sqdn did undertake some night flying training (including Ship-Controlled Approaches), enabling its pilots to become deck-qualified in day or night conditions. Deck landings at night were admirably described by the Squadron pilots as "Docking in Space", but the training proved to be of great benefit later on. Owing to some signs of salt-water corrosion emerging, the three 656 Sqdn Scouts were flown from 'Europic Ferry' to 'Elk' on 11 May, where they were stored below decks until 17 May. In the interim period 656 Sqdn took XR627 ('DO' 3 CBAS) on temporary charge, permitting John Greenhalgh to carry out sight familiarisation flights to 'Canberra' on 12 May and 'Stromness' on 13 May. Rich Walker undertook a similar flight to 'Canberra' on 14 May. On 19 May 'Europic Ferry' was marking time on the edge of the TEZ, enabling each Scout to test-fire one SS.11 round at sea in final preparation for the San Carlos landings. At 0400Z on 20 May, the vessel began to head for the Falkland Islands at full speed; Operation "Sutton" was then well and truly under way.

Just prior to dawn on 21 May, 'Europic Ferry' sailed into Falkland Sound and took up position in San Carlos Water. Scouts XT637 (Walker) and XT649 (Greenhalgh) were airborne at 1100Z to support 2 PARA in ferrying supplies ashore and conducting armed reconnaissance. Each Scout flew in excess of eight hours during the day (to 2000Z). XR628 (Kalinski) was tasked to support 3 PARA but was not called upon, so flew miscellaneous duties and later assisted the other two in recovering 40 SAS soldiers to 'Intrepid' from the Goose Green area. 'Europic Ferry' was ordered to sail out of Falkland Sound at 0200Z on 22 May in anticipation of dawn Argentine air-raids. The

Scouts had been returned to the ship for overnight parking (except XR627 which rejoined 'B' Flt/3 CBAS and remained ashore) and thus 656 Sqdn remained at sea for several days until the vessel returned to San Carlos at dawn on 26 May. 656 Sqdn then took up a position ashore, settling into a temporary base at the foot of the Sussex Mountains just south-west of Head of the Bay House (UC 598800). Squadron kit plus 200 drums of aviation fuel was airlifted ashore, providing 656 Sqdn and 3 CBAS with enough fuel for their initial operations, including the 2 PARA advance on Camilla Creek House (27 May) and on to Darwin and Goose Green (28 May) [see also 3 CBAS notes]. Two 656 Sqdn Scouts (XT637 and XT649) were converted to the CASEVAC role for 2 PARA's assault on 28 May, operating continuously throughout the day (following the loss of 3 CBAS Scout XT629) until an hour after last light. Later, at 0200Z on 29 May, Capt J.Young ('B' Company, 2 PARA) was found to be seriously injured close to the Argentine line of defence. Although both were desperately tired, Greenhalgh and Walker (with LCpl Gammon) flew XT649 forward. Despite a total blackout, the extreme cold, and the Scout running very short of fuel, Capt Young was evacuated back to the makeshift field hospital at Ajax Bay. That dramatic flight from the front-line and landing at Ajax Bay was made in complete darkness and by dead reckoning navigation, an action which certainly saved the officer's life and for which Greenhalgh was later awarded the DFC.

## 656 SQDN HQ & MAIN PARTY

Immediately following the dispatch of the Squadron Advanced Section and the replacement of the low mod state aircraft, the remainder of 656 Sqdn moved to Sennybridge with the 5th Infantry Brigade for Exercise "Welsh Falcon". Composition of the Brigade had changed dramatically following the deployment of 2 PARA and 3 PARA to the South Atlantic as part of the 3rd Commando Brigade, RM. In order to build up its depleted strength, two Battalions of Guards were transferred to the 5th Infantry Brigade, which by 16 April consisted of the following:

| | |
|---|---|
| *2nd Battalion Scots Guards* | *(2 SG)* |
| *1st Battalion Welsh Guards* | *(1 WG)* |
| *1st Battalion 7th Duke of Edinburgh's Own Gurkha Rifles* | *(1/7 GR)* |

Three Scout AH.1's (XV130, XV139, XW282) and six Gazelle AH.1's (XX377, XX409, XZ290, XZ314, XZ321, ZA728) were flown from Netheravon to Southampton docks on 8 May for loading aboard 'Baltic Ferry' and 'Nordic Ferry' respectively. Departure from Southampton took place during the early hours of 9 May, when 'Baltic Ferry' sailed at 0001Z and was followed by 'Nordic Ferry' an hour later. The 656 Sqdn Main Party personnel embarked the 'Queen Elizabeth 2' on 12 May (with most of 5 Inf Bde), together with last-minute stores.

Under the watchful eyes of Soviet "trawlers", the two ferries docked briefly at Freetown, Sierra Leone, at 2100Z on 16 May before continuing their passage south. 'Queen Elizabeth 2' sailed on to Ascension Island, from where a high-speed dash to Grytviken, South Georgia began on 22 May with arrival on 27 May. With the liner at anchor in calm water, Squadron personnel were transferred to 'Canberra' early on 28 May using 'Junella' as a ferry between the two ships. After a brief stay in the TRALA, 'Canberra' sailed into San Carlos Water on 2 June to off-load 5th Infantry Brigade and 656 Sqdn personnel. In the meantime, 'Baltic Ferry' had arrived in San Carlos Water early on 1 June, from where the three Scouts flew off to rendezvous with a 2 PARA detachment close to the Squadron's Advanced Section base (UC 598800). With the arrival of its HQ, the Advanced Section of three Scouts that had been attached to 3 CBAS since 7 May reverted to parent Squadron control, an event which officially took place on 1 June. Similarly, 2 PARA transferred from the 3rd Commando Brigade back to its parent 5th Infantry Brigade on that date. 'Nordic Ferry' anchored off San Carlos settlement at 1030Z on 3 June. In high winds and almost continuous rain the Gazelles flew off to Clam Valley at 1400Z.

As the Squadron HQ settled in at Clam Valley, one Scout (XT637) was deployed to the Brigade HQ on 2 June. The remaining five helicopters were tasked to support the 2 PARA assault against Swan Inlet House (UC 885568) on the same date. For that operation, both XR628 (Sgt R.Kalinski/LCpl J.J.Rigg) and XT649 (Capt J.G.Greenhalgh/Cpl M.Lord) had reverted to the ATGW role to support the leading troops, each Scout having a paratrooper armed with a sub-machine gun positioned at the open door. The other Scouts (XV130, XV139, XW282) were flown in the utility role, also with doors removed and each with four men from 6 Platoon/'B' Company 2 PARA on board. Both XR628 and XT649 fired two SS.11's in the assault as a "softening-up" manoeuvre, Cpl Lord scoring one hit whilst his second missile suffered a wire-break. Similarly, one of the SS.11's fired from XR628 proved to be a "rogue", while a second attempt was hampered by a failure of the latch release mechanism. In fact, Swan Inlet House was later found to be unoccupied and it was from there that Major Crossland made his famous telephone call to Fitzroy to discover that Argentine forces had apparently withdrawn from there as well as Bluff Cove settlement. 2 PARA immediately made a daring move forward to Fitzroy Ridge aboard the 18 Sqdn Chinook ZA718, which was escorted by a pair of Scouts. From Fitzroy Ridge, Scout XR628 (Kalinski/Rigg) then moved a 2 PARA reconnaissance platoon forward to Bluff Cove. A number of other Scout AH.1's flew further elements of 2 PARA forward from Goose Green.

It was at about that time that intelligence reports had confirmed the presence in Stanley of an Argentine land-based Exocet missile launcher. Fearing it to be mobile, Scout XT649 (Greenhalgh) was tasked on 5 June to overfly the many islands east of Bluff Cove as a precautionary measure in preparation for the planned deployment of the two Guards Regiments by LSL from San Carlos. As it transpired, the Exocet launcher never left the Port Stanley area. Although 656 Sqdn HQ remained at Clam Valley, both Gazelle and Scout Flights moved to Goose Green on 5 June. Routine aircraft maintenance was still carried out

by the 70 Aircraft Workshops Detachment at Clam Valley.

The Squadron's only loss of life occurred during the night of 5/6 June. At 2030Z Gazelle AH.1 XX377 (SSgt C.A.Griffin/LCpl S.J.Cockton) was tasked with flying some Signals Squadron personnel to Mount Pleasant Peak in order to site a REBRO Station there as part of an operation to establish a forward communications link between 5 Inf Bde and 2 PARA (who were previously out of communication at night). After flying forward and inserting the Station, the Gazelle returned to Goose Green to refuel and await further tasking. However, by about 0200Z on 6 June the Station had stopped functioning, so the Signals Squadron CO (Major M.Forge) requested a Gazelle to take SSgt Baker and himself forward with spares and fuel. XX377 was again tasked and, with the same crew, departed Goose Green at 0350Z. However at 0408Z, at a point some two miles south of Mount Pleasant Peak and in an area not declared fully clear of the enemy, it sustained a direct missile strike to the rear fuselage/fenestron area. At the time reports suggested that a British ship had fired a Sea Dart missile which brought down an AAC helicopter *(one such report appeared in " 'Canberra' The Great White Whale Goes To War")* but subsequent research by the authors has failed to confirm this. XX377 was flying at between 70 and 200 feet above ground level at the time and all four occupants were killed instantly in the crash which followed immediately after the missile strike. Later on 6 June, 656 Sqdn's HQ moved from Clam Valley to Darwin, taking up residency in several barns, unoccupied houses and a greenhouse. Tasks for that day included a Gazelle reconnaissance of the beached Argentine patrol boat 'Rio Iguazu' at Button Bay on the north side of Choiseul Sound (UC 775500).

Immediately following their arrival on the Islands, the Gurkhas (1/7 GR) had positioned to Goose Green and commenced patrols in areas to the south and south-east of the settlement as part of a "clearing houses from the map" operation. By implementing a systematic search of all barns and houses, areas were gradually declared "safe". For several days, 656 Sqdn Scouts inserted Gurkha patrols at a number of points in order to clear Arrow Harbour House (UC 660470) on Pondi Ridge, Torcida Point (UC 750460) and Lively Island (UC 990380). The weather had improved on 7 June and at 1705Z, just after another patrol had been inserted on Lafonia, a Gurkha patrol reported enemy activity at Egg Harbour House (UC 365513) and called for helicopter support. Scout XV139 (Sgt I.Roy/Cpl M.Johns) flew forward to a nearby ridge, by which time the Argentine soldiers had been seen to evacuate the house and run into a nearby gully. Having temporarily lost sight of the enemy, Ian Roy radioed the Squadron HQ and requested an observation helicopter, whereupon Gazelle XX409 (Capt P.G.Piper/LCpl L.Beresford) flew forward and landed behind the ridge alongside the Scout. Ian Roy pointed out to Philip Piper the area in which the enemy was hiding, then flew XV139 back to Goose Green to refuel as he foresaw that there would be a long drawn out operation. In the meantime, Philip Piper and Les Beresford took-off in XX409 and circled the gully (out of firing range) for some 10 to 12 minutes and then took up a position to the west which would have enabled them to see any further

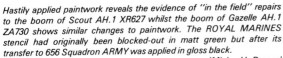

Hastily applied paintwork reveals the evidence of "in the field" repairs to the boom of Scout AH.1 XR627 whilst the boom of Gazelle AH.1 ZA730 shows similar changes to paintwork. The ROYAL MARINES stencil had originally been blocked-out in matt green but after its transfer to 656 Squadron ARMY was applied in gloss black.
*(Michael I. Draper)*

When news of the attack against 'Sir Tristram' in Port Pleasant reached the 3 CBAS 'B' Flight Commander, Capt J. Niblett, he flew aboard on 11.6.82 to retrieve crew's personal kit that had been stored below deck. Just before departing Niblett photographed his Scout AH.1 (XP902) against the twisted and still smouldering structure.
*(Capt J. P. Niblett, RM)*

XV130 Scout AH.1 of 656 Squadron prepares for take-off from the Scout Flight base at Goose Green on 7.6.82. This view illustrates well the configuration of 'Utility' Scouts with rear doors removed and with the Underslung Load Hook visible beneath the cabin. However, just behind the pilot's seat is the SS.11 Guidance System box which identifies '130 as being, in reality, an ATGW variant but with missiles temporarily removed.
*(815 Sqdn 'Exeter' Flight)*

On 2.7.82 656 Squadron Gazelle AH.1 XX409 began to run short of fuel towards the end of a routine tasking, at which point Capt P. Piper radioed 'Exeter' for assistance. The ship's Lynx HAS.2 was speedily hangared so as to allow '409 to make what is believed to have been the first deck landing by an AAC helicopter onto a Type 42 Destroyer. 'Exeter' was moored alongside 'Stena Seaspread' at the time during a series of diving operations in San Carlos Water.
*(815 Sqdn 'Exeter' Flight)*

movement by the enemy. When XV139 returned from Goose Green, it was closely followed by XW282 (Capt S.M.Drennan/LCpl J.Gammon), while back at base preparations were under way to fly more of the Gurkhas forward on board two 825 Sqdn Sea Kings. With three Army helicopters in position, it was agreed locally that they would move in slowly towards the gully. Cpl Johns (in XV139) fired one SS.11 missile and scored a direct hit against what was reported by Philip Piper to be the enemy position, but as Sam Drennan (in XW282) overflew a different part of the gully, so eight Argentine troops ran out with their arms up to surrender without a fight. What was believed to have been "the enemy looking forlornly out to sea", and therefore subjected to a HELARM attack, turned out to be simply an outcrop of rocks! Sam Drennan landed immediately to permit John Gammon to disarm the Argentines, but as Gammon leapt from the Scout and then over a small fence, his trouser belt buckle snapped. A somewhat curious spectacle followed as John Gammon directed his captives with a sub-machine gun under one arm, the other free hand being used to hold his trousers up! The situation was not made any easier when, a few minutes later, the AAC crews handed over their prisoners to the Gurkhas. None of the pilots spoke Spanish and not one of the Gurkhas present was fluent in English! All the same, those problems were satisfactorily overcome, and amongst the captured weaponry was a Mauser sniper rifle and a SA-7 missile and launcher (the latter was subsequently placed on display in the Museum of Army Flying at Middle Wallop).

The improvement in weather conditions on 7 June was welcomed as 656 Sqdn HQ plans involved a move forward to Fitzroy. However, the lack of support helicopters (Chinook/Sea King) forced a postponement of that move. The position remained the same on 8 June, but on that day an increase in enemy air activity disrupted all tasking of the available helicopters. An early afternoon air attack by the Argentines on 8 June against the anchorage in Port Pleasant succeeded in hitting 'Sir Tristram' and 'Sir Galahad'. The two ships, which had brought the Guards from San Carlos, were abandoned (on fire and with UXB's below decks). Casualties were heavy, especially aboard 'Sir Galahad', and Squadron Scouts and Gazelles were tasked with CASEVAC duties from Fitzroy to Ajax Bay.

8 June was also remembered by 656 Sqdn as the day on which "Dick Klink's Donkey" stopped over MacPhee Pond. At 1850Z news reached the Squadron HQ that Dick Kalinski and Julian Rigg (in Scout XR628) had earlier been forced to take avoiding action from a formation of five Grupo 5 A-4B Skyhawks to the south-west of Fitzroy. Kalinski had simply (and quickly) gone to ground and remained stationary in the hover several feet above MacPhee Pond (VC 018551). When all seemed clear, Kalinski climbed away to resume tasking, but as he did so XR628 appeared to suffer a tail rotor drive-shaft failure. With control lost, he made an immediate forced-landing — into the pond. Luckily it was a fresh water pond and only four feet deep, but nevertheless XR628 sat with the cockpit floor under a foot of water. Although relatively easy to extract, the continued lack of heavy-lift helicopters prevented its rescue, so the Scout remained in MacPhee Pond for three days (during which period

REME technicians removed the AF120 sight and engine). It was eventually airlifted back to Fitzroy by Sea King at 1930Z on 11 June, then to San Carlos in similar fashion two days later.

656 Sqdn HQ (together with Gazelle and Scout Flights) finally moved forward to Fitzroy early on 9 June in company with 5 Inf Bde HQ. Even at that stage, there was still confusion in off-loading Brigade stores and supplies, partly because of Argentine air attacks and a general shortage of LCU's and Mexeflotes. Limited fuel stocks also caused a number of problems, and for several days 656 Sqdn was forced to curtail all tasking at last light pending fuel replenishment. Continuous resupply sorties by the Scout Flight into forward areas created many hazardous situations for the aircrew. One such operation involved XV139 on 9 June when Ian Roy was tasked with delivering some supplies to a Scots Guards Reconnaissance Platoon at Port Harriet House (VC 300677) and to collect the Platoon CO. Just before the Scout attempted to land, the house came under heavy enemy mortar fire as a result of which the patrol withdrew with two casualties. During the brief bombardment, Ian Roy held off just out of range. When the shelling ceased he flew in to extract the Guards, but on passing close to Port Harriet Point his helicopter was subjected to an Argentine Blowpipe attack. The missile fortunately missed by some 25 yards and impacted into nearby high ground (it was possible that a second Blowpipe was fired at XV139 on that sortie, but details remain unclear). A large piece of the Blowpipe's casing was later presented to Ian Roy as a reminder that he had led a charmed life on that occasion.

Whilst the Scout and Gazelle Flights moved to Fitzroy on 9 June, those helicopters tasked with battle operations were forced to locate refuelling facilities away from base. One such facility was provided at the Port San Carlos Harrier strip where, on 9 June, Gazelle ZA728 (Sgt G.H.Keates/LCpl J.A.Coley) narrowly avoided certain disaster following prompt action by an alert pilot. Graham Keates had positioned to the strip for a rotors-running refuel, but midway through the operation (with the refueller standing on the skids) Keates noticed an Air Portable Fuel Cell begin to roll down a gentle slope towards ZA728. Keates lifted off the helicopter by inches only, in order to "take the weight of the helicopter off the skids but not to impede the refuelling", and turned it through 60° as well. The APFC continued to roll downhill and appeared to miss the Gazelle "by inches" before coming to rest some distance away. The refueller, wearing ear-defenders throughout the operation, remained totally unaware of the situation, as did Cpl Coley who was studying his charts at the time in readiness for resuming the Flight Plan. With the refuelling complete, ZA728 took-off to carry on with its tasking. It was not until the crew returned to base at the end of the day that they noticed that the starboard vertical stabiliser had actually been damaged by the APFC. The damage had not produced any adverse effects on flying characteristics, however!

Before departure from the United Kingdom, a decision had been taken to fit SNEB 68mm rocket packs to 656 Sqdn Gazelles in the same manner as those fitted to the 3 CBAS aircraft. Sufficient packs (and spares) had been acquired in time for the Squadron departure from Southampton, but as a result of an apparent oversight,

*656 Squadron Scout AH.1 XV139 awaits the imminent arrival of a 2nd Scots Guards "walking wounded" party on the morning of 14.6.82 at Goat Ridge. Clearly visible is the Infra Red Shield fitted to deflect exhaust heat into the main rotor-blade downwash as part of a standard anti-heat seeking missile defence system. Just visible beneath the cabin can be seen the Underslung Load Hook.*
*(Paul R. G. Haley, 'SOLDIER')*

*The partially burnt-out wreckage of 3 CBAS 'B' Flight Scout AH.1 XT629/DR lies inverted after becoming the victim of a Grupo 3 Pucara attack on 28.5.82. The Scout had been en route to the Goose Green battlefront at the time in order to retrieve the bodies of Col H. Jones and others. Sadly Pilot Lt R. Nunn was killed outright but amazingly his Aircrewman, Sgt R. Belcher, survived with severe leg injuries.*
*(R. McLeod)*

*A new meaning to the term "Squadron Floater"? In fact 656 Squadron Scout AH.1 XR628/DO stands in 4 feet of fresh water on the edge of Mac-Phee Pond after Sgt Kalinski and Cpl J. Rigg were forced to take avoiding action from Argentine fighter aircraft on 8.6.82, whilst at the same time the Scout suffered a main gearbox failure. The missing port door was put to good use by the crew and later by a repair team who paddled to and from the shore without even getting their feet wet!*
*(Cpl J. Rigg, AAC)*

only the pods had been loaded aboard 'Nordic Ferry'. The stores booms had been loaded elsewhere and were not found until after the Squadron arrived in the Falkland Islands. The booms were eventually located on 4 June, but in view of a pending move by the Gazelle Flight from the San Carlos area to Goose Green, it had been decided to send the armament packs on to that location where an Aircraft Maintenance Group would fit them "in the field". In high winds, the first two boom kits were underslung beneath XX409 for transfer to Goose Green, but shortly after take-off the load began to swing violently. Close to losing control of their helicopter, the crew (Philip Piper and Les Beresford) were forced to jettison the cargo, both kits being written-off as a result. It was subsequently decided to dispatch the packs by road, but not before further problems (mainly associated with the weather) had been overcome. The first 656 Sqdn Gazelle AH.1 was eventually fitted with a stores boom and pod overnight on 7/8 June. The 68mm rockets did not, however, arrive until late on 9 June, by which time most of the Gazelles were heavily committed to operations. It was not until midday on 10 June that the installation was completed and a test firing was carried out at a group of rocks in Choiseul Sound.

10 and 11 June were relatively quiet days for 656 Sqdn as preparations were being finalised for a major assault by 3 Cdo Bde against Two Sisters, Mount Harriet and Mount Longdon. Resupply and maintenance of Rapier sites positioned around Fitzroy received high priority, as did the supply of fuel and stores to forward-based units. That stretched the logistics system almost to breaking point. Two Scouts (XT637 and XT649) were placed under the temporary operational control of 3 CBAS for the battle, supporting 2 PARA and a detachment of 1 WG. By dawn on 12 June plans had been sealed for the Scots Guards' assault on Tumbledown and for the Gurkhas to pass through to take Mount William, while the Welsh Guards (in reserve) were tasked with moving further forward to capture Sapper Hill. Severely low fuel stocks limited any early tasking on 13 June, but despite that the Squadron successfully carried out resupply of stores and troop lifts in preparation for another night attack. As if to add to the Squadron's problems, the 3 Cdo Bde HQ at Estancia House was heavily attacked by Grupo 5 A-4B Skyhawks around 1515Z whilst Scout XT637 and Gazelle ZA728 were both positioned there. ZA728 (Keates/Coley) had flown to a position adjacent to Estancia House (VC 195742) for a crew briefing prior to proceeding forward to Two Sisters and Mount Harriet. Minutes later, Scout XT637 (operating in support of 3 PARA) landed close to the Gazelle in order to collect two Daily Express journalists and fly them forward to the front-line. Fortunately, both crews were out of their helicopters when the Skyhawks attacked, as bomb-blast damaged the Scout's top canopy while debris holed the tail rotor and dented the rear boom in several places. Blast also shattered the cockpit perspex on ZA728 and damaged the fin and rear boom area, whilst other reports tell of the ground being lifted by the blast which caused damage to the Gazelle's belly panels. Both damaged helicopters were airlifted back to San Carlos later in the day for repairs at the 70 Aircraft Workshop REME facility, although a number of factors hindered their immediate return to service. In the case of

the Gazelle, while the boom and fin were repaired overnight, perspex did not become available until mid-July. Similarly, panel damage sustained by the Scout was repaired overnight but return to flight status was hampered by a total lack of spare tail rotors. Ultimately, the REME Detachment struck a deal with one of the Ship's Flights, an Army VHF radio being "swopped" for a spare Wasp HAS.1 rotor blade.

At 2359Z on 13 June a noisy night attack signalled the start of 2nd Scots Guards' assault on Tumbledown. Despite the intensity of artillery support fire, they encountered heavy opposition. It was not until 2 PARA succeeded in advancing along Wireless Ridge to a position overlooking Moody Brook that artillery fire was able to be directed with some degreee of accuracy. In direct support of the Wireless Ridge battle, Scout XW282 (Greenhalgh/Gammon) flew several CASEVAC sorties under intense artillery fire and in extremely bad weather conditions. At 0406Z, XW282 landed at Fitzroy with the first two battle casualties from 2 PARA before continuing to extract more wounded soldiers for several hours during the night. At dawn, 656 Sqdn began launching CASEVAC sorties from Tumbledown. The first call was received by the Regimental Aid Post at Goat Ridge when it appeared that a Gurkha and three Scots Guardsmen were lying seriously injured on the east slope of Tumbledown, within sight and range of Argentine positions on the outskirts of Stanley. The extent of their injuries and the rocky terrain prevented a stretcher party from carrying the men to a safe collection point. Scout XV139 (Drennan/Rigg) was tasked with their extraction and flew forward from Goat Ridge in some of the most appalling weather conditions witnessed during the conflict. Sam Drennan was subsequently awarded the DFC for that successful CASEVAC. Part of his citation reads as follows:

*"In the assault the battalion was subjected to continuous, accurate enemy small-arms and artillery fire. Despite this, Captain Drennan repeatedly volunteered to fly forward to evacuate very seriously wounded casualties who required immediate medical attention and who could not have survived movement by stretcher over the extremely rough ground of Tumbledown. In order to reach the wounded on the battalions front line, on at least three separate occasions he had to move to exposed forward-slope positions in full view of the enemy. He was personally responsible for the evacuation of 16 casualties from Tumbledown under extremely difficult conditions. Flying under fire, over difficult mountainous terrain, in extremely turbulent winds and heavy snow showers, Captain Drennan repeatedly put his own life at risk."*

One Scout sortie had been mounted at 2345Z on 13 June to rescue a Welsh Guardsman suffering from severe pneumonia on Sapper Hill. Once again Scout XV139 (Drennan/Rigg) was tasked and flew forward despite a strong south-easterly wind, frequent heavy snow showers and no moonlight. Sam Drennan found the conditions on Sapper Hill so appalling that on at least one occasion XV139 was almost blown into the rocky hillside. Not making his task any easier was the fact that the Guards had not illuminated a landing site and the only lights seen

The classic CASEVAC portrait: with rotors still running a stretcher party has opened the starboard pod, the cover being visible to the lower left, and removed the casualty for treatment. At the same time a replacement stretcher is positioned in order to allow the Scout to return to the battle area with the minimum of delay. In this view XT637/DV of 656 Squadron is at Ajax Bay with 2 PARA casualties from Goose Green. Pilot Sgt D. Kalinski awaits the signal to take-off.
*(Paul R. G. Haley, 'SOLDIER')*

Unlike Gazelles of 3 CBAS those of 656 Squadron always operated with their doors on. XZ290 is seen here, early on 14.6.82, taking on a wounded Scots Guardsman at the Goat Ridge Regimental Aid Post. Space limitations did not allow for the stretcher to be loaded and injured soldiers sometimes faced an uncomfortable, though welcome, flight to the Field Hospital. Note that XZ290 is not, by this late stage, fitted with an IR Shield.
*(Paul R. G. Haley, 'SOLDIER')*

XX412/(C)Y Gazelle AH.1 of 3 CBAS 'C' Flight, seen at Teal Inlet on 5.6.82 whilst supporting the overland move by 3 PARA from San Carlos to Teal. Note that the flotation packs had, by then, been removed as they considerably reduced the Gazelle's payload ability.
*(via Major A. Eames, RM)*

42 Commando RM HQ operated from a Volvo BV202 vehicle and trailer. In this view, taken on the rugged terrain of Mount Kent, a Gazelle AH.1 of 3 CBAS 'M' Flight is positioned close by whilst the crew attend a briefing before continuing their tasking.
*(via Major A. Eames, RM)*

by the aircrew were thought to have been an Argentine Land Rover, itself lost and groping its way through the snowstorm. Eventually, Drennan was forced to return to base at 0100Z owing to the Scout's low fuel state. At 0125Z he tried again, that time successfully, and finally returned to Fitzroy with the injured Guardsman at 0225Z. CASEVAC flights from Tumbledown continued throughout 14 June and included the rescue of several Argentine troops who clearly displayed their relief at being captured by the British.

At 1300Z on 14 June, 2 PARA received orders to move off Wireless Ridge and to advance beyond the deserted Moody Brook Barracks towards Stanley. 'D' Company, in the most forward position, came under heavy artillery fire from an Argentine 105mm battery which was dug in near Stanley Racecourse. In addition, a large number of enemy troops were seen to be on the move in an apparent attempt to reinforce Sapper Hill to the south-east, while hundreds more were fleeing towards Stanley itself. 2 PARA requested Harrier support but bad weather precluded such action. In the meantime, Scout XW282 (Greenhalgh/Gammon) had completed its 2 PARA CASEVAC duties on the northern spur of Wireless Ridge, during which both crew members had observed the Argentine defensive positions. Greenhalgh sought clearance to refit his aircraft with SS.11 missiles and to attack "targets of opportunity" close to Stanley. Permission was duly granted and during the sortie John Gammon fired four SS.11's at retreating Argentine infantry ahead of the 2 PARA advance and to silence enemy gun emplacements (two 3 CBAS Scouts followed up to complete the final offensive sortie of the campaign). Squadron activity had reached a frantic pace by midday on 14 June. Continuous calls for CASEVAC flights, urgent replenishment missions, and liaison work, placed a heavy demand on all available helicopters and aircrew, but by 1550Z that day unconfirmed reports told of white flags being raised in Port Stanley (negotiations began later but became protracted).

As the British forces entered Stanley, 656 Sqdn crews flew into Port Stanley Racecourse where several CAB601 UH-1H's were found still to be in flyable condition. Two had been crudely repainted with whitewash for Argentine CASEVAC duties, one of which (AE-409) was "impressed" into service by 656 Sqdn to support 5 Inf Bde. No attempt was made to repaint the UH-1H, but its serial was painted out and replaced by a large "656", that move being to avoid confusion between the "Huey" and Gazelle XX409. The period immediately after the ceasefire enabled 656 Sqdn to take stock of its aircraft. CAT.2 Scout XR628 (the helicopter which had force-landed in MacPhee Pond) was airlifted onto 'Elk' for passage back to the United Kingdom with 3 CBAS, while two Gazelle AH.1's (XW893 and XX444) that had arrived at Port William aboard 'Contender Bezant' for 3 CBAS on 23 June were handed over to 656 Sqdn, as was 3 CBAS Gazelle ZA730. Three Scouts (XP907, XR629, XV141) which had arrived on 27 June aboard 'Astronomer' as Battle Casualty Replacements were also taken onto 656 Sqdn charge. By then, the Squadron had 16 helicopters which comprised Scout AH.1's XP907, XR629, XT637, XT649, XV130, XV139, XV141 and XW282 plus Gazelle AH.1's XW893, XX409, XX444, XZ290, XZ314, XZ321, ZA728

and ZA730, in addition to the CAB601 UH-1H AE-409 which continued to be flown in support of 5 Inf Bde until 13 July (when it was flown by Mike Sharpe onto a Mexeflote at the stern of 'Atlantic Causeway' in San Carlos Water to be returned to the United Kingdom).

By mid-July, Army Air Corps strength on the Falkland Islands had been reduced to Garrison Force size which consisted of eight Scouts AH.1's and four Gazelles AH.1's, so the surplus aircraft were accordingly returned to the United Kingdom. Four Gazelles (XX409, XX444, XZ314 and ZA728) were embarked on 'Tor Caledonia' and dispatched on 31 July along with two Scouts (XT649 and XV130), the latter having been replaced by two new arrivals from the United Kingdom (XV121 and XW799). The Squadron's Operation "Corporate" tour came to an end at the end of July when 657 Sqdn personnel arrived on the Islands. The official change-over date was 2 August when 657 Sqdn simply took over 656 Sqdn's Scouts and Gazelles.

After a period of leave, 656 Sqdn resumed its normal tasking at Netheravon with the two Scouts returned aboard 'Tor Caledonia' plus four more aircraft taken on charge from storage at Wroughton (XP905, XT646, XV124, XW281). Three of the repatriated Gazelles (XX409, XX444 and XZ314) also remained on Squadron strength, later augmented by two new aircraft from store at Wroughton (ZA772 and ZA775).

---

*Aircrew with 656 Sqdn during Operation "Corporate" and their awards:*

### Pilots

*Major C.S.Sibun AAC (OC) MID.*
**Scout Flt:** *Capt S.M.Drennan AAC DFC; Capt J.G.Greenhalgh RCT\* DFC; Lt T.S.Ward-Booth AAC; WO2 M.J.Sharpe AAC MID; Sgt I.Roy RE MID; Sgt R.Kalinski PARA\* MID; Sgt R.J.Walker AAC\* MID.*

**Gazelle Flt:** *Capt A.P.Bourne RA MID; Capt P.G.Piper RA; SSgt C.A.Griffin AAC (KIA); Sgt G.H.Keates REME; Sgt P.G.Moran AAC; Sgt J.R.A.Sutherland AAC.*

### Aircrewmen

**Scout Flt** *(Air Gunners):* *Cpl M.Johns AAC\*; Cpl M.Lord AAC; LCpl S.Cholerton REME\*; LCpl J.Gammon PARA\*; LCpl I.Mousette AAC; LCpl J.J.Rigg AAC MID.*
**Gazelle Flt** *(Observers):* *Sgt K.D.Beveridge AAC; LCpl L.Beresford AAC; LCpl S.J.Cockton AAC (KIA); LCpl J.A.Coley REME; LCpl N.S.Fraser AAC; LCpl S.A.Long AAC.*

---

Scout Pilots and Air Gunners marked * were deployed as the Squadron Advanced Section aboard 'Europic Ferry' (temporarily attached to 3 CBAS from 7 May to 1 June 1982). The remaining Scout personnel travelled south aboard 'Baltic Ferry', while all Gazelle pilots and aircrew sailed south aboard 'Nordic Ferry'. After the arrival in the Falkland Islands of the Squadron Main Party, Lt Ward-Booth was appointed as one of two Brigade Liaison Officers, thus assuming a non-flying role. The second BLO was Capt R.W.Twist, RRF who at that time was the Squadron's second in command. Capt Drennan, who had sailed aboard 'Queen Elizabeth 2' with Major Sibun

(having only joined 656 Sqdn on the day of its departure) replaced Lt Ward-Booth as a pilot with the Scout Flight. WO2 Sharpe also acted as the Sqdn QHI and, following the Argentine surrender, he flew Scouts and Gazelles as well as the impressed Ejercito UH-1H AE-409.

# BATTLE CASUALTY REPLACEMENTS

In order to support the Army and Marine light helicopter force in the Falkland Islands, a number of Gazelle AH.1's and Scout AH.1's were placed to Battle Casualty Replacement (BCR) status. That essentially involved selecting suitable aircraft, nominally in pairs and presumably with low hours since last overhaul, and effecting an immediate modifications update prior to them being sent to Middle Wallop for immediate dispatch to the Task Force.

## GAZELLE AH.1

The first two Gazelles were placed to BCR status on 25 May. XW893 of 658 Sqdn had been earmarked for Northern Ireland duties as part of a decision to increase the permanent establishment of Gazelles in the province from eight to eleven, but ZA773 was released from Wroughton on 25 May to replace it. The second Gazelle (XX444) was one of two ARWS machines that had been processed through Fleetlands over the period 15-19 April for Radar Altimeter fit, the other one (XZ314) having been issued to 656 Sqdn for dispatch aboard 'Nordic Ferry' with the main Squadron party. Both XW893 and XX444 were later conveyed by road from Middle Wallop to Lyneham and departed as airfreight on 27 May, as detailed in the main text (possibly aboard LTW Hercules C.3 XV303 which left for Dakar and Ascension that night). Two more Gazelles (XW849/V and XX450/F) were drawn from ARWS stock and placed to BCR status. XW849 had been at Fleetlands since 5 May undergoing a routine mods programme, while XX450 was flown to Fleetlands for "Corporate" mods on 24 May. Both aircraft were out-shopped on 27 May, returning to Middle Wallop the same day for fitment of I-Band Transponders (XW849 by road due to a faulty clutch). With all ARWS markings removed, both were hangared and deemed "ready to move" on 28 May. Replacement Gazelles ZA737 and ZA768 were subsequently released by Wroughton to ARWS. Finally, on 28 May two additional Gazelles (XW888/C, XW889/D) were flown from Middle Wallop to Fleetlands for Radar Altimeter fit, returning on 2 June for further mods. They completed the Gazelle BCR stock, both being declared "ready to move" at 1800Z on 4 June.

## SCOUT AH.1

As shown in the individual service histories, the initial three BCR Scouts all came from 657 Sqdn, although not in a straightforward manner. XR629 was flown from Oakington to Middle Wallop during May as part of a direct allocation there for modifications (including Nitesun). XV141, earmarked for 657 Sqdn (ex-Wroughton reserve), was flown to Middle Wallop on 5 May for similar mods. Both were declared "ready to move" at 1800Z on 27 May. Third of the initial batch was the ex-3 CBAS Utility Scout XP907, originally allocated to 657 Sqdn in exchange for XV140 but which had in fact been flown to Middle Wallop on 4 April for restoration to ATGW status. That work, along with other mods which included fixtures for flotation equipment, was completed on 4 June. All three helicopters (XP907, XR629 and XV141) left Middle Wallop at 1400Z on 7 June for Devonport and their transit south aboard 'Astronomer'. The second batch of three BCR Scouts included two more 657 Sqdn aircraft. XT644 and XV123 had progressed to Middle Wallop for sundry mods before joining XP907 in being declared "ready to move" on 4 June. The third involved D&T Sqdn Scout AH.1 XT632 which had been placed to BCR stock and deemed as "ready to move" on 28 May.

Two Scouts were also placed at BCR Reserve status and formed part of a contract with Westland Helicopters to embody fixed-fittings for flotation equipment (Mod 1027) in the same manner as XP907. XW799, which had just completed a major overhaul at 70 Aircraft Workshops and had been ferried to Wroughton on 13 May, was dispatched by road to Weston-super-Mare on 20 May. The second (XV121), which had been held in store at Wroughton since arriving from 659 Sqdn on 12 January, was sent to Weston-super-Mare on 3 June for the same flotation equipment fit. XW799 and XV121 returned to Middle Wallop by road on 2 July and 6 July respectively.

With the surrender of Argentine forces on the Falkland Islands on 14 June, the BCR helicopters were stood down. Gazelles XW849 and XX450 stayed at Middle Wallop and were subsequently allotted to 3 CBAS at Yeovilton on 1 July to cover for shortfalls, as all of the Marines aircraft were undergoing major overhauls. XW888 and XW889 simply remained on ARWS charge and resumed their normal training duties. Of the Scouts, XT632 resumed duties with the D&T Sqdn while XT644 and XV123 returned to 657 Sqdn. The latter pair remained within the United Kingdom, despite the fact that Squadron personnel relieved 656 Sqdn in the South Atlantic during August. The two flotation gear equipped Scouts (XW799 and XV121) did progress to the Falkland Islands, however. Following their transfer from Middle Wallop to Lyneham, they were airfreighted out on 11 July by LTW Hercules, to be joined later by several other similarly equipped Scouts.

# INDIVIDUAL AIRCRAFT DETAILS

Under normal circumstances, 3 CBAS aircraft were allotted two-letter call-signs, with Gazelles being prefixed 'C' and Scouts being prefixed 'D'. Codes were derived from the call-signs, but only the second letter was applied to the aircraft in White on the fin (Gazelle) or rear cabin panel (Scout) and repeated in White on the nose panel (although on several Scouts the latter was in Black). The system was devised in such a manner that no two helicopters would have the same second letter. In the individual aircraft details which follow, call-signs/code letters are shown as '(C)K' (taking Gazelle XX376 as an example), indicating that the radio call-sign was 'CK' but that only the letter 'K' was actually carried on the airframe. Suffix letters were permanently allocated to the 3 CBAS flights as follows: 'A' Flight used 'F', 'G' and 'H'; 'C' Flight used 'X', 'Y' and 'Z'; 'M' Flight used 'K', 'L' and 'M'; whilst the Scouts of 'B' Flight used 'P', 'Q', 'R', 'S', 'T' and 'U'. The letters 'A', 'B' and 'C' were reserved for further spare aircraft to cover for temporary shortfalls in Flight strengths, and were generally described as being allotted to HQ Flight. In fact, because Gazelle strength was one short of establishment, the letter 'C' remained vacant until allotted to a captured Agusta A-109A at the end of the campaign. Not surprisingly, some Gazelles were exchanged between Flights at the time of departure which upset the normally strict sequence of Flight radio call-sign allocation.

656 Sqdn, on the other hand, did not use code letters. They used radio call-signs instead which were assigned to pilots rather than helicopters. The three Advanced Section Scouts were allotted, and carried, a locally-devised code sequence, but that was abandoned when the Section was absorbed into 3 CBAS operational control, whereupon they adopted two-letter codes and call-signs within the sequence detailed above. When 656 Sqdn entered the battle, pilot/aircraft call-signs were allotted within the sequence '1A', '1B' etc for the Gazelle Flight and '2A', '2B' etc for the Scout Flight, but no external evidence of those combinations appeared on the aircraft.

Instructions to erase external markings by overpainting were complied with immediately before departure from the United Kingdom. That included, on 3 CBAS Scouts, the application of a Matt Black rectangular block over the White ROYAL MARINES legend and code letters. There were, of course, exceptions and slight variations. The fact that the work was carried out at NASU Yeovilton over the weekend of 3/4 April probably accounted for XP902 escaping the treatment (as it was undergoing an ECU

change at Middle Wallop at the time). A subsequent and half-hearted attempt was made to scratch out the White lettering on XP902, but it was still very much in evidence throughout the campaign. Unit pride probably accounted for the fact that the two ex-657 Sqdn Scout AH.1's had their ARMY legend "blocked out" in Matt Black, but it was thought that (initially at least) one of them operated with only the letters 'A' and 'Y' erased. The tail rotor danger warning was also "blocked out" on all Scouts except XP902, although the tail rotors themselves retained their high-visibility Black and White stripes. A subsequent and further variation was to befall Scout XR627 as a result of the Ajax Bay incident. Initially, all markings had been "blocked out" in the United Kingdom in accordance with earlier instructions, but after shrapnel damage to its boom had been repaired, the Black/Green camouflage pattern was restored by crude brush painting over the erased titles. The removal of code letters from Scouts produced a fleet of virtually anonymous aircraft (except for XW616 whose nose code 'P' remained in evidence throughout), so full two-letter call-signs were applied in Black just below the starboard windscreen panel. The three 656 Sqdn Advanced Section Scouts used the 'D' sequence, their codes ranging between 'DN' and 'DV'. Some of those code letters suffered from weathering, however, and only very close scrutiny of XW615 at the end of the campaign revealed that it had at one stage carried the code 'DS'.

Some of the 3 CBAS Gazelles had earlier been given Black ROYAL MARINES titles with only their fin codes remaining White. Those helicopters were also treated to a similar toning down of external markings, however. For Operation "Corporate", all White lettering and codes were overpainted in Matt Black although fin and nose letters still remained visible after that treatment. XZ326 retained its previous ARWS code 'W' as that did not duplicate any existing 3 CBAS code, but the ARMY legend on its boom was "blocked out" in Green. The 656 Sqdn Gazelles required no alteration to their external colours or markings and operated as normal. One notable exception, however, was ZA730. In the same manner as XZ326, it had the ROYAL MARINES titles "blocked out" in Green, but after transfer from 3 CBAS to 656 Sqdn in June 1982, ARMY titling was superimposed in Black over the Green block. ZA730 operated in that manner until after its return to the United Kingdom in December 1983.

---

## GAZELLE

**XW893 AH.1**

On 29.3.82 with 658 Sqdn at Netheravon, uncoded. Flown to Fleetlands for Phase I/II mods update 13.4.82, then allotted to the

Northern Ireland Regt but not delivered. Flown instead to Middle Wallop on 24.5.82 and assigned to BCR 25.5.82 with immediate issue to 3 CBAS as a replacement for XX402. Taken to Lyneham by road 27.5.82, departing the same day by LTW Hercules for Ascension where it was immediately transferred to 'Contender Bezant' for departure 3.6.82. Off-loaded at Port Stanley on 18.6.82 and

delivered to 3 CBAS for 'A' Flight, call-sign (CX) allotted although no code applied externally (note that the call-sign would normally apply to 'C' Flt aircraft). With the pending return of 3 CBAS to the UK, it was transferred to 656 Sqdn and flown from Port Stanley to Fitzroy 23.6.82. Handed over to 657 Sqdn on 2.8.82 until 2.12.82 when formally issued to the Garrison Army Air Sqdn

FI. That allocation covered operations by 658 Sqdn, 651 Sqdn and 654 Sqdn. Departed Port Stanley 10.4.84 aboard 'Sand Shore', arriving at Marchwood 5.5.84. Off-loaded 8.5.84 and removed by road to Middle Wallop 9.5.84 for survey.

## XX376 AH.1

On 29.3.82 with 3 CBAS 'M' Flt at Arbroath coded '(C)K'. Flown to Marchwood on 5.4.82 for loading aboard 'Sir Percivale', sailing with the ship the next day. Flown off to Ascension 20.4.82 to have SNEB 68mm rocket pack fitted. Resumed transit to Falklands on 30.4.82 aboard LSL 'Sir Percivale' for Operation "Sutton". Transferred to 'C' Flight 22.5.82 to compensate for "D-Day" losses (no call-sign change). Loaded aboard 'Elk' 23.6.82 at the conclusion of the campaign, returning to Devonport 12.7.82. Collected by MARTSU 14.7.82 and taken to Netheravon, arriving there by 15.7.82 on 70 Aircraft Workshops REME transport. To Middle Wallop on 3.8.82 for major overhaul and repair.

## XX377 AH.1

On 29.3.82 with 3 CBAS coded '(C)L' (and in theory allocated to 'M' Flight) but was midway through a major modification programme at Fleetlands. Earmarked for the Northern Ireland Regiment as part of a planned increase in Gazelle establishment in Ulster (but still officially to remain on 3 CBAS strength). Reportedly delivered from Fleetlands to Ulster 26.4.82. Reallocated to 656 Sqdn (believed due to its high mod-state), collected by the unit from Middle Wallop 29.4.82 and flown to Netheravon. *(XZ320/T of ARWS was later issued to the Northern Ireland Regt as its replacement, being replaced within ARWS by XZ340 ex-656 Sqdn)* Flown to Southampton docks 8.5.82 from Netheravon for loading aboard 'Nordic Ferry', sailing with the ship on 9.5.82. Off-loaded to Clam Valley near San Carlos settlement 3.6.82.

Tasked to take spares and fuel from Goose Green to Mount Pleasant Peak 6.6.82 where a REBRO Station had become unserviceable. Whilst still 2 miles south of the peak it sustained a missile strike (unconfirmed reports suggest that a British ship had fired the missile). Flying at between 70 and 200ft AGL at the time, it crashed immediately. All four occupants, SSgt Griffin (pilot), LCpl Cockton (aircrewman), Major Forge (Signals Sqdn CO) and SSgt Baker (Signals Sqdn) were killed on impact. *(NB: XX377 was the only 656 Sqdn Gazelle not fitted with a SNEB 68mm rocket pack).*

## XX380 AH.1

On 29.3.82 with 3 CBAS 'M' Flt, probably at Arbroath, coded '(C)M'. Had progressed to Plymouth by 5.4.82 when it was flown to Marchwood (via Middle Wallop) for loading aboard 'Sir Percivale', sailing later that day. Flown off to Ascension 20.4.82 to have SNEB 68mm rocket pack fitted. Resumed transit to the Falklands on 30.4.82 aboard 'Sir Percivale' for Operation "Sutton". At the conclusion of the campaign it was loaded aboard 'Elk' 23/24.6.82 for return to the UK, arriving at Devonport 12.7.82. Collected by MARTSU 14.7.82 for transport by road to

Netheravon, where it arrived on 15.7.82. To Middle Wallop on 3.8.82 for major overhaul and repair.

## XX402 AH.1

On 29.3.82 with 3 CBAS 'A' Flt at Coypool coded '(C)G'. Transferred to 'C' Flt and flown aboard 'Sir Galahad' at Devonport on 5.4.82, sailing with the ship the next day. Flown off to Ascension c20.4.82 to have SNEB 68mm rocket pack fitted. Resumed transit to the Falklands on 30.4.82 aboard 'Sir Galahad' for Operation "Sutton". Fitted with a GPMG in the port doorway for self-defence purposes.

Immediately following the loss of XX411 to enemy small-arms fire on 21.5.82, it was sent to the Port San Carlos area to obtain more information about those Argentine positions. While flying at 70ft AGL, it was hit from starboard and below by small-arms fire from Compania 'C' of RgtInf25 (the same Argentine unit which had brought down XX411) and crashed into a hillside near Clam Creek (UC 640922). The pilot (Lt Francis) and aircrewman (LCpl Griffin) were both killed.

## XX409 AH.1

On 29.3.82 with ARWS at Middle Wallop coded 'AA'. Delivered to Netheravon 23.4.82 for 656 Sqdn and then flown to Southampton docks on 8.5.82 for loading aboard 'Nordic Ferry', sailing with the ship next day. Off-loaded to Clam Valley, San Carlos on 3.6.82. At the conclusion of 656 Sqdn's tour it was loaded aboard 'Tor Caledonia' for return to the UK. Sailed with the ship from Port William on 1.8.82, arriving at Felixstowe 20.8.82 with a damaged canopy, presumably sustained after the Argentine surrender. Taken by road to Netheravon 21.8.82 for storage until transferred to Middle Wallop during 10.82 for overhaul and repair.

## XX411 AH.1

On 29.3.82 with 3 CBAS 'C' Flt at Coypool coded '(C)X'. Flown aboard 'Sir Galahad' at Devonport 5.4.82, sailing with the ship the next day. Flown off to Ascension c20.4.82 to have SNEB 68mm rocket pack fitted. Resumed transit to the Falklands aboard 'Sir Galahad' 30.4.82 for Operation "Sutton". For self-defence purposes a GPMG was fitted in the port doorway with both of the port doors removed.

On 21.5.82, whilst being flown by Sgt Evans (pilot) and Sgt Candlish (observer), it was tasked to act as an armed escort for 846 Sqdn Sea King HC.4 ZA296 which was taking supplies ashore. As the two aircraft passed Fanning Head and Hospital Point and beyond Port San Carlos settlement, the Sea King crew realised their error in being too far forward and broke off to the west. The Gazelle crew did not realise what had happened until it was too late. As their aircraft turned to port it was hit in the tail rotor and engine/gearbox area by small-arms fire from an Ejercito unit, Compania 'C' of RgtInf25. Sgt Evans ditched the helicopter successfully into Port San Carlos (approximately UC 632922), despite having been wounded, and both aircrew were able to scramble clear and swim ashore before it sank. Unfortunately, the pilot later died from

his wounds.

The wreck of XX411 was lifted from the sea and taken to Port Stanley during 10.82 (possibly by Chinook) for a survey by 657 Sqdn, after which it was loaded aboard the 'Sapele' for shipment to the UK. The ship arrived at Hull on 5.11.82 and the wreck was taken by road to Middle Wallop 7.11.82 where it was allocated to Battle Damage Repair. The fenestron and SNEB aimer ("candle") were used in a Falklands display at the Museum of Army Flying, the former subsequently being passed on to the Fleet Air Arm Museum.

## XX412 AH.1

On 29.3.82 with 3 CBAS 'C' Flt at Coypool coded '(C)Y'. Flown aboard 'Sir Galahad' at Devonport 5.4.82, sailing with the ship the next day. Flown off to Wideawake c20.4.82 for fitting of SNEB 68mm rocket pack. Resumed transit to the Falklands aboard 'Sir Galahad' 30.4.82 for Operation "Sutton". For self-defence it was fitted with a GPMG in the rear port doorway.

Damaged by enemy surface-to-air fire near Port San Carlos on 21.5.82, but immediate temporary repairs were carried out after its return to 'Sir Galahad' (the tail rotor was replaced and bullet holes were masked, enabling it to continue operations). It amassed the highest total of flying hours for the type (143.7) during the period of the conflict.

At the conclusion of the campaign it was loaded aboard 'Elk' on 23.6.82 and returned to Devonport 12.7.82. Collected by MARTSU 14.7.82 for conveyance to Netheravon, where it arrived by 70 Aircraft Workshops REME transport on 15.7.82. Taken by road to Middle Wallop 20.7.82 for display at "Army Air 82" in damaged condition and subsequently repaired by 70 Aircraft Workshops REME.

## XX413 AH.1

On 29.3.82 with 3 CBAS 'M' Flt at Arbroath coded '(C)Z', although theoretically a 'C' Flt machine (no doubt acting as a temporary replacement for XX377 while the latter was at Fleetlands). Flown to Middle Wallop on 4.4.82 and then to Marchwood on 5.4.82 for loading aboard 'Sir Percivale', sailing with the ship that day for Lyme Bay. Flown from the ship to Lee-on-Solent and back on 6.4.82. Flown off to Ascension 20.4.82 for fitting of SNEB 68mm rocket pack. Resumed its transit to the Falklands aboard 'Sir Percivale' 30.4.82 for Operation "Sutton". At the conclusion of the campaign it was loaded aboard 'Elk' on 23.6.82 and returned to Devonport 12.7.82. Collected by MARTSU 14.7.82 for conveyance to Netheravon where it arrived on 15.7.82. Taken by road to Middle Wallop 29.7.82 for major overhaul and repair.

## XX444 AH.1

On 29.3.82 with ARWS at Middle Wallop coded 'K'. Flown to Fleetlands 15.4.82 to have a Radar Altimeter fitted. Out-shopped on 19.4.82 and returned to ARWS charge but not subsequently flown by the unit. Along with XW893, placed to Battle Casualty Replacement stock (replaced at ARWS by ZA769). Released to 3 CBAS to replace XX411 and conveyed to Lyneham by road on

XX411/(C)X Gazelle AH.1 of 3 CBAS at the Beaver Slipway, Stanley on 20.10.82 after being recovered from Port San Carlos where it had been shot down by enemy small-arms fire during a recce tasking on 21.5.82. Of interest are the rear seat belts that had been tightly knotted in order not to interfere with the floor-mounted GPMG, nor to flap uncontrollably during 'doors-off' operations. Although damage was extensive as a result of the crash, salt corrosion was later found to have been minimal.

(Richard Gardner)

XW849 Gazelle AH.1 was for a short period designated as a Battle Casualty Replacement towards the latter stages of "Corporate" but was not, in fact, shipped south. Seen here at RAF Wyton 31.7.82 whilst on 3 CBAS charge (but still with ARMY titling) '849 displays all of the essential campaign modifications: IR Shield to deflect exhaust heat, stores boom with SNEB 68mm rocket pod, missile "candle" aiming post, and flotation pack attached to the landing skids. (Peter J. Cooper)

**Left** XX412 Gazelle AH.1 of 3 CBAS 'C' Flight displays, at Middle Wallop 24.7.82 several "Corporate" modifications; the protective GPMG in the port doorway and the SNEB 68mm rocket pod. The outer clasp is used for holding 4in slow-falling flares (more usually known as "Wallop Bangers") but these were not used. **Centre** Aiming of rockets by the crew was achieved by lining up a scratch mark on the canopy with a plastic "candle" mounted on the ARC340 aerial. **Right** Single action or ripple firing of rockets was controlled from a panel hastily added to the main cockpit instrument display, as seen on XX411.

(Peter J. Cooper (centre); Michael I. Draper (left/right))

*Within ten days of the Argentine surrender units of 3rd Commando Brigade RM began returning to the United Kingdom. In this view an unidentified 846 Squadron Sea King HC.4 lifts a 3CBAS Gazelle AH.1 (believed to be XX413/(C)Z) from Port Stanley Racecourse to 'Elk' on 23.6.82. Another Gazelle AH.1 (ZA776/(C)H) awaits transfer whilst to the left can be seen the Bell 212 H-83.*

(Lt D. Balchin, RN)

27.5.82 for airlift to Wideawake by Hercules, leaving the same day. Transferred to 'Contender Bezant', sailing from Ascension on 28.5.82. Delivered to 3 CBAS 'A' Flt on 18.6.82 and allocated call-sign (CE). Transferred to 656 Sqdn and flown from Port Stanley to Fitzroy 23.6.82. At the conclusion of the Squadron's tour, it was loaded aboard 'Tor Caledonia' for return to the UK. Sailed with the ship from Port William on 1.8.82, arriving at Felixstowe on 20.8.82. Taken by road to Netheravon on 21.8.82.

*While on operations in the Falkland Islands it received the logo "One Eye The Wasp" [see 829 Sqdn]*

### XZ290 AH.1

On 29.3.82 with ARWS at Middle Wallop coded 'J'. Delivered to Netheravon 27.4.82 for 656 Sqdn. Flown to Southampton docks on 8.5.82 for loading aboard 'Nordic Ferry', sailing with the ship 9.5.82. Off-loaded 3.6.82 to Clam Valley, San Carlos. At the conclusion of the campaign, handed over to 657 Sqdn on 2.8.82 and later to the Garrison Army Air Sqdn FI on 2.12.82. That allocation was to cover subsequent operations by 658 Sqdn, 651 Sqdn and 654 Sqdn. Returned to the UK aboard 'Fin Siff', arriving at Portsmouth 26.7.84. Off-loaded for overnight parking at Lee-on-Solent and conveyed by road to 70 Aircraft Workshops REME at Middle Wallop on 27.7.84 for engine removal and survey.

### XZ314 AH.1

On 29.3.82 with ARWS at Middle Wallop coded 'O'. Flown to Fleetlands 15.4.82 to have a Radar Altimeter fitted. Out-shopped on 19.4.82 to Middle Wallop and delivered to 656 Sqdn 22.4.82 in exchange for XZ332 (by which time the ARWS code had been removed). Flown from Netheravon to Southampton docks 8.5.82 for loading aboard 'Nordic Ferry', sailing with the ship the next day. Off-loaded to Clam Valley, San Carlos on 3.6.82.

Suffered slight damage at Estancia House on 13.6.82 during an attack by Grupo 5 Skyhawks.

On completion of 656 Sqdn's tour of duty, it was loaded aboard 'Tor Caledonia' for return to the UK. Sailed with the ship from Port William on 1.8.82, arriving at Felixstowe 20.8.82. Taken by road to Netheravon on 21.8.82.

### XZ321 AH.1

On 29.3.82 with ARWS at Middle Wallop coded 'Z'. Code removed, it was delivered to Netheravon 21.4.82 for 656 Sqdn in exchange for XZ346. Flown to Southampton docks on 8.5.82 for loading aboard 'Nordic Ferry', sailing with the ship 9.5.82. Off-loaded to Clam Valley, San Carlos on 3.6.82. At the conclusion of the campaign, it was handed over to 657 Sqdn on 2.8.82, then subsequently to the Garrison Army Air Sqdn FI (that allocation

covering operations by 658 Sqdn, 651 Sqdn and 654 Sqdn). Eventually loaded aboard the 'Sand Shore' 24.12.83 for shipment to the UK, arriving at Marchwood 24.1.84 prior to transfer by road to Middle Wallop on 25.1.84 for a survey. Taken to Wroughton by road 1.2.84.

*At some stage during its Falklands tour, the serial was applied in Dayglo Red beside the starboard fuel filler inlet.*

### XZ326 AH.1

On 29.3.82 with ARWS at Middle Wallop coded 'W'. Having fixed fittings for flotation equipment, it was issued to 3 CBAS 3.4.82 to make up for a shortfall in their Gazelle establishment (flown from Middle Wallop to Coypool for 'A' Flt that day). The fact that it also had the uprated Astazou IIIN2 engine was apparently overlooked in the haste to dispatch the RM force and thus this Gazelle was "non-standard" to 3 CBAS. Flown aboard 'Sir Geraint' at Devonport on 5.4.82, sailing with the ship the next day. The Dayglo Red ARWS fin patch was removed and the aircraft coded '(C)W' (the code letter 'W' being applied to the nose in Black). Flown off to Ascension c20.4.82 to have a SNEB 68mm rocket pack fitted.

Experienced a total engine failure 29.4.82 while flying over the sea off Ascension and force-landed on the beach, suffering minor damage. It was airlifted to 'Sir Geraint' by Sea

359

King for repairs to a faulty gauge.

Resumed its transit aboard 'Sir Geraint' on 30.4.82 until transferred to 'Sir Tristram' 20.5.82 for Operation "Sutton".

Damaged by the down draught from an 18 Sqdn Chinook at Port Stanley on 17.6.82 and declared CAT.3. Loaded aboard 'Elk' on 23.6.82 for return to the UK, arriving at Devonport on 12.7.82. Collected by MARTSU on 14.7.82, but taken by road to Middle Wallop by 70 Aircraft Workshops REME transport where it arrived 15.7.82 for major overhaul and repair.

## ZA728 AH.1

On 29.3.82 with 3 CBAS HQ Flt at Coypool coded '(C)A'. Not shipped with the main CBAS group, reportedly due to lack of space aboard the LSL's. Temporarily stored at Bickleigh until flown to Netheravon 19.4.82 for 656 Sqdn (XZ329 acting as crew-ferry), thence to Middle Wallop for final attention by 70 Aircraft Workshops. Believed to have received a replacement boom at that stage which would explain the "clean removal" of ROYAL MARINES titles and the adoption of ARMY instead. Returned to Netheravon on 22.4.82 and then flown to Southampton docks 8.5.82 for loading aboard 'Nordic Ferry', sailing with the ship the next day. Off-loaded to Clam Valley, San Carlos on 3.6.82.

Sustained slight damage at the Port San Carlos Harrier FOB on 9.6.82 during a rotors-running refuelling. On 13.6.82 it was flown to a position near Estancia House for crew briefing prior to flying forward to Two Sisters and Mount Harriet. The area was attacked by Grupo 5 A-4B Skyhawks some 15 minutes after it had landed. Bomb blast shattered the cockpit perspex and damaged the fin and rear boom area. Airlifted back to San Carlos for repairs; the boom and fin were repaired overnight but canopy perspex did not become available until mid-7.82 so the Gazelle was grounded.

Flown aboard 'Tor Caledonia' on 29.7.82 for return to the UK. Sailed with the ship from Port William on 1.8.82, arriving at Felixstowe on 20.8.82. Removed by road to Netheravon on 21.8.82 for temporary storage, then transferred by road to Middle Wallop on 13.10.82 for a major overhaul and repairs by 70 Aircraft Workshops REME.

## ZA730 AH.1

On 29.3.82 with 3 CBAS 'A' Flt at Coypool coded '(C)F'. Flown aboard 'Sir Geraint' at Devonport on 5.4.82, sailing with the ship the next day. Flown off to Ascension c20.4.82 to have a SNEB 68mm rocket pack fitted, resuming transit to the Falklands aboard 'Sir Geraint' 30.4.82 until transferred to 'Sir Tristram' on 20.5.82 for Operation "Sutton". Transferred to 656 Sqdn at the end of the campaign and delivered from Stanley to Fitzroy 23.6.82 (reportedly due to there being insufficient space for it aboard 'Elk'). Subsequently transferred to 657 Sqdn on 2.8.82 and later to the Garrison Army Air Sqdn FI on 2.12.82 (that allocation covering subsequent operations by 658 Sqdn, 651 Sqdn and 654 Sqdn). Eventually shipped back to the UK, arriving at Middle Wallop 16.12.83. Af-

ter a survey by 70 Aircraft Workshops it was transferred by road to Wroughton for storage on 10.1.84.

## ZA776 AH.1

On 29.3.82 with 3 CBAS 'A' Flt at Coypool coded '(C)H'. Flown aboard 'Sir Geraint' at Devonport on 5.4.82, sailing with the ship the next day. Flown off to Ascension c20.4.82 to have a SNEB 68mm rocket pack fitted. Resumed transit to the Falklands 30.4.82 aboard 'Sir Geraint' until transferred to 'Sir Tristram' on 20.5.82 for Operation "Sutton". At the end of the campaign it was loaded aboard 'Elk' on 23.6.82 and departed 24.6.82 for the UK. Arrived at Devonport 12.7.82 and collected by MARTSU 14.7.82 for transfer by road to Netheravon, where it arrived on 16.7.82. Taken to Middle Wallop by road on 26.7.82 for a major overhaul and repair.

---

## SCOUT

### XP902 AH.1

On 29.3.82 with 3 CBAS 'B' Flt at Coypool coded '(D)T'. Flown to Middle Wallop on 3.4.82 for an ECU and AF120 Sight change. Flown aboard 'Fearless' at Portsmouth on 6.4.82 for transit to Ascension. Full code 'DT' applied in Black and all other marks partially erased by "scraping". Transferred to 'Sir Tristram' on 28.4.82 for transit south to the Falklands, moving again 20.5.82 to 'Stromness' for Operation "Sutton". At the end of the campaign it was loaded aboard 'Elk' on 23/24.6.82 and returned to the UK, arriving at Devonport on 12.7.82. Taken by road to Netheravon 14.7.82 and later by road to Wroughton on 3.9.82 for storage.

### XP907 AH.1

On 29.3.82 with 3 CBAS 'B' Flt at Coypool coded '(D)U' (utility variant). Flown to Yeovilton 4.4.82 and allotted to 657 Sqdn in exchange for ATGW variant XV140. Flown to Middle Wallop 4.4.82 for restoration to ATGW status by MARTSU, involving replacement of the entire cabin with that from XR630 (ex-AETW Battle Damage). Allotment to 657 Sqdn later cancelled; placed to BCR. Released to 3 CBAS and taken to Devonport 7.6.82 for shipment aboard 'Astronomer' as a replacement for XT629, but issued to 656 Sqdn upon arrival at Port William 27.6.82 as a replacement for XR628. At the end of 656 Sqdn's tour it was handed over to 657 Sqdn on 2.8.82 until transferred to the Garrison Army Air Sqdn FI on 2.12.82 for operation by 658 Sqdn personnel. With the arrival of 651 Sqdn (personnel and Lynx AH.1's) during 6.83, it was loaded aboard 'Sir Geraint' and sailed with the ship from Port Stanley 10.6.83 to arrive at Marchwood c4.7.83. Taken by road to Middle Wallop 4.7.83 for survey by 70 Aircraft Workshops. Remained at Middle Wallop until loaned to 658 Sqdn early in 1984.

### XR627 AH.1

On 29.3.82 with 3 CBAS 'B' Flt at Coypool coded '(D)Q'. Flown to Yeovilton on 4.4.82 for mods and removal of codes before being flown aboard 'Fearless' at Portsmouth on 6.4.82 for transit to Ascension. Full code 'DQ' applied in Matt Black. Transferred to

'Sir Tristram' on 28.4.82, but returned to 'Fearless' 29.4.82 for onward transit to the Falklands. Transferred to 'Europic Ferry' 11.5.82 for use by the 656 Sqdn Detachment, remaining aboard the ship for Operation "Sutton".

Sustained slight shrapnel damage on 27.5.82 whilst undergoing a gearbox change at Ajax Bay (repaired by 30.5.82, its boom brush-painted to restore the camouflage pattern but service titling was not reapplied).

At the end of the campaign it was loaded aboard 'Elk' on 23/24.6.82, returning to Devonport on 12.7.82. Taken by road to Netheravon 14.7.82 and later to Wroughton on 3.9.82 for storage. During a major inspection at Wroughton late-1983, shrapnel (presumably from the Ajax Bay incident) was found still to be lodged in the rear cabin area.

### XR628 AH.1

On 29.3.82 with 656 Sqdn at Netheravon, uncoded. Flown to Southampton docks 21.4.82 and dispatched aboard 'Europic Ferry' on 22.4.82 as part of the Squadron Advanced Section. Coded 'C' in Dayglo Red 23.4.82. 'Europic Ferry' arrived at Freetown 2.5.82, departed 4.5.82 and arrived off Ascension 7.5.82 (on which date the Section was re-titled 5 Flt/3 CBAS). Recoded 'DO' in Matt Black and departed Ascension 7.5.82, still aboard 'Europic Ferry'. Flown to 'Elk' on 11.5.82 for covered storage until 17.5.82 when returned to 'Europic Ferry'. Positioned ashore 26.5.82 but reverted to 656 Sqdn charge on 1.6.82.

Made a forced-landing in MacPhee Pond, East Falkland on 8.6.82, where it was temporarily abandoned until airlifted to Fitzroy by 846 Sqdn Sea King HC.4 on 11.6.82 and then on to San Carlos settlement on 13.6.82.

Declared CAT.2 and placed aboard 'Elk' in 23/24.6.82 for return to the UK. Arrived at Devonport on 12.7.82 and collected by MARTSU 14.7.82 for transport to Netheravon, where it arrived by 70 Aircraft Workshops REME transport on 15.7.82. Taken by road to Wroughton on 2.9.82 for storage.

### XR629 AH.1

On 29.3.82 with 657 Sqdn at Oakington. Flown to Middle Wallop for mods (which included Nitesun) on 27.5.82 and allotted to BCR the same day. Conveyed to Devonport on 7.6.82, loaded aboard 'Astronomer' and left with the ship on 8.6.82. Issued to 656 Sqdn upon arrival at Port William 27.6.82. Transferred to 657 Sqdn 2.8.82 until issued to the Garrison Army Air Sqdn FI on 2.12.82 (at that time operated by personnel from 658 Sqdn). With the arrival of 651 Sqdn (personnel and Lynx AH.1's) during 6.83, it was loaded aboard 'Sir Geraint' and sailed with the ship from Port Stanley on 10.6.83, arriving at Marchwood c4.7.83. Taken by road to Middle Wallop on 4.7.83 for a survey by 70 Aircraft Workshops prior to transfer by road to Wroughton for storage on 2.8.83.

### XT629 AH.1

On 29.3.82 with 3 CBAS 'B' Flt at Coypool

656 Squadron Scout AH.1 XT649/DN displays well the hastily applied call-sign beneath the starboard windscreen panel. Of the Squadron's Scouts only the three Advanced Section examples adopted codes/call-signs with the 3 CBAS sequence. '649 escaped battle damage and remained on Squadron strength after 656 returned to Netheravon where this view was taken on 24.8.82. To the left can be seen XV130 while in the background are Gazelles XZ314 and XX444.
(Peter J. Cooper)

ZA728 Gazelle AH.1 of 656 Squadron at Netheravon on 24.8.82 after its return from the Falklands with obvious signs of battle damage repairs. On 13.6.82 '728 had sustained shrapnel and blast damage and the three fin patches bear witness to repairs by the San Carlos AMG. An almost certain disaster had been avoided earlier when, on 9.6.82, '728 had a close shave with an Air Portable Fuel Cell which damaged the vertical stablizer (see inset view).(Peter J. Cooper)

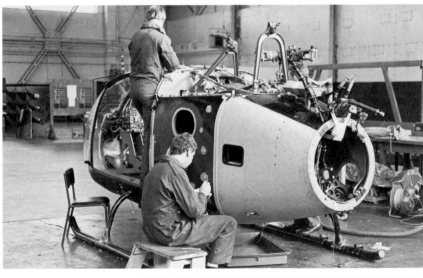

ZA728 Gazelle AH.1 finally entered 70 Aircraft Workshops, REME at Middle Wallop on 13.10.82 for a 'Post "Corporate" Overhaul and Repair' and is seen here midway through that programme which virtually involved a complete rebuild. Subsequently it emerged with full 3 CBAS insignia for return to ROYAL MARINES charge.
(Michael I. Draper)

coded '(D)R'. Flown to Yeovilton on 4.4.82 for mods and removal of codes before being flown aboard 'Fearless' at Portsmouth on 6.4.82 for transit to Ascension. Full code 'DR' applied in Matt Black. Transferred to 'Sir Tristram' on 28.4.82 but returned to 'Fearless' 29.4.82. Cross-ferried to 'Elk' c11.5.82 for storage below decks. Moved from 'Elk' to 'Europic Ferry' 17.5.82 until positioned aboard 'Stromness' 20.5.82 for Operation "Sutton".

Whilst being positioned for a CASEVAC task to the Goose Green area it was shot down less than 1 mile south-east of Camilla Creek House (UC 656649) on 28.5.82 by a Grupo 3 Pucara flown by Teniente Gimenez (almost certainly A-537). The pilot (Lt Nunn) was killed while the aircrewman (Sgt Belcher) was injured. The wreckage was used for spares recovery during the remainder of the conflict and remained "in situ" until 12.8.84 when it was airlifted (in three loads) by Scout AH.1 XR632 (WO2 W Couper/SSgt Douglas) and dropped into Grantham Sound, approximately one mile east of Rabbit Island.

**XT637 AH.1**

On 29.3.82 in storage at Wroughton. Released to 656 Sqdn on 16.4.82 to replace XT626. Flown to Southampton docks from Netheravon on 21.4.82 and departed aboard 'Europic Ferry' 22.4.82 as part of the Sqdn Advanced Section. Coded 'F' in Dayglo Red on 23.4.82. 'Europic Ferry' arrived at Freetown on 2.5.82, departed on 4.5.82 and arrived off Ascension 7.5.82 (on which date the Section was retitled 5 Flt/3 CBAS). Recoded 'DV' in Matt Black. Left Ascension 7.5.82, still aboard 'Europic Ferry'. Flown to 'Elk' on 11.5.82 for covered storage until 17.5.82 when it returned to 'Europic Ferry'. Positioned ashore 26.5.82 but reverted to 656 Sqdn HQ charge on 1.6.82.

Sustained blast and shrapnel damage to its top canopy and rear boom 13.6.82 during an attack by Grupo 5 Skyhawks at Estancia House. Airlifted by Sea King to San Carlos that day for repair by the 70 Aircraft Workshops Detachment. Resumed operations with 656 Sqdn some days later.

Handed over to 657 Sqdn on 2.8.82 until transferred to the Garrison Army Air Sqdn FI on 2.12.82 (at that time manned by 658 Sqdn personnel). With the arrival of 651 Sqdn (personnel and Lynx AH.1's) during 6.83, it was loaded aboard 'Sir Geraint' and sailed with the ship from Port Stanley 10.6.83, arriving at Marchwood c4.7.83. Taken by road to Middle Wallop on 4.7.83 for a survey by 70 Aircraft Workshops prior to transfer by road to storage at Wroughton on 2.8.83.

**XT649 AH.1**

On 29.3.82 with 656 Sqdn at Netheravon. Flown to Southampton docks on 21.4.82 and sailed aboard 'Europic Ferry' 22.4.82 as part of the Squadron Advanced Section. Coded 'A' in Dayglo Red 23.4.82. The ship arrived at Freetown on 2.5.82, left 4.5.82 and arrived off Ascension 7.5.82 (on which date the Section was retitled 5 Flt/3 CBAS). Recoded 'DN' in Matt Black. Sailed from Ascension aboard 'Europic Ferry' on 7.5.82. Flown to 'Elk' 11.5.82 for covered storage, returning to

'Europic Ferry' on 17.5.82. Positioned ashore 26.5.82 but reverted to 656 Sqdn charge on 1.6.82. At the end of the Squadron's tour it was embarked on 'Tor Caledonia' 29.7.82, sailing with the ship for the UK from Port William on 1.8.82. Arrived at Felixstowe on 20.8.82 and taken by road to Netheravon on 21.8.82. Following routine servicing and repairs, it returned to 656 Sqdn, remaining in strength until replaced by a Lynx AH.1. Flown to Wroughton on 3.11.83 for storage.

**XV130 AH.1**

On 29.3.82 with 656 Sqdn at Netheravon. Flown to Southampton Docks 8.5.82 and dispatched aboard 'Baltic Ferry' on 9.5.82. Offloaded at San Carlos settlement 1.6.82.

Sustained damage from Chinook down draught at Fitzroy 16.6.82. Airlifted aboard 'Tor Caledonia' by 820 Sqdn Sea King HAS.5 c29.7.82 for return to the UK, arriving at Felixstowe on 20.8.82 and taken by road to Netheravon 21.8.82. Following routine servicing and repairs, it returned to 656 Sqdn, remaining on strength until replaced by a Lynx AH.1. Ferried to Wroughton 3.11.83 for storage.

**XV139 AH.1**

On 29.3.82 with 656 Sqdn at Netheravon. Flown to Southampton docks 8.4.82 and dispatched aboard 'Baltic Ferry' 9.4.82. Offloaded at San Carlos 1.6.82.

On 9.6.82 during a tasking to Port Harriet House, it was fired at and narrowly missed by an Argentine Blowpipe missile which passed within 25 yards and impacted into nearby ground. The pilot (Sgt Roy) was later presented with the remains of the Blowpipe as a war trophy.

Handed over to 657 Sqdn on 2.8.82 but, with the arrival during 12.82 of 658 Sqdn as the Garrison Army Air Sqdn FI, it was picketed out at Port Stanley to await shipment back to the UK. Eventually embarked on 'Baltic Ferry' during 3.83, arriving at Felixstowe on 12.4.83. Taken by road to Middle Wallop 13.4.83 for survey by 70 Aircraft Workshops prior to transfer by road to storage at Wroughton on 27.4.83.

**XV140 AH.1**

On 29.3.82 with 657 Sqdn at Oakington. Flown to Yeovilton 4.4.82 upon issue to 3 CBAS as a replacement for XP907. Flown to Marchwood 5.4.82 for loading aboard 'Sir Lancelot', sailing with the ship that day for Ascension. Coded 'DU' in Matt Black with ARMY titles blocked out in Matt Black. A Radar Altimeter was fitted aboard 'Sir Lancelot' between 1.5.82 and 3.5.82, prior to Operation "Sutton". At the conclusion of the campaign it was loaded aboard 'Elk' on 23/24.6.82 and returned to Devonport 12.7.82. Collected by MARTSU 14.7.82 for conveyance to Netheravon, where it arrived (by 70 Aircraft Workshops REME low-loader) 15.7.82. Taken by road to Wroughton 2.9.82 for storage.

**XV141 AH.1**

On 29.3.82 in storage at Wroughton. Released

to 657 Sqdn and flown to Middle Wallop 5.5.82 for mods update. Placed to BCR stock and declared "ready to move" on 27.5.82. Taken by road to Devonport 7.6.82 for loading aboard 'Astronomer', sailing with the ship on 8.6.82. Issued to 656 Sqdn on arrival at Port William on 27.6.82, until handed over to 657 Sqdn on 2.8.82 at the end of 656 Sqdn's tour. Following the arrival of 658 Sqdn as the Garrison Army Air Sqdn FI on 2.12.82 it was picketed out at Port Stanley to await shipment back to the UK. Eventually embarked 'Baltic Ferry' during 3.83 and arrived at Felixstowe on 12.4.83. To Middle Wallop by road 13.4.83 for a survey by 70 Aircraft Workshops prior to transfer by road to Wroughton 27.4.83 for storage.

**XW282 AH.1**

On 29.3.82 in store at Wroughton. Released to 656 Sqdn and flown out to Netheravon 16.4.82. Flown to Southampton docks 8.5.82 for loading aboard 'Baltic Ferry', sailing with the ship on 9.5.82. Off-loaded at San Carlos settlement on 1.6.82. At the conclusion of 656 Sqdn's tour it was handed over to 657 Sqdn 2.8.82 until transferred to the Garrison Army Air Sqdn FI on 2.12.82 (at that time manned by 658 Sqdn personnel). After the arrival of 651 Sqdn (personnel and Lynx AH.1's) in 6.83 it was loaded aboard 'Sir Geraint' and sailed with the ship from Port Stanley on 10.6.83, arriving at Marchwood c4.7.83. Taken by road to Middle Wallop on 4.7.83 for a survey by 70 Aircraft Workshops prior to transfer by road to storage at Wroughton on 2.8.83.

**XW615 AH.1**

On 29.3.82 with 657 Sqdn at Oakington. Flown to Yeovilton 4.4.82 for issue to 3 CBAS as a replacement for XP893. Flown to Marchwood 5.4.82 for loading aboard 'Sir Lancelot', sailing with the ship that day for Ascension. Coded 'DS' in Matt Black with ARMY titles blocked out in Matt Black. Continued south aboard 'Sir Lancelot' for Operation "Sutton". At the conclusion of the campaign it was loaded aboard 'Elk' 23/24.6.82 for return to the UK and arrived at Devonport 12.7.82. Taken by road to Netheravon 14.7.82 and later to Wroughton on 3.9.82 for storage.

**XW616 AH.1**

On 29.3.82 with 3 CBAS 'B' Flt at Coypool coded '(D)P'. Flown to Yeovilton on 4.4.82 for mods and overpainting of ROYAL MARINES titles and codes in Matt Black, then to Marchwood on 5.4.82 for loading aboard 'Sir Lancelot', departing with the ship 6.4.82 for Ascension. Full code 'DP' applied in Matt Black, but code 'P' on nose still clearly visible after earlier repainting. Continued south aboard 'Sir Lancelot' for Operation "Sutton". Conveyed to San Carlos (Blue Beach) for ECU and hydraulic repairs by the 70 Aircraft Workshops Detachment on 17.6.82. Air-tested 20.6.82 and returned to Port Stanley where it was loaded aboard 'Elk' 23/24.6.82 for return to the UK. Arrived at Devonport 12.7.82 and collected by MARTSU 14.7.82 for transport by road to Netheravon where it arrived (by 70 Aircraft Workshops REME low-loader) on 15.7.82. Taken by road to Wroughton on 3.9.82 for storage.

# VULCAN

# 44, 50 & 101 SQUADRONS

By the end of March 1982 the Royal Air Force Vulcan B.2 fleet had been reduced to three squadrons, all based at Waddington. The type's withdrawal from operational service was expected to have been accomplished by the end of June 1982 when 44 Sqdn, 50 Sqdn and 101 Sqdn would also have disbanded. The Falklands conflict was to substantially change these plans, however, leading to the Vulcan's use in anger for the first time in nearly 25 years of service. Personnel at Waddington were placed on standby on 9 April for possible action in the South Atlantic. The Station's Engineering Wing was given the task of bringing the Air-to-Air Refuelling equipment up to operational standard on 10 of the aircraft so that aircrew could receive training in AAR techniques as soon as possible (the Vulcans all had refuelling probes, but the equipment had not been used for many years). Six of the ten aircraft were selected for possible deployment to the South Atlantic as follows:

| XL391 | 101 Sqdn | XM607 | 44 Sqdn |
| XM597 | 101 Sqdn | XM612 | 44 Sqdn |
| XM598 | 50 Sqdn | XM654 | 50 Sqdn |

They were the only remaining Vulcan B.2's which still had both forward and aft Skybolt missile attachment points and the refrigeration ducting for that missile running through their wings. In the event, XM654 remained on normal flying duties and was not used for Operation "Corporate". Five crews were selected, two from 50 Sqdn, one each from 44 Sqdn and 101 Sqdn, plus another from the recently-disbanded 9 Sqdn. All had taken part in a "Red Flag" exercise at Nellis AFB, Nevada (USA) during February 1982, one of the main factors behind their selection. The five aircraft were given improved navigational equipment by fitting the Carousel INS. The first such modification was carried out at Marham as the Victor K.2 fleet already used that equipment (XM597 was probably the aircraft concerned as it was seen flying from Marham on 18 April). The aircraft were also given extra ECM equipment in the shape of Westinghouse AN/ALQ-101 jamming pods carried on locally-devised underwing py-

lons, the associated wiring using the Skybolt missile refrigeration ducts mentioned earlier. Training in conventional bombing tactics began during mid-April, while AAR training was carried out with the Victor K.2's from Marham between 14-17 April. None of the five aircraft selected for use on Operation "Corporate" had been resprayed in the latest "wraparound" camouflage scheme, all of them still wearing the older Matt Dark Green and Matt Medium Sea Grey camouflage with Light Aircraft Grey undersides. Modifications to their colour schemes during the working-up period involved the application of a coat of Dark Sea Grey over the Light Aircraft Grey undersides and the removal of squadron insignia from the fin.

The first two Vulcans departed Waddington for Wideawake at 0900Z on 29 April (XM598 flown by Sqdn Ldr R.J.Reeve and crew with XM607 flown by Flt Lt W.F.M.Withers and crew), while a third (XM597) was launched as an airborne spare but later returned to base. The two primary aircraft flew non-stop south to Ascension Island supported by Victor K.2's from Marham, each Vulcan requiring two in-flight refuellings during the journey before landing at Wideawake at 1800Z. Sqdn Ldr A.C.Montgomery became the Detachment Commander on Ascension Island with responsibility for all of the Vulcan crews deployed there.

The first of the "Black Buck" missions (code-name for the Vulcan sorties from Ascension Island) were directed against the runway at Stanley Airport, the intention being that the airfield should be denied to high performance fighter aircraft. The first strike ("Black Buck 1") was launched from Wideawake around midnight (GMT) on 30 April/1 May. XM598 (Sqdn Ldr Reeve and crew) was designated as the primary aircraft, with XM607 (Flt Lt Withers and crew) in reserve and due to return once the primary aircraft had successfully completed its first AAR. The take-off of eleven Victors and two Vulcans (XM598 at slot 11 and XM607 at slot 13) began at 2350Z with a one minute departure interval, an impressive operation carried out in complete darkness as all thirteen aircraft had their navigation lights switched off. The captain's direct vision window on XM598 was slammed shut on departure but refused to seal properly, so the crew were

# VULCAN B.2 XM607 44 SQUADRON

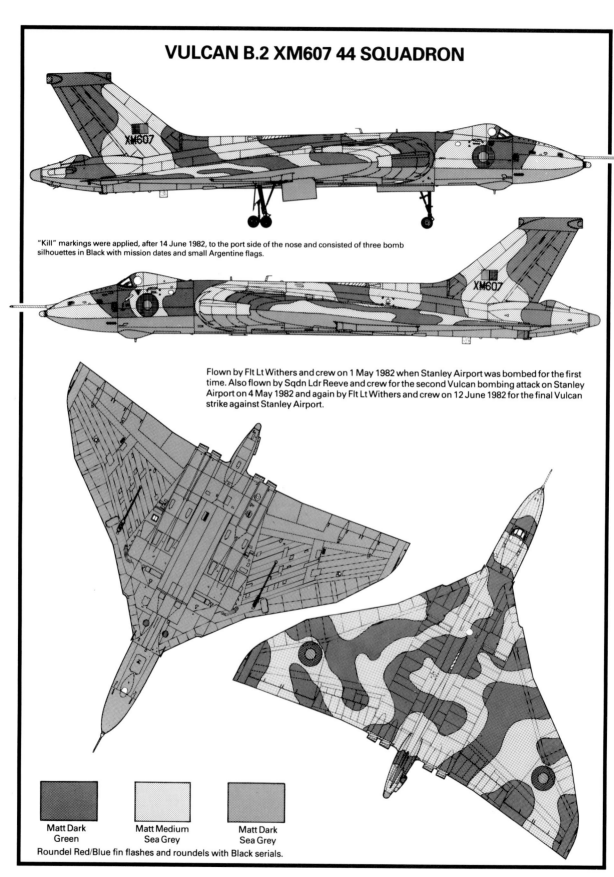

"Kill" markings were applied, after 14 June 1982, to the port side of the nose and consisted of three bomb silhouettes in Black with mission dates and small Argentine flags.

Flown by Flt Lt Withers and crew on 1 May 1982 when Stanley Airport was bombed for the first time. Also flown by Sqdn Ldr Reeve and crew for the second Vulcan bombing attack on Stanley Airport on 4 May 1982 and again by Flt Lt Withers and crew on 12 June 1982 for the final Vulcan strike against Stanley Airport.

Matt Dark
Green

Matt Medium
Sea Grey

Matt Dark
Sea Grey

Roundel Red/Blue fin flashes and roundels with Black serials.

unable to pressurise the aircraft. It was therefore decided that XM598 would return to Wideawake and that XM607 would continue with the mission. Martin Withers' crew comprised Fg Off P.L.Taylor (Co-pilot) with Flt Lts R.D.Wright (Nav-Radar), G.C.Graham (Nav-Plotter), H.Prior (AEO) and R.J.Russell (an AAR Instructor from Marham). Descent to low level took place some 300 miles from the target, with a last-minute climb to 10,000ft for the bomb-run across the Airport. At about two miles before the target was reached, the Vulcan's bombing computer set the release mechanism in motion and all 21 1,000lb bombs were released over a period of five seconds. They were dropped in a line which ran diagonally across the runway, standard tactics to ensure that at least one bomb would hit it. The codeword "Superfuse" was transmitted at 0746Z to indicate a successful mission ("Rhomboid" would have been sent to signify the opposite) and the Vulcan reversed course to begin its long return flight to Ascension Island, eventually landing at Wideawake at 1452Z on 1 May.

That raid effectively signalled the end of efforts to resolve the dispute with Argentina by diplomatic means and the six-week struggle to retake the Islands by force commenced. The attack came very much as a surprise to the enemy troops on the ground at Port Stanley, the Vulcan's RWR only picking up transmissions from an Argentine Skyguard fire-control radar as the bombs were about to leave the aircraft. This was promptly jammed by Hugh Prior using the ALQ-101 pod carried under the starboard wing. Only one of the bombs had struck the runway itself while another hit the runway edge, but the remainder caused some damage to the Airport's facilities. More important was the fact that it confirmed to the Argentines that the Royal Air Force was able to launch such a raid at extended range. Targets on the Argentine mainland were therefore under similar threat and this attack reinforced the views of those who feared such reprisals by the British.

A repeat performance by XM607 was launched at 2345Z on 3 May ("Black Buck 2"), Sqdn Ldr Reeve's crew comprising Flt Lts D.T.Dibbens (Co-pilot), M.A.Cooper (Nav-Radar), J.Vinales (Nav-Plotter), B.J.Masefield (AEO) and P.A.Standing (AARI). The aircraft took-off at slot three in the mass launch of bombers and tankers (reserve XM598 departed at slot five but was not required on that occasion). The raid followed the same profile as the previous one except that the final bombing run was made at 16,000ft, but none of the 21 bombs dropped at 0830Z on 4 May caused any damage to the runway. XM607 was turned back towards Ascension Island and the return trip to Wideawake was accomplished without incident.

XM598 and XM607 were flown back to Waddington on 7 May, but XM607 returned south to Wideawake on 15 May in time for the next raid ("Black Buck 3") which was planned for the following day. XM607 and XM612 were designated as the primary and reserve aircraft respectively (the latter having arrived from Waddington on 14 May), but in the event the mission was cancelled after both port pylons had been removed from the aircraft (the crews had erroneously thought that the pylons caused excessive drag). XM607 was flown back to Waddington on 20 May, followed by XM612 on 23 May.

Back in the United Kingdom, thoughts turned to arming the Vulcan with missiles to counter the Argentine radars sited on the Islands. The main threat was posed by two surveillance radars: a Westinghouse AN/TPS-43F (operated by the FAA's Grupo 2 de Vigilancia y Control) which had gone on-line near Stanley Airport on 6 April but was moved into the town itself during the night of 13/14 April for protection (a "decoy" antenna was left on Sapper Hill), and the Ejercito-operated Cardion TPS-44 positioned close to Stanley on the Airport road. Others used by the Argentines included Skyguard and Super Fledermaus fire control radars linked to both FAA and Ejercito Oerlikon 35mm twin-barrelled anti-aircraft guns. Initial missile trials involved Martel (already used by the Royal Air Force) which was first flown on the underwing hard-points of XM597 on 4 May with live firing trials over the Cardigan Bay range two days later. Even though those trials were successful, it was decided that the AGM-45 Shrike would be used instead. The latter missile was supplied by the United States Air Force and visits to Waddington by Shrike-equipped F-4G Phantoms from the 52ndTFW at Spangdahlem, West Germany between 19-23 May were no doubt connected with that. Trials with first two and then four Shrikes (two on each pylon) were flown, after which the Vulcans chosen for the role were deployed south to Ascension Island. XM598 (the reserve aircraft) arrived at Wideawake on 26 May followed by XM597 (the primary aircraft) on 27 May.

Launch of the first anti-radar Vulcan mission armed with Shrike missiles ("Black Buck 4") was planned for midnight on 28 May. XM597 departed on time crewed by Sqdn Ldr C.N.McDougall (Pilot), Fg Off C.Lackman (Co-pilot) plus Flt Lts D.Castle (Nav-Radar), B.Smith (Nav-Plotter), R.Trevaskus (AEO) and B.Gardner (sixth man, another Vulcan pilot). Unfortunately, the aircraft was forced to return to Wideawake five hours into the mission after the lead Victor's HDU failed. "Black Buck 5" followed shortly before midnight on 30 May using the same aircraft and crew, the Westinghouse AN/TPS-43F surveillance radar at Port Stanley being the mission's target. The flight proceeded as planned and the Vulcan descended to 300ft some 200 miles from the Falkland Islands before climbing to 16,000ft at 20 miles to commence its run-in to the target, having already broken radio-silence to co-ordinate a Sea Harrier strike with the Task Force. As the Vulcan climbed, so its RWR picked up the AN/TPS-43F transmissions, but they promptly ceased as the Argentines appeared to switch off the radar. The Grupo 2 VYCA personnel were in fact trying to confuse the bomber crew by reducing the signal strength of their radar in order to make the aerial appear further away from the aircraft than it really was, thereby hopefully drawing the Vulcan within range of anti-aircraft guns. Some 40 minutes passed before Sqdn Ldr MacDougall's crew picked up radar transmissions again and could pinpoint the source. Both Shrikes were launched at approximately 0845Z on 31 May and homed on it, the radar ceasing transmissions at the moment the missiles hit the ground. The first one struck the ground 10 to 15 yards from the radar aerial causing minor damage to its intended target, while the second came down some distance away. The Vulcan crew assumed at the time that the radar had been hit, but it was operational again 24 hours later; a

**Above** *Vulcan B.2 XM607 is seen at its Waddington base on 1.7.82 after it had returned from Wideawake immediately following the cease-fire on 14.6.82. The mission markings (**Inset**) were applied to the port side of the nose radome after the Vulcan had returned from the South Atlantic and they depict three black bomb silhouettes falling onto three Argentine flags, the date of each raid appearing beneath.*

*(Terry Senior; (**Inset**) Peter J. Cooper)*

**Left** *XM597 was the only other Vulcan B.2 to have been used in anger against Argentine forces and it is here seen under tow at Waddington on 1.7.82. The inset views show a "zap" applied by a visiting USAF C-5A crew at Wideawake; the mission markings applied to the port side of the nose radome depict two black Shrike missile silhouettes with the Argentine flag above and mission dates below together with a Brazilian flag. The third inset shows the hastily-adapted underwing pylons.*

*(Terry Senior; (**Insets**) Michael I. Draper ("zap"/pylons) and Peter J. Cooper (mission markings)).*

revetment was subsequently built to protect it from any further blast damage.

The same aircraft and crew were launched from Wideawake for "Black Buck 6" late on 2 June, this time armed with four Shrikes instead of two for another strike against the same radar. The raid followed the same profile as the previous one, the AN/TPS-43F radar being switched off as the Vulcan commenced its final run-in during the early hours of 3 June. Once again, some 40 minutes were spent waiting overhead for this or any other radar to be switched on and, shortly after the start of a dummy descent towards the airfield, the aircraft's RWR picked up an Ejercito Skyguard radar. Two Shrikes were launched, destroying the radar which had been acting as a fire control unit for one of the GADA601 anti-aircraft batteries close to Port Stanley. Four Argentine soldiers (an officer, one NCO and two conscripts) were killed by the direct hit. After another short delay in the hope that the AN/TPS-43F radar might be switched on again, the Vulcan and its crew were forced to leave the area due to their critical fuel state. Assisted by a Nimrod MR.2, XM597 made a successful rendezvous with its Victor tanker about half-way back to Wideawake. However, the tip of the Vulcan's refuelling probe broke off during the AAR and the crew were forced to divert to the nearest available airfield, which was at Rio de Janeiro in Brazil. Refuelling had been taking place at 20,000ft and the crew quickly calculated that the aircraft would not even reach the coast if it remained at that altitude, so low was their fuel state. Neil McDougall climbed the Vulcan to 40,000ft, where it burned fuel more economically, and the two unused Shrikes were fired off. One of the missiles failed to fire, however, and remained attached to the pylon as there was no other system for releasing it. All classified documents were collected together, placed inside a hold-all and jettisoned through the crew entry door after the cabin had been de-pressurised and the crew had put on oxygen masks. There was some delay in getting the crew door shut again, but the problem was overcome when the door was at last sealed and the cabin was repressurised. Initial conversation with Brazilian ATC was somewhat evasive as the crew sought to conceal their identity while diplomatic channels were contacting Embassy staff at Rio de Janeiro.

Eventually arrangements were made with ATC for an emergency diversion to Rio's Galeao Airport and the "four-jet" commenced an initial descent to 20,000ft as it approached the coast (Neil McDougall was not prepared to go lower until committed to a landing). The runway was sighted six miles out, clearance to make a straight-in approach for a downwind landing obtained, then a very steep spiral descent was commenced with airbrakes out and throttles closed. The descent was exceptionally well judged by the pilot, the Vulcan being lined up for landing passing 800ft one and a half miles out (although going at twice its normal approach speed!). The nose was raised to slow the aircraft down for a perfect landing. 2,000lbs of fuel remained when the Vulcan's engines were shut down, less than would have been required for an overshoot and one circuit. The "hung-up" missile was made safe by the crew, then impounded by the Brazilian authorities along with the aircraft. The crew were very well treated by the Brazilians and were soon offered the opportunity to return home, but they elected to stay until the aircraft was released. That eventually occurred on 10 June when they flew XM597 (minus Shrike) to Ascension Island. A new refuelling probe was fitted prior to the aircraft's return flight to Waddington on 13 June.

The final Vulcan sortie, "Black Buck 7", was mounted by XM607 during the night of 11 June, the aircraft having returned from Waddington on 10 June. Martin Withers' crew was the same as for "Black Buck 1", except that the AARI on that occasion was Peter Standing. It was to be another conventional bombing mission aimed at the facilities on Stanley Airport rather than the runway, and was accomplished successfully. XM598 and XM607 returned to Waddington on 14 June and the type's gradual withdrawal from RAF service was recommenced.

> *Vulcan aircrew involved in the "Black Buck" raids during Operation "Corporate" and their awards:*
>
> *Sqdn Ldr C.N.McDougall RAF DFC; Sqdn Ldr R.J.Reeve RAF; Flt Lt D.Castle RAF; Flt Lt M.A.Cooper RAF; Flt Lt D.T.Dibbens RAF; Flt Lt B.Gardner RAF; Flt Lt G.C.Graham RAF MID; Flt Lt B.J.Masefield RAF; Flt Lt H.Prior RAF MID; Flt Lt R.J.Russell RAF AFC MID; Flt Lt B.Smith RAF; Flt Lt P.A.Standing RAF QCVSA; Flt Lt R.Trevaskus RAF; Flt Lt J.Vinales RAF; Flt Lt W.F.M.Withers RAF DFC; Flt Lt R.D.Wright RAF MID; Fg Off C.Lackman RAF; Fg Off P.L.Taylor RAF MID.*

# POST-CONFLICT TANKER CONVERSIONS

101 Sqdn disbanded on 4 August, followed by 44 Sqdn on 21 December, leaving 50 Sqdn as the only Vulcan unit to survive into 1983 after its aircraft had received a new lease of life directly resulting from the War with Argentina. The need for extra air-refuelling capacity soon became evident as the ageing Victor K.2 fleet struggled to cope with the demands made on it for fuel from newly probe-equipped Nimrod and Hercules aircraft in addition to its previous customers. The VC-10 tanker conversion project, while fairly advanced, could not be brought forward sufficiently to fill the gap in capacity, so the Vulcan and Hercules were selected for conversion to the tanker role during the conflict as an interim solution to the problem. The Vulcan was already able to carry up to three long-range fuel tanks in its bomb bay, giving it a total fuel capacity of some 96,000lbs. Six aircraft (XH558, XH560, XH561, XJ825, XL445 and XM571) were selected for tanker conversion and sent to British Aerospace at Wood-

ford to receive the necessary modifications to their plumbing plus the fitment of Flight Refuelling's Mk.17B HDU into the redundant ECM tailcone (a box-like fairing was added to the underside to improve the airflow over the lower part of the HDU). They emerged as Vulcan K.2's, the prototype being XH561 which made its first test flight after conversion on 18 June. Each aircraft's colour scheme was modified as well, much of the underside being repainted White (the trailing edge of the wings and most of the fuselage from the mid-point backwards), while Dayglo Red and Black lines were applied to assist receiver aircraft in lining up on the drogue. The HDU's were all eventually to be used in the VC-10 tanker programme so the Vulcan K.2's progressively lost their air-refuelling capability as the VC-10 K.2's began to leave the conversion line at Filton during 1983. XJ825 was the first Vulcan K.2 to have its HDU removed (on 4 May 1983), while enough VC-10 tankers had been delivered to 101 Sqdn at Brize Norton by 31 March 1984 to permit 50 Sqdn to disband at Waddington on that date, having flown over 3,000 hours on the Vulcan K.2.

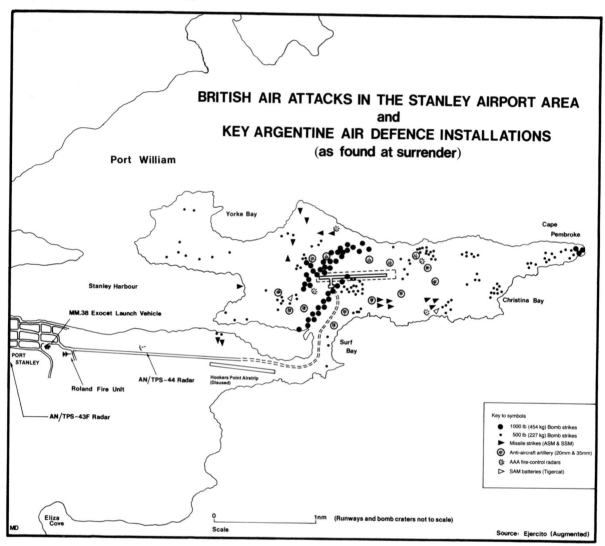

## INDIVIDUAL AIRCRAFT DETAILS

**XH558** K.2       *Not deployed south*

On 29.3.82 with 44 Sqdn at Waddington (as a B.2). To BAe Woodford 30.6.82 for tanker conversion and first flown as a K.2 on 3.9.82. Delivered from Woodford to 50 Sqdn at Waddington on 12.10.82. Flown to A&AEE Boscombe Down 25.10.82 for trials, returning to 50 Sqdn on 30.11.82. Withdrawn from use at Waddington on 31.3.84.

**XH560** K.2       *Not deployed south*

On 29.3.82 with 44 Sqdn at Waddington (as a B.2). To BAe Woodford 15.6.82 for tanker conversion and first flown as a K.2 on 16.8.82. Delivered from Woodford to 50 Sqdn at Waddington on 23.8.82. Withdrawn from use at Waddington on 31.3.84.

**Above** *Vulcan tanker XH561 of 50 Squadron is seen at Waddington on 1.7.82, the day that the K.2 conversion was officially revealed to the Press. Although somewhat "Heath Robinson" in appearance, the HDU "skip"* (**Inset**) *caused little change in the aircraft's performance apart from demanding revised angles of attack for landing and take-off due to reduced ground clearance. Much of the IFR fit was in fact recessed into the ECM bay in the tailcone.*

*(Terry Senior;* (**Inset**) *Peter J. Cooper)*

**Below** *Of those helicopters seen in this view aboard 'Atlantic Conveyor' shortly before the Exocet missile attack on 25.5.82, only the Chinook HC.1 ZA718/BN of 18 Squadron (foreground) survived; all of the Wessex helicopters went down with the ship. The inset view shows the charred remains of ZA706/BT on the rear deck just before the ship eventually sank. This Chinook had been fitted with rotor-blades and would have been the second to leave the container ship but for the attack.*

*(Ministry of Defence)*

**XH561** K.2         *Not deployed south*

On 29.3.82 with 50 Sqdn at Waddington (as a B.2). To BAe Woodford on 4.5.82 for tanker conversion and first flown as the prototype K.2 on 18.6.82 (two sorties). A third flight on 20.6.82 involved refuelling trials with a Nimrod (dry) and a Victor (wet). A further sortie on 22.6.82 included AAR trials with a Victor and a Vulcan (B.2 XM654 flown by Sqdn Ldr McDougall). Delivered from Woodford to 50 Sqdn at Waddington on 23.6.82, flying the unit's first sortie on 30.6.82 (refuelling Vulcan B.2 XM607 flown by Sqdn Ldr Reeve). Displayed to the Press at Waddington on 1.7.82. Withdrawn from use at Waddington 31.3.84 and flown to Catterick 14.6.84 for burning by the Fire School (allocated Maintenance Serial 8809M on 22.3.84).

**XJ825** K.2         *Not deployed south*

On 29.3.82 with 101 Sqdn at Waddington (as a B.2). To BAe Woodford on 11.5.82 for tanker conversion and first flown as a K.2 on 29.6.82. Delivered from Woodford to 50 Sqdn at Waddington on 1.7.82. Withdrawn from use at Waddington on 31.3.84 and later used for battle damage repair training on the airfield (allocated Maintenance Serial 8810M on 22.3.84).

**XL391** B.2         *Not deployed south*

On 29.3.82 with 101 Sqdn at Waddington. Selected for Operation "Corporate" use; Squadron markings removed and undersides repainted Matt Dark Sea Grey. Used during the working-up period but not deployed operationally, remaining at Waddington. Transferred to 44 Sqdn 21.6.82 and then retired at Waddington when 44 Sqdn disbanded on 21.12.82. Flown to Blackpool on 16.2.83 for preservation.

**XL445** K.2         *Not deployed south*

On 29.3.82 with 44 Sqdn at Waddington (as a B.2). To BAe Woodford on 25.5.82 for tanker conversion and first flown as a K.2 on 22.7.82. Delivered to Waddington for 50 Sqdn at the end of its first flight. Withdrawn from use at Waddington 31.3.84 and flown to Lyneham on 5.4.84 for crash rescue duties (allocated Maintenance Serial 8811M on 22.3.84).

**XM571** K.2         *Not deployed south*

On 29.3.82 with 101 Sqdn at Waddington (as a B.2). To BAe Woodford on 11.5.82 for tanker conversion and first flown as a K.2 on 13.7.82. Delivered to A&AEE Boscombe Down on 15.7.82, still wearing 101 Sqdn markings. To Waddington for maintenance on 24.8.82, returning to Boscombe Down on 1.9.82 in 50 Sqdn markings. Delivered to 50 Sqdn at Waddington on 25.10.82. Withdrawn from use there on 31.3.84 and flown to Gibraltar 9.5.84 for crash rescue duties (allocated Maintenance Serial 8812M on 22.3.84).

**XM597** B.2

On 29.3.82 with 101 Sqdn at Waddington. Selected for Operation "Corporate" use; Squadron markings removed and undersides repainted Matt Dark Sea Grey. One of two

Vulcans converted to carry anti-radar missiles, carrying out trials with Martel on 4/5.5.82 prior to being equipped with Shrike (the missile eventually chosen). Deployed to Wideawake on 27.5.82.

Flown by Sqdn Ldr McDougall and crew, it departed Wideawake late on 28.5.82 for the first planned Shrike missile raid ("Black Buck 4"), but the failure of a Victor HDU caused its cancellation five hours into the mission and it landed back at Wideawake during the early hours of 29.5.82. The same crew left Wideawake late on 30.5.82 for "Black Buck 5", the Argentine AN/TPS-43F radar at Port Stanley being attacked with two Shrikes at 0845Z on 31.5.82 after the aircraft had loitered for some 40 minutes attempting to pinpoint its target. The first missile hit the ground 10-15 yards from the aerial causing minor damage, while the second missile impacted some distance away (the radar was serviceable again 24 hours later). The aircraft and its crew returned safely to Wideawake later on 31.5.82.

Another Shrike raid ("Black Buck 6") was launched from Wideawake late on 2.6.82 (flown once again by Sqdn Ldr McDougall and crew), this time armed with four missiles instead of two. The AN/TPS-43F remained switched off for the duration of the loiter but a GADA601 Skyguard fire-control radar was engaged instead and destroyed (killing four soldiers). During the return flight to Wideawake on 3.6.82 the aircraft's refuelling probe broke while tanking from a Victor, causing an enforced diversion to Galeao Airport at Rio de Janeiro in Brazil. One of two unused Shrikes was jettisoned but the other "hung up" and was impounded by the Brazilian authorities (along with the aircraft) after a spectacular diving approach to Galeao Airport. Flown to Ascension on 10.6.82 after release by the Brazilian authorities and fitted with a new refuelling probe.

Flown back to Waddington on 13.6.82. Transferred to 44 Sqdn on 1.7.82 then to 50 Sqdn on 24.12.82 (44 Sqdn having disbanded on 21.12.82). Continued in service until 50 Sqdn disbanded at Waddington on 31.3.84 and then flown to East Fortune on 12.4.84 for the Royal Scottish Museum of Flight.

*After return to the UK, "kill" markings were applied to the port side of the nose, consisting of two Shrike missile silhouettes in Black with mission dates, along with a Brazilian flag.*

**XM598** B.2

On 29.3.82 with 50 Sqdn at Waddington. Selected for Operation "Corporate" use; Squadron markings removed and undersides repainted Matt Dark Sea Grey. Deployed to Wideawake on 29.4.82.

Launched as the primary aircraft for "Black Buck 1" around midnight on 30.4.82 but was forced to return to Ascension with pressurisation problems early on 1.5.82 (XM607 completed the mission).

Returned to Waddington on 7.5.82 and then flown back to Wideawake on 26.5.82 as a spare aircraft for the anti-radar "Black Buck" raids. Left Wideawake for Waddington on 14.6.82, being transferred to 44 Sqdn on

22.6.82. Retired at Waddington when 44 Sqdn disbanded there on 21.12.82. Flown out to Cosford on 20.1.83 for the Aerospace Museum (allocated Maintenance Serial 8778M on 4.1.83).

**XM607** B.2

On 29.3.82 with 44 Sqdn at Waddington. Selected for Operation "Corporate" use; Squadron markings removed and undersides repainted Matt Dark Sea Grey. Deployed to Wideawake on 29.4.82.

Flown by Flt Lt Withers and crew, it departed Wideawake around midnight on 30.4.82 as reserve aircraft for the first bombing raid against Stanley Airport. Took over as the primary aircraft when XM598 (Sqdn Ldr Reeve and crew) was forced to abort with pressurisation problems. 21 bombs dropped on the airfield at 0746Z on 1.5.82, of which one actually struck the runway. Returned safely to Wideawake at 1452Z.

Departed Wideawake at 2345Z on 3.5.82 for "Black Buck 2" (flown by Sqdn Ldr Reeve and crew), a second attempt to put the runway at Stanley Airport out of action. 21 bombs were dropped at 0830Z on 4.5.82 but none hit the runway. The aircraft returned safely to Wideawake that day.

Flown to Waddington 7.5.82 then back to Wideawake on 15.5.82 for the aborted "Black Buck 3" raid on 16.5.82. Dispatched to Waddington once again on 20.5.82.

Deployed to Ascension for the last time on 10.6.82. Flown by Flt Lt Withers and crew, it departed Wideawake late on 11.6.82 for the final conventional bombing sortie against Stanley Airport on 12.6.82 ("Black Buck 7"). The aircraft returned safely to Wideawake.

Flown back to Waddington on 14.6.82. 44 Sqdn disbanded on 21.12.82 and the aircraft was retired at Waddington for gate-guard duties (allocated Maintenance Serial 8779M on 4.1.83).

*After return to the UK, "kill" markings were applied to the port side of the nose, consisting of three bomb silhouettes in Black with mission dates.*

**XM612** B.2

On 29.3.82 with 44 Sqdn at Waddington. Selected for Operation "Corporate" use; Squadron markings removed and undersides repainted Matt Dark Sea Grey. Deployed to Ascension on 14.5.82 but was not used on operational missions. Flown back to Waddington on 23.5.82, remaining with 44 Sqdn although it never regained their Squadron markings. Retired at Waddington when the unit disbanded on 21.12.82. Flown out to Norwich on 30.1.83 for preservation.

**XM654** B.2         *Not deployed south*

On 29.3.82 with 50 Sqdn at Waddington. Selected for Operation "Corporate" use; Squadron markings removed and undersides repainted Matt Dark Sea Grey. Not deployed operationally. Remained at Waddington with 50 Sqdn until withdrawn from use in 7.82. Broken-up on the airfield 14-17.12.82.

# HARRIER

The Harrier GR.3 made a valuable contribution to the overall success of Operation "Corporate". Originally envisaged as attrition replacements for the Royal Navy Sea Harrier fleet, the aircraft were in fact put to good use alongside their naval counterparts, taking over most of the low-level ground-attack tasks. Most sorties during the amphibious landings phase were airborne alert missions, many of them being used for reconnaissance as very little opposition was encountered. Their services were called upon more during the retaking of Darwin and Goose Green where they had a decisive effect on the outcome. During the final phase of the fighting they were mainly tasked with battlefield air interdiction sorties in the hills to the west of Port Stanley. Frequent attacks on the runway at Stanley Airport served only to prove how ineffective 1,000lb bombs can be when delivered at low level and how difficult it is to achieve results when loft-bombing without the assistance of INAS and the aircraft's weapon aiming computer (which was not programmed for that sort of delivery). The arrival of LGB's late in the conflict provided a significant improvement in results, provided that a FAC on the ground was in the right place and equipped to illuminate the target. The aircraft itself was shown to be able to withstand much in the way of battle damage, virtually all of the Harriers being hit by small arms fire at some stage during the conflict. 1(F) Sqdn also proved its ability to deploy aircraft over great distances and to operate with limited facilities in an alien environment. Operation "Corporate" saw the first operational use of land-based Royal Air Force aircraft from an aircraft carrier since World War II.

# 1(F) SQUADRON

1 (Fighter) Squadron received a warning order on 8 April directing it to prepare for carrier operations in the South Atlantic. The Squadron was committed to Operation "Corporate" as it was recognised that the relatively small Sea Harrier force was bound to suffer losses. The Royal Air Force Harrier GR.3 was the only suitable aircraft available for attrition replacement and its early deployment to the theatre would also relieve the Fleet Air Arm aircraft of some of their ground-attack tasks, thus allowing them to concentrate more on air defence. 1(F) Sqdn was totally self-reliant when deployed in peacetime and that capability of "bare base" operations meant that it was ideally suited for deployment to the South Atlantic.

Initial plans were that its aircraft would sail south aboard 'Atlantic Conveyor' on 22/23 April, members of the Squadron having inspected the vessel at Liverpool the previous week to confirm that its foredeck would support limited Harrier operations with only a few modifications. In the event it was decided that the Harriers would be flown south to Ascension Island before joining the vessel, permitting a further 10 days of working-up time in the United Kingdom, so 'Atlantic Conveyor' sailed without them.

The Squadron's complement of Harriers at the end of March 1982 was as follows:

| GR.3 | XV787/02 | XW767/06 | XZ963/14 | XZ130/27 |
|------|----------|----------|----------|----------|
|      | XW919/03 | XZ989/07 | XV778/16 | XZ129/29 |
|      | XV752/04 | XV751/08 | XV755/20 |          |
|      | XZ992/05 | XZ964/09 | XW769/24 |          |
| T.4  | XW925/17 |          |          |          |

Unit markings had been removed from the nose and tail of several 1(F) Sqdn aircraft in March during filming of the BBC Television serial "Squadron". XV755, XV787, XW919, XZ989 and XZ992 were involved in filming at Lyneham between 23-25 March but work on that project ceased when the unit was placed on standby. Some of the aircraft continued to operate without unit markings during April, but the task was transferred to the Gutersloh-based squadrons and several of their aircraft were involved in filming at Wildenrath during May (once again with unit markings removed). The Harriers deployed to the Task Force all departed wearing the individual aircraft code in Red on the fin and outriggers but the 1(F) Sqdn badge on the nose was painted over. The unit's complement of GR.3's increased during the working-up period, a total of eight additional aircraft being taken on strength as follows:

As the aircraft were to be based in 'Hermes', the Squadron's pilots were given training time on the ski-jump at Yeovilton with two or three jumps each between 14 and 23 April. Dissimilar Air Combat Training was also carried out during the working-up period, five Harrier GR.3's (XW767, XW919, XZ129, XZ133 and XZ963) being detached to Binbrook on 15 April to fly against the resident Lightnings. Welcome assistance from the French meant that 1(F) Sqdn crews were able to carry out DACT against one of the aircraft types that they were likely to encounter in the South Atlantic. The Armee de l'Air dispatched ECT.2/2 Mirage IIIBE 261/2-ZF to Coningsby from Dijon-Longvic during the morning of 22 April, Noratlas 83/63-KF from ET.63 arriving via Cambrai in support. The two-seat Mirage flew several sorties against Harrier GR.3's on 22/23 April before leaving for Metz late on the second day (its support Noratlas flying direct to Dijon). Aeronavale Super Etendards were also involved in DACT missions, but those aircraft did not land in the United Kingdom.

While the Squadron's aircrew prepared for maritime operations, the maintenance personnel at Wittering concerned themselves with the task of making the GR.3's carrier-compatible. A team from the MoD and BAe Kingston drew up a list of the required modifications between 14 and 16 April and work commenced the following week. Tie-down rings were fitted to outrigger legs, minor changes made to steering and nozzle control mechanisms, holes were drilled in certain strategic places to allow salt water to drain out while other areas received protection against salt water corrosion. BAe dispatched an initial batch of 12 I-Band Transponders (equipment already carried by Sea Harriers which enabled them to be positively identified on radar) between 22 April and 1 May, later fitted to the underside of each aircraft's nose Laser Ranger and Marked Target Seeker. In an attempt to overcome the problem of setting up the Harrier GR.3's INAS on a rolling deck, BAe and Ferranti designed a trolley-mounted device called Ferranti Inertial Rapid Alignment Equipment (FINRAE) which could be plugged in to the aircraft on start up to feed positional data into the INAS. Despite the amount of work involved, the system did not provide the degree of accuracy required for operational use in the South Atlantic, so the primary method of navigation employed by 1(F) Sqdn was visual.

It was decided that the aircraft should have an Air-to-Air Missile capability. BAe worked on that problem and produced a simple but ingenious modification kit by 21 April which allowed the GR.3's outboard wing pylons to take either AIM-9G Sidewinder missiles, bombs (BL-755 Cluster Bomb Units, Pave Way Laser-Guided Bombs or 1,000lb High Explosive Bombs) or the Fleet Air Arm's two-inch rocket pods (the GR.3's own uninsulated SNEB 68mm rocket pods being unsuitable for carrier operations

due to the high electro-magnetic forces aboard ship). A 30 minute conversion time to the missile fit was achieved, although a further 90 minutes was also required for safety checks. The kit received MoD approval on 22 April and the first Sidewinder conversion was completed at Wittering on 28 April, the aircraft (XZ989) being flown to A&AEE Boscombe Down by Flt Lt J.Rochfort the next day. GR.3's XV789, XZ130 and XZ972 (from Wittering, in company with XZ993/AU loaned from 3 Sqdn) plus XZ989 (from Boscombe Down) arrived at Valley on 30 April for live firing trials which took place over the Cardigan Bay ranges on 1/2 May. A total of 18 kits was produced by BAe for use in the South Atlantic operations. Further additions to the GR.3's normal weapons inventory included various electronic countermeasures systems, one of which was a radar jammer named "Blue Eric" installed in the front of a converted Aden cannon pod. Nine pods had been modified by 21 May, only two weeks after the initial planning had commenced. Another modification which surfaced late in the working-up period was the equipping of the Harriers with an ALE-40 cartridge dispenser for infra-red decoy flares on the underside of the fuselage aft of the airbrake. That modification was not cleared in time for the first six aircraft sent south, which had to make do with bundles of chaff attached to the airbrake and bomb-release mechanisms.

LTW Hercules C.1 XV191 and C.3 XV303 departed Wittering on 1 May bound for Ascension Island (via Gibraltar and Dakar) with 40 maintenance personnel aboard. Five Harriers (XV787, XV789, XZ972, XZ989 and XZ997) were positioned to St Mawgan during the morning of 2 May, of which XV789, XZ972 and XZ989 departed the following morning on the 4,600 mile flight to Wideawake. They were refuelled en route by Victor K.2's from Marham, while 42 Sqdn Nimrod MR.1 XV249 operated from Freetown in Sierra Leone to provide SAR cover. For the nine and a quarter hour ferry flight, each of the GR.3's carried two 330 gallon ferry tanks on the inboard pylons and two empty 100 gallon tanks on the outboard pylons, the latter being for eventual use in combat. All three successfully completed the journey, XZ989 non-stop followed by XV789 and XZ972 after a short technical stop at Banjul in The Gambia. Two more Harriers were flown from Wittering to St Mawgan on the morning of 3 May (XZ963 and XZ988), followed by XZ132 that evening. The morning of 4 May saw the departure south from St Mawgan of XV787, XZ963 and XZ997, of which XZ963 and XZ997 completed the journey to Wideawake non-stop, but XV787 suffered from technical problems and was forced to divert to Porto Santo (Madeira) where it landed at 1250Z. That aircraft was flown to Gibraltar on 8 May and returned to Wittering via Istres two days later. Two more GR.3's (XW919 and XZ129) positioned from Wittering to St Mawgan during the afternoon of 4 May, leaving for Ascension Island the next morning accompanied by XZ132 and XZ988. Three completed the journey non-stop while the fourth GR.3 (XZ132) completed its journey on 6 May after an enforced diversion to Banjul.

The first deployment from the United Kingdom to Ascension Island can be summarised thus:

| Aircraft | Left Wittering | Arrived Wideawake |
|---|---|---|
| XV787/02 | 1200Z on 2 May | (ret'd Wittering) |
| XW919/03 | 1500Z on 4 May | 1830Z on 5 May |
| XZ989/07 | 1005Z on 2 May | 1845Z on 3 May |
| XZ963/14 | 1100Z on 3 May | 1830Z on 4 May |
| XZ129/29 | 1345Z on 4 May | 1830Z on 5 May |
| XZ997/31 | 1015Z on 2 May | 1830Z on 4 May |
| XV789/32 | 1005Z on 2 May | 2215Z on 3 May |
| XZ972/33 | 1005Z on 2 May | 2215Z on 3 May |
| XZ988/34 | 1015Z on 3 May | 1830Z on 5 May |
| XZ132/36 | 2015Z on 3 May | 1230Z on 6 May |

Six GR.3's (XV789, XZ963, XZ972, XZ988, XZ989 and XZ997) embarked 'Atlantic Conveyor' off the Island on 6 May, landing on a specially-built pad just aft of the forward mast and then taxying between the container "walls" for parking. While the containers did provide a degree of protection for the aircraft, further measures were taken to ensure that they were not exposed to salt water spray. Unlike the Sea Harrier, which was designed from the outset for the maritime environment, the GR.3 had several components made from magnesium which reacts with salt water to induce corrosion. Once aboard ship, each aircraft's engine was given an anti-corrosion spray and sealed. The pylons and undercarriage were then liberally covered with PX28 (a protective coating) before the entire aircraft was wrapped in a "Driclad" plastic cover to protect it from the elements.

Due to the high value placed on facilities at Ascension Island, the remaining Harriers (XW919, XZ129 and XZ132) were armed with AIM-9G Sidewinder missiles for air defence duties at Wideawake until the first 29(F) Sqdn Phantom FGR.2's arrived on 24 May. The Harrier GR.3 had no radar to aid night interceptions, so the aircrew were issued with Night-Vision Goggles which apparently worked very well! 1(F) Sqdn personnel manned that detachment until relieved by 4 Sqdn crews on 21 May.

Wg Cdr P.T.Squire (Officer Commanding), Sqdn Ldr R.D.Iveson and 18 maintenance personnel under Flt Lt B.Mason embarked 'Atlantic Conveyor' on 7 May, on which date Sqdn Ldrs P.Harris and J.J.Pook with Flt Lts J.Glover, M.W.J.Hare, A.Harper and J.Rochfort embarked 'Norland', both ships sailing south from Ascension Island later that day. Four of the six Harriers were flown from 'Atlantic Conveyor' to 'Hermes' on 18 May and Peter Squire (XZ972) was first to land aboard the carrier at 1630Z. He was followed by John Rochfort (XV789), Peter Harris (XZ988) and Jerry Pook (XZ997). Tony Harper (XZ963) accomplished the journey on 19 May in XZ963, while the sixth GR.3 (XZ989 flown by John Rochfort again) completed its journey on 20 May. The last two aircraft both made refuelling stops aboard 'Invincible' as 'Hermes' was by then out of VTOL flight range from 'Atlantic Conveyor'.

The total of Harrier GR.3's at Wideawake had increased to nine by 30 May. XV762, XV778, XW767, XZ133 and XZ992 were positioned from Wittering to St Mawgan on the afternoon of 28 May, four of them being flown to Ascension Island on 29 May (XV778, XW767,

XZ133 and XZ992). XV762 followed the next day accompanied by XW924 which had been positioned to St Mawgan from Wittering early on 29 May. That final part of the Squadron's deployment from the United Kingdom to Ascension Island can be summarised thus:

| Aircraft | Left Wittering | Arrived Wideawake |
|---|---|---|
| XZ992/05 | 1500Z on 28 May | 1810Z on 29 May |
| XW767/06 | 1525Z on 28 May | 1835Z on 29 May |
| XZ133/10 | 1510Z on 28 May | 1810Z on 29 May |
| XV778/16 | 1505Z on 28 May | 1810Z on 29 May |
| XW924/35 | 0750Z on 29 May | 1950Z on 30 May |
| XV762/37 | 1515Z on 28 May | 1835Z on 30 May |

Of those, XV778 and XZ133 arrived aboard 'Hermes' on 1 June after an epic flight lasting 8hrs 20mins, flown by Flt Lts M.Beech and M.M.MacLeod respectively. Each Harrier was supported by four Victors, the only diversion "airfield" available en route being 'Engadine', positioned about half-way between Ascension Island and the Task Force. Two more GR.3's (XW919 flown by Flt Lt R.Boyens and XZ992 flown by Flt Lt N.Gilchrist) followed at 1700Z on 8 June after a flight lasting 7hrs 50mins. On this occasion, Ross Boyens' aircraft suffered a failure of some navigational instruments so Nick Gilchrist led the way. Four more aircraft (XV762, XW767, XW924 and XZ129) were loaded aboard 'Contender Bezant' off Ascension Island on 3 June but they did not see operational use during the conflict. The ship arrived on station to the east of the TEZ on 10 June, accompanied by 'Norland' which brought their aircrew, but the Harriers were not disembarked prior to the Argentine surrender on 14 June. The one remaining (15th) GR.3 which reached Wideawake was XZ132, but it suffered from incurable fuel leaks and was later returned to the United Kingdom. The 1(F) Sqdn aircraft available for use in the conflict were therefore:

| | | | | |
|---|---|---|---|---|
| **From 20 May** | XV789 | XZ963 | XZ972 | XZ988 |
| | XZ989 | XZ997 | | |
| **From 1 June** | XV778 | XZ133 | | |
| **From 8 June** | XW919 | XZ992 | | |

**From 10 June** XV762 XW767 XW924 XZ129
*Note: these four aircraft did not see action prior to the surrender on 14 June.*

Missions began soon after the arrival of the initial aircraft aboard 'Hermes' on 18 May. Each pilot flew at least twice on 19 May during the Squadron's operational work-up, the aircraft carrying AIM-9G's for use in the air-to-air role. Peter Squire and Tony Glover flew the first sortie of the day and were tasked while airborne with intercepting a Grupo 1 Boeing 707 estimated to be some 180 miles northeast of the Task Force. Although unsuccessful, that mis-

An embarrassing and almost catastrophic incident aboard 'Hermes' was narrowly avoided on 21.5.82 when Flt Lt John Rochfort returned to the carrier at 1450Z after an armed reconnaissance mission over the San Carlos beach-head. His Harrier GR.3, XZ997/31, landed close to the edge of the flight-deck, so near in fact that the port outrigger ended up in the catwalk. Fortunately the aircraft was stabilised and then hoisted back onto the deck by the ground-crews and suffered no serious damage as a result. XZ997 still carries a full bomb load, John Rochfort having been unable to find a suitable target during the sortie.          (Ministry of Defence)

With a full weapons load, Sqdn Ldr Peter Harris begins his brief take-off run from 'Hermes' for an attack against the Port Stanley area on 30.5.82. The Harrier GR.3, XZ989/07, carries a 1,000lb bomb on the starboard outer pylon and a Paveway LGB on the port outer pylon but it was not until two weeks later that Paveway was used with successful results. Within 24 hours of this photograph XZ989 held the somewhat dubious distinction of being the only airworthy Harrier GR.3 aboard 'Hermes' although, fortunately, that situation was short-lived.

(Flt Lt D. H. S. Morgan, RAF)

This photograph of Pebble Island airfield, taken from an 801 Squadron Sea Harrier FRS.1 on 21.5.82, shows the disposition of the six Pucaras, three (of four) Mentors and the Skyvan destroyed or disabled in the SAS raid on 15.5.82. The Pucaras are arrowed and the Mentors ringed. The Skyvan's tail fins are clearly visible.          (Royal Navy)

This reconnaissance photograph taken from an 801 Squadron Sea Harrier FRS.1 on 31.5.82 shows Stanley Airport. Bomb craters (from Vulcan raids), the control tower (on the south side of the runway) and apron are clearly visible. Closer scrutiny reveals five Pucaras and a number of other types including an Islander to the north of the runway. On the south side, at the eastern threshold, three swept-wing aircraft are discernable. They are MB-339A's of 1 Escuadrilla de Ataque.

(Royal Navy)

sion saw the Squadron's first operational involvement. The Sidewinders were removed at the end of the day and the aircraft dedicated to the ground attack and reconnaissance roles to which they were best suited, permitting the Sea Harriers to concentrate mainly on air defence.

The first offensive mission was launched from the carrier at 1500Z on 20 May, when Peter Squire led Bob Iveson and Jerry Pook in a successful CBU attack against a fuel dump at Fox Bay East on West Falkland, their GR.3's recovering to 'Hermes' at 1545Z. An armed reconnaissance mission by Jerry Pook (XZ988) and Mark Hare (XZ963) was carried out at dawn on 21 May after the SAS had notified the carrier of possible targets to the north of Mount Kent. The two Harriers made a surprise attack on several CAB601 helicopters at that location; their first pass was not successful, but Chinook AE-521 was destroyed and Puma AE-501 badly damaged by Aden cannon fire from Hare's GR.3 in subsequent passes, while UH-1H AE-417 (which was about to take-off) escaped with damage to a rotor blade (later repaired). The Argentines claim that the two Harriers made seven passes over their camp where another dozen CAB601 helicopters were hidden! Hare's GR.3 was hit by small-arms fire but it had been repaired by the following morning.

The second mission of the day was not quite so successful. Bob Iveson (XZ997) and Jeff Glover (XZ972) were launched from 'Hermes' at 1156Z, but Iveson had to abort the mission due to problems with his aircraft's undercarriage and landed back aboard the carrier at 1212Z. He had been a last-minute replacement for Peter Squire (XV789), whose aircraft had developed a fault before departure. Glover continued alone to provide air support for troops in the area of San Carlos, but his services were not called upon. He was instructed to carry out a low-level photo-reconnaissance run over suspected enemy positions at Port Howard (West Falkland) which he accomplished successfully although nothing was seen. He was then asked to repeat the run. After a delay of about 15 minutes, Glover covered the same area again but on that occasion the enemy was ready for him. At about 1300Z his aircraft was hit by a Blowpipe SAM, believed to have been fired by a soldier of the Argentine Special Forces unit deployed at Port Howard (Compania de Comandos 601). The Harrier rolled through some 300° and a wing had folded before Glover had time to eject, his parachute not being fully deployed when he hit the water. The aircraft crashed into the ground close to Packe's Port Howard while its pilot landed in the water between Packe's and Port Howard and was picked up by Argentine soldiers in a rowing boat. Glover suffered a broken left arm, shoulder and collar-bone and a badly bruised face. He was well looked after by the Argentines, being flown by helicopter to Goose Green during the night of 22 May and then to Stanley during the night of 23 May, before being taken out to Comodoro Rivadavia on the mainland the next day by a Grupo 1 C-130. Glover was not released by the Argentines until 8 July.

Peter Harris (XZ988) and John Rochfort (XZ997) left 'Hermes' at 1345Z on 21 May to carry out an armed reconnaissance of the landing area at San Carlos, returning to the ship an hour later, the GR.3's still carrying their bombs. Harris landed safely at 1445Z but Rochfort's arrival at 1450Z was less successful, his GR.3 ending up

with its port outrigger in the catwalk. The aircraft was lifted back on deck, undamaged. Indeed, it was being flown by Mark Hare a few hours later in company with Jerry Pook (XZ989) for an hour-long mission which was launched from the carrier at 1900Z.

Four GR.3's armed with CBU's were launched at 1701Z on 22 May for another armed reconnaissance mission searching for Pucaras at Weddell airstrip, Darwin and Goose Green. Flown by Jerry Pook (XZ997), Bob Iveson (XZ963), Peter Harris (XZ989) and John Rochfort (XV789), the GR.3's bombed POL dumps and Pucara aircraft at Goose Green, some of the latter having been damaged in previous air raids. The Goose Green attack encountered heavy anti-aircraft fire but the Harriers came through unscathed, Iveson returning to the carrier without having released his bombs. Peter Squire and Tony Harper carried out an armed reconnaissance mission over Dunnose Head later that day (taking-off from 'Hermes' at 1924Z) as a prelude to the following morning's bombing mission.

Attacks against airstrips were a priority at that time so four GR.3's flown by Peter Squire (XZ997), Peter Harris (XZ963), Mark Hare (XZ989) and Tony Harper (XZ988) were launched at first light (1216Z) on 23 May to drop 1,000lb bombs on Dunnose Head. No aircraft were found, but the landing strip was attacked anyway as it was suspected (incorrectly) that it might have been used by the Grupo 1 C-130's on resupply flights from the mainland. Damage was caused to buildings and one local resident suffered injuries, but the strip itself remained untouched. Mark Hare visited the settlement at the end of hostilities to apologise for the damage caused, the residents having been forced to move to Chartres after some of the buildings at Dunnose Head were destroyed. Ironically, the airstrip was never used by the Argentines; their resupply flights "disappeared" from radar in that vicinity but the aircraft used terrain masking and continued on to Port Stanley. Pook (XZ989) and Rochfort (XZ963) mounted another armed reconnaissance mission between 1530Z and 1645Z, flying over troop emplacements in the areas around Chartres and Port Howard, while four GR.3's were launched at 1854Z to attack the airstrip at Pebble Island with CBU's and retarded 1,000lb bombs. Again, that was to prevent its possible use by aircraft on resupply flights from the mainland. Peter Squire (XZ988), Tony Harper (XZ989), Jerry Pook (XZ997) and John Rochfort (XZ963) all returned safely to 'Hermes' after the mission. 24 May saw the Squadron's first attack on Stanley Airport. Two 800 Sqdn Sea Harriers (XZ496 and ZA191) provided defence suppression armed with radar airburst VT bombs immediately prior to Bob Iveson (XZ997) and Tony Harper (XZ989) making an attack on the runway with retarded 1,000lb bombs. Peter Squire (XZ988) and Mark Hare (XV789) followed some 20 seconds later with the same type of weapons, but the runway survived the attack even though it was hit by three of the 12 bombs. The four GR.3's recovered to the carrier between 1258Z and 1300Z. That day saw the arrival with the Task Force of Laser-Guided Bombs, but at that stage there were no Forward Air Controllers or markers to illuminate targets for them.

A further attack on Stanley Airport by Jerry Pook (XZ988), Peter Harris (XZ989), Peter Squire (XV789) and

John Rochfort (XZ997) launched at about 1420Z on 25 May caused little significant damage, the quartet being supported again by two 800 Sqdn Sea Harriers (XZ455 and ZA191). Peter Squire (XZ989) and John Rochfort (XZ997) were launched for another armed reconnaissance mission at 1631Z, only 90 minutes after they had returned from the previous attack on Port Stanley, while Peter Harris (XZ988) and Mark Hare (XV789) took-off at 1728Z for yet another attack on the Airport. Both pairs landed safely back aboard 'Hermes', the first two without having dropped their bombs and the second two with the news that at least three of the six bombs dropped had missed their target. Peter Harris (still in XZ988) was only aboard the carrier for an hour before taking-off again for yet another mission against Stanley Airport, again in company with two 800 Sqdn Sea Harriers (XZ460 and ZA194). The trio launched from 'Hermes' at 1927Z, proceeded to Stanley Airport and tossed their bombs before recovering to 'Hermes' at 2041Z. The crews came back from this mission having sighted "Super Etendards" on the airfield, but they were in fact 1 Escuadrilla Aermacchi MB-339A's. The greatest misfortune to befall the Squadron on 25 May, however, was the loss to an Exocet missile of 'Atlantic Conveyor' with its large store of CBU's and 1,000lb bombs as well as other Squadron equipment.

Several sorties were flown in support of the advancing ground forces in the Port Stanley area on 26 May. Jerry Pook (XZ988) and John Rochfort (XZ963) launched from 'Hermes' at 1233Z on one such mission, but Pook was forced to return after 30 minutes with his IFF unserviceable. Without that piece of equipment functioning properly, he was as likely to be shot down by British forces as he was by the Argentines. Peter Squire (XZ989) was launched for a solo toss-bomb attack on Stanley Airport at 1659Z, but one of his three bombs hung-up and was later jettisoned. Extensive cloud cover prevented the results of that mission being confirmed. Jerry Pook (XZ989) and Mark Hare (XZ988) attacked a CAB601 Puma on the ground near Mount Kent while they were on an armed reconnaissance mission, having launched from the carrier at 1756Z. The helicopter was destroyed by Pook's CBU's, but it was in fact the same Puma (AE-501) which had been put out of action by Mark Hare on 21 May.

27 May saw further attacks on Port Stanley and Goose Green involving all seven pilots. Bob Iveson (XZ988) and Mark Hare (XV789) were launched from 'Hermes' at 1612Z to search for and attack two 105mm guns and troop emplacements at Goose Green and Darwin in support of 2 PARA's advance. During their first pass they saw nothing (no FAC being available to guide them), but on the second they dropped CBU's on a company-sized position. During a follow-up pass with Aden cannon, Iveson's Harrier was hit, probably by 35mm Oerlikon shells. The fire warning light came on, the controls froze and the aircraft began to lose hydraulic pressure. Even though the engine continued to run, the fire grew in intensity and Iveson was forced to eject some 40 seconds after being hit. The aircraft fireballed on hitting the ground about seven miles west of Goose Green settlement (UC 519594), while its pilot landed behind the enemy lines. Jerry Pook (XV789) took-off from the carrier at 1920Z on a solo photo-reconnaissance mission to try and locate Iveson, but returned to 'Hermes' an hour later having had no success. Bob Iveson was eventually picked up by 3 CBAS Gazelle XX380 three days later, none the worse for his experience, having successfully evaded capture in the unoccupied Paragon House about seven miles west northwest of Goose Green. After a night-stop at the Brigade HQ, he was flown back to 'Hermes' by Sea King.

An armed reconnaissance mission over Douglas Settlement (East Falkland) was carried out on 28 May, followed by an attack against enemy positions on Mount Kent. Bad weather prevented attacks on the Goose Green and Darwin areas until early evening, when an urgent request for air support was received from the advancing troops. Peter Harris (XZ989) and Tony Harper (XZ997) were detailed for the job, but Jerry Pook (XV789) volunteered to join them as well. The ground FAC briefed the pilots on their targets as they ran in, the most important being a 35mm AA gun emplacement on the promontory at Goose Green. The Argentines were using the AA gun as an effective artillery piece against the advancing soldiers of 2 PARA. Harris and Harper dropped CBU's while Pook fired 72 two-inch rockets from his two pods in the successful attack. It provided a great boost to morale for the hardpressed, but resolute, British troops as well as playing a crucial part in hastening the Argentine surrender there the following morning.

The Port Stanley area received further GR.3 attacks on 29 May, although bad weather restricted operations. Peter Squire (XZ989) and Mark Hare (XZ997) carried out a rocket attack in the area of Mount Kent, while Peter Harris (XZ963) carried out an unsuccessful search for radar sites reported to the north of the town.

30 May was a bad day for 1(F) Sqdn as another Harrier GR.3 was lost. Two pairs were launched during the morning on bombing missions in the Port Stanley area, followed later by a four-aircraft formation which included aircraft armed with LGB's, the first time that they had been used in the conflict. Flown by Peter Harris (XZ989), Tony Harper (XZ997), Jerry Pook (XZ963) and John Rochfort (XV789), the four GR.3's took-off from 'Hermes' between 1435Z and 1438Z, the first two for an LGB attack in the Port Stanley area and the second pair armed with two-inch rocket pods to search for helicopters reported on the ground west of the town. The LGB raid was unsuccessful due to the lack of a FAC, while the other two encountered a column of Argentine troops and Pook's aircraft was hit by small-arms fire. They continued the search for enemy helicopters, but none was located so instead an artillery position was attacked with their rockets. On heading back towards 'Hermes', Pook was informed by his wingman that XZ963 seemed to be venting fuel. Both GR.3's climbed to cruise height, but the leak in Pook's aircraft worsened. All stores were jettisoned, but it became clear that the Harrier would not make it back to the carrier. With fuel gauges indicating empty, Pook descended to 10,000ft then ejected at 1520Z some 30 miles from 'Hermes'. He landed in the sea, inflated and then got into his dinghy, but was in the water for less than 10 minutes before being rescued by 826 Sqdn Sea King XZ571 which had been dispatched in the direction of the two Harriers even before Pook had ejected. John Rochfort returned to 'Hermes' at 1528Z, followed by the other pair from the unsuccessful LGB attack at

# HARRIER GR.3 XZ989/07 1(F) SQUADRON

Flown by Sqdn Ldr Pook on 26 May 1982 when he destroyed the already damaged CAB601 Compania de Asalto 'A' Puma AE-501.

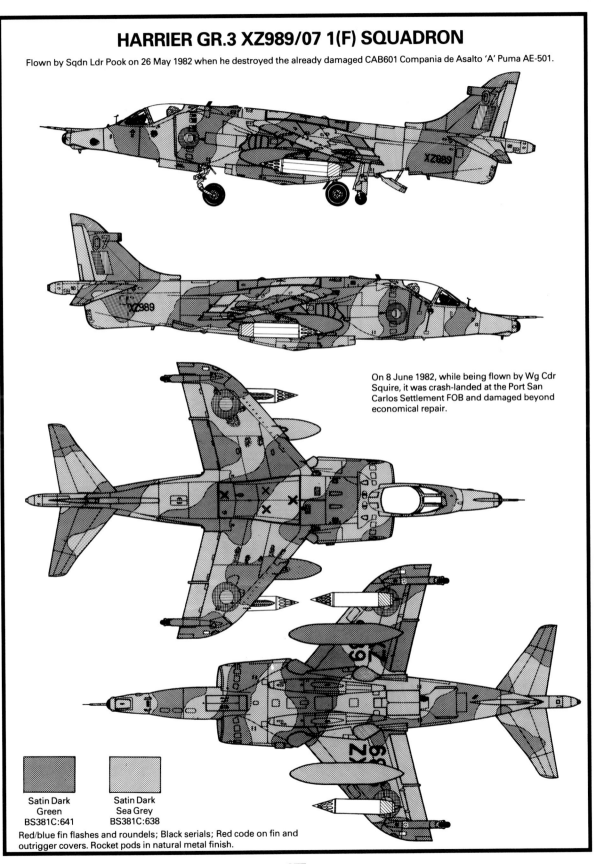

On 8 June 1982, while being flown by Wg Cdr Squire, it was crash-landed at the Port San Carlos Settlement FOB and damaged beyond economical repair.

Satin Dark Green
BS381C:641

Satin Dark Sea Grey
BS381C:638

Red/blue fin flashes and roundels; Black serials; Red code on fin and outrigger covers. Rocket pods in natural metal finish.

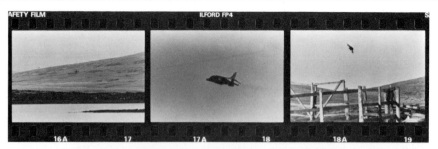

Taken from Estancia House on East Falkland (reportedly on 21.5.82), this dramatic sequence of photographs shows an unidentified 1(F) Squadron Harrier GR.3 attacking Argentine positions on Mount Kent. If the date is correct, the pall of smoke visible in Frame 22 may well be from the CAB601 Chinook AE-521 which was destroyed in the raid that morning. The Harriers involved were XZ963/14 and XZ988/34.

*(via Flt Lt R. Robinson, RAF)*

Harrier GR.3 XZ989/07 of 1(F) Squadron suffered an engine failure during its final approach to the FOB, north-west of Port San Carlos settlement, on 8.6.82. Wg Cdr Peter Squire was shaken but otherwise unhurt in the crash-landing that followed. XZ989, seen here "in situ" immediately afterwards, was later moved to Port Stanley where it remained until airlifted to Ascension Island by LTW Hercules on 20.11.82 for onward conveyance to the United Kingdom by Heavylift Belfast. *(815 Sqdn 'Exeter' Flight)*

In low-visibility markings and with weapons fitted, the Harrier GR.3 takes on a somewhat fearsome appearance. This unidentified aircraft is armed with AIM-9G Sidewinder missiles at a snow-covered RAF Stanley on 6.7.82. An abandoned Pucara, A-513, is in the background. In spite of its armament, this Harrier was about to undertake a most inoffensive, but fundamentally important, role – that of snow clearance!

*(815 Sqdn 'Exeter' Flight)*

1540Z. Peter Squire and Tony Harper later carried out an armed reconnaissance mission in the vicinity of Mount Kent, but the Argentine troop concentrations they expected to find had moved on.

With only three GR.3's then available, 1 Sqdn was to suffer further bad luck on 31 May which by nightfall would leave it with just one serviceable machine (XZ989). Another attack on Stanley Airport was attempted during the morning by Tony Harper (XV789, armed with LGB's), Peter Harris (XZ989, bombs) and John Rochfort (XZ997, rockets) but, once again, no FAC was available. At 1430Z a further report of "Super Etendards" at the eastern end Stanley Airport's runway was received, so a hurried operation was mounted. Peter Squire (XV789) and Mark Hare (XZ997) took-off at 1452Z for a rocket attack against these targets, two 800 Sqdn Sea Harriers (XZ496 and XZ500 armed with toss bombs) providing support. The two Harrier GR.3's successfully recovered to the carrier about an hour later but had suffered battle-damage which put them out of action for the next day or two. Peter Harris took-off in the one available GR.3 at 1647Z for an attack in the Mount Usborne area, accompanied by three 800 Sqdn Sea Harriers (XZ455 and XZ460 with bombs plus ZA191 with LGB's). That was to be yet another attempt to gain success with LGB's, Harris trying to use the GR.3's laser designator to illuminate the target for weapons aboard Lt Morrell's Sea Harrier. However, the planned target near Mount Usborne was too adjacent to British troops, so another target in the Port Stanley area was chosen instead. The results (if any) remain unconfirmed, but the mission served to prove that a ground FAC with the appropriate target designator would have to be in position before an LGB mission could be expected to meet with any success. XV789 required an engine change following the day's activities. A Pegasus 103 had been lost with the sinking of 'Atlantic Conveyor', so the first major problem was to locate another within the Task Force as the Sea Harrier's Pegasus 104 was not compatible. One was later located aboard 'Intrepid' and ferried by helicopter to the carrier. Both Royal Navy and Royal Air Force personnel carried out the engine change in short bursts of activity over the next three days when they could be spared from the more pressing operational tasks.

Bad weather affected flying on 1 June. Peter Squire (XZ989) joined Flt Lt Ball (in 800 Sqdn Sea Harrier XZ457) on a reconnaissance flight that afternoon, the pair launching from the carrier at 1700Z and recovering at 1810Z. However, the most important event of the day for 1(F) Sqdn was the arrival aboard 'Hermes' at 1732Z of two replacement GR.3's direct from Ascension Island (Mike Beech and Murdo MacLeod flying XV778 and XZ133 respectively).

The FOB at Port San Carlos was completed by the Royal Engineers on 2 June, 10ft by 2ft strips of aluminium having been laid by hand to make an 850ft runway. There was also a metal pad for vertical take-off/landing, plus parking space for four aircraft (the original intention was to have parking space for 10 aircraft but a large quantity of material was lost with the sinking of 'Atlantic Conveyor'). Aviation fuel was kept in floating bags moored at the shoreline, to be pumped ashore using a small pipeline to the strip. 1(F) Sqdn crews nicknamed the FOB "Sid's Strip" after its CO, Sqdn Ldr

B.S.Morris AFC (it was known as "HMS Sheathbill" to Royal Navy pilots).

Bad weather continued to disrupt the flying but Jerry Pook (XZ989) and Murdo MacLeod (XZ133) managed to get airborne for a 45 minute sortie during the morning of 2 June armed with rockets to support the ground forces. The weather continued to affect flying until 5 June, when two 800 Sqdn Sea Harriers became the first aircraft to make use of the FOB. Bob Iveson led a pair of GR.3's in shortly afterwards, flying once again after his ejection the previous week. He in fact stayed locally for two nights, not returning to 'Hermes' until 7 June. Deploying the Harriers to the FOB meant that their INAS could at last be set up properly, although the aircraft returned to the safety of 'Hermes' each evening. Peter Squire (XZ997) and Mike Beech (XZ989) were launched from 'Hermes' at 1850Z in company with two 800 Sqdn Sea Harriers (XZ457 and XZ500) to search for ground-launched Exocet missiles south-west of Port Stanley but none was found.

Jerry Pook (XZ989) and Murdo MacLeod (XZ133) departed 'Hermes' some 240 miles east of Port Stanley at 1200Z on 6 June to position to the FOB, further attacks in the Stanley area being carried out that day along with another reconnaissance mission looking for ground-launched Exocet missiles. The GR.3's spent much of 7 June waiting at the FOB for calls upon their services which never came, as there was little contact between the British and Argentine troops. The day saw Bob Iveson grounded with back problems which had resulted from his earlier ejection. He was dispatched to Ascension Island aboard 'British Trent' on 11 June, arriving at Wittering aboard a 207 Sqdn Devon on 24 June after the transit by 10 Sqdn VC-10 from Wideawake to Brize Norton. He was the first 1(F) Sqdn pilot to return home.

Four aircraft were launched from the carrier at 1315Z on 8 June, but once again no suitable targets could be found so they were directed to land at the FOB. The first three landed safely, but the fourth GR.3 (XZ989 flown by Peter Squire) suffered a partial engine failure on approach and crash-landed on the grass adjacent to the strip. The aircraft careered straight across the metal runway and came to rest straddling a slit trench. Squire was shaken but uninjured, while the Harrier itself was damaged beyond the capabilities of the local repair teams and later robbed for spares.

Two further reinforcements landed aboard 'Hermes' direct from Wideawake at 1700Z on 8 June, flown by Ross Boyens (XW919) and Nick Gilchrist (XZ992). The FOB had been repaired and was operational once again by first light on 9 June. Several GR.3 sorties were launched from Port San Carlos during the day against Argentine positions on Sapper Hill and Mount Longdon, encountering intense ground fire. Murdo MacLeod's aircraft was hit following rocket attacks against 155mm gun emplacements, but he was not aware how seriously until his return to 'Hermes'. Small-arms fire had severed hydraulic lines to the extent that his undercarriage would not lower properly and had to be blown down.

Harrier GR.3's XZ992 (Peter Harris) and XZ997 (Nick Gilchrist) were dispatched from 'Hermes' to the FOB at 1131Z on 10 June to await instructions but were not called upon. Peter Squire (XV789) and Mark Hare (XV778) flew a photo-reconnaissance mission over the front line west of Port Stanley, taking-off from 'Hermes' at 1300Z. They crossed the coast near Fitzroy and then split up, Squire going north past the western edge of the town while Hare flew north-east past Two Sisters and Mount Longdon, both at low level. Having returned from the FOB, XZ992 (John Rochfort) and XZ997 (Nick Gilchrist) departed 'Hermes' at 1631Z armed with LGB's. They were accompanied by Jerry Pook in XV789 and Ross Boyens in XV778 (both armed with bombs), but all four later returned to the carrier with weapons intact as there was no FAC in place to illuminate a target for them. Peter Squire (in XZ997) and Murdo MacLeod (XV778) launched at 1854Z for a CBU attack on troop concentrations in the area west of Stanley, the targets having been provided by the photo-reconnaissance mission earlier in the day. They both experienced intense small-arms fire and MacLeod's Harrier suffered damage to wiring as one bullet passed right through the cockpit area. The aircraft was unserviceable for the next couple of days while that was repaired.

Several sorties against Argentine positions were launched on 11 June, once again into intense small-arms fire. Tony Harper (XZ997) and Nick Gilchrist (XW919) took-off from 'Hermes' at 1122Z for an LGB attack on Port Stanley. The next pair to launch, Jerry Pook (XV789) and Mike Beech (XZ992), departed at 1148Z but returned after 20 minutes following IFF failure in XV789. Some two hours later, Ross Boyens (XZ992) and John Rochfort (XW919) took-off to bomb Argentine troop positions but Rochfort had problems shortly after departure and was forced to jettison his bombs. He was able to continue with the mission armed only with Aden cannon. Jerry Pook (XV789) and Mike Beech (XZ133) followed at 1450Z with an attack on Mount Harriet, while Peter Harris (XV789) and Nick Gilchrist (XZ997) left the carrier at 1810Z for a CBU attack in the Port Stanley area. Peter Squire (XZ992) and Mark Hare (XZ133) performed the final mission of the day, launching at 1823Z armed with 1,000lb bombs for an attack on gun emplacements near Mount Longdon. Three Blowpipe missiles were fired at them; the first two fell well short, but the third finally exploded some 100ft above Harris' GR.3 (an unnerving experience!).

There were six sorties during the morning of 12 June against Argentine troop concentrations on Sapper Hill. Ross Boyens (XZ133) and Mike Beech (XV778) took-off at 1145Z, intending to land at Port San Carlos after their mission, but the FOB was out of action due to ice and fog so they had to return to 'Hermes'. Peter Harris (XV789) and Murdo MacLeod (XW919) departed together at 1400Z and MacLeod was hit once again by small-arms fire. The damage was slightly more serious that time, as a bullet had passed through a hot-air duct causing a fire to start when the Harrier was slowed to the hover. The aircraft was landed successfully on board 'Hermes' at 1510Z, however, and the fire was extinguished. XW919 played no further part in the fighting (although it was eventually patched up by the BDR team), being transferred to 'Contender Bezant' for return to Wittering after hostilities ceased. The final GR.3 launch of the day involved Tony Harper (XZ133) and Nick Gilchrist (XV778).

By 12 June, one of the GR.3's had been modified to enable it to carry two Shrike anti-radar missiles, but in the event that option was never exercised.

The first successful LGB attack took place on 13 June when Peter Squire (XZ997) attacked a Company HQ on Tumbledown, there being a FAC in position to mark the target on that occasion. The first LGB tossed at the target fell short but the second scored a direct hit minutes later. Wingman Mark Hare (XZ133) followed up with CBU's, the pair returning to Hermes at 1530Z at the end of the hour-long mission. Jerry Pook carried out a similarly successful LGB attack on a 105mm gun emplacement near Moody Brook during the afternoon, accompanied by John Rochfort.

Ross Boyens (XV789) and Murdo MacLeod (XV778) departed the FOB at 1132Z on 14 June, but bad weather prevented any further sorties for the next few hours. The weather subsequently improved to enable Peter Harris (XZ997 with LGBs) and Nick Gilchrist (XZ133 with CBU's) to depart 'Hermes' at 1500Z for another attack on Sapper Hill. They made contact with the FAC, only to be told to hold off as white flags had been seen in Port Stanley. The surrender followed at 1555Z and the two GR.3's returned to 'Hermes' with their bomb loads intact, landing at 1625Z.

That concluded 1(F) Sqdn's contribution to the war effort. A total of 150 sorties were flown from 'Hermes' and the Port San Carlos FOB between 18 May and 14 June, of which 126 were operational tasked sorties over the Falkland Islands. The Squadron was reported to have been grounded by bad weather on only two and a half days throughout the period, with few tasked sorties being aborted due either to weather or aircraft unserviceabilities. Following the surrender, 1(F) Sqdn's role changed to that of air defence and AIM-9G Sidewinders were fitted once again. There was a rotation of pilots on 21 June, most of the original personnel being returned to Wittering aboard 115 Sqdn Andover XS596 on 7 July after their arrival by VC-10 at Brize Norton. Flying thereafter included practice radar-controlled intercepts, air combat training and several flag-waving sorties over the Islands. The GR.3's took part in a Task Force air defence exercise on 27 June, during which they defended the Fleet against attacking Sea Harriers.

26 June saw an advance party from 1(F) Sqdn take up residence at Stanley Airport prior to the aircraft and personnel aboard 'Hermes' disembarking to rudimentary facilities there on 4 July, thus enabling the carrier to continue her homeward journey. The four additional machines aboard 'Contender Bezant' (by then anchored off Port Stanley) followed over the next two days. Those aircraft formed what became unofficially known as the Harrier Detachment (HarDet), RAF Stanley (as the Airport had been renamed). XZ133 was damaged during a gale on 28 July when a portable hangar collapsed onto it, while XV778, XW767 and XZ997 suffered minor storm damage on the same date. A gradual rotation of aircraft was commenced, the first to return to the United Kingdom being those which had suffered damage (XW919, XZ133 and XZ989). By the end of the year, only six aircraft from the original 14 Harriers sent to the Falkland Islands were still in residence at RAF Stanley (all of which returned during the course of 1983).

The Task Force flagship 'Hermes' reveals a crowded flight-deck of mixed Harrier variants in this, perhaps, unusual view of the carrier, taken just hours before the Argentine surrender on 14.6.82. Although still tied down, 1(F) Squadron Harrier GR.3's XZ997/31 and XV789/32 (in the foreground) are fully armed and ready for immediate dispatch. Amongst the Sea Harriers towards the stern two other GR.3's, XZ133/10 and XV778/16, take a well-earned rest. *(Ministry of Defence)*

Being prepared for an LGB mission from 'Hermes' on 14.6.82 is 1(F) Squadron Harrier GR.3 XZ997/31. The patches applied to the upper surface of the aircraft's port wing by the battle-damage repair teams are indicative of the amount of small-arms fire that the Harrier was able to absorb, yet still remain operational. *(Ministry of Defence)*

1(F) Sqdn handed over responsibility for the Detachment to 4 Sqdn (under Wg Cdr McKeon) on 10 November. All three Royal Air Force Harrier GR.3 squadrons and 233 OCU subsequently provided personnel on a rotational basis, the turn of 1(F) Sqdn coming once more on 16 August 1983. The HarDet was officially redesignated 1453 Flight four days later on 20 August 1983, unit markings consisting of a yellow letter code on the fin with the Falkland Islands shield on the nose. The official opening of the new airport at Mount Pleasant (East Falkland) on 12 May 1985, with its ability to accept long-range, widebodied tanker/transport aircraft, enabled the Flight to be disbanded that month and its aircraft were withdrawn to the United Kingdom.

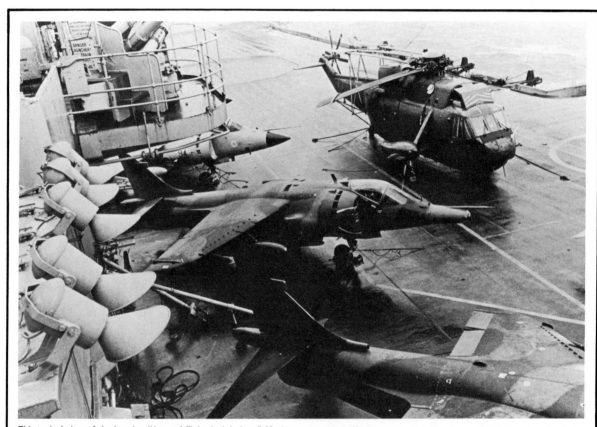

*This typical view of the heaving 'Hermes' flight-deck in late 5.82 shows aircraft of 1(F) Squadron, 800 Squadron and 826 Squadron. Both the Harrier GR.3, XV789/32 (centre), and Sea Harrier FRS.1, ZA194 '94', had earlier arrived in the TEZ on 'Atlantic Conveyor' and each subsequently achieved a measure of fame. In Lt Martin Hale's hands the Sea Harrier destroyed a Grupo 6 de Caza Dagger on 23.5.82, while the RAF Harrier suffered battle damage on 31.5.82 severe enough to warrant an engine change on 'Hermes'. The Sea King HAS.5 is ZA131 '–/(1)33'.*

*(Ministry of Defence)*

# INDIVIDUAL AIRCRAFT DETAILS

**XV762** GR.3

On 29.3.82 with 233 OCU at Wittering coded 'G'. Transferred to 1(F) Sqdn during 4.82 and recoded '37' in Red on fin/outriggers but minus Squadron badge on nose. Flown to St Mawgan from Wittering on 28.5.82 and then on to Wideawake on 30.5.82. Embarked 'Contender Bezant' off Ascension 3.6.82, sailing south with her the same day. Arrived in the TEZ on 10.6.82 but remained aboard ship and not used prior to the surrender on 14.6.82. Disembarked to RAF Stanley on/by 6.7.82 to join the other 1(F) Sqdn aircraft which had moved ashore from 'Hermes' on 4.7.82. The detachment subsequently became known as the HarDet. Current 31.12.82 (allocated code 'A') but had returned to Wittering for 1(F) Sqdn before the HarDet was redesignated 1453 Flight on 20.8.83.

**XV778** GR.3

On 29.3.82 with 1(F) Sqdn at Wittering coded '16'. Squadron badge on the nose removed prior to being positioned from Wittering to St Mawgan on 28.5.82 and then on to

Wideawake on 29.5.82. Flown from Wideawake direct to 'Hermes' in the TEZ on 1.6.82.

Flown by Flt Lt MacLeod, it suffered damage to cockpit wiring on 10.6.82 when hit by small-arms fire during a CBU attack west of Port Stanley (repaired on 'Hermes' during the next couple of days).

Disembarked to RAF Stanley with 1(F) Sqdn on 4.7.82, the detachment subsequently becoming known as the HarDet. Sustained minor storm damage 28.7.82, later repaired. Current on 31.12.82 (allocated code 'H') but had returned to Wittering for 1(F) Sqdn before the HarDet was redesignated 1453 Flight on 20.8.83.

### XV787 GR.3

On 29.3.82 with 1(F) Sqdn at Wittering, minus code and Squadron marks for filming of the TV serial "Squadron" (allocated code '02'). Involved in ski-jump training at Yeovilton 14.4.82 and 21.4.82. Flown from Wittering to St Mawgan 2.5.82, leaving for Wideawake on 4.5.82. Suffered technical problems while en route and diverted to Porto Santo, Madeira. Spares arrived aboard Hercules C.1 XV177 on 6.5.82 and, following repairs, it was flown to Gibraltar on 8.5.82. Returned to Wittering (via Istres) on 10.5.82.

### XV789 GR.3

On 29.3.82 with 4(F) Sqdn at Gutersloh coded 'F'. Transferred to 1(F) Sqdn and flown to Wittering on 16.4.82 with XZ997/E. Recoded '32' in Red on fin and outriggers but minus Squadron badge on the nose. To Valley for AIM-9G test firings 30.4.82. Positioned from Wittering to St Mawgan on 2.5.82, continuing to Wideawake via Banjul on 3.5.82. Embarked 'Atlantic Conveyor' off Ascension on 6.5.82, sailing with the ship for the TEZ on 7.5.82. Flown off to 'Hermes' on 18.5.82.

Piloted by Sqdn Ldr Pook, it took part in a successful three-aircraft attack on enemy gun positions at Goose Green on 28.5.82, playing a crucial part in hastening the Argentine surrender there the following morning.

Flown by Wg Cdr Squire, it suffered battle damage during a rocket attack in the Port Stanley area on 31.5.82. Repairs and an engine change were accomplished aboard 'Hermes'.

Disembarked to RAF Stanley with 1(F) Sqdn on 4.7.82, the detachment subsequently becoming known as the HarDet. Current 31.12.82 (allocated code 'F') but returned to Gutersloh for 4(F) Sqdn before the HarDet was redesignated 1453 Flight on 20.8.83.

### XW767 GR.3

On 29.3.82 with 1(F) Sqdn at Wittering coded '06'. Operated from Binbrook for DACT on 15.4.82 and from Yeovilton for ski-jump training on 15.4.82 and 19.4.82. Squadron badge on the nose removed prior to being positioned to St Mawgan from Wittering on 28.5.82 and then on to Wideawake on 29.5.82. Embarked 'Contender Bezant' off Ascension on 3.6.82 and sailed south with the ship later the same day. Arrived in the TEZ on 10.6.82

but remained aboard the vessel and was not used operationally prior to the surrender on 14.6.82. Disembarked on/by 6.7.82 to RAF Stanley, joining the other 1(F) Sqdn aircraft which had moved ashore on 4.7.82 from 'Hermes', the detachment subsequently becoming known as the HarDet. Suffered minor storm damage 28.7.82, later repaired. Crashed into the sea off Cape Pembroke on 6.11.82 after engine failure, Wg Cdr Squire ejecting safely.

### XW919 GR.3

On 29.3.82 with 1(F) Sqdn at Wittering minus code and Squadron marks for filming of the TV serial "Squadron" (allocated code '03'). Operated from Binbrook for DACT on 15.4.82 and from Yeovilton for ski-jump training on 14, 17, 20 and 23.4.82. The fin-code was reapplied prior to it being flown from Wittering to St Mawgan on 4.5.82 and then to Wideawake on 5.5.82. Remained at Wideawake on air defence duties until three 29(F) Sqdn Phantom FGR.2's arrived from Coningsby on 24/26.5.82. Flown non-stop to 'Hermes' from Wideawake 8.6.82.

Damaged by small-arms fire on 12.6.82 while being flown by Flt Lt MacLeod in an attack on Sapper Hill. Part of the rear fuselage caught fire on final approach to 'Hermes' but the aircraft landed safely. The fire was extinguished and the aircraft patched up, but it took no further part in the conflict.

Transferred from 'Hermes' to 'Contender Bezant' for return to the UK, sailing with the ship from Port William on 13.7.82 to arrive at Southampton on 1.8.82. Off-loaded and departed by road to Wittering on 2.8.82, arriving there 4.8.82 for repair.

### XW924 GR.3

On 29.3.82 with 233 OCU at Wittering coded 'H'. Transferred to 1(F) Sqdn during 4.82 and recoded '35' in Red on fin/outriggers but minus Squadron badge on nose. Flown to St Mawgan from Wittering on 29.5.82 and then on to Wideawake 30.5.82. Embarked 'Contender Bezant' off Ascension on 3.6.82 and sailed south with her the same day. Arrived in the TEZ on 10.6.82 but remained aboard the ship and not used prior to the surrender on 14.6.82. Disembarked to RAF Stanley on/by 6.7.82, joining the other 1(F) Sqdn aircraft which had moved ashore from 'Hermes' on 4.7.82, the detachment subsequently became known as the HarDet. Suffered an inadvertent Sidewinder release on 13.7.82 during take-off, both AIM-9G's being fired simultaneously. The starboard missile hit the ground harmlessly but the port one flew for some 400 yards before breaking up on hitting the ground; 11 soldiers working at the runway edge sustained injuries from the fragments. Current with the HarDet during 12.82 (allocated code 'B') but shipped to Ascension for return to the UK, arriving at Wittering aboard Heavylift Belfast G-BEPS on 11.1.83.

### XZ129 GR.3

On 29.3.82 with 1(F) Sqdn at Wittering coded '29'. Operated from Yeovilton for ski-jump training 14.4.82 and from Binbrook for DACT 15.4.82. Squadron badge on the nose was removed prior to being flown to St

Mawgan on 4.5.82 and then to Wideawake 5.5.82. Remained on air defence duties at Wideawake until the arrival of three 29(F) Sqdn Phantom FGR.2's from Coningsby on 24/26.5.82. Embarked 'Contender Bezant' off Ascension on 3.6.82, sailing south with the vessel the same day. Arrived in the TEZ on 10.6.82 but remained aboard ship and not used prior to the surrender on 14.6.82. Disembarked on/by 6.7.82 to RAF Stanley, joining the other 1(F) Sqdn aircraft which had moved ashore from 'Hermes' on 4.7.82. The detachment subsequently became known as the HarDet. Current 31.12.82 (allocated code 'M') but shipped to Ascension for return to the UK, arriving at Wittering aboard Heavylift Belfast G-BEPE on 26.1.83.

### XZ132 GR.3

On 29.3.82 with 233 OCU at Wittering coded 'A'. Transferred to 1(F) Sqdn during 4.82 and recoded '36' in Red on fin/outriggers but minus Squadron badge on nose. Flown to St Mawgan from Wittering on 3.5.82 and to Banjul on 5.5.82, completing its transit to Wideawake the following day. Suffered from incurable fuel leaks and was later returned to Wittering (date not known). No further involvement in South Atlantic operations.

### XZ133 GR.3

On 29.3.82 with 233 OCU at Wittering coded 'P'. Transferred to 1(F) Sqdn during 4.82 and recoded '10' in Red on fin/outriggers but minus Squadron badge on nose. Operated from Binbrook on 15.4.82 for DACT. Flown from Wittering to St Mawgan on 28.5.82 and then to Wideawake 29.5.82. Flown non-stop from Wideawake to 'Hermes' in the TEZ on 1.6.82.

Armed with CBU's, it was flown by Flt Lt Gilchrist on 1(F) Sqdn's last sortie of the War on 14.6.82, accompanying Sqdn Ldr Harris in XZ997 armed with LGB's. The attack was called off by the FAC when white flags were seen in Port Stanley.

Disembarked to RAF Stanley with 1(F) Sqdn on 4.7.82, the detachment subsequently becoming known as the HarDet. Suffered CAT.4 damage in a storm on 28.7.82 when a portable hangar collapsed on top of it. Transferred to 'Invincible' in Port William by 18 Sqdn Chinook ZA720/BG on 25.8.82 for return to the UK. Airlifted off to Culdrose 16.9.82 (the day before 'Invincible' arrived at Portsmouth) by 18 Sqdn Chinook ZA710/BC. Left by road for Wittering on 11.10.82, arriving there on 13.10.82 for repair.

### XZ963 GR.3

On 29.3.82 with 1(F) Sqdn at Wittering coded '14'. Flown to Yeovilton for ski-jump training on 15, 16, 19 and 21.4.82 and to Binbrook for DACT on 15.4.82. Squadron badge on the nose removed prior to being flown to St Mawgan from Wittering 3.5.82 and then to Wideawake 4.5.82. Embarked 'Atlantic Conveyor' off Ascension on 6.5.82, sailing with the ship for the TEZ on 7.5.82. Flown off to 'Hermes' on 19.5.82.

Flown on an armed reconnaissance mission by by Flt Lt Hare on 21.5.82 (accompanied by Sqdn Ldr Pook in XZ988) during which some Ejercito helicopters were strafed in the vicinity

The first 1(F) Squadron Harrier GR.3 to return to the United Kingdom after the cease-fire was XW919/03 which had sustained heavy small-arms fire damage to internal systems on 12.6.82. Declared non-effective, it had been shipped back aboard 'Contender Bezant' and is seen here inside the ship's ''hangar'' just hours after arriving at Southampton on 1.8.82. Shortly afterwards the Harrier was lifted onto the quayside prior to its departure by road to Wittering the following day. (Michael I. Draper)

AIM-9G-equipped Harrier GR.3 XZ129/29, operating with the ''HARDET'' at RAF Stanley on 19.10.82, is seen parked on temporary matting. This aircraft was one of four reinforcements which had been sent south from Ascension Island aboard 'Contender Bezant' but had failed to see combat even though the ship had arrived in the TEZ on 10.6.82. It remained aboard the vessel (with the other three) until after the 1(F) Squadron GR.3's aboard 'Hermes' had disembarked to Stanley Airport on 4.7.82.

(Richard Gardner)

The Victor K.2 detachment at Wideawake performed outstandingly in assisting the Vulcan ''Black Buck'' raids against Stanley Airport and undertaking other very long-range missions. Seen at Wideawake on 1.5.82, XL232 wears the badge of 232 OCU, the training unit which utilised aircraft from both 55 and 57 Squadrons as required.

(Mel James)

Victor K.2 XL189, also seen at Wideawake on 1.5.82, sports 57 Squadron's old ''Heinz Baked Beans'' unit marking which was in the process of being superseded by the more representative blue/red Phoenix insignia. (Mel James) of Mount Kent. Hare destroyed CAB601 Chinook AE-521 and damaged Puma AE-501 with cannon fire while UH-1H AE-417 escaped with damage to one rotor blade.

Involved in a four-aircraft formation attack against the airstrip at Dunnose Head on 23.5.82 (flown by Sqdn Ldr Harris) which resulted in the destruction of some of the settlement and injury to one of the local inhabitants.

On 30.5.82, while being flown by Sqdn Ldr Pook in search of enemy helicopters which had been reported west of Port Stanley, it was hit by small-arms fire resulting in a fuel leak. The pilot was forced to eject into the sea some 30 miles short of 'Hermes' (east of the Falklands) when the aircraft ran out of fuel. Pook was rescued by 826 Sqdn Sea King XZ571 after less than 10 minutes in the water.

### XZ972 GR.3

On 29.3.82 with 233 OCU at Wittering coded 'L'. Transferred to 1(F) Sqdn during 4.82 and recoded '33' in Red on fin/outriggers but minus Squadron badge on nose. Sent to Valley for AIM-9G trial firings on 30.4.82. Deployed from Wittering to St Mawgan on 2.5.82 and then on to Wideawake (via Banjul) 3.5.82. Embarked 'Atlantic Conveyor' off Ascension on 6.5.82, sailing with the ship for the TEZ on 7.5.82. Flown off to 'Hermes' on 18.5.82, being the first GR.3 to arrive aboard the carrier.

Became the Squadron's first casualty on 21.5.82 while being flown by Flt Lt Glover on a solo armed reconnaissance mission over Port Howard on West Falkland. Hit by a Blowpipe SAM (believed fired by a soldier from the Argentine Special Forces unit, CC601); the pilot ejected safely before the aircraft crashed into the ground at Packe's Port Howard. He came down in the water between Packe's and Port Howard and was picked up as a PoW by Argentine soldiers in a rowing boat. Eventually transferred to the Argentine mainland, he was not released until 8.7.82. The remains of XZ972 were still present at Packe's Port Howard in late 1983.

### XZ988 GR.3

On 29.3.82 with 233 OCU at Wittering coded 'N'. Transferred to 1(F) Sqdn during 4.82 and recoded '34' in Red on fin/outriggers but minus Squadron badge on nose. Deployed from Wittering to St Mawgan on 3.5.82 and then to Wideawake on 5.5.82. Embarked 'Atlantic Conveyor' off Ascension on 6.5.82, sailing with the ship for the TEZ on 7.5.82. Flown off to 'Hermes' by Sqdn Ldr Harris 18.5.82.

Flown by Sqdn Ldr Pook on 21.5.82 when he and Flt Lt Hare (in XZ963) strafed CAB601 helicopters near Mount Kent. Hare's GR.3 destroyed Chinook AE-521, damaged Puma AE-501 and superficially damaged a rotor blade on UH-1H AE-417.

Involved in a four-aircraft formation attack against the airstrip at Dunnose Head on 23.5.82 (flown by Flt Lt Harper) which resulted in the destruction of some of the settlement and injury to one of the local inhabitants.

Used on the Squadron's first attack against

---

Stanley Airport on 24.5.82 armed with retarded 1,000lb bombs (flown by Wg Cdr Squire).

Hit by gunfire (almost certainly 35mm Oerlikon) on 27.5.82 during its third attack run over Goose Green in support of 2 PARA's advance, Sqdn Ldr Iveson ejecting safely seconds before the aircraft exploded on hitting the ground about seven miles west of Goose Green settlement (UC 519594). The pilot came down behind enemy lines but managed to avoid capture at Paragon House (seven miles west north-west of Goose Green) until picked up by 3 CBAS Gazelle XX380 three days later. The remains of XZ988 were still present at the crash site on 11.8.85.

### XZ989 GR.3

On 29.3.82 with 1(F) Sqdn at Wittering minus code and Squadron marks for filming of the TV serial "Squadron" (allocated code '07'). Operated from Yeovilton for ski-jump training on 16.4.82. Flown to A&AEE Boscombe Down from Wittering 29.4.82 for acceptance of the AIM-9G fit and then on to Valley the next day for test firings over the Cardigan Bay ranges. The fin-code was reapplied before deployment to St Mawgan on 2.5.82 for transit to Wideawake on 3.5.82. Embarked 'Atlantic Conveyor' off Ascension on 6.5.82, sailing with the ship for the TEZ 7.5.82. Flown off to 'Hermes' on 20.5.82.

Involved in a four-aircraft formation attack against the airstrip at Dunnose Head on 23.5.82 (flown by Flt Lt Hare) which resulted in the destruction of some of the settlement and injury to one of the local inhabitants.

Took part in the Squadron's first attack on Stanley Airport with retarded 1,000lb bombs on 24.5.82, flown by Flt Lt Harper.

A CAB601 Puma was attacked by Sqdn Ldr Pook on 26.5.82 in the vicinity of Mount Kent, and was later identified as AE-501 which had been damaged by Flt Lt Hare in the raid on 21.5.82. The Puma was completely destroyed by his CBU's.

Flown by Wg Cdr Harris, it took part in a successful three-aircraft attack on enemy gun positions at Goose Green on 28.5.82, playing a crucial part in hastening the Argentine surrender there the following morning.

Suffered loss of power while landing at the Port San Carlos FOB on 8.6.82, the aircraft hitting the strip very hard and skidding to a halt (Wg Cdr Squire, the pilot, was shaken but not injured). Damaged beyond the resources of the BDR team and used as a spares source. Moved to RAF Stanley by 18 Sqdn Chinook after the ceasefire and then flown to Wideawake aboard LTW Hercules C.1P XV290 on 20.11.82. Transferred to Heavylift Belfast G-BFYU and arrived at Wittering on 23.11.82. Removed to BAe Dunsfold by 15.3.83 for assessment but eventually classified as CAT.5. Still at Dunsfold 10.1.85 when the Maintenance Serial 8849M was allocated it, pending transfer to Gütersloh for Ground Instruction duties.

### XZ992 GR.3

On 29.3.82 with 1 Sqdn at Wittering minus

---

code and Squadron marks for filming of the TV serial "Squadron" (allocated code '05'). Fin-code reapplied prior to being flown non-stop to Goose Bay in Canada on 13.4.82 for a "Maple Flag" exercise at CFB Cold Lake in company with seven other Harriers from the RAF Germany Squadrons. Returned to the UK at Lossiemouth via Keflavik with the RAFG aircraft on 6.5.82 (no Victor support being available), parting company with the others there to fly back to Wittering. Deployed to St Mawgan on 28.5.82 and then to Wideawake on 29.5.82 before being flown non-stop to 'Hermes' in the TEZ on 8.6.82. Disembarked to RAF Stanley with the Squadron on 4.7.82, the detachment subsequently becoming known as the HarDet. Shipped to Ascension for return to the UK, arriving at Wittering on 16.11.82 aboard Heavylift Belfast G-BFYU.

### XZ997 GR.3

On 29.3.82 with 4(F) Sqdn at Gütersloh coded 'E'. Transferred to 1(F) Sqdn and flown to Wittering on 16.4.82 with XV789/F. Recoded '31' in Red on fin and outriggers but minus Squadron badge on the nose. Involved in ski-jump training at Yeovilton 19.4.82 and 22.4.82. Flown to St Mawgan 2.5.82 and then to Wideawake 4.5.82. Embarked 'Atlantic Conveyor' off Ascension on 6.5.82, sailing with the ship for the TEZ 7.5.82. Flown off to 'Hermes' on 18.5.82.

Suffered no damage at all in an incident on 21.5.82 when, flown by Flt Lt Rochfort, it landed back aboard 'Hermes' after an armed reconnaissance mission but ended up with one outrigger in the catwalk. Lifted back on deck, undamaged.

Took part in a four-aircraft formation attack against the airstrip at Dunnose Head on 23.5.82 (flown by Wg Cdr Squire) which resulted in the destruction of some of the settlement and injury to one of the local inhabitants.

Involved in the Squadron's first attack on the runway at Stanley Airport on 24.5.82, armed with retarded 1,000lb bombs (piloted by Sqdn Ldr Iveson).

Flown by Flt Lt Harper, it took part in a successful three-aircraft attack on enemy gun positions at Goose Green on 28.5.82, playing a crucial part in hastening the Argentine surrender there the following morning.

Carried out the first successful LGB sortie on 13.6.82 when Wg Cdr Squire attacked an enemy position on Tumbledown, scoring a direct hit with his second bomb. Took-off from 'Hermes' at 1500Z on 14.6.82 (flown by Wg Cdr Squire again) for an LGB attack in the Port Stanley area, accompanied by Nick Gilchrist in XZ133. This attack was called off by the FAC when white flags were seen in Port Stanley at 1555Z and the GR.3 landed back aboard the carrier with LGB's intact at 1625Z.

Disembarked to RAF Stanley with 1(F) Sqdn on 4.7.82, the unit subsequently becoming known as the HarDet. Current 31.12.82 (allocated code 'E') but had returned to Gütersloh for 4(F) Sqdn before the HarDet was redesignated 1453 Flight on 20.8.83.

The 'Atlantic Conveyor' Chinook HC.1 consignment consisted of ZA719/BM, ZA718/BN, ZA707/BP, ZA716/BQ (centre) and ZA706/BT and all five arrived at HMS Drake, Plymouth on 23.4.82. This photograph was taken prior to their embarkation in Plymouth Sound two days later.
(R. Hill)

One of the more mundane tasks which befell 'Bravo November' after the cease-fire on 14.6.82 was the collection of Argentine prisoners-of-war from outlying areas, some of whom are seen here being taken aboard on 16.6.82 during a rotors-running ground stop at Stanley Racecourse. (Lt S. A. George, RN)

By avoiding the Exocet attack on 'Atlantic Conveyor', as well as surviving several later incidents, the Chinook HC.1 ZA718/BN was subsequently, and appropriately, tagged "THE SURVIVOR". The inscription was applied in matt black just aft of the cockpit, on the starboard side.
(Michael I. Draper)

When 'Contender Bezant' arrived at Southampton Docks on 23.9.82 it brought three Wessex HU.5's, two Pucaras and three Chinook HC.1's, one of which was ZA718/BN. Early the following morning the Chinook was off-loaded to the quayside prior to its eventual return to Odiham. (Michael I. Draper)

# CHINOOK

## 18 SQUADRON

18 Sqdn's reformation parade took place at Odiham on 24 February, just over one month before Argentina invaded the Falkland Islands. The unit had previously been equipped with the Wessex HC.2 at Gutersloh, West Germany but was stood down in December 1980 pending its re-equipment with the Chinook HC.1. Training on the new type commenced during July 1981 at Odiham in the expectation that the Squadron would return to Gutersloh during 1982, but in the event this move was delayed by nearly a year due to involvement in Operation "Corporate". The unit had received the following aircraft by 29 March:

| | | |
|---|---|---|
| ZA719/BM | ZA670/BS | ZA683/BX |
| ZA718/BN | ZA706/BT | ZA682/BY |
| ZA707/BP | ZA705/BU | ZA681/BZ |
| ZA716/BQ | ZA679/BV | |
| ZA711/BR | ZA680/BW | |

Commanded by Wg Cdr A.J.Stables, 18 Sqdn received notice on 6 April of its intended inclusion in the forces being assembled for Operation "Corporate". That date found ZA670, ZA679 and ZA716 detached to Culdrose, providing some much-needed heavy-lift capability during the massive task of transferring personnel and stores to the various ships assembling at Devonport as part of the Task Force. Flown by Sqdn Ldr B.Freeman and Flt Lt D.Morgan, ZA679 airlifted a five-ton propeller bearing to 'Invincible' (which had sailed from Portsmouth the previous day), thus saving the carrier a visit to Devonport for repairs. ZA706 joined the trio on 7 April. An initial quantity of five Chinooks was prepared for deployment to the South Atlantic over the next two weeks, all "Batch 2" aircraft which had carbon-fibre rotor blades and the pressure refuelling system fitted as standard. Various modifications were carried out during that period, including installation of Omega and Radar Warning Receivers. The aircraft retained their Matt Dark Green and Matt Dark Sea Grey camouflage with Matt Black undersides, but they were covered with an anti-corrosion coating which did give the camouflage a darker appearance. The

Black ROYAL AIR FORCE titles and codes were also retained, along with the Squadron badge on the rear pylon. Only one Royal Air Force Chinook squadron was in existence at the time so it was considered unnecessary to remove what was already a fairly low-visibility unit marking. One additional aircraft which joined the unit during that period was ZA715, delivered to Odiham from Fleetlands on 19 April to take up the code 'BL'.

The Squadron's first deployment began during the morning of 23 April when the following were flown from Odiham to the Royal Navy Barracks at Plymouth (HMS Drake) with crew-ferry ZA715:

| | | |
|---|---|---|
| ZA719/BM | ZA707/BP | ZA706/BT |
| ZA718/BN | ZA716/BQ | |

Accompanied by six 848 Sqdn Wessex HU.5's, all five Chinooks embarked 'Atlantic Conveyor' on 25 April. A small air and groundcrew detachment (under Sqdn Ldr K.Smith) also embarked the converted container ship, while the rest of the deployed Squadron personnel were flown out from Brize Norton to Wideawake (via Dakar) by 10 Sqdn VC-10 C.1 and embarked 'Norland' off the Island on 7 May for passage south to the Total Exclusion Zone. 'Atlantic Conveyor' sailed for Freetown in Sierra Leone on 25 April, eventually arriving off Ascension Island on 5 May. ZA707 was disembarked to help with the massive VERTREP operation being conducted from Wideawake. The Chinook was on task within 90 minutes of leaving the ship and remained on the Island until embarked on 'Contender Bezant' at the end of the month. During that three-week period, ZA707 flew 100 hours with no significant unserviceability, on one day managing to lift 350 tonnes of equipment to Task Force shipping. The other four Chinooks departed south from Ascension Island on 7 May aboard 'Atlantic Conveyor', having been joined by eight 809 Sqdn Sea Harrier FRS.1's and six 1(F) Sqdn Harrier GR.3's. The fixed-wing aircraft were all transferred to 'Invincible' and 'Hermes' when the ship joined the Task Force on 18 May, after which work commenced on preparing the four Chinooks for disembarkation.

Squadron personnel spent much of 25 May refitting rotor blades to two of the four Chinooks (ZA706 and ZA718), a very difficult operation due to the lack of suitable lifting gear. A fork-lift truck was employed on this task, the only suitable piece of machinery available on board. Work on ZA718 had been completed by late afternoon and, following engine runs, it was flown off to begin resupply flights to nearby shipping. At 1936Z, while about 90 miles north-east of Port Stanley (at 50°37′S 56°10′W), 'Atlantic Conveyor' was hit in the port quarter by one of two Exocets which had been launched from a pair of CANA Super Etendards. The missile struck close to the waterline and fire spread out of control, enveloping the ship in dense black smoke. Within 30 minutes it became clear that the damage control parties were fighting a losing battle and the order to abandon ship was given. 12 personnel lost their lives in the attack, including the Ship's Master (Captain Ian North), although all of the 18 Sqdn personnel aboard escaped without injury. F/Sgt Brian Jopling (one of the Chinook air loadmasters) was manning a machine gun position on the bridge at the time of the attack. He was one of the last to leave after the order to abandon ship had been given and was subsequently awarded the Queen's Gallantry Medal for saving the lives of several of his colleagues in the extremely cold water. ZA718 recovered to 'Hermes' but the three Chinooks still aboard (ZA716 and ZA719 on the forward deck and ZA706 on the rear deck) were destroyed along with six Wessex HU.5's and a Lynx HAS.2, although most of the fires had burned themselves out by the following day. The ship was still afloat on 28 May and, having been assessed as salvageable, was taken under tow by the tug 'Irishman', but she broke her back and sank two days later in bad weather.

ZA718 operated from 'Hermes' on 26 May and then disembarked to Landing Site Whale (the joint 845/846 Sqdn FOB north of San Carlos near Old House Creek) that evening to join the main party of 18 Sqdn personnel who had gone ashore from 'Fearless' during the morning. Under Wg Cdr Tony Stables, the main party had sailed south from Ascension Island with 2 PARA aboard 'Norland', remaining aboard that ship during the landings in San Carlos Water on 21 May to take over air defence duties (with four GPMG's) once the troops had been disembarked. During the numerous enemy air raids that followed, Squadron personnel claim to have put many rounds into a Grupo 5 Skyhawk which bombed 'Antelope' on 23 May *[see Grupo 5 notes]*. The detachment was transferred by landing craft from 'Norland' to 'Fearless' the same evening.

18 Sqdn personnel spent the following two days (24/25 May) aboard 'Fearless', once again supplementing the ship's defences with GPMG's. It was reported to have been a member of the Squadron who first coined the phrase "Bomb Alley" to describe the air raids in San Carlos Water (subsequently used in a signal and gained widespread use throughout the Task Force and the Press back in the United Kingdom). The detachment moved ashore to the Old House Creek FOB on 26 May to be joined by "Bravo November" (ZA718) later in the day, flown in from 'Hermes' by Flt Lts J.Kennedy and A.Tailby.

Having lost three-quarters of his complement of aircraft, Tony Stables was forced to rethink his deployment plans. He decided that a detachment under Sqdn Ldr R.U.Langworthy (consisting of two 4-man crews, 13 groundcrew and four Joint Helicopter Support Unit technicians) would remain ashore to operate "Bravo November", while the remaining personnel would embark 'Europic Ferry' to sail with her for the TRALA and await the arrival of replacement helicopters from the United Kingdom. Many problems faced Dick Langworthy, particularly as all specialist tools and spares for ZA718 had been consumed by the fire on board 'Atlantic Conveyor', but despite various unserviceabilities (including windscreen wipers, cockpit instruments, etc) the aircraft remained available throughout the campaign. His immediate tasks upon disembarkation included the ferrying of stores and ammunition to the front line and the transport of Argentine PoW's from Goose Green to Ajax Bay.

In the evening of 30 May, an SAS patrol discovered that the enemy had withdrawn most of its troops from the area around Mount Kent. It was decided to insert 85 troops from 'K' Company 42 Cdo, three 105mm field guns and 22 tonnes of ammunition into the position after dark by helicopter, using NVG techniques. Three 846 Sqdn Sea King HC.4's airlifted in troops to take the position, while ZA718 (flown by Dick Langworthy and Flt Lt A.A.Lawless) followed up with a load consisting of two 105mm field guns and 22 men all carried internally plus the additional 105mm field gun as an underslung load. Its rear undercarriage sank into the peat upon landing, so the helicopter had to be kept in a low hover to enable the cargo ramp to be lowered. After the troops and guns had been unloaded, the Chinook commenced its low-level return flight to the new Squadron FOB at Port San Carlos settlement (the detachment having redeployed there that day from Old House Creek). However, the weather had deteriorated and at one point ZA718 flew into a snow shower during which the forward visibility fell almost to zero. Travelling low and fast, the Chinook descended slightly and struck the surface of one of the creeks between Estancia House and Teal Inlet. That slowed the helicopter down, but fortunately Dick Langworthy recovered from the situation and managed to fly the helicopter clear of the water. The return flight to Port San Carlos settlement was continued thereafter at a higher altitude! An inspection after landing revealed that very little damage had been caused.

During the afternoon of 2 June, following the famous telephone call which Major Crossland made to Fitzroy confirming that Argentine troops had vacated the settlement, ZA718 (flown by Flt Lt N.J.Grose and Fg Off C.Miller) was used to advance men from 2 PARA forward from Goose Green towards the position. With seats folded against the side, 81 fully-armed paratroops were crammed into the helicopter for its first mission. That was well above the manufacturer's advertised troop-carrying capability! The second mission involved 75 fully-armed paratroops and both were conducted in poor visibility with a low cloudbase over an area that had not been fully confirmed as clear of enemy troops. The result, however, was that the British ground forces were then within 10 miles of Port Stanley.

"Bravo November" continued to prove its worth as the

advance continued, ferrying ammunition and supplies forward to the troops on the front line in exchange for PoW's and casualties (64 injured troops were ferried from Fitzroy to 'Uganda' in one sortie on 8 June after the attacks on LSL's 'Sir Tristram' and 'Sir Galahad'). Its heavy-lift capabilities were also called upon on 7 June when damaged 846 Sqdn Sea King HC.4 ZA310 and 825 Sqdn Sea King HAS.2A XV696 were airlifted back to their respective FOB's at Fern Valley Creek (about one mile north of San Carlos settlement) and San Carlos settlement from outlying sites. Both Sea Kings had been damaged on landing earlier in the conflict, ZA310 north of Fanning Head on 23 May and XV696 at Lookout Hill on 4 June. On 13 June, rotor downwash from ZA718 temporarily put the Harrier FOB close to Port San Carlos settlement out of action when some of the metal planking lifted, causing the diversion to 'Fearless' and 'Intrepid' of two 800 Sqdn Sea Harriers. In 109 flying hours between 27 May and 14 June (the day of the surrender), "Bravo November" had carried some 2,150 troops (including 550 PoW's and 95 CASEVAC cases) plus in excess of 550 tonnes of stores and equipment.

Back in the United Kingdom, 18 Sqdn gained five more Chinook HC.1's by the end of May: ZA713 (13 May), ZA714 (25 May) and ZA717 (30 April) all arrived from temporary store at Fleetlands, ZA708 returned from A&AEE Boscombe Down on 27 May, while ZA720 was delivered in following its journey by sea from Boeing Vertol, the manufacturer. The aircraft took up the codes 'BJ', 'BH', 'BK', 'BE' and 'BG' respectively. A second batch of Chinooks was dispatched to the South Atlantic during the month:

| | | |
|---|---|---|
| ZA713/BJ | ZA715/BL | ZA705/BU |

ZA713 and ZA715 were both flown to the Royal Navy Barracks (HMS Drake) at Plymouth on 19 May (along with crew-ferry ZA717) while ZA705 followed on 20 May. The trio embarked 'Contender Bezant' on 20 May along with a Sea King HAS.2 and two Wasp HAS.1's, sailing with the ship that day for a RAS in Start Bay. At about midday on 21 May the vessel departed Start Bay for the South Atlantic (via Freetown 28/29 May) to arrive at Ascension Island on 31 May. ZA707 was embarked from Wideawake during the stopover (along with four Harrier GR.3's and two Gazelle AH.1's), the ship finally sailing for the TEZ at 1200Z on 3 June accompanied by 'St Edmund'. After a rendezvous with 'Europic Ferry' 500 miles east of the Falkland Islands on 9 June, ZA705 was flown ashore by Tony Stables and Flt Lt R.L.Hill on 14 June. ZA707 attempted to follow that day (flown by Sqdn Ldr M.Dudgeon and Fg Off S.Falla) but diverted to 'Europic Ferry' about 10 minutes after take-off following a spurious radio transmission warning of a dogfight over 'Hermes' (the carrier was to have been used for a refuelling stop en route to the Port San Carlos FOB). The Chinook finally managed to depart 'Europic Ferry' on 16 June after a Force 11 gale had died down. The remaining pair disembarked 'Contender Bezant' to the Port San Carlos FOB on 18 June after the ship had sailed into Stanley Harbour, ZA713 being flown by Flt Lt B.Mansfield and Flt Lt R.Neville while ZA715 was flown by Flt Lt P.Norton and Fg Off T.Fauchon.

Following the loss of the helicopters aboard 'Atlantic Conveyor' on 25 May, three more 18 Sqdn Chinooks were prepared for shipment to the South Atlantic as attrition replacements:

| | | |
|---|---|---|
| ZA720/BG | ZA714/BH | ZA717/BK |

On 6 June, accompanied by crew-ferry ZA711, these three helicopters were flown from Odiham to the Royal Navy Barracks at Plymouth (HMS Drake) to embark 'Astronomer', a container ship which had been undergoing conversion for use as a helicopter carrier and repair facility at Devonport since 1 June. The vessel sailed into Plymouth Sound on the evening of 7 June and embarked five Wessex HU.5's, four Scout AH.1's and Chinook HC.1 ZA717 before darkness prevented any further activity (as it was, it took until midnight for the Chinook to be de-bladed and positioned in the "hangar" on her forward deck). She sailed at 0100Z on 8 June to rendezvous with 'Black Rover' for a practice RAS off Portland Bill (carried out between 0700Z and 0800Z), following which the remaining helicopters (ZA714, ZA720 and further Wessex HU.5's) were embarked in Lyme Bay. 'Astronomer' sailed for Ascension Island at 1400Z on 8 June, the three Chinooks being wrapped in canvas covers during the journey south by the 21-strong Royal Air Force contingent aboard. Their covered rear pylons protruded from the hangar and the Ship's Master (Captain H.S.Bladon) passed a comment that they looked like three "Yogi Bears". Almost inevitably the canvas covers had eyes, ears and noses applied in the appropriate places! The ship crossed the equator on 15 June and Chinook ZA714 was bladed-up that day, making a test-flight in the afternoon. The aircraft left for Wideawake at approximately 1630Z on 16 June to make arrangements for the ship's stay at Ascension Island, 'Astronomer' herself arriving in Clarence Bay at 1800Z to berth alongside 'Alvega' for bunkering. The ship began to receive VERTREP helicopters from 0900Z the next morning and finally sailed south from the Island during the morning of 18 June (having left ZA714 at Wideawake). She arrived in the TRALA on 26 June, taking up station close to 'Eburna' and in sight of 'Hermes', then entered Port William Sound at 0500Z on 27 June to anchor just north of West Tussac Island. The two Chinooks had their blades refitted and were flown off to the FOB at Port San Carlos settlement, ZA720 on 27 June followed by ZA717 on 29 June.

The replacement aircraft from 'Contender Bezant' and 'Astronomer' were all kept very busy in the massive clearing up operation, even though they had arrived on the scene too late to see any action prior to the Argentine surrender on 14 June. Their initial tasking involved the transporting of aviation fuel for the Fleet Air Arm helicopters. Up to 10,000 gallons were ferried 60 miles each day (in all some 200,000 gallons) until refuelling facilities at Stanley Airport became available. The fuel was carried in APFCs, a Sea King being able to airlift one whereas the Chinook could carry four (even six on one occasion when two were suspended beneath each hook). The 18 Sqdn aircraft were used to embark troops and equipment (including damaged helicopters and many of the Argentine "trophies") for transport back to the United Kingdom. They also supplemented the minimal port facilities at Port Stanley by offloading containers and other equipment from ships arriving from the United Kingdom.

While all of the 18 Sqdn Chinooks sent to the South Atlantic during the war have since returned to the United Kingdom, they have been replaced by others sent south to continue operations in the Islands. The detachment moved from the FOB at Port San Carlos to a new site at Kelly's Garden close to San Carlos settlement on 23/24 March 1983, having become (unofficially) known as the Falkland Islands ChinDet. Official designation as 1310 Flight occurred on 20 August 1983, the unit adopting a Penguin as its insignia and taking up single-letter codes in Black. At the time of writing, the aircraft and crews continue to be rotated between the Islands and the United Kingdom at regular intervals.

The 33rd and last Chinook HC.1 (ZA721) was delivered to Odiham on 8 June 1982 following its arrival at Seaforth Docks, Liverpool by container ship. The gradual build-up of Chinook-qualified personnel enabled the second squadron (7 Sqdn) to reform on the helicopter three months later on 1 September, while 18 Sqdn's move back to Gutersloh finally took place during April/May 1983. It was evident, however, that the 30 surviving Chinooks would be insufficient to meet the demands of two squadrons, a detachment in the Falkland Islands and an OCU, so further orders were placed with the manufacturer.

Three attrition replacements were to be followed by five additional aircraft, the first of the former (ZD574) arriving at Odiham during July 1984. The War had seen the first operational use of the pressure refuelling system and the triple hook system. The latter in particular was a great asset, meaning that several small, easily prepared loads could be carried at the same time. The Chinook had a smaller undercarriage "footprint" than its naval counterparts (both Sea King and Wessex), enabling it to operate from most ships in the Task Force which were equipped with a helicopter deck.

---

*18 Sqdn aircrew during Operation "Corporate" and their awards:*

Wg Cdr A.J.Stables RAF (OC); Sqdn Ldr M.Dudgeon RAF; Sqdn Ldr R.U.Langworthy RAF AFC DFC; Sqdn Ldr K.Smith RAF; Flt Lt N.J.Grose RAF AFC; Flt Lt R.L.Hill RAF; Flt Lt A.T.Jones RAF MID; Flt Lt J.Kennedy RAF; Flt Lt A.A.Lawless RAF; Flt Lt B.Mansfield RAF; Flt Lt R.Neville RAF; Flt Lt P.Norton RAF; Flt Lt A.Tailby RAF; Fg Off S.Falla RAF; Fg Off T.Fauchon RAF; Fg Off C.Miller RAF MID; Fg Off A.Strachan RAF; MALM A.C.Rogers RAF; MALM J.G.Savidge RAF; F/Sgt I.Gutteridge RAF; F/Sgt B.W.Jopling RAF QGM; Sgt M.Bridge RAF; Sgt R.A.Clement RAF; Sgt P.J.Gibson RAF; Sgt G.Rogan RAF; Sgt D.F.A.Maxwell RAF; Sgt S.J.Sheldon RAF; Sgt D.C.Watson RAF.

---

# INDIVIDUAL AIRCRAFT DETAILS

**ZA705** HC.1

On 29.3.82 with 18 Sqdn at Odiham coded 'BU'. Flown to the RN Barracks, Plymouth (HMS Drake) on 20.5.82 and embarked 'Contender Bezant' in Plymouth Sound the same day. Sailed with the ship for the South Atlantic from nearby Start Bay on 21.5.82 (via Ascension 31.5-3.6.82). Disembarked to the FOB at Port San Carlos settlement on 14.6.82 (via a refuelling stop aboard 'Hermes') and used on general transport duties during the clearing up operation after the Argentine surrender. Transported the damaged 848 Sqdn 'D' Flt Wessex XT486 from 'Glamorgan' to the Port San Carlos settlement FOB on 19.6.82. Re-embarked 'Contender Bezant' 3.9.82 at Port William and sailed with her for the UK on 6.9.82, arriving at Southampton on 23.9.82. Off-loaded 24.9.82 and taken to Odiham by MARTSU transport on 3.10.82.

**ZA706** HC.1

On 29.3.82 with 18 Sqdn at Odiham coded 'BT'. Joined ZA670, ZA679 and ZA716 at Culdrose on 7.4.82 helping to load Task Force shipping. Flown from Odiham to the RN Barracks, Plymouth (HMS Drake) on 23.4.82 and embarked 'Atlantic Conveyor' in Plymouth Sound on 25.4.82, sailing with her that day for the South Atlantic (via Ascension 5-7.5.82).

On 25.5.82, whilst the ship was some 90 miles north-east of Port Stanley (at 50°37′S 56°10′W) en route to Falkland Sound, 'Atlantic Conveyor' was hit by an Exocet missile (one of two launched from a pair of 2 Escuadrilla Super Etendards) and caught fire. The Chinook (positioned on the rear deck) was consumed by the fire, its remains sinking with the ship on 30.5.82.

**ZA707** HC.1

On 29.3.82 with 18 Sqdn at Odiham coded 'BP'. Flown to the RN Barracks, Plymouth (HMS Drake) on 23.4.82 and embarked 'Atlantic Conveyor' in Plymouth Sound on 25.4.82, sailing with her that day for Ascension. Flown off to Wideawake 5.5.82 to help with the heavy VERTREP tasks between the Island and the ships of the Task Force until the end of 5.82. Embarked 'Contender Bezant' off the Island and sailed with her for the TEZ on 3.6.82. Flown off 14.6.82 en route to the Port San Carlos settlement FOB but diverted to 'Europic Ferry' some 10 minutes after take-off following a spurious air raid warning. Stranded aboard the ship for two days due to Force 11 gales, but finally managed to complete its journey ashore on 16.6.82. Remained at the Port San Carlos FOB until embarked on 'Astronomer' 14.11.82 for return to the UK, arriving at

Devonport on 3.12.82. Disembarked to a compound at the Granby Gate entrance to the dockyard and left by road for Odiham on 9.12.82, arriving there the following day.

**ZA713** HC.1

On 29.3.82 in store at Fleetlands, uncoded. Flown from Fleetlands to Odiham on 13.5.82 for 18 Sqdn and coded 'BJ'. To the RN Barracks, Plymouth (HMS Drake) 19.5.82 and embarked 'Contender Bezant' in Plymouth Sound the following day. Sailed with the ship for the South Atlantic from nearby Start Bay on 21.5.82 (via Ascension 31.5-3.6.82). Disembarked to the FOB at Port San Carlos settlement on 18.6.82 after the ship had entered Stanley Harbour. Used on general transport duties during the massive clearing up operation after the Argentine surrender. Remained with the ChinDet until embarked on 'Leicesterbrook' 20.3.83 and sailed with her for the UK, arriving at Barry on 27.4.83. Disembarked and left by road for Odiham on 3.5.83, arriving there the following day.

**ZA714** HC.1

On 29.3.82 in store at Fleetlands, uncoded. Flown from Fleetlands to Odiham on 25.5.82 for 18 Sqdn and coded 'BH'. To the RN Barracks, Plymouth (HMS Drake) on 6.6.82 and

**Above** *Chinook HC.1's ZA705/BU and ZA714/BH also returned to Southampton on 'Contender Bezant' and both are seen here on the quayside on 25.9.82 immediately after off-loading. The dull and somewhat shabby appearance of these Chinooks is due to their having been sprayed with a PX32 protective film to prevent salt corrosion during the voyage home. Both departed for Odiham by road.* (Peter J. Cooper)

**Above** *Modifications undertaken to those Chinook HC.1's that were deployed to the South Atlantic included the fitting of radar-warning receivers. This equipment was mounted in two radomes, each with 180°-plus field-of-view to provide comprehensive detection of threat radars. These two views show (top) the forward radome mounted low on the nose and (immediately above) the aft radome high on the trailing edge of the rear pylon.* (Michael I. Draper)

**Left** *Chinook HC.1 ZA705/BU lifted the damaged 848 Squadron 'D' Flight Wessex HU.5 XT486 '–/XR' off 'Glamorgan' on 19.6.82 to the Port San Carlos settlement FOB after it had suffered earlier storm damage on the destroyer.* (A. B. Walsh) embarked 'Astronomer' in Lyme Bay on 8.6.82, sailing with the ship that day for Ascension. Test-flown on 15.6.82 and then disembarked to Wideawake on 16.6.82, remaining there for VERTREP duties until the arrival of 'Contender Bezant' from the Falklands on 14.9.82. Departed with the vessel on 15.9.82 for return to the UK, arriving at Southampton 23.9.82. Off-loaded the following day and removed by road to Odiham on 3.10.82.

### ZA715 HC.1

On 29.3.82 in store at Fleetlands, uncoded. Flown from Fleetlands to Odiham on 19.4.83 for 18 Sqdn and coded 'BL'. To the RN Barracks, Plymouth (HMS Drake) 19.5.82 and embarked 'Contender Bezant' in Plymouth Sound the following day. Sailed with the ship for the South Atlantic from nearby Start Bay 21.5.82 (via Ascension 31.5-3.6.82). Disembarked to the FOB at Port San Carlos settlement on 18.6.82 after the ship had entered Stanley Harbour. Used on general transport duties during the massive clearing up operation after the Argentine surrender. Remained with the ChinDet until flown aboard 'Leicesterbrook' on 20.3.83, sailing with her for the UK to arrive at Barry on 27.4.83. Disembarked and left by road for Odiham on 5.5.83, arriving there on 7.5.83.

### ZA716 HC.1

On 29.3.82 with 18 Sqdn at Odiham coded 'BQ'. At Culdrose 6.4.82 with ZA670 and ZA679, helping to load Task Force shipping. Flown from Odiham to the RN Barracks, Plymouth (HMS Drake) on 23.4.82 and embarked 'Atlantic Conveyor' in Plymouth Sound on 25.4.82, sailing with her that day for the South Atlantic (via Ascension 5-7.5.82).

On 25.5.82, whilst the ship was some 90 miles north-east of Port Stanley (at 50°37′S 56°10′W) en route to Falkland Sound, 'Atlantic Conveyor' was hit by an Exocet missile (one of two launched from a pair of 2 Escuadrilla Super Etendards) and caught fire. The Chinook (positioned on the forward deck) was consumed by the fire, its remains sinking with the ship on 30.5.82.

### ZA717 HC.1

On 29.3.82 in store at Fleetlands, uncoded. Flown from Fleetlands to Odiham on 30.4.82 for 18 Sqdn and coded 'BK'. To the RN Barracks, Plymouth (HMS Drake) on 6.6.82 and embarked 'Astronomer' in Plymouth Sound

7.6.82. Sailed to Lyme Bay with the ship that night before continuing to the South Atlantic 8.6.82 (via Ascension 16-18.6.82). Disembarked to the FOB at Port San Carlos settlement on 29.6.82 after the ship had anchored in Port William Sound two days earlier. Used on general transport duties during the massive clearing up operation following the Argentine surrender. Remained with the ChinDet until embarked on 'Leicesterbrook' on 21.3.83 to sail with her for the UK, arriving at Barry 27.4.83. Disembarked and flown to Odiham on 29.4.83.

### ZA718 HC.1

On 29.3.82 with 18 Sqdn at Odiham coded 'BN'. Flown to the RN Barracks, Plymouth (HMS Drake) on 23.4.82 and embarked 'Atlantic Conveyor' in Plymouth Sound on 25.4.82, sailing with her that day for the South Atlantic (via Ascension 5-7.5.82). Prepared for flight 25.5.82 while the ship was en route to San Carlos Water. Crewed by Flt Lt Kennedy, Flt Lt Tailby, MALM Savidge and Sgt Gibson, it was fortuitously airborne when the ship was hit by one of two Exocet missiles launched by a pair of 2 Escuadrilla Super Etendards. Landed aboard 'Hermes', operating from the carrier on 26.5.82 before disembarking to the joint 845/846 Sqdn FOB near Old House Creek (some 2 miles north of San Carlos settlement) that evening in support of the ground forces. Moved to the Port San Carlos settlement FOB on 30.5.82.

Suffered minor damage late on 30.5.82 while being flown by Sqdn Ldr Langworthy and Flt Lt Lawless when it struck the surface of a creek between Estancia House and Teal Inlet during a snowstorm while returning from Mount Kent to the FOB at Port San Carlos settlement.

Flown by Flt Lt Grove and Fg Off Miller, it transported 81 fully-armed paratroops in one mission from Goose Green to Fitzroy on 2.6.82 (over twice the normal troop complement).

Airlifted two disabled Sea Kings on 7.6.82: 846 Sqdn HC.4 ZA310 from a position north of Fanning Head to the 846 Sqdn FOB at Fern Valley Creek and 825 Sqdn HAS.2A XV696 from Lookout Hill to the 825 Sqdn FOB at San Carlos settlement.

Its rotor downwash damaged the Harrier FOB close to Port San Carlos settlement on 13.6.82, causing two 800 Sqdn Sea Harriers to divert to 'Fearless' and 'Intrepid'.

Used on general transport duties during clearing up operations following the Argentine surrender on 14.6.82 until it embarked 'Contender Bezant' on 4.9.82 and sailed with the ship from Port William on 6.9.82 for the UK. Arrived with the vessel at Southampton on 23.9.82, disembarked and taken by road to Odiham on 4.10.82.

*By the time of its return to the UK, it had acquired the name "The Survivor" in Black on the nose.*

### ZA719 HC.1

Arrived at Southampton on delivery from the USA aboard 'Atlantic Span' on 20.3.82 and flown to Odiham on 22.3.82 for 18 Sqdn, taking up the code 'BM'. Flown to the RN Barracks, Plymouth (HMS Drake) on 23.4.82 and embarked 'Atlantic Conveyor' in Plymouth Sound on 25.4.82, sailing with her that day for the South Atlantic (via Ascension 5-7.5.82).

On 25.5.82, whilst the ship was some 90 miles north-east of Port Stanley (at 50°37′S 56°10′W) en route to Falkland Sound, 'Atlantic Conveyor' was hit by an Exocet missile (one of two launched from a pair of 2 Escuadrilla Super Etendards) and caught fire. The Chinook (positioned on the forward deck) was consumed by the fire, its remains sinking with the ship on 30.5.82.

### ZA720 HC.1

On 29.3.82 with Boeing Vertol at Ridley, Pennsylvania (USA) prior to delivery. Flown aboard 'Atlantic Champagne' at Newark (New Jersey) on 9.5.82 and sailed with the ship for the UK. Disembarked and flown to Odiham (seen there unmarked on 3.6.82) for issue to 18 Sqdn, taking up the code 'BG'. Flown to the RN Barracks, Plymouth (HMS Drake) on 6.6.82 and embarked 'Astronomer' in Lyme Bay on 8.6.82, sailing with the ship for the South Atlantic the same day (via Ascension 16-18.6.82). Disembarked to the FOB at Port San Carlos settlement on 27.6.82 after the vessel had anchored in Port William Sound that day. Used on general transport duties during the massive clearing up operation following the Argentine surrender. Transferred with the ChinDet from the Port San Carlos FOB to Kelly's Garden 24.3.83 prior to embarking 'Leicesterbrook' on 28.3.83 for return to the UK, sailing with the ship to arrive at Barry on 27.4.83. Disembarked and flown to Odiham on 30.4.83.

*Chinook HC.1 ZA707/A illustrates the indigenous marking of 1310 Flight which consists of a Black and White penguin applied to the rear rotor pylon. Seen at Odiham 1.8.84, ZA707 had just returned from the Falkland Islands for overhaul and return to 7 Squadron. (T. E. Stone)*

# VICTOR

## 55 & 57 SQUADRONS

With the closest airfield available for use by the British forces being on Ascension Island, some 3,900 miles north of the Falklands, it was clear from the outset of Operation "Corporate" that the Victor tanker fleet would have a supporting role to play in any attempt to retake the Islands. 24 Victor B.2's had been involved in a protracted conversion programme to K.2 tanker configuration during the years 1970 to 1978 (eventually completed by Hawker Siddeley Aviation at Woodford), these being the only strategic tankers in operational service with the Royal Air Force at the time of the Argentine invasion. Nine VC-10's were undergoing conversion to this role by British Aerospace at Filton, but the first of these (K.2 ZA141) did not make its first flight until 22 June 1982 and it was impracticable to accelerate the programme. Of the original Victor K.2's, XL513 had been destroyed in a take-off accident at Marham on 28 September 1976, while the remaining 23 aircraft were still in service with 55 Sqdn and 57 Sqdn at Marham on 29 March 1982 as follows:

| 55 Sqdn | XH671 | XL188 | XL233 |
|---------|-------|-------|-------|
|         | XH675 | XL190 | XL511 |
|         | XL161 | XL191 | XM715 |
|         | XL162 | XL232 | XM717 |
| 57 Sqdn | XH669 | XL160 | XL192 |
|         | XH672 | XL163 | XL231 |
|         | XH673 | XL164 | XL512 |
|         | XL158 | XL189 |       |

There were, in fact, three operational Victor K.2 units at the time, the third being 232 OCU which borrowed aircraft from the other two squadrons to fulfil its training role (XL232 of 55 Sqdn carrying the 232 OCU badge as a "representative aircraft" for the unit). All of the Victor K.2's wore standard Matt Dark Green and Medium Sea Grey camouflage, White undersides, Red/Blue roundels and fin-flash with Dayglo Red stripes under the wing-tips and on the underwing pods. The aircraft all retained their squadron markings on the fin during the subsequent deployment to Ascension Island.

Training in the Maritime Radar Reconnaissance role began immediately as this was to be the first task in which the Victors would be employed, while three crews (under Sqdn Ldr J.G.Elliott, Sqdn Ldr M.D.Todd and Sqdn Ldr R.Tuxford) were chosen to practice low-level photo-reconnaissance missions. XL192 was used by all three crews for PR missions over Scotland on 14/15 April while XL163, XL164 and XL189 were used on 16 April. The aircraft had the ability to carry out both PR and MRR tasks in addition to Air-to-Air Refuelling, cameras having been reinstalled into the noses of several K.2's. The type's radar also received some modifications, while Carousel inertial navigation sets (subsequently replaced by Omega) were installed to provide the very accurate navigational information required for long-range flights over water. The last major pre-"Corporate" mission carried out by the Victor tanker fleet involved the transatlantic deployment of eight Harrier GR.3's from Wittering to Goose Bay on 13 April, en route to a "Maple Flag" exercise at CFB Cold Lake, Alberta. XH669 (57 Sqdn) and XH671, XL232, XM717 (all 55 Sqdn) returned to Marham from Goose Bay two days later. Many of the subsequent routine AAR tasks were assumed by United States Air Force KC-135A's operating from their bases at Mildenhall and Fairford.

Meanwhile, the two Victor squadrons prepared for deployment to the South Atlantic. An advance operations and ground crew party had arrived at Wideawake Airfield on Ascension Island during the early hours of 18 April. The first five tankers arrived direct from Marham later the same day (XL163, XL189, XL192, XL511 and XM715), to be followed by four more on 19 April (XH671, XL164, XL188 and XL232) to give the detachment an initial complement of nine aircraft. Each Victor which deployed direct from Marham was itself refuelled by another before leaving United Kingdom airspace, thereby ensuring that it would have sufficient fuel for the nine-hour transit flight with reserves in case of diversion. Gp Capt J.S.B.Price ADC (Marham's Station Commander) arrived at Wideawake on 18 April to become Senior Royal Air Force Officer, Ascension Island. Wg Cdr D.W.Maurice-Jones (Wing Commander Operations at Marham) took up the post of Victor Detachment Commander at Wideawake, but he was relieved on 22 April by

Wg Cdr A.W.Bowman MBE (OC 57 Sqdn).

The first operational mission carried out by the Victor detachment at Wideawake involved an MRR sortie to South Georgia on 20 April. XL192 was the designated aircraft, crewed by Sqdn Ldr J.G.Elliott (Captain), Fg Off R.Evans (Co-Pilot), Sqdn Ldr A.I.B.Beedie (Nav-Radar), Sqdn Ldr M.R.Buxey (Nav-Plotter), Flt Lt R.C.Chappell (AEO) and Sqdn Ldr A.Cowling (MRR Specialist). Take-off took place just before 0400Z accompanied by four supporting tankers, the final AAR of the outbound leg being accomplished some 2,000 miles south of Ascension Island. John Elliott and crew continued south until they arrived in the vicinity of South Georgia, descending from 43,000ft to 18,000ft for a radar search of the area which took 90 minutes and covered in excess of 150,000 square miles. Once their work had been completed, XL192 was climbed to cruising altitude for the journey back to Wideawake. Meanwhile, four more tankers had been launched to provide the K.2 with fuel for its return journey. XL192 safely completed its MRR mission having covered a distance in excess of 7,000 miles, establishing a record for a long-range operational reconnaissance flight (only to be exceeded by Nimrods later in the conflict!). The list below details the nine Victor K.2's involved, their commanders and hours flown:

| MRR aircraft | | |
|---|---|---|
| XL192 | Sqdn Ldr J.G.Elliott | 14hrs 45mins |
| **Outbound tankers** | | |
| XH671 | Sqdn Ldr M.D.Todd | 2hrs 45mins |
| XL163 | Sqdn Ldr R.Tuxford | 3hrs 40mins |
| XM715 | Sqdn Ldr F.Milligan | 3hrs 55mins |
| XL189 | Flt Lt A.M.Skelton | 8hrs 40mins |
| **Return tankers** | | |
| XL163 | Sqdn Ldr F.Milligan | 3hrs 45mins |
| XL188 | Sqdn Ldr R.Tuxford | 3hrs 50mins |
| XL164 | Sqdn Ldr M.D.Todd | 8hrs 00mins |
| XL511 | Wg Cdr C.C.B.Seymour | 8hrs 05mins |

Similar MRR missions were conducted overnight on 22/23 April by XL163 (Sqdn Ldr Todd and crew, airborne for 14 hrs 5 mins) and on 24/25 April by XL189 (Wg Cdr Seymour and crew, airborne for 14hrs 5mins). Those three sorties were able to provide the small Task Group led by 'Antrim' with very important information on the whereabouts of all shipping, icebergs and pack-ice in the vicinity of South Georgia prior to and during Operation "Paraquat" (the retaking of the Island, successfully concluded on 26 April).

Those Victors still at their Norfolk base during the latter part of April were kept occupied in support of other aircraft deploying south to Ascension Island as well as providing AAR training for Vulcan crews. XH675 (55 Sqdn) and XL231 (57 Sqdn) carried out practice AAR's with 809 Sqdn Sea Harriers on 21 April (XL231 again on 22 April) prior to the latter's deployment to Wideawake at the end of April for ferrying to the South Atlantic aboard 'Atlantic Conveyor'. XL231 was particularly busy during late April and early May, being used as a "hack" aircraft for the transfer of spares, documents and personnel. It was also that Victor which undertook the first refuelling trials with the newly-probed Nimrod MR.2P (at Woodford on 28 April) and Hercules C.1P (at Boscombe Down on 1 May). Both of those were ground trials, the first airborne link-ups being carried out by the same Victor on 29 April and 2 May respectively. XL233 and XL191 were collected from the maintenance unit at St Athan on 15 April and 24 April respectively upon completion of major overhauls, but no Victors could be spared to replace them until XL231 was released on 12 May. The maintenance staff at St Athan put that Victor through a major overhaul in the record time of three weeks, the aircraft returning to 57 Sqdn on 7 June in exchange for XM717 whose overhaul was completed in a similar period.

Six additional Victors had been deployed to Wideawake by the end of the month, comprising XH672 (on 23 April), XL162 (25 April), XL233 (25 April), XH669 (29 April), XL512 (30 April) and XM717 (30 April), thus bringing the detachment to a complement of 14 aircraft (XM715 having returned to Marham via Dakar on 26 April). On 29 April four aircraft (XH675, XL158, XL160 and XL512 all from/to Marham) refuelled Vulcan B.2's XM598 and XM607 during their deployment from Waddington to Wideawake, while on 30 April four more aided the transit of six 809 Sqdn Sea Harriers from Yeovilton to Banjul en route to Wideawake. That involved XL158 and XM715 on round trips from/to Marham, and XL160 and XL191 which accompanied the Sea Harriers south to Banjul. The latter two Victors also performed a mission out of Banjul the next day to cover the final leg of their journey to Ascension Island. Another pair of Sea Harriers followed 24 hours behind, supported by XH675 (Marham-Banjul) and XM715 (Marham-Marham). They completed the journey to Wideawake on 2 May with assistance from XH675 on a round trip from Banjul. XL160 returned to Marham that day while XH675 and XL191 followed on 3 May and 7 May respectively.

The increase in Victors on the Island was required for the first "Black Buck" Vulcan bombing raid, mounted from Wideawake during the night of 30 April/1 May. The raids were masterpieces of strategic planning, calling for at least 15 Victor sorties and 18 different AAR's just to get one Vulcan to Port Stanley and back. The stream departure of 11 Victor K.2's (XH669, XH672, XL162, XL163, XL188, XL189, XL192, XL232, XL511, XL512 and XM717) and two Vulcan B.2's (XM598, XM607) for "Black Buck 1" commenced at 2350Z on 30 April. Two of the Victors were airborne reserves, one of which was used on the mission when another tanker suffered problems with its HDU. As the mission progressed, Victors began to leave the formation at regular intervals and return to Wideawake. All went well until only three tankers and one Vulcan, XM607, remained (XM598 having returned to Wideawake after developing a fault). XL512 (Flt Lt A.M.Skelton and crew) developed a fuel leak as it pulled clear from an AAR for the return flight and another K.2 had to be scrambled from Wideawake to refuel it. XH669

(Flt Lt S.Biglands and crew) and XL189 (Sqdn Ldr R.Tuxford and crew) continued south with the Vulcan. Bob Tuxford's aircraft refuelled the bomber and then gave Steve Biglands' tanker more fuel prior to turning for home, but the receiving Victor's probe broke soon after initial contact (the whole operation being carried out in heavy turbulence above bad weather). The two Victors accordingly swopped places, Tuxford taking back on board as much fuel from Biglands' aircraft as he could before sending the latter home to Ascension Island. Tuxford's drogue received a test "prod" from the Vulcan before this was done, however, just to make sure that the tip of Biglands' probe was not still inside the basket. The final Vulcan refuelling took place some 3,000 miles south of Ascension Island. XL189 was by now considerably lower on fuel than expected, so the final transfer to the Vulcan was terminated early. Despite this, the tanker did not have enough fuel left to reach Wideawake and the crew calculated that they might well have to ditch the aircraft about 400 miles south of the Island unless another Victor could be scrambled to refuel them. A radio call to arrange such assistance might well have compromised the entire mission, so Bob Tuxford maintained radio-silence until the bomber had transmitted its code-word signifying successful completion of the raid. Only then did he call for help and additional Victors were scrambled from Wideawake to meet him. Tuxford was awarded the Air Force Cross as a result of this mission, while his crew (Sqdn Ldr E.F.Wallis MBE, Flt Lt M.E.Beer, Flt Lt J.N.Keable and Flt Lt G.D.Rees) all received the Queen's Commendation for Valuable Service in the Air. The listing below accounts for all of the tankers involved in "Black Buck 1", their captains and hours flown:

### Outbound tankers

| | | |
|---|---|---|
| XL163 | Sqdn Ldr F.Milligan | 1hr 10mins |
| XL192 | Flt Lt N.J.Brooks | 4hrs 5mins |
| XL232 | Sqdn Ldr J.G.Elliott | 4hrs 15mins |
| XH672 | Sqdn Ldr M.D.Todd | 4hrs 20mins |
| XM717 | Sqdn Ldr B.R.Neal | 4hrs 20mins |
| XL511 | Wg Cdr C.C.B.Seymour | 4hrs 40mins |
| XL162 | Flt Lt S.P.Hamilton | 5hrs 20mins |
| XL512 | Flt Lt A.M.Skelton | 8hrs 10mins |
| XL188 | Sqdn Ldr A.M.Tomalin | 8hrs 30mins |
| XH669 | Flt Lt S.Biglands | 12hrs 15mins |
| XL189 | Sqdn Ldr R.Tuxford | 14hrs 5mins |

### Return tankers

| | | |
|---|---|---|
| XL163 | Sqdn Ldr F.Milligan | 1hr 25mins |
| XL192 | Flt Lt A.J.Barrett | 2hrs 55mins |
| XL233 | Sqdn Ldr M.D.Todd | 3hrs 25mins |
| XH671 | Flt Lt S.O.Jones | 5hrs 20mins |
| XL511 | Wg Cdr C.C.B.Seymour | 5hrs 40mins |
| XL232 | Sqdn Ldr J.G.Elliott | 6hrs 10mins |
| XH672 | Sqdn Ldr B.R.Neal | 9hrs 20mins |

XL160 deployed to Ascension Island via Banjul on 3 May in time for "Black Buck 2" which was mounted that night, involving another mass take-off from Wideawake. Every Victor on the Island was involved in the operation, either on the outbound or return legs. On that occasion, the long-distance flights were performed by XL192 (Flt Lt Skelton and crew, 11hrs 50mins) and XH669 (Sqdn Ldr Milligan and crew, 14hrs 00mins). Following its return from that mission, XL232 left for Marham the same day (via Banjul).

The next major operation for the tanker fleet involved the deployment of nine 1(F) Sqdn Harrier GR.3's from St Mawgan to Wideawake between 3 May and 6 May. Victors involved in that exercise included XL160 on 3 May (Marham-Banjul, continuing to Wideawake that day), XM715 on 4 May (Marham-Banjul, returning the same day), XH673 and XM715 on 5 May (both Marham-Banjul), plus XM715 on 6 May (Banjul-Banjul). XH673 and XM715 both returned to Marham later on 6 May. The following day saw much activity between Ascension Island and the United Kingdom as the two "Black Buck" Vulcan B.2's returned home, therefore permitting a reduction in Victor numbers as well. XL160, XL233 and the two Vulcans flew direct to their respective bases at Marham and Waddington, supported by XL164 and XM717 (both on round trips from Wideawake) with XH671 and XL163 which both flew to Banjul before completing the return transit to Marham on 8 May. Some of the vacant apron area at Wideawake was taken up by the arrival of the first Nimrod MR.2P on 7 May, deployed non-stop from Kinloss. The first extended-range Nimrod MRR patrol was carried out by XV227 on 9 May with Victors XH669, XL188 and XL189 in support. Nimrod MRR missions were flown almost daily over the next two weeks as intelligence was gathered on Argentine shipping movements prior to Operation "Sutton". XV232 deployed south from Kinloss on 9 May with XL163 in support (operating from/to Marham), the first to use AAR during the transit to Wideawake, while another followed on 13 May (refuelled by XL163 once again). Some of the Nimrod MRR flights mounted from Wideawake during that period required large numbers of Victor missions in support. One such sortie on 15 May was airborne for 19hrs 5mins and covered in excess of 8,300 miles, exceeding the previous record established by Victor XL189 on 20 April. The mission required the following tankers to be launched (listed in sequence of sortie length):

| | | |
|---|---|---|
| XL189 | Sqdn Ldr R.Tuxford | 0hrs 50mins |
| *XL162* | Flt Lt P.M.Millikin | 3hrs 40mins |
| XL512 | Flt Lt A.J.Barrett | 3hrs 45mins |
| XM717 | Wg Cdr C.C.B.Seymour | 3hrs 45mins |
| *XL162* | Flt Lt P.M.Millikin | 3hrs 50mins |
| *XL511* | Sqdn Ldr J.G.Elliott | 4hrs 00mins |
| XM715 | Sqdn Ldr M.D.Todd | 5hrs 10mins |
| XH672 | Flt Lt A.D.Richardson | 7hrs 35mins |
| XL191 | Flt Lt S.P.Hamilton | 7hrs 35mins |
| *XL511* | Flt Lt P.G.Heath | 7hrs 40mins |
| XL188 | Sqdn Ldr F.Milligan | 8hrs 40mins |
| XH669 | Flt Lt A.M.Skelton | 11hrs 10mins |

*Note that XL162 and XL511 flew twice, being used on both the outbound and return legs.*

An even longer MRR mission on 20/21 May covered 8,453 miles in 18hrs 51mins, for which 14 support Victor missions were launched.

Further changes to the Victor fleet on Ascension Island included the arrival direct from Marham of XH673 (12 May), XH671 (13 May), XM715 (13 May), XL160 (14 May), XL232 (16 May), XL233 (17 May) and XL163 (18 May), while XL191 flew Marham-Dakar on 13 May supporting a Vulcan and then completed its journey to the Island on 14 May. Those which returned home during the same period were XL192 (13 May via Dakar) and XL189 (18 May via Banjul).

The departure of 'Atlantic Conveyor' from Ascension Island on 7 May with its immensely valuable cargo of Harriers, Sea Harriers and helicopters also provided trade for the deployed Victor force. One 809 Sqn Sea Harrier was kept on full alert aboard the container ship in case it came under attack. In the event, the services of that aircraft were not called upon, but Victors were launched every day from 10 May to 13 May as a contingency, carrying out progressively longer missions as the ship made its way south towards the TEZ. The final such sortie on 13 May saw Sqdn Ldr Tuxford airborne in XH672 for 11hrs 50mins with three other Victors in support. Vulcan XM612 redeployed south from Waddington late on 13 May (refuelled by XL191 en route from Marham to Dakar and XH675 and XM715 on round trips from Marham), followed by XM607 24 hours later (refuelled by XH675, XL163 and XL232 all on round trips from Marham). "Black Buck 3", planned for 16 May, was later cancelled and the two Vulcans returned to Waddington on 20 May and 23 May.

The arrival of the first Hercules C.1P at Wideawake heralded the beginning of another sphere of operations for the Victor tanker fleet, that of refuelling long-range air-drop flights between Ascension Island and ships in the TEZ. Those missions began on 16 May with a 6,300 mile round trip by XV200, the Hercules remaining airborne for 24hrs 05mins. Three Victors provided fuel on the outbound leg (XH671, XL162 and XL512) while three more provided fuel for the return on 17 May (XH669, XL188 and XM717). Hercules C.1P XV179 remained airborne for 26 hours on 28/29 May during an air-drop to 'Active' and similar air-refuelled Hercules missions were launched on a regular basis until well after the Argentine surrender on 14 June.

The next significant operation involving the Victor fleet was the deployment of three 29(F) Sqdn Phantom FGR.2's from Coningsby to Wideawake for air defence duties on the Island. XV468 and XV484 were flown south on 24 May supported by XL192 (Marham-Dakar, returning on 25 May), XH675 and XL159 (both from/to Marham), while XV466 followed on 26 May with XL192 (Marham-Dakar) and XL159 (from/to Marham) in support. XL192 continued to Wideawake the same day and relieved XH669 which flew to Marham via Dakar on 28 May. Similar support was provided to Vulcan B.2's XM598 and XM597 which deployed south from Waddington on 26/27 May, the tankers operating from/to Marham. Six 1(F) Sqdn Harrier GR.3's were deployed from St Mawgan to Wideawake on 29/30 May, XL158 flying south with them as far as Dakar on both days (returning each evening) while XH669 and XL189

provided additional fuel on round trips from Marham. "Black Buck 4", the first anti-radar Vulcan sortie, was launched from Wideawake during the night of 28/29 May, but had to be cancelled several hours into the mission after the lead Victor's HDU became unserviceable. "Black Buck 5" during the night of 30/31 May was more successful and involved the support of 18 Victor missions, Sqdn Ldr Tomalin and crew in XL163 covering the greatest distance (they were airborne for 13hrs 10mins). XL232 returned to Marham on 31 May by way of Dakar, leaving 16 Victors on the Island at the beginning of June.

1(F) Sqdn Harrier GR.3's XV778 and XZ133 were flown from Wideawake direct to 'Hermes' in the TEZ on 1 June, involving support from eight Victors on round trips from the Island. XM717 (Flt Lt Jones and crew) and XH672 (Flt Lt Millikin and crew) covered the greatest distance with the Harriers, remaining airborne for 11hrs 35mins and 11hrs 45mins respectively. A similar operation was mounted on 8 June for the transfer of Harriers XW919 and XZ992 from Wideawake direct to the carrier. The next "Black Buck" raid involved Vulcan B.2 XM597, taking-off for another anti-radar sortie overnight on 2/3 June. 14 Victor missions were flown to ensure that the bomber reached its target safely, Flt Lt Biglands and crew in XL189 covering the greatest distance with 13hrs 15mins spent in the air. His aircraft had already been airborne for 8hrs 40mins in transit from Marham to Wideawake on 2 June, proving that miracles were being performed by the ground crews in keeping the ageing aircraft in the air. All did not go well on the Vulcan's return from "Black Buck 6" as the bomber's probe broke during the final AAR, forcing a diversion to Rio de Janeiro, Brazil. The last Vulcan raid took place during the night of 11/12 June when XM607 (which had returned to Ascension Island on 10 June) took-off from Wideawake for "Black Buck 7", a conventional bombing sortie against Stanley Airport. The longest Victor mission on that occasion lasted 13hrs 40mins, being flown by Flt Lt Richardson and crew in XL160.

The Argentine surrender on 14 June had little immediate effect on the pace of Victor operations from Wideawake as there was still a requirement for extended-range Nimrod and Hercules sorties south from Ascension Island. Further arrivals from Marham during the month were XH669 (12 June via Dakar), XL161 (7 June), XL189 (2 June), XL231 (14 June on its first deployment south) and XL232 (26 June). Those returning to the United Kingdom were XH671 (27 June via Dakar), XH672 (15 June via Dakar), XL163 (23 June via Dakar), XL164 (8 June), XL188 (27 June), XM715 (13 June via Dakar but returned south on 26 June) and XM717 (3 June via Dakar). The departure of the last Nimrod MR.2P from the Island on 18 August and the reopening of Stanley Airport as RAF Stanley after repair work at the end of that month permitted a reduction in the number of Victors detached to Wideawake, particularly as the first of six hurriedly-converted Hercules tankers had arrived on Ascension Island by that time.

Albeit on a smaller scale than during the conflict, the Victor fleet continued to provide sterling service in the South Atlantic until the opening of the new airfield at Mount Pleasant in the Falkland Islands on 12 May 1985.

As the new runway was able to accept long-range wide-bodied jets which were capable of reaching the Islands without the need for AAR, the Victor detachment on Ascension Island was finally withdrawn. The last aircraft dispatched to the South Atlantic was XL163 of 57 Sqdn which arrived at Wideawake on 12 March 1985. It returned to Marham on 10 June 1985, flown back by Wg Cdr Martin Todd (OC 55 Sqdn) who, as a Squadron Leader with 57 Sqdn, had been the pilot of XL189, the first Victor deployed to Ascension Island on 18 April 1982.

continued

*Ldr B.R.Neal RAF; Sqdn Ldr F.Tiernan RAF; Sqdn Ldr M.D.Todd RAF QCVSA; Sqdn Ldr A.M.Tomalin RAF; Sqdn Ldr R.Tuxford RAF AFC: Flt Lt A.J.Barrett RAF; Flt Lt S.Biglands RAF; Flt Lt N.J.Brooks RAF; Flt Lt P.H.Gausden RAF; Flt Lt S.P.Hamilton RAF; Flt Lt K.L.Handscomb RAF; Flt Lt P.G.Heath RAF; Flt Lt S.O.Jones RAF; Flt Lt P.M.Millikin RAF; Flt Lt J.V.Poole RAF; Flt Lt A.D.Richardson RAF; Flt Lt B.Russell RAF; Flt Lt A.M.Skelton RAF; Flt Lt P.A.Standing RAF.*

*55 and 57 Sqdns' Victor captains deployed to Wideawake during Operation "Corporate" and their awards:*

*Wg Cdr C.C.B.Seymour RAF: Sqdn Ldr J.G.Elliott RAF MID; Sqdn Ldr D.A.Foulger RAF; Sqdn Ldr A.M.Lovett RAF; Sqdn Ldr F.Milligan RAF; Sqdn*

continued

*Other aircrew from 55 and 57 Sqdns deployed to Wideawake during Operation "Corporate" who received awards:*

*Sqdn Ldr E.F.Wallis MBE RAF QCVSA; Flt Lt M.E.Beer RAF QCVSA; Flt Lt J.N.Keable RAF QCVSA; Flt Lt G.D.Rees RAF QCVSA.*

*The Victor K.2 tanker fleet continued to fly support sorties from Ascension Island until 6.85. XH672 of 57 Squadron, seen here at Wideawake in 4.83, was one of those aircraft that had earlier flown "Black Buck" missions and supported long-range Nimrod operations and Sea Harrier deployments. XM717 of 55 Squadron is seen beyond.*

*(M. D. Howley)*

# INDIVIDUAL AIRCRAFT DETAILS

**XH669** K.2

On 29.3.82 with 57 Sqdn at Marham. Deployed to Goose Bay, Canada on 13.4.82 in support of Harrier GR.3's en route from Wittering to CFB Cold Lake for an exercise. Returned to Marham on 15.4.82 and then flown non-stop to Wideawake on 29.4.82. Tanker missions from there included: the first two "Black Buck" Vulcan B.2 bombing raids overnight on 30.4/1.5.82 and 3/4.5.82; the first Nimrod MR.2P sortie on 9.5.82; contingency cover on 11/12.5.82 for the alert 809 Sqdn Sea Harrier FRS.1 aboard 'Atlantic Conveyor' and the recovery of the first Hercules C.1P air-drop mission from the TEZ on 17.5.82. Returned to Marham via Dakar on 28.5.82. Flown on round trips from/to

Marham on 29/30.5.82 to refuel 1(F) Sqdn Harrier GR.3's en route from St Mawgan to Wideawake. Deployed to Wideawake again (via Dakar) on 12.6.82, from where subsequent tanker missions included supporting Nimrod MR.2P and Hercules C.1P sorties from the Island on 13/14.6.82. Returned to Marham post-30.6.82.

**XH671** K.2

On 29.3.82 with 55 Sqdn at Marham. Deployed to Goose Bay, Canada on 13.4.82 in support of Harrier GR.3's en route from Wittering to CFB Cold Lake for an exercise. Returned to Marham on 15.4.82 and then flown non-stop to Wideawake on 19.4.82.

Subsequent tanker missions from there included the MRR sortie by XL192 of 57 Sqdn on 20.4.82 and the second "Black Buck" Vulcan bombing raid overnight on 3/4.5.82. Flown to Banjul on 7.5.82 in support of a Vulcan redeployment, returning to Marham the following day. Carried out one mission from Marham on 12.5.82 for Hercules C.1P crew training before deploying to Wideawake again non-stop on 13.5.82. Subsequent tanker missions from there included: the outbound leg of the first Hercules C.1P air-drop mission to the TEZ 16.5.82; the deployment of two 1(F) Sqdn Harrier GR.3's from Ascension to 'Hermes' in the TEZ on 1.6.82 and the "Black Buck 6" Vulcan B.2 anti-radar sortie on 3.6.82. Returned to Marham via Dakar on 27.6.82.

**XH672** K.2

On 29.3.82 with 57 Sqdn at Marham. Flown non-stop to Wideawake on 23.4.82, from where subsequent tanker missions included: the first two "Black Buck" Vulcan B.2 bombing raids overnight on 30.4/1.5.82 and 3/4.5.82; contingency cover on 11/12/13.5.82 for the alert 809 Sqdn Sea Harrier FRS.1 aboard 'Atlantic Conveyor'; the first Nimrod MR.2P reconnaissance mission off the Argentine coast on 15.5.82; the deployment of two 1(F) Sqdn Harrier GR.3's from Ascension to 'Hermes' in the TEZ on 1.6.82 and the last two "Black Buck" Vulcan B.2 sorties on 3.6.82 and 12.6.82. Returned to Marham via Dakar on 15.6.82.

**XH673** K.2

On 29.3.82 with 57 Sqdn at Marham. Carried out several receiver training sorties from Marham during 4.82 (Vulcan) and early 5.82 (Hercules and Nimrod). Deployed to Banjul on 5.5.82, refuelling 1(F) Sqdn Harrier GR.3's en route from St Mawgan to Wideawake. Returned to Marham on 6.5.82. Not flown again until deployed non-stop to Wideawake on 12.5.82, subsequent tanker missions from there including support for the deployment of two 1(F) Sqdn Harrier GR.3's from Ascension to 'Hermes' in the TEZ on 1.6.82 and the "Black Buck 6" Vulcan B.2 anti-radar sortie on 3.6.82. Returned to Marham post-30.6.82.

**XH675** K.2      *Not deployed to Ascension*

On 29.3.82 with 55 Sqdn at Marham. Supported the deployment of Vulcan B.2's from Waddington to Wideawake on 29.4.82 (operating from/to Marham). Deployed to Banjul on 1.5.82, refuelling 809 Sqdn Sea Harrier FRS.1's en route from Yeovilton to Ascension. Carried out a round trip from Banjul in support of the same aircraft on 2.5.82 before returning to Marham 3.5.82. Remained at Marham for the rest of the conflict, missions including several training sorties with Nimrods during early 5.82. Operating from/to Marham, it supported the deployment of Vulcan B.2's (13/14.5.82), Phantom FGR.2's (24.5.82) and a Hercules C.1P (14.6.82) from the UK to Ascension prior to the Argentine surrender on 14.6.82.

**XL158** K.2      *Not deployed to Ascension*

On 29.3.82 with 57 Sqdn at Marham. Supported the deployment of Vulcan B.2's from Waddington to Wideawake on 29.4.82, 809 Sqdn Sea Harrier FRS.1's from Yeovilton to Wideawake on 30.4.82 and 1(F) Sqdn Harrier GR.3's from St Mawgan to Wideawake on 5.5.82 (operating from/to Marham). Carried out several training sorties with Nimrods during 5.82. Deployed to Dakar on 29/30.5.82 (returning each evening), supporting the deployment of 1(F) Sqdn Harrier GR.3's from St Mawgan to Wideawake. Remained at Marham for the rest of the conflict where missions included several training sorties with Hercules C.1P's.

**XL160** K.2

On 29.3.82 with 57 Sqdn at Marham. Supported the deployment of Vulcan B.2's from Waddington to Wideawake on 29.4.82 (operating from/to Marham). Deployed to Banjul on 1.5.82, refuelling 809 Sqdn Sea Harrier FRS.1's en route from Yeovilton to Ascension. Carried out a round trip from Banjul in support of the same aircraft on 2.5.82 before returning to Marham on 2.5.82. Deployed from Marham to Wideawake via Banjul on 3.5.82, supporting the deployment of 1(F) Sqdn Harrier GR.3's from St Mawgan to Ascension. Subsequent tanker missions from Wideawake included supporting the second "Black Buck" Vulcan B.2 bombing raid overnight 3/4.5.82. Returned to Marham non-stop on 7.5.82, supporting the redeployment of a Vulcan B.2. Flown back to Wideawake non-stop on 14.5.82 and subsequent tanker missions from there included supporting the final "Black Buck" Vulcan B.2 bombing raid on 12.6.82. Returned to Marham post-30.6.82.

**XL161** K.2

On 29.3.82 with 55 Sqdn undergoing maintenance at Marham. Test-flown 3.6.82 and carried out its first mission on 5.6.82 (Hercules C.1P training as well as mutuals (Victor-to-Victor training) with XH675). Flown non-stop to Wideawake on 7.6.82 and subsequent tanker missions from there included supporting the deployment of two 1(F) Sqdn Harrier GR.3's from Ascension to 'Hermes' in the TEZ on 8.6.82. Returned to Marham post-30.6.82.

**XL162** K.2

On 29.3.82 with 55 Sqdn at Marham. Flown non-stop to Wideawake on 25.4.82 and subsequent tanker missions from there included: the first two "Black Buck" Vulcan B.2 bombing raids overnight on 30.4/1.5.82 and 3/4.5.82; the first Nimrod MR.2P reconnaissance mission off the Argentine coast on 15.5.82; the outbound leg of the first Hercules C.1P air-drop mission to the TEZ on 16.5.82; the deployment of two 1(F) Sqdn Harrier GR.3's from Ascension to 'Hermes' in the TEZ on 1.6.82 and the last two "Black Buck" Vulcan B.2 sorties on 3/12.6.82. Returned to Marham post-30.6.82.

**XL163** K.2

On 29.3.82 with 57 Sqdn at Marham. Carried out MRR/PR training over Scotland on 16.4.82 and flown to Wideawake non-stop on 18.4.82. Refuelled XL192 when that Victor carried out the first MRR mission to South Georgia on 20.4.82.

Overnight on 22/23.4.82, flown by Sqdn Ldr Todd and crew, it carried out the second long-range MRR mission to South Georgia which lasted 14hrs 5mins.

Further tanker missions from Wideawake included support for the first two "Black Buck" Vulcan B.2 bombing raids overnight on 30.4/1.5.82 and 3/4.5.82 (the latter after an air test on 2.5.82). Flown to Banjul on 7.5.82 (supporting the redeployment of a Vulcan B.2 to Waddington) and returned to Marham the following day. While based at Marham it supported the deployment to Ascension of two Nimrod MR.2P's (9/13.5.82) and a Vulcan B.2 (14.5.82). Flown back to Wideawake non-stop on 18.5.82, from where subsequent tanker missions included supporting the "Black Buck 5" and "Black Buck 6" Vulcan B.2 sorties overnight on 30/31.5.82 and 3.6.82. Returned to Marham via Dakar on 23.6.82.

**XL164** K.2

On 29.3.82 with 57 Sqdn at Marham. Carried out MRR/PR training over Scotland on 16.4.82 and flown to Wideawake non-stop on 19.4.82. Subsequent tanker missions from there included: the MRR sortie by XL192 of 57 Sqdn on 20.4.82; the "Black Buck 2" Vulcan B.2 bombing raid overnight on 3/4.5.82; the redeployment of a Vulcan B.2 to Waddington on 7.5.82; contingency cover for the alert 809 Sqdn Sea Harrier FRS.1 aboard 'Atlantic Conveyor' on 10/11/12.5.82 and the "Black Buck 6" Vulcan B.2 sortie on 3.6.82. Returned to Marham non-stop on 8.6.82.

**XL188** K.2

On 29.3.82 with 55 Sqdn at Marham. Flown to Wideawake non-stop on 19.4.82, subsequent tanker missions from there including: the MRR sortie by XL192 of 57 Sqdn on 20.4.82; the first two "Black Buck" Vulcan B.2 bombing raids overnight on 30.4/1.5.82 and 3/4.5.82; the first Nimrod MR.2P on 9.5.82; contingency cover for the alert 809 Sqdn Sea Harrier FRS.1 aboard 'Atlantic Conveyor' on 10/13.5.82; the first Nimrod MR.2P reconnaissance mission off the Argentine coast on 15.5.82; the return leg of the first Hercules C.1P air-drop mission to the TEZ on 17.5.82 and the deployment of two 1(F) Sqdn Harrier GR.3's from Ascension to 'Hermes' in the TEZ on 8.6.82. Returned to Marham non-stop on 27.6.82.

**XL189** K.2

On 29.3.82 with 57 Sqdn at Marham. Carried out MRR/PR practice over Scotland on 16.4.82 and flown to Wideawake non-stop on 18.4.82 (the first Victor deployed to Ascension). Refuelled XL192 when that Victor carried out the first MRR mission to South Georgia on 20.4.82.

Overnight on 24/25.4.82, flown by Wg Cdr Seymour and crew, it carried out the third long-range MRR sortie to South Georgia which lasted 14hrs 5mins.

Flown by Flt Lt Tuxford and crew, it supported "Black Buck 1" overnight on 30.4/1.5.82, the first Vulcan B.2 bombing raid against Stanley Airport. Remained airborne for 14hrs 5mins, travelling the furthest distance with the bomber and carrying out the last southbound refuelling 3,000 miles from Ascension *[see text for further relevant details about the mission.]*

Subsequent tanker missions from Wideawake included: the second "Black Buck" Vulcan B.2 bombing raid overnight on 3/4.5.82; the first Nimrod MR.2P sortie on 9.5.82 and the first Nimrod MR.2P reconnaissance mission off the Argentine coast on 15.5.82. Returned to Marham (via Banjul) on 18.5.82 and while based there it supported the deployment to Ascension of 29(F) Sqdn Phantom FGR.2's on 24/26.5.82 and 1(F) Sqdn Harrier GR.3's on 29/30.5.82. Redeployed non-stop to Wideawake on 2.6.82, from where subsequent tanker missions included supporting the "Black Buck 6" Vulcan B.2 sortie on 3.6.82. Returned to Marham post-30.6.82.

**XL190** K.2      *Not deployed to Ascension*

On 29.3.82 with 55 Sqdn at Marham. No record of the aircraft having flown at all during Operation "Corporate". Reported to have been undergoing maintenance at Marham throughout the period.

**XL191** K.2

On 29.3.82 with 55 Sqdn at Marham. Deployed to Banjul on 30.4.82, refuelling 809 Sqdn Sea Harrier FRS.1's en route from Yeovilton to Ascension. Carried out a round trip from Banjul in support of the same aircraft in 1.5.82 before returning to Marham on 7.5.82. Flown to Dakar on 13.5.82, supporting the deployment of a Vulcan B.2 from Waddington to Ascension, and then continued to Wideawake on 14.5.82. Subsequent tanker missions from Wideawake included supporting the first Nimrod MR.2P reconnaissance mission off the Argentine coast on 15.5.82 and the "Black Buck 6" Vulcan B.2 anti-radar sortie on 3.6.82. Returned to Marham post-30.6.82.

**XL192** K.2

On 29.3.82 with 57 Sqdn. Carried out practice MRR/PR missions over Scotland 14/15.4.82 and flown to Wideawake non-stop on 18.4.82.

On 20.4.82, flown by Sqdn Ldr Elliott and crew, it carried out the first long-range MRR mission to South Georgia which lasted 14hrs 45mins (a record for operational long-range reconnaissance flights, broken later in the War by Nimrod MR.2P's). Some 150,000 square miles were mapped, the mission (and two subsequent ones by XL163 23/24.4.82 and XL189 24/25.4.82) providing valuable information on shipping, icebergs and pack-ice prior to and during Operation "Paraquat" (the retaking of South Georgia).

Subsequent tanker missions from Wideawake included supporting the first two "Black Buck" Vulcan B.2 bombing raids overnight on 30.4/1.5.82 and 3/4.5.82 and providing contingency cover on 12/13.5.82 for the alert 809 Sqdn Sea Harrier FRS.1 aboard 'Atlantic Conveyor' before being flown back to Marham via Dakar on 13.5.82. Deployed to Dakar on 24.5.82, supporting two 29(F) Sqdn Phantom FGR.2's en route from Coningsby to Ascension. Returned to Marham on 25.5.82 and then deployed to Dakar again on 26.5.82 in support of a third 29(F) Sqdn Phantom FGR.2 en route to Ascension. Continued to Wideawake the same day, from where subsequent tanker missions included support for the deployment of two 1(F) Sqdn Harrier GR.3's from Ascension to 'Hermes' in the TEZ on 1.6.82 and the "Black Buck 6" Vulcan B.2 anti-radar sortie 3.6.82. Returned to Marham post-30.6.82.

**XL231** K.2

On 29.3.82 with 57 Sqdn at Marham. Very active on general support duties throughout 4.82. One seven-day period saw it visit Yeovilton on 19.4.82, Waddington on 20.4.82, Kinloss and Yeovilton on 22.4.82,

Waddington and Lyneham on 23.4.82, Waddington on 24.4.82 and Kinloss and Waddington on 25.4.82, while on 21.4.82 it had carried out a training flight with 809 Sqdn Sea Harrier FRS.1's. To Woodford for Nimrod MR.2P ground link-up trials on 28.4.82, returning to Marham on 29.4.82 after carrying out the first Nimrod MR.2P AAR that day. To Boscombe Down 1.5.82 for Hercules C.1P ground link-up trials, returning the same day. Carried out the first Hercules C.1P AAR on 2.5.82 during a sortie from Marham, during which it also supported 1(F) Sqdn Harrier GR.3's deploying from St Mawgan to Ascension. Involved in further Hercules C.1P receiver training 6-8.5.82 before being dispatched from Marham to St Athan on 12.5.82 for major overhaul. Servicing was completed in record time and it was flown back to Marham on 7.6.82, undertaking an air test from there on 9.6.82. Missions were performed from Marham on 10/13.6.82 before it was flown to Wideawake non-stop on 14.6.82, supporting the deployment of a Hercules C.1P from Lyneham to the Island. Returned to Marham post-30.6.82.

**XL232** K.2

On 29.3.82 with 55 Sqdn at Marham (wearing the markings of 232 OCU). Deployed to Goose Bay, Canada on 13.4.82 in support of Harrier GR.3's en route from Wittering to CFB Cold Lake for an exercise. Returned to Marham on 15.4.82 and then flown non-stop to Wideawake on 19.4.82. Subsequent tanker missions from there included supporting the first two "Black Buck" Vulcan B.2 bombing raids overnight on 30.4/1.5.82 and 3/4.5.82. Returned to Marham (via Banjul) on 4.5.82 and while there it supported the deployment of a Vulcan B.2 from Waddington to Ascension on 14.5.82. Redeployed to Wideawake non-stop on 16.5.82, from where subsequent tanker missions included assisting the recovery of a Nimrod MR.2P from a long-range reconnaissance sortie 18.5.82. Returned to Marham via Dakar on 31.5.82 and not flown again until after the Argentine surrender on 14.6.82.

**XL233** K.2

On 29.3.82 undergoing major overhaul at St Athan. Returned to Marham for 55 Sqdn 15.4.82 and carried out an air test on 23.4.82 before deploying non-stop to Wideawake on 25.4.82. Subsequent tanker missions from there included supporting the second "Black Buck" Vulcan B.2 bombing raid overnight on 3/4.5.82. Returned non-stop to Marham on 7.5.82, supporting the redeployment of a Vulcan B.2 from Ascension to Waddington. Flown back to Wideawake non-stop on 17.5.82, from where subsequent tanker missions included supporting the deployment of two 1(F) Sqdn Harrier GR.3's from Ascension to 'Hermes' in the TEZ on 1.6.82 and the "Black Buck 6" Vulcan B.2 anti-radar sortie on 3.6.82. Returned to Marham post-30.6.82.

**XL511** K.2

On 29.3.82 with 55 Sqdn at Marham. Flown non-stop to Wideawake on 18.4.82. Refuelled XL192 when that Victor carried out the first MRR mission to South Georgia on 20.4.82. Further tanker missions from Wideawake included: the first two "Black Buck" Vulcan B.2 bombing raids overnight on 30.4/1.5.82 and

3/4.5.82; contingency cover for the alert 809 Sqdn Sea Harrier FRS.1 aboard 'Atlantic Conveyor' on 13.5.82; the first Nimrod MR.2P reconnaissance mission off the Argentine coast on 15.5.82 and the "Black Buck 7" Vulcan B.2 bombing raid on 12.6.82. Returned to Marham post-30.6.82.

**XL512** K.2

On 29.3.82 with 57 Sqdn at Marham. Supported the deployment of two Vulcan B.2's from Waddington to Ascension on 29.4.82. Flown to Wideawake non-stop on 30.4.82 and subsequent tanker missions from there included: the "Black Buck 1" Vulcan B.2 bombing raid overnight 30.4/1.5.82; the first Nimrod MR.2P reconnaissance mission off the Argentine coast on 15.5.82; the outbound leg of the first Hercules C.1P air-drop mission to the TEZ on 16.5.82; the deployment of two 1(F) Sqdn Harrier GR.3's from Ascension to 'Hermes' in the TEZ on 1.6.82 and the "Black Buck 6" Vulcan B.2 anti-radar sortie on 3.6.82. Returned to Marham post-30.6.82.

**XM715** K.2

On 29.3.82 with 55 Sqdn at Marham. Flown non-stop to Wideawake on 18.4.82. Refuelled XL192 when that Victor carried out the first MRR mission to South Georgia on 20.4.82. Returned to Marham (via Dakar) on 26.4.82 and while based there it supported the deployment of 809 Sqdn Sea Harrier FRS.1's from Yeovilton to Ascension on 30.4.82 and 1.5.82. Flown to Banjul and back on 4.5.82 in support of 1(F) Sqdn Harrier GR.3's deploying from St Mawgan to Ascension. Returned to Banjul on 5.5.82 with further Harrier GR.3's, carrying out a round trip from Banjul in support of the same aircraft on 6.5.82 (flown back to Marham later that day). Supported the deployment of a Vulcan B.2 from Waddington to Ascension on 13.5.82 on a round trip from Marham before being flown non-stop to Wideawake later that day. Subsequent tanker missions from Wideawake included supporting the first Nimrod MR.2P reconnaissance mission off the Argentine coast on 15.5.82 and the "Black Buck 6" Vulcan B.2 anti-radar sortie on 3.6.82. Returned to Marham via Dakar on 13.6.82.

**XM717** K.2

On 29.3.82 with 55 Sqdn at Marham. Deployed to Goose Bay, Canada on 13.4.82 in support of Harrier GR.3's en route from Wittering to CFB Cold Lake for an exercise. Returned to Marham on 15.4.82. Flown non-stop to Wideawake on 30.4.82, from where subsequent tanker missions included: the first two "Black Buck" Vulcan B.2 bombing raids overnight on 30.4/1.5.82 and 3/4.5.82; the redeployment of a Vulcan B.2 to Waddington on 7.5.82; contingency cover for the alert 809 Sqdn Sea Harrier FRS.1 aboard 'Atlantic Conveyor' on 11.5.82; the first Nimrod MR.2P reconnaissance mission off the Argentine coast on 15.5.82; the return leg of the first Hercules C.1P air-drop mission to the TEZ 17.5.82; the deployment of two 1(F) Sqdn Harrier GR.3's from Ascension to 'Hermes' in the TEZ on 1.6.82 and the "Black Buck 6" Vulcan B.2 anti-radar sortie on 3.6.82. Returned to Marham via Dakar later on 3.6.82 before being flown to St Athan for major overhaul on 7.6.82.

*Nimrod MR.2P XV227 of the Kinloss Wing is seen at Wideawake on 16.5.82, a week after the first IFR-probed aircraft was deployed to the Island. At that time the aircraft had yet to be modified to carry Sidewinder missiles on underwing pylons for self-defence, the system not being cleared for operational use until 28.5.82.* (Mel James)

*Kinloss Wing Nimrod MR.2P XV239 displays the underwing Sidewinder installation to good advantage while performing at the Wyton Open Day on 31.7.82. Up to four missiles could be carried, each pylon being able to carry two as seen on XV234 at Brize Norton on 18.6.83 (**Lower Right**). Typical of the many modification programmes which were rushed through during the early stages of the conflict, the Nimrod's IFR probe (**Lower Left**) proved to be a functional, if aesthetically unpleasing, addition to the airframe. (Peter J. Cooper)*

# NIMROD

## 42(TB) SQUADRON

On 4 April, HQ 18 (Maritime) Group directed 42 (Torpedo Bomber) Sqdn at St Mawgan to prepare two Nimrod MR.1's, three crews and supporting ground-crew for deployment to Ascension Island for an unspecified period, thus beginning the maritime patrol aircraft's involvement in Operation "Corporate". At that time, 42(TB) Sqdn was using the following Nimrod MR.1's:

| | | | |
|---|---|---|---|
| XV226 | XV244 | XV249 | XV262 |
| XV233 | XV245 | XV258 | |

All except XV262 had been resprayed in the new camouflage scheme which consisted of Hemp upper surfaces and Light Aircraft Grey undersides. The roundels were Red/Blue (except for those under the wings which were Red/White/Blue) while the serials were in Black (the last two digits being repeated on the nose and fin). XV262 was still awaiting a respray, retaining the earlier colour scheme which consisted of White upper surfaces, Light Aircraft Grey undersides, 'D' Class Red/White/Blue roundels and Black serials (the last two digits repeated as above). The Nimrod fleet was at that time progressively being updated to MR.2 standard by British Aerospace at Woodford, which involved installation of the more capable Searchwater radar. 120 Sqdn and 206 Sqdn at Kinloss had already completed conversion to the MR.2, while 201 Sqdn on the same station was in the process of conversion. 236 OCU had moved from St Mawgan to Kinloss on 1 April to begin transition, leaving 42(TB) Sqdn as the last operator of the MR.1.

XV244 (Flt Lt S.C.Smith and Crew 1) and XV258 (Sqdn Ldr M.A.Norris and Crew 4) left St Mawgan for Lajes in the Azores on 5 April, completing their respective transits to Ascension Island the following day when the first aircraft landed at Wideawake at 1755Z. The third crew (Crew 8 under Flt Lt J.G.Turnbull) was split between the two Nimrods for the journey from St Mawgan to Wideawake.

Under the command of Wg Cdr D.L.Baugh, the detachment flew its first operational sortie from Wideawake on 7 April when Flt Lt Turnbull and crew took-off in XV258 for a surface surveillance and submarine support mission which lasted for 6hrs 10mins. A similar mission by Sqdn Ldr Norris and crew on 9 April saw the same aircraft airborne for 6hrs 45mins. With accommodation on the Island at a premium, Flt Lt Smith and crew returned to the United Kingdom that day following the decision that the Squadron's task could be achieved with two crews. XV244 performed its first operational mission on 10 April, Flt Lt Turnbull and crew taking the aircraft south from Ascension Island on surface surveillance duties which lasted 8hrs 30mins. XV244 carried out similar taskings on 11 April (Flt Lt Turnbull and crew, airborne for 9hrs 50mins), 12 April (Sqdn Ldr Norris and crew, airborne for 9hrs 30mins), 14 April (Sqdn Ldr Norris and crew, airborne for 9hrs) and 15 April (Sqdn Ldr Norris and crew, airborne for 9hrs 10mins). These sorties concluded 42(TB) Sqdn's operations from Wideawake and two Kinloss Wing Nimrod MR.2's arrived on the Island (on 13 April and 17 April) to assume the maritime surveillance task. MR.1 XV258 (Flt Lt Turnbull and crew) flew Wideawake-Dakar-Gibraltar on 13 April, completing the flight to St Mawgan on 15 April, while XV244 (Flt Lt C.Montgomery and Crew 4) left Wideawake for Lajes on 17 April to arrive at St Mawgan the following day. Wg Cdr Baugh (by then the Senior Royal Air Force Officer, Ascension Island) and Sqdn Ldr Norris remained at Wideawake until 12 May to assist with operations from the Island, Wg Cdr Baugh subsequently being awarded the OBE for his work during this period.

Apart from a 4hr torpedo modification trial flight from St Mawgan by XV249 (Flt Lt Turnbull and Crew 8) on 27 April, 42(TB) Sqdn's subsequent involvement in Operation "Corporate" missions was limited to providing SAR cover for the Harrier deployments to Ascension Island. Looking after the southerly part of the single-engined fighters' long over-water transit to Wideawake, XV249 (Sqdn Ldr R.Piper and Crew 5) deployed from St Mawgan to Freetown in Sierra Leone on 1 May. The aircraft flew SAR sorties from there on 3, 4, 5 and 6 May before recovering to St Mawgan on 7 May. The northerly part of the Harriers' transit was watched over by missions launched from St Mawgan on 3 May (Flt Lt I.Scott and Crew 3 in XV244), 4 May (Flt Lt C.Montgomery and

Crew 4 in XV244) and 5 May (Flt Lt N.E.Jones and Crew 6 in XV245). Similar sorties were launched at the end of the month, XV249 (Flt Lt A.J.Stacey and Crew 9) flying missions from Dakar in Senegal on 26, 29 and 30 May.

Back in the United Kingdom, 42(TB) Sqdn's Nimrod MR.1 fleet relieved the Kinloss Wing MR.2's of all SAR commitments as well as much of their routine fishery patrol missions for the duration of the conflict. The Squadron did visit Ascension Island again after the surrender, deploying one Nimrod and two crews to Wideawake from 17 August to 5 November to provide SAR cover during the early days of the Hercules "air bridge" to Port Stanley.

> *42(TB) Sqdn Nimrod captains deployed to Wideawake, Dakar and Freetown during Operation "Corporate" and their awards:*
>
> *Wg Cdr D.L.Baugh RAF OBE; Sqdn Ldr M.A.Norris RAF (and Crew 4); Sqdn Ldr R.Piper RAF (and Crew 5); Flt Lt S.C.Smith RAF (and Crew 1); Flt Lt A.J.Stacey RAF (and Crew 9); Flt Lt J.G.Turnbull RAF (and Crew 8).*

# 51 SQUADRON

Operating from Wyton, the activities of 51 Sqdn's fleet of three reconnaissance Nimrod R.1's (XW664, XW665 and XW666) were, and still are (at the time of writing), rarely commented upon by official sources, although it has been admitted that the Squadron did participate in Operation "Corporate". The fact that XW664 was seen shortly after the surrender sporting an IFR probe [see *photograph*] would tend to confirm that particular aircraft's involvement, but no further details have come to light. Similarly, it has not been possible to confirm reports that a small number of Canberra PR.9's operated by 39 Sqdn at Wyton were also involved in the conflict (the Squadron officially disbanded on 28 May 1982).

# 120, 201 & 206 SQUADRONS

120, 201 and 206 Sqdns all flew the updated Nimrod MR.2 from Kinloss at the start of Operation "Corporate", the aircraft themselves being pooled for use by each Squadron as required. Some unmodified Nimrod MR.1's were also still present awaiting their turn to join the conversion line at Woodford, but those aircraft were not involved in the deployment to Ascension Island. Nimrod MR.2's available to the three Squadrons were as follows:

| | | | |
|---|---|---|---|
| XV227 | XV236 | XV243 | XV260 |
| XV228 | XV237 | XV253 | |
| XV230 | XV239 | XV254 | |
| XV232 | XV241 | XV255 | |

The aircraft were all painted in the standard Hemp and Light Aircraft Grey colour scheme [*refer to the 42 Sqdn notes for details*]. An additional machine (XV256) had been lost in an accident, while XV229 and XZ284 were retained for trials at BAe Woodford and A&AEE Boscombe Down respectively. Newly-converted MR.2's which emerged from the Woodford production line during or shortly after Operation "Corporate" included XV234, XV238, XV247 and XV248.

Two Kinloss Wing Nimrod MR.2's arrived at Wideawake on 13 April and 17 April (believed to have been XV230 and XV255 respectively) to replace the 42 Sqdn MR.1's. They commenced operations almost immediately, XV230 being used to drop secret orders concerning Operation "Paraquat" (the retaking of South Georgia) to 'Antrim' on 15.4.82 while the vessel was en route south from Ascension Island. Wg Cdr D.Emmerson (OC 206 Sqdn) arrived at Wideawake on 21 April and assumed the role of Nimrod Detachment Commander. Missions undertaken by the Maritime Reconnaissance crews under his command then fell into three main categories, the most frequent and least glamorous being the defence of Ascension Island. As the South Atlantic staging post was crucial to the British Forces, it was considered a particularly attractive target to the Argentines for either air or sea attack or raids by Special Forces. For this reason the sea around the Island was constantly patrolled by Nimrods co-operating with the Royal Navy guard-ship. The other two mission categories involved reconnaissance and escort duties. The former covered the investigation of surface contacts and the carrying out of anti-submarine sweeps ahead of the various elements of the Task Force moving south towards the Falkland Islands (confined to a radius of about 2,000 miles from Wideawake until the advent of in-flight refuelling), while the latter involved acting as a communications link between Victor tankers and their receivers (and equipped for SAR should that be required). Wg Cdr Emmerson captained a Nimrod which was launched during the night of 30 April/1 May to assist the first "Black Buck" Vulcan raid against Stanley Airport, its radar aiding the link-up between Victors and Vulcan while its advanced communications fit enabled the operations room on Ascension Island to be kept up-to-date with rendezvous and fuel transfer information.

In the United Kingdom, preliminary discussions on the feasibility of equipping Nimrod MR.2's with an air-to-air refuelling capability had taken place, British Aerospace at Woodford being given instructions to proceed with the necessary modifications on 14 April. A refuelling probe was fitted to trials MR.2 XV229, along with a small ventral fin to improve handling qualities, and this aircraft took to the air for the first time on 27 April. The aircraft did not receive the necessary internal "plumbing" and was used as an aerodynamic test-bed only. 57 Sqdn Victor K.2 XL231 flew to Woodford the following day for ground trials with XV229, while the Nimrod itself was flown to Kinloss on 30 April for "dry" AAR training. The first fully operational refuelling system was installed in XV238 (the 14th Nimrod MR.2, still present on the conversion line at Woodford), that aircraft being used for acceptance trials at A&AEE Boscombe Down which resulted in the modification being cleared for use on 5 May. Small finlets above and below the tailplane were incorporated on that and all subsequent aircraft to receive the modification, the type being redesignated MR.2P. 16 aircraft were so modified during or shortly after the conflict:

| | | | |
|---|---|---|---|
| XV227 | XV234 | XV239 | XV253 |
| XV228 | XV236 | XV243 | XV254 |
| XV230 | XV237 | XV247 | XV255 |
| XV232 | XV238 | XV248 | XV260 |

The first extended-range flight by the type took place on 6 May when XV238 (Flt Lt A.Mellville Jackson and 206 Sqdn Crew 3, accompanied by AARI Sqdn Ldr E.Banfield from the A&AEE) took-off at 2200Z for a 20-hour mission.

Nimrod MR.2P XV227 deployed non-stop from Kinloss to Wideawake on 7 May without the help of AAR. This aircraft carried out the first AAR-assisted mission from Wideawake two days later, being flown some 2,750 miles south south-west of Ascension Island by Flt Lt D.J.Ford and 206 Sqdn Crew 5 (AARI Sqdn Ldr N.R.J.Wingate AFC) to provide anti-submarine cover for Task Force ships heading towards the Falkland Islands. The Nimrod took-off at 0930Z and was airborne for 12hrs 45mins. The same aircraft flew the first long-range sortie from Ascension Island on 12 May (Flt Lt C.Moncaster and 201 Sqdn Crew 1; AARI Flt Lt M.G.Christy), taking-off at 0605Z for a flight which lasted 14hrs 35mins and reached as far south as 45° South. MR.2P XV232 (Flt Lt J.A.Cowan and 201 Sqdn Crew 7, AARI Sqdn Ldr J.Rudin) left Kinloss at 0930Z on 9 May for the first AAR-assisted deployment from the United Kingdom to Ascension Island, arriving at Wideawake 10hrs 25mins later. That aircraft was involved in two record-breaking sorties from the Island. On 15 May it took-off at 0805Z with Flt Lt Cowan and 201 Sqdn Crew 7 (AARI Sqdn Ldr Rudin; Wg Cdr Emmerson also aboard) for a long-range reconnaissance flight which lasted 19hrs 5mins, extensive cloud cover having prevented the use of satellite-derived information. The Nimrod was flown south to a point 150 miles north of Port Stanley and then west until approximately 60 miles off the Argentine coast. XV232 then tracked north-east at between 7,000ft and 12,000ft parallel with the coast and its Searchwater radar was used to survey a strip 400 miles wide and 1,000 miles long, confirming that all Argentine warships were still successfully blockaded in port by the threat of British nuclear-powered submarines. It was a fine day and the aircraft was vulnerable during some segments of that flight, but XV232 was successfully recovered to Wideawake without incident after a total of three AAR's and having travelled 8,300 miles. Similar extended-range reconnaissance flights were tasked regularly during the next few days, culminating in the second record-breaking flight by XV232 during the night of 20/21 May just prior to the landings at San Carlos. Flt Lt Ford and 206 Sqdn Crew 5 (AARI Sqdn Ldr Wingate; Wg Cdr Emmerson aboard once again) departed Wideawake at 1715Z in the aircraft and followed a similar course to the one that had been flown on 15 May. Although on this occasion the Nimrod was airborne for 18hrs 50mins (15mins less than the earlier flight) it covered a greater distance (8,453 miles), the furthest travelled in one sortie by any aircraft during Operation "Corporate" and one of the longest combat missions of all time.

Other modifications were carried out to the basic Nimrod MR.2 airframe once it became apparent that the aircraft would not be operating entirely on ASW missions under the conditions of complete air superiority envisaged in the North Atlantic environment for which the type was designed and for which its crews had been trained. Air combat training against friendly fighters commenced on 3 May, while the engineers at Woodford were given the task of equipping the aircraft with a defensive air-to-air missile capability. The Nimrod had been designed with under-wing hard-points and a prototype had undertaken trials with Martel anti-shipping missiles some 12 years previously, so the task was to design suitable pylons for the attachment of Sidewinder missiles and their associated wiring. MR.2 XV229 was used for the trial installation, making its first flight after modification on 26 May. Acceptance checks of the AIM-9 fit were completed on 28 May. MR.2P XV232 (back from Ascension Island) became the first aircraft to enter service on 31 May, the first deployment to Wideawake taking place on 5 June.

Further additions to the Nimrod MR.2's normal weaponry included clearance for the use of BL755 CBU's and 1,000lb HE bombs following the fitment of a makeshift bomb-sight. Modifications were also carried out to the weapons bay to allow the carriage of AGM-84A Harpoon anti-shipping missiles which were provided by the United States. Nimrod MR.2P XV234 first flew after Harpoon conversion on 10 June and acceptance checks were completed two days later. MR.2P XV237 became the first aircraft to enter service (on 19 June), the first deployment to Wideawake taking place on 2 July, well after the surrender.

Some 111 Nimrod sorties were launched from Wideawake in support of Operation "Corporate", but activities continued from Ascension Island for some time after the surrender. MR.2P XV234 (Flt Lt Moncaster and 201 Sqdn Crew 1) performed the final Kinloss Wing sortie from Wideawake on 17 August, the aircraft and crew leaving the Island for Gibraltar the following day prior to returning to Kinloss at 1010Z on 19 August.

120, 201 and 206 Sqdn Nimrod captains deployed to Wideawake during Operation "Corporate" included the following (with their awards):

*continued*

*continued*

Wg Cdr D.Emmerson RAF AFC; Flt Lt J.A.Cowan RAF (and 201 Sqdn Crew 7); Flt Lt D.J.Ford RAF (and 206 Sqdn Crew 5); Flt Lt C.J.Moncaster RAF (and 201 Sqdn Crew 1).

# INDIVIDUAL AIRCRAFT DETAILS

**XV227** MR.2P

On 29.3.82 with the Kinloss Wing as a Nimrod MR.2. Converted to MR.2P by fitment of an IFR probe. Deployed from Kinloss to Wideawake non-stop 7.5.82 (the first MR.2P to arrive on Ascension). Carried out the first AAR-assisted surveillance sortie from the Island on 9.5.82 and the first long-range patrol on 12.5.82 (airborne for 14hrs 15mins and reached as far south as 45°S). Still present at Wideawake on 16.5.82; subsequently returned to Kinloss.

**XV228** MR.2

On 29.3.82 with the Kinloss Wing. Known to have been deployed to Wideawake during Operation "Corporate" (noted there on 1.5.82). Subsequently returned to the UK for MR.2P conversion.

**XV230** MR.2

On 29.3.82 with the Kinloss Wing. Deployed to Wideawake (believed to have been on 13.4.82) with XV255 to replace the 42(TB) Sqdn MR.1 detachment and used to drop secret orders concerning Operation "Paraquat" to 'Antrim' on 15.4.82 (the vessel being en route from Ascension to South Georgia). Returned to the UK for MR.2P conversion and then redeployed to Wideawake (noted there 18.5.82). Subsequently returned to Kinloss.

**XV232** MR.2P

On 29.3.82 with the Kinloss Wing as a Nimrod MR.2. Converted to MR.2P by fitment of an IFR probe. Deployed from Kinloss to Wideawake non-stop 9.5.82 (the first AAR-assisted deployment).

On 15.5.82, flown by Flt Lt Cowan and 201 Sqdn Crew 7, it carried out a very long-range mission to survey Argentine coastal waters, travelling 8,300 miles in 19hrs 5mins. A similar mission by the same aircraft on 20/21.5.82 (flown by Flt Lt Ford and 206 Sqdn Crew 5) covered 8,453 miles in 18hrs 50mins, one of the furthest travelled combat sorties of all time.

Returned to the UK for AIM-9 Sidewinder conversion and was the first to enter service at Kinloss on 31.5.82.

**XV243** MR.2P

On 29.3.82 with the Kinloss Wing as a Nimrod MR.2. Converted to MR.2P by fitment of an IFR probe. Known to have been deployed to Wideawake during Operation "Corporate" (noted there 18.5.82).

**XV244** MR.1

On 29.3.82 with 42(TB) Sqdn at St Mawgan. Flown from St Mawgan to Lajes 5.4.82 and on to Wideawake 6.4.82. Carried out surface surveillance missions from Ascension on 10, 11, 12, 14 and 15.4.82. Left Wideawake for Lajes on 17.4.82, returning to St Mawgan on 18.4.82.

**XV247** MR.2P

On 29.3.82 with the Kinloss Wing as a Nimrod MR.2. Converted to MR.2P by fitment of an IFR probe. Known to have been deployed to Wideawake during Operation "Corporate" (noted there on 21.5.82).

**XV249** MR.1

On 29.3.82 with 42(TB) Sqdn at St Mawgan. Flown from St Mawgan to Freetown 1.5.82 to provide SAR cover for the 1(F) Sqdn Harrier GR.3 deployments to Ascension. Carried out SAR missions from Freetown on 3, 4, 5 and 6.5.82 before returning to St Mawgan on 7.5.82. Deployed to Dakar at the end of the month to provide similar cover for a Phantom and more Harriers en route from the UK to Ascension, flying SAR missions on 26, 29 and 30.5.82 before returning to St Mawgan.

**XV255** MR.2

On 29.3.82 with the Kinloss Wing. Deployed to Wideawake (believed on 17.4.82) with XV230 to replace the 42(TB) Sqdn MR.1 detachment. Subsequently returned to the UK for MR.2P conversion.

**XV258** MR.1

On 29.3.82 with 42(TB) Sqdn at St Mawgan. Flown from St Mawgan to Lajes 5.4.82 and on to Wideawake 6.4.82. Carried out surface surveillance and submarine support missions from Ascension on 7/9.4.82. Left Wideawake for Gibraltar (via Dakar) on 13.4.82, returning to St Mawgan on 15.4.82.

**XV260** MR.2

On 29.3.82 with the Kinloss Wing. Known to have been deployed to Wideawake during Operation "Corporate" (noted there on 1.5.82). Subsequently returned to the UK for MR.2P conversion.

**XW664** R.1

On 29.3.82 with 51 Sqdn at Wyton. Noted at Wyton on 26.4.82. Believed to have been involved in Operation "Corporate" missions but no details known. Had gained an IFR probe by the time of the Argentine surrender on 14.6.82.

*51 Squadron's involvement in Operation "Corporate" was not confirmed officially until the unit received its South Atlantic Honours. Nimrod R.1 XW664 was the only one of the Squadron's three aircraft to gain an IFR probe during the conflict and is presumed, therefore, to have taken part. Its operating base and duration of deployment remain, at the time of writing, something of a mystery.*

*(Colin Johnson)*

# HERCULES

# 24, 30, 47 & 70 SQUADRONS

At the end of March 1982 the Royal Air Force had available to it a total of 54 Hercules transports, operated in a pooled fleet by 24, 30, 47 and 70 Sqdns at Lyneham. Those four units comprised the Lyneham Transport Wing, 242 OCU (the co-located Hercules training unit) borrowing LTW aircraft as required. The aircraft on strength were as follows:

| C.1 | XV177 XV189 XV199 XV210 XV222 XV298 |
| --- | --- |
| | XV178 XV190 XV201 XV211 XV291 XV299 |
| | XV181 XV191 XV203 XV213 XV292 XV300 |
| | XV182 XV192 XV204 XV214 XV293 XV302 |
| | XV185 XV193 XV205 XV215 XV295 XV304 |
| | XV186 XV195 XV206 XV217 XV296 XV306 |
| | XV187 XV196 XV209 XV218 XV297 XV307 |
| | |
| C.3 | XV176 XV197 XV207 XV220 XV290 XV303 |
| | XV183 XV202 XV219 XV221 XV294 XV305 |

66 Hercules C.1's were purchased for Royal Air Force use in the mid-1960's. Four of them had been lost in accidents prior to the start of Operation "Corporate" (XV180, XV194, XV198 and XV216), while one aircraft (XV208) had been modified for use by the Meteorological Research Flight at RAE Farnborough and redesignated a Hercules W.2. Mid-1979 saw the initiation of a programme to increase the fuselage length of 30 of the Hercules C.1's by 15 feet, the modified aircraft being redesignated Hercules C.3's. The first (XV223) was converted by Lockheed in the United States and became a trials aircraft, remaining with A&AEE Boscombe Down throughout Operation "Corporate", while all subsequent conversions were carried out by Marshall of Cambridge (Engineering) Ltd at Teversham. The Company had completed 12 aircraft by the end of March 1982, while XV188 (the 13th) was returned to Lyneham on 1 April followed by XV301 (the 14th) on 19 May. XV184 (the 15th) and XV212 (the 16th) remained under conversion at Teversham for the duration of the conflict with Argentina and were joined by XV217 on 5 April when that aircraft was delivered from Lyneham to become the Company's 17th conversion. Two Hercules C.1's (XV179 and XV200) were undergoing major over-

haul at Cambridge at the start of the conflict but both returned to the LTW (after modification — see later) in time to see service prior to the surrender. All of the aircraft were in standard Matt Dark Green and Dark Sea Grey camouflage with Light Aircraft Grey undersides, Red/Blue roundels and fin-flash, plus serials in Black. White ROYAL AIR FORCE titles were carried on the forward fuselage while the last three digits of the serial were repeated in White on the nose and fin.

Four Hercules C.1's (XV189, XV196, XV304 and XV306) departed Lyneham for Gibraltar on 2 April, thereby commencing the type's involvement in Operation "Corporate". During the next few days an "air bridge" was established between the United Kingdom and Ascension Island, with daily departures from Lyneham reaching a peak of 16 on 29 April (nine to Dakar, one to Banjul and six to Gibraltar) as the requirement to transport stores and equipment to ships en route to the South Atlantic increased.

Another valuable mission performed by the Hercules fleet was that of air-drops to the Task Force ships en route to and in the South Atlantic. Those operations commenced during the third week of April using standard Hercules C.1's, but it had already become clear that the type's range would have to be extended to cater for the requirement to carry out personnel and supply drops to shipping as far south as the Total Exclusion Zone. Using cylindrical auxiliary tanks which had been in storage since the retirement of most of the Andover and Argosy transport fleets, Lyneham's Engineering Wing devised a two-tank installation inside the forward fuselage by 20 April which increased the endurance of the Hercules C.1 by some three to four hours. A similar four-tank installation was developed to permit even longer-range missions, but that configuration resulted in a substantial payload reduction and was therefore of use only for high value air-drops at extreme range from Ascension Island. Aircraft which received the long-range tanks were, for convenience, referred to as LR2's or LR4's, depending upon the number of tanks installed.

The first extended-range Hercules C.1 to be deployed was XV196, the aircraft leaving Lyneham late on 4 May for a non-stop overnight flight to Wideawake. The first

**Above** *One major development during Operation "Corporate" was the installation of refuelling probes in RAF Hercules. The prototype Hercules C.1P conversion, XV200, is seen here in early 5.82 taking on fuel from Victor K.2 XL231 (of 57 Squadron) during acceptance checks at A&AEE Boscombe Down. Only six of these probe-equipped aircraft had been converted before the Argentine surrender on 14.6.82.* (Ministry of Defence)

**Left** *Ascension Island to Port Stanley requires approximately 13 flying hours of a Hercules and a number of IFR sorties. Here, some four hours out of Wideawake and southbound on 13.10.82, is a Hercules C.1P flown by a 47 Squadron crew. It is about to make contact with the basket of Hercules C.1K XV296 (flown by a 30 Squadron crew). Some 24,000lb of fuel was taken on board by the Hercules C.1P during this refuelling.*
(Richard Gardner)

**Left** *Hercules C.1K XV296 was one of the original batch of four C.1's that were converted to C.1K tanker configuration by Marshall of Cambridge. The prototype was actually XV296 and it made its first flight on 8.6.82. It is seen here on 13.10.82 between Wideawake and Stanley, posing for the camera before returning to Ascension Island following the refuelling of a Hercules C.1P en route to RAF Stanley.* (Richard Gardner)

**Far Left** *XV179 was the second Hercules C.1 to receive the refuelling probe modification. Most of the probes used in the modification programme were redundant Belfast and Vulcan items.* **Left** *C.1K tanker conversions required the fitting of an HDU and associated "traffic lights" into the rear cargo door as seen here on XV192.*
(Peter J. Cooper)

mission (to 'Plymouth') was launched at 0055Z on 7 May and lasted 18 hours, although the air-drop itself had to be cancelled due to bad weather. A more successful flight the following day resulted in drops to 'Plymouth', 'Irishman' and 'Yorkshireman' with XV196 remaining airborne for 17hrs 10mins on that occasion. Three more missions were performed from Wideawake by the aircraft and its 47 Sqdn Special Forces crew before returning non-stop to Lyneham on 16 May. Prior to the surrender on 14 June, 47 Sqdn (both Main and Special Forces elements) carried out the majority of air-drop missions launched from Wideawake, including all of the extended-range sorties, while the remainder were performed by 70 Sqdn. The other two units (24 Sqdn and 30 Sqdn) were not trained in the tactical support role and concentrated on the more routine, but equally important, airlift between the United Kingdom and Ascension Island. The only other long-range Hercules C.1 deployed to the South Atlantic for any length of time was XV291, flown non-stop from Lyneham to Wideawake on 15 May. Its activities included a 16hr 40min round trip to 'Leeds Castle' which was launched at 0735Z on 18 May and crewed by 47 Sqdn's Main element. The aircraft was flown back to Lyneham via Gibraltar on 24 May.

In the United Kingdom, Marshall of Cambridge had commenced design work on 15 April on an in-flight refuelling probe installation for the Hercules C.1 in order to further increase the aircraft's range. XV200, already at the company's Cambridge facility on major overhaul, was chosen, as the first aircraft to receive the modification (Mod 5308). The probe was mounted on top of the fuselage above the cockpit, offset slightly to starboard, while the associated plumbing was faired-in along the fuselage roof to the trailing edge of the starboard wing root. The work was completed in ten days and the aircraft made its first test flight from Cambridge on 28 April before delivery to A&AEE Boscombe Down the following day for acceptance checks. 57 Sqdn Victor K.2 XL231 was flown from Marham to Boscombe Down on 1 May for ground link-up trials, while the same tanker (on a round trip from and to Marham) was used the next day for the first aerial coupling with XV200. A 20 knot difference between the maximum cruising speed of the Hercules and the minimum cruising speed of the Victor in level flight was overcome by developing a unique AAR procedure. Both aircraft were put into a 500ft per minute rate of descent for the refuelling, which would typically last for about 15 minutes. On 5 May XV200 was delivered to Lyneham for crew training prior to its deployment non-stop to Wideawake on 14 May. All aircraft which received the modification were redesignated Hercules C.1P's. A total of 16 were converted, of which six (XV179, XV196, XV200, XV206, XV218 and XV291) were completed before the Argentine surrender on 14 June. The second such conversion was XV179 which had arrived at Cambridge on 23 March for a major overhaul (delivery to Lyneham occurred on 13 May), while those which followed all arrived at Cambridge in LR2 configuration and were, for convenience, referred to as PLR2's. Details of the 16 conversions follow, giving the dates of arrival at and departure from Cambridge:

| Serial | In | Out | Serial | In | Out |
|--------|------|--------|--------|--------|--------|
| XV200 | 2 Mar | 29 Apr | XV187 | 6 Jul | 20 Jul |
| XV179 | 23 Mar | 13 May | XV298 | 6 Jul | 23 Jul |
| XV218 | 13 May | 25 May | XV300 | 9 Aug | 3 Sep |
| XV196 | 17 May | 31 May | XV195 | 9 Aug | 7 Sep |
| XV206 | 21 May | 3 Jun | XV205 | 8 Sep | 30 Sep |
| XV291 | 25 May | 9 Jun | XV292 | 3 Sep | 11 Oct |
| XV210 | 13 Jun | 29 Jun | XV191 | 9 Aug | 25 Oct |
| XV211 | 21 Jun | 6 Jul | XV185 | 30 Sep | 25 Oct |

Flt Lt H.C.Burgoyne of 47 Sqdn Special Forces element commanded the first air-refuelled mission ("Cadbury 1") from Ascension Island on 16 May, his crew comprising Flt Lt R.L.Rowley (co-pilot), Flt Lt J.D.Cunningham (navigator) and Flt Sgt S.E.Sloan (engineer). Harold Burgoyne was awarded the AFC as a result of his involvement in that 6,300 mile sortie, launched from Wideawake at 0245Z (the rest of his crew received Queen's Commendations for Valuable Service in the Air). The outbound leg was supported by Victor K.2's XH671 (55 Sqdn), XL162 (55 Sqdn) and XL512 (57 Sqdn), Burgoyne's AFC citation stating that 1,000lbs of stores and eight parachutists were successfully dropped to 'Antelope' within the TEZ. Victor K.2's XH669 (57 Sqdn), XL188 (55 Sqdn) and XM717 (55 Sqdn) provided fuel for the return leg, the Hercules finally touching down on Wideawake's runway at 0250Z on 17 May.

C.1P XV179 was flown non-stop from Lyneham to Wideawake on 19 May to operate alongside XV200, performing its first mission ("Cadbury 2") two days later. The aircraft left Wideawake at 0140Z on 21 May for an air-drop to 'Alacrity', returning at 0040Z on 22 May. By 6 June those two aircraft had carried out 11 missions into the TEZ, each lasting at least 20 hours. XV196 (in fact the fourth conversion) left Lyneham for Gibraltar on 5 June en route to Wideawake to become the third resident Hercules C.1P, taking-off at 0405Z on 6 June for its first operational sortie (a 24hr 5min flight to 'Minerva'). XV218 deployed non-stop from Lyneham to Wideawake on 13 June, the last C.1P to see service during the conflict. It took-off at 0430Z on 14 June for its first air-drop mission from the Island and was still airborne when the Argentine forces surrendered. The other two C.1P conversions which were completed by Marshall's before the surrender did not in fact deploy south until after 14 June (XV206 on 15 June and XV291 on 18 June, both non-stop from Lyneham). Missions to both shipping and the Falkland Islands themselves continued after the surrender. Flt Lt T.Locke and his 70 Sqdn crew set an endurance record on 18 June, their Hercules C.1P remaining airborne for 28hrs 4mins during a supply drop to a Rapier battery close to Port Stanley.

Regardless of whether in-flight refuelling was used or not, each air-drop mission mounted from Ascension Island during the conflict was allocated a girl's name (progressing in alphabetical order) to identify it. For example, Hercules C.1 XV291 performed Airdrop "Helen" to 'Leeds Castle' on 18 May, followed by C.1 XV297 on Airdrop "Ingrid" to 'Avenger' on 21 May, C.1P XV179 on Airdrop "Julie" to 'Alacrity' on 21 May and C.1P XV200 on Airdrop "Katie" to 'Olna' and 'Anco Charger' on 23 May. This system of identification continued even after Flt Lt J.Norfolk and crew carried out the first flight into the reopened Stanley Airport on 24 June (for example, the mission to Stanley Airport from Wideawake on 26 June was named Airland "Violet").

The table below lists all known air-refuelled "Cadbury" sorties mounted from Wideawake between 16 May and 14 June:

| Date | Serial | Airdrop | Out | Back |
|------|--------|---------|------|------|
| 16 May | XV200 | not known | 0245Z | 0250Z (17 May) |
| 21 May | XV179 | "Julie" | 0140Z | 0040Z (22 May) |
| 23 May | XV200 | "Katie" | 0855Z | 1030Z (24 May) |
| 24 May | XV179 | "Lara" | 0650Z | 0255Z (25 May) |
| 25 May | XV200 | "Mary" | 0720Z | 0500Z (26 May) |
| 26 May | XV179 | "Nora" | 0520Z | 0550Z (27 May) |
| 28 May | XV179 | "Olive" | 0340Z | 0540Z (29 May) |
| 29 May | XV200 | not known | 0345Z | 0410Z (30 May) |
| 1 Jun | XV179 | "Ursula" | 0355Z | 0410Z (2 Jun) |
| 2 Jun | XV200 | "Vera" | 0340Z | 0340Z (3 Jun) |
| 4 Jun | XV179 | "Wilma" | 0400Z | 1230Z (4 Jun) |
| 5 Jun | XV179 | "Wilma II" | 0640Z | 0630Z (6 Jun) |
| 6 Jun | XV196 | "Xaviera" | 0405Z | 0410Z (7 Jun) |
| 7 Jun | XV179 | "Yvonne" | 0425Z | 0445Z (8 Jun) |
| 9 Jun | XV179 | "Zara" | 0510Z | 0550Z (10 Jun) |
| 10 Jun | XV200 | "Alison" | 0440Z | 0540Z (11 Jun) |
| 11 Jun | XV196 | not known | 0420Z | 0430Z (12 Jun) |
| 13 Jun | XV179 | "Elaine" | 0435Z | 0545Z (14 Jun) |
| 14 Jun | XV218 | "Gina" | 0430Z | 0435Z (15 Jun) |

*Airdrop "Wilma" on 4 June was aborted due to one of the Victor K.2's having an unserviceable HDU.*

Hercules C.1P XV291 carried out the last mission into RAF Stanley on 14 August before the runway was closed to allow extension and repair work to be carried out. Sorties over the following two weeks thus had to revert to airdrops, although an "air snatch" system was also used to permit the pick-up of mail from the Islands. Devised at short notice by the Joint Air Transport Establishment at Brize Norton, it involved trailing a grappling hook on 150ft of nylon rope from the rear cargo door of the Hercules to engage a loop of nylon rope suspended between two 22ft poles positioned 50ft apart on the ground. The aircraft would run in at 50ft to make the snatch and the mail bag (attached to the loop by another 150ft of nylon rope) would then be winched up into the Hercules. Some 30 operational snatches were carried out before services to RAF Stanley were able to resume on 29 August (C.1P XV200 being the first movement that day on the reopened runway).

In the United Kingdom, Marshall of Cambridge was asked to carry out two further Hercules modification projects on 30 April. The first (Mod 5309) involved the installation of CMA 771 Omega precise navigation equipment into those aircraft which would be carrying out long-range over-water air-drop missions from Ascension Island. Hercules C.1P XV179 (the second probe-equipped machine) was the first to receive that equipment, making

its first flight from Cambridge on 12 May. The second project involved a trial to determine the suitability of the type as a tanker aircraft. Hercules C.1 XV296 was delivered to Cambridge from Lyneham on 1 May in LR4 configuration to become the prototype conversion (Mod 5310). A Flight Refuelling Ltd Mk.17B HDU was mounted inside the aircraft on the rear cargo loading ramp, while the drogue itself was faired-in (along with the AAR signal lights) on the exterior of the door. The installation was designed so that the fuselage could remain pressurised while the drogue was not deployed (it would have taken too long to develop a system that enabled the aircraft to remain pressurised even when refuelling). The fuel was drawn from the aircraft's main tanks rather than auxiliary tanks carried in the cabin. Designated a Hercules C.1K, XV296 made its first test flight from Cambridge on 8 June, during which the drogue was successfully deployed. Following another test flight on 10 June, the aircraft was delivered to the A&AEE at Boscombe Down on 11 June for the first "dry" contact, carried out that day with a Harrier. Buffeting was experienced during the operation so XV296 was returned to Cambridge on 15 June for further modifications. Hercules C.3 XV199 was borrowed from Lyneham for the day on 17 June. Accompanied by Marshall's own Cessna Citation G-BFRM as a photographic chase aircraft, it made a test flight from Cambridge with wool-tufting attached to the rear fuselage in order to identify the passage of the airflow around the rear cargo door. The buffeting problem was duly resolved by the addition of strakes to the underside of the cargo loading ramp. XV296 was test-flown again on 17/18/20/21 June, the flight on 21 June involving the first successful "wet" contact with a Buccaneer. The Hercules C.1K returned to Boscombe Down on 22 June for further refuelling trials involving Hercules, Nimrod, Phantom and Sea Harrier aircraft during the next week. It was flown back to Cambridge from Boscombe Down on 29 June before eventual delivery to Lyneham on 5 July for entry into service.

Initially, only four Hercules C.1's received the modification, none of them seeing operational service before the Argentine surrender on 14 June. The period of time that each aircraft spent undergoing conversion at Cambridge was as follows:

| Serial | In | Out | Serial | In | Out |
|--------|-----|------|--------|------|------|
| XV296 | 1 May | 5 Jul | XV204 | 12 Jun | 21 Jul |
| XV201 | 28 Apr | 15 Jul | XV192 | 21 Jun | 26 Jul |

A further contract received later in 1982 called for the modification of two more aircraft. XV203 and XV213 were dispatched to Cambridge during December 1982 for conversion, returning to Lyneham on 4 March 1983 and 10 March 1983 respectively. The tanker aircraft were used almost exclusively in the South Atlantic to refuel the "air bridge" Hercules C.1P's operating between Wideawake and RAF Stanley and the Harriers and Phantoms deployed to the Falkland Islands. The detachment of Hercules C.1K's and C.1P's at RAF Stanley gained the designation 1312 Flight on 20 August 1983.

To provide an indication of how valuable the Hercules fleet was to the overall success of Operation "Corporate", the type had clocked up over 13,000 flying hours (including some 44 air-drop missions) by the Argentine surrender on 14 June. Its adaptability was significantly advantageous, the aircraft gaining modifications to increase its range enabling it to successfully perform additional roles required by the very nature of a War fought in a maritime environment so far from home.

*A complete list of Lyneham Transport Wing aircrew involved in Operation "Corporate" is not available. The names given below are those who gained awards during the conflict (all from 47 Sqdn):*

*Sqdn Ldr A.M.Roberts RAF AFC; Flt Lt H.C.Burgoyne RAF AFC; Flt Lt J.D.Cunningham RAF QCVSA; Flt Lt R.L.Rowley RAF QCVSA; Flt Sgt S.E.Sloan RAF QCVSA.*

# INDIVIDUAL AIRCRAFT DETAILS

While the LTW Hercules fleet was heavily committed in support of Operation "Corporate" throughout the period of the conflict, there is insufficient significant data available on each aircraft to warrant the inclusion of Individual Aircraft Histories.

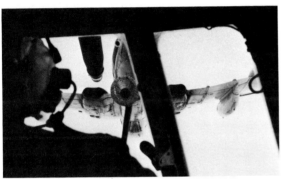

**Above Left** *Flown by a 47 Squadron crew, a Hercules C.1P is about to link up with Victor K.2 XH671 (of 55 Squadron) some seven hours after leaving Ascension Island for RAF Stanley on 13.10.82. The connection between Victor and Hercules was difficult at the best of times and had to be accomplished during a shallow descent. At a speed of 235 knots, some 18,000lb of fuel was transferred during this descent from 16,000 to 9,000ft.*
**Above Right** *The Victor K.2 XH671, framed by the port cockpit window, poses for the camera before returning to Wideawake. (Richard Gardner)*

*Hercules C.1's fitted with extra fuel tanks in the fuselage undertook a number of long-range air-drop sorties to Task Force shipping prior to the appearance of the first Hercules C.1P's. This C.1, operating from Wideawake, is about to make a drop into the South Atlantic.*
*(Ministry of Defence)*

*The stretched Hercules C.3's did not receive any of the refuelling modifications undergone by other marks. The fifteen C.3's in service by 14.6.82 were primarily used to ferry supplies between the United Kingdom and Ascension Island. XV303 is seen at Lyneham on 1.2.83.*
*(Peter J. Cooper)*

**Top** *Seen here at the Brize Norton Air Day on 12.6.82, XV107 was one of two VC-10 C.1's that were used to fly the survivors of 'Sheffield' to Brize Norton on 28.5.82. The Red Cross markings were only worn by those VC-10's that collected casualties from Uruguay but the aircraft continued to carry the markings on the forward fuselage and under the wings until well after the cease-fire.* *(Chris Farman)*

**Centre and Lower** *VC-10 C.1 XV105 (of 10 Squadron) is seen arriving at Brize Norton from Wideawake (via Dakar) on 24.6.82 with survivors of the attacks on 'Sir Galahad' and 'Sir Tristram'. Amongst other notable passengers was Sqdn Ldr Bob Iveson of 1(F) Squadron, the first Harrier GR.3 pilot to return to the United Kingdom from "Corporate" operations. For this and all similar flights bringing men home from the Falklands, ground-crews and other station personnel formed a guard of honour. The arrival of a VC-10 was thus always greeted with dignity, respect and great emotion.* *(Michael I. Draper)*

# VC-10

# 10 SQUADRON

Commanded by Wg Cdr O.G.Bunn MBE, 10 Sqdn was involved in the conflict from the very beginning. Based at Brize Norton, its fleet consisted of 13 VC-10 C.1 long-range strategic transports which had entered service with the Squadron during 1966. All were subsequently named after servicemen who had been awarded the Victoria Cross:

| | |
|---|---|
| XR806 | *George Thompson* |
| XR807 | *Donald Garland VC and Thomas Gray VC* |
| XR808 | *Kenneth Campbell VC* |
| XR810 | *David Lord VC* |
| XV101 | *Lance Hawker VC* |
| XV102 | *Guy Gibson VC* |
| XV103 | *Edward Mannock VC* |
| XV104 | *James McCudden VC* |
| XV105 | *Albert Ball VC* |
| XV106 | *Thomas Mottershead VC* |
| XV107 | *James Nicolson VC* |
| XV108 | *William Rhodes-Moorhouse VC* |
| XV109 | *Arthur Scarfe VC* |

The 14th machine (XR809) became G-AXLR and was converted into a flying test-bed for the Rolls Royce RB.211 engine and then later scrapped, but the remaining aircraft were all on Squadron strength on 29 March and available for use throughout the conflict. The VC-10's were still painted in the same basic colour scheme in which they had been delivered, consisting of a White top and Grey undersides with a Blue cheat-line along the line of the cabin windows. The last three digits of the serial were repeated above the fin-flash, while the aircraft name appeared in a blue scroll above the cheatline just in front of the forward crew entry door.

10 Sqdn's first visit to the South Atlantic came as early as 3 April when XV106 was dispatched from Brize Norton to Montevideo in Uruguay (via a technical stop at Ascension Island) to collect the Governor of the Falkland Islands, Rex Hunt, and the captured Royal Marines from NP8901, who had all been flown to the Uruguayan capital by Argentine transport aircraft the same day. The VC-10 left Montevideo's Carrasco International Airport on 4 April and, after another technical stop at Ascension Island, arrived at Brize Norton during the morning of 5 April. XV109 flew from Brize Norton to Wideawake late on 5 April and returned the following day, the first of many transport flights by VC-10, Hercules and chartered civil aircraft involved with the build-up of stores, equipment and personnel on that essential British staging post in the South Atlantic. The VC-10 flights to Ascension Island became more frequent from mid-April, with four or five flights in each direction on some days, most of which staged via Dakar (Senegal) or Banjul (The Gambia).

An incident on 18 April involved XV102 which was parked immediately in front of chartered British Airways Boeing 707 G-ASZF at Wideawake. At 2210Z, as the VC-10 began to taxi out for its return flight to Brize Norton via Dakar, the jet efflux from its four Rolls Royce Conways blew the steps positioned by the forward passenger door of the Boeing 707 into the leading edge of the wing, causing some damage. That was patched up and the Boeing 707 eventually flew back to Heathrow.

As the build-up increased, 10 Sqdn became more and more involved in Operation "Corporate" at the expense of some of its other commitments. The regular service from Brize Norton to Washington was, however, increased from twice weekly to an average of four times weekly. Many of the additional flights used call-signs in the same ranges as those allocated to VC-10's employed on the more obvious Operation "Corporate" missions to Wideawake, including XV108 on 23 April which took Foreign Secretary Francis Pym to Washington for last ditch talks with the US Secretary of State, Alexander Haig. There were also flights to Pope AFB, North Carolina (Fort Bragg) by XV102 on 13 May and XR807 on 14 May, and to Wurtsmith AFB, Michigan by XV103 on 5 June, but the significance of those missions is not known.

Some 35 Falkland Islands inhabitants arrived by air at Montevideo on 14 April, having been deported by the Argentines. They were flown out by XR807, arriving at Brize Norton early on 18 April. The unit's next visit to Uruguay was to collect the 22 Royal Marines who had surrendered to the Argentines on South Georgia, along with a further seven from NP8901 who had initially managed to evade capture on the Falklands Islands. These commandos had been taken to the General Roca Military Academy at Comodoro Rivadavia in Argentina, where they were held as PoW's. On 18 April they were taken by air to Montevideo with 13 scientists who had been working for the British Antarctic Survey on South Georgia. XV106 returned to Brize Norton non-stop from Wideawake with all of them in the early hours of 21 April. The subsequent recapture of South Georgia on 25 April resulted in some 180 Argentine prisoners (both civilian and military) being taken by sea to Ascension Island for onward transfer to Argentina. They arrived off the Island aboard 'Tidespring' on 12 May, were transferred to Wideawake, and then are believed to have been flown to Montevideo the following day by 10 Sqdn VC-10. That operation was supervised by the International Red Cross and the VC-10 was suitably marked with a Red Cross on a White square applied to each side of the forward fuselage and to the underside of each wing.

Survivors from the attack on 'Sheffield' were taken from the TEZ to Ascension Island aboard the tanker 'British Esk' before being flown home from Wideawake to Brize Norton on 27 May by two 10 Sqdn VC-10's. XR807 arrived at Brize Norton with 137 passengers, followed by XV103 with another 134. Neither of these aircraft carried Red Cross markings as they were only worn by the VC-10's involved in aeromedical evacuation flights from Uruguay.

Little of the Squadron's contribution to Operation "Corporate" became publicly known until the three survey vessels 'Hecla', 'Hydra' and 'Herald' began their shuttle service as ambulance ships between the TEZ and Montevideo, taking wounded personnel from the hospital ship 'Uganda' to Uruguay for onward air transportation to the United Kingdom. Once again, the whole operation was monitored by the International Red Cross and each of the VC-10's involved sported the Red Cross markings mentioned earlier. 'Hecla' performed the first of the ambulance services, arriving at Montevideo on 2 June with 18 injured British personnel and 24 Argentine prisoners from the 'Narwal', of whom the latter were to be handed back to the Argentine authorities. XV108 arrived the same day to collect the 18 wounded, nine of whom were survivors from 'Sheffield'. The VC-10 returned to Brize Norton the following day, having staged through Wideawake.

'Hydra' arrived at Montevideo on 6 June with 51 wounded aboard, but on that occasion there was a short delay as the VC-10 was diverted to another airfield due to fog. It received unfortunate publicity when a consignment of combat aircraft equipment was discovered to have been inadvertently left aboard after it had departed Wideawake for Uruguay. 134 survivors from 'Atlantic Conveyor' were taken to Ascension Island aboard the tanker 'British Tay' and then transferred to Wideawake for their return

flight to the United Kingdom. XV102 performed that flight, staging through Dakar to arrive at Brize Norton during the afternoon of 7 June. 'Herald' carried out the next ambulance run to Montevideo on 13 June with 61 wounded aboard, 28 of whom were stretcher cases. They were transferred the same day to XV108 which arrived at Brize Norton during the morning of 14 June after a technical stop at Wideawake.

Ambulance flights continued after the ceasefire on 14 June. 'Hecla' made her second visit to the Uruguayan capital on 14 June carrying 61 wounded from 'Sir Tristram' and 'Sir Galahad', of whom three were stretcher cases. They all arrived at Brize Norton on 17 June, care of 10 Sqdn. 'Hydra' followed four days after 'Hecla' with more than 80 wounded soldiers from the Welsh Guards and 2/3 PARA, who were returned to Brize Norton on 19 June aboard XV104 and XR810. Rex Hunt departed from the Squadron's Oxfordshire base on 23 June for Ascension Island en route to the Falkland Islands to assume his new role as Civil Commissioner. At Wideawake he transferred to a Hercules and arrived at Port Stanley on 25 June. The Squadron continued to carry out aeromedical evacuation flights to Uruguay, meeting 'Herald' (24 June) and 'Hydra' (29 June, 12/13 July) to bring back more wounded servicemen, but more of the unit's workload was by then being directed towards the return of soldiers who were collecting on Ascension Island in ever increasing numbers. Four VC-10's and a chartered DC-10 from British Caledonian Airways brought back 700 men from 2/3 PARA to Brize Norton on 6 July, a further four VC-10's were involved in the return of 440 men from 45 Cdo to Arbroath on 8 July (XV106 via Dakar to Leuchars) and 9 July (XR810, XV101, XV109 via Dakar to Leuchars), plus another four VC-10's on 29 July which returned 350 Welsh Guardsmen to Brize Norton.

By the end of July, the tasking situation was showing signs of returning to normal for 10 Sqdn, but the considerable British presence on Ascension Island and in the Falkland Islands meant that Wideawake would still receive regular resupply flights by the Squadron for the foreseeable future. As with the operations of Lyneham's Hercules fleet, little was publicised at the time concerning 10 Sqdn's VC-10 activities, but it is questionable whether the momentum of Operation "Corporate" could have been maintained without the lifeline provided between the United Kingdom and Ascension Island by these two aircraft types.

---

*Operation "Corporate" involved all 10 Sqdn VC-10 crews. Individuals have not been identified.*

---

# INDIVIDUAL AIRCRAFT DETAILS

---

While all 13 of 10 Sqdn's VC-10 C.1's were heavily committed in support of Operation "Corporate" throughout the period of the conflict, there is insufficient significant data available on each of the aircraft to warrant the inclusion of Individual Aircraft Histories.

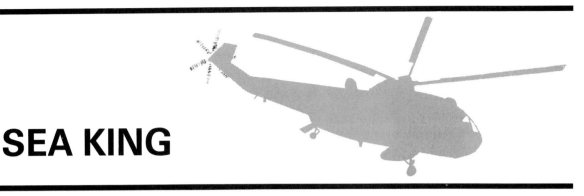

# SEA KING

## 202 SQUADRON

Two officers and eight ratings arrived at Wideawake Airfield, Ascension Island on 6 April aboard an LTW Hercules to form the nucleus of Naval Party 1222, tasked with setting up a forward logistics base on the Island. They were to receive stores, personnel, equipment, ammunition and helicopters from the United Kingdom and arrange their transhipment south to the Falkland Islands. The number of personnel involved in this operation grew as activity at Wideawake increased, NP1222 eventually becoming an element of the Combined British Forces Support Unit at Wideawake. Two 845 Sqdn Wessex HU.5's were allocated to the airfield for HDS and VERTREP duties, followed by an 846 Sqdn Sea King HC.4, but the departure south of the latter aboard 'Elk' in early May left the helicopter fleet at Wideawake desperately short of capacity, even though helicopters which belonged to the various Ships' Flights in transit were being put to good use. As all suitable Royal Navy helicopters had already been allocated to other Operation "Corporate" tasks, the Royal Air Force made good the deficiency by supplying a Sea King HAR.3 (and a Chinook HC.1) to be based at Wideawake.

With the exception of one aircraft retained by Westland Helicopters for trials (XZ587), on 29 March the entire fleet of Sea King HAR.3's was in service with 202 Sqdn, one of two Air-Sea Rescue squadrons under the Search and Rescue Wing located at Finningley:

| | | | | |
|---|---|---|---|---|
| XZ585 | XZ589 | XZ592 | XZ595 | XZ598 |
| XZ586 | XZ590 | XZ593 | XZ596 | XZ599 |
| XZ588 | XZ591 | XZ594 | XZ597 | ZA105 |

The unit operated four two-aircraft detachments ('A' Flight at Boulmer, 'B' Flight at Brawdy, 'C' Flight at Coltishall, 'D' Flight at Lossiemouth), plus a Training Flight with 706 Sqdn at Culdrose. The helicopters were painted Gloss Yellow overall with 'D' Class roundels and Black titles. The Sea King selected for deployment to Ascension Island was XZ593 which had arrived at Finningley on 29 April from Lossiemouth for attention by the SAR Engineering Wing. It was prepared for shipment

south by air, leaving Finningley aboard Heavylift Belfast G-BFYU for Freetown and Wideawake on 8 May. Two four-man crews under Flt Lt M.J.Carlyle arrived on 9 May to operate the aircraft, a third (replacement) crew following on 14 June. After reassembly by NP1222 personnel, XZ593 was put to work on both SAR and logistical support missions alongside 18 Sqdn Chinook HC.1 ZA707 which had disembarked on 5 May from the 'Atlantic Conveyor'. Along with the two Wessex HU.5's, those two helicopters provided a balanced fleet, enabling each VERTREP mission to be tasked to suit a particular ship's deck size or stores handling capability. Although tasked by NP1222, each helicopter's parent squadron maintained overall control of both aircraft and aircrew.

Overnight on 12/13 May, XZ593 carried out the transfer of 69 Argentine PoW's (captured on South Georgia) and 16 guards from 'Tidespring' to Wideawake for onward passage to Montevideo in Uruguay. The movement of stores and 150 personnel from 'Dumbarton Castle' to 'Queen Elizabeth 2', plus the recovery of six CASEVAC cases from the latter, accounted for 8hrs 15mins flying by the helicopter on 20 May. VERTREP and HDS missions continued to keep the Sea King fully occupied, typical examples of those being 12hrs 5mins flown on 1 June during the replenishment of 'Contender Bezant', 'St Edmund' and 'Tor Caledonia', while four hours were flown on 3 June during a night replenishment of 'British Tay'. With no Chinook available on 7 June, XZ593 was used to transport a 7,126lb liquid oxygen bowser from Wideawake to 'Dumbarton Castle'. The aircraft was stripped of all unnecessary equipment for that flight, while minimum fuel and crew were carried. Operations from Wideawake continued following the Argentine surrender on 14 June, including a noteworthy CASEVAC mission lasting 5hrs 55mins on 15 June to the submarine 'Spartan' which included a refuelling stop aboard 'Leeds Castle' during the return flight. The submarine had been on patrol continuously for 100 days without fresh food, so, on the outbound leg, XZ593 transported (along with the mail) sufficient strawberries and cream for the entire crew!

The aircraft's Ascension Island operations came to an end on 7 September when it embarked 'Invincible' for the

*202 Squadron Sea King HAR.3 XZ593 was delivered to Wideawake by Heavylift Belfast on 9.5.82 in order to assist with the massive task of transferring stores and equipment to Task Force ships. It is seen here visiting 'Astronomer' when the ship passed Ascension Island in mid-6.82. The two "Yogi Bear" Chinooks (ZA720/BG and ZA717/BK), in transit to the Falkland Islands, are clearly visible in the background*
*(T. & J. Harrison Ltd)*

*Sea King HAR.3 XZ592 was resprayed in the low-visibility Matt Grey scheme with Black titles before being flown from Finningley to Southampton Docks on 4.8.82 for the journey south to Port Stanley. XZ592, with XZ591 and ZA105 (both of which are just visible in the background), is seen tightly positioned inside the "hangar" on 'Contender Bezant' shortly before the ship sailed from Southampton on 7.8.82.*
*(Michael I. Draper)*

*Following their arrival in the Falkland Islands, the three 202 Squadron Sea King HAR.3's were given the codes 'SA' (XZ592), 'SB' (ZA105, pictured here on 15.10.82) and 'SC' (XZ591) and they formed the Falklands "SARDET" at Navy Point. Aircrew were initially drawn from 202 Squadron 'C' Flight at Coltishall. The arrival of these aircraft allowed many of the Royal Navy Sea Kings in the Falklands theatre to return to their more normal anti-submarine role.      (Richard Gardner)*

journey back to the United Kingdom. SAR missions were flown from the carrier on 10 and 13 September, but the aircraft was flown off to Brawdy on 17 September before the vessel arrived at Portsmouth later that same day. XZ593 finally returned to Finningley on 27 September for attention by the SAR Engineering Wing.

After the Argentine surrender it was decided that a permanent detachment of Sea King HAR.3's would be sent to the Falkland Islands for SAR and general transport duties. Accordingly, personnel from 202 Sqdn 'C' Flight at Coltishall prepared for deployment to the South Atlantic, while three helicopters (XZ591, XZ592, ZA105) were resprayed at Finningley in a low-visibility scheme which consisted of Dark Sea Grey overall with Black titles and Red/Blue roundels. Each aircraft was flown to Wyton for attention by the Electronic Warfare Avionics Unit prior to embarkation. All three Sea Kings left Finningley on 4 August to embark 'Contender Bezant' that day at Southampton Docks, sailing with the ship for the South Atlantic on 7 August. After she arrived in Port William on 25 August, the helicopters were off-loaded to Navy Point and gained the Black codes 'SC', 'SA' and 'SB' respectively, these being the radio call-signs allocated to each aircraft to make them compatible with others using the Army's ARC 340 radio net. The detachment commenced its general transport duties as 202 Sqdn 'C' Flight, although after one year's operations (during which the Sea Kings were rotated with others dispatched south from the United Kingdom) it was redesignated 1564 Flight on 20 August 1983.

---

*202 Sqdn aircrew at Wideawake during Operation "Corporate":*

*Flt Lt M.J.Carlyle RAF (Det Cdr); Sqdn Ldr R.A.Cross RAF; Flt Lt G.D.Clements RAF; Flt Lt P.A.Cunningham RAF; Flt Lt P.Martin RAF; Flt Lt S.Mould RAF; Flt Lt R.Newton RAF; Flt Lt M.Ternouth RAF; Flt Lt G.D.Wright RAF; MAEOp P.Williams RAF; MALM W.R.Griffiths RAF; MALM K.T.Mursell RAF; MALM V.S.Oliver RAF.*

---

# INDIVIDUAL AIRCRAFT DETAILS

**XZ591** HAR.3          *Deployed post-14.6.82*

On 14.6.82 with the SAR Engineering Wing at Finningley in standard Gloss Yellow Rescue scheme. Resprayed in the low-vis Dark Sea Grey scheme on 20.7.82. To Wyton 23.7.82 for mods by the EWAU, returning to Finningley 29.7.82. Flown aboard 'Contender Bezant' at Southampton Docks on 4.8.82, sailing with her for Portsmouth on 7.8.82. Left Portsmouth with the ship on 8.8.82 for the South Atlantic, arriving in Port William on 25.8.82. Disembarked to Navy Point and coded 'SC' for 202 Sqdn 'C' Flt. Used for SAR and general transport duties until it embarked 'Sir Percivale' for passage back to the UK, arriving at Marchwood (Southampton) with the ship on 9.5.83. Transferred by road to Finningley, arriving there on 13.5.83.

**XZ592** HAR.3          *Deployed post-14.6.82*

On 14.6.82 with the SAR Engineering Wing at Finningley in standard Gloss Yellow Rescue scheme. Resprayed in the low-vis Dark Sea Grey scheme 22.7.82. Flown to Wyton on 26.7.82 for mods by the EWAU, returning to Finningley 30.7.82. Flown aboard 'Contender Bezant' at Southampton Docks on 4.8.82, sailing with her for Portsmouth on 7.8.82. Departed Portsmouth with the ship on 8.8.82 for the South Atlantic, arriving in Port William on 25.8.82. Disembarked to Navy Point and coded 'SA' for 202 Sqdn 'C' Flt. Used for SAR and general transport duties until it embarked 'Sir Geraint' for passage back to the UK, arriving at Marchwood (Southampton) with the ship c4.7.83. Transferred by road to Finningley, arriving there on 11.7.83.

**XZ593** HAR.3

On 29.3.82 with 202 Sqdn 'D' Flt at Lossiemouth. Flown to the SAR Engineering Wing at Finningley on 29.4.82 and prepared for shipment to Ascension by air. Departed Finningley aboard Heavylift Belfast G-BFYU on 8.5.82 and arrived at Ascension (via Freetown) the same day. Commenced VERTREP and HDS operations from Wideawake which continued after the Argentine surrender on 14.6.82. Embarked 'Invincible' 7.9.82 for re-turn to the UK, flying off to Brawdy on 17.9.82 prior to the carrier's arrival at Portsmouth the same day. Returned to the SAR Engineering Wing at Finningley 27.9.82 having flown a total of 327hrs 50mins between 8.5.82 and 17.9.82.

**ZA105** HAR.3          *Deployed post-14.6.82*

On 14.6.82 with the SAR Engineering Wing at Finningley in standard Gloss Yellow Rescue scheme. To Wyton 15.7.82 for mods by the EWAU, returning to Finningley 26.7.82. Resprayed in the low-vis Dark Sea Grey scheme on 30.7.82. Flown aboard 'Contender Bezant' at Southampton Docks on 4.8.82, sailing with her for Portsmouth on 7.8.82. Left Portsmouth with the ship on 8.8.82 for the South Atlantic, arriving in Port William on 25.8.82. Disembarked to Navy Point and coded 'SB' for 202 Sqdn 'C' Flt. Used on SAR and general transport duties until it embarked 'Sir Percivale' for passage back to the UK, arriving at Marchwood (Southampton) on 9.5.83. Transferred by road to Finningley, arriving there 12.5.83.

After an 8hr 45min flight from Ascension Island to RAF Stanley with seven air refuellings en route, 29(F) Squadron Phantom FGR.2 XV468/W is seen here taxying from the runway. Its arrival on 17.10.82 marked the handing-over of the air defence duties from the 1(F) Squadron Harriers to the Phantoms. XV468, the first to arrive, was crewed by Wg Cdr Ian Macfadyen, the Phantom Detachment Commander, and Sqdn Ldr Pete Simpson. The squadron markings on this particular aircraft consist of the White code 'W' on the nose-wheel door and two solid White bars on either side of the roundel.          (Richard Gardner)

Phantom FGR.2 XV466/E (of 29(F) Squadron) is seen here about to take the arrestor gear at RAF Stanley upon its arrival from Wideawake on 18.10.82. The runway at Stanley, although some 6,000ft in length, was fitted with arrestor equipment for the Phantom operations; the first arrested landing pulled the aircraft up in 700ft. Note that the aircraft is fully armed with both Skyflashes and Sidewinder missiles. Squadron markings on this Phantom consist of a White code 'E' on the nose-wheel door and the 29(F) Squadron badge on the nose beneath the cockpit.
(Richard Gardner)

Pucara A-515 made its first flight as ZD485 from Boscombe Down on 28.4.83 and its only public appearance was at the International Air Tattoo, Greenham Common, on 23/24.7.83. Here Sqdn Ldr Russ Peart makes a low flypast prior to landing there on 21.7.83. The A&AEE did little to change the original camouflage which, on A-515, was the version that the FAA ultimately considered to be most appropriate for the Malvinas theatre.
(Peter J. Cooper)

# PHANTOM

## 29(F) SQUADRON

29 (Fighter) Squadron operated the Phantom FGR.2 from Coningsby at the start of Operation "Corporate", the following aircraft being active with the unit at the end of March 1982:

| | | | |
|---|---|---|---|
| XV489/A | XV491/F | XV478/J | XV468/W |
| XV421/B | XV419/G | XV473/L | |
| XV484/C | XV442/H | XT909/M | |
| XV466/E | XV424/I | XT896/T | |

Most of the aircraft had been resprayed in the standard air defence three-tone Grey scheme, with toned-down Light Blue/Pink roundels and fin-flash plus White serials, but with full colour unit markings and Red fin-codes (repeated in Red on the nose-wheel door). XV489/A, XV421/B, XV473/L and XV468/W were still in the older camouflage scheme which consisted of Matt Dark Green and Dark Sea Grey upper surfaces, Light Aircraft Grey undersides, Red/Blue roundels and fin-flash plus Black serials. Of these, XV473/L and XV468/W were resprayed in the three-tone Grey scheme at St Athan during the course of Operation "Corporate", returning to 29(F) Sqdn and taking up the same codes again.

The Squadron returned from Armament Practice Camp at Akrotiri in Cyprus on 1 April and received notice of its impending involvement in Operation "Corporate" later that month. The unit was tasked with the preparation and deployment to Ascension Island of three Phantom FGR.2's. The aircraft were to be used in their customary air defence role to help protect that important South Atlantic staging post from possible air attack. Three aircraft in the three-tone Grey scheme were chosen for the detachment, their Squadron insignia having been removed and the code being worn only on the nose-wheel door. XV484/C and XV468/W were flown from Coningsby to Wideawake on 24 May, followed by XV466/E on 26 May (the latter being flown by Sqdn Ldr P.R.Morley who assumed the role of Detachment Commander). The nine and a half hour non-stop flights were carried out with the aid of Victor K.2's XH675 (55 Sqdn, Marham-Marham), XL189 (57 Sqdn, Marham-Marham), XL192 (57 Sqdn, Marham-Dakar) on 24 May and XL189 (57 Sqdn,

Marham-Marham), XL192 (57 Sqdn, Marham-Dakar) on 26 May. Remaining alert on the long overwater transit was a problem for the Phantom aircrew, particularly for Sqdn Ldr Morley and his navigator (Flt Lt J.R.Millo) on their solo flight. They whiled away the hours working through a "Daily Telegraph" crossword book, passed with some difficulty between the front and rear cockpits!

The Quick Reaction Alert commitment on the Island was taken over from 1(F) Sqdn on 25 May and maintained until the detachment was stood down on 14 July, a month after the Argentine surrender. Alert aircraft were scrambled on several occasions to identify unknown air and surface contacts. Two Soviet Tu-20 "Bears" were intercepted by Sqdn Ldr Morley and Fg Off N.J.Marks in XV484 on 11 July, the intruders being interested in the return passage of 'Hermes' to the United Kingdom. Those crews not on QRA flew whenever possible during the detachment, both by day and by night, but they were always mindful of the fact that there was no other runway available within 1,000 miles and that Wideawake had no instrument recovery facilities or runway arrester gear. The crews had at first been given some disused accommodation half-way up Green Mountain at Two Boats settlement but, because of its distance from the airfield and the need to get reserve alert crews to their aircraft in the shortest possible time, the detachment was one of the first to move into "Concertina City" when that temporary accommodation area was erected close to the airfield.

The detachment ceased QRA duties on 14 July and the three Phantoms were then prepared for their return flights to Coningsby. All were flown back non-stop with support once again from the Victor K.2 fleet, XV484 completing the journey on 18 July followed by XV466 on 19 July and XV468 on 20 July.

The Squadron's involvement in South Atlantic operations did not cease with the end of this detachment, however. Following the Argentine surrender on 14 June, it became clear that air defence aircraft would be required to protect the Falkland Islands for the foreseeable future and 29(F) Sqdn was earmarked for eventual deployment to Port Stanley. The Airport's existing 4,100ft runway was not long enough to permit operations by the Phantom, so AM2 matting acquired from the United States was used to extend it by 2,000ft (the operation being completed in mid-October). Nine of the Squadron's aircraft were prepared for deployment during September as follows:

| | | |
|---|---|---|
| XV402/A | XV466/E | XV426/Q |
| XV484/C | XV419/G | XV464/U |
| XV423/D | XV474/P | XV468/W |

Several of the aircraft were recent acquisitions by the Squadron, all being in the three-tone Grey scheme with most unit insignia removed apart from the Red code on the nosewheel door.

The Phantoms began to congregate on Ascension Island in mid-September to await the reopening of RAF Stanley's runway (XV484/C, XV423/D, XV419/G and XV474/P having arrived at Wideawake by 18 September). 17 October saw 29(F) Sqdn take over responsibility for air defence of the Falkland Islands from the Sea Harrier FRS.1's of 809 Sqdn (supplemented by the Sidewinder-equipped Harrier GR.3's of 1(F) Sqdn) with the arrival that day from Ascension Island of XV468/W, flown by Wg Cdr I.D.Macfadyen (who became Detachment Commander) and navigated by Sqdn Ldr G.P.Simpson. The remaining eight aircraft completed the transit from Wideawake during the following week. The unit's tour in the South Atlantic was completed at the end of 1983 when 23 Sqdn from Wattisham took over responsibility for the same aircraft on a permanent basis, 29(F) Sqdn gaining new Phantoms during January 1984 to enable operations from Coningsby to recommence.

The reduction in the quantity of Phantoms available for the air defence of the United Kingdom once the nine aircraft had been dispatched to Port Stanley was made good by the purchase from United States Navy surplus stocks of 15 F-4J's. These aircraft were taken from storage at Davis-Monthan AFB in Arizona during late 1983 and sent to the Naval Air Rework Facility at North Island, San Diego (California) for major overhaul, delivery to the United Kingdom taking place between August 1984 and January 1985. The 15 Phantoms (ZE350 to ZE364) were flown to Wattisham for use by the reactivated 74 Sqdn.

*29(F) Sqdn aircrew deployed to Wideawake during Operation "Corporate":*

*Sqdn Ldr P.R.Morley RAF, Flt Lt A.K.Cairncross RAF, Flt Lt P.R.Marskell RAF, Flt Lt J.B.Megarry RAF, Fg Off P.J.Courtenage RAF (all pilots); Sqdn Ldr R.W.D.Trotter RAF, Flt Lt R.Cook RAF, Flt Lt W.Davies RAF, Flt Lt R.Jones RAF, Flt Lt J.R.Millo RAF (all navigators).*

# INDIVIDUAL AIRCRAFT DETAILS

**XV466** FGR.2

On 29.3.82 with 29(F) Sqdn coded 'E', on Armament Practice Camp at Akrotiri, Cyprus. Returned to Coningsby on 1.4.82. Squadron markings removed (except code in Red on nose-wheel door) prior to being flown direct from Coningsby to Wideawake on 26.5.82 for air defence duties (refuelled en route by Victors from Marham). The detachment was stood down on 14.7.82 and the aircraft prepared for return to the UK. Flown non-stop from Wideawake to Coningsby on 19.7.82.

**XV468** FGR.2

On 29.3.82 allocated to 29(F) Sqdn at Coningsby coded 'W', still wearing the older camouflage scheme. Noted undergoing respray at St Athan early 5.82 and returned to Coningsby in the three-tone Grey scheme. Minus Squadron marks and with the code in Red on the nose-wheel door only, it was flown direct from Coningsby to Wideawake on 24.5.82 and refuelled en route by Victors from Marham. The detachment was stood down on 14.7.82 and the aircraft prepared for return to the UK. Flown non-stop to Coningsby on 20.7.82.

*Redeployed to Wideawake during 9.82 with eight others from the unit (including XV466 and XV484) to await the completion of runway extension work at RAF Stanley. Crewed by Wg Cdr Macfadyen (pilot) and Sqdn Ldr Simpson (navigator), it became the first of those aircraft to land at RAF Stanley when flown non-stop from Wideawake on 17.10.82 for air defence duties.*

**XV484** FGR.2

On 29.3.82 with 29(F) Sqdn coded 'C', on Armament Practice Camp at Akrotiri, Cyprus. Returned to Coningsby on 1.4.82. Squadron markings removed (except code in Red on nose-wheel door) prior to being flown direct to Wideawake from Coningsby on 24.5.82 for air defence duties (refuelled en route by Victors from Marham). The detachment was stood down on 14.7.82 and the aircraft prepared for return to the UK. Flown non-stop from Wideawake to Coningsby on 18.7.82.

**Part 2**
# appendices

# BRITISH AIRWAYS, TRADEWINDS AIRWAYS & HEAVYLIFT CARGO AIRLINES

Wideawake airfield on Ascension Island received some 535 inbound air transport movements during Operation "Corporate". While most of those flights involved 10 Sqdn VC-10's and Lyneham Transport Wing Hercules, a small but significant portion of the 6,000 tons of freight delivered to the South Atlantic staging post was flown in courtesy of chartered civilian aircraft.

Boeing 707's G-ASZF of British Airways (flight number "BA3624") and G-SAIL of Tradewinds Airways (flight number "IK507") arrived at Wideawake from Marham on 18 April with ground equipment for the 55 Sqdn and 57 Sqdn Victors which were deployed to the Island from that date. However, the rest of the civilian contribution came from Heavylift Cargo Airlines and its fleet of ex-Royal Air Force Belfast strategic freighters. Five of them had been purchased by Heavylift, becoming G-BEPE, G-OHCA, G-HLFT, G-BFYU and G-BEPS. Three of them had entered service with the airline by the start of Operation "Corporate". The Company was no stranger to Ministry of Defence contracts, the Belfasts frequently being called upon to carry outsize military cargoes similar to those which they had been used to transporting in their previous service life.

G-BEPE was diverted to Yeovilton late on 3 April while on its way back to the Company's Stansted base. It performed the first MoD charter on 4 April by transporting two 845 Sqdn Wessex HU.5's to Ascension Island via Dakar. By 9 April G-BEPE and G-BFYU had both made two trips to Wideawake from Yeovilton carrying a total of six 845 Sqdn Wessex HU.5's and one 846 Sqdn Sea King HC.4. G-BFYU departed Finningley for Freetown on 8 May en route to Wideawake with a 202 Sqdn Sea King HAR.3, while G-BEPS made two further flights from Yeovilton to Ascension Island (via Freetown) on 6 May and 9 May with further 845 Sqdn Wessex HU.5's. Those flights which carried helicopters are summarised below, giving date, aircraft, flight number and route as well as details of the helicopters carried:

| | | |
|---|---|---|
| **4 April** G-BEPE | "NP652" from Yeovilton *(Wessex HU.5s XT468, XT765 of 845 Sqdn)* | |
| **5 April** G-BFYU | "NP654" from Yeovilton *(Wessex HU.5s XT464, XT473 of 845 Sqdn)* | |

*continued*

| | | |
|---|---|---|
| **7 April** G-BFYU | "NP656" from Yeovilton *(Sea King HC.4 ZA312 of 846 Sqdn)* | |
| **8 April** G-BEPE | "NP658" from Yeovilton *(Wessex HU.5s XT451, XT460 of 845 Sqdn)* | |
| **6 May** G-BEPS | "NP690" from Yeovilton *(Wessex HU.5s XT450, XT459 of 845 Sqdn)* | |
| **8 May** G-BFYU | "NP694" from Finningley *(Sea King HAR.3 XZ593 of 202 Sqdn)* | |
| **9 May** G-BEPS | "NP692" from Yeovilton *(Wessex HU.5s XS491, XT761 of 845 Sqdn)* | |

The Belfast was used for several more "Corporate" charters to Ascension Island during April and May 1982, most of the flights carrying aircraft ground equipment. They included G-BFYU "NP660" from Stansted on 17 April, G-BEPE "NP664" from Kinloss on 24 April, G-BFYU "NP680" from Waddington on 25 April, G-BEPS "NP682" from Lyneham on 27 April, G-BFYU "NP684" from Brize Norton on 29 April, G-BEPS "NP686" from Coningsby on 1 May, G-BFYU "NP688" from Lyneham on 4 May, G-BEPE "NP696" from Stansted on 10 May, G-BFYU "NP698" from Stansted on 11 May and G-BEPS "NP602" from Lyneham on 17 May.

MoD charters continued to be placed with the airline after the Argentine surrender on 14 June. By the end of October a regular service had been commenced through Brize Norton to Ascension Island via Dakar. Several of the return flights brought back 1(F) Sqdn Harrier GR.3's to Wittering, including XZ992 on 16 November and XZ989 on 23 November (both in G-BFYU), XW924 on 11 January 1983 (in G-BEPS) and XZ129 on 26 January 1983 (in G-BEPE). In fact, the Heavylift Belfast fleet had proved extremely useful to the MoD before, during and after Operation "Corporate", arguably demonstrating how short-sighted the original decision to retire the aircraft from Royal Air Force service had been.

— *continued*

# THE DEPARTURE OF THE TASK FORCE

| Vessel: | From: | | Date: | Vessel: | From: | | Date: |
|---|---|---|---|---|---|---|---|
| HMS ENDURANCE | (on station) | (2) | — | HMS HYDRA | Portsmouth | | 24.4.82 |
| RFA FORT AUSTIN | "Springtrain" | | 29.3.82 | ANCO CHARGER | Fawley | | 24.4.82 |
| HMS SPARTAN | Gibraltar | | 1.4.82 | ATLANTIC CONVEYOR | | | |
| HMS SPLENDID | Faslane | | 1.4.82 | | Devonport | (4) | 25.4.82 |
| HMS ANTRIM | "Springtrain" | (1)(2) | 2.4.82 | BRITISH WYE | Devonport | | 25.4.82 |
| HMS ARROW | "Springtrain" | (1) | 2.4.82 | EUROPIC FERRY | Portland | (4) | 25.4.82 |
| HMS BRILLIANT | "Springtrain" | (1)(2) | 2.4.82 | HMS ONYX | Gosport | | 26.4.82 |
| HMS COVENTRY | "Springtrain" | (1) | 2.4.82 | HMS INTREPID | Portland | (4) | 26.4.82 |
| HMS GLAMORGAN | "Springtrain" | (1) | 2.4.82 | RFA BAYLEAF | Devonport | | 26.4.82 |
| HMS GLASGOW | "Springtrain" | (1) | 2.4.82 | BRITISH AVON | Devonport | | 26.4.82 |
| HMS PLYMOUTH | "Springtrain" | (1)(2) | 2.4.82 | NORLAND | Portsmouth | (4) | 26.4.82 |
| HMS SHEFFIELD | "Springtrain" | (1) | 2.4.82 | RFA TIDEPOOL | (see main text) | (4) | 27.4.82 |
| RFA APPLELEAF | "Springtrain" | (1) | 2.4.82 | HMS CORDELLA | Portland | | 27.4.82 |
| RFA TIDESPRING | "Springtrain" | (1)(2) | 2.4.82 | HMS FARNELLA | Portland | | 27.4.82 |
| RFA SIR TRISTRAM | Belize | (5) | 2.4.82 | HMS JUNELLA | Portland | | 27.4.82 |
| HMS CONQUEROR | Faslane | | 4.4.82 | HMS NORTHELLA | Portland | | 27.4.82 |
| HMS COURAGEOUS | Faslane | | 4.4.82 | HMS PICT | Portland | | 27.4.82 |
| RMAS TYPHOON | Portland | | 4.4.82 | HMS LEEDS CASTLE | Portsmouth | | 29.4.82 |
| HMS INVINCIBLE | Portsmouth | (3) | 5.4.82 | RFA SIR BEDIVERE | Marchwood | | 29.4.82 |
| HMS HERMES | Portsmouth | (3) | 5.4.82 | IRIS | Devonport | | 29.4.82 |
| HMS ALACRITY | Devonport | (3) | 5.4.82 | HMS DUMBARTON CASTLE | | | |
| HMS ANTELOPE | Devonport | (3)(5) | 5.4.82 | | Portland | | 1.5.82 |
| RFA OLMEDA | Devonport | (3) | 5.4.82 | RMAS GOOSANDER | Rosyth | | 2.5.82 |
| RFA PEARLEAF | Portsmouth | (3) | 5.4.82 | HMS AMBUSCADE | Gibraltar | | 3.5.82 |
| RFA BRAMBLELEAF | Mombasa, Kenya | | 5.4.82 | HMS VALIANT | Faslane | | 3.5.82 |
| RFA SIR PERCIVALE | Marchwood | (5) | 5.4.82 | LYCAON | Southampton | | 4.5.82 |
| HMS FEARLESS | Portsmouth | (4) | 6.4.82 | ALVEGA | Portsmouth | | 5.5.82 |
| RFA RESOURCE | Rosyth | (3) | 6.4.82 | HMS EXETER | Antigua | | 7.5.82 |
| RFA SIR GALAHAD | Devonport | (5) | 6.4.82 | EBURNA | St Anna Bay, WI | | 8.5.82 |
| RFA SIR GERAINT | Devonport | (5) | 6.4.82 | SAXONIA | Devonport | | 8.5.82 |
| RFA SIR LANCELOT | Marchwood | (5) | 6.4.82 | BALTIC FERRY | Southampton | | 9.5.82 |
| RFA STROMNESS | Portsmouth | (4) | 7.4.82 | NORDIC FERRY | Southampton | | 9.5.82 |
| HMS BROADSWORD | Gibraltar | (3) | 8.4.82 | HMS ACTIVE | Devonport | (7) | 10.5.82 |
| HMS YARMOUTH | Gibraltar | (3) | 8.4.82 | HMS ANDROMEDA | Devonport | (7) | 10.5.82 |
| CANBERRA | Southampton | (6) | 9.4.82 | HMS AVENGER | Devonport | (7) | 10.5.82 |
| ELK | Southampton | (6) | 9.4.82 | HMS BRISTOL | Portsmouth | (7) | 10.5.82 |
| BRITISH TAY | Devonport | | 9.4.82 | HMS MINERVA | Devonport | (7) | 10.5.82 |
| IRISHMAN | Portsmouth | | 10.4.82 | HMS PENELOPE | Devonport | (7) | 10.5.82 |
| SALVAGEMAN | Portsmouth | | 10.4.82 | RFA ENGADINE | Devonport | (7) | 10.5.82 |
| BRITISH ESK | Portland | | 11.4.82 | RFA OLNA | Portsmouth | (7) | 10.5.82 |
| YORKSHIREMAN | Portsmouth | | 13.4.82 | HMS CARDIFF | Gibraltar | (7) | 12.5.82 |
| BRITISH TAMAR | Milford Haven | | 14.4.82 | BALDER LONDON | Portsmouth | | 12.5.82 |
| RFA BLUE ROVER | Portsmouth | | 16.4.82 | QUEEN ELIZABETH 2 | | | |
| STENA SEASPREAD | Portsmouth | | 16.4.82 | | Southampton | | 12.5.82 |
| BRITISH TRENT | Isle of Grain | | 17.4.82 | RFA FORT GRANGE | Devonport | | 14.5.82 |
| BRITISH TEST | Gibraltar | | 18.4.82 | ATLANTIC CAUSEWAY | | | |
| HMS ARDENT | Devonport | (6) | 19.4.82 | | Devonport | | 14.5.82 |
| HMS ARGONAUT | Devonport | (6) | 19.4.82 | WIMPEY SEAHORSE | Devonport | | 16.5.82 |
| RFA PLUMLEAF | Portland | | 19.4.82 | BRITISH TAMAR | Gibraltar | | 17.5.82 |
| RFA REGENT | Portland | | 19.4.82 | ST EDMUND | Devonport | | 19.5.82 |
| FORT TORONTO | Southampton | | 19.4.82 | TOR CALEDONIA | Southampton | | 20.5.82 |
| UGANDA | Gibraltar | | 19.4.82 | CONTENDER BEZANT | | | |
| HMS HECLA | Gibraltar | | 20.4.82 | | Devonport | | 21.5.82 |
| BRITISH DART | Loch Striven | | 22.4.82 | GEESTPORT | Portsmouth | | 21.5.82 |
| HMS HERALD | Portsmouth | | 24.4.82 | RFA BRAMBLELEAF | Portland | | 23.5.82 |

| Vessel: | From: | Date: | | |
|---|---|---|---|---|
| SCOTTISH EAGLE | Milford Haven | 24.5.82 | (1) | Advanced Group |
| BRITISH ENTERPRISE III | | | (2) | South Georgia Group |
| | Rosyth | 26.5.82 | (3) | Carrier Group |
| STENA INSPECTOR | Charleston, SC | 6.6.82 | (4) | 'Fearless' Group (from Ascension); merged with (6) |
| ASTRONOMER | Devonport | 8.6.82 | | 10.5.82 |
| LAERTES | Devonport | 8.6.82 | (5) | LSL Group (from Ascension); merged with (4) & (6) |
| AVELONA STAR | Portsmouth | 10.6.82 | | 16.5.82 to complete the Amphibious Forces |
| G A WALKER | Devonport | 10.6.82 | (6) | 'Canberra' Group (from Ascension) |
| ST HELENA | Portland | 13.6.82 | (7) | 'Bristol' Group |
| HMS BRECON | Portland | 13.6.82 | | |
| HMS LEDBURY | Portland | 13.6.82 | | |

'Invincible' and 'Hermes' go to war. *(Peter J. Cooper)*

# UNITED KINGDOM SHIPPING

This appendix details the ships of the Royal Navy including the deployment and movements of those military and civilian vessels involved in the Task Force.

The first part describes the status of the Royal Navy, Royal Fleet Auxiliary, Royal Maritime Auxiliary Service and Royal Corps of Transport fleets as they were on 29 March 1982. The changes and orders for new ships which occurred as a result of the conflict have been included for the sake of completeness. The second part is divided into various sections, giving individual details of the service vessels and Ships Taken Up From Trade (STUFT) deployed both before and after the Argentine surrender (up to 31 December 1982). Other sections deal with captured and recaptured vessels, merchant vessels taken up from trade to replace RFA ships deployed to the South Atlantic, and with other ships which became involved in the conflict. Finally, a checklist giving departure dates for shipping involved in the Task Force is included as a quick reference.

# ROYAL NAVY

## AIRCRAFT CARRIERS

'Hermes' Class; converted to the dual ASW/Commando role in 1976/77; refit for Sea Harrier operations in 1980; relegated to alongside training role 4.84. Armed with Seacat SAM system.

| R12 | HMS HERMES | Commissioned 18.11.59 |
|-----|------------|----------------------|

'Invincible' Class. Sea Dart SAM system.

| R05 | HMS INVINCIBLE | Commissioned 11.7.80 |
|-----|----------------|----------------------|
| R06 | HMS ILLUSTRIOUS | *Commissioned 20.6.82* |
| R09 | HMS ARK ROYAL | *Commissioned 1.11.85* |

## SUBMARINES

'Resolution' Class; nuclear-powered Ballistic Missile submarine. Armed with Polaris A3 SLBM's and 21 inch torpedoes.

| S22 | HMS RESOLUTION | Commissioned 2.10.67 |
|-----|----------------|----------------------|
| S23 | HMS REPULSE | Commissioned 28.9.68 |
| S26 | HMS RENOWN | Commissioned 15.11.68 |
| S27 | HMS REVENGE | Commissioned 4.12.69 |

'Trafalgar' Class; torpedo-armed, nuclear-powered Fleet submarines.

| S113 | HMS TRAFALGAR | *Commissioned 27.5.83* |
|------|---------------|------------------------|
| S114 | HMS TURBULENT | *Commissioned 28.4.84* |
| S115 | HMS TIRELESS | *Commissioned 5.10.85* |
| S116 | HMS TORBAY | *To commission 1986* |
| S117 | HMS TALENT | |
| S118 | HMS TACTICIAN | |

'Valiant' Class; nuclear-powered Fleet submarines. Armed with Mk.8 and 21 inch Tigerfish torpedoes; to receive two Harpoon SSM systems.

| S102 | HMS VALIANT | Commissioned 18.7.66 |
|------|-------------|----------------------|
| S103 | HMS WARSPITE | Commissioned 18.4.67 |

'Churchill' Class; nuclear-powered Fleet submarines. Armed with 21 inch Tigerfish torpedoes; to receive two Harpoon SSM systems.

| S46 | HMS CHURCHILL | Commissioned 15.7.70 |
|-----|---------------|----------------------|
| S48 | HMS CONQUEROR | Commissioned 9.11.71 |
| S50 | HMS COURAGEOUS | Commissioned 16.10.71 |

'Swiftsure' Class; nuclear-powered Fleet submarines. Armed with 21 inch Tigerfish torpedoes; to receive two Harpoon SSM systems.

| S108 | HMS SOVEREIGN | Commissioned 11.7.74 |
|------|---------------|----------------------|
| S109 | HMS SUPERB | Commissioned 13.11.76 |
| S110 | HMS SCEPTRE | Commissioned 14.2.78 |
| S111 | HMS SPARTAN | Commissioned 22.9.79 |

| | | |
|---|---|---|
| S112 | HMS SPLENDID | Commissioned 21.3.81 |
| S126 | HMS SWIFTSURE | Commissioned 17.4.73 |

'Oberon' Class; diesel-electric Patrol submarines. Armed with 21 inch torpedoes. 'Opossum' had a modified bow and was first of the 'Opossum' class.

| | | |
|---|---|---|
| S09 | HMS OBERON | Commissioned 24.2.61 |
| S10 | HMS ODIN | Commissioned 3.5.62 |
| S11 | HMS ORPHEUS | Commissioned 25.11.60 |
| S12 | HMS OLYMPUS | Commissioned 7.7.62 |
| S13 | HMS OSIRIS | Commissioned 11.1.64 |
| S14 | HMS ONSLAUGHT | Commissioned 14.8.62 |
| S15 | HMS OTTER | Commissioned 20.8.62 |
| S16 | HMS ORACLE | Commissioned 14.2.63 |
| S17 | HMS OCELOT | Commissioned 31.1.64 |
| S18 | HMS OTUS | Commissioned 5.10.63 |
| S19 | HMS OPOSSUM | Commissioned 5.6.64 |
| S20 | HMS OPPORTUNE | Commissioned 29.12.64 |
| S21 | HMS ONYX | Commissioned 20.11.67 |

'Porpoise' Class; diesel-electric Patrol submarines. Armed with 21 inch torpedoes. S01 paid off in 6.82.

| | | |
|---|---|---|
| S01 | HMS PORPOISE | Commissioned 17.4.58 |
| S07 | HMS SEALION | Commissioned 25.7.61 |
| S08 | HMS WALRUS | Commissioned 10.2.61 |

## DESTROYERS

'County' Class; carried one Wessex HAS.3. Armed with Exocet SSM and Seaslug II SAM systems plus 4.5 inch and 20mm guns. D19/20 re-equipped with Lynx HAS.2 after the conflict. D18 paid off 4.84 (sold to Chile).

| | | |
|---|---|---|
| D18 | HMS ANTRIM | Commissioned 14.7.70 |
| D19 | HMS GLAMORGAN | Commissioned 11.10.66 |
| D20 | HMS FIFE | Commissioned 21.6.66 |

Type 82, 'Bristol' Class; flight-deck but no helicopter assigned. Armed with Sea Dart SAM and Ikara ASM systems plus 4.5 inch and 20mm guns.

| | | |
|---|---|---|
| D23 | HMS BRISTOL | Commissioned 31.3.73 |

Type 42, 'Sheffield' Class; one Lynx carried. Armed with Sea Dart SAM system, 4.5 inch and 20mm guns plus Mk.46 torpedoes. Survivors fitted with extra guns after the conflict.

| | | |
|---|---|---|
| D80 | HMS SHEFFIELD | Commissioned 16.2.75 |
| D86 | HMS BIRMINGHAM | Commissioned 3.12.76 |
| D87 | HMS NEWCASTLE | Commissioned 23.3.78 |
| D88 | HMS GLASGOW | Commissioned 24.5.79 |
| D108 | HMS CARDIFF | Commissioned 24.9.79 |
| D118 | HMS COVENTRY | Commissioned 20.10.78 |

Type 42, Batch 2; one Lynx carried. Armed with Sea Dart SAM system, 4.5 inch and 20mm guns plus Mk.46 torpedoes. Fitted with extra guns after the conflict.

| | | |
|---|---|---|
| D89 | HMS EXETER | Commissioned 19.9.80 |
| D90 | HMS SOUTHAMPTON | Commissioned 31.10.81 |
| D91 | HMS NOTTINGHAM | *Commissioned 6.4.83* |
| D92 | HMS LIVERPOOL | *Commissioned 9.7.82* |

Type 42, Batch 3 (stretched); to carry one Lynx helicopter.

| | | |
|---|---|---|
| D95 | HMS MANCHESTER | *Commissioned 16.12.82* |
| D96 | HMS GLOUCESTER | *Commissioned 16.5.85* |
| D97 | HMS EDINBURGH | *To commission 17.12.85* |
| D98 | HMS YORK | *Commissioned 9.8.85* |

## FRIGATES

Type 22, 'Broadsword' Class, Batch 1; carried one Lynx but able to carry two. Armed with Exocet SSM and Seawolf SAM systems plus 40mm guns.

| | | |
|---|---|---|
| F88 | HMS BROADSWORD | Commissioned 3.5.79 |
| F89 | HMS BATTLEAXE | Commissioned 28.3.80 |
| F90 | HMS BRILLIANT | Commissioned 15.5.81 |
| F91 | HMS BRAZEN | *Commissioned 2.7.82* |

Type 22, 'Broadsword' Class (stretched), Batch 2; three under construction (plus one more laid down 3.83). As a result of the conflict orders were placed for two additional Batch 2 (stretched) vessels.

| | | |
|---|---|---|
| F92 | HMS BOXER | *Commissioned 22.12.83* |
| F93 | HMS BEAVER | *Commissioned 13.12.84* |
| F94 | HMS BRAVE | *To commission 1985* |
| F95 | HMS LONDON | *To commission 1986* |
| | HMS SHEFFIELD | *To commission 1987* |
| | HMS COVENTRY | *To commission 1987* |

Type 22, 'Broadsword' Class (stretched), Batch 3; four ordered post-conflict.

| | | |
|---|---|---|
| F99 | HMS CORNWALL | *To commission 1987* |
| | HMS CUMBERLAND | |
| | HMS CHATHAM | |
| | HMS (name not known) | |

Type 21, 'Amazon' Class; one Lynx carried (except HMS Active which carried one Wasp). Armed with Exocet SSM and Seacat SAM systems, 4.5 inch and 20mm guns, plus Mk.46 Torpedoes.

| | | |
|---|---|---|
| F169 | HMS AMAZON | Commissioned 11.5.74 |
| F170 | HMS ANTELOPE | Commissioned 19.7.75 |
| F171 | HMS ACTIVE | Commissioned 17.6.77 |
| F172 | HMS AMBUSCADE | Commissioned 5.9.75 |
| F173 | HMS ARROW | Commissioned 29.7.76 |
| F174 | HMS ALACRITY | Commissioned 2.7.77 |
| F184 | HMS ARDENT | Commissioned 13.10.77 |
| F185 | HMS AVENGER | Commissioned 15.4.78 |

Type 12, 'Rothesay' Class; one Wasp carried. Armed with Seacat SAM system, 4.5 inch guns and Limbo ASW mortar (except for the unarmed F108). HMS Lowestoft and HMS Londonderry both converted to trials ships (no helicopters). Disposals announced during 1981: F106/113/115/129 (all 1982), F108 (1983) and F107 (1984). As a direct result of the conflict, HMS Lowestoft was refitted for service 4-6.82, while disposals were amended as follows: F106 (1982), F108/113/129 (all 1984) and F101/103/107/115/126 (all 1985).

| F101 | HMS YARMOUTH | Commissioned 26.3.60 |
|------|--------------|----------------------|
| F103 | HMS LOWESTOFT | Commissioned 18.10.61 |
| F106 | HMS BRIGHTON | Commissioned 28.9.61 |
| F107 | HMS ROTHESAY | Commissioned 23.4.60 |
| F108 | HMS LONDONDERRY | Commissioned 22.7.60 |
| F113 | HMS FALMOUTH | Commissioned 25.7.61 |
| F115 | HMS BERWICK | Commissioned 1.6.61 |
| F126 | HMS PLYMOUTH | Commissioned 11.5.61 |
| F129 | HMS RHYL | Commissioned 31.10.60 |

Type 12, 'Whitby' Class. One retained for use as a training ship (due to be withdrawn during 1985 following its replacement by 'Leander' Class frigate HMS Juno).

| F43 | HMS TORQUAY | Commissioned 10.5.56 |
|-----|-------------|----------------------|

'Leander' Class, Batch 1 conversion (Ikara); one Wasp carried. Armed with Seacat SAM and Ikara ASM systems, 40mm guns and Limbo ASW mortar. Disposals announced during 1981: F39 (1983) and F10/15 (1984). As a result of the conflict the disposals were rescinded. F104 sold to New Zealand 18.7.83 as HMNZS Southland and F114 later paid off 31.3.85. Additional dates given below are the Ikara conversion completion dates.

| F10 | HMS AURORA (3.76) | Commissioned 9.4.64 |
|-----|-------------------|---------------------|
| F15 | HMS EURYALUS (3.76) | Commissioned 16.9.64 |
| F18 | HMS GALATEA (9.74) | Commissioned 25.4.64 |
| F38 | HMS ARETHUSA (4.77) | Commissioned 24.11.63 |
| F39 | HMS NAIAD (7.75) | Commissioned 15.3.65 |
| F104 | HMS DIDO (10.78) | Commissioned 18.9.63 |
| F109 | HMS LEANDER (12.72) | Commissioned 27.3.63 |
| F114 | HMS AJAX (9.73) | Commissioned 10.12.63 |

'Leander' Class, Batch 2 conversion (Exocet); one Lynx carried. Armed with Exocet SSM and Seacat SAM systems, 40mm guns and Mk.32 torpedoes. Conversion of HMS Juno was halted to be refitted to the training role, due to be completed during 1985. The additional dates given are Exocet conversion completion dates.

| F28 | HMS CLEOPATRA (11.75) | Commissioned 17.8.67 |
|-----|-----------------------|----------------------|
| F40 | HMS SIRIUS (10.77) | Commissioned 15.6.66 |
| F42 | HMS PHOEBE (4.77) | Commissioned 15.4.66 |
| F45 | HMS MINERVA (3.79) | Commissioned 14.5.66 |
| F47 | HMS DANAE (9.80) | Commissioned 7.9.67 |
| F52 | HMS JUNO | Commissioned 18.7.67 |
| F56 | HMS ARGONAUT (3.80) | Commissioned 17.8.67 |
| F127 | HMS PENELOPE (1.82) | Commissioned 31.10.63 |

Broadbeam 'Leander' Class. F57/58/60/71/75 made up Batch 3 conversion (Exocet and Seawolf); one Lynx carried. Armed with Exocet SSM and Seawolf SAM systems, 40mm guns plus Mk.32 torpedoes (F58/60/71 all under conversion on 29.3.82). F12/16/69/70/72 all unconverted; one Wasp carried. Armed with Seacat SAM system, 4.5 inch and 20mm guns plus Limbo ASW mortar. HMS Bacchante was sold to New Zealand during 1982 (handed over 1.10.82 as HMNZS Wellington). The additional dates given below are conversion completion dates.

| F12 | HMS ACHILLES | Commissioned 9.7.70 |
|-----|--------------|---------------------|
| F16 | HMS DIOMEDE | Commissioned 2.4.71 |
| F57 | HMS ANDROMEDA (12.80) | Commissioned 2.12.68 |
| F58 | HMS HERMIONE (12.83) | Commissioned 11.7.69 |
| F60 | HMS JUPITER (8.83) | Commissioned 9.8.69 |
| F69 | HMS BACCHANTE | Commissioned 17.10.69 |
| F70 | HMS APOLLO | Commissioned 28.5.72 |
| F71 | HMS SCYLLA (11.84) | Commissioned 12.2.70 |
| F72 | HMS ARIADNE | Commissioned 10.2.73 |
| F75 | HMS CHARYBDIS (6.82) | Commissioned 2.6.69 |

Type 81, 'Tribal' Class; one Wasp carried. Armed with Seacat SAM system, 4.5 inch and 20mm guns plus Limbo ASW mortar. All were in reserve with the Standby Squadron at Chatham except HMS Ashanti in use as a harbour training ship at Portsmouth. As a result of the conflict F122/124/133 were refitted and recommissioned 24.7.82, 9.8.82 and 17.7.82 respectively (F119/125/131 all being stripped for spares). The remainder were put up for disposal. F122 and F133 were paid off 29.3.84 followed by F124 30.3.84, all three of them being sold to Indonesia during 1984.

| F117 | HMS ASHANTI | Commissioned 23.11.61 |
|------|-------------|-----------------------|
| F119 | HMS ESKIMO | Commissioned 21.2.63 |
| F122 | HMS GURKHA | Commissioned 13.2.63 |
| F124 | HMS ZULU | Commissioned 17.4.64 |
| F125 | HMS MOHAWK | Commissioned 29.11.63 |
| F131 | HMS NUBIAN | Commissioned 9.10.62 |
| F133 | HMS TARTAR | Commissioned 26.2.62 |

---

### ASSAULT SHIPS

'Fearless' Class. Able to carry five Wessex HU.5's, four LCM(9) and four LCVP landing craft. Armed with Seacat SAM system and 40mm guns. HMS Intrepid was held in reserve and due for disposal in 1982, while HMS Fearless was due for disposal in 1984. Both were reprieved as a result of the conflict.

| L10 | HMS FEARLESS | Commissioned 25.11.65 |
|-----|--------------|-----------------------|
| L11 | HMS INTREPID | Commissioned 11.3.67 |

## ICE PATROL VESSEL

Converted to this role during 1967/1968 (previously the 'Anita Dan'). Carried two Wasps. Armed with 20mm guns. Due for disposal during 1982 but reprieved as a direct result of the conflict.

**A171  HMS ENDURANCE**     Commissioned 1968

## SURVEY VESSELS

'Hecla' Class; one Wasp carried. HMS Herald was Improved 'Hecla' Class.

| | | |
|---|---|---|
| **A133  HMS HECLA** | Commissioned | 8.9.65 |
| **A137  HMS HECATE** | Commissioned | 20.12.65 |
| **A138  HMS HERALD** | Commissioned | 31.10.74 |
| **A144  HMS HYDRA** | Commissioned | 4.5.66 |

In addition there were seven coastal and inshore survey vessels on strength in 1982.

## REPAIR & MAINTENANCE VESSELS

'Head' Class. In reserve since 1972.

| | | |
|---|---|---|
| **A134  HMS RAME HEAD** | Commissioned | 18.8.45 |
| **A191  HMS BERRY HEAD** | Commissioned | 30.5.45 |

## SUPPORT VESSELS

Submarine tender.

**A236  HMS WAKEFUL**

Diving support ship; on charter.

**SEAFORTH CLANSMAN**  Commissioned 4.78

Seabed operations vessel. Launched 19.5.81 but completion delayed.

**K07  HMS CHALLENGER**     *Commissioned 3.8.84*

## MINE COUNTER MEASURES VESSELS

'Hunt' Class minesweepers. Armed with 40mm Bofors gun. Nine more under construction or on order at the time of the conflict.

| | | |
|---|---|---|
| **M29  HMS BRECON** | Commissioned | 21.3.80 |
| **M30  HMS LEDBURY** | Commissioned | 11.6.81 |

There were also 31 other MCM vessels and one minelayer in use with the RN and RN Reserve in 1982.

## FISHERY PROTECTION VESSELS

'Castle' Class. Able to operate one Sea King but no hangar facilities. Armed with 40mm Bofors gun.

| | | |
|---|---|---|
| **P258  HMS LEEDS CASTLE** | Commissioned | 27.10.81 |
| **P265  HMS DUMBARTON CASTLE** | | |
| | Commissioned | 26.3.82 |

In addition there were 17 patrol craft of various Classes on strength in 1982.

## OTHER VESSELS

The RN was also responsible for the Royal Yacht Britannia (A00).

# ROYAL FLEET AUXILIARY

The Royal Fleet Auxiliary was operated by the Director of Fuel, Movements and Victualling and formed part of the RN Supply and Transport Service (RNSTS) within the MoD (Navy). The RNSTS provided all logistic support for the RN and was civilian-manned by Merchant Navy personnel.

## HELICOPTER SUPPORT SHIP

Able to carry up to six helicopters.

**K08  RFA ENGADINE**     Commissioned 15.12.67

## FLEET TANKERS — LARGE

'Ol' Class; able to carry two Sea Kings.

| | | |
|---|---|---|
| **A122  RFA OLWEN** | Commissioned | 21.6.65 |
| **A123  RFA OLNA** | Commissioned | 1.4.66 |
| **A124  RFA OLMEDA** | Commissioned | 18.10.65 |

'Later Tide' Class; able to carry two Sea Kings. RFA Tidepool en route to the Chilean Navy during 4.82, RFA Tidespring withdrawn in 1984.

| | | |
|---|---|---|
| **A75  RFA TIDESPRING** | Commissioned | 18.1.63 |
| **A76  RFA TIDEPOOL** | Commissioned | 28.6.63 |

## FLEET TANKERS — SMALL

'Rover' Class; first three re-engined 1974.

| A268 | RFA GREEN ROVER | Commissioned | 15.8.69 |
| A269 | RFA GREY ROVER | Commissioned | 10.4.70 |
| A270 | RFA BLUE ROVER | Commissioned | 15.7.70 |
| A271 | RFA GOLD ROVER | Commissioned | 22.3.74 |
| A273 | RFA BLACK ROVER | Commissioned | 23.8.74 |

## SUPPORT TANKERS

'New Leaf' Class; large bulk tankers with limited RAS capability, no flight-deck. All were ex-commercial vessels on charter to the MoD.

| A79 | RFA APPLELEAF | Commissioned | 1979 |
| A81 | RFA BRAMBLELEAF | Commissioned | 1979 |
| A109 | RFA BAYLEAF | Commissioned | 1982 |

'Old Leaf' Class; small chartered tankers, no flight-deck.

| A77 | RFA PEARLEAF | Commissioned | 1.60 |
| A78 | RFA PLUMLEAF | Commissioned | 7.60 |

## FLEET REPLENISHMENT SHIPS

'Fort' Class; able to carry four Sea Kings.

| A385 | RFA FORT GRANGE | Commissioned | 6.4.78 |
| A386 | RFA FORT AUSTIN | Commissioned | 11.5.79 |

'Resource' Class; able to carry two Wessex.

| A480 | RFA RESOURCE | Commissioned | 16.5.67 |
| A486 | RFA REGENT | Commissioned | 6.6.67 |

## STORES SUPPORT SHIPS

'Ness' Class; helicopter deck but no hangar.

A345 leased to the United States Navy during 9.81 (purchased by them in 9.82 as USNS Spica); A344 sold to the United States Navy in 4.83 as USNS Saturn.

| A344 | RFA STROMNESS | Commissioned | 21.3.67 |
| A345 | RFA TARBATNESS | Commissioned | 10.8.67 |

## LANDING SHIPS, LOGISTIC

Able to carry 534 troops, plus 16 tanks and 34 other vehicles.

| L3004 | RFA SIR BEDIVERE | Commissioned | 17.5.67 |
| L3005 | RFA SIR GALAHAD | Commissioned | 17.12.66 |
| L3027 | RFA SIR GERAINT | Commissioned | 12.7.67 |
| L3029 | RFA SIR LANCELOT | Commissioned | 18.1.64 |
| L3036 | RFA SIR PERCIVALE | Commissioned | 22.3.68 |
| L3505 | RFA SIR TRISTRAM | Commissioned | 14.9.67 |

Due to the loss of 'Sir Galahad' and the damage done to 'Sir Tristram' during the conflict, two Ro-Ro vessels were chartered as replacements for two years from 14.1.83. Formerly 'Grey Master' (Norway) and 'Lakespan Ontario' (Canada), they were commissioned on 26.3.83 as 'Sir Caradoc' (L3522) and 'Sir Lamorak' (L3532) respectively. The subsequently repaired 'Sir Tristram' was restored to RFA service c9.10.85.

# ROYAL MARITIME AUXILIARY SERVICE

The Royal Maritime Auxiliary Service had over 400 powered vessels and was administered by the Director of Marine Service (Naval), providing marine services at the various Naval bases. Two RMAS vessels were deployed during "Corporate":

## OCEAN TUG

| A95 | RMAS TYPHOON | Commissioned 1960 |

## MOORING, SALVAGE & BOOM VESSEL

| A165 | RMAS GOOSANDER | Commissioned 10.9.73 |

# ROYAL CORPS OF TRANSPORT

The Royal Corps of Transport was fundamentally tasked with all aspects relating to movement affecting the Army by land, sea and air (other than tactical movement or transport organic to a particular unit). The Corps officially came into being on 15 July 1965 by a retitling of the Royal Army Service Corps (RASC) and a fusion of various responsibilities which had previously been carried out by either the RASC or the Royal Engineers. Administrative changes which took place after 1965 included the formation of 73 Sqdn RCT at Port Stanley after the retaking of the Falkland Islands. Responsibilities of the RCT include the operation of Marchwood Military Port at Southampton.

The RCT operated a variety of landing craft, the largest of which were the LCL's 'Ardennes' (L4001) and 'Arakan' (L4003), eight 'Avon' Class Ramp Powered Lighters (RPL's) as well as various tugs, launches and other craft under logistical control of ports or beachheads. Two 'Mulberry' Class landing craft were deployed to the Falkland Islands following the Argentine surrender.

---

## LANDING CRAFT, RAMPED

L105　ARROMANCHES
L106　ANTWERP

---

# INDIVIDUAL SHIP DETAILS

---

## RN, RFA & RMAS SHIPS DEPLOYED PRE-15 JUNE 1982

### ACTIVE

*Cdr P.C.B.Canter RN*

Sailed south from Devonport with the 'Bristol' Group on 10.5.82, passed Ascension 18/19.5.82 and entered the TEZ 25.5.82. Began duties in the Task Force screen 150-180 miles east of Port Stanley by day and detached inshore for bombardment and convoy protection into San Carlos Water by night. Detached to the TRALA 28.5.82 for repairs and arrived in San Carlos Water 31.5.82 with essential supplies for 'Arrow'. Involved in heavy bombardment of Moody Brook and Tumbledown areas, contributing to the Argentine surrender. Detached to San Carlos Water 17.6.82, then to Port William 1.7.82 for guardship duties until 8.7.82 when she rejoined the CVBG. Moved to San Carlos Water on 14.7.82 for final repairs, visiting the memorial to 'Antelope' and 'Ardent' at San Carlos before sailing for the UK on 15.7.82 (via Ascension 23/24.7.82), arriving at Devonport on 3.8.82.

### ALACRITY

*Cdr C.J.S.Craig RN (awarded DSC)*

Left Devonport 5.4.82 for the South Atlantic (via Ascension 16-18.4.82), becoming one of the first ships in the TEZ established on 30.4.82. Commenced bombardment duties off Port Stanley on 1.5.82 and received minor damage from a Grupo 6 Dagger in the day's only effective air raid. While entering Falkland Sound on 11.5.82, the Argentine supply ship 'Isla de los Estados' was discovered heading for Port Howard. 'Alacrity' fired on the ship with her 4.5 inch gun, causing her to explode and sink. Detached from the TEZ on 2.6.82 for repairs to her main engines and sailed for the UK on 6.6.82 (via Ascension). Arrived at Devonport on 24.6.82, being the first ship to return. Her 4.5 inch gun required a new barrel, the old one having been worn out after firing over 500 rounds during the bombardments.

### AMBUSCADE

*Cdr P.J.Mosse RN*

Arrived Devonport late 2.82 from Gulf Patrol and deployed 9.4.82 to arrive at Gibraltar

13.4.82 for guard-ship duties. Ordered further south 28.4.82 and left Gibraltar 3.5.82 (via Ascension 11.5.82). Entered the TEZ 22.5.82. Involved in the bombardment of Argentine shore positions during which the ship came under attack from howitzers at Sapper Hill on 30.5.82. Moved to San Carlos Water 27.6.82 for repairs, departing the TEZ 5.7.82 to transport a detachment of Scots Guards to South Georgia. Sailed from there to the UK on 7.7.82. Arrived at Devonport 24.7.82 having covered 29,226 miles during Operation "Corporate".

### ANDROMEDA

*Capt J.L.Weatherall RN*

Sailed south from Devonport on 10.5.82 with the 'Bristol' Group (via Ascension 18/19.5.82) and entered the TEZ 25.5.82, joining the CVBG overnight. Acted as escort to 'Invincible' throughout the conflict and entered San Carlos Water 15.6.82. Escorted 'Canberra' into Port Stanley harbour to collect PoW's 16.6.82 and rejoined 'Invincible' 18.6.82. Visited South Georgia 15-22.8.82 before sailing for the UK, arriving at Devonport 10.9.82.

### ANTELOPE

*Cdr N.J.Tobin RN (awarded DSC)*

Sailed south from Devonport 5.4.82, detaching from the CVBG 9.4.82 to join the 'Fearless' Group as escort to Ascension. At Ascension 21-29.4.82 and on 24.4.82 intercepted the Argentine merchant ship 'Rio de la Plata' while she was attempting to shadow 'Canberra' near the island. Continued south as escort to the LSL's but detached 1.5.82 to rendezvous with 'Antrim' 6.5.82 and exchange escort roles. 'Antelope' accompanied 'Tidespring' back to Ascension with PoW's (staying there 12-15.5.82). Sailed south once again and entered the TEZ on 22.5.82, joining the ships in San Carlos Water. The Flight's Lynx attacked the Argentine merchant vessel 'Rio Carcarana' off Port King with two Sea Skua missiles on 23.5.82 and set the ship ablaze. In the course of two attacks by Grupo 5 A-4B Skyhawks on 23.5.82 she was struck by two bombs which failed to explode and by one of the aircraft (C-242) which hit the main mast top before being brought down by an unidentified SAM. One bomb exploded while being defused, tearing a large hole in the starboard side. The ship then caught fire and was abandoned, after which she blew up and sank

in San Carlos Water. Only the bows and stern were still visible on 24.5.82. The ship's company embarked that day in 'Norland' for passage to South Georgia, where they were transferred to 'Queen Elizabeth 2' for passage back to the UK, arriving at Southampton 11.6.82.

### ANTRIM

*Capt B.G.Young RN (awarded DSO)*

Sailed from Portsmouth on 17.3.82 for Exercise "Springtrain" and dispatched south on 2.4.82. Ordered to South Georgia 7.4.82 for Operation "Paraquat" (via Ascension 10-12.4.82), carrying out a rendezvous with 'Endurance' on 14.4.82 and arriving in position off South Georgia on 21.4.82. Troops put ashore that day by 'Antrim' Flt (737 Sqdn) and 845 Sqdn 'E' Flt, but taken off again 22.4.82 due to weather conditions (with the loss of both 845 Sqdn Wessex HU.5's). On 25.4.82 'Antrim' Flt spotted and took part in the attack on the Argentine submarine 'Santa Fe'. The enemy surrendered South Georgia on 26.4.82 and the ship sailed for Ascension 2.5.82 to escort 'Tidespring' with PoW's. Handed over that duty to 'Antelope' 6.5.82 and returned south as escort to the LSL's, joining the Amphibious Group on 16.5.82 for the landings on 21.5.82. On that date she was twice attacked by Grupo 6 Daggers and was hit by a 1,000lb bomb which, although failing to explode, caused considerable damage. Sailed from the AOA on 22.5.82 for repairs, rejoining the CVBG 23.5.82. Detached to South Georgia 25.5.82, arriving there on 27.5.82 to collect Maj Gen J.Moore for transfer to 'Fearless' on 29.5.82. Detached again 31.5.82 and arrived at South Georgia on 2.6.82 to act as guardship before sailing for the UK 29.6.82 (via Ascension 7.7.82) to arrive at Portsmouth 17.7.82.

### APPLELEAF

*Capt G.P.A.McDougall RFA*

Sailed from Gibraltar 2.4.82 upon detachment south from Exercise "Springtrain", beginning refuelling duties on 11.4.82. Joined the Task Force 14.5.82 to operate as a refuelling station at 25°S until early 6.82 when she exchanged positions with 'Plumleaf' at 40°S. Refuelled many ships passing north and south before sailing for the UK 25.7.82 to arrive at Rosyth after anchoring initially in Kirkcaldy Bay on 9.8.82.

## ARDENT

*Cdr A.W.J.West RN (awarded DSC)*

Sailed from Devonport 19.4.82 (via Ascension 29.4.-6.5.82), escorting the 'Canberra' Group south from the Island. Joined the 'Fearless' Group on 10.5.82 and the LSL's on 16.5.82 to complete the build up of amphibious forces on the edge of the TEZ before leading them into Falkland Sound for the landings 21.5.82. Commenced bombardment of Goose Green and Darwin and, while in Grantham Sound, was attacked by a Grupo 5 A-4B Skyhawk and then by three Grupo 6 Daggers. The latter attack seriously damaged the ship and destroyed her Lynx; she was then evacuated to the protection of other warships off North West Island. Within forty minutes she was attacked again by two flights of 3 Escuadrilla A-4Q Skyhawks and in those final attacks the ship was hit by two 500lb bombs which set the aft end ablaze and caused her to list heavily. The crew abandoned ship and the vessel sank off North West Island in Falkland Sound (51°35′S 59°13′W) during the evening of 22.5.82.

## ARGONAUT

*Capt C.H.Layman MVO RN (awarded DSO)*

On sea trials when ordered to the South Atlantic, sailing from Devonport on 19.4.82 (via Ascension 28.4.-6.5.82). Escorted the Amphibious Group from Ascension and entered Falkland Sound on 20.5.82 for the landings. On radar picket duty off Jersey Point 21.5.82 when damaged in successive air raids by a 1 Escuadrilla MB-339A and two waves of Grupo 6 Daggers which rendered the engines and steering unserviceable. During the raids a Grupo 6 Dagger (C-428) was shot down by a SAM, possibly a Seacat fired from either 'Argonaut' or 'Plymouth', but more likely a Seawolf from 'Broadsword'. Towed clear by 'Plymouth' with two unexploded bombs aboard but was declared operational again 26.5.82 after the bombs had been defused. Relieved by 'Minerva' as the AAWC in San Carlos Water 29.5.82 and sailed east for repairs. Sent back to the UK for repairs on 5.6.82 (via Ascension on 16.6.82) to arrive at Devonport on 26.6.82.

## ARROW

*Cdr P.J.Booterstone RN (awarded DSC)*

Sailed from Gibraltar on 26.3.82 for Exercise "Springtrain" but ordered to the South Atlantic on 2.4.82, becoming one of the first ships in the Advanced Group. At Ascension 11-14.4.82. Entered the TEZ 1.5.82 to commence bombardment of Stanley Airport that same day. As she withdrew with 'Alacrity' and 'Glamorgan' they were attacked by three Grupo 6 Daggers, 'Arrow' receiving minor damage from cannon fire. Rescued survivors from 'Sheffield' 4.5.82 after she was hit by an Exocet. Ordered into San Carlos Water on 23.5.82 for an indefinite period due to cracks in her superstructure. Survived two weeks in "bomb alley" before joining the CVBG 7.6.82. Departed for the UK on 18.6.82 (via Ascension 26.6.82) and arrived at Devonport on 7.7.82.

## AVENGER

*Capt H.M.White RN*

In a DED period at Devonport before sea trials at Portland 26.4.-5.5.82. Sailed south from Devonport 10.5.82 (via Ascension on 18/19.5.82) with the 'Bristol' Group. Entered the TEZ 25.5.82, joining the Task Force that night to be tasked with bombardment duties. Attacked by Grupo 4 A-4C's on 30.5.82 in the mistaken belief that she was 'Invincible' but no damage was sustained. Entered San Carlos Water on 31.5.82, detaching on 8.6.82 to hold inshore West Falkland by day and patrol for ships/aircraft involved in enemy resupply missions by night. Accepted the surrender of enemy forces at Fox Bay on 15.6.82 and her Flight was engaged in area searches of West Falkland until 23.6.82. To Port Stanley 24.6.82 for guardship duties until 23.8.82 when she sailed for the UK via Dakar, arriving at Devonport on 10.9.82.

## BAYLEAF

*Capt A.E.T.Hunter RFA*

Accepted by the RFA on 25.3.82 and sailed from Devonport on 26.4.82 for the South Atlantic on her maiden operational voyage (via brief sea trials at Portland and a visit to Gibraltar). Refuelled from 'Anco Charger' off Ascension on 8.5.82 and sailed south to join the CVBG overnight 25/26.5.82 with the 'Bristol' Group. Began tanker duties with the Task Force, refuelling 'Queen Elizabeth 2' and supporting the carriers, topping up from the civilian fuel tankers as and when required. Sailed for the UK, arriving at Devonport 31.8.82.

## BLUE ROVER

*Capt D.A.Reynolds RFA*

At Gibraltar late 3.82 participating in Exercise "Springtrain". Transferred all her stores to ships heading east then sailed for the UK to dock at Portsmouth on 6.4.82. Re-stored and converted to carry aviation fuel before departing on 16.4.82 for Ascension, where further stores were taken on. Refuelled the LSL's then left for South Georgia, arriving on 9.5.82 to join 'Endurance' as support for the garrison and to warn approaching vessels of icebergs. Arrived in San Carlos Water 1.6.82 to unload ammunition before sailing on 3.6.82 to spend two weeks refuelling various ships of the Task Force, firstly in the Sound and then in the TRALA 8-16.6.82. She moved to Port Stanley to continue refuelling duties after the surrender until being ordered back to the UK on 28.6.82, arriving at Portsmouth on 17.7.82.

## BRAMBLELEAF

*Capt M.S.J.Farley RFA*

On Gulf Patrol during 4.82 and at Mombasa, Kenya 5.4.82 when ordered direct to South Georgia (via the Cape of Good Hope) to provide forward fuel support for Operation "Paraquat". During fuel transfer to 'Tidespring' on 23.4.82 a submarine alert forced an emergency breakaway which damaged equipment on 'Brambleleaf'. Fuel transfer was completed on 24.4.82 and the ship

sailed for the UK and repairs, arriving at Portland by 15.5.82. Sailed south once more on 23.5.82. On station 28.8.82 with 'Illustrious' and remained there until returning to Gibraltar on 16.12.82.

## BRECON

*Cdr P.A.Fish RN*

Departed Rosyth 15.5.82 for Portland, continuing south from there on 13.6.82 to arrive at Port Stanley on 10.7.82. To Ajax Bay 14.7.82 then returned to Port Stanley on 25.7.82. Spent five weeks on operations to clear Argentine minefields around the Islands. Sailed for the UK on 13.8.82 and arrived at Rosyth on 15.9.82.

## BRILLIANT

*Capt J.F.Coward RN (awarded DSO)*

Sailed from Gibraltar 26.3.82 to take part in Exercise "Springtrain" and ordered south 2.4.82 with the Advanced Group. At Ascension 11-14.4.82. Detached to South Georgia on 22.4.82 for Operation "Paraquat", her Flight's two Lynx being involved in the attack on the Argentine submarine 'Santa Fe' on 25.4.82. Sailed from South Georgia 28.4.82 to join 'Invincible' as escort. Detached 1.5.82 for ASW action with 'Yarmouth' north-east of the Islands, but the suspected submarine ('San Luis') was not found. Relieved 'Broadsword' on picket duty off Port Stanley 10.5.82 and became the first vessel to use the Seawolf in anger on 12.5.82, shooting down two Grupo 5 A-4B Skyhawks (C-246 and C-208), while a third (C-206) crashed into the sea while taking avoiding action. On 15.5.82 her Flight attacked the 'Bahia Buen Suceso' at Fox Bay but without success. Rejoined the CVBG 16.5.82 until transferred to the Amphibious Group 20.5.82 and to San Carlos 21.5.82 where she received minor cannon fire damage from Grupo 6 Daggers. In company with the 'Yarmouth', she intercepted the motor vessel 'Monsunen' 22.5.82 which was driven ashore 23.5.82 under pursuit from the two frigates. Rejoined 'Hermes' as escort 23-27.5.82 (rescuing survivors from the 'Atlantic Conveyor' 25.5.82) before detaching for repairs. Rejoined the CVBG on 30.5.82 to act as escort to 'Invincible' by day and to the supply ships in the AOA by night. Took part in Operation "Canbelow" from 6-8.6.82, attempting to intercept Argentine bomber and resupply aircraft operating at night. Detached east on 9.6.82 to escort 'St Edmund', 'Contender Bezant' and 'Europic Ferry' to Port William until rejoining the CVBG on 17.6.82. Relieved by 'Broadsword' 22.6.82 and sailed east, finally leaving for the UK 23.6.82 (via Ascension 30.6.82) to arrive at Devonport on 13.7.82.

## BRISTOL

*Capt A.Grose RN*

At Portsmouth 6.4.82 ready for sea trials, fitted with the Fleet Satellite Communications System. Sailed south from Portsmouth 10.5.82 (via Ascension 18/19.5.82) and entered the TEZ on 25.5.82, joining the CVBG 26.5.82. Assumed the role of Flagship 2.7.82 from 'Hermes' when Rear Admiral Derek Refell took over from Rear Admiral

Woodward. Handed over her Flagship duties to 'Illustrious' on 28.8.82 and sailed for the UK on 31.8.82 (via Ascension 6-7.9.82), arriving at Portsmouth on 17.9.82.

## BROADSWORD

*Capt W.R.Canning ADC RN (awarded DSO)*

Left Gibraltar 26.3.82 for Exercise "Springtrain", but recalled to prepare for Gulf Patrol. Departed Gibraltar for Naples 5.4.82 but recalled yet again, returning there on 6.4.82. Sailed 8.4.82 to join the CVBG 11.4.82 as escort to 'Hermes'. At Ascension 16-18.4.82 and entered the TEZ 1.5.82. Commenced radar picket duty off Port Stanley until relieved by 'Brilliant' 10.5.82 to bombard shore positions. Detached 14.5.82 for the Pebble Island operations, returning the next day. Detached 17.5.82 with 'Invincible' at high speed to the west for a covert operation off the South American mainland in total darkness and radio-silence. Returned on 18.5.82 to rendezvous with the Amphibious Group, acting as Escort Commander for the landings on 21.5.82. Operating off Fanning Head she received minor cannon fire damage in an early Grupo 6 Dagger raid. During this attack one of her Seawolf missiles is thought to have brought down Grupo 6 Dagger C-428, although the Seacats of 'Argonaut' and 'Plymouth' have also been credited with the kill by some sources. Tasked to operate in the "missile trap" to the north of Pebble Island on 22.5.82. She was bombed on 25.5.82 by Grupo 5 A-4B Skyhawks while still engaged on those operations; one bomb bounced off the sea, in through the hull and up through the flight-deck, taking the nose off Lynx HAS.2 XZ729 before landing in the sea on the other side without exploding. She rejoined the CVBG on 26.5.82, carrying out a rendezvous with 'Baltic Ferry', 'Canberra' and 'Tidepool' on 1.6.82 and escorting them into San Carlos Water. In San Carlos Water again later in the month for repairs/maintenance inshore before relieving 'Brilliant' as escort to 'Hermes' 22.6.82. Sailed from Port William on 3.7.82 and departed with 'Hermes' for the UK on 4.7.82. Detached 15.7.82 for Gibraltar, eventually arriving at Devonport on 23.7.82.

## CARDIFF

*Capt M.G.T.Harris RN*

On patrol in the Persian Gulf when the conflict began. Ordered to the South Atlantic and sailed from Mombasa, Kenya 20.4.82 for Gibraltar, arriving 7.5.82. Sailed on 12.5.82 to join the 'Bristol' Group 14.5.82. At Ascension 18/19.5.82. Joined the CVBG on 26.5.82 to take over duties shelling the Port Stanley area from the damaged 'Glasgow'. Reported to have fired two Sea Darts early on 6.6.82 at an unidentified and slow-moving aircraft heading east towards Fitzroy settlement, but no hit confirmed. Escorted 'Canberra' from San Carlos Water to Port William 16.6.82 and remained as her escort until 25.6.82. After the surrender some of her crew took over the captured patrol vessel 'Islas Malvinas' and renamed her 'HMS Tiger Bay'. Relieved by 'Birmingham' and then sailed for the UK 7.7.82 (via Ascension 18.7.82), arriving at Portsmouth on 28.7.82.

## CONQUEROR

*Cdr C.L.Wreford-Brown RN (awarded DSO)*

Sailed south from Faslane 4.4.82 and arrived off South Georgia 19.4.82. Headed for the CVBG 23.4.82 but ordered back to South Georgia to find and sink the Argentine submarine 'Santa Fe' reported in the area. Arrived off Grytviken 25.4.82 and patrolled north of the Island until leaving for the CVBG 28.4.82. Ordered to station 170 miles southwest of the Falkland Islands for surveillance of the Argentine cruiser 'General Belgrano' and her escorts, detecting the group at long range on 30.4.82. On 2.5.82 she fired three Mk.8 torpedoes at the 'General Belgrano', scoring two hits (the third struck the 'Hipolito Bouchard' but failed to explode). Dived and ran deep following a depth charge attack by 'Piedra Bueno' and later returned to the position of the attack before entering the TEZ 4.5.82. Ordered north 9.5.82 and then proceeded north-east to escort the Amphibious Force coming south. Moved west 31.5.82 to survey reported movement of enemy surface ships southward within the Argentine 12-mile limit and patrolled 20-30 miles off the mainland before closing to 6 miles off the Gulf of Matias on 9.6.82. Moved further south 11-14.6.82 before leaving for the UK 15.6.82. Arrived at Faslane on 3.7.82 flying the "Jolly Roger" (in accordance with service custom after the sinking of an enemy ship).

## COURAGEOUS

*Cdr R.T.N.Best RN*

Arrived back at Faslane on 2.4.82 after a 302 day deployment but was ordered straight to the South Atlantic, sailing on 4.4.82 to patrol between the Argentine mainland and the Falklands. Returned to the UK, arriving at Faslane on 13.8.82.

## COVENTRY

*Capt D.Hart-Dyke MVO RN*

Sailed from Portsmouth on 17.3.82 for Exercise "Springtrain", for which she left Gibraltar on 26.3.82, but was ordered south on 2.4.82 (at Ascension 11-14.4.82). Entered the TEZ 1.5.82 and on 3.5.82 her Flight's Lynx attacked and severely damaged the Argentine patrol boat 'Alferez Sobral'. While off Choiseul Sound 3.5.82 shot down CAB601 Puma AE-505 with a Sea Dart. Relieved on picket duty off Port Stanley 10.5.82 by 'Glasgow'. Tasked with 'Broadsword' to operate as a "missile trap" to the north of Pebble Island on 22.5.82, lying in wait to ambush enemy aircraft. She remained on station until 25.5.82 when, after bringing down Grupo 5 A-4B Skyhawk C-244 and Grupo 4 A-4C Skyhawk C-304 with Sea Darts, she was hit by bombs from Grupo 5 Skyhawks which ruptured her port hull. The ship capsized shortly afterwards and sank.

## DUMBARTON CASTLE

*Lt Cdr N.D.Wood RN*

Sailed from Rosyth (her home port) on 26.4.82 for Portsmouth to be fitted with communications equipment and a desalination plant. Arrived at Portsmouth on 30.4.82 and

sailed 1.5.82 for Portland en route to the South Atlantic. Began duties at Ascension on 11.5.82 as a despatch vessel ferrying stores between vessels of the Task Force. Made two round trips from Ascension to South Georgia, the TRALA and the Falklands, being noted at Port William on 19.6.82 and South Georgia 23.6.82. Sailed north from Ascension to the UK, visiting Gibraltar 13.8.82 and arriving at Rosyth 20.8.82.

## ENDURANCE

*Capt N.J.Barker RN (awarded CBE)*

Sailed from Portsmouth 13.10.81 on what should have been her last deployment to the South Atlantic and Antarctica. Arrived at Port Stanley 19.3.82 and was due back in the UK 5.5.82. Sailed for South Georgia 21.3.82 following the landing of the scrap metal merchants, her Flight inserting an observation post there on 24.3.82. The Marine detachment was disembarked to Grytviken on 31.3.82 and the observation post taken off. The ship then sailed for Port Stanley but returned eastwards on 1.4.82 after the invasion. Initially she stayed away from the Falklands and South Georgia because of her limited capability. Sailed north on 5.4.82 to rendezvous with 'Antrim', 'Plymouth' and 'Tidespring' 14.4.82 after embarking troops from 'Fort Austin' 12.4.82. Off South Georgia 21.4.82 for Operation "Paraquat" and her Flight joined the attack on the submarine 'Santa Fe' on 25.4.82. To Leith 26.4.82 to take the surrender of the enemy garrison and remained on station. Assisted in the recovery of steel plate from the old whaling stations for use by the repair group late 5.82. Sailed from South Georgia on 17.6.82 for Southern Thule and Operation "Keyhole", for which she embarked a Wessex HU.5 of 848 Sqdn 'E' Flight. The surrender was secured on 20.6.82 and the ship returned to South Georgia on 24.6.82. Sailed 16.7.82 for a week's stay at Port Stanley before departing for the UK, arriving at Chatham on 20.8.82.

## ENGADINE

*Capt D.F.Freeman RFA*

Embarked 847 Sqdn 'A' Flt and a maintenance crew from 825 Sqdn then sailed from Devonport 10.5.82 on her first visit to the southern hemisphere. Routed via Gibraltar on 15.5.82 and Ascension 25/26.5.82, entering the TEZ 6.6.82 and the TRALA on 7.6.82. To San Carlos Water 9.6.82 to operate as a Wessex support ship and as a refuelling platform for the land-based helicopters. Moved to Port William on 27.6.82. Sailed from there for the UK on 7.7.82, calling briefly at San Carlos to collect 825 Sqdn personnel and damaged Sea King HAS.2A XV696. She passed Ascension 18.7.82 and arrived at Devonport on 30.7.82. The ship performed 450 deck fuellings and received 1,606 deck landings during Operation "Corporate".

## EXETER

*Capt H.M.Balfour MVO RN*

Sailed from Portsmouth 16.3.82 for duties as West Indies guardship and still there 29.4.82 despite Argentine claims that she was ablaze after hitting a mine! Dedicated to the Task

Although subjected to a determined attack by Grupo 5 de Caza A-4B Skyhawks in San Carlos Water on 23.5.82, 'Antelope' suffered relatively limited damage from the two bombs that struck her. Both failed to detonate and she is seen here after the attack (with her 815 Squadron Lynx XZ723 (321) still embarked) but before an attempt was made to defuse the first of the bombs. The attempt failed and a huge blast and subsequent fire consumed the frigate. Following magazine explosions, the ship broke her back and early the following day she sank. (Ministry of Defence)

Grupo 5 de Caza Skyhawks also destroyed 'Coventry'. A combination of equipment failure, errors of judgement and ill luck allowed the aircraft of Teniente Velasco to bomb her with some precision and her hull was ruptured by three 1,000lb bombs. 'Coventry' capsized one hour later, taking many men and the 815 Squadron Lynx XZ242 with her. She went down, some 10 miles north of Pebble Island, in the late afternoon of 25.5.82.
(Ministry of Defence)

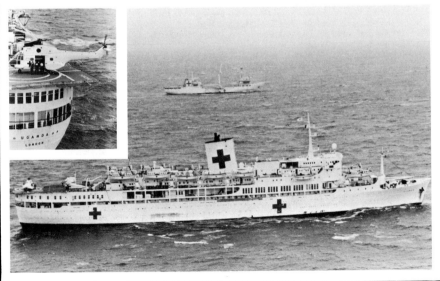

The P & O Cruise Liner 'Uganda' (foreground) was hastily converted into a hospital ship in early 4.82. Although not assigned her own helicopter, she was regularly visited by those of other vessels. She is seen here operating in the Red Cross Box with 'Bahia Paraiso', transferring Argentine casualties to Armada hospital ship via the latter's Puma helicopter (Inset). The Puma, presumed to be a CAB601 example supplied by the Ejercito, remained anonymous to the end of the conflict! (Ministry of Defence)

Force 7.5.82 as a result of the loss of 'Sheffield' and sailed from St John's, Antigua the same day. At Ascension on 14.5.82 and entered the TEZ on 21.5.82 to begin duties as a jammer picket 20 miles west of the CVBG. Shot down two Grupo 4 A-4C Skyhawks (C-301 and C-310) with Sea Darts during their attack on 'Avenger' 30.5.82. Shot down Grupo 2 Learjet 35A T-24 on 7.6.82 and Grupo 2 Canberra B.62 B-108 on 14.6.82, both with Sea Darts. She departed north for return to the UK on 7.7.82 (via Ascension on 18.7.82) and arrived at Portsmouth on 28.7.82.

## FEARLESS

*Capt E.S.J.Larken RN (awarded DSO)*

Sailed south from Portsmouth 6.4.82 with HQ 3 Cdo Bde and three 3 CBAS Scouts, embarking three 846 Sqdn Sea Kings from Portland on passing down the English Channel. Arrived at Ascension 17.4.82 and spent three weeks in assault training before continuing south 8.5.82. Joined by the 'Canberra' Group on 10.5.82 and made a rendezvous with the LSL's on the edge of the TEZ on 16.5.82 to complete the Amphibious Group. To San Carlos Water 21-27.5.82 for the landings, gunfire from the ship bringing down Grupo 5 A-4B Skyhawk C-215 on the latter date. Returned to San Carlos Water on 30.5.82. Her landing-craft L703 'Foxtrot 4' was attacked and sunk in Choiseul Sound on 8.6.82 by a Grupo 5 A-4B Skyhawk. To San Carlos Water once more on 13.6.82 and moved to Port William on 17.6.82, finally departing Port Stanley for the UK on 24.6.82 with four 846 Sqdn Sea Kings and two captured CAB601 A-109A's. She arrived at Devonport on 13.7.82 to disembark the Marines and aircraft before docking at Portsmouth on 14.7.82.

## FORT AUSTIN

*Cdre S.C.Dunlop CBE RFA (awarded DSO)*

Diverted from Exercise "Springtrain", sailing from Gibraltar on 29.3.82 to replenish 'Endurance' in the South Atlantic (having left 824 Sqdn 'B' Flt at RAF North Front). Arrived at Ascension 6.4.82 and embarked three 815 Sqdn Lynx HAS.2's followed by 845 Sqdn 'B' Flt on 7/8.4.82, sailing on 9.4.82 for the rendezvous with 'Endurance' 12.4.82. Set course northwards on 13.4.82, carrying out Lynx transfers to other ships on 17.4.82, and arrived at Ascension on 21.4.82. Departed south once more 23.4.82, entering the TEZ on 3.5.82 to operate as a helicopter maintenance base. Entered Falkland Sound on 21.5.82 for the landings and remained on station until departing for the UK from the TRALA on 7.6.82 (via Ascension 16.6.82), arriving at Devonport on 28.6.82.

## FORT GRANGE

*Capt D.G.M.Averill CBE RFA*

Departed Devonport 14.5.82 with 824 Sqdn 'C' Flt embarked after completing her refit one month early. Entered the TEZ 3.6.82 to rendezvous with the CVBG and spent eight days replenishing 25 vessels of the Task Force. Entered San Carlos Water to resupply the beachhead and ships, being used as a 24-hour helicopter refuelling station. Took on stores

from STUFT vessels for resupply to the Task Force and shore bases. Lost one Sea King on 11.7.82 during a VERTREP mission to 'Leeds Castle'. At Port Stanley 17.7.82 and remained on station until sailing north from the TEZ 17.9.82 en route to the UK. Disembarked 'C' Flight to Culdrose on 2.10.82 before arriving at Devonport on 3.10.82.

## GLAMORGAN

*Capt M.E.Barrow ADC RN (awarded DSO)*

Sailed from Portsmouth 17.3.82 for Exercise "Springtrain" but ordered to the South Atlantic 2.4.82, arriving at Ascension 11.4.82. Detached north 14.4.82 to meet the CVBG and then returned to Ascension 16.4.82. Continued south 18.4.82 and commenced her first bombardment action on 1.5.82, but when withdrawing from the Port Stanley area she suffered minor underwater damage from bombs which narrowly missed her during a Grupo 6 Dagger counter-attack. Detached 14.5.82 for the Pebble Island operations and on 16.5.82 for Operation "Tornado" until 21.5.82, but continued to detach each night for bombardment of the Port Stanley area. Entered Falkland Sound 22.5.82. Detached to the TRALA 30.5-11.6.82 for repairs and maintenance plus duties as TRALA "manager". Left 11.6.82 for NGS duties but hit 12.6.82 by a land-launched Exocet missile which destroyed the ship's Wessex HAS.3 and hangar. Fires were brought under control and she was back in service 36 hours later. Visited San Carlos Water 18.6.82. Sailed for the UK on 21.6.82 (via Ascension 29.6.82) and arrived at Portsmouth 10.7.82. Fired 1,450 4.5 inch rounds during the conflict (more than any other vessel) and seven Seaslugs.

## GLASGOW

*Capt A.P.Hoddinott OBE RN*

Sailed from Gibraltar 26.3.82 for participation in Exercise "Springtrain" but ordered to the South Atlantic 2.4.82 (via Ascension 11-14.4.82). Made a rendezvous with the CVBG on 23.4.82 and became the first surface vessel to enter the TEZ 1.5.82. Her Flight's Lynx attacked and severely damaged the Argentine patrol boat 'Alferez Sobral' on 3.5.82. During an attack by Grupo 5 A-4B Skyhawks off Port Stanley on 12.5.82 she was struck by a 500lb bomb which passed through both sides of the hull without exploding. Withdrawn to the edge of the TEZ for repairs before departing for the UK on 27.5.82 with her engines and propellers under manual control. Passed Ascension on 7.6.82 and arrived at Portsmouth 19.6.82 for a refit and repairs.

## GOOSANDER

*Capt A.MacGregor RMAS*

Sailed from Rosyth 2.5.82 for the South Atlantic and arrived at Ascension to lay and maintain mooring buoys for the ships using the Island's waters. Departed Ascension for the UK and arrived back at Rosyth 11.8.82.

## HECLA

*Capt G.L.Hope RN*

Sailed on 2.3.82 for a five-month deployment

in the North Atlantic and arrived at Gibraltar on 8.4.82 for a two week maintenance period. Ordered south on 14.4.82 and converted/repainted for the CASEVAC role before sailing 20.4.82. At Ascension 2/3.5.82. Joined the hospital ship 'Uganda' on 3.5.82 at a holding position some 1,500 miles south-west of Ascension, but ordered to the TEZ at full speed following the loss of 'Sheffield' 4.5.82, operating from the Red Cross Box (RCB) from 14.5.82. Detached from the RCB to Montevideo, Uruguay on 29.5.82 and arrived there 2.6.82 with the first British and Argentine casualties for repatriation. Returned to the RCB on 6.6.82 and then made a second trip to Montevideo with further casualties by 14.6.82. Sailed for the UK from a position 4 to 5 miles north of Falkland Sound on 29.6.82, arriving at Devonport on 29.7.82.

## HERALD

*Cdr R.I.C.Halliday RN*

Returned home to Portsmouth 7.4.82 for leave after six months on survey work in the Red Sea and Gulf of Oman. Tasked for Operation "Corporate" on 15.4.82, converted/repainted at Portsmouth for the CASEVAC role, and sailed 24.4.82. Diverted to Rio de Janeiro, Brazil on 14.5.82 with a sick seaman, arriving/departing 18.5.82, and then entered the RCB some 40 miles north of Falkland Sound on 25.5.82. Sailed from the RCB 8.6.82 to disembark casualties at Montevideo, Uruguay 13.6.82. Embarked further casualties alongside 'Uganda' in Grantham Sound 19.6.82 for disembarkation at Montevideo on 24/25.6.82. Transported 161 casualties in the two trips. Sailed for the UK (via Ascension 5.7.82), returning to Portsmouth on 21.7.82.

## HERMES

*Capt L.E.Middleton ADC RN (awarded DSO)*

Commenced embarkation of 800 (including integrated element of 899), 826 and 846 Sqdns plus part of 42 Cdo 'A' Coy on 2.4.82 from Portsmouth on 5.4.82 (1045Z) and arrived at Ascension 16.4.82 having embarked Rear Admiral John "Sandy" Woodward ("Springtrain" Commander) from 'Glamorgan' on 15.4.82 as the Task Force Commander. Departed Ascension on 18.4.82 as Flagship and entered the TEZ on 1.5.82. Operated east of the Falklands to minimise the chances of enemy air attacks. Detached on 14.5.82 for the Pebble Island operations, returning the next day. Remained on station until the Flagship role was transferred to 'Bristol' on 2.7.82. Entered Port William Sound on 3.7.82 to launch aircraft for a victory flypast over Port Stanley. Sailed for the UK on 4.7.82 via Ascension 11.7.82 and disembarked six Sea Harriers 19.7.82 from the Bay of Biscay. Arrived at Portsmouth on 21.7.82 and the remaining aircraft were disembarked the next day.

## HYDRA

*Cdr R.J.Campbell RN*

The vessel returned to Portsmouth on 4.3.82 after a six month deployment to the Caribbean. Tasked for Operation "Corporate" on 15.4.82 in the CASEVAC role, she was converted/repainted at Portsmouth and sailed south on 24.4.82 (via Ascension 8.5.82). Joined 'Uganda' on the edge of the TEZ 19.5.82, entering the RCB on 22.5.82. Detached east on 25.5.82 to collect casualties from 'Canberra', which were in turn transferred to 'Uganda' on 26.5.82 in the RCB. Sailed for Montevideo, Uruguay on 2.6.82 with casualties, arriving on 6.6.82. Diverted to stand by the Liberian tanker 'Hercules' which had been bombed by Grupo 2 Canberra B.62's on 8.6.82. To Grantham Sound 11.6.82 and embarked Red Cross delegates on 12.6.82 from the Argentine hospital ship 'Bahia Paraiso'. Sailed for Montevideo on 14.6.82, arriving 18.6.82, but returned to Port William on 23.6.82. To Montevideo again 24.6-5.7.82 and 7-17.7.82 (anchored there 29.6.82 and 12/13.7.82). Anchored in Port William Sound on 17.7.82. Moved to Port Stanley 18.7.82 and then made two round Falkland trips 26.7-5.8.82 and 11-19.8.82. Sailed from Port Stanley for the UK on 27.8.82, arriving at Portsmouth 24.9.82. Carried 251 casualties to Montevideo on her four trips.

## INTREPID

*Capt P.G.V.Dingemans RN (awarded DSO)*

At Portsmouth during 3.82 being de-stored prior to disposal, but hurriedly re-stored. Sailed from Portsmouth on 15.4.82 for work-up at Portland and then departed for the South Atlantic on 26.4.82 with two 845 Sqdn 'E' Flt Wessex HU.5's. One 846 Sqdn Sea King was embarked from Culdrose as the vessel passed down the English Channel. Arrived at Ascension 5.5.82 and transferred 845 Sqdn 'E' Flt to 'Tidepool' that day. Embarked two Wessex HU.5's of 845 Sqdn 'D' Flt on 7.5.82 before sailing south with the 'Fearless' Group. Carried out a rendezvous with the LSL's 16.5.82 on the edge of the TEZ. She embarked four 846 Sqdn Sea Kings on 19.5.82 and entered Falkland Sound on 21.5.82 for the assault. Landed 2 SG at Bluff Cove on 2.6.82. From 17-23.6.82 the ship was involved in assisting the civilian authorities in returning Island life to normal. Moved to Port William on 23.6.82 and embarked 29 Cdo Regt RA, sailing from Port Stanley on 26.6.82 for the UK with four 846 Sqdn Sea Kings aboard. Arrived at Devonport 13.7.82 to disembark troops and aircraft before docking at Portsmouth on 14.7.82.

## INVINCIBLE

*Capt J.J.Black MBE RN (awarded DSO)*

Arrived at Portsmouth 22.3.82 after participation in NATO Exercise "Alloy Express" off Norway. Embarked 801 (including integrated element of 899) and 899 Sqdns before sailing south from Portsmouth on 5.4.82 (at 1015Z) via Ascension 16-18.4.82. Entered the TEZ on 1.5.82 and operated east of the Falklands to minimise the chances of enemy air attacks. Detached on 17.5.82 with 'Broadsword' at high speed to the west for a covert operation off the South American mainland and returned 18.5.82. Remained on station after the surrender until she sailed north for a period of rest and recuperation from 17-30.6.82. Returned to the CVBG to relieve 'Hermes' and to provide fighter cover until relieved in turn by 'Illustrious'. Visited San Carlos Water 18.8.82 and entered Port William on 24.8.82

before departing for the UK on 28.8.82 (via Ascension 6/7.9.82) to arrive at Portsmouth on 17.9.82 after 166 days at sea, the longest period ever for continuous Carrier operations at sea (beating the USS Eisenhower's previous record by 13 days). During that period the vessel sailed 51,660 miles. 801 Sqdn flew off 17.9.82 followed by 820 Sqdn on 18.9.82.

## LEDBURY

*Lt Cdr A.Rose RN*

Sailed from Rosyth 15.5.82 for Portland, leaving on 7.6.82 for Portsmouth but returned to Portland the next day. Sailed for the South Atlantic on 13.6.82. Arrived at Port Stanley on 10.7.82 and spent five weeks on operations to clear Argentine minefields around the Falklands, moving to Ajax Bay 14.7.82 before returning to Port Stanley 25.7.82. Sailed for the UK on 13.8.82 to arrive at Rosyth 15.9.82.

## LEEDS CASTLE

*Lt Cdr C.F.B.Hamilton RN*

Arrived at Newcastle on 22.4.82 during North Sea patrol and ordered back to Rosyth, docking on 23.4.82. Moved to Portsmouth 26.4.82 to be fitted with communications equipment and a desalination plant on 27/28.4.82 before sailing for the South Atlantic via Portland on 29.4.82 (via Ascension 9-11.5.82). Entered the TEZ on 21.5.82 and began her role as a despatch vessel. Sailed for South Georgia on 25.5.82, arriving 27.5.82 to act as a fuel station for helicopters cross-decking stores and vehicles between 'Canberra', 'Norland' and 'Queen Elizabeth 2'. Sailed for Ascension 29.5.82 and arrived there on 6.6.82 to be detailed as the Island guardship for three weeks. Departed for the Falklands on 29.6.82, arriving at Port Stanley on 12.7.82 and Port San Carlos on 13.7.82 before returning to Port Stanley on 15.7.82. Sailed from there on 18.7.82, joining the CVBG on 19.7.82 and then moved to South Georgia on 20.7.82. Arrived at Grytviken 22.7.82 before departing for the UK 24.7.82 via Ascension (and Gibraltar 13-15.8.82), arriving at Rosyth 20.8.82 after sailing 26,944 miles.

## MINERVA

*Cdr S.H.G.Johnston RN*

At Devonport for a refit 3/4.82 but that was postponed and the ship prepared for deployment. She sailed from Devonport with the 'Bristol' Group on 10.5.82 for the South Atlantic (via Ascension 18/19.5.82) and entered the TEZ on 26.5.82. Relieved the damaged 'Argonaut' as AAWC in San Carlos Water on 29.5.82 and her Flight boarded the Argentine hospital ship 'Bahia Paraiso' 31.5.82 to inspect her. Joined the CVBG 3.6.82 but returned to San Carlos Water on 8.6.82 with 'Engadine' and the MCM trawlers. Sailed for Port William 16.6.82 and relieved by 'Penelope' on 14.7.82. Left for the UK on 15.7.82 (via Ascension 23/24.7.82) to arrive at Devonport on 3.8.82.

## OLMEDA

*Capt G.P.Overbury RFA (awarded OBE)*

Left Devonport for the South Atlantic on

5.4.82 with 824 Sqdn 'A' Flt and joined the CVBG on 6.4.82. Arrived at Ascension on 16.4.82 and departed 18.4.82, entering TEZ on 1.5.82 to begin her tanker duties around the Task Force. Detached on 16.6.82 for South Georgia en route to Operation "Keyhole", embarking 'M' Coy 42 Cdo at South Georgia 18.6.82 before arriving off Southern Thule 20.6.82 for the assault and retaking of the dependency. Refuelled 'Yarmouth' on 21.6.82 at latitude 59°15' South, probably the most southerly RAS ever carried out by the Royal Navy. Ordered back to the UK 21.6.82 (via Ascension 30.6/1.7.82) and disembarked 'A' Flt to Culdrose 10.7.82 before docking at Devonport on 12.7.82.

## OLNA

*Capt J.A.Bailey RFA*

Sailed from Portland on 22.2.82 for Gibraltar with 772 Sqdn 'C' Flt and 824 Sqdn 'B' Flt embarked, the latter being transferred to RAF North Front for Exercise "Springtrain" before 'Olna' departed to join Gulf Patrol. At Mombasa, Kenya on 5.4.82 but ordered to the UK, arriving at Portland on 22.4.82 to re-store before sailing on 26.4.82 for Portsmouth (arriving the next day). Embarked 848 Sqdn 'B' Flt and sailed south on 10.5.82 (via Ascension 18/19.5.82). Entered the TEZ 25.5.82 and commenced tanker duties 29.5.82 in the CVBG before departing to San Carlos Water 7.6.82. Detached to the TRALA 10.6.82 to re-fuel from STUFT tankers and moved to San Carlos Water on 13.6.82. Sailed to the TRALA again 16.6.82 before anchoring in Port William Sound on 20.6.82. Moved to San Carlos Water the next day and returned to Port William on 27.6.82. Sailed to ride out a storm on 30.6.82, returned on 1.7.82 and detached to the CVBG 8.7.82. Present in San Carlos Water 28.7-2.8.82 and 11/12.8.82 and arrived at Port William 13.8.82. Sailed on 17.8.82 for the CVBG, detaching 21.8.82 to a position 800 miles north of the Falklands to refuel 'Illustrious' on 24.8.82. Joined by 'Invincible' on 31.8.82 and began her journey back to the UK. Passed Ascension 6/7.9.82 and disembarked 'B' Flt on 16.9.82 before arriving at Portsmouth on 17.9.82, having carried out 143 RAS operations to 54 ships.

## ONYX

*Lt Cdr A.J.Johnson RN*

Sailed from Gosport on 26.4.82 for the South Atlantic, the only diesel-electric submarine to be deployed during the conflict. Believed to have been used to "take off" Special Forces personnel from the Argentine mainland near the Rio Grande naval air base. She struck an uncharted rock which damaged two torpedo tubes, jamming a torpedo inside one of them. Sailed for the UK and arrived at Gosport on 18.8.82.

## PEARLEAF

*Capt J.McCulloch RFA*

Sailed south from Portsmouth on 5.4.82 carrying Heavy Furnace Fuel Oil for 'Hermes', the only RN vessel to use it. She carried out RAS refuelling trials with 'Canberra' off Ascension on 22.4.82 and departed the Island with the LSL's, joining the

'Fearless' Group on 16.5.82. Relieved 'Blue Rover' as station tanker at South Georgia on 4.6.82 until she moved north on 18.6.82 to refuel other ships en route to and from the Falklands. Remained on station until sailing for the UK via Gibraltar 2-9.8.82 to arrive at Devonport 13.8.82.

## PENELOPE

*Cdr P.V.Rickard RN*

Recommissioned on 22.1.82 after conversion and commenced sea trials from 12-15.4.82 and 19.4-5.5.82. She sailed south from Devonport with the 'Bristol' Group on 10.5.82 (via Ascension 18/19.5.82). Entered the TEZ on 25.5.82 and joined the CVBG overnight. Detached to San Carlos Water 30.5.82 and assisted the damaged 'Argonaut'. Detached 1.6.82 to the north-east of the Falklands to collect an air-drop which included the new CO of 2 PARA, Lt Col David Chaundler. She rejoined the CVBG on 3.6.82. To San Carlos Water on 4.6.82 for escort duties until 14.6.82, although she was detached on 9.6.82 for a clandestine operation on an island north of West Falkland. Her Flight attacked the coastal patrol craft 'Rio Iguazu' in Choiseul Sound 13.6.82. Moved to Port Stanley late 6.82 until she sailed on 23.8.82 for the UK via Dakar, arriving at Devonport 10.9.82.

## PLUMLEAF

*Capt R.W.M.Wallace RFA*

The ship had completed her commitment to Exercise "Springtrain" on 6.4.82 and was preparing for Far East deployment with 'Broadsword' and 'Yarmouth' when ordered to conduct RAS trials with 'Canberra' and 'Elk' 10/11.4.82. Arrived at Portland 12.4.82 for last-minute stores before departing on 19.4.82 for the South Atlantic (via Ascension 1-3.5.82). Joined the LSL group 11.5.82 before transferring most of her remaining fuel load to 'Pearleaf' and returning north to refuel from 'British Dart'. Headed south again to refuel the 'Bristol' Group before taking up position at 40°S as a refuelling station. Exchanged position with 'Appleleaf' in early 6.82, moving to 25°S for two weeks, then returned to Ascension for two days late 6.82. Directed to station off the Canary Islands as a tanker for the ships returning and their replacements heading south. Carried out her final RAS operations 10.7.82 with 'Fearless' and 'Intrepid' before arriving at Gibraltar on 22.7.82. Based at Gibraltar on RAS duties until she returned to Portsmouth on 26.8.82, having issued 20,000 tons of fuel in 55 RAS operations and received 11,000 tons in refuellings from the BP tankers.

## PLYMOUTH

*Capt D.Pentreath RN (awarded DSO)*

Ordered to the South Atlantic on 2.4.82 from Exercise "Springtrain". Detached from the Advanced Group on 7.4.82 for South Georgia and Operation "Paraquat" (via Ascension 10-12.4.82). Joined 'Endurance' 14.4.82 and was in position off South Georgia 21.4.82. Her Flight was involved in the attack on the Argentine submarine 'Santa Fe' on 25.4.82 and the surrender of South Georgia was signed aboard on 26.4.82. Joined the CVBG 29.4.82

and entered the TEZ on 1.5.82. She was detached to the LSL Group 8.5.82 as an escort, merging with the 'Fearless' Group on 16.5.82 to complete the Amphibious Group. Acted as escort to the landings on 21.5.82. Some sources believe that a Seacat launched from 'Plymouth' or 'Avenger' brought down the Grupo 6 Dagger C-428 that day. A Seawolf from 'Broadsword' is a more likely candidate. She commenced bombardment support until 29.5.82, rejoining the CVBG on 30.5.82. Returned to San Carlos Water on 1.6.82 for day air defence and night patrol duties until 8.6.82 when seriously damaged in an air attack by Grupo 6 Daggers which caused a 6° list. Detached to the east 9.6.82 for repairs and returned to Port Stanley on 14.6.82 to resume bombardment duties which were cancelled following the surrender. She entered Port Stanley on 17.6.82, moved to San Carlos on 18.6.82 and then rejoined the CVBG on 20.6.82. Sailed for the UK (via Ascension 29.6.82 and Gibraltar 7-9.7.82) and arrived at Rosyth on 14.7.82 for a refit. Fired 909 4.5 inch shells and nine Seacat missiles during the conflict.

## REGENT

*Capt J.Logan RFA*

Departed south from Portland on 19.4.82 with 848 Sqdn 'A' Flt embarked, arriving at Ascension 29.4.82. Sailed on 2.5.82, entering the TEZ on 12.5.82 to commence her replenishment duties. She detached on 8.6.82 for South Georgia (arriving there on 11.6.82) as her Flight was required to embark 'Olmeda' for Operation "Keyhole" (the recapture of Southern Thule). The Flight returned 24.6.82 and the ship transitted the TEZ 28.6-1.7.82 to rejoin the CVBG. Anchored off Port Stanley 6-13.7.82 and operated in Berkeley Sound from 13.7-24.8.82. Returned to the UK (via Ascension), 'A' Flt disembarking on 12.9.82 before the ship arrived at Rosyth on 15.9.82.

## RESOURCE

*Capt B.A.Seymour RFA*

Departed Rosyth on 6.4.82 with 845 Sqdn 'A' Flt and part of 'Z' Coy 45 Cdo embarked, completing her stores VERTREP off Culdrose 7.4.82. Arrived at Ascension 17.4.82 and departed the next day. Carried out a rendezvous with 'Canberra' on 23.5.82 170 miles north north-east of Port Stanley to VERTREP stores and ammunition for unloading in San Carlos Water on 24.5.82. At South Georgia on 2.6.82 and operating in the TRALA on 8.6.82. Arrived at Port Stanley 17.6.82 before sailing for South Georgia 26.6.82. Arrived there 27.6.82 and then left for the UK (via Ascension 29.6-8.7.82), docking at Devonport on 19.7.82.

## SHEFFIELD

*Capt J.F.T.G.Salt RN*

Sailed from Portsmouth 19.11.81 for Gulf Patrol and due back 6.4.82 after participation in Exercise "Springtrain", for which she left Gibraltar on 26.3.82. Diverted to the South Atlantic on 2.4.82 as part of the Advanced Group (via Ascension 11-14.4.82), taking over command of the Group when 'Brilliant' detached to South Georgia on 22.4.82. Hit by a 2

Escuadrilla Super Etendard-launched Exocet missile on 4.5.82 while on forward radar picket duty 70 miles south-east of Port Stanley (52°46′S 57°07′W). The missile failed to explode on impact, but fires from its burning fuel got out of control and the ship was abandoned (21 crew died as a result of the attack). Taken in tow by 'Yarmouth' on 9.5.82 for safe harbour at South Georgia but sank on 10.5.82 in stormy seas (53°04′S 56°56′W).

## SIR BEDIVERE

*Capt P.J.McCarthy RFA (awarded OBE)*

Returned to Marchwood from a West Indies deployment before sailing for the South Atlantic on 29.4.82 (via Ascension 8-13.5.82). Entered the TEZ 18.5.82 and arrived in San Carlos Water on 23.5.82. Rejoined the CVBG 26.5.82 but had returned to San Carlos Water by 2.6.82 for resupply of the beachhead and remained there until 15.6.82. Moved to Port William 16.6.82 and still there 25.6.82, remaining on station in the Islands for general resupply duties. Finally sailed from San Carlos 25.10.82 with 64 coffins for re-burial in the UK, arriving at Marchwood on 16.11.82.

## SIR GALAHAD

*Capt P.J.G.Roberts RFA (awarded DSO)*

Left Devonport 6.4.82 for the South Atlantic with three 3 CBAS Gazelle AH.1's embarked, arriving at Ascension on 19/20.4.82. Departed 29.4.82 and (with the Amphibious Group) joined the Task Force on 19.5.82. Entered San Carlos Water on 21.5.82 for the landings and was still there 24.5.82 when hit by a 500lb bomb which failed to explode (it was later lifted overboard). Embarked the Welsh Guards on 7.6.82 and moved to Port Pleasant, but on 8.6.82 she was attacked by Grupo 5 A-4B Skyhawks and hit by two bombs which caused fires and set off ammunition, severely damaging the ship. Towed out to sea by 'Typhoon' on 24.6.82 to be sunk as a war grave on 26.6.82.

## SIR GERAINT

*Capt D.E.Lawrence RFA (awarded DSC)*

Left Devonport 6.4.82 for the South Atlantic with three 3 CBAS Gazelle AH.1's and part of 'Z' Coy 45 Cdo embarked, arriving at Ascension 19/20.4.82. Departed 29.4.82 and joined the main Task Force on 19.5.82 as part of the Amphibious Group. Took part in the initial assault landings in San Carlos Water 21.5.82 and in the subsequent resupply missions. Departed for the UK late 6.82 and arrived at Marchwood on 23.7.82.

## SIR LANCELOT

*Capt C.A.Purtcher-Wydenbruck RFA (awarded OBE)*

Left Marchwood 6.4.82 for the South Atlantic with three 3 CBAS Gazelle AH.1's and part of HQ Coy 45 Cdo embarked, arriving at Ascension 19/20.4.82. Continued south on 29.4.82 to join the Amphibious Group before a rendezvous with the main Task Force on 19.5.82. Took part in the initial assault landings 21.5.82, remaining on resupply missions. During an enemy air raid on 24.5.82 the ship was hit by a bomb which failed to explode, but caused fires and damaged her aft end. Once repaired with the bomb removed, she continued operations until going alongside 'Stena Seaspread' by 23.6.82 for further repairs which were completed on 28.6.82. Sailed for the UK 26.7.82, arriving at Portsmouth on 18.8.82.

## SIR PERCIVALE

*Capt A.F.Pitt RFA (awarded DSC)*

Left Marchwood 5.4.82 with three 3 CBAS Gazelle AH.1's and part of HQ Coy 45 Cdo, anchoring overnight in Lyme Bay. Joined the other LSL's off Plymouth 6.4.82 and sailed for the South Atlantic, arriving at Ascension 19/20.4.82. Sailed on 29.4.82 to join the Amphibious Group, arriving with the main Task Force on 19.5.82. Entered San Carlos Water 21.5.82 for the initial assault landings at Ajax Bay. Rejoined the CVBG 25.5.82 and helped to search for and rescue survivors from 'Atlantic Conveyor'. Returned to San Carlos Water and embarked 300 PoW's 30.5.82 for accommodation, but they were disembarked on 31.5.82 for the ship to make a priority trip to Teal Inlet with 600 troops. Sailed 2.6.82 for Teal Inlet and acted as a key refuelling facility, making several more trips from San Carlos to Teal Inlet. 57 helicopters were refuelled on 5.6.82 alone. Moved to Port Stanley on 16.6.82, the first ship to enter the port after the surrender, after which she provided accommodation for three days of rest for 45 Cdo. Took personnel from 'C' and 'M' Flts of 3 CBAS from Teal to Stanley on 23.6.82. Made a further trip to Teal before sailing for the UK on 28.6.82 (via Ascension on 8.7.82) to arrive at Marchwood 23.7.82.

## SIR TRISTRAM

*Capt G.R.Green RFA (awarded DSC)*

Departed Belize 2.4.82 and joined the Amphibious Force, arriving at Ascension by 20.4.82 and departing on 29.4.82 with two 3 CBAS Scout AH.1's embarked from the other vessels. Joined the main Task Force on 19.5.82, taking part in the initial assault landings at San Carlos on 21.5.82. Landed the Scots Guards at Fitzroy on 2.6.82 in company with 'Fearless'. Moved the Welsh Guards to Fitzroy on 8.6.82 but, whilst unloading, was attacked by Grupo 5 A-4B Skyhawks and was struck by two bombs which failed to explode. Suffered small fires and damage to the aft end and was initially abandoned. Later repaired and towed by 'Typhoon' to Port Stanley during 6.82 for use as an alongside accommodation ship. In 5.83 she was loaded onto the semi-submersible heavy-lift ship 'Dan Lifter' at Stanley, sailing for the UK on 16.5.83 and arriving in the Tees on 13.6.83. Unloaded 14.6.83 and towed by the tug 'Cragsider' from the Tees to the Tyne on 15.6.83 for a survey prior to refit and repair. Returned to RFA service c9.10.85

## SPARTAN

*Cdr J.B.Taylor RN (MID)*

Operating from Gibraltar on Exercise "Springtrain" when ordered south. Exchanged practice torpedoes for live ones from 'Oracle' at Gibraltar before sailing 1.4.82. Off Port

Stanley 12.4.82 (the first submarine in the MEZ), her task being to blockade the port. Returned to Devonport on 24.7.82 having spent three months submerged.

## SPLENDID

*Cdr R.C.Lane-Nott RN (MID)*

Sailed south from Faslane on 1.4.82. Tasked with surveillance of the Argentine carrier '25 de Mayo' and patrol duties off the Argentine coast. Returned to the UK, arriving at Devonport 12.6.82.

## STROMNESS

*Capt J.B.Dickinson RFA (awarded OBE)*

Left Portsmouth 7.4.82 for the South Atlantic with part of 'Z' Coy 45 Cdo embarked along with 2,750 tons of equipment. Arrived at Ascension by 20.4.82, departing south with the 'Fearless' Group on 8.5.82 to join the LSL's on the edge of the TEZ 16.5.82. First RFA vessel to enter Falkland Sound on 21.5.82 for the landings. Remained in San Carlos Water for six days and then sailed for South Georgia with survivors from 'Coventry', who were transferred to the 'Queen Elizabeth 2' on 28.5.82 in exchange for 400 troops plus ammunition and Rapier missiles from 'Lycaon'. Returned to San Carlos early 6.82 to unload, then present in the TRALA 5-14.6.82 for VERTREP operations, mainly to 'Canberra'. Returned to South Georgia to re-store from 'Saxonia' for four days then arrived at Port William by 25.6.82. Sailed for the UK late 6.82 with 45 Cdo (who disembarked at Ascension 7/8.7.82 for the flight home), arriving at Portsmouth on 19.7.82.

## TIDEPOOL

*Capt J.W.Gaffrey RFA*

Sold to the Chilean Navy and, after a refit on the Tyne, was on delivery with a joint Royal Navy/Chilean Navy crew when the conflict began. Loaned back to the Royal Navy by Chile, whose crew were replaced by RN personnel. Took on stores at Curacao and arrived at Ascension 27.4.82. 845 Sqdn 'E' Flt transferred from 'Intrepid' 5.5.82 and sailed south with the ship 6.5.82. Joined the 'Fearless' Group on 11.5.82 and then the LSL's 16.5.82 on the edge of the TEZ. Entered the TEZ on 18.5.82 and suffered a minor collision with 'Ambuscade' on 22.5.82 during tanker duties. Detached to San Carlos Water 1/2.6.82 and then in the TRALA from 8-13.6.82. Remained on station until handed over to Chile during 8.82, the Royal Navy crew returning to Gatwick Airport on 16.8.82. Carried out 114 fuel and ammunition transfers during the deployment.

## TIDESPRING

*Capt S.Redmond RFA (awarded OBE)*

Departed Portsmouth on 15.3.82 for Exercise "Springtrain" but was detached to the South Atlantic 2.4.82. She was ordered to South Georgia 7.4.82 for Operation "Paraquat", arriving at Ascension 10.4.82 to embark 845 Sqdn 'C' Flt on 11.4.82 before continuing south the following day. Carried out a ren-

dezvous with 'Endurance' 14.4.82 and in position off South Georgia 21.4.82. Both Wessex HU.5's of 'C' Flt were lost 22.4.82 during the recovery of troops from the Fortuna Glacier in bad weather. After the surrender of South Georgia she embarked PoW's on 27.4.82 and sailed for Ascension (arriving on 12.5.82). Embarked two replacement Wessex HU.5's 15.5.82 and sailed south once more 16.5.82 to enter the TEZ on 27.5.82, commencing tanker duties around the Task Force. 'C' Flt transferred to 'Hermes' on 3.7.82 and the ship sailed for the UK (via Ascension), arriving at Portsmouth on 22.7.82.

## TYPHOON

*Capt J.N.Morris RMAS (until 21.7.82)*
*Capt B.Stephens RMAS (from 21.7.82)*

Sailed from Portland 4.4.82 with Naval Party 1810 embarked, arriving at Ascension by 20.4.82 to spend 12 days providing fresh water to the Task Force ships. Sailed for South Georgia and arrived at Grytviken by 27.5.82. Remained there for a month helping to pump out the Argentine submarine 'Santa Fe' (from which she recovered the battle ensign) and transferring the Gurkhas, Welsh and Scots Guards on 27/28.5.82 from 'Queen Elizabeth 2' to 'Canberra'. Operating in the TRALA 12.6.82. Moved to the Falklands to take the still burning 'Sir Galahad' in tow 24.6.82 for sinking 26.6.82 as a war grave. Later towed 'Sir Tristram' to Stanley for use as an accommodation ship. Ferried stores, water and a total of 1,500 troops between the Task Force ships. Sailed from the Falklands early 9.82 and arrived at Portsmouth on 24.9.82.

## VALIANT

*Cdr T.M.Le Marchand RN (MID)*

Sailed south from Faslane on 3.5.82 for patrol duties off the Argentine coast. Returned to the UK, arriving at Faslane on 29.7.82.

## YARMOUTH

*Cdr A.Morton RN (awarded DSC)*

Taking part in Exercise "Springtrain" and due for Far East deployment, she sailed from Gibraltar on 5.4.82 for Naples, but was ordered to return and arrived back at Gibraltar on 6.4.82. Sailed south on 8.4.82 to rendezvous with the 'Fearless' Group the next day and then detached towards the CVBG 10.4.82 (reached on 11.4.82). At Ascension 16-18.4.82 and entered the TEZ 1.5.82. Detached with 'Brilliant' for ASW action to the north-east of the Falklands when the suspected submarine ('San Luis') was not found. Rejoined the CVBG on 2.5.82 and helped to rescue survivors from 'Sheffield' on 4.5.82. Detached 8.5.82 to locate the abandoned hulk of 'Sheffield', taking her in tow on 9.5.82, but she rolled over and sank on 10.5.82. Made a rendezvous with the Amphibious Group on 19.5.82, acting as escort during the landings on 21.5.82. On AAW station in San Carlos Water 22.5-1.6.82. Accompanied by 'Brilliant', she intercepted the Argentine motor vessel 'Monsunen' on 22.5.82 and drove it aground. Rejoined the CVBG on 5.6.82 and tasked with bombardment duties until the surrender on 14.6.82. Sailed 15.6.82 for the retaking of Southern Thule and then returned to Port Stanley 25.6.82 with PoW's. Took part in the "Falktrain" programme from 27.6.82 before sailing for the UK 7.7.82 (via Ascension 16/17.8.82), arriving at Rosyth 28.7.82. Fired over 1,000 4.5 inch rounds during the campaign (some 32 tons of shells).

## CAPTURED ARGENTINE AND RECAPTURED FALKLAND ISLANDS SHIPPING

### FALKLAND SOUND *(1967) 494 GRT*

A Merchant Oil Rig Tender, previously named 'Yehuin' and owned by Geomatter SA of Buenos Aires. Commandeered by the Argentine Armada for work in the Falklands during 4.82, but captured by British forces on 15.6.82 and taken over by a crew from 'Fearless' 18.6.82. Renamed 'Falkland Sound' (although affectionately known as the 'Black Pig') and operated around Port Stanley and Port William until 2.7.82, including a shuttle service from Port William to 'Canberra' 21/22.6.82 ferrying troops for return to the UK. Handed over to another RN crew 2.7.82; later operated by NP1242.

### FORREST *(1967) 144 GRT*

A Motor Cargo Ship owned by the Falkland Islands Government. Left Port Stanley 1.4.82 to carry out a radar watch on the sea approaches. Reported radar contacts approaching in the early hours of 2.4.82 and the Argentines invaded shortly thereafter. Commandeered by the Argentine forces, returning to British control after the surrender on 14.6.82. Operated a shuttle service at Port William, taking PoW's (16.6.82) and British troops (22/23.6.82) to 'Canberra'. Carried out various other military duties before return to normal operations.

### MONSUNEN *(1957) 230 GRT*

A Motor Cargo Ship owned by the Falkland Islands Company and commandeered by the Argentine forces 4.82 to ferry troops and equipment within the Falkland Islands. Intercepted by 'Brilliant' & 'Yarmouth' Flight helicopters 23.5.82 in Choiseul Sound and run aground to be abandoned by the Argentine crew on the south-east coast of East Falkland near Goose Green/Lively Sound. After being beached on 23.5.82 she was towed to Darwin by 'Forrest' on 24.5.82. Salvaged by the Royal Navy and taken over by 4.6.82, under command of an officer from 'Fearless', to ferry British troops from Goose Green to Bluff Cove early 6.82 and later to carry out inter-island duties (used to rescue survivors from the 'Fearless' LCU 'Foxtrot 4' on 8.6.82).

### TIGER BAY

*Lt S.Hambrook RN*

A Z-28 patrol craft built in West Germany during 1979 for the Prefectura Naval Argentina (PNA) as the 'Islas Malvinas' and in use with the Argentine forces in the Falklands. Damaged on 1.5.82 by GPMG attack from 'Alacrity' Flight's Lynx whilst sheltering near Lively Island and returned to Port Stanley. Captured there following the surrender,

repaired, then put into operation by a crew from 'Cardiff' who renamed the ship 'HMS Tiger Bay'. Repaired with parts from sister ship 'Rio Iguazu' (attacked 22.5.82 by Sea Harriers and 13.6.82 by 'Penelope' Flight's Lynx) which was too badly damaged to be of use. Later transferred to NP1242 and used for general maintenance. Loaded on board the heavy-lift ship 'Dyvi Swan' 8.83 for return to the UK and off-loaded in the Solent 8.9.83 to be towed into Portsmouth.

## RN, RFA & RCT SHIPS DEPLOYED 15 JUNE — 31 DECEMBER 1982

### AMAZON

*Cdr I.Garnett RN*

Left Devonport 2.8.82 for the South Atlantic as an escort for 'Illustrious'. Returned to the UK to arrive at Devonport on 19.11.82.

### ANTRIM

*Capt B.G.Young RN*

Sailed from Portsmouth 8.11.82 on her second visit to the South Atlantic. Patrolled until returned to Portsmouth on 25.3.83.

### ANTWERP *Operated by the RCT*

Loaded aboard 'Strathewe' which left Southampton for the South Atlantic 28.6.82. Arrived at Port William on 17.7.82 where 'Antwerp' was unloaded and used as a general Army transport around the Islands until 8.83 when she was loaded aboard the heavy-lift vessel 'Dyvi Swan'. Returned to the UK and was off-loaded in the Solent on 8.9.83 to be towed to Portsmouth.

### APOLLO

*Cdr C.M.Sloane RN*

Sailed from Devonport on 18.6.82 for the South Atlantic, joining 'Invincible' on 7.7.82 and noted at Port Stanley 15.7.82. Sailed for the UK, arriving at Devonport 17.10.82 with cracks in her superstructure due to the heavy sea conditions.

### ARIADNE

*Cdr D.Evans RN*

Departed from Devonport on 8.11.82 for the South Atlantic and patrolled until she returned to Devonport 25.3.83.

### ARROMANCHES *Operated by the RCT*

Loaded aboard 'Strathewe' which left Southampton for the South Atlantic 28.6.82. Arrived at Port William on 17.7.82 where 'Arromanches' was unloaded and used as a general Army transport around the Islands until 8.83 when she was loaded aboard the heavy-lift vessel 'Dyvi Swan'. Returned to the UK and was off-loaded in the Solent on 8.9.83 to be towed to Portsmouth.

### BACCHANTE

*Cdr A.C.Lyddon RN*

Sailed from Portsmouth on 17.5.82 for Gibraltar to be held in reserve for the Task Force. Departed Gibraltar 20.6.82 for a rendezvous with the 'Birmingham' Group, proceeding with them to the South Atlantic and joining the CVBG on 7.7.82. Patrolled until she sailed for the UK, arriving at Portsmouth 30.8.82 flying her paying-off pennant. Handed over to the RNZN on 1.10.82 as 'HMNZS Wellington' and departed 11.10.82 on passage to New Zealand.

### BATTLEAXE

*Capt D.Nolan RN*

Left Devonport on 2.8.82 for the South Atlantic as an escort for 'Illustrious' and arrived in the Falklands area 24.8.82. Patrolled until she left for the UK 24.10.82 (via Gibraltar 12/13.11.82), arriving at Devonport on 19.11.82.

### BIRMINGHAM

*Cdr J.E.Culley RN*

After a year long refit (completed 3.82) and work-up, she sailed from Portsmouth 18.6.82 for the South Atlantic, joining 'Invincible' 7.7.82. Patrolled until she left for home, arriving at Portsmouth on 17.10.82.

### BRAZEN

*Capt N.F.Dingemans RN*

Commissioned on 2.7.82 and after work-up sailed from Devonport on 6.10.82 for the South Atlantic to relieve 'Battleaxe' off the Falklands on 24.10.82. Patrolled until mid-12.82 when she sailed for the UK via Gibraltar, arriving at Devonport 6.1.83.

### CHARYBDIS

*Cdr N.Westberg RN*

Recommissioned on 6.8.82. Departed Devonport 8.11.82 for the South Atlantic and patrolled the Falklands until leaving for the UK via Dakar and Madeira, arriving at Devonport 25.3.83.

### DANAE

*Cdr G.L.D.W.Gough RN*

Left Devonport on 18.6.82 for the South Atlantic and joined 'Invincible' 7.7.82. Remained on station until she returned to Devonport 17.10.82.

### DIOMEDE

*Cdr W.L.T.Peppe RN*

Departed Portsmouth 22.6.82 for the South Atlantic and joined 'Invincible' 7.7.82. Returned to the UK to arrive at Portsmouth 17.10.82.

### FORT AUSTIN

*Capt R.M.Thorn RFA*

Left Devonport 26.8.82 on her second trip south. Embarked 848 Sqdn 'C' Flt from 'Olwen' 27.9.82 (transferred to 845 Sqdn aboard 'Illustrious' 16.10.82). Returned to the UK and anchored in Plymouth Sound 17.12.82.

## FORT GRANGE

*Capt D.G.M.Averill RFA*

Sailed from Devonport 19.11.82 and embarked four 826 Sqdn Sea Kings off Culdrose on 21.11.82. On station 31.12.82 with the aircraft operating as a Flight from RAF Stanley. Returned to the UK and arrived at Devonport 24.6.83.

## GLASGOW

*Capt A.P.Hoddinott OBE RN*

Repaired and refitted (including the addition of two twin Oerlikon 30mm and two single Oerlikon 20mm guns) and departed Portsmouth 6.9.82 on her second trip to the South Atlantic. Returned to the UK to arrive at Portsmouth 20.12.82.

## HECATE

*Lt Cdr B.W.Miller RN*

Repainted grey overall and fitted with two 20mm guns at Devonport during 6.82. To Portland for a short work-up and then sailed 23.7.82 from the Portland sea areas to the South Atlantic as a temporary ice patrol vessel while 'Endurance' returned to the UK for a refit. Departed the Falklands during 1.83, sailing around Cape Horn and visiting Talcahuano, Chile before proceeding north through the Pacific Ocean and the Panama Canal to Antigua. Returned to Devonport on 18.2.83.

## ILLUSTRIOUS

*Capt J.Slater RN*

Fitted with two Vulcan Phalanx CIWS guns and arrived at Portsmouth 21.6.82, having commissioned at sea the previous day. Worked-up at Portland from 24.6.82 and departed Portsmouth on 2.8.82 for the South Atlantic, embarking 809 Sqdn Sea Harriers, 814 Sqdn Sea King HAS.5's and 824 Sqdn Sea King AEW.2's the same day in the English Channel. Took on stores off Ascension 16.8.82 and relieved 'Invincible' 28.8.82, taking over from 'Bristol' as the South Atlantic Force Flagship. Sailed from the Falklands late 10.82 and returned to the UK via Puerto Rico and the USA (Fort Lauderdale and Philadelphia). Disembarked her aircraft in Mounts Bay on 6/7.12.82 and returned to Portsmouth on 8.12.82.

## LIVERPOOL

*Capt F.Grenier RN*

Left Portsmouth on 8.11.82 for the South Atlantic and remained on station until she departed for Devonport on 28.3.83.

## MINERVA

*Cdr A.N.Law RN*

Sailed from Devonport 29.11.82 on her second visit to the South Atlantic and remained on patrol until she departed for the UK, returning to Devonport on 24.3.83.

## NEWCASTLE

*Capt A.D.Hutton RN*

Left Portsmouth 6.9.82 for the South Atlantic and remained on station until returning to Portsmouth on 20.12.82.

## OLMEDA

*Capt G.P.Overbury RFA (awarded OBE)*

Left Devonport on 6.9.82 for her second trip to the South Atlantic and remained on station until returning to Devonport on 19.12.82.

## OLWEN

*Capt J.McLaughlin RFA*

Undergoing a refit at Gibraltar early 1982 and departed 7.6.82 upon completion. Arrived at Devonport 10.6.82 and embarked 848 Sqdn 'C' Flt before sailing south on 16.6.82. Arrived at Ascension 28.6.82, continuing south on 9.7.82 with 'Norland'. Arrived in the Falklands on 20.7.82 and embarked the changeover garrison for South Georgia, departing 22.7.82 to arrive at Grytviken on 24.7.82. Returned to Port Stanley 26.7.82 and joined the CVBG the next day. Operated in the CVBG until 6.8.82 and from 10-17.8.82, 21-30.8.82, 2-6.9.82, 8.9.82, 17-25.9.82, anchoring at Port San Carlos 7-10.8.82, Berkeley Sound 18-20.8.82, 31.8/1.9.82, 7.9.82, 9-16.9.82 and at Port San Carlos 26.9.82. Transferred 'C' Flt to 'Fort Austin' on 27.9.82 before sailing for the UK, arriving at Devonport on 25.10.82.

## PHOEBE

*Cdr W.F.G.Griffin RN*

Departed Devonport 6.9.82 for the South Atlantic and remained on station until returning to Devonport on 19.12.82.

## SIRIUS

*Cdr P.J.Melson RN*

Rededicated 24.6.82 at Devonport following a refit there. Departed Devonport 6.9.82 for the South Atlantic but had to put into Gibraltar for two days for repairs after hitting a whale in the Bay of Biscay. Patrolled in Falklands Waters until returning to Devonport 19.12.82.

## SOUTHAMPTON

*Capt H.G.De Courcy-Ireland RN*

Left Portsmouth on 18.6.82 for the South Atlantic and joined 'Invincible' 7.7.82. Remained on station until returning to Portsmouth 17.10.82.

## TIDESPRING

*Capt S.Redmond RFA (awarded OBE)*

Refit commenced at Gibraltar 15.8.82 upon arrival from Portsmouth. Departed Gibraltar for the UK upon completion, arriving at Devonport 17.10.82. Sailed 25.10.82 for sea trials and then departed direct to the South Atlantic, embarking one 826 Sqdn Sea King HAS.5 on 8.11.82. The helicopter joined the four from 'Fort Grange' as a Flight at RAF Stanley, the ship returning to Rosyth 25.3.83.

# SHIPS TAKEN UP FROM TRADE

In compiling the following list of Ships Taken Up From Trade (STUFT) during the conflict, it became apparent that the prefix letters often quoted elsewhere, such as MV (Motor Vessel), RMS (Royal Mail Steamship), SS (Steamship), etc., are in fact obsolete and bear little relationship to the particular vessel's peacetime role or means of propulsion. The vessels involved in Operation "Corporate" embraced a wide variety of roles, from Merchant Tankers to Merchant Tugs, from Cruise Liners to Roll-on Roll-off ("Ro-Ro") Ferries, and from Cable Ships to Offshore Support Vessels. For this reason, prefix letters are not used in the following listing, but each vessel's peacetime and wartime role is indicated in order to acquaint the reader with the mammoth size of the operation. In addition to the year of launching, GRT and Captain's name, details of the embarked Naval Party have also been included (where known and applicable).

# INDIVIDUAL SHIP DETAILS

## ALVEGA (1977) 33,329 GRT

*Capt A.Lazenby*

A Motor Tanker chartered from Silver Line. Sailed from Le Havre to Portsmouth 1.5.82 and fitted with RAS gear, departing 5.5.82 for Ascension. Used as a base storage tanker at Ascension until 9.83 when she was replaced by the Cunard tanker 'Lucerna'. Moved to San Carlos as base tanker and remained on MoD until returned to Rosyth 21.3.84.

## ANCO CHARGER (1973) 15,568 GRT

*Capt B.Hatton*

A Motor Tanker chartered 18.4.82 from Panocean. Arrived at Portsmouth 18.4.82 and fitted with RAS gear before moving on to Fawley 22.4.82 to take on aviation fuel. Departed 24.4.82 for the South Atlantic (via Ascension 5-8.5.82). Operated in the TRALA before entering San Carlos Water 27.6.82 to reprovision and spend a month on duty as a refuelling station. Sailed 28.7.82 for the UK, arriving Portsmouth 16.8.82. To Fawley on 24.8.82, leaving 25.8.82 for the Falklands for use as a short-term storage and supply tanker. Sailed from the Falklands for St Anna Bay (West Indies), arriving on 2.12.82. Sailed for the UK and then departed Solent anchorage 11.1.83 for the South Atlantic again, remaining on MoD charter until 3.84.

## ASTRONOMER (1977) 27,867 GRT

*Capt H.S.Bladen*
*NP2140 (Lt Cdr R.Gainsford RN)*

A Motor Container Ship, requisitioned from the Harrison Line at Felixstowe 28.5.82 following the loss of 'Atlantic Conveyor'. Sailed 30.5.82 and arrived at Plymouth 31.5.82 for conversion to a helicopter carrier and repair facility (hangar, two 20mm guns, chaff launchers, Unifoxer). Sailed south on 8.6.82 (via Ascension 16-18.6.82) with Wessex, Chinook and Scout helicopters, joining the CVBG 26.6.82. Anchored at Port William on 27.6.82 and commenced her helicopter support role on 2.7.82 with the arrival of two damaged Wessex HU.5's for attention by MARTSU (embarked due to the impending departure of 'Atlantic Causeway' and 'Contender Bezant'). Remained on station, moving to San Carlos in 8.82 until her departure for Devonport c14.11.82, arriving 3.12.82 with Wessex HU.5's, a Chinook and a captured CAE UH-1H. Moved to Falmouth on 8.12.82 for refit and return to her owners.

*Converted to helicopter carrier/support ship with the leased US Navy Arapaho system installed. Re-chartered by the MoD 22.4.83 for two years and renamed RFA Reliant (A131) at Birkenhead on 16.11.83.*

## ATLANTIC CAUSEWAY (1969) 14,946 GRT

*Capt M.H.C.Twomey*
*NP1990 (Cdr R.P.Seymour RN)*

A Steam Ro-Ro Container Ship requisitioned from Cunard/ACL 3.5.82 while en route from the USA to Southampton. Diverted to Antwerp, arriving 4.5.82 to unload as most of her cargo was destined for the Continent. Sailed on 5.5.82 and arrived at Plymouth 6.5.82 for conversion to the helicopter support role (including hangar, flight-deck, RAS gear, SATCOM). Moved to Plymouth Sound 13.5.82 to embark Wessex and Sea King helicopters. Departed for the South Atlantic on 14.5.82 (via Freetown 19/20.5.82), joining 'Queen Elizabeth 2' off Ascension 22.5.82. Entered the TEZ 29.5.82 and landed Gurkhas in San Carlos Water overnight 1-2.6.82 before departing east 2.6.82 to the TRALA. To San Carlos again 8/9.6.82 to embark casualties from 'Sir Tristram' and 'Sir Galahad', then moved east again. To Port William 17.6.82 and then to San Carlos Water 12.7.82 before leaving for the UK on 13.7.82 with Sea King and Wessex helicopters plus four "trophies" (two Pucaras and two UH-1H's). Passed Ascension 20-21.7.82 and arrived at Mounts Bay 27.7.82, disembarking Sea Kings before docking at Devonport later that day. Departed Plymouth on 31.7.82 and returned to her owners.

## ATLANTIC CONVEYOR (1970) 14,946 GRT

*Capt I.H.North (awarded posthumous DSC)*
*NP1840 (Capt M.H.G.Layard RN, awarded CBE)*

A Steam Ro-Ro Container Ship requisitioned 14.4.82 from Cunard/ACL whilst laid-up at Liverpool. Left for Plymouth 15.4.82, arriving on 16.4.82 for conversion to the aircraft and helicopter support role (including flight-deck, RAS gear, SATCOM). Embarked Wessex and Chinook helicopters 24.4.82, sailing on 25.4.82 for the South Atlantic (via Freetown 2.5.82). Arrived at Ascension 5.5.82 and embarked Sea Harriers and Harriers from Wideawake, departing on 7.5.82 with the 'Fearless' Group. Joined the LSL's on the edge of the TEZ 16.5.82 and joined the CVBG 18.5.82 for transfer of Sea Harriers and Harriers to the two carriers. Whilst 90 miles north-east of Port Stanley (50°38′S 56°08′W) en route to San Carlos Water at 1936Z on 25.5.82, the ship was hit by an Exocet launched by one of two attacking 2 Escuadrilla Super Etendards. The missile struck the port side and exploded, causing fires. The ship was abandoned with the loss of 12 crew, a Lynx, three Chinook and six Wessex helicopters, plus a large quantity of tents, spares and ammunition. Still afloat 28.5.82 when assessed as salvageable. Taken in tow by the tug 'Irishman' but broke her back on 30.5.82 during bad weather. The forward section sank immediately while the aft section had to be sunk by naval gunfire.

## AVELONA STAR (1975) 9,784 GRT

*Capt H.Dyer*

A Motor Refrigerated Cargo Ship chartered 28.5.82 from Blue Star Line for transport of food. Left Sheerness for Portsmouth 30.5.82, arriving 31.5.82 for fitting of helipad and RAS gear. Sailed on 10.6.82 for the South Atlantic (via Ascension 19.6.82) and joined the CVBG 1.7.82. Entered San Carlos Water on 4.7.82, moving to Port Stanley by 15.7.82. Used as a "floating supermarket", alternating between the San Carlos and Port Stanley areas, receiving supplies from 'Geestport' and 'Saxonia'. Left Port Stanley 11.11.82 for Ascension, continuing north 20.11.82 to arrive at Portsmouth on 29.11.82. To Liverpool 4.12.82, arriving there on 6.12.82. Returned to Portsmouth on 24.1.83 and made four trips to and from the Falkland Islands before being returned to her owners during 5.84.

## BALDER LONDON (1976) 19,976 GRT

*Capt K.J.Wallace*

A Motor Tanker chartered 12.5.82 from Lloyds Industrial Leasing for fleet refuelling. Sailed from Tenerife on 1.5.82, arriving at Portsmouth 7.5.82 for fitting of RAS gear. Sailed on 12.5.82 for the South Atlantic. In San Carlos Water late 6.82 when it refuelled 'Anco Charger'. Remained on station until sailing for the UK late 7.82, arriving at Plymouth 15.8.82. Left Plymouth on 26.8.82 and returned to her owners.

*Taken on long-term charter by the MoD during 3.84 and renamed RFA Orangeleaf.*

## BALTIC FERRY (1978) 6,455 GRT

*Capt E.Harrison*
*NP1960 (Lt Cdr G.B.Webb RN)*

A Motor Ro-Ro Ferry requisitioned from Townsend Thoreson on 1.5.82 for transport of troops and helicopters. Left Felixstowe 2.5.82 and arrived at Portsmouth on 3.5.82, moving to Southampton on 5.5.82. Embarked part of 5th Infantry Brigade and 656 Sqdn Scout AH.1 helicopters and then sailed for the South Atlantic on 9.5.82, having been fitted with two helipads able to accommodate up to two Sea Kings (plus SATNAV/SATCOM equipment and RAS gear). Passed Ascension 20.5.82 and joined the CVBG, detaching 1.6.82 to San Carlos Water to offload helicopters. In the TRALA 9-12.6.82, San Carlos Water 15.6.82 and Port William 17-25.6.82. Over 400 landings had been made on her helicopter deck by 2.7.82. Remained in the Falklands until 23.3.83 when she left Port Stanley for the UK with three Scouts, arriving at Felixstowe on 12.4.83. Sailed on 13.4.83 for a refit at North Shields followed by return to commercial service.

## BRITISH AVON (1972) 15,540 GRT

*Capt J.W.M.Guy*

A Motor Tanker, chartered from BP 20.4.82 for fleet refuelling. Arrived at Portsmouth that day for fitting of RAS gear before moving to Plymouth 22.4.82. Departed for the South Atlantic on 26.4.82 to refuel the RFA's, returning 5.6.82 to Portsmouth. To Portland 11.6.82 before sailing south again on 14.6.82 for further refuelling operations. Returned to the UK, arriving at Rosyth on 28.12.82 before moving to Grangemouth 8.1.83 on return to her owners.

## BRITISH DART (1972) 15,650 GRT

*Capt J.A.N.Taylor*

A Motor Tanker, chartered from BP on arrival at Portsmouth 9.4.82 for fitting of RAS gear. Sailed 11.4.82 for Loch Striven to load but delayed by technical problems. Sailed south from Loch Striven 22.4.82 for fleet refuelling and arrived at Ascension 4.5.82. Left the next day for a holding position midway between Ascension and the Falklands to refuel the RFA's 15-31.5.82. Joined the CVBG 31.5.82 to collect mail, returning to Ascension 18.6.82. Arrived at Plymouth on 2.7.82, departing 16.7.82 to reach Grangemouth on 19.7.82 for return to commercial service.

## BRITISH ENTERPRISE III (1965) 1,595 GRT

*Capt D.Grant*
*NP2090 (Lt Cdr B.E.M.Reynell RN)*

A Motor Offshore Ship, requisitioned on 18.5.82 from British Underwater Engineering at Dundee for use as a dispatch vessel. Sailed to Rosyth that day for conversion, departing 26.5.82 for the South Atlantic. Still on station 16.7.82 when the ship's Gemini was rescued off a beach by 'Leeds Castle'. Arrived at Portsmouth on 29.8.82, moving to Leith 5.9.82 for return to commercial service.

## BRITISH ESK (1973) 15,644 GRT

*Capt G.Barber*

A Motor Tanker, chartered from BP on 6.4.82 for fleet refuelling. She had sailed from Hamburg on 5.4.82, arriving at Portland 7.4.82 for fitment of RAS gear. Departed on 11.4.82 for a rendezvous with the Task Force 14.5.82 to refuel the RFA vessels 16.5.82 650 miles east north-east of Stanley. Arrived at Ascension on 26.5.82 with 311 personnel aboard, including 262 survivors from 'Sheffield'. Docked at Portsmouth 8.6.82 to reload. Sailed south again on 14.6.82, making visits to Saint Helena 20-22.9.82, 8.12.82, 23-28.12.82, 18-22.2.83 and 11-13.4.83. They were interspersed with refuellings at sea (for ships heading to/from the Falklands) and visits to Ascension. Returned to Campbeltown during 4.83, moving to Grangemouth on 30.4.83. Remained on charter into 1984.

## BRITISH TAMAR (1973) 15,642 GRT

*Capt W.H.Hare*

A Motor Tanker chartered from BP on 6.4.82 for fleet refuelling. Arrived at Portsmouth 9.4.82 for fitting of RAS gear, leaving on 10.4.82 to load fuel. Arrived at Milford Haven 13.4.82 from Grangemouth, departing

14.4.82 for the South Atlantic (via Madeira 18.4.82), reaching Ascension on 28.4.82. Moved to a holding area south-west of Ascension to refuel Task Force ships, including a world record 52 hour 40 minute pump-over to 'Plumleaf'. Returned to Ascension then sailed north to Gibraltar to reload, arriving 14.5.82. Left 17.5.82 for the South Atlantic once more. To Saint Helena 8-10.8.82 before returning north to Gibraltar 24.8.82 via Ascension. Departed 6.9.82 for the South Atlantic once again and accompanied 'Lowestoft' on a "tour" of Ascension Island, Tristan da Cunha and Saint Helena. At Saint Helena 15-19.12.82 before returning to Ascension and then to Portsmouth 20.6.83. Remained on charter into 1984.

## BRITISH TAY (1973) 15,650 GRT

*Capt P.T.Morris*

A Motor Tanker, chartered from BP on 6.4.82 for fleet refuelling. Arrived at Plymouth that day from Swansea for loading and fitting of RAS gear, departing 9.4.82 for the South Atlantic (via Ascension). Proceeded to the tanker holding area and refuelled the RFA's. Took survivors from 'Atlantic Conveyor' to Ascension. Returned to Plymouth 16.6.82 and left for the South Atlantic again on 25.6.82. Arrived at Portland 17.10.82 (via Las Palmas 9.10.82) then left for Plymouth on 25.10.82, arriving there the next day. Sailed for the South Atlantic again on 4.11.82. Departed Ascension early 1.83 for St Anna Bay, West Indies 10/11.1.83 then to Portsmouth, arriving 24.1.83. Remained on charter until the end of 6.83 when returned to commercial service.

## BRITISH TEST (1972) 15,653 GRT

*Capt T.A.Oliphant*

A Motor Tanker, chartered from BP to be used for fleet refuelling upon arrival at Portsmouth on 9.4.82 from Rouen. Sailed 11.4.82 and arrived at Gibraltar 15.4.82. Left 18.4.82 for Ascension, arriving 27.4.82. Continued further south to the tanker holding area and later took survivors from 'Sir Galahad' back to Ascension. Remained on station until it returned to Portsmouth 4.7.82. Departed 17.7.82 to arrive at Grangemouth on 22.7.82 for return to commercial service.

## BRITISH TRENT (1973) 15,653 GRT

*Capt P.R.Walker*

A Motor Tanker, chartered from BP on 12.4.82 at Portsmouth for fleet refuelling and fitted with RAS gear. Sailed from Portsmouth to Fawley on 13.4.82 before departing 15.4.82 for the Isle of Grain (arrived there the same day). Departed 17.4.82, arriving at Ascension on 29.4.82 before sailing further south. Operated in the TRALA until c10.6.82 when she sailed for Ascension with survivors from 'Sir Tristram', subsequently arriving at Portland on 5.7.82. Sailed for the South Atlantic again 7.82, returning to Portland from Ascension on 23.10.82. Sailed 4.11.82 for third trip south, returning to Rosyth 15.2.83. Remained on charter until 10.83 when she was returned to commercial service.

## BRITISH WYE (1974) 15,649 GRT

*Capt D.M.Rundle (awarded OBE)*

A Motor Tanker chartered from BP on 20.4.82 at Portsmouth for fleet refuelling and fitted with RAS gear. Arrived at Plymouth 22.4.82, departing 25.4.82 for the South Atlantic (via Ascension 5.5.82). Bombed by a Grupo 1 Hercules on 29.5.82 while at position 47°54'S 39°19'W, one bomb bouncing off her deck and the rest missing completely. Operated in the TRALA until she returned to Portland 11.7.82. Sailed on 22.7.82, was present in Singapore Roads 18-21.8.82 and then left for Bahrain. Sailed 3.9.82 for Loch Striven via Mombasa 12/13.9.82, arriving 2.10.82. Left 5.10.82 on return to commercial service.

## CANBERRA (1961) 44,807 GRT

*Capt D.J.Scott-Masson (awarded CBE)*
*NP1710 (Capt C.P.O.Burne RN, awarded CBE)*

A Turbo-electric Cruise Liner, requisitioned from P & O while cruising in the Mediterranean en route to Southampton. Called at Gibraltar on 4.4.82 to embark a military planning party flown out from the UK (notice of requisition was served on 5.4.82 off Portugal). Arrived at Southampton on 7.4.82 for troopship conversion, including the addition of two helicopter landing pads and RAS gear. Embarked 2,000 troops from 3 PARA, 40 Cdo and 42 Cdo and sailed on 9.4.82. Carried out RAS trials with 'Plumleaf' on 11.4.82 and then continued south to Ascension (via Freetown on 17.4.82), arriving on 20.4.82. Exercised with the LCU's 1-5.5.82 before leaving for the TEZ on 6.5.82, joining the 'Fearless' Group 10.5.82, the LSL's 16.5.82 and the CVBG 18.5.82. Cross-decked 40 Cdo to 'Fearless' and 3 PARA to 'Intrepid' 220 miles east north-east of Stanley on 19.5.82. Entered Falkland Sound on 21.5.82 for the landings at San Carlos. Sailed on 22.5.82 to a position 130 miles north-east of Stanley until 25.5.82 when she sailed for South Georgia. Arrived at Grytviken 27.5.82 to embark 5 Inf Bde from 'Queen Elizabeth 2' before sailing 28.5.82 to rejoin the CVBG 1.6.82. To San Carlos Water 2.6.82 and disembarked the troops 2/3.6.82. Entered the TRALA 5.6.82 and remained there until 14.6.82. To San Carlos Water once again, arriving 15.6.82 to embark PoW's, moving to Port William on 16.6.82 to take on more PoW's, making a total of 4,167 PoW's aboard by 17.6.82. Departed 18.6.82 for Puerto Madryn (Argentina), arriving the next day to disembark PoW's before returning to Port William on 20.6.82. Embarked men of 42 and 45 Cdo before moving to San Carlos Water on 24.6.82 for 42 Cdo to embark. Sailed from Port William for the UK on 25.6.82. Replenished off Ascension 3.7.82, arriving at Southampton on 11.7.82 for refit and return to commercial service.

## CONTENDER BEZANT (1981) 11,445 GRT

*Capt A.MacKinnon*
*NP2050 (Lt Cdr D.H.N.Yates RN)*

A Motor Ro-Ro Container Ship chartered from Sea Containers 12.5.82 for use as an aircraft and helicopter carrier. Left Le Havre 14.5.82 for Plymouth, arriving 15.5.82 for conversion (hangar and flight-deck). Sea King, Wasp and Chinook helicopters were embarked on 20.5.82. The ship moved to Start Bay later that day before sailing for the South Atlantic 21.5.82 (via Freetown 28/29.5.82) and arrived at Ascension on 31.5.82 to embark a Chinook, Gazelles and some Harrier GR.3's. Sailed on 3.6.82, arriving on station east of the TEZ 10.6.82. To Port William 17.6.82 to unload. Sailed for the UK 13.7.82 (via Ascension 21-22.7.82), having embarked a battle-damaged Harrier GR.3, and arrived Southampton at 1.8.82 to reload. Embarked three Sea King HAR.3's before departing 7.8.82 for Portsmouth, sailing south again the same day. Arrived at Port William 25.8.82 and then sailed for the UK on 6.9.82 (via Ascension 14/15.9.82) with Wessex and Chinook helicopters plus two captured Pucaras embarked. Returned to Southampton on 23.9.82, unloaded and then sailed to Falmouth on 27.9.82 for a refit followed by return to commercial service.

*Purchased by the MoD on 1.3.84 for a two-year conversion to a helicopter and VTOL aircraft training ship as a replacement for 'Engadine' in 1986.*

**EBURNA** *(1979) 19,763 GRT*

*Capt J.C.Beaumont*

A Motor Tanker, chartered from Shell (UK) at Invergordon on 13.4.82 for fleet refuelling, having sailed from Hamburg 11.4.82. She arrived at Plymouth on 18.4.82 for fitting of RAS gear. Departed 20.4.82 for St Anna Bay (West Indies), arriving there on 7.5.82. Sailed for the South Atlantic on 8.5.82 to operate in the TRALA for three weeks. Arrived at Rosyth 31.7.82, sailing 19.8.82 on return to commercial service.

**ELK** *(1977) 5,463 GRT*

*Capt J.P.Morton (awarded CBE)*
*NP1720 (Cdr A.S.Ritchie RN, awarded OBE)*

A Motor Ro-Ro Cargo Ship, requisitioned for the transport of aircraft and arms. Arrived at Middlesborough from Helsingborg 5.4.82. Received notice of requisition and sailed the same day for Southampton, arriving 6.4.82. Converted to carry Army vehicles and given RAS gear. Embarked part of HQ Coy 45 Cdo before departing 9.4.82 for the South Atlantic (via Freetown on 17.4.82). Arrived at Ascension 20.4.82 where the sides of her upper deck were cut away to facilitate operations by helicopters. Sailed on 6.5.82 with the 'Canberra' Group, joining the 'Fearless' Group 10.5.82, the LSL's 16.5.82 and the CVBG on 19.5.82 as a second-line supply ship. She entered San Carlos Water overnight on 27/28.5.82 to unload vehicles and ammunition. Made two more night runs 30/31.5.82 before anchoring 4-7.6.82. Sailed to the TRALA 7.6.82 and remained there until 12.6.82, returning to San Carlos Water on 13.6.82. Moved troops of the Commando Logistic Regt to Port Stanley 20.6.82 then loaded Gazelle and Scout helicopters of 3 CBAS on 23/24.6.82. Departed Port Stanley 24.6.82 for the UK, passing Ascension 3.7.82 to arrive at Devonport 12.7.82. Sailed for the Tyne on 16.7.82 (via Portsmouth 17-20.7.82), arriving there on 21.7.82 for overhaul. Returned to commercial service on 12.8.82.

**EUROPIC FERRY** *(1968) 4,190 GRT*

*Capt W.J.C.Clarke (awarded OBE)*
*NP1860 (Lt Cdr C.E.K.Roe RN)*

A Motor Ro-Ro Ferry, requisitioned 19.4.82 at Southampton from Townsend Thoreson and modified to the troop transport role (fitted with RAS gear and SATNAV/SATCOM equipment). Embarked Scout AH.1's from 656 Sqdn 21.4.82 and sailed 22.4.82 for Portland with part of 2 PARA. Carried out RAS practice with 'Grey Rover' before departing on 25.4.82 for the South Atlantic (via Freetown 2-4.5.82 and Ascension 7/8.5.82). Left Ascension with the 'Fearless' Group, joining the LSL's on 16.5.82 on the edge of the TEZ. Entered San Carlos Water 21.5.82 (the smallest vessel in the assault) to land 80 troops, departing later in the day. Remained at sea until returned to San Carlos Water at dawn on 26.5.82 to complete unloading, departing 27.5.82 to rejoin the CVBG. Sailed to the TRALA 29.5.82, remaining there until 9.6.82. Helped 'Contender Bezant' with the transfer of Chinooks to the Islands and loaded equipment for return to the UK, departing 25.6.82. Arrived at Southampton on 17.7.82 to unload, sailing 26.7.82 to Avonmouth for refit and return to commercial service.

**FORT TORONTO** *(1981) 19,982 GRT*

*Capt R.I.Kinnier*

A Motor Tanker, chartered from Canadian Pacific 7.4.82. Left Aarhus (Denmark) that day, arriving at Southampton on 10.4.82 for fitting of RAS gear. Loaded with fresh water before her departure on 19.4.82, arriving at Ascension on 29.4.82. Sailed for the South Atlantic in early May, noted with the LSL group 16.5.82 and operated independently to supply water to ships of the Task Force. Operated in the TRALA 6-10.6.82, arriving at Port William 17.6.82 to remain in the Port Stanley area as a base water supply tanker. Returned to the UK during 4.84 and returned to commercial service.

**G.A.WALKER** *(1973) 18,744 GRT*

*Capt E.C.Metham*

A Motor Tanker, chartered from Canadian Pacific on 20.4.82 and arrived at the Isle of Grain on 27.4.82. Sailed for Plymouth on 28.4.82 but returned to the Isle of Grain on 2.5.82. Fitted with RAS gear and intended to be used as a support tanker, but initially retained in European waters to replace RFA's. Left for Gibraltar 3.5.82, arriving 8.5.82. Departed 10.5.82 for Rotterdam and return to her owners, arriving on 15.5.82. Sailed on 16.5.82 for Loch Striven (via Tail of Bank), arriving 21.5.82. Departed 23.5.82 for Rotterdam, arriving 26.5.82 to be re-chartered. Left for Rosyth on 28.5.82, arriving there on 29.5.82, then moved on to Portsmouth (arriving on 5.6.82). To Plymouth on 7.6.82 (arrived 9.6.82) and departed 10.6.82 for the South Atlantic. Arrived at Port Stanley late 6.82 to be used as a base fuel tanker until she returned to Portsmouth 27.9.84.

**GEESTPORT** *(1982) 7,730 GRT*

*Capt G.F.Foster*
*NP1920 (2/O R.Bourne RFA)*

A Motor Refrigerated Cargo Ship requisitioned from Geest Line at Avonmouth on 7.5.82 for transport of food. Sailed 7.5.82, arriving at Portsmouth on 9.5.82 for conversion (helipad, RAS gear) and loading. Left for the South Atlantic on 21.5.82, retaining a mostly West Indian crew (one of the few exceptions to the British-only crew rule). Arrived at South Georgia 11.6.82 to transfer stores to the RFA's. To the CVBG 21.6.82, San Carlos Water 22.6.82 and moved to Port William by 25.6.82. Departed Port Stanley 3.8.82 and arrived at Portsmouth 19.8.82. To Avonmouth 23.8.82 for a refit prior to return to commercial service.

**IRIS** *(1976) 3,874 GRT*

*Capt A.Fulton (awarded OBE)*
*NP1870 (Lt Cdr J.Bithell RN)*

A Motor Cable Ship, requisitioned on 24.4.82 from British Telecom for use as a dispatch vessel. She sailed from Southampton to Plymouth on 27.4.82 for conversion (helipad, RAS gear, SATCOM, 2 x 20mm Oerlikon guns), departing on 29.4.82 for the South Atlantic. Loaded extra supplies and a RM detachment at Ascension before arriving at Grytviken (South Georgia) 25.5.82. Loaded steel recovered from the whaling station at Stromness 26.5.82 (the steel was held for use in ship repairs) and sailed to join the Task Force 30.5.82 on dispatch duties. Returned to South Georgia and then back to Ascension, arriving 19.6.82 for minor engine repairs. Rejoined the Task Force 4.7.82, visiting San Carlos and Port Stanley before returning to Ascension 23.7.82 for a crew change (NP2820 to replace NP1870). Carried out further duties in the South Atlantic before returning to Southampton on 30.11.82. Sailed 4.12.82 to Glasgow for a refit and return to owners.

**IRISHMAN** *(1978) 686 GRT*

*Capt W.Allen*

A Motor Tug, requisitioned from United Towing on 7.4.82 while at Flushing. To Portsmouth on 8.4.82 and sailed on 10.4.82. At Ascension 24.4-3.5.82 and arrived at Tristan da Cunha 10.5.82. Departed 16.5.82, entering the TRALA on 24.5.82. Involved in the attempts to salvage 'Atlantic Conveyor' 26-28.5.82 before moving to South Georgia (arrived 7.6.82). To Port Stanley 19.6.82 for harbour operations and clearance work with RN divers, also being involved in the salvaging of 'Sir Tristram' and 'Bahia Buen Suceso'. Sailed for the UK (via Ascension 13.10.82) to arrive at Hull on 29.10.82. Sailed on 31.10.82 to the Tyne for a refit and return to commercial service. Re-chartered 3.83 for more South Atlantic service and still in use late 1984.

**LAERTES** *(1976) 11,804 GRT*

*Capt H.T.Reid*

A Motor Cargo Ship, requisitioned from the China Mutual Steamship Company 28.5.82 for the transport of ammunition. Left Belfast 28.5.82 for Plymouth, arriving on 29.5.82 to load (also fitted with RAS gear). Sailed 8.6.82 for the Falklands (via Ascension 17-19.6.82), arriving at Port William 3.7.82 to unload. Completed unloading in San Carlos Water during 7.82. Sailed for the UK on 3.8.82, returning to Plymouth 21.8.82. Left for Barry 31.8.82 and return to her owners.

## LYCAON (1976) 11,804 GRT

*Capt H.R.Lawton*
*NP1900 (Lt Cdr D.J.Stiles RN)*

A Motor Cargo Ship, chartered on 26.4.82 from the China Mutual Steamship Company after arriving at Falmouth on 14.4.82 to be laid up. Sailed for Southampton on 26.4.82 (arrived 27.4.82). Loaded and given RAS gear plus SATCOM equipment and then sailed 4.5.82 for South Georgia (arriving 28.5.82) to transfer her cargo of ammunition and Rapier missile rounds to 'Stromness'. Sailed to the TRALA on 11.6.82 and then anchored in San Carlos Water 15.6.82 before moving to Port William on 20.6.82. Her crew was relieved on 22.8.82 and she remained on station until her departure from Port Stanley for the UK, passing Ascension 2.4.83 to arrive at Hull 21.4.83. Remained on charter until she arrived at Falmouth on 20.7.83 to be laid up. Re-chartered for further South Atlantic work between 10.83 and 5.84.

## NORDIC FERRY (1978) 6,455 GRT

*Capt R.Jenkins*
*NP1950 (Lt Cdr M.St.J.D.A.Thorburn RN)*

A Motor Ro-Ro Ferry, requisitioned on 1.5.82 from Townsend Thoresen at Europoort, Netherlands. Sailed from Felixstowe on 3.5.82 for Portsmouth, arriving there on 4.5.82. Moved to Southampton 6.5.82 where her conversion was completed (two helipads, RAS gear plus SATNAV/SATCOM equipment). Embarked six 656 Sqdn Gazelle AH.1's 8.5.82 prior to sailing on 9.5.82 for the South Atlantic (via Freetown on 16.5.82) with part of 5 Inf Bde. Passed Ascension 20.5.82, joining the CVBG before detaching to Ajax Bay 3.6.82 to unload helicopters to Clam Valley. She remained on station until her departure from Port Stanley early 7.82 with 2nd Btn The Scots Guards. Arrived off South Georgia on 8.7.82 to embark Royal Marines and then sailed for Ascension and the UK, arriving at Southampton on 29.7.82. Sailed for a refit on the Tyne 31.7.82 before returning to commercial service on 25.8.82.

## NORLAND (1974) 12,988 GRT

*Capt D.A.Ellerby (awarded CBE)*
*NP1850 (Cdr C.J.Esplin-Jones RN, awarded OBE)*

A Motor Ro-Ro Ferry, requisitioned on 16.4.82 from P & O North Sea Ferries. Arrived at Hull on 17.4.82, departing on 21.4.82 to arrive at Portsmouth 22.4.82 for the fitting of two helipads plus SATNAV and SATCOM equipment. Embarked part of 2 PARA and sailed on 26.4.82 (via Freetown 4.5.82) to arrive at Ascension on 7.5.82. Left the same day to join the 'Fearless' Group, meeting the LSL's on 16.5.82, and claims to have been the first ship in San Carlos Water on 21.5.82 for the landings. Unloaded and sailed that evening to the holding area north-east of Stanley. She entered San Carlos Water again on 23.5.82 to unload more troops and embark survivors from 'Antelope', then returned to the holding area on 24.5.82 before her departure to South Georgia on 25.5.82. Arrived at Grytviken

27.5.82 to embark 5 Inf Bde from 'Queen Elizabeth 2'. Sailed on 28.5.82 for San Carlos Water, arriving 1.6.82 to unload before embarking PoW's 2.6.82 and sailing to join the CVBG. Back to San Carlos Water 6.6.82 to take on more PoW's the next day. Sailed for Montevideo (Uruguay) on 7.6.82 with 1,012 PoW's aboard, arriving there on 12.6.82 to disembark them. Departed 13.6.82 and returned to San Carlos Water 17.6.82 to embark a further 1,000 PoW's. Sailed 18.6.82 for Port Stanley to collect more PoW's. Left for Puerto Madryn (Argentina) on 19.6.82 with 2,047 PoW's, arriving 21.6.82. Unloaded and then returned to Port Stanley 23.6.82 to embark 2 and 3 PARA for return to the UK. Sailed on 25.6.82 and arrived at Ascension 5.7.82. Unloaded and then embarked Queen's Own Highlanders, departing south again 9.7.82. Made several trips between Ascension and Port Stanley until 1.83 (apart from a spell during 11.82 when the ship suffered from engine trouble and the shuttle was taken over by 'St Edmund'). Sailed from Port Stanley on 6.1.83 en route to the UK via Ascension and Tenerife, arriving off Hull on 31.1.83. Entered Hull docks on 1.2.83 for an official welcome, sailing again on 3.2.83 to Immingham for a refit and return to commercial service.

## QUEEN ELIZABETH 2 (1968) 67,140 GRT

*Capt P.Jackson*
*NP1980 (Capt N.C.H.James RN)*

A Steam Passenger Liner which was requisitioned from Cunard on 3.5.82 upon arrival at Southampton from Philadelphia (USA). Three helicopter decks were fitted, along with RAS gear, and she embarked 5 Inf Bde along with two 825 Sqdn Sea King HAS.2A's before sailing 12.5.82. Passed close to but out of sight of Ascension 22.5.82 before joining 'Atlantic Causeway' later the same day. Sailed to South Georgia and anchored in Cumberland Bay East on 27/28.5.82. Her troops were transferred to 'Stromness', 'Canberra' and 'Norland' in exchange for 629 survivors from 'Ardent', 'Antelope' and 'Coventry'. She sailed for the UK on 29.5.82 to arrive at Southampton 11.6.82 for a refit and return to commercial service.

## ST EDMUND (1974) 8,987 GRT

*Capt M.J.Stockman*
*NP2060 (Lt Cdr A.M.Scott RN)*

A Motor Ro-Ro Ferry, requisitioned from British Rail Sealink UK at Harwich on 12.5.82 and sailed that day for Plymouth. Arrived there 13.5.82 for conversion (including two helipads, SATNAV/SATCOM equipment, RAS gear and extra water/fuel tanks). Departed south on 19.5.82 (via Ascension) arriving in the TRALA early 6.82. Joined the CVBG 15.6.82 and proceeded to Port William 16.6.82. Departed Port Stanley on 5.7.82 with 500 senior PoW's and arrived at Puerto Madryn (Argentina) on 14.7.82 to unload. Returned to Port Stanley and put to use as an accommodation ship 10.8.82 (replaced 'Norland' on the Ascension shuttle service during 11.82). Sailed from Port Stanley early 2.83 for the UK, via Ascension 16.2.83 and Las Palmas 21/22.2.83, arriving in the Solent 25.2.83. Sailed 26.2.83 and arrived at Wallsend-on-Tyne on 28.2.83 for a refit and

sold to the MoD as 'HMS Keren' (28.4.83). Remained in service with a merchant navy crew as MV 'Keren', still in use on the Falkland Islands-Ascension service during late 1984.

## ST HELENA (1963) 3,150 GRT

*Capt M.L.M.Smith*
*NP2100 (Lt Cdr D.N.Heelas RN)*

A Motor Cargo Vessel requisitioned from Curnow Shipping 22.5.82 after arrival at Avonmouth from Tenerife. Sailed for Portsmouth the same day, arriving on 24.5.82 for conversion (helipad, RAS gear, SATCOM/SATNAV equipment, 4 x 20mm Oerlikon guns). Sailed to Portland 10.6.82 for work-up as a minesweeper support vessel, sailing for the South Atlantic 13.6.82 to arrive off Port Stanley on 10.7.82. To Ajax Bay on 14.7.82, returning to Port Stanley 25.7.82. Her role in the Falklands was to set up and maintain a Trisponder System for accurate navigational assistance, for which an 829 Sqdn Wasp HAS.1 Flight was embarked. She departed from Port Stanley 13.8.82 and returned to Rosyth on 16.9.82. Sailed to Southampton for a refit (arrived 24.9.82), leaving 27.10.82 to arrive in the Tees on 29.10.82. Departed 2.11.82 for the Falklands (via St.Helena 21.11.82). Returned to the UK via Ascension, arriving at Falmouth 11.6.83 for a refit and return to commercial service.

## SALVAGEMAN (1980) 1,598 GRT

*Capt A.J.Stockwell*

A Motor Tug, requisitioned on 6.4.82 from United Towing whilst lying at Aberdeen. Arrived at Portsmouth on 8.4.82, departing on 10.4.82 for the South Atlantic. Arrived at Ascension 23.4.82, Tristan da Cunha 2.5.82 and South Georgia 7.5.82. Ordered to assist 'Sheffield' on 8.5.82 but the destroyer sank before the tug's arrival. Worked in the TRALA with battle-damaged ships and then sent to South Georgia on 7.6.82 from where the ship sailed on 17.6.82 for Southern Thule and Operation "Keyhole" (the Master acting as a witness to the surrender 20.6.82). Returned to South Georgia and carried out salvage work from 28.6.82 on captured submarine 'Santa Fe' at Grytviken, moving the vessel to Hestesletten in Cumberland Bays. Sailed 15.7.82 for Port Stanley, arriving there 19.7.82 for harbour operations and clearance work. Departed for the UK, arriving at Hull 22.6.84 for a refit. Following trials, she moved to the Pool of London 17-22.9.84 to receive her Falkland Battle Honours. Left for Southampton and Portsmouth, sailing on 6.10.84 for further duty in the South Atlantic.

## SAXONIA (1972) 12,029 GRT

*Capt H.Evans*

A Motor Refrigerated Cargo Ship chartered from Cunard 28.4.82 for transport of food. Sailed from Bremerhaven on 29.4.82, arriving at Portsmouth 30.4.82 for conversion (helipad, RAS gear, SATNAV/SATCOM equipment). Moved to Plymouth 7.5.82 and arrived 8.5.82, departing south the same day. Arrived at South Georgia on 23.5.82 to transfer stores to RFA's and then sailed for the UK on 13.6.82, arriving at Portsmouth 28.6.82. Reloaded and sailed 20.7.82 for another trip to the South Atlantic, this time to the Falklands. Slightly damaged 17.9.82 when she ran aground on the north side of Port William. Sailed for the UK and arrived at Portsmouth 27.10.82, sailing on 2.11.82 for North Shields. Arrived there on 3.11.82 for a refit and return to commercial service. Re-chartered 1.84 for further South Atlantic service.

## SCOTTISH EAGLE (1980) 32,995 GRT

*Capt A.Terras*

A Motor Tanker, chartered from King Line 12.5.82 while en route New York to Portsmouth. Arrived on 15.5.82 for fitting of RAS gear and SATCOM equipment, departing 19.5.82 for Milford Haven (arrived 21.5.82). Loaded and then sailed 24.5.82 to arrive at South Georgia 18.6.82, becoming a base storage tanker. Moved to the Falklands 14.7.82 and still in use 8.83 as a base fuel ship. Departed Port Stanley on 26.9.83 and arrived at Plymouth on 23.10.83 for a refit and return to commercial service.

## STENA INSPECTOR (1980) 6,061 GRT

*Capt D.Ede*
*NP2010 (Capt P.J.Stickland RN)*

A Diesel-electric Off-shore Support Vessel which was chartered 25.5.82 from Stena Caribbean upon arrival at Savannah, GA. Moved to Charleston, SC 1.6.82 for modifications (including SATNAV/SATCOM equipment and a heavy machine shop). Sailed for the South Atlantic 6.6.82 (via Ascension 21.6.82 and St.Helena 28.6.82) with NP2010 embarked. Made two trips from the Falklands to St Helena before sailing to South Georgia to assist with the salvage of the captured submarine 'Santa Fe' during 7.82. Moved to Port William, arriving there 26.7.82 for ship repair and support duties until 10.83 when she sailed for the UK, arriving at Glasgow on 13.11.83 for a refit.

*Purchased by the MoD for maintenance duties in the South Atlantic and, in 1984, renamed RFA Diligence (A132).*

## STENA SEASPREAD (1980) 6,061 GRT

*Capt N.Williams*
*NP1810 (Capt P.Badcock RN, awarded CBE)*

A Diesel-electric Off-shore Support Vessel, requisitioned on 8.4.82 from Stena Atlantic and recalled from the Thistle oilfield. Arrived at Peterhead 10.4.82 and then sailed for Portsmouth the next day, arriving on 12.4.82 for loading and modifications (including a heavy machine shop and SATNAV/SATCOM equipment). Sailed on 16.4.82 for the South Atlantic (via Ascension 28.4.82) and arrived at South Georgia 16.5.82, moving to the TRALA on 20.5.82. Carried out damage repairs to 11 Royal Navy ships plus routine repairs to 24 more, attending to four captured ships as well. Moved to San Carlos Water 17.6.82 until sailing on 25.7.82 for the UK, arriving at Portsmouth 18.8.82. She was re-chartered from 1.9.82 for use in the diving support role for recovery work on the wrecks around the Falklands. On trials from Portsmouth 13-15.9.82 before sailing on 16.9.82 for the Falklands. Recovered equipment and other items from

sunken ships, including the well-known cross of nails from 'Coventry'. She returned to Portsmouth on 28.1.83 and then sailed to Avonmouth on 12.2.83 for a refit and return to commercial service.

## TOR CALEDONIA (1977) 5,056 GRT

*Capt A.Scott*
*NP2020 (Lt Cdr J.G.Devine RN)*

A Motor Ro-Ro Cargo Vessel, requisitioned 18.5.82 from Tor Line, having arrived at Southampton from Rotterdam two days earlier. Fitted with RAS gear, loaded with vehicles and Rapier missiles and then sailed on 20.5.82 for Ascension, arriving there on 31.5.82. Sailed on 2.6.82 and entered the TRALA 12.6.82 for stores transfer. To Port William on 17.6.82 to complete unloading. Surplus 656 Sqdn helicopters were loaded 29.7.82 at Port Stanley and she sailed 1.8.82, also carrying captured Argentine CH-47C, Puma, Pucara and UH-1H aircraft. Arrived off Portsmouth 19.8.82, from where the CH-47C and Puma were airlifted to RNAY Fleetlands by an RAF Chinook HC.1. Left the same day for Felixstowe, arriving 20.8.82 to unload. Sailed 24.8.82 for the Tyne and a refit prior to return to commercial service. Re-chartered for use as a stores ship at Port Stanley, sailing from Hull on 1.2.83 and returned to Felixstowe 8.5.84.

## UGANDA (1952) 16,907 GRT

*Capt J.G.Clark*
*NP1830 (Cdr A.B.Gough RN and Surgeon Cdr A.J.Rintoul RN)*

A Steam Cruise Liner, requisitioned on 10.4.82 from P & O whilst in Alexandria, Egypt. Arrived at Naples on 13.4.82 to disembark 1,000 school children. Sailed on 14.4.82 for Gibraltar, arriving 16.4.82 for conversion to a hospital ship (including helipad, SATCOM equipment, RAS gear). Repainted white overall with Red Cross markings, sailing south 19.4.82 (via Ascension 28.4-1.5.82). Entered the Red Cross Box (RCB) 11.5.82. Embarked casualties from the three ambulance ships 'Hecla', 'Herald' and 'Hydra' during 5/6.82, entering Falkland Sound 29.5.82 to collect casualties from the Goose Green battles. Carried out a rendezvous with the Argentine hospital ship 'Bahia Paraiso' for casualty transfers on 4.6.82, 10.6.82 and 16.6.82. Present in Grantham Sound on 11.6.82, 14.6.82 and 19.6.82; at Port William on 24.6.82. Later in the month she carried out a rendezvous with Argentine hospital ship 'Almirante Irizar'. The last Argentine casualties were transferred on 13.7.82, on which date she was de-registered as a hospital ship. The Red Crosses were deleted on 14.7.82, the doctors and surgeons having treated 730 cases (150 Argentine) and carried out some 504 operations. She embarked Gurkhas in Grantham and Falkland Sounds 15/16.7.82, having taken on the troopship role, and sailed from Port William on 18.7.82 for the UK. Arrived at Southampton 9.8.82 to unload and then sailed 11.8.82 to arrive at North Shields 13.8.82 for a refit prior to return to commercial service. Re-chartered for two years from 16.1.83 for the Falklands-Ascension service with NP2230 embarked. Left the Falkland Islands for the last time on 4.4.85 en route to the UK and return to her

owners.

## WIMPEY SEAHORSE (1982) 1,599 GRT

*Capt M.J.Slack (awarded OBE)*
*NP2000 (CO not known)*

A Motor Offshore Support Vessel/Tug, requisitioned 4.5.82 from Wimpey Marine for use as a mooring ship. Arrived at Rosyth 5.5.82 for modifications (SATCOM equipment, RAS gear) and left 13.5.82 to complete loading at Plymouth. She sailed south on 16.5.82 (via Ascension 29.5.82), arriving at South Georgia on 8.6.82. Laid moorings in Stromness harbour, Leith harbour and off Grytviken. Sailed to Port Stanley 22.7.82 to lay moorings there and in Port William. Left for the UK on 12.8.82 and arrived at Portsmouth on 4.9.82. Sailed to Southampton on 8.9.82 for a refit and return to commercial service.

## YORKSHIREMAN (1978) 686 GRT

*Capt P.Rimmer*

A Motor Tug, requisitioned 7.4.82 from United Towing whilst towing a barge to the Magnus oilfield. She was diverted to Lerwick and then moved to Portsmouth on 12.4.82 for the fitting of communications equipment. Sailed 13.4.82 for Ascension, arriving on 27.4.82. Worked from there until sailing on 3.5.82 for Tristan da Cunha (arriving 10.5.82). Left 16.5.82 and entered the TRALA 24.5.82 before moving to South Georgia on 7.6.82. Assisted with the salvage of the Argentine submarine 'Santa Fe' during 6/7.82. Arrived at Port Stanley 19.7.82 for harbour operations and clearance work with RN divers. Remained on station until sailing from Port Stanley for the UK late 6.83 (via Ascension). Arrived at Hull on 23.7.83 before proceeding to Wallsend on 26.7.83 for refit and return to commercial service.

---

## STUFT COMMISSIONED FOR ROYAL NAVY SERVICE

---

## CORDELLA (1973) 1,238 GRT

*Lt Cdr M.C.G.Holloway RN*

A Motor Freezer Trawler which was requisitioned on 11.4.82 at Hull from J.Marr & Son and arrived at Rosyth 16.4.82 for conversion to minesweeping duties. To Portland on 26.4.82 for work-up and commissioned as HMS 'Cordella' with the 11th MCMS. Departed on 27.4.82 for the South Atlantic (via Ascension 11.5.82). At Grytviken, South Georgia on 27/28.5.82 to transfer troops from 'Queen Elizabeth 2' to 'Canberra' and 'Norland'. Entered the TRALA c7.6.82 to carry out minesweeping duties 21.6-10.7.82 (noted at Port Stanley 12.7.82). Sailed for the UK (via Gibraltar 3-5.8.82), returning to Rosyth 11.8.82. Decommissioned and dispatched to the Humber Graving Dock at Immingham for a refit and return to her owners.

**FARNELLA** *(1972) 1,207 GRT*

*Lt R.J.Bishop RN*

A Motor Freezer Trawler, requisitioned 11.4.82 at Hull from J.Marr & Son and sailed on 12.4.82 to Rosyth for conversion to minsweeping duties. To Portland 26.4.82 for work-up and commissioned as 'HMS Farnella' with the 11th MCMS. Departed on 27.4.82 for the South Atlantic (via Ascension 11.5.82). At Grytviken, South Georgia 27/28.5.82 to help transfer troops from 'Queen Elizabeth 2' to 'Canberra' and 'Norland'. She carried out minesweeping duties between 21.6.82 and 10.7.82 and was then noted at Port Stanley 12.7.82 before sailing for the UK (via Gibraltar 3-5.8.82). She arrived at Rosyth on 11.8.82, was de-commissioned and commenced a refit before being returned to commercial service.

**JUNELLA** *(1975) 1,615 GRT*

*Lt Cdr M.Rowledge RN*

A Motor Fish Factory Trawler requisitioned 11.4.82 at Hull from J.Marr & Son and arrived at Rosyth on 15.4.82 for conversion to the minesweeping role, being commissioned for RN service as 'HMS Junella' with the 11th MCMS. Left Rosyth 26.4.82 for work-up at Portland and then sailed for the South Atlantic the next day (via Ascension 11.5.82). At Grytviken, South Georgia 27/28.5.82 to transfer troops from 'Queen Elizabeth 2' to 'Canberra' and 'Norland'. To the Falklands for minesweeping duties from 21.6-10.7.82 and noted at Port Stanley 12.7.82. Sailed for the UK (via Gibraltar 3-5.8.82), arriving at Rosyth on 11.8.82 with an Argentine mine aboard for examination. De-commissioned and dispatched to Humber Graving Dock at Immingham for a refit and return to her owners.

**NORTHELLA** *(1973) 1,238 GRT*

*Lt Cdr J.P.S.Greenop RN*

A Motor Freezer Trawler requisitioned 11.4.82 at Hull from J.Marr & Son and arrived at Rosyth on 13.4.82 for conversion to the minesweeping role, being commissioned as 'HMS Northella' with the 11thMCMS. Sailed to Portland on 26.4.82 for work-up, leaving for the South Atlantic the next day (via Ascension 11.5.82). At Grytviken, South Georgia 27/28.5.82 for transfer of troops from 'Queen Elizabeth 2' to 'Canberra' and 'Norland'. Entered the TRALA c7.6.82 before commencing minesweeping duties off Port Stanley 21.6-10.7.82. Noted there 12.7.82 before sailing for the UK (via Gibraltar 3-5.8.82) and arrived at Rosyth 11.8.82. De-commissioned and sailed for a refit and return to her owners. Taken up once more in 10.83 to become a target vessel based at Faslane.

**PICT** *(1973) 1,478 GRT*

*Lt Cdr D.G.Garwood RN (MID)*

A Motor Freezer Trawler requisitioned 16.4.82 from British United Trawlers at Hull and arrived at Rosyth 20.4.82 for conversion to the minesweeping role. Commissioned as 'HMS Pict' with the 11th MCMS, sailing to Portland on 26.4.82 for work-up. Departed

for Ascension on 27.4.82 (arriving 11.5.82) and then continued south. At Grytviken, South Georgia 27/28.5.82 to transfer troops from 'Queen Elizabeth 2' to 'Canberra' and 'Norland'. Joined the TRALA c7.6.82 and in San Carlos Water 15.6.82 before moving to Port Stanley 16.6.82 for minesweeping work from 21.6-10.7.82. Left for the UK (via Gibraltar 3-5.8.82) and arrived at Rosyth 11.8.82. De-commissioned and sailed for a refit and return to her owners.

---

### STUFT DEPLOYED
### 15 JUNE — 31 DECEMBER 1982

**ANNETTE S** *(1972) 499 GRT*

A Motor Cargo Vessel. Most of its available cargo space chartered from Sigrid M. Sorenson of Denmark. Departed from the Tees 17.11.82 for the Falklands, after which she sailed to Santos, Brazil (arriving 15.1.83).

**BRITISH FORTH** *(1973) 15,540 GRT*

A Motor Tanker chartered from BP for fleet refuelling which left the Tyne on 25.6.82 for Portsmouth, arriving 30.6.82. Sailed 5.7.82 for Ascension and then returned to the UK, arriving at Portland 27.7.82. Left for Gibraltar 2.8.82 then returned to the UK, arriving at Loch Striven on 14.8.82. Sailed again 16.8.82 for Invergordon and then the South Atlantic. Remained on station until departing for the UK during 2.83, arriving at Rosyth 2.3.83. Remained on charter until 12.83 when she returned to commercial service.

**CEDARBANK** *(1976) 11,282 GRT*

A Motor Cargo Ship chartered from the Bank Line 12.6.82 upon arrival at Southampton from Hampton Roads, VA (USA). Loaded with prefabricated huts and sailed 24.6.82 for the Falklands. Arrived back at Hull 8.9.82 and returned to commercial service.

**CUNARD COUNTESS** *(1976) 17,495 GRT*

A Motor Passenger Ship chartered from Cunard 10.82 to take over from 'Norland' on the Ascension-Falklands shuttle service. Departed San Juan (Puerto Rico) via Barbados 3.11.82 for Ascension. Made her last round trip Ascension to Montevideo (Uruguay) during 4.83 to collect the bereaved relatives for their Falklands visit. Arrived at Malta 4.5.83 for a refit and return to commercial service.

**FERNCARRIER** *(1975 'Kollbris') 39,039 GRT*

A Motor Semi-submersible Heavy-lift Vessel chartered from Fearnley and Eger, Norway (in fact a conversion of the tanker 'Kollbris'). Loaded the accommodation barge 'Safe Dominia' at Gothenburg and then sailed 18.11.82 on her maiden voyage. Arrived at Southampton 22.11.82 and loaded two RMAS launches (HLD27 ex-Portsmouth and HL7025 ex-Chatham). Departed 23.11.82 for the South Atlantic, arriving at Port Stanley 15.12.82. Unloaded the 'Safe Dominia' on 20.12.82 and sailed the same day for Pascagoula, MS (USA).

**FORT EDMONTON** *(1975) 18,782 GRT*

A Motor Tanker chartered from Canadian Pacific which departed Europoort 22.10.82 to arrive at Rosyth 24.10.82. Left 28.10.82 and arrived at Antwerp 30.10.82. Sailed 2.11.82 for Ascension as an aviation fuel base ship. Replaced by 'Maersk Ascension' in early 8.83 and departed for the UK, arriving at Portland 20.8.83. Left for Gibraltar 2.9.83 and returned to commercial service.

**FORT ROUGE** *(1980) 19,982 GRT*

A Motor Tanker chartered from Canadian Pacific to carry fresh water. Departed Rio de Janeiro (Brazil) 23.8.82 for the Falklands. Returned to Southampton 26.9.82 and sailed 6.10.82 for a second trip to the Falklands. Departed to San Nicolas Bay (Netherlands Antilles), arriving 18.12.82, and returned to commercial service.

**LEICESTERBROOK** *(1977) 1,599 GRT*

A Motor Cargo Vessel chartered from F.T.Everard & Sons which sailed from Falmouth 11.12.82 for Port Stanley (via Helsingborg 14-23.12.82, Corunna 1-6.1.83, St.Vincent 13.1.83). Returned to the UK, arriving at Barry 27.4.83 with four 18 Sqdn Chinooks. Departed 28.4.83 and returned to commercial service. Re-chartered late 5.83 for further trips to the Falklands (still in use late 1984).

**LINNE** *(1979) 5,551 GRT*

A Motor Ro-Ro Cargo Ship chartered from Brostrums Rederi AB for a one-way trip to the Falklands with prefabricated housing in 12.82.

**MYRMIDON** *(1980) 16,482 GRT*

A Motor Cargo Ship chartered from Ocean Transport & Trading Co. Arrived on the Tees 22.6.82 for loading. Departed 2.7.82 for the Falklands and then returned to the UK, arriving at Tilbury on 28.10.82 for return to commercial service.

**RANGATIRA** *(1972) 9,387 GRT*

*Capt P.Liddell*
*NP2070 (Cdr D.H.Lines RN)*

A Motor Ro-Ro Passenger/Cargo Ship which had been laid up at Falmouth by the Union Steamship Company since 5.7.81. Chartered 15.5.82 for use as an accommodation ship, sailing to Plymouth 23.5.82 for conversion (RAS gear, SATCOM/SATNAV equipment, 4 x Oerlikon 20mm guns, helipad). Carried out trials on 31.5.82 and then departed on 14.6.82, arriving at Southampton 15.6.82 to load. Left for the South Atlantic on 19.6.82 and arrived off Port Stanley 11.7.82. Put to use as an accommodation ship. On station, receiving over 1,000 helicopter landings on her deck by 12.82. Finally sailed for the UK 25.9.83, arriving at Devonport 18.10.83. Later moved on to Belfast and returned to her owners.

**SAFE DOMINIA**

An Accommodation Barge chartered from the Consafe Group, Sweden for use in the Falklands. Loaded aboard 'Ferncarrier' at

Gothenburg, sailing on 18.11.82 for Southampton and Port Stanley. The ship arrived on 15.12.82 and the barge was offloaded 20.12.82 at Port Stanley. Still in use during 1984.

**SAINT BRANDAN** *(1976) 931 GRT*

A Motor Ro-Ro Ferry chartered from J.A.Gardner & Co of Glasgow. Departed Ardrossan on 27.8.82, arriving at Portsmouth 30.8.82. Sailed on 4.9.82 for the Falklands. Returned to the UK during the summer of 1984.

**SAND SHORE** *(1970) 2,848 GRT*

A Motor Ro-Ro Vessel chartered from Nils Hugosand, Oslo and sailed from Hull to the Tees on 13.9.82. Departed 19.9.82 for the South Atlantic and operated on the Ascension-Port Stanley shuttle service until she returned to the UK, arriving at Southampton 22.10.83. Left 31.10.83 for Port Stanley, returning to Southampton on 24.1.84. Sailed again 5.2.84 for Port Stanley then back again to Southampton 5.5.84. Remained on MoD charter operating between Marchwood and Antwerp until late 1984.

**SAPELE** *(1980) 9,140 GRT*

A Motor Cargo Vessel chartered from Elder Dempster in 7.82 and arrived in the Tees 18.7.82 to be loaded. Sailed 24.7.82 for Port Stanley. Left for the UK, arriving at Hull on 5.11.82 with a wrecked 3 CBAS Gazelle embarked. Returned to her owners after unloading.

**STRATHEWE** *(1978) 12,598 GRT*

*Capt S.T.S.Household*
*NP2150 (Lt Cdr R.H.Hewland RN)*

A Motor Cargo Ship, chartered from P & O while en route from Dubai to Dar-es-Salaam. Diverted to the UK on 3.6.82, unloading her cargo at Malta before arrival at Southampton on 17.6.82 for conversion (RAS gear, SATNAV/SATCOM equipment, Unifoxer, etc). The RCT landing craft 'Antwerp' and 'Arromanches' were loaded aboard before her departure on 28.6.82 for Port William where she arrived on 17.7.82 to unload. Returned to the UK, arriving at Middlesborough 26.8.82 to take aboard pontoons and prefabricated huts. Sailed for the Falklands again on 6.9.82 (via Sheerness 7.9.82). Arrived at Port Stanley 25.9.82 but was damaged 11.10.82 when she dragged her anchor during high winds. Left Port Stanley during 11.82 carrying LCU's from 'Intrepid' (L706 'T1' and L707 'T2') to arrive at Hull on 12.12.82. Sailed 17.12.82 for the Tyne, arriving on 18.12.82 for a refit and return to commercial service. Sold to the Sealift Co of Monrovia as the 'Lindenbels', sailing on 30.1.83 for Norrkoping (Sweden).

# STUFT FOR NON-SOUTH ATLANTIC DUTIES IN 1982

*The following vessels are all Motor Tankers and were chartered during 1982 to replace the RFA tankers away in the South Atlantic.*

**BRITISH FERN** *(1964) 13,252 GRT*

Chartered from BP 4.82 for fleet refuelling. Arrived Bahrain from Salalah 20.4.82 and departed 22.4.82 to arrive at Gibraltar 10.5.82. Returned to commercial service by 19.5.82.

**BRITISH HAZEL** *(1964) 12,964 GRT*

Chartered from BP 4.82 to operate in UK waters.

**BRITISH IVY** *(1965) 13,271 GRT*

Chartered from BP during 4.82. Left Bahrain on 13.4.82 and arrived at Gibraltar on 29.4.82. Departed 5.5.82, returning to commercial service by 19.5.82.

**BRITISH VINE** *(1965) 13,408 GRT*

Chartered from BP during 4.82 to operate in UK waters. Chartered again in 7.82 and 8.82.

**CORONA** *(1976) 4,899 GRT*

Chartered from Backman & Sonner Rederi, Donso (Sweden) 20.4.82 to transport fuel to and from RN facilities around the UK. Returned to commercial service late 8.82.

**CORTINA** *(1981) 6,499 GRT*

Chartered from owners of 'Corona' (as above) to replace that ship from late 8.82 to mid-9.82.

**ESSO AVON** *(1981) 1,599 GRT*

Chartered from Esso for UK coastal duties 4-6.82.

**ESSO FAWLEY** *(1967) 11,064 GRT*

Chartered from Esso 4-6.82 for UK coastal duties, including a visit to Gibraltar 26-28.4.82.

**ESSO MILFORD HAVEN** *(1967) 10,902 GRT*

Chartered from Esso during 4.82 for UK coastal duties.

**ESSO PENZANCE** *(1971) 2,178 GRT*

Chartered from Esso 8.82 for UK coastal duties.

**FINNANGER** *(1975) 21,267 GRT*

Chartered from Westfall-Larsen, Norway, arriving at Portland on 15.4.82 from St Anna Bay (West Indies). Departed 17.4.82 to Mounts Bay, arriving at Hamburg 19.4.82.

Left 21.4.82 to arrive at Lome (Togo) on 4.5.82 and then sailed 5.5.82 for Gibraltar. Arrived 17.5.82 and departed 18.5.82 for Skikda (Algeria). Arrived there 23.5.82 for return to commercial service.

**HANS MAERSK** *(1982) 8,952 GRT*

Chartered from Moller of Copenhagen for UK coastal duties during 5/6.82. Re-chartered for further coastal duties 10-12.82, visiting Gibraltar 16/17.11.82. Left Antwerp on 13.12.82 for Ascension, making many round trips to the Island from various ports. Renamed 'Maersk Harrier' under the British flag 2.84 and still in use late 1984.

**LUMINETTA** *(1972) 14,925 GRT*

Chartered from Cunard during 4/5.82 to refuel RN ships in the Persian Gulf after 'Olna' was ordered back to the UK. At Bahrain 16-21.4.82 and then sailed for Singapore Roads, arriving 3.5.82. Left 10.5.82 and returned to Bahrain on 24.5.82.

**NATALIE** *(1981) 1,101 GRT*

Chartered from First Maritime K.K. (Japan) to deliver fuel from Milford Haven to Plymouth during 5.82.

**ORIONMAN** *(1975) 3,623 GRT*

Chartered 20.4.82 from Rowbotham Tankships for UK coastal duties between refineries and RN bases, including Gibraltar. Returned to commercial service late 5.82.

**O.T.ACID** *(1981) 5,721 GRT*

Chartered from Johanssen Lars/OT Rederierna for UK tanker duties. Left Swansea 30.9.82 for Portland, arriving 1.10.82. Left 4.10.82 and at Portsmouth 5/6.10.82 then Portland again 6/7.10.82 when she was returned to the owners and sailed for Hamburg.

**VINGA POLARIS** *(1981) 6,117 GRT*

Chartered from the Johansson Group, Sweden for UK coastal duties during 5.82.

# OTHER SHIPPING

**HERCULES** *(1971) 99,827 GRT*

American-registered Steam Tanker (*not UK owned or chartered*) operated by United Carriers Inc. Sailed from St Croix (VI) in ballast en route around Cape Horn to Valdez, Alaska. While 480 miles east of the Falklands on 8.6.82, she was bombed by two Grupo 2 Canberras and damaged. Diverted to Rio de Janeiro for survey and anchored south of Ilha Rosa due to the discovery of an unexploded bomb aboard. Towed out to sea by the tug 'Smit Lloyd III' on 17/18.7.82 and sunk 290 miles east of Florianopolis (Brazil) on 20.7.82, following the decision that it was too hazardous to remove the bomb. The ship took six hours to sink.

**Part 3**

# FALKLAND ISLANDS, THE DEPENDENCIES

and

# BRITISH ANTARCTIC TERRITORY

*Floating sedately in calm waters near Port San Carlos settlement (reportedly in 9.36) is S1818, a Fairey IIIF of 718 (Catapult) Flight. Based on 'Exeter', aircraft and ship were visiting Port Stanley at the time. Forty-six years later, and in far less peaceful circumstances, 'Exeter' Flight's Lynx HAS.2, XZ723, regularly overflew the same stretch of water.* (A. and S. Cameron)

*Sixteen years after being ditched in shallow water, towed clear and then abandoned at nearby Salvador settlement, East Falkland, the former 'Endurance' Flight Whirlwind HAR.9 XM666 'ED/(4)48' was still resident in 8.85 albeit in dilapidated condition. During the conflict it is reported to have disconcerted a number of Argentine pilots!* (via R. and J. McLeod)

*Seen here, floating in Stanley Harbour, is XV859 an SR.N6 Winchester 6 hovercraft of Naval Party 8902. The Unit was based at Moody Brook from 10.67 to 5.72 and their "Hoovercraft" was popular with the Islanders because of its ability to carry freight or passengers over the worst of terrain.* (J. S. Wright)

# AVIATION IN THE FALKLAND ISLANDS, DEPENDENCIES & BRITISH ANTARCTIC TERRITORY

With few exceptions, the only aeroplanes seen in the Falkland Islands before, during or immediately after World War II were floatplanes or amphibians such as Fairey IIIF's, Seafoxes, Walruses and Sea Otters from visiting Royal Navy warships. One exception, reportedly seen over the Islands in the early 1930's, was an unknown type of seaplane from the French vessel 'Jeanne d'Arc' which had anchored at Port Stanley while cruising in Falklands' waters.

During World War II only one military aircraft is known to have been based in the Islands and its presence is interesting. In January 1942 the British feared that the Falkland Islands, because of their strategic position between the Pacific and Atlantic Oceans, might be invaded, not by Argentina but by Japan. That month a small "Task Force" was prepared in the Caribbean and dispatched to the South Atlantic. The "Force" consisted of a tanker and a Walrus amphibian (W2738) of 710 Sqdn 'Y' Flight, at that time based in the seaplane-carrier 'Albatross' which remained in the Caribbean. 'Y' Flight's "Task" was to patrol to the south and south-west of the Falkland Islands and give warning of any approaching Japanese ships.

Tied down to the deck of the tanker, the Walrus was shipped to Port Stanley from where it eventually commenced daily patrols. However, no invasion fleet was seen before W2738 (christened "Audrey III") was lost on 1 March 1942 when, shortly after take-off from Stanley Harbour, the engine stopped. An attempted landing in an inlet near the town resulted in the Walrus bouncing twice on the water before turning over onto its back. The pilot (S/Lt Trevor David) and his crew were unhurt, but "Audrey III" was a total wreck. It is not known if the aircraft was replaced and the patrols resumed, but available evidence suggests not.

Few British military aircraft appear to have visited the Islands between the end of World War II and the mid-1950's. From then until the Argentine invasion the most usual types seen were helicopters, notably the Whirlwinds of the ice patrol vessel 'Protector' and the Whirlwinds or Wasps of her successor, 'Endurance'.

On 17 October 1969, while 'Endurance' was engaged in a hydrographic survey of the Port Salvador area of East Falkland, one of her Whirlwind HAR.9's (XM666 'ED/(4)48') ran out of fuel while ferrying, of all items, drums of AVTUR from Rincon Grande to Salvador settlement. It was ditched in shallow water close to the settlement and, with the aid of a vehicle, was eventually hauled clear and sleighed to the settlement where it was surveyed, stripped of all useful parts and then abandoned.

The substantially complete hulk was still at Gibraltar Station, Salvador settlement, in August 1985.

An unusual, useful and reasonably long-term military resident of the Falkland Islands was an SR.N6 Winchester 6 hovercraft (XV859). It arrived at Port Stanley as deck cargo on 'Aes' in October 1967 and belonged to Naval Party 8902, a unit formed to assess the suitability of the type in a surface communications and support role. NP8902 and its hovercraft were sent to the Falklands because the Islands were considered to be the ideal environment for such an assessment. Based and hangared at Moody Brook near Port Stanley, the "Hoovercraft" (as it was referred to by the Islanders) circumnavigated the Islands on more than one occasion during the years it was there and visited nearly every "Camp" settlement at least once during its stay. The SR.N6 was very popular with the Islanders, who appreciated its flexibility and passenger and freight carrying capacity. For them it was an ideal vehicle to supplement the FIGAS Beaver floatplanes. However, following an accident in which it was severely damaged, XV859 and NP8902 were returned to the United Kingdom in May 1972 and not replaced, much to the disappointment of the Islanders.

As recounted elsewhere, civil aviation arrived in the Falkland Islands in 1948 in the form of two Austers, followed by other types in later years as the internal air services developed. An attempt made in 1952 to start a flying-boat service between the Islands and the United Kingdom came to nothing and it was not until 1971 that an external air service was established with Argentina using FAA Albatross amphibians. In 1972 the first FAA/LADE services linking Port Stanley with Comodoro Rivadavia by F-27 Friendship landplanes became possible with the opening of the Hookers Point airstrip. Situated near the town, the Argentine-operated facility had been paid for, and constructed by, Argentina and its presence was viewed with great suspicion by many Islanders. Stanley Airport, on the Cape Pembroke peninsular, replacing Hookers Point, became operational in December 1977 (but was not officially opened until May 1979), and for the first time jet airliners (FAA/LADE F-28 Fellowships) linked the Islands with the South American mainland. The service was suspended shortly after the Argentine invasion. Naturally, after the conflict, the LADE flights were not resumed and Islanders had to wait until May 1985 before it was possible to leave the Falklands on a commercial flight. However, it was not now to Argentina but to the United Kingdom (via Ascension Island) on a British Airways Boeing 747.

The first privately-owned Falkland Islands' aircraft, a Cessna 172M, was delivered in 1974 and it was followed two years later by a second. A third example, a Cessna 172P owned by the then Governor, Rex Hunt, arrived in January 1982 but did little flying before the Argentine invasion. All three were damaged during the conflict and then vandalised. The two Cessna 172M's were replaced in 1983 by Cessna F172's.

Prior to the invasion a few foreign-registered aircraft visited the Islands. Some, like the Argentine Cessna 172 in 1964, the DC-4 in 1966 and the Aero Commander in 1968

were unwelcome, but others, like the two Canadian Cansos which landed in Stanley Harbour in the mid-1950's en route to Antarctica and Chilean and American "light twins", helped to show that although the Falkland Islands were remote, they were not totally isolated.

Since the 1982 conflict, aviation in the Falkland islands has changed fundamentally. Jet fighters, jet transports and helicopters of all sizes are common sights. It would be pleasant to think that their crews might still be "treated to goose pie" when visiting remote settlements (as were their floatplane-flying predecessors, according to one settlement diary). Perhaps they are?

# FALKLAND ISLANDS INTERNAL AIR SERVICES

Those acquainted with the needs of small and isolated settlements such as those which exist on the Falkland Islands will know that the aeroplane or helicopter can, and does, provide one of the essential lifelines which enable such communities to survive. Within the United Kingdom, the air-ambulance services that were established in the Highlands and Islands of Scotland during the 1920's and 1930's are now considered to be a part of everyday life. Similar opinion prevails in the Falkland Islands, although domestic flying did not start until 1948 and owed its inception more to the concept of the Flying Doctor Service in Australia rather than to any British influence (the latter influence was to come much later).

The origin of internal air services in the Falkland Islands can be traced back to November 1946 when Miles Clifford (later Sir Miles) was appointed Governor. He soon concluded that all forms of communication within the Islands were in urgent need of review as none of them fully met the requirements or aspirations of the population. Inter-island shipping was reliable but infrequent, while the existing telephone and radio-telephone links required expansion and replacement by more modern equipment. Paved road surfaces were restricted to Port Stanley, whilst elsewhere in the "Camp" *(from the Spanish word "Campo" meaning "Countryside"; used by the Islanders to describe anywhere outside the confines of Port Stanley)* the "roads" were merely tracks, their condition varying from reasonable to bad. (Paradoxically, there were many motor vehicles on the Islands including, at that time, Bren Gun Carriers left behind by the departing British Forces at the end of World War II.) Feelings of isolation were most keenly felt by the Islanders in times of serious illness or injury, because there was no quick method of transporting patients to hospital in Port Stanley. Instead, they were subjected to the rigours of long and uncomfortable sea or overland journeys.

Although the Islands were self-supporting with good prospects for profitable sheep farming, Clifford was of the opinion that a population of about 2,000 people could not create sufficient revenue (in spite of a recently-applied Export Tax on the Islands' products) to build and maintain a reasonable network of roads which would provide the basis for good overland communication on East and

West Falkland. Shipping services could be improved but would do little to speed up communication. More positively, he was sure that modern radio and telephone links could be provided at reasonable cost and substantially reduce the feelings of isolation in the more remote settlements, especially those on the west coast of West Falkland. The problem of moving sick and injured people as quickly as possible to hospital in Port Stanley had yet to be resolved.

March 1947 saw Miles Clifford make his first trip to the Antarctic Dependencies, aboard the Falkland Islands' vessel 'Fitzroy'. During the journey he read an article about the Australian Flying Doctor Service in an issue of "Reader's Digest" and the seed for a similar scheme in the Falkland Islands was sown. In the course of his visits to various Antarctic bases, he was impressed with the wind-driven generators used to charge the survey teams' radio batteries. He realised that such generators could be used on the Falkland Islands where strong winds were a normal feature of the weather.

The concepts of an air-ambulance or flying doctor service and modern transceivers located in the Camp settlements and Port Stanley were discussed with others on his return to the Islands. Naturally, there were sceptics and dissenters as well as supporters of his ideas. Miles Clifford, however, was by then convinced of the need to introduce aviation into the Islands and during a visit to London in the summer of 1948 he initiated, on behalf of the Falkland Islands Government (but under the auspices of FIDS, the Falkland Islands Dependencies Survey), the purchase of two Austers and the employment of a pilot, V.H.Spencer, to fly them from Port Stanley Racecourse. The Racecourse was the only reasonably long and moderately flat area in Port Stanley from which a light aircraft could take-off and land.

Two ex-military Austers were bought for £700 each and were British-registered as G-AJCH and G-AJCI on 18 August. Accompanied by a supply of spare parts, the two aircraft were shipped to Port Stanley in November aboard the Antarctic survey ship 'John Biscoe'. Upon arrival, G-AJCH was assembled as quickly as possible by P.Bruce-Hill (a FIDS employee formerly with Auster Aircraft Limited) in a partially-built, roofless hangar and prepared for a historic flight.

Dawn on 19 December 1948 heralded a beautiful sunny day. That morning, Vic Spencer started the Auster's Lycoming engine, taxied the aircraft onto the Racecourse and took-off into the clear blue sky. It was soon apparent that he was relishing every moment of the flight as he put the aeroplane through its paces — much to the consternation of some of the as-yet-unconvinced onlookers. Satisfied with his, and the Auster's, performance, Vic flew back overhead the Racecourse, made an approach, gently touched down, taxied in and switched off the engine. Miles Clifford's vision of aviation in the Falkland Islands had become reality.

Another significant milestone was passed on 24 December that year. Stewart Slessor, then Senior Medical Officer in Port Stanley, requested the services of the Auster and its pilot. A little girl, Sandra Short, living at North Arm settlement in southern East Falkland, had fallen seriously ill with Peritonitis and needed immediate hospital treatment. A telephone call to the settlement Farm Manager established that there was a suitable local landing site, that sheep skins mounted and pegged on sticks would identify the runway and that smoke from a small fire lit nearby would indicate the wind direction. The flight was successful and within three hours of the request for aid the youngster was in Port Stanley being operated on and her life saved. At long last — and on Christmas Eve of all days — the concept of an air-ambulance service had been vindicated and most sceptics silenced.

On 3 March 1949 the second Auster, duly assembled, made its initial flight from the Racecourse, while a few days later G-AJCH and G-AJCI were reregistered as VP-FAA and VP-FAB to become the first two aircraft on the Falkland Islands Civil Aircraft Register. Official paperwork recording the fact was not issued until 26 September that year and VP-FAB is believed to have flown for some time beyond that date still marked as G-AJCI. In the case of VP-FAA, an even longer period was to pass before its Falkland Islands registration was applied. That was because on 7 April 1949 G-AJCH suffered a landing accident at the San Carlos settlement airstrip, overturning when the mainwheels sank into the soft surface, and had to be shipped back to Port Stanley and from there to the United Kingdom for repairs. However, by then it had been realised that floatplanes were potentially more useful in the Islands due to the lack of suitable airstrips and the proximity of water to all the farming communities and their woolsheds. Most, if not all, of the settlements had landing stages for the inter-island ships to which floatplanes could be moored to load or unload mail, passengers and a limited amount of freight. Thus, the Falkland Islands Government decided that whilst VP-FAA was away for repair the opportunity would be taken to convert it to a floatplane. Meanwhile, VP-FAB would be retained as a landplane for the foreseeable future.

By the year's end a total of 28 passengers had been carried, of whom eight were private individuals and the remainder Government officers on official business. It was a small but significant start to an enterprise which began as an air-ambulance service but which would gradually evolve into FIGAS, the Falkland Islands Government Air Service.

In May 1950, VP-FAB was joined by another Auster (VP-FAC) and a Noorduyn Norseman (VP-FAD), both of which were configured as floatplanes and had previously been operated by FIDS in Antarctica. The Norseman was a particularly useful acquisition as it could carry up to ten persons. It was the last of its type to be built and, with the Auster, had been purchased for FIDS in 1949 for a specific rescue mission in Marguerite Bay, Graham Land in the Antarctic [see British Antarctic Territory notes]. The Auster and the Norseman were at first loaned to, but later purchased by, the Falkland Islands Government.

Not surprisingly, the exact date on which the air service became known as FIGAS has proved impossible to determine, for the acronym started as an idea of Vic Spencer's and was gradually adopted more by useage than by any official pronouncement. The first confirmed reference to it is on 23 June 1951 when VP-FAA, recently returned from its rebuild and floatplane conversion in the United Kingdom, was test-flown from Stanley Harbour. Shortly before that flight Vic had had a "winged penguin" motif with the letters "FIGAS" below it painted on to the Auster's freshly-doped blue fuselage.

With the arrival of VP-FAA, FIGAS then had four aircraft on its inventory. This increased capacity enabled the fledgling air service to develop and passengers began to be carried on a slightly more regular basis rather than ad hoc. However, it was not until after the introduction of the Islander aircraft in 1979 that anything remotely resembling a scheduled passenger service was contemplated. The FIGAS order of priorities has always been clearly defined, namely: medical or air-ambulance requirements; postal duties; conveyance of Falkland Islands Government officers on official business and the carriage of passengers and freight.

The postal delivery service, often referred to as the "mail drop", involved (and still involves) an aircraft making low, slow passes over a settlement while the pilot or a passenger literally dropped the weighted hessian bags of letter-mail to the ground through an open door or window. The collection of mail bound for the United Kingdom or elsewhere abroad was more complicated than the delivery service. That was because outbound mail from the Falkland Islands in the years prior to 1971 (when the external air service was first established) was taken eleven times a year by 'Fitzroy' (and latterly 'Darwin') to Montevideo in Uruguay for onward distribution. In the case of East Falkland, FIGAS made no special arrangements for collecting outgoing mail because letters and packages could be sent overland to Port Stanley or collected by the relatively frequent flights calling at such places as Darwin and North Arm settlements. Remote West Falkland had far fewer flights to its settlements, so FIGAS undertook a special mail collection trip eleven times a year to Fox Bay and either Hill or Roy Coves. Those flights were planned to take place three days prior to 'Fitzroy' (or 'Darwin') sailing from Port Stanley, thus allowing a margin for bad weather or aircraft unserviceability. Islanders in outlying settlements on West Falkland, knowing when a FIGAS mail aircraft was due, were able to send their letters or packages overland, or by small boat, to reach Fox Bay or Hill or Roy Coves in time for the collection.

The involvement of aircraft in the postal service was a great boon to the Islanders, but the medical and air-ambulance flights were infinitely more important to the widely dispersed population living, for the most part, in very isolated communities. As in the case of Sandra Short, availability of an aircraft often meant the difference between life or death to a person who was critically ill or injured, and that could sometimes involve FIGAS committing all of its resources to one request for aid.

The following case, which happened whilst Capt J.Kerr was a FIGAS pilot, illustrates just such a situation. At 4 o'clock one morning he received a telephone call from the SMO in Port Stanley. A shepherd at Goose Green, East Falkland had a knife wound in the stomach and immediate assistance was required. An aircraft was quickly prepared for ambulance duty and a medical officer flown to the scene of the accident. After an examination he decided that the patient could not be moved and that an emergency operation was essential. The aircraft was dispatched to Port Stanley to collect an operating team and equipment. That accomplished, the aircraft was sent back to Port Stanley with a sample of the injured man's blood for grouping and cross-matching. The aeroplane returned with a supply of suitable blood, but by the time it arrived the patient needed oxygen and more blood than had been anticipated. A second FIGAS aircraft had to be used to deliver the oxygen and an additional quantity of plasma, and then remain available to provide any further assistance. Following the successful emergency operation, the patient and medical team were flown to Port Stanley in the late afternoon, but it was 7 o'clock that evening before both aircraft had been washed down and hangared.

Hardly a week passed without a medical or air-ambulance flight being requested, and often it would occur two or three times in one week. For many years, especially during the predominantly Beaver era from 1953 to 1979, there were only two aircraft on the FIGAS inventory at any one time. The impracticability of establishing a conventional scheduled passenger service as well as providing the air ambulances with a fleet of only two aeroplanes can readily be appreciated.

The efficiency of the medical flights, and FIGAS operations as a whole, improved immeasurably with the installation of modern radio communications equipment at the settlements and in the aircraft. As mentioned previously, Miles Clifford's views on the radios, batteries and generators he had seen during his visits to the Antarctic bases had been discussed with others upon his return to Port Stanley. Eventually, a requirement for the necessary equipment (modified to local needs) was submitted to the Crown Agents in London for sanction and purchase. Approval was given and, in due course, the first of the newly-manufactured transceivers, batteries and associated wind-driven generators arrived in the Islands and soon every farm settlement was equipped. The transceivers had two frequencies, one of which (4.5 Megacycles) could be used to contact Port Stanley hospital (via the town's Wireless/Telegraph station) for advice, help or an air ambulance. The other frequency (2 Megacycles), often referred to in the Islands as the "Farmyard", was used for inter-settlement chat, substantially reducing any feelings of isolation in the Camp communities. FIGAS aircraft were fitted with compatible 4.5 Megacycle radios so that the pilots could contact settlements to advise them of such matters as arrival times for mail-drops. Conversely,

Islanders were not encouraged to talk directly to FIGAS aircraft except in emergencies or to pass essential information. To request seats, potential passengers radioed Port Stanley and their requirements were passed on to the FIGAS office. Even in 1985 this is still done and each evening the local Falkland Islands domestic radio station broadcasts the passenger lists for the following day and the settlements to be visited.

In the early years the only hangarage available was a small building for the landplanes (located a few yards north of the Racecourse at its western end), but it was totally inadequate for the later Auster and Norseman floatplanes. Initially, they remained in the open, protected from the worst of the weather by being parked in a revetment at the head of the slipway. Eventually, a Robin-type hangar was procured in the United Kingdom and erected on the southern shore of Stanley Harbour about 150 yards north of the landplane hangar. Latterly, the landplane hangar was used for the storage of aircraft spares and sundry other equipment.

Miles Clifford had been involved in the 1949 purchase of the Norseman for FIDS and, whilst in Canada, he was able to witness a demonstration of the new DHC-2 Beaver floatplane. Suitably impressed, he realised that here, at last, was an aircraft ideally suited to the Falkland Islands' environment. He resolved to buy one for FIGAS as soon as possible.

The first FIGAS Beaver, dismantled and packed in two crates, was shipped to Port Stanley from Canada in June/July 1953 aboard 'Fitzroy'. It was reassembled under the supervision of two de Havilland (Canada) engineers and test-flown by one of that company's pilots before being handed over to FIGAS in August. On the 20th of that month the Beaver was officially, but incorrectly, registered as VP-FAE instead of VP-FAF [see British Antarctic Territory notes and the Individual Aircraft Details of Hornet Moth VP-FAE].

Soon after the Beaver arrived, the Norseman was withdrawn from service with irreparable advanced corrosion in the main undercarriage legs, engine bearers and other metal components. The airframe was eventually scuttled in Stanley Harbour, but the floats were retained for many years as the basis of a raft used in the Harbour. Of the three Austers, VP-FAB had been airworthy until at least 30 October 1951 but was withdrawn from use before the end of the year and stored (dismantled as a spares' source) in the landplane hangar; VP-FAC was retired at the same time as the Norseman (and for the same reason) and joined VP-FAB; the original Auster, VP-FAA, soldiered on until 1956.

A second Beaver from Canada arrived crated at Port Stanley aboard 'Fitzroy' in late August 1955. Supervised by de Havilland (Canada) personnel, it was unpacked and assembled in the floatplane hangar prior to its acceptance test flight from Stanley Harbour on 29 September by Jim Kerr. Because of the incorrect registration letters applied to the first Beaver (which had yet to be realised and rectified), the second one had been allotted the markings VP-FAF instead of VP-FAG. Both errors were corrected (on paper at least) on 21 August 1956 when H.Bennett, the Falkland Islands Registrar General, officially altered the allocations to VP-FAF and VP-FAG. However, photo-

Creating wake in Ajax Bay, San Carlos Water in 5.50 is Auster 5 floatplane VP-FAC. It had been loaned that month to FIGAS by FIDS and was later purchased by the FI Government for the Air Service. (V. H. Spencer)

Photographed from 'Fitzroy' (date unknown) is the FIGAS Norseman 5 VP-FAD, taxying at Goose Green, East Falkland. It remained in service with FIGAS until c8.53 when advanced metal corrosion caused it to be withdrawn from use. (V. H. Spencer)

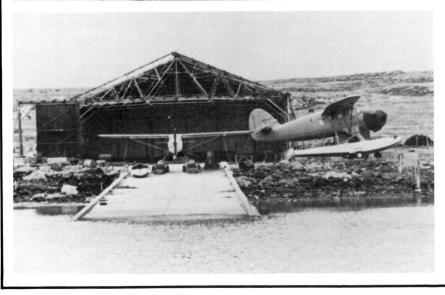

Viewed from Stanley Harbour in 1951, the Robin-type floatplane hangar is seen under construction. The Norseman 5 VP-FAD is parked in front of it and the Auster 5 VP-FAC is on the slipway. Thirty-one years later the same hangar served as an Argentine mortuary.

(V. H. Spencer)

451

graphic and verbal evidence shows that both Beavers retained their original markings (VP-FAE and VP-FAF) throughout their service with FIGAS. (As late as October 1984 a wing marked VP-FAE was lying dumped in the grass at Moody Brook.)

The last commercial flight by the Auster VP-FAA took place on 24 April 1956, but it was retained as a training aircraft until June when, because of extensive corrosion in the fuselage and tail framework, it was withdrawn from use. VP-FAA was reportedly burnt on a pyre near the slipway in 1957 along with the fuselage remains of VP-FAB and VP-FAC.

From 1956 until 1979, FIGAS gradually developed and improved its Beaver floatplane operations. That included the carriage of passengers arriving at, or departing from, Port Stanley on the external air service provided by Argentine military aircraft from 1971 *[see Falkland Islands External Air Services notes]*. No more than two Beavers were on charge at any one time, but losses, disposals and their subsequent replacements accounted for a further five of these sturdy floatplanes (VP-FAH, VP-FAK, VP-FAL, VP-FAT and VP-FAV) being delivered between 1958 and 1979.

There was no fixed route structure for the Beaver operations which, by at least 1976, covered some 36 different settlements. Instead, an "on demand" service was established so that passengers and freight could be collected and deposited according to a particular day's bookings. All flights were, of course, subject to weather and sea states, but generally most aircraft reached their destinations on the desired days. Fares for resident Islanders were subsidised by the Falkland Islands Government, but non-residents paid the full rate. In 1958 560 passengers were carried, a substantial increase over the 1949 figure of 28.

In addition to the normal, but repairable, damage and corrosion that floatplanes operating from the sea are susceptible to, there were three incidents between August 1953 and April 1982 in which Beavers were damaged beyond repair. VP-FAF (actually VP-FAG), flown by Capt G.Toye, was involved in a take-off accident at the Moro, Douglas Station, East Falkland on an unknown date sometime between October 1957 and May 1958. Although it capsized and sank (fortunately without casualties), the aircraft was recovered and returned to Port Stanley aboard 'Shackleton'. However, it had been so badly handled during the salvage operation that it was deemed to be beyond economical repair and was broken up for scrap and spares.

VP-FAL, which was delivered to the Falkland Islands in March 1967, also capsized and sank after a taxying accident on 10 August 1976 at New Island, one of the most westerly islands of West Falkland. Relief pilot J.Levine and his passengers were not injured but, because of damage incurred during the recovery and extensive engine and airframe corrosion, VP-FAL was scrapped. Two months later, on 14 October, sister aircraft VP-FAK tipped over and sank following a landing accident at Mare Harbour, East Falkland, in which the pilot (Capt I.T.Campbell MBE) was killed and the passenger slightly injured. The Beaver, carried by the tide, eventually beached itself inverted on Johnsons Island at the entrance to Mare Harbour. VP-FAK was salvaged and brought back aboard 'Monsunen' to Port Stanley, where it was

hangared pending the accident investigation. By the time this had been completed the aircraft was so badly corroded that it had to be scrapped. Surprisingly, a wing from the aircraft was noted lying in the grass at Moody Brook in October 1984, while the fuselage was reported to be outside the AAC facility on Murray Heights, Port Stanley, at about the same time.

In 1977 a review committee, consisting mainly of FIGAS personnel, was formed to consider suitable types of aircraft for future operations in the Islands. A number of options were considered, including the Australian-built GAF Nomad, the Canadian DHC-6 Twin Otter and the British BN-2 Islander — all of them twin-engined. The possibility of adding a third Beaver floatplane to the FIGAS inventory was not discounted, although there was a general (but by no means unanimous) feeling that the air service should gradually evolve into a landplane operation. Landplanes were considered to be more economical than floatplanes and easier to maintain as they were less prone to salt water corrosion. Another important consideration was that the Beaver was by then out of production and any subsequent acquisition would have to be via the second-hand market. Nobody was very keen on being dependant upon that source for the long-term future of FIGAS.

On paper the Nomad looked reasonable, as did the Islander, but the preferred type was the Twin Otter which had gained a good reputation with the British Antarctic Survey Flight who had successfully operated several examples since 1968 in the most extreme of weather conditions. However, the review committee accepted that it, and the Nomad, with their turboprop engines, were too expensive and too sophisticated for the FIGAS maintenance facilities. Either type would also require a substantial increase on the forecasted passenger and freight traffic if the projected financial operating losses were to be kept to a minimum.

Enquiries concerning the 10-seat piston engined Islander revealed that it was proving rugged and economical on the Scottish Highlands and Islands routes where it operated into airstrips of a type proposed for the Falkland Islands settlements. The passenger and freight capacity appeared to be suitable for the Islands and its maintenance requirements were well within the capabilities of the then current FIGAS facilities.

Accordingly, one Islander was ordered, to be paid for by the United Kingdom Overseas Development Administration. Registered VP-FAY, it departed Bembridge, Isle of Wight, on 12 September 1979 and arrived at the new Stanley Airport via North and South America on 4 October. It was based and hangared at the new Airport which had been officially opened on 1 May that year, replacing the temporary aerodrome at nearby Hookers Point.

If Islander operations proved viable, FIGAS intended to gradually phase out floatplane services over a number of years. However, before that could happen, all the farm settlements in the Camp needed suitable airstrips. In some cases the sites of the old Auster strips could be restored, but the vast majority needed to be created from uncultivated land. Settlements were provided with new radio equipment, generators, windsocks, money and advice on how to drain, prepare and construct grass runways. By the time the Islander had been delivered, a small number of new and restored airstrips were available for use.

During the three months prior to December 1979, Capt A.D.Alsop of Loganair Ltd (a successful and experienced Islander operator in the Scottish Highlands and Islands) visited the Falkland Islands to make an assessment of available strips and those being, or about to be, prepared. Their quality ranged from "Excellent" to "Very Good" and "Good" with only a few in the "Acceptable-to-Poor" classification. The settlement farm managers and their staff had listened carefully to the advice they had been given on drainage and surface preparation and over the next few years a network of 41 grass and hard-beach landing sites became available.

Capt Alsop recommended a properly scheduled, but flexible, route structure for the Islander in order to provide the best possible service for the Islands' inhabitants, increase aircraft utilisation and create additional income for FIGAS. The proposed structure was based on three radial routes between Port Stanley and pre-notified destinations, to be operated on specific days (subject to bookings) with optional stops en route on the outbound and inbound legs. Additionally, an "inner circle" route starting and finishing at Port Stanley was also suggested which would operate subject to aircraft availability. These and other proposals concerning the administration of the air service were considered by FIGAS and a number were implemented, albeit some of them in modified form. The Beavers continued to operate on an "on demand" basis to settlements which did not yet have airstrips. They also provided a back-up service to the Islander when it was unserviceable or undergoing scheduled maintenance.

3,870 passengers were carried by FIGAS in the year ending December 1979 and load factors continued to improve between January 1980 and the end of March 1982. Many passengers used these FIGAS passenger flights in conjunction with the LADE Fokker F-27 and F-28 services between Stanley Airport and Comodoro Rivadavia in Argentina [see Falkland Islands External Air Services notes]. All of that came to an abrupt halt with the Argentine invasion in the early hours of 2 April 1982.

Before progressing to the Argentine occupation of the Falkland Islands and its repercussions on FIGAS operations, mention must be made of long-serving aircraft engineers such as Maurice Smith, Dave Jones and Vernon Steen and those pilots employed by the Air Service during the pioneering years before April 1982.

Vic Spencer's last flight for FIGAS (in the Norseman) was on 18 January 1952 and nine days later he departed the Falkland Islands for the United Kingdom. His successor, Capt S.Halls, only stayed a short while before being replaced by Capt F.Deverell. In 1953 J.S.R.Huckle, who had been Harbour Master at Port Stanley, was sent to Hamble in the United Kingdom for pilot training and whilst there he met Jim Kerr, but it was not until 16 September 1954 that they met again. On that occasion it was in Port Stanley, by which time John Huckle was head of the Harbour and Aviation Departments (and a FIGAS pilot) and Capt Kerr had just arrived to replace Frank Deverell. Huckle resigned as FIGAS pilot and administrator in June 1956 and the following month saw Kerr appointed as Head of the Aviation Department (later retitled Director of Civil Aviation), a post that he held until September 1980.

Capt G.Toye replaced John Huckle as a FIGAS pilot and for a period during 1957-58 there were three pilots: Kerr, Toye and a Falkland Islander, Capt I.T.Campbell. Ian Campbell had been taught to fly by Jim Kerr before gaining his CPL at Hamble and returning to the Islands to fly the Beavers. Capt Toye had departed by early 1958 and FIGAS operations continued with only two pilots, Jim Kerr and Ian Campbell, until the latter was killed in October 1976.

Following the death of Ian Campbell and the subsequent AID enquiry, FIGAS was recommended to employ three, and not two, pilots for its operations. Capts R.Hooper and D.Emsley were recruited but Hooper later left and was replaced by Capt J.Ayers on 24 June 1978. In time, Emsley departed and his place was taken by Capt I.White in February 1980. During the period of these comings and goings, Eddie Anderson, a young Islander, was selected for pilot training and joined FIGAS after obtaining his CPL. At the time of writing he was still with FIGAS flying twin-engined Islanders.

After nearly 26 years with FIGAS, Jim Kerr left the Falkland Islands on 26 May 1980 for terminal leave and retirement in the United Kingdom. Having resigned in May, John Ayers departed just over five weeks later, on 2 July. By April 1982 the FIGAS pilots were Anderson, White and Selwood (who had joined FIGAS just over a year before). Capts Ian White and Mike Selwood later left FIGAS and by mid-1985 the Air Service had four resident pilots: Eddie Anderson, Andy Alsop, Ian McPhee and Mike Goodwin (another Falkland Islander).

During the evening of 1 April 1982 a FIGAS pilot flew VP-FAY from the Airport to the Racecourse ready for a dawn reconnaissance flight in response to reports that Argentine ships were approaching the Islands. That proposed flight was pre-empted by the invasion. Following the Argentine landings, the Islander was flown back to the Airport by a reluctant FIGAS pilot where it was immediately impressed into Argentine service.

A number of sorties were made to outlying settlements for various propaganda and military reasons. For example, mail was flown to Goose Green shortly after the invasion and when the Islander arrived there the Argentine flight crew made great play of pointing out that the mail delivery demonstrated their non-hostile intentions and that normality had returned! VP-FAY was noted on 11 April overflying Darwin and Goose Green and landing at Fox Bay East, West Falkland, after two aborted approaches.

A military mission took place on 23 April when it was flown to Pebble Island (reportedly by a LADE pilot). Upon arrival, one of the passengers proceeded to carefully inspect the grass runways before departing again in the Islander. The inspection was obviously satisfactory because, the next day, a Prefectura Skyvan landed to off-load men and materials prior to the deployment of four Mentors from 4 Escuadrilla on 29 April and, subsequently, Grupo 3 Pucaras.

The FIGAS Islander was resident at the Airport on 1 May when the 800 Sqdn Sea Harriers attacked at 1110Z. It was badly damaged by bomb-blast or cannon fire (probably both), to the extent that the fuselage was severed. Subsequent shelling and attacks by Vulcans, Sea Harriers and Harriers merely added to the damage and by the time of the surrender of the Argentine forces late on 14 June, it was in a dilapidated state. Subsequent pilfering and vandalism did not improve matters. The propellers and engines were eventually removed and returned to the United Kingdom for assessment and overhaul, but the airframe, being beyond redemption, was dumped on the edge of the airfield (it was still there, near the FIGAS hangar, in June 1985).

At the outset of the conflict the two FIGAS Beavers were resident at the floatplane hangar. VP-FAT was demolished whilst parked outside the hangar on 11/12 June during British bombardments. VP-FAV, which had been sitting on the slipway, was also damaged, but not as extensively as VP-FAT. However, any hopes of making it airworthy again were dashed on 28 July 1982 when it was blown over onto its back and completely wrecked during a 70 knot gale.

The War and its immediate aftermath had left FIGAS without aeroplanes, so Vernon Steen, Eddie Anderson and Gerald Cheek (the Islands' Director of Civil Aviation) suggested to anyone who would listen that it might be a sensible and prudent idea to make airworthy one of the captured CAB601 UH-1H helicopters for FIGAS use. If achieved, it would reduce the number of civilian missions being demanded of the British Forces' helicopters.

A suitable example (AE-424), minus many parts which had been filched by souvenir hunters or vandals, was taken to the floatplane hangar from the Racecourse where it had been left after the Argentine surrender. FIGAS staff then started work to make it serviceable, recovering instruments and radios which had been removed from AE-424 and other UH-1H's by unauthorised persons — ostensibly for "safe keeping"! Quite naturally, FIGAS' efforts attracted the attention of "desirables" (those who offered to help) and "undesirables" (those who wanted to take the helicopter away!).

Shortly after FIGAS commenced work on AE-424, they were visited by Lt Cdr R.C.Caesley, the AEO of 820 Sqdn based in 'Invincible' with Sea King HAS.5 helicopters. After looking over the rudimentary facilities available to FIGAS (including a severely shell and shrapnel-holed, sieve-like hangar), an offer of practical help was made. Volunteers from the Squadron (notably CPO A.R.Downham and PO G.A.Pilch) would help restore the UH-1H to a flyable condition so that it could be ferried to 'Invincible'. Aboard the carrier it would be stripped down, inspected, missing parts replaced where possible and, finally, repainted in FIGAS colours (LAEM I.R.Nicholl would be responsible for the respray). On 18 August 1982 AE-424, by then known as "Hernandez", was ready and Lt Cdr Keith Dudley (820 Sqdn's Senior Pilot who had been trained to fly UH-1D's during an exchange posting in West Germany) flew it that day to 'Invincible' which was then in San Carlos Water. What happened next is best described by "Hernandez" himself (courtesy of 820 Sqdn and the Editor of "FLIGHT DECK" magazine):

*"Allo Amigos, I been told that I can tella you my life story (de Inglish she gets better every day no?). I was born in America, but I dont remember very much about that as I was very young. I went to work in Argentina (my mother I dont thinka she likes me very much — funny I dont remember her) where I have lots of nice friends, many Hueys and Chinooks. Anyway, I digesting, back to my story, so de next thing I know I am flying over mucha water which looksa very cold. Things happen very quickly after that, de next thing I know I am sitting in a bog, and people are pulling me apart. But I very lucky as funny man with glasses — I think he called Deps (Deputy AEO) — he comes over to me and after much poking around my private parts, sucking of the teeth and shaking of the head, he bring along his boys — they nice boys — who go all over me putting me to rights and things. My radios, they got back from the local radio hams, my dials and things they got from poor wrecked friends.*

*Then this very strange man he come — I no understand him, he says things like Gott und Himmel and Dumpkoff, I think he called de Senile Parrot (Senior Pilot). Anyway he start me up and fly me away to his mother. He very strange man his mother she very big and painted grey and made of steel (I suppose it no wonder he goes around saying dumpkoff all the time). Well dis Senile Parrot his mother she got a warm heart with lots of room and friendly faces. Here they have another man who take a great interest in me, he called Aeeoh. Well he knows of many people he say who do nothing but siesta all de time and he going to get them to do something useful for a change, he say they called Peelots. Well anyway these peelots come and rub me all over with bits of black paper and splash water everywhere, this makes the Aeeoh man very happy. Well after the peelots are finished rubbing me all over, the nice men come and repaint me in the latest fashion, I now red all over with FIGAS painted on in white. One of the peelots he ask the Aeeoh man what this FIGAS mean and he say many things about peelots but he also say it means Falkland Islands Government Air Service, but my name Hernandez, oh well at least I got a nice warm place to sleep in so I not complaining. Then one day I go back on top of the Senile Parrots mother and he and some man with a light blue beret start me up and fly me ashore. Some of my nice new friends I make on mother fly with me to say goodbye. I feel very sad to leave my new friends but I sure to make plenty new ones with the people with light blue berets."*

Gracias, "Hernandez"! 26 August was the date that the UH-1H, by then registered and painted as VP-FBD, was flown from the carrier back to the FIGAS floatplane hangar. For that flight there were two pilots, Lt Cdr Dudley and Maj R.E.Connel CF, a Canadian exchange pilot with 657 Sqdn AAC who had many flying hours on the type. Because 820 Sqdn and 'Invincible' were about to depart for the United Kingdom, and because FIGAS did not have any helicopter pilots, 657 Sqdn (and Maj Connel in particular) had volunteered to fly mail and a limited amount of freight in VP-FBD to the Camp settlements. Unfortunately, only two such flights were made before it was grounded. The MoD was unhappy about military pilots flying a "civil" helicopter — and an uncertificated one at that! 657 Sqdn continued to undertake mail flights but used its own helicopters. Although the MoD decision appeared to be bureaucratic, it really was not — at least not completely. In the immediate aftermath of the War a blind eye was turned to various activities, but eventually a return to normality and regulations was essential and that inevitably applied to 657 Sqdn and its involvement with the UH-1H (even though the Huey really belonged to the MoD and not FIGAS).

After much deliberation it was decided by FIGAS (and others) that the helicopter's airframe, mechanics and electrics should be thoroughly surveyed. An inspection by Ian McLeod (an Islander) on behalf of Bristow Helicopters (a United Kingdom-based company which had offered to help renovate the machine) revealed damage to the port rear skid support frames which was consistent with the UH-1H having suffered a heavy landing at some stage. More deliberation by FIGAS and the Falkland Islands Government resulted in a decision being made to send the helicopter to Bristow's Redhill (near London, United Kingdom) maintenance base where the main gearbox, rotor-head and airframe would be overhauled. There was even talk of replacing VP-FBD with one of the airworthy examples which had been shipped back to the United Kingdom by the British Forces, but that came to nothing.

VP-FBD was prepared for the sea journey and carried by an 18 Sqdn Chinook to an awaiting ship, but that was as far as it went. The decision to take it to the United Kingdom was rescinded and "Hernandez" was airlifted back to the floatplane hangar. Sir Rex Hunt, the Civil Commissioner, decided after further deliberation and advice that it would remain in the Falkland Islands, not as a commercial helicopter but as a future museum piece. In retrospect, it was the correct decision. Although initially there were ample spare parts on the Islands, the cost to FIGAS of operating such an uneconomical military helicopter and certifying it to carry fare-paying passengers would have made the whole venture a financial impracticability. Following a long period of outside storage close to the floatplane hangar and later at Moody Brook, VP-FBD was moved into the old hovercraft hangar there in August 1984 and was still resident in June 1985.

During August 1982, FIGAS purchased a second-hand Beaver in Canada to replace one of those lost as a result of the conflict. The original intention had been to obtain the turboprop version because AVGAS was becoming increasingly difficult to obtain. However, it was not to be and by the end of 1982 a landplane, piston-engined Beaver (VP-FBE) had been shipped to the Islands. It was converted to a floatplane and flight-tested on 20 January 1983 prior to entering service with FIGAS.

Two new piston-engined Islanders (VP-FBF and VP-FBG), replacements for the ill-fated VP-FAY and the other lost Beaver, were purchased for FIGAS using Rehabilitation Funds provided by the United Kingdom and on 4 January 1983 the crated aircraft departed Ridham Docks, Gravesend, aboard the 'Kirsten Smits' bound for Port Stanley. The ship arrived in Stanley Harbour on 16 February and by late March the Islanders had been off-loaded, assembled and test-flown from RAF Stanley (the renamed Stanley Airport).

With the FIGAS inventory thus restored to three aircraft, the next problem was to repair war-damaged airstrips and provide new ones at those settlements in the Camp still without them. By late October 1984 that had been achieved and floatplane operations finally ceased. It was fortunate that the airstrips were ready by then because the Beaver's floats had become corroded and needed replacing. VP-FBE was then converted to a landplane which meant that the 1977 objective of a landplane-only fleet had finally been achieved, in spite of an unscheduled interruption to the master plan in 1982!

In March 1985 the Beaver was advertised for sale and the following month it departed Port Stanley aboard 'Bransfield' for Grimsby in the United Kingdom, where it was off-loaded and stored awaiting a buyer. A third Islander ordered to replace it was being worked on in October 1985 at the Pilatus Britten-Norman factory at Bembridge for delivery to the Falkland Islands at the end of the year. By way of a reminder of the 1982 War, and the short-lived existence of the FIGAS UH-1H, the third Islander was allocated that helicopter's registration — VP-FBD.

The future of FIGAS seems assured, with a fleet of three modern and economical Islanders, a network of good airstrips throughout the Islands, and a steady annual increase in passenger, mail and freight traffic. Although the new Royal Air Force-operated aerodrome at Mount Pleasant (about 23 miles south-west of Port Stanley) with its 8,497ft main runway was officially opened on 12 May 1985, FIGAS remain based at RAF Stanley where the hangarage has been increased to cater for the new Islander.

For the immediate future FIGAS, other than on special occasions, does not plan to operate out of RAF Mount Pleasant but, should the need arise, it could provide feeder flights for Falkland Islanders, tourists and others travelling to and from the United Kingdom in such types as Boeing 747's and Lockheed Tristars — a far cry from the initial flight by an Auster on 19 December 1948.

*The first aircraft purchased by FIGAS after the conflict was the Beaver VP-FBE. Delivered in 12.82, it remained in service (initially as a floatplane and latterly as a landplane) until 1985 when it was withdrawn from use at RAF Stanley and flown to the Racecourse for disposal. Following this engine-run on the slipway outside the floatplane hangar in 1.85, the engine was inhibited and the aircraft dismantled and crated for shipping to the United Kingdom. The tundra tyres are for soft surface operations.* (V. Steen)

# FALKLAND ISLANDS EXTERNAL AIR SERVICES

Although the concept of a Catalina or Canso service to Montevideo in Uruguay had been proposed by Miles Clifford and others, it was not until 1951 that a real attempt was made to establish an external air service. Aquila Airways Limited, a flying-boat operator based at Southampton, was contacted by L.W.H.Young (the then Managing Director of the Falkland Islands Company) and asked about the possibility of using Sunderlands to operate a service between the United Kingdom and the Falkland Islands. A feasibility study revealed that a Sunderland could complete the journey between Southampton Water and Stanley Harbour in six stages, taking eight or nine days.

A survey flight was arranged for April 1952 (FIC's centenary year), allowing time for the necessary planning to be completed. In the late evening of 20 April, with Capt Douglas Pearson in command, Sunderland III G-AGJN took-off from Southampton Water carrying nine passengers and crew on the first leg to Funchal (Madeira). During the morning of 22 April it departed there for Sal (Cape Verde Islands), continuing to Natal and Rio de Janeiro (Brazil) on 25 April before reaching Montevideo in

the evening of 26 April. After a stopover of forty hours, G-AGJN was airborne again on 28 April for the final eight-hour journey to Stanley Harbour where it alighted later that day.

The aircraft's arrival was cause for much celebration but, after four days of socialising and discussing the flight with what seemed to be the entire population of the Islands, Capt Pearson, his crew and 16 passengers departed in the Sunderland on 2 May for the reciprocal flight to the United Kingdom. The flying-boat eventually landed on Southampton Water in the mid-afternoon of 8 May after a very successful round trip of 18,000 miles. The survey had proved that an air service to the Falkland Islands was a practical proposition. Moreover, with careful planning and reduced stopover times en route, the flight-time in each direction could be shortened to three or four days. Unfortunately, for reasons that have never been fully explained, the service was not implemented and it was to be 19 years before an external air service became a reality.

Following a "Joint Statement", initialled by the United Kingdom and Argentina on 1 July 1971 and formally

*Moored in the choppy waters of Stanley Harbour sometime between 28.4 and 2.5.52 is Aquila Airways' Sunderland III, G-AGJN. In spite of the flying boat's successful route-proving flight from Southampton, no air service was established between the Falklands and the United Kingdom until 1985 when British Airways commenced Boeing 747 flights from RAF Mount Pleasant to RAF Brize Norton.*

*(via Orlean Bonner)*

*The Argentine-British "Joint Declaration of Buenos Aires 1 July 1971" allowed Argentina to operate an air service between Port Stanley and, normally, Comodoro Rivadavia using the HU-16B Albatross amphibians of I Escuadron de Busqueda y Salvamento. This photograph of BS-03 in Stanley Harbour was taken in 11.72, about the time that the Argentine-constructed temporary airstrip at Hookers Point (near Port Stanley) came into operation and the Albatross service ceased.* *(J. S. Wright)*

signed by both nations on 8 August that year, a temporary air service was initiated between Port Stanley and Comodoro Rivadavia in Argentina using HU-16B Albatross amphibians of the FAA's Search and Rescue unit, 1 Escuadron de Busqueda y Salvamento. The possibility of such a service had arisen after a successful Albatross flight was made to Port Stanley in February 1971 to evacuate a seriously ill lighthouse keeper to Argentina for an emergency operation. Albatross BS-02 operated the first official passenger flight on 3 July 1971.

The implementation of the air service was welcomed by many Islanders, but the involvement of Argentina was treated with suspicion by some of them, especially when they learned that Argentina had been given permission to build a temporary airstrip at Hookers Point (near Port Stanley) so that FAA/LADE Friendship airliners could replace the amphibians. The aluminium matting airstrip, initially 2,625ft long but later extended to 3,281ft, was to remain in use until an airport constructed by the United Kingdom on the Cape Pembroke peninsula came into operation in 1977. The Hookers Point airstrip was opened

on 15 November 1972 and LADE flights operated from there until December 1977, when they were transferred to Stanley Airport with its 4,100ft runway (although the Airport was not officially opened until 1 May 1979). The temporary airstrip remained available for use by light aircraft, diversions or emergency landings until the night of 1/2 November 1978, when a high wind uprooted the matting runway and many large sections received irreparable damage. The Friendships eventually gave way to Fellowships and the once or twice-weekly service continued until the Argentine invasion on 2 April 1982, after which the LADE services continued on a once-weekly basis until 27 April when all Argentine flights from the mainland to Port Stanley were suspended. When FAA flights resumed in early May, they were undertaken by C-130's; the LADE services were not resumed.

After the War a new aerodrome was constructed at Mount Pleasant (south-west of Port Stanley) and from May 1985 the Islanders had, at last, an air service to the United Kingdom.

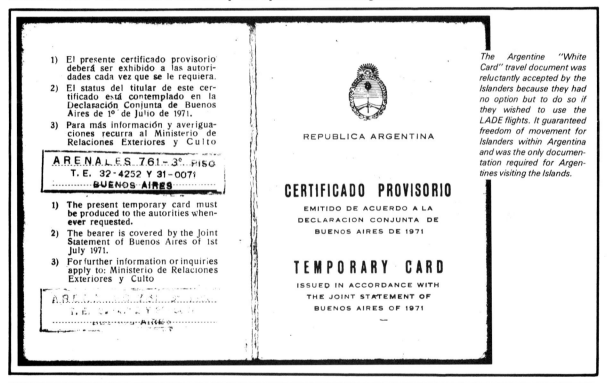

The Argentine "White Card" travel document was reluctantly accepted by the Islanders because they had no option but to do so if they wished to use the LADE flights. It guaranteed freedom of movement for Islanders within Argentina and was the only documentation required for Argentines visiting the Islands.

# FALKLAND ISLANDS ARGENTINE INCURSIONS

Prior to April 1982 an Argentine invasion of the Falkland Islands had always been a possibility although, to many distant observers, the threat seemed improbable. The Islanders, however, realised how vulnerable their Islands were and that only token resistance would be possible should Argentina decide to seek sovereignty by force. Moreover, many Islanders held serious reservations

concerning the British Government's reaction to such an invasion. Would military force be used to oust the Argentines, or would London treat it as "fait accompli" and come to an accommodation with Buenos Aires?

During 1963 and 1964 there was a resurgence of Argentine interest in the Islands and dormant passions were aroused in the Argentine population by their government when a "Malvinas Day" and other measures were announced. Although such measures were probably intended to do little more than propagate emotive discussion about liberating "Las Islas Malvinas" from British colonial rule, they may have led directly to three bizarre aviation-related incidents on the Falkland Islands. Each demonstrated the hot-headedness of some Argentines and the vulnerability of the Islands.

In September 1964 an Argentine-registered Cessna 172 (identity unknown) flown by one Miguel Fitzgerald landed on Port Stanley Racecourse. An Argentine flag was planted and a written proclamation of Argentine sovereignty handed to a bemused Islander before the Cessna took-off to return to Argentina. The Argentine Government publicly dissociated itself from the event.

Two years later a far less amusing incident occurred. At 1245Z on 28 September an unfamiliar sound was heard in Port Stanley as a DC-4 (LV-AGG) of Aerolineas Argentinas, trying to remain below cloud, made several low passes over the town. Eventually the pilot commenced a westerly approach to, and a landing on, the Racecourse. The DC-4 narrowly missed a grandstand before touching down about 100 yards beyond and skidding to a halt 400 yards later (having hit two telephone poles on the way). No sooner did it come to rest than the starboard undercarriage started to sink into soft ground. LV-AGG had been on a domestic flight between Buenos Aires and Rio Gallegos when it was hijacked by an armed Argentine nationalist group known as "El Condor" and the pilot forced to fly the aircraft to Port Stanley. The number of people on board varies according to different accounts, but it appears that there was a crew of six and probably 45 passengers of whom either 18 or 26 (including one woman and a photographer) belonged to, or sympathised with, "El Condor".

On the Racecourse, a detachment of Royal Marines arrived in a Land Rover as some of the occupants emerged from the aircraft wearing anoraks and hoods and brandishing Mauser sub-machine guns. The Marines had

The largest aircraft ever likely to land on Port Stanley Racecourse was a hijacked Aerolineas Argentinas DC-4 (LV-AGG) which unexpectedly arrived on 28.9.66. On board were members of the "El Condor" group who had come to liberate "Las Malvinas". The aircraft sank into the soft ground to its starboard wing-tip but when photographed here it had been raised ready for take-off. It managed to get airborne safely although the clearance between wing-tips and grandstands was in the order of only two feet!
(J. Leonard)

In 11.68 the Aero Commander LV-JGE, owned by the Argentine newspaper "Cronica", landed in rough ground alongside the Eliza Cove road to the south-east of Port Stanley, damaging its undercarriage. The three occupants, fanatical Argentine nationalists, had arrived to confront Lord Chalfont (who was visiting the Falklands) about Argentine sovereignty of "Las Islas Malvinas". The three were taken to 'Endurance' in 'Endurance' Flight's Whirlwind HAR.9, XL898 'ED/(4)49', where they were held in custody. Eventually they, and their aircraft, were shipped back to Argentina.
(J. Leonard and J. S. Wright)

little option but to surrender. No sooner had they done so than the "El Condor" leader (a slim-hipped, blonde-haired and blue-eyed woman in her middle twenties) came forward to address the officer-in-charge of the Marines. Unfortunately her English was poor and a male hijacker was ushered to the front to inform the officer that the "El Condor" group had come to liberate the "Malvinas" and its population from British rule. He was politely informed by the officer, and locals present, that the Islanders had no desire to be liberated from British rule. When translated, this statement caused consternation among the hijackers and for a few minutes they seemed undecided on their next action.

Events became more unpleasant when the Marines were taken on board as hostages while the hijackers argued. Eventually, the passengers were allowed off and, after further heated discussions, the pilot was ordered to fly the hijackers back to Argentina. However, when the engines were started and full power was applied, the aircraft became bogged down to its axles. This was perhaps fortunate because there was later said to be only 20 minutes worth of fuel left in its tanks.

The drama ended later in the day when a local priest, acting as a mediator, negotiated the surrender of the hijackers and the release of the Marines on the promise that the hijackers would be allowed to return unhindered to Argentina. The following day an Argentine merchant vessel (with marines on board) came into Falklands' waters and took the "El Condor" group back to Argentina where they were each sentenced to 15 years imprisonment. The somewhat shaken passengers were also repatriated by sea. It took three days to raise LV-AGG clear of the mud and, with 1,600 gallons of fuel on board, the DC-4 managed to take-off on 8 October and return safely to Argentina.

A third uninvited aircraft arrived in November 1968 while Lord Chalfont (then Minister of State at the Foreign and Commonwealth Office) was in the Falkland Islands to explain to the Islanders the policy that the British Government had been pursuing in recent discussions with Argentina concerning the Islands. Knowing that Lord Chalfont and press reporters following his visit were in Port Stanley, Hector Garcia, editor of the Argentine newspaper "Cronica", decided to fly to the Islands to confront the Minister in the presence of reporters with questions pertaining to Argentine sovereignty of "Las Malvinas". Garcia was a consistently fanatical nationalist who, a few years later, would announce that he had recruited 20,000 volunteers to invade the Falkland Islands. (The response of the Argentine military government of the day was to shut down the newspaper for a year.) Garcia was also the photographer who had accompanied the "El Condor" hijackers to Port Stanley in the DC-4.

Piloted by none other than Miguel Fitzgerald, Garcia and an unknown passenger were flown to Port Stanley in the newspaper's Aero Commander, LV-JGE. On arriving overhead Port Stanley, Fitzgerald circled the town at least twice before deciding not to land on the Racecourse where the aircraft might become bogged down. Instead, he elected to land on a straight section of the Eliza Cove gravel road stretching south-east from Port Stanley to the Cove. The road was very narrow and although one mainwheel briefly touched it, the Aero Commander actually landed in rough ground alongside and stopped with one wheel in a ditch and a badly damaged undercarriage.

Within a few minutes of the aircraft grinding to a halt a Whirlwind HAR.9 (XL898) from 'Endurance' landed nearby bringing armed Royal Marines. Coincident with the helicopter, a Land Rover containing Lord Chalfont and other officials arrived. As no-one quite knew what to expect, there was considerable relief when the aircraft's occupants proved to be three unarmed, if voluble, civilians. Despite protestations, the Argentines were flown to 'Endurance' in the Whirlwind and detained there. Garcia never achieved his public confrontation with Lord Chalfont, but was eventually interviewed by incredulous press reporters who could scarcely believe that the editor of a newspaper could be directly involved in such a fiasco. Shortly afterwards, the three Argentines and their damaged and dismantled Aero Commander were shipped back to Argentina.

Thus ended the third of three unpleasant, unnecessary and, as it transpired, related incidents which did nothing to improve the already strained relationship between Argentina, the Falkland Islands and the United Kingdom. Strident editorials stressing Argentine sovereignty claims (and in some cases advocating invasion) continued to appear in "Cronica" and other Argentine newspapers and journals. Perhaps, in retrospect, it was inevitable that there would eventually be another incursion. It occurred, on 2 April 1982.

# THE DEPENDENCIES & BRITISH ANTARCTIC TERRITORY

Space limitations prevent anything more than a brief description of aviation activity in the Falkland Islands Dependencies and British Antarctic Territory. Indeed, the past 43 years have provided enough information to devote a book to the subject, ranging from South Georgia-based whaling companies using Walrus amphibians and S-55 helicopters for spotting whales to accounts of ski-equipped aircraft operations from snow and ice airstrips in Antarctica. However, for the purposes of this book, aviation details must be restricted to the activities of the Falkland Island Dependencies Survey and its successor, the British Antarctic Survey, both of which used aircraft registered in the Falkland Islands. Detailed histories of their aeroplanes can be read elsewhere in this book but, in order to appreciate them, some background explanation of the origins of FIDS and BAS is necessary.

In response to the Argentine annexation on 8 February 1942 of a segment of British territory in Antarctica (an

BRITISH ANTARCTIC SURVEY STATIONS

Permanent stations

| FARADAY | | |
|---|---|---|
| Argentine Islands | Lat | 65°15'S |
| (geophysical observatory) | Long | 64°16'W |

| GRYTVIKEN* | | |
|---|---|---|
| Cumberland East Bay | Lat | 54°17'S |
| South Georgia | Long | 36°30'W |
| (biological and geophysical station) | | |

| BIRD ISLAND | | |
|---|---|---|
| South Georgia | Lat | 54°00'S |
| (biological station) | Long | 38°03'W |

| HALLEY † | | |
|---|---|---|
| Coats Land | Lat | 75°35'S |
| (geophysical observatory) | Long | 26°46'W |

| ROTHERA | | |
|---|---|---|
| Adelaide Island | Lat | 67°34'S |
| (earth sciences air base) | Long | 68°08'W |

| SIGNY | | |
|---|---|---|
| Signy Island | Lat | 60°43'S |
| South Orkney Islands | Long | 45°36'W |
| (biological laboratory) | | |

Field stations (summer only)

| DAMOY | | |
|---|---|---|
| Dorian Bay | Lat | 64°49'S |
| Wiencke Island | Long | 63°31'W |
| (air facility) | | |

| FOSSIL BLUFF | | |
|---|---|---|
| Alexander Island | Lat | 71°20'S |
| (earth sciences air facility) | Long | 68°17'W |

\* Closed temporarily
† Situated on a floating ice shelf moving westward at about 0.8km per year.

*When the Antarctic area of what had been administered as the Falkland Islands Dependencies was retitled British Antarctic Territory in 1962, FIDS became BAS. BAS aircraft then adopted their construction numbers as identities rather than using Falkland Islands civil registrations. Otter "294" was formerly VP-FAK (although actually VP-FAI!). Of interest is the "Bass Ales" style of lettering on the engine cowling and the roundel. The c/n is on the fin and beneath the port wing.*
*(British Antarctic Survey)*

area of land and sea between 25°W and 68°34'W which included Deception Island in the South Shetland Islands), the warship 'Carnarvon Castle' was sent to Deception Island. The Union Flag was raised in January 1943 and all signs of Argentine occupancy were removed, but the event caused the British Government to review its rights in the area and how it would preserve them. Moreover, the strategic importance of the area had to be considered, especially as the political situation in Argentina at the time — the middle of World War II — made it undesireable for that nation to have control of the southern half of Drake Passage (between South America and Antarctica), perhaps allowing German merchant "raider" ships access to sheltered Antarctic harbours. Despite more pressing priorities elsewhere, the Royal Navy was tasked with sending a small, military-orientated scientific force under the code name Operation "Tabarin" to establish British bases. By February 1944 two were in being, one on Deception Island and the other at Port Lockroy on Wiencke Island, close to the Graham Land Peninsula (later renamed the Antarctic Peninsula). During the next two years more bases, or Stations as they came to be known, were created and, aside from any military requirements, the scientific potential of Antarctica began to be realised. Control of "Tabarin" passed to the Colonial Office at the end of World War II and the organisation was renamed as the Falkland Islands Dependencies Survey (British-administered areas of Antarctica were part of the Falkland Islands Dependencies at that time).

The vagaries of the Antarctic environment and its effect on all forms of surface transport inevitably led to the use of aircraft. FIDS obtained its first aeroplane, a ski-equipped Auster J/1 Autocrat (G-AIBI), in 1946. A small hangar was built at the FIDS Station on Stonington Island (Marguerite Bay, Graham Land) in preparation for its arrival on 'Trepassey' in late February or early March 1947. The crated aircraft was rafted ashore and hauled onto the beach where it was unpacked, assembled, christened "Ice Cold Katy" and put to work. Unfortunately, "Katy" was destroyed on 15 September that year when a ski hit a projecting lump of ice, causing her to turn over onto her back. The replacement, a second-hand Hornet Moth biplane (G-ADMO), arrived at Deception Island on 21 February 1948 and, like its predecessor, was rafted ashore. However, because no skis had come with the aeroplane, G-ADMO was a useless asset and remained crated on the beach. A packing case which reportedly contained the skis was eventually traced, but upon opening was found to contain stove pipes!

The Hornet Moth was later registered in the Falkland Islands as VP-FAE and shipped to Port Stanley in March 1950, remaining in storage in a hangar (crated and still marked as G-ADMO) until burned in 1957. *[Details of VP-FAE and subsequent Falklands-registered aircraft that served with FIDS (and later BAS) are included in the Individual Aircraft Details which follow this section].*

Aircraft did not constitute a regular, or integral, part of FIDS/BAS activities until the purchase of a Beaver and an Otter in 1959/60. An airstrip and hangar were constructed on Deception Island, which was to become the centre of aircraft operations for the next eight years, and facilities at the Station were made adequate for aircraft to be serviced and wintered there. Regrettably, the airstrip and base had to be vacated in December 1967 due to a volcanic eruption on the Island. The air facility was moved south to Adelaide Station (on Adelaide Island), but it was not practical to maintain the newly-acquired Twin Otter aircraft there. They were flown to the Northern Hemisphere

In formation over the English countryside near their Fairoaks "winter quarters" in early 10.83 or late 9.84 are the three BAS Twin Otters VP-FAZ, VP-FBB and VP-FBC. Soon after the photograph was taken they departed on their annual "migration" to Rothera Station on Adelaide Island in British Antarctic Territory.
*(British Antarctic Survey)*

for maintenance and wintering (initially to Canada, but latterly to the United Kingdom) at the end of each summer's operations. The snow and ice airstrip at Adelaide Station deteriorated with time and the air facility was moved to Rothera Station (also on Adelaide Island), about 40 miles to the north-east. That Station was still the hub of BAS operations in 1985.

The most radical political event to take place in Antarctica occurred in 1959 when the Antarctic Treaty was signed by the United Kingdom and 11 other nations. The Treaty led to much more friendly co-operation, and considerably less squabbling about territorial claims, between countries possessing Antarctic bases. The Antarctic portion of what had previously been administered as the Falkland Islands Dependencies was designated British Antarctic Territory in 1962 and FIDS was redesignated as the British Antarctic Survey. Because the Territory was no longer part of the Falkland Islands Dependencies,

Falklands' registration letters ceased to appear on BAS aircraft and construction numbers were used for identification instead (the aeroplanes on charge between 1962 and early 1968 never leaving the Territory). However, with the demise of Deception Island Station and the procurement of aeroplanes which required servicing outside the Territory, BAS aircraft had to be registered somewhere in order to permit ferry flights to and from Antarctica via South America. They could have been registered in the United Kingdom but, as the Governor of the Falkland Islands was also High Commissioner of the Territory, it was decided to resume the tradition of registering aircraft in the Falkland Islands (where BAS had an office). By 1985 the Survey had three Twin Otters in its inventory (VP-FAZ, VP-FBB and VP-FBC) and, as this book was being finalised, they were being prepared at their United Kingdom winter quarters at Fairoaks for the annual pilgrimage south to Antarctica and another season supporting BAS field and scientific parties.

# FALKLAND ISLANDS CIVIL AIRCRAFT REGISTER & INDIVIDUAL AIRCRAFT DETAILS

*Abbreviations & acronyms used and their meanings*

| | |
|---|---|
| *AAL* | *Auster Aircraft Limited, Rearsby, UK.* |
| *AOP* | *Air Observation Post.* |
| *BAS* | *British Antarctic Survey.* |
| *CAC* | *Cessna Aircraft Company, Wichita, Kansas, USA.* |
| *CCF* | *Canadian Car and Foundry Company Limited, Montreal, Quebec, Canada.* |
| *Cert* | *Certificate.* |
| *c/n* | *construction number.* |
| *Dept* | *Department.* |
| *DHC* | *de Havilland Aircraft Company (Canada) Limited and de Havilland Aircraft of Canada Limited, Downsview, Ontario, Canada.* |
| *FIDS* | *Falkland Islands Dependencies Survey.* |
| *FIGAS* | *Falkland Islands Government Air Service.* |
| *FI Govt* | *Falkland Islands Government.* |
| *IAVB* | *Intreprinderea de Avioane Bucuresti.* |
| *IRMA* | *Intreprinderea de Reparat Material Aeronautic.* |
| *JEA* | *Jersey European Airways Limited.* |
| *MAL* | *Mann Aviation Limited.* |
| *MU* | *Maintenance Unit.* |
| *NERC* | *Natural Environment Research Council.* |
| *PBN* | *Pilatus Britten-Norman Limited, Bembridge, Isle of Wight, UK.* |
| *PFAG* | *Pilatus Flugzeugwerke Aktiengesellschaft, Stans, Switzerland.* |
| *RCAF* | *Royal Canadian Air Force.* |
| *Regd* | *Registered.* |
| *Regn* | *Registration.* |
| *RNoAF* | *Royal Norwegian Air Force.* |
| *SBAC* | *Society of British Aerospace Companies Limited.* |
| *SPRI* | *Scott Polar Research Institute, Cambridge, UK.* |
| *WFU* | *Withdrawn From Use.* |
| *WOC* | *Written Off Charge.* |

**VP-FAA** *Auster 5*      *c/n 2054*

Civilianised (believed by AAL) RAF AOP.5 TW510, bought on behalf of the FI Govt by FIDS (purchase details completed 10.9.48) and regd as G-AJCH on 18.4.48. Crated and shipped on 'John Biscoe' from Southampton to Port Stanley during 11.48. Reassembled at its Port Stanley Racecourse base and test-flown from there by V.H.Spencer on 19.12.48 prior to the initial air ambulance flight 24.12.48. Although allotted the regn VP-FAA c6.3.49, the FI Regn Cert to that effect (cancelling G-AJCH on the British Civil Aircraft Register) was not issued until 26.9.49. The aircraft was still marked as G-AJCH (but using VP-FAA as a call-sign) on 7.4.49 when, on landing at San Carlos settlement airstrip,

the mainwheels sank into soft ground causing the aeroplane to overturn and sustain damage to the fin and fuselage. V.H.Spencer, the pilot, was uninjured but the aircraft had to be shipped to Port Stanley and from there to AAL in the UK (date unknown) for repair and conversion to a floatplane. Repaired and converted, VP-FAA was returned by ship to FIGAS at Port Stanley and, after reassembly, test-flown from Stanley Harbour by V.H.Spencer on 23.6.51. Following its last commercial flight (by J.Kerr) on 24.4.56 the aircraft was retained as a trainer until WFU 6.56 due to extensive corrosion in the tail and fuselage framework. Subsequently broken up and burned in early 1957 with VP-FAB, VP-FAC and VP-FAE (G-ADMO). Regn cancelled on 4.2.57.

**VP-FAB** *Auster 4*      *c/n 817*

Civilianised (believed by AAL) RAF AOP.4 MS951, bought on behalf of the FI Govt by FIDS (purchase details completed 7.9.48) and regd as G-AJCI on 18.8.48. Crated and shipped on 'John Biscoe' from Southampton to Port Stanley during 11.48. Reassembled at its Port Stanley Racecourse base and test-flown from there on 3.3.49 by V.H.Spencer. Although the regn VP-FAB was allotted c6.3.49 and was subsequently used as a call-sign, the aircraft reportedly remained marked as G-AJCI until an unknown date after 26.9.49 when the FI Regn Cert confirming the VP-FAB allocation was issued, thereby cancelling G-AJCI on the British Civil Aircraft Register. Retained as a landplane and,

following its last known flight on 30.10.51, was WFU by FIGAS. Dismantled and stored in a hangar as a spares source until burned in early 1957 with VP-FAA, VP-FAC and VP-FAE (G-ADMO). Regn cancelled on 4.2.57.

**VP-FAC** *Auster 5*                    *c/n 1813*

RAF AOP.5 TW476, bought ex-storage at 20MU Aston Down by AAL on 30.5.49 against a FIDS order for a civilianised floatplane conversion to be used on an Antarctic rescue mission. Regd VP-FAC and painted as such by 25.8.49 when ready for its initial test-flight as a landplane. Flown to Beaumaris, Anglesey on 30.8.49 for 6.45hrs of floatplane trials by Auster test pilot L.Leetham before returning to Rearsby as a landplane on 16.9.49. Departed (crated) on 'John Biscoe' from Southampton 12.10.49 for Deception Island, South Shetlands, where it was unloaded, assembled and then air-tested on 18.12.49. Flown as a floatplane from there to the Argentine Islands to rendezvous with (and be based on) 'John Biscoe'. Piloted by Flt Lt J.Lewis, it reconnoitred open sea routes around ice floes and clear water areas close to Stonington Island in Marguerite Bay, Graham Land before the 11 persons marooned on the Island were rescued in three groups by Norseman VP-FAD and 'John Biscoe' between 30.1.50 and 11.2.50. VP-FAC returned to Deception Island on 19.2.50 where it was dismantled and crated prior to being shipped to Port Stanley on 'John Biscoe', arriving there 3.3.50. Off-loaded, reassembled by FIDS and then loaned to the FI Govt after their pilot (V.H.Spencer) had been checked-out by Flt Lt Lewis on 7.5.50. Sold to FIGAS in 11.51 and remained in service until c8.53 when WFU because of airframe corrosion. Dismantled and stored in a hangar as a spares source until burned in early 1957 with VP-FAA, VP-FAB and VP-FAE (G-ADMO). Regn cancelled on 4.2.57.

**VP-FAD** *Norseman 5*                *c/n N29-45*

Last production aircraft, purchased by FIDS from CCF in 1949 for an Antarctic rescue mission. Regd VP-FAD and painted as such be-

fore being crated and shipped to the UK. Departed on 'John Biscoe' from Southampton 12.10.49 for Deception Island, South Shetlands, where it was unloaded, assembled as a floatplane and then air-tested on 28.12.49. Flown to the Argentine Islands and operating from there on 30.1.50 and 6.2.50 its pilot (Pt Off P.St Louis RCAF) flew the aircraft to Stonington Island in Marguerite Bay, Graham Land, to rescue (in two groups) five of the 11 men marooned on the Island. Returned to Deception Island to be dismantled and crated prior to being shipped to Port Stanley on 'John Biscoe', arriving there 3.3.50. Off-loaded and assembled by FIDS and then loaned to the FI Govt after their pilot (V.H.Spencer) had been type-checked by Pt Off St Louis on 2.6.50. Sold to FIGAS later that year and remained in service until c8.53 when WFU due to advanced corrosion in main undercarriage legs, engine bearers and other metal components. Dismantled and stored in the floatplane hangar until early 1957 when the airframe was scuttled in Stanley Harbour. The floats, however, were retained for many years as part of a raft. Regn cancelled on 4.2.57.

**VP-FAE** *DH.87B Hornet Moth*        *c/n 8086*

Purchased by FIDS from a Danish owner (to replace J/1 Autocrat G-AIBI — *see text*) and regd as G-ADMO 26.11.47 (previous identity OY-DTI). Overhauled at Hatfield and, following a test-flight from there, was crated and shipped from Southampton on 'John Biscoe' to Deception Island, Antarctica, arriving there on 21.2.48. Although unloaded onto the beach there was no point in unpacking it because, due to a loading oversight, no skis had been sent with the aircraft. On 26.9.49, while still located at Deception Island, a FI Regn Cert was issued allocating the regn VP-FAE to the aeroplane, thereby cancelling G-ADMO on the British Civil Aircraft Register. Remained snowbound in packing cases until shipped on 'John Biscoe' to Port Stanley (arriving 3.3.50) where the crated machine was off-loaded and stored in the landplane hangar. When eventually partially unpacked, an inspection revealed that dampness had affected the plywood construction and some

glued joints. Although no longer airworthy, VP-FAE (still marked as G-ADMO) languished in storage until early 1957 when it was burned with VP-FAA, VP-FAB and VP-FAC. Regn cancelled on 4.2.57.

*The aircraft's log books were still in existence as late as 1979 in the Aviation Dept office on Govt Jetty, Port Stanley.*

**VP-FAF** *DHC-2 Beaver*              *c/n 500*

Purchased new from DHC by the FI Govt for FIGAS and shipped (crated) on 'Fitzroy' to Port Stanley 6/7.53. Under DHC supervision it was unloaded, assembled and then test-flown (by a DHC pilot) from Stanley Harbour prior to handover to FIGAS in 8.53. Due to a regn allocation error, the aircraft had been delivered painted as VP-FAE instead of VP-FAF. By 21.8.56 the mistake had been realised but the aeroplane remained marked as VP-FAE until at least 6.6.67, the date of its last known flight for FIGAS. About then it was sold to L.J.Dorney of Mexico City, Mexico and regd N17597. Departed (crated) on 'Darwin' in late 1967 or early 1968 (reportedly still marked as VP-FAE) for Montevideo, Uruguay, and onward trans-shipment. Regn (VP-FAF) was cancelled on 15.3.68. As late as 11.84 a spare (or replaced) wing marked VP-FAE was lying in the grass at Moody Brook near Port Stanley.

**VP-FAG** *DHC-2 Beaver*              *c/n 828*

Purchased new from DHC by the FI Govt for FIGAS and shipped (crated) on 'Fitzroy' to Port Stanley, arriving there in late 8.55. Under DHC supervision, it was unpacked and assembled as a floatplane prior to its acceptance test-flight from Stanley Harbour by J.Kerr on 29.9.55. Due to a regn allocation error, the aircraft had been delivered painted as VP-FAF instead of VP-FAG. Although the mistake was realised, and amended regn paperwork issued on 21.8.56, the aircraft remained marked as VP-FAF. While being piloted by G.Toye sometime between 11.57 and 3.58, it capsized and sank in a take-off at the Moro, Douglas Station, East Falkland (there were no casualties). Salvaged and shipped on 'Shackleton' to

Port Stanley but, having been badly damaged during recovery, was deemed to be "beyond economical repair" and reduced to spares and scrap. Regn not cancelled until 15.3.68.

**VP-FAH** *DHC-2 Beaver*                    *c/n 1129*

Purchased new from DHC by the FI Govt for FIGAS as a replacement for VP-FAG. Crated and shipped on 'Fitzroy' to Port Stanley, arriving there in 7.58. Unpacked and assembled as a floatplane prior to being flight-tested from Stanley Harbour by J.Kerr on 19.8.58. Remained in service until at least 5.1.67, the date of its last known flight for FIGAS. Sold c6.67 to L.J.Downey of Mexico City, Mexico and regd N17598. Departed (crated) on 'Darwin' in late 1967 or early 1968 (reportedly still marked as VP-FAH) for Montevideo, Uruguay, and onward trans-shipment. FI regn cancelled on 15.3.68.

**VP-FAI** *DHC-3 Otter*                    *c/n 294*

Bought new from DHC by FIDS and painted in error as VP-FAK (VP-FAK had been reserved for future FIGAS use). Departed (crated) on 'Kista Dan' from Southampton 18.12.59 for Deception Island, South Shetlands, arriving there on 26.1.60. Unpacked, assembled, fitted with wheels/skis and test-flown by 3.2.60. Flown south to the Argentine Islands 18.3.60 and then to Horseshoe Island in Marguerite Bay on 19.3.60 for relief operations before returning to Deception Island on 27.3.60 to be hangared and serviced during the winter. (From then until 3.67 the aircraft was normally based at Adelaide Station on Adelaide Island for FIDS/BAS support flights during the summer months, returning to Deception Island each winter for maintenance and storage.) Damaged in a series of gales at Deception Island from 2-10.10.61 but repaired 11/12.10.61. On 30.10.61 a FI Regn Cert was issued confirming the aircraft to be VP-FAI but the airframe markings were not altered. Following an ownership change from FIDS to BAS on 1.1.62, the aeroplane was painted in BAS livery (to comply with the creation of British Antarctic Territory on 1.3.62). The new colour-scheme included removal of the regn and application of its c/n as an identity (in black to the fin and underside of the port wing at least). Remained marked like that until grounded and WOC at its Deception Island base in 3.67 due to extensive corrosion in the fuselage.

**VP-FAJ** *DHC-2 Beaver*                    *c/n 1342*

Purchased new from DHC by FIDS and departed Southampton (crated) 18.12.59 on 'Kista Dan' for Deception Island, South Shetlands, arriving there on 26.1.60. After assembly on the ship (and a test-flight as a floatplane on 7.2.60), it sailed with her for the Argentine Islands on 8.2.60 to be based aboard for ice-reconnaissance flights. While anchored in high winds off the Argentine Islands on 12.3.60, 'Kista Dan' (with the Beaver on her foredeck) and 'John Biscoe' drifted so close to each other that the aircraft's protruding port wing was torn off when 'John Biscoe' hit it. The aeroplane was off-loaded at Deception Island c1.4.60 and by 8.60 (following receipt of a new wing brought from Port Stanley by 'John Biscoe') it had been repaired and the floats replaced by wheels/skis. On 16.9.60, having landed on sea-ice off the Argentine Is-

lands, Flt Lt R.Lord was taxying the aircraft clear of the marked runway when the ski-undercarriage broke through thin ice. Recovery proved impossible, but the wings, fin and most internal fittings were removed before the fuselage sank. The salvaged parts and the redundant floats were later sold to the FI Govt as spares for the FIGAS Beavers.

**VP-FAJ** *DHC-3 Otter*                    *c/n 377*

Bought new from DHC in 11.60 by FIDS (to replace Beaver VP-FAJ) and painted in error as VP-FAL (no regn had been allocated to it and VP-FAL had been reserved for future FIGAS use). Crated and shipped on 'Kista Dan' from Southampton to Deception Island, South Shetlands, arriving there on 11.1.61. Unloaded, assembled, fitted with wheels/skis and then test-flown on 21.1.61. (From then until 12.67 the aircraft was normally based at Adelaide Station on Adelaide Island for FIDS/BAS support flights during the summer months, returning to Deception Island each winter for maintenance and storage.) Ownership of the aircraft changed from FIDS to BAS on 1.1.62 and on 1.3.62 a FI Regn Cert was issued declaring it to be VP-FAJ (a reissue of the Beaver regn). The aeroplane remained marked as VP-FAL until it was painted in BAS livery (to comply with the creation of British Antarctic Territory on 1.3.62). The new colour-scheme included removal of the regn and application of its c/n as an identity (in black to the fin and underside of the port wing at least). Remained marked like that until 28.12.64 when the tail ski was ripped off, the undercarriage struts driven up through the airframe and the rear fuselage twisted in a landing accident at Adelaide Station. The pilot (Flt Lt E.J.Skinner) was unhurt but the aircraft, which had fallen some 30ft into a dip in the snow and ice not been seen from the air, was deemed to be "beyond economical repair" and WOC. The unused FI regn (VP-FAJ) was cancelled on 13.6.65.

**VP-FAK** *DHC-2 Beaver*                    *c/n 1664*

Purchased new from DHC by the FI Govt for FIGAS and, accompanied by Beaver VP-FAL, was flown as a landplane to Port Stanley Racecourse (via South America) in 3.67. Converted to a floatplane and flight-tested from Stanley Harbour by I.T.Campbell in early 6.67 (pre 13.6). Remained in service with FIGAS until 14.10.76 when it capsized and sank while landing at Mare Harbour, East Falkland. The pilot, I.T.Campbell, was drowned and the passenger slightly injured. Carried by the tide, the superficially-damaged aircraft beached itself inverted on Johnsons Island at the entrance to Mare Harbour. Recovered and taken to Port Stanley aboard 'Monsunen' on 17.10.76. A combination of damage sustained during the salvage operation, and corrosion which developed while hangared awaiting the outcome of the accident investigation, led to the aircraft being declared "beyond economical repair" and it was reduced to spares and scrap. In 10.84 a wing from the aircraft was seen lying in the grass at Moody Brook and the fuselage was reported to be outside the AAC hangar on Murray Heights, Port Stanley.

**VP-FAL** *DHC-2 Beaver*                    *c/n 1666*

Purchased new from DHC by the FI Govt for

FIGAS and, accompanied by Beaver VP-FAK, was flown as a landplane to Port Stanley Racecourse (via South America) in 3.67. Converted to a floatplane and flight-tested from Stanley Harbour by J.Kerr on 13.6.67. Remained in FIGAS service until 10.8.76 when it capsized and sank (without casualties) in a taxying accident at New Island, West Falkland, while being flown by a relief pilot (J.Levine). Recovered and shipped to Port Stanley where, as a result of damage sustained during the salvage operation, it was declared "beyond economical repair" and reduced to spares and scrap. All (or part) of the fuselage was reported to be dumped outside the float-plane hangar on 16.8.82, while on 18.5.83 a wing marked VP-FAL was noted in the grass at Moody Brook near Port Stanley.

**VP-FAM** *DHC-3 Otter*                    *c/n 395*

A former RNoAF aircraft (60-395) purchased by Halle & Peterson, Oslo c30.8.67 which, on being sold to NERC for BAS, was erroneously painted as VP-FAM (no regn had been allocated to it by the FI Registrar of Aircraft). The RNoAF serial was retained on the fin. Departed (crated) on 'Perla Dan' from Southampton on 29.11.67 for Deception Island, South Shetlands, where it arrived late 12.67. Not unpacked there as the base had been evacuated after a volcanic eruption on 4.12.67. Instead, it was transported aboard 'Perla Dan' to Grytviken, South Georgia (arriving 2.1.68) and was stored there until collected by 'Endurance' and returned to Deception Island in 12.68. Unloaded, assembled, fitted with wheels/skis and flight-tested prior to being flown south to Adelaide Station, Adelaide Island, on 6.2.69 for BAS support duties. On 3.3.69, following engine failure about 30 miles north-east of Stonington Island (Graham Land), it force-landed in a badly crevassed area and was sufficiently damaged to be WOC.

**VP-FAM** *DHC-2 Turbo-Beaver*
                                        *c/n 1670-TB40*

Purchased from DHC by NERC for BAS (previously CF-WSC) and departed Downsview on 22.11.69 in company with Twin Otter VP-FAO, routing via South America to Adelaide Staion on Adelaide Island where it landed on 7.12.69. Supported BAS field parties until 25.3.70 when it departed Adelaide Station for servicing and storage at DHC Downsview, arriving there on 4.4.70. Returned to Adelaide Station (via Punta Arenas in Chile) in mid-12.70 for BAS summer operations before flying back to Downsview in early 4.71. On 10.2.71 a FI Regn Cert was issued confirming the aircraft's regn. At the end of 11.71 it arrived at Adelaide Station from Downsview and, following a season of BAS support flights (mostly to/from Fossil Bluff on Alexander Island), it departed Adelaide Station on 20.3.72 and arrived at Downsview on 28.3.72. Its regn was cancelled 14.4.72 upon being sold to DHC as CF-BLX.

**VP-FAN** *Not allocated.*

**Unregistered** *PC6/B1-H2 Turbo-Porter*
                                        *c/n 619*

Purchased new from PFAG by NERC for BAS and delivered (crated) to Southampton for shipment on 'Perla Dan' to Deception Island, South Shetlands, arriving there on 8.1.67. Unloaded, assembled and fitted with wheels/skis before being test-flown 13.1.67. No regn allotted to it by the FI Registrar of Aircraft and all references to it having been allocated or painted as VP-FAN are erroneous. As an identity, the c/n was worn in large digits on both sides of the fin. Flown south to Adelaide Station, Adelaide Island, on 26.1.67 for BAS support flights, returning to Deception Island 6.3.67 for servicing and storage. Flight-tested on 15.8.67 and flown to Adelaide Station 18.8.67. From there it was used to resupply or establish a chain of five BAS depots between Fossil Bluff on Alexander Island and Stonington Island in Graham Land. As it was about to get airborne on 26.2.68 from a patch of ice at the junction of the Miller and Meiklejohn Glaciers in Palmer Land, a weld in the port undercarriage leg fractured and the ski turned outwards, causing the aircraft to slew violently. The pilot (Flt Lt J.Ayers) and his two passengers were unhurt but the tail ski was torn off. An attempted wheeled take-off from the same ice patch on 1.3.68 nearly ended in disaster when the starboard wheel broke through the ice crust and the aircraft briefly tipped onto its nose before crashing back onto the ice, twisting the rear fuselage. The aircraft was WOC and the uninjured pilot and passengers were not rescued until 21.12.68!

*The place where the Turbo-Porter crashed was named "Porter Nunatak" by Flt Lt Ayers and is still referred to by that title.*

**VP-FAO** *DHC-6 Twin Otter Series 200*
c/n 152

Ordered new from DHC by NERC for BAS on 1.9.67 and first flew at Downsview 20.9.68 prior to handover to BAS on 11.10.68 (regn worn only on the upper and lower wing surfaces). Flown via South America and Deception Island, South Shetlands (3.12.68) to Adelaide Station, Adelaide Island, where it arrived on 4.12.68. After a summer season supporting BAS field operations, it departed Adelaide Station at the end of 3.69 en route to Downsview for maintenance and storage (the first FIDS/BAS/NERC aircraft not to be wintered and serviced in Antarctica). Left Downsview on 22.11.69 for Adelaide Station and landed there 7.12.69. Following a series of glaciological radio echo-sounding flights, it took-off from Adelaide Station on 25.3.70 en route to Downsview, arriving there 4.4.70. Flown to Adelaide Station in mid-12.70 for BAS duties, returning to Downsview in 4.71 for servicing and disposal. On 10.2.71 a FI Regn Cert was issued confirming it to be VP-FAO, but the regn was cancelled 15.6.71 upon sale of the aircraft as F-BRPC to Air Paris, Orly, France.

**VP-FAP** *DHC-6 Twin Otter Series 300*
c/n 333

Ordered new from DHC by NERC for BAS on 3.7.71 and noted on the Downsview production line 1.9.71. A FI Regn Cert confirming it to be VP-FAP was issued on 23.9.71. Handed over to BAS on 10.11.71 and departed for Adelaide Station, Adelaide Island, arriving there at the end of 11.71. After

a series of glaciological radio echo-sounding equipment trials and BAS support flights, it left Adelaide Station on 20.3.72 for Downsview, arriving 28.3.72. Following servicing and storage there, it left on 3.10.72 for Adelaide Station and, after a delay at Punta Arenas in Chile (8-12.10.72) due to bad weather over the Antarctic Peninsula, it arrived at its destination (via Palmer Station, Anvers Island 12.10.72) on 13.10.72. Flown later that day by Flt Lt B.J.Conchie to Stonington Island off Graham Land to collect a sick geologist and take him back to Adelaide Station before flying him to Rio Gallegos, Argentina (via Punta Arenas) on 14.10.72; from there the geologist was flown in an Argentine military aircraft to hospital in Buenos Aires. On returning to Adelaide Station, VP-FAP supported BAS operations until 26.2.73 when it left for Downsview, arriving there for its annual overhaul on 4.3.73. Departed Adelaide Station 6.10.73 and, after its arrival there on 16.10.73, was engaged in BAS support flights until it left for Downsview again on 28.2.74. Returned to Adelaide Station on 18.10.74 and, after the summer, arrived back at Downsview 15.3.75. Left Downsview on 8.10.75, arriving at Adelaide Station c17.10.75 from where, in addition to normal BAS flights, it was used to transport men and materials to a new air facility being constructed at Rothera Station (also on Adelaide Island) to replace the one at Adelaide Station. Departed Adelaide Station in 3.76 for Downsview and, after its annual servicing and storage period, was flown to Rothera Station where it landed on 7.11.76. On 21.1.77, in poor visibility at Gomez Nunatak (south of King George VI Sound), the aircraft was flown into a snow slope when the pilot (P.Prattis) mistook it for a flat landing site. The engines and avionics were salvaged but the aircraft was WOC and not recovered.

**VP-FAQ** *DHC-6 Twin Otter Series 300*
c/n 347

Ordered new from DHC by NERC for BAS on 25.4.72 (to replace Turbo-Beaver VP-FAM) and issued with a FI Regn Cert on 22.8.72. Handed over to BAS on 2.10.72 and reached Adelaide Station, Adelaide Island on 29.10.72. Used mainly in support of Fossil Bluff Station, Alexander Island before leaving Adelaide Station on 26.2.73 for Downsview, arriving there 4.3.73 for servicing and storage. Departed Downsview on 6.10.73, landing at Adelaide Station 16.10.73, and flown in support of BAS operations until it left Adelaide Station 28.2.74 for Punta Arenas in Chile en route to Downsview for wintering. Returned to Adelaide Station on 18.10.74 and departed there 5.3.75 for Downsview, where it landed on 15.3.75. About 5.75 it was leased to the University of Nebraska for a five-week ice-sheet survey in Greenland on behalf of the US National Science Foundation. Arrived at Adelaide Station from Downsview on 4.11.75 and during that season, in addition to normal BAS support flights, it was used to transport men and materials to a new air facility being constructed at Rothera Station (also on Adelaide Island) to replace the airstrip at Adelaide Station. Departed Adelaide Station in 3.76 for Downsview and, after servicing, was chartered for work in Oman by Taylor Woodrow (International) Limited for three months (including 5.76). After returning to Downsview for maintenance it left for

Rothera Station, arriving there on 7.11.76. Upon arrival it was leased out for ten weeks to the US Ross Ice Shelf Project but, following the loss of VP-FAP on 21.1.77, was recalled to rescue the pilot and crew of the crashed aircraft and fly them to Rothera. Left Rothera for Downsview at the end of 2.77 and returned at the end of 10.77. In late 3.78 the nosewheel leg and the airframe were damaged beyond local repair when the pilot tried to take-off with a full load from a very rough surface at Rothera. Nobody on board was injured, but the aeroplane had to be dismantled and loaded onto 'Bransfield' which departed for the UK (via the Falklands) on 24.3.78, arriving at Southampton 23.5.78. Off-loaded and transported to MAL at Fairoaks for repairs. Air-tested there 25.9.78 and flown to Biggin Hill on 4.10.78, from where it departed 5.10.78 to route via North and South America to Rothera Station, landing there on 14.11.78. Left Rothera Station on 2.3.79 for the UK and leased to Loganair (a Glasgow-based airline) from c29.3.79. Returned off lease to MAL at Fairoaks on 6.9.79 for maintenance before leaving for Biggin Hill on 11.9.79 en route to Rothera Station (via Toronto where it was noted on 18.9.79), arriving there in late 11.79. Departed Rothera Station on 26.2.80 for Downsview and Calgary, Canada. At the latter location its BAS titles were removed prior to it leaving on 27.3.80 for the UK and a further period of lease to Loganair until 5.9.80. On that date it took-off from Biggin Hill for Rothera Station, where it landed on 23.11.80. Departed Rothera Station on 3.3.81 for the UK and leased to JEA (a Jersey-based airline) from 15.4.81. Remained on lease to JEA until sold to the Company on 27.4.82 as G-BKBC.

**VP-FAR** *Cessna 172M*
c/n 63016

Purchased new from CAC in 1974 (ex temporary regn N13827) by R.A.M.Pitaluga of Gibraltar Station, Salvador, East Falkland and seen at Wichita 3.74 awaiting delivery to Port Stanley in 4.74. After arrival, it was test-flown from Hookers Point airstrip (near Port Stanley) on 14.5.74 before moving to Salvador. Following the Argentine invasion on 2.4.82, the owner was interned in Port Stanley (shortly before 1.5.82) and his aircraft grounded at Stanley Airport. On 1.5.82 it was badly damaged during the 800 Sqdn Sea Harrier raid and further damaged in subsequent British shelling and bombing attacks. When inspected post-14.6.82, the starboard wing had been severed but the aircraft was considered to be repairable. Still unrepaired at RAF Stanley in 6.85.

**VP-FAS** *Cessna 172M*
c/n 66573

Purchased new from CAC in 1976 (ex temporary regn N80403) by the Chartres Sheep Farming Company Limited and based at Chartres, West Falkland. On 1.4.82 the pilot, W.H.Luxton (Director of the Company), flew the aircraft from Chartres to Stanley Airport, where it remained following the Argentine invasion on 2.4.82. Suffered bomb-blast and shrapnel damage from the many British bombing and shelling attacks. Derelict at the Airport post-14.6.82 and the hulk was still resident at RAF Stanley in 6.85.

**VP-FAT** *DHC-2 Beaver*
c/n 1098

Purchased second-hand in Canada (ex

Rob Pitaluga's Cessna 172M, shown here at RAF Stanley in late 7.82, was one of three (the others were VP-FAS and VP-FBA) damaged during the conflict and subsequently vandalised. Various plans to restore VP-FAR and VP-FBA had failed to materialise by mid-1985.

(815 Sqdn 'Exeter' Flight)

Islander VP-FAY was impressed into Argentine service after the invasion on 2.4.82. Its military career came to an abrupt end at Stanley Airport on 1.5.82 when the fuselage was severed by a CBU dropped, almost certainly, from 800 Squadron Sea Harrier FRS.1 ZA192 '92' of Flt Lt Dave Morgan. Much of the damage visible in this post-war photograph was caused by vandals and not weapons.

(Lt D. Balchin, RN)

Parked alongside the slipway at the FIGAS Beaver hangar in early 7.82 is the "battle-damaged" VP-FAV. Although assessed as repairable, any thoughts of restoration were dashed on 28.7.82 when it was wrecked in a gale. (S. Van Tromp)

C-GUIH) by the FI Govt for FIGAS and, configured as a landplane, was flown via South America to Hookers Point airstrip (near Port Stanley), arriving there on 7.11.76. Flown from there to the Racecourse on 9.11.76 and stored in the nearby floatplane hangar pending delivery of floats from Canada. Once converted, it remained in FIGAS service until permanently grounded after the Argentine invasion on 2.4.82. Demolished by British bombardments on 11/12.6.82 while parked outside the floatplane hangar. Its remains were gradually disposed of during 1982/83.

**VP-FAU** *Not allocated.*

**VP-FAV** *DHC-2 Beaver*                    *c/n 1233*

Purchased second-hand in Canada (ex C-GUHH) by the FI Govt for FIGAS and flown as a floatplane to Port Stanley (via South America), landing in Stanley Harbour on 6.12.76. Remained in FIGAS service until permanently grounded after the Argentine invasion on 2.4.82. Extensively shrapnel-damaged while parked on the slipway by the floatplane hangar during British bombardments on 11/12.6.82. Assessed as repairable, it was blown over onto its back in a gale on 28.7.82 and completely wrecked. The crumpled fuselage, devoid of fin and regn, was noted dumped outside the floatplane hangar on 18.5.83 and again on 18.9.84.

**VP-FAW** *DHC-6 Twin Otter Series 300*
                                              *c/n 546*

Ordered new from DHC by NERC for BAS on 26.4.77 (to replace VP-FAP) and first flew at Downsview 27.6.77 prior to handover to BAS on 11.7.77. Arrived at Rothera Station, Adelaide Island, at the end of 10.77 and undertook BAS support flights until it departed in 3.78 for Biggin Hill in the UK (via South and North America). Noted there on 27.3.78 prior to being leased to Loganair (a Glasgow-based airline) until 13.9.78 when it arrived at Fairoaks from Aberdeen off lease for maintenance by MAL. Departed for Biggin Hill 12.10.78 and left there on 18.10.78 for Rothera Station, where it landed on 14.11.78. On 2.3.79 it took-off from Rothera Station en route to the UK, arriving at Glasgow 29.3.79 on lease to Loganair. Arrived at Biggin Hill off lease 7.9.79 and was flown to MAL at Fairoaks on 10.9.79 for final preparations prior to flying out to Biggin Hill 11.9.79 en route to Rothera Station (via Toronto where it was seen on 18.9.79), which it reached in late 11.79. Left Rothera Station on 26.2.80 for Downsview and Calgary, Canada. At the latter location its BAS titles were removed before it took-off on 27.3.80 for the UK and a period of lease to Loganair until 5.9.80. On that date it departed Biggin Hill for Rothera Station, where it should have arrived on 23.11.80. However, it was delayed at Punta Arenas in Chile, initially with wheel/ski hydraulic problems and then by bad weather over the Antarctic Peninsula, and did not arrive at its destination until late 12.80. In late 2.81, the nose and nosewheel ski were badly damaged when the aircraft hit a hard sastrugi on take-off from the Mount Charity (Eternity Range) area. Local repair was not possible and it was dismantled, crated and (c7.3.81) put aboard 'Bransfield' which then sailed for Southampton, arriving there on 13.5.81. Off-loaded and

taken by road to MAL at Fairoaks for repairs. Upon completion it was leased to JEA (a Jersey-based airline) in 7.81, returning to Fairoaks on 7.9.81 for maintenance. Flown to Biggin Hill 4.10.81 en route to Rothera Station, where it arrived in mid-10.81. At Rothera Station on 18.11.81 both it and VP-FAZ were torn from their tie-down ropes in gales and overturned. The two badly-damaged aircraft were dismantled, crated and put on board 'Bransfield' to be returned to the UK. At the time of the Argentine invasion of the Falklands on 2.4.82 the ship was in Argentine coastal waters, but she proceeded to Faraday in the Argentine Islands and then, keeping south of 60°S (within the Treaty area), sailed east to the South Sandwich Islands before turning north for Southampton, where she berthed on 11.5.82. VP-FAW (and VP-FAZ) were taken to MAL at Fairoaks for damage assessment (noted there 29.5.82). VP-FAW was eventually WOC and its hulk was seen in a jig at Fairoaks on 17.12.84 awaiting scrapping (parts from it having been used to rebuild VP-FAZ). Still present on 6.8.85.

**VP-FAX** *Not allocated.*

**VP-FAY** *BN-2A-27 Islander*              *c/n 872*

Built in Bucharest, Romania, by IRMA and test-flown there on 29.9.78 before being ferried as G-BFNN to Bembridge 10.12.78 for selling, painting and fitting out. Bought by the UK Overseas Development Administration for FIGAS and departed Bembridge on 12.9.79 for Port Stanley (via North and South America), landing at Stanley Airport 4.10.79. Flown during the evening of 1.4.82 from the Airport to the Racecourse so that a reconnaissance flight could be made from there at dawn on 2.4.82. That dawn flight was pre-empted by the Argentine invasion. Instead, the aircraft was flown back to Stanley Airport and impressed into Argentine service. Known Argentine-operated flights included one to Fox Bay East, West Falkland on 11.4.82 and another to Pebble Island airstrip, West Falkland on 23.4.82 (reportedly flown by a LADE pilot to assess the airstrip's suitability for use by such combat types as Mentors and Pucaras). The fuselage was severed by bomb-blast or cannon-fire (or both) during the 800 Sqdn Sea Harrier attack on 1.5.82 and it was further damaged by shrapnel in subsequent British shelling and bombing. Noted derelict (minus salvageable parts) at RAF Stanley in 5.83 and 6.85.

*Total airframe hours 917.45, including 30.30 flown by Argentine pilots.*

**VP-FAZ** *DHC-6 Twin Otter Series 310*
                                              *c/n 748*

Ordered new from DHC by NERC for BAS on 2.3.81. Accepted by BAS on 29.5.81 and later that year was flown to Rothera Station, Adelaide Island, arriving in early 11.81. While lashed down at Rothera Station airstrip on 18.11.81, both it and VP-FAW were torn from their tie-down ropes in gales and overturned. The badly damaged aircraft was dismantled, crated and loaded on 'Bransfield' in 3.82 before she sailed for Punta Arenas, Chile and the Falklands en route to the UK. At the time of the Argentine invasion of the Falklands on 2.4.82 the ship was in Argentine coastal waters, but she proceeded to Faraday

in the Argentine Islands and then, keeping south of 60°S (within the Antarctic Treaty area), sailed east to the South Sandwich Islands before turning north for Southampton, where she berthed on 11.5.82. VP-FAZ (and VP-FAW) were taken to MAL at Fairoaks for damage assessment (noted there on 29.5.82). After substantial repairs (using parts from VP-FAW) which involved rejigging and installation of a new empennage, it was restored to flying condition and flight-tested on 15.8.83. Flown out to Biggin Hill on 7.10.83 and departed there on 10.10.83 for Rothera Station (accompanied by VP-FBB and VP-FBC, the first time that three BAS aircraft had been deployed together to Antarctica) but was delayed at Punta Arenas by bad weather at its destination and did not reach there until the beginning of 11.83. It left for the UK in mid-3.84 and arrived at Fairoaks on 29.3.84. After servicing by MAL, the aircraft was stored until flown to Farnborough on 29.8.84 for the SBAC exhibition and display, returning to Fairoaks 11.9.84. On 29.9.84 it took-off for Biggin Hill and departed there 1.10.84 for Rothera Station, where it arrived on 25.10.84. Left Rothera Station on 16.3.85 and arrived at Fairoaks (via Cambridge) on 27.3.85. After its annual service, and the fitting of new equipment, the aircraft was stored prior to leaving for Biggin Hill on 20.9.85 en route to Rothera Station, where it landed on 7.10.85.

**VP-FBA** *Cessna 172P*                    *c/n 75309*

Purchased from CAC (ex temporary regn N62603) by the Governor of the Falkland Islands, R.M.Hunt, and ferried to Port Stanley in 1.82 to be based at Stanley Airport. Impressed by the Argentines following the invasion on 2.4.82. The aircraft was parked at the Airport during the 800 Sqdn Sea Harrier raid on 1.5.82 and suffered bomb-blast and shrapnel-damage during that and later British shelling and bombing attacks. Inspection post-14.6.82 showed that it might be repairable, but seen almost derelict at RAF Stanley in 6.85.

*Total airframe hours 96.00, but it is not known how many of those were flown by Argentine pilots.*

**VP-FBB** *DHC-6 Twin Otter Series 310*
                                              *c/n 783*

Ordered new from DHC by NERC for BAS on 22.1.82. Test-flown at Downsview as C-GDKL before handover to BAS on 19.3.82. Noted at Toronto on 28.4.82 still marked as C-GDKL but with VP-FBB taped over. Flown to the UK, arriving at Fairoaks on 1.6.82 prior to being leased to JEA (a Jersey-based airline) c6.7.82. Returned to Fairoaks off lease 2.8.82 for servicing before flying out to Biggin Hill 6.10.82 and setting off from there on 7.10.82 for Rothera Station, Adelaide Island, where it landed on 20.10.82. Left Rothera Station in mid-3.83 and arrived back at Fairoaks 29.3.83 for maintenance. Leased to the SPRI, it was flown to Biggin Hill on 8.4.83 and from there to Spitzbergen for survey work. Returned to Fairoaks off lease on 10.5.83, from where it made a number of flights prior to leaving for Biggin Hill on 7.10.83. On 10.10.83 it departed there for Rothera Station (accompanied by VP-FAZ and VP-FBB, the first time that three BAS aircraft had been deployed together to Antarctica) but was delayed at Punta Arenas in Chile by bad weather at its destination and did not reach there until the beginning of 11.83. It left for the UK in mid-3.84 to be overhauled by MAL at Fairoaks (arriving 29.3.84) prior to storage there. Flown to Biggin Hill on 25.9.84 and departed there 1.10.84 for Rothera Station, where it landed on 25.10.84. After the summer BAS support flights it took-off from Rothera Station on 16.3.85 and arrived back at Fairoaks on 28.3.85 for maintenance and the fitting of new equipment. After a period of storage, the aircraft was flown to Cambridge on 28.5.85 and from there to Le Bourget, Paris for the "Air Salon". Returned to Fairoaks (via Cambridge) on 10.6.85 and remained there until 20.9.85 when it left for Biggin Hill en route to Rothera Station, where it arrived on 7.10.85.

**VP-FBC** *DHC-6 Twin Otter Series 310*
*c/n 787*

Ordered new from DHC by NERC for BAS on 22.1.82 and first flew from Downsview 12.3.82 marked as C-GDIU (a temporary test regn) before handover on 19.3.82. Seen at Toronto 28.4.82 still marked as C-GDIU but with VP-FBC taped over. Arrived at Cambridge on 6.5.82 and by 30.5.82 was on lease to JEA (a Jersey-based airline). The lease having ended, it was flown from Leavesden to Fairoaks on 25.9.82 for servicing by MAL. Departed 6.10.82 for Kidlington (via Wycombe Air Park) and set off from there on 7.10.82 en route to Rothera Station, Adelaide Island, arriving on 20.10.82. Left there in mid-3.83 for MAL at Fairoaks, where it landed on 29.3.83. On 7.10.83 it was flown out to Biggin Hill and departed there 10.10.83 for Rothera Station, Adelaide Island (accompanied by VP-FAZ and VP-FBB, the first time that three BAS aircraft had deployed together to Antarctica) but was delayed at Punta Arenas in Chile because of bad weather at its destination and did not reach there until the beginning of 11.83. It left for the UK in mid-3.84 to be overhauled at Fairoaks (arriving 29.3.84) prior to storage there. Flown to Biggin Hill on 29.9.84 and departed there 1.10.84 for Rothera Station, where it landed on 25.10.84. After the summer BAS support flights it took-off from Rothera Station on 16.3.85 and arrived back at Fairoaks on 28.3.85 for maintenance and the fitting of new

equipment. After a period of storage, the aircraft left for Biggin Hill on 20.9.85 en route to Rothera Station, where it arrived on 7.10.85.

**VP-FBD** *UH-1H Iroquois*
*c/n 13934*

A former CAB601 helicopter (AE-424) captured in good condition on Port Stanley Racecourse by British forces and later renovated for FIGAS use *[see CAB601 notes and Iroquois Individual Aircraft Details]*.

**VP-FBD** *BN-2B-26 Islander*
*c/n 2160*

Built in Bucharest, Romania by IAVB and test-flown there on 29.3.83 before being ferried as G-BKJK to PBN, Bembridge on 20.7.84 for selling, painting and fitting out. Bought by the FI Govt for FIGAS (replacing VP-FBE) and allotted the regn VP-FBD previously allocated to (and worn by) the FIGAS UH-1H. During 10/11.85 the aircraft was being prepared at Bembridge and Hurn (painting) for shipment to Port Stanley during 12.85.

**VP-FBE** *DHC-2 Beaver*
*c/n 1568*

Purchased second-hand in Canada (ex C-GNGN) by the FI Govt for FIGAS. On 18.10.82 the Canadian regn was cancelled and the aircraft crated and shipped to Port Stanley on 'Aes' in 12.82. Unpacked, assembled as a floatplane and then flight-tested from Stanley Harbour 20.1.83. Noted at RAF Stanley on 18.10.84 (having recently been converted to a landplane) and continued to fly from there until WFU in 1.85 and advertised for sale. Dismantled and crated before departing on 2.4.85 aboard 'Bransfield' for Grimsby in the UK, arriving there 4.5.85. Unloaded and stored in Grimsby pending sale (probably to Canada). Still stored (crated) in mid-9.85 awaiting a buyer.

**VP-FBF** *BN-2B-27 Islander*
*c/n 2125*

Built in Bucharest, Romania by IAVB and test-flown there on 24.1.82 before being ferried as G-BJEK to PBN, Bembridge 23.2.82 for selling, painting and fitting out. Purchased for FIGAS using Falkland Islands Rehabilitation Funds provided by the UK. Both it and VP-FBG were dismantled and crated before

being transported from Bembridge to Ridham Dock, Gravesend and loaded on 'Kirsten Smits' which sailed on 4.1.83 and arrived in Stanley Harbour 16.2.83. Between 28.2 and 4.3.83, the crates were airlifted by 18 Sqdn Chinook to RAF Stanley where VP-FBF was unpacked, assembled and then flight-tested on 28.3.83 before entering service. Still operated by FIGAS in 9.85 and based at RAF Stanley.

**VP-FBG** *BN-2B-26 Islander*
*c/n 2126*

Built in Bucharest, Romania by IAVB and test-flown there on 30.1.82 before being ferried as G-BJOJ to PBN, Bembridge 9.3.82 for selling, painting and fitting out. Purchased for FIGAS using Falkland Islands Rehabilitation Funds provided by the UK. Both it and VP-FBF were dismantled and crated before being transported from Bembridge to Ridham Dock, Gravesend and loaded on 'Kirsten Smits' which sailed on 4.1.83 and arrived in Stanley Harbour 16.2.83. Between 28.2 and 4.3.83, the crates were airlifted by 18 Sqdn Chinook to RAF Stanley where VP-FBG was unpacked, assembled and then flight-tested on 25.3.83 before entering service. Still operated by FIGAS in 9.85 and based at RAF Stanley.

**VP-FBH** *Cessna F172N*
*c/n F.2024*

Purchased by the Chartres Sheep Farming Company Limited, Chartres, West Falkland from Rogers Aviation, Cranfield, UK (ex G-BIRJ) to replace VP-FAS. Seen crated at Cranfield on 17.1.83 shortly before shipment to Port Stanley. Assembled by FIGAS at RAF Stanley in 4.83 to be based at Chartres and still in use there in 9.85.

**VP-FBI** *Not allocated.*

**VP-FBJ** *Cessna F172P*
*c/n F.2083*

Purchased by R.M.Pitaluga of Gibraltar Station, Salvador, East Falkland from Westair, Cranfield, UK (ex G-BHKG) to replace VP-FAR. Seen crated at Cranfield on 17.1.83 shortly before shipment to Port Stanley. Assembled by FIGAS at RAF Stanley in 4.83 to be based at Salvador. Seriously damaged (propeller, mainplane and fin) in a taxying accident in a high wind at Salvador on 23.9.85. To be repaired by FIGAS at RAF Stanley.

# FALKLAND ISLANDS — WAR LOSSES

To be read in conjunction with the Falkland Islands Civil Aircraft Register & Individual Aircraft Details. Where relevant, reference should also be made to the history of FIGAS [see Falkland Islands Internal Air Services]. Losses are listed by type in date and time order. The number in the left-hand column is cumulative, leading to the final total of Falkland Islands aircraft losses.

| **BN-2A ISLANDER** | | | *Loss 1* |
|---|---|---|---|
| 1 | VP-FAY | FIGAS | *1.5.82* | *c1110Z* |

| **DHC-2 BEAVER** | | | *Loss 1* |
|---|---|---|---|
| 2 | VP-FAT | FIGAS | *11/12.6.82* | *unknown* |

| **CESSNA 172M/172P** | | | *Losses 3* |
|---|---|---|---|
| 3 | VP-FAR | R.M.Pitaluga | *1.5.82 et seq* |
| 4 | VP-FAS | Chartres Sheep Farming Co Ltd | *1.5.82 et seq* |
| 5 | VP-FBA | FI Governor, R.Hunt | *1.5.82 et seq* |

# GLOSSARY

*The full Spanish meaning of each Argentine abbreviation is given in italics, followed by the English translation in parentheses.*

| | |
|---|---|
| **AAA** | Anti-Aircraft Artillery. |
| **AAC** | Army Air Corps. |
| **A&AEE** | Aeroplane and Armament Experimental Establishment. |
| **AAM** | Air-to-Air Missile. |
| **AAR** | Air-to-Air Refuelling. |
| **AARI** | Air-to-Air Refuelling Instructor. |
| **AAW** | Anti-Aircraft Warfare. |
| **AAWC** | Anti-Aircraft Warfare Controller. |
| **ACE** | Allied Command Europe. |
| **ACM** | Air Combat Manoeuvres/Manoeuvring. |
| **Active Sonar** | see "Sonar". |
| **ADC** | Aide-de-camp (officer acting as confidential assistant to a senior officer). |
| **ADEX** | Air Defence Exercise. |
| **AEM** | Air Engineering Mechanic. |
| **AEO** | Air Engineering Officer. |
| **AETW** | Aircraft Engineering Training Wing. |
| **AEW** | Airborne Early Warning. |
| **AFB** | Air Force Base. |
| **AFC** | Air Force Cross. |
| **AGL, agl** | Above Ground Level. |
| **AGM-45A** | see "Shrike". |
| **AI** | Aircraft Interception. |
| **AI** | Ascension Island. |
| **AID** | Accident Investigation Department. |
| **AIU** | Accident Investigation Unit. |
| **AIM-9B, AIM-9G, AIM-9L** | see "Sidewinder". |
| **ALE-40** | Tracor chaff and flare dispenser. |
| **AMG** | Advanced Maintenance Group. |
| **AMRAAM** | Advanced Medium Range Air-to-Air Missile. |
| **AN/ALQ-101** | Westinghouse electronic countermeasures equipment (podded). |
| **AN/TPS-43F** | Westinghouse three-dimensional long range surveillance radar. |
| **AN/TPS-44** | Cardion tactical surveillance radar. |
| **AOA** | Amphibious Operations Area. |
| **AOC** | Air Officer Commanding. |
| **APFC** | Air Portable Fuel Cell. |
| **AQ** | Army Quartermaster. |
| **ARA** | *Armada Republica Argentina* (Republic of Argentina Navy). |
| **Armada** | Navy. |
| **ARWS** | Advanced Rotary Wing Squadron. |
| **AS.12** | Aerospatiale Air-to-Surface missile (wire-guided). |
| **ASM** | Air-to-Surface Missile. |
| **ASM** | Anti-Submarine Missile. |
| **ASV** | Air-to-Surface-Vessel (aircraft search radar for detecting vessels on the surface of the sea). |
| **ASW** | Anti-Submarine Warfare. |
| **ATC** | Air Traffic Control. |
| **ATGW** | Anti-Tank Guided Weapon. |
| **auw** | All up weight. |
| **AVGAS** | Aviation Gasoline (high octane petrol used by piston-engined aircraft). |
| **AWI** | Air Warfare Instructor. |
| | |
| **BA** | *Brigada Aerea* (Air Brigade). |
| **BA** | Buenos Aires. |
| **BAC** | British Aircraft Corporation. |
| **BAe** | British Aerospace. |
| **BAM** | *Base Aerea Militar* (Military Air Base). |
| **BAMMLV** | *Base Aerea Militar Malvinas* (Military Air Base Malvinas). |
| **BAN** | *Base Aeronaval* (Naval Air Base). |
| **BAS** | British Antarctic Survey. |
| **BBC** | British Broadcasting Corporation. |
| **BCR** | Battle Casualty Replacement. |

| | |
|---|---|
| **Bde** | Brigade. |
| **BDR** | Battle Damage Repair. |
| **Belouga** | Matra BLG.66 battlefield dispersion cluster package (cluster bomblets). |
| **Bergen** | Type of rucksack. |
| **BIM** | *Brigada Infanteria Marina* (Marine Infantry Brigade). |
| **BL755** | Hunting cluster bomb unit. |
| **BLO** | Brigade Liaison Officer. |
| **Blowpipe** | Short Brothers surface-to-air missile (shoulder-launched). |
| **BMA** | Brigade Maintenance Area. |
| **BoB** | Battle of Britain. |
| **Bofors** | Bofors 40mm anti-aircraft gun used by the Royal Navy in L/60 and L/70 versions. |
| **Btn** | Battalion. |
| **BuAer** | Bureau of Aeronautics (United States Navy). |
| | |
| **Ca** | *Compania* (Company). |
| **CAAG601** | *Compania de Aviacion de Apoyo General 601* (General Support Aviation Company 601). |
| **CAB601** | *Battalon de Aviacion de Combate 601* (Combat Aviation Battalion 601). |
| **CAE** | *Comando Aviacion del Ejercito* (Army Aviation Command). |
| **CANA** | *Comando Aviacion Naval Argentina* (Argentine Naval Aviation Command). |
| **Candle** | Unofficial name for the white candle-shaped plastic aiming point attached to the nose-mounted ARC340 radio aerial on Army Air Corps Gazelle AH.1's for use in aiming SNEB rockets. |
| **CAP** | Combat Air Patrol. |
| **Capt** | Captain. |
| **CASEVAC** | Casualty Evacuation. |
| **CASEX** | Combined Anti-Submarine Exercise. |
| **CAT.** | Category; degree of damage to British military aircraft ranging from CAT.1 (minor) to CAT.5 (write-off). |
| **CB** | Companion (of the Order) of the Bath. |
| **CBAS** | Commando Brigade Air Squadron. |
| **CBE** | Commander (of the Order) of the British Empire. |
| **CBU** | Cluster Bomb Unit. |
| **CCA** | Carrier Controlled Approach. |
| **Cdo** | Commando. |
| **CdoAeDef** | *Comando Aereo de Defensa* (Air Defence Command). |
| **CdoAeEstr** | *Comando Aereo Estrategico* (Strategic Air Command). |
| **CdoFAS** | *Comando de la Fuerza Aerea Sur* (Southern Air Force Command). |
| **CdoAeTr** | *Comando Aereo de Transporte* (Air Transport Command). |
| **Cdr** | Commander. |
| **CEOPECON** | *Centro de Operaciones Conjuntas* (Combined Operations Centre). |
| **CEV** | *Centro de Ensayos en Vuelo* (Flight Test Centre). |
| **CF** | Canadian Forces. |
| **CFB** | Canadian Forces Base. |
| **Chaff** | Radar reflecting material used to confuse missiles and radar. |
| **Chancha** | "Mother Sow" (Argentine slang term for the KC-130H tanker). |
| **ChinDet** | Chinook Detachment. |
| **CINCFC** | Commander-in-Chief Fleet Commendation. |
| **CIC** | *Centro de Informacion y Control* (Information and Control Centre). |
| **CIVGAS** | Civilian Gasoline; standard civilian petrol, equal to 3-star grade. |
| **CIWS** | Close-In Weapons System. |
| **CLFFI** | Commander Land Forces Falkland Islands. |
| **CMG** | Companion (of the Order) of St Michael and St George. |
| **CNIE** | *Comision Nacional de Investigationes Especiales* (National Commission of Special Investigations). |
| **Co** | Company. |
| **CO** | Commanding Officer. |
| **COA** | Carrier Operating Area. |
| **COIN** | Counter Insurgency. |
| **COMAW** | Commander Amphibious Warfare. |
| **Comm** | Commodore. |
| **COST** | Continuation Operational Sea Trials. |
| **Coy** | Company. |
| **Cpl** | Corporal. |

| | |
|---|---|
| **CPL** | Commercial Pilot's Licence. |
| **CPOACMN** | Chief Petty Officer Aircrewman. |
| **CSgt** | Colour Sergeant. |
| **CTI** | Chief Tactical Instructor. |
| **CVBG** | Carrier Battle Group; the "V" in "CV" is used in naval aviation terminology to signify an aircraft carrier equipped with "heavier-than-air" aircraft. |
| **Cymbeline** | Thorn-EMI mortar locating radar used by the British Army. |
| | |
| **DA** | Direct Action (Bomb). |
| **DACT** | Dissimilar Air Combat Training. |
| **DED** | Docking and Essential Defects. |
| **DEFA** | Groupement Industriel des Armements Terrestres (GIAT) 30mm aircraft cannon (DEFA553). |
| **Det** | Detachment. |
| **DFC** | Distinguished Flying Cross. |
| **DFM** | Distinguished Flying Medal. |
| **DLP** | Deck Landing Practice. |
| **DNAW** | Directorate of Naval Air Warfare. |
| **DoD** | Department of Defense (United States). |
| **DSC** | Distinguished Service Cross. |
| **DSM** | Distinguished Service Medal. |
| **DSO** | Distinguished Service Order. |
| **D&T** | Demonstration and Trials. |
| | |
| **EAM** | *Escuela de Aviacion Militar* (Military Aviation School). |
| **EAN** | *Estacion Aeronaval* (Naval Air Station). |
| **ECM** | Electronic Countermeasures. |
| **ECU** | Engine Change Unit. |
| **Ejercito** | Army. |
| **Elta** | Israeli-manufactured Elta Electronics point defence alert radar (target acquisition with anti-aircraft artillery). |
| **ELINT** | Electronic Intelligence. |
| **Esc** | *Escuadrilla* (Flight or Squadron). Normally it means "Flight", but in Argentine Naval Aviation Command (CANA) use it means "Squadron". |
| **ESM** | Electronic Support (or Surveillance) Measures (the interception and analysis of radar and radio emissions from sources beyond radar range). |
| **ETPS** | Empire Test Pilots School. |
| **EWAU** | Electronic Warfare Avionics Unit. |
| **Exocet** | Aerospatiale sea-skimming missile in MM.38 (surface-to-surface) and AM.39 (air-to-surface) versions. |
| | |
| **FAA** | Fleet Air Arm. |
| **FAA** | *Fuerza Aerea Argentina* (Argentine Air Force). |
| **FAAM** | Fleet Air Arm Museum. |
| **FAB** | Forca Aerea Brasileira (Brazilian Air Force). |
| **FAC** | Forward Air Controller. |
| **FAP** | Fuerza Aerea Peruana (Peruvian Air Force). |
| **FAU** | Fuerza Aerea Uruguaya (Uruguayan Air Force). |
| **FCACMN** | Fleet Chief Aircrewman. |
| **FDO** | Fighter Direction Officer. |
| **FDO** | Flight Deck Officer. |
| **FEEE601GN** | *Formacion de Empleos Especiales del Escuadron 601 de Gendarmerie Nacional* (Specially Deployed Formation of 601 Squadron, National Gendarmerie). |
| **Fg Off** | Flying Officer. |
| **FI** | Falkland Islands. |
| **FIDS** | Falkland Islands Dependencies Survey. |
| **FIGAS** | Falkland Islands Government Air Service. |
| **FIM-92A** | see "Stinger". |
| **FINRAE** | Ferranti Inertial Navigation Reference and Attitude Equipment. |
| **FIPZ** | Falkland Islands Protection Zone (replacing the Total Exclusion Zone) established by the British Government at 1500Z on 22 July 1982 following the British announcement on 12 July of a de facto cessation of hostilities between the United Kingdom and Argentina. The outer limit was a circle of 150 nautical miles radius from 51°40'S 59°30'W (the same centre |

point used for the previous Total and Maritime Exclusion Zones). All unidentified ships and aircraft approaching or entering the Zone were to be investigated and those belonging to the Argentine military kept away from the Falkland Islands. The Protection Zone was still in existence as at August 1985.

| | |
|---|---|
| FIR | Front-line Immediate Replacement. |
| FLIR | Forward Looking Infra-Red. |
| Flt | Flight. |
| Flt Cdr | Flight Commander. |
| Flt Lt | Flight Lieutenant. |
| FMA | *Fabricar Militar de Aviones* (Military Aircraft Factory). |
| FMS | Foreign Military Sales (United States). |
| FOB | Forward Operating Base. |
| FOD | Foreign Object Damage. |
| FOF | Flag Officer Flotilla. |
| FPB | Fast Patrol Boat. |
| FONAC | Flag Officer Naval Air Command. |
| FRADU | Fleet Requirements and Air Direction Unit. |
| F/Sgt | Flight Sergeant. |
| FTS | Flying Training School. |
| | |
| GA | Georgia (United States). |
| GADA | *Grupo de Artilleria de Defensa Aerea* (Air Defence Artillery Group; GADA101, GADA601 and GADA602 were deployed to the Falkland Islands). |
| GAF | Government Aircraft Factories (Australia). |
| GCB | Knight Grand Cross (of the Order) of the Bath. |
| GG | Grenadier Guards. |
| GMT | Greenwich Mean Time (see "Z"). |
| GOE | *Grupo de Operaciones Especiales* (Special Operations Group). |
| Gp Capt | Group Captain. |
| GPMG | General Purpose Machine Gun (7.62mm). |
| GPU | Ground Power Unit. |
| GrAeExplRec1 | *Grupo Aereo de Exploracion y Reconocimiento 1* (Air Group 1, Investigation and Reconnaissance). |
| G2VYCA | *Grupo 2 de Vigilancia y Control Aereo* (Group 2, Air Surveillance and Control). |
| GRT | Gross Registered Tonnage. |
| | |
| HarDet | Harrier Detachment. |
| HDS | Helicopter Delivery Service. |
| HDU | Hose Drum Unit. |
| HE | High Explosive. |
| Heads | Naval slang term for toilets. |
| HELARM | Helicopter, Armed; an armed helicopter tasking. |
| HIE | Helicopter Installed Equipment; the instrumentation and electronics package associated with a specific weapons system. |
| HIFR | Helicopter In-Flight Refuelling. |
| Hi-lo-hi | High-low-high; type of mission profile for aircraft. |
| HMAV | Her Majesty's Auxiliary Vessel. |
| HMNZS | Her Majesty's New Zealand Ship. |
| HMS | Her Majesty's Ship. |
| HQ | Headquarters. |
| HRH | His Royal Highness. |
| HrMS | Haar Majesteits Schip (Her Majesty's Ship — Netherlands). |
| HUD | Head-Up Display. |
| HUEY, Huey | Slang name for the Bell UH-1 helicopter derived from its original United States Army designation (HU-1) and the cartoon character "Baby Huey". |
| | |
| IAI | Israel Aircraft Industries. |
| I-Band Transponder | A receiver/transmitter (operating within the I-Band of frequencies) fitted to ships and aircraft which, upon interrogation by an I-Band primary radar signal, automatically emits a pre-coded reply pulse which is displayed on the radar screen as a series of decodeable slashes alongside the primary radar target. |
| IDF/AF | Israeli Defence Force/Air Force. |
| IFF | Identification, Friend or Foe. |

| | |
|---|---|
| **IFR** | In-Flight Refuelling. |
| **Ikara** | British Aerospace Dynamics ship-launched, rocket-propelled, anti-submarine acoustic torpedo carrier (designed to a specification of the Department of Defence Support, Australia). |
| **ILS** | Instrument Landing System. |
| **Inf Bde** | Infantry Brigade. |
| **INAC** | *Instituto Nacional de Aviacion Civil* (National Institute of Civil Aviation). |
| **INAS** | Inertial Navigation-Attack System. |
| **INMARISAT** | see "MARISAT". |
| **INS** | Inertial Navigation System. |
| **IR** | Infra Red. |
| **IRCC** | International Red Cross Commission. |
| | |
| **JATE** | Joint Air Transport Establishment. |
| **JP-1** | Jet Propellant-1; incorrect Argentine use of the designation when referring to JET A-1 kerosene turbojet and turboprop aircraft fuel. |
| **JSTU** | Joint Services Trials Unit. |
| **Junglies** | Royal Navy slang term for the Royal Marines and their Wessex and Sea King helicopters. |
| | |
| **KCB** | Knight Commander (of the Order) of the Bath. |
| **KIA** | Killed In Action. |
| | |
| **LACMN** | Leading Aircrewman. |
| **LADE** | *Lineas Aereas del Estado* (State Airlines). |
| **LAEM** | Leading Air Engineering Mechanic. |
| **LAPADS** | Lightweight Acoustic Processing and Display System. |
| **LCL** | Landing Craft, Large. |
| **LCM** | Landing Craft, Medium. |
| **LCpl** | Lance Corporal. |
| **LCU** | Landing Craft, Utility. |
| **LCVP** | Landing Craft, Vehicle and Personnel. |
| **LEPUS** | Type of flare, originally manufactured by Bofors. |
| **LGB** | Laser-Guided Bomb. |
| **LMG** | Light Machine Gun. |
| **Low-vis** | Low-visibility (pertaining to markings and camouflage schemes). |
| **LOX** | Liquid Oxygen. |
| **LPD** | Landing Platform, Dock. |
| **LRMTS** | Laser Ranger and Marked Target Seeker. |
| **LSL** | Landing Ship, Logistic. |
| **Lt** | Lieutenant. |
| **Lt Cdr** | Lieutenant Commander. |
| **Lt Col** | Lieutenant Colonel. |
| **LTW** | Lyneham Transport Wing. |
| **LVTP** | Landing Vehicle, Tracked, Personnel. |
| | |
| **MACC** | Military Aid to Civil Community. |
| **MAD** | Magnetic Anomaly Detector. |
| **MAEOp** | Master Air Electronics Operator. |
| **Maj** | Major. |
| **MALM** | Master Air Loadmaster. |
| **MARISAT** | International commercial Maritime Satellite communications system. |
| **MARTSU** | Mobile Aircraft Repair, Transport and Salvage Unit. |
| **MASDC** | Military Aircraft Storage and Disposition Center (United States). |
| **MASH** | Mobile Army Surgical Hospital (United States). |
| **MBE** | Member (of the Order) of the British Empire. |
| **MC** | Military Cross. |
| **MCM** | Mine Countermeasures. |
| **MCMS** | Mine Countermeasures Squadron. |
| **MDAP** | Mutual Defence Assistance Programme/Mutual Defense Assistance Program. |
| **MEDEVAC** | Medical Evacuation. |
| **MEXEFLOTE** | Military Engineering Experimental Establishment-designed multi-purpose motorised pontoon. |
| **MEZ** | Maritime Exclusion Zone around the Falkland Islands announced by the British Government on 7 April 1982 and effective from 0400Z on 12 April 1982. The outer limit of the |

Zone was a circle of 200 nautical miles radius from 51°40'S 59°30'W (a position in Falkland Sound considered to be the centre of the Falkland Islands). From the time and date stated, any Argentine warships or Argentine naval auxiliaries found within the Zone were to be treated as hostile and therefore liable to attack by British forces.

| | |
|---|---|
| **MID** | Mention in Despatches. |
| **Milan** | Missile d'Infanterie Leger Antichar; wire-guided anti-tank missile system under the production management of Euromissile. |
| **Mile, miles** | Nautical Miles (within the context of this book). |
| **Mne** | Marine. |
| **MO** | Medical Officer. |
| **MoD** | Ministry of Defence. |
| **MoD(PE)** | Ministry of Defence (Procurement Executive). |
| **Mods** | Modifications. |
| **MR** | Maritime Reconnaissance. |
| **MRR** | Maritime Radar Reconnaissance. |
| **MS** | Mississippi (United States). |
| **MV** | Motor Vessel. |
| **MVO** | Member of the Royal Victorian Order. |
| **NAS** | Naval Air Station (United States). |
| **NASU** | Naval Aircraft Support Unit. |
| **NATIU** | Naval Aircraft Trials Installation Unit. |
| **NATO** | North Atlantic Treaty Organisation. |
| **NAVEX** | Navigation Exercise. |
| **NAVHARS** | Navigation, Heading and Attitude Reference System. |
| **NCO** | Non-Commissioned Officer. |
| **NERC** | Natural Environment Research Council. |
| **NGS** | Naval Gunfire Support. |
| **NITESUN, Nitesun** | Powerful helicopter-borne searchlight. |
| **nm** | Nautical Mile (see also "Mile"). |
| **NTM** | Notice To Move. |
| **Nunatak** | Rocky crag or small mountain surrounded by a glacier or ice sheet. |
| **NVG** | Night Vision Goggles. |
| **OBE** | Officer (of the Order) of the British Empire. |
| **OC** | Officer Commanding. |
| **OCU** | Operational Conversion Unit. |
| **Oerlikon** | Oerlikon-Buhrle anti-aircraft guns used by the British (20mm single barrel) and Argentine (35mm twin barrel) forces. |
| **Omega** | Very Low Frequency hyperbolic lattice global navigation system based on eight transmitting stations located worldwide. The position of an aircraft (or ship) is determined by the on-board Omega equipment automatically selecting the three best signals and calculating the intersection point. |
| **OTHT** | Over The Horizon Targeting. |
| **PARA, Para** | Parachute; as in 2 PARA (2nd Battalion The Parachute Regiment). |
| **Passive Sonar** | see "Sonar". |
| **Paveway** | Family of laser-guided bombs emanating from the PAVE WAY programme established by the United States Air Force with Texas Instruments as prime contractor. |
| **Picket Ship** | A ship detached from the main body of the fleet to watch or listen for warning of enemy presence or attack. |
| **PBN** | Pilatus Britten-Norman Limited. |
| **PNA** | *Prefectura Naval Argentina* (Argentine Coastguard) |
| **PNG** | Passive Night Goggles; image-intensifying goggles used during Operation "Corporate" by some 846 Sqdn pilots for night-flying operations. Some modifications were required to the associated Sea King HC.4 helicopters. |
| **POACMN** | Petty Officer Aircrewman. |
| **POL** | Petrol, Oil, Lubricants. |
| **PoW** | Prisoner of War. |
| **PR** | Photographic Reconnaissance. |
| **Pt Off** | Pilot Officer. |
| **QCVSA** | Queen's Commendation for Valuable Service in the Air. |

| | | |
|---|---|---|
| **QGM** | Queen's Gallantry Medal. | |
| **QHI** | Qualified Helicopter Instructor. | |
| **QRA** | Quick Reaction Alert. | |
| **R530** | Matra air-to-air missile. | |
| **R550** | Matra Magic air-to-air missile. | |
| **RA** | Royal Artillery. | |
| **RACA** | *Representaciones Aero Comerciales Argentinas* (Argentine Commercial Aviation Representation). | |
| **RADALT** | Radio Altimeter. | |
| **RAE** | Royal Aircraft Establishment. | |
| **RAF** | Royal Air Force. | |
| **RAFG** | Royal Air Force Germany. | |
| **RAN** | Royal Australian Navy. | |

**Rank Equivalents (Officers)**

| ARMADA | | ROYAL NAVY |
|---|---|---|
| | No direct equivalent | Admiral of the Fleet |
| *Almirante* | (Admiral) | Admiral |
| *Vicealmirante* | (Vice-Admiral) | Vice-Admiral |
| *Contraalmirante* | (Rear Admiral) | Rear Admiral |
| | No direct equivalent | Commodore |
| *Capitan de Navio* | (Warship Captain) | Captain |
| *Capitan de Fragata* | (Frigate Captain) | Commander |
| *Capitan de Corbeta* | (Corvette Captain) | Lieutenant-Commander |
| *Teniente de Navio* | (Warship Lieutenant) | Lieutenant |
| *Teniente de Fragata* | (Frigate Lieutenant) | Sub-Lieutenant |
| *Teniente de Corbeta* | (Corvette Lieutenant) | Acting Sub-Lieutenant |
| *Guardiamarina* | (Naval Guard) | Midshipman |

When suffixed "IM" the Armada rank is that of an officer of the *Infanteria de Marina* (Marines).

| EJERCITO | | ARMY & ROYAL MARINES |
|---|---|---|
| | No direct equivalent | Field Marshal |
| *Teniente General* | (Lieutenant General) | General |
| *General de Division* | (Division General) | Lieutenant-General |
| *General de Brigada* | (Brigade General) | Major-General |
| | No direct equivalent | Brigadier |
| *Coronel* | (Colonel) | Colonel |
| *Teniente Coronel* | (Lieutenant Colonel) | Lieutenant-Colonel |
| *Mayor* | (Major) | Major |
| *Capitan* | (Captain) | Captain |
| *Primer Teniente* | (First Lieutenant) | Lieutenant |
| *Teniente* | (Lieutenant) | No direct equivalent |
| *Subteniente* | (Sub-Lieutenant) | Second Lieutenant |

It should be noted that many Army Air Corps and Royal Marines pilots hold the ranks of Warrant Officer or Sergeant. It is believed that no operational pilots of the Comando Aviacion Ejercito hold a rank lower than that of Teniente.

| FUERZA AEREA | | ROYAL AIR FORCE |
|---|---|---|
| | No direct equivalent | Marshal of the Royal Air Force |
| *Brigadier General* | (Brigadier General) | Air Chief Marshal |
| *Brigadier Mayor* | (Brigadier Major) | Air Marshal |
| *Brigadier* | (Brigadier) | Air Vice-Marshal |
| | No direct equivalent | Air Commodore |
| *Comodoro* | (Commodore) | Group Captain |
| *Vicecomodoro* | (Vice-Commodore) | Wing Commander |
| *Mayor* | (Major) | Squadron Leader |
| *Capitan* | (Captain) | No direct equivalent |
| *Primer Teniente* | (First Lieutenant) | Flight Lieutenant |
| *Teniente* | (Lieutenant) | Flying Officer |
| *Alferez* | (Ensign) | Pilot Officer |

| | |
|---|---|
| **RAS** | Replenishment At Sea (resupply taking place between two ships during passage at sea). |
| **RASC** | Royal Army Service Corps. |
| **Rapier** | British Aerospace Dynamics surface-to-air missile. |
| **RCB** | Red Cross Box; a defined, agreed and promulgated hostility-free area within which hospital ships can operate without fear of attack by combating nations. |
| **RCT** | Royal Corps of Transport. |
| **REBRO** | Relay Broadcast. |
| **Regt** | Regiment. |
| **Retard** | Method of bomb delivery by which a parachute slows down the bomb after release. |
| **REME** | Royal Electrical and Mechanical Engineers. |
| **RFA** | Royal Fleet Auxiliary. |
| **RgtInf** | *Regimentaria de Infanteria* (Infantry Regiment). |
| **RM** | Royal Marines. |
| **RMAS** | Royal Maritime Auxiliary Service. |
| **RN** | Royal Navy. |
| **RNAS** | Royal Naval Air Station. |
| **RNAY** | Royal Naval Air Yard. |
| **RNR** | Royal Navy Reserve. |
| **RNSTS** | Royal Navy Supply and Transport Service. |
| **RNZN** | Royal New Zealand Navy. |
| **Ro-Ro** | Roll-on Roll-off cargo vessel. |
| **RP** | Rocket Projectile. |
| **Roland** | Euromissile mobile surface-to-air missile. |
| **RRF** | Royal Regiment of Fusiliers. |
| **RVR** | Runway Visual Range. |
| **RWR** | Radar Warning Receiver. |
| **SA-7** | Soviet-manufactured surface-to-air missile, shoulder-launched in Argentine use. Known to NATO as "Grail" but once widely referred to as "Strela" (Arrow). |
| **SACEUR** | Supreme Allied Commander Europe (NATO). |
| **SAM** | Surface-to-Air Missile. |
| **SAR** | Search And Rescue. |
| **SARBE** | Search And Rescue Beacon Equipment (any aircraft with a VHF/UHF homer can receive the equipment's automatically transmitted signal. Later models of SARBE allow voice-over transmissions to be made. |
| **SARH** | Semi-Active Radar Homing. |
| **SAS** | South African Ship. |
| **SAS** | Special Air Service. |
| **Sastrugi** | Fluted ridges carved by the wind on a snow surface; they may vary in size from a few inches to five feet high and lie parallel to the prevailing wind. |
| **SATCOM** | Satellite Communications System. |
| **SATNAV** | Satellite Navigation System. |
| **SBS** | Special Boat Squadron. |
| **SC** | South Carolina (United States). |
| **SCA** | Ship Controlled Approach. |
| **SCCBS** | *Sub-Centros de Control de Busqueda y Salvamento* (Search and Rescue Sub-Centre Control). |
| **Seacat** | Short Brothers shipborne surface-to-air missile (GWS-20). |
| **Sea Dart** | British Aerospace Dynamics shipborne surface-to-air missile (GWS-30). |
| **Sea Eagle** | British Aerospace Dynamics air-to-surface missile. |
| **Searchwater** | Thorn EMI ARI5980 long-range maritime surveillance radar. |
| **Sea Skua** | British Aerospace Dynamics all-weather, helicopter-launched, sea-skimming anti-ship guided weapon. |
| **Seaslug** | British Aerospace Dynamics shipborne surface-to-air missile. |
| **Seawolf** | British Aerospace Dynamics shipborne surface-to-air missile (GWS-25). |
| **Sgt** | Sergeant. |
| **Shafrir** | Rafael Armament Development Authority air-to-air missile. |
| **SHQ** | Squadron Headquarters. |
| **Shrike** | Texas Instruments AGM-45A air-to-surface anti-radiation missile. |
| **SHSU** | Sea Harrier Support Unit. |
| **Sidewinder** | Ford Aerospace/Raytheon AIM-9 air-to-air missile. |
| **SITREP** | Situation Report. |
| **Skyguard** | Contraves all-weather fire control system used in conjunction with anti-aircraft artillery |

| | against low-flying aircraft. |
|---|---|
| **SLBM** | Submarine-Launched Ballistic Missile. |
| **S/Lt** | Sub-Lieutenant. |
| **SMO** | Senior Medical Officer. |
| **SNEB** | Brandt Armements 68mm unguided pod-launched rockets. |
| **SOBS** | *Seccion Operativa de Busqueda y Salvamento* (Search and Rescue Operations Section). |
| **Sonar** | Sound Navigation and Ranging; a system for underwater detection of objects by emitted or reflected sound waves. Passive Sonar detects sound waves while Active Sonar transmits sound waves and detects those waves reflected back to source. |
| **SP** | Senior Pilot. |
| **Sqdn** | Squadron. |
| **Sqdn Ldr** | Squadron Leader. |
| **SS** | Steamship. |
| **SSgt** | Staff Sergeant. |
| **SSM** | Surface-to-Surface Missile. |
| **SS.11** | Aerospatiale Surface-to-Surface missile (wire-guided). Used by the British in the Air-to-Surface role from some types of Royal Navy and Army Air Corps helicopters. The correct designation is AS.11 but the British armed forces still refer to it by the prefix letters of the surface-based version. |
| **STANAVFORLANT** | Standing Naval Force Atlantic (NATO). |
| **Stingray** | Marconi acoustic homing lightweight torpedo. |
| **Stinger** | General Dynamics FIM-92A shoulder-launched surface-to-air missile. |
| **STUFT** | Ships Taken Up From Trade (requisitioned merchant vessels). |
| **SUE** | Super Etendard. |
| **Superfledermaus** | Contraves anti-aircraft fire control system used in conjunction with anti-aircraft artillery against low-flying aircraft. |
| **SWATEX** | Submarine Warfare Air Training Exercise. |
| **TACAN** | Tactical Air Navigator; ground-based VHF omni-directional navigation aid associated with Distance Measuring Equipment (DME). |
| **TANS** | Tactical Air Navigation System; self-contained, computerised Doppler navigation equipment installed in aircraft. |
| **TEZ** | Total Exclusion Zone around the Falkland Islands announced by the British Government on 28 April 1982 and effective from 1100Z on 30 April 1982. The outer limit was the same as for the Maritime Exclusion Zone established on 12 April 1982. However, from the time and date stated the Zone applied not only to Argentine warships and Argentine naval auxiliaries but also to any other ship, whether naval or merchant vessel, which was operating in support of the illegal occupation of the Falkland Islands by Argentine forces. The Zone also applied to any aircraft, whether military or civil, which was operating in support of the illegal occupation. Any ship or any aircraft which was found within the Zone without due authority from the Ministry of Defence in London was regarded as operating in support of the illegal occupation and therefore regarded as hostile and liable to attack by British forces. In addition, Port Stanley airport was considered to be closed from the time and date stated and any aircraft on the ground in the Falkland Islands was regarded as being present in support of the illegal occupation and accordingly was liable to attack. On 7 May 1982 Argentina was told that from that date any of its warships or military aircraft more than 12 nautical miles from the Argentine coast would be treated as hostile and dealt with as appropriate (a move made necessary by the proximity of Argentine bases, the threat posed by Argentine carrier-borne aircraft and the ability of hostile forces to approach undetected in bad weather and at low level). |
| **TF** | Task Force. |
| **TG** | Task Group. |
| **TICM** | Thermal Imaging Common Module; an infra-red device associated with the identification of heat-producing targets. |
| **Tigercat** | Short Brothers ground-to-air missile close-range defence system. |
| **Tigerfish** | GEC-Marconi Mk.24 wire-guided, acoustic-homing torpedo. |
| **TOAS** | *Teatro de Operaciones del Atlantico Sur* (Theatre of Operations, South Atlantic). |
| **TPS-43, TPS-44** | see "AN/TPS-43" and "AN/TPS-44". |
| **TRALA** | Tug, Repair and Logistic Area; initially known as the "TARA" (Tug and Repair Area). |
| **TVS** | Television South (a British television company). |
| **UHF** | Ultra High Frequency. |
| **UK** | United Kingdom. |
| **Unifoxer** | A towed noise-generator used to decoy acoustic homing torpedoes. |

| | |
|---|---|
| **UNIMOG** | Mercedes-Benz all purpose, go anywhere vehicle. |
| **USA** | United States of America. |
| **USAF** | United States Air Force. |
| **USMC** | United States Marine Corps. |
| **USN** | United States Navy. |
| **USNS** | United States Navy Ship (Fleet Auxiliary Vessel). |
| **USS** | United States Ship. |
| **UXB** | Unexploded Bomb. |
| | |
| **VA** | Virginia (United States). |
| **VC** | Victoria Cross. |
| **VERTREP** | Vertical Replenishment. |
| **VHF** | Very High Frequency. |
| **VIP** | Very Important Person. |
| **VLF** | Very Low Frequency. |
| **VOR** | Very High Frequency Omni-directional Range (VHF navigation aid). |
| **VT** | Variable Time; used in connection with bombs which have fuses or other trigger mechanisms set to detonate at different times. |
| **VTOL** | Vertical Take-Off and Landing. |
| | |
| **wef** | With effect from. |
| **Wg Cdr** | Wing Commander. |
| **WHL** | Westland Helicopters Limited. |
| **WI** | West Indies. |
| **WO2** | Warrant Officer Class II. |
| | |
| **YPF** | *Yacimientos Petroliferos Fiscales* (Argentine State Oil Company which has, amongst other roles, financial responsibility for the exploitation of oil reserves). |
| | |
| **Z** | An abbreviation for Greenwich Mean Time (commonly called "Zulu" Time from the international phonetic alphabet word used for the letter "Z"). |
| **Zap** | Slang term for unofficial logos, badges or names affixed to an aircraft. |
| **Zuni** | 68mm unguided pod-launched rockets. |
| | |
| **2/O** | Second Officer. |

The transformation of "Hernandez" from AE-424 to VP-FBD.

. . . . . . untouched on Port Stanley Racecourse.

. . . . . . during rub-down in 'Invincible'.

. . . . . . the finished product.

(Top) *S. Van Tromp;*
(Others) *Lt S. A. George, RN*

480

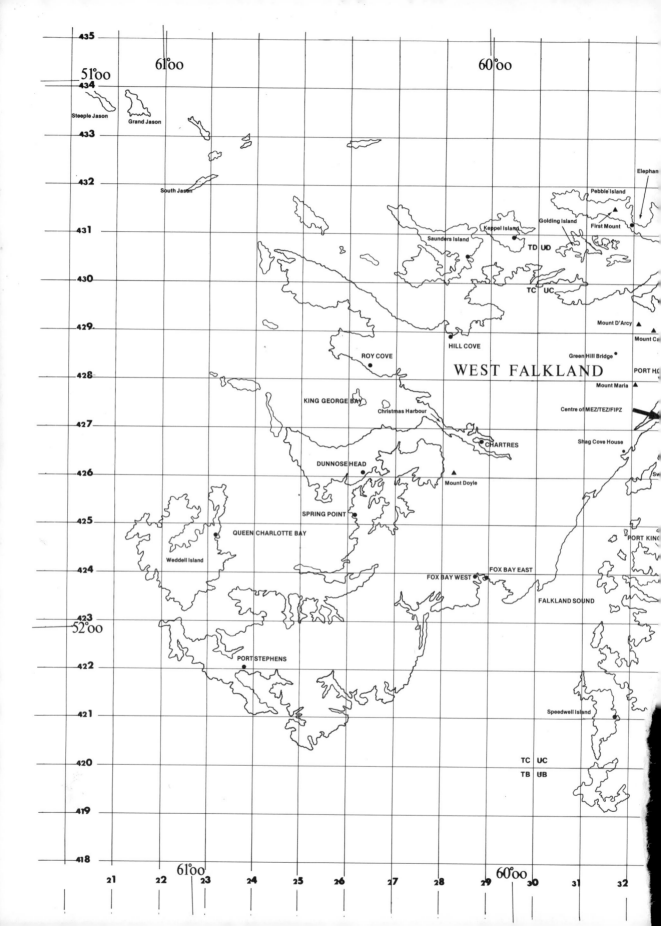

435

434

Steeple Jason

Grand Jason

433

432

South Jason

Elephan

Pebble Island

431

Keppel Island          Golding Island      First Mount

Saunders Island                        TD UD

430                                                  TC   UC

429                                              Mount D'Arcy

Mount Ca

HILL COVE

ROY COVE          Green Hill Bridge

428                    WEST FALKLAND          PORT H

Mount Maria

KING GEORGE BAY                        Centre of MEZ/TEZ/FIPZ

427        Christmas Harbour

CHARTRES          Shag Cove House

426    DUNNOSE HEAD

Mount Doyle          Sw

425

SPRING POINT

QUEEN CHARLOTTE BAY                        PORT KING

Weddell Island

424                              FOX BAY EAST

FOX BAY WEST

FALKLAND SOUND

423
52°oo

422    PORT STEPHENS

Speedwell Island

421

420                    TC   UC
                       TB   UB

419

418